P9-CLE-820

HISTORICAL ATLAS

WILLIAM R. SHEPHERD

Late Professor of History, Columbia University

Eighth Edition, 1956

This edition contains all maps of the Seventh Revised and Enlarged Edition and a special supplement of historical maps for the period since 1929 prepared by C. S. Hammond & Company

Published by
The Colonial Offset Co., Inc.
Pikesville, Maryland

Sole Distributors
Barnes & Noble, Inc.
New York, N. Y.

Library of Congress Card Catalogue No. Map 56-4

To T. S.
my life's companion
who induced me to go forth
and see the world

Printed in the United States of America

PREFACE TO THE EIGHTH EDITION

Long a classic in its field, the Shepherd Atlas was out of print for many years, but remained in constant demand. Since the plates, originally made in Germany, were destroyed, this edition was printed by offset lithography. A special supplementary section of historical maps for the period since 1929 was prepared for the new edition by C. S. Hammond & Company.

In his preface to the Seventh Edition, 1929, the author expressed appreciation to Professor Charles H. Haskins, Harvard University; Professor Charles M. Andrews, Yale University; his colleagues, Professors Austin P. Evans, William Linn Westermann and Harry J. Carman, Columbia University; Mr. Harry W. Martin, Horace Mann Boy's School, New York; Dr. Isaiah Bowman and Mr. W. L. G. Joerg, the American Geographical Society; Principal C. Grant Robertson, Birmingham University; Honorary Professor T. F. Tout, Manchester University; Mr. L. Cecil Jane, Aberystwyth College, University of Wales; and the officials of the Library of the British Museum, in particular Mr. F. D. Sladen, Superintendent of the Reading Room.

For suggestions helpful in the preparation of the Eighth Edition, the publisher wishes to thank Mr. James M. Darley, Chief Cartographer of the National Geographic Society; Professor Walther Kirchner, University of Delaware; Professor John A. Krout, Vice President and Provost, Columbia University; Professor Bert James Loewenberg, Sarah Lawrence College; Professor Thomas C. Mendenhall, Yale University; Professor Marshall Smelser, University of Notre Dame.

ACKNOWLEDGMENT

Among the works consulted in the preparation of the Atlas the following have been especially serviceable:

R. Altamira y Crevea, Historia de España y de la civilización española. (4 vols. Madrid, 1909—1911)

E. Ambrosius ed., Andrees Allgemeiner Handatlas. (8th ed. 2d imp. Leipzig, 1924)

F. M. Anderson and A. S. Hershey, Handbook for the diplomatic history of Europe, Asia and Africa, 1870—1914. (Washington, 1918)

K. Andree, Geographie des Welthandels. (3 vols. Frankfort, 1910—1913)

Archiv für Eisenbahnwesen. (Berlin, 1878 . . . .)

E. M. Avery, A history of the United States and its people. (7 vols. Cleveland, 1904—1910)

J. G. Bartholomew, An Atlas of economic geography. (London, 1914)

J. G. Bartholomew ed., The Times survey atlas of the world. (London, 1922)

C. R. Beazley, The dawn of modern geography. (3 vols. London, 1897—1906)

E. Bonvalot, Le Tiers État d'après la charte de Beaumont-en-Argonne et ses filiales. (Paris, 1884)

I. Bowman, The new world. (Yonkers, 1926)

J. H. Breasted, A history of Egypt from the earliest times to the Persian conquest. (2d ed. New York, 1909)

J. Brunhes, Human Geography. (New York, 1920)

—, La géographie de l'histoire. (Paris, 1921)

J. Buchan ed., A history of the great war. (4 vols. New York, 1922)

The Cambridge ancient history. (6 vols. Cambridge, 1923 . . . .)

The Cambridge history of British foreign policy, 1783—1919. (3 vols. Cambridge, 1922—1923)

The Cambridge medieval history (5 vols. Cambridge, 1911 . . . .)

The Cambridge modern history (13 vols. Cambridge, 1902—1912).

The Cambridge modern history atlas. (2d ed. Cambridge, 1924)

A del Cantillo, Tratados, convenios y declaraciones de paz y de comercio. (Madrid, 1843)

H. M. Chadwick, The origin of the English nation. (Cambridge, 1907)

C. U. J. Chevalier, Répertoire des sources historiques du moyen-âge; Pt. II: topo-bibliographie. (2 vols. Paris, 1894—1903)

The Colonial Office list. (London, 1862 . . . .)

J. S. Corbett, Drake and the Tudor navy. (2 vols. London, 1899)

H. W. C. Davis, England under the Normans and Angevins. (London, 1915)

E. Debes ed., Neuer Handatlas über alle Teile der Erde. (4th ed. 2d imp. Leipzig, 1914)

L. Dominian, The frontiers of language and nationality in Europe. (New York, 1917)

G. Droysen, Allgemeiner historischer Handatlas. (Leipzig, 1886)

E. M. Earle, Turkey, the great powers and the Bagdad railway. (New York, 1923)

C. Errera, L'epoca delle grandi scoperte geografiche. (Milan, 1902)

Europäischer Geschichtskalender. (Munich, 1860 . . .)

H. J. Fleure, Human geography in western Europe. (2d ed. London, 1919)

—, The treaty settlement of Europe. (London, 1921)

E. Florez, España sagrada. (51 vols. Madrid, 1747—1879)

Foreign Affairs. (New York, 1922)

E. A. Freeman, Historical geography of Europe. (2 vols. 3d ed. London, 1903)

A García Cubas, Cuadro geográfico, estadístico, descriptivo e histórico de los Estados Unidos Mexicanos. (Mexico, 1884)

The Geographical Journal. (London, 1893 . . . .)

The Geographical Review (New York, 1916 . . . .)

W. Götz, Die Verkehrswege im Dienste des Welthandels. (Stuttgart, 1888)

—, Historische Geographie: Beispiele und Grundlinien. (Leipzig, 1904)

A. B. Hart ed., The American nation: a history from original sources by associated scholars. (28 vols. New York, 1904—1918)

C. H. Haskins and R. H. Lord, Some problems of the peace conference. (Cambridge, Mass., 1920)

F. J. Haverfield, The Roman occupation of Britain. (Oxford, 1924)

A. J. Herbertson and O. J. R. Howarth eds., The Oxford survey of the British Empire. (6 vols. Oxford, 1914)

E. Hertslet ed., China treaties (3d ed. London, 1908)

—, The map of Africa by treaty (3d ed. 3 vols. London, 1909)

—, The map of Europe by treaty. (4 vols. London, 1875, 1891)

K. Heussi and H. Mulert, Atlas zur Kirchengeschichte. (Tübingen, 1905)

W. v. Heyd, Histoire du commerce du Levant au moyen-âge. (2 vols. Leipzig, 1885—1886)

ACKNOWLEDGMENT

A. Himly, Histoire de la formation territoriale des états de l'Europe centrale. (2 vols. Paris, 1876)

T. H. Holdich, Boundaries in Europe and the Near East. (London, 1918)

L. Hugues, Cronologia delle scoperte e delle esplorazioni geografiche dall' anno 1492 a tutto il secolo XIX. (Milan, 1903)

C. Huelsen, The Roman forum. (2d ed. Rome, 1909)

W. W. Hunter, History of British India. (2 vols. London, 1899—1900)

P. Huvelin, Essai historique sur le droit des marchés et des foires. (Paris, 1897)

The imperial gazetteer of India. 3d ed. 26 vols. Oxford, 1907—1909)

C. Joppen, Historical atlas of India. (London, 1914)

J. S. Keltie, The partition of Africa. (2d ed. London, 1895)

H. and R. Kiepert, Formae orbis antiqui. (Berlin, 1901 . . . .)

C. G. de Koch and M. S. F. Schoell, Histoire abrégée des traités de paix entre les puissances de l'Europe depuis la paix de Westphalie. (15 vols. Paris, 1817—1818)

C. Kretschmer, Die Entdeckung Amerikas in ihrer Bedeutung für die Geschichte des Weltbildes. (Berlin, 1892)

C. de Lannoy and H. van der Linden, Histoire de l'expansion coloniale des peuples européens. (2 vols. Brussels, 1907—1911)

J. N. Larned ed., History for ready reference. (7 vols. Springfield, 1913)

E. Lavisse, Histoire de France depuis les origines jusqu'à la révolution. (9 vols. Paris, 1900 to 1911)

Lippincott's new gazetteer. (Philadelphia, 1916)

W. J. Loftie, London. (3d ed. London, 1892)

A. Longnon, Atlas historique de la France. (Paris, 1907)

C. Lucas ed., A historical geography of the British colonies. (12 vols. Oxford, 1905 to 1925)

K. von Martens and F. de Cussy, Recueil manuel et pratique de traités, conventions et autres actes diplomatiques. (7 vols. Leipzig, 1846 to 1857)

L. de Mas-Latrie, Trésor de chronologie d'histoire et de géographie pour l'étude et l'emploi des documents du moyen-âge. (Paris, 1889)

E. Mc Clure, Historical church atlas. (London, 1897)

H. R. Mill, The international geography. (New York, 1909)

C. F. R. de Montalambert, The monks of the west from Saint Benedict to Saint Bernard. (6 vols. New York, 1896)

R. Muir and G. Philip, Philips' New historical atlas for students. (5th ed. London, 1923)

J. Murdoch and I. Yamagata, A history of Japan. (2 vols. Yokohama, 1903, 1910)

D. P. Myers, Manual of collection of treaties. (Cambridge, Mass., 1922)

H. Nissen, Italische Landeskunde. (2 vols. Berlin, 1883—1902)

A. E. Nordenskiöld, Facsimile atlas to the early history of cartography. (London, 1889)

A. Oakes and R. B. Mowat eds., The great European treaties of the nineteenth century. (Oxford, 1918)

C. W. C. Oman, England before the Norman conquest. (5th ed. London, 1921)

E. L. Oxenham, Historical atlas of the Chinese Empire. (London, 1898)

P. Pelet, Atlas des colonies françaises. (Paris 1900—1902)

A. Petermanns Mitteilungen aus Justus Perthes' geographischer Anstalt über wichtige neue Erforschungen auf dem Gesamtgebiete der Geographie. (Gotha, 1855 . . . .)

O. F. Peschel, Geschichte des Zeitalters der Entdeckungen. (Stuttgart, 1858)

H. Pirenne, Medieval cities. (Princeton, 1925)

E. Porritt, The unreformed House of Commons. (2 vols. Cambridge, 1903)

R. L. Poole ed., Historical atlas of modern Europe. (Oxford, 1896—1902)

B. Poten ed., Handwörterbuch der Militärwissenschaften. (5 vols. Leipzig, 1877—1880)

F. W. Putzgers Historischer Schul-Atlas (48th ed. Leipzig, 1928)

H. Rashdall, The universities of Europe in the middle ages. (2 vols. Oxford, 1895)

O. Reclus, Atlas de la plus grande France. (Paris, 1913)

F. P. W. von Richthofen, China: Ergebnisse eigener Reisen und darauf gegründeter Studien. (5 vols. Berlin, 1877—1912)

E. K. A. Riehm, Handwörterbuch des biblischen Altertums. (2 vols. Leipzig, 1898)

W. Z. Ripley, The races of Europe. (New York, 1910)

C. G. Robertson and J. G. Bartholomew, An historical atlas of modern Europe from 1789 to 1922. (2d ed. London, 1924)

ACKNOWLEDGMENT

C. G. Robertson and J. G. Bartholomew, Historical and modern atlas of the British Empire (with supplement, London, 1905, 1924)

H. T. Robinson, Colonial chronology. (London, 1892)

Royal Asiatic Society of Great Britain and Ireland, Journal. (London, 1834 . . . .)

—, Transactions. (London, 1827 . . . .)

Royal Colonial Institute, Proceedings. (London, 1869 . . . .)

Royal Geographical Society, Journal. (London, 1831 . . . .)

S. Ruge, Die Entwicklung der Kartographie von Amerika bis 1570. (Gotha, 1892)

F. Schrader, Atlas de géographie historique. (Paris, 1911)

F. Seebohm, The English village community. (4th ed. London, 1905)

E. C. Semple, American history and its geographic conditions. (New York, 1903)

W. H. Siebert, The underground railroad from slavery to freedom. (New York, 1898)

W. Sievers, Süd- und Mittelamerika. (3d ed. Leipzig, 1914)

G. A. Smith and J. G. Bartholomew, Atlas of the historical geography of the Holy Land. (London, 1915)

C. von Spruner and T. Menke, Handatlas für die Geschichte des Mittelalters und der neueren Zeit. (Gotha, 1871—1880)

C. von Spruner, Historisch-geographischer Handatlas zur Geschichte Asiens, Afrikas, Amerikas und Australiens. (Gotha, 1855)

The statesman's year-book. (London, 1864 . . . .)

Stielers Handatlas. (Gotha, 1925)

A. M. H. J. Stokvis, Manuel d'histoire, de généalogie et de chronologie de tous les états du globe . . . (3 vols. Leyden, 1888—1893)

A. Supan, Die territoriale Entwicklung der europäischen Kolonien. (Gotha, 1906)

P. Teleki, Atlas zur Geschichte der Kartographie der japanischen Inseln. (Budapest, 1909)

H. W. V. Temperley, ed., A history of the peace conference of Paris. (5 vols. London, 1920 to 1921)

L. Thorndike, The history of medieval Europe. (New York, 1917)

M. Torrente, Historia de la revolución hispanoamericana. (3 vols. Madrid, 1829—1830)

The treaties of peace. (2 vols. New York, 1924)

U. S. Bureau of the Census, Statistical atlas of the United States. (Washington, 1903, 1914, 1925)

P. Vidal de la Blache, Histoire et géographie: atlas général Vidal-Lablache. (Paris, 1922)

P. Vinogradoff, The growth of the manor (rev. ed. London, 1911)

—, Villainage in England. (Oxford, 1892)

L. Vivien de Saint-Martin, Atlas universel de géographie (rev. ed. Paris, 1923)

E. A. Walker, Historical atlas of South Africa. (London, 1922)

World atlas of commercial geology: Pt. I, Distribution of mineral production. (Washington, 1921)

World missionary atlas. (London, 1925)

J. K. Wright, Geographical lore at the time of the crusades. (New York, 1924)

H. Yule, Cathay and the way thither (new ed. 4 vols. London, 1915—1916)

A. Zimmermann, Die europäischen Kolonien. (5 vols. Berlin, 1896—1903)

New York, March 1928

W. R. S.

CONTENTS

	PAGE
Physical Map of Europe, Western Asia and Northern Africa	2. 3
Mycenean Greece and the Orient, 2100—1300 B. C. Inset: Reference Map of the Nile Delta.	4
The Assyrian Empire and the Region about the Eastern Mediterranean, 850—625 B. C.	5
Reference Map of Ancient Palestine Insets: Plan of Jerusalem. Dominions of David and Solomon (1025—953 B. C.). Palestine under the later Kings (953—722 B. C.). Palestine under Joshua and the Judges (1250—1125 B. C.).	6. 7
The Orient 600—500 B. C. The Oriental Empires about 600 B. C. The Persian Empire about 500 B. C.	8
The Beginnings of Historic Greece, 700—600 B. C.	8
Vicinity of Troy. The Shores of the Propontis. Plan of Olympia	9
Reference Map of Ancient Greece. Northern Part	10. 11
Greek and Phoenician Settlements in the Mediterranean Basin, about 550 B. C.	12
Greece at the Time of the War with Persia, 500—479 B. C. The Athenian Empire at its Height (about 450 B. C.)	13
Reference Map of Ancient Greece. Southern Part Inset: Crete.	14. 15
Reference Map of Attica. Plan of Thermopylæ, 480 B. C. Inset: Harbors of Athens.	16
Greece at the Beginning of the Peloponnesian War (431 B. C.). Greece under Theban Headship (362 B. C.)	17
The Macedonian Empire, 336—323 B. C. Insets: The Ætolian and Achaian Leagues. Plan of Tyre.	18. 19
Kingdoms of the Diadochi After the Battle of Ipsus (301 B. C.). At the Beginning of the Struggle with Rome (about 200 B. C.).	18. 19
Reference Map of Asia Minor under the Greeks and Romans	20
Plan of Imperial Rome	22
Plan of Athens Inset: Plan of the Acropolis of Athens.	23
Plan of Republican Rome	23
Republican Forum. Imperial Forums	24
Reference Map of Ancient Italy. Northern Part	26. 27
The Growth of Roman Power in Italy to 218 B. C.	29
Reference Map of Ancient Italy. Southern Part Insets: Vicinity of Naples. Plan of Syracuse.	30. 31
Rome and Carthage at the Beginning of the Second Punic War, 218 B. C.	32
The Growth of Roman Power in Asia Minor I, after the Treaty of Apamea, 188 B. C.; II, before the outbreak of the Mithradatic Wars, 90 B. C.; III, as organized by Pompey, 63 B. C.	33
Territorial Expansion of Rome Insets: Plan of Carthage. Vicinity of Rome. Plan of Alexandria.	34. 35

CONTENTS

PAGE

Reference Map of the European Provinces of the Roman Empire 38. 39
Insets: Gaul in the Time of Cæsar. The Rhine Country in Roman Times. Country about the Lower Danube in Roman Times.

The Roman Empire about 395 42. 43

Economic Map of the Ancient World 44

Migrations and Conquests, 150—1066 45

Development of Christianity to 1300 46. 47

The Roman and Hunnic Empires about 450 48

Physical Map of the British Isles 49

The Germanic Kingdoms and the East Roman Empire in 486 50

Roman Britain about 410. Britain about 600 51

The Germanic Kingdoms and the East Roman Empire, 526—600 52
The Germanic Kingdoms and the East Roman Empire in 526. Europe and the East Roman Empire, 533—600.

The Califate in 750 53

Growth of Frankish Power, 481—814 53

The Carolingian and Byzantine Empires and the Califate about 814 54. 55
Inset: Northern Austrasia about 814.

Disruption of the Carolingian Empire, 843—888 56

The Peoples of Europe about 900 57

Europe and the Byzantine Empire about 1000 58. 59

England in the Eighth and Ninth Centuries 60
England in the Eighth Century. England in the Ninth Century.

France about 1035 61

Central Europe, 919—1125 62. 63

Italy about 1050 64
Inset: The Patrimony of St. Peter.

Danish Dominions, 1016—1241 64

England 1087—1154 65

PAGE

Europe and the Mediterranean Lands about 1097 66. 67
Inset: Europe and the Mediterranean Lands by Religions about 1097.

Asia Minor and the States of the Crusaders in Syria, about 1140 68
Insets: Palestine. Plan of Jerusalem about 1187.

France, 1154—1184 69
Inset: Domain, Fiefs and Suzerains of the Count of Champagne in the Twelfth Century.

Europe and the Mediterranean Lands about 1190 70. 71
Inset: Guelf, Hohenstaufen and Ascanian Domains in Germany about 1176.

The Holy Roman Empire under the Hohenstaufen, 1138—1254 72

The Mediterranean Lands after 1204 73

The British Isles, 1200—1450. Plan of London about 1300. Vicinity of London, 1200—1600 74. 75

France in 1328 76
Inset: The Chief Wool-raising Districts of England and Wool-manufacturing Towns of Flanders, Artois and Brabant.

Europe, 1360—1400 77

Central Europe in 1378 78. 79
Inset: Dominions of Ottocar of Bohemia.

Spread of German Settlements to the Eastward, 800—1400 80
Inset: The March of Lusatia.

The Great Schism, 1378—1417 81

France in 1453 81

Spain, 910—1492 82. 83
Spain in 910. Spain in 1037. Spain in 1150. Spain, 1212—1492.

England and France, 1455—1494 84

Decline of the March of Brandenburg under the Houses of Wittelsbach and Luxemburg, 1320—1415 85

The Wettin Lands, 1221—1485 85
Inset: Temporary break-up of the Wettin Lands about 1300.

Central Europe about 1477 86. 87

CONTENTS

	PAGE
Decline of German Power in the Baltic Region, 1380—1560	88
The Byzantine Empire, 1265—1355	89
I. The Byzantine Empire in 1265. II. The Byzantine Empire and the Ottoman Turks in 1355.	
Italy about 1494	90
Insets: The Milanese under the Visconti, 1339 - 1402. The Republic of Florence, 1300—1494.	
The Swiss Confederation, 1291—1513	91
The Mongol Dominions, 1227—1405	92
The Ottoman Empire, 1451—1481. Constantinople	93
Ecclesiastical Map of Western Europe in the Middle Ages	94. 95
Inset: Vicinity of Naples.	
Plan of Rome in the Middle Ages	96
The Roman Suburbicarian (Cardinal) Bishoprics about the 12th Century	96
Ecclesiastical Map of the British Isles in the Middle Ages	97
Mediaeval Commerce (Europe)	98. 99
Insets: England. Hanseatic League in Northern Germany.	
Rural Deaneries	100
Part of the bishopric of Winchester showing rural deaneries and religious houses during the Middle Ages.	
Mediaeval Universities	100
Ground-Plan of a Monastery (St. Gall, Switzerland)	101
Mediaeval Industry (Western Europe)	102. 103
Plan of a Mediaeval Manor	104
Enfranchisment of Mediaeval Towns	104A
Expansion of the Charter of Beaumont-en-Argonne, 1182—1300.	
Mediaeval Commerce (Asia)	104B. 104C
Inset: India.	
Europe in 1490	104D
The West Indies and Central America, 1492—1525	105
Inset: Watling's Island.	
The Conquest of Mexico, 1519—1521	106
The Expansion of Europe, 1340—1600	107—110
The Conquest of Peru, 1531-1533	111
The Portuguese Colonial Dominions in India and the Malay Archipelago, 1498—1580	112
The Imperial Circles about 1512	113
Central Europe about 1547	114. 115
Insets: Principality of Orange. Wettin Lands, 1485—1554.	
The Religious Situation in Europe about 1560	116
The Religious Situation in Central Europe about 1560. The Religious Situation in Europe about 1560.	
The Netherlands, 1559—1609	117
Europe about 1560	118. 119
The Religious Situation in Central Europe about 1618	120
Sweden about 1658	120
Principal Seats of War in Europe, 1618—1660	121
Treaty Adjustments, 1648—1660	121
1. Treaty of Westphalia, 1648. 2. Treaty of the Pyrenees, 1659; Peace of Roeskilde-Oliva, 1658, 1660.	
Central Europe about 1648	122. 123
Europe in 1648	124
Principal Seats of War in Europe, 1672—1699	125
Treaty Adjustments, 1668—1699	125
Treaties of Aix-la-Chapelle, Nimwegen, St. Germain, Ryswick, Carlowitz.	
Extension of the French Frontiers, 1601—1789	126
England an Ireland, 1485—1688	127
England and Wales, 1485—1688. Ireland, 1550—1653. Ecclesiastical England, 1534—1547.	
Scotland, 1488—1688	128
The Ottoman Empire, 1481—1683	128A
The Expansion of Europe, 1600—1700	128B. 128C
Insets: Partition of Guiana and the West Indies. India. The Establishment of Dutch Power in the Malay Archipelago, 1602—1641. Guinea Coast.	

CONTENTS

	PAGE
Principal Seats of War in Europe, 1700—1721	129
Europe about 1740 Inset: The Growth of Savoy, 1418—1748.	130. 131
Principal Seats of War, 1740—1763 Inset: Spain. West Africa. West Indies. Canada. India.	132
Treaty Adjustments, 1713—1763 Treaties of Utrecht, Rastatt, Baden, Stockholm, Frederiksborg, Nystad, Passarowitz, Vienna, Belgrade, Breslau, Dresden, Aix-la-Chapelle, Paris, Hubertusburg. Insets: Acadia and Newfoundland. Eastern North America.	133
Central Europe about 1786	134. 135
The Expansion of Europe, 1700—1763 Insets: The West Indies, 1700—1763. Cook's Voyages in the Southern Pacific.	136
India, 1700—1792	137
The Growth of Russia in Europe, 1300—1796	138. 139
Typical German States before and since the French Revolution	
I. Baden. Insets: County of Sponheim. Lordship of Grävenstein. Baden since 1801.	142
II. Wurtemberg Insets: County of Horburg and Lordship of Reichenweier. Principality-County of Montbéliard. Wurtemberg since 1495.	143
France in 1789 The "Gouvernements". The Generalities or Intendancies. The Salt tax and the Customs. Laws and Courts.	146. 147
Ecclesiastical Map of France, 1789 and 1802	148
France in 1791	148
Plans of Versailles and Paris in 1789	149
Napoleon's Campaign in Egypt, 1798	150
Northern Italy, 1796 (for the campaigns of 1796—1805)	150
Germany and Italy in 1803	151
Germany and Italy in 1806	151
Treaty Adjustments, 1810—1812 Insets: India. Cape Colony.	152
Principal Seats of War, 1788—1815 Insets: India. Egypt. Napoleon's Campaign in Russia, 1812.	153
Central Europe in 1812 Inset: Europe in 1812.	154. 155
The Waterloo Campaign. Europe in 1815 Plan of the Waterloo Campaign, June 16—18, 1815. Europe in 1815.	156
Treaty Adjustments, 1814, 1815 Inset: Fortresses along the French Frontier.	157
Central Europe, 1815—1866	158. 159
The German Zollverein (Customs Union) 1828—1872 1828—1834. After 1834.	160
Germany, 1866—1919	161
Italy, 1815—1924	161
Industrial England since 1750	162
England and Wales in 1832	163
The Ottoman Empire, 1683—1913 Insets: Southwestern Crimea, 1854. Plan of Sevastopol, 1854—1855.	164
Peoples of Southeastern Europe and Asia Minor in 1913	165
Europe, 1871—1914	166. 167
Peoples of Austria-Hungary in 1914	168
The World at War, 1914—1918	168A
Principal Seats of War, 1914—1918	168B
The Western European Front, 1914—1918	168C
Treaty Adjustments, 1919—1926	168D

CONTENTS

PAGE

Treaty Adjustments 1919—1926. The Rhineland 168E

Europe in 1928 168F. 168G

Peoples of Central Europe in 1928 168H
Inset: South Tyrol.

The Near East since 1913. I. 168J. 168K

The Near East. II. 168L
Proposed Partitions of the Ottoman Empire, 1915, 1916. The Dardanelles. Partitions of Thrace. 1878—1923. The Religious Situation.

The Growth of European and Japanese Dominions in Asia since 1801 170. 171
Inset: Vicinity of Peking.

Australia and New Zealand since 1788 172

The Partition of Africa 174. 175
Insets: The Suez Canal and Lower Egypt. The Boer Republics till 1902. The Spanish Zone in Morocco.

Distribution of European Languages 176

European, African and Asiatic Migration 177

The World in 1929 179—182

Localities in Western Europe, connected with American History 184

Localities in England, connected with American History 185

Physical Map of North America 186. 187

The Indians in the United States to 1905 188

Reference Map of the New England Colonies, 1607—1760 189
Insets: Rhode Island. Vicinity of Boston. Vicinity of New York.

European Exploration and Settlement in the United States, 1513—1776 190. 191
Inset: Principal English Grants, 1606—1665.

Reference Map of the Middle Colonies, 1607—1760 192
Inset: Settlements on the Delaware River.

Reference Map of the Southern Colonies, 1607—1760 193
Inset: Settlements on the James River. The Georgian Coast.

PAGE

The British Colonies in North America, 1763—1775 194
Inset: Middle Colonies.

Campaigns of the American Revolution, 1775—1781 195
Insets: Vicinity of Boston (1775—1776). The West and South, 1778—1781.

The United States, 1783—1803 196
Insets: The State of Franklin, 1784—1788. Early Distribution of the Public Lands (Ohio).

Territorial Expansion of the United States since 1803 198. 199
Insets: Alaska. Hawaii. Guam. Samoa Islands. Wake Island. Midway Island. Virgin Islands. Porto Rico. The Philippine Islands.

Campaigns of the War of 1812 200
Campaigns of the War of 1812. The Southwest. Vicinity of Washington in 1814.

Campaigns of the Mexican War, 1846—1847 201
Inset: Route from Vera Cruz to Mexico.

The Organization of Territories in the United States since 1803 202. 203
I. 1803—1810. II. 1810—1835. III. 1835—1855. IV. Since 1855.

Slavery and the Staple Agricultural Products in the Southern States, 1790—1860 204

Slavery and Emancipation in the United States, 1777—1865 206. 207
Inset: The Region South of the Great Lakes.

Seat of the Civil War, 1861—1865 204
Inset: Vicinity of Gettysburg.

Westward Development of the United States 210. 211

Canada and Newfoundland 212
Inset: The Arbitration Boundary between Canada and Alaska.

Mexico, Central America and the West Indies 213
Inset: Central Mexico.

South America 214. 215
Inset: South America about 1790.

Hispanic America, 1828—1929 216
Inset: The Chilean—Peruvian—Bolivian Frontier.

CONTENTS

Maps, since 1929, prepared by C. S. Hammond & Company

Europe, 1930-1939 218

The Far East, 1930-1941 218

European Theater of War
1939-1945 219

Far Eastern Theater of War
1939-1945 219

The World at War, 1939-1945 ...... 220. 22

The World of the United Nations
and the Cold War, 1945-1955 .... 222. 22

Retreat of Colonialism in the
Postwar Period 224. 22

Europe in 1955 22

Scale 1:30 000 000
Miles.
Areas above 5000 feet
" " 1600 "
" " 600 "
" below " "
" " sea-level
Desert
ATLANTIC OCEAN
BRITISH ISLES
ICELAND
Mt. Hecla
ARCTIC
Arctic Circle
Lofoten Is.
SCANDINAVIAN HIGHLANDS
SCANDINAVIAN PENINSULA
GULF OF BOTHNIA
Faroe Is.
Shetland Is.
Orkney Is.
The Hebrides
Grampian Mts.
Central Plain
IRISH SEA
Pennine Chain
Welsh Mts.
Central Plain
NORTH SEA
JUTLAND PENINSULA
Zealand
BALTIC SEA
Lands End
English Channel
Strait of Dover
GREAT LOWL
Elbe R.
Oder R.
Vistula R.
Rhine R.
Seine R.
Loire R.
PLAIN OF FRANCE
Erzgebirge
Plain of Bohemia
C. Finisterre
BAY OF BISCAY
Danube R.
CARPATHIAN MTS.
Cantabrian Mts.
PYRENEES
Mt. Blanc
THE ALPS
Mte Rosa
Plain of Lombardy
Rhone R.
Po R.
Hungarian Plain
Douro (Duero) R.
IBERIAN PENINSULA
Tagus R.
Spanish Plateau
Ebro R.
Wallachian Plain
Danube R.
C. St. Vincent
Sierra Morena
Guadalquivir R.
Sierra Nevada
Balearic Is.
Corsica
SARDINIA
APENNINES
ITALIAN PENINSULA
ADRIATIC SEA
BALKAN MTS.
BALKAN PENINSULA
Madeira Is.
Strait of Gibraltar
C. Spartel
Mt. Vesuvius
MEDITERRANEAN
GRECIAN PENINSULA
MOREA PENINSULA
Isthmus of Corinth
AEGEAN
SICILY
Mt. Etna
Strait of Messina
Malta
Crete
CANARY IS.
ATLAS MOUNTAINS
THE TELL
ALGERIAN PLATEAUS
Oasis of Wargla
ALGERIAN SAHARA
Oases of Tuat
Barka Plateau
LIBYAN DESERT
SAHARA
Oases of Fezzan
Oases of Kufra
TIBESTI HIGHLANDS
Oasis of Kawar
Niger River
L. CHAD
Longitude West of Greenwich 0 Longitude East of Greenwich

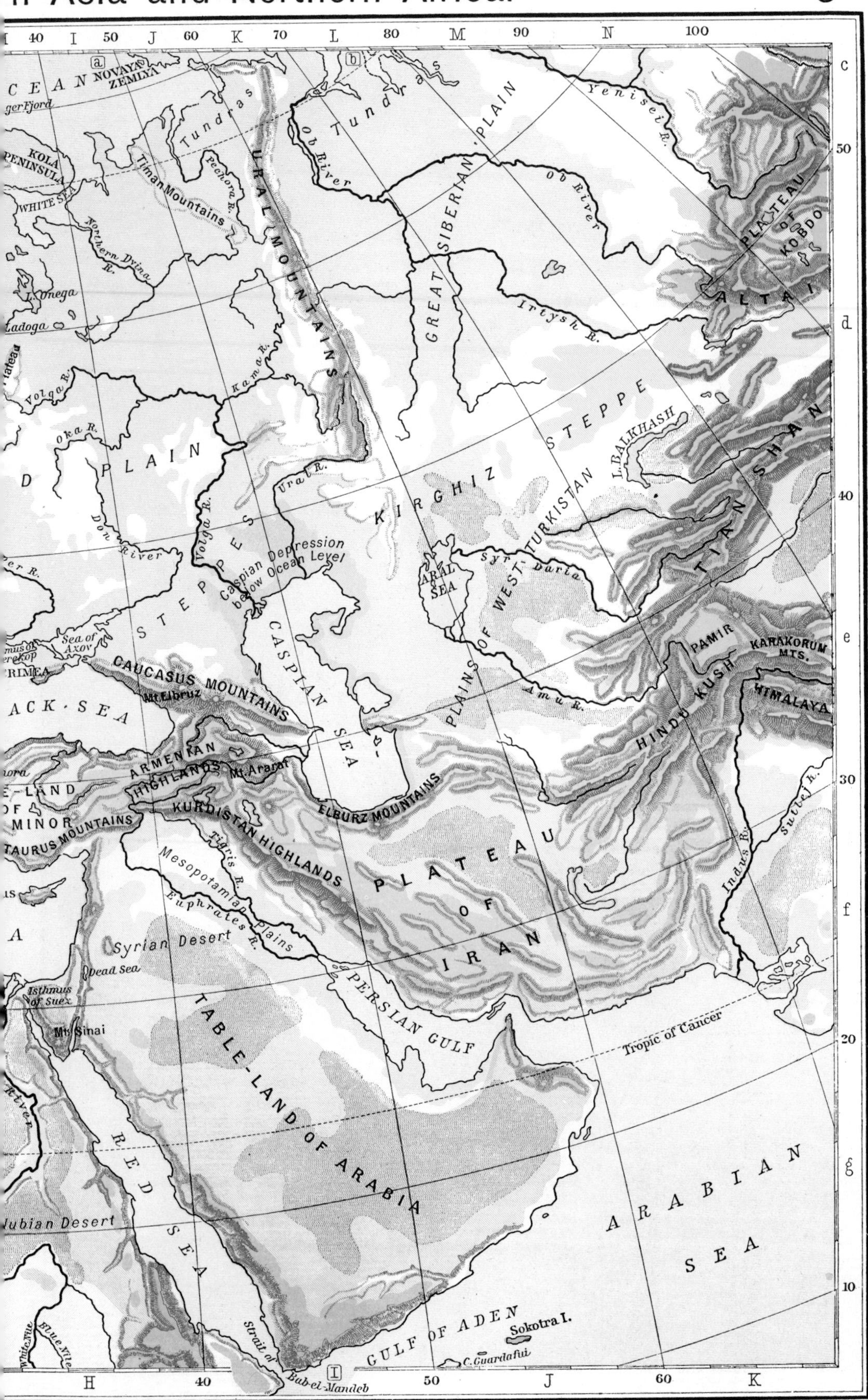
NOVAYA ZEMLYA
KOLA PENINSULA
WHITE SEA
Timan Mountains
URAL MOUNTAINS
Tundras
Ob River
GREAT SIBERIAN PLAIN
Yenisei R.
PLATEAU OF KOBDO
ALTAI
Irtysh R.
L. Onega
Ladoga
Volga R.
Kama R.
Oka R.
PLAIN
Don River
Ural R.
STEPPES
Caspian Depression below Ocean Level
KIRGHIZ STEPPE
L. BALKHASH
ARAL SEA
Syr Daria
PLAINS OF WEST TURKISTAN
TIAN SHAN
PAMIR
KARAKORUM MTS.
HIMALAYA
HINDU KUSH
Amu R.
Sea of Azov
CRIMEA
CAUCASUS MOUNTAINS
Mt. Elbruz
CASPIAN SEA
BLACK SEA
ARMENIAN HIGHLANDS
Mt. Ararat
KURDISTAN HIGHLANDS
ELBURZ MOUNTAINS
TAURUS MOUNTAINS
PLATEAU OF IRAN
Tigris R.
Euphrates R.
Mesopotamian Plains
Syrian Desert
Dead Sea
Isthmus of Suez
Mt. Sinai
PERSIAN GULF
Tropic of Cancer
Indus R.
Sutlej R.
TABLE-LAND OF ARABIA
RED SEA
Nubian Desert
ARABIAN SEA
GULF OF ADEN
Sokotra I.
C. Guardafui
Strait of Bab-el-Mandeb
Blue Nile
White Nile

Mycenean Greece and The Orient, 2100—1300 B.C.

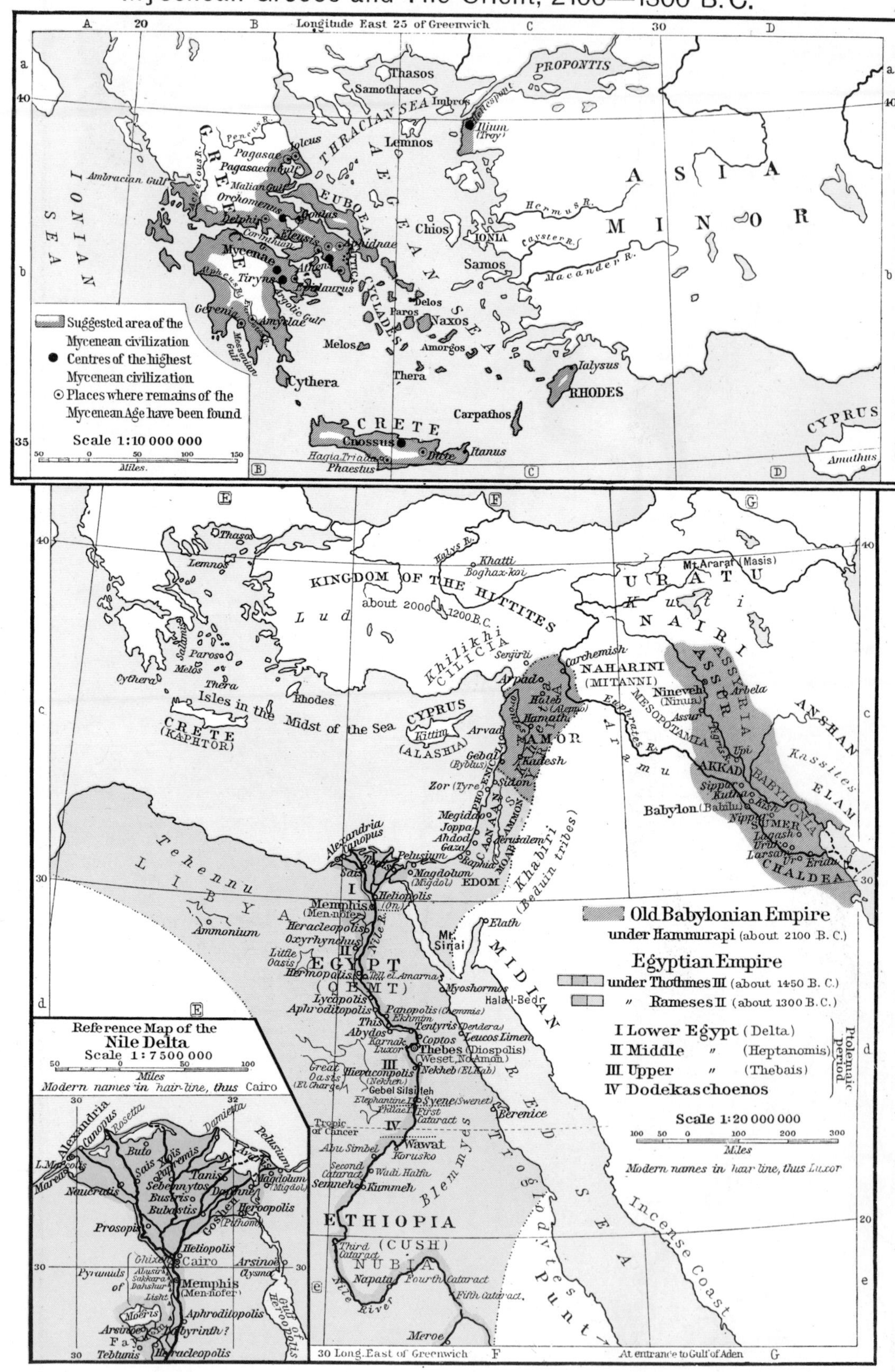

The Assyrian Empire and the Region about the Eastern Mediterranean, 850—625 B.C. 5

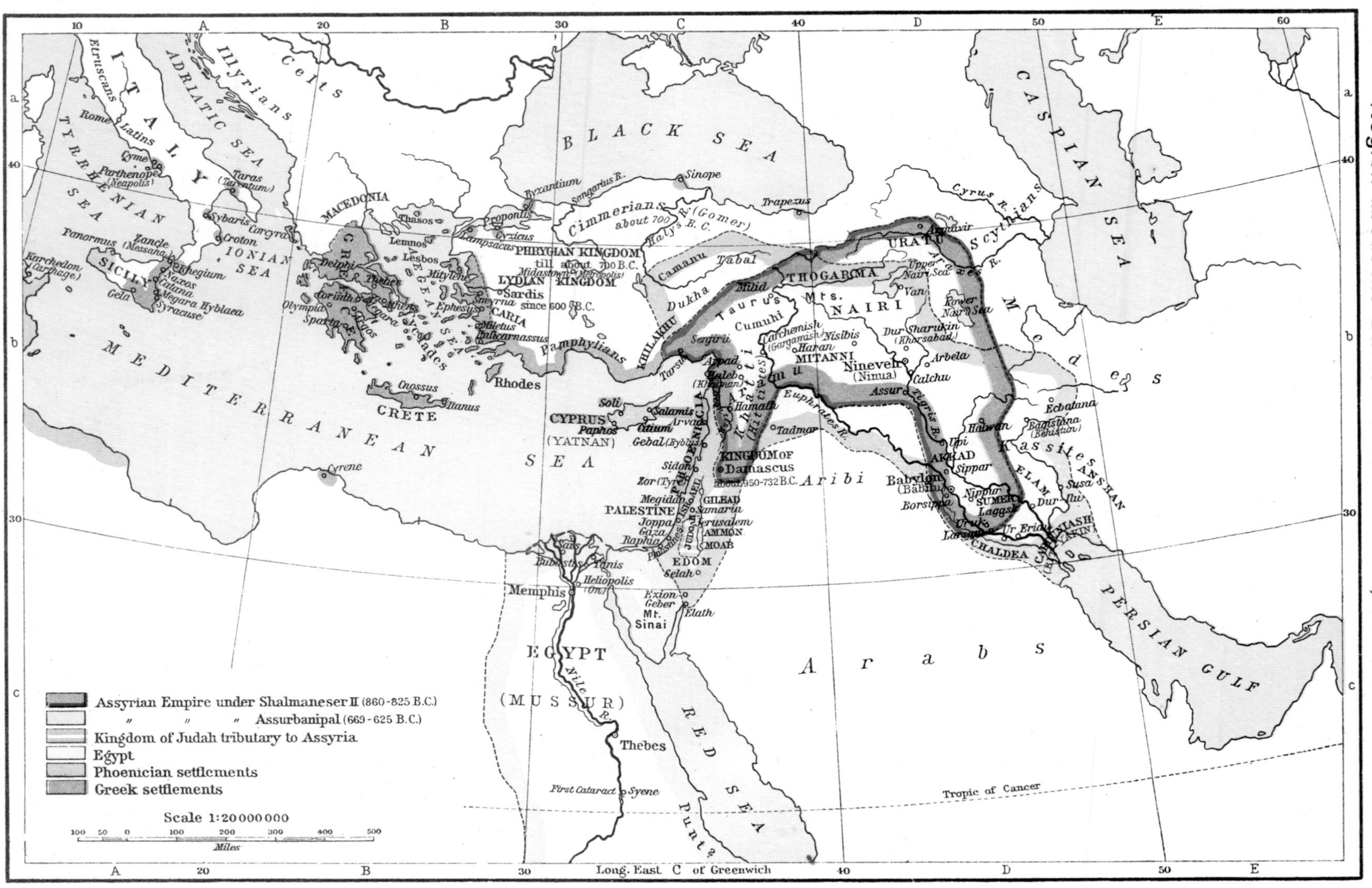

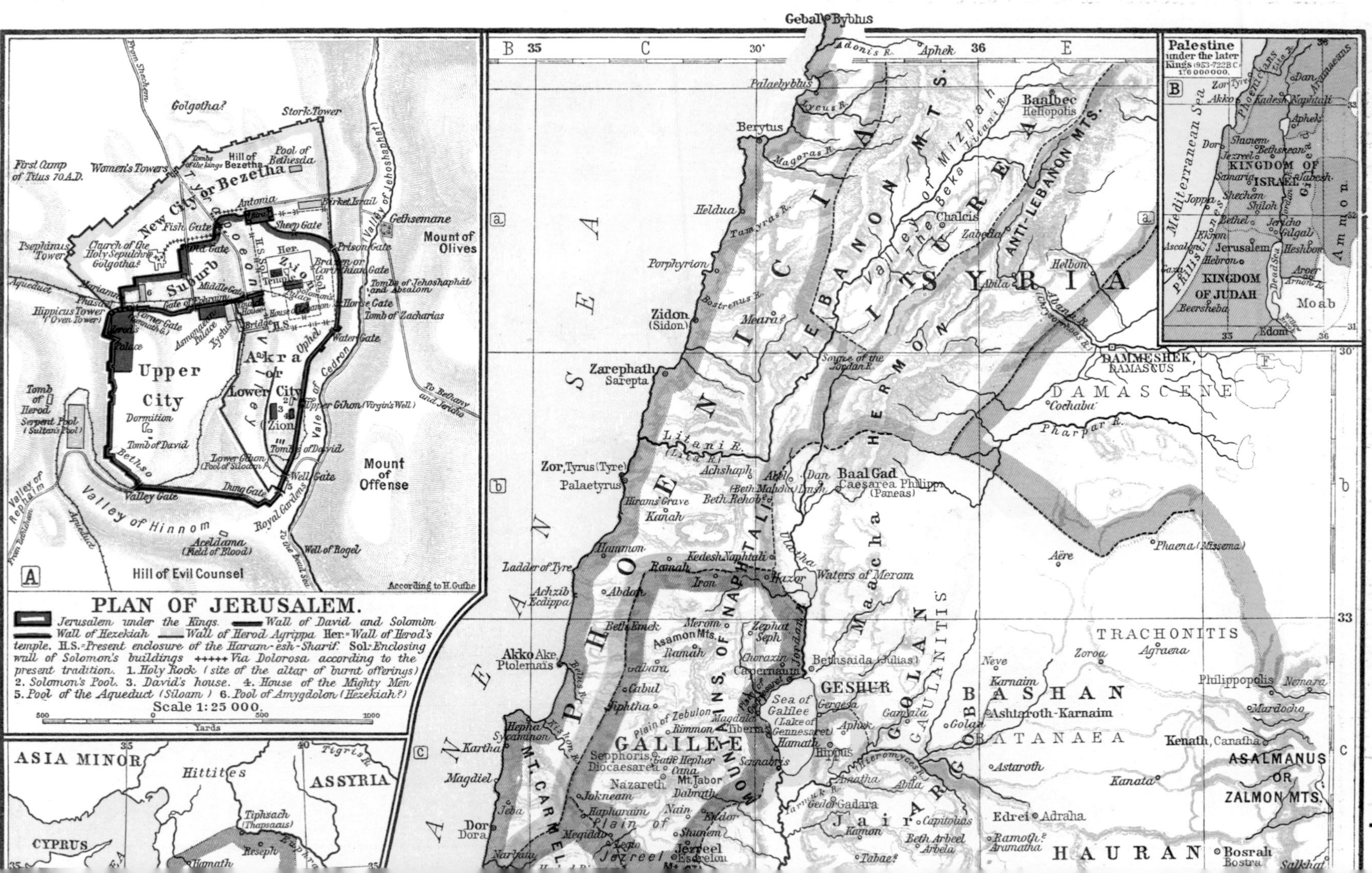
Palestine under the later Kings (953-722 B.C.) 1:6 000 000.
KINGDOM OF ISRAEL
KINGDOM OF JUDAH
Mediterranean Sea
Ammon
Moab
Edom
PLAN OF JERUSALEM.
Jerusalem under the Kings. Wall of David and Solomon. Wall of Hezekiah. Wall of Herod Agrippa. Her: Wall of Herod's temple. H.S.=Present enclosure of the Haram-esh-Sharif. Sol: Enclosing wall of Solomon's buildings. +++++ Via Dolorosa according to the present tradition. 1. Holy Rock (site of the altar of burnt offerings) 2. Solomon's Pool. 3. David's house. 4. House of the Mighty Men 5. Pool of the Aqueduct (Siloam) 6. Pool of Amygdalon (Hezekiah?)
Scale 1:25 000
Yards
According to H. Guthe
Upper City
Akra or Lower City
Zion
Suburb
New City or Bezetha
Mount of Olives
Mount of Offense
Hill of Evil Counsel
Valley of Hinnom
Valley of Jehoshaphat
Gethsemane
Golgotha?
Aceldama (Field of Blood)
LEBANON MTS.
ANTI-LEBANON MTS.
HERMON
PHOENICIA
SYRIA
ITURAEA
DAMASCENE
TRACHONITIS
BATANAEA
BASHAN
GAULANITIS
GOLAN
GESHUR
GALILEE
MOUNTAINS OF NAPHTALI
HAURAN
ASALMANUS OR ZALMON MTS.
MT. CARMEL
Sea of Galilee (Lake of Gennesaret)
DAMMESHEK, DAMASCUS
Zidon (Sidon)
Zarephath Sarepta
Zor, Tyrus (Tyre) Palaetyrus
Akko Ake, Ptolemais
Berytus
Gebal Byblus
Baalbec Heliopolis
Baal Gad Caesarea Philippi (Paneas)
Nazareth
Dor Dora
ASIA MINOR
ASSYRIA
CYPRUS
Hittites

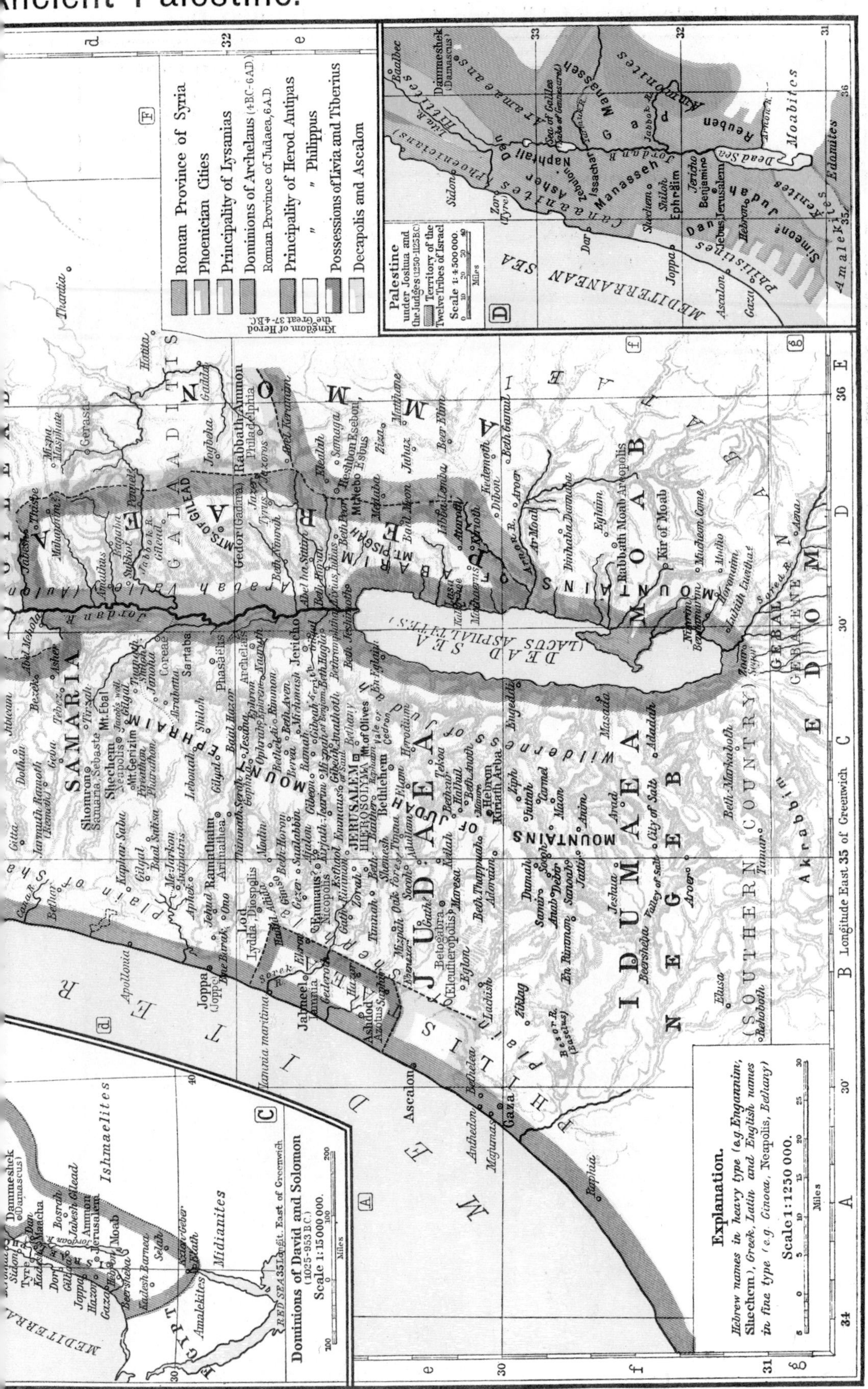
Roman Province of Syria
Phoenician Cities
Principality of Lysanias
Dominions of Archelaus (4 B.C.-6 A.D.)
Roman Province of Judaea, 6 A.D.
Principality of Herod Antipas
" " Philippus
Possessions of Livia and Tiberius
Decapolis and Ascalon
Kingdom of Herod the Great 37-4 B.C.
Palestine under Joshua and the Judges (1250-1125 B.C.)
Territory of the Twelve Tribes of Israel
Scale 1:4500000.
Dominions of David and Solomon (1025-953 B.C.)
Scale 1:15000000.
Explanation.
Hebrew names in heavy type (e.g. Engannim, Shechem), Greek, Latin and English names in fine type (e.g. Ginaea, Neapolis, Bethany)
Scale 1:1250000.
Longitude East 35 of Greenwich
SAMARIA
JUDAEA
IDUMAEA
DEAD SEA
MEDITERRANEAN SEA
MOAB
EDOM

8 The Orient, 600—500 B. C.
The Beginnings of Historic Greece, 700—600 B. C.

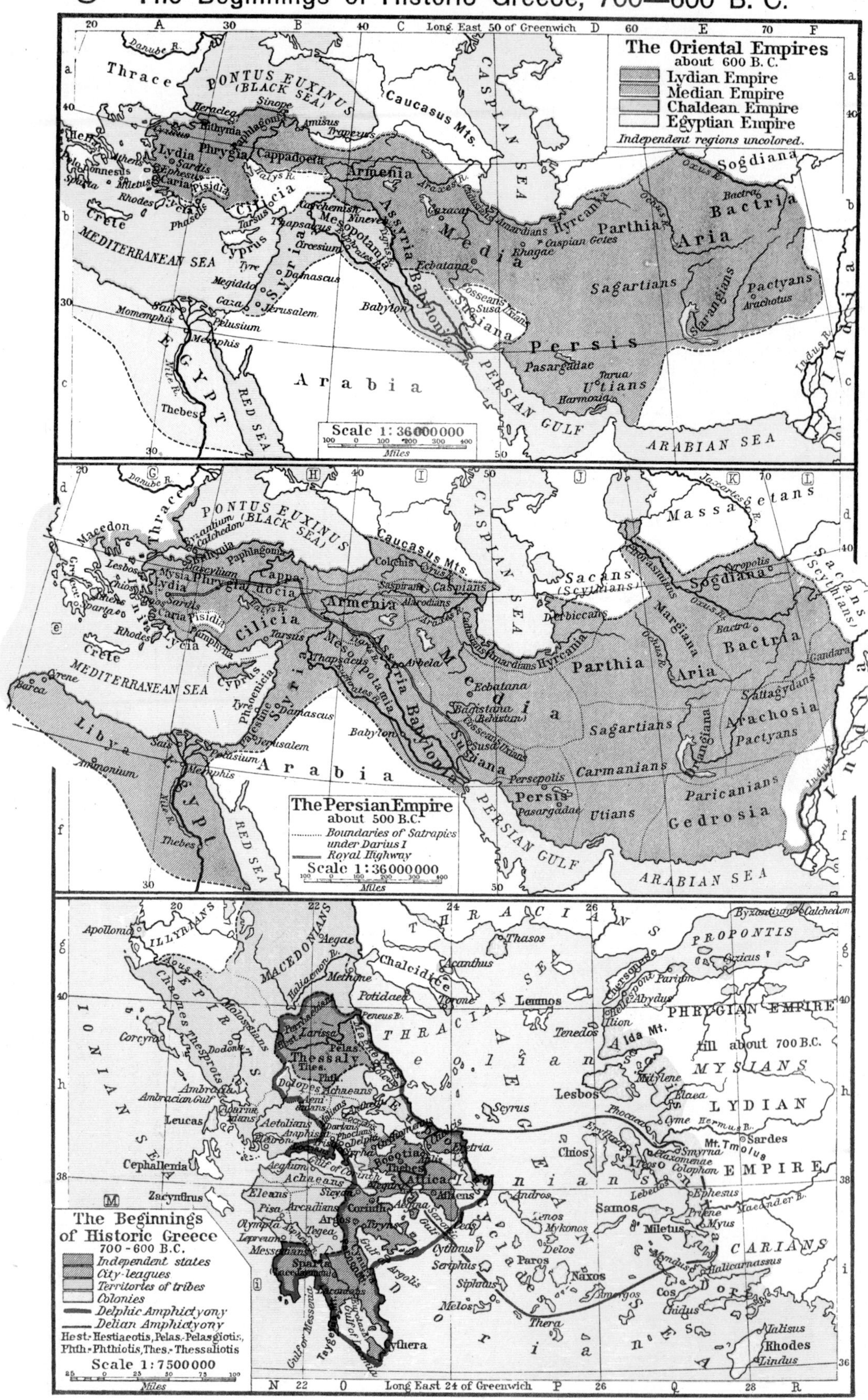

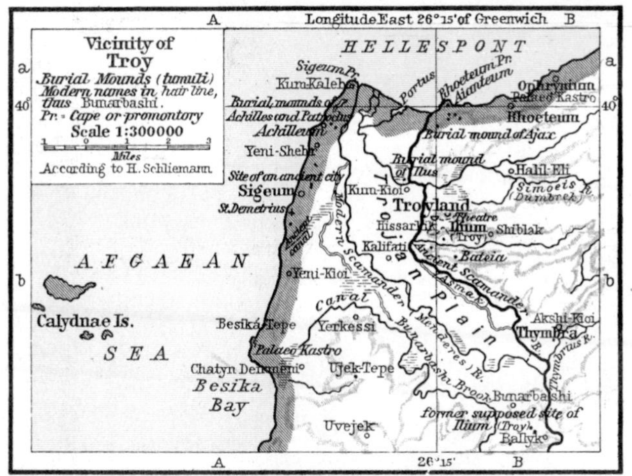
Vicinity of Troy
Burial Mounds (tumuli)
Modern names in hair line, thus Bunarbashi.
Pr. = Cape or promontory
Scale 1:300000
Miles
According to H. Schliemann
Longitude East 26°15' of Greenwich
HELLESPONT
AEGAEAN
SEA
Calydnae Is.
Besika Bay
Sigeum
Troyland
Ilium
Trojan plain
Thymbra
Rhoeteum
Ophrynium
Burial mound of Ajax
Burial mound of Ilus
Burial mounds of Achilles and Patroclus
Achilleum
Site of an ancient city
Ancient Scamander
Modern Scamander
Bunarbashi
former supposed site of Ilium (Troy)
Hissarlik
Kum-Kaleh
Yeni-Shehr
Yeni-Kioi
Besika-Tepe
Palaeo Kastro
Ujek-Tepe
Uvejek
Ballyk
Kalifatli
Shiblak
Halil-Eli
Akshi-Kioi
Yerkessi
Chatyn Dermeni
Bateia
Simoeis R. (Dumbrek)
Menderes R.
Bunarbashi Brook
Thymbrius R.
Portus
Rhoeteum Pr.
Aianteum
Sigeum Pr.
St. Demetrius
canal

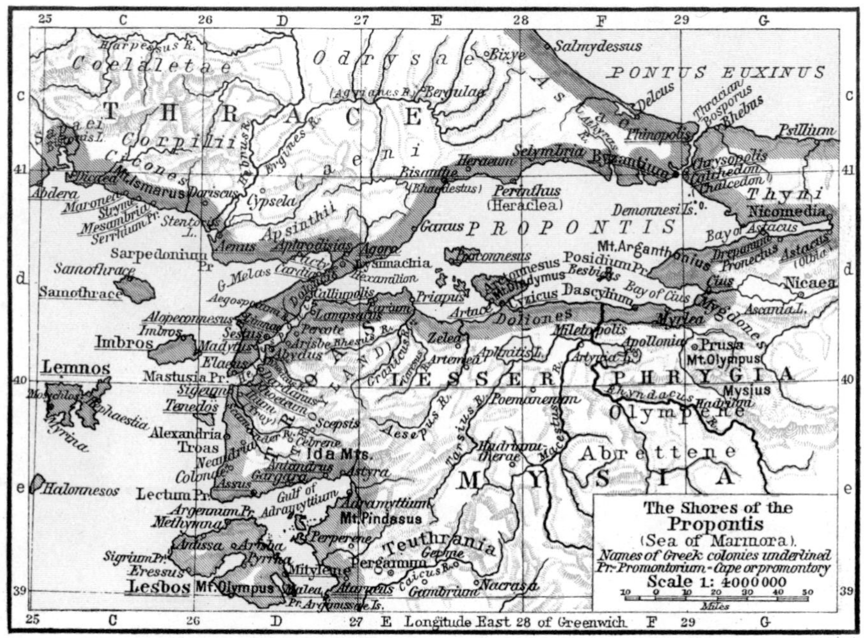
The Shores of the Propontis
(Sea of Marmora).
Names of Greek colonies underlined
Pr. Promontorium, = Cape or promontory
Scale 1: 4000000
Miles
Longitude East 28 of Greenwich
THRACE
PROPONTIS
PONTUS EUXINUS
Odrysae
Caeni
Coelaletae
Corpilii
Cicones
Apsinthii
Thyni
LESSER PHRYGIA
MYSIA
Abrettene
Olympene
Teuthrania
Dolionés
Mygdones
Byzantium
Chalcedon
Chrysopolis
Selymbria
Perinthus (Heraclea)
Heraeum
Bisanthe (Rhaedestus)
Salmydessus
Bizye
Phinopolis
Nicomedia
Astacus
Nicaea
Cius
Myrlea
Prusa
Mt. Olympus
Apollonia
Miletopolis
Cyzicus
Dascylium
Artace
Proconnesus
Priapus
Parium
Lampsacus
Callipolis
Lysimachia
Cardia
Agora
Aphrodisias
Aenus
Doriscus
Maronea
Abdera
Samothrace
Imbros
Lemnos
Tenedos
Sigeum
Ilium
Abydus
Sestus
Madytus
Elaeus
Alexandria Troas
Assus
Lectum Pr.
Ida Mts.
Antandrus
Gargara
Adramyttium
Gulf of Adramyttium
Mt. Pindasus
Pergamum
Lesbos
Mytilene
Methymna
Antissa
Eressus
Mt. Olympus
Halonnesos
Zelea
Scepsis
Cebrene
Aesepus R.
Granicus R.
Tarsius R.
Macestus R.
Caicus R.
Hadrianutherae
Poemanenum
Hadriani
Mysius
Ascania L.
Demonnesi Is.
Mt. Arganthonius
Posidium Pr.
Bay of Cius
Hebrus R.
Chersonese
Hexamilion
Aegospotami
Percote
Arisbe
Dardanus
Rhoeteum
Neandria
Colonae
Hamaxitus
Mastusia Pr.
Sarpedonium Pr.
Stentoris L.
Serrhium Pr.
Mesambria
Stryme
Ismarus
Cypsela
Hebrus R.
Bergulae
Rhebas
Psillium
Thracian Bosporus
Delcus
Atyra
Garus
Drepanum
Pronectus
Sigrium Pr.
Argennum Pr.
Perperene
Gryneia
Gambrium
Nacrasa
Atarneus
Malea
Pr. Argennusae Is.
Pyrrha
Arisba
Myrina
Hephaestia
Moschylus
Melas G.
Artemea
Aphnitis L.
Miletopolis
Artynia L.
Rhyndacus R.
Astyra
Apollonia

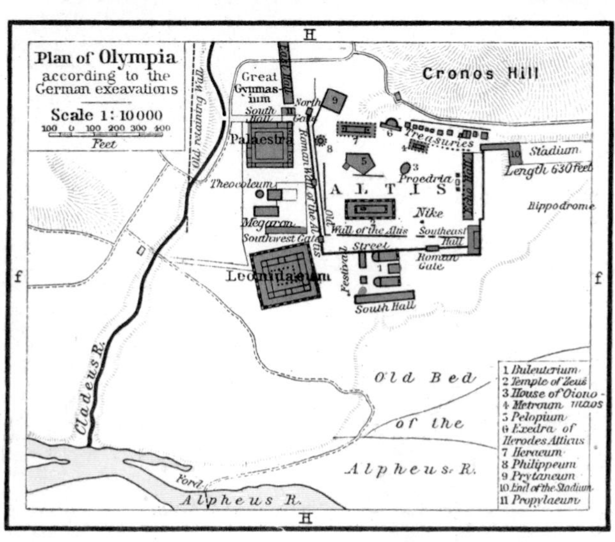
Plan of Olympia
according to the German excavations
Scale 1: 10000
Feet
Cronos Hill
ALTIS
Great Gymnasium
South Hall
North Gate
Palaestra
Theocoleum
Megaron
Southwest Gate
Leonidaeum
Roman Wall of the Altis
Wall of the Altis
Treasuries
Stadium
Length 630 Feet
Hippodrome
Proedria
Nike
Southeast Hall
Street
Roman Gate
Festival Gate
South Hall
Old Retaining Wall
Cladeus R.
Old Bed of the Alpheus R.
Alpheus R.
Ford
1 Buleuterium
2 Temple of Zeus
3 House of Oionomaos
4 Metroum
5 Pelopium
6 Exedra of Herodes Atticus
7 Heraeum
8 Philippeum
9 Prytaneum
10 End of the Stadium
11 Propylaeum

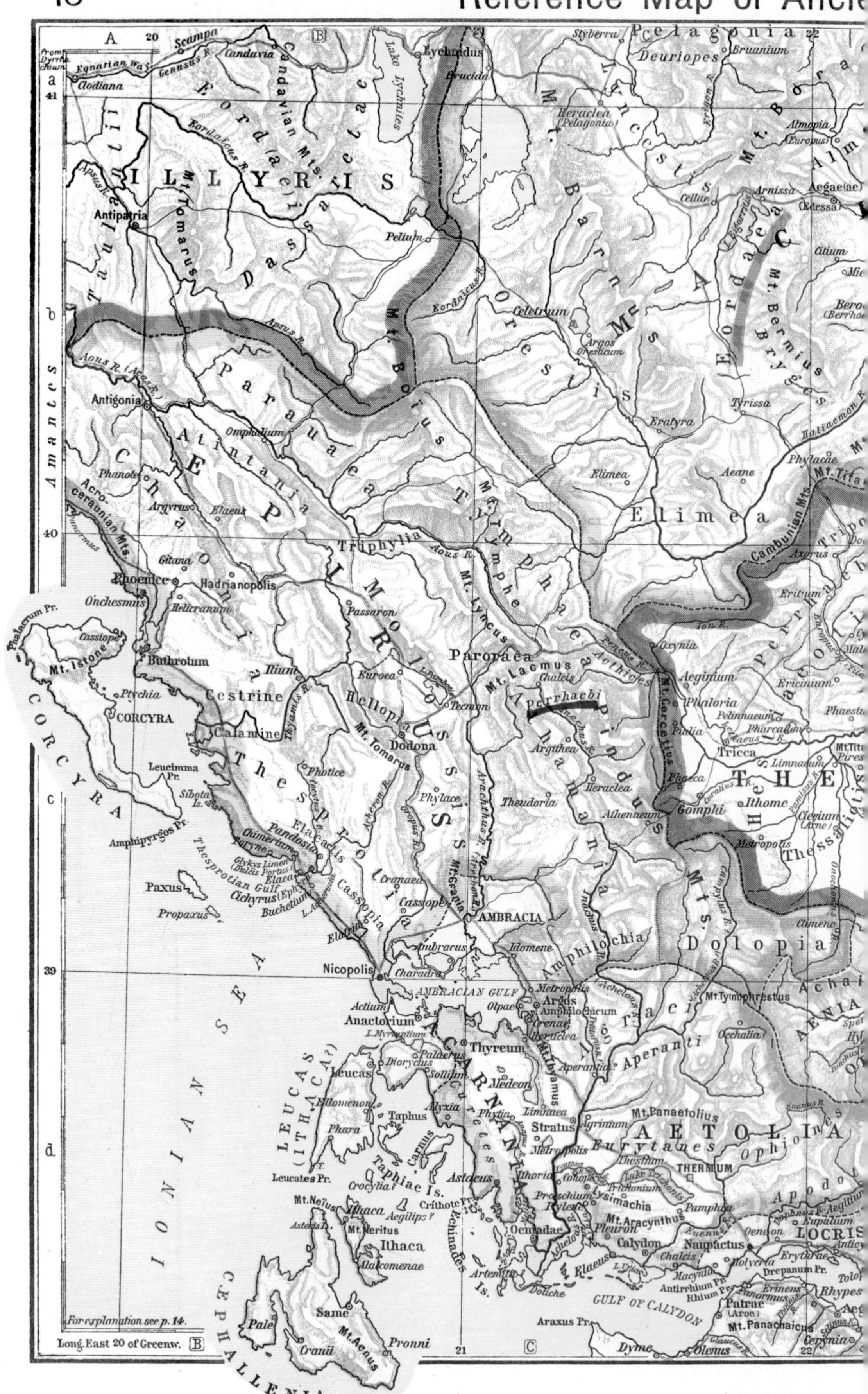

THRACIAN SEA
AEGEAN SEA
THERMAIC GULF
STRYMONIC GULF
ACANTHIAN GULF
SINGITIC GULF
TORONAIC GULF
PAGASAEAN GULF
MALIAN GULF
EUBOIC GULF
GULF OF CORINTH
CHALCIDICE
MAGNESIA
EUBOEA
BOEOTIA
PHOCIS
THASOS
Mygdonia
Bisaltia
Crestonia
Edones
Odomanti
Pieria
Amphaxitis
Bottice
Pallene (Phlegra)
Sithonia
Acte
Thessalonica
Therma
Amphipolis
Potidaea (Cassandrea)
Olynthus
Stagirus (Stagira)
Acanthus
Neapolis
Crenides (Philippi)
Serrhae
Larissa
Pherae
Pagasae
Demetrias
Sciathus
Peparethus
Icus
Scyrus
Chalcis
Eretria
Thebes
Delphi
Chersonesus Pr.
Caphereus Pr.

Greek and Phoenician Settlements in the Mediterranean Basin, about 550 B. C.

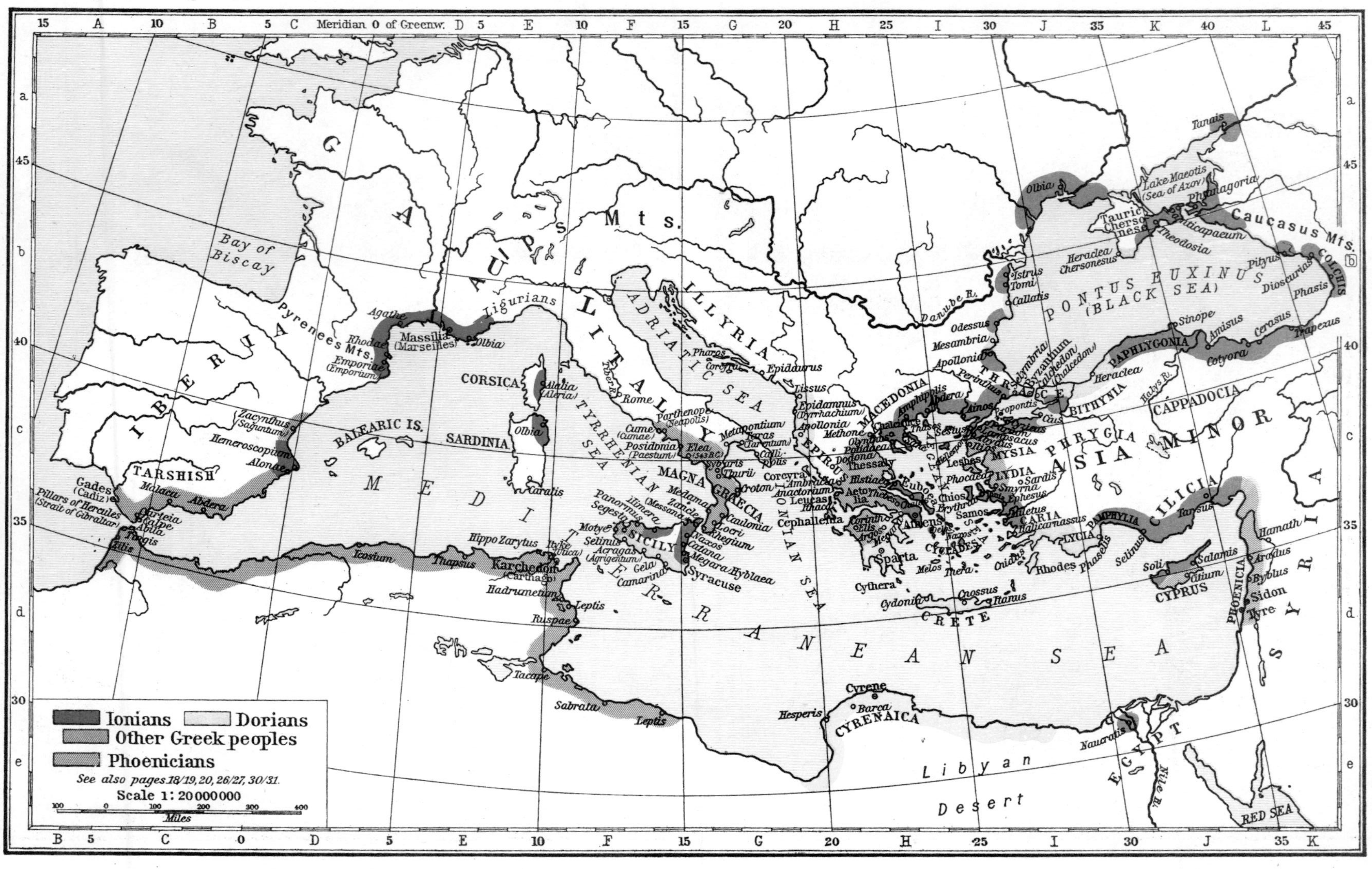

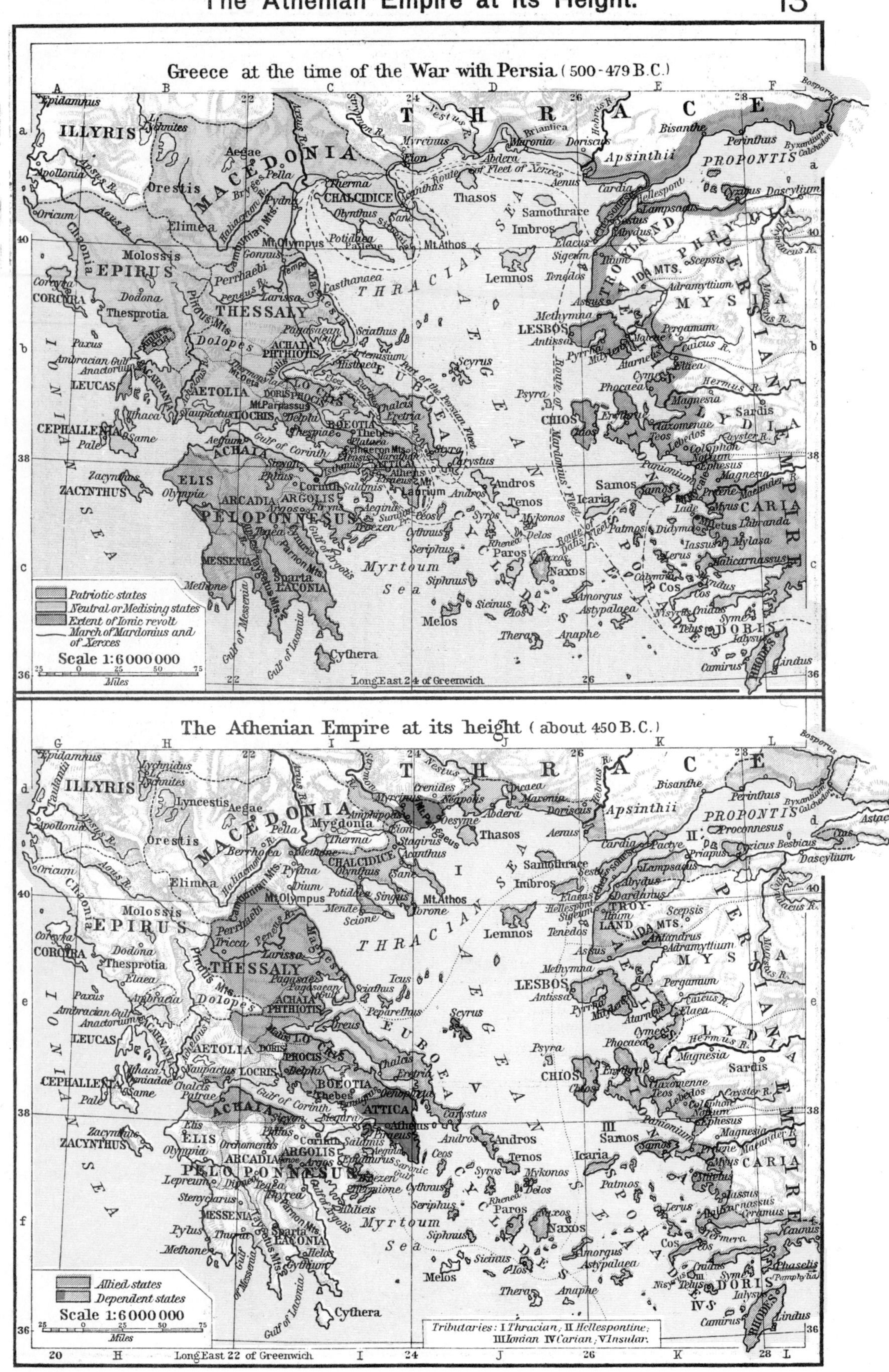
Greece at the time of the War with Persia (500-479 B.C.)
Patriotic states
Neutral or Medising states
Extent of Ionic revolt
March of Mardonius and of Xerxes
Scale 1:6000000
Miles
Long. East 24 of Greenwich
The Athenian Empire at its height (about 450 B.C.)
Allied states
Dependent states
Scale 1:6000000
Miles
Tributaries: I Thracian; II Hellespontine; III Ionian; IV Carian; V Insular.
Long. East 22 of Greenwich
THRACE
MACEDONIA
ILLYRIS
EPIRUS
THESSALY
PELOPONNESUS
THRACIAN SEA
AEGEAN SEA
IONIAN SEA
Myrtoum Sea
PROPONTIS
PERSIAN EMPIRE

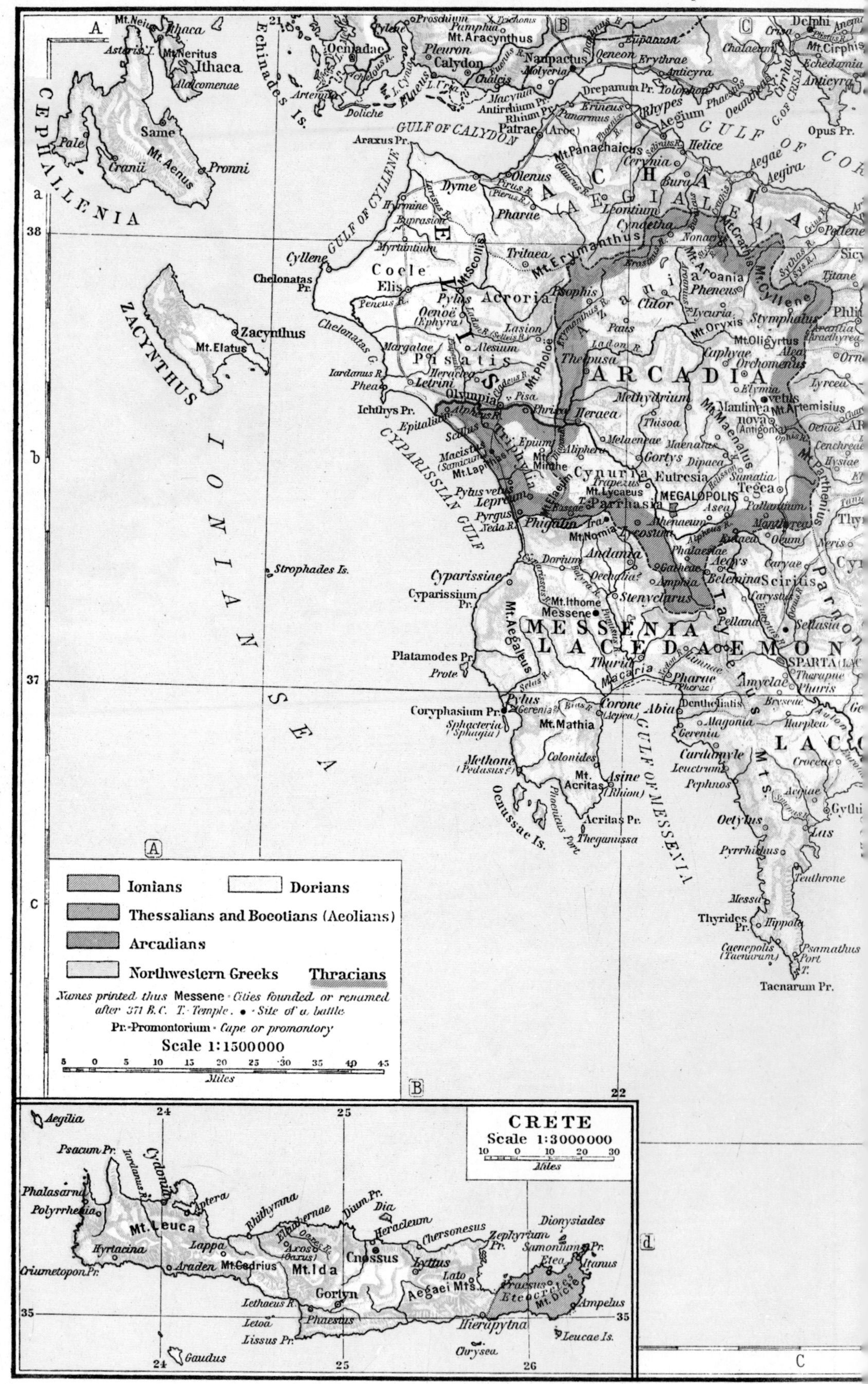
CEPHALLENIA
Ithaca
ZACYNTHUS
IONIAN SEA
Echinades Is.
GULF OF CALYDON
GULF OF CYLLENE
CYPARISSIAN GULF
GULF OF MESSENIA
ACHAIA
ELIS
ARCADIA
MESSENIA
LACEDAEMON
Strophades Is.
Oenussae Is.
Ionians
Dorians
Thessalians and Boeotians (Aeolians)
Arcadians
Northwestern Greeks
Thracians
Names printed thus Messene - Cities founded or renamed after 371 B.C. T.- Temple. • - Site of a battle
Pr.-Promontorium - Cape or promontory
Scale 1:1500000
Miles
CRETE
Scale 1:3000000
Miles
Cydonia
Mt. Leuca
Mt. Ida
Cnossus
Gortyn
Phaestus
Hierapytna
Aegaei Mts.
Gaudus

AEGEAN SEA
BOEOTIA
THEBES
ATTICA
ATHENS
MEGARIS
MEGARA
SARONIC GULF
AEGINA
EUBOEA
CHALCIS
Eretria
Marathon
ANDROS
TENOS
CEOS
CYTHNUS
SYROS
CYCLADES
SERIPHUS
SIPHNUS
PAROS
MELOS
MYRTOUM SEA
GULF OF ARGOLIS
CRETAN SEA
CRETE
Cydonia
Hydrea
Troezen
Epidaurus
Cythera
Aegilia
Long. East 23 of Greenwich

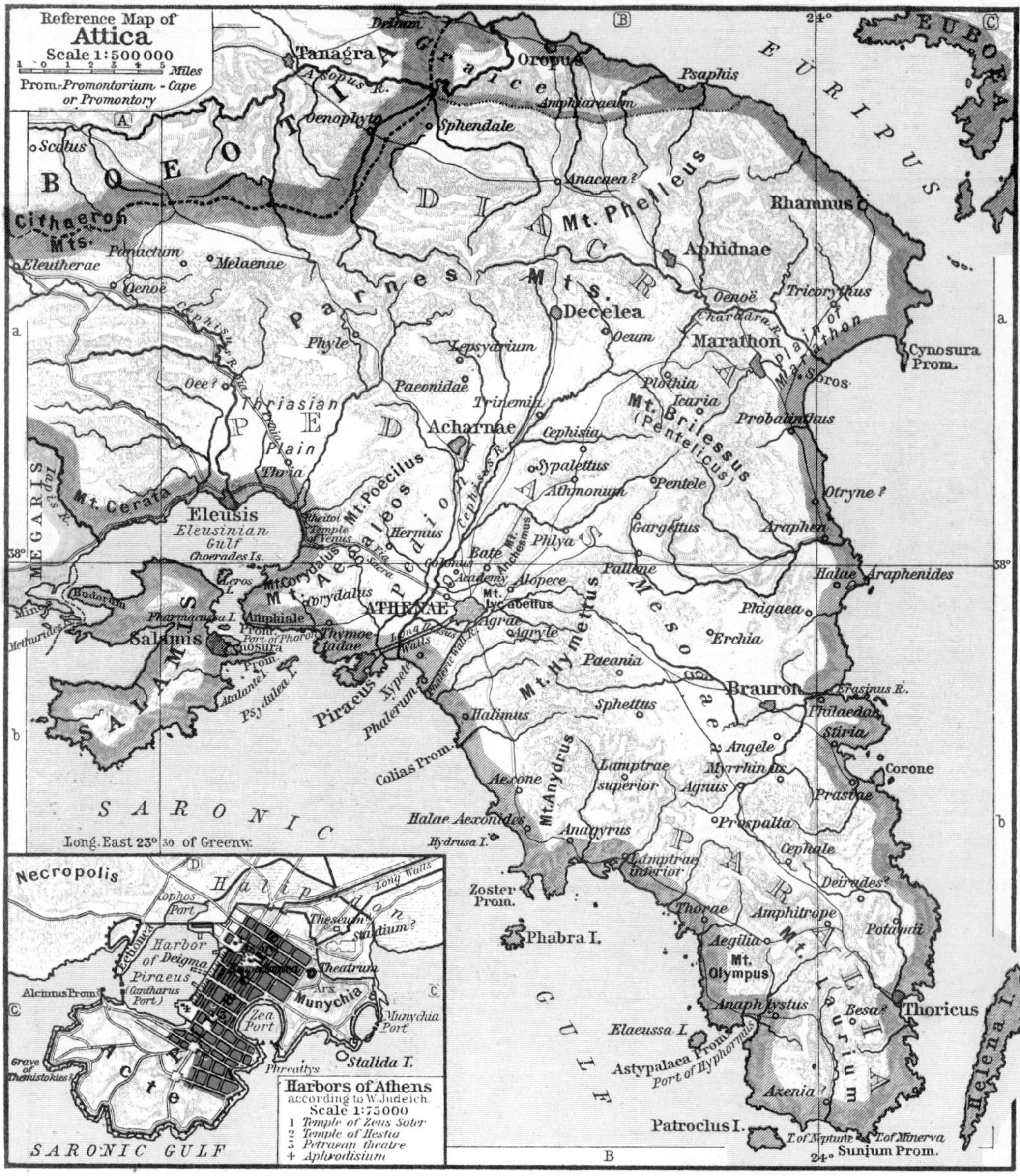

Reference Map of
Attica
Scale 1:500 000
Miles
Prom.: Promontorium - Cape or Promontory
Harbors of Athens
according to W. Judeich.
Scale 1:75000
1 Temple of Zeus Soter
2 Temple of Hestia
3 Petraean theatre
4 Aphrodisium
Long. East 23° 30 of Greenw.
BOEOTIA
Cithaeron Mts.
Parnes Mts.
Mt. Phelleus
Mt. Brilessus (Pentelicus)
Mt. Hymettus
Mt. Aegaleos
Mt. Poecilus
Mt. Cerata
Mt. Corydalus
Mt. Laurium
Mt. Olympus
MEGARIS
SALAMIS
EURIPUS
EUBOEA
SARONIC GULF
ATHENAE
Eleusis
Eleusinian Gulf
Thriasian Plain
Piraeus
Phalerum
Marathon
Plain of Marathon
Decelea
Acharnae
Aphidnae
Rhamnus
Oropus
Tanagra
Psaphis
Amphiaraeum
Sphendale
Oenophyta
Scolus
Eleutherae
Panactum
Melaenae
Oenoë
Phyle
Lepsydrium
Paeonidae
Trinemia
Cephisia
Sypalettus
Athmonum
Pentele
Gargettus
Phlya
Pallene
Alopece
Agryle
Paeania
Sphettus
Erchia
Brauron
Halae Araphenides
Araphen
Otryne ?
Probalinthus
Cynosura Prom.
Tricorythus
Oeum
Plothia
Icaria
Halimus
Colias Prom.
Aexone
Halae Aexonides
Anagyrus
Lamptrae superior
Lamptrae interior
Agnus
Myrrhinus
Angele
Prospalta
Cephale
Prasiae
Steiria
Philaedae
Corone
Deirades
Potamii
Amphitrope
Thorae
Aegilia
Anaphlystus
Besa
Thoricus
Helena I.
Zoster Prom.
Phabra I.
Elaeussa I.
Astypalaea Prom.
Port of Hyphormus
Patroclus I.
Azenia
T. of Neptune
T. of Minerva
Sunium Prom.
Hydrusa I.
Psyttalea I.
Atalante I.
Budorum
Necropolis
Cophos Port
Harbor of Deigma
Piraeus (Cantharus Port)
Alcimus Prom.
Eetionea
Zea Port
Munychia
Munychia Port
Theatrum
Theseum
Stadium ?
Long Walls
Stalida I.
Phreattys
Grave of Themistokles ?
Acte
SARONIC GULF

Plan of Thermopylae 480 B.C.
Scale 1:400000
Miles
Lamia
Phalara
Coast line in the time of Herodotus
MALIAN GULF
Spercheus R.
Anticyra
Alluvial Deposit
Present coast
Present course
Dyras R.
Malian Plain
Melas R.
Persian Camp
Trachis
Heraclea
OETA MTS.
Asopus R.
West defile
Thermopylae
Phocian Wall
Alpeni
Nicaea
Scarphea
Thronium
Anthela
Hot springs
Amphictionium
Trachinian Cliffs
LOCRIS
MALIS
Anopaea Mts.
Path followed by Persians
5730 ft.
Tarphe
MT. CALLIDROMUS
DORIS
PHOCIS
Pharygae
22° 30' Long. East of Greenw.

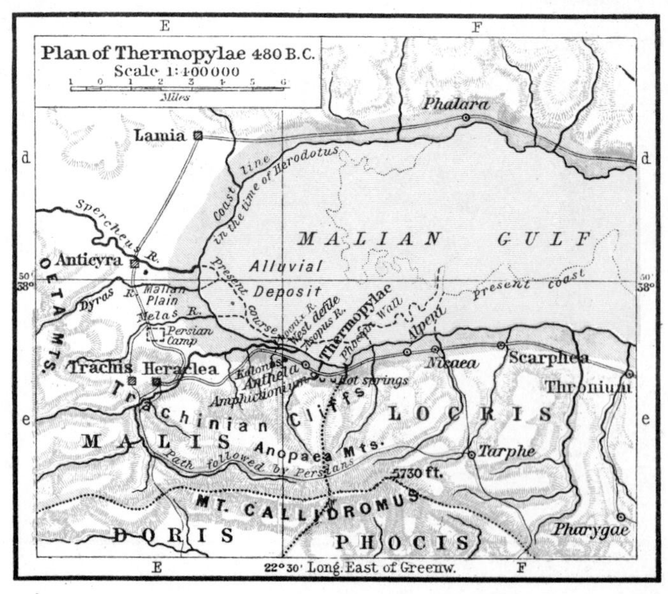

Greece at the Beginning of the Peloponnesian War. Greece under Theban Headship.

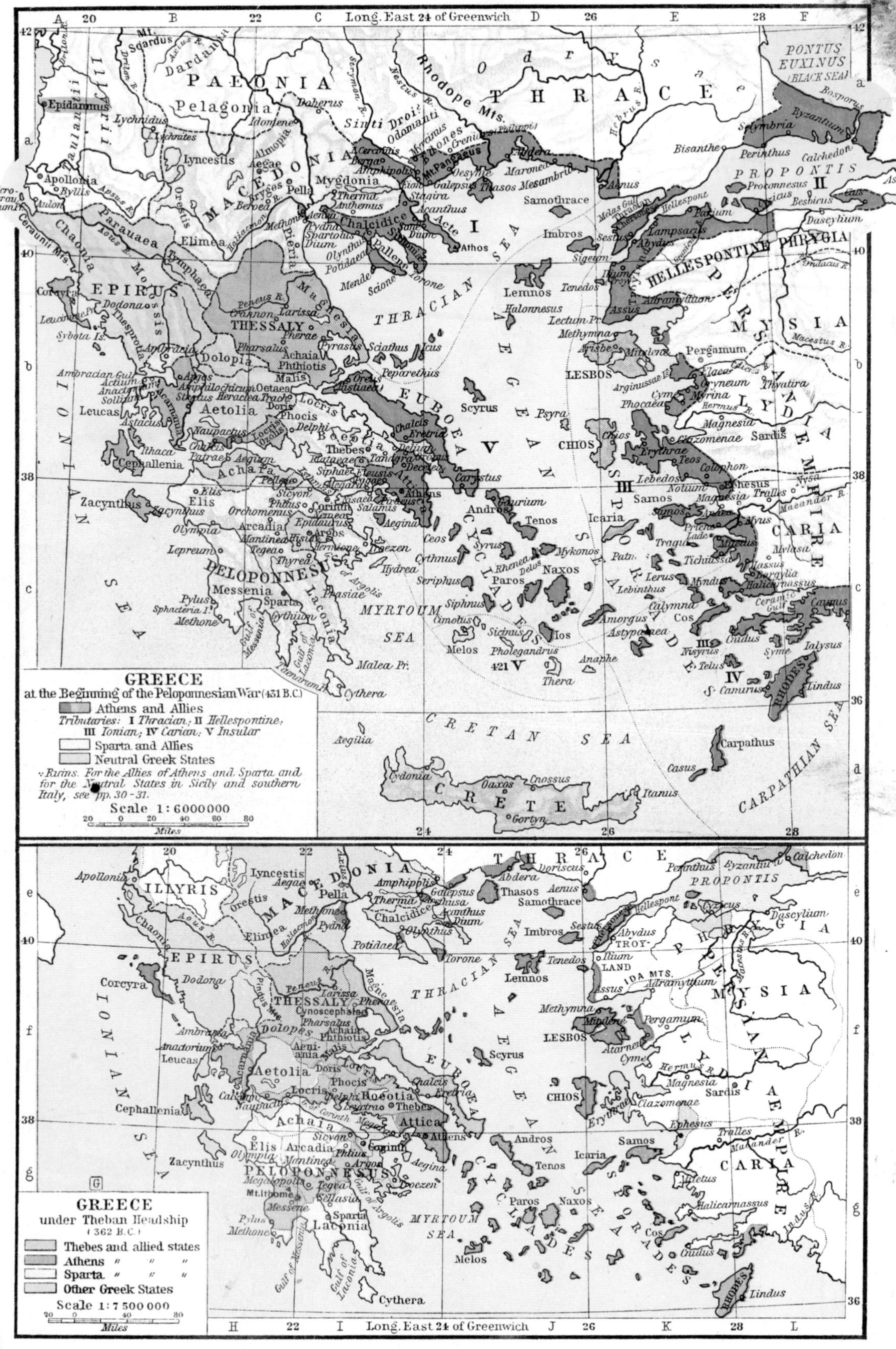

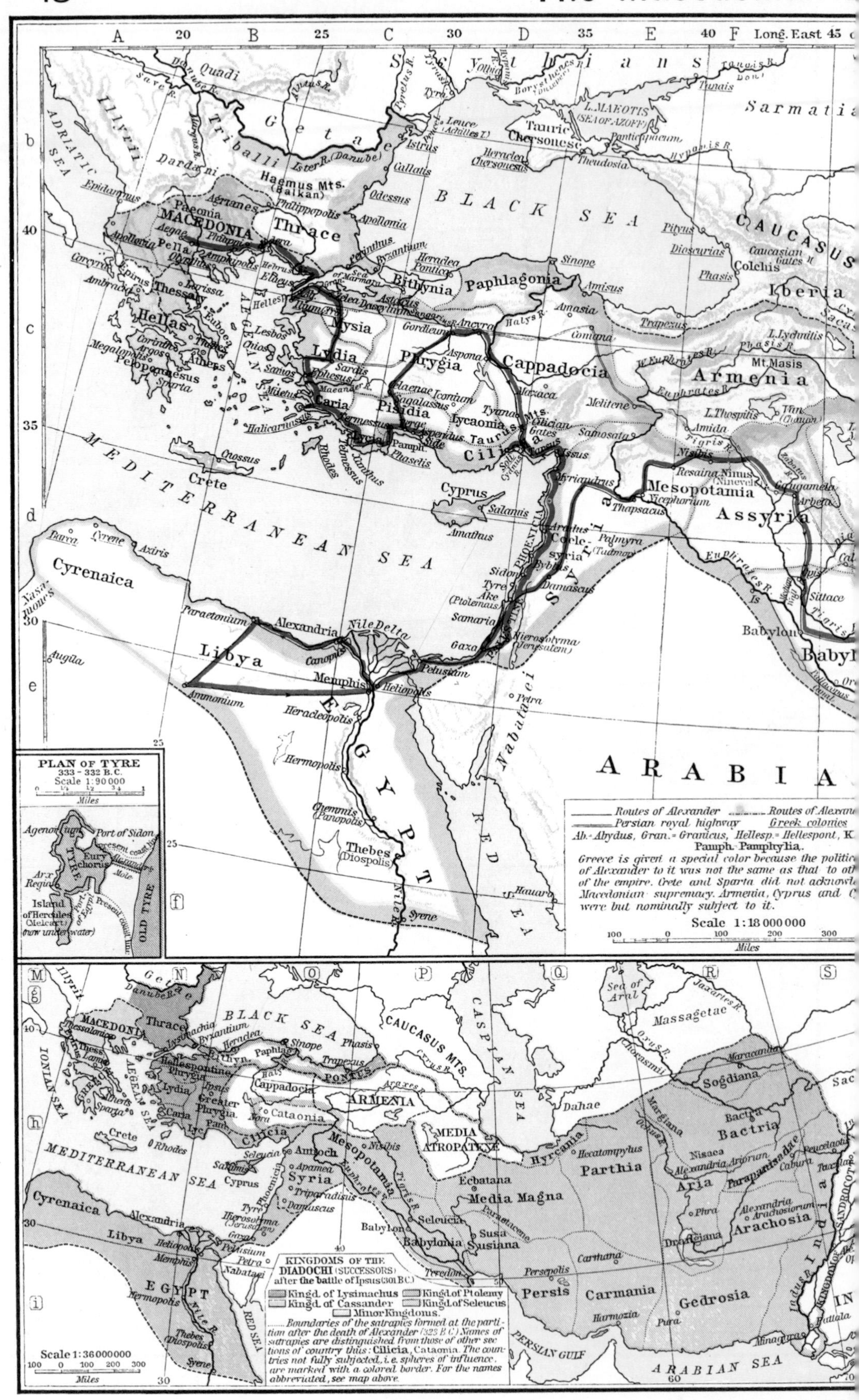

Long. East 45
Scythians
Quadi
Getae
Triballi
Ister R. (Danube)
Illyrii
Dardani
ADRIATIC SEA
Epidamnus
Haemus Mts. (Balkan)
Agrianes
Philippopolis
Paeonia
MACEDONIA
Aegae
Pella
Philippi
Abdera
Thrace
Apollonia
Amphipolis
Olynthus
Corcyra
Epirus
Ambracia
Thessaly
Larissa
Hellas
Euboea
Thebes
Corinth
Argos
Athens
Megalopolis
Peloponnesus
Sparta
Lesbos
Chios
Samos
Miletus
Ephesus
Sardis
Lydia
Mysia
Caria
Halicarnassus
Rhodes
Crete
Cnossus
Ilium (Troy)
Hellespont
Propontis or Sea of Marmara
Byzantium
Perinthus
Heraclea Pontica
Bithynia
Paphlagonia
Sinope
Amisus
Amasia
Comana
Gordieum
Ancyra
Halys R.
Phrygia
Cappadocia
Mazaca
Iconium
Sagalassus
Pisidia
Lycaonia
Tyana
Taurus Mts.
Cilician Gates
Cilicia
Tarsus
Issus
Lycia
Pamphylia
Phaselis
Side
Aspendus
Perge
Telmessus
Xanthus
BLACK SEA
Odessus
Callatis
Istrus
Tyras
Olbia
Leuce (Achilles I.)
Tauric Chersonese
Heraclea Chersonesus
Theudosia
L. MAEOTIS (SEA OF AZOFF)
Panticapaeum
Tanais
Sarmatia
Borysthenes R. (Dnieper)
Hypanis R.
Pityus
Dioscurias
Phasis
Colchis
CAUCASUS
Caucasian Gates
Iberia
Trapezus
Armenia
Mt. Masis
Euphrates R.
Melitene
Samosata
Amida
Tigris R.
Nisibis
Resaina
Ninus (Nineveh)
Gaugamela
Arbela
Mesopotamia
Nicephorium
Thapsacus
Assyria
Syria
Myriandrus
Cyprus
Salamis
Amathus
Aradus
Coele-syria
Palmyra (Tadmor)
Byblus
Sidon
Tyre
Damascus
Ake (Ptolemais)
Samaria
PHOENICIA
PALESTINE
Gaza
Hierosolyma (Jerusalem)
Babylon
Sittace
Opis
MEDITERRANEAN SEA
Cyrenaica
Barca
Cyrene
Axiris
Nasamones
Paraetonium
Alexandria
Nile Delta
Canopus
Pelusium
Libya
Memphis
Heliopolis
Ammonium
Augila
EGYPT
Heracleopolis
Hermopolis
Chemmis (Panopolis)
Thebes (Diospolis)
Nile R.
Syene
Petra
Nabataei
RED SEA
Hauara
ARABIA
PLAN OF TYRE 333 - 332 B.C.
Scale 1:90 000
Miles
Agenorium
Port of Sidon
present coast line
Eurychorus
TYRE
Alexander's Mole
Arx Regia
Port of Egypt
Island of Hercules (Melcart) (now under water)
Present coast line
OLD TYRE
Routes of Alexander
Routes of Alexander
Persian royal highway
Greek colonies
Ab.- Abydus, Gran.= Granicus, Hellesp.= Hellespont, K
Pamph. Pamphylia.
Greece is given a special color because the politic of Alexander to it was not the same as that to ot of the empire. Crete and Sparta did not acknowl Macedonian supremacy. Armenia, Cyprus and C were but nominally subject to it.
Scale 1:18 000 000
Miles
Getae
Danube R.
Illyrii
MACEDONIA
Thessalonica
Thrace
Lysimachia
Byzantium
Heraclea
Sinope
Phasis
Bithyn.
Paphlag.
Trapezus
PONTUS
IONIAN SEA
AEGEAN SEA
Hellespontine Phrygia
Lydia
Greater Phrygia
Caria
Lyc.
Pam.
Cappadocia
Cataonia
Cilicia
ARMENIA
Araxes R.
CAUCASUS MTS.
Cyrus R.
CASPIAN SEA
Sea of Aral
Jaxartes R.
Massagetae
Oxus R.
Chorasmii
Maracanda
Sogdiana
Bactra
Bactria
Margiana
Dahae
MEDIA ATROPATENE
Hyrcania
Hecatompylus
Parthia
Nisaea
Alexandria Ariorum
Aria
Parapamisadae
Cabura
Thess.
Lamia
GREECE
Athens
Sparta
Crete
Rhodes
MEDITERRANEAN SEA
Seleucia
Salamis
Cyprus
Antioch
Apamea
Syria
Triparadisus
Phoenicia
Tyre
Damascus
Hierosolyma (Jerusalem)
Gaza
Mesopotamia
Nisibis
Euphrates R.
Tigris R.
Ecbatana
Media Magna
Paraetacene
Babylon
Seleucia
Babylonia
Susa
Susiana
Teredon
Persepolis
Persis
Carmania
Carmana
Harmozia
Gedrosia
Pura
Phra
Alexandria Arachosiorum
Arachosia
Drangiana
Indus R.
Pattala
Minagara
PERSIAN GULF
ARABIAN SEA
Cyrenaica
Alexandria
Libya
Heliopolis
Memphis
Pelusium
Petra
Nabataei
EGYPT
Hermopolis
Nile R.
Thebes (Diospolis)
Syene
RED SEA
KINGDOMS OF THE DIADOCHI (SUCCESSORS) after the battle of Ipsus (301 B.C.)
Kingd. of Lysimachus
Kingd. of Ptolemy
Kingd. of Cassander
Kingd. of Seleucus
Minor Kingdoms.
Boundaries of the satrapies formed at the partition after the death of Alexander (323 B.C.) Names of satrapies are distinguished from those of other sections of country thus: Cilicia, Cataonia. The countries not fully subjected, i.e. spheres of influence, are marked with a colored border. For the names abbreviated, see map above.
Scale 1:36 000 000
Miles

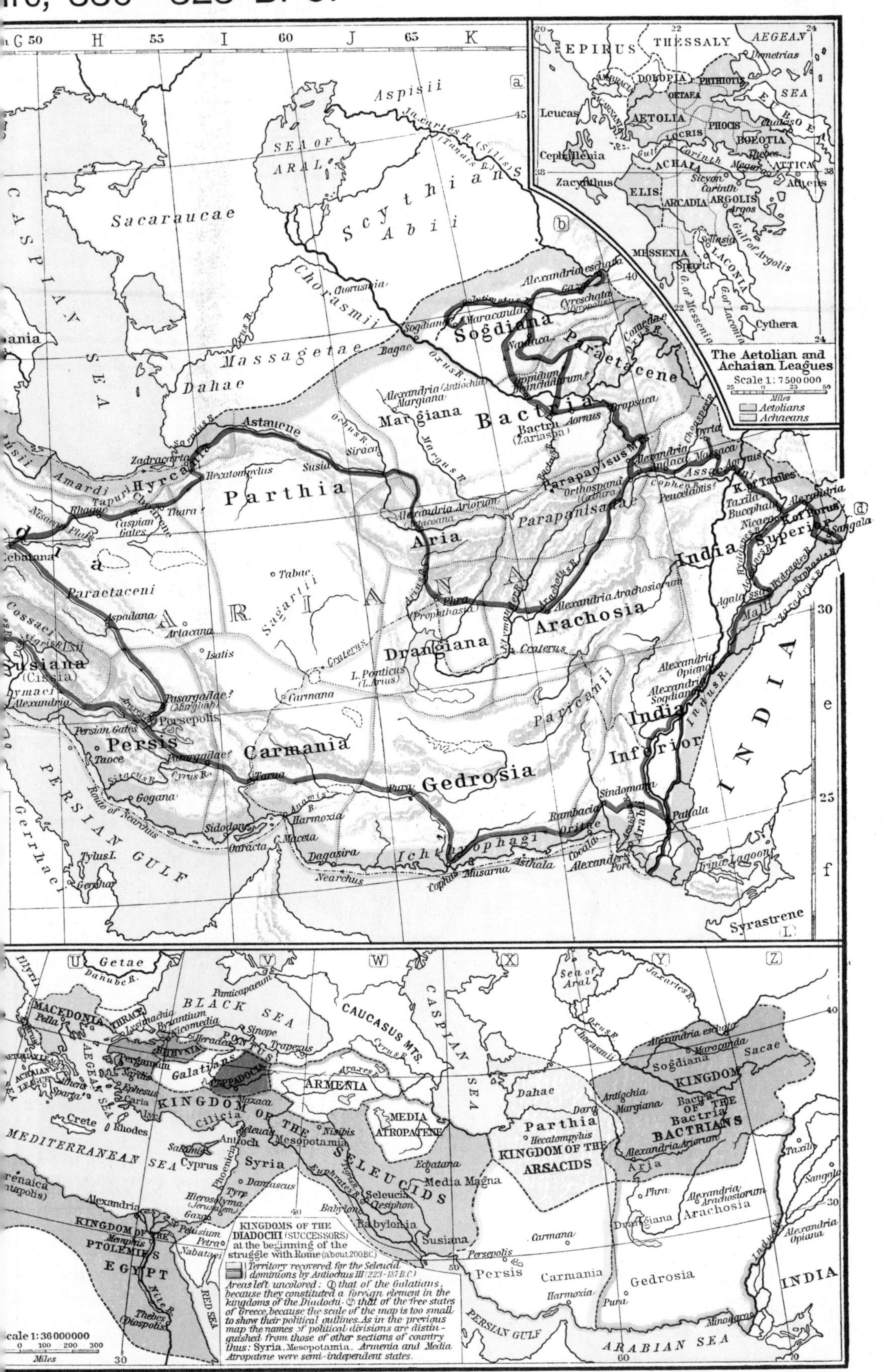

SEA OF ARAL
Sacaraucae
Scythians
Abii
Aspisii
Jaxartes R. (Tanais R.) (Silis)
CASPIAN SEA
Chorasmii
Massagetae
Dahae
Sogdiana
Maracanda
Alexandria eschata
Cyreschata
Paraetacene
Bactria
Bactra (Zariaspa)
Aornus
Drapsaca
Margiana
Alexandria (Antiochia) Margiana
Astauene
Hyrcania
Zadracarta
Amardi
Tapuri
Parthia
Hecatompylus
Susia
Caspian Gates
Ecbatana
Paraetaceni
Aria
Alexandria Ariorum
Artacoana
Parapanisadae
Parapanisus Mts.
Ortospana
Alexandria
Peucelaotis
K. of Taxiles
Taxila
Bucephala
Nicaea
Sangala
India Superior
India Inferior
INDIA
Arachosia
Alexandria Arachosiorum
Phra
(Prophthasia)
Drangiana
L. Ponticus (L. Arius)
ARIANA
Sagartii
Tabae
Isatis
Aspadana
Artacana
Carmana
Carmania
Susiana (Cissia)
Elymaei
Pasargadae
Persepolis
Persian Gates
Persis
Taoce
Gogana
Harmozia
Gedrosia
Pura
Parycanii
Ichthyophagi
Oritae
Rambacia
Arabii
Patala
Sindomana
Alexander's Port
Cocala
Musarna
Nearchus
Route of Nearchus
PERSIAN GULF
Gerrhaei
Tylus I.
Syrastrene
Malli
Alexandria Opiana
Alexandria Sogdiorum
Indus R.

EPIRUS
THESSALY
AEGEAN SEA
DOLOPIA
PHTHIOTIS
OETAEA
AETOLIA
LOCRIS
PHOCIS
BOEOTIA
EUBOEA
Leucas
Cephallenia
Zacynthus
ACHAIA
Gulf of Corinth
Sicyon
Corinth
Megara
ATTICA
Athens
Thebes
ELIS
ARCADIA
ARGOLIS
Argos
MESSENIA
Sparta
LACONIA
Cythera
The Aetolian and Achaian Leagues
Scale 1: 7 500 000
Miles
Aetolians
Achaeans

Getae
Danube R.
MACEDONIA
Pella
THRACE
Lysimachia
Byzantium
Nicomedia
BLACK SEA
Panticapaeum
Sinope
PONTUS
Heraclea
BITHYNIA
Trapezus
Pergamum
Galatians
CAPPADOCIA
CAUCASUS MTS.
ARMENIA
ACHAIAN LEAGUE
Athens
Sparta
Sardis
Ephesus
Caria
Rhodes
Crete
AEGEAN SEA
MEDITERRANEAN SEA
KINGDOM OF THE SELEUCIDS
Cilicia
Seleucia
Antioch
Cyprus
Syria
Phoenicia
Tyre
Damascus
Hierosolyma (Jerusalem)
Gaza
Mesopotamia
Nisibis
Euphrates R.
Tigris R.
Seleucia
Ctesiphon
Babylon
Babylonia
Susiana
MEDIA ATROPATENE
Ecbatana
Media Magna
Persepolis
Persis
Carmania
Harmozia
Gedrosia
Pura
Dahae
Parthia
Hecatompylus
KINGDOM OF THE ARSACIDS
Sea of Aral
Jaxartes R.
Oxus R.
Chorasmii
Alexandria eschata
Maracanda
Sogdiana
Sacae
KINGDOM OF THE BACTRIANS
Bactra
Bactria
Antiochia Margiana
Alexandria Ariorum
Aria
Phra
Drangiana
Alexandria Arachosiorum
Arachosia
Taxila
Sangala
Alexandria Opiana
Indus R.
Minnagara
INDIA
ARABIAN SEA
PERSIAN GULF
Alexandria
KINGDOM OF THE PTOLEMIES
EGYPT
Memphis
Pelusium
Petra
Nabataei
Nile R.
Thebes (Diospolis)
RED SEA
Cyrenaica
Cale 1: 36 000 000
Miles
KINGDOMS OF THE DIADOCHI (SUCCESSORS) at the beginning of the struggle with Rome (about 200 B.C.)
Territory recovered for the Seleucid dominions by Antiochus III (223-187 B.C.)
Areas left uncolored: ① that of the Galatians, because they constituted a foreign element in the kingdoms of the Diadochi; ② that of the free states of Greece, because the scale of the map is too small to show their political outlines. As in the previous map the names of political divisions are distinguished from those of other sections of country thus: Syria, Mesopotamia. Armenia and Media Atropatene were semi-independent states.

Reference Map of Asia Minor under the Greeks and Romans.

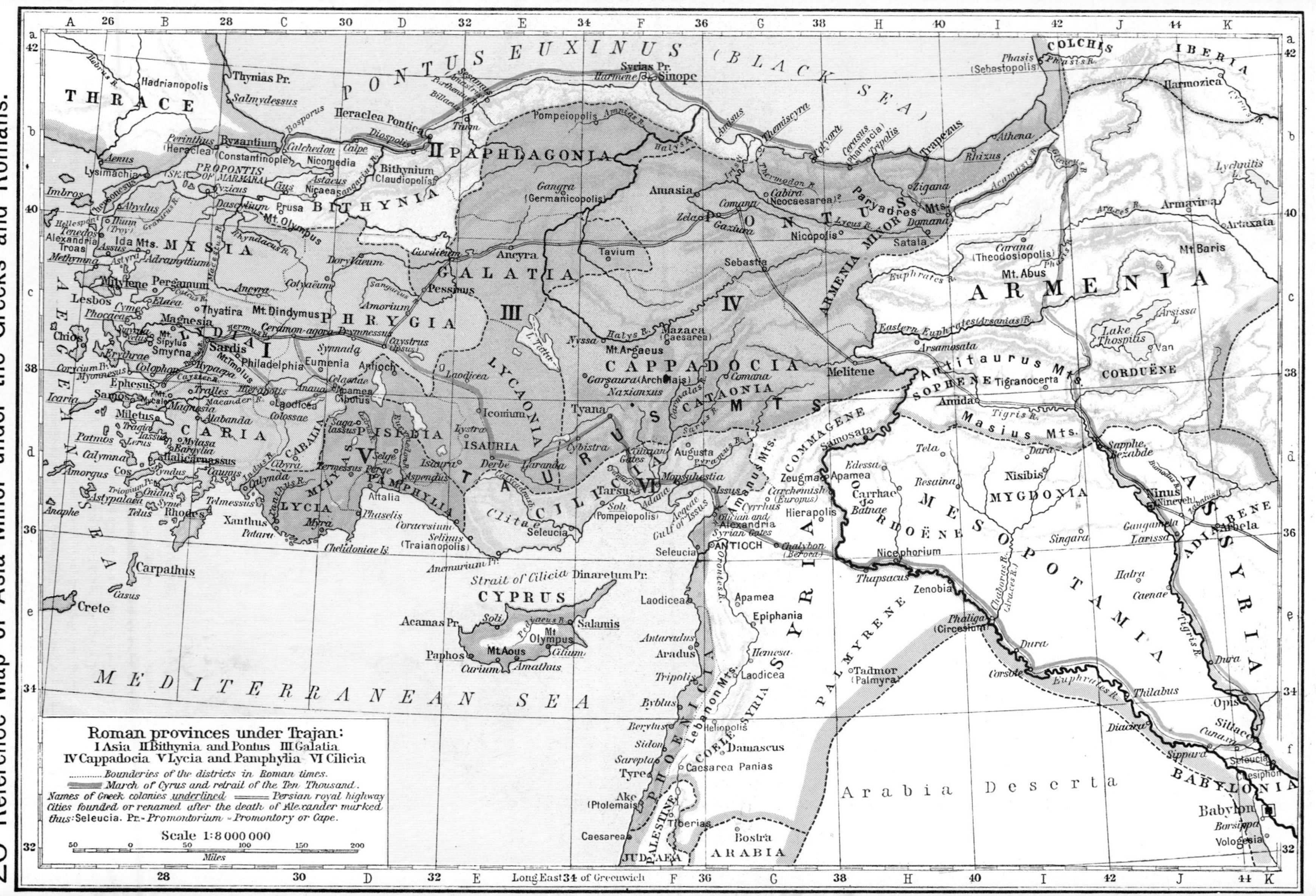

Plans o

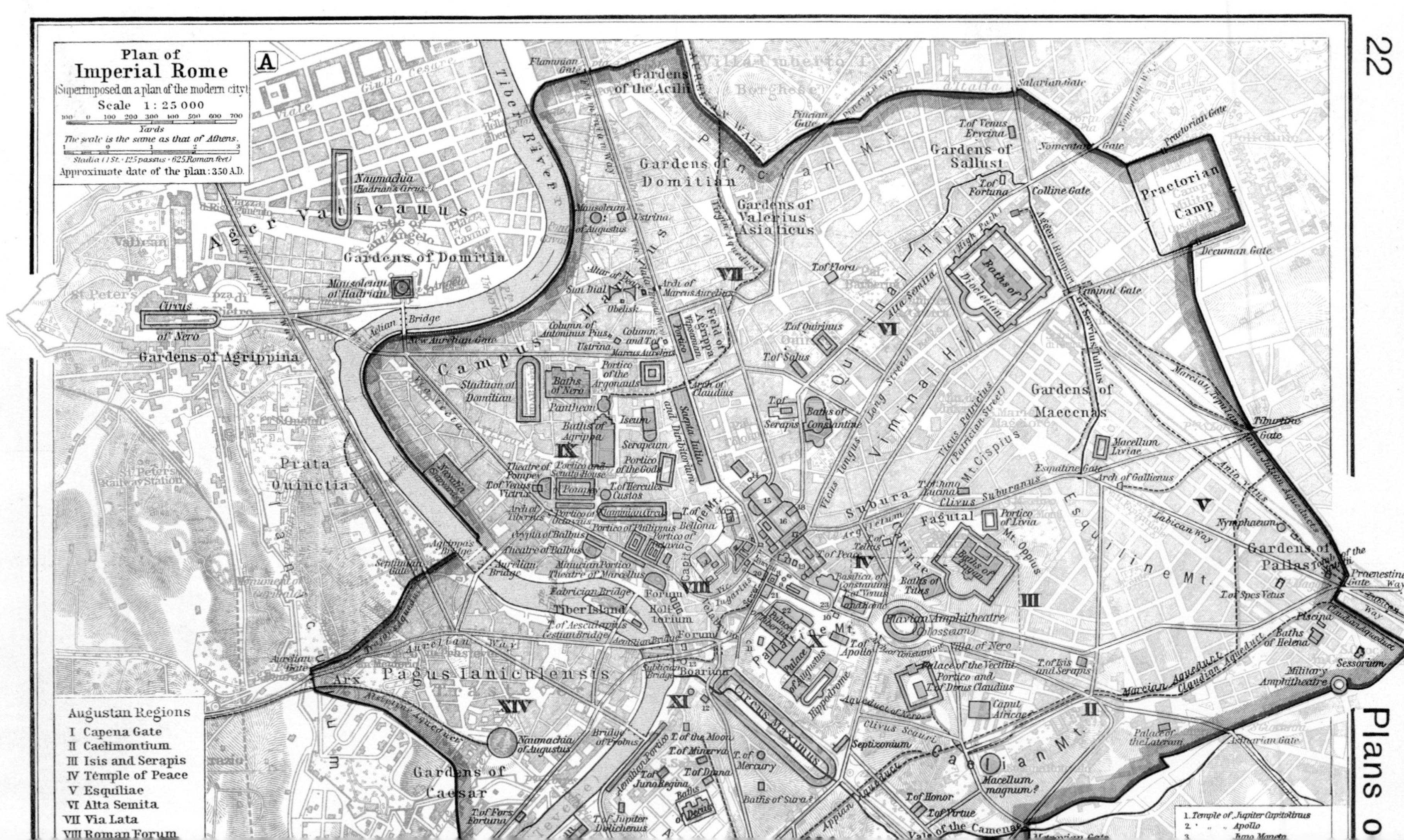
A
Plan of
Imperial Rome
(Superimposed on a plan of the modern city)
Scale 1 : 25 000
Yards
The scale is the same as that of Athens.
Approximate date of the plan: 350 A.D.
Augustan Regions
I Capena Gate
II Caelimontium
III Isis and Serapis
IV Temple of Peace
V Esquiliae
VI Alta Semita
VII Via Lata
VIII Roman Forum
1. Temple of Jupiter Capitolinus
Praetorian Camp
Baths of Diocletian
Field of Agrippa
Circus Maximus
Flavian Amphitheatre (Colosseum)
Tiber River
Campus Martius
Gardens of Sallust
Gardens of Maecenas
Gardens of Domitia
Gardens of Agrippina
Gardens of Caesar
Gardens of Domitian
Gardens of the Acilii
Gardens of Valerius Asiaticus
Gardens of Pallas
Circus of Nero
Mausoleum of Hadrian
Mausoleum of Augustus
Pantheon
Baths of Nero
Baths of Trajan
Tiber Island
Pagus Ianiculensis
Ager Vaticanus
Prata Quinctia
Viminal Hill
Quirinal Hill
Esquiline Mt.
Caelian Mt.
Palatine Mt.

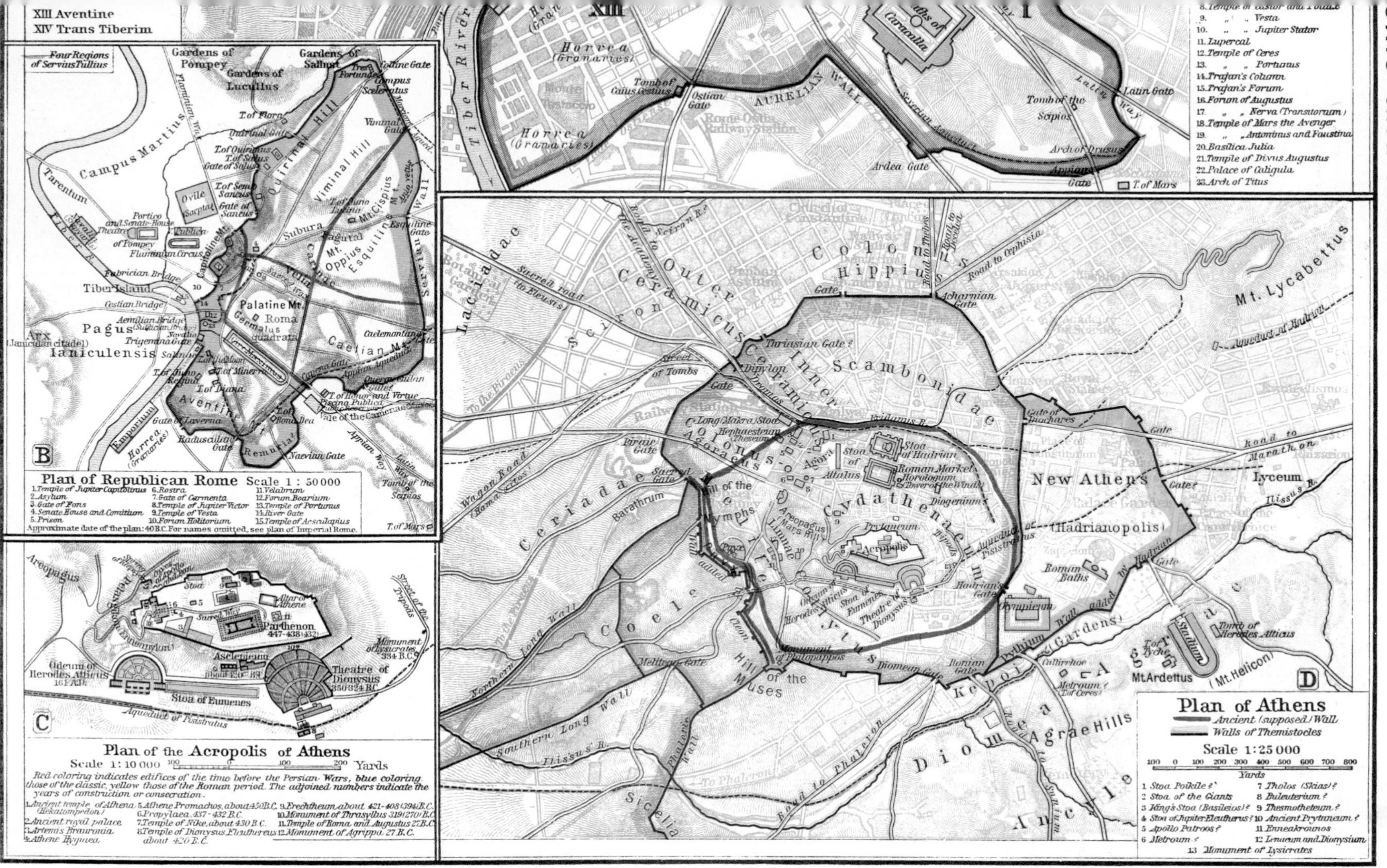
XIII Aventine
XIV Trans Tiberim
9. " " Vesta
10. " " Jupiter Stator
11. Lupercal
12. Temple of Ceres
13. " " Portunus
14. Trajan's Column
15. Trajan's Forum
16. Forum of Augustus
17. " " Nerva (Transitorium)
18. Temple of Mars the Avenger
19. " " Antoninus and Faustina
20. Basilica Julia
21. Temple of Divus Augustus
22. Palace of Caligula
23. Arch of Titus
Horrea (Granaries)
Tomb of Caius Cestius
Ostian Gate
AURELIAN WALL
Rome-Ostia Railway Station
Tomb of the Scipios
Latin Gate
Arch of Drusus
Ardea Gate
T. of Mars
Four Regions of Servius Tullius
Gardens of Pompey
Gardens of Lucullus
Gardens of Sallust
Campus Martius
Tarentum
Viminal Hill
Palatine Mt.
Roma Quadrata
Caelian Mt.
Aventine
Pagus Ianiculensis
Tiber Island
Emporium
Plan of Republican Rome Scale 1 : 50000
1. Temple of Jupiter Capitolinus
2. Asylum
3. Gate of Fons
4. Senate House and Comitium
5. Prison
6. Rostra
7. Gate of Carmenta
8. Temple of Jupiter Victor
9. Temple of Vesta
10. Forum Holitorium
11. Velabrum
12. Forum Boarium
13. Temple of Portunus
14. River Gate
15. Temple of Aesculapius
Approximate date of the plan: 40 B.C. For names omitted, see plan of Imperial Rome.
Areopagus
Parthenon 447-438 (432)
Odeum of Herodes Atticus 161 A.D.
Asclepieum
Theatre of Dionysus 350-324 B.C.
Stoa of Eumenes
Aqueduct of Pisistratus
Monument of Lysicrates 334 B.C.
Street of the Tripods
Plan of the Acropolis of Athens
Scale 1:10 000 Yards
Red coloring indicates edifices of the time before the Persian Wars, blue coloring those of the classic, yellow those of the Roman period. The adjoined numbers indicate the years of construction or consecration.
1. Ancient temple of Athena (Hekatompedon)
2. Ancient royal palace
3. Artemis Brauronia
4. Athene Hygiaea
5. Athene Promachos, about 450 B.C.
6. Propylaea 437-432 B.C.
7. Temple of Nike, about 430 B.C.
8. Temple of Dionysus Eleuthereus about 420 B.C.
9. Erechtheum about 421-408 (394) B.C.
10. Monument of Thrasyllus 319 (270) B.C.
11. Temple of Roma and Augustus 27 B.C.
12. Monument of Agrippa 27 B.C.
Laciadae
Outer Ceramicus
Colonus Hippius
Scambonidae
Inner Ceramicus
Cydathenaeum
Ceriadae
Coele
Collytus
Acropolis
Hill of the Muses
Mt. Lycabettus
New Athens (Hadrianopolis)
Lyceum
Stadium
Mt. Ardettus
Diomea
Agrae Hills
Plan of Athens
Ancient (supposed) Wall
Walls of Themistocles
Scale 1:25 000
Yards
1 Stoa Poikile?
2 Stoa of the Giants
3 King's Stoa (Basileios)?
4 Stoa of Jupiter Eleutherus?
5 Apollo Patroos?
6 Metroum?
7 Tholos (Skias)?
8 Buleuterium?
9 Thesmotheteum?
10 Ancient Prytaneum?
11 Enneakrunos
12 Lenaeum and Dionysium
13 Monument of Lysicrates

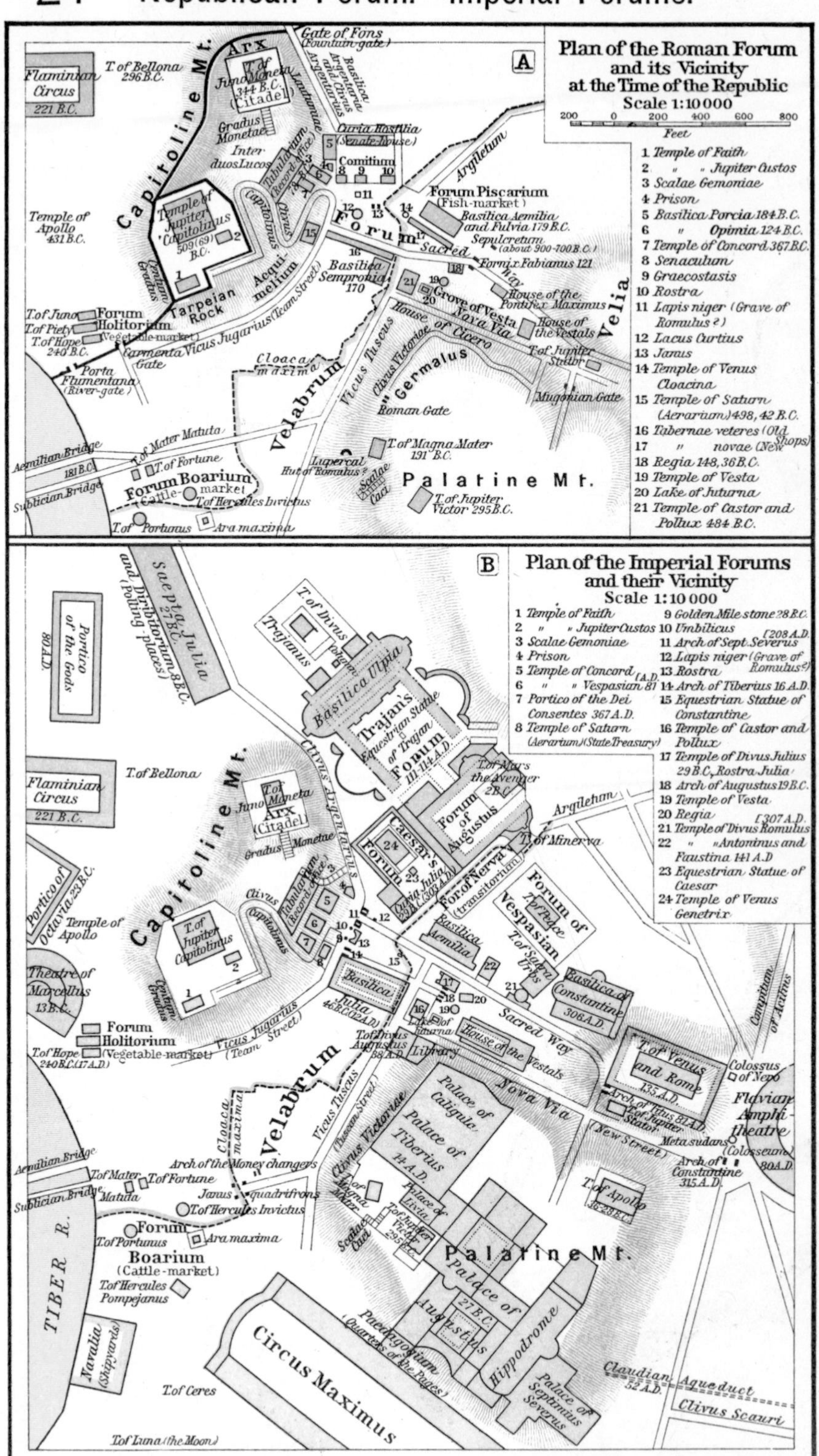

The dates given are those of the construction or consecration of the buildings.

Helvetii
RAETIA
TRANSPADANE GAUL
PENNINE ALPS
GRAIAN ALPS
COTTIAN ALPS
MARITIME ALPS
LIGURIA
CISPADANE
GULF OF GENOA
CORSICA
TYRRHEN
Augusta Taurinorum
(Taurasia)
Mediolanium
(Milan)
Cremona
Placentia
Genua
(Genoa)
Luna
Pisae
Alalia
(Aleria)
Ilva (Aethalia)
Scale 1:2 500 000
Miles
Greek colonies
Phoenician colonies
Roman colonies before the civil wars (See also p. 29)
Of the two northern boundaries of Italy and of Etruria, the more southerly is that of the period before Augustus, and the more northerly that of the period after Augustus.
Modern names of passes thus [Julier]
Pr.-Promontorium - Cape or promontory
Long. East 10 of Greenwich

NORICUM
CARNIC ALPS
TRIDENTINE ALPS
JULIAN VENETIAN
Mt. Caruanca
Carni
VENETIA
Veneti
PANNONIA
Latovici
ALPS DALMATIA
Iapydes
ISTRIA
Liburni
ILLYRICUM
GULF OF TERGESTE
GULF OF FLANONA
ADRIATIC SEA
GAUL
Lingones
MOUNTAINS
Ager Gallicus
Senones
UMBRIA
PICENUM
Praetutti
Mt. Fiscellus
Vestini
Frentani
Marrucini
Paeligni
Marsi
Aequi
Hernici
Caraceni
Sabini
ETRURIA
SEA
Aguontum
Teurnia
Sebatum
Littamum
[Kreuzberg]
[Plöken]
Loncium
Santicum
Virunum
Iuenna
Colatio
Celeia
Atrans
Emona
Nauportus
Longaticum
Acervo
Neviodunum
Praetorium Latovicorum
Metulum
Sublavio
Pons Drusi
Bauzanum
Endidae
Tridentum
Ausugum
Feltria
Bellunum
Laebactes
Iulium Carnicum
Larix
Osopus
Forum Iulii
Aquileia
Mt. Ocra [Alpis Iulia]
Tergeste
Concordia
Opitergium
Ceneta
Acelum
Tarvisium
Altinum
Vicetia
Patavium
Aponus
Ateste
Verona
Portus Aedro
Brundulum
Atria
Hostilia
Anneianum
Piranum
Agida
Neapolis
Parentium
Ruginium
Pullaria
Pola (Col. Pietas Iulia)
Polaticum Pr.
Nesactium
Piquentum
Tarsatica
Flanona
Alvona
Fulfinium
Curicum
Crexi
Apsorus
Arba
Ortopla
Vegia
Senia
Avendo
Arupium
Aenona
Iader
Asseria
Lissa
Mentorides Is.
Portunata
Celadussae Is.
Ad Padum
Spina
Spineticum Ostium
Forum Gallorum
Bonomia (Felsina)
Claterna
Forum Cornelii
Faventia
Ravenna
Classes
Padusa R.
Rubicon R.
Forum Livii
Forum Popili
Caesena
Ariminum
Sarsina
Mevaniola
[La Futa]
Faesulae
Florentia
Pisaurum
Forum Fortunae (Iulia Fanestris)
Sena Gallica
Ancona
Cumerum Pr.
Numana
Potentia
Auximum
Pitinum Pisaurense
Sestinum
Urbinum
Forum Sempronii
[Furlo P.]
Pitinum Mergens
Cales
Sentinum
Tifernum Tiberinum
Iguvium
[Scheggia P.]
Attidium
Helvillum
Arretium
Cortona
L. Trasimenus
Perusia
Asisium
Clusium
Hispellum
Fulginiae
Trebiae
Nursia
Mt. Tetrica
Asculum
Interamnia
Hadria
Castrum novum
Truentinum
Firmum
Cupra Maritima
Castellum Firmanum
Spoletium
Carsulae
Interamna
Tuder
Volsinii vet. novi
L. Volsiniensis
Ameria
Narnia
Ocriculum
Reate
Amiternum
Aufinum
Teate
Ortona
Aternum
Pinna
Corfinium
Alba Fucens
Lake Fucinus
Marruvium
Sulmo
Iuvanum
Histonium
Buca
Bovianum vetus
Terventum
Aufidena
Cosa
Saturnia
Tarquinii
Graviscae
Centumcellae
Castrum novum
Caere
Pyrgi
Veii
Falerii
Mt. Soracte
Nepete
Sutrium
Blera
Tibur
Praeneste
Tusculum
ROME
Ostia
Portus Augusti

The Growth of Roman Power in Italy to 218 B.C.

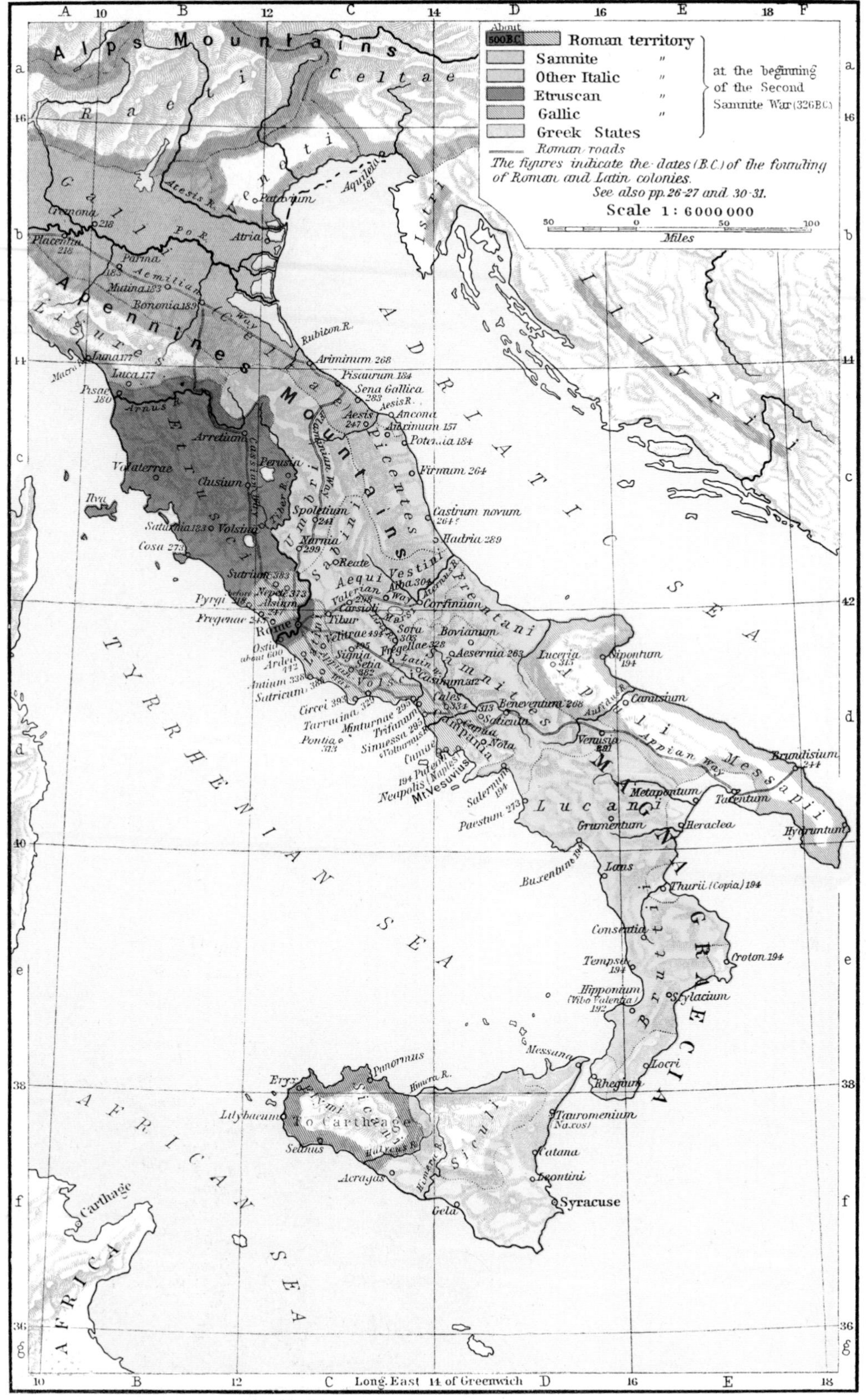

TYRRHENIAN SEA
SICILY
CAMPANIA
ROME
Ostia
Tusculum
Praeneste
Antium
Circei
Tarracina
Pontiae Is.
Pithecussae Is.
Aenaria
Capreae
BAY OF NAPLES
BAY OF PAESTUM
Paestum
Neapolis
Capua
Beneventum
Liparaeae (Aeoliae or Vulcaniae) Is.
Ustica
Aegates (Aegusae) Is.
Lilybaeum
Panormus (Palermo)
Agrigentum
Syracuse
Messana
Mt. Etna
NEBRODES MTS.
HERAEAN MOUNTAINS
Longitude East 13 of Greenwich

ADRIATIC SEA
GULF OF TARENTUM
GULF OF SCYLACIUM
IONIAN SEA
MAGNA GRAECIA
APULIA
CALABRIA
BRUTTIUM
ILLYRICUM
Barium
Brundisium
Tarentum (Taras)
Metapontum
Heraclea
Sybaris
Thurii (Col. Copia)
Croton
Petelia
Scolacium (Scylacium)
Caulonia
Locri Epizephyrii
Hydruntum
Callipolis
Dyrrhachium (Epidamnus)
Apollonia
Vicinity of Naples
Phlegraean Fields
Mt. Gaurus
Cyme Cumae
Naples
Palaeopolis
Astroni
Forum Vulcani (Solfatara)
Dicaearchia, Puteoli
Baiae
Nesis
Pausilypum
Harbor of Misenum
Prom. of Misenum
Scale 1:300000
Miles
Present area of Naples
Modern names in hair line
Plan of Syracuse
At the time of the Peloponnesian War (431-404 B.C.)
Extension under Dionysius I (405-367 B.C.)
Trogilus Port
TYCHA
ACHRADINA
Labdalum
Euryalus EPIPOLAE
NEAPOLIS
Temenites
Little Harbor
ORTYGIA (NASOS)
Lysimelia Marsh
Great Harbor
Olympieum
POLICHNE
Dascon
PLEMMYRIUM
Scale 1:200000
1 Arethusa Spring
2 Temple of Athene
3 " " Artemis
4 Citadel of Dionysius
5 Pentapylum
6 Forum
7 Stone quarries (Latomiae)
8 Roman amphitheatre
9 Greek theatre
10 Heracleum
11 Hexapylum
12 Temple of Demeter and Persephone
Neapolis Allies of Athens
Syracuse " " Sparta
Croton Neutral States
during the Peloponnesian War (431-404 B.C.)
For scale and explanation, see p. 26-27.

Rome and Carthage at the Beginning of the Second Punic War, 218 B. C.

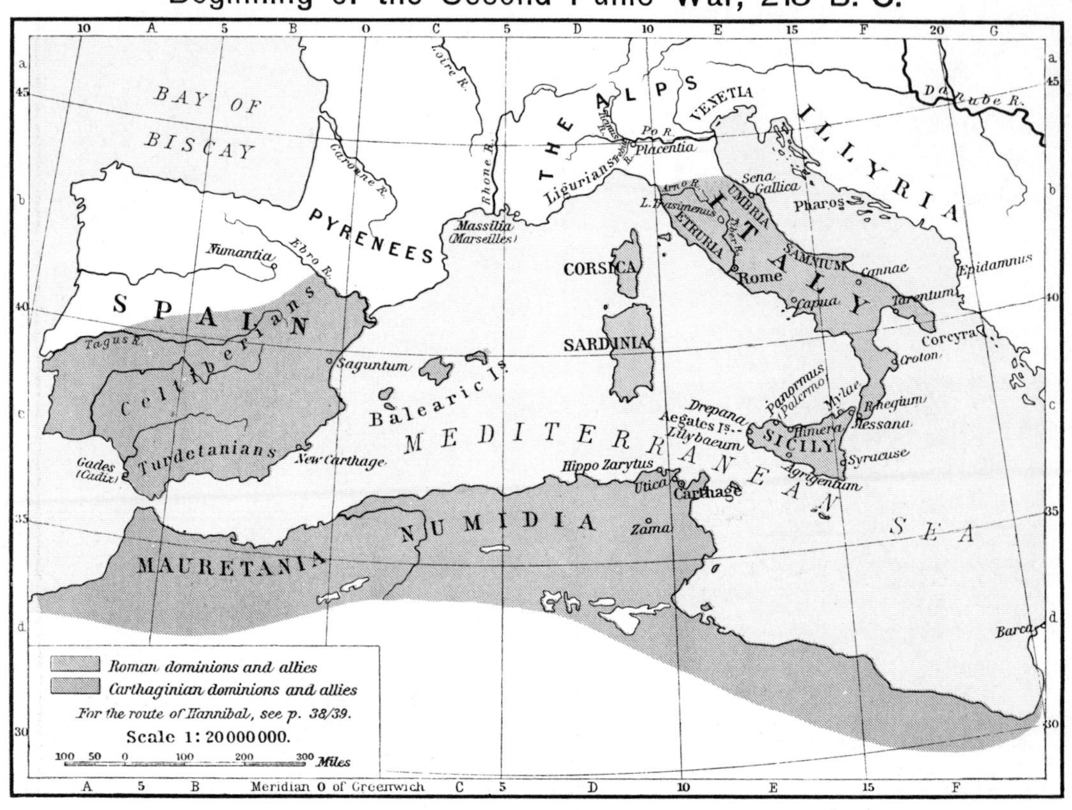

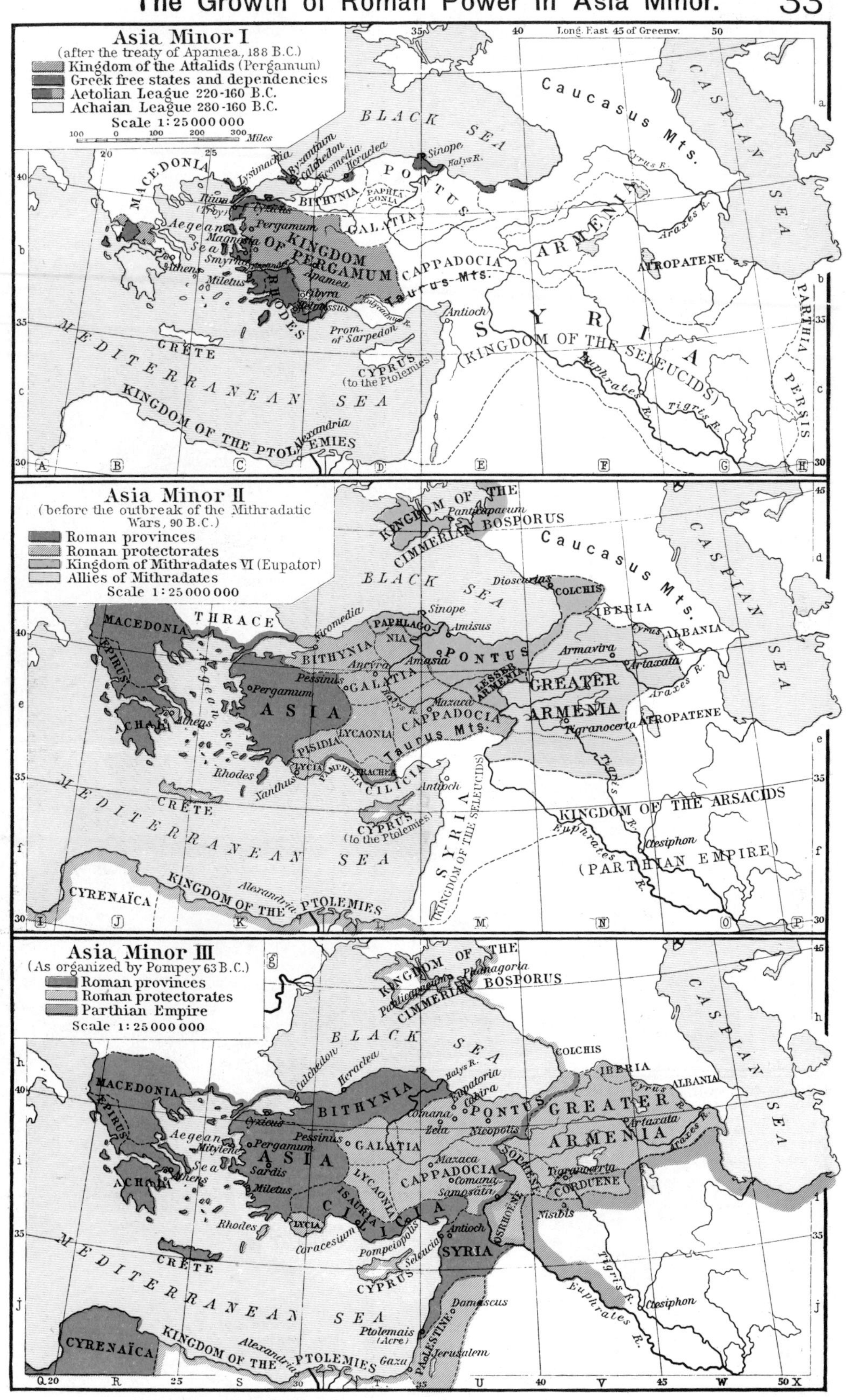
Asia Minor I
(after the treaty of Apamea, 188 B.C.)
Kingdom of the Attalids (Pergamum)
Greek free states and dependencies
Aetolian League 220-160 B.C.
Achaian League 280-160 B.C.
Scale 1:25 000 000
BLACK SEA
Caucasus Mts.
CASPIAN SEA
MACEDONIA
BITHYNIA
PONTUS
GALATIA
KINGDOM OF PERGAMUM
CAPPADOCIA
ARMENIA
ATROPATENE
Taurus Mts.
RHODES
SYRIA (KINGDOM OF THE SELEUCIDS)
PARTHIA
PERSIS
CRETE
CYPRUS (to the Ptolemies)
MEDITERRANEAN SEA
KINGDOM OF THE PTOLEMIES
Asia Minor II
(before the outbreak of the Mithradatic Wars, 90 B.C.)
Roman provinces
Roman protectorates
Kingdom of Mithradates VI (Eupator)
Allies of Mithradates
Scale 1:25 000 000
KINGDOM OF THE CIMMERIAN BOSPORUS
COLCHIS
IBERIA
ALBANIA
THRACE
MACEDONIA
EPIRUS
ACHAIA
ASIA
BITHYNIA
PAPHLAGONIA
PONTUS
GALATIA
CAPPADOCIA
LESSER ARMENIA
GREATER ARMENIA
LYCAONIA
PISIDIA
LYCIA
PAMPHYLIA
TRACHEA
CILICIA
SYRIA (KINGDOM OF THE SELEUCIDS)
KINGDOM OF THE ARSACIDS (PARTHIAN EMPIRE)
CYRENAÏCA
KINGDOM OF THE PTOLEMIES
Asia Minor III
(As organized by Pompey 63 B.C.)
Roman provinces
Roman protectorates
Parthian Empire
Scale 1:25 000 000
KINGDOM OF THE CIMMERIAN BOSPORUS
COLCHIS
IBERIA
ALBANIA
MACEDONIA
EPIRUS
ACHAIA
ASIA
BITHYNIA
PONTUS
GALATIA
GREATER ARMENIA
CAPPADOCIA
SOPHENE
CORDUENE
OSRHOENE
LYCAONIA
ISAURIA
LYCIA
CILICIA
SYRIA
PALESTINE
CYPRUS
CRETE
CYRENAÏCA
MEDITERRANEAN SEA
KINGDOM OF THE PTOLEMIES

Plan of Carthage
Scale 1:300 000
Miles
1. Trade harbor
2. War harbor (Cothon)
3. Forum
4. Byrsa (Citadel)
5. Temple of Esmun
6 (Aesculapius)
6. Amphitheatre
7. Circus
8. Theatre.
Megara
Magalia
i.e. New city
Old city
Scipio's camp
Scipio's mole
STAGNUM TUNETICUM
(BAY OF TUNIS)
Taenia
Meridian 0 of Greenw.
Sitones
Mt. Saevo
Thule I.?
Ebudae Is. (Hebrides)
Orcades Is. (Orkneys)
Suiones
SCATINAVIA (SCANDINAVIA)
Goths
CALEDONIA (SCOTLAND)
Wall of Antoninus or Severus
80 A.D.
HIBERNIA (IRELAND)
Eblana
Hadrian's Wall
NORTH SEA
CIMBRIC CHERSONESE (DENMARK)
Brigantes
Eburacum (York)
Deva
Viroconium
Lindum
BRITAIN
Isca
Londinium (London)
Cassiterides Is.?
ENGLISH CHANNEL
Friesians
Chauci
Batavians
Lombards
Cherusci
Semnones
Viruni
Burgund
Sugambri
Colonia Agrippina
Chatti
GERMANIA
GERMANIA INFERIOR
Augusta Treverorum
Rotomagus
BELGICA
Lutetia
Durocortorum
Argentoratum
LUGUDUNENSIS
Liger (Loire) R.
Hermunduri
Marcomanni
Regina Castra
Quadi
Vindobona
Augusta Vindelicorum
Lauriacum
VINDELICIA
RAETIA
NORICUM
Avaricum
Augustodunum
Vesontio
GAUL
AQUITANIA (AQUITAINE)
Lugdunum
Burdigala
BAY OF BISCAY
Aventicum
Curia
Virunum
Mediolanum (Milan)
CISALPINE
GAUL
Aquileia
Emona
Cremona
Placentia
Genua (Genoa)
Vienna
Tolosa
NARBONENSIS
Nemausus
Arelate
Narbo
Massilia (Marseilles)
Cantabri
Astures
GALLAECIA
Bracara
TARRACONENSIS
Numantia
Ebro R.
Salmantica
Celtiberians
Ilerda
Caesaraugusta
SPAIN
LUSITANIA
Durius (Duero) R.
Olisipo
Tagus R.
Emerita Augusta
Toletum
Anas R.
Tarraco
Dertosa
Saguntum
Valentia
IBERIAN SEA
Corduba
Hispalis
Munda
FARTHER BAETICA
Gades (Cadiz)
New Carthage
Malaca
Pityusae
BALEARIC IS.
CORSICA
Aleria
SARDINIA
Caralis
Rome
ITALY
Pisae
Ariminum
Ancona
Corfinium
Capua
Neapolis (Naples)
Canusium
Tarentum
Croton
Messana
Tauromenium
Syracuse
SICILY
Lilybaeum
Agrigentum
Cossyra
ADRIATIC
TYRRHENIAN SEA
Salonae
Pharus
MEDITERRANEAN SEA
Tingis
Lixus
Rusaddir
Iol, Caesarea
Icosium
Saldae
MAURETANIA TINGITANA
MAURETANIA CAESARIENSIS
42 A.D.
Hippo Regius
Cirta
NUMIDIA
Zama
Utica
Carthage
Hadrumetum
Ruspina
Thapsus
Thenae
Theveste
Thelepte
Capsa
Lopadusa
Melita
SYRTIS MINOR
Meninx
Sabrata
Oea
TRIPOLIS
Leptis major
PROCONSULAR AFRICA
42 A.D.
GAETULIA
SYRTIS M.
Garamantes
IONIA
SICILI
ATLANTIC OCEAN
Plan of Alexandria
according to Puchstein
Scale 1:100 000
Mile
Myrmex
Pharos (lighthouse)
GREAT HARBOR
Lochias
Regia
Jewish Quarter
Gate of the Sun (Canopic Gate)
Pharos I.
Heptastadium
Museum
PORTUS EUNOSTUS (OLD PORT)
Posidium
Theatre
Bruchium
Dromos
Gate of the Moon
Rhakotis
LAKE MAREOTIS
1. Palace harbor
2. Antirrhodus I.
3. Timonium
4. Harbor of Cibotus
5. Ancient } mouth of the
6. Present } Nile canal
7. Serapeum and Pompey's Pillar
8. Temple of Neptune
9. Nile canal
Present shore.
Abbreviations:
P.A. Pennine Alps
M.A. Maritime Alps
K.C. Kingdom of Cottius
Scale 1:20 000 000
Miles
Long

Vicinity of Rome
Scale 1:1000000
Miles
Main roads and branch roads
Aqueducts. (A)
1. Milvian Bridge
2. Virgin Aqueduct
3. Appian Aqueduct
4. Ferentinian Grove
5. T. of Jupiter Latiaris
6. Trajan's Aqueduct
7. Hadrian's Villa.
ROME
Veii
Caere
Alsium
Fregenae
Port of Augustus
Port of Claudius
Port of Trajan
Ostia
Vicus Augustanus
Laurentum
Lavinium
Ardea
Ager Romanus
Ager Solonius
Lanuvium
Aricia
Alba Longa
Tusculum
Praeneste
Tibur
Gabii
Fidenae
Crustumerium
Nomentum
Eretum
Cures
Feronia
Capena
Sabate Lake Sabatinus
Carsioli
Anagnia
Signia
Cora
Norba
Velitrae
Artena
Tellenae
Bovillae
Corioli
Sassula
Aefula
Pedum
Labicum
Mt. Algidus
Mt. Albanus
Flaminian Way
Salarian Way
Tiburtine Way
Valerian Way
Latin Way
Appian Way
Ostian Way
Aurelian Way
Portus Way
Praenestine Way
Fenni
SARMATIA
Budini
Huns
Vonedae
Bastarnae
Navari
Roxolani
Alazones
Alans
Aorsi
Utii
Borysthenes (Dnieper) R.
Tanaïs (Don) R.
Rha (Volga) R.
Tyras R.
Olbia
Tyra
Tanaïs
Lake Maeotis (Sea of Azov)
Panticapaeum
Phanagoria
Maeotae
Siracae
Sindi
Heniochi
Zichi
Abasgi
Legae
Caucasus Mts.
Tauric Chersonese (Crimea)
Theodosia
Heraclea
KINGDOM OF THE CIMMERIAN BOSPORUS
BLACK SEA
CASPIAN SEA
DACIA
107-275 A.D.
Potaïssa
Getae
Troesmis
Tomis
LOWER MOESIA
Ister (Danube) R.
Naïssus
Sardica
THRACE
Apollonia
Adrianopolis
Philippopolis
Byzantium (Constantinople)
Nicomedia
Chalcedon
BITHYNIA
PAPHLAGONIA
Sinope
Amasia
PONTUS
Gangra
Ancyra
GALATIA
Trapezus
Dioscurias
Phasis (Sebastopolis)
COLCHIS
IBERIA
ALBANIA
Albana
Moschi
SACASENE
Lychnitis L.
Armavira
Artaxata
Araxes R.
ARMENIA
115-117 A.D.
Matianus L.
MEDIA ATROPATENE
Gazaca
Thospitis L.
CORDUENE
SOPHENE
Amida
Tigranocerta
ADIABENE
Ninus (Nineveh)
Arbela
ASSYRIA
115-117 A.D.
Ecbatana
Nisibis
115-363 A.D.
Hatra
Edessa
OSRHOENE
Carrhae
MESOPOTAMIA
Nicephorium
Artemita
EMPIRE OF THE PARTHIANS
Ctesiphon
Seleucia
Tigris R.
Babylon
BABYLONIA
115-117 A.D.
Euphrates R.
Susa
Agaraei
MYSIA
Pergamum
ASIA
133
PHRYGIA
Sardis
LYDIA
Miletus
CARIA
PISIDIA
Iconium
LYCAONIA
PAMPHYLIA
LYCIA
43 A.D.
Rhodes
CAPPADOCIA
17 A.D.
Caesarea
Melitene
COMMAGENE
CILICIA
Anthemusias
Antioch
Apamea
COELE-SYRIA
Emesa
Palmyra
275 A.D.
SYRIA
Salamis
CYPRUS
58
PHOENICIA
Damascus
Tyre
Bostra
106 A.D.
Caesarea
Hierosolyma (Aelia Capitolina) (Jerusalem)
PALESTINE
Gaza
Pelusium
Petra
ARABIA
Nabataei
Aelana
68 A.D.
Alexandria
Saïs
Sebennytus
Arsinoe
Memphis
EGYPT
30
Nile R.
Hermopolis
RED SEA
Ammonium
MARMARICA
20
CYRENAICA
75
Cyrene
Apollonia
CRETE
67
Carpathus
ACHAIA
146
Athens
Sparta
AEGEAN SEA
Lemnos
Pharsalus
Pydna
MACEDONIA
Philippi
Thessalonica
THESSALY
Apulum
Sarmizegetusa
Roman territory at the beginning of the 1st. Punic War (264 B.C.)
Acquired as a result of the 1st. Punic War (238 B.C.)
Acquired up to the end of the 2nd. Punic War (201 B.C.)
" up to 133 B.C.
" up to the death of Caesar (44 B.C.)
" " " " " " Augustus (14 A.D.)
" " " " " " Marcus Aurelius (180 A.D.)
Boundaries of the Roman provinces before the time of Diocletian
Imperial
Senatorial
Provinces
Colored border indicates countries semi-independent. Unless accompanied by the letters A.D., the figures given are those of the date of acquisition B.C. The shifting of imperial and senatorial provinces from one control to the other is not indicated, except by an occasional double underlining, thus CYPRUS
...d capitals of the four divisions under Diocletian, 284-305 A.D.
Greenwich
25
30
35
40

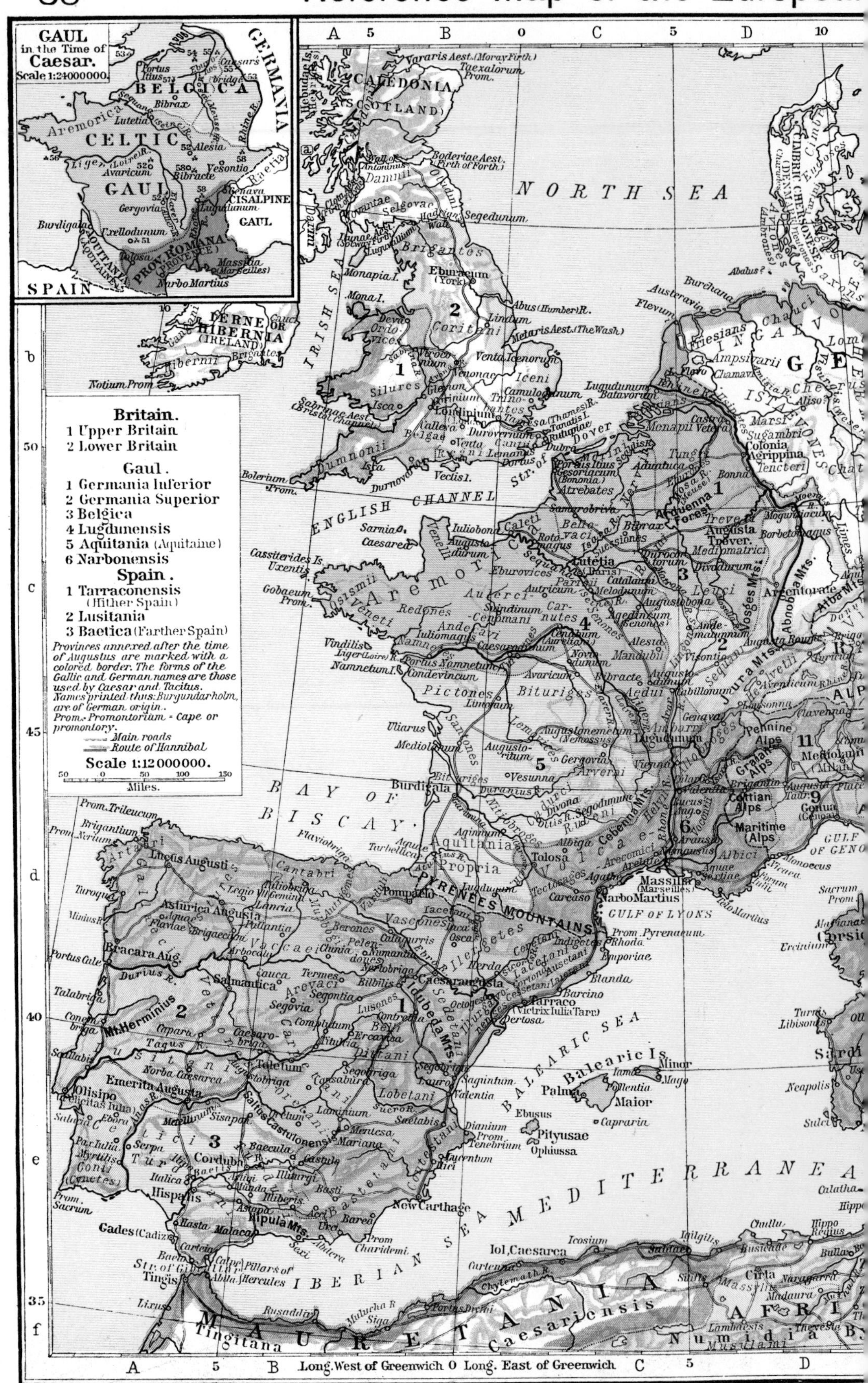
GAUL
in the Time of
Caesar.
Scale 1:24000000.
GERMANIA
BELGICA
CELTIC
GAUL
Aremorica
AQUITANIA
PROV. ROMANA
(PROVENCE)
CISALPINE
GAUL
SPAIN
Lutetia
Bibrax
Alesia
Vesontio
Avaricum
Bibracte
Gergovia
Lugdunum
Genava
Burdigala
Tolosa
Massilia (Marseilles)
Narbo Martius
Rhine R.
Britain.
1 Upper Britain
2 Lower Britain
Gaul.
1 Germania Inferior
2 Germania Superior
3 Belgica
4 Lugdunensis
5 Aquitania (Aquitaine)
6 Narbonensis
Spain.
1 Tarraconensis
(Hither Spain)
2 Lusitania
3 Baetica (Farther Spain)
Provinces annexed after the time of Augustus are marked with a colored border. The forms of the Gallic and German names are those used by Caesar and Tacitus.
Names printed thus: Burgundarholm, are of German origin.
Prom. = Promontorium = Cape or promontory.
Main roads
Route of Hannibal
Scale 1:12000000.
Miles.
CALEDONIA
(SCOTLAND)
NORTH SEA
IRISH SEA
HIBERNIA
(IRELAND)
Eburacum (York)
Londinium
ENGLISH CHANNEL
Str. of Dover
BAY OF BISCAY
Aremorica
Lutetia (Paris)
Lugdunum
Aquitania
PYRENEES MOUNTAINS
GULF OF LYONS
Massilia (Marseilles)
Narbo Martius
BALEARIC SEA
Balearic Is.
Emerita Augusta
Toletum
Corduba
Hispalis
Gades (Cadiz)
New Carthage
Str. of Gibraltar
Pillars of Hercules
IBERIAN SEA
MEDITERRANEAN
MAURETANIA
Tingitana
Caesariensis
Numidia
Long. West of Greenwich 0 Long. East of Greenwich

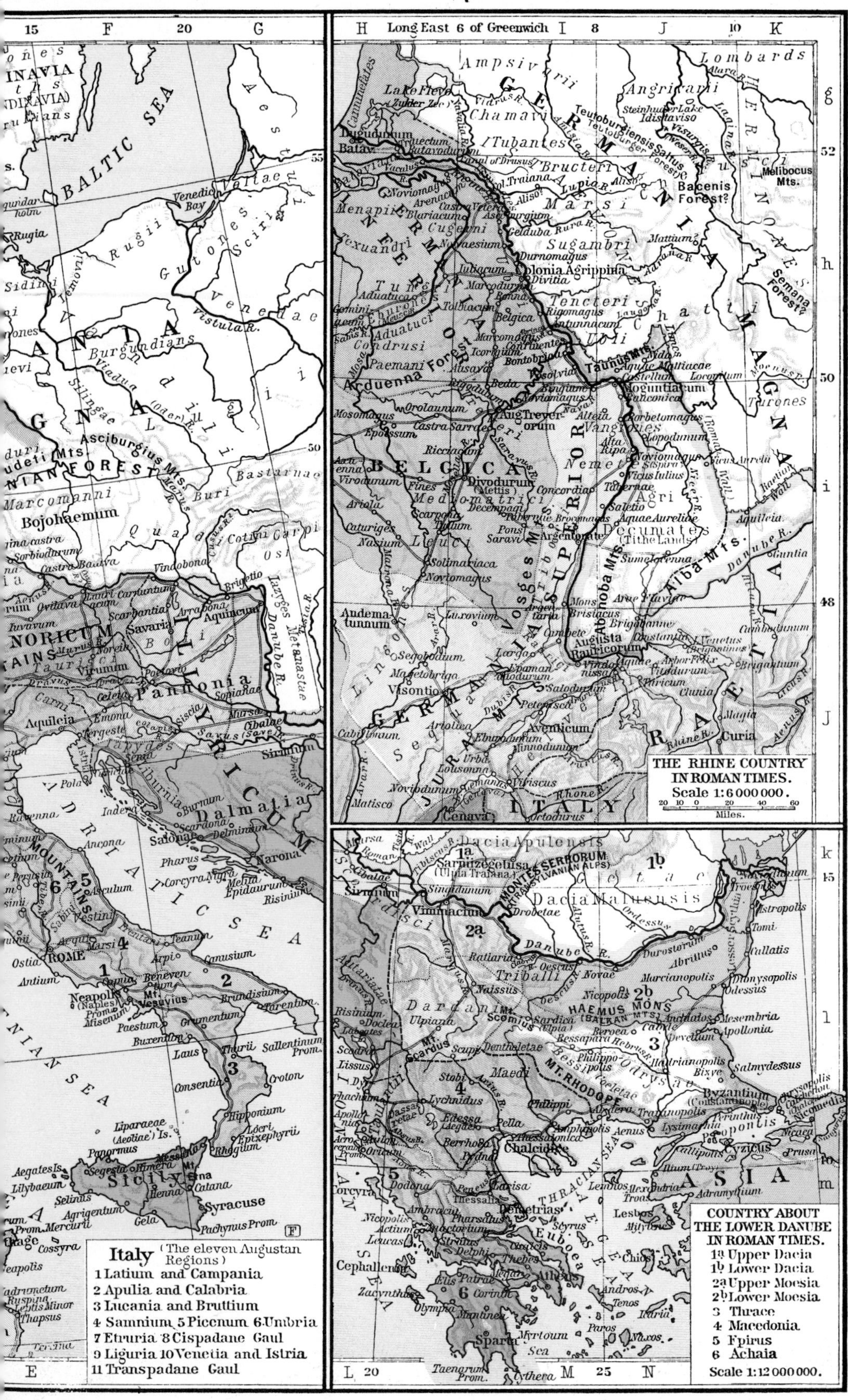
THE RHINE COUNTRY IN ROMAN TIMES.
Scale 1:6 000 000.
Miles.
Long East 6 of Greenwich
GERMANIA MAGNA
GERMANIA INFERIOR
GERMANIA SUPERIOR
BELGICA
RAETIA
ITALY
Colonia Agrippina
Mogontiacum
Augusta Treverorum
Divodurum
Argentorate
Augusta Rauricorum
Vosges Mts.
Jura Mts.
Taunus Mts.
Arduenna Forest
Teutoburgiensis Saltus
Agri Decumates (Tithe Lands)
COUNTRY ABOUT THE LOWER DANUBE IN ROMAN TIMES.
1a Upper Dacia
1b Lower Dacia
2a Upper Moesia
2b Lower Moesia
3 Thrace
4 Macedonia
5 Epirus
6 Achaia
Scale 1:12 000 000.
Dacia Apulensis
Dacia Malvensis
HAEMUS MONS (BALKAN MTS.)
MT. RHODOPE
Byzantium (Constantinople)
Thessalonica
Athens
Sparta
ASIA
Italy (The eleven Augustan Regions)
1 Latium and Campania
2 Apulia and Calabria
3 Lucania and Bruttium
4 Samnium 5 Picenum 6 Umbria
7 Etruria 8 Cispadane Gaul
9 Liguria 10 Venetia and Istria
11 Transpadane Gaul
BALTIC SEA
NORICUM
Pannonia
ILLYRICUM
Dalmatia
ROME
Neapolis (Naples)
Sicily
Syracuse
Bojohaemum
Marcomanni
Burgundians
Gutones
Vistula R.
Danube R.

ATLANTIC OCEAN
NORTH SEA
BAY OF BISCAY
ENGLISH CHANNEL
CAEDONIA
HIBERNIA
BRITAIN
D. OF GAUL
Wall of Hadrian
York
Lincoln
Caerleon upon Usk
St. Albans
Colchester
London
Frisians
Saxons
Franks
Thuringians
Burgundians
Lombards
Alamanni
Jutes
DENMARK
Angles
Tongres
Soissons
Rouen
Reims
Cologne
Trèves
Paris
Châlons
Verdun
Worms
Metz
Nantes
Sens
Toul
Strasburg
Tours
Poitiers
Bourges
Besançon
Vindonissa
Geneva
Lyons
Vienne
Bordeaux
Toulouse
Narbonne
Arles
Marseilles
Nicaea
PYRENEES
Ratisbon
Passau
Lorch
Vienna
Augsburg
Salzburg
D. OF ITALY
Como
Bergamo
Brescia
Milan
Verona
Aquileia
Turin
Pavia
Po R.
Genoa
Bologna
Ravenna
Pisa
Florence
APENNINES
ADRIATIC SEA
Corsica
ROME
Ostia
D. OF THE CITY OF ROME
MARE TYRRHENUM
Naples
Brindisi
Taranto
Sardinia
Cagliari
Messina
Palermo
Sicily
Syracuse
WEST ROMAN EMPIRE
PREFECTURE OF GAUL
D. OF SPAIN
Braga
Leon
Astorga
Duero R.
Calahorra
Saragossa
Avila
Tagus R.
Merida
Evora
Toledo
Guadiana R.
Cordova
Castulo
Sevilla
Italica
Guadalquivir R.
Faro
Elvira
Tucci
Mentesa
Malaga
Cadiz
Baza
Cartagena
Urci
Gerona
Barcelona
Tarragona
Balearic Is.
MEDITERRANEAN SEA
Caesarea Mauretaniae
D. OF AFRICA
PREFECTURE OF ITALY
Tipasa
Milevis
Calama
Hippo Regius
Sitifis
Cirta
Tagaste
Bagai
Sicca
Carthage
P. OF AFRICA
Hadrumetum
Thapsus
Ruspe
Sufes
Vita
Leptis magna
ATLAS
Mauretanians
Limits of the Roman Empire
Boundaries of dioceses
Boundaries of provinces
Seat of a patriarchate
Seat of a metropolitanate (archbishopric)
Seat of a bishopric
D.- DIOCESE; P.- PROCONSULATE
Scale 1:20000000
Miles
Long. West of Greenwich 0 Long. East of Greenwich

Provinces
PREFECTURE OF GAUL
DIOCESE OF SPAIN
1. Baetica, 2. Lusitania, 3. Galicia,
4. Tarraconensis, 5. Carthaginiensis,
6. Mauretania Tingitana
7. Balearic Isles.
DIOCESE OF GAUL
1. Viennensis, 2. Lugdunensis,
3.4, Germania I. II,
5.6, Belgica I. II,
7. Maritime Alps,
8. Pennine and Graian Alps,
9. Maxima Sequanorum,
10.11, Aquitaine I. II,
12. Novempopulana,
13.14, Narbonnensis I. II,
DIOCESE OF BRITAIN
1. Maxima Caesariensis, 2. Valentia,
3.4, Britain I. II,
5. Flavia Caesariensis.
PREFECTURE OF ITALY
DIOCESE OF AFRICA
1. Byzacium, 2. Numidia,
3. Tripolitana,
4. Mauretania Sitifensis
5. Mauretania Caesariensis
DIOCESE OF THE CITY OF ROME
1. Campania, 2. Tuscany and Umbria,
3 Picenum Suburbicarium, 4. Sicily,
5. Apulia and Calabria,
6. Bruttia and Lucania,
7. Samnium, 8. Sardinia,
9. Corsica, 10. Valeria.
DIOCESE OF ITALY
1. Venetia and Istria,
2. Aemilia, 3. Liguria,
4. Flaminia and Picenum Annonarium, 5. Cottian Alps,
6.7, Raetia I. II, 8. Pannonia II,
9. Savia, 10. Pannonia I, 11. Dalmatia,
12. Noricum mediterraneum,
13. Noricum ripense,
14. Valeria ripensis
PROCONSULATE OF AFRICA
PREFECTURE OF ILLYRICUM
DIOCESE OF MACEDONIA
1. Macedonia, 2. Crete, 3. Thessaly,
4. Epirus vetus, 5. Epirus nova,
6. Macedonia Salutaris.
DIOCESE OF DACIA
1. Dacia mediterranea, 2. Moesia I,
3. Praevalitana, 4. Dardania,
5. Dacia ripensis.
PROCONSULATE OF ACHAIA
PREFECTURE OF THE EAST
DIOCESE OF EGYPT
1. Upper Libya, 2. Lower Libya,
3. Thebais, 4. Egypt, 5. Arcadia,
6. Augustamnica.
DIOCESE OF THE EAST
1. Palestine I, 2. Phoenicia,
3. Syria I, 4. Cilicia I,
5. Cyprus, 6. Palestine II,
7. Palestine Salutaris,
8. Phoenicia Libani,
9. Eufratensis, 10. Syria Salutaris,
11. Osrhoëne, 12. Mesopotamia,
13. Cilicia II, 14. Isauria,
15. Arabia.
DIOCESE OF PONTUS
1. Bithynia, 2. Galatia,
3. Paphlagonia, 4. Honorias,
5. Galatia Salutaris,
6.7, Cappadocia I. II,
8. Helenopontus,
9. Pontus Polemoniacus,
10.11, Armenia I. II,
DIOCESE OF ASIA
1. Pamphylia, 2. Lydia,
3. Caria, 4. Lycia,
5. Lycaonia, 6. Pisidia,
7. Phrygia Pacatiana,
8. Phrygia Salutaris.
DIOCESE OF THRACE
1. Europe, 2. Thrace,
3. Haemimontium,
4. Rhodope, 5. Moesia II,
6. Scythia.
PROCONSULATE OF ASIA

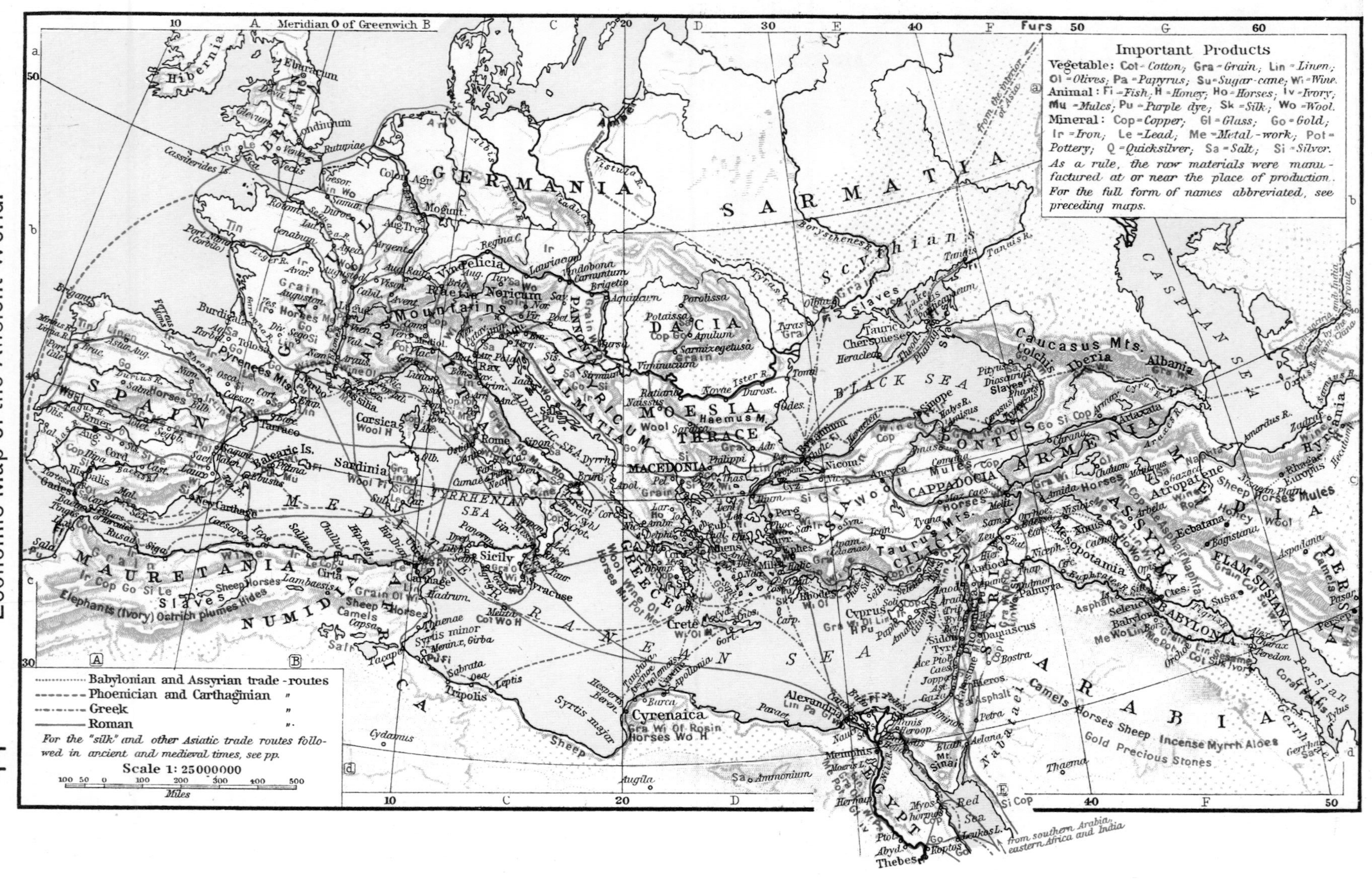
Important Products
Vegetable: Cot-Cotton; Gra-Grain; Lin-Linen; Ol-Olives; Pa-Papyrus; Su-Sugar-cane; Wi-Wine.
Animal: Fi-Fish; H-Honey; Ho-Horses; Iv-Ivory; Mu-Mules; Pu-Purple dye; Sk-Silk; Wo-Wool.
Mineral: Cop-Copper; Gl-Glass; Go-Gold; Ir-Iron; Le-Lead; Me-Metal-work; Pot-Pottery; Q-Quicksilver; Sa-Salt; Si-Silver.
As a rule, the raw materials were manufactured at or near the place of production.
For the full form of names abbreviated, see preceding maps.
Meridian 0 of Greenwich
Furs
Hibernia
BRITAIN
GERMANIA
SARMATIA
Scythians
DACIA
MOESIA
THRACE
MACEDONIA
BLACK SEA
CASPIAN SEA
Caucasus Mts.
ARMENIA
CAPPADOCIA
ASSYRIA
BABYLONIA
SPAIN
MAURETANIA
NUMIDIA
AFRICA
MEDITERRANEAN SEA
Cyrenaica
Alexandria
EGYPT
ARABIA
Babylonian and Assyrian trade-routes
Phoenician and Carthaginian "
Greek "
Roman "
For the "silk" and other Asiatic trade routes followed in ancient and medieval times, see pp.
Scale 1: 25000000
Miles
from southern Arabia, eastern Africa and India

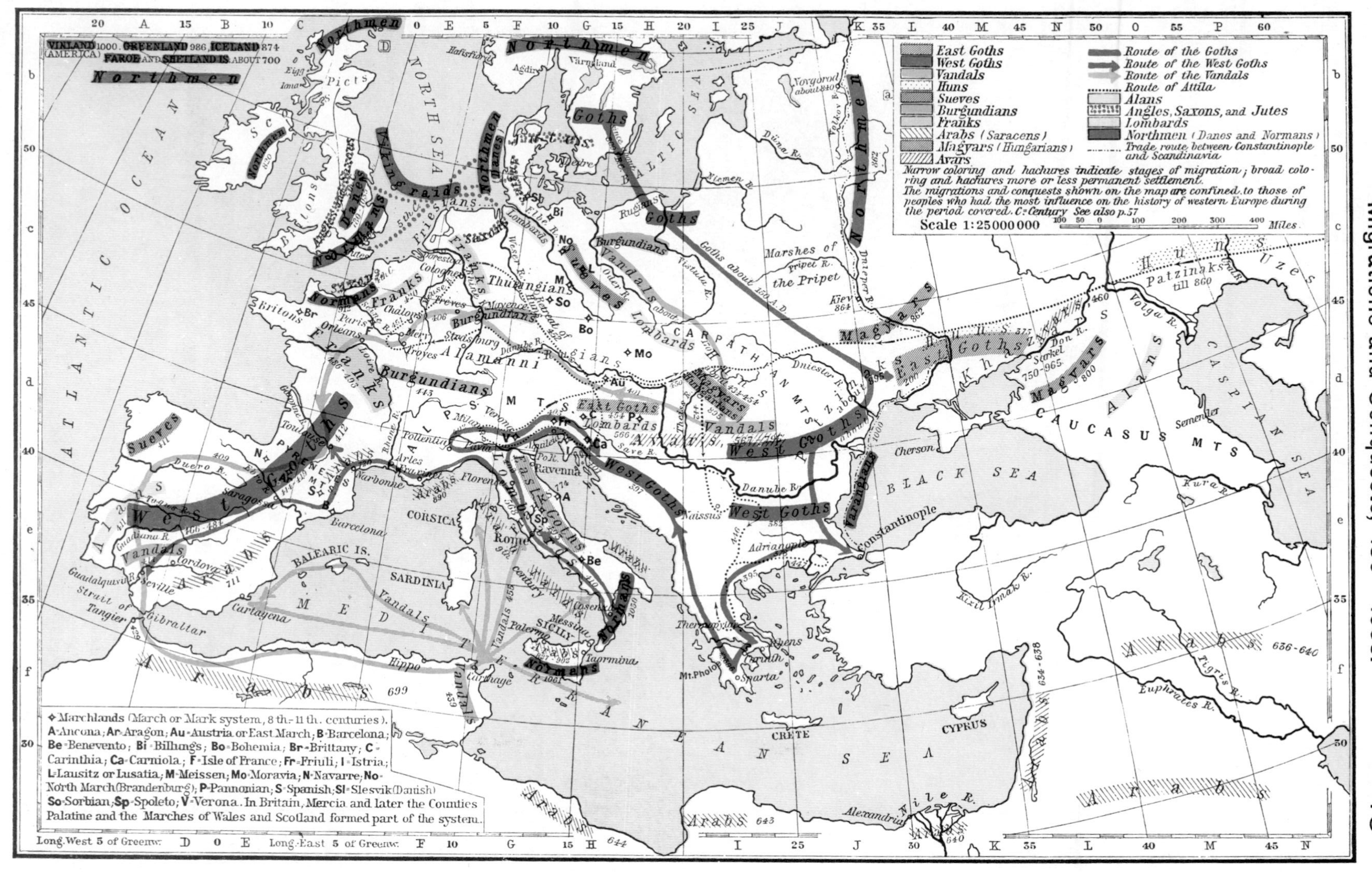
VINLAND 1000. GREENLAND 986 ICELAND 874
(AMERICA) FAROE AND SHETLAND IS. ABOUT 700
Northmen
East Goths
West Goths
Vandals
Huns
Sueves
Burgundians
Franks
Arabs (Saracens)
Magyars (Hungarians)
Avars
Route of the Goths
Route of the West Goths
Route of the Vandals
Route of Attila
Alans
Angles, Saxons, and Jutes
Lombards
Northmen (Danes and Normans)
Trade route between Constantinople and Scandinavia
Narrow coloring and hachures indicate stages of migration; broad coloring and hachures more or less permanent settlement.
The migrations and conquests shown on the map are confined to those of peoples who had the most influence on the history of western Europe during the period covered. C: Century See also p.57
Scale 1:25000000
Miles
✧ Marchlands (March or Mark system, 8 th.-11 th. centuries). A-Ancona; Ar-Aragon; Au-Austria or East March; B-Barcelona; Be-Benevento; Bi-Billungs; Bo-Bohemia; Br-Brittany; C-Carinthia; Ca-Carniola; F-Isle of France; Fr-Friuli; I-Istria; L-Lausitz or Lusatia; M-Meissen; Mo-Moravia; N-Navarre; No-North March (Brandenburg); P-Pannonian; S-Spanish; Sl-Slesvik (Danish) So-Sorbian; Sp-Spoleto; V-Verona. In Britain, Mercia and later the Counties Palatine and the Marches of Wales and Scotland formed part of the system.
ATLANTIC OCEAN
NORTH SEA
BALTIC SEA
BLACK SEA
CASPIAN SEA
MEDITERRANEAN SEA
CAUCASUS MTS
CARPATHIAN MTS
Viking raids
Marshes of the Pripet
Constantinople
Long. West 5 of Greenw.
Long. East 5 of Greenw.

ATLANTIC OCEAN
NORTH SEA
IRELAND
Christianity introduced by St. Patrick 440-493
Iona
Christianity introduced from Ireland by St. Columba 563
Picts
STRATHCLYDE
NORTHUMBRIA
WALES
MERCIA
EAST ANGLIA
CORNWALL
WESSEX
ESSEX
SUSSEX
KENT
Canterbury
London
Augustine 597-604
Roman Britain, partially Christianized in 3d Century. Christianity subsequently uprooted in England by Anglo-Saxon invasions of 5th and 6th Centuries
English Channel
Frisians
Saxons
Thuringians
Wends
Abotrites
Pomeranians
BOHEMIA
Czechs
MORAVIA
PANNONIA
ILLYRICUM
Franks
GAUL
Christianity introduced in 496
Paris
Soissons
Poitiers
Limoges
Bordeaux
Toulouse
Narbonne
Marseilles
Burgundians
Alamanni
Bavarians
Vosges
Alps
Lombards
Arians in 5th Century, Catholics in 7th Century
Milan
Venice
Ravenna
Pisa
Florence
Rome
Monte Cassino
Pozzuoli
Salerno
Apennines
ADRIATIC SEA
CORSICA
SARDINIA
SICILY
MELITA
Bay of Biscay
Pyrenees
Sueves
Arians in the 5th Century, Catholics in 550
SPAIN
Visigoths
Arians in the 4th Century, Catholics in 589
Lisbon
Toledo
Cordova
Seville
Malaga
Cartagena
Barcelona
Tarragona
Strait of Gibraltar
MAURETANIA
NUMIDIA
Caesarea
Hippo Regius
Carthage
Leptis Magna
MEDITERRANEAN
Northern Limit of Mohammedanism
From the Seventh Century
Norwegians
Oslo
Swedes
GOTHIA
Introduced by Ansgar and his successors (829-1000)
Danes
Extent of Christianity about 600 (pontificate of Gregory I, the Great, 590 - 604)
Area Christianized 600 - 800
" " 800 - 1100
" " 1100 - 1300
Damascus Churches of the apostolic period (33 - 100)
Nicaea Principal churches of the post apostolic period (100-311)
Alexandria / Antioch Mission centres in both periods
Journeys of the Apostle Paul
Peoples converted from Arianism to Catholicism
Figures indicate approximate dates of conversion to Christianity
Scale 1 : 20 000 000
Miles
Long.

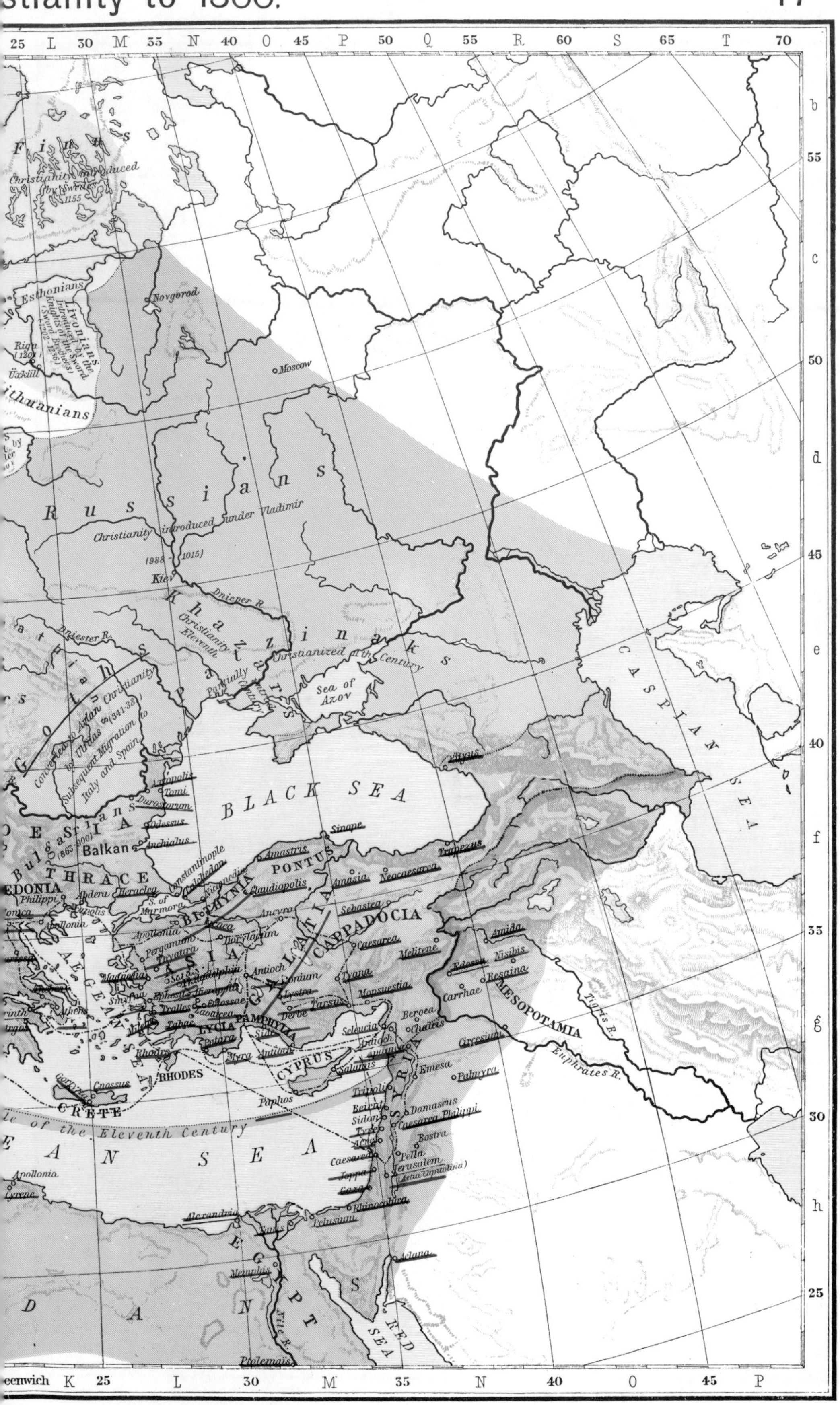
Christianity introduced by Swedes 1155
Esthonians
Livonians
Novgorod
Riga
Moscow
Lithuanians
Russians
Christianity introduced under Vladimir (988–1015)
Kiev
Dnieper R.
Dniester R.
Khazars
Petchenegs
Christianized 11th Century
Sea of Azov
Goths
Converted to Arian Christianity by Ulfilas (341-381)
Subsequent Migration to Italy and Spain
BLACK SEA
Bulgaria (865-900)
Balkan
Tomi
Odessus
Anchialus
Sinope
Amastris
PONTUS
Trapezus
THRACE
Constantinople
Chalcedon
Heraclea
Philippi
S. of Marmora
BITHYNIA
Nicomedia
Claudiopolis
Amasia
Neocaesarea
Sebastea
CAPPADOCIA
GALATIA
Ancyra
Nicaea
Dorylaeum
Pergamum
Thyatira
ASIA
Philadelphia
Antioch
Iconium
Lystra
Derbe
Caesarea
Melitene
Tyana
Mopsuestia
Tarsus
Smyrna
Ephesus
Hierapolis
Colossae
Laodicea
Tralles
Miletus
LYCIA
PAMPHYLIA
Patara
Myra
Rhodus
RHODES
Cnossus
Gortyna
CRETE
AEGEAN SEA
Seleucia
Antioch
CYPRUS
Salamis
Paphos
Beroea
Chalcis
Edessa
Amida
Nisibis
Resaina
Carrhae
MESOPOTAMIA
Tigris R.
Circesium
Euphrates R.
Emesa
Palmyra
SYRIA
Tripoli
Beirut
Sidon
Tyre
Acre
Damascus
Caesarea Philippi
Bostra
Pella
Caesarea
Joppa
Jerusalem (Aelia Capitolina)
Gaza
Rhinocolura
Pelusium
Alexandria
Apollonia
Cyrene
Memphis
Aelana
EGYPT
Nile R.
RED SEA
Ptolemais
CASPIAN SEA
of the Eleventh Century
MEDITERRANEAN SEA
Greenwich

The Roman and Hunnic Empires about 450.

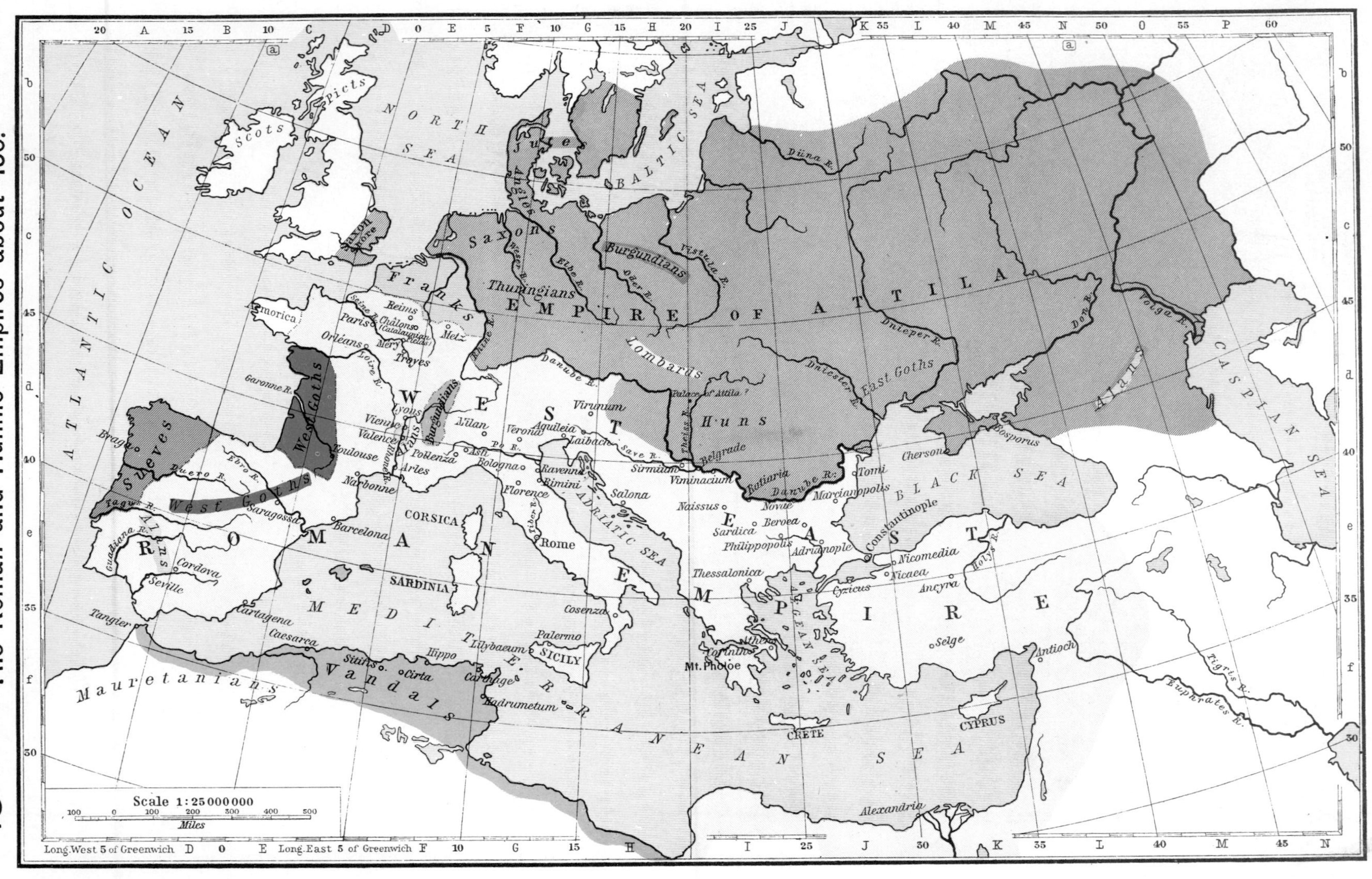

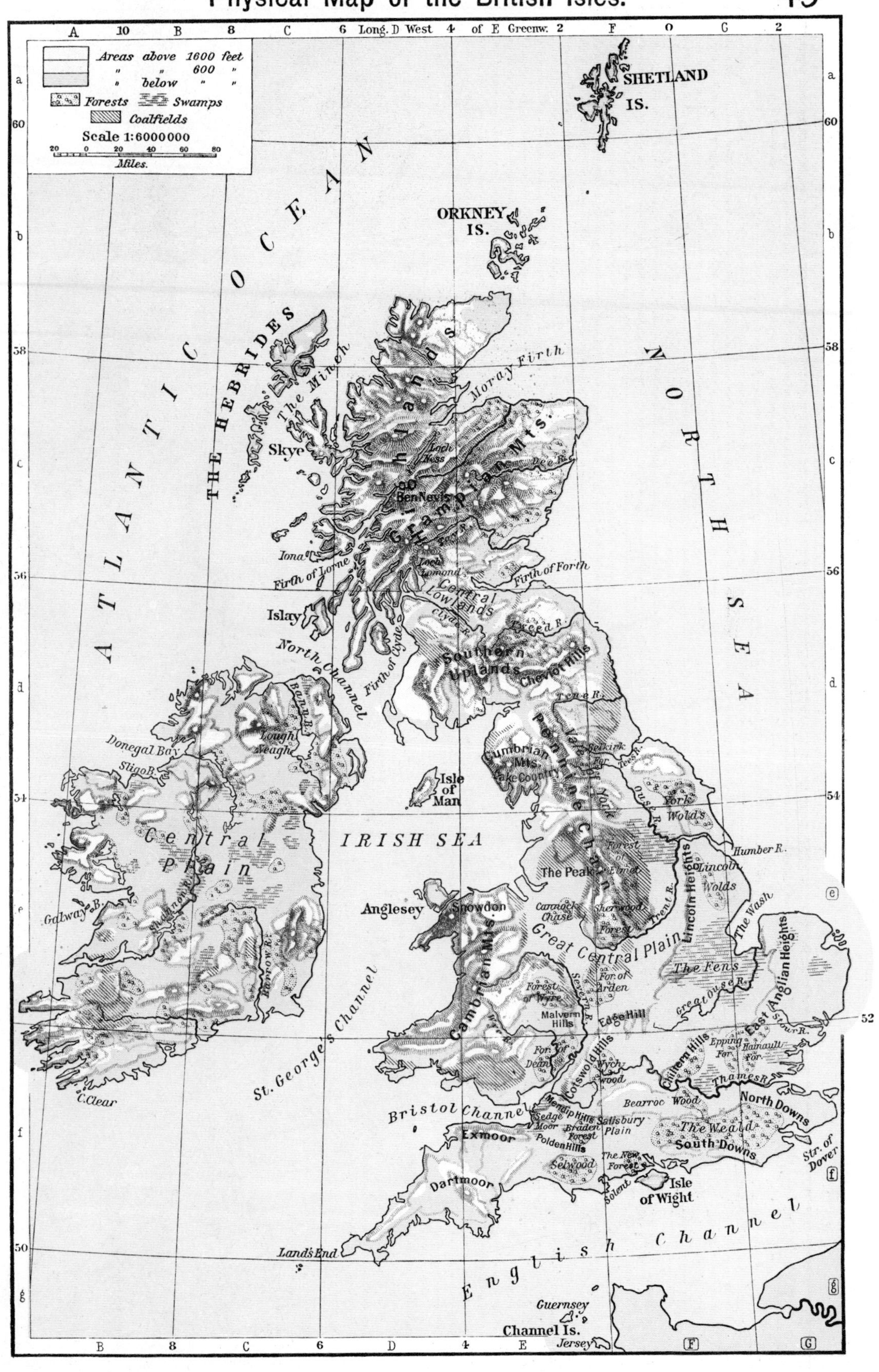
Areas above 1600 feet
" " 600 "
" below " "
Forests
Swamps
Coalfields
Scale 1:6000000
Miles.
Long. D West of E Greenw.
SHETLAND IS.
ORKNEY IS.
ATLANTIC OCEAN
THE HEBRIDES
The Minch
Moray Firth
NORTH SEA
Skye
Loch Ness
Ben Nevis
Grampian Mts.
Dee R.
Iona
Firth of Lorne
Loch Lomond
Firth of Forth
Central Lowlands
Islay
Clyde R.
Tweed R.
North Channel
Firth of Clyde
Southern Uplands
Cheviot Hills
Tyne R.
Donegal Bay
Sligo B.
Lough Neagh
Bann R.
Isle of Man
Cumbrian Mts.
Lake Country
Vale of York
Tees R.
York Wolds
Humber R.
Central Plain
IRISH SEA
The Peak
Forest of Elmet
Lincoln Heights
Lincoln Wolds
The Wash
Galway B.
Shannon R.
Anglesey
Snowdon
Cannock Chase
Sherwood Forest
Trent R.
Great Central Plain
The Fens
East Anglian Heights
Barrow R.
Cambrian Mts.
St. George's Channel
Forest of Wyre
For. of Arden
Great Ouse R.
Malvern Hills
Severn R.
Edge Hill
Stour R.
Chiltern Hills
Epping For.
Hainault For.
For. of Dean
Cotswold Hills
Wychwood
Thames R.
C. Clear
Bristol Channel
Mendip Hills
Sedge Moor
Braden Forest
Salisbury Plain
Bearroc Wood
North Downs
The Weald
South Downs
Exmoor
Polden Hills
Selwood
The New Forest
Str. of Dover
Dartmoor
Solent
Isle of Wight
English Channel
Land's End
Guernsey
Channel Is.
Jersey

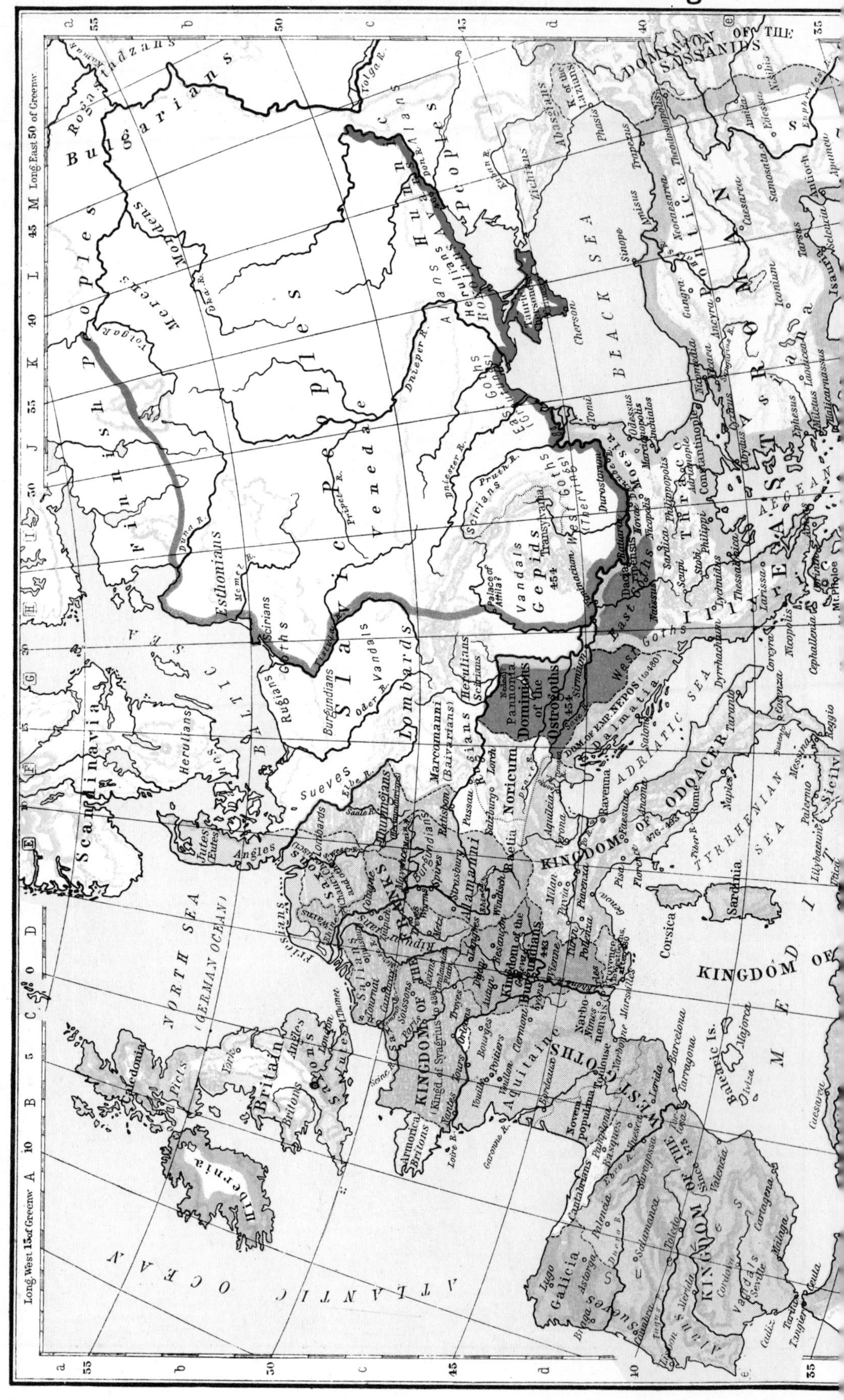

BLACK SEA
NORTH SEA
(GERMAN OCEAN)
ATLANTIC OCEAN
ADRIATIC SEA
TYRRHENIAN SEA
AEGEAN
Scandinavia
Hibernia
Britain
Caledonia
Picts
Britons
Angles
Saxons
Jutes
Esthonians
Finnish Peoples
Bulgarians
Slavic Peoples
Venedae
Lombards
Sueves
Rugians
Burgundians
Herulians
Marcomanni (Baivarians)
Noricum
Pannonia
Dominions of the Ostrogoths
Vandals
Gepids
Scirians
Dacia
Moesia
Thrace
Illyria
Dalmatia
KINGDOM OF ODOACER
KINGDOM OF THE FRANKS
KINGDOM (Kingd. of Syagrius)
Kingdom of the Burgundians
Alamanni
Aquitaine
West Goths
Galicia
Sicily
Sardinia
Corsica
Balearic Is.
Constantinople
Ravenna
Rome
Naples
Milan
Marseilles
Toulouse
Barcelona
Tarragona
Valencia
Carthagena
Malaga
Seville
Cordova
Toledo
Salamanca
Lugo
Astorga
Armorica
Paris
Soissons
Orleans
Tours
Nantes
Bourges
Lyons
Vienne
Mainz
Cologne
Treves
Metz
Strasburg
Ratisbon
Passau
Salzburg
Aquileia
Verona
Florence
Pisa
Sinope
Trapezus
Chersonese
Ephesus
Tarsus
Antioch
Ancyra
Iconium
DOMINION OF THE SASSANIDS

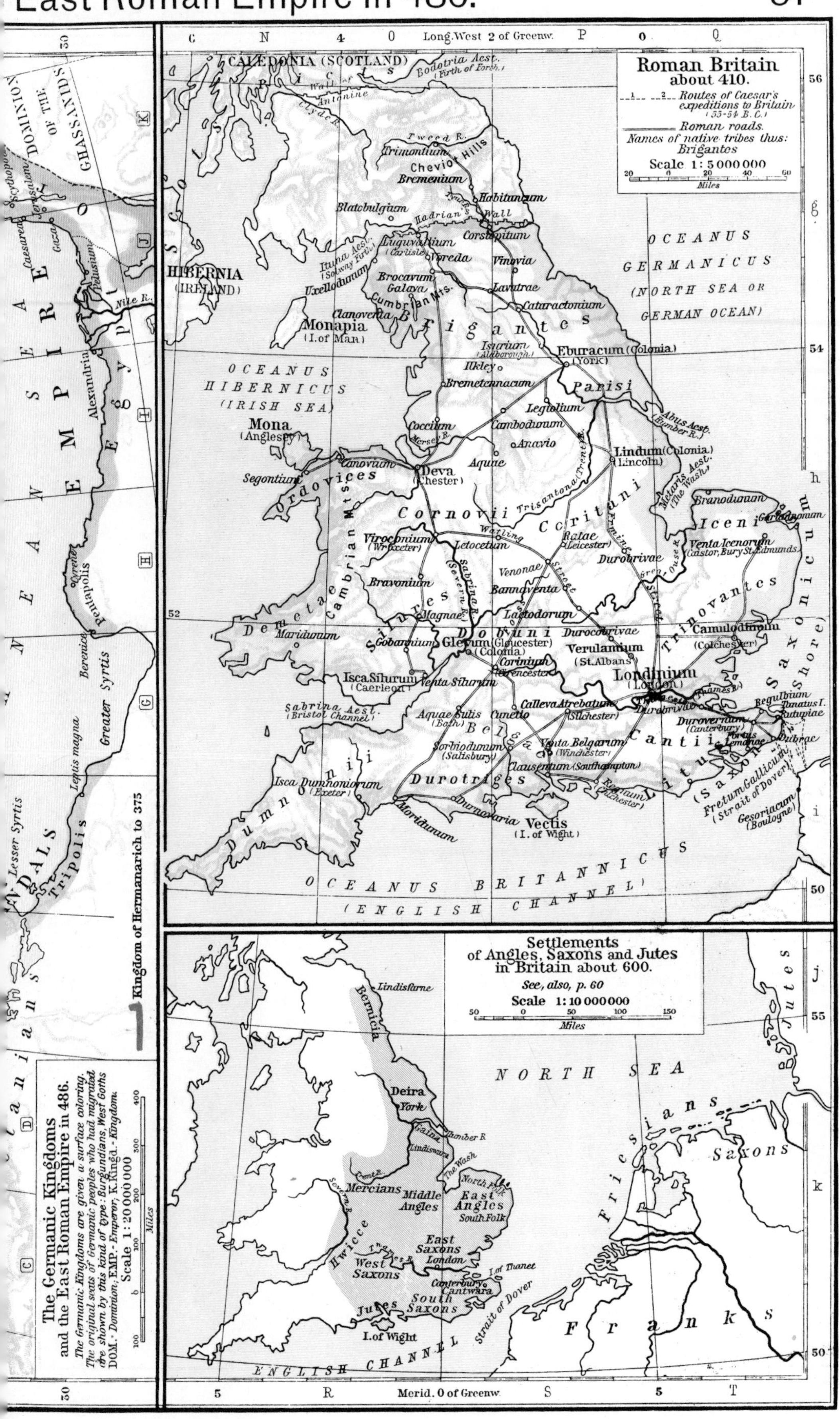
Roman Britain
about 410.
Routes of Caesar's expeditions to Britain (55-54 B.C.)
Roman roads.
Names of native tribes thus: Brigantes
Scale 1: 5 000 000
Miles
Settlements
of Angles, Saxons and Jutes
in Britain about 600.
See, also, p. 60
Scale 1: 10 000 000
Miles
The Germanic Kingdoms
and the East Roman Empire in 486.
The Germanic Kingdoms are given a surface coloring. The original seats of Germanic peoples who had migrated are shown by this kind of type: Burgundians, West Goths
DOM.-Dominion, EMP.-Emperor, K.Kingd.-Kingdom.
Scale 1: 20 000 000
Kingdom of Hermanarich to 375
DOMINION OF THE GHASSANIDS
CALEDONIA (SCOTLAND)
HIBERNIA (IRELAND)
Monapia (I. of Man)
OCEANUS HIBERNICUS (IRISH SEA)
Mona (Anglesey)
OCEANUS GERMANICUS (NORTH SEA OR GERMAN OCEAN)
Eburacum (Colonia) (York)
Lindum (Colonia) (Lincoln)
Deva (Chester)
Londinium (London)
Verulamium (St. Albans)
Camulodunum (Colchester)
Glevum (Gloucester) (Colonia)
Isca Silurum (Caerleon)
Vectis (I. of Wight)
OCEANUS BRITANNICUS (ENGLISH CHANNEL)
Fretum Gallicum (Strait of Dover)
Gesoriacum (Boulogne)
Brigantes
Cornovii
Coritani
Iceni
Trinovantes
Dobuni
Silures
Demetae
Ordovices
Belgae
Cantii
Durotriges
Dumnonii
Parisi
NORTH SEA
Bernicia
Deira
Mercians
Middle Angles
East Angles
East Saxons
West Saxons
South Saxons
Jutes
Hwicce
Frisians
Saxons
Franks
ENGLISH CHANNEL
Strait of Dover
I. of Wight
Merid. 0 of Greenw.
Long. West 2 of Greenw.

52 The Germanic Kingdoms and the East Roman Empire, 526—600.

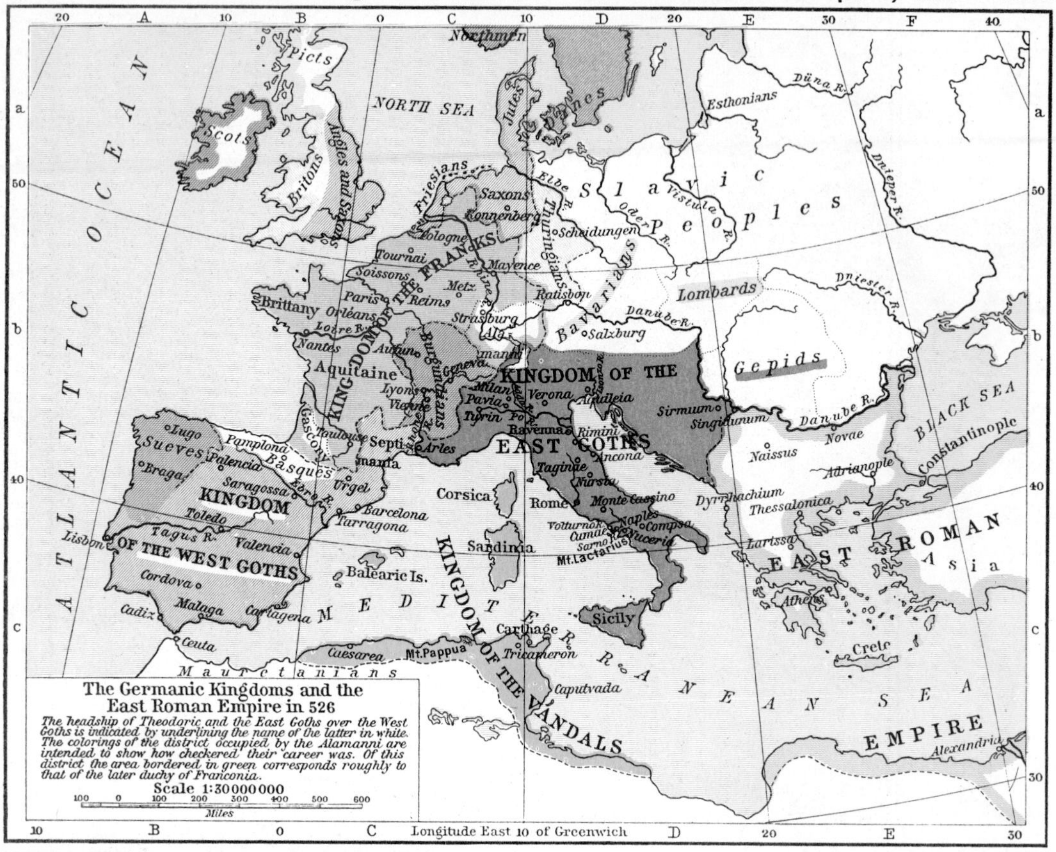

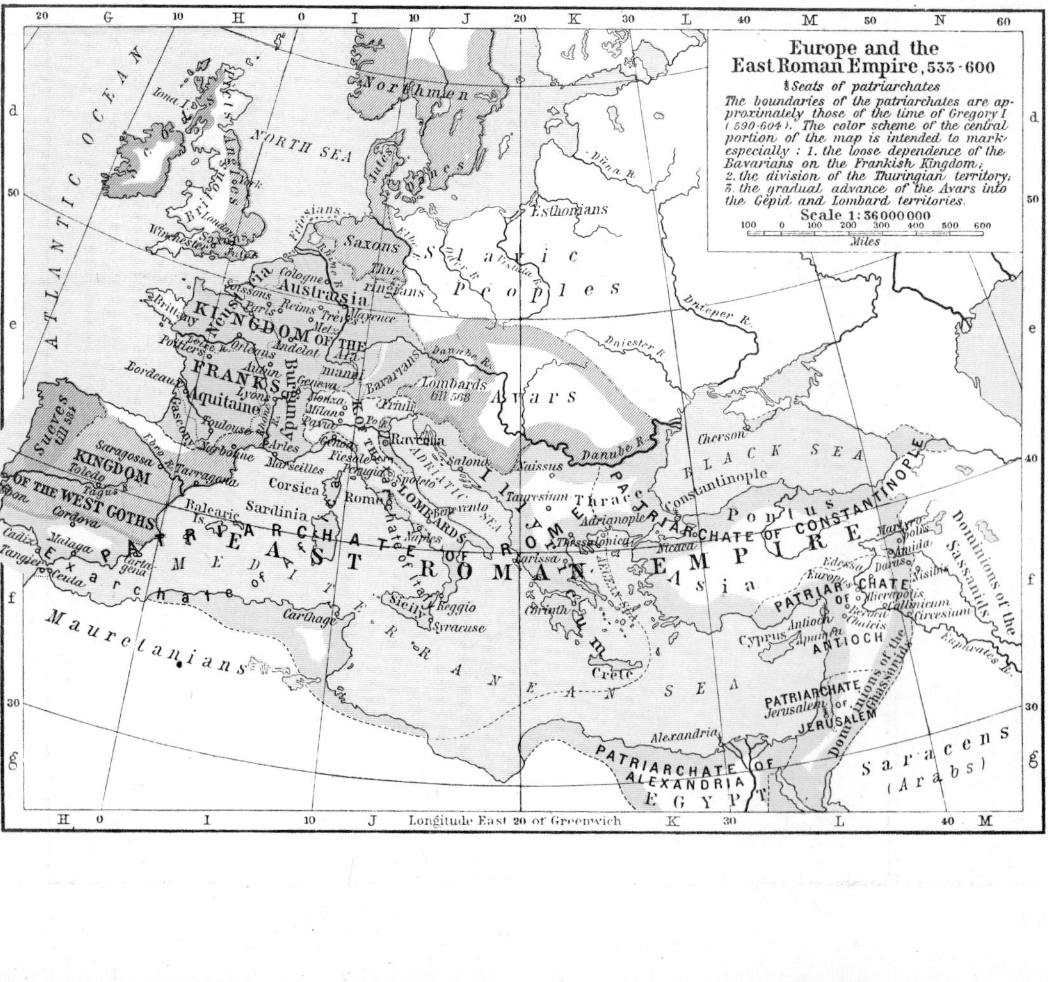

The Germanic Kingdoms and the East Roman Empire in 526

The headship of Theodoric and the East Goths over the West Goths is indicated by underlining the name of the latter in white. The colorings of the district occupied by the Alamanni are intended to show how checkered their career was. Of this district the area bordered in green corresponds roughly to that of the later duchy of Franconia.

Scale 1:30000000

100 0 100 200 300 400 500 600 Miles

Longitude East 10 of Greenwich

Europe and the East Roman Empire, 533-600

‡ *Seats of patriarchates*

The boundaries of the patriarchates are approximately those of the time of Gregory I (590-604). The color scheme of the central portion of the map is intended to mark especially: 1. the loose dependence of the Bavarians on the Frankish Kingdom; 2. the division of the Thuringian territory; 3. the gradual advance of the Avars into the Gepid and Lombard territories.

Scale 1:36000000

100 0 100 200 300 400 500 600 Miles

Longitude East 20 of Greenwich

The Califate in 750. Growth of Frankish Power, 481—814.

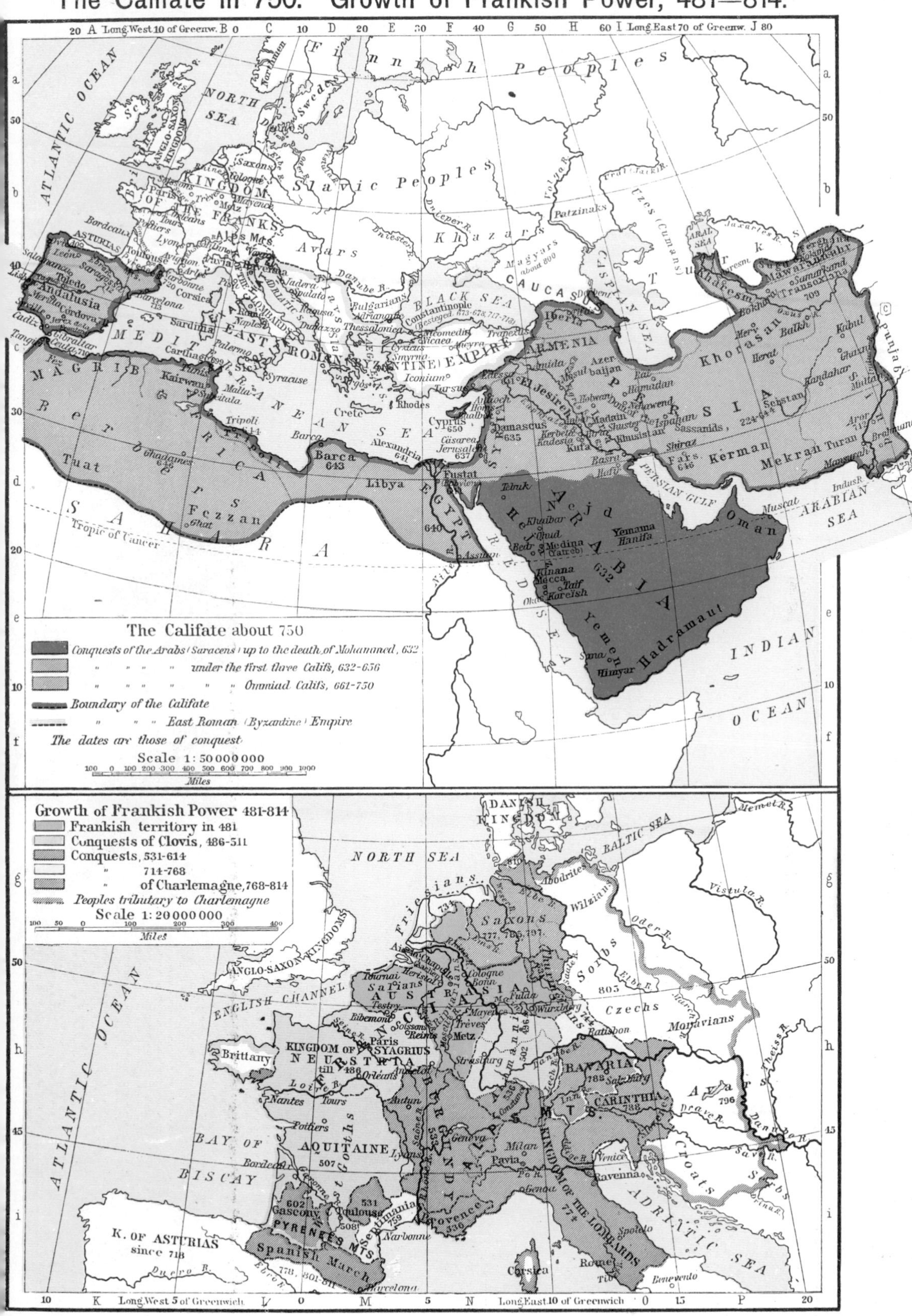

The Carolingian Empire
Slavic peoples tributary to Charlemagne
Slavs
Celts
The Byzantine Empire
The Califate
Boundary of the Patrimony of St. Peter, as determined in 774
Frontier station for trade with Slavs and Avars thus: Schesel
Site of important event thus: Poitiers
Seat of an archbishopric
" " a bishopric
In the East Frankish dominions about the end of the ninth century
Monastery
Castle or stronghold
Scale 1: 20 000 000
Miles
Long. West 5 of Greenwich
ATLANTIC OCEAN
NORTH SEA
Shetland Is.
Orkney Is.
The Hebrides
Iona
DANISH KINGDOM
ANGLO-SAXON KINGDOMS
Wales
London
Winchester
Canterbury
AUSTRASIA
NEUSTRIA
BRITTANY
AQUITAINE
GASCONY
BURGUNDY
ALAMANNIA
BAVARIA
BOHEMIA
CARINTHIA
Saxons
Lombardy
Provence
Septimania
Spanish March
KINGDOM OF ASTURIAS
OMMIAD EMIRATE OF CORDOVA
Cordova
Seville
Granada
Toledo
Lisbon
Oporto
Cadiz
Strait of Gibraltar
Tangier
Balearic Is.
Majorca
Minorca
Corsica
SARDINIA
SICILY
Palermo
Messina
Syracuse
Malta
Tripoli
Rome
Ravenna
Duchy of Spoleto
DUCHY OF BENEVENTO
Naples
Barcelona
Narbonne
Marseilles
Poitiers
Roncesvalles
Tours
Paris
Reims
Aachen
Cologne
Frankfurt
Magdeburg
Schesel
Bremen
Slavs
Swedes
MEDITERRANEAN
TYRRHENIAN SEA
ADRIATIC SEA
DOMINION OF THE IDRISIDS (since 788)
DOMINION OF THE AGHLABIDS (since 800)
CALIFATE OF
Kairwan

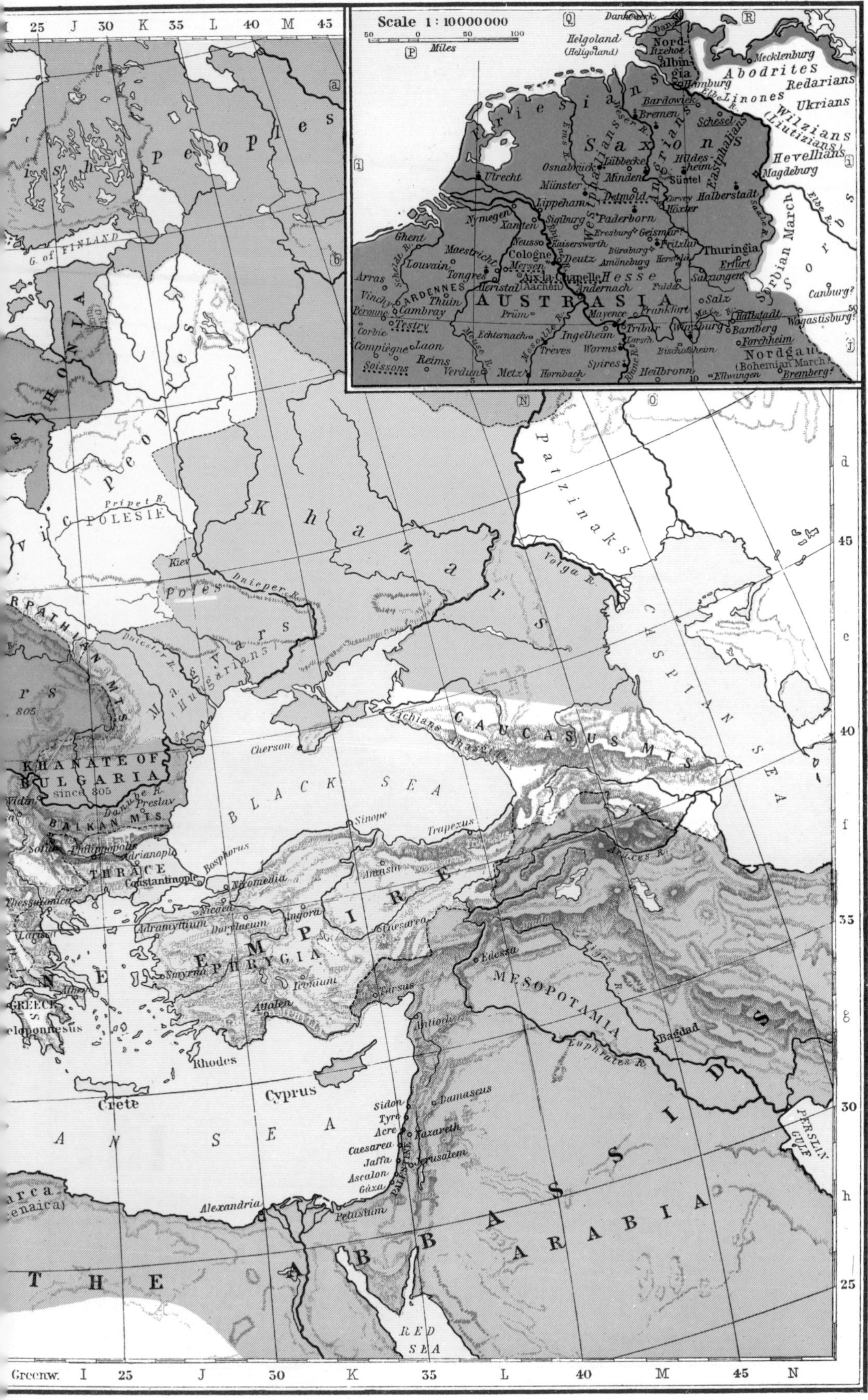
Scale 1 : 10000000
Miles
Helgoland (Heligoland)
Nord-Albingia
Itzehoe
Hamburg
Mecklenburg
Abodrites
Redarians
Ukrians
Linones
Wilzians (Liutizians)
Hevellians
Magdeburg
Frisians
Saxons
Bardowiek
Bremen
Schesel
Westphalians
Angrians
Eastphalians
Osnabrück
Lübbecke
Minden
Hildesheim
Süntel
Utrecht
Münster
Detmold
Halberstadt
Lippeham
Corvey
Höxter
Nymegen
Xanten
Sigiburg
Paderborn
Eresburg
Geismar
Fritzlar
Ghent
Maestricht
Neuss
Kaiserswerth
Büraburg
Thuringia
Erfurt
Louvain
Tongres
Cologne
Deutz
Amöneburg
Hersfeld
Mersen
Aix la Chapelle (Aachen)
Hesse
Salzungen
Arras
Heristal
Andernach
Fulda
ARDENNES
Thuin
AUSTRASIA
Salz
Vinchy
Cambray
Prüm
Mayence
Frankfort
Halbstadt
Peronne
Testry
Tribur
Würzburg
Bamberg
Corbie
Echternach
Ingelheim
Lorsch
Forchheim
Compiègne
Laon
Treves
Worms
Bischofsheim
Nordgau (Bohemian March)
Reims
Spires
Soissons
Verdun
Metz
Hornbach
Heilbronn
Ellwangen
Bremberg
Serbian March
Sorbs
Canburg?
Wogastisburg?
Elbe R.
Saale R.
Main R.
Rhine R.
Moselle R.
Meuse R.
Scheldt R.
Ems R.
Weser R.
Peoples
G. of FINLAND
ESTHONIA
Pripet R.
POLESIE
Kiev
Dnieper R.
Poles
Khazars
Avars
Magyars (Hungarians)
Dniester R.
CARPATHIAN MTS.
805
KHANATE OF BULGARIA since 805
Vidin
Danube R.
Preslav
BALKAN MTS.
Sofia
Philippopolis
Adrianople
THRACE
Constantinople
Bosphorus
Thessalonica
Larissa
GREECE
Peloponnesus
Cherson
BLACK SEA
Sinope
Trapezus
Amisus
Nicomedia
Nicaea
Angora
Adramyttium
Dorylaeum
Caesarea
EMPIRE
PHRYGIA
Smyrna
Iconium
Attalea
Tarsus
Antioch
Rhodes
Crete
Cyprus
SEA
Patzinaks
Volga R.
CASPIAN SEA
Lichians
Abasgians
CAUCASUS MTS.
Araxes R.
Edessa
MESOPOTAMIA
Tigris R.
Euphrates R.
Bagdad
PERSIAN GULF
Sidon
Tyre
Acre
Damascus
Nazareth
Caesarea
Jaffa
Jerusalem
Ascalon
Gaza
PALESTINE
Alexandria
Pelusium
Cyrenaica
THE ABBASSIDS
ARABIA
RED SEA
Greenw.
I 25 J 30 K 35 L 40 M 45 N
d 45 e 40 f 35 g 30 h 25

Disruption of the Carolingian Empire, 843—888.

The Peoples of Europe about 900.

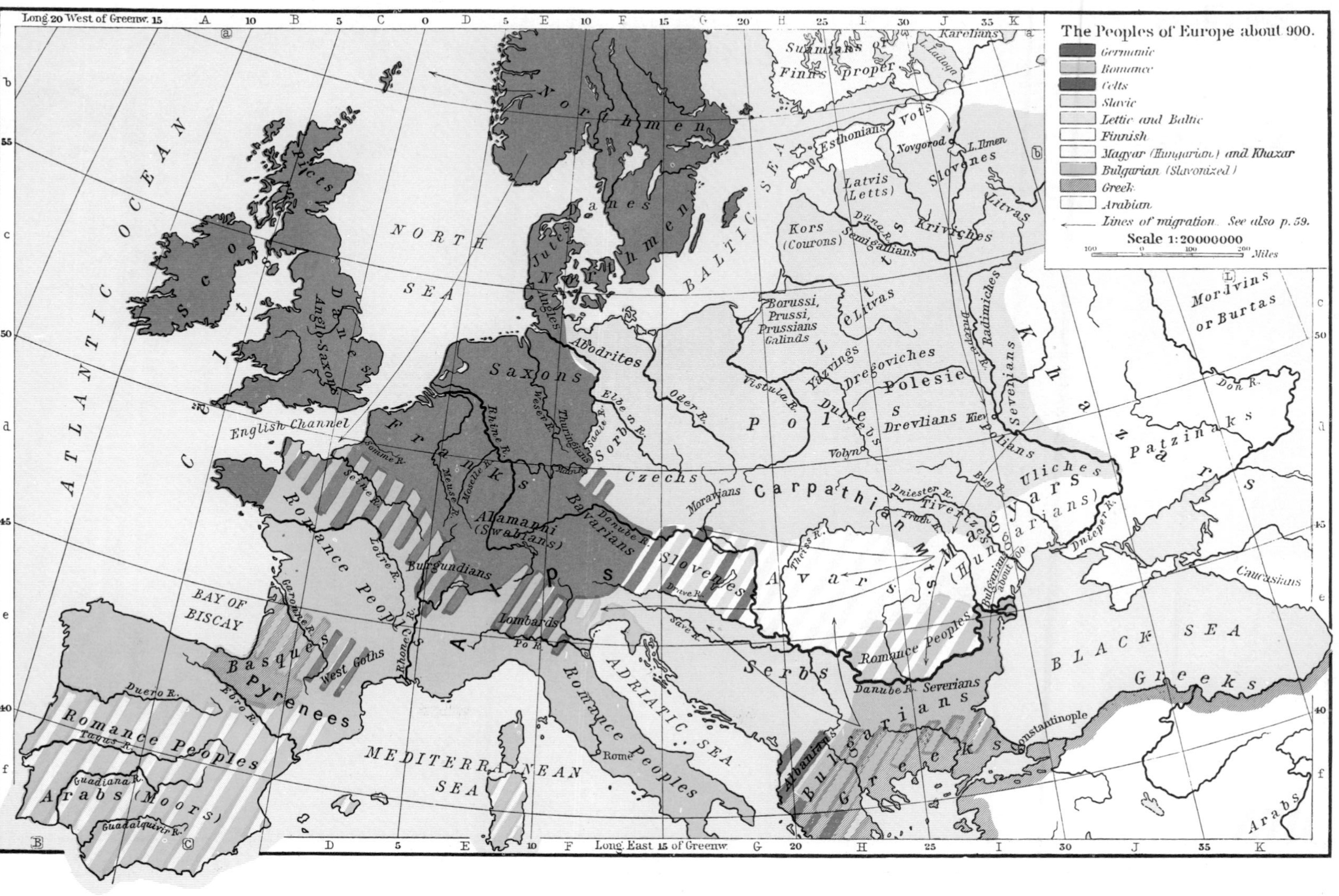

Route of the Varangians.
Scale 1:15000000
Miles.
C. County; D.-Duchy; D.M.-Danish March; K-Kingdom; M: March; Sax.M.- Saxon March; Th.-Theme.
ATLANTIC OCEAN
NORTH SEA
ENGLISH CHANNEL
KINGDOM OF NORWAY
Tonsberg
KINGDOM OF DENMAR
Ribe
Roeskilde
Slesvik
Hamburg
Bremen
SCOTLAND
Edinburgh
IRELAND
Dublin
Cork
WALES
Cardiff
Chester
ENGLAND
Durham
York
Norwich
Oxford
London
Thames R.
Canterbury
Boulogne
C. OF FLANDERS
FRIESLAND
Osnabrück
Utrecht
D. OF SAXONY
Minden
Paderborn
Magdeburg
D. OF LOWER LORRAINE
Aix-la-Chapelle
Cologne
D. OF WEST FRANCONIA
Frankfort
Worms
Metz
D. OF UPPER LORRAINE
Strasburg
ALSACE
Rhine R.
D. OF NORMANDY
Rouen
C. OF BRITTANY
Nantes
Paris
C. OF CHAMPAGNE
Rheims
Troyes
D. OF Orléans
D. OF FRANCIA
Loire R.
Tours
Poitiers
Bourges
FRANCE
D. OF AQUITAINE
Limoges
Bordeaux
Langres
D. OF BURGUNDY
Autun
Besançon
Basel (Bale)
Constance
D. OF ALAMANNIA (SWABIA)
Augsburg
D. OF BAVARIA
Regensburg
NORDGAU
KINGDOM OF BURGUNDY
Lyons
Vienne
Geneva
Avignon
Arles
Marseilles
Nice
LOMBARDY
Milan
Bergamo
Pavia
Susa
Genoa
Parma
Modena
Bologna
Venice
Ravenna
Pisa
Florence
TUSCIA
Siena
SPOLETO
STATES OF THE CHURCH
Rome
Gaeta
Naples
D. OF GASCONY
C. OF TOULOUSE
Toulouse
Narbonne
Nimes
PYRENEES MTS.
C. OF BARCELONA
Barcelona
Bayonne
K. OF NAVARRE
Pamplona
Aragon
Burgos
CASTILE
Asturias
Oviedo
Leon
KINGDOM OF LEON
Zamora
Duero R.
Salamanca
Saragossa
Lerida
Ebro R.
Tagus R.
Toledo
Lisbon
Cuenca
CALIFATE OF CORDOVA
SARACENIC POSSESSIONS
Guadiana R.
Cordova
Guadalquivir R.
Sevilla
Valencia
Murcia
Cartagena
Malaga
Strait of Gibraltar
Tangier
Balearic Isles
CORSICA
End of ninth century
SARDINIA
MEDITERRANEAN
Palermo 831
Mazara 827
Algiers
Biserta
Tunis
Kairwan
Mehdiya
DOMINION OF THE FATIMIDES
Dates are those of Saracenic conquest or possession.
Long. West 5 of Greenwich
Long. East 5 of Greenwich

Route of the Varangians
Esthonians
Livonians
Lithuanians
Prussians
Novgorod
L. Ilmen
Veps
Merians
Bulgars
Muromans
Mordvins or Burtas
Smolensk
RUSSIA
Minsk
Pinsk
Chernigov
Kiev
Dnieper R.
Pripet R.
Duna R.
Niemen R.
Oka R.
Volga R.
Donetz R.
Don R.
Kuban R.
Danzig
DUCHY OF POLAND
CHROBATIA
Cracow
Plock
Gnesen
Belz
Halicz
Dniester R.
Bug R.
Patzinaks
CARPATHIAN MTS.
KINGDOM OF HUNGARY
Territory in dispute between Transylvania Hungary and the Patzinaks
Pressburg (Pozsony)
Erlau (Eger)
Gran (Esztergom)
Maros R.
Theiss R.
Pruth R.
Danube R.
Nicopolis
Mitrovica Sirmium
Belgrade (Beograd)
SERVIA
Ragusa (Dubrovnik)
Dioclea
DALMATIA disputed with Venice
Vidin
Nissa (Niš)
Sofia
Skoplje
Tirnovo
Peristhlava
Varna
THEME OF THE BALKAN MTS. HAEMIMONS
THEME OF THE PHILIPPOPOLIS
STRYMON
Adrianople
TH. OF THRACE
THEME OF MACEDONIA
Constantinople
TH. OF SALONICA
THESSALONICA
THEME OF DYRRHACHIUM
Dyrrhachium
Okhrida (Ohrid)
Kastoria
Larissa
THEME OF HELLAS
Athens
NICOPOLIS
CEPHALENIA
THEME OF PELOPONNESUS
Corinth
Argos
THEME OF THE AEGEAN ISLANDS
BYZANTINE EMPIRE
Bari 842-870
Brindisi
Taranto 846-882, 927
Chandax
TH. OF CRETE
CAUCASUS MTS.
Cherson
THEME OF CHERSON (conquered by the Varangians 988)
BLACK SEA
Sinope
Trapezus
Amastris
Heraclea
TH. OF PAPHLAGONIA
Gangra
ARMENIAC THEME
Amasia
THEME OF CHALDIA
Colonea
TH. OF COLONEA
TH. OF MESOPOTAMIA
Sebastea
TH. OF SEBASTEA
BUCELLARIAN TH.
Claudiopolis
OPTIMATON
Nicomedia
Nicaea
Cyzicus
Prusa
Ancyra
OPSICIAN THEME
Adramyttium
Dorylaeum
Amorium
ANATOLIC THEME
Iconium
THEME CHARSIANON
Caesarea
THEME OF CAPPADOCIA
Podandus
TH. OF LYCANDOS
THEME OF CILICIA
Tarsus
Seleucia
TH. OF SELEUCIA
THEME OF ANTIOCH
Antioch
Aleppo
Edessa
Euphrates R.
DOMINION OF THE HAMDANIDS
THRACESIAN THEME
Mitylene
Sardis
Smyrna
Ephesus
TH. OF THE CIBYRRHAEOTS
Side
Attalea
Myra
Constantia
Paphos
TH. OF CYPRUS
Tripoli
Homs
Damascus
SYRIA
Acre
Jerusalem
AEGEAN SEA

England in the Eighth and Ninth Centuries.

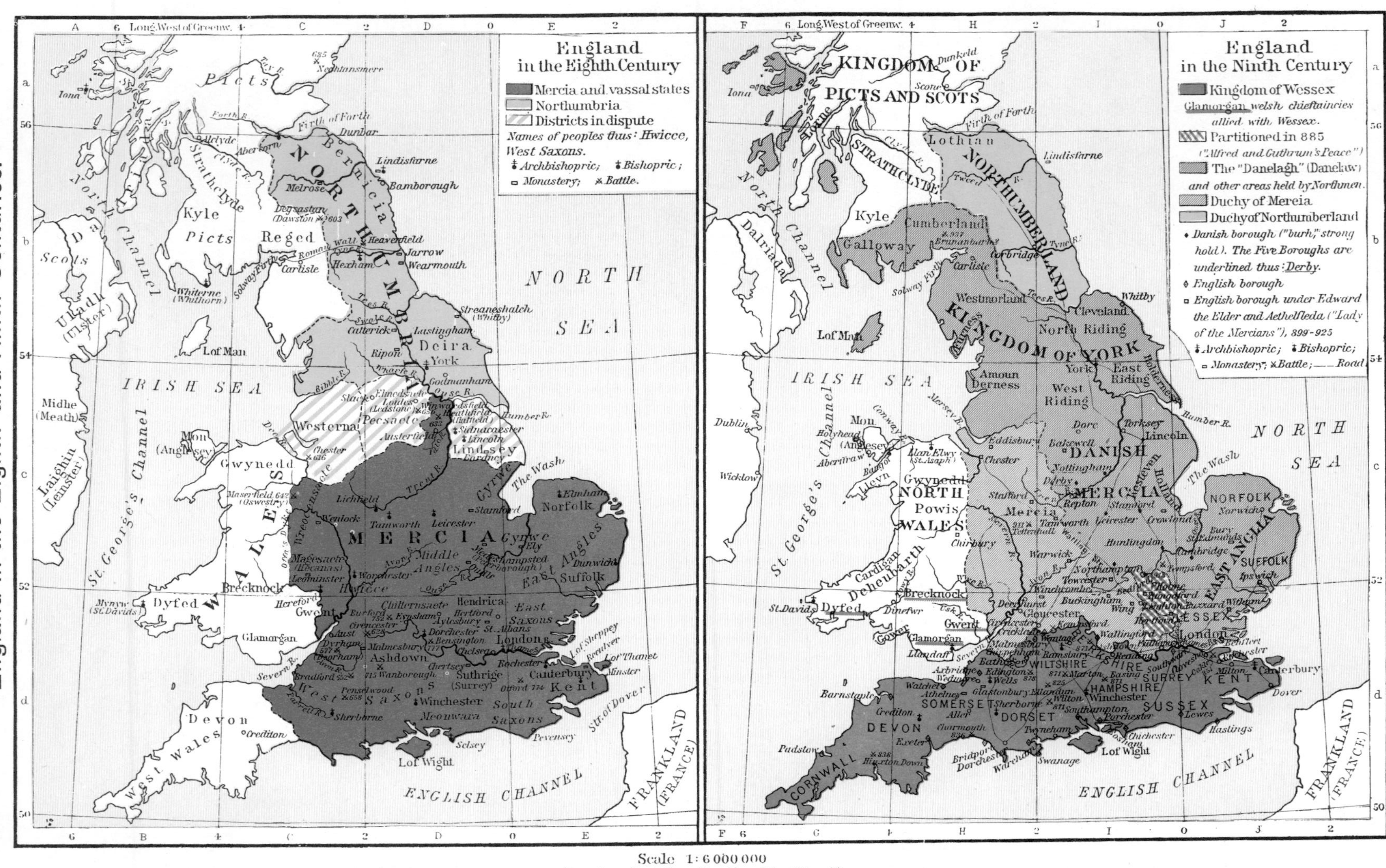

France about 1035.

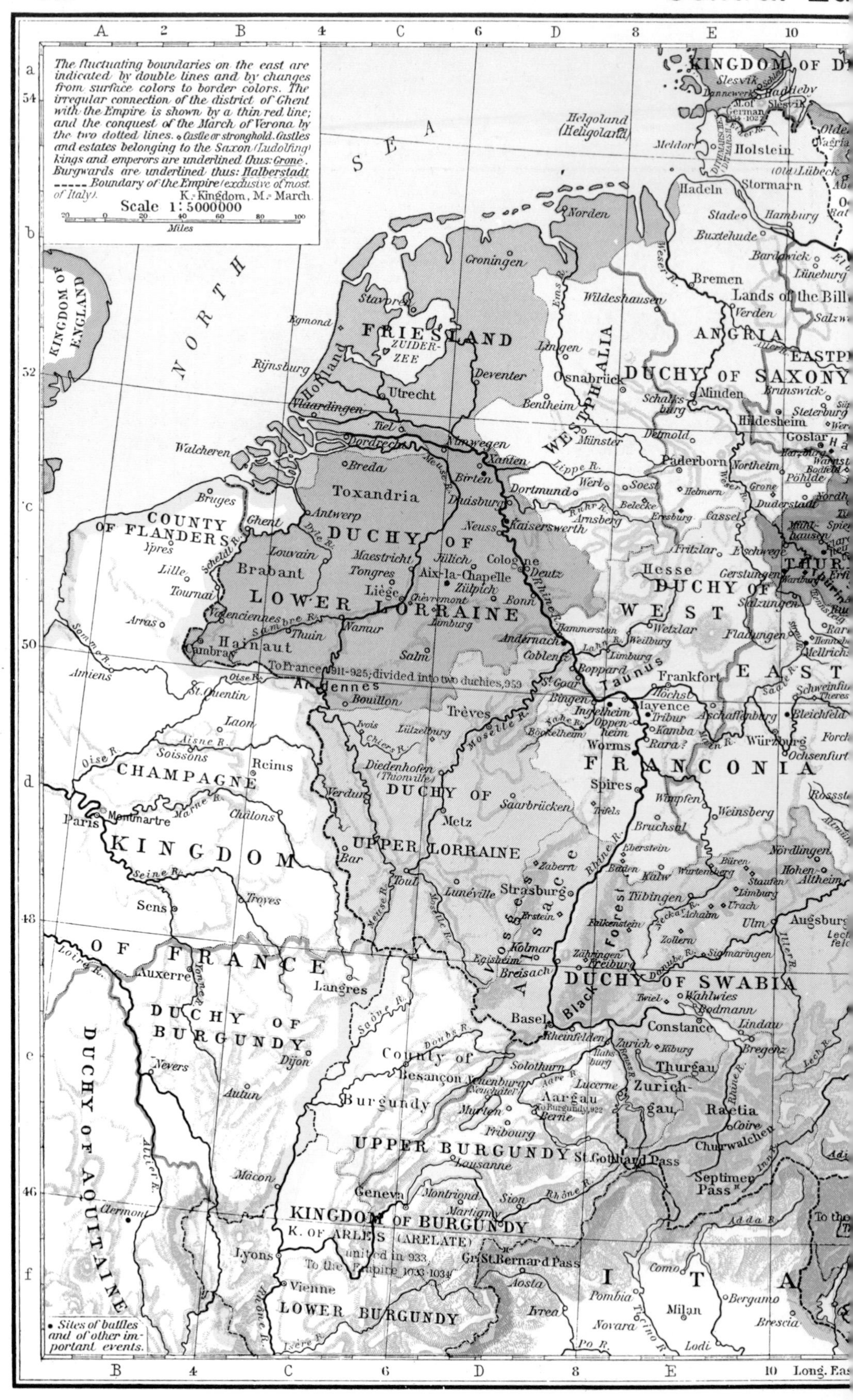
The fluctuating boundaries on the east are indicated by double lines and by changes from surface colors to border colors. The irregular connection of the district of Ghent with the Empire is shown by a thin red line; and the conquest of the March of Verona by the two dotted lines. ∘ Castle or stronghold. Castles and estates belonging to the Saxon (Ludolfing) kings and emperors are underlined thus: Grone. Burgwards are underlined thus: Halberstadt
---- Boundary of the Empire (exclusive of most of Italy).
K. = Kingdom, M. = March.
Scale 1: 5000000
Miles
• Sites of battles and of other important events.
NORTH SEA
KINGDOM OF ENGLAND
KINGDOM OF D
Helgoland (Heligoland)
Holstein
Hamburg
Bremen
FRIESLAND
ZUIDER-ZEE
Groningen
Utrecht
Deventer
Holland
Vlaardingen
Walcheren
Nimwegen
Xanten
WESTPHALIA
DUCHY OF SAXONY
ANGRIA
Osnabrück
Minden
Münster
Paderborn
Hildesheim
Toxandria
Antwerp
Bruges
Ghent
COUNTY OF FLANDERS
Ypres
Lille
Tournai
Arras
DUCHY OF LOWER LORRAINE
Brabant
Louvain
Maestricht
Tongres
Liège
Aix-la-Chapelle
Cologne
Deutz
Duisburg
Kaiserswerth
Dortmund
Hainaut
Cambrai
Valenciennes
Namur
Ardennes
To France 911-925; divided into two duchies, 959
Bouillon
Trèves
Coblenz
Andernach
Hesse
DUCHY OF WEST FRANCONIA
Frankfort
Mayence
Worms
Spires
Würzburg
EAST
Amiens
St. Quentin
Laon
Soissons
Reims
CHAMPAGNE
Paris
Montmartre
Châlons
KINGDOM OF FRANCE
Sens
Troyes
Auxerre
Langres
Verdun
Metz
DUCHY OF UPPER LORRAINE
Toul
Bar
Lunéville
Saarbrücken
Strasburg
Alsace
Vosges
Black Forest
Breisach
Basel
DUCHY OF SWABIA
Tübingen
Ulm
Augsburg
Constance
Lindau
Bregenz
Zurich
Thurgau
Zurich-gau
Raetia
Coire
Churwalchen
Septimer Pass
St. Gotthard Pass
DUCHY OF BURGUNDY
Dijon
Nevers
Autun
DUCHY OF AQUITAINE
Clermont
County of Burgundy
Besançon
Aargau
Berne
Lucerne
UPPER BURGUNDY
Lausanne
Geneva
Sion
Mâcon
KINGDOM OF BURGUNDY
K. OF ARLES (ARELATE)
United in 933,
To the Empire 1033-1034
Gr. St. Bernard Pass
Lyons
Vienne
LOWER BURGUNDY
Aosta
Ivrea
Novara
Milan
Bergamo
Brescia
Lodi
ITA
Rhine R.
Rhône R.
Moselle R.
Meuse R.
Seine R.
Marne R.
Loire R.
Saône R.
Danube R.
Po R.
Long. East

BALTIC SEA
Rügen
Arkona
Julin (Jomsburg)
Kolberg
Danzig
Prussians
Belgard
Wollin
Usedom
Demmin
Wolgast
MARCH
POMERANIA
Stettin
Redarians
Rhetra?
Garz
Ukrians
Pyritz
Nakel
Wilzians (Liutizians)
Prizlawa
Havelberg
Hevellians
NORTH MARCH (NORDMARK)
Brandenburg
Gnesen
Posen
Lebus
Krossen
EAST MARCH (OSTMARK)
Jüterbog
Zerbst
Lusatians
March of Lusatia
Dobrilugk
POLAND
Kingdom, 1025
Glogau
Liegnitz
Breslau
Sagan
Niemitsch
Halle
Merseburg
Strehla
Milzienians
March of Meissen
MARCH OF THURINGIA
Görlitz
Bautzen
Meissen
Dalaminzians
Dohna
Zeitz
Schweidnitz
Nimptsch
Warthe
Glatz
Under Poland since 999
CHROBATIA
Cracow
Miriquidi
Leitmeritz
Melnik
Brüx
Saaz
Nimburg
Bunzlau
Prague
Wyschehrad
Leitomischl
DUCHY OF BOHEMIA
Under Poland, 1003-1004
Olmütz
MORAVIA
Under Poland, 1003-1029
Brünn
Pilsen
Leuchtenberg
Klattau
Netolitz
Ratisbon
Böhmerwald
Znaym
Trencsin
Mailberg
BAVARIAN EAST MARCH (OSTMARK) (MARGRAVATE OF AUSTRIA)
Passau
Linz
Melk
Krems
Tulln
Pöchlarn
St. Pölten
Vienna
Hainburg
Presburg
Hungarian 907-955
Duchy, 1156
Wels
Steier
Mühldorf
DUCHY OF BAVARIA
Salzburg
Traungau
Ödenburg (Sopron)
Pitten
HUNGARY
Buda (Ofen)
MARCH OF
Established 970?
Eppenstein
Hengstburg
Detached from Carinthia, 1035
Friesach
CARINTHIA
DUCHY OF CARINTHIA
Villach
Detached from Bavaria, 976
From 1055 M. OF STYRIA 1180, Duchy
Souna
Friuli
MARCH OF VERONA
to Carinthia, 976
Aquileia
Grado
Laibach
MARCH OF CARNIOLA
Trieste
Detached from Carinthia 1040
MARCH OF ISTRIA
Duchy of Venice
CROATIA
Oder R.
Warthe R.
Vistula R.
Pilica R.
Elbe R.
Danube R.
Drave R.
Save R.
Mur R.
Raab R.
Theiss R.
Waag R.
Gran R.
March R.
Thaya R.
Enns R.
Inn R.
Isar R.
Salzach R.
Neisse R.
Bober R.
Spree R.
Leitha R.

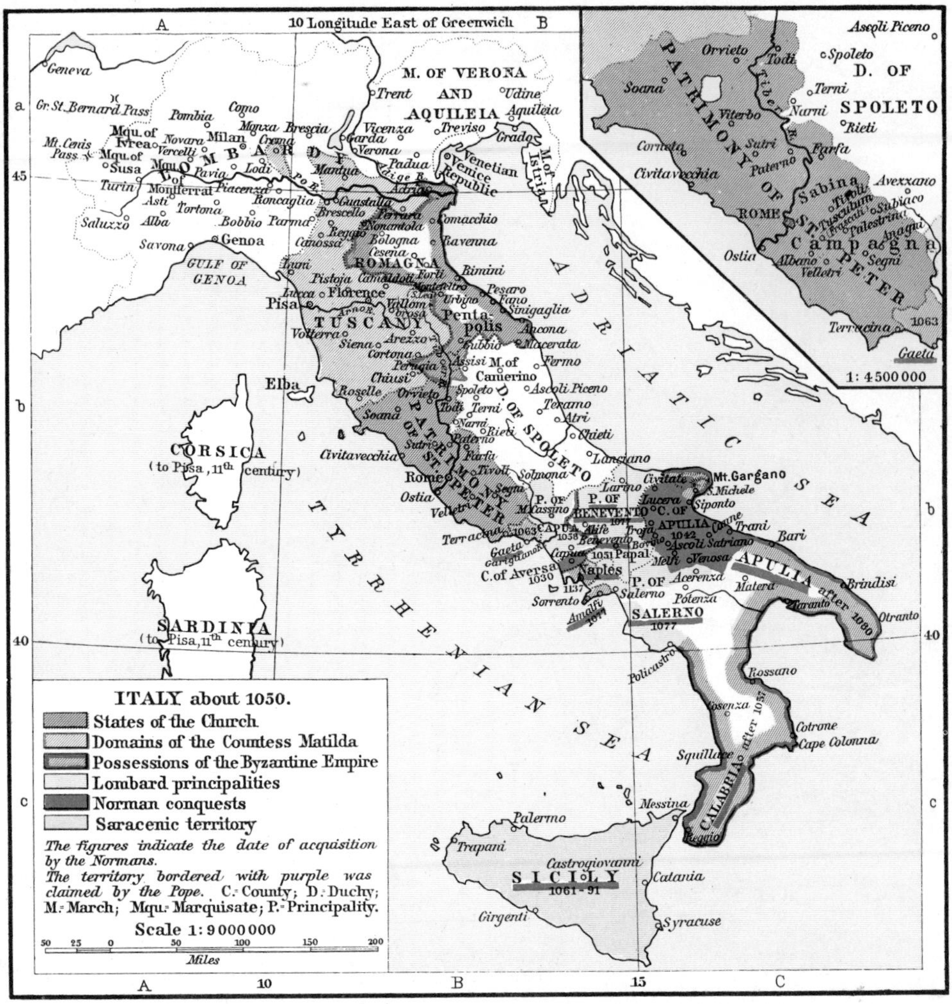

Italy about 1050. Dominions of Cnut, 1014—1035.

ITALY about 1050.

- States of the Church
- Domains of the Countess Matilda
- Possessions of the Byzantine Empire
- Lombard principalities
- Norman conquests
- Saracenic territory

The figures indicate the date of acquisition by the Normans.
The territory bordered with purple was claimed by the Pope. C.: County; D.: Duchy; M.: March; Mqu.: Marquisate; P.: Principality.

Scale 1: 9 000 000

50 25 0 50 100 150 200
Miles

10 Longitude East of Greenwich

M. OF VERONA AND AQUILEIA
LOMBARDY
Venetian Republic
ROMAGNA
TUSCANY
Pentapolis
M. of Camerino
D. OF SPOLETO
PATRIMONY OF ST. PETER
P. OF BENEVENTO
C. OF APULIA
APULIA after 1080
SALERNO 1077
CALABRIA after 1057
SICILY 1061-91
CORSICA (to Pisa, 11th century)
SARDINIA (to Pisa, 11th century)
ADRIATIC SEA
TYRRHENIAN SEA
GULF OF GENOA

Inset: PATRIMONY OF ST. PETER; D. OF SPOLETO; Sabina; Campagna; ROME; 1063; 1: 4 500 000

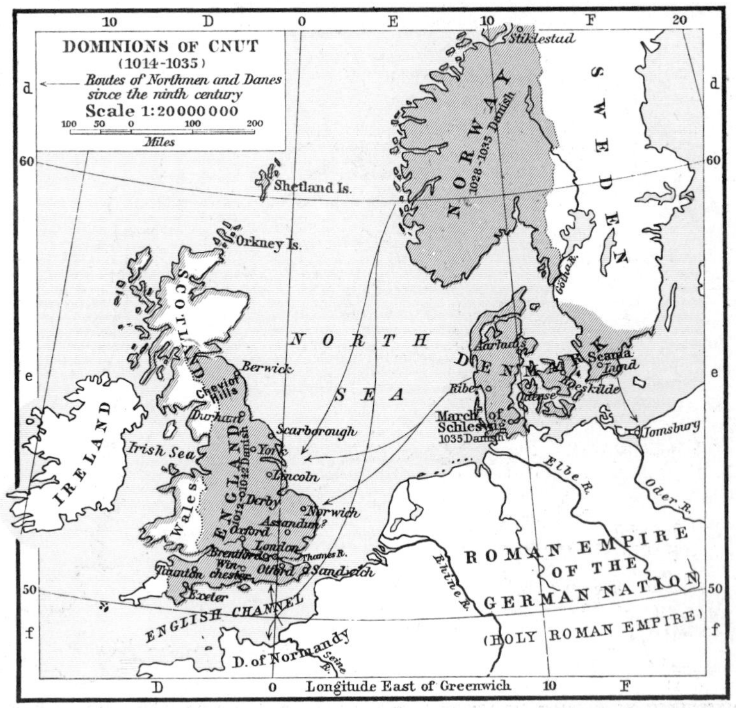

England, 1087—1154.

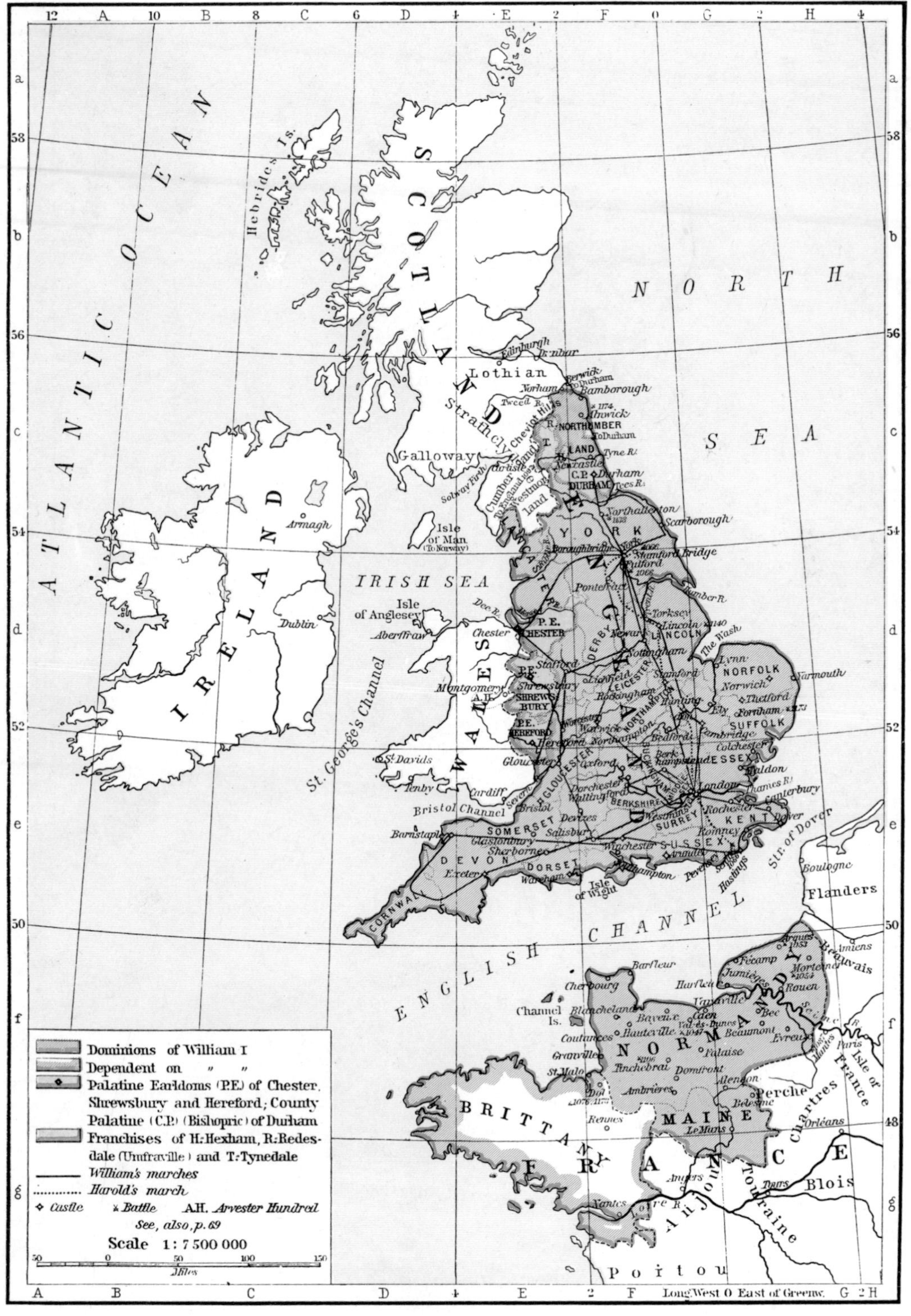

Routes of the leaders of the first Crusade
(1096-1099)
Godfrey of Bouillon
Adhemar of Puy and Raymond of Toulouse
Bohemond and Tancred
Robert of Flanders and Hugh of Vermandois
Route of the combined forces. C.-County; D.-Duchy; P.-Principality.
Scale 1:20 000 000
Miles
ATLANTIC OCEAN
NORTH SEA
KINGDOM OF NORWAY
KINGDOM OF SWEDEN
GOTHLAND
KINGDOM OF DENMARK
KINGDOM OF SCOTLAND
IRELAND
KINGDOM OF ENGLAND
WALES
DUCHY OF POMERANIA
ROMAN EMPIRE OF THE GERMAN NATION
(HOLY ROMAN EMPIRE)
KINGDOM OF FRANCE
Normandy
Maine
Vermandois
Flanders
KINGDOM OF BURGUNDY
KINGDOM OF LEON
COUNTY OF PORTUGAL
KINGDOM OF CASTILE
KINGDOM OF NAVARRE
KINGDOM OF ARAGON
COUNTY OF BARCELONA OR CATALONIA
DOMINION OF THE ALMORAVIDS 1060-1147
KINGDOM OF CROATIA
DALMATIA
ADRIATIC SEA
TYRRHENIAN SEA
NORMAN PRINCIPALITY
Corsica (to Pisa)
SARDINIA (to Pisa)
Balearic Is.
MEDITERRANEAN
C. OF SICILY
Malta 1090 to Sicily
DOMINION OF THE HAMMADITES
Zeirids
CALIFATE OF
Gulf of Gabes
Tripoli
The Growth of Islamic Power, 632-1097
Scale 1:90,000000
Under Mohammed, up to 632
632 - 700
701 - 800
801 - 900
To 1097
Byzantine Empire
Persia
Arabia
Magrib
Spain
France
Italy
Egypt

Europe and the Mediterranean Lands by Religions about 1097.
Christians:
Belonging to the Roman Church
" " " Greek "
Mohammedans:
Under the Calif of Bagdad (Abbasid)
" " " Cairo (Fatimite)
Dates are those of conversion to Christianity
Scale 1: 40 000 000
Miles
Meridian of Greenwich
ATLANTIC OCEAN
NORTH SEA
BALTIC SEA
NORWAY about 1000
SWEDEN about 1000
DENMARK
IRELAND
SCOTLAND
ENGLAND
Canterbury
Finns
Novgorod
Letts
Lithuanians
Pomeranians 12 cent.
Prussians
Polock
Vitebsk
Smolensk
Russians about 1000
Chernigov
Kiev
Poles
Cracow
Czechs
GERMANY
Mayence
Reims
FRANCE
BURGUNDY
Salzburg
Gran (Esztergom)
Hungarians about 1000
Cumans
LEON
CASTILE
SPAIN
Toledo
Cordova
DOM. OF THE ALMORAVIDS
DOM. OF THE HAMMADITES
ITALY
Rome
NORMAN PRINCIPALITIES
MEDITERRANEAN SEA
BLACK SEA
BYZANTINE EMPIRE
Constantinople
Armenians
CALIFATE OF BAGDAD (ABBASID)
Nestorians
Antioch
Bagdad
Jerusalem
Alexandria
Cairo
CALIFATE OF CAIRO (FATIMITE)
Volga R.
Kama R.
Don R.
Dnieper R.
Dniester R.
Danube R.
Pskov
LITHUANIA
Minsk
Pinsk
Halicz
Cumans about 1050
Sea of Asov
Bosporus
Khazars
Ossetes (Alans?)
Gothia
Cherson
CASPIAN SEA
Georgia
Tiflis
Shirvan
Kura R.
Kars
Ani
Trebizond
Sinope
BYZANTINE EMPIRE
Patzinaks
Philippopolis
Adrianople
Constantinople
Chalcedon
MACEDONIA
Thessalonica
Gallipolis
Nicomedia
Nicaea
Angora
Amasia
Neocaesarea
Theodosiopolis
Erzerum
Manzikert
Armenia
Tabriz
Azerbaijan
Kurdistan
DOMINIONS OF THE SELJUK TURKS
Danishmend
SULTANATE OF ROUM
Dorylaeum
Pergamum
Sardis
Smyrna
Philadelphia
Ephesus
Laodicea
Philomelium
Iconium
Caesarea
Heraclea
Attalia
Tarsus
Seleucia
Myra
Rhodes
Armenian Petty States
Melitene
Amida
Edessa
Mardin
Marash
Harran
DOMINION OF MOSUL
Mosul (Seljuk 1055)
El Jesireh
Aleppo
Antioch
Shahr Zor
Hamadan
Tigris R.
Bagdad (Seljuk 1055)
Euphrates R.
Iraq
Homs (Emesa)
SYRIA
Nicosia
Cyprus
Limasol
Tripoli
Beirut
Sidon
Tyre
Acre
Damascus (Seljuk 1076)
Jaffa
Ascalon
Gaza
Jerusalem
Fatimite 969, Seljuk 1071, Fatimite 1098.
Dead Sea
PALESTINE
ARABIA
Candia
Crete
AEGEAN SEA
Damietta
Alexandria
El Arish
Cairo
(FATIMITE)
EGYPT
Nile R.
RED SEA

Asia Minor and the States of the Crusaders in Syria, about 1140.

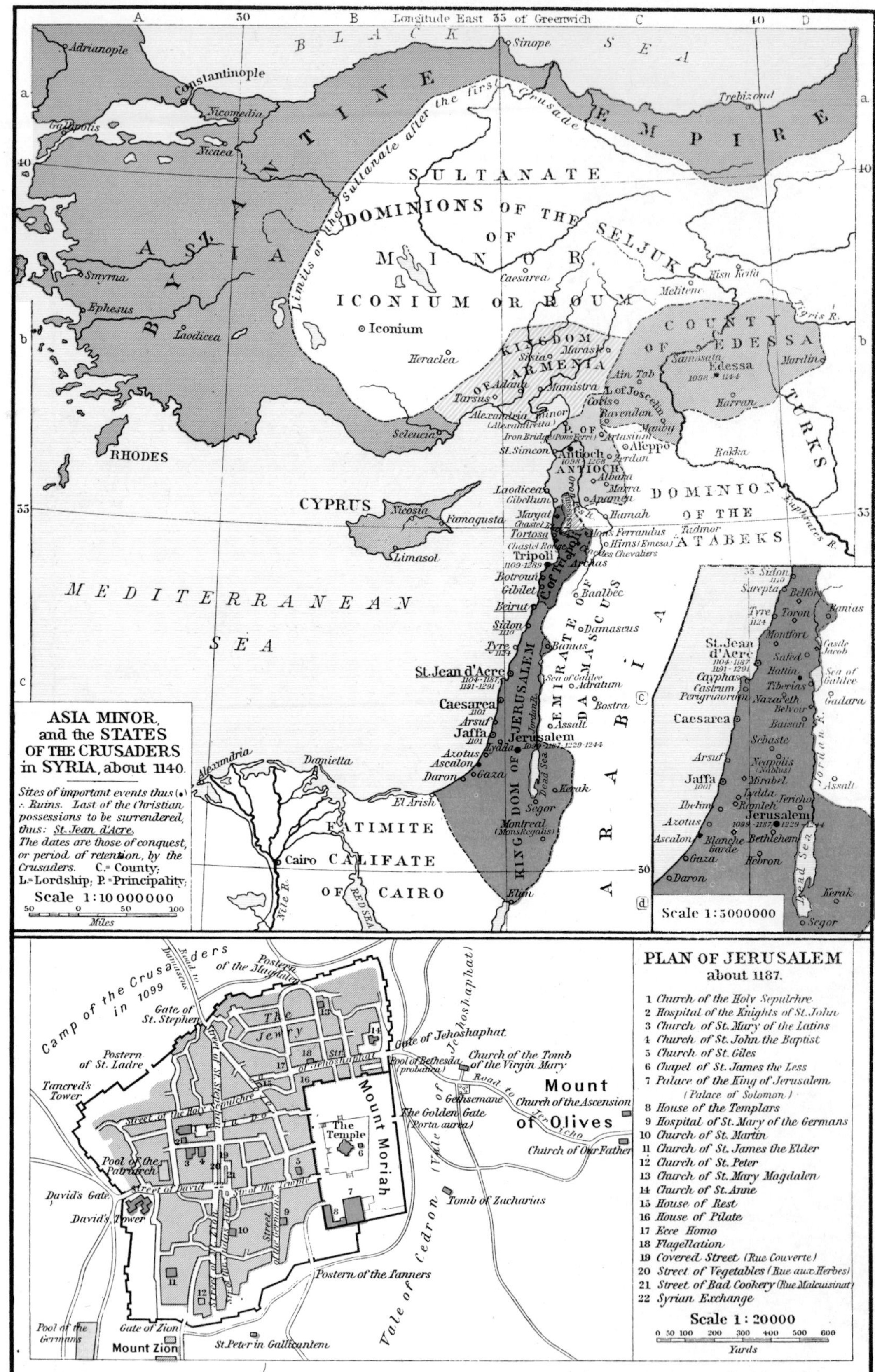

Royal Domain
Other fiefs
English possessions
English dominions held of the French Crown
B.- BISHOPRIC; C.- COUNTY; D.- DUCHY;
K.- KINGDOM; M.- MARQUISATE;
S.- SEIGNIORY; V.- VISCOUNTY.
Scale 1: 7 500 000
See also, p. 70
Domain, Fiefs and Suzerains of the Count of Champagne in the Twelfth Century.
Held of the
Emperor as suzerain
King of France
Duke of Burgundy
Archbishop of Reims
Sens
Bishop of Autun
Auxerre
Langres
Abbot St. Denis
B.- BISHOPRIC; C.- COUNTY;
S.- SEIGNIORY; V.- VISCOUNTY.
Comp.- Compiègne; Prém.- Prémontré;
Montm.- Montmorency.
Scale 1: 5000000

ATLANTIC OCEAN
NORTH SEA
KINGDOM OF NORWAY
KINGDOM OF DENMARK
KINGDOM OF SCOTLAND
IRELAND
Anglo-Norman Colonies
KINGDOM OF ENGLAND
ENGLISH CHANNEL
Aberdeen
Perth
Edinburgh
Berwick
Carlisle
Durham
York
Chester
Leicester
Northampton
Oxford
London
Canterbury
Southampton
Exeter
Milford
Waterford
Wexford
Dublin
Limerick
Tönsberg
Calmar
Lund
Rügen
Hamburg
Bremen
Stettin
Utrecht
Brunswick
Posen
HOLY ROMAN EMPIRE
KINGDOM OF GERMANY
Cologne
Bruges
Ghent
Boulogne
Rouen
Paris
Reims
Mayence
Treves
Metz
Spires
Prague
Nuremberg
Ratisbon
Strasburg
Augsburg
Vienna
Basel
Constance
Salzburg
KINGDOM OF FRANCE
Orleans
Clairvaux
Tours
Poitiers
Bourges
Vezelay
Clermont
Limoges
Bordeaux
Lyons
Toulouse
Narbonne
Arles
Marseilles
Geneva
Turin
Milan
Pavia
Alessandria
Genoa
Trent
Aquileia
Verona
Venice
Croatia
KINGDOM OF ITALY
Ravenna
Florence
Pisa
Ancona
Rome
Naples
Salerno
Bari
Taranto
ADRIATIC SEA
DALMATIA
Zara
Spalato
Corsica
Sardinia
Balearic Is.
NORMAN KINGDOM OF THE TWO SICILIES
Palermo
Messina
Reggio
Syracuse
Malta
KINGDOM OF CASTILE
KINGDOM OF LEON
KINGDOM OF PORTUGAL
K. OF NAVARRE
KINGDOM OF ARAGON
Santiago de Compostela
Oviedo
Leon
Burgos
Valladolid
Oporto
Coimbra
Salamanca
Saragossa
Lerida
Barcelona
Tarragona
Tudela
Santarem
Lisbon
Talavera
Toledo
Alcantara
Merida
Badajoz
Cuenca
Valencia
Calatrava
Silves
Seville
Cordova
Játiva
Murcia
Jaén
Granada
Cadiz
Malaga
Almeria
Algeciras
Gibraltar
Tangier
Ceuta
Tetuan
DOMINIONS OF THE ALMOHADS
MEDITERRANEAN SEA
Richard's Fleet
Philip Augustus Fleet
Melilla
Oran
Tenes
Algiers
Bugia (Bougie)
Bona
Tunis
Setif
Constantine
Tlemsen
Fez
Morocco
Kairwan
Mahedia
Gabes
Tripoli
Sirt
De Cl.=De Clare; De Co.=De Courcy; De L.=De Lacy (Anglo-Norman Earldoms in Ireland); DOM.=Dominion; K.=Kingdom; PRINC.=Principality; W.M.E.=Welsh Marcher Earldoms; W.P.=Welsh Principalities.
Crusade of Louis VII and Conrad III (1147-1149)
Crusade of Richard I, Philip II (Augustus) and Frederick I (Barbarossa) (1189-1191)
Scale 1:20000000
Miles
Long. West 5 of Greenwich
Long. East 5 of Greenwich

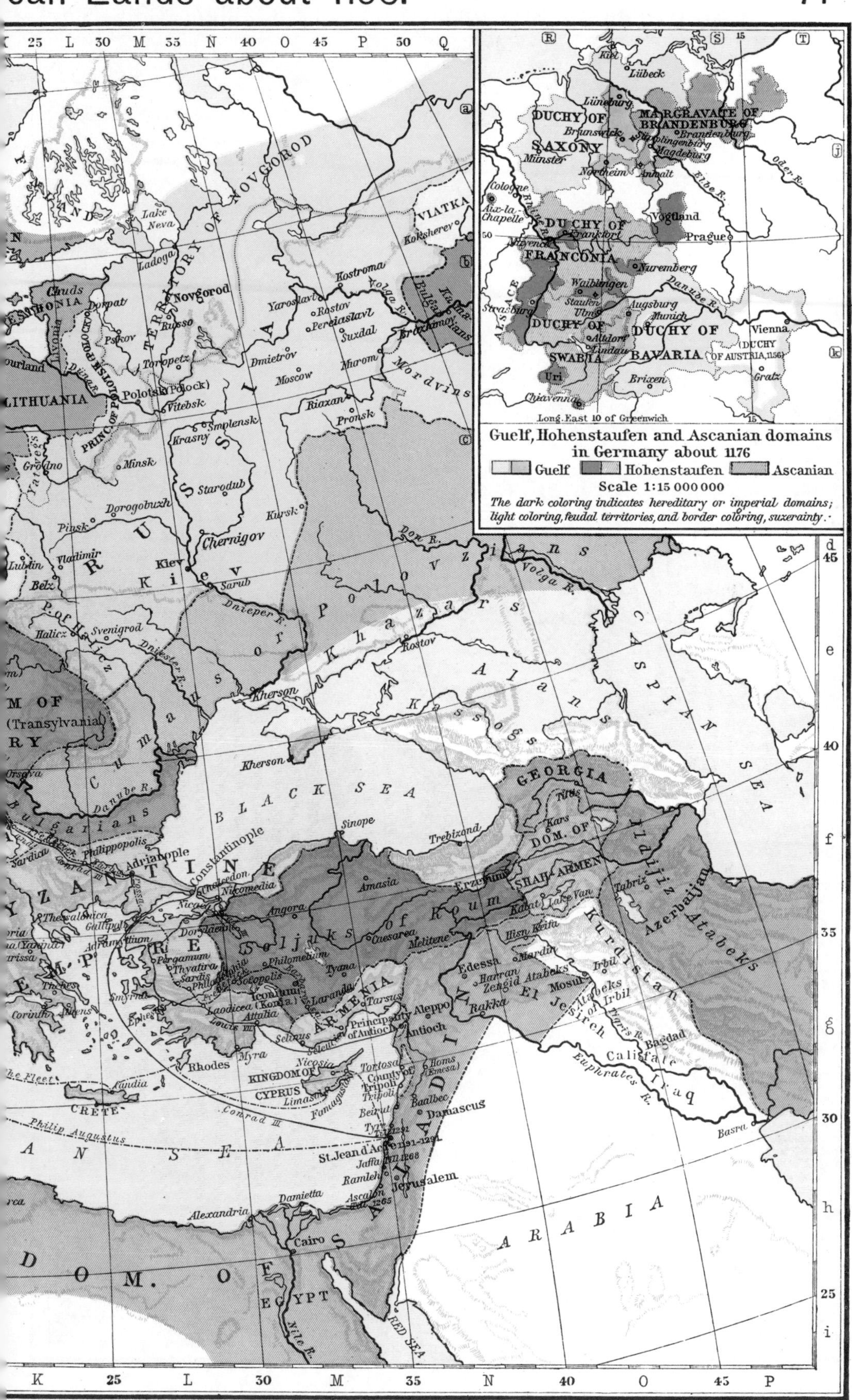

Guelf, Hohenstaufen and Ascanian domains in Germany about 1176
Guelf
Hohenstaufen
Ascanian
Scale 1:15 000 000
The dark coloring indicates hereditary or imperial domains; light coloring, feudal territories, and border coloring, suzerainty.
Long. East 10 of Greenwich
DUCHY OF SAXONY
MARGRAVATE OF BRANDENBURG
DUCHY OF FRANCONIA
DUCHY OF SWABIA
DUCHY OF BAVARIA
(DUCHY OF AUSTRIA, 1156)
ALSACE
Kiel
Lübeck
Lüneburg
Brunswick
Brandenburg
Magdeburg
Münster
Northeim
Anhalt
Cologne
Aix-la-Chapelle
Vogtland
Frankfort
Prague
Nuremberg
Waiblingen
Staufen
Ulm
Strasburg
Augsburg
Munich
Altdorf
Lindau
Vienna
Uri
Brixen
Gratz
Chiavenna
Rhine R.
Elbe R.
Oder R.
Danube R.
TERRITORY OF NOVGOROD
Novgorod
Lake Ladoga
Lake Neva
VIATKA
Koksherev
Kostroma
Volga R.
Yaroslavl
Rostov
Pereiaslavl
Suzdal
Murom
Moscow
Dmietrov
Riazan
Pronsk
Mordvins
Bulgarians
Pskov
Dorpat
Livonia
Courland
LITHUANIA
Polotsk
Vitebsk
Smolensk
Krasny
Minsk
Grodno
Starodub
Kursk
Dorogobuzh
Pinsk
Chernigov
Kiev
Vladimir
Lublin
Belz
Sarub
RUSSIA
Halicz
Svenigrod
Dnieper R.
Dniester R.
Don R.
Polovzians
Khazars
Rostov
Kherson
Alans
Kassogs
Cumans
CASPIAN SEA
BLACK SEA
GEORGIA
Kars
DOM. OF SHAH-ARMEN
Tabriz
Lake Van
Azerbaijan Atabeks
Kurdistan
Erzerum
Trebizond
Sinope
Amasia
Seljuks of Roum
Caesarea
Melitene
Angora
Constantinople
Chalcedon
Nicomedia
Adrianople
Philippopolis
Sardica
Bulgarians
Danube R.
BYZANTINE EMPIRE
Thessalonica
Gallipoli
Pergamum
Thyatira
Sardis
Philadelphia
Philomelium
Sozopolis
Iconium (Konia)
Laodicea
Smyrna
Ephesus
Attalia
Laranda
Tyana
Tarsus
ARMENIA
Seleucia
Selinus
Principality of Antioch
Antioch
Aleppo
Edessa
Harran
Zengid Atabeks
Mosul
Irbil
Atabeks of Irbil
El Jesireh
Rakka
Mardin
Hisn Keifa
Tigris R.
Euphrates R.
Bagdad
Califate
Iraq
Basra
Rhodes
Myra
KINGDOM OF CYPRUS
Nicosia
Limassol
Famagusta
Tortosa
County of Tripoli
Tripoli
Homs (Emesa)
Baalbec
Damascus
Beirut
Tyre
St. Jean d'Acre
Jaffa
Ramleh
Jerusalem
Ascalon
Damietta
Alexandria
Cairo
EGYPT
Nile R.
RED SEA
SALADIN
ARABIA
Candia
CRETE
Philip Augustus
Conrad III
Louis VII
Corinth
Athens
Thebes
Orsova
(Transylvania)

72 The Holy Roman Empire under the Hohenstaufen, 1138—1254.

CASPIAN SEA
BLACK SEA
ADRIATIC SEA
AEGEAN SEA
MEDITERRANEAN SEA
KINGDOM OF GEORGIA
Alans
RUSSIA
Cumans
KINGDOM OF HUNGARY
K. OF BULGARIA 1203
EMPIRE OF TREBIZOND
EMPIRE OF NICAEA
SULTANATE OF ICONIUM OR ROUM
K. OF ARMENIA
K. OF CYPRUS (LUSIGNANS)
K. OF JERUSALEM
CALIPHATE OF BAGDAD
ARABIA
DOMINIONS OF THE AYYUBIDS
CRETE Venetian, 1212
Despotat of Epirus
Albania
K. OF THESSALONICA
KINGDOM OF THE TWO SICILIES
SICILY
SARDINIA
Corsica
States of the Church
K. OF ITALY
HOLY ROMAN EMPIRE
K. OF GERMANY
K. OF ARLES
KINGDOM OF FRANCE
K. OF ARAGON
Balearic Is.
DOM. OF THE ALMOHADS 1129 - 1270
(MUWAHHIDS)
Fourth crusade, 1202-1204
Crusade of Frederick II, 1228-1229
Crusades of Louis IX, 1248-1254 and 1270
Venetian possessions
Genoese cities after 1261 (thus Pera)
Scale 1:18 000 000
Miles
C.-County; D.-Duchy; Dom.-Dominion; Emp.-Empire; K.-Kingdom; P.-Principality.
Longitude East 25 of Greenwich

Ireland
Clans and families thus: O'Reilly
Archbishopric Bishopric
Borough Castle
Scale 1:6 000 000
Miles
ATLANTIC OCEAN
CONNAUGHT
ULSTER
Tyrone
Meath
LEINSTER
Leix
MUNSTER
Thomond
Desmond
Dublin
Armagh
Drogheda
Wexford
Waterford
Limerick
Cork
Kinsale
Galway
North Channel
Scotland
Scale 1:600
THE HEBRIDES
Ceded by Norway 1266
Caithness
Sutherland
Ross
Moray Firth
ELGIN
BANFF
ABERDEEN
KINCARDINE
FORFAR OR ANGUS
PERTH
FIFE
STIRLING
LOTHIAN
BERWICK
DUMFRIES
Firth of Clyde
Firth of Forth
ENGLAND
England and Wales
Abbey represented in the House of Lords
Borough returning members to House of Commons
Castle Battle BERKS.=Berks
Cinque Ports thus: Hastings
Scale 1:4 000 000
ISLE OF MAN
Ceded by Norway 1266
IRISH SEA
NORTH SEA
CUMBERLAND
WESTMORLAND
PALATINATE OF DURHAM
NORTHUMBERLAND
YORK
COUNTY PALATINE OF LANCASTER (1377)
COUNTY PALATINE OF CHESTER
ANGLESEY
PRINCIPALITY OF WALES
DERBY
NOTTINGHAM
LINCOLN
NORFOLK
SUFFOLK
ESSEX
KENT
SUSSEX
SURREY
HAMPSHIRE
DORSET
DEVON
CORNWALL
SOMERSET
WILTSHIRE
BERKS
OXFORD
GLOUCESTER
HEREFORD
SHROPSHIRE
STAFFORD
WARWICK
LEICESTER
NORTHAMPTON
CAMBRIDGE
HUNTINGDON
BUCKINGHAM
BEDFORD
HERTFORD
MIDDLESEX
London
ST. GEORGE'S CHANNEL
BRISTOL CHANNEL
ENGLISH CHANNEL
Strait of Dover
Isle of Wight
Meridian 0 of Greenw.

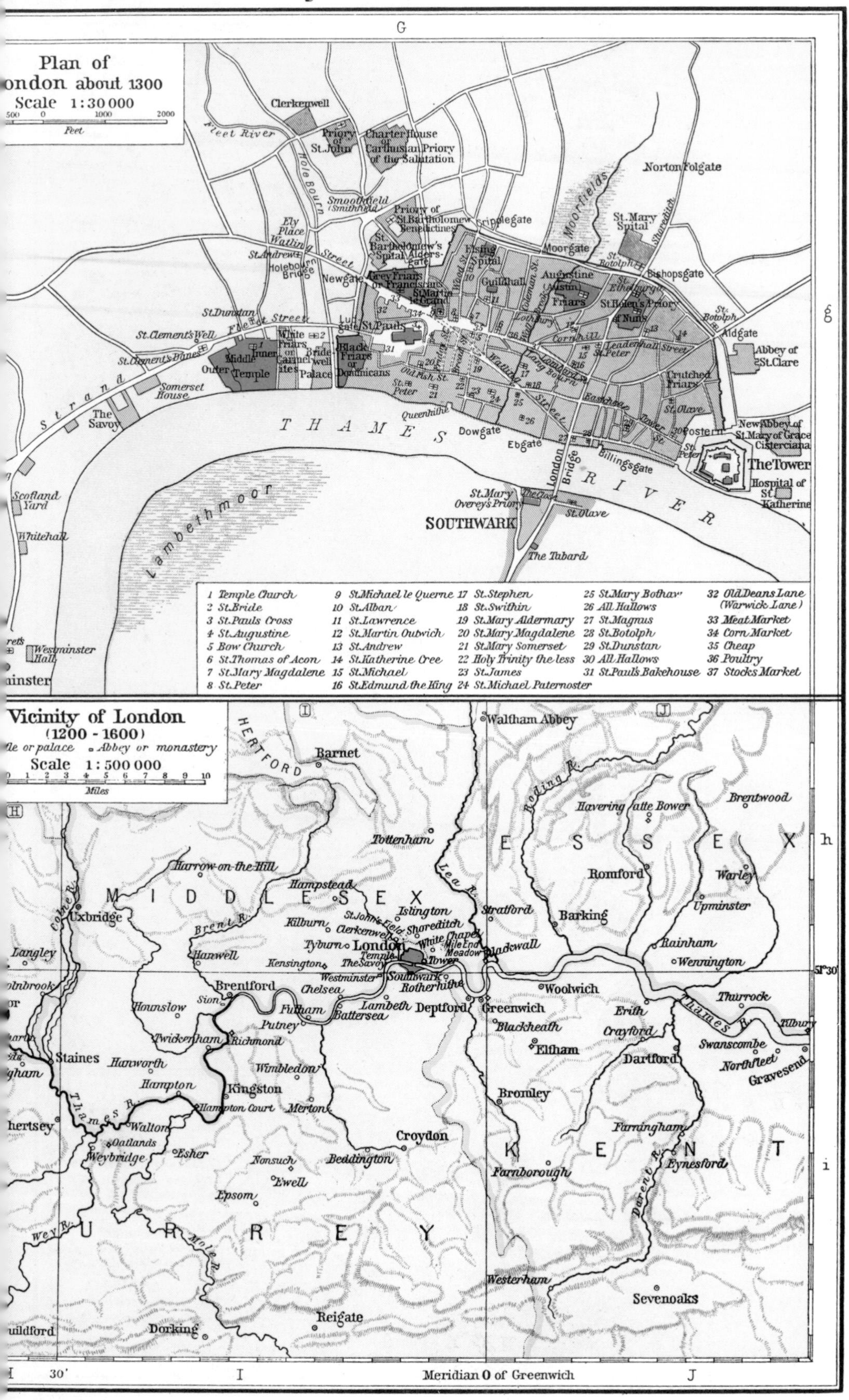

Plan of
ondon about 1300
Scale 1:30 000
Feet
1 Temple Church
2 St.Bride
3 St.Pauls Cross
4 St.Augustine
5 Bow Church
6 St.Thomas of Acon
7 St.Mary Magdalene
8 St.Peter
9 St.Michael le Querne
10 St.Alban
11 St.Lawrence
12 St.Martin Outwich
13 St.Andrew
14 St.Katherine Cree
15 St.Michael
16 St.Edmund the King
17 St.Stephen
18 St.Swithin
19 St.Mary Aldermary
20 St.Mary Magdalene
21 St.Mary Somerset
22 Holy Trinity the less
23 St.James
24 St.Michael Paternoster
25 St.Mary Bothaw
26 All Hallows
27 St.Magnus
28 St.Botolph
29 St.Dunstan
30 All Hallows
31 St.Paul's Bakehouse
32 Old Deans Lane (Warwick Lane)
33 Meat Market
34 Corn Market
35 Cheap
36 Poultry
37 Stocks Market
Clerkenwell
Priory of St.John
Charter House of Carthusian Priory of the Salutation
Fleet River
Hole Bourn
Norton Folgate
Moorfields
St.Mary Spital
Smoothfield (Smithfield)
Priory of St.Bartholomew Benedictines
Cripplegate
Moorgate
Bishopsgate
Aldgate
Abbey of St.Clare
Ely Place
Watling Street
Holebourn Bridge
Newgate
Grey Friars or Franciscans
Guildhall
Augustine (Austin) Friars
St.Helen's Priory of Nuns
St.Dunstan
Fleet Street
St.Clement's Well
St.Clement's Danes
White Friars or Carmelites
Bridewell Palace
Black Friars or Dominicans
St.Pauls
Inner Temple
Middle Temple
Outer Temple
Strand
Somerset House
The Savoy
Crutched Friars
St.Olave
Postern
New Abbey of St.Mary of Grace Cisterciana
The Tower
Hospital of St.Katherine
Queenhithe
Dowgate
Ebgate
Billingsgate
London Bridge
Thames River
Lambethmoor
Scotland Yard
Whitehall
Westminster Hall
St.Mary Overey's Priory
St.Olave
Southwark
The Tabard
Vicinity of London (1200-1600)
Scale 1:500 000
Miles
Waltham Abbey
Barnet
Hertford
Havering atte Bower
Brentwood
Tottenham
Essex
Romford
Warley
Upminster
Middlesex
Harrow-on-the-Hill
Hampstead
Islington
Stratford
Barking
Uxbridge
Brent R.
Kilburn
Clerkenwell
Shoreditch
Tyburn
London
White Chapel
Mile End Meadow
Blackwall
Rainham
Wennington
Langley
Hanwell
Kensington
The Savoy
Temple
Tower
Westminster
Southwark
Rotherhithe
Woolwich
Brentford
Chelsea
Thurrock
Hounslow
Sion
Fulham
Lambeth
Battersea
Deptford
Greenwich
Erith
Putney
Blackheath
Crayford
Tilbury
Twickenham
Richmond
Eltham
Dartford
Swanscombe
Staines
Hanworth
Wimbledon
Northfleet
Gravesend
Hampton
Kingston
Bromley
Thames R.
Hampton Court
Merton
Walton
Croydon
Farningham
Oatlands
Weybridge
Esher
Nonsuch
Beddington
Kent
Farnborough
Eynesford
Ewell
Darent R.
Epsom
Wey R.
Surrey
Mole R.
Westerham
Sevenoaks
Reigate
Dorking
Meridian 0 of Greenwich

France in 1328.

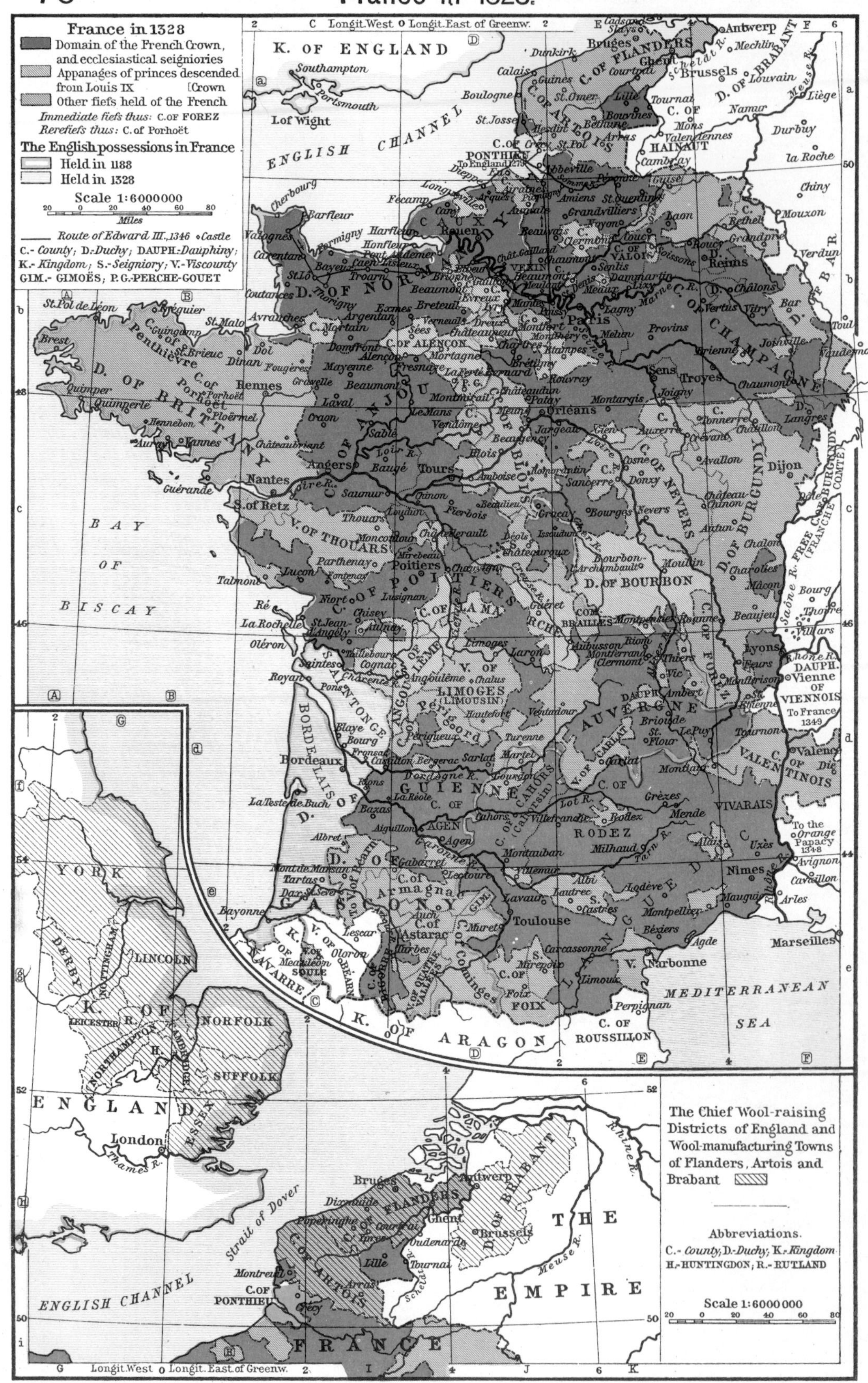

Boundary of the Empire
English possessions in France, 1360
Calais " " " " 1400
House of Anjou
" " Luxemburg (in addition to Hungary)
Bosnia Under shifting supremacy
DENMARK, NORWAY, SWEDEN under the Union of Calmar, 1397
B.E.= Byzantine Empire in 1400; C.= County; D.= Duchy;
K.= Kingdom; P.= Principality; Rep.= Republic
Scale 1:25000000
Miles

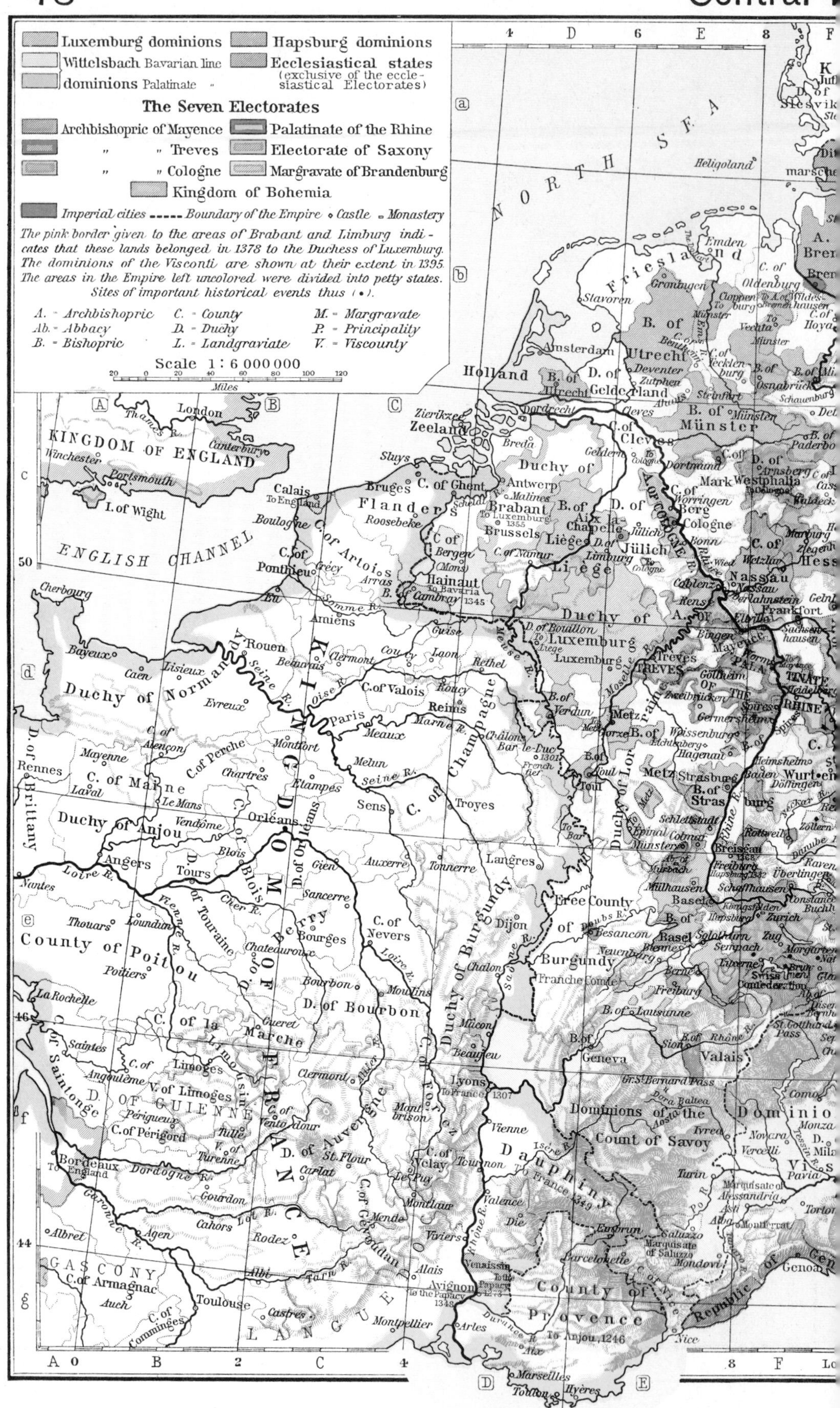
Luxemburg dominions
Hapsburg dominions
Wittelsbach Bavarian line
dominions Palatinate "
Ecclesiastical states
(exclusive of the ecclesiastical Electorates)
The Seven Electorates
Archbishopric of Mayence
" " Treves
" " Cologne
Palatinate of the Rhine
Electorate of Saxony
Margravate of Brandenburg
Kingdom of Bohemia
Imperial cities
Boundary of the Empire
Castle
Monastery
The pink border given to the areas of Brabant and Limburg indicates that these lands belonged in 1378 to the Duchess of Luxemburg.
The dominions of the Visconti are shown at their extent in 1395.
The areas in the Empire left uncolored were divided into petty states.
Sites of important historical events thus (•).
A. = Archbishopric
Ab. = Abbacy
B. = Bishopric
C. = County
D. = Duchy
L. = Landgraviate
M. = Margravate
P. = Principality
V. = Viscounty
Scale 1 : 6 000 000
Miles
NORTH SEA
KINGDOM OF ENGLAND
ENGLISH CHANNEL
KINGDOM OF FRANCE
Duchy of Normandy
County of Poitou
Duchy of Anjou
D. of Guienne
Languedoc
Gascony
C. of Champagne
Duchy of Burgundy
Free County of Burgundy
Dauphiny
County of Provence
Dominions of the Count of Savoy
Duchy of Luxemburg
Flanders
Brabant
Holland
Zeeland
Friesland
Hainaut
Duchy of Lorraine
Valais

BALTIC SEA
Bornholm
Möen
Falster
Fehmern
P. of Rügen
To Pomerania, 1325
Stralsund
Greifswald
Wolgast
Kolberg
B. of Kammin
Kammin
Stolp
Lauenburg
Danzig
Königsberg
Braunsberg
Ermeland
Elbing
Dirschau
Pomerelia
To Teutonic Order, 1310
Domain of the Teutonic Order
Marienburg
Marienwerder
Neustettin
Rostock
Wismar
Schwerin
Güstrow
Mecklenburg
D. of Schwerin
Parchim
D. of Pomerania
Schivelbein
Stargard
Stettin
Prenzlau
Ukermark
Neumark
Flatow
Bromberg
Kulm
Thorn
Kujavia
Inowrazlaw
Wloclawek
Masovia
Dobrzyn
Plock
Gnesen
Radziejow
Brest
Posen
KINGDOM OF POLAND
Warsaw
Peisern
Poland and Lithuania under the same ruling house, 1386
Macijowice
Prignitz
Ruppin
MARGRAVATE OF BRANDENBURG
Bavarian, 1324-1373
Altmark
Stendal
Tangermünde
Havelberg
Berlin
Cölln
Küstrin
Schwerin
B. of Lebus
Frankfort
Schwiebus
Oder R.
Brandenburg
Fürstenwalde
Magdeburg
Zinna
P. of Dessau
Wittenberg
ELECTORATE OF SAXONY
Margravate of Lusatia
Luxemburg (Bohemian) 1368
Kottbus
Krossen
Sagan
P. of Glogau
Sorau
Halberstadt
Anhalt
Ballenstedt
Nordhausen
Merseburg
Halle
Leipzig
M. of Osterland
Meissen
M. of Meissen
Dresden
Dohna
Luxemburg (Bohemian) 1320
Bautzen
Görlitz
Duchy of
P. of Liegnitz
P. of Öls
Kalisz
Petrikau
Radom
Wielun
P. of Breslau
To Luxemburg, 1335
Jauer
Schweidnitz
P. of Brieg
Münsterberg
P. of Oppeln
Czenstochova
Silesia
Siewierz
Under Luxemburg (Bohemian) suzerainty, since beginning of the 14th century
Ratibor
Auschwitz
Cracow
Tarnow
Vistula R.
Zator
Lucka
Walden
Pleissnerland
Freiberg
Zittau
Aussig
Wartenberg
Leitmeritz
Glatz
Graupen
Plauen
Kaaden
Bilin
Melnik
Königgrätz
Jägerndorf
P. of Troppau
Pardubitz
Kolin
Carlsbad
Eger
Prague
Wyschehrad
Kuttenberg
Leitomischl
P. of Teschen
KINGDOM OF BOHEMIA
To Luxemburg, 1310
Olmütz
Iglau
Margravate of Moravia
To Luxemburg, 1310
Brünn
Znaim
Pilsen
Nepomuk
Pisek
Neuhaus
Budweis
Rosenberg
Weitra
Eggenburg
Laa
Duchy of
Dürnkrut
Marchfeld
Krems
Freistadt
Linz
Mauerbach
Vienna
St. Pölten
Austria
Hapsburg, 1282
Baden
Kulmbach
Bamberg
UPPER PALATINATE
Nuremberg
Ratisbon
D. of Bavaria-Straubing
Straubing
B. of Passau
Ingolstadt
Landshut
D. of Bavaria
Freising
D. of Munich
Bavaria-Munich
Landshut
Salzburg
A. of Salzburg
Hallein
Berchtesgaden
Tyrol
Innsbruck
Landeck
Brenner Pass
Lienz
Gmünd
D. of Carinthia
Hapsburg, 1335
Klagenfurt
Villach
Bleiberg
B. of Brixen
Boxen
Trent
Patriarchate of Aquileia
Udine
Aquileia
Belluno
Görz
D. of Carniola
Hapsburg, 1282, 1335
Laibach
Cilli
Wendish March
Trieste
Duchy of Styria
Judenburg
Friesach
Bruck
Gratz
Vordernberg
Semmering Pass
Neuberg
Kapfenberg
Rohitsch
Agram
Ödenburg
Güns
Güssing
Pressburg
Tyrnau
Neutra
Trentschin
Kremnitz
Schemnitz
Altsohl
Liptau
Käsmark
Leutschau
Kaschau
Neudorf
Altendorf
Gran
Erlau
Raab
Buda (Ofen)
Pest
KINGDOM OF HUNGARY
Luxemburg 1386
Vesprem
Danube R.
Theiss R.
Szegedin
Drave R.
Mur R.
Save R.
Croatia
KINGDOM OF BOSNIA
Dalmatia
Zara
To the Venetian Republic
Pola
Venetian Republic
Venice
Chioggia
Treviso
Padua
Vicenza
Verona
Della Scala Dominions
Carrara
Mantua
Po R.
Ferrara
Este
Modena
Bologna
Ravenna
Forli
Cesena
Rimini
Pesaro
Ancona
PAPAL STATES
Florence
Arno R.
Dominions of Ottocar of Bohemia
Egerland 1266
Eger R.
Elbe R.
Oder R.
Bohemia
Moravia
Moldau R.
March R.
Waag R.
Inn R.
Danube R.
Austria 1251
1254
Styria
Carinthia 1269
1260
Carniola 1269
Drave R.
Save R.
Mur R.
Bohemia and Moravia
Acquisitions of Ottocar
Scale 1 : 12 000 000

Spread of German Settlements to the Eastward, 800—1400.

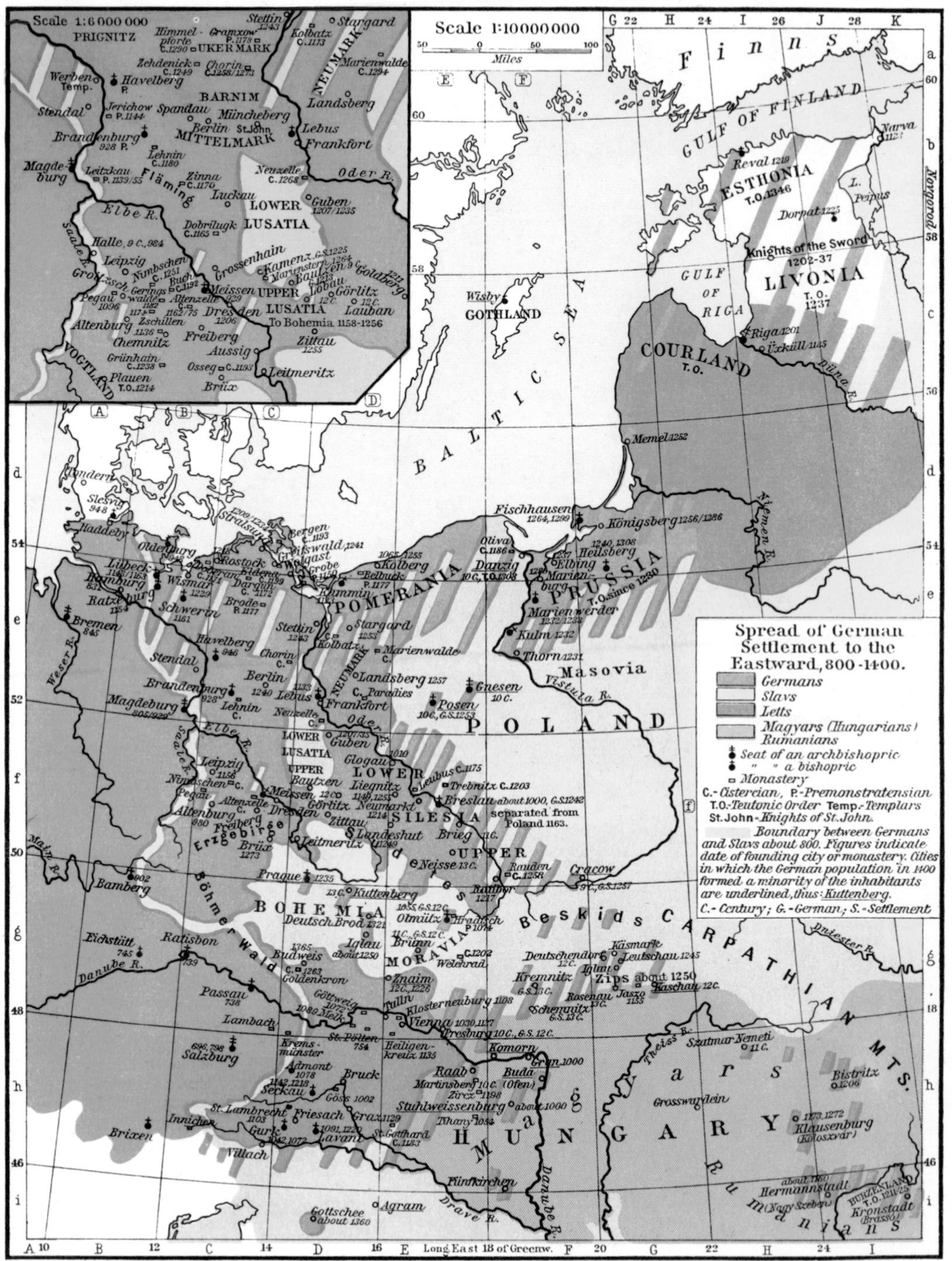

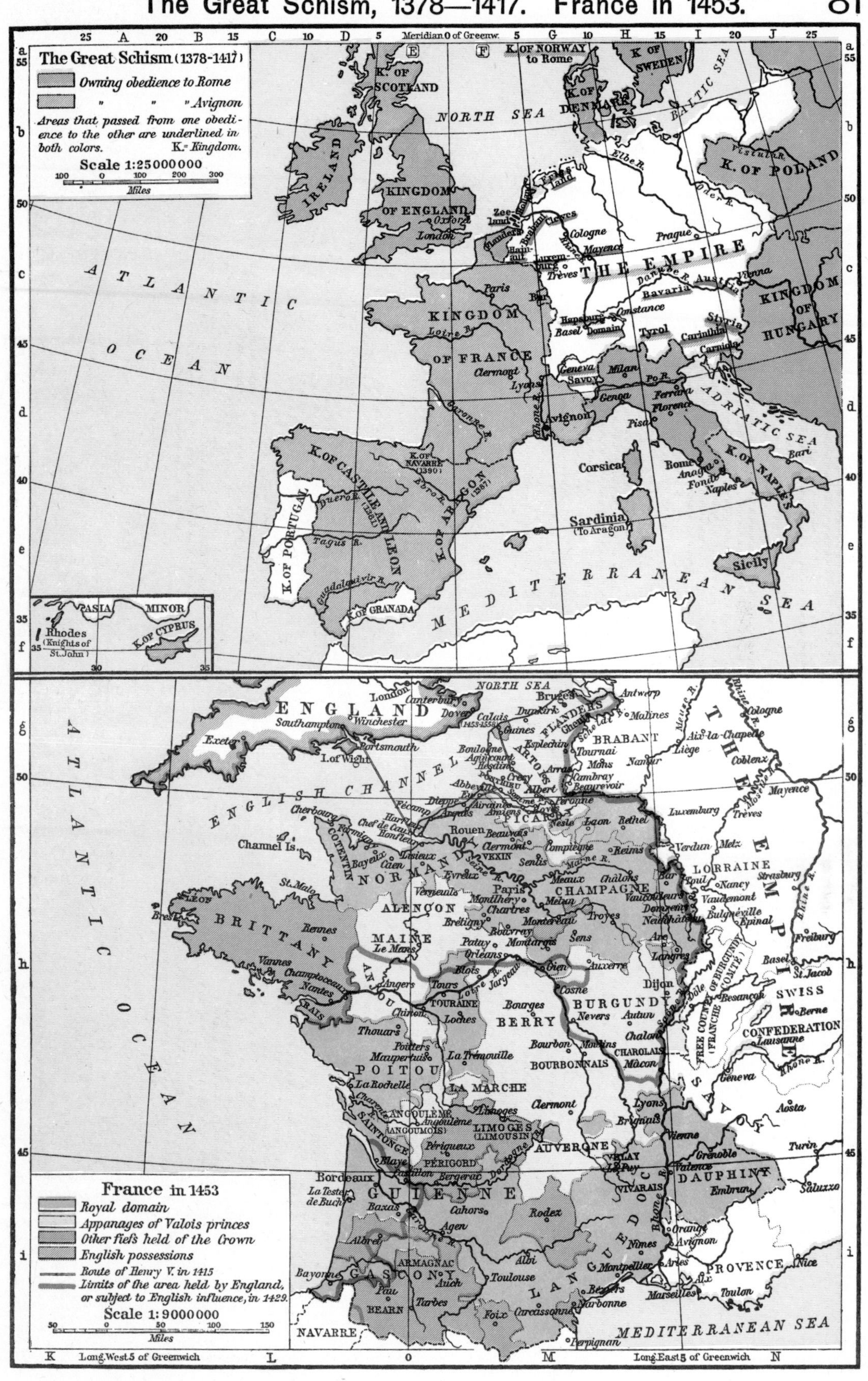
The Great Schism (1378-1417)
Owning obedience to Rome
" " " Avignon
Areas that passed from one obedience to the other are underlined in both colors. K.= Kingdom.
Scale 1:25000000
Miles
ATLANTIC OCEAN
NORTH SEA
BALTIC SEA
K. OF SCOTLAND
IRELAND
KINGDOM OF ENGLAND
K. OF NORWAY to Rome
K. OF SWEDEN
K. OF DENMARK
K. OF POLAND
THE EMPIRE
KINGDOM OF HUNGARY
KINGDOM OF FRANCE
K. OF CASTILE AND LEON
K. OF PORTUGAL
K. OF ARAGON
K. OF NAVARRE
K. OF GRANADA
K. OF NAPLES
ADRIATIC SEA
MEDITERRANEAN SEA
Corsica
Sardinia (To Aragon)
Sicily
ASIA MINOR
K. OF CYPRUS
Rhodes (Knights of St. John)
France in 1453
Royal domain
Appanages of Valois princes
Other fiefs held of the Crown
English possessions
Route of Henry V. in 1415
Limits of the area held by England, or subject to English influence, in 1429.
Scale 1:9000000
Miles
ENGLAND
ENGLISH CHANNEL
ATLANTIC OCEAN
BRITTANY
NORMANDY
PICARDY
ARTOIS
FLANDERS
BRABANT
CHAMPAGNE
LORRAINE
ALENÇON
MAINE
ANJOU
TOURAINE
BERRY
BURGUNDY
FREE COUNTY OF BURGUNDY (FRANCHE COMTÉ)
SWISS CONFEDERATION
THE EMPIRE
POITOU
LA MARCHE
BOURBONNAIS
CHAROLAIS
SAVOY
ANGOULÊME (ANGOUMOIS)
SAINTONGE
LIMOGES (LIMOUSIN)
AUVERGNE
PÉRIGORD
VELAY
VIVARAIS
DAUPHINY
GUIENNE
GASCONY
ARMAGNAC
BEARN
LANGUEDOC
PROVENCE
NAVARRE
MEDITERRANEAN SEA
Long. West 5 of Greenwich
Long. East 5 of Greenwich

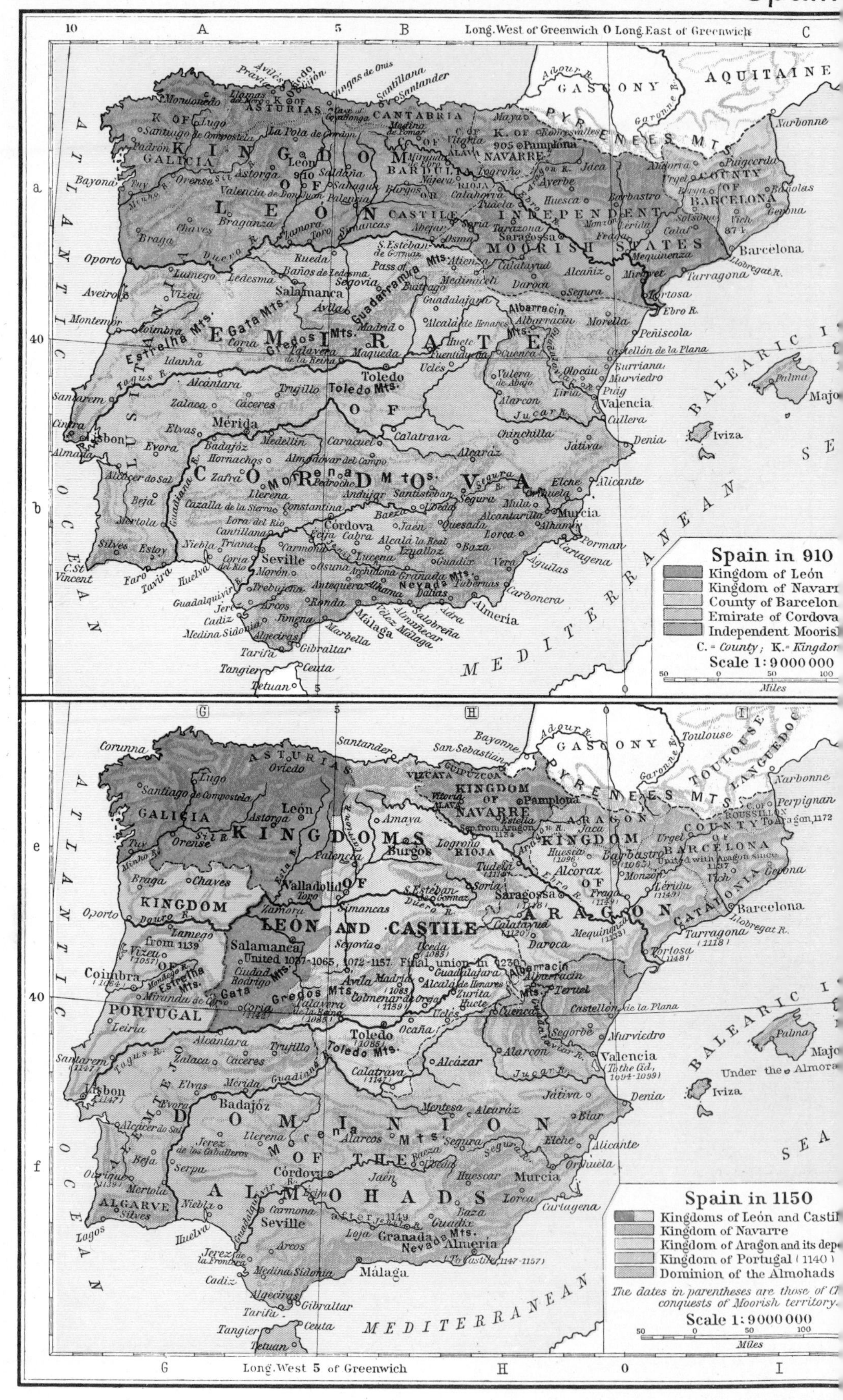
Long. West of Greenwich 0 Long. East of Greenwich
Spain in 910
Kingdom of León
Kingdom of Navarr
County of Barcelon
Emirate of Cordova
Independent Moorisl
C. = County; K. = Kingdor
Scale 1: 9 000 000
Miles
KINGDOM OF LEON
K. OF GALICIA
K. OF ASTURIAS
CANTABRIA
K. OF NAVARRE
COUNTY OF BARCELONA
INDEPENDENT MOORISH STATES
EMIRATE OF CORDOVA
PYRENEES MTS.
GASCONY
AQUITAINE
ATLANTIC OCEAN
MEDITERRANEAN SEA
BALEARIC IS.
Gata Mts.
Estrelha Mts.
Gredos Mts.
Guadarrama Mts.
Toledo Mts.
Sierra Morena
Nevada Mts.
Spain in 1150
Kingdoms of León and Castil
Kingdom of Navarre
Kingdom of Aragon and its dep
Kingdom of Portugal (1140)
Dominion of the Almohads
The dates in parentheses are those of Ch
conquests of Moorish territory.
Scale 1: 9000000
Miles
KINGDOMS OF LEÓN AND CASTILE
United 1037-1065, 1072-1157. Final union in 1230
KINGDOM OF NAVARRE
KINGDOM OF ARAGON
KINGDOM OF PORTUGAL
COUNTY OF BARCELONA
CATALONIA
TOULOUSE
LANGUEDOC
GALICIA
ASTURIAS
ALGARVE
DOMINION OF THE ALMOHADS
Under the Almora
Long. West 5 of Greenwich

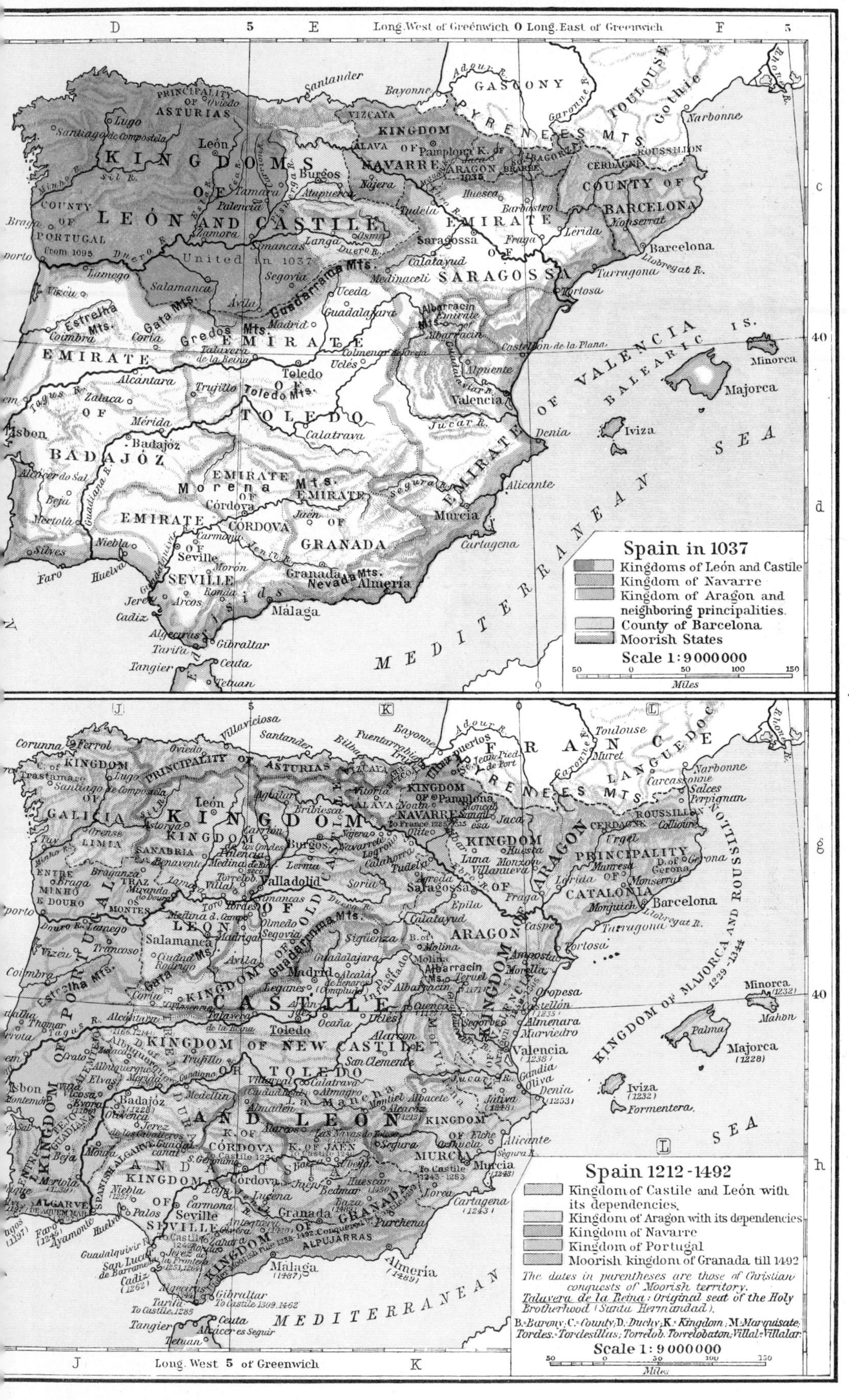

Long. West of Greenwich 0 Long. East of Greenwich
Spain in 1037
Kingdoms of León and Castile
Kingdom of Navarre
Kingdom of Aragon and neighboring principalities.
County of Barcelona
Moorish States
Scale 1: 9000000
Miles
KINGDOMS OF LEÓN AND CASTILE
United in 1037
KINGDOM OF NAVARRE
EMIRATE OF SARAGOSSA
COUNTY OF BARCELONA
EMIRATE OF TOLEDO
EMIRATE OF BADAJÓZ
EMIRATE OF CÓRDOVA
EMIRATE OF GRANADA
EMIRATE OF SEVILLE
EMIRATE OF VALENCIA
BALEARIC IS.
MEDITERRANEAN SEA
Spain 1212-1492
Kingdom of Castile and León with its dependencies.
Kingdom of Aragon with its dependencies
Kingdom of Navarre
Kingdom of Portugal
Moorish kingdom of Granada till 1492
The dates in parentheses are those of Christian conquests of Moorish territory.
Talavera de la Reina: Original seat of the Holy Brotherhood (Santa Hermandad).
B.=Barony; C.=County; D.=Duchy; K.=Kingdom; M.=Marquisate; Tordes.=Tordesillas; Torrelob.=Torrelobaton; Villal.=Villalar.
Scale 1: 9000000
Miles
Long. West 5 of Greenwich
KINGDOM OF CASTILE AND LEON
KINGDOM OF NEW CASTILE
KINGDOM OF ARAGON
KINGDOM OF NAVARRE
PRINCIPALITY OF CATALONIA
KINGDOM OF VALENCIA
KINGDOM OF MAJORCA AND ROUSSILLON 1229-1344
KINGDOM OF GRANADA
KINGDOM OF PORTUGAL
FRANCE
LANGUEDOC
MEDITERRANEAN SEA

England and France, 1455—1494.

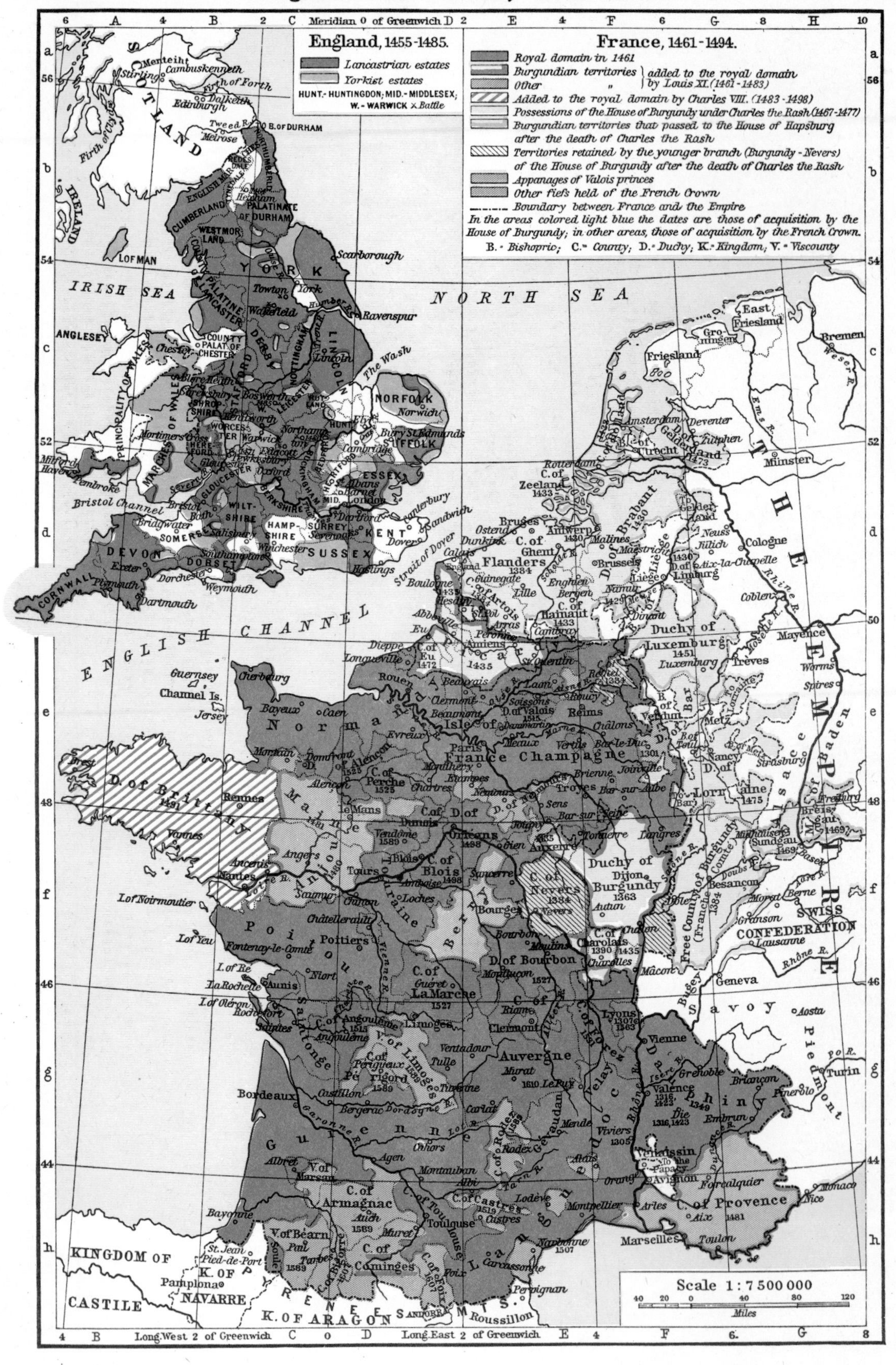

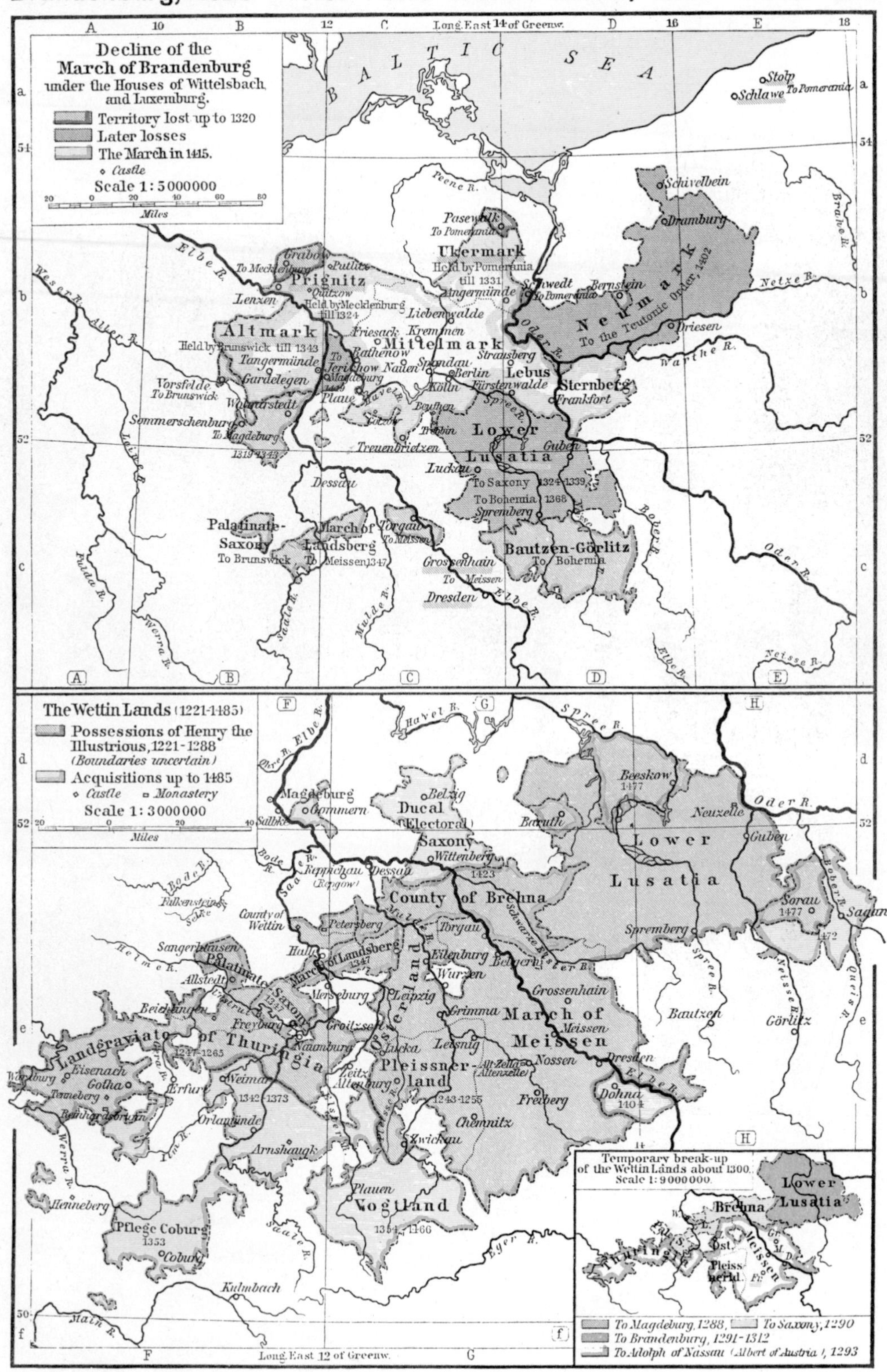
Decline of the March of Brandenburg under the Houses of Wittelsbach and Luxemburg.
Territory lost up to 1320
Later losses
The March in 1415.
Castle
Scale 1: 5000000
Miles
BALTIC SEA
Altmark
Prignitz
Mittelmark
Ukermark
Neumark
To the Teutonic Order, 1402
Lower Lusatia
Bautzen-Görlitz
Palatinate-Saxony
March of Landsberg
The Wettin Lands (1221-1485)
Possessions of Henry the Illustrious, 1221-1288 (Boundaries uncertain)
Acquisitions up to 1485
Castle
Monastery
Scale 1: 3000000
Miles
Ducal (Electoral) Saxony
County of Brehna
Landgraviate of Thuringia
March of Meissen
Pleissnerland
Osterland
Vogtland
Pflege Coburg
Temporary break-up of the Wettin Lands about 1300. Scale 1: 9000000.
To Magdeburg, 1288,
To Saxony, 1290
To Brandenburg, 1291-1312
To Adolph of Nassau (Albert of Austria), 1293
Long. East 12 of Greenw.

Meridian 0 of Greenw.
NORTH SEA
ENGLISH CHANNEL
KINGDOM OF ENGLAND
KINGDOM OF FRANCE
Dominions of the House of Hapsburg
Dominions of the House of Burgundy
Possessions of Charles the Rash
" " the Burgundy-Nevers line
The possessions of Charles the Rash held of the French Crown are given a wide border; those of the Burgundy-Nevers line, similarly, a narrow border.
Ecclesiastical States
Imperial Cities
Boundary of the Empire
The two colorings given to the Bohemian region are intended to show that in 1477 a Polish Jagellon was reigning in Bohemia; and that Moravia and Silesia were subject to Hungary, but were reunited with Bohemia in 1490. The areas in the Empire left uncolored were divided into petty states.
Abbreviations
A: Archbishopric; Ab: Abbacy; B: Bishopric; C: County; D: Duchy; Lg: Landgraviate; M: Margravate; Marq: Marquisate; P: Principality; Pal: Palatinate; Rep: Republic; Castle; Monastery.
Scale 1:6 000 000
Miles

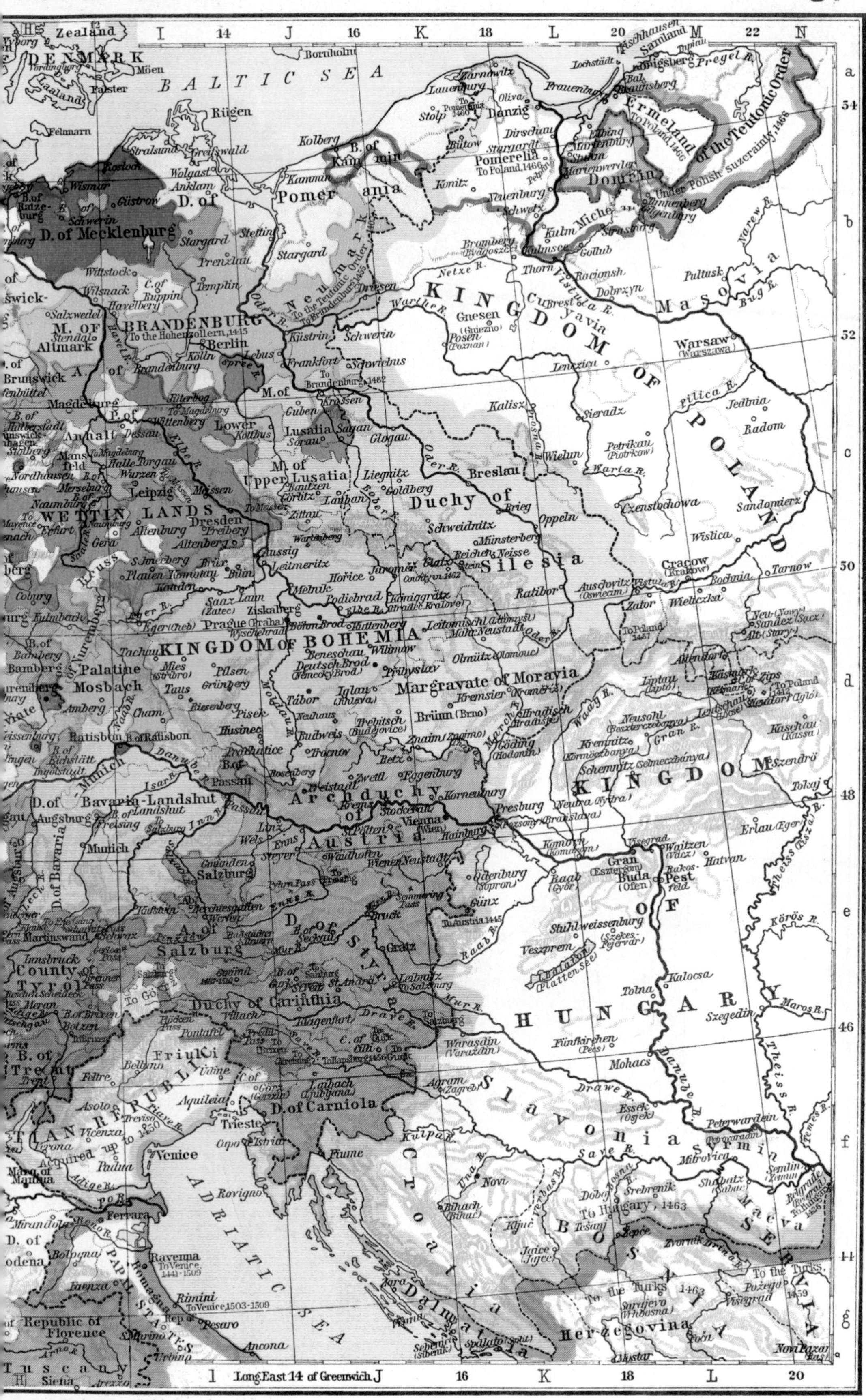

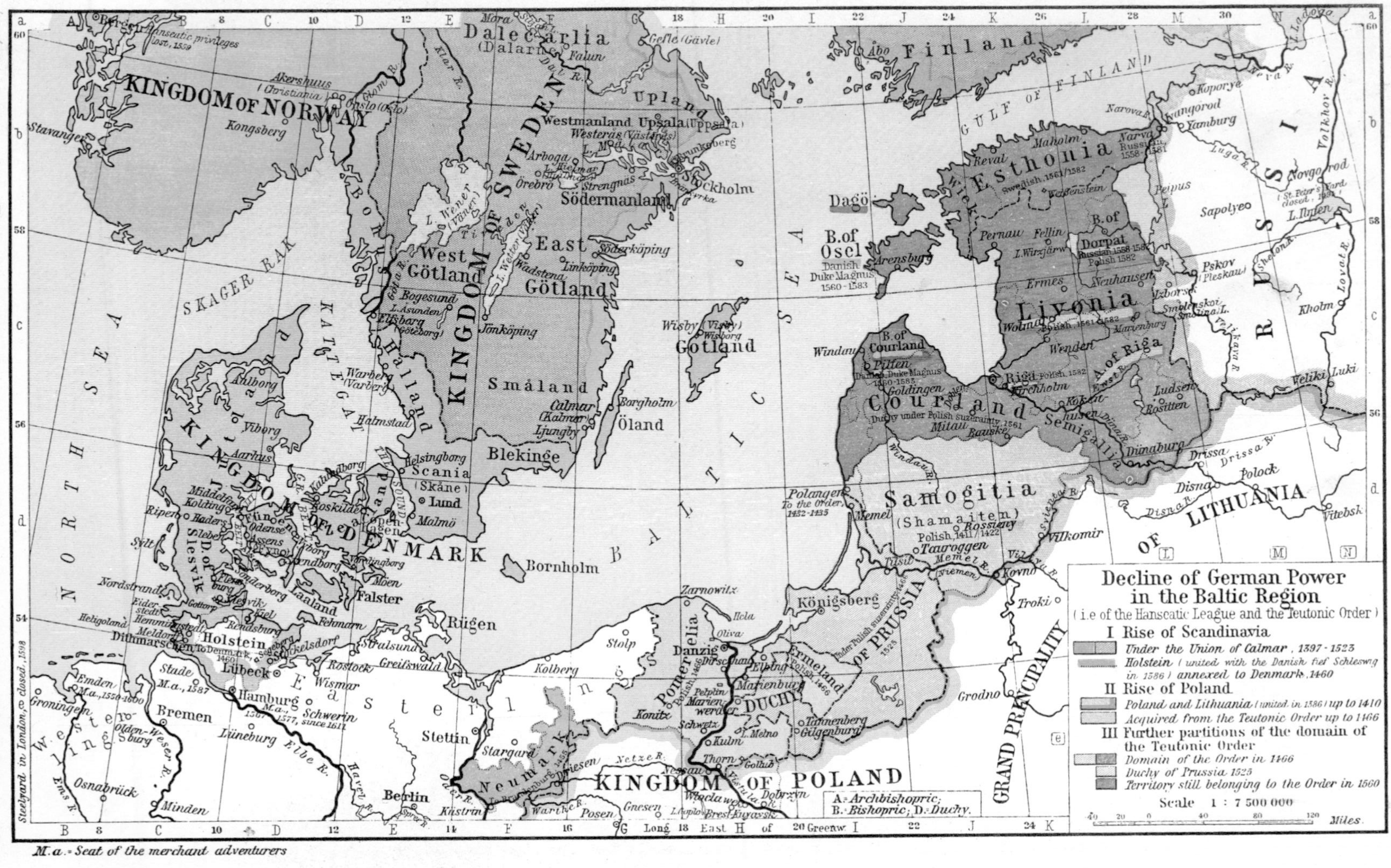

M.a. = Seat of the merchant adventurers

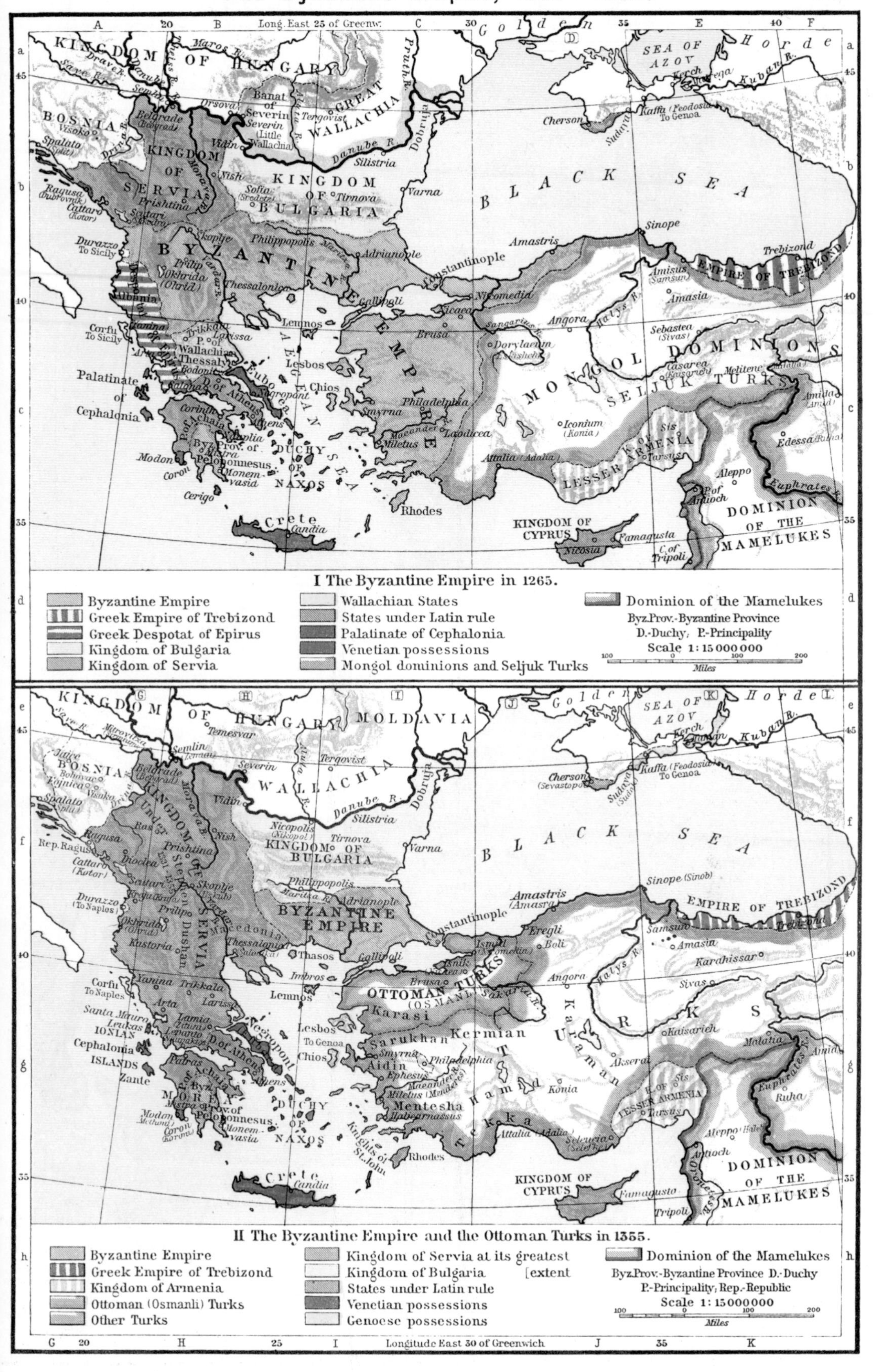
I The Byzantine Empire in 1265.
Byzantine Empire
Greek Empire of Trebizond
Greek Despotat of Epirus
Kingdom of Bulgaria
Kingdom of Servia
Wallachian States
States under Latin rule
Palatinate of Cephalonia
Venetian possessions
Mongol dominions and Seljuk Turks
Dominion of the Mamelukes
Byz.Prov.-Byzantine Province
D.-Duchy; P.-Principality
Scale 1: 15 000 000
Miles
II The Byzantine Empire and the Ottoman Turks in 1355.
Byzantine Empire
Greek Empire of Trebizond
Kingdom of Armenia
Ottoman (Osmanli) Turks
Other Turks
Kingdom of Servia at its greatest extent
Kingdom of Bulgaria
States under Latin rule
Venetian possessions
Genoese possessions
Dominion of the Mamelukes
Byz.Prov.-Byzantine Province D.-Duchy
P.-Principality; Rep.-Republic
Scale 1: 15 000 000
Miles
Longitude East 30 of Greenwich

The Milanese under the Visconti, 1339-1402.
Dominions of Azzo Visconti (1329-1339)
Acquired by Luchino and Giovanni Visconti (1339-54)
" " Bernabò and Galeazzo Visconti (1354-85)
" " Gian Galeazzo Visconti (1385-1402)
Areas given a border coloring are those which became dowries for Visconti heiresses, or were otherwise lost, before 1402.
Scale 1: 5000000
Miles
The Republic of Florence, 1300-1494.
Boundaries of the Tuscan States in 1300
The Republic of Florence:
In 1300
Acquired, 1300 - 1377
" ,1377 - 1433
" ,1433 - 1494
Protected States
Scale 1: 5000000
Miles
In the States of the Church the areas given a surface coloring of violet were under effective control.
SWITZERLAND
Tyrol
Carinthia
Carniola
DUCHY OF SAVOY
DUCHY OF MILAN
VENETIAN
REP. OF GENOA
REP. OF FLORENCE
REP. OF SIENA
Umbria
The Marches
Abruzzi
Molise
Capitanata
Campania
Principati
Basilicata
KINGDOM OF THE TWO SICILIES
Sicily
Corsica (To Genoa)
Elba
Lipari or Aeolian Is.
Rome
Naples
Venice
Florence
Milan
Genoa
Malta

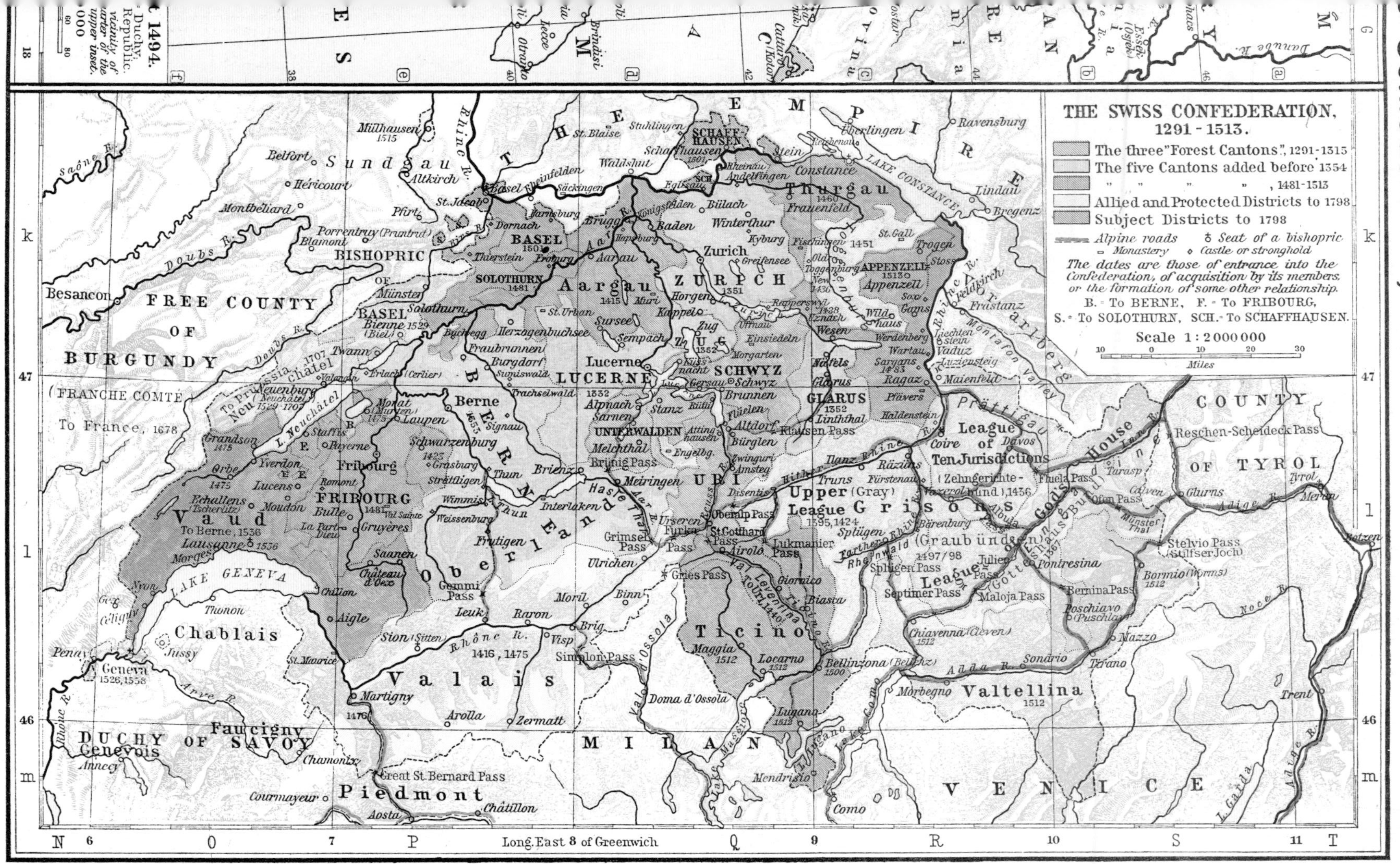
THE SWISS CONFEDERATION, 1291 - 1513.
The three "Forest Cantons", 1291-1315
The five Cantons added before 1354
" " " , 1481-1513
Allied and Protected Districts to 1798
Subject Districts to 1798
Alpine roads
Seat of a bishopric
Monastery
Castle or stronghold
The dates are those of entrance into the Confederation, of acquisition by its members, or the formation of some other relationship.
B. - To BERNE, F. - To FRIBOURG,
S. - To SOLOTHURN, SCH. - To SCHAFFHAUSEN.
Scale 1:2000000
Miles
Long. East 8 of Greenwich

The Mongol Dominions, 1227—1405.

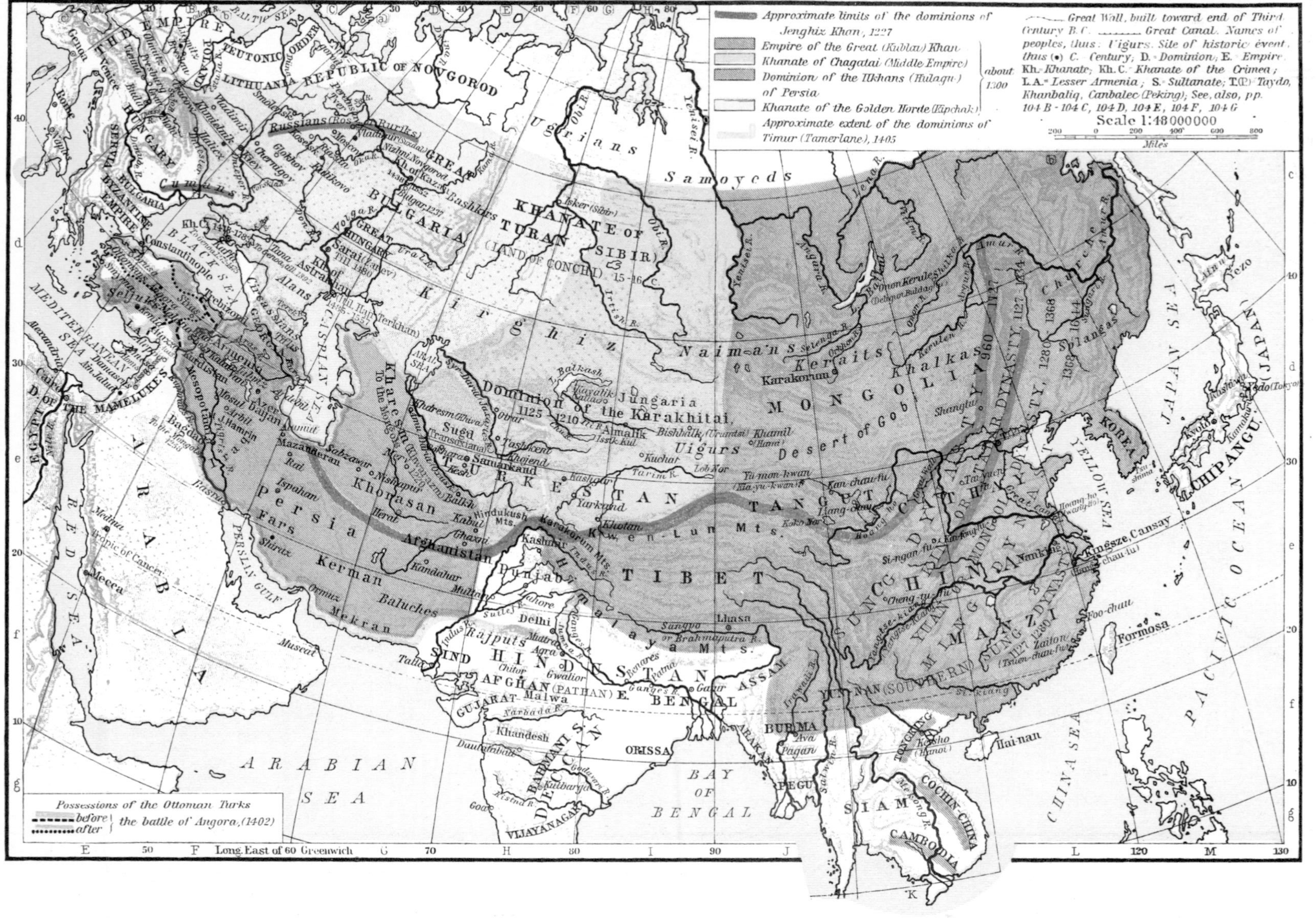

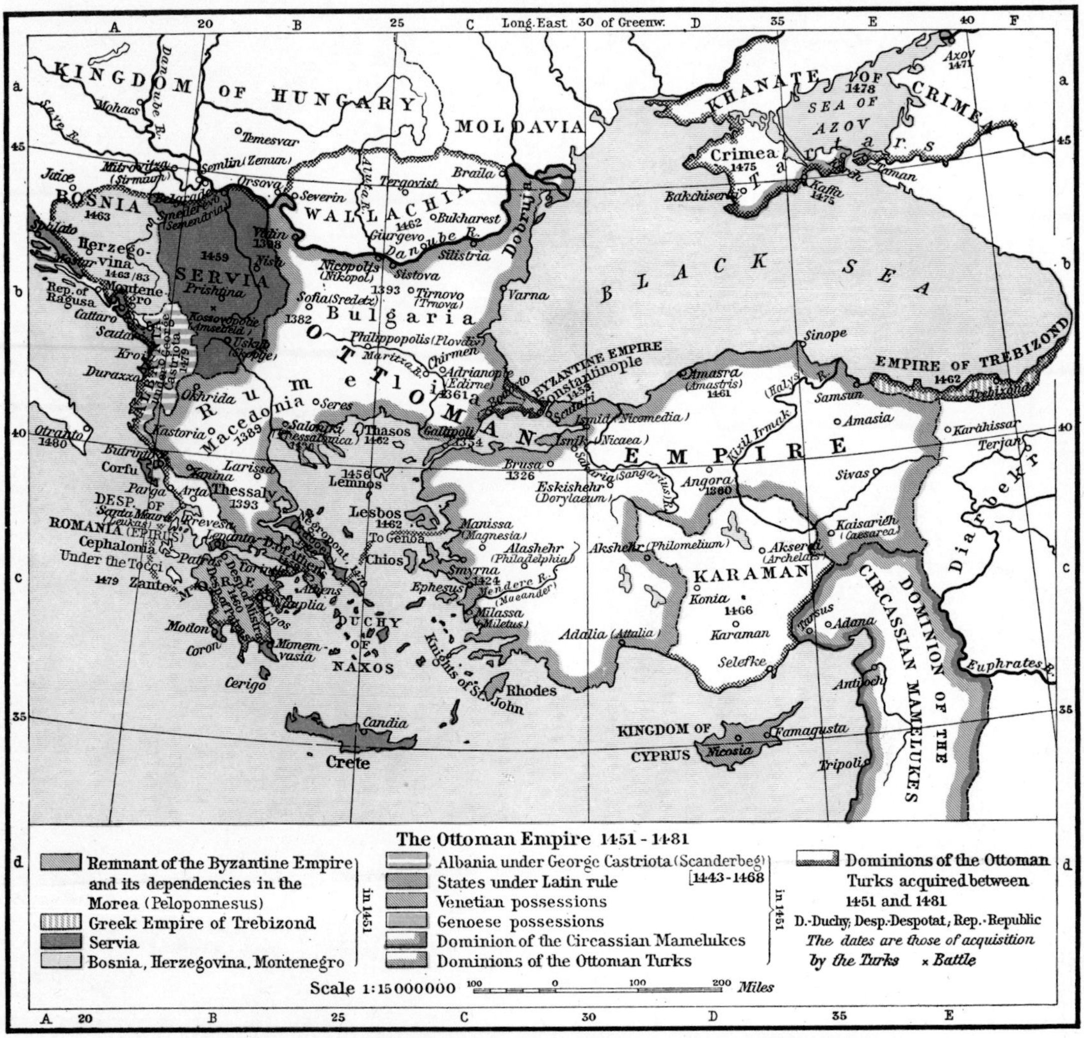

Long. East 30 of Greenw.
KINGDOM OF HUNGARY
MOLDAVIA
KHANATE OF CRIMEA
SEA OF AZOV
Azov 1471
Tatars
Crimea 1475
Kaffa 1475
Bakhchiserai
Mohacs
Save R.
Danube R.
Temesvar
Semlin (Zemun)
Mitrovitza (Sirmium)
Jaice
BOSNIA 1463
Belgrade
Semendria
Orsova
Severin
WALLACHIA
Tergovist
Braila
Bukharest
1462
Giurgevo
Danube R.
Silistria
Dobruja
Herzegovina 1463/83
Rep. of Ragusa
Montenegro
Cattaro
Scutari
Duraxxo
SERVIA 1459
Prishtina
Kossovopolje
Uskub (Skopje)
Vidin 1398
Nish
Nicopolis (Nikopol)
Sistova
Tirnovo (Trnova)
1393
Sofia (Sredetz)
1382
Bulgaria
Varna
BLACK SEA
Philippopolis (Plovdiv)
Maritza R.
Chirmen
Adrianople (Edirne) 1361
BYZANTINE EMPIRE
Constantinople 1453
Scutari
Ismid (Nicomedia)
Isnik (Nicaea)
OTTOMAN EMPIRE
Rumelia
Macedonia 1389
Ochrida
Seres
Salonika (Thessalonica)
Thasos 1462
Gallipoli
Kastoria
Otranto 1480
Butrinto
Corfu
Parga
Arta
Janina
Larissa
Thessaly 1393
Lemnos 1456
Lesbos 1462
To Genoa
Chios
DESP. OF ROMANIA (EPIRUS)
Santa Maura (Leukas)
Prevesa
Cephalonia
Under the Tocci
1479
Zante
Patras
Negropont 1470
Lepanto
Dchy. of Athens
Corinth
Athens
Nauplia
Argos
Mistra
Modon
Coron
Monemvasia
Cerigo
DUCHY OF NAXOS
Knights of St. John
Rhodes
Candia
Crete
Brusa 1326
Eskishehr (Dorylaeum)
Sakaria (Sangarius) R.
Manissa (Magnesia)
Alashehr (Philadelphia)
Smyrna 1424
Ephesus
Mendere R. (Maeander)
Milassa (Miletus)
Akshehr (Philomelium)
Angora 1360
Amasra (Amastris) 1461
Sinope
Halys R.
Kizil Irmak
Samsun
Amasia
EMPIRE OF TREBIZOND
1462
Trebizond
Karahissar
Terjan
Sivas
Kaisarieh (Caesarea)
Aksera (Archelais)
KARAMAN
Konia 1466
Karaman
Selefke
Adalia (Attalia)
Tarsus
Adana
Antioch
Diarbekr
Euphrates R.
DOMINION OF THE CIRCASSIAN MAMELUKES
KINGDOM OF CYPRUS
Nicosia
Famagusta
Tripoli
The Ottoman Empire 1451 - 1481
in 1451: Remnant of the Byzantine Empire and its dependencies in the Morea (Peloponnesus); Greek Empire of Trebizond; Servia; Bosnia, Herzegovina, Montenegro
Albania under George Castriota (Scanderbeg) [1443 - 1468
in 1451: States under Latin rule; Venetian possessions; Genoese possessions; Dominion of the Circassian Mamelukes; Dominions of the Ottoman Turks
Dominions of the Ottoman Turks acquired between 1451 and 1481
D.-Duchy; Desp.-Despotat; Rep.-Republic
The dates are those of acquisition by the Turks × Battle
Scale 1:15000000 100 0 100 200 Miles

Valley of the Sweet Waters of Europe
Wall of old (Greek) Byzantium (?)
Wall of Constantine (330)
Double Wall of Theodosius II (408-450)
Wall of Heraclius (626-641)
Wall of mediaeval Galata
Wall of the New Seraglio
Yildiz Kiosk
Mosque of Ayyub
The Lycus
Kosmidion (Ayyub)
Golden Horn (Chrysokeras)
St. Dimitri
Dolma Baghcheh
Cheragan Palace
Beshiktash (Diplokionion)
Palace of Blachernae
Palace of the Hebdomon (Tekfour Serai)
Kassim Pasha
Yeni Shehr
Fundoukli (Aianteion)
Gate of Charisius (Adrianople Gate)
Phanariot Quarter
PERA
Tophane
BOSPORUS
Christ Tower
GALATA (SYCAE)
Church of the Apostles (Mosque of Mohammed II)
Seraglio Point
So-called Tower of Leander
Barrier Chain (1453)
SCUTARI (CHRYSOPOLIS)
Gate of St. Romanus (Cannon Gate)
Gate of Rhegion (Rhegion)
Old Janizary Quarter
The Lycus
Aqueduct of Valens
Sheik-ul Islam
Mosque of Suleiman
Sublime Porte
Old Seraglio
New Seraglio
Acropolis of Greek Byzantium
Forum of Constantine
Hippodrome (Atmeidan)
Imperial Palace
Bucoleon Palace
Gate of Selymbria (Silivri) (Spring Gate)
Port of Eleutherius (Theodosius)
SEA OF MARMORA
Golden Gate
Castle of the Seven Towers (Yedi Kouleh)
KADIKEUI (CHALCEDON)
CONSTANTINOPLE
Scale 1:125000 0 ½ 1 1½ Miles
Byzantine names in thin type, thus: Cosmidion. 1 - St. Sophia 2 - Statue of Justinian 3 - Serpent Column 4 - Burnt Column (of Constantine) 5 - Mosque of Bajazet 6 - Mosque of Sultan Valideh 7 - Grave of the last Byzantine emperor 8 - Greek Patriarchate 9 - Prison of Anemas 10 - Old (Mahmoud) Bridge 11 - New (Valideh) Bridge 12 - Tomb of Khair-ed-Din Barbarossa 13 - Column of Arcadius. —— Route over which the ships of Mohammed II. were drawn.

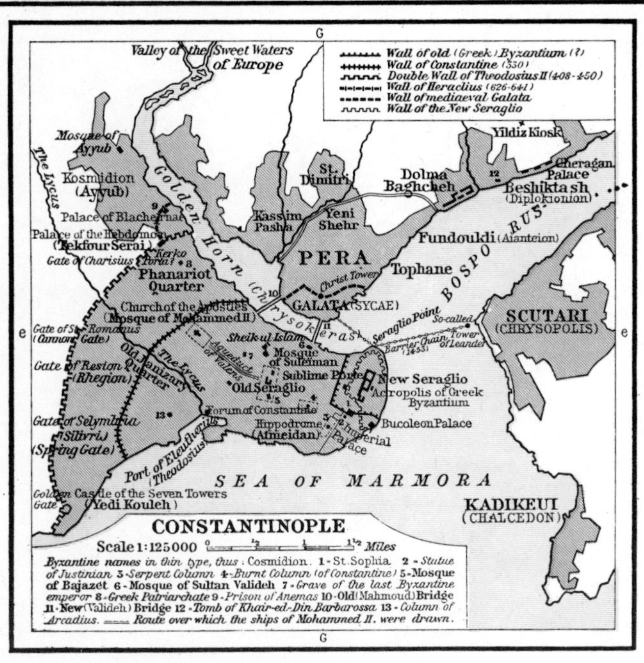

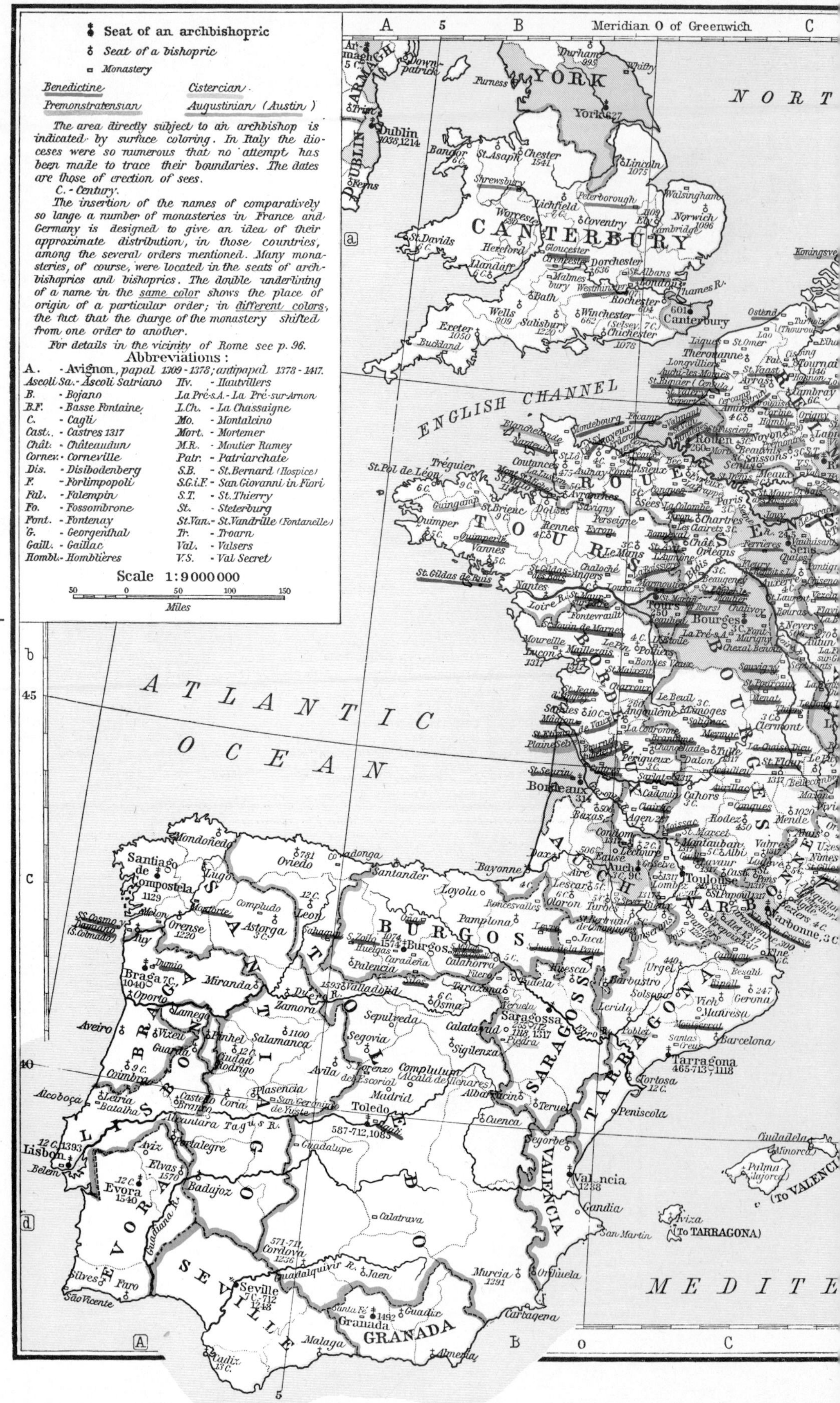
Seat of an archbishopric
Seat of a bishopric
Monastery
Benedictine
Cistercian
Premonstratensian
Augustinian (Austin)
The area directly subject to an archbishop is indicated by surface coloring. In Italy the dioceses were so numerous that no attempt has been made to trace their boundaries. The dates are those of erection of sees.
C. - Century.
The insertion of the names of comparatively so large a number of monasteries in France and Germany is designed to give an idea of their approximate distribution, in those countries, among the several orders mentioned. Many monasteries, of course, were located in the seats of archbishoprics and bishoprics. The double underlining of a name in the same color shows the place of origin of a particular order; in different colors, the fact that the charge of the monastery shifted from one order to another.
For details in the vicinity of Rome see p. 96.
Abbreviations:
A. - Avignon, papal 1309-1378; antipapal 1378-1417.
Ascoli Sa. - Ascoli Satriano
B. - Bojano
B.F. - Basse Fontaine
C. - Cagli
Cast. - Castres 1317
Chât. - Châteaudun
Cornev. - Corneville
Dis. - Disibodenberg
F. - Forlimpopoli
Fal. - Falempin
Fo. - Fossombrone
Font. - Fontenay
G. - Georgenthal
Gaill. - Gaillac
Hombl. - Homblières
Hv. - Hautvillers
La Pré-s.A. - La Pré-sur-Arnon
L.Ch. - La Chassaigne
Mo. - Montalcino
Mort. - Mortemer
M.R. - Moutier Ramey
Patr. - Patriarchate
S.B. - St. Bernard (Hospice)
S.G.i.F. - San Giovanni in Fiori
S.T. - St. Thierry
St. - Steterburg
St.Van. - St. Vandrille (Fontanelle)
Tr. - Troarn
Val. - Valsers
V.S. - Val Secret
Scale 1:9000000
50 0 50 100 150
Miles
Meridian 0 of Greenwich
YORK
CANTERBURY
ENGLISH CHANNEL
ATLANTIC OCEAN
ROUEN
TOURS
BORDEAUX
BOURGES
AUCH
NARBONNE
BURGOS
SANTIAGO
BRAGA
TOLEDO
SARAGOSSA
TARRAGONA
VALENCIA
LISBON
EVORA
SEVILLE
GRANADA
MEDITE

BALTIC SEA
Bishopric of the Pomeranians
RIGA
MAGDEBURG
GNESEN
To GNESEN about 1200
TO MAYENCE
PRAGUE, after 1344
SALZBURG
GRAN
KALOCSA
AQUILEIA
MILAN
RAVENNA
GENOA
SPALATO
ZARA
ADRIATIC SEA
ROME
RAGUSA
BARI
TORRES
ORISTANO
CAGLIARI
PALERMO
MESSINA
MONREALE
REGGIO
To GENOA
To PISA
CAPUA
BENEVENTO
NAPLES
SORRENTO
AMALFI
SALERNO
ANEAN SEA
VENICE
Cologne
Mayence
Prague
Cracow
Breslau
Vistula R.
Oder R.
Elbe R.
Danube R.
Drave R.
Trent
Verona
Florence
Pisa
Lucca
Siena
Naples
Brindisi
Otranto
Taranto
Cattaro
Antivari
Durazzo
Belgrade
Palermo
Messina
Cagliari
Ajaccio 6 C.

Plan of Rome in the Middle Ages. The Roman Suburbicarian Bishoprics.

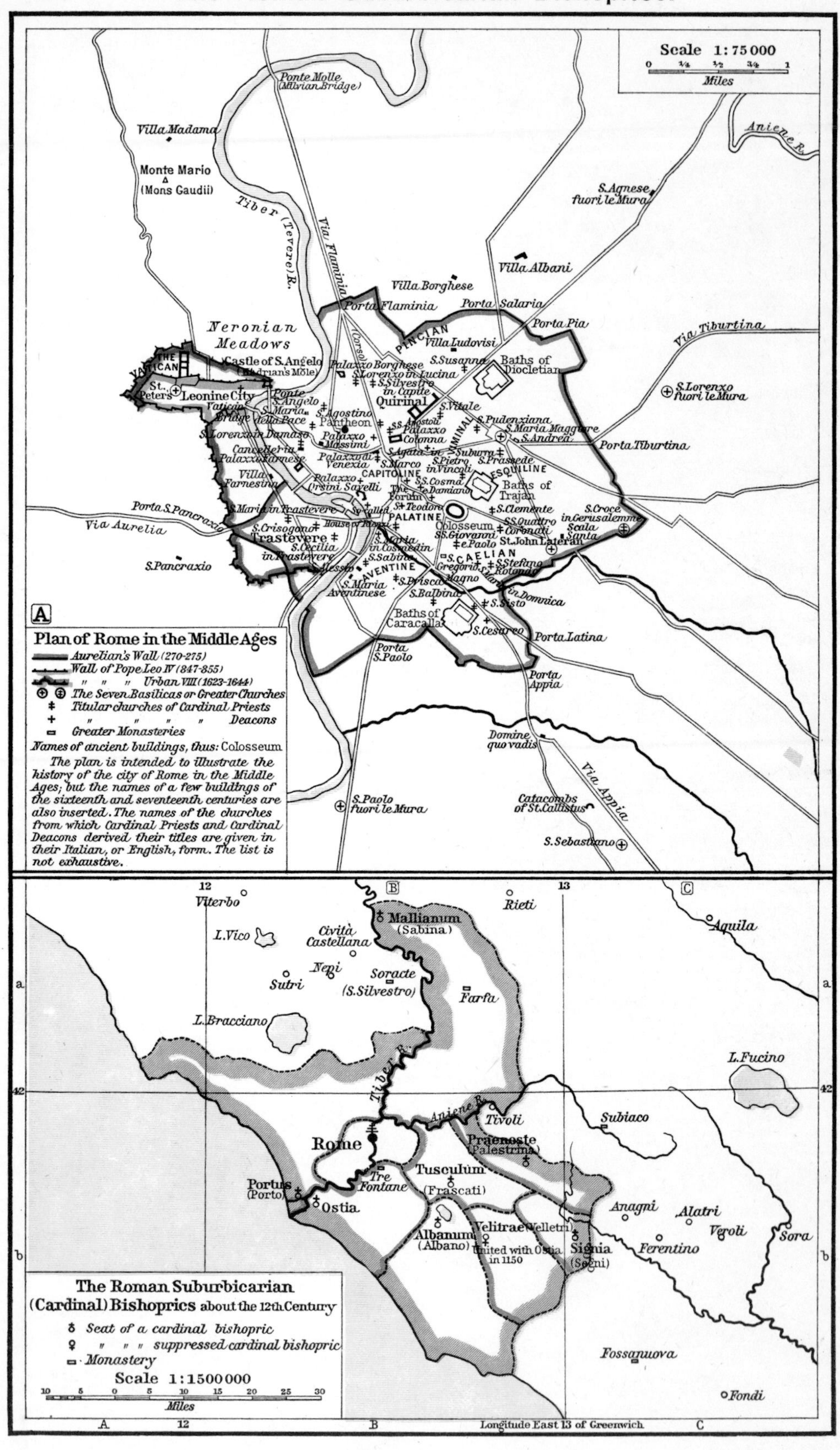

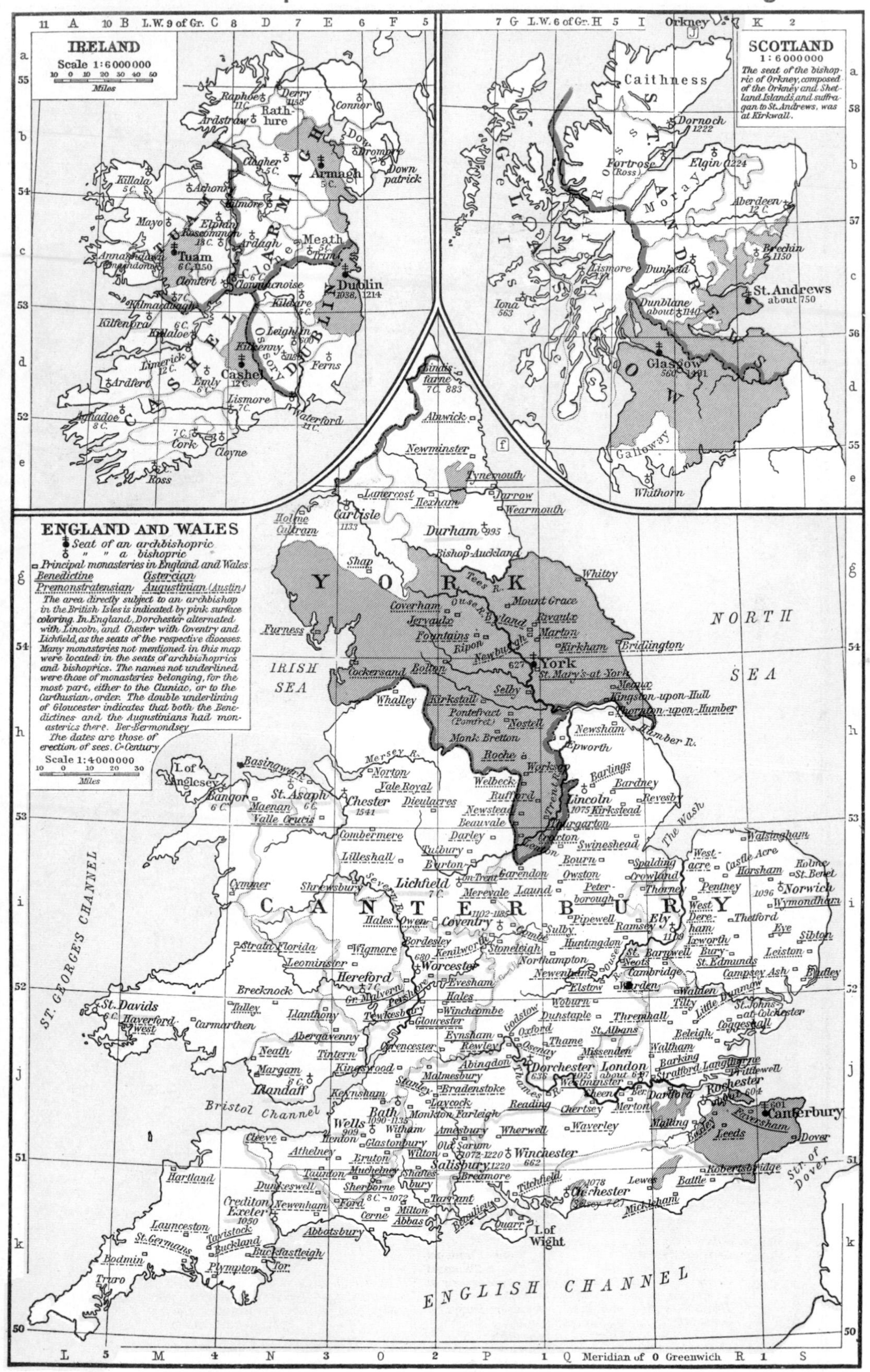
IRELAND
Scale 1:6000000
Miles
SCOTLAND
1:6000000
The seat of the bishopric of Orkney, composed of the Orkney and Shetland Islands and suffragan to St. Andrews, was at Kirkwall.
ENGLAND AND WALES
Seat of an archbishopric
" " a bishopric
Principal monasteries in England and Wales
Benedictine
Cistercian
Premonstratensian
Augustinian (Austin)
The area directly subject to an archbishop in the British Isles is indicated by pink surface coloring. In England, Dorchester alternated with Lincoln, and Chester with Coventry and Lichfield, as the seats of the respective dioceses. Many monasteries not mentioned in this map were located in the seats of archbishoprics and bishoprics. The names not underlined were those of monasteries belonging, for the most part, either to the Cluniac, or to the Carthusian, order. The double underlining of Gloucester indicates that both the Benedictines and the Augustinians had monasteries there. Ber-Bermondsey
The dates are those of erection of sees. C=Century
Scale 1:4000000
Miles
ARMAGH
TUAM
CASHEL
DUBLIN
ST. ANDREWS
GLASGOW
YORK
CANTERBURY
IRISH SEA
NORTH SEA
ST. GEORGE'S CHANNEL
Bristol Channel
ENGLISH CHANNEL
Str. of Dover
Armagh
Dublin
Tuam
Cashel
St. Andrews
Glasgow
York
Canterbury
Meridian of 0 Greenwich

1 : 10 000 000
I. of Man
IRISH SEA
Dublin
(Donnybrook)
Anglesey
Preston
Ormskirk
York
Hull
Doncaster
Grimsby
Humber R.
Horncastle
Chester
Nottingham
The Wash
Boston
Stamford
Norwich
Leicester
Lynn
St. Ives
Yarmouth
Coventry
Stourbridge
Bury
St. Edmunds
Market Harborough
Northampton
Cambridge
Ipswich
Chelmsford
Abingdon
Westminster
Wallingford
Bristol
Devizes
London
Salisbury
Winchester
Southampton
Exeter
Portsmouth
ATLANTIC OCEAN
To Iceland
Bergen
NORWAY
To Kholmogory
Trondhjem
Oslo
SKAGER RAK
GERMAN OCEAN
SEA OF ENGLAND
OR
WEST SEA
(NORTH SEA)
SCOTLAND
IRELAND
Irish Sea
Falkirk
Edinburgh
Berwick
Carlisle
Ballinasloe
Dublin
Chester
Boston
Hull
Stourbridge
Bristol
Southampton
Winchester
London
To the Baltic
Lübeck
Hamburg
Bremen
Stralsund
Stettin
Danzig
Brunswick
Münster
Magdeburg
Berlin
Posen
Frankfort
Cologne
Dortmund
Erfurt
Leipzig
Frankfort on the Main
THE EMPIRE
Nuremberg
Bamberg
Prague
Ratisbon
Passau
Vienna
Ulm
Augsburg
Constance
Munich
Salzburg
Worms
Spire
Strasburg
Bruges
Ghent
Antwerp
ENGLISH CHANNEL
To Spain and Portugal
FRANCE
Paris
Rouen
Caen
Rennes
Nantes
Orléans
Chartres
Tours
Troyes
Provins
Poitiers
La Rochelle
Limoges
Clermont
Lyons
Bordeaux
Toulouse
Montpellier
Nîmes
Narbonne
Marseilles
Beaucaire
Besançon
Basel
Lucerne
St. Gothard
Geneva
ALPS
Milan
Turin
Genoa
Pavia
Verona
Venice
Padua
Trent
Piacenza
Modena
Bologna
Ferrara
Pisa
Florence
Viterbo
Rome
Naples
Amalfi
Bari
Brindisi
Messina
Syracuse
SICILY
CORSICA
SARDINIA
THE APENNINES
SEA OF ROCHELLE
(BAY OF BISCAY)
To England
To Spanish ports
Venetian galleys in the 14th century
PORTUGAL
SPAIN
PYRENEES MTS
Corunna
Santiago de Compostela
León
Burgos
Pamplona
Bilbao
Oporto
Valladolid
Medina del Campo
Palencia
Segovia
Avila
Saragossa
Barcelona
Tortosa
Lisbon
Toledo
Alcalá de Henares
Cuenca
Valencia
Cáceres
Seville
Cordova
Murcia
Alicante
Cartagena
Granada
Malaga
Almeria
Cadiz
Tarifa
Gibraltar
Strait of Gibraltar
Tangier
Ceuta
Balearic Is.
Palma
To North Africa
To Egypt
To France and Italy
MITERETANE
(MEDITERRANEAN)
To the Canary Islands
Fez
Oran
Algiers
Setif
Tunis
Kairwan
Mogador
ATLAS MTS.
MAGRIB
AFRICA
Tafilet
Tripoli
Ghadames
Sirt
Sella
Areas of relatively dense population
" " moderate sized "
Land routes (by navigable rivers, also)
Mongol Baltic trade route
Sea routes
" " of the Hanseatic League (Hansa)
" " " " Venetians
" " " " Genoese
In possession, also, of most of the commerce in the Black Sea.
Lübeck Centres of the Hanseatic League
Bergen Foreign offices of the " "
Soest Cities belonging to " "
Dieppe Foreign cities in which the Hanseatic League, or any of its members, possessed trading privileges
Principal markets and fairs
Alpine passes
Roman missionary archbishopric
" " bishopric
Nestorian metropolitanate
in the fourteenth century
Fland.-Flanders
Thour.-Thourout
Mediaeval names in hair-line, thus: MITERETANE,
Bambilonia Names of peoples, thus: Bashkirs
See, also, pp. 102-103, 104 B-104 C and 104 G
Scale 1 : 20 000 000
Miles
Long.

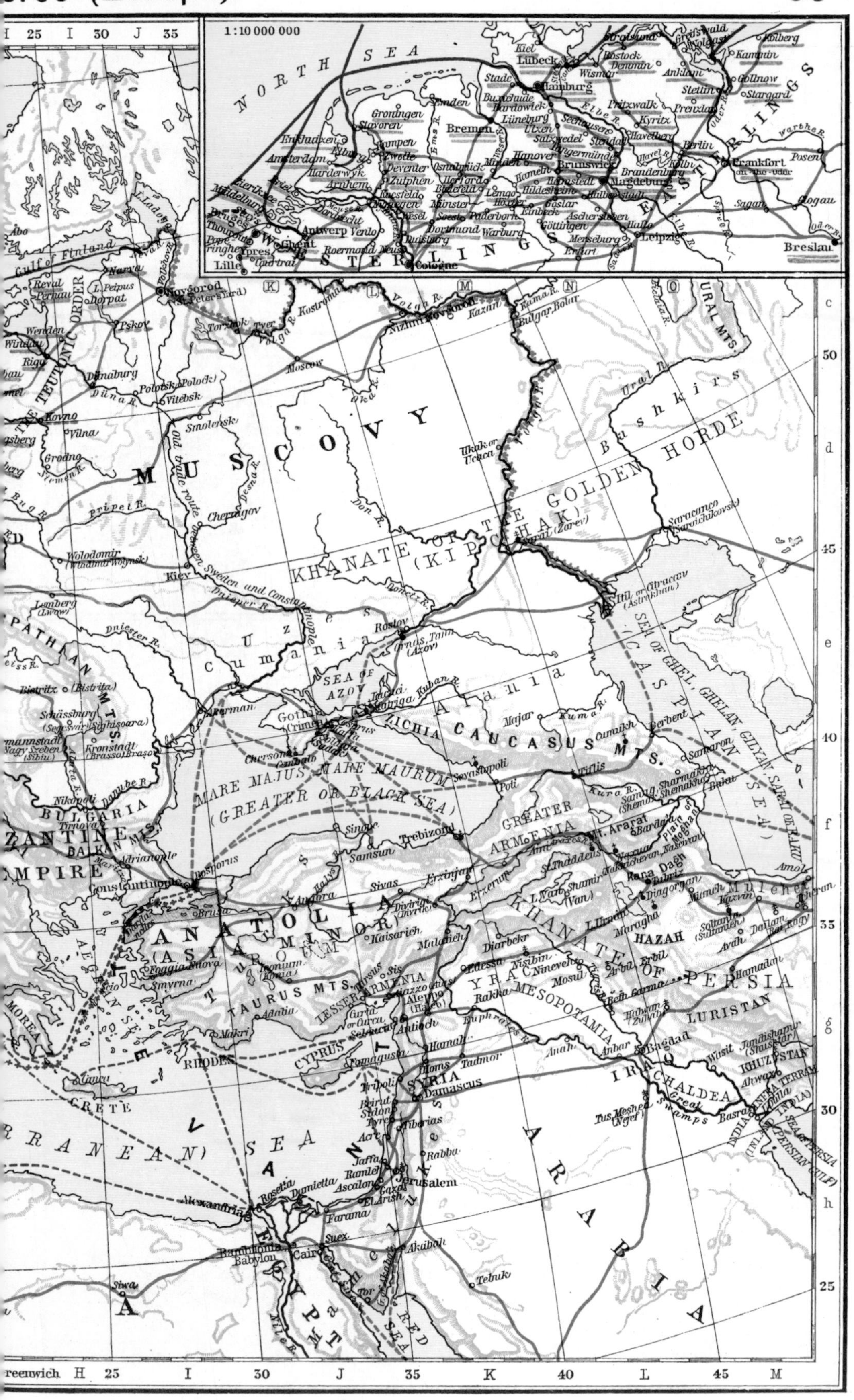
1:10 000 000
NORTH SEA
EASTERLINGS
MUSCOVY
KHANATE OF THE GOLDEN HORDE
(KIPCHAK)
MARE MAJUS MARE MAURUM
(GREATER OR BLACK SEA)
CAUCASUS MTS.
SEA OF GHEL, GHELAN, GILYAN, SARAI OR BAKU
(CASPIAN SEA)
ANATOLIA
(ASIA MINOR)
KHANATE OF PERSIA
MESOPOTAMIA
ARABIA
SYRIA
CYPRUS
CRETE
RHODES
BULGARIA
BYZANTINE EMPIRE
TAURUS MTS.
LESSER ARMENIA
GREATER ARMENIA
CHALDEA
IRAQ
LURISTAN
KHUZISTAN
Constantinople
Trebizond
Alexandria
Cairo
Jerusalem
Damascus
Bagdad
Novgorod
Moscow
Kiev
Lübeck
Hamburg
Bremen
Cologne
Breslau
Greenwich H 25 I 30 J 35 K 40 L 45 M

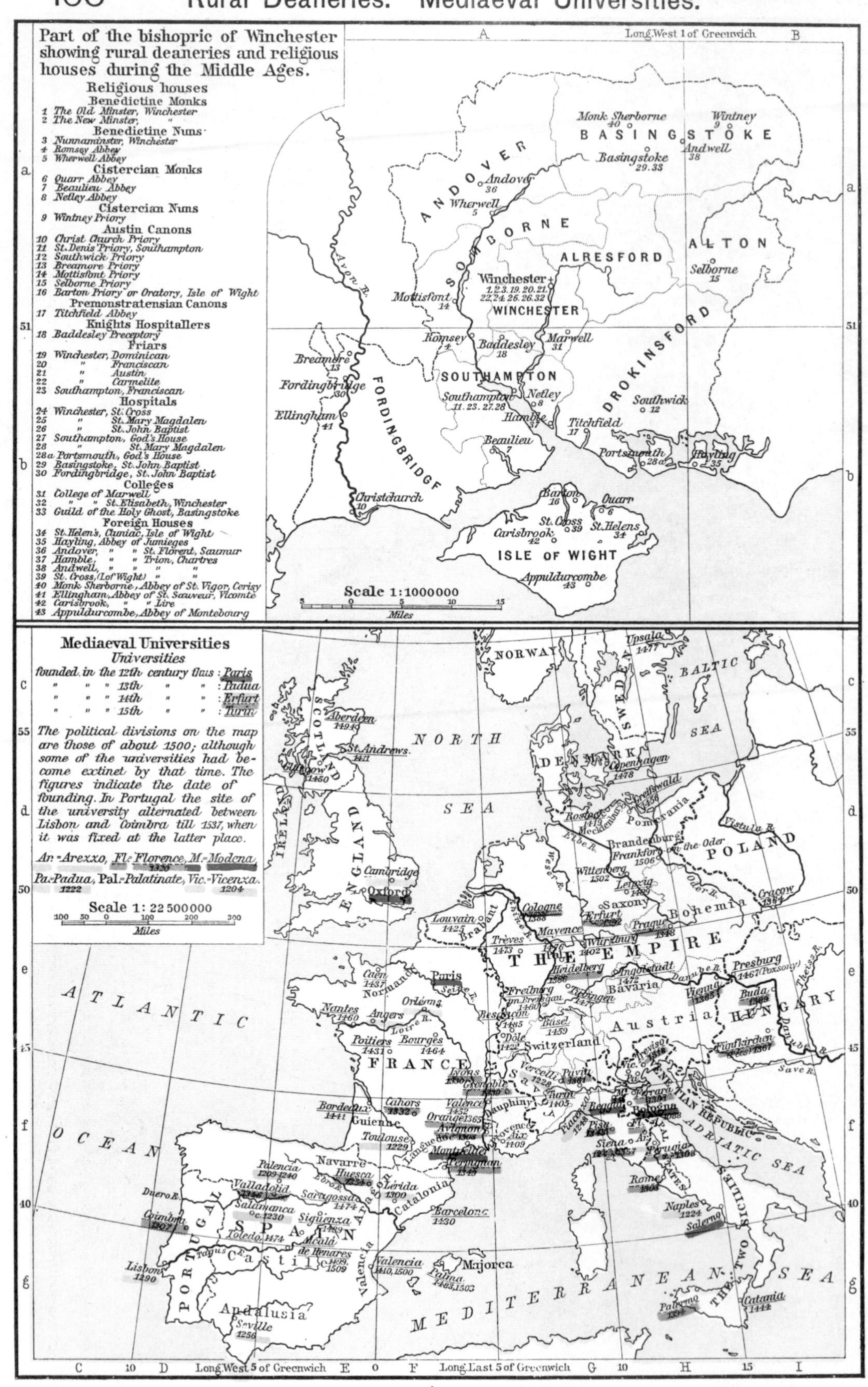
Part of the bishopric of Winchester showing rural deaneries and religious houses during the Middle Ages.
Religious houses
Benedictine Monks
1 The Old Minster, Winchester
2 The New Minster, "
Benedictine Nuns
3 Nunnaminster, Winchester
4 Romsey Abbey
5 Wherwell Abbey
Cistercian Monks
6 Quarr Abbey
7 Beaulieu Abbey
8 Netley Abbey
Cistercian Nuns
9 Wintney Priory
Austin Canons
10 Christ Church Priory
11 St. Denis Priory, Southampton
12 Southwick Priory
13 Breamore Priory
14 Mottisfont Priory
15 Selborne Priory
16 Barton Priory or Oratory, Isle of Wight
Premonstratensian Canons
17 Titchfield Abbey
Knights Hospitallers
18 Baddesley Preceptory
Friars
19 Winchester, Dominican
20 " Franciscan
21 " Austin
22 " Carmelite
23 Southampton, Franciscan
Hospitals
24 Winchester, St. Cross
25 " St. Mary Magdalen
26 " St. John Baptist
27 Southampton, God's House
28 " St. Mary Magdalen
28a Portsmouth, God's House
29 Basingstoke, St. John Baptist
30 Fordingbridge, St. John Baptist
Colleges
31 College of Marwell
32 " " St. Elisabeth, Winchester
33 Guild of the Holy Ghost, Basingstoke
Foreign Houses
34 St. Helen's, Cluniac, Isle of Wight
35 Hayling, Abbey of Jumieges
36 Andover, " " St. Florent, Saumur
37 Hamble, " " Trion, Chartres
38 Andwell, " " " "
39 St. Cross, (I. of Wight) " "
40 Monk Sherborne, Abbey of St. Vigor, Cerisy
41 Ellingham, Abbey of St. Sauveur, Vicomte
42 Carisbrook, " " Lire
43 Appuldurcombe, Abbey of Montebourg
Long. West 1 of Greenwich
BASINGSTOKE
ANDOVER
SOMBORNE
ALRESFORD
ALTON
WINCHESTER
DROKINSFORD
SOUTHAMPTON
FORDINGBRIDGE
ISLE OF WIGHT
Scale 1:1000000
Miles
Mediaeval Universities
Universities
founded in the 12th century thus: Paris
" " " 13th " " : Padua
" " " 14th " " : Erfurt
" " " 15th " " : Turin
The political divisions on the map are those of about 1500; although some of the universities had become extinct by that time. The figures indicate the date of founding. In Portugal the site of the university alternated between Lisbon and Coimbra till 1537, when it was fixed at the latter place.
Ar.=Arezzo, Fl.=Florence, M.=Modena, Pa.=Padua, Pal.=Palatinate, Vic.=Vicenza.
Scale 1: 22 500 000
Miles
ATLANTIC OCEAN
NORTH SEA
BALTIC SEA
MEDITERRANEAN SEA
ADRIATIC SEA
THE EMPIRE
FRANCE
SPAIN
PORTUGAL
POLAND
HUNGARY
ENGLAND
SCOTLAND
IRELAND
NORWAY
SWEDEN
DENMARK
Long. West 5 of Greenwich
Long. East 5 of Greenwich

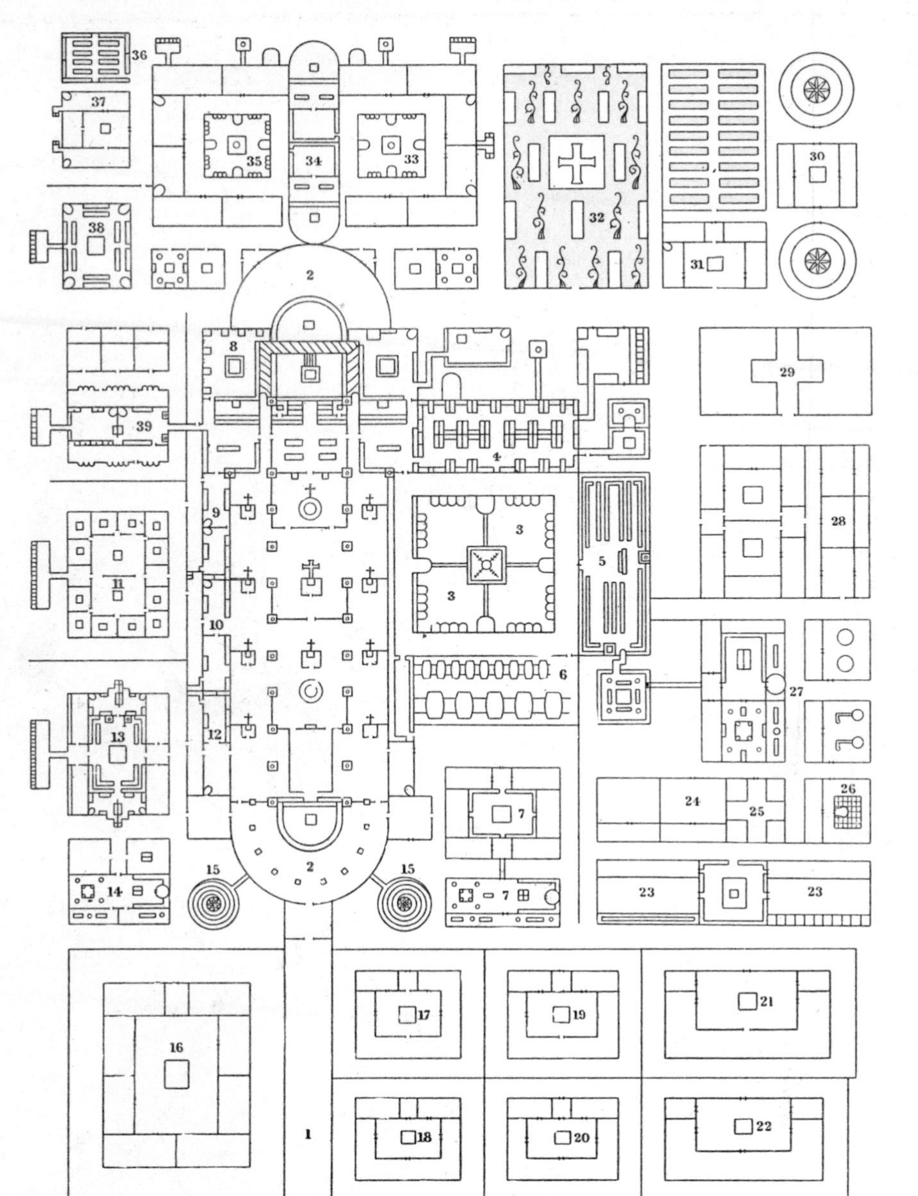

Explanation

This ground-plan is a reduced copy from the ninth century original preserved in the present monastery library. It represents an ideal Benedictine house, and was probably not carried out in complete detail. The enclosure, surrounded by a wall, was about four hundred feet long by about three hundred wide. - 1. *Entrance to the church from outside the walls.* 2. *Church with two apses and numerous altars.* 3. *Main cloister, showing arches.* 4. *Dormitory above; room with heating apparatus below.* 5. *Refectory below; wardrobe above.* 6. *Cellar with storehouses above.* 7. *House for pilgrims and poor travellers, with brewery and bakery adjoining.* 8. *Writing-room below; library above.* 9. *Living-room and dormitory for visiting monks.* 10. *Schoolmaster's lodging.* 11. *School-room for ordinary pupils with lodgings for the teachers.* 12. *Porter's lodge.* 13. *Quarters for guests of quality.* 14. *Brewery and bakery belonging to* 13. 15. *Towers with spiral staircases, overlooking the whole place.* 16. *Large building of unknown use.* 17. *Sheep-stall.* 18. *Servants' quarters.* 19. *Goat-stall with goatherds' quarters.* 20. *Swine-stall with swineherds' quarters.* 21. *Cattle-shed with cowherds' quarters.* 22. *Horse-barn with grooms' quarters.* 23. *Stable for mares and oxen with hay-lofts above and quarters for servants in the middle.* 24. *Workshops of coopers and turners.* 25. *Storehouse for brewery-grain.* 26. *Fruit-drying house.* 27. *Brewery and bakery for the resident monks, showing mortars and hand-mills.* 28. *Workshops of shoemakers, saddlers, sword and shield-makers, carvers, tanners, goldsmiths, blacksmiths, fullers.* 29. *Granary and threshing-floor.* 30. *House of poultry-keeper; hen-house and goose-pen adjoining.* 31. *House of the gardener; kitchen-garden adjoining. The original gives names of vegetables on the several beds.* 32. *Burying-ground.* 33. *Cloister and living-rooms of the "oblati" and their teacher, and of convalescents.* 34. *Church for the novices and the ill.* 35. *Cloister and living-rooms, especially for the seriously ill.* 36. *Hospital-garden.* 37. *Physician's quarters, apothecary-shop and rooms for patients.* 38. *Additional building for surgical purposes.* 39. *Abbot's house, showing entrance to church and to main cloister.*

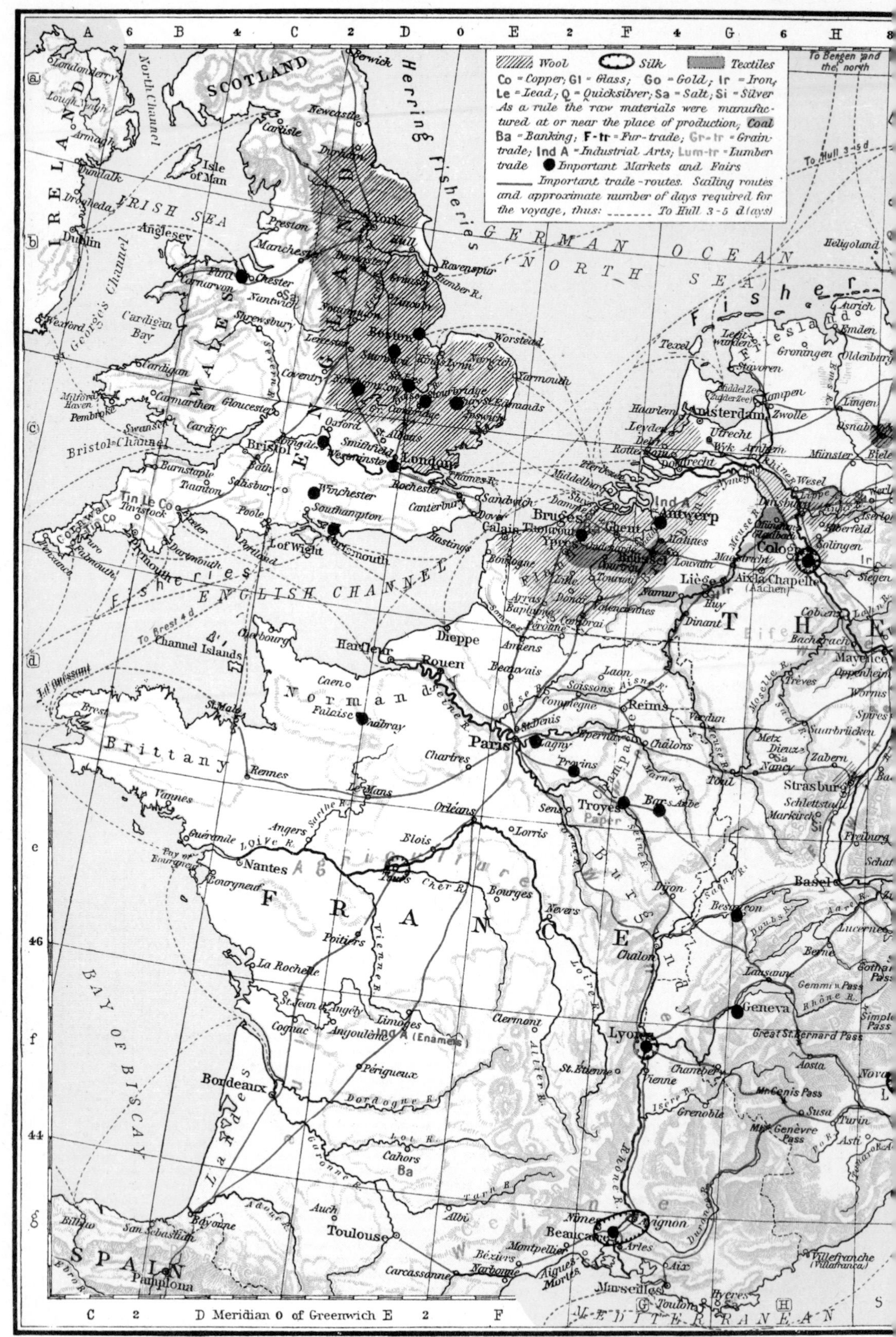

Scale 1:7000000

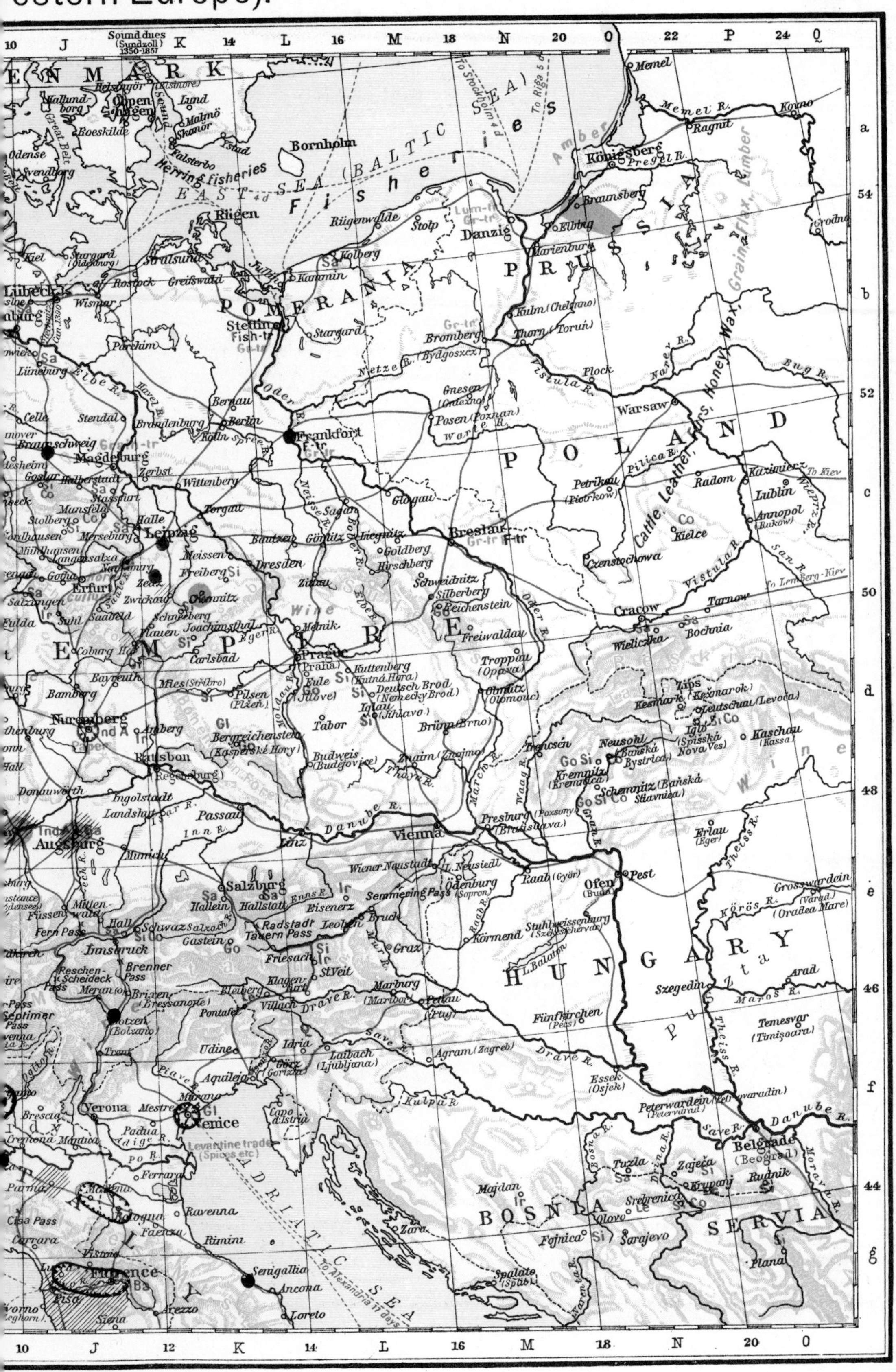

Plan of a Mediaeval Manor.

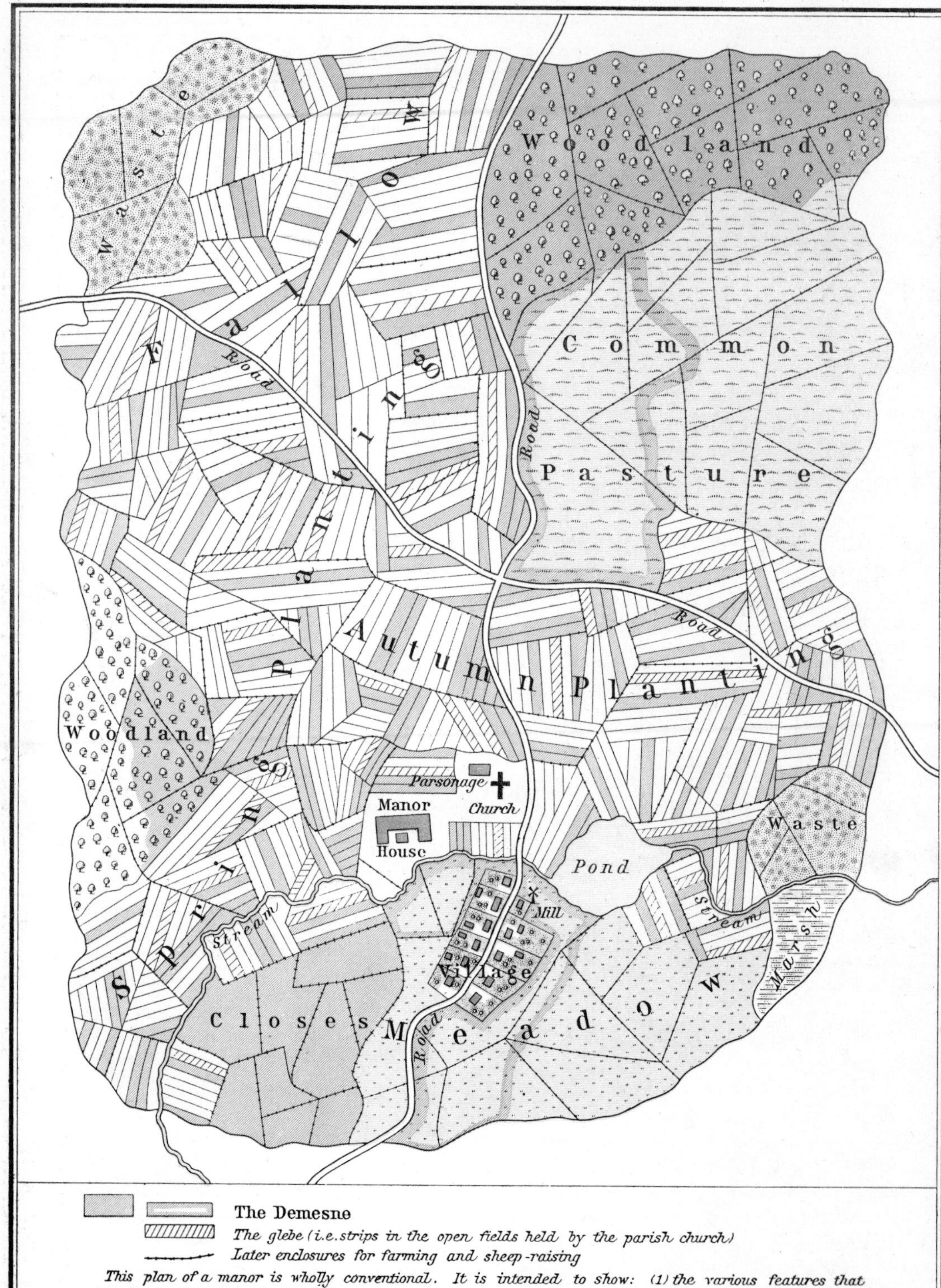

The Demesne

The glebe (i.e. strips in the open fields held by the parish church)

Later enclosures for farming and sheep-raising

This plan of a manor is wholly conventional. It is intended to show: (1) the various features that might be found in English manors (or vills) of the mediaeval period; (2) the more important changes in the agricultural system which occurred in England from the fourteenth century onward. Many of these manorial features, of course, appeared in similar domains on the continent.

Enfranchisement of Mediaeval Towns: Expansion of the Charter of Beaumont-en-Argonne, 1182—1300.

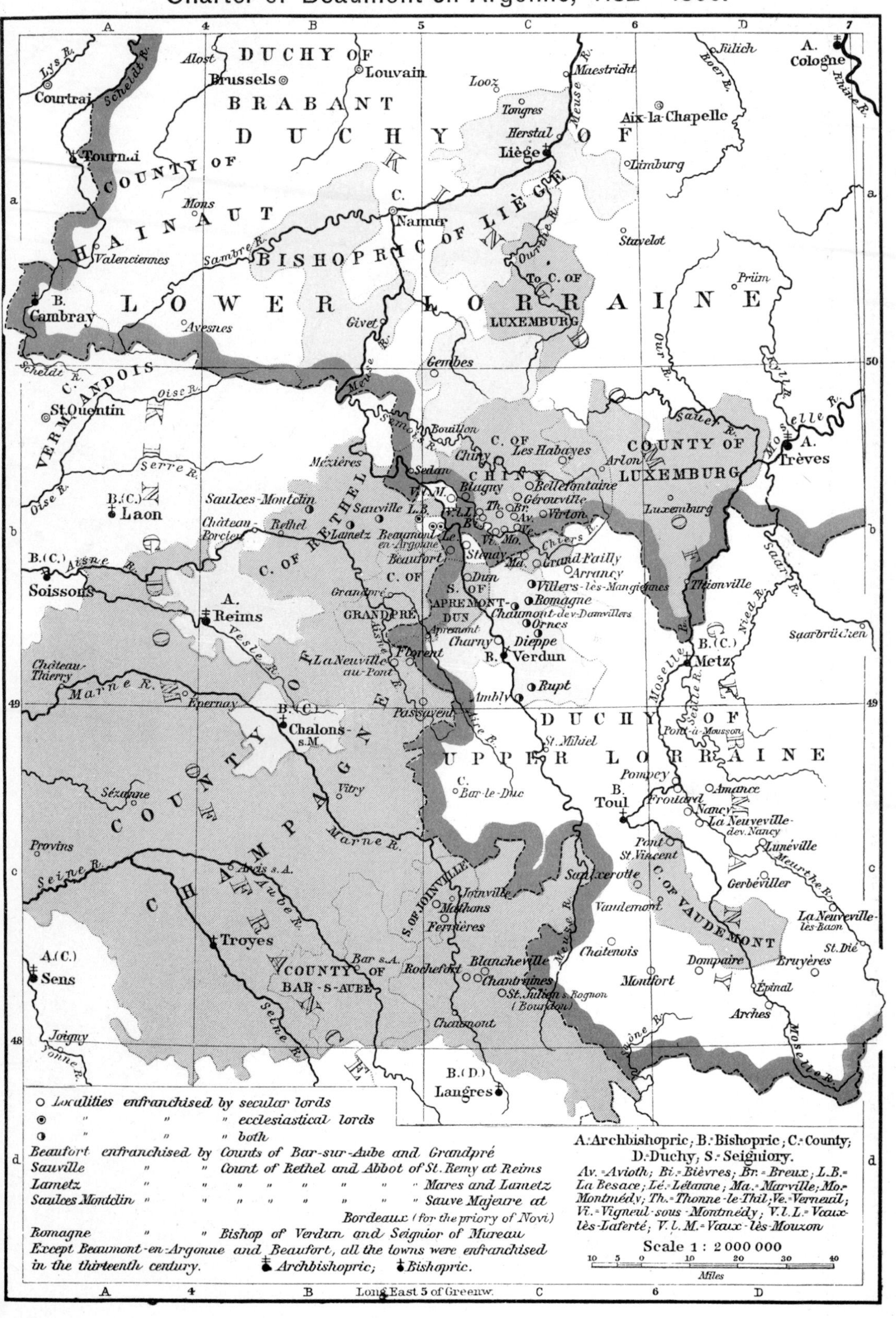

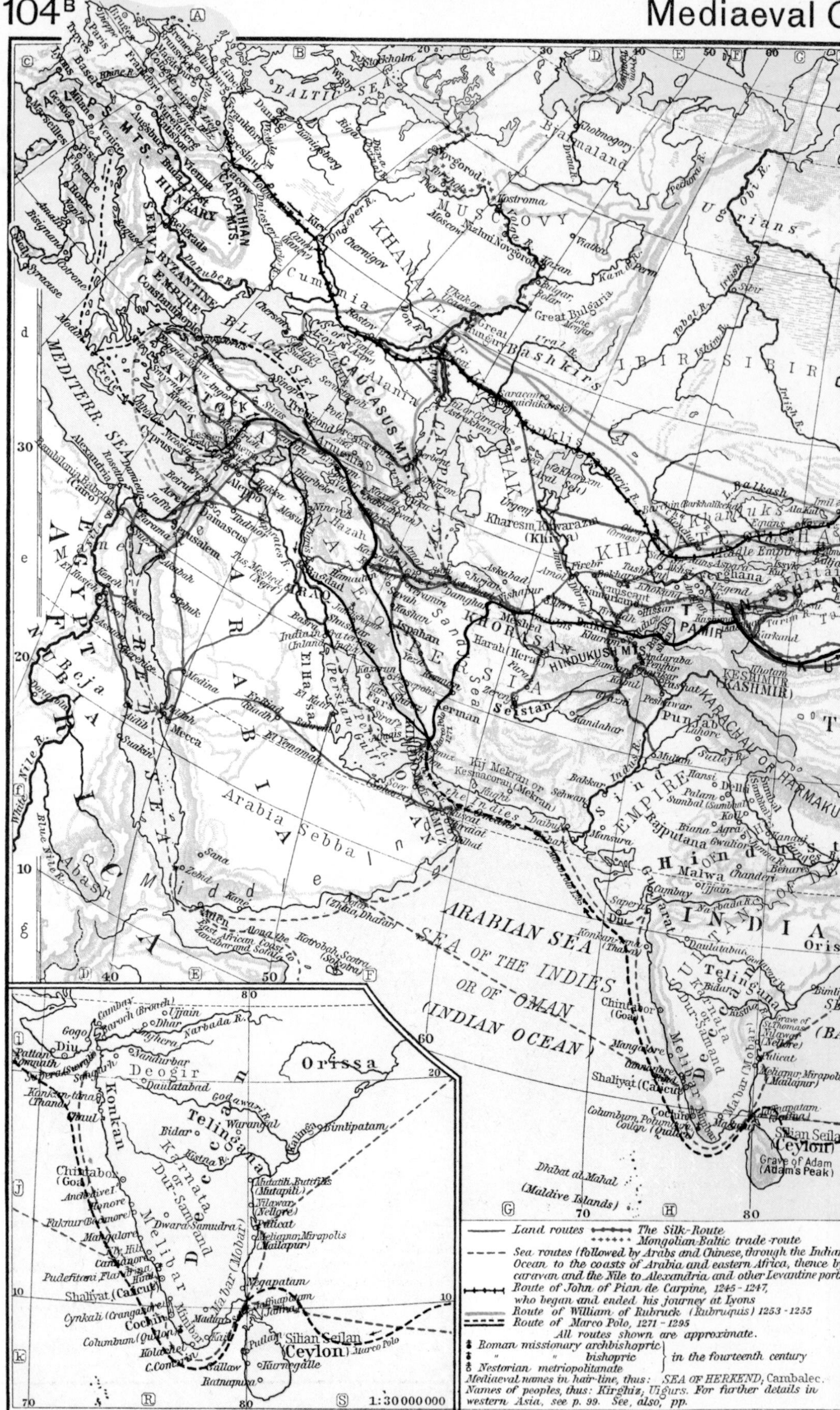

Scale 1:40 000 000

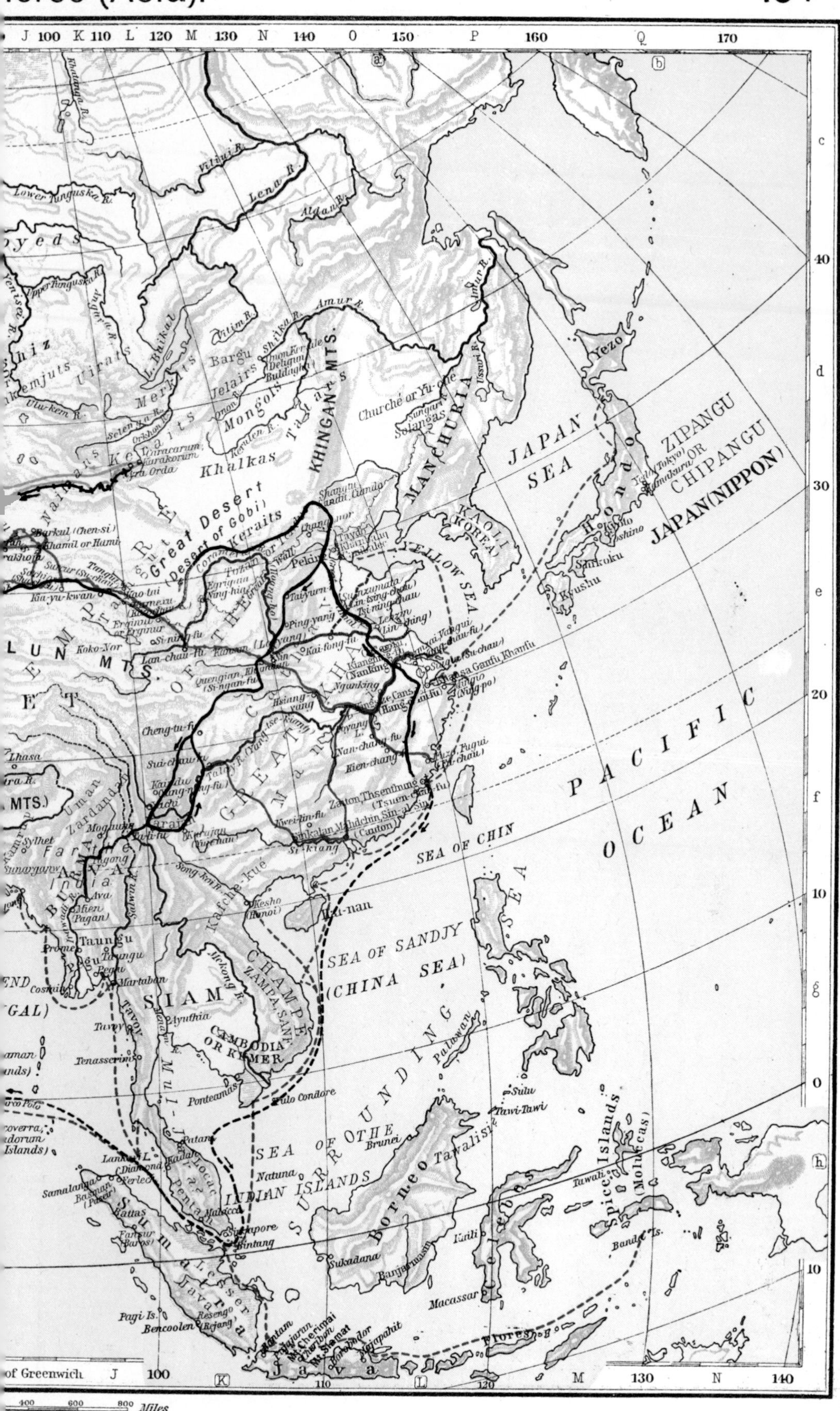
JAPAN SEA
ZIPANGU OR CHIPANGU
JAPAN (NIPPON)
Yezo
Hondo
Kiushu
Sikoku
Yedo (Tokyo)
Kamakura
Kioto
MANCHURIA
KAOLI (KOREA)
YELLOW SEA
KHINGAN MTS.
Great Desert (Desert of Gobi)
Keraits
Mongols
Khalkas
Tatars
Merkits
Bargu
Jelairs
Uirats
Lena R.
Amur R.
Vitim R.
Aldan R.
Lower Tunguska R.
Upper Tunguska R.
L. Baikal
Karakorum
Churche or Yu-che
Solangas
Peking
Kai-fong-fu
Lan-chau-fu
Koko-Nor
Cheng-tu-fu
Lhasa
MTS.
Nan-chang-fu
Kien-chang-fu
Zayton, Thsenthung (Tsuen-chau-fu)
Kinkalan, Mahachin, Sin-al-Sin (Canton)
SEA OF CHIN
PACIFIC OCEAN
SEA OF SANDJY (CHINA SEA)
SEA OF OTHE INDIAN ISLANDS
SURROUNDING SEA
SIAM
CHAMPE
CAMBODIA OR KHMER
Ayuthia
Tenasserim
Pegu
Martaban
Taungu
Ava
Pagan
Prome
Hai-nan
Kesho (Hanoi)
Palawan
Sulu
Tawi-Tawi
Borneo
Brunei
Sukadana
Banjarmasin
Macassar
Celebes
Spice Islands (Moluccas)
Banda Is.
Flores
Java
Sumatra
Malacca
Singapore
Bintang
Bencoolen
Pagi Is.
Natuna
Pulo Condore
Ponteamas
Patani
of Greenwich
Miles

Europe in 1490.

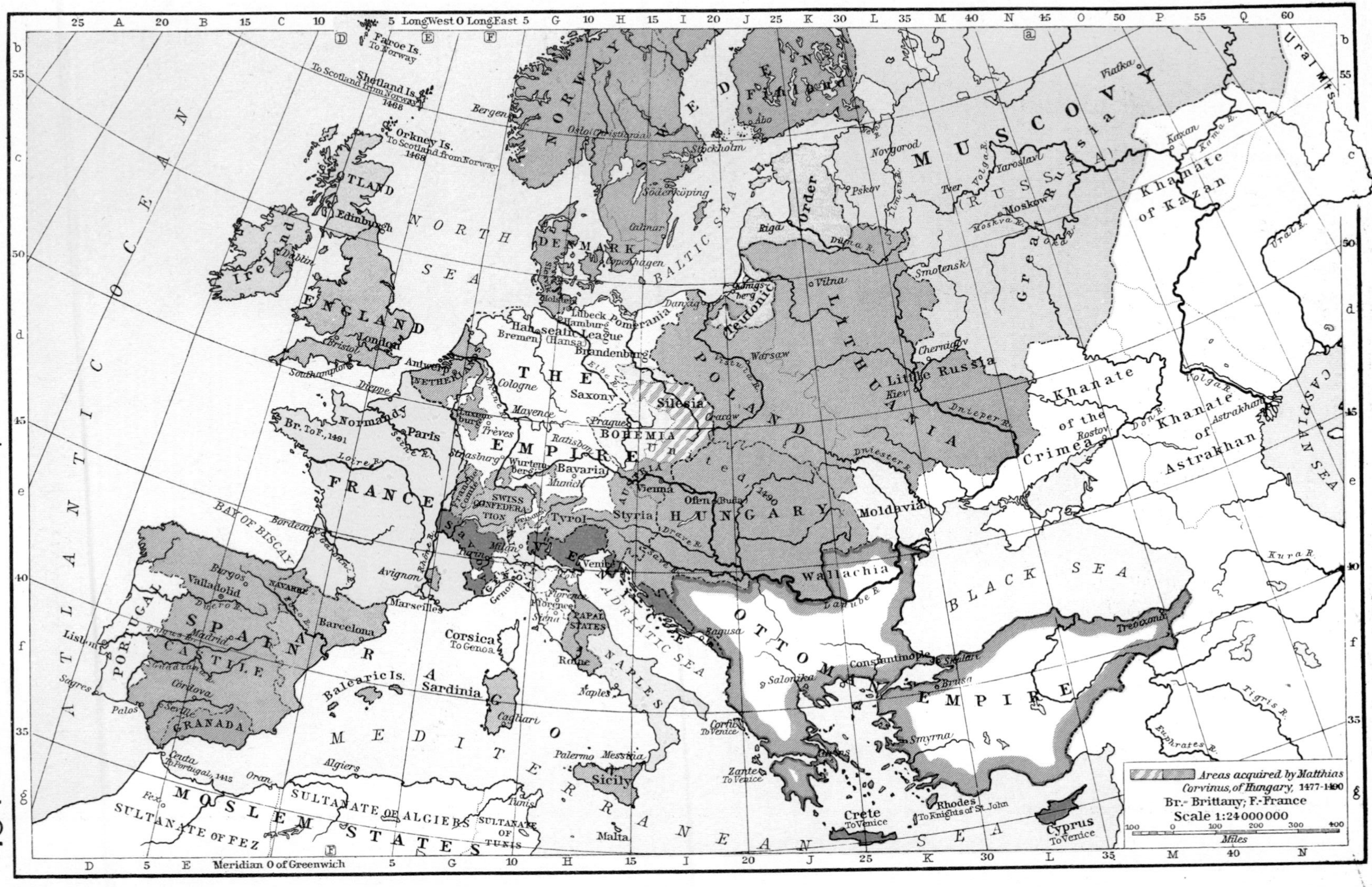

The West Indies and Central America, 1492—1525.

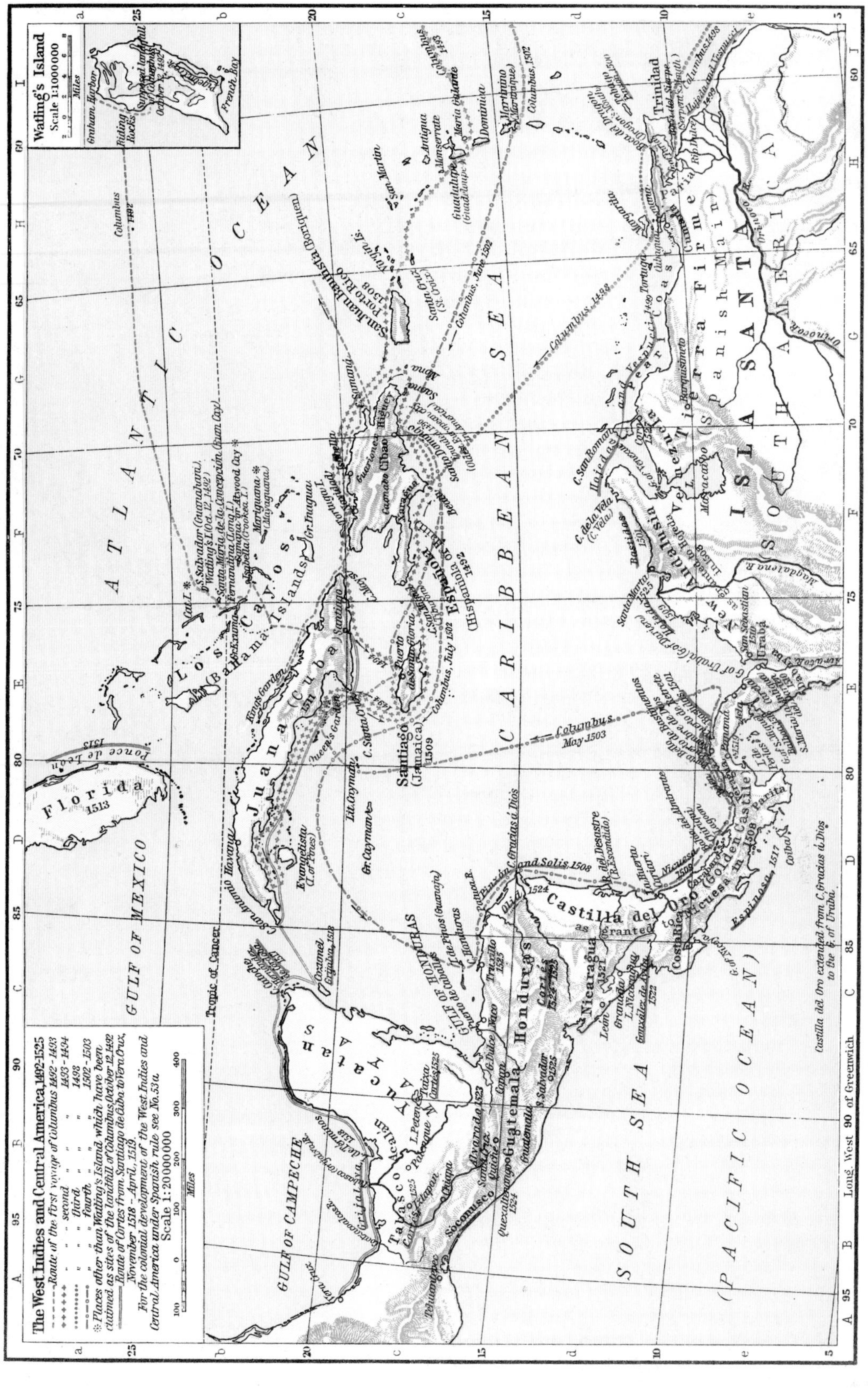

The Conquest of Mexico, 1519—1521.

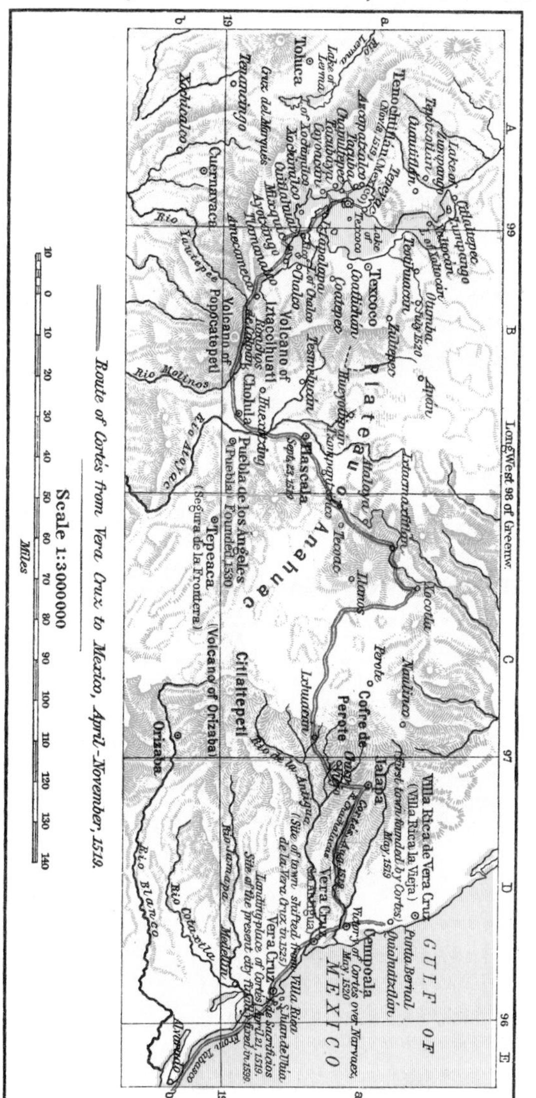

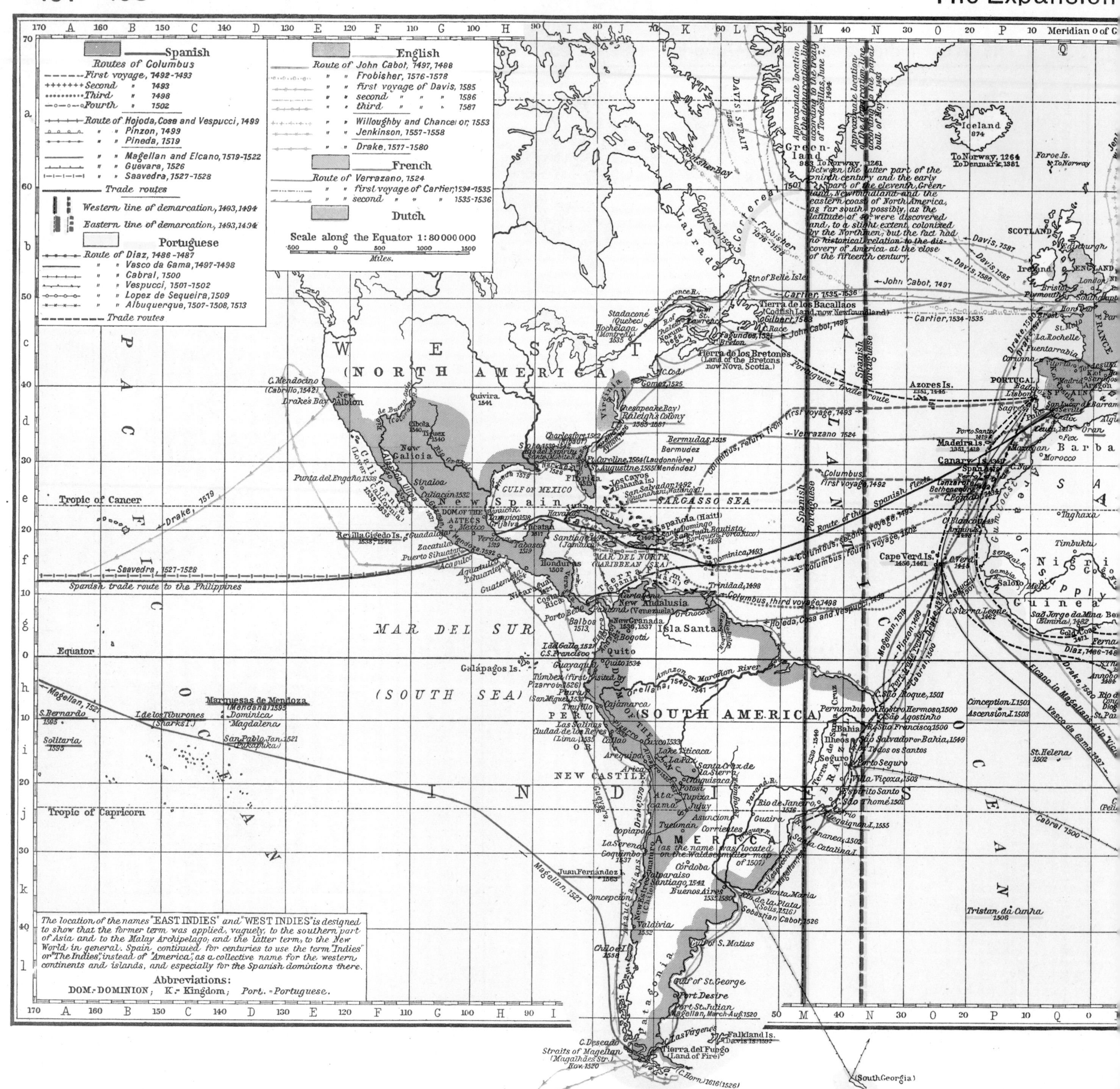
Spanish
Routes of Columbus
First voyage, 1492-1493
Second 1493
Third 1498
Fourth 1502
Route of Hojoda, Cosa and Vespucci, 1499
Pinzon, 1499
Pineda, 1519
Magellan and Elcano, 1519-1522
Guevara, 1526
Saavedra, 1527-1528
Trade routes
Western line of demarcation, 1493, 1494
Eastern line of demarcation, 1493, 1494
Portuguese
Route of Diaz, 1486-1487
Vasco da Gama, 1497-1498
Cabral, 1500
Vespucci, 1501-1502
Lopez de Sequeira, 1509
Albuquerque, 1507-1508, 1513
Trade routes
English
Route of John Cabot, 1497, 1498
Frobisher, 1576-1578
first voyage of Davis, 1585
second 1586
third 1587
Willoughby and Chancellor, 1553
Jenkinson, 1557-1558
Drake, 1577-1580
French
Route of Verrazano, 1524
first voyage of Cartier, 1534-1535
second 1535-1536
Dutch
Scale along the Equator 1: 80 000 000
Miles.
Between the latter part of the ninth century and the early part of the eleventh, Greenland, Newfoundland and the eastern coast of North America, as far south possibly as the latitude of 40° were discovered and, to a slight extent, colonized by the Northmen; but the fact had no historical relation to the discovery of America at the close of the fifteenth century.
The location of the names "EAST INDIES" and "WEST INDIES" is designed to show that the former term was applied, vaguely, to the southern part of Asia and to the Malay Archipelago; and the latter term, to the New World in general. Spain continued for centuries to use the term "Indies" or "The Indies", instead of "America", as a collective name for the western continents and islands, and especially for the Spanish dominions there.
Abbreviations:
DOM. = DOMINION; K. = Kingdom; Port. = Portuguese.
NORTH AMERICA
SOUTH AMERICA
MAR DEL SUR
(SOUTH SEA)
PACIFIC OCEAN
ATLANTIC OCEAN
WEST INDIES
Tropic of Cancer
Equator
Tropic of Capricorn
GULF OF MEXICO
SARGASSO SEA
New Spain
NEW CASTILE
Iceland
Greenland
Labrador
DAVIS STRAIT
SCOTLAND
Ireland
ENGLAND
FRANCE
PORTUGAL
SPAIN
Guinea
Spanish trade route to the Philippines
Meridian 0 of Greenwich

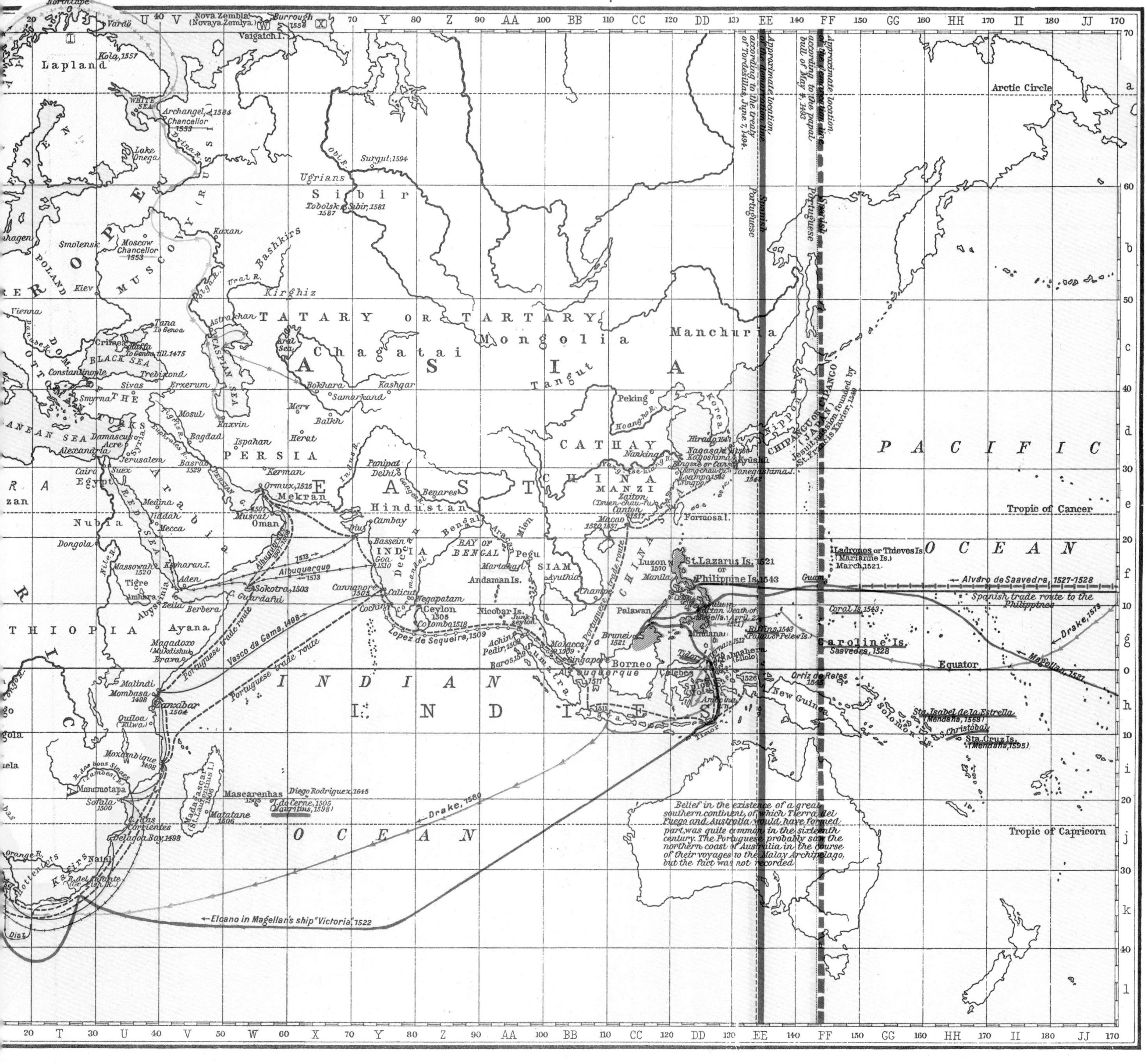

The Conquest of Peru, 1531—1533.

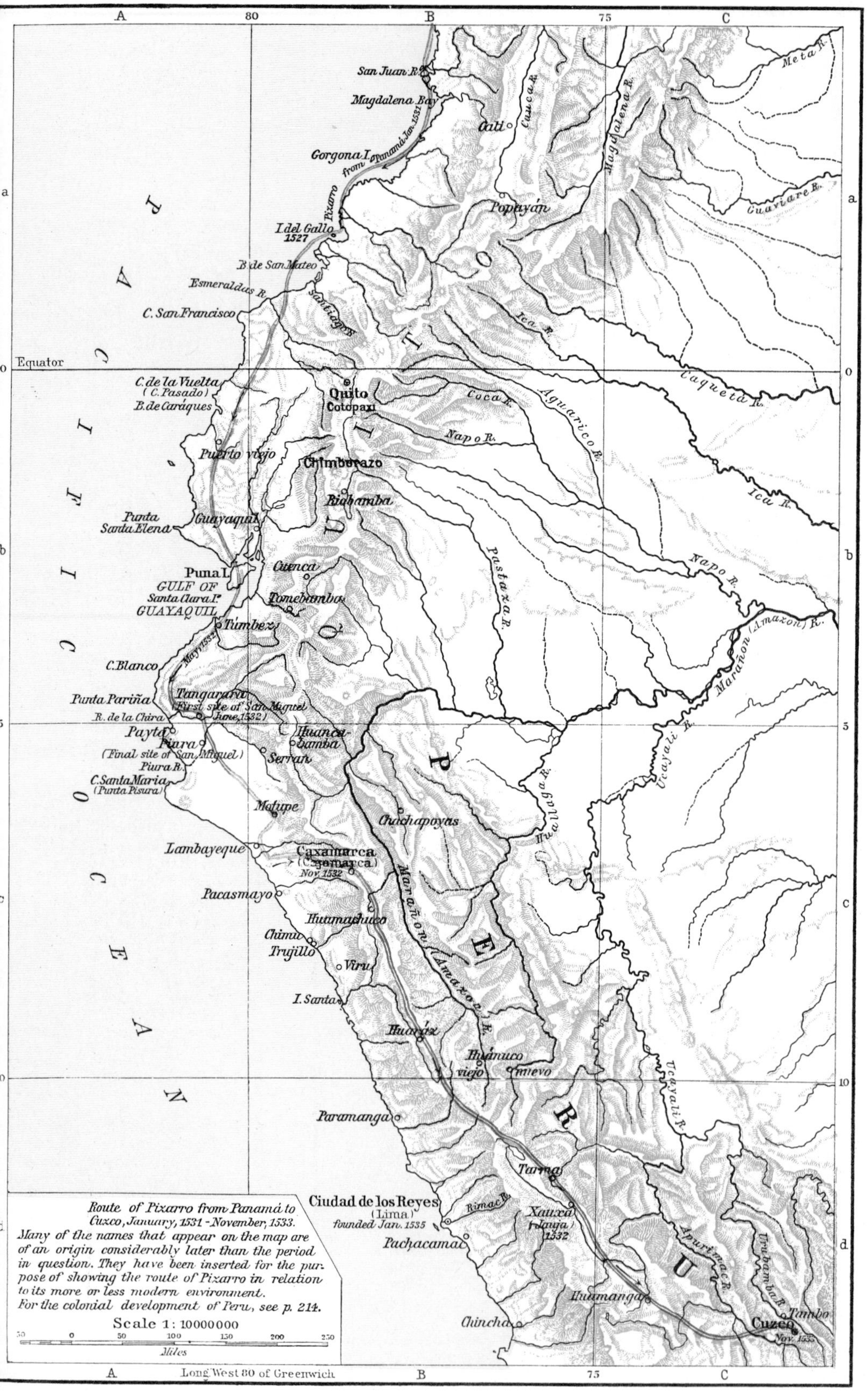

Route of Pizarro from Panamá to Cuzco, January, 1531 - November, 1533.
Many of the names that appear on the map are of an origin considerably later than the period in question. They have been inserted for the purpose of showing the route of Pizarro in relation to its more or less modern environment.
For the colonial development of Peru, see p. 214.

Scale 1: 10000000

Long. West 80 of Greenwich

The Portuguese Colonial Dominions in India and the Malay Archipelago, 1498—1580.

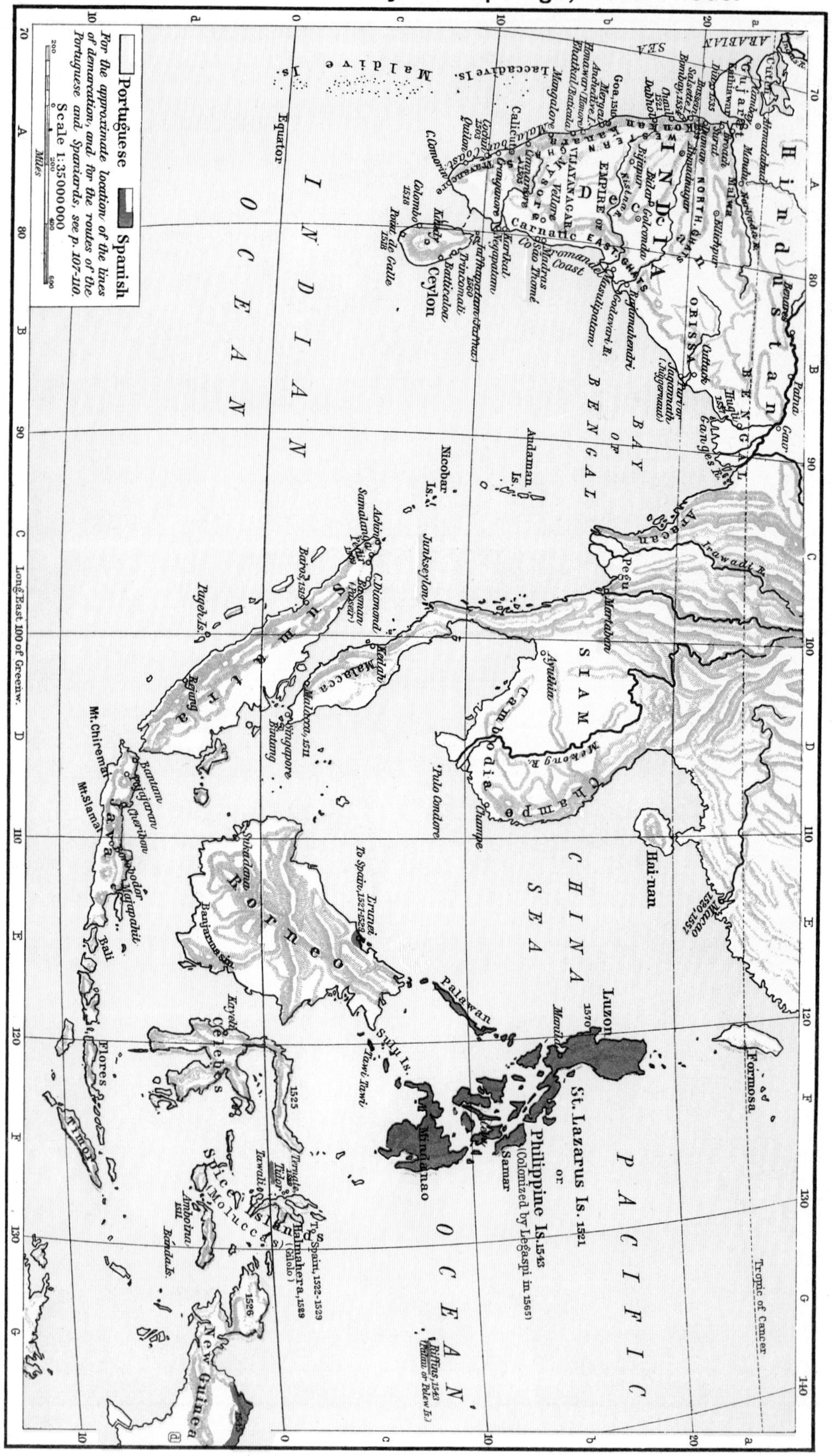

Portuguese — Spanish

For the approximate location of the lines of demarcation, and for the routes of the Portuguese and Spaniards, see p. 107-110.

Scale 1:35000000

Long. East 100 of Greenw.

The Imperial Circles about 1512.

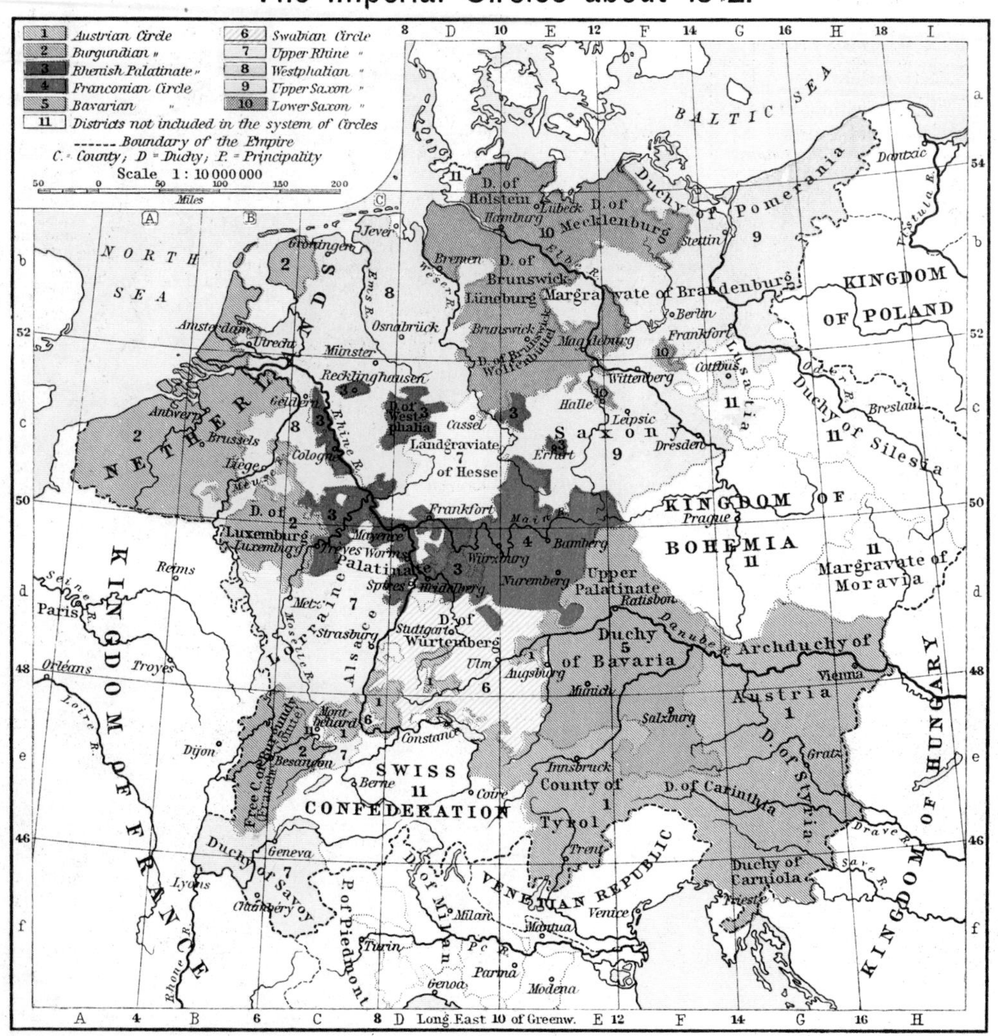

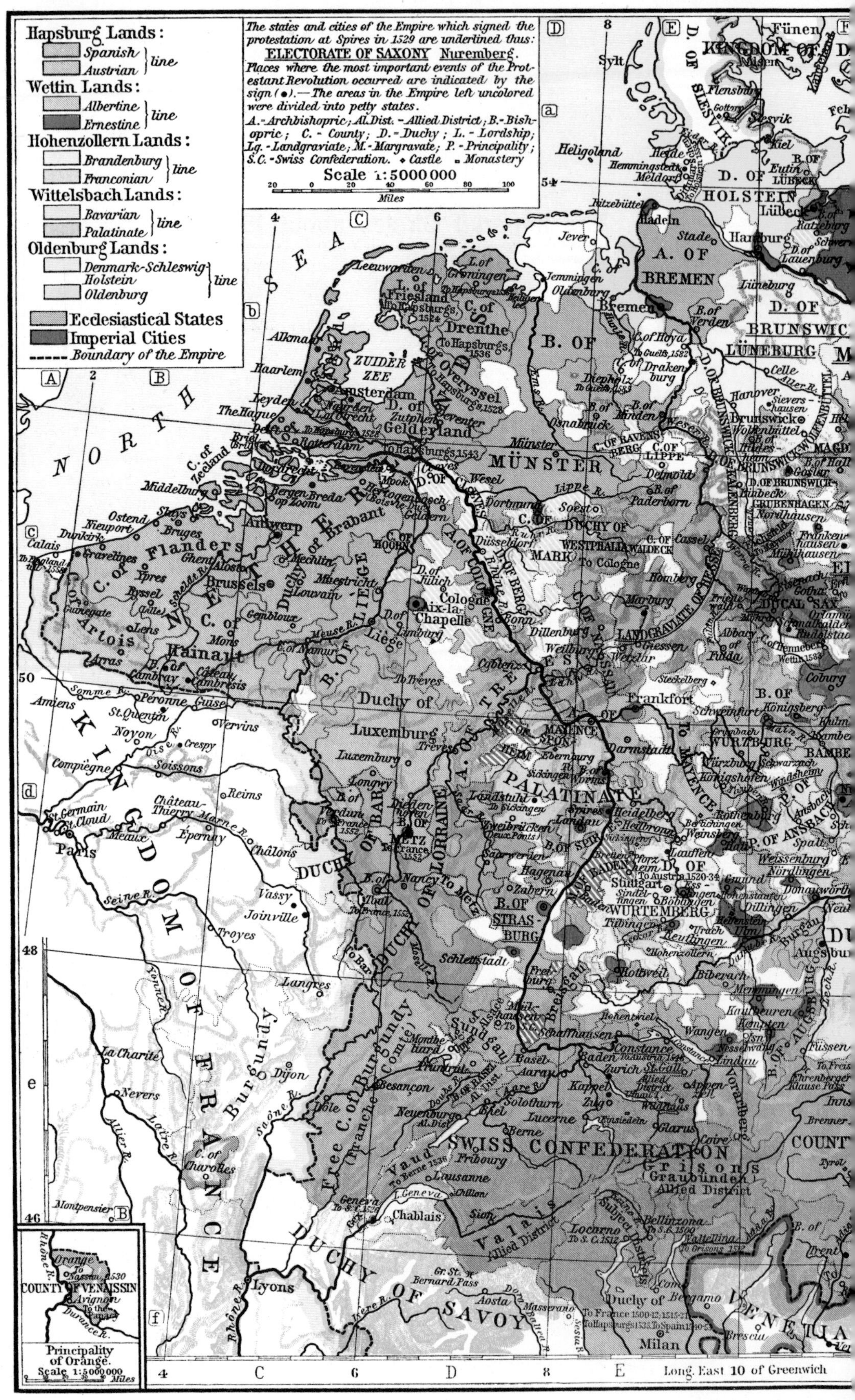
Hapsburg Lands:
Spanish line
Austrian line
Wettin Lands:
Albertine line
Ernestine line
Hohenzollern Lands:
Brandenburg line
Franconian line
Wittelsbach Lands:
Bavarian line
Palatinate line
Oldenburg Lands:
Denmark-Schleswig-Holstein line
Oldenburg
Ecclesiastical States
Imperial Cities
Boundary of the Empire
The states and cities of the Empire which signed the protestation at Spires in 1529 are underlined thus: ELECTORATE OF SAXONY Nuremberg.
Places where the most important events of the Protestant Revolution occurred are indicated by the sign (●).— The areas in the Empire left uncolored were divided into petty states.
A.-Archbishopric; Al.Dist.-Allied District; B.-Bishopric; C.-County; D.-Duchy; L.-Lordship; Lg.-Landgraviate; M.-Margravate; P.-Principality; S.C.-Swiss Confederation. ◆ Castle ▪ Monastery
Scale 1:5000000
Miles
NORTH SEA
KINGDOM OF FRANCE
NETHERLANDS
C. of Flanders
Duchy of Brabant
C. of Artois
Hainaut
Duchy of Luxemburg
PALATINATE
MÜNSTER
SWISS CONFEDERATION
DUCHY OF SAVOY
DUCHY OF LORRAINE
Free C. of Burgundy (Franche Comté)
Burgundy
A. OF BREMEN
HOLSTEIN
D. OF SLESVIK
LANDGRAVIATE OF HESSE
D. OF WURTEMBERG
B. OF STRASBURG
Principality of Orange.
COUNTY OF VENAISSIN
Scale 1:5000000
Long. East 10 of Greenwich

BALTIC SEA
KINGDOM OF POLAND
DUCHY OF PRUSSIA
KINGDOM OF BOHEMIA
To Austria, 1526
MARGRAVATE OF MORAVIA
DUCHY OF SILESIA
ARCHDUCHY OF AUSTRIA
HUNGARY
TURKISH HUNGARY
To the Turks, 1541
BAVARIA
DUCHY OF STYRIA
DUCHY OF CARINTHIA
DUCHY OF CARNIOLA
Wettin Lands
1485-1554
Border coloring of the bishoprics (B.) indicates the protectorate under which they stood
Scale 1:6000000
Lands ruled by the (Ernestine) Elector of Saxony in 1521 (according to Leipsic Treaty of 1485)
Albertine Lands (1521)
Transferred from Ernestine to Albertine by Wittenberg Capitulation (1547)
Ernestine after W. Cap.
To Bohemia after W. Cap.
Transferred from Albertine to Ernestine by Naumburg Treaty (1554)

The Religious Situation in Europe about 1560.

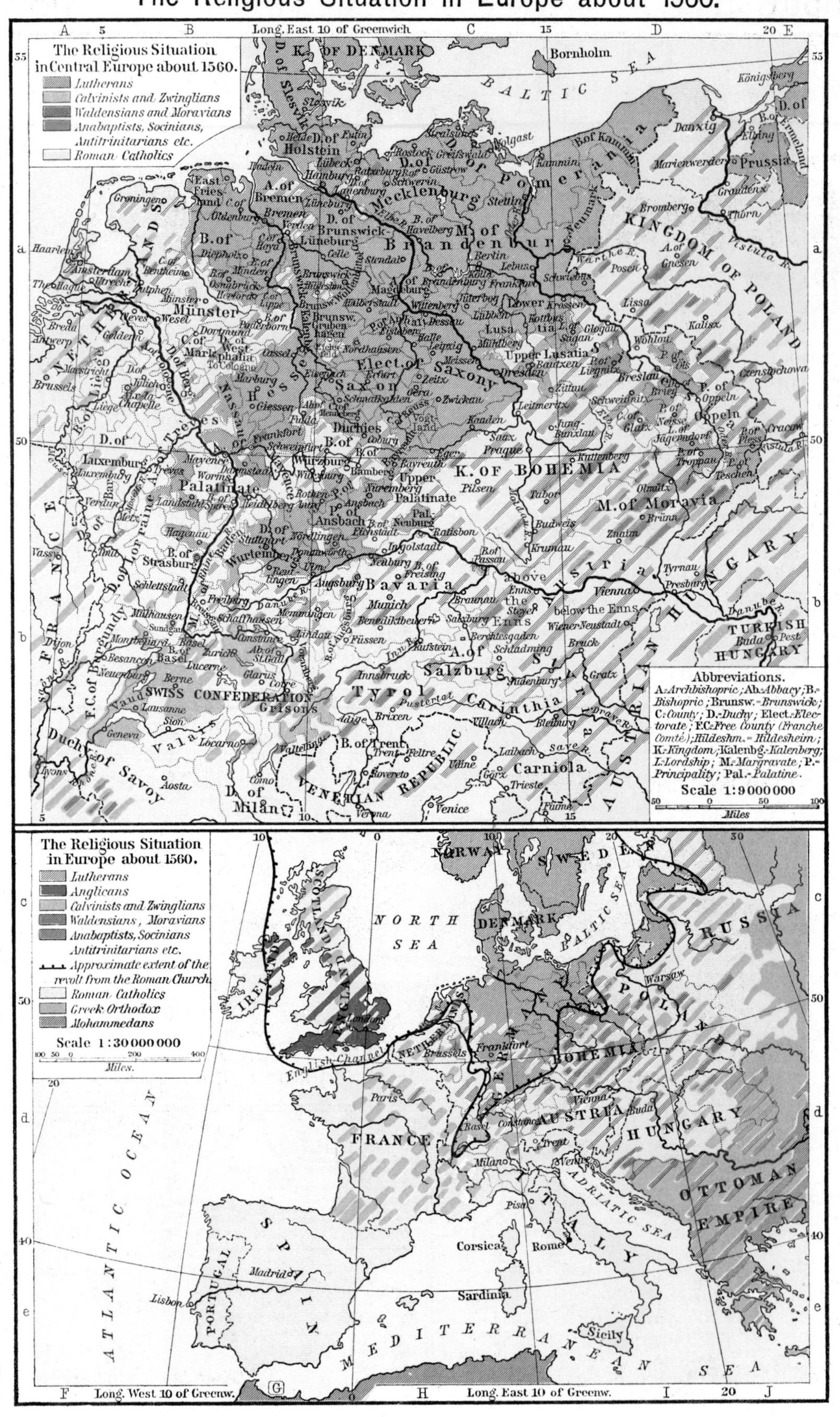

The Netherlands, 1559—1609.

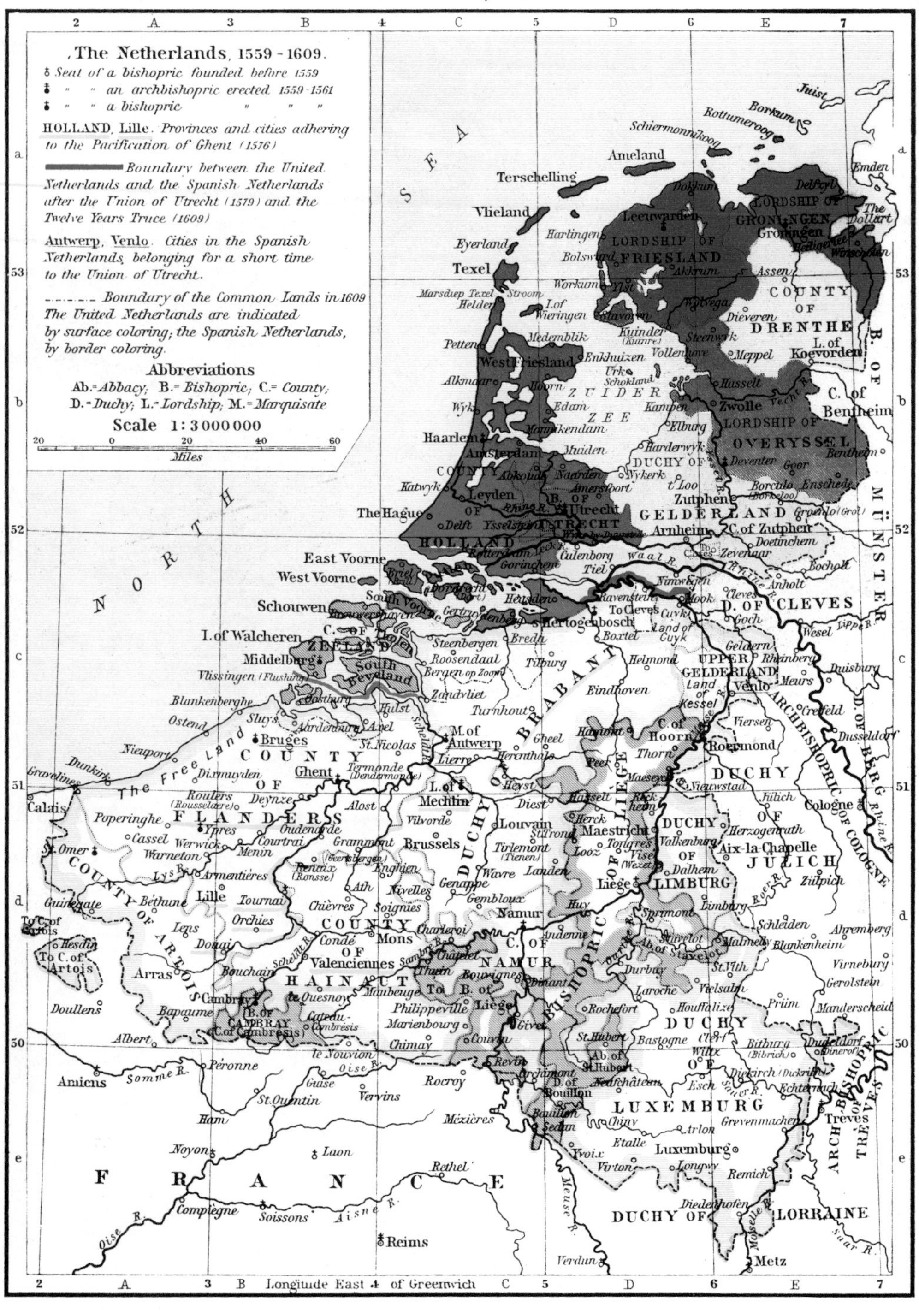

Meridian 0 of Greenwich
Long. West 0 Long. East
KINGDOM OF NORWAY
Shetland Is.
Orkneys
The Hebrides
KINGDOM OF SCOTLAND
Inverness
Aberdeen
Perth
St. Andrews
Firth of Forth
Dunbar
Berwick
Flodden
Northumberland
NORTH SEA
Ulster
Connaught
Armagh
IRELAND
Galway
Limerick
Munster
Cork
Waterford
Dublin
Donegal Bay
Dingle Bay
September
Aug. 23
Aug. 12
Solway Firth
Carlisle
Westmorland
York
KINGDOM OF ENGLAND
Leicester
Peterborough
Norwich
Wales
Gloucester
Coventry
Oxford
Cambridge
London
Canterbury
Dover
Plymouth
Portsmouth
Lizard Head
July 29
ENGLISH CHANNEL
July 31
Aug. 4
Aug. 8
Guernsey
Jersey
Cherbourg
ATLANTIC OCEAN
September and October
Amsterdam
The Hague
Utrecht
NETHERLANDS
Bruges
Ghent
Flanders
Artois
Calais
Brussels
Aix-la-Chapelle
Liège
Cologne
Marburg
Munster
Cassel
Bremen
Hamburg
Oldenburg
Brunswick
Magdeburg
Eisleben
Erfurt
Leipzig
SAXONY
Schwerin
Lübeck
Holstein
Schleswig
K. OF DENMARK
Jutland
Copenhagen
Stavanger
Bergen
Aggershuus
Oslo
Kongsberg
Bohus
Halland
THE EMPIRE
Frankfort
Mayence
Luxemburg
Metz
Lorraine
Spires
Nuremberg
Stuttgart
Ratisbon
Strasburg
BAVARIA
Munich
Augsburg
Salzburg
Innsbruck
Tyrol
Carinthia
Rouen
Brest
Brittany
Rennes
Le Mans
Paris
Noyon
Soissons
Meaux
Château Thierry
Châlons
Verdun
Vassy
Joinville
Nemours
Orléans
Blois
Amboise
Tours
Nantes
Moncontour
Poitiers
La Rochelle
KINGDOM OF FRANCE
Bourges
Romorantin
La Charité
Langres
Burgundy
Franche Comté
Besançon
Bern
Zurich
Basel
SWISS CONFEDERATION
Geneva
Lyons
Clermont
Limoges
Montpensier
Jarnac
Cognac
Coutras
Bordeaux
Bergerac
Albret
Bayonne
Béarn
Toulouse
Montauban
Rodez
Languedoc
Orange
Avignon
Aigues mortes
Narbonne
Marseilles
Provence
Toulon
Nice
Dauphiny
Grenoble
D. OF SAVOY
Turin
Pinerolo
Saluzzo
Milan
Pavia
Genoa
Parma
Modena
Mantua
Verona
Padua
Venice
VENETIAN
Ferrara
Bologna
Florence
Lucca
Pisa
Siena
Urbino
Ancona
PAPAL STATES
Perugia
Spoleto
Piombino
Presidios To Spain
Civitavecchia
Viterbo
Rome
Gaeta
Naples
Corsica To Genoa
Bastia
K. OF SARDINIA
Sassari
Cagliari
BAY OF BISCAY
Bay of Ferrol July 16
July 22
Corunna
Santiago
Santander
Bilbao
Leon
Burgos
K. of Navarre
Pamplona
Valladolid
Zamora
Salamanca
Segovia
Saragossa
Aragon
Lérida
Montserrat
Barcelona
Tarragona
Tortosa
Madrid
Toledo
Alcalá de Henares
Escorial
KINGDOM OF SPAIN
Castile
Valencia
Játiva
Calatrava
Cordova
Seville
Granada
Malaga
Almeria
Murcia
Cartagena
Cadiz
Gibraltar
Ceuta
Tangier
Algarve
Faro
Palos
Oporto
Braganza
Douro R.
Coimbra
PORTUGAL
K. OF PORTUGAL To Spain
Lisbon
Setúbal
Badajoz
Balearic Is.
Minorca
Majorca
Iviza
MEDIT
FEZ AND MOROCCO
BARBARY STATES
ALGERIA
TUNIS
Tlemsen
Oran To Spain
Melilla To Spain
Algiers
Bona To Spain
Bizerta
Goletta
Tunis
Palermo
Girgenti
Sicily
Malta To Knights of St. John

Possessions of the House of Hapsburg:
Spanish line
Austrian line
in surface coloring
European empire of Charles V about 1526
Possessions of the House of Bourbon:
Hereditary lands of Henry of Bourbon-Navarre (later Henry IV.)
Lands of Charles of Bourbon-Montpensier (the Constable)
The underlining of Metz, Toul and Verdun indicates that, while these cities legally formed part of the Empire after 1552, they were actually held by France.
Montferrat belonged to Mantua, and the papal territory of Ferrara to Modena.
Sites of important events are indicated by the sign (•)
Route of the Armada 1588.
× Battle ∘ Castle ▪ Monastery
Abbreviations:
D.=Duchy. Dom.=Domain. K.=Kingdom.
L.N.=Lower Navarre. M.=Margravate.
P.=Principality. Rep.=Republic. U.N.=Upper Navarre.
Scale 1:15 000 000
100 0 100 200
Miles
MUSCOVITE DOMINIONS
(RUSSIA)
GRAND PRINCIPALITY OF LITHUANIA
KINGDOM OF POLAND
KHANATE OF THE CRIMEA
ASTRAKHAN To Russia, 1557
OTTOMAN EMPIRE
BLACK SEA
SEA OF AZOV
P. OF TRANSYLVANIA
P. OF MOLDAVIA
P. OF WALLACHIA
K. OF HUNGARY
DOM. OF THE TEUTONIC ORDER
RUMELIA
CYPRUS To Venice
CRETE To Venice

The Religious Situation in Central Europe about 1618. Sweden about 1658.

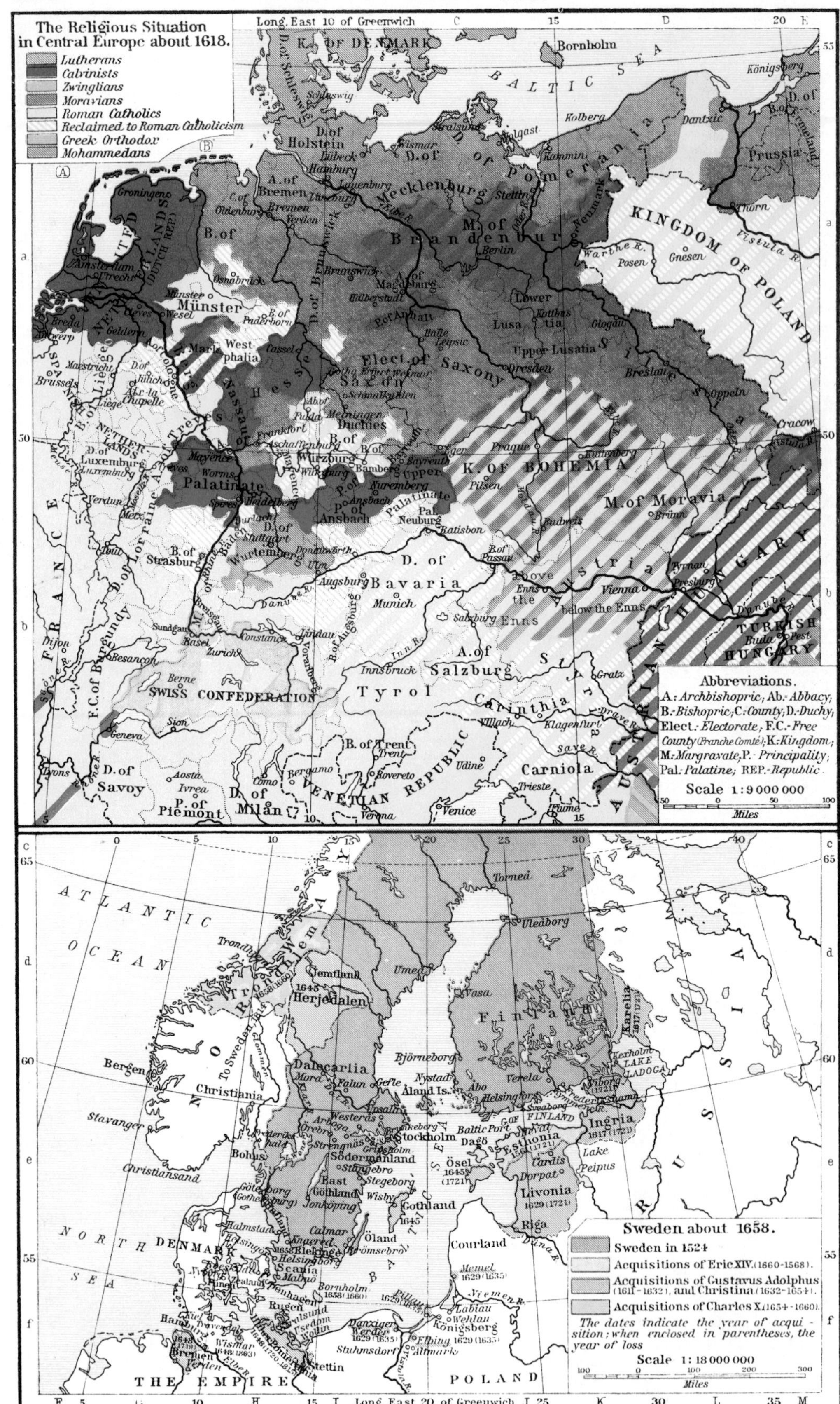

Principal Seats of War, 1618—1660.
Treaty Adjustments, 1648—1660.

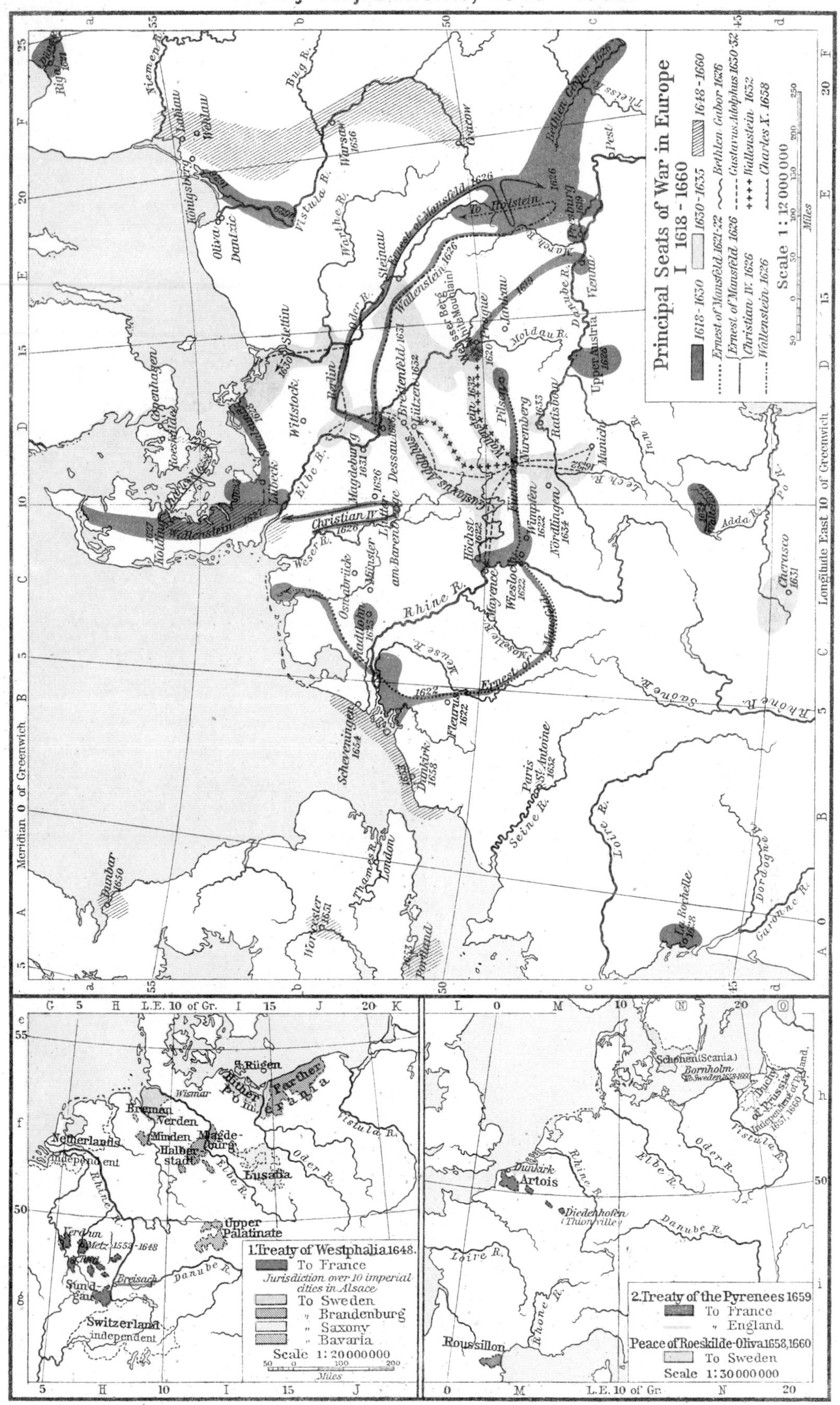

N O R T H S E A
KINGDOM OF FRANCE
UNITED NETHERLANDS
Independent of the Empire 1648
SPANISH NETHERLANDS
Flanders
Artois
To France 1659
SWITZERLAND
Independent of the Empire 1648
Grisons
DUCHY OF SAVOY
PRINCIPALITY OF PIEDMONT
Duchy of Milan
HOLSTEIN
SLESVIK
DUCHY OF LÜNEBURG
MÜNSTER
LANDGRAVIATE OF HESSE-CASSEL
DUCHY OF WESTPHALIA
DUCHY OF WURTEMBERG
Franche Comté
To France 1678
To France, 1601
Heligoland
To Holstein-Gottorp
Norwich
Amsterdam
Rotterdam
Utrecht
The Hague
Antwerp
Brussels
Ghent
Bruges
Ostend
Dunkirk
Calais
Lille
Cambray
Namur
Liège
Aix-la-Chapelle
Cologne
Düsseldorf
Coblenz
Frankfort
Mayence
Worms
Spires
Heidelberg
Mannheim
Darmstadt
Würzburg
Stuttgart
Tübingen
Strasburg
Breisach
Metz
Nancy
Toul
Verdun
Sedan
Reims
Laon
Soissons
Noyon
Compiègne
Amiens
St. Quentin
Paris
St. Germain-en-Laye
Meaux
Châlons
Troyes
Fontainebleau
Langres
Dijon
Besançon
Chalon
Lyons
Geneva
Lausanne
Berne
Lucerne
Zurich
Basel
Constance
Bourges
Nevers
Montluçon
Clermont
St. Étienne
Bremen
Hamburg
Lübeck
Hanover
Brunswick
Osnabrück
Minden
Paderborn
Cassel
Marburg
Fulda
Groningen
Emden
Oldenburg
Verden
Flensburg
Kiel
Rendsburg
Lyons
Aosta
Como
Bergamo
Brescia
Locarno
Lugano
Chiavenna
Sion
Annecy
Chambéry
B 4 C 6 D 8 E 10 Long. East F
A 2 B 4 C 6 D 8 E
54
50
48
46

BALTIC SEA
KINGDOM OF POLAND
Great Poland
DUCHY OF PRUSSIA
Ermeland
Pomerania
Farther Pomerania
Neumark
Ukermark
Mittelmark
Lower Lusatia
Upper Lusatia
ELECTORATE OF SAXONY
DUCHY OF SILESIA
KINGDOM OF BOHEMIA
MARGRAVATE OF MORAVIA
ARCHDUCHY OF AUSTRIA
BELOW THE ENNS
ABOVE THE ENNS
DUCHY OF STYRIA
DUCHY OF CARINTHIA
DUCHY OF CARNIOLA
KINGDOM OF HUNGARY
OTTOMAN EMPIRE
Königsberg
Danzig
Stettin
Berlin
Posen
Warsaw
Praga
Cracow
Breslau
Dresden
Leipzig
Prague
Vienna
Presburg
Linz
Salzburg
Gratz
Trieste
Hapsburg Lands:
Austrian line
Spanish line
Hohenzollern Lands:
Brandenburg line
Franconian line
Wettin Lands:
Albertine line
Ernestine line
Wittelsbach Lands:
Bavarian line
Palatinate line
Oldenburg Lands:
Denmark (royal portion) and Oldenburg
Holstein-Gottorp (ducal portion)
Ecclesiastical States
Imperial Cities
Boundary of the Empire
The chief territorial changes in the seventeenth century are indicated by narrow colored borders. The color scheme, furthermore, shows how the Saxon portion of the County of Henneberg, held in common by the Albertines and the Ernestines till 1660, was divided between them at that time; also, how the County of Sponheim, held in common by Baden and the Palatinate, was divided between them in 1707 and 1776. The areas in the Empire left uncolored were divided into petty states.
Sites of the most important battles and diplomatic negotiations are given the sign ●
The states and cities to which the Edict of Restitution (1629) applied are underlined, thus: Strasburg
Abbreviations
A.=Archbishopric. A.Z.=Anhalt-Zerbst. Ab.=Abbacy. B.=Bishopric. Bav.=Bavaria. Brand.=Brandenburg. C.=County. D.=Duchy. Fr.W.C.=Frederick William Canal. H.C.=Hesse-Cassel. L.=Lordship. Lg.=Landgraviate. M.=Margravate. Meck.=Mecklenburg. P.=Principality. Pal.=Palatinate
◇ Castle. ▭ Monastery.
Scale 1:5 000 000
20 0 20 40 60 80 100
Miles.

Europe in 1648.

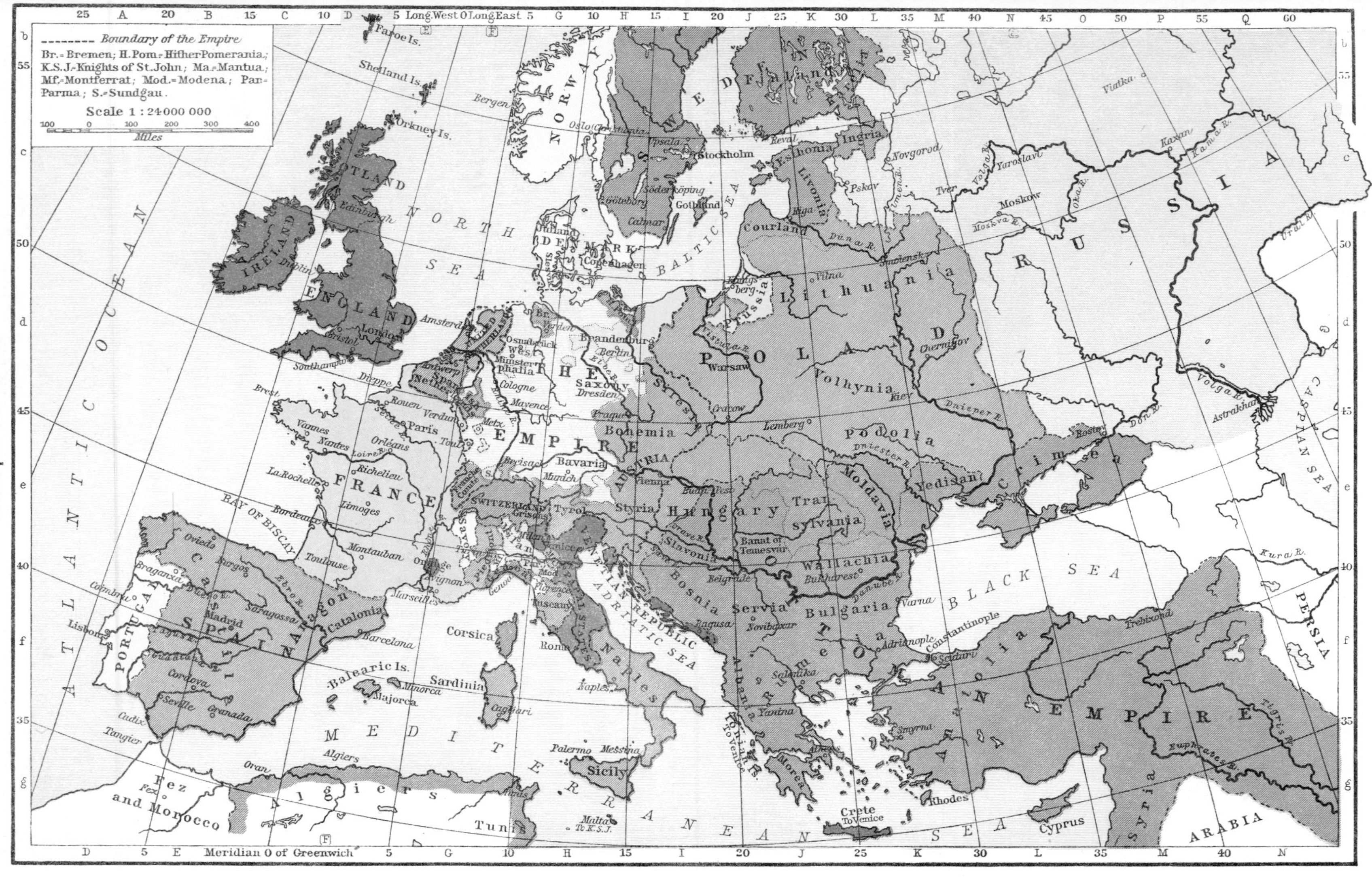

Principal Seats of War in Europe, 1672—1699.
Treaty Adjustments, 1688—1699.

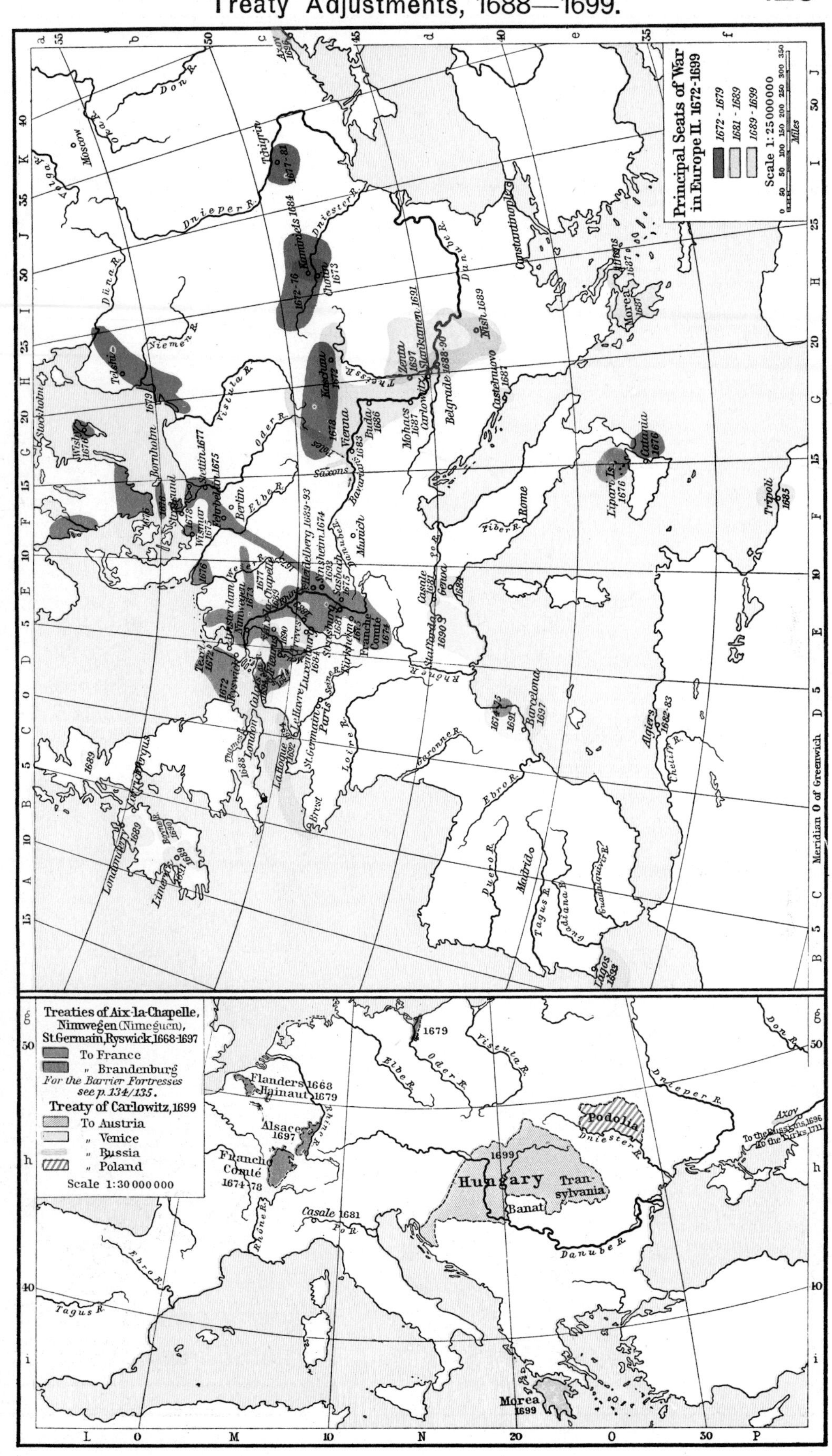

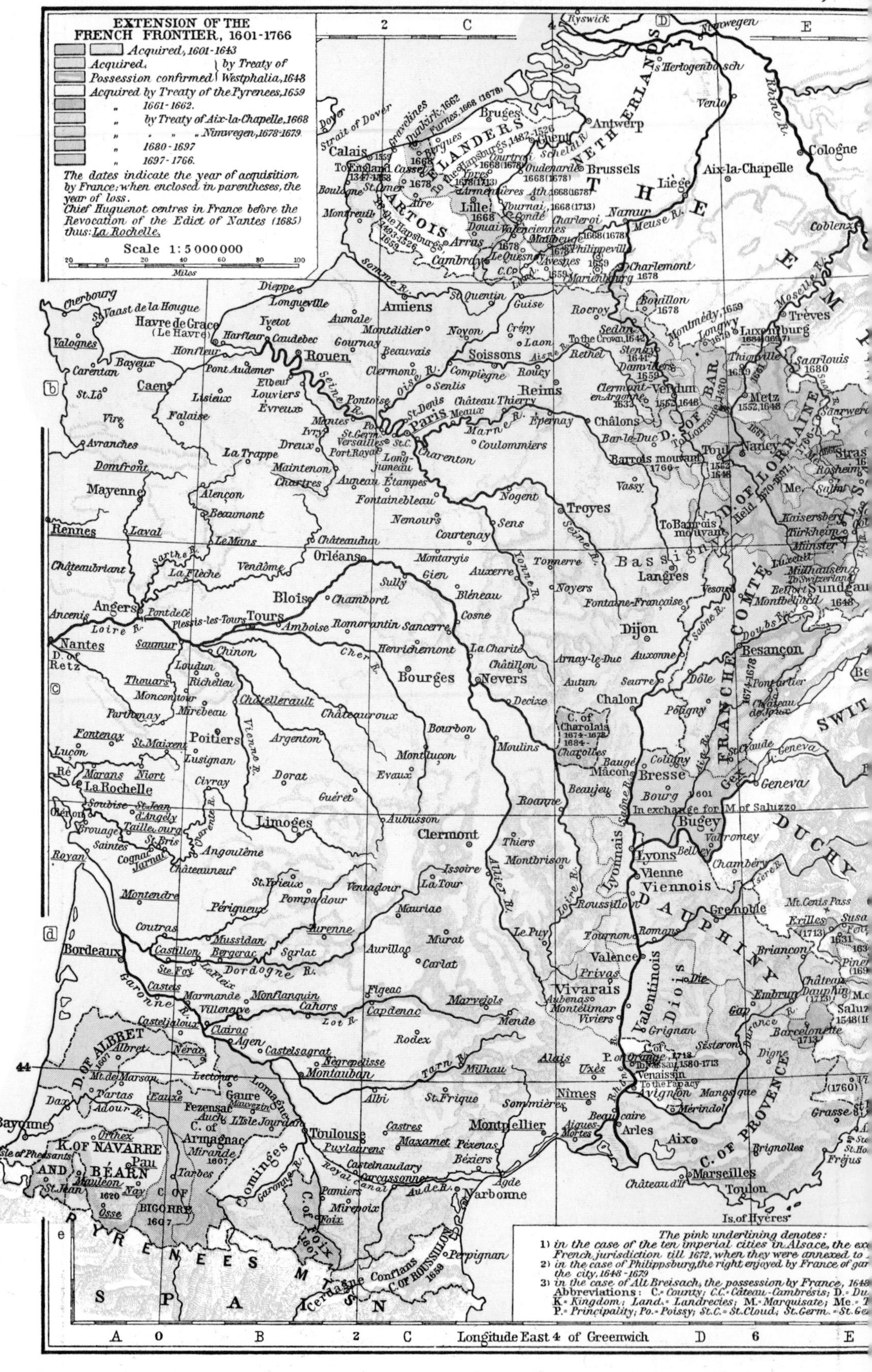
EXTENSION OF THE FRENCH FRONTIER, 1601-1766
Acquired, 1601-1643
Acquired, Possession confirmed } by Treaty of Westphalia, 1648
Acquired by Treaty of the Pyrenees, 1659
" 1661-1662.
" by Treaty of Aix-la-Chapelle, 1668
" " " Nimwegen, 1678-1679.
" 1680-1697
" 1697-1766.
The dates indicate the year of acquisition by France; when enclosed in parentheses, the year of loss.
Chief Huguenot centres in France before the Revocation of the Edict of Nantes (1685) thus: La Rochelle.
Scale 1:5 000 000
Miles
The pink underlining denotes:
1) in the case of the ten imperial cities in Alsace, the exc
French jurisdiction till 1672, when they were annexed to
2) in the case of Philippsburg, the right enjoyed by France of gar
the city, 1648-1679
3) in the case of Alt Breisach, the possession by France, 1648
Abbreviations: C.= County; C.C.= Câteau-Cambrésis; D.= Du
K.= Kingdom; Land.= Landrecies; M.= Marquisate; Me.= T
P.= Principality; Po.= Poissy; St.C.= St.Cloud; St.Germ.= St.Ge
Longitude East 4 of Greenwich
FLANDERS
ARTOIS
THE NETHERLANDS
THE EMPIRE
D. OF BAR
D. OF LORRAINE
FRANCHE COMTÉ
DAUPHINY
C. OF PROVENCE
DUCHY
SWIT
Bassigny
Bresse
Bugey
Gex
Lyonnais
Viennois
Valentinois
Diois
Vivarais
D. OF ALBRET
K. OF NAVARRE AND BÉARN
BIGORRE 1607
C. OF FOIX 1607
Comminges
Armagnac
C. OF ROUSSILLON 1659
PYRENEES MTS
SPAIN
Paris
Calais
Dunkirk, 1662
Gravelines
Bruges
Antwerp
Brussels
Ghent
Lille 1668
Douai
Arras
Cambrai
Namur
Liège
Aix-la-Chapelle
Cologne
Coblenz
Trèves
Luxemburg
Metz
Nancy
Toul
Verdun
Sedan
Amiens
Rouen
Havre de Grace (Le Havre)
Caen
Cherbourg
Rennes
Nantes
Angers
Orléans
Blois
Tours
Poitiers
La Rochelle
Limoges
Bordeaux
Toulouse
Montauban
Montpellier
Nîmes
Avignon
Arles
Aix
Marseilles
Toulon
Grenoble
Lyons
Dijon
Besançon
Geneva
Chambéry
Troyes
Reims
Soissons
Bourges
Nevers
Clermont
Narbonne
Perpignan
Bayonne
Pau
Loire R.
Seine R.
Garonne R.
Dordogne R.
Rhône R.
Saône R.
Rhine R.
Meuse R.
Moselle R.
Somme R.
Marne R.
Oise R.
Lot R.
Tarn R.
In exchange for M. of Saluzzo
To the Papacy
Is. of Hyères
Strait of Dover

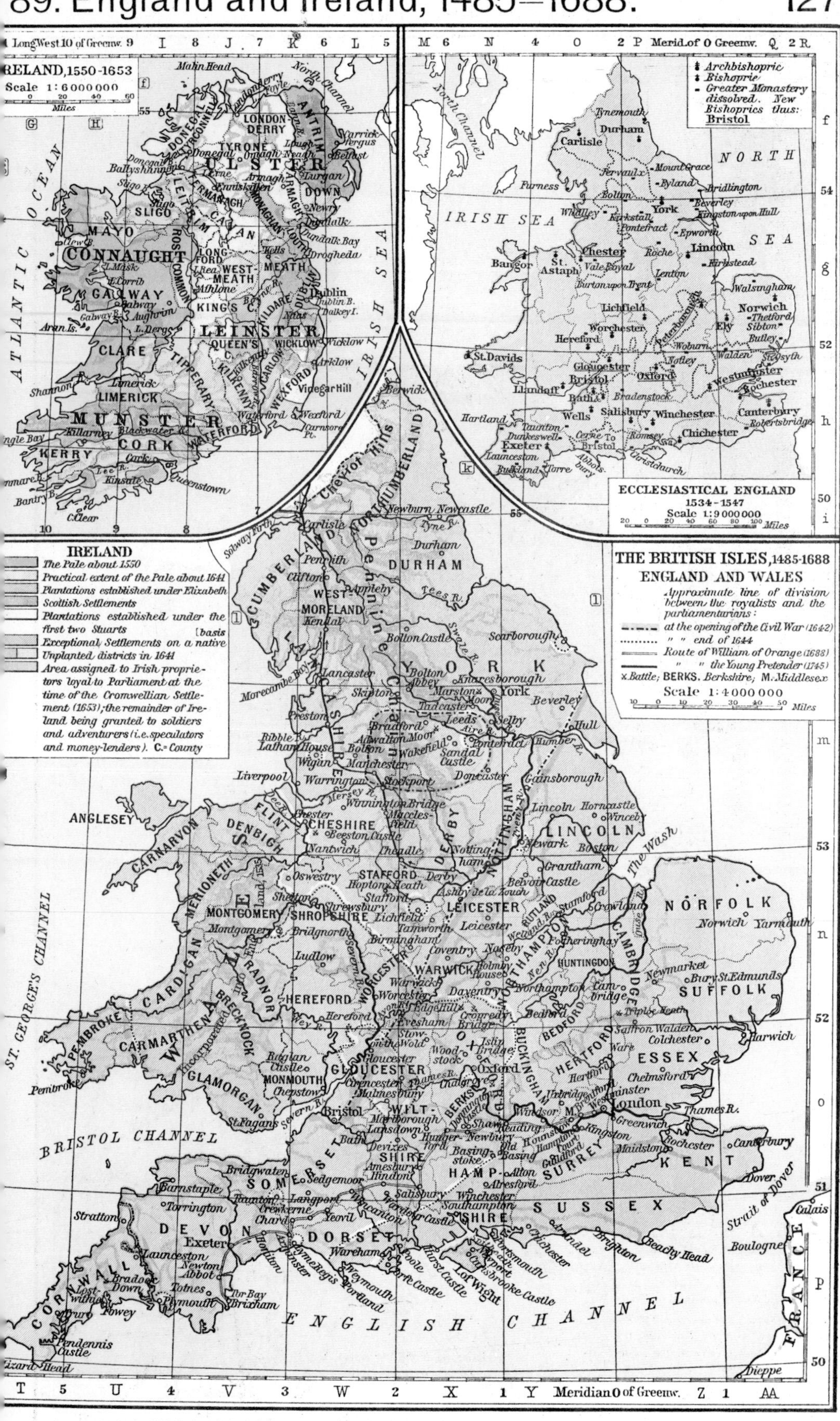
IRELAND, 1550-1653
Scale 1: 6 000 000
Miles
IRELAND
The Pale about 1550
Practical extent of the Pale about 1641
Plantations established under Elizabeth
Scottish Settlements
Plantations established under the first two Stuarts
Exceptional Settlements on a native basis
Unplanted districts in 1641
Area assigned to Irish proprietors loyal to Parliament at the time of the Cromwellian Settlement (1653); the remainder of Ireland being granted to soldiers and adventurers (i.e. speculators and money-lenders). C.= County
ULSTER
CONNAUGHT
LEINSTER
MUNSTER
DONEGAL
TYRONE
LONDON-DERRY
ANTRIM
DOWN
ARMAGH
MONAGHAN
SLIGO
MAYO
GALWAY
CLARE
LIMERICK
KERRY
CORK
WATERFORD
WEXFORD
WICKLOW
KILKENNY
TIPPERARY
KING'S C.
QUEEN'S C.
WEST-MEATH
LONGFORD
ROSCOMMON
Dublin
Belfast
Drogheda
Vinegar Hill
ATLANTIC OCEAN
IRISH SEA
North Channel
Archbishopric
Bishopric
Greater Monastery dissolved. New Bishoprics thus: Bristol
ECCLESIASTICAL ENGLAND 1534-1547
Scale 1: 9 000 000
Miles
NORTH SEA
Carlisle
Durham
York
Lincoln
Chester
Lichfield
Norwich
Ely
Worchester
Hereford
Gloucester
Oxford
Bristol
Westminster
Rochester
Canterbury
Wells
Salisbury
Winchester
Chichester
Exeter
St. Davids
Bangor
St. Asaph
Llandaff
THE BRITISH ISLES, 1485-1688
ENGLAND AND WALES
Approximate line of division between the royalists and the parliamentarians:
at the opening of the Civil War (1642)
" " end of 1644
Route of William of Orange (1688)
" " the Young Pretender (1745)
x Battle; BERKS. Berkshire; M. Middlesex
Scale 1: 4 000 000
Miles
NORTHUMBERLAND
CUMBERLAND
WESTMORELAND
DURHAM
YORK
LANCASHIRE
CHESHIRE
DERBY
NOTTINGHAM
LINCOLN
NORFOLK
SUFFOLK
ESSEX
KENT
SUSSEX
SURREY
HAMPSHIRE
DORSET
DEVON
CORNWALL
SOMERSET
WILTSHIRE
BERKS
GLOUCESTER
OXFORD
BUCKINGHAM
HERTFORD
BEDFORD
CAMBRIDGE
HUNTINGDON
NORTHAMPTON
RUTLAND
LEICESTER
WARWICK
WORCESTER
STAFFORD
SHROPSHIRE
HEREFORD
MONMOUTH
ANGLESEY
CARNARVON
DENBIGH
FLINT
MERIONETH
MONTGOMERY
CARDIGAN
RADNOR
PEMBROKE
CARMARTHEN
BRECKNOCK
GLAMORGAN
WALES
London
Marston Moor
Naseby
Edgehill
Sedgemoor
Worcester
Newbury
ST. GEORGE'S CHANNEL
BRISTOL CHANNEL
ENGLISH CHANNEL
Strait of Dover
The Wash
FRANCE
Calais
Boulogne
Dieppe
Meridian 0 of Greenw.

Scotland, 1488—1688.

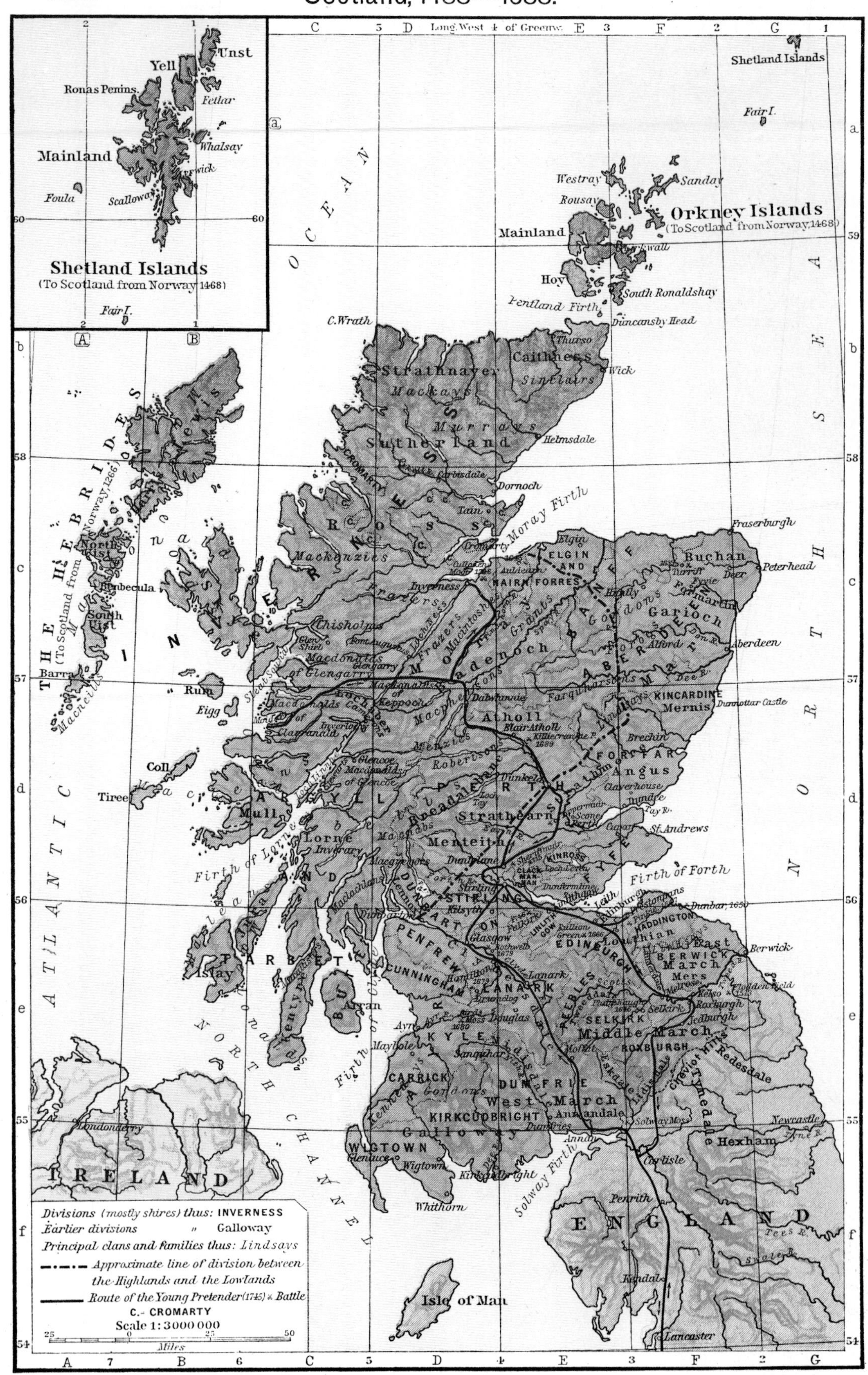

The Ottoman Empire, 1481—1683.

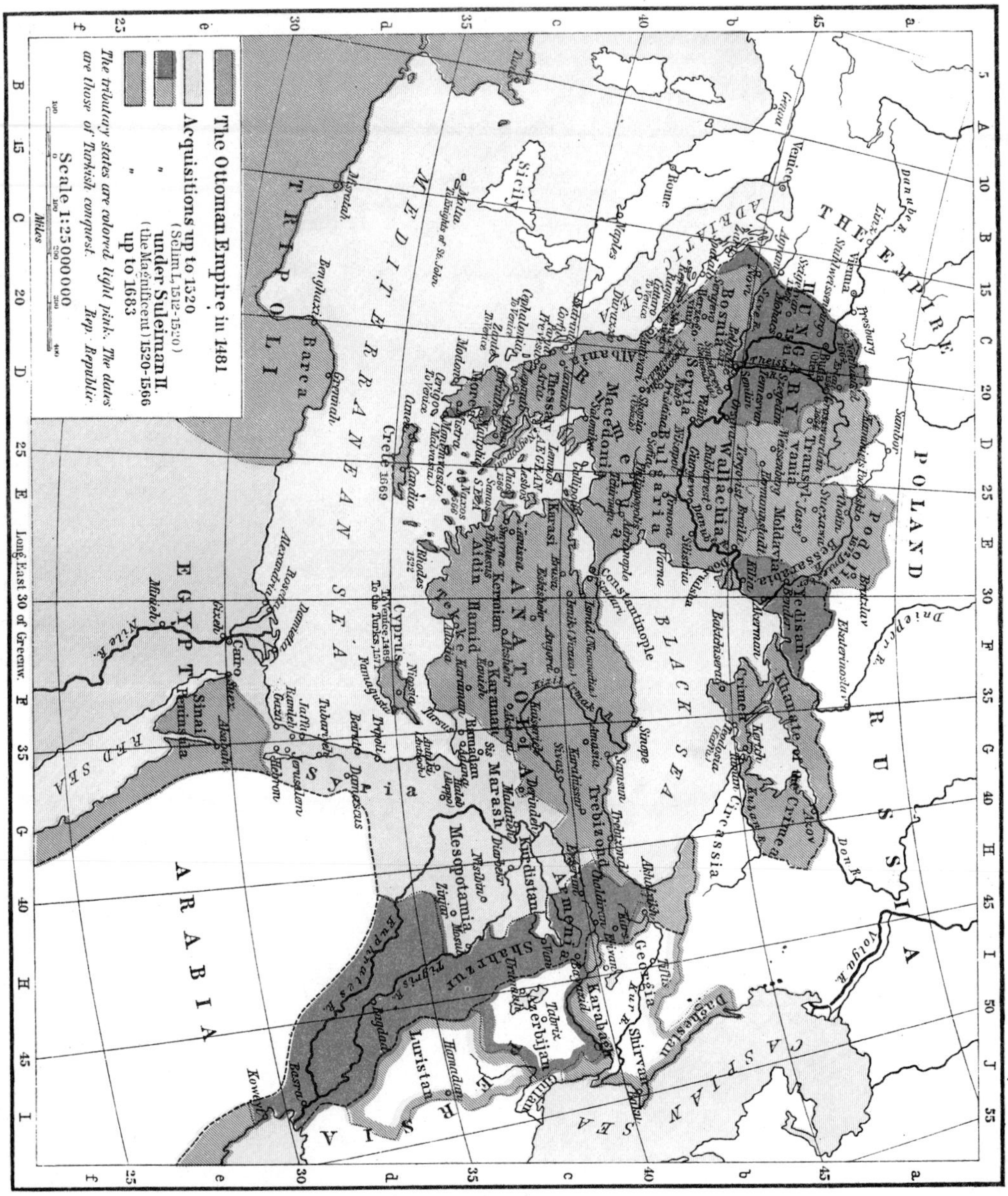

The Expansion o

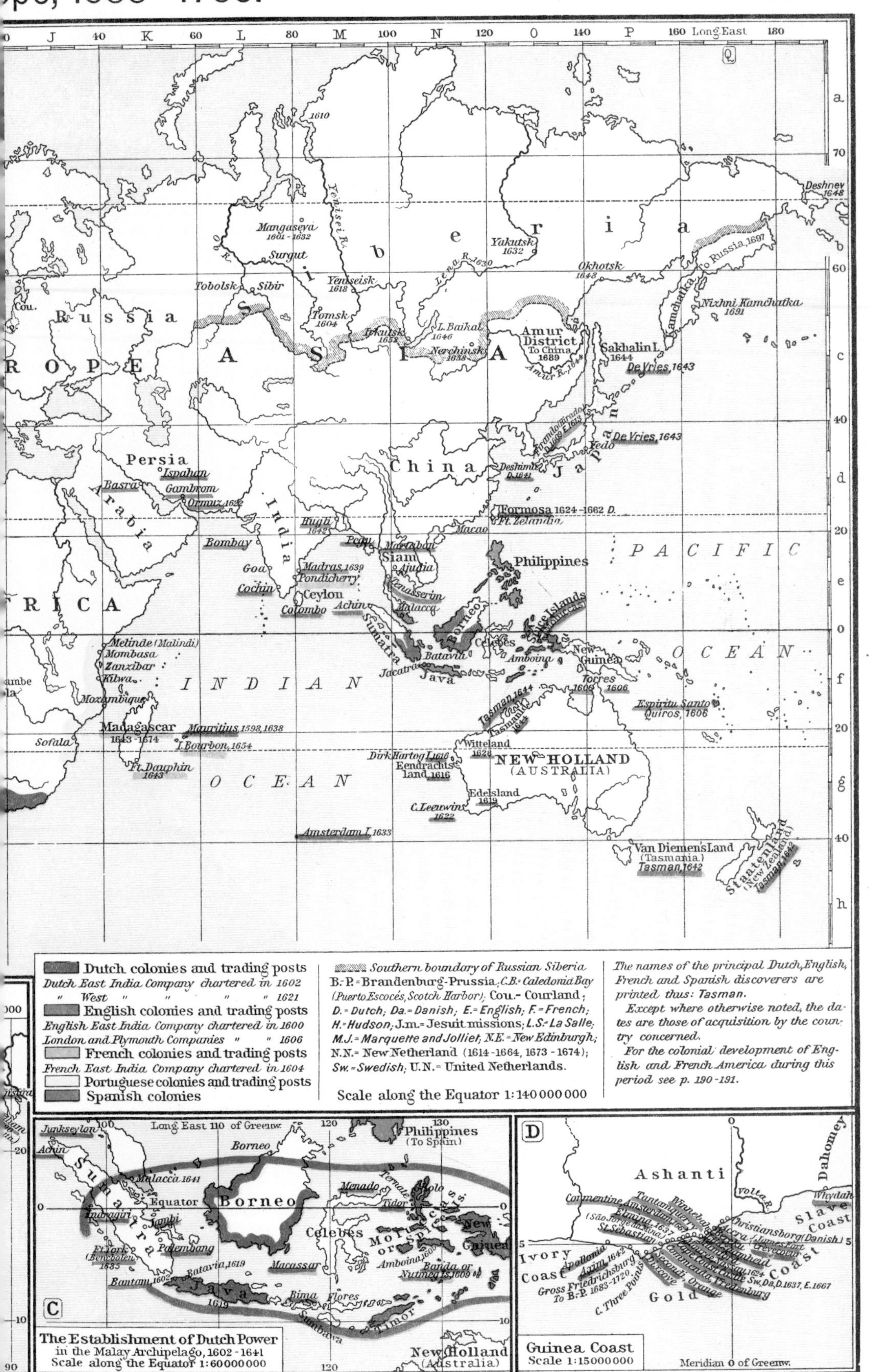
Dutch colonies and trading posts
Dutch East India Company chartered in 1602
" West " " " 1621
English colonies and trading posts
English East India Company chartered in 1600
London and Plymouth Companies " " 1606
French colonies and trading posts
French East India Company chartered in 1604
Portuguese colonies and trading posts
Spanish colonies
Southern boundary of Russian Siberia
B.-P. = Brandenburg-Prussia; C.B. = Caledonia Bay (Puerto Escocés, Scotch Harbor); Cou. = Courland; D. = Dutch; Da. = Danish; E. = English; F. = French; H. = Hudson; J.m. = Jesuit missions; L.S. = La Salle; M.J. = Marquette and Jolliet; N.E. = New Edinburgh; N.N. = New Netherland (1614-1664, 1673-1674); Sw. = Swedish; U.N. = United Netherlands.
Scale along the Equator 1:140000000
The names of the principal Dutch, English, French and Spanish discoverers are printed thus: Tasman.
Except where otherwise noted, the dates are those of acquisition by the country concerned.
For the colonial development of English and French America during this period see p. 190-191.
Siberia
Russia
ASIA
China
Japan
Persia
Arabia
India
AFRICA
INDIAN OCEAN
PACIFIC OCEAN
NEW HOLLAND (AUSTRALIA)
Van Diemen's Land (Tasmania) Tasman, 1642
Staatenland (New Zealand) Tasman, 1642
Philippines
C
The Establishment of Dutch Power in the Malay Archipelago, 1602-1641
Scale along the Equator 1:60000000
D
Guinea Coast
Scale 1:15000000
Ashanti
Dahomey
Ivory Coast
Gold Coast
Slave Coast

Principal Seats of War in Europe, 1700—1721.

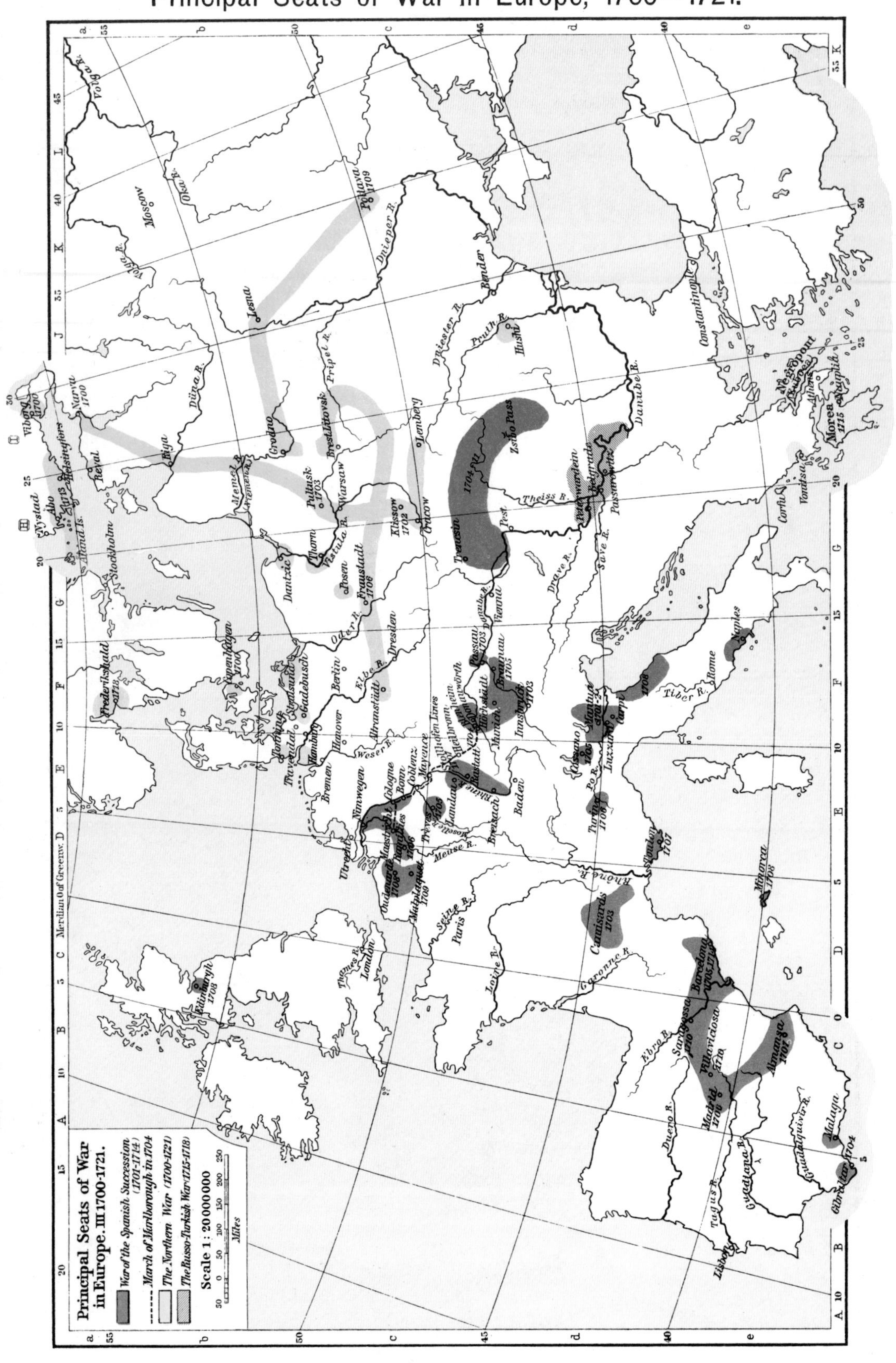

The Growth of Savoy, 1418-1748
The County of Savoy about 1280
Domain of the Duchy of Savoy in 1418
Territory acquired up to 1435
" " " " 1531
" lost " " 1536
" acquired " " 1601
" lost " " 1601
" acquired " " 1631
" " " " 1714
" " " " 1738
" " " " 1748
For other acquisitions of Savoy between 1714 and 1721, see the main map.
Co.- Cocconato Gr.- Crescentino
Scale 1:4000000
Miles
Free County of Burgundy
SAVOY
PIEDMONT
FRANCE
Valais
Vaud
Geneva
Lyons
Chambéry
Grenoble
Turin
Milan
Genoa
Nice
Alessandria
Pavia
Casale
Saluzzo
Aosta
G. of Genoa
NORTH SEA
ENGLAND
ENGLISH CHANNEL
UNITED NETHERLANDS
Austrian Netherlands
KINGDOM OF FRANCE
BAY OF BISCAY
ATLANTIC OCEAN
KINGDOM OF SPAIN
K. OF PORTUGAL
Catalonia
Balearic Is
Minorca
Majorca
Gibraltar To England 1704
FEZ AND MOROCCO
ALGERIA
SWITZERLAND
K. OF SARDINIA
Long. West 5 of Greenwich
Long. East 5 of Greenwich

KINGDOM OF SWEDEN
Finland
Stockholm
Gothland
Öland
BALTIC SEA
Ingria
Esthonia
Livonia
D. OF COURLAND
Polish Livonia
St. Petersburg
RUSSIAN EMPIRE
Govt. of Novgorod
Govt. of Moscow
Govt. of Smolensk
Govt. of Voronezh
Govt. of Biel-gorod
Govt. of Kiev
Cossacks of the Don
Zaporogian Cossacks
Ukraine
Lithuania
KINGDOM OF POLAND
Volhynia
Little Poland
Great Poland
Podolia
K. OF PRUSSIA
Königsberg
Danzig
Warsaw
Silesia
SAXONY
Bohemia
Moravia
AUSTRIA
Vienna
Styria
Carinthia
Carniola
KINGDOM OF HUNGARY
Gr. P. of Transylvania
Banat
Moldavia
Bessarabia
Yedisan
Crimea
SEA OF AZOV
Wallachia
Bulgaria
Servia
Bosnia
Herzegovina
Montenegro
REP. OF RAGUSA
Rumelia
Albania
Levadia
Morea
Crete
OTTOMAN EMPIRE
Anatolia
Constantinople
BLACK SEA
KINGDOM OF THE TWO SICILIES
Sicily
Malta
VENETIAN REPUBLIC
House of Bourbon
House of Hapsburg-Lorraine
Kingdom of Prussia and its dependencies
House of Savoy
Boundary of the Empire
Castle or Fortress
Monastery
Abbreviations.
A.= Austria. D.= Duchy. Govt.= Government. GR.D.= Grand Duchy. Gr.P.= Grand Principality. H.= Holstein-Gottorp. K.= Kingdom. P.= Principality. REP.= Republic.
Sites of battles, diplomatic negotiations and other events of historical importance are indicated by the sign (•).
Scale 1:15000000
Miles

Principal Seats of War, 1740—1763.

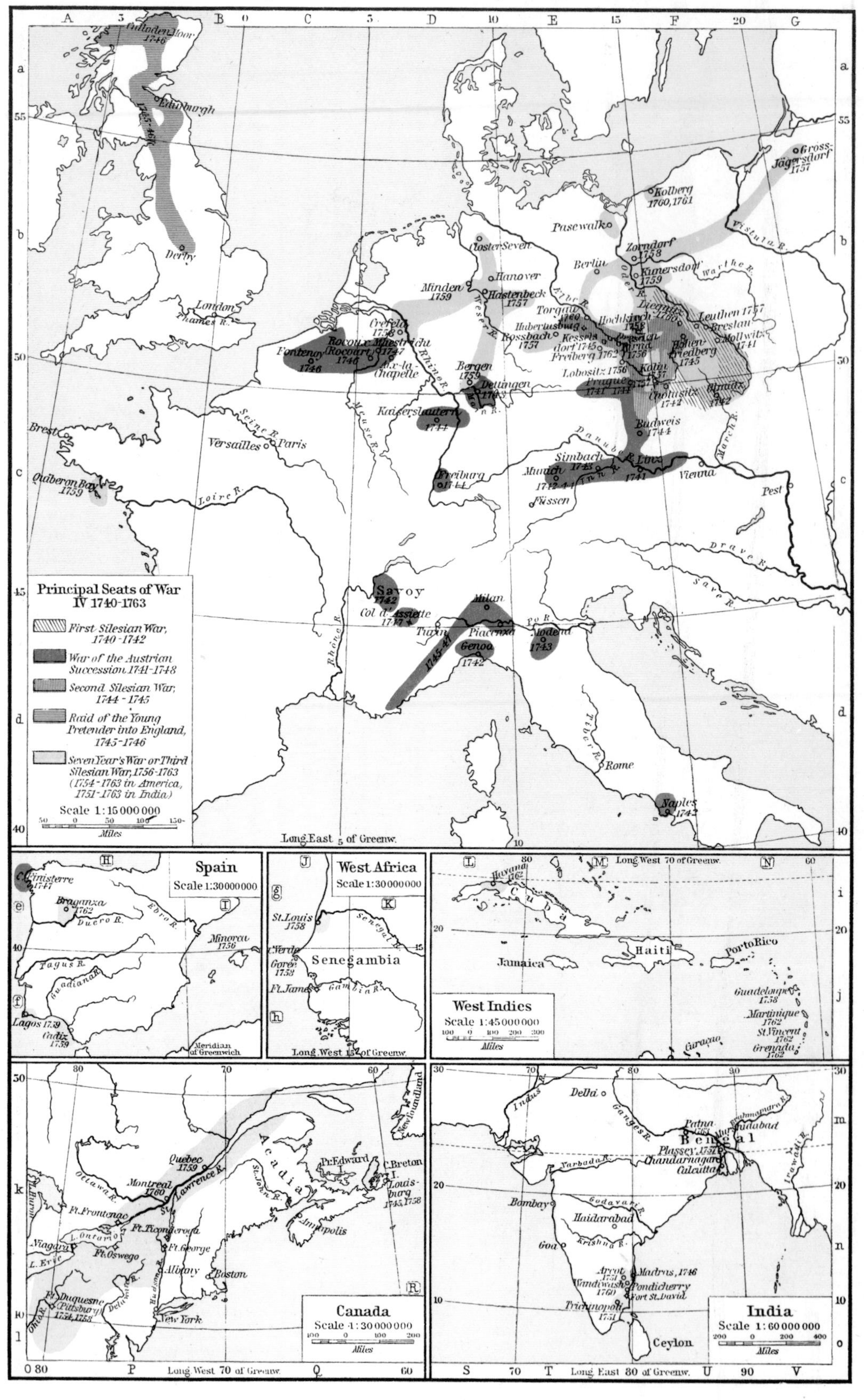

Treaty Adjustments, 1713—1763.

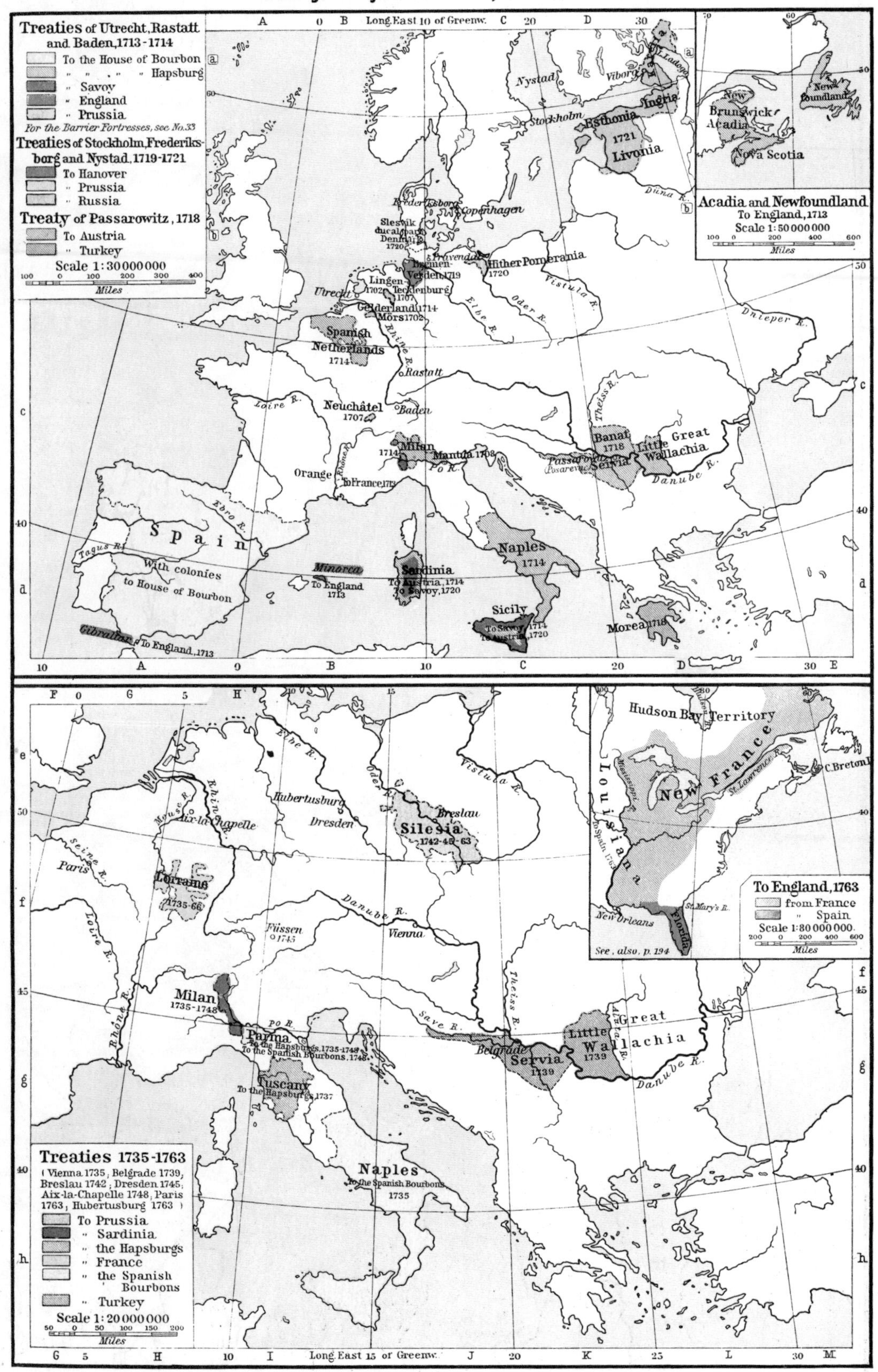

NORTH SEA
UNITED NETHERLANDS
AUSTRIAN NETHERLANDS
KINGDOM OF FRANCE
SWITZERLAND
ELECTORATE OF HANOVER
MÜNSTER
HESSE-CASSEL
PALATINATE
WURTEMBERG
K. OF SARDINIA
Piedmont
Heligoland
Cuxhaven
Hamburg
Lübeck
Holstein
Bremen
Emden
Groningen
Helder
Amsterdam
Zuider Zee
The Hague
Rotterdam
Utrecht
Deventer
Arnheim
Antwerp
Ghent
Bruges
Ostend
Dunkirk
Calais
Boulogne
Dover
Brussels
Louvain
Maestricht
Liège
Aix-la-Chapelle
Cologne
Jülich
Lille
Tournay
Douai
Arras
Valenciennes
Mons
Namur
Amiens
Abbeville
Laon
Compiègne
Soissons
Reims
Paris
Versailles
Châlons
Verdun
Metz
Toul
Nancy
Lunéville
Strasburg
Troyes
Langres
Dijon
Besançon
Nevers
Bourges
Montluçon
Clermont-Ferrand
St. Etienne
Lyons
Chalon
Geneva
Lausanne
Berne
Lucerne
Zurich
Basel
Constance
Frankfort
Mannheim
Heidelberg
Stuttgart
Würzburg
Hanover
Brunswick
Göttingen
Cassel
Marburg
Darmstadt
Milan
Como
Bergamo
Brescia
Turin
Long. East 10 of Greenwich

BALTIC SEA
KINGDOM OF PRUSSIA
East Prussia
Ermeland
West Prussia
Netze District
New East Prussia
To Prussia, 1795
South Prussia
To Prussia, 1793
KINGDOM OF POLAND
West Galicia
To Austria, 1795
New Silesia
To Prussia, 1795
K. of Galicia
To Austria, 1772
Hither Pomerania
Farther Pomerania
Neumark
Ukermark
Mittelmark
Lower Lusatia
Upper Lusatia
D. of Prussia
Silesia
Austrian Silesia
KINGDOM OF BOHEMIA
M. of Moravia
Archduchy of Austria
Below the Enns
Above the Enns
Inn Quarter
To Austria, 1779
A. OF SALZBURG
D. of Styria
D. of Carinthia
D. of Carniola
Istria
To Venice
Croatia
Slavonia
KINGDOM OF HUNGARY
Friuli
Königsberg
Danzig
Stettin
Berlin
Posen
Warsaw
Breslau
Dresden
Prague
Vienna
Cracow
Hapsburg Lands
Hohenzollern Lands:
Prussia
Franconian line
Wettin Lands:
Albertine
Ernestine
Wittelsbach Lands:
Bavaria (Palatinate-Sulzbach)
Palatinate-Zweibrücken (Deux Ponts)
Oldenburg Lands:
Denmark (royal portion)
Holstein-Gottorp (ducal portion) and Oldenburg
Ecclesiastical States
Imperial Cities
Boundary of the Empire.
Barrier Fortresses are underlined thus: Ypres.
Stollhofen and Weissenburg lines.
The chief territorial changes in the eighteenth century are indicated by narrow colored borders.
Sites of the most important battles and diplomatic negotiations are given the sign (•).
The areas in the Empire left uncolored were divided into petty states.
Abbreviations:
A. = Archbishopric; A. Z. = Anhalt-Zerbst; B. = Bishopric; Br. C. = Bromberg Canal; C. = County; D. = Duchy; Fr. W. C. = Frederick William Canal; H. C. = Hesse-Cassel; K. Kingdom; Lg. = Landgraviate; M. = Margravate; Meckl. = Mecklenburg; N. = Nassau; P. = Principality.
Castle or fortress
Monastery
Scale 1 : 5 000 000
Miles

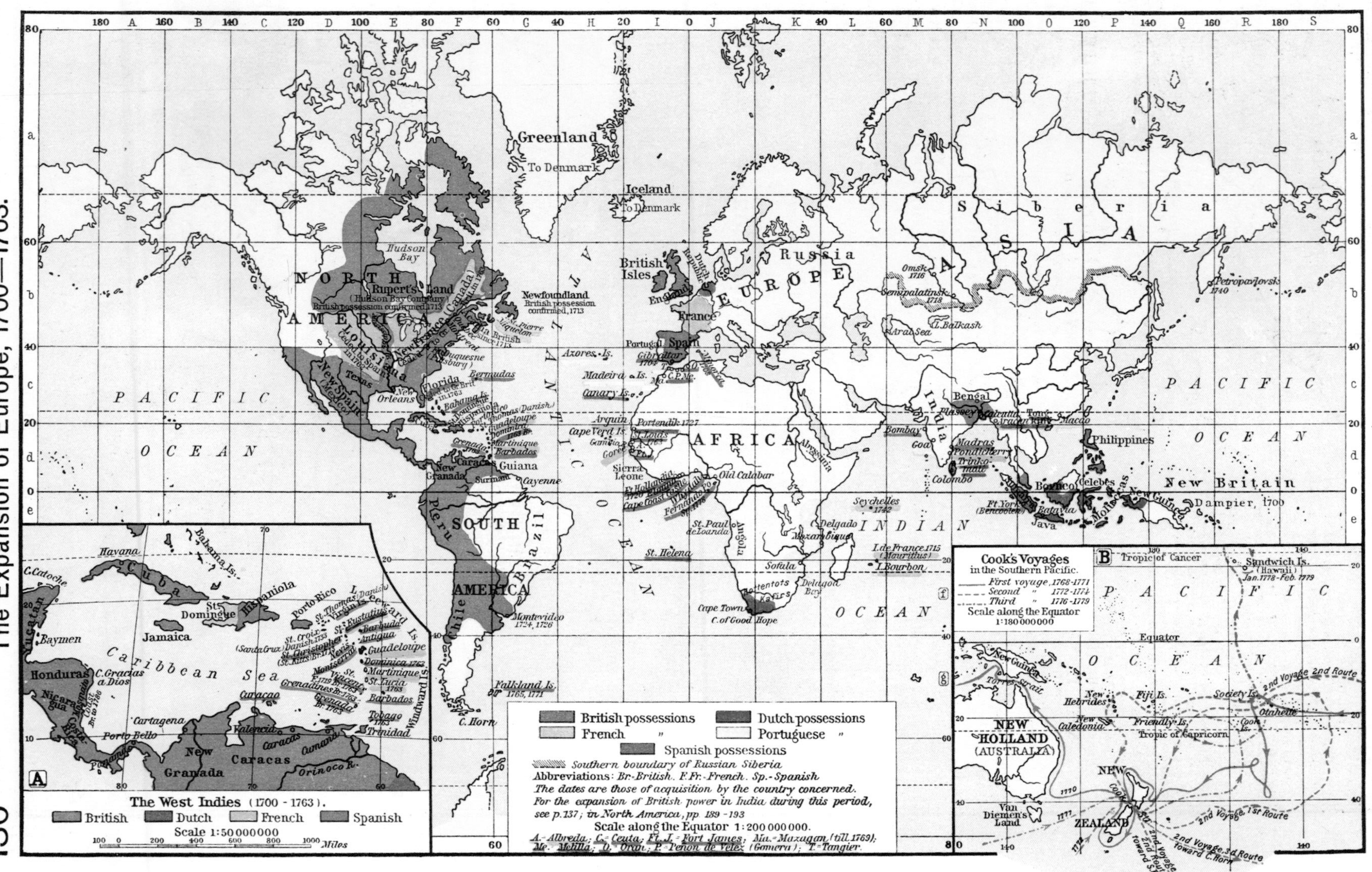

Greenland
To Denmark
Iceland
To Denmark
British Isles
England
France
Spain
Portugal
EUROPE
Russia
ASIA
Siberia
Omsk 1716
Semipalatinsk 1718
Aral Sea
L. Balkash
Petropavlovsk 1740
NORTH AMERICA
Hudson Bay
Rupert's Land
(Hudson Bay Company)
British possession confirmed 1713
Louisiana
New Spain (Mexico)
Texas
New Orleans
Florida
Bermudas
Newfoundland
British possession confirmed, 1713
Azores Is.
Madeira Is.
Canary Is.
Arguin
Portendik 1727
Cape Verd Is.
Sierra Leone
Old Calabar
AFRICA
Abyssinia
St. Paul de Loanda
Angola
Sofala
Mozambique
Delagoa Bay
Cape Town
C. of Good Hope
St. Helena
Seychelles 1742
I. de France 1715 (Mauritius)
I. Bourbon
INDIAN OCEAN
India
Bengal
Bombay
Goa
Madras
Pondicherry
Colombo
Philippines
Borneo
Celebes
Java
Batavia
Moluccas
New Guinea
New Britain
Dampier, 1700
PACIFIC OCEAN
ATLANTIC OCEAN
Guiana
Cayenne
New Granada
SOUTH AMERICA
Brazil
Peru
Chile
Montevideo 1724, 1726
Falkland Is. 1765, 1771
C. Horn
A
The West Indies (1700 - 1763).
British
Dutch
French
Spanish
Scale 1:50 000 000
Miles
Havana
Cuba
Bahama Is.
Hispaniola
St. Domingue
Porto Rico
Jamaica
Caribbean Sea
Honduras
C. Gracias a Dios
Baymen
Nicaragua
Cartagena
Porto Bello
Curaçao
New Granada
Caracas
Orinoco R.
Guadeloupe
Dominica 1763
Martinique
St. Lucia
Barbados
Tobago
Trinidad
Windward Is.
Leeward Is.
British possessions
Dutch possessions
French "
Portuguese "
Spanish possessions
Southern boundary of Russian Siberia
Abbreviations: Br.-British. F.Fr.-French. Sp.-Spanish.
The dates are those of acquisition by the country concerned.
For the expansion of British power in India during this period, see p. 137; in North America, pp. 189 - 193
Scale along the Equator 1:200 000 000.
B
Cook's Voyages in the Southern Pacific.
First voyage 1768-1771
Second " 1772-1774
Third " 1776-1779
Scale along the Equator 1:180 000 000
Tropic of Cancer
Sandwich Is. (Hawaii) Jan. 1778 - Feb. 1779
Equator
Tropic of Capricorn
New Hebrides
New Caledonia
Fiji Is.
Friendly Is.
Society Is.
Otaheite
Cook Is.
NEW HOLLAND (AUSTRALIA)
Van Diemen's Land
NEW ZEALAND
2nd Voyage 1st Route
2nd Voyage 2nd Route
2nd Voyage 3d Route toward C. Horn

India, 1700—1792.

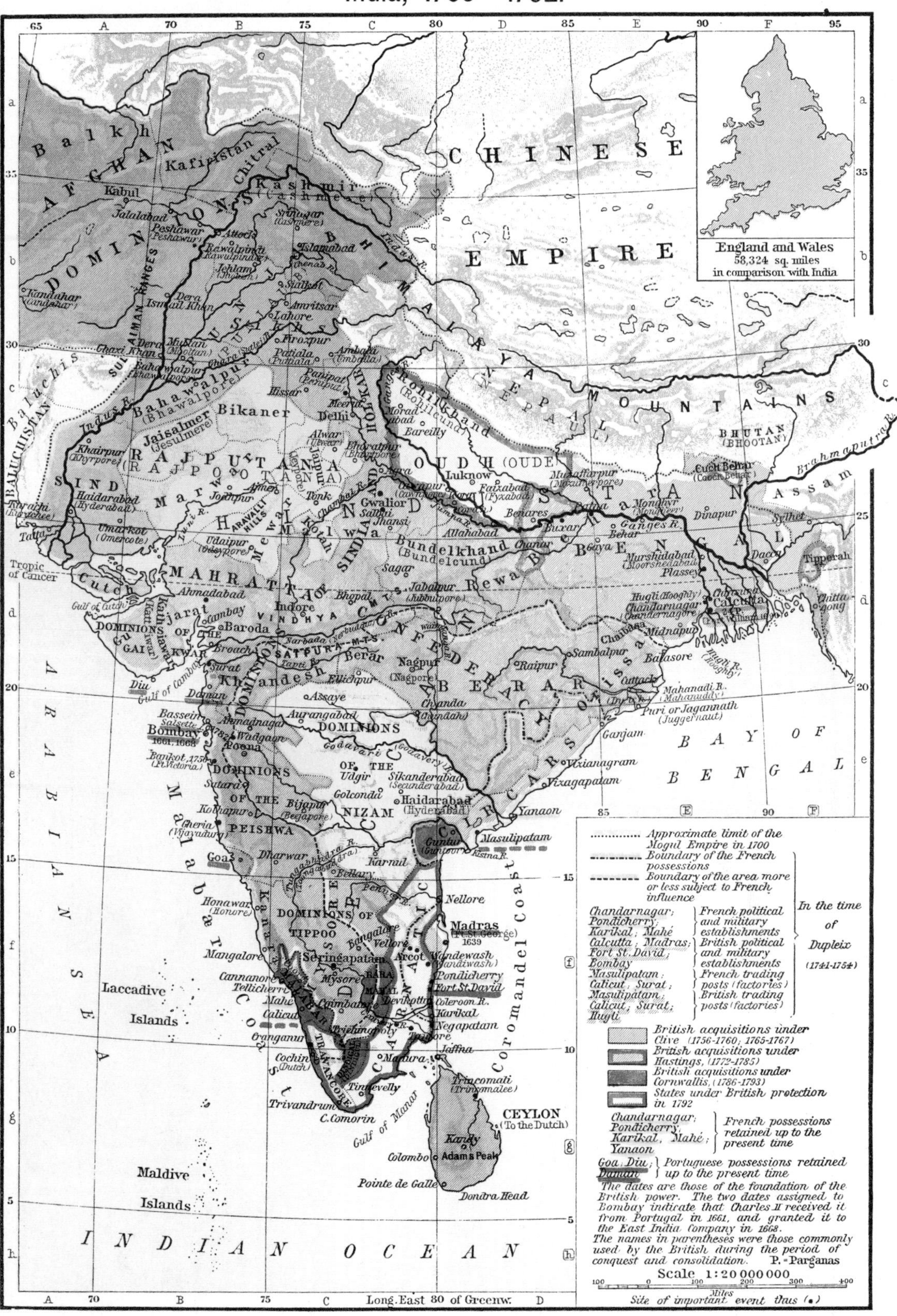

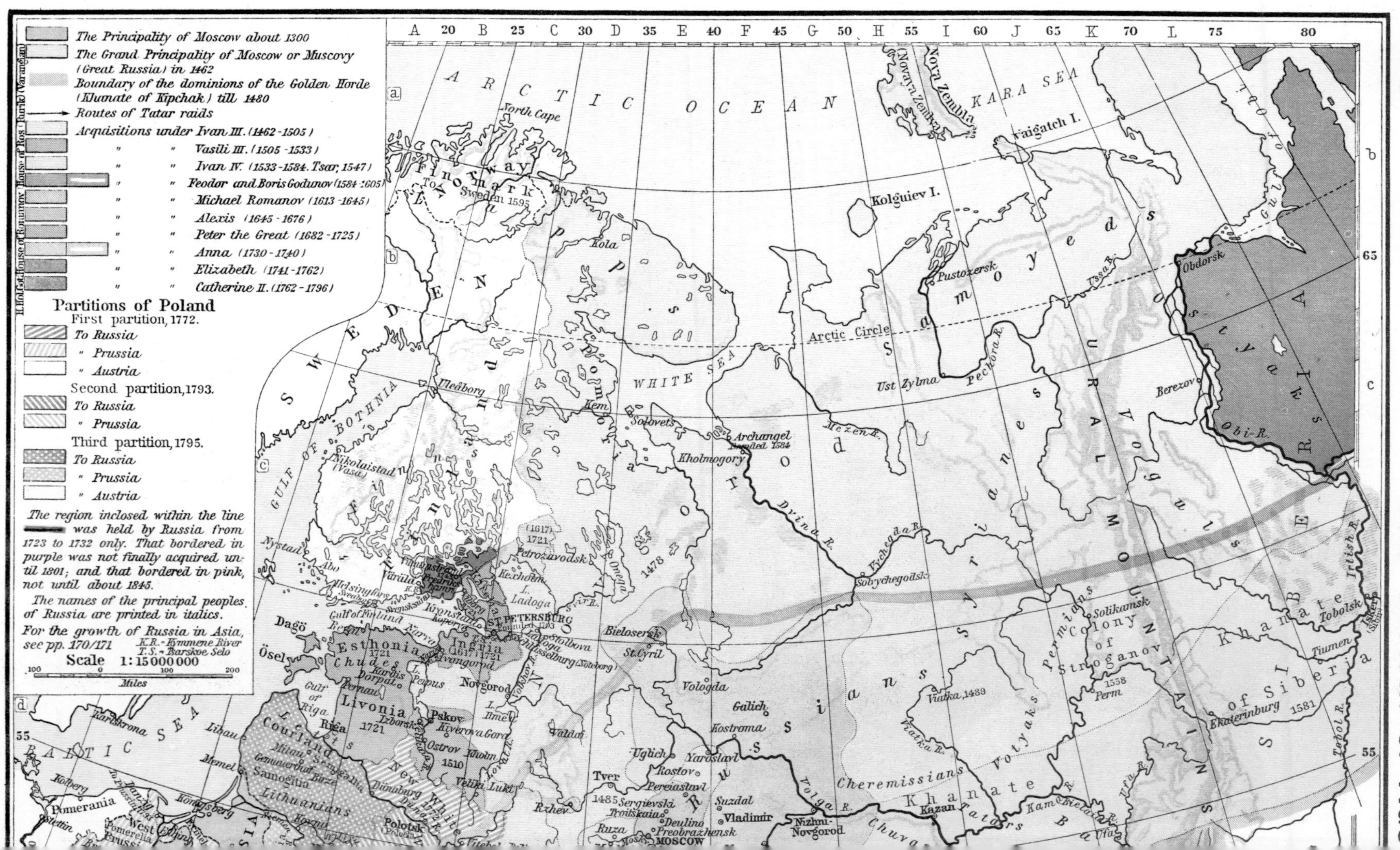
The Principality of Moscow about 1300
The Grand Principality of Moscow or Muscovy (Great Russia) in 1462
Boundary of the dominions of the Golden Horde (Khanate of Kipchak) till 1480
Routes of Tatar raids
Acquisitions under Ivan III. (1462-1505)
" " Vasili III. (1505-1533)
" " Ivan IV. (1533-1584. Tsar, 1547)
" " Feodor and Boris Godunov (1584-1605)
" " Michael Romanov (1613-1645)
" " Alexis (1645-1676)
" " Peter the Great (1682-1725)
" " Anna (1730-1740)
" " Elizabeth (1741-1762)
" " Catherine II. (1762-1796)
Partitions of Poland
First partition, 1772.
To Russia
" Prussia
" Austria
Second partition, 1793.
To Russia
" Prussia
Third partition, 1795.
To Russia
" Prussia
" Austria
The region inclosed within the line was held by Russia from 1723 to 1732 only. That bordered in purple was not finally acquired until 1801; and that bordered in pink, not until about 1845.
The names of the principal peoples of Russia are printed in italics.
For the growth of Russia in Asia, see pp. 170/171
K.R. - Kymmene River
T.S. - Barskoe Selo
Scale 1:15000000
Miles
ARCTIC OCEAN
KARA SEA
WHITE SEA
URAL MOUNTAINS
GULF OF BOTHNIA
BALTIC SEA
SWEDEN
Arctic Circle
Kolguiev I.
Vaigatch I.
North Cape
Archangel
Kholmogory
Solovets
Pustozersk
Ust Zylma
Berezov
Obdorsk
Sobychegodsk
Vologda
Galich
Kostroma
Yaroslavl
Rostov
Pereiaslavl
Suzdal
Vladimir
Nizhni-Novgorod
Kazan
Tver
Uglich
Novgorod
Pskov
Riga
ST. PETERSBURG
Esthonia
Livonia
Courland
Ingria
Lithuanians
Cheremissians
Votyaks
Perm
Solikamsk
Ekaterinburg
Tobolsk
Tiumen
Colony of Stroganov
Khanate of Siberia
Dagö
Ösel

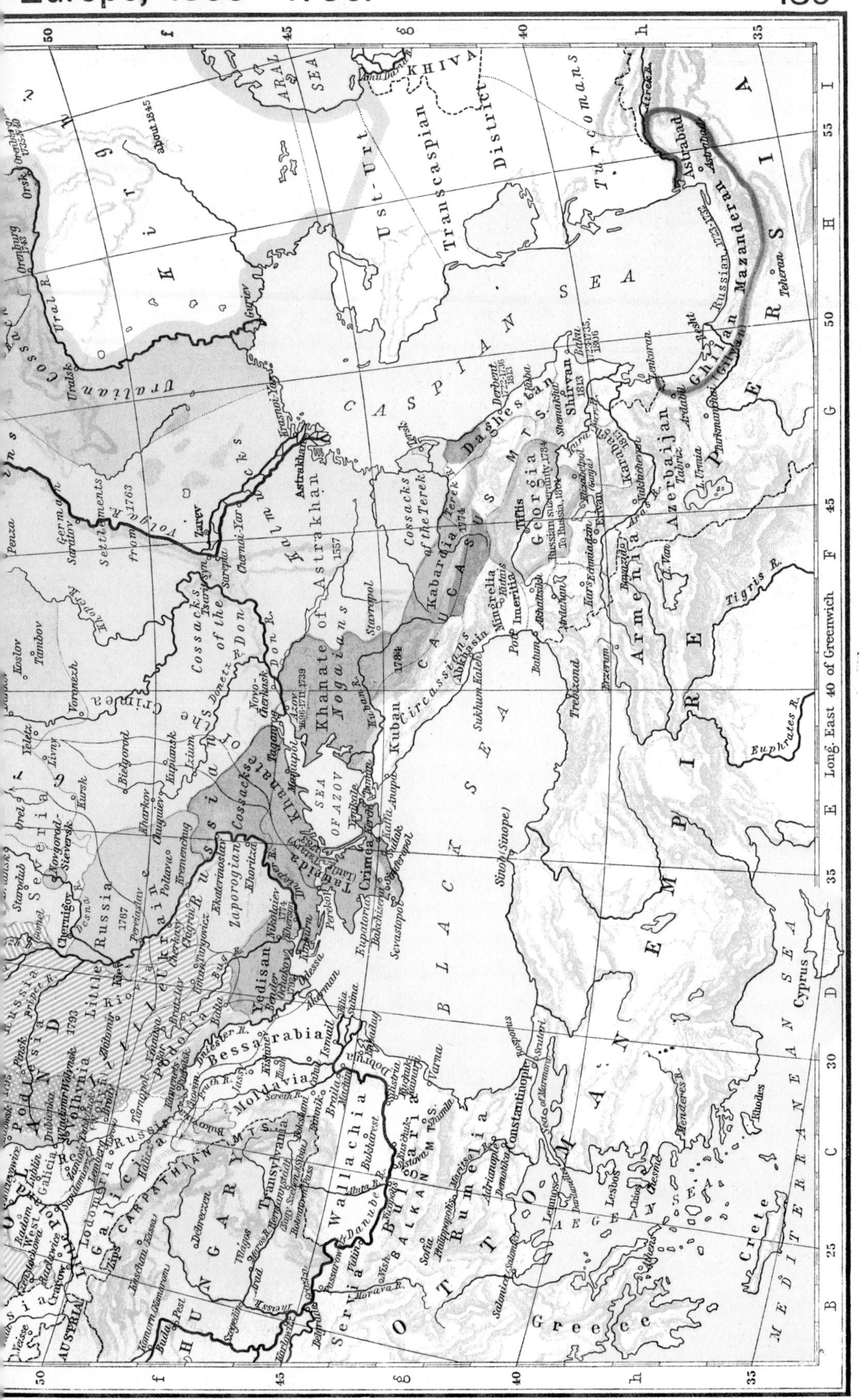
ARAL SEA
KHIVA
Ust-Urt
Transcaspian District
CASPIAN SEA
Astrakhan
Khanate of Astrakhan
Cossacks of the Terek
Kabardia
Daghestan
Georgia
Mingrelia
Imeritia
Shirvan
Azerbaijan
Armenia
Mazanderan
Ghilan
PERSIA
Teheran
Astrabad
BLACK SEA
SEA OF AZOV
Crimea
Khanate of the Crimea
Kuban
Circassians
Abkhasia
Cossacks of the Don
Zaporogian Cossacks
Yedisan
Little Russia
Bessarabia
Moldavia
Wallachia
Transylvania
HUNGARY
Rumelia
Bulgaria
Constantinople
OTTOMAN EMPIRE
Greece
Crete
Cyprus
Rhodes
MEDITERRANEAN SEA
Long. East 40 of Greenwich

Typical German States befor[e]

I. Baden.

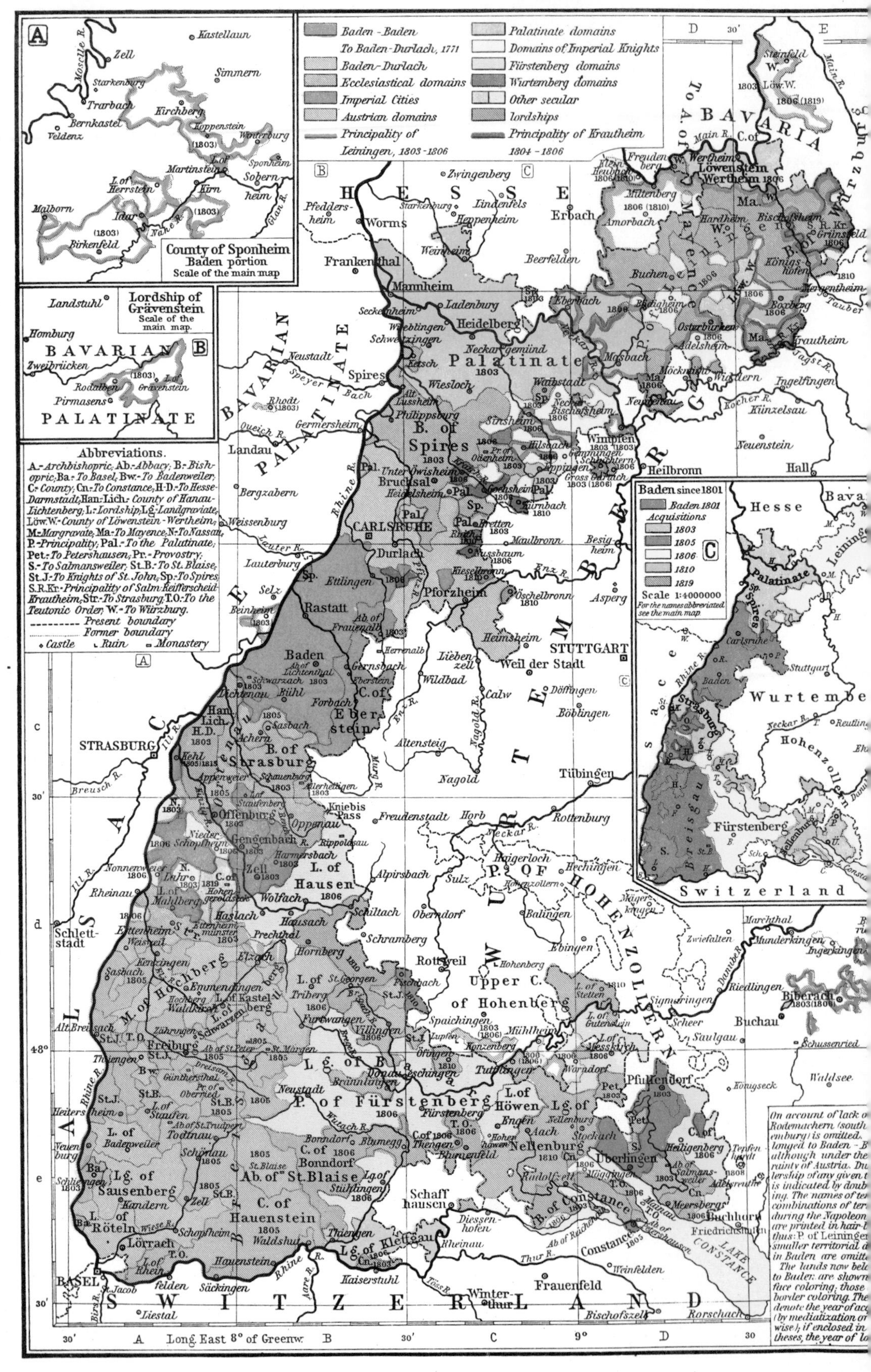

On account of lack o[f space]... Rodemachern (south... emburg) is omitted.... longed to Baden-B... although under the... rainty of Austria. Du... lership of any given t... is indicated by doub... ing. The names of ter... combinations of ter... during the Napoleon... are printed in hair-l... thus: P. of Leininge[n]... smaller territorial a... in Baden are omitte... The lands now belo... to Baden are shown... face coloring; those... border coloring. The... denote the year of acq... (by mediatization or... wise); if enclosed in... theses, the year of lo...

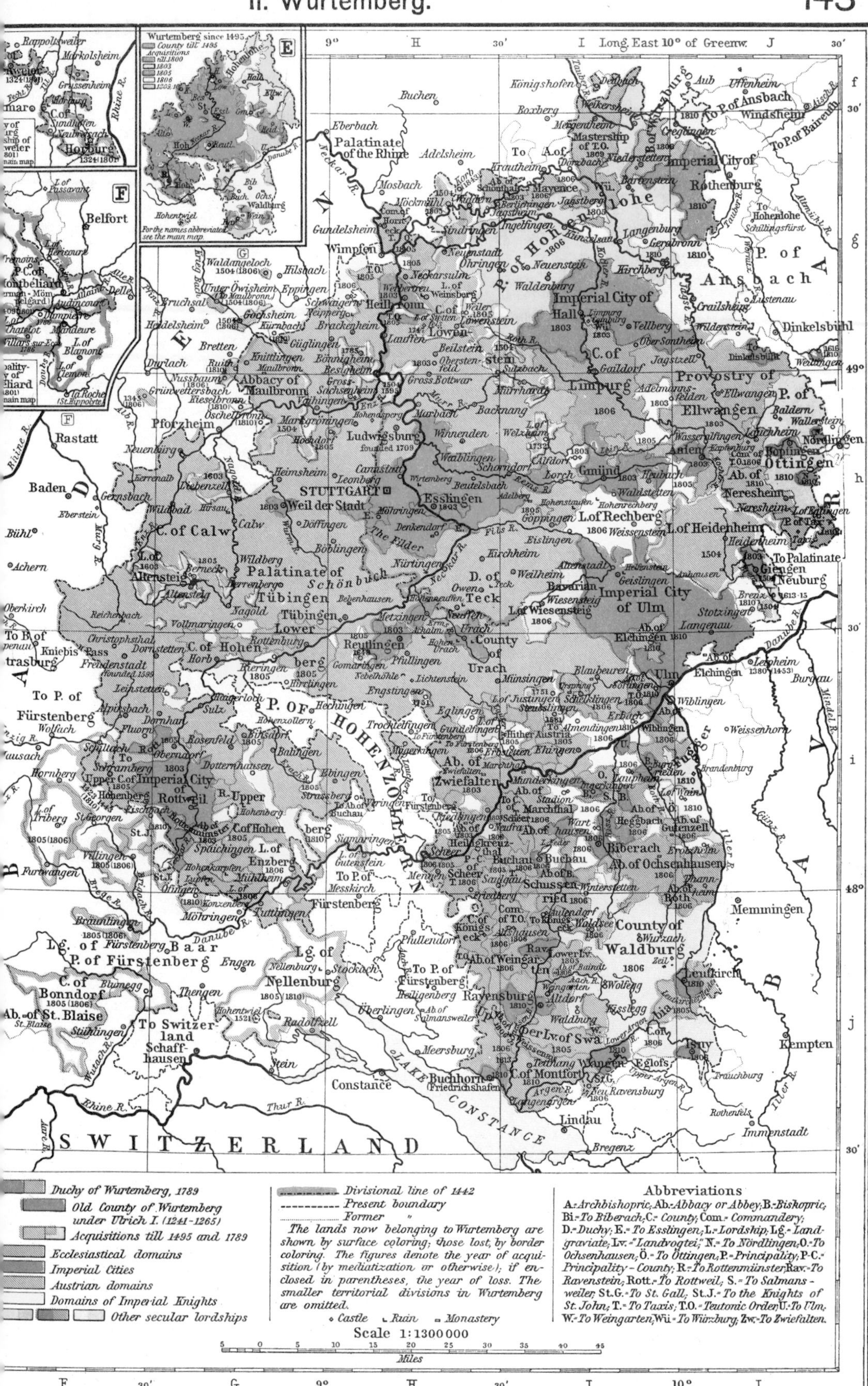
Wurtemberg since 1495
SWITZERLAND
STUTTGART
Lake Constance
Duchy of Wurtemberg, 1789
Old County of Wurtemberg under Ulrich I. (1241-1265)
Acquisitions till 1495 and 1789
Ecclesiastical domains
Imperial Cities
Austrian domains
Domains of Imperial Knights
Other secular lordships
Divisional line of 1442
Present boundary
Former "
The lands now belonging to Wurtemberg are shown by surface coloring; those lost, by border coloring. The figures denote the year of acquisition (by mediatization or otherwise); if enclosed in parentheses, the year of loss. The smaller territorial divisions in Wurtemberg are omitted.
Castle
Ruin
Monastery
Abbreviations
A.=Archbishopric; Ab.=Abbacy or Abbey; B.=Bishopric; Bi.=To Biberach; C.=County; Com.=Commandery; D.=Duchy; E.=To Esslingen; L.=Lordship; Lg.=Landgraviate; Lv.="Landvogtei;" N.=To Nördlingen; O.=To Ochsenhausen; Ö.=To Öttingen; P.=Principality; P-C.=Principality-County; R.=To Rottenmünster; Rav.=To Ravenstein; Rott.=To Rottweil; S.=To Salmansweiler; St.G.=To St. Gall; St.J.=To the Knights of St. John; T.=To Taxis; T.O.=Teutonic Order; U.=To Ulm; W.=To Weingarten; Wü.=To Würzburg; Zw.=To Zwiefalten.
Scale 1:1300000
Miles

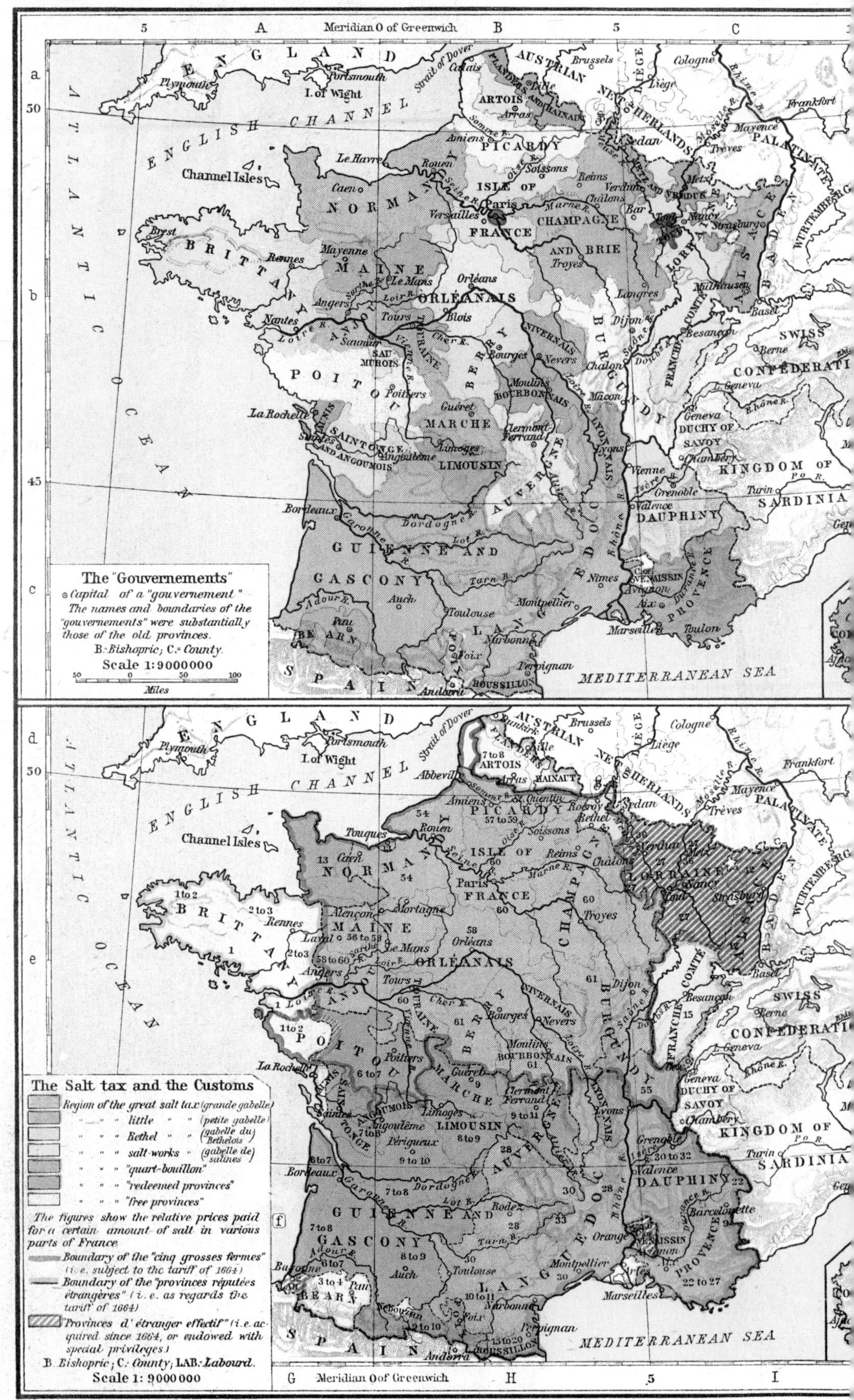
Meridian 0 of Greenwich
The "Gouvernements"
Capital of a "gouvernement"
The names and boundaries of the "gouvernements" were substantially those of the old provinces.
B.=Bishopric; C.=County.
Scale 1:9000000
Miles
The Salt tax and the Customs
Region of the great salt tax (grande gabelle)
" " " little " " (petite gabelle)
" " " Bethel " " (gabelle du Rethelois)
" " " salt-works " (gabelle de salines)
" " " "quart-bouillon"
" " " "redeemed provinces"
" " " "free provinces"
The figures show the relative prices paid for a certain amount of salt in various parts of France.
Boundary of the "cinq grosses fermes" (i.e. subject to the tariff of 1664)
Boundary of the "provinces réputées étrangères" (i.e. as regards the tariff of 1664)
"Provinces d' étranger effectif" (i.e. acquired since 1664, or endowed with special privileges)
B. Bishopric; C. County; LAB. Labourd.
Scale 1: 9000000
ENGLAND
ENGLISH CHANNEL
ATLANTIC OCEAN
MEDITERRANEAN SEA
Channel Isles
I. of Wight
Plymouth
Portsmouth
Strait of Dover
AUSTRIAN NETHERLANDS
Brussels
LIÉGE
Cologne
Frankfort
PALATINATE
BADEN
WURTEMBERG
SWISS CONFEDERATION
DUCHY OF SAVOY
KINGDOM OF SARDINIA
SPAIN
BRITTANY
NORMANDY
PICARDY
ARTOIS
ISLE OF FRANCE
CHAMPAGNE AND BRIE
LORRAINE
ALSACE
MAINE
ORLÉANAIS
ANJOU
TOURAINE
BERRY
NIVERNAIS
BURGUNDY
FRANCHE COMTÉ
POITOU
MARCHE
LIMOUSIN
AUVERGNE
BOURBONNAIS
LYONNAIS
DAUPHINY
PROVENCE
LANGUEDOC
GUIENNE AND GASCONY
BÉARN
ROUSSILLON
SAINTONGE AND ANGOUMOIS
Paris
Versailles
Rouen
Caen
Le Havre
Rennes
Brest
Nantes
Angers
Le Mans
Tours
Orléans
Blois
Bourges
Poitiers
La Rochelle
Limoges
Bordeaux
Toulouse
Montpellier
Nîmes
Marseilles
Toulon
Lyons
Dijon
Besançon
Strasburg
Nancy
Metz
Reims
Troyes
Amiens
Arras
Sedan
Grenoble
Perpignan
Andorra

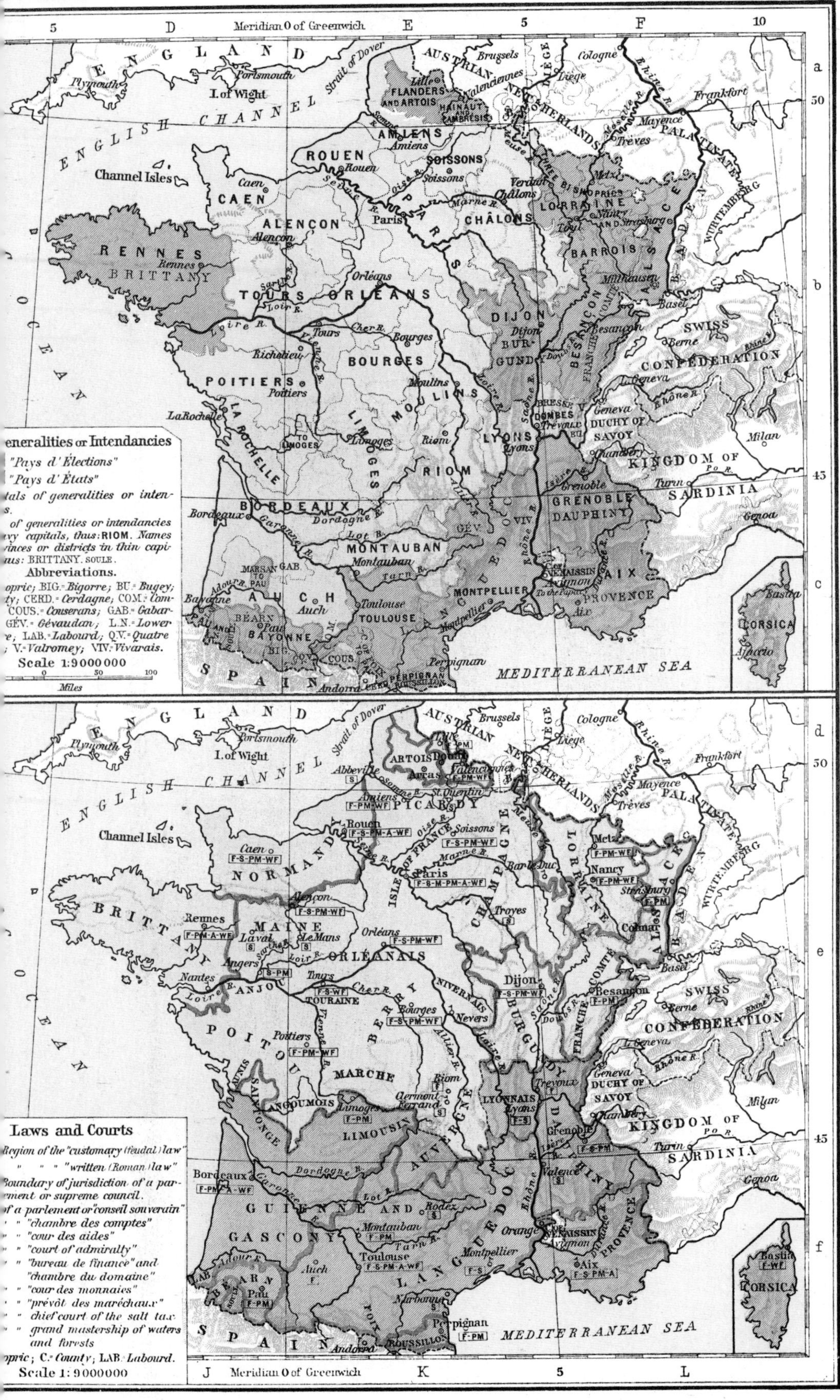
Meridian 0 of Greenwich
ENGLAND
ENGLISH CHANNEL
Strait of Dover
Plymouth
Portsmouth
I. of Wight
Channel Isles
AUSTRIAN NETHERLANDS
Brussels
LIÉGE
Liége
Cologne
Frankfort
Mayence
Trèves
PALATINATE
WURTEMBERG
BADEN
FLANDERS AND ARTOIS
HAINAUT AND CAMBRÉSIS
Lille
Valenciennes
AMIENS
Amiens
ROUEN
Rouen
SOISSONS
Soissons
CAEN
Caen
ALENCON
Alençon
PARIS
Paris
CHÂLONS
Châlons
Verdun
Metz
THREE BISHOPRICS
LORRAINE AND BARROIS
Nancy
Toul
ALSACE
Strasburg
Mülhausen
Basel
RENNES
Rennes
BRITTANY
TOURS
ORLÉANS
Orléans
Tours
Richelieu
BOURGES
Bourges
POITIERS
Poitiers
La Rochelle
LA ROCHELLE
LIMOGES
Limoges
MOULINS
Moulins
RIOM
Riom
DIJON
Dijon
BURGUNDY
BESANÇON
Besançon
FRANCHE COMTÉ
LYONS
Lyons
BRESSE
DOMBES
Trévoux
SWISS CONFEDERATION
Berne
Geneva
DUCHY OF SAVOY
Chambéry
KINGDOM OF SARDINIA
Turin
Milan
Genoa
GRENOBLE
Grenoble
DAUPHINY
BORDEAUX
Bordeaux
MONTAUBAN
Montauban
MARSAN
GAB.
AUCH
Auch
Bayonne
BÉARN
Pau
BAYONNE
BIG.
Q.V.
COUS.
TOULOUSE
Toulouse
LANGUEDOC
MONTPELLIER
Montpellier
VIV.
GÉV.
VENAISSIN
Avignon
To the Papacy
AIX
Aix
PROVENCE
Perpignan
ROUSSILLON
Andorra
SPAIN
MEDITERRANEAN SEA
CORSICA
Bastia
Ajaccio
OCEAN
Rhine R.
Rhône R.
Loire R.
Seine R.
Garonne R.
Dordogne R.
Lot R.
Tarn R.
Marne R.
Oise R.
Somme R.
Saône R.
Allier R.
Cher R.
Vienne R.
Sarthe R.
Po R.
Generalities or Intendancies
"Pays d'Élections"
"Pays d'États"
Capitals of generalities or intendancies
Names of generalities or intendancies in heavy capitals, thus: RIOM. Names of provinces or districts in thin capitals: BRITTANY. SOULE.
Abbreviations.
BIG.= Bigorre; BU.= Bugey; CERD.= Cerdagne; COM.= Comminges; COUS.= Couserans; GAB.= Gabardan; GÉV.= Gévaudan; L.N.= Lower Navarre; LAB.= Labourd; Q.V.= Quatre Vallées; V.= Valromey; VIV.= Vivarais.
Scale 1:9000000
0 50 100
Miles
ARTOIS
Douai
Arras
Abbeville
St. Quentin
PICARDY
NORMANDY
ISLE OF FRANCE
CHAMPAGNE
Bar le Duc
Troyes
Colmar
Laval
Le Mans
Angers
MAINE
ORLÉANAIS
Nantes
ANJOU
TOURAINE
BERRY
NIVERNAIS
Nevers
POITOU
AUNIS
SAINTONGE
ANGOUMOIS
MARCHE
LIMOUSIN
Clermont-Ferrand
AUVERGNE
LYONNAIS
Valence
Orange
GUIENNE AND GASCONY
Rodez
Narbonne
FOIX
F-S-PM-A-WF
F-PM-WF
F-S-PM-WF
F-S-M-PM-A-WF
F-PM-A-WF
S-PM
F-S-WF
F-PM
F-S-PM-A
F-S
F-WF
Laws and Courts
Region of the "customary (feudal) law"
" " " "written (Roman) law"
Boundary of jurisdiction of a parlement or supreme council.
Seat of a parlement or "conseil souverain"
" " "chambre des comptes"
" " "cour des aides"
" " "court of admiralty"
" " "bureau de finance" and "chambre du domaine"
" " "cour des monnaies"
" " "prévôt des maréchaux"
" " chief court of the salt tax
" " grand mastership of waters and forests
Bishopric; C.= County; LAB.= Labourd.
Scale 1:9000000

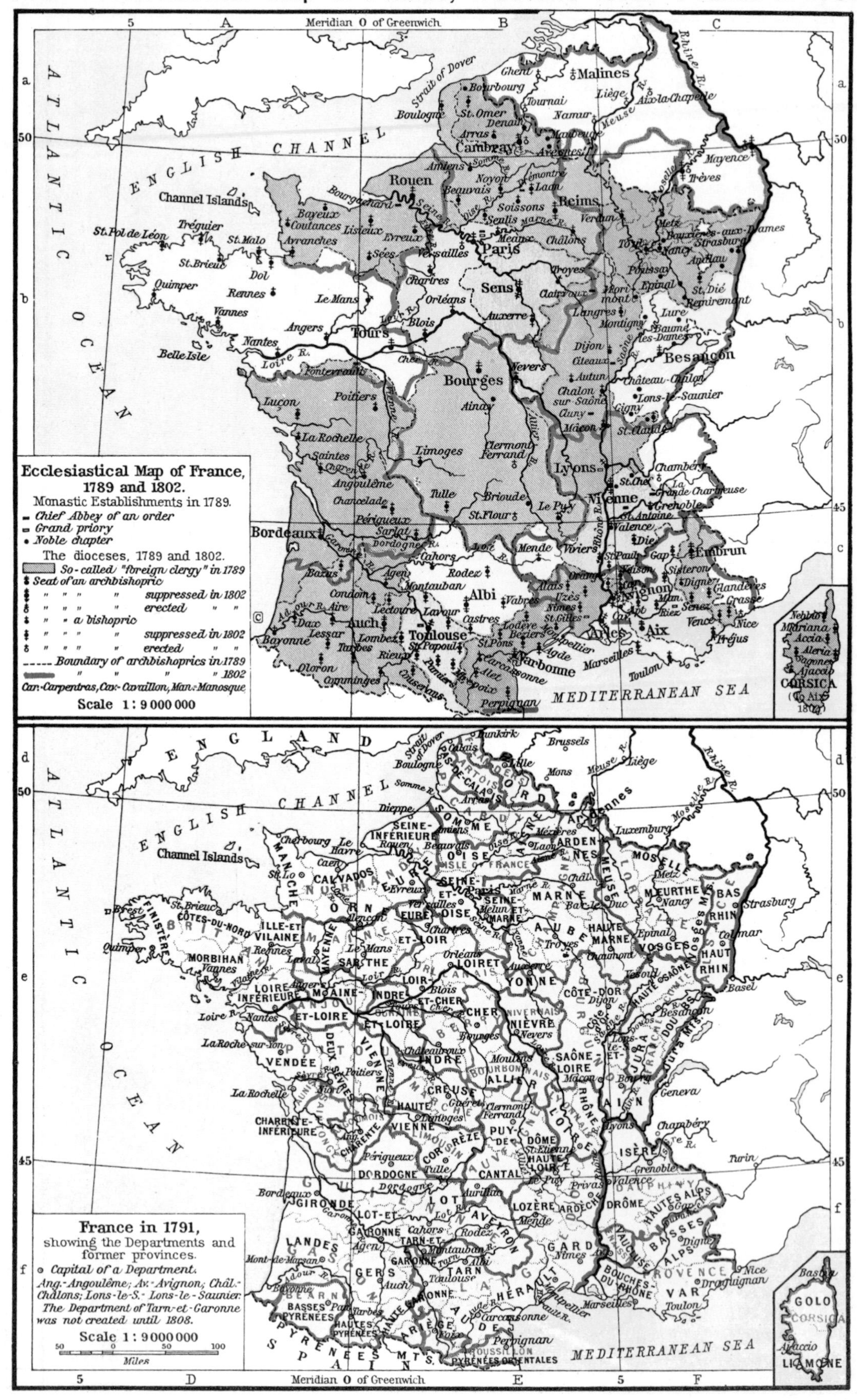
Ecclesiastical Map of France, 1789 and 1802.
Monastic Establishments in 1789.
Chief Abbey of an order
Grand priory
Noble chapter
The dioceses, 1789 and 1802.
So-called "foreign clergy" in 1789
Seat of an archbishopric
" " " " suppressed in 1802
" " " " erected " "
" " a bishopric
" " " " suppressed in 1802
" " " " erected " "
Boundary of archbishoprics in 1789
" " " " 1802
Car.-Carpentras, Cav.-Cavaillon, Man.-Manosque
Scale 1 : 9 000 000
ENGLISH CHANNEL
ATLANTIC OCEAN
MEDITERRANEAN SEA
CORSICA
France in 1791,
showing the Departments and former provinces.
Capital of a Department.
Ang.-Angoulême; Av.-Avignon; Châl.-Châlons; Lons-le-S.-Lons-le-Saunier.
The Department of Tarn-et-Garonne was not created until 1808.
Scale 1 : 9 000 000
Miles
ENGLAND
SPAIN
Meridian 0 of Greenwich

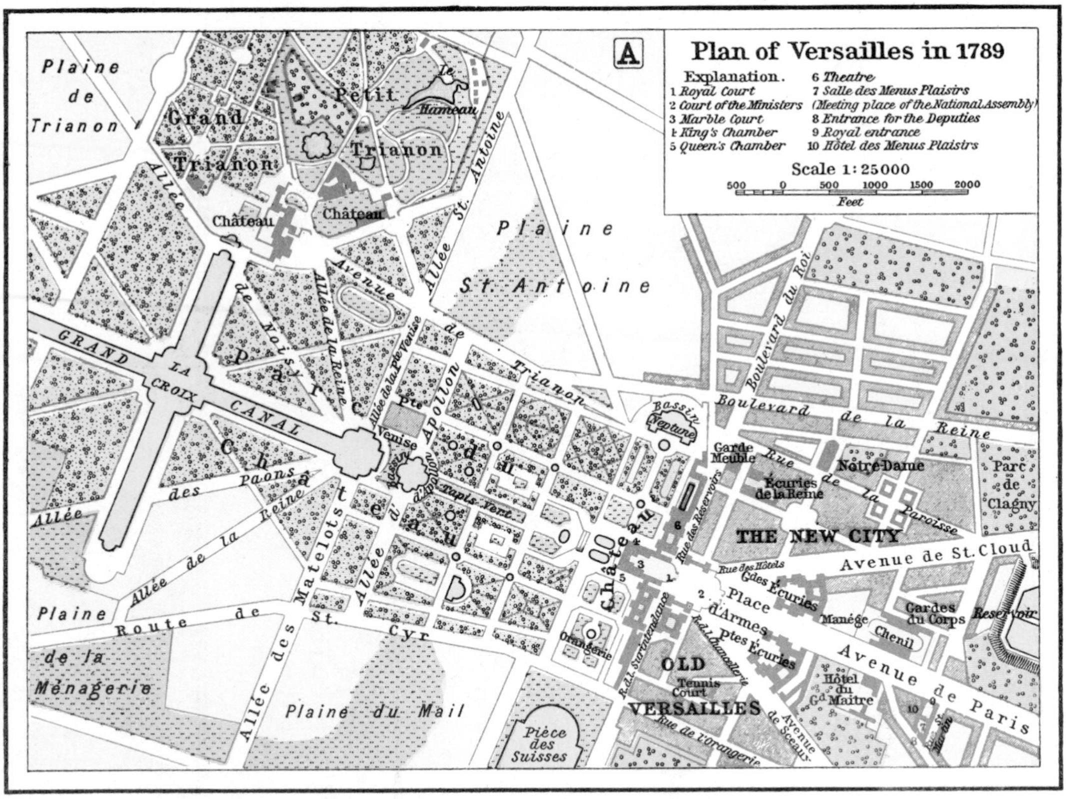

Plan of Versailles in 1789
Explanation.
1 Royal Court
2 Court of the Ministers
3 Marble Court
4 King's Chamber
5 Queen's Chamber
6 Theatre
7 Salle des Menus Plaisirs (Meeting place of the National Assembly)
8 Entrance for the Deputies
9 Royal entrance
10 Hôtel des Menus Plaisirs
Scale 1:25000
500 0 500 1000 1500 2000
Feet
A
Plaine de Trianon
Grand Trianon
Petit Trianon
Le Hameau
Château
Château
Allée St. Antoine
Plaine St. Antoine
Avenue de Trianon
Allée de Noisy
Allée de la Reine
Parc du Château
GRAND CANAL
LA CROIX
Allée des Paons
Allée de la Reine
Allée des Matelots
Allée d'Apollon
Bassin d'Apollon
Tapis Vert
Pte. Venise
Bassin de Neptune
Boulevard du Roi
Boulevard de la Reine
Garde Meuble
Rue de la Paroisse
Notre Dame
Écuries de la Reine
Parc de Clagny
THE NEW CITY
Avenue de St. Cloud
Rue des Réservoirs
Château
Rue des Hôtels
Gdes Écuries
Place d'Armes
Ptes Écuries
Manége
Gardes du Corps
Reservoir
Chenil
Avenue de Paris
Orangerie
OLD VERSAILLES
Tennis Court
Hôtel du Gd Maître
Avenue de Sceaux
Rue de l'Orangerie
Plaine Route de St. Cyr
Plaine de la Ménagerie
Plaine du Mail
Allée des Matelots
Pièce des Suisses

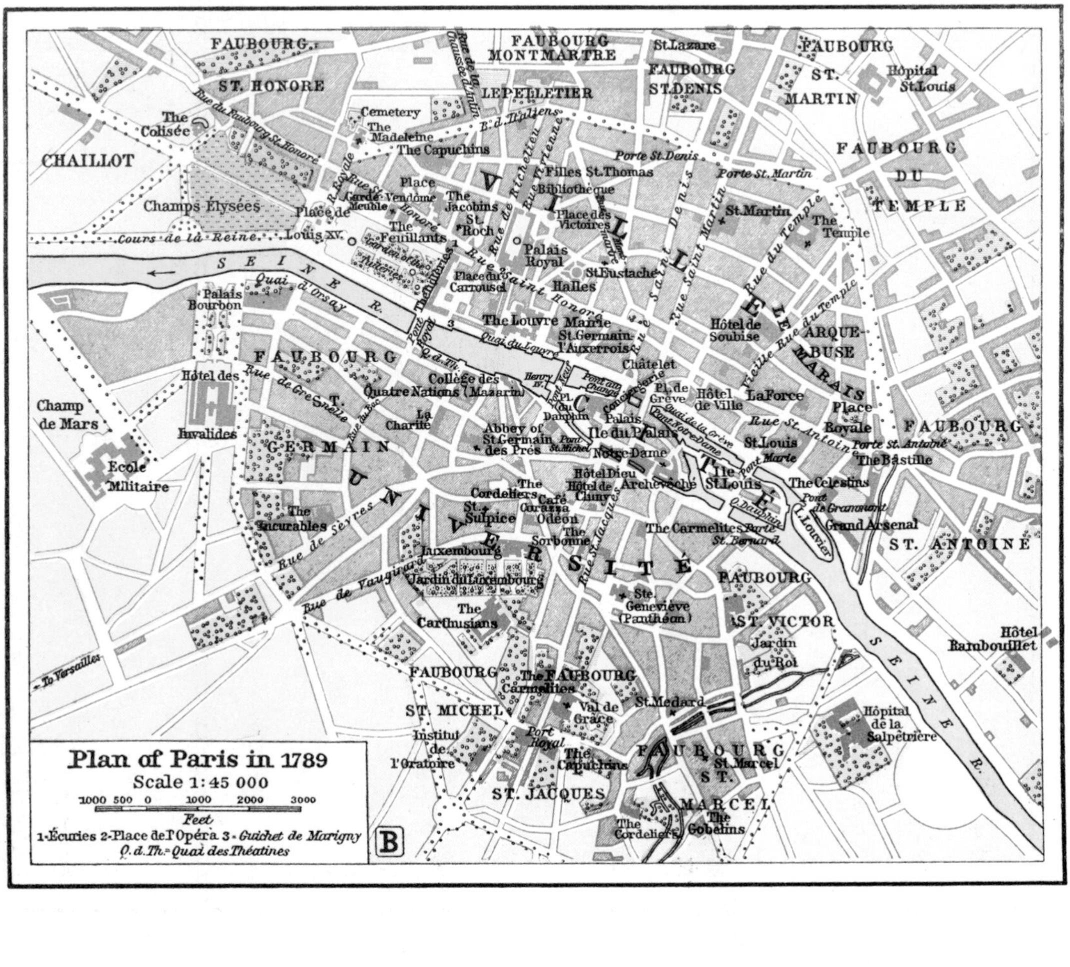

Plan of Paris in 1789
Scale 1:45 000
1000 500 0 1000 2000 3000
Feet
1-Écuries 2-Place de l'Opéra 3-Guichet de Marigny
Q.d.Th.-Quai des Théatines
B
FAUBOURG ST. HONORE
FAUBOURG MONTMARTRE
St. Lazare
FAUBOURG ST. DENIS
FAUBOURG ST. MARTIN
Hôpital St. Louis
LEPELLETIER
Cemetery
The Madeleine
The Capuchins
The Colisée
CHAILLOT
Rue du Faubourg St. Honoré
B.d. Italiens
Porte St. Denis
Porte St. Martin
FAUBOURG DU TEMPLE
Filles St. Thomas
Bibliothèque
Place Vendome
Garde Meuble
The Jacobins
St. Roch
Place des Victoires
St. Martin
The Temple
Champs Élysées
Place de Louis XV.
Cours de la Reine
The Feuillants
Jardin des Tuileries
Palais Royal
VILLE
St. Eustache
Halles
Place du Carrousel
Rue St. Honoré
SEINE R.
Quai d'Orsay
Palais Bourbon
The Louvre
Mairie
St. Germain l'Auxerrois
Hôtel de Soubise
ARQUEBUSE
Quai du Louvre
Châtelet
FAUBOURG ST. GERMAIN
Hôtel des Invalides
Collège des Quatre Nations (Mazarin)
Pont au Change
Pl. de Grève
Hôtel de Ville
LaForce
LE MARAIS
Rue de Grenelle
La Charité
Place Royale
Champ de Mars
Abbey of St. Germain des Prés
Pl. Dauphin
Palais
Ile du Palais
CITÉ
Notre Dame
St. Louis
FAUBOURG
Porte St. Antoine
The Bastille
Ecole Militaire
Hôtel Dieu
Archevêché
Ile St. Louis
The Celestins
Pont de Gramont
Grand Arsenal
The Cordeliers
St. Sulpice
Café Corazza
Odéon
Hôtel de Cluny
The Incurables
Rue de Sèvres
The Sorbonne
The Carmelites
Porte St. Bernard
ST. ANTOINE
Luxembourg
Jardin du Luxembourg
UNIVERSITÉ
FAUBOURG ST. VICTOR
Rue de Vaugirard
Ste. Geneviève (Panthéon)
Jardin du Roi
The Carthusians
Hôtel Rambouillet
To Versailles
FAUBOURG ST. MICHEL
The FAUBOURG
Carmelites
Val de Grace
St. Medard
Hôpital de la Salpêtrière
Institut de l'Oratoire
Port Royal
The Capuchins
FAUBOURG ST. MARCEL
St. Marcel
ST. JACQUES
The Cordeliers
The Gobelins
SEINE R.

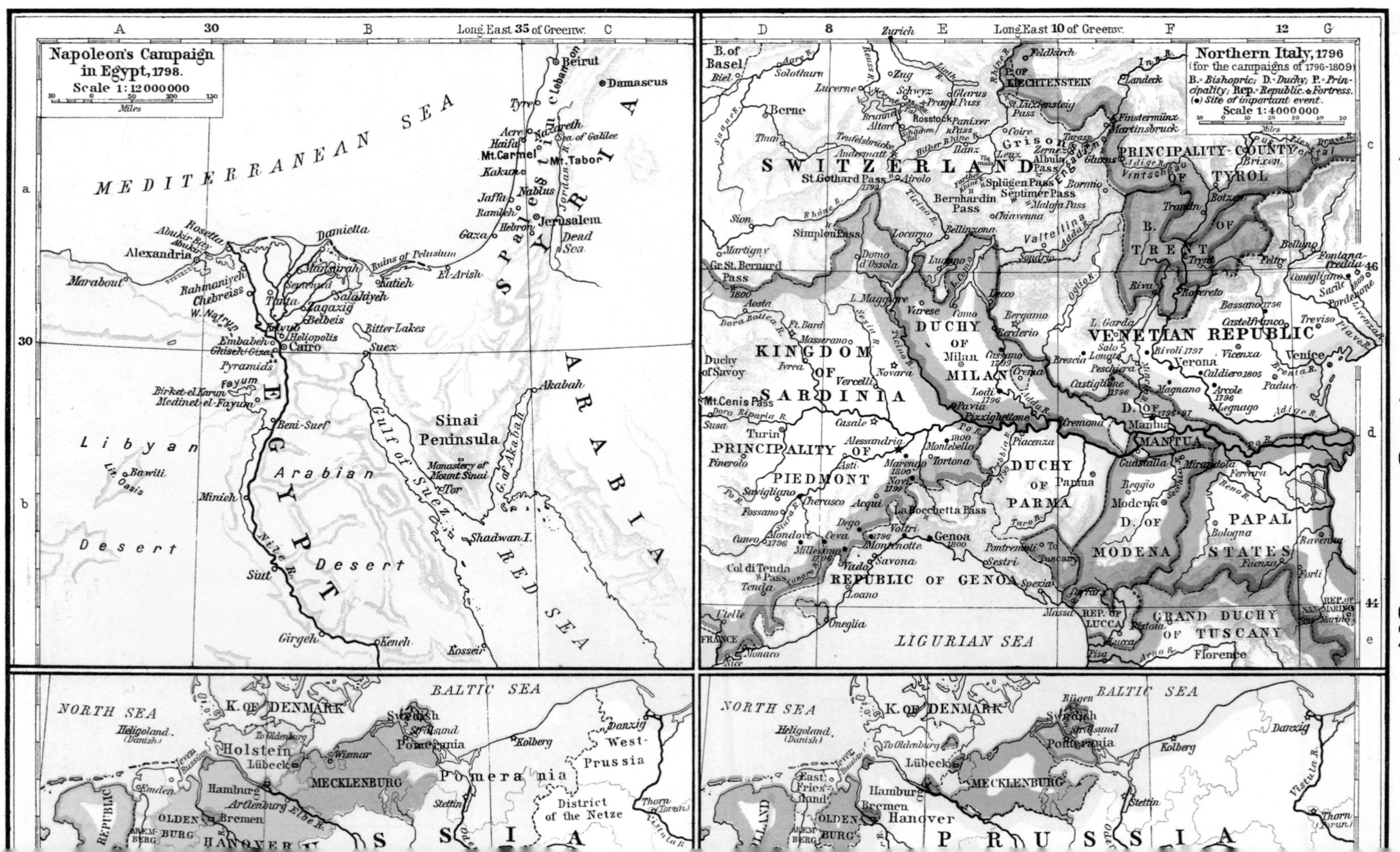
Napoleon's Campaign in Egypt, 1798.
Scale 1:12000000
Miles
MEDITERRANEAN SEA
Alexandria
Rosetta
Damietta
Cairo
Pyramids
Suez
Sinai Peninsula
Gulf of Suez
RED SEA
ARABIA
SYRIA
EGYPT
Libyan
Desert
Arabian
Jaffa
Acre
Jerusalem
Damascus
Beirut
Northern Italy, 1796
(for the campaigns of 1796-1809)
B.: Bishopric; D.: Duchy; P.: Principality; Rep.: Republic. ✠ Fortress.
(•) Site of important event.
Scale 1:4000000
SWITZERLAND
KINGDOM OF SARDINIA
DUCHY OF MILAN
VENETIAN REPUBLIC
PRINCIPALITY-COUNTY OF TYROL
PIEDMONT
DUCHY OF PARMA
D. OF MODENA
PAPAL STATES
GRAND DUCHY OF TUSCANY
REPUBLIC OF GENOA
LIGURIAN SEA
NORTH SEA
BALTIC SEA
K. OF DENMARK
MECKLENBURG
PRUSSIA

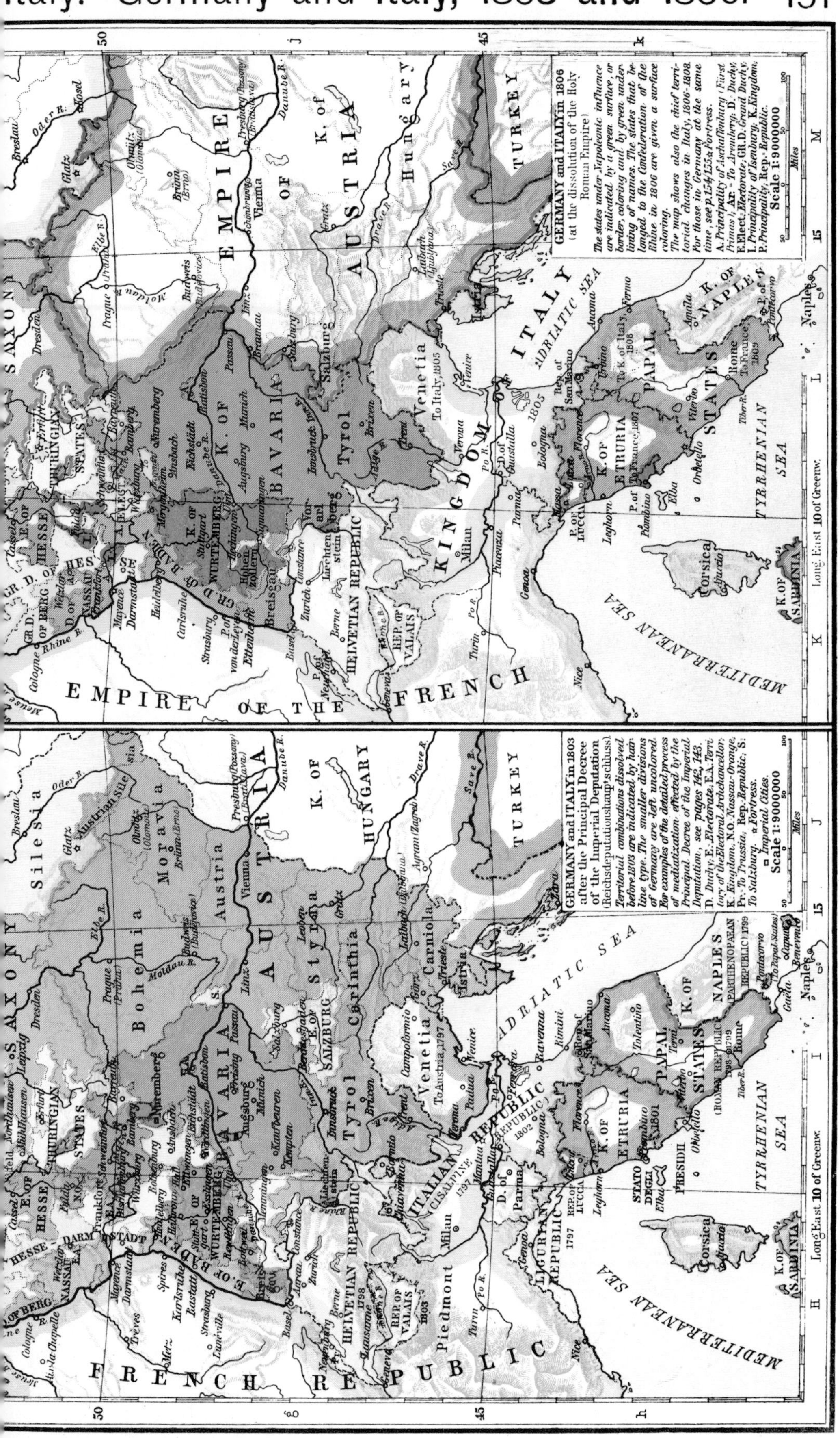
GERMANY and ITALY in 1806
(at the dissolution of the Holy Roman Empire)
The states under Napoleonic influence are indicated by a green surface, or border, coloring and by green underlining of names. The states that belonged to the Confederation of the Rhine in 1806 are given a surface coloring.
The map shows also the chief territorial changes in Italy, 1806-1808. For those in Germany at the same time, see p. 154/155. ☆ Fortress.
A. Principality of Aschaffenburg (Fürst Primas); Ar. = To Arenberg; D. Duchy; E. Elect. = Electorate; GR. D. Grand Duchy; I. Principality of Isenburg; K. Kingdom; P. Principality; Rep. Republic.
Scale 1:9000000
Miles
GERMANY and ITALY in 1803
after the Principal Decree of the Imperial Deputation
(Reichsdeputationshauptschluss).
Territorial combinations dissolved before 1803 are indicated by hair line type. The smaller divisions of Germany are left uncolored. For examples of the detailed process of mediatization effected by the Principal Decree of the Imperial Deputation, see pages 142, 143.
D. Duchy; E. Electorate; E.A. Territory of the Electoral Archchancellor; K. Kingdom; N.O. Nassau-Orange; Pr. To Prussia; Rep. Republic; S: To Salzburg. ☆ Fortress. ▫ Imperial Cities.
Scale 1:9000000
Miles
EMPIRE OF THE FRENCH
FRENCH REPUBLIC
KINGDOM OF ITALY
ITALIAN REPUBLIC
EMPIRE OF AUSTRIA
AUSTRIA
TURKEY
TYRRHENIAN SEA
MEDITERRANEAN SEA
ADRIATIC SEA

Treaty Adjustments, 1801—1812.

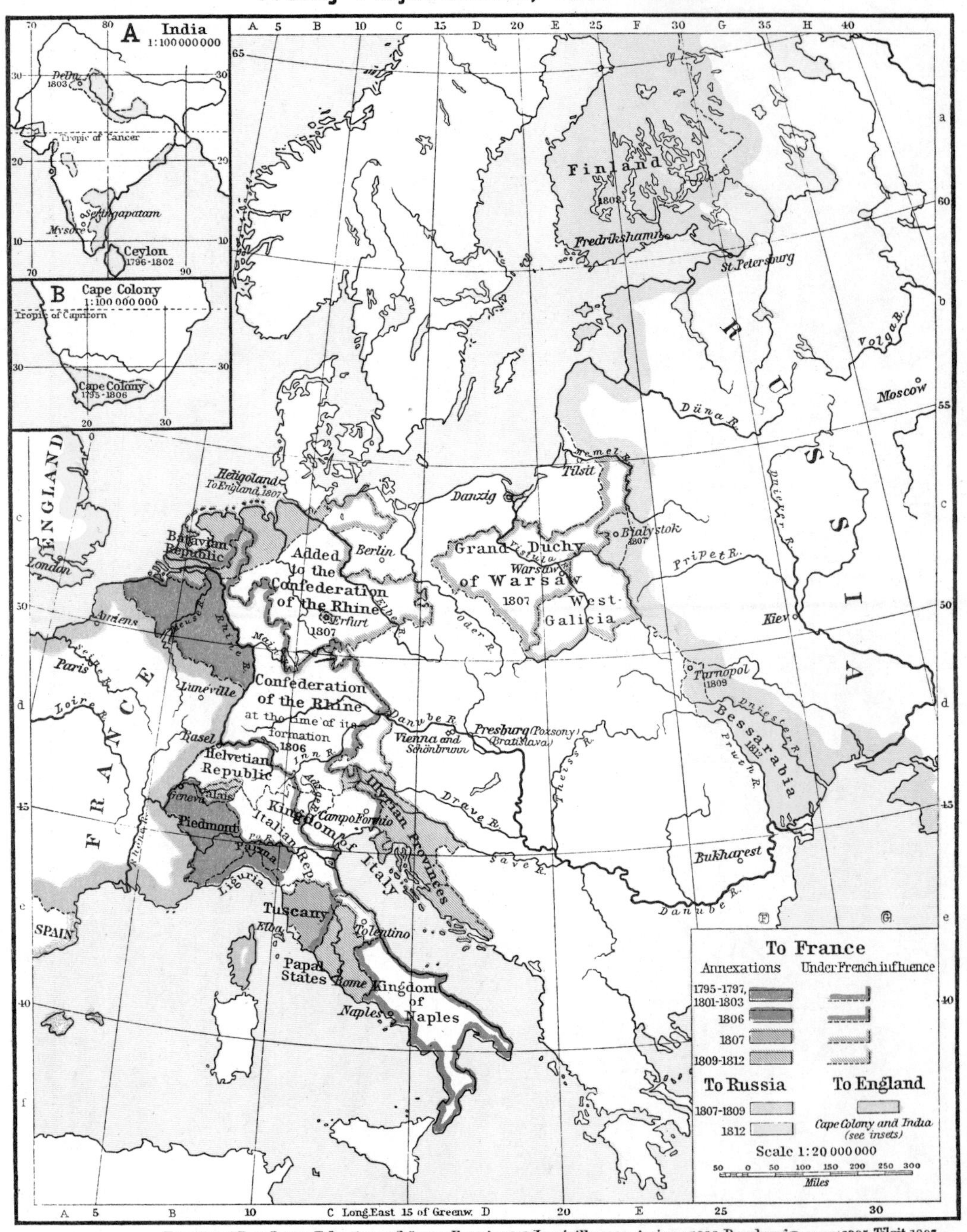

Treaties of Basel, 1795; Tolentino and Campo Formio, 1797; Lunéville, 1801; Amiens, 1802; Presburg (Pozsony), 1805; Tilsit 1807; Fredrikshamn and Vienna (Schönbrunn), 1809; Bukharest, 1812.

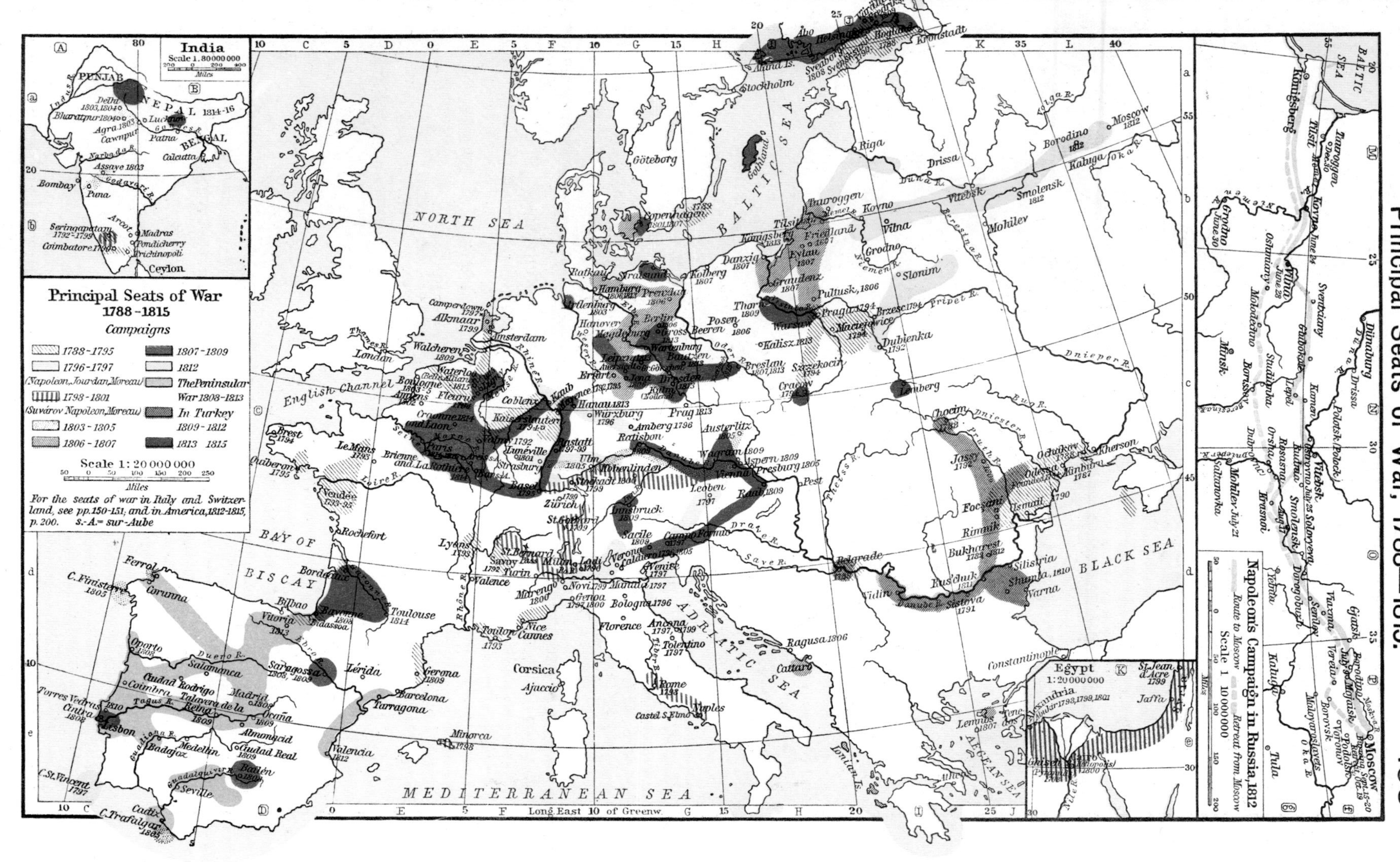
Principal Seats of War
1788-1815
Campaigns
1788-1795
1796-1797
(Napoleon, Jourdan, Moreau)
1798-1801
(Suvárov Napoleon, Moreau)
1803-1805
1806-1807
1807-1809
1812
The Peninsular War 1808-1813
In Turkey 1809-1812
1813 1815
Scale 1: 20 000 000
Miles
For the seats of war in Italy and Switzerland, see pp. 150-151; and in America, 1812-1815, p. 200. s.-A.= sur-Aube
India
Scale 1: 80 000 000
PUNJAB
NEPAL 1814-16
BENGAL
Delhi 1803, 1804
Bhurtpur 1804
Agra 1803
Cawnpur
Lucknow
Patna
Calcutta
Assaye 1803
Bombay
Puna
Seringapatam 1792-1799
Coimbatore 1790
Arcot
Madras
Pondicherry
Trichinopoli
Ceylon
NORTH SEA
BALTIC SEA
BAY OF BISCAY
English Channel
MEDITERRANEAN SEA
ADRIATIC SEA
BLACK SEA
AEGEAN SEA
Long. East 10 of Greenw.
Stockholm
Åland Is.
Åbo
Helsingfors
Sveaborg 1808
Kronstadt
Göteborg
Gotland
Copenhagen 1801, 1807
Riga
Drissa
Borodino 1812
Moscow 1812
Kaluga
Smolensk 1812
Vitebsk
Mohilev
Tauroggen
Tilsit
Kovno
Vilna
Grodno
Slonim
Königsberg
Friedland 1807
Eylau 1807
Danzig 1807
Kolberg 1807
Graudenz
Thorn 1809
Pultusk, 1806
Warsaw
Praga 1794
Brzesc 1794
Maciejowice 1794
Dubienka 1792
Posen
Kalisz 1813
Breslau 1807, 1813
Szczekocin 1794
Cracow
Lemberg
Stralsund
Hamburg
Lübeck
Hanover
Magdeburg
Berlin
Leipzig
Bautzen 1813
Dresden
Jena
Erfurt
Hanau 1813
Würzburg 1796
Amberg 1796
Ratisbon
Prag 1813
Austerlitz 1805
Wagram 1809
Aspern 1809
Vienna
Presburg 1805
Raab 1809
Leoben 1797
Hohenlinden
Stockach 1800
Ulm 1805
Rastatt
Lunéville 1801
Strasburg
Basel 1795
Zürich 1799
St. Gotthard
Innsbruck 1809
Sacile 1809
Campo Formio 1797
Venice 1797
Verona
Caldiero
Mantua 1797
Lodi
Milan
Marengo 1800
Novi 1799
Genoa 1797, 1800
Bologna 1796
Florence
Ancona 1797, 1799
Tolentino 1797
Rome 1798
Naples
Castel S. Elmo
Ragusa 1806
Cattaro
Corsica
Ajaccio
Minorca 1798
Nice
Cannes
Toulon 1793
St. Bernard Pass
Turin
Valence
Lyons 1793
Amsterdam
Alkmaar 1799
Camperdown 1797
Walcheren 1809
Waterloo
Boulogne
Amiens 1802
Fleurus
Coblenz
Mainz
Kaiserslautern 1794
Valmy 1792
Craonne 1814 and Laon
Paris
Brienne and La Rothière 1814
Arcis-s.-A.
London
Brest 1794
Quiberon 1795
Le Mans 1793
Vendée 1793-95
Rochefort
Bordeaux
Bayonne 1808
Toulouse 1814
Bilbao
Vitoria 1813
Ferrol
C. Finisterre 1805
Corunna
Oporto 1809
Salamanca
Saragossa 1808, 1809
Lérida
Gerona 1809
Barcelona
Tarragona
Valencia 1812
Ciudad Rodrigo
Coimbra
Talavera de la Reina 1809
Madrid
Ocaña 1809
Almonacid
Torres Vedras 1810
Cintra 1808
Lisbon
Badajoz
Medellin 1809
Ciudad Real
Bailén 1808
Seville
Cadiz
C. Trafalgar 1805
C. St. Vincent 1797
Belgrade
Pest
Vidin
Rustchuk
Silistria
Shumla, 1810
Varna
Sistova 1791
Bukharest 1812
Rimnik
Focsani
Ismail 1790
Odessa
Ochakov
Kinburn 1787
Kherson
Jassy 1792
Chocim
Constantinople
Lemnos 1807
Ionian Is.
Egypt
1:20 000 000
Alexandria
Abukir 1798, 1799, 1801
St. Jean d'Acre 1799
Jaffa
Napoleon's Campaign in Russia, 1812
Route to Moscow
Retreat from Moscow
Scale 1 : 10 000 000
Miles
Dünaburg
Polotsk (Polock)
Kamen
Glubokoje
Sventziany
Lepel
Studianka
Borissov
Minsk
Molodechno
Oshmiany
Vilna June 28
Kovno June 24
Grodno June 30
Tauroggen Dec. 30
Königsberg
Ostrovno July 25
Rudnia
Rosasna
Orsha
Dubrovno
Mohilev July 21
Saltanovka
Krasnoi
Smolensk
Solovyeva
Dorogobuzh
Yelnia
Semlev
Viazma
Gjatsk
Borodino
Mojaisk
Vereia
Borovsk
Maloyaroslavets
Kaluga
Tula
Moscow Sept. 15-20
Podolsk
Voronov
Oka R.
Moskva R.

NORTH SEA
UNITED KINGDOM
K. OF DENMARK
Zealand
Holstein
D. OF MECKLENB
KINGDOM OF WESTPHALIA
GR.D. OF BERG
D. OF NASSAU
HESSE
FRANKFORT
SAXON DUCHIES
GR.D. OF SCHWEINFURT
WURZBURG
BADEN
K. OF WURTEMBERG
K. OF BAVA
EMPIRE OF THE FRENCH
SWITZERLAND
Tyrol
KINGDOM OF ITALY
Paris
Brussels
Antwerp
Amsterdam
Rotterdam
Cologne
Hamburg
Hanover
Frankfort
Strasburg
Lyons
Geneva
Milan
Turin
Genoa
Munich
Nuremberg
Bamberg
Augsburg
Ulm
Innsbruck
To France, 1810
Long. East 10 of Greenwich

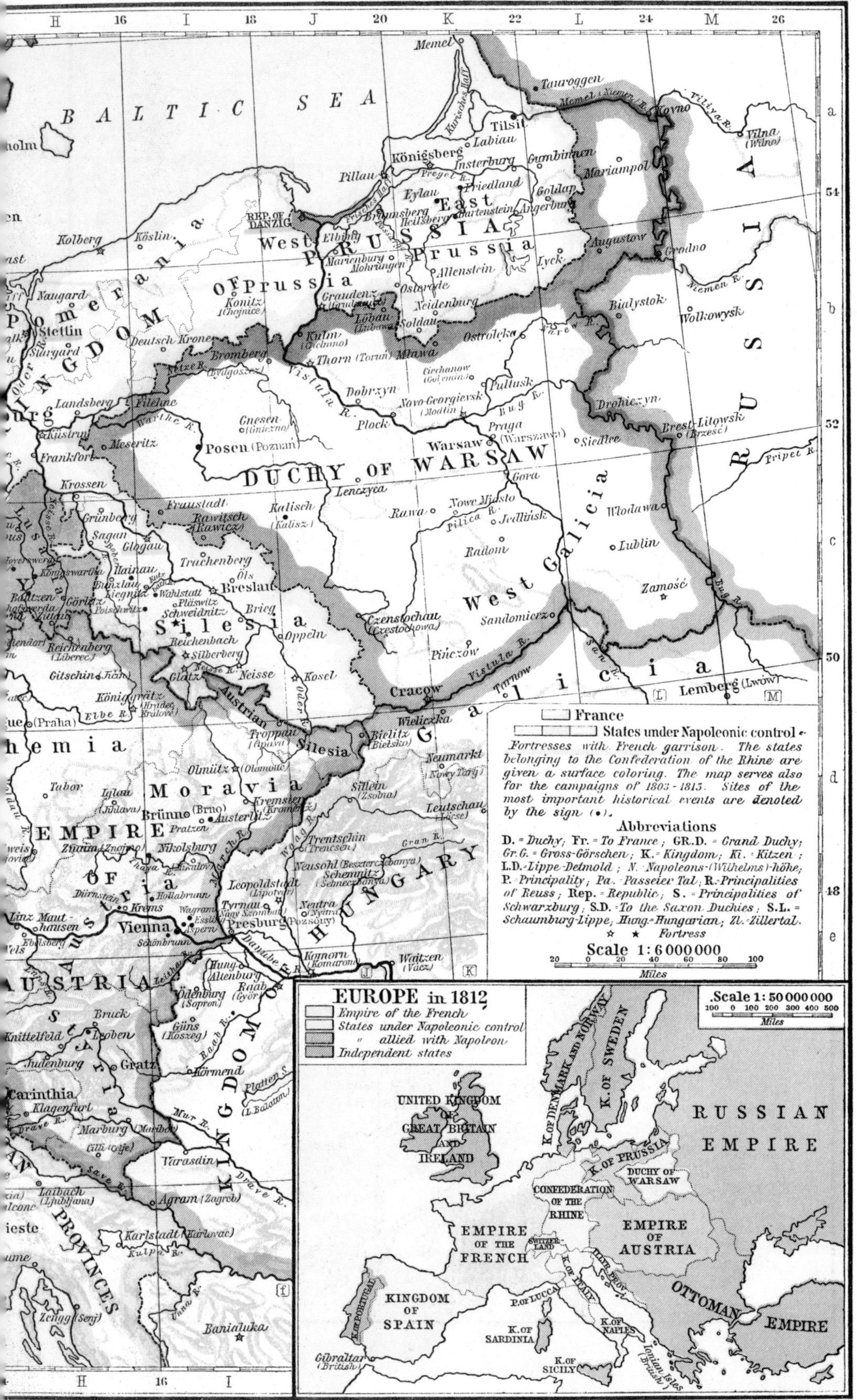
BALTIC SEA
KINGDOM OF PRUSSIA
Pomerania
West Prussia
East Prussia
DUCHY OF WARSAW
West Galicia
Galicia
RUSSIA
Silesia
Austrian Silesia
Bohemia
Moravia
EMPIRE OF AUSTRIA
HUNGARY
KINGDOM OF HUNGARY
Styria
Carinthia
PROVINCES
REP. OF DANZIG
Memel
Tauroggen
Tilsit
Königsberg
Kovno
Vilna (Wilno)
Mariampol
Grodno
Bialystok
Wolkowysk
Warsaw
Praga (Warszawa)
Brest-Litowsk (Brześć)
Posen (Poznań)
Thorn (Toruń)
Kalisch (Kalisz)
Breslau
Cracow
Lublin
Zamość
Lemberg (Lwów)
Vienna
Presburg (Pozsony)
Brünn (Brno)
Austerlitz
Wagram
Agram (Zagreb)
Laibach (Ljubljana)
Banialuka
France
States under Napoleonic control
Fortresses with French garrison. The states belonging to the Confederation of the Rhine are given a surface coloring. The map serves also for the campaigns of 1805-1815. Sites of the most important historical events are denoted by the sign (•).
Abbreviations
D. = Duchy; Fr. = To France; GR.D. = Grand Duchy; Gr.G. = Gross-Görschen; K. = Kingdom; Ki. = Kitzen; L.D. = Lippe-Detmold; N. Napoleons-(Wilhelms)-höhe; P. Principality; Pa. Passeier Tal; R. Principalities of Reuss; Rep. = Republic; S. = Principalities of Schwarzburg; S.D. = To the Saxon Duchies; S.L. = Schaumburg-Lippe; Hung. = Hungarian; Zi. = Zillertal.
☆ ★ Fortress
Scale 1:6 000 000
Miles
EUROPE in 1812
Empire of the French
States under Napoleonic control
" allied with Napoleon
Independent states
Scale 1:50 000 000
Miles
UNITED KINGDOM OF GREAT BRITAIN AND IRELAND
K. OF DENMARK AND NORWAY
K. OF SWEDEN
RUSSIAN EMPIRE
K. OF PRUSSIA
DUCHY OF WARSAW
CONFEDERATION OF THE RHINE
EMPIRE OF THE FRENCH
SWITZERLAND
EMPIRE OF AUSTRIA
K. OF ITALY
ILLYR. PROV.
KINGDOM OF SPAIN
K. OF PORTUGAL
P. OF LUCCA
K. OF SARDINIA
K. OF NAPLES
K. OF SICILY
OTTOMAN EMPIRE
Gibraltar (British)
Ionian Isles (British)

The Waterloo Campaign. Europe in 1815.

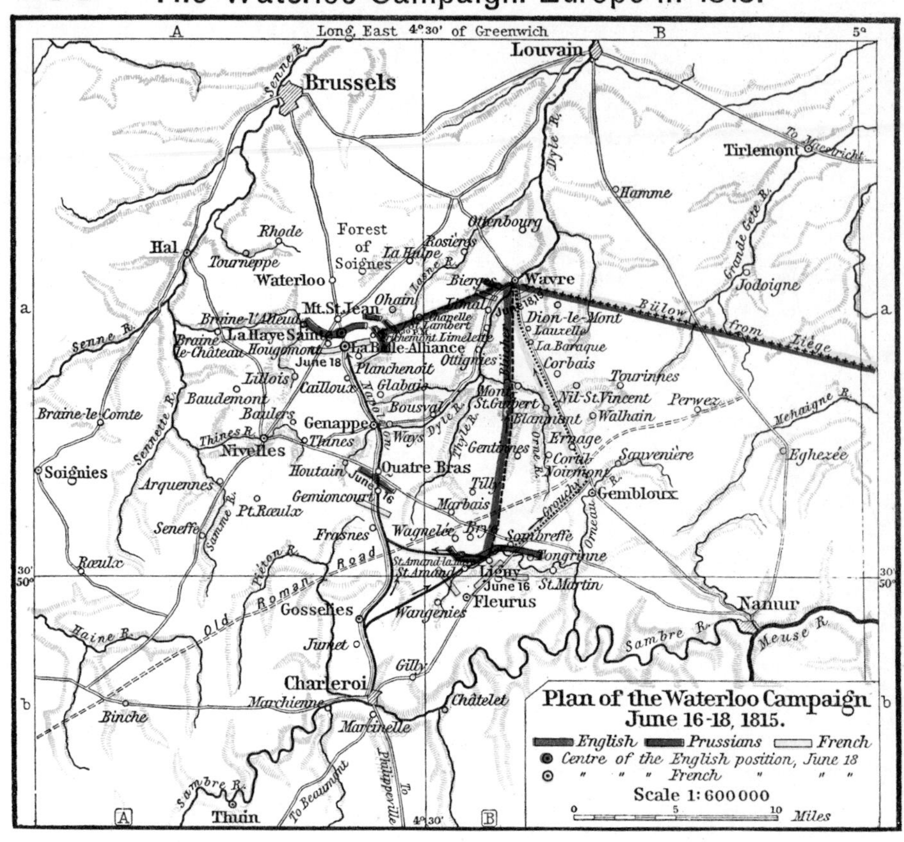

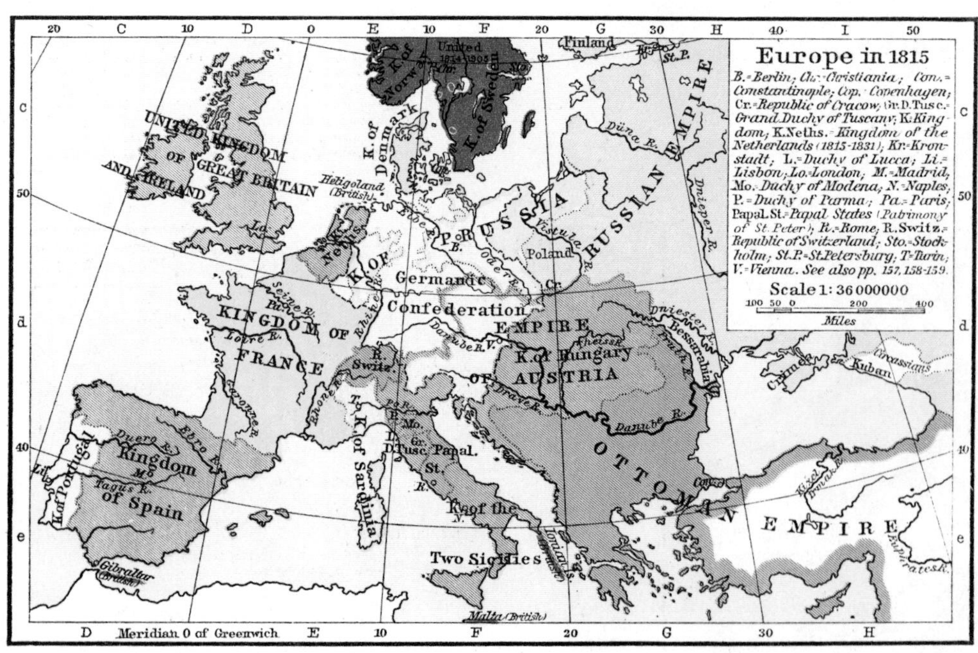

To Austria
To Prussia
" Bavaria
" Hanover
" Baden
" Wurtemberg
" Denmark
" Russia
" Sardinia
" Switzerland
Malta To Great Britain
The Austrian Netherlands united with the former Dutch Republic as the Kingdom of the Netherlands.- The Grand Duchy of Luxemburg, under the personal rule of the King of the Netherlands, was a member of the Germanic Confederation.
United with Sweden as the Kingdom of Sweden and Norway.
The states belonging to the Germanic Confederation are given a surface coloring. See also pp. 158-159
Scale 1: 12 000 000
Miles
KINGDOM OF SWEDEN AND NORWAY, 1814-1905
NORTH SEA
BALTIC SEA
DENMARK
Jutland
Heligoland British 1814-1890
GERMANIC CONFEDERATION
PRUSSIA
KINGDOM OF POLAND
EMPIRE OF AUSTRIA
HUNGARY
Bohemia
Moravia
Galicia
Tyrol
SWITZERLAND
FRANCE
K. OF SARDINIA
Lombardy
Venetia
Tuscany
Papal States
KINGDOM OF THE TWO SICILIES
OTTOMAN EMPIRE
Bosnia
Servia
ADRIATIC SEA
MEDITERRANEAN SEA
Corsica (To France)
Sardinia
Balearic Is. (To Spain)
Malta (British)
Ionian Is. Republic under British protection till 1863-1864, then to Greece
L. East 15 of Greenwich
★ French frontier fortress held by the Allies, 1815
☆ Fortress of the Germanic Confederation
The four Free Cities thus : Hamburg
K.-Kingdom; Lux.-Luxemburg; Prov.-Province;
R.-Republic ; Ras.-Rastatt
(Austrian) Netherlands till 1795
Netherlands 1815
LUXEMBURG
Rhine Prov. To Prussia 1815
Palatinate To Bavaria, 1815
FRANCE
Scale 1: 6 000 000
Miles
★ French frontier fortress held by the Allies, 1815
Eastern boundary of France in 1792
" " " " " 1814
" " " " " 1815

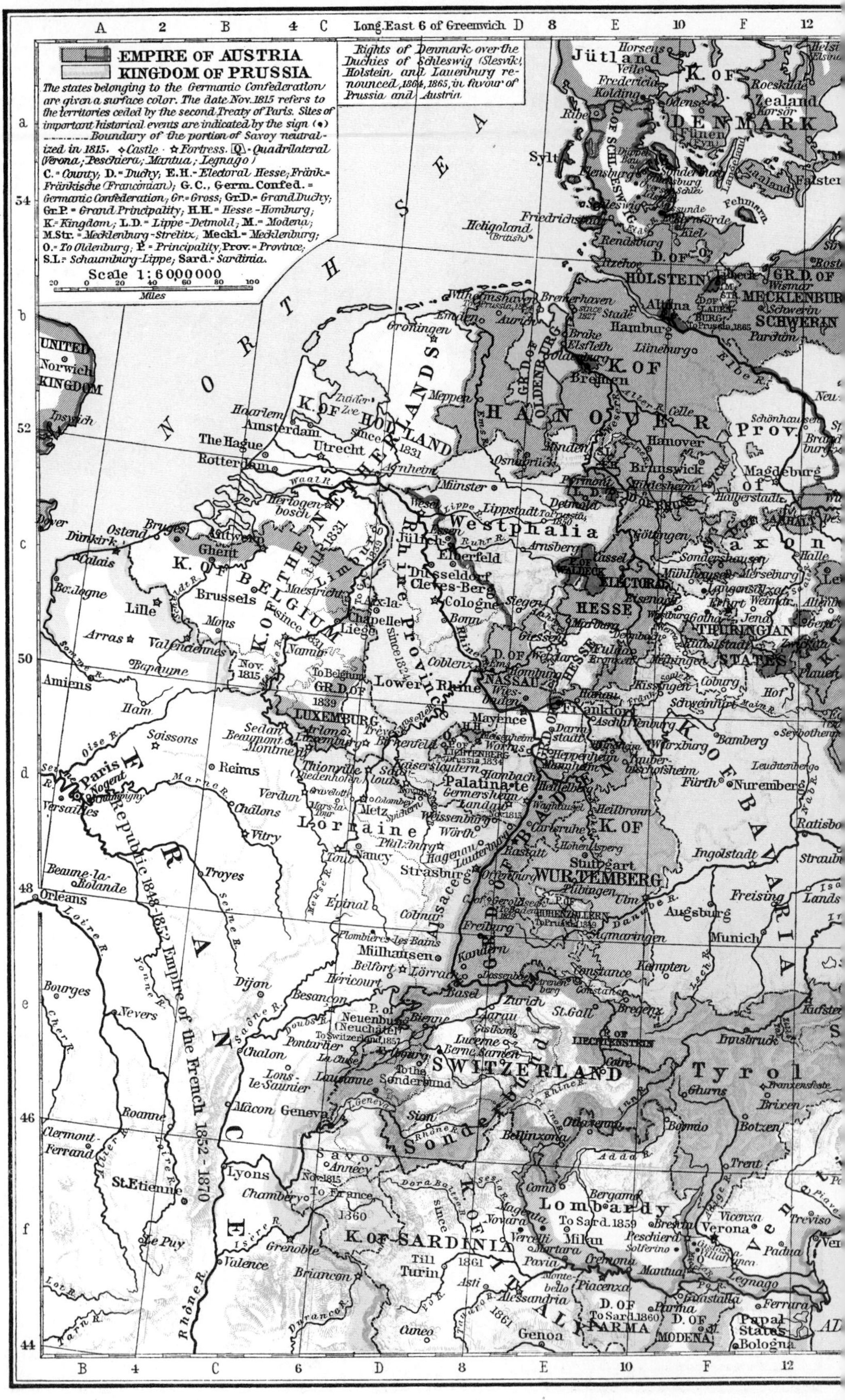
Long. East 6 of Greenwich
EMPIRE OF AUSTRIA
KINGDOM OF PRUSSIA
The states belonging to the Germanic Confederation are given a surface color. The date Nov. 1815 refers to the territories ceded by the second Treaty of Paris. Sites of important historical events are indicated by the sign (•)
Boundary of the portion of Savoy neutralized in 1815. Castle. Fortress. Q. = Quadrilateral (Verona; Peschiera; Mantua; Legnago)
C. = County; D. = Duchy; E.H. = Electoral Hesse; Fränk. = Fränkische (Franconian); G. C., Germ. Confed. = Germanic Confederation; Gr. = Gross; Gr.D. = Grand Duchy; Gr.P. = Grand Principality; H.H. = Hesse-Homburg; K. = Kingdom; L.D. = Lippe-Detmold; M. = Modena; M.Str. = Mecklenburg-Strelitz; Meckl. = Mecklenburg; O. = To Oldenburg; P. = Principality; Prov. = Province; S.L. = Schaumburg-Lippe; Sard. = Sardinia.
Scale 1:6000000
Miles
Rights of Denmark over the Duchies of Schleswig (Slesvik), Holstein and Lauenburg renounced, 1864, 1865, in favour of Prussia and Austria
NORTH SEA
K. OF DENMARK
Jütland
Zealand
D. OF SCHLESWIG
D. OF HOLSTEIN
Heligoland (British)
GR. D. OF MECKLENBURG SCHWERIN
K. OF HANOVER
GR. D. OF OLDENBURG
UNITED KINGDOM
K. OF HOLLAND
THE NETHERLANDS
Amsterdam
The Hague
Rotterdam
Utrecht
K. OF BELGIUM
Brussels
Antwerp
Ghent
Westphalia
Rhine Province
Cologne
Düsseldorf
Coblenz
ELECTORAL HESSE
NASSAU
Frankfort
THURINGIAN STATES
K. OF BAVARIA
Nuremberg
K. OF WURTEMBERG
Stuttgart
GR. D. OF BADEN
GR. D. OF LUXEMBURG
Palatinate
Lorraine
Alsace
Strasburg
FRANCE
Paris
Republic 1848-1852
Empire of the French 1852-1870
Lyons
SWITZERLAND
Sonderbund
Tyrol
Lombardy
Milan
K. OF SARDINIA
Turin
Genoa
K. OF ITALY
D. OF PARMA
D. OF MODENA
Venetia
Papal States
Bologna

BALTIC SEA
Bornholm
Memel
Rossieny
Vilkomir
Tilsit
Kovno
Vilna (Wilno)
Königsberg
Eydtkuhnen
Virballen (Virbalis)
Gumbinnen
Lithuania
East Prussia
united 1824-1878
West Prussia
Danzig
Elbing
Marienburg
Marienwerder
Köslin
Kolberg
Allenstein
Augustowo
Grodno
Lomza
Tykocin
Bialystok
Slonim
Ostrolenka (Ostroleka)
Graudenz (Grudziadz)
Stargard
Schneidemühl
Thorn (Torun)
Bromberg (Bydgoszcz)
Rypin
K. of Poland (by the Congress of Vienna)
Pultusk
Modlin (Novogeorgievsk)
Plock
Wloclawek
Bielsk
Brest-Litowsk (Brzesc)
Landsberg
Gnesen (Gniezno)
Radziejow
Küstrin
Frankfort
Posen (Poznan)
Wreschen
Warsaw
Wola
Praga
Siedlce
Schroda
Rogasin
Xions (Ksiaz)
Lissa (Leszno)
Koschmin (Kozmin)
Kalisch (Kalisz)
Lódz
Warka
Deblin
Ivangorod
Kowel
Volhynia
Petrikau (Piotrkow)
Radom
Lublin
Chelm
Glogau
Guben
RUSSIA
RUSSIAN EMPIRE
Oels
Breslau
Liegnitz
Görlitz
Schweidnitz
Czenstochau (Czestochowa)
Kielce
Sandomierz
Zamosc
Red Russia
Landeshut
Silberberg
Oppeln
Busk
Glatz
Neisse
Kosel
Ratibor
Republic of Cracow
Vistula R.
Tarnow
Jaroslaw
Przemysl
Lemberg (Lwow)
Galicia
Silesia
Teschen
To the Germ. Confed. since 1818
Neu Sandec (Nowy Sacz)
Dukla
Dniester R.
Stanislau (Stanislawow)
Pardubitz
Bohemia
Troppau (Opava)
Olmütz (Olomouc)
Iglau (Jihlava)
Kremsier
Moravia
Brünn (Brno)
Spielberg
Nikolsburg
Zips
Leutschau (Löcse)
Eperjes
CARPATHIAN MTS.
Budamer
Munkács
Neusohl (Besztercebanya)
Kremnitz
Altsohl (Zolyom)
Schemnitz (Selmecz)
Kaschau (Kassa)
Iglo
Lower Austria
Tyrnau
Leopoldstadt
Losoncz
Miskolcz
Tokay
Vienna
Presburg (Pozsony)
Gänserndorf
Krems
Danube R.
KINGDOM OF HUNGARY
Kapolna
Komorn (Komarom)
Waitzen (Vacs)
Gyöngyös
Hatvan
Gödöllö
Tisza-Füred
Debreczen
Wieselburg
Csorna
Raab (Györ)
Ödenburg (Sopron)
Buda (Ofen)
Pest
Czegléd
Szolnok
Grosswardein (Varad)
Szamos-Ujvar
Dees (Dej)
Bistritz
Sächsisch-Reen
Steinamanger
Stuhlweissenburg (Szekesfehervar)
Kecskemét
Klausenburg (Kolozsvar, Cluj)
Gr. P. of Transylvania
Maros-Vasarhely
Csik-Szereda
Gratz
Styria
Földvar
Csongrád
Szentes
Transylvania
Schässburg
Carinthia
Klagenfurt
Marburg (Maribor)
Nagy-Kanizsa
Tolna
Paks
Szegedin
Arad
Világos
Karlsburg (Alba Iulia)
Mediasch
Mühlbach
Hermannstadt
Kronstadt
Fogaras
Cilli
Varasdin
Fünfkirchen (Pécs)
Maria Theresiopel (Szabadka)
Szöreg
Kikinda
Temesvár
Lugos
Déva
Broos
Vizakna
Rotenturm Pass
Törzburg Pass
Tömös Pass
Carniola
Agram (Zagreb)
Zombor
Hegyes
Becse
Banat
Eisernthor Pass (Iron Gate)
Illyria
Croatia
Slavonia
Essek (Osijek)
Voivodina
Peterwardein (Petervárad)
Werschitz (Versecz)
Weisskirchen
Mehadia
Wallachia
Adelsberg
Fiume
Karlstadt
Poxsega
Karlowitz
Slavonian Military Frontier
Banat Military Frontier
Croatian Military Frontier
Zengg (Senj)
Banjaluka
Bosnia
Belgrade
Pancsova
SERVIA
Principality, 1817
Craiova
Danube R.
PRINCIPALITY OF RUMANIA, 1859

The German Zollverein (Customs-Union), 1828—1872.

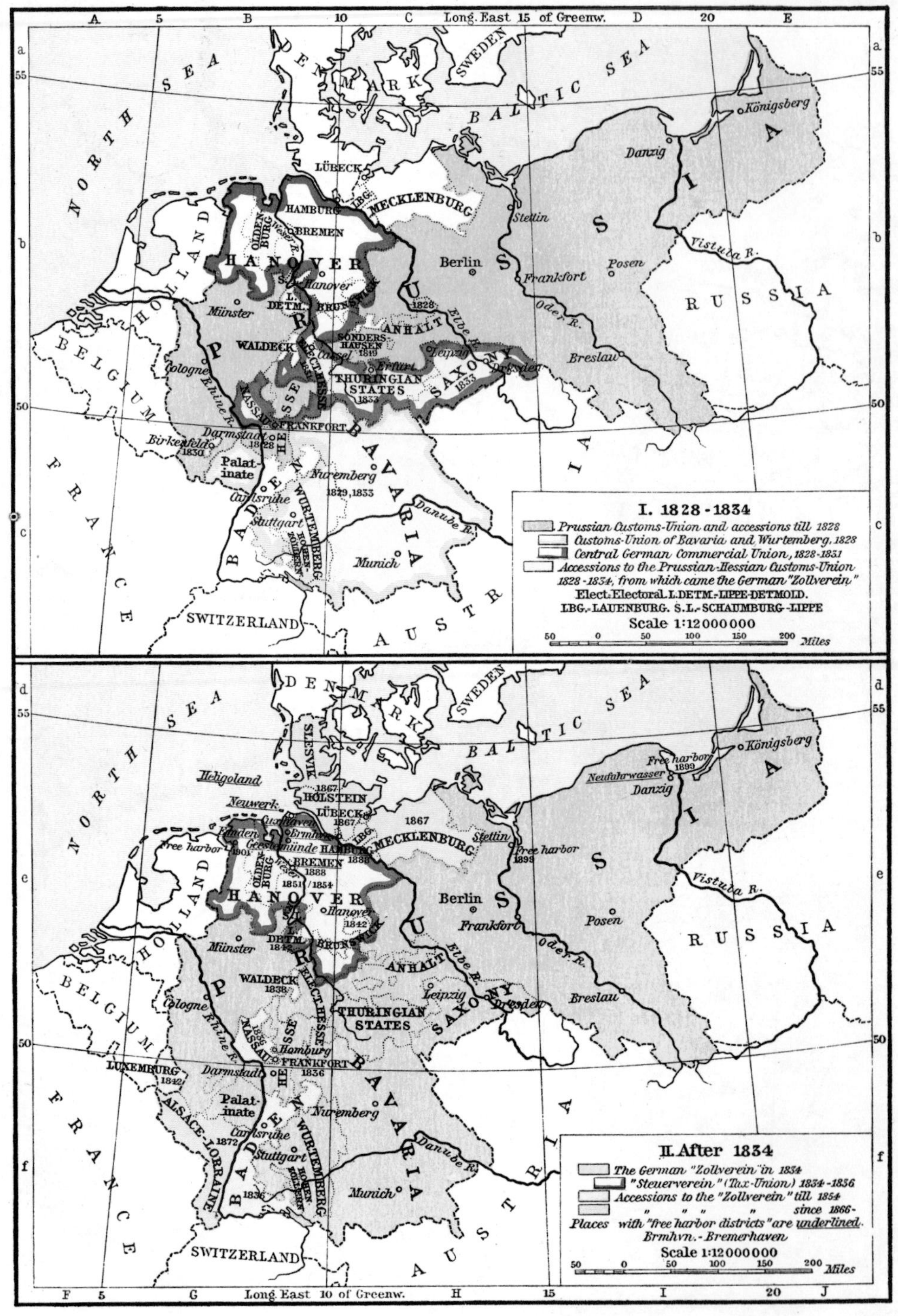

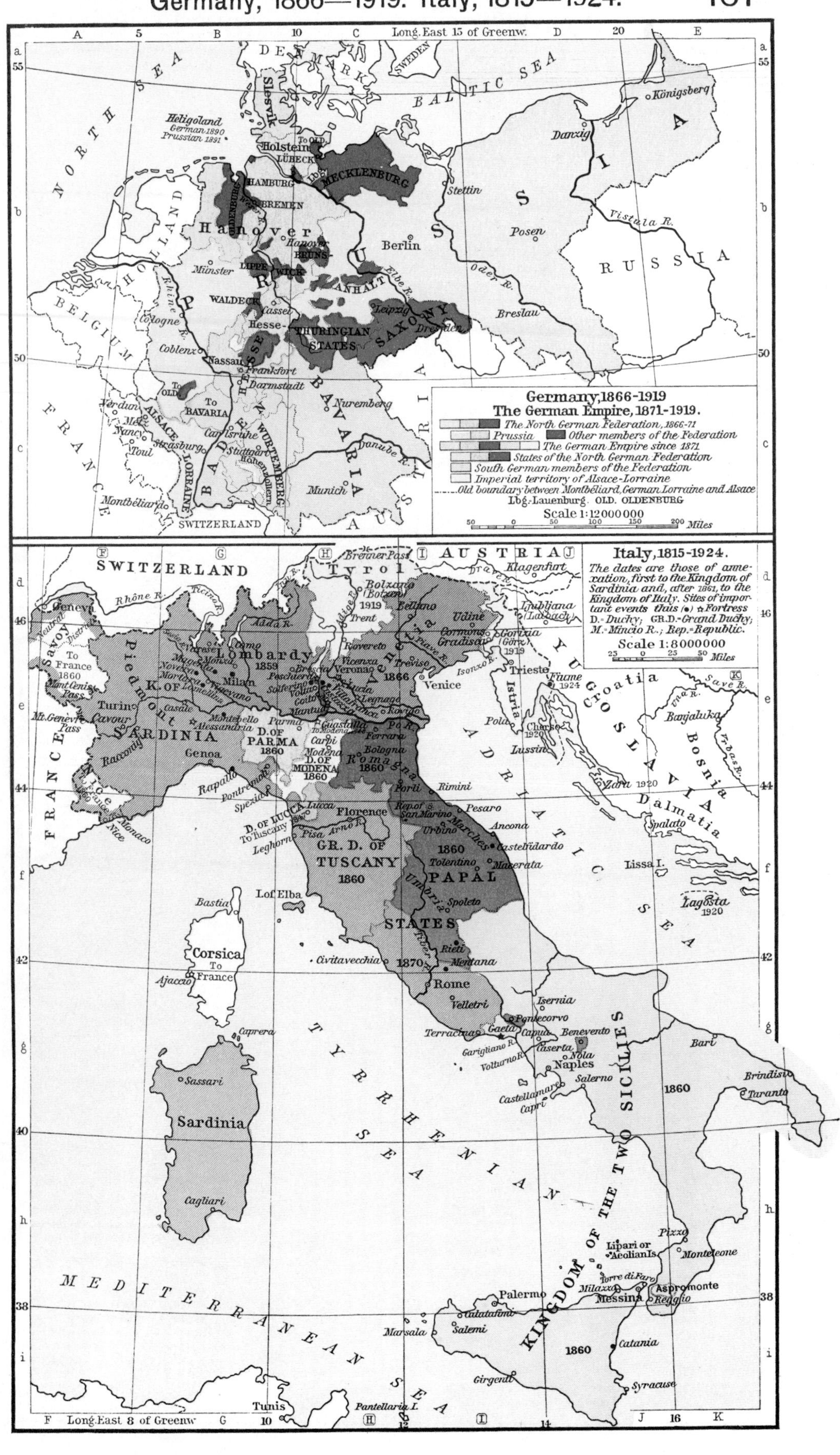
Germany, 1866-1919
The German Empire, 1871-1919.
The North German Federation, 1866-71
Prussia
Other members of the Federation
The German Empire since 1871
States of the North German Federation
South German members of the Federation
Imperial territory of Alsace-Lorraine
Old boundary between Montbéliard, German Lorraine and Alsace
Lbg.-Lauenburg. OLD. OLDENBURG
Scale 1:12000000
Miles
Italy, 1815-1924.
The dates are those of annexation, first to the Kingdom of Sardinia and, after 1861, to the Kingdom of Italy. Sites of important events thus (•) ☆ Fortress
D. = Duchy; GR.D. = Grand Duchy; M. = Mincio R.; Rep. = Republic.
Scale 1:8000000
Miles
NORTH SEA
BALTIC SEA
PRUSSIA
RUSSIA
BELGIUM
FRANCE
SWITZERLAND
AUSTRIA
BAVARIA
SAXONY
MECKLENBURG
Hanover
KINGDOM OF SARDINIA
GR. D. OF TUSCANY
PAPAL STATES
KINGDOM OF THE TWO SICILIES
ADRIATIC SEA
TYRRHENIAN SEA
MEDITERRANEAN SEA
YUGOSLAVIA
Corsica To France
Sardinia

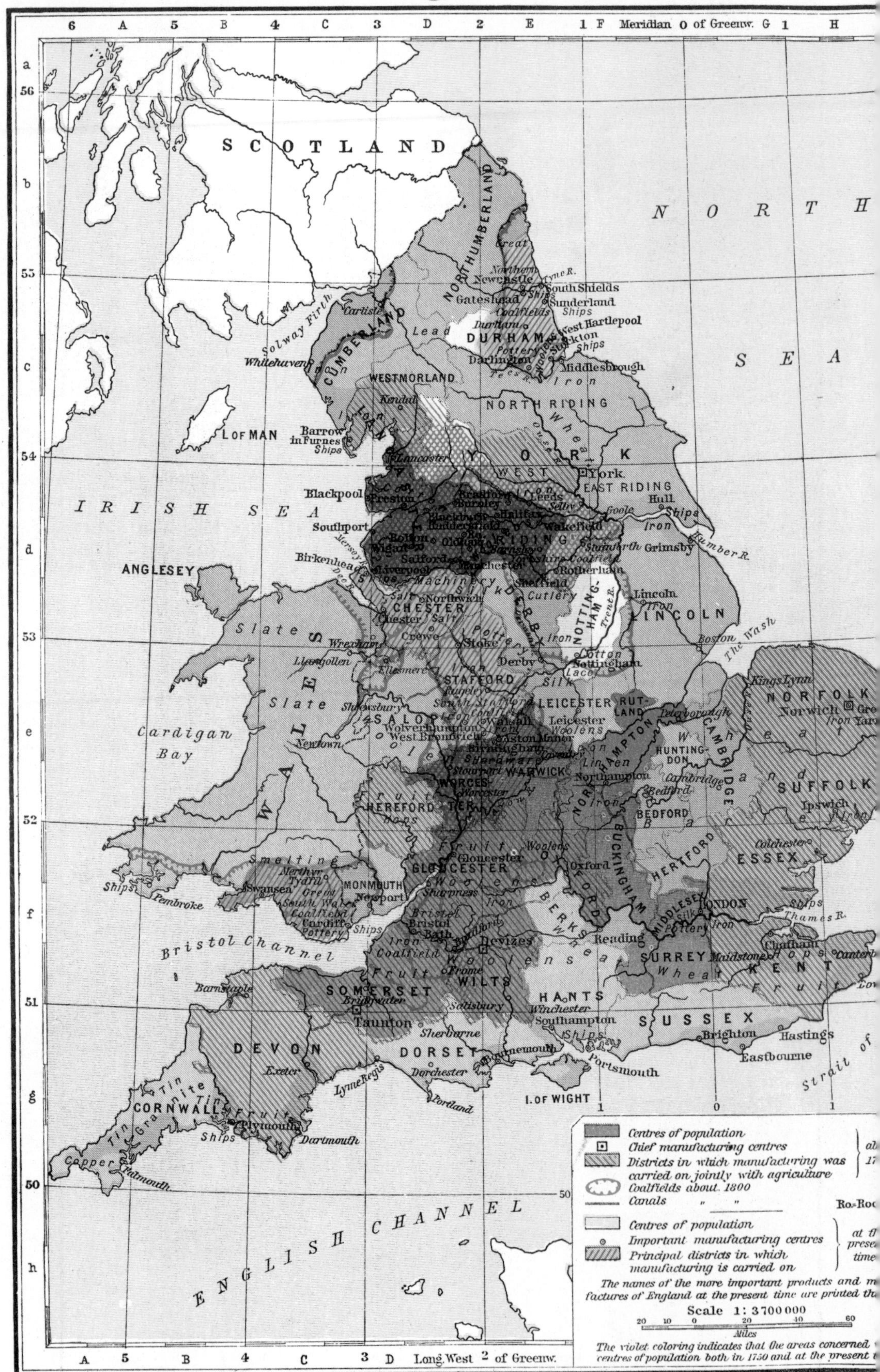
Meridian 0 of Greenw.
Long. West 2 of Greenw.
SCOTLAND
NORTH SEA
IRISH SEA
I. OF MAN
ANGLESEY
WALES
Cardigan Bay
Bristol Channel
ENGLISH CHANNEL
Strait of
Solway Firth
NORTHUMBERLAND
CUMBERLAND
DURHAM
WESTMORLAND
NORTH RIDING
YORK
WEST
EAST RIDING
RIDING
LANCASTER
CHESTER
DERBY
NOTTINGHAM
LINCOLN
STAFFORD
SALOP
LEICESTER
RUTLAND
NORFOLK
SUFFOLK
CAMBRIDGE
HUNTINGDON
NORTHAMPTON
WARWICK
WORCESTER
HEREFORD
MONMOUTH
GLOUCESTER
OXFORD
BUCKINGHAM
BEDFORD
HERTFORD
ESSEX
MIDDLESEX
BERKS
SURREY
KENT
SUSSEX
HANTS
WILTS
SOMERSET
DORSET
DEVON
CORNWALL
I. OF WIGHT
Carlisle
Whitehaven
Newcastle
Gateshead
South Shields
Sunderland
West Hartlepool
Stockton
Durham
Darlington
Middlesbrough
Kendal
Barrow in Furness
Lancaster
York
Blackpool
Preston
Bradford
Leeds
Burnley
Blackburn
Halifax
Huddersfield
Wakefield
Southport
Bolton
Wigan
Oldham
Barnsley
Salford
Manchester
Liverpool
Birkenhead
Selby
Goole
Hull
Grimsby
Rotherham
Sheffield
Northwich
Chester
Crewe
Wrexham
Llangollen
Ellesmere
Stoke
Derby
Nottingham
Lincoln
Boston
The Wash
King's Lynn
Norwich
Great Yarmouth
Shrewsbury
Newtown
Wolverhampton
West Bromwich
Walsall
Birmingham
Aston Manor
Coventry
Stourport
Worcester
Leicester
Peterborough
Northampton
Cambridge
Bedford
Ipswich
Colchester
Merthyr Tydfil
Swansea
Pembroke
Newport
Cardiff
Gloucester
Sharpness
Oxford
Bristol
Bath
Devizes
Frome
Reading
London
Maidstone
Chatham
Canterbury
Barnstaple
Bridgwater
Taunton
Salisbury
Winchester
Southampton
Brighton
Hastings
Eastbourne
Sherborne
Bournemouth
Portsmouth
Dorchester
Exeter
Lyme Regis
Portland
Plymouth
Dartmouth
Falmouth
Coal
Coalfields
Coalfield
Iron
Ships
Lead
Wheat
Salt
Machinery
Cutlery
Pottery
Slate
Cotton
Lace
Silk
Woolens
Linen
Hardware
Fruit
Hops
Smelting
Tin
Granite
Copper
Yorkshire Coalfield
South Staffordshire Coalfield
South Wales Coalfield
Tyne R.
Tees R.
Ouse R.
Mersey R.
Dee R.
Trent R.
Humber R.
Thames R.
Centres of population
Chief manufacturing centres
Districts in which manufacturing was carried on jointly with agriculture
Coalfields about 1800
Canals " "
Centres of population
Important manufacturing centres
Principal districts in which manufacturing is carried on
The names of the more important products and
factures of England at the present time are printed
Scale 1: 3 700 000
Miles
The violet coloring indicates that the areas concerned
centres of population both in 1750 and at the present

Meridian 0 of Greenw.
Ab. = Abingdon
Am. = Amersham
And. = Andover
Ayl. = Aylesbury
B.A. = Bere Alston
Blet. = Bletchingley
Chelt. = Cheltenham
Chipp = Chippenham
Ch.Wyc. = Chipping Wycombe
Chr. = Christchurch
Cirenc. = Cirencester
Crick. = Cricklade
E. = East
E.S. = East Surrey
Finsb. = Finsbury
Gat. = Gatton
Greenw. = Greenwich
Gr.M. = Great Marlow
Guildf. = Guildford
Heyt. = Heytesbury
Hind. = Hindon
Hudd. = Huddersfield
Kidderm. = Kidderminster
Lamb. = Lambeth
Lisk. = Liskeard
Malm. = Malmesbury
Marlb. = Marlborough
Maryleb. = Marylebone
MIDD. = Middlesex
Milb. = Milborne Port
N. = North
New Wood. = New Woodstock
NOTT. = Nottingham
Old S. = Old Sarum
Petersf. = Petersfield
Read. = Reading
S. = South
Salf. = Salford
Salisb. = Salisbury
Sherb. = Sherborne
Southw. = Southwark
Tewkesb. = Tewkesbury
W. = West
Wall. = Wallingford
Warr. = Warrington
W.B. = Wootton Bassett
We. = Wendover
Westm. = Westminster
Winch. = Winchester
Wolv. = Wolverhampton
Worc. = Worcester
ENGLAND AND WALES
showing the system of representation in the House of Commons before and after the Reform Act of 1832
Haslemere — Borough returning two members before 1832 } disfranchised in 1832
Higham Ferrers — " one member " "
St. Ives — " that had its representation reduced in 1832
Birmingham — " enfranchised in 1832, and returning two members
Tynemouth — " " " " " one member
Nottingham — " returning two members before and after 1832
Abingdon — " " one member " " " "
OXFORD — County " three members after 1832
BEDFORD — " " two " " "
SOUTH DEVON — Division of county returning two members after 1832.
Before 1832 each county in England returned two members, and each county in Wales one member; after 1832 nine counties in Wales, only, returned one member.
Scale 1:3700000
Miles

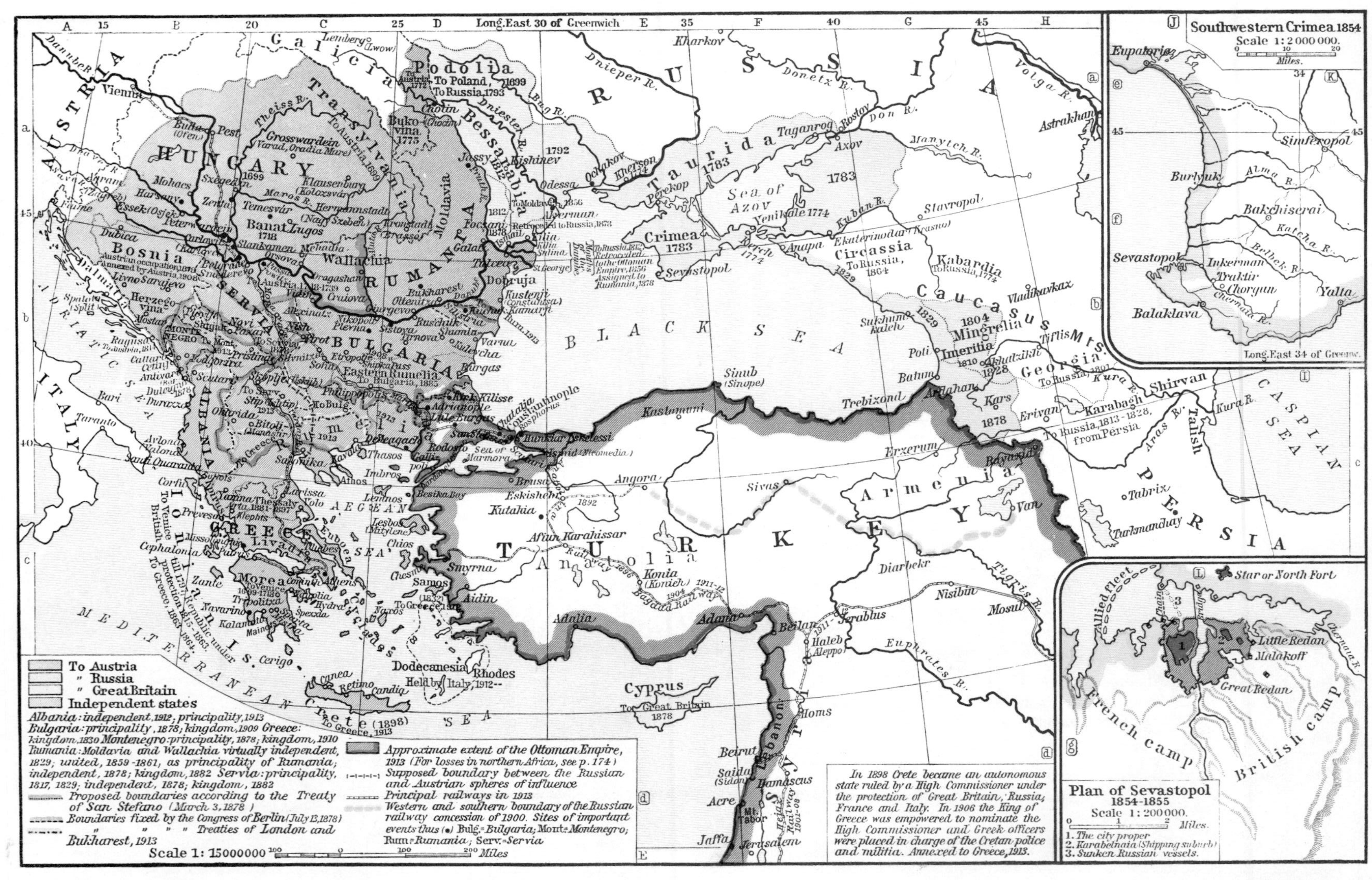
Southwestern Crimea 1854
Scale 1:2 000 000.
Plan of Sevastopol 1854-1855
Scale 1:200000.
1. The city proper
2. Karabelnaia (Shipping suburb)
3. Sunken Russian vessels.
French camp
British camp
Allied fleet
CASPIAN SEA
PERSIA
BLACK SEA
RUSSIA
TURKEY
Anatolia
Armenia
Caucasus
Bessarabia
Transylvania
HUNGARY
BULGARIA
SERVIA
ALBANIA
GREECE
RUMANIA
AUSTRIA
ITALY
MEDITERRANEAN SEA
AEGEAN SEA
Crimea
Cyprus
Crete (1898)
In 1898 Crete became an autonomous state ruled by a High Commissioner under the protection of Great Britain, Russia, France and Italy. In 1906 the King of Greece was empowered to nominate the High Commissioner and Greek officers were placed in charge of the Cretan police and militia. Annexed to Greece, 1913.
To Austria
" Russia
" Great Britain
Independent states
Albania: independent, 1912; principality, 1913
Bulgaria: principality, 1878; kingdom, 1909 Greece: kingdom, 1830 Montenegro: principality, 1878; kingdom, 1910
Rumania: Moldavia and Wallachia virtually independent, 1829; united, 1859-1861, as principality of Rumania; independent, 1878; kingdom, 1882 Servia: principality, 1817, 1829; independent, 1878; kingdom, 1882
Proposed boundaries according to the Treaty of San Stefano (March 3, 1878)
Boundaries fixed by the Congress of Berlin (July 13, 1878)
" " " Treaties of London and Bukharest, 1913
Approximate extent of the Ottoman Empire, 1913 (For losses in northern Africa, see p. 174)
Supposed boundary between the Russian and Austrian spheres of influence
Principal railways in 1913
Western and southern boundary of the Russian railway concession of 1900. Sites of important events thus (•) Bulg.=Bulgaria, Mont.=Montenegro; Rum.=Rumania, Serv.=Servia
Scale 1: 15000000

Peoples of Southeastern Europe and Asia Minor in 1913.

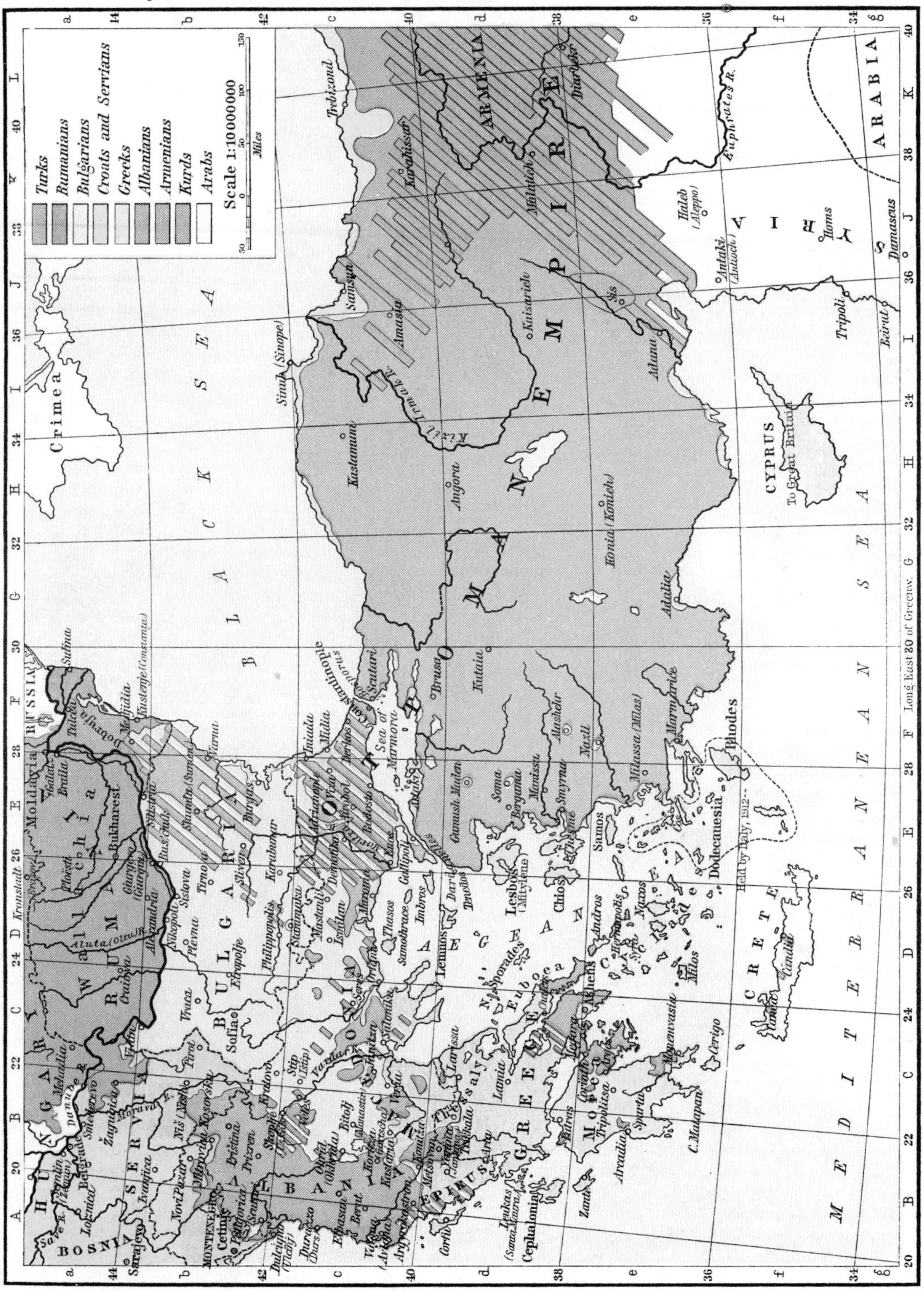

Turks
Rumanians
Bulgarians
Croats and Servians
Greeks
Albanians
Armenians
Kurds
Arabs

Scale 1:10000000

50 0 50 100 150 Miles

Long. East 30 of Greenw.

Illinois, 56,650 sq. miles in comparison with Europe
Meridian 0 of Greenwich
Jan Mayen
Arctic Circle
Iceland (To Denmark)
A T L A N T I C O C E A N
Faröe Is. (To Denmark)
Orkney Is.
Shetland Is.
The Hebrides
Malin Head
Valencia I.
IRELAND
Sligo
Dublin
Cork
GREAT BRITAIN
Inverness
Aberdeen
Dundee
Edinburgh
Glasgow
Newcastle
Leeds
Hull
Sheffield
Manchester
Liverpool
Birmingham
Cardiff
Bristol
Portsmouth
London
Str. of Dover
ENGLISH CHANNEL
Channel Is.
NORTH SEA
Kristiansund
Aalesund
Dovre Fjeld
Bergen
Christiania
Stavanger
Egersund
The Naze
Kristiansand
Arendal
Laurvik
SKAGER RAK
Kattegat
Göteborg
Copenhagen
Esbjerg
Heligoland (To Germany, 1890)
Bornholm
Hamburg
Bremen
Hanover
Berlin
Stettin
Magdeburg
Leipzig
Düsseldorf
Cologne
Cassel
Chemnitz
Dresden
Halle
Amsterdam
The Hague
Rotterdam
Antwerp
Brussels
Lille
Le Havre
Brest
Rennes
Le Mans
Rouen
Amiens
Reims
Paris
Versailles
Orleans
Angers
Nantes
Nancy
Troyes
Poitiers
La Rochelle
Limoges
Angoulême
Bordeaux
Clermont
St. Etienne
Lyons
Besançon
Grenoble
Cevennes
Toulouse
Nimes
Marseilles
Perpignan
Toulon
Nice (To France 1860)
Monaco
FRANCE
Nuremberg
Stuttgart
Munich
Augsburg
Vienna
Gratz
Pilsen
Brünn
Olmütz
AUSTRIA
Berne
SWITZERLAND
Milan
Turin
Genoa
Parma
Bologna
Venice
Trieste
Florence
Leghorn
Ancona
ADRIATIC SEA
ITALY
Rome
Naples
Mt. Vesuvius
Taranto
Foggia
Corsica
Ajaccio
Sardinia
Sassari
Cagliari
TYRRHENIAN SEA
Palermo
Messina
Sicily
Catania
Reggio
Malta (Brit.)
IONIAN
C. Ortegal
Corunna
C. Finisterre
Santiago
Vigo
Oporto
Braga
Coimbra
Lisbon
Setúbal
C. St. Vincent
Lagos
Tavira
PORTUGAL
Santander
Bilbao
Pamplona
Vitoria
Valladolid
Burgos
Léon
Salamanca
Madrid
Saragossa
Lerida
Catalonia
Gerona
Barcelona
Tarragona
Tortosa
Toledo
Valencia
Castellon de la Plana
Badajoz
Sierra Morena
Cordova
Seville
Huelva
Ciudad Real
Albacete
Murcia
Alicante
Cartagena
Granada
Sierra Nevada
Malaga
Cadiz
Algeciras
Gibraltar (Brit.)
Almeria
Tangier
Ceuta (Sp.)
Melilla (Sp.)
SPAIN
Pyrenees
Andorra
Balearic Is.
Majorca
Minorca
Iviza
Palma
Formentera
MEDITERRANEAN
Algiers
Oran
Bougie
Constantine
Bone
Tunis
TUNIS
Fr. Prot. 1881
Kairwan
ALGERIA
To France, 1830
Rabat
Casablanca
Fez
MOROCCO
French Protectorate, 1912
Marakesh (Marocco)
Bosnia
Sarajevo
Dalmatia
Agram (Zagreb)
Lofoten Is.
West Fiord
Bernösand
Sundsvall
Karlstad
Jönköping
Kalmar
Halmstad
Hälsingborg
Malmö
Aalborg
Aarhus
Kiel
Lübeck
Posen
Breslau

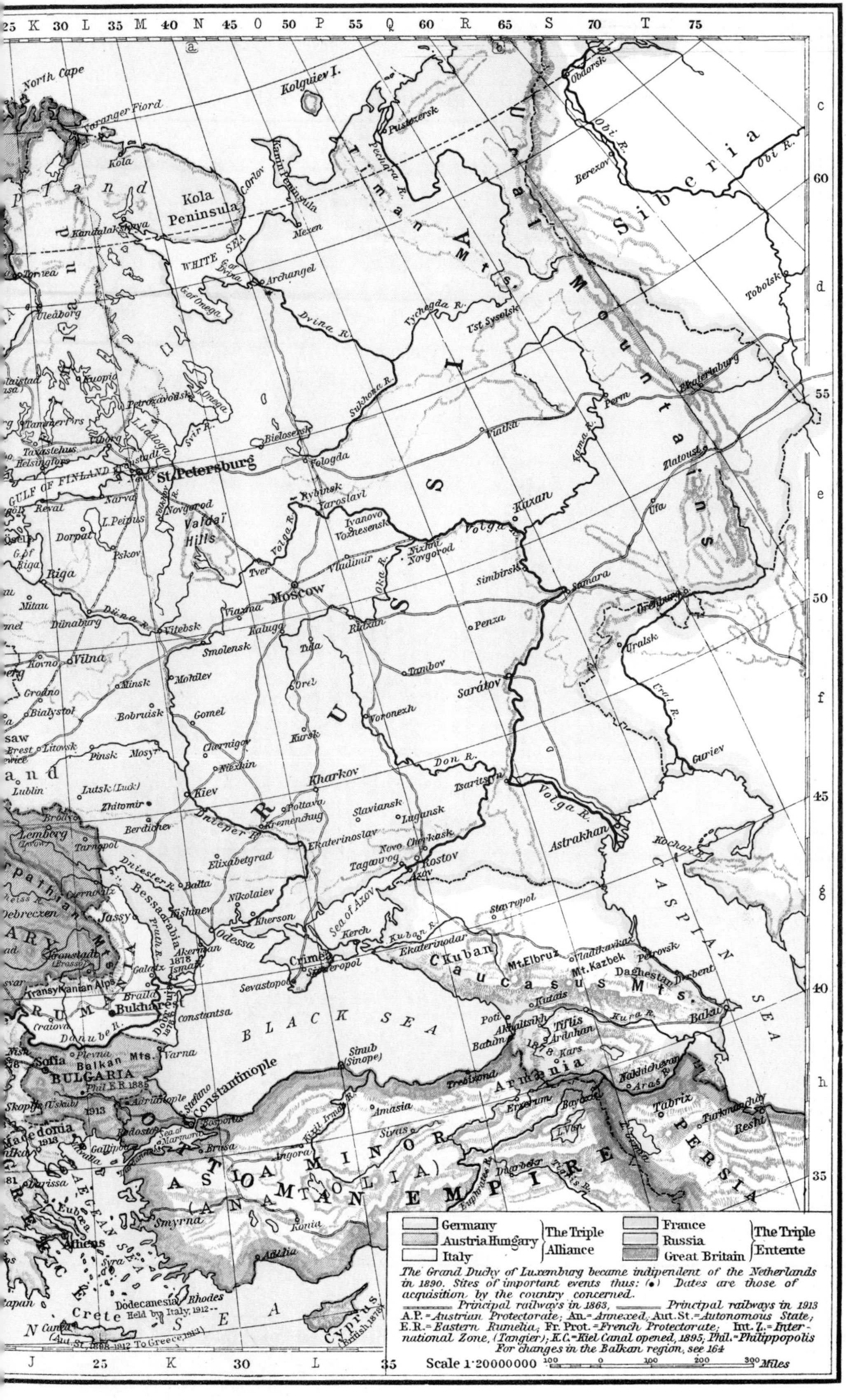
Germany
Austria Hungary
Italy
The Triple Alliance
France
Russia
Great Britain
The Triple Entente
The Grand Duchy of Luxemburg became indipendent of the Netherlands in 1890. Sites of important events thus: (•) Dates are those of acquisition by the country concerned.
Principal railways in 1863, Principal railways in 1913
A.P.=Austrian Protectorate; An.=Annexed; Aut.St.=Autonomous State; E.R.=Eastern Rumelia; Fr. Prot.=French Protectorate; Int. Z.=International Zone, (Tangier); K.C.=Kiel Canal opened, 1895; Phil.=Philippopolis
For changes in the Balkan region, see 164
Scale 1:20000000
100 0 100 200 300 Miles
North Cape
Kolguiev I.
Varanger Fiord
Kola
Kola Peninsula
Kanin Peninsula
Pustozersk
Pechora R.
Mezen
WHITE SEA
Archangel
G. of Onega
Dvina R.
Tychegda R.
Ust Sysolsk
Obdorsk
Obi R.
Berezov
Siberia
Tobolsk
Ural Mountains
Timan Mts.
Uleaborg
Kuopio
Petrozavodsk
L. Onega
L. Ladoga
Svir R.
Bielosersk
Sukhona R.
Viatka
Perm
Kama R.
Ekaterinburg
Zlatoust
Ufa
Tavastehus
Helsingfors
Viborg
Kronstadt
GULF OF FINLAND
St. Petersburg
Vologda
Reval
Narva
Novgorod
L. Peipus
Valdai Hills
Dorpat
Pskov
Ösel
G. of Riga
Riga
Rybinsk
Yaroslavl
Ivanovo Voznesensk
Kazan
Volga R.
Nizhni Novgorod
Vladimir
Tver
Moscow
Oka R.
Simbirsk
Samara
Orenburg
Mitau
Dünaburg
Düna R.
Vitebsk
Viazma
Kaluga
Riazan
Penza
Uralsk
Smolensk
Tula
Tambov
Kovno
Vilna
Grodno
Minsk
Mohilev
Orel
Saratov
Ural R.
Bialystok
Bobruisk
Gomel
Voronezh
Brest Litovsk
Pinsk
Mosyr
Kursk
Chernigov
Nezhin
Don R.
Guriev
Lublin
Lutsk (Luck)
Zhitomir
Kiev
Kharkov
Tsaritsyn
Poltava
Kremenchug
Slaviansk
Lugansk
Astrakhan
Brody
Berdichev
Dnieper R.
Lemberg
Tarnopol
Ekaterinoslav
Novo Cherkask
Taganrog
Rostov
Azov
Elizabetgrad
Dniester R.
Balta
Bessarabia
Nikolaiev
Kishinev
Jassy
Kherson
Odessa
Sea of Azov
Kerch
Kuban R.
Stavropol
Ekaterinodar
Kuban
Crimea
Simferopol
Sevastopol
Mt. Elbruz
Vladikavkaz
Mt. Kazbek
Petrovsk
Daghestan
Derbent
Caucasus Mts.
CASPIAN SEA
Kutais
Poti
Tiflis
Akhaltsikh
Ardahan
Batum
Kars
Kura R.
Baku
Akerman
Ismail
Galatz
Braila
Bukharest
Craiova
Danube R.
Dobruja
Constantsa
BLACK SEA
Sinub (Sinope)
Varna
Sofia
Plevna
Balkan Mts.
BULGARIA
Phil. E.R. 1885
Adrianople
Stefano
Constantinople
Trebizond
Armenia
Nakhichevan
Aras R.
Tabriz
Turkmanchay
Resht
Erzerum
Bayazid
L. Van
Amasia
Kizil Irmak R.
Bosporus
Rodosto
Sea of Marmora
Gallipoli
Brusa
Sivas
Angora
ASIA MINOR (ANATOLIA)
OTTOMAN EMPIRE
Euphrates R.
Diarbekr
Tigris R.
PERSIA
Macedonia
Skoplje (Üskub)
1913
AEGEAN SEA
Larissa
Euboea
Athens
Smyrna
Konia
Adalia
Syra
Dodecanesia
Rhodes
Held by Italy, 1912
Crete
Canea
(Aut. St. 1898-1912 To Greece, 1913)
Cyprus (British, 1878)
SEA
J 25 K 30 L 35
25 K 30 L 35 M 40 N 45 O 50 P 55 Q 60 R 65 S 70 T 75
c 60 d 55 e 50 f 45 g 40 h 35

Peoples of Austria-Hungary in 1914.

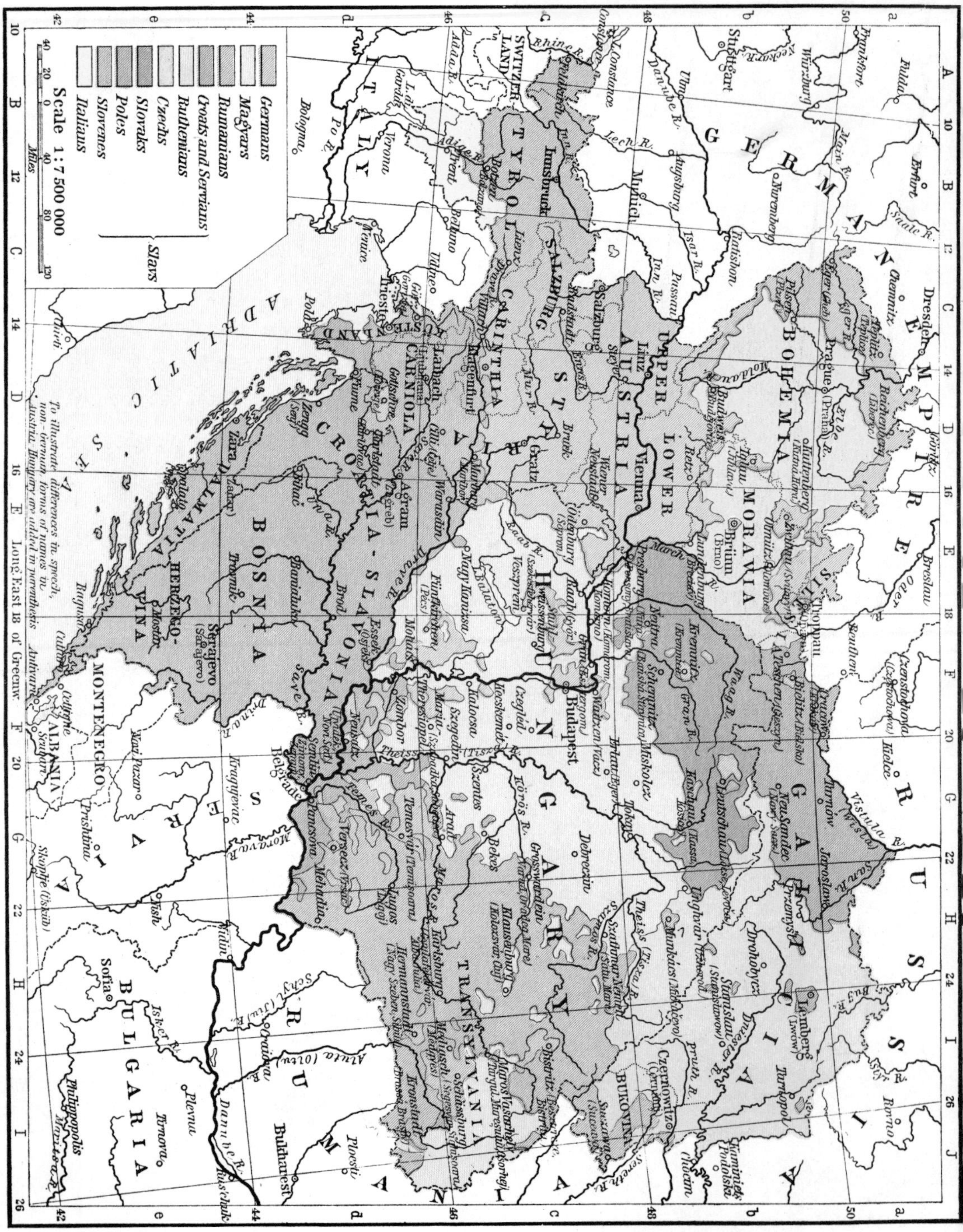

Germans
Magyars
Rumanians
Croats and Servians
Ruthenians
Czechs
Slovaks
Poles
Slovenes
Italians

Slavs

Scale 1:7 500 000

Miles

To illustrate differences in speech, non-German forms of names in Austria-Hungary are added in parenthesis.

The World at War, 1914—1918.

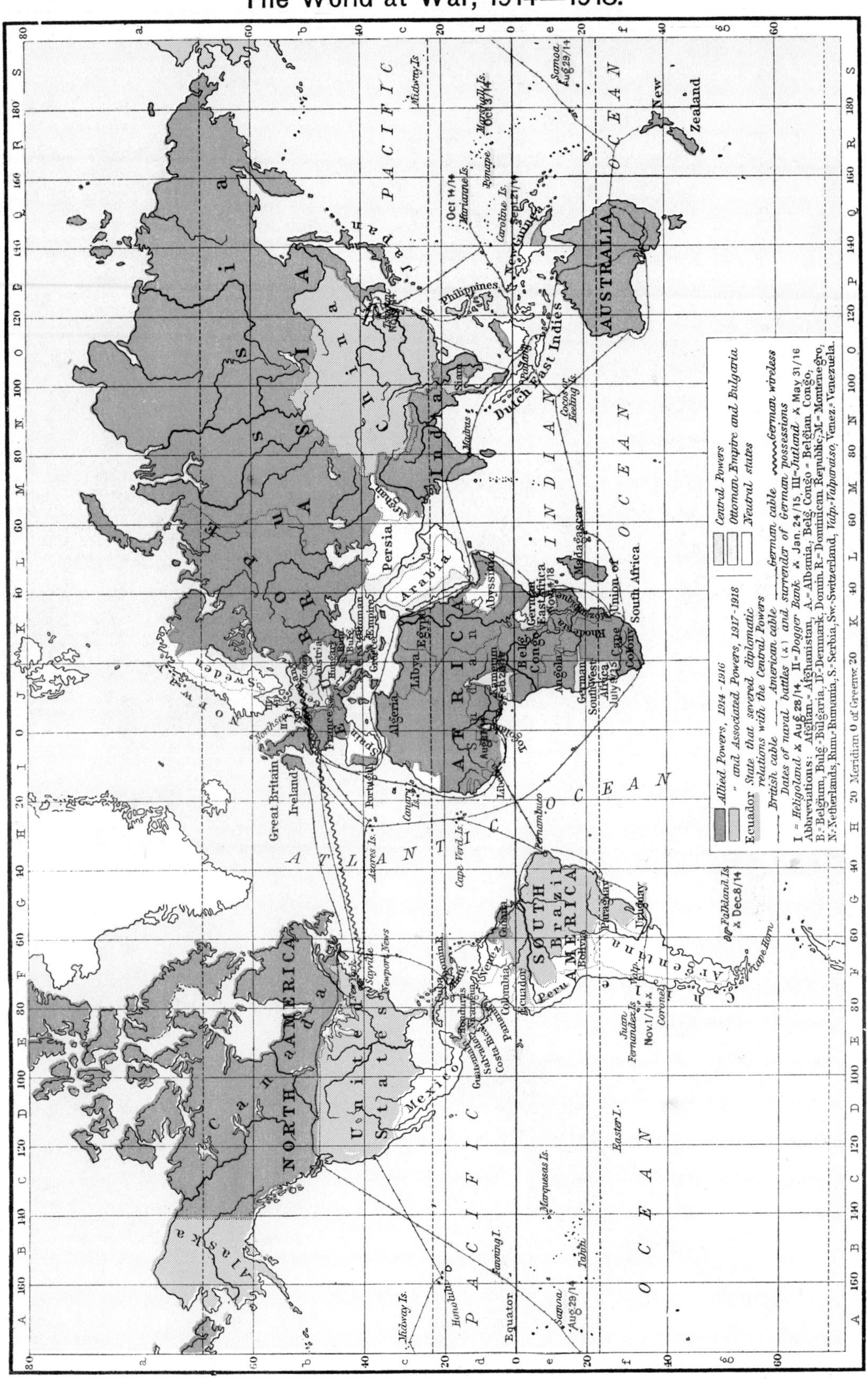

Principal Seats of War, 1914—1918.

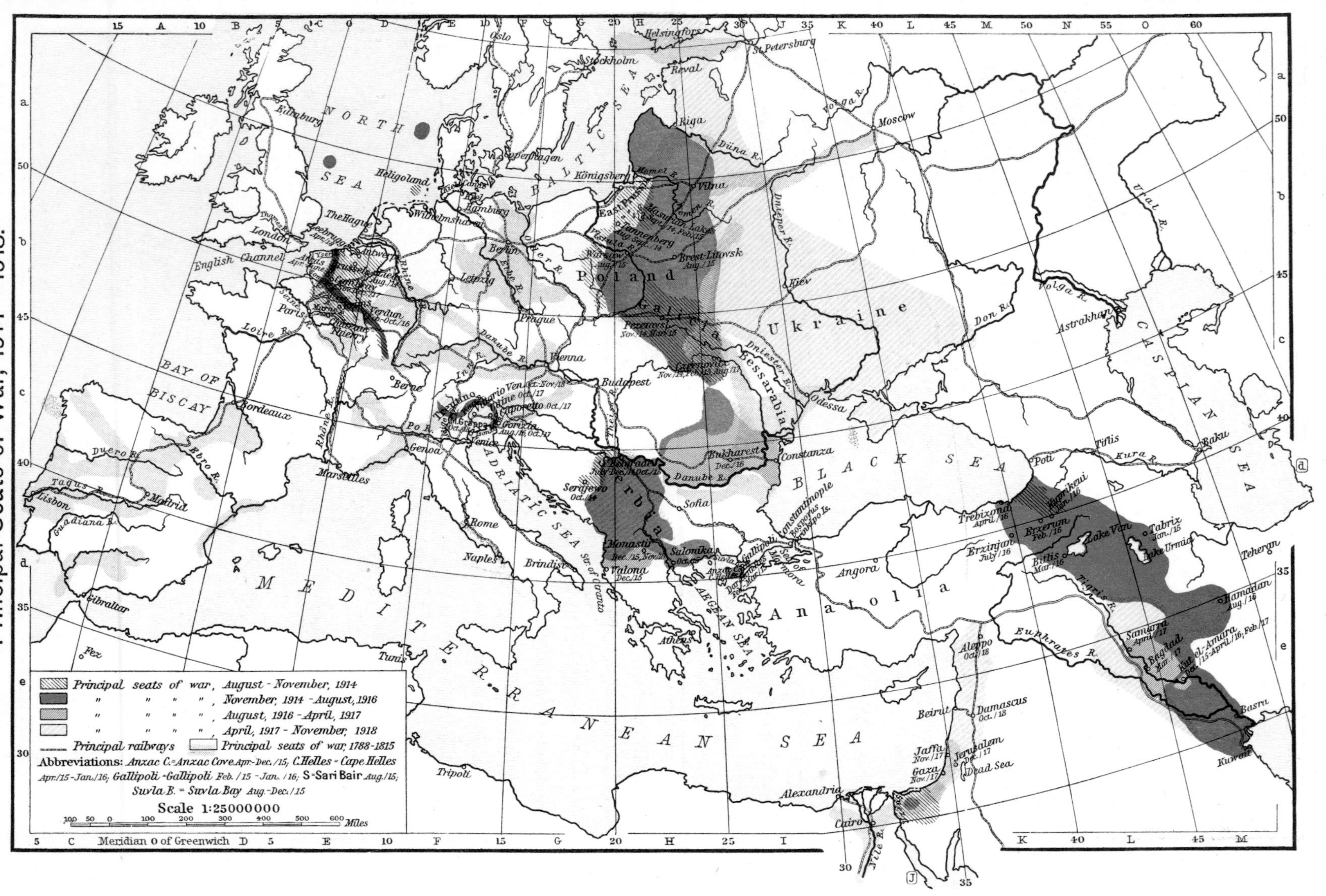

The Western European Front, 1914—1918.

Treaty Adjustments, 1919—1926.

For the Rhineland see p 168E

Treaty Adjustments, 1919—1926. The Rhineland.

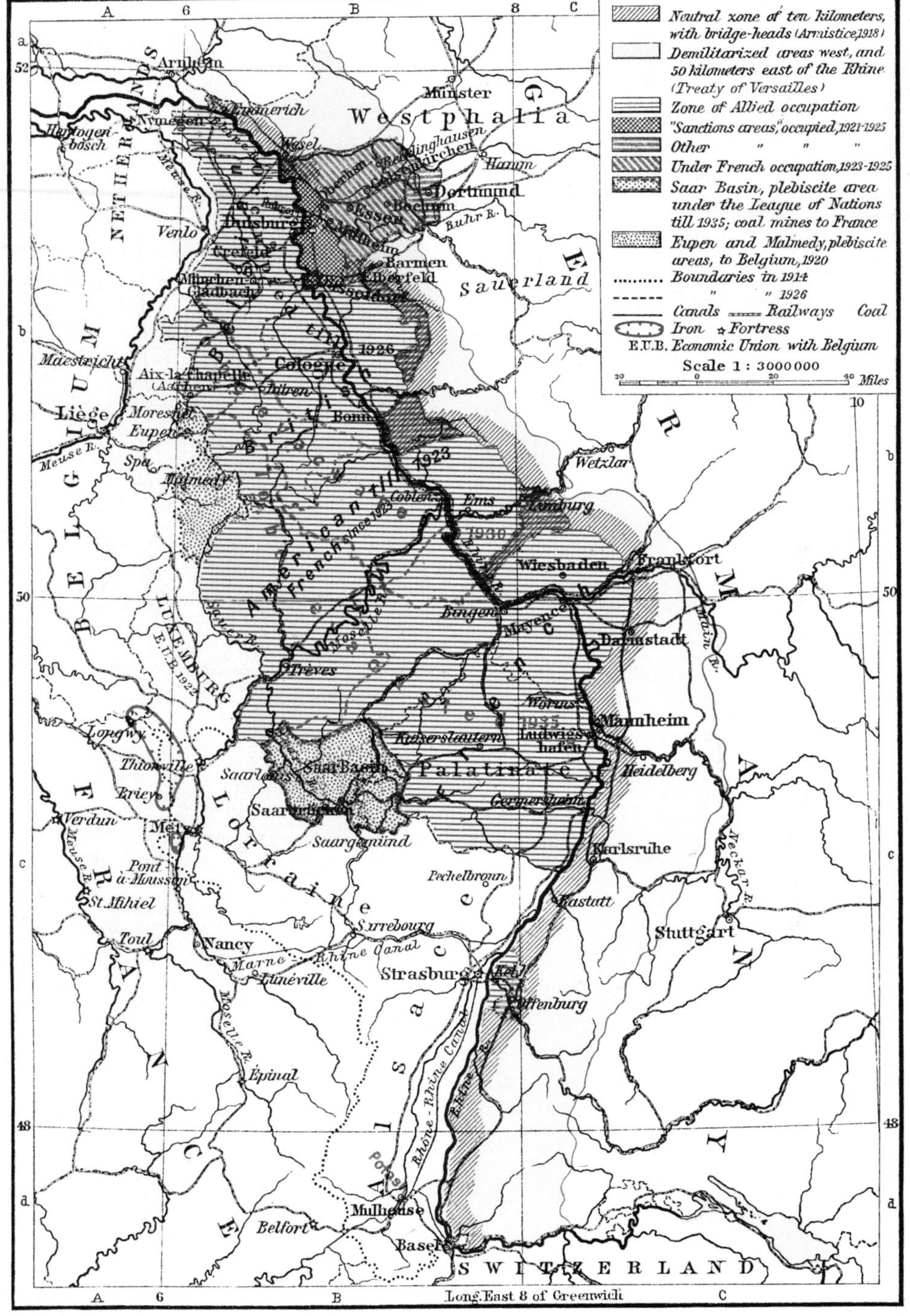

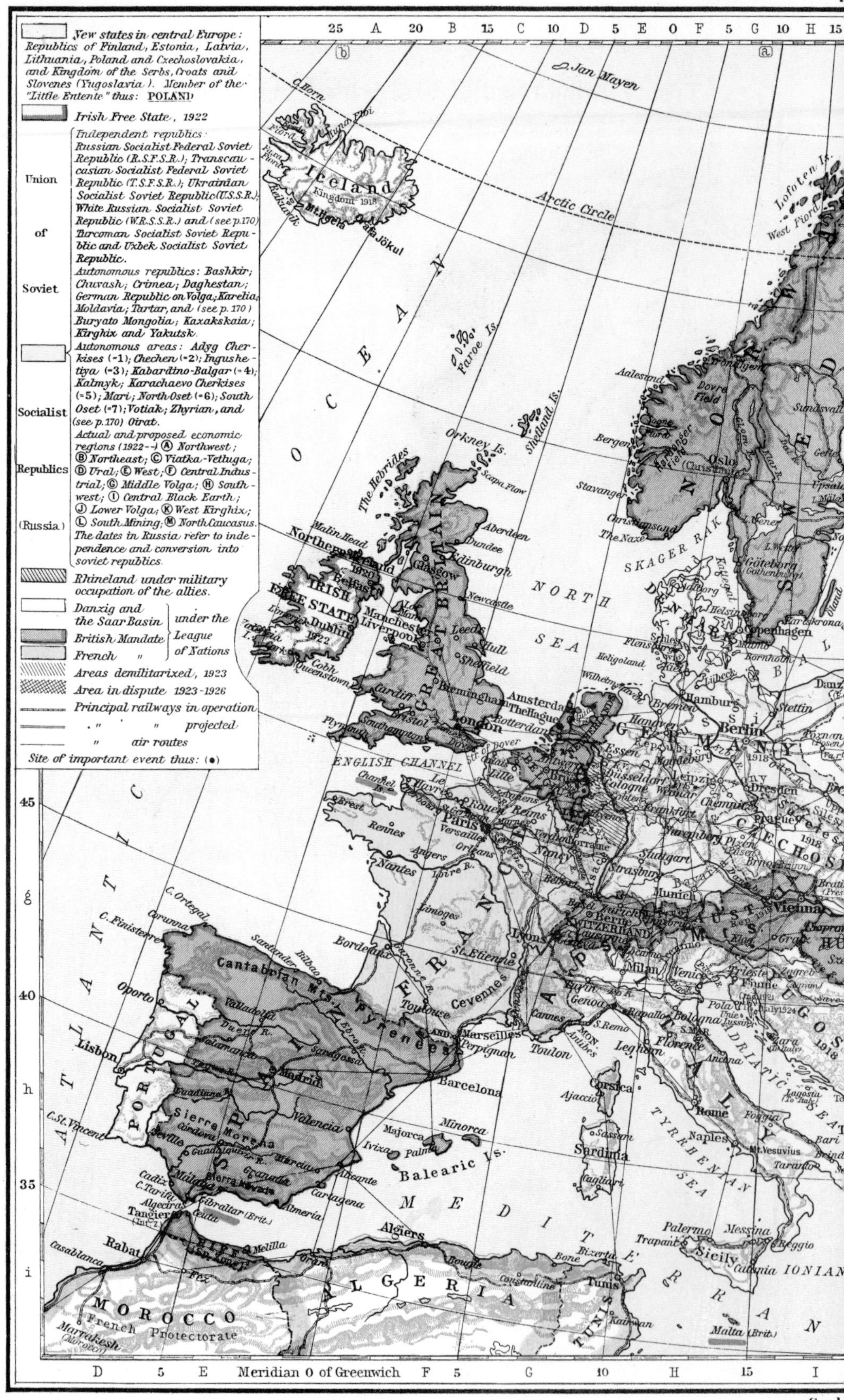
New states in central Europe: Republics of Finland, Estonia, Latvia, Lithuania, Poland and Czechoslovakia, and Kingdom of the Serbs, Croats and Slovenes (Yugoslavia). Member of the "Little Entente" thus: POLAND
Irish Free State, 1922
Union of Soviet Socialist Republics (Russia)
Independent republics: Russian Socialist Federal Soviet Republic (R.S.F.S.R.); Transcaucasian Socialist Federal Soviet Republic (T.S.F.S.R.); Ukrainian Socialist Soviet Republic (U.S.S.R.); White Russian Socialist Soviet Republic (W.R.S.S.R.) and (see p.170) Turcoman Socialist Soviet Republic and Uzbek Socialist Soviet Republic.
Autonomous republics: Bashkir; Chuvash; Crimea; Daghestan; German Republic on Volga; Karelia; Moldavia; Tartar, and (see p. 170) Buryato Mongolia; Kazakskaia; Kirghiz and Yakutsk.
Autonomous areas: Adyg Cherkises (-1); Chechen (-2); Ingushetiya (-3); Kabardino-Balgar (-4); Kalmyk; Karachaevo Cherkises (-5); Mari; North Oset (-6); South Oset (-7); Votiak; Zhyrian, and (see p.170) Oirat.
Actual and proposed economic regions (1922--) Ⓐ Northwest; Ⓑ Northeast; Ⓒ Viatka-Vetluga; Ⓓ Ural; Ⓔ West; Ⓕ Central Industrial; Ⓖ Middle Volga; Ⓗ Southwest; Ⓘ Central Black Earth; Ⓙ Lower Volga; Ⓚ West Kirghiz; Ⓛ South Mining; Ⓜ North Caucasus. The dates in Russia refer to independence and conversion into soviet republics.
Rhineland under military occupation of the allies.
Danzig and the Saar Basin
British Mandate
French "
under the League of Nations
Areas demilitarized, 1923
Area in dispute 1923-1926
Principal railways in operation
" " projected
" air routes
Site of important event thus: (•)
Jan Mayen
Iceland
Kingdom 1918
Arctic Circle
Lofoten Is.
Faroe Is.
Shetland Is.
Orkney Is.
The Hebrides
ATLANTIC OCEAN
NORTH SEA
GREAT BRITAIN
IRISH FREE STATE
Northern Ireland
London
Paris
FRANCE
SPAIN
PORTUGAL
Madrid
Lisbon
Berlin
GERMANY
SWITZERLAND
ITALY
Rome
Corsica
Sardinia
Sicily
Balearic Is.
MEDITERRANEAN
ALGERIA
MOROCCO
French Protectorate
TUNIS
Malta (Brit.)
Gibraltar (Brit.)
ENGLISH CHANNEL
Meridian 0 of Greenwich

Abbreviations.
AND.=Andorra; E.=Eupen; Erf.=Erfurt; F.C.T.=Free City and Territory; F.D.R.=Federal Democratic Republic; Ind.=Independent; Int.Z.=International Zone (Tangier); Klag.=Klagenfurt; L.=Liechtenstein; Lith.=Lithuania; LUX.=Luxembourg; M.=Malmedy; MON.=Monaco; R.V.=Ruhr Valley; S.MAR.=San Marino; S.B.=Saar-Basin; Y.=Ypres; Ys.=Yugoslavia.
UNION OF SOVIET SOCIALIST REPUBLICS, 1922
RUSSIAN SOCIALIST FEDERAL SOVIET REPUBLIC, 1918
SIBERIA
RUSSIA
UKRAINE 1918, 1920
WHITE RUSSIA
Kazakskaia 1925
Kola Peninsula
Karelia 1923
FINLAND 1917
ESTONIA 1918
LATVIA 1918
LITHUANIA
RUMANIA
BULGARIA
TURKEY
ANATOLIA
Republic 1923
SYRIA
French Mandate 1920
MESOPOTAMIA
British Mandate 1920
IRAQ
PERSIA
TRANSCAUCASIA 1922
Georgia 1918, 1921
Armenia 1918, 1921
Azerbaijan 1918, 1920
Caucasus Mts.
BLACK SEA
CASPIAN SEA
AEGEAN SEA
Crimea 1921
Bessarabia
Moldavia 1924
Kalmyk 1920
Daghestan 1921
Bashkir 1919
Tartar 1920
Votiak 1920
Chuvash 1925
Ural Mts.
Timan Mts.
Moscow
Leningrad (Petrograd)
Archangel
Kiev
Kharkov
Odessa
Rostov
Tiflis
Baku
Angora
Constantinople
Smyrna
Athens
Bukharest
Sofia
Damascus
Bagdad
Cyprus (Brit.)
Crete
Dodecanese (To Italy, 1923)
Rhodes
Samara
Kazan
Astrakhan
Tsaritsyn
Saratov
Orenburg
Perm
Sverdlovsk (Ekaterinburg)
Tobolsk
Obdorsk
Vologda
Tver
Smolensk
Minsk
Vilnius (Vilna)
Kaunas (Kovno)
Riga
Tallinn (Reval)
Helsingfors
Gulf of Finland
White Sea
Kolguiev I.
North Cape
K 30 L 35 M 40 N 45 O 50 P 55 Q 60 R 65 S
J 25 K 30 L 35 M 40 N
60 55 50 45 40 35
d e f g h i

Peoples of Central Europe in 1929.

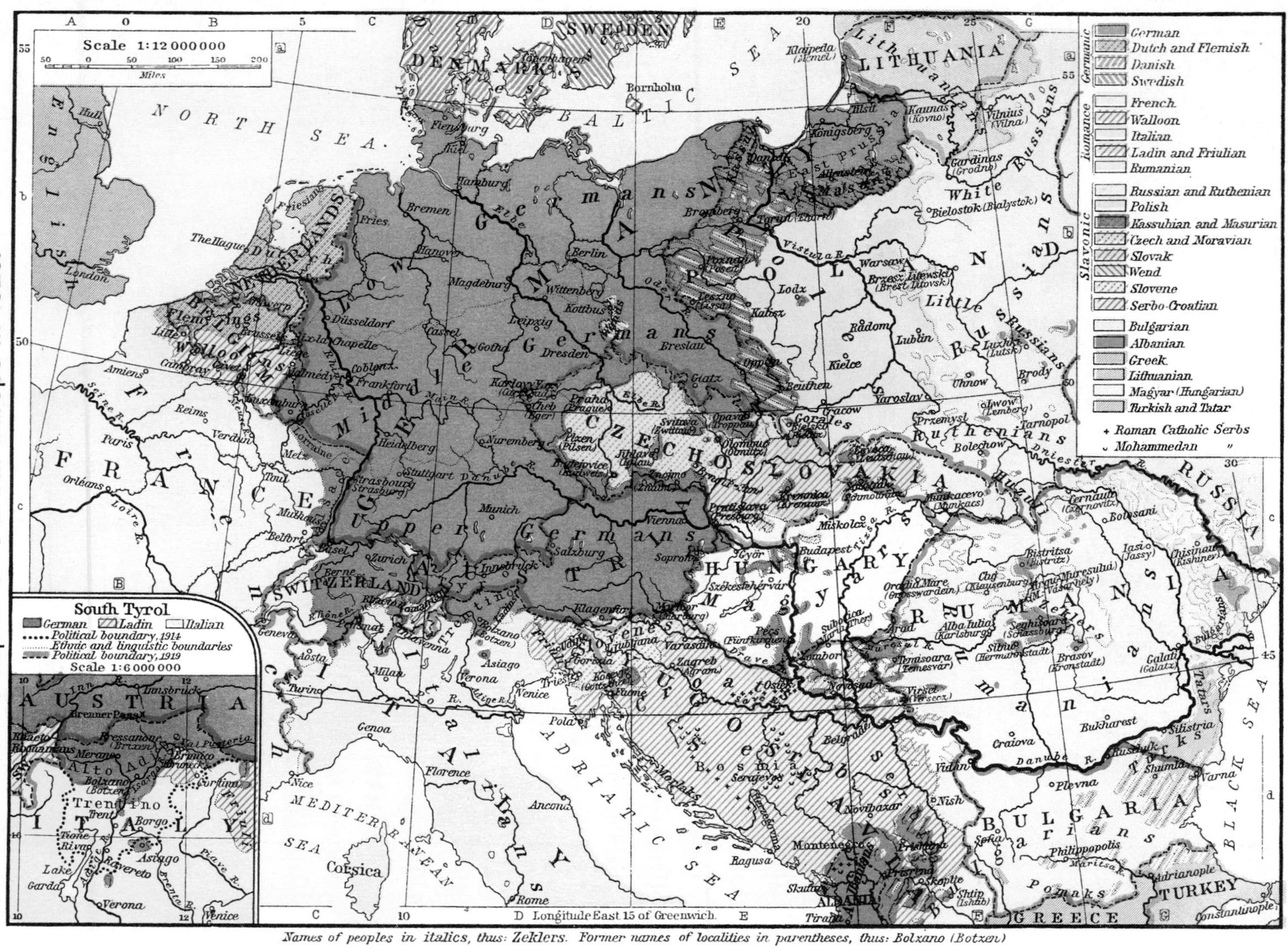

Names of peoples in italics, thus: Zeklers. Former names of localities in parentheses, thus: Bolzano (Botzen)

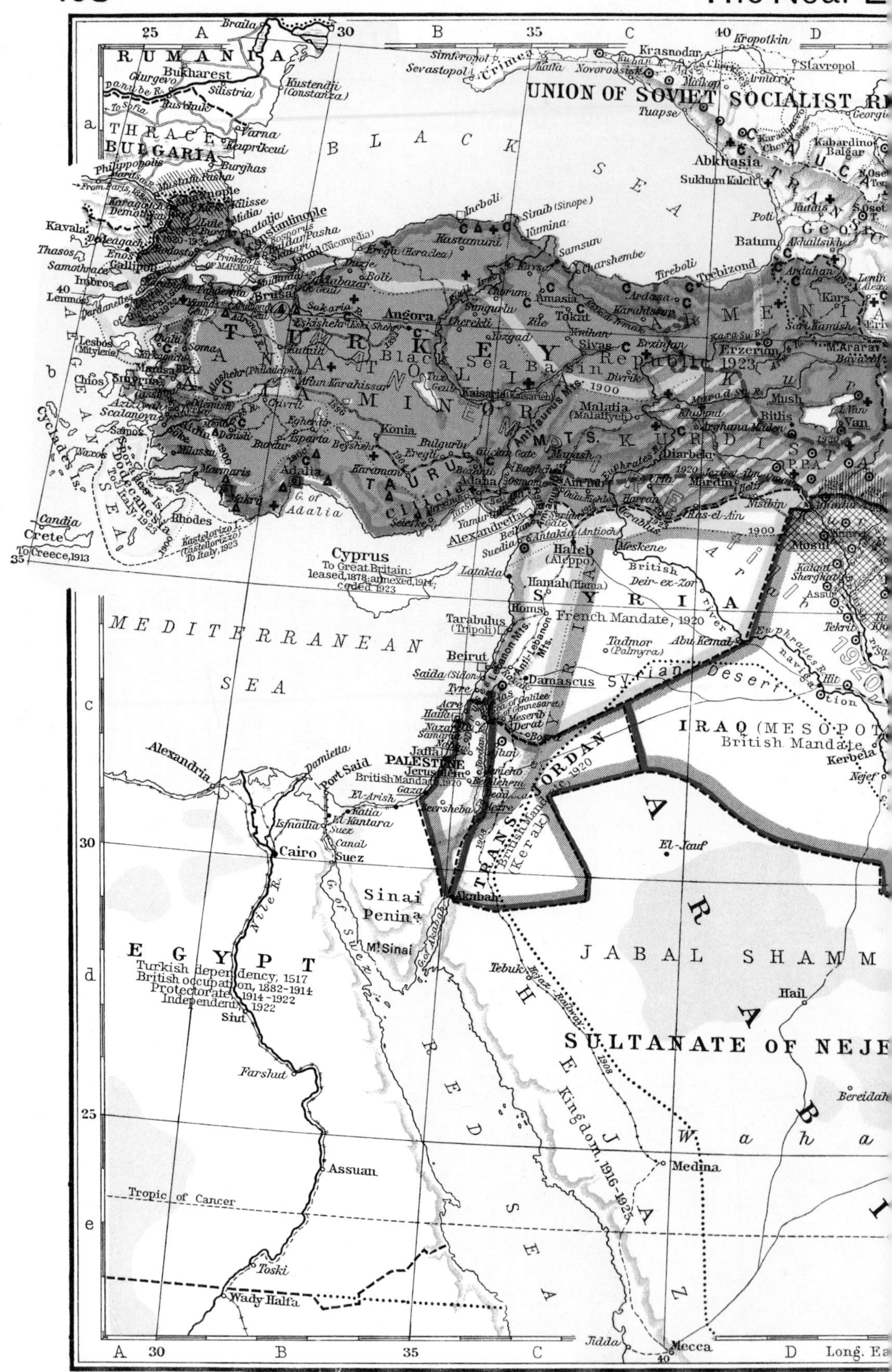
RUMANIA
UNION OF SOVIET SOCIALIST R
BLACK SEA
BULGARIA
TURKEY
ASIA MINOR
MEDITERRANEAN SEA
Cyprus
To Great Britain: leased,1878; annexed,1914; ceded 1923
SYRIA
French Mandate, 1920
IRAQ (MESOPOT
British Mandate
PALESTINE
British Mandate, 1920
TRANS JORDAN
EGYPT
Turkish dependency, 1517
British occupation, 1882-1914
Protectorate, 1914-1922
Independent, 1922
SULTANATE OF NEJE
HEJAZ Kingdom, 1916-1925
RED SEA
JABAL SHAMM
ARABIA
Tropic of Cancer

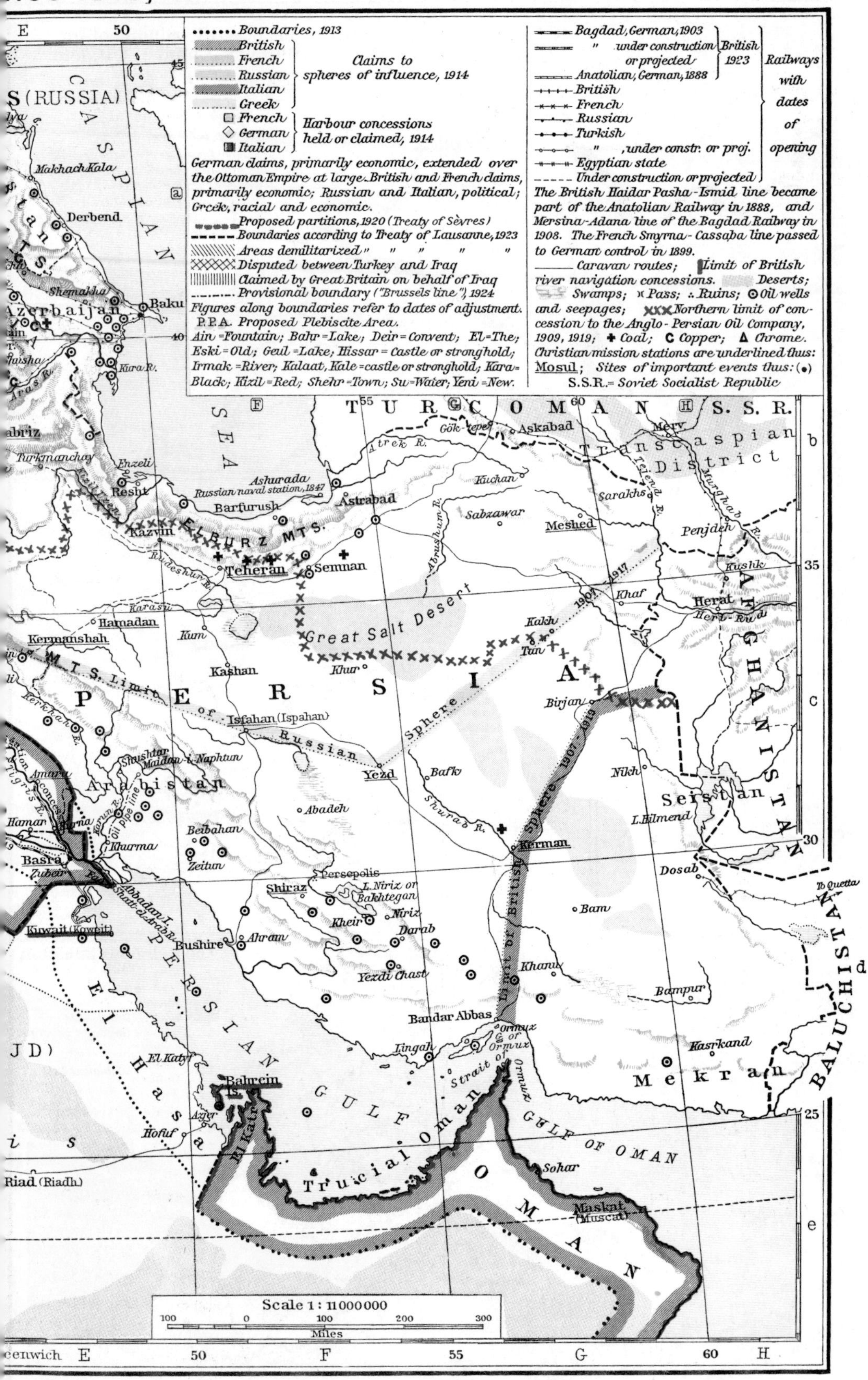
Boundaries, 1913
British
French
Russian
Italian
Greek
Claims to spheres of influence, 1914
French
German
Italian
Harbour concessions held or claimed, 1914
German claims, primarily economic, extended over the Ottoman Empire at large. British and French claims, primarily economic; Russian and Italian, political; Greek, racial and economic.
Proposed partitions, 1920 (Treaty of Sèvres)
Boundaries according to Treaty of Lausanne, 1923
Areas demilitarized " " " "
Disputed between Turkey and Iraq
Claimed by Great Britain on behalf of Iraq
Provisional boundary ("Brussels line"), 1924
Figures along boundaries refer to dates of adjustment.
P.P.A. Proposed Plebiscite Area.
Ain = Fountain; Bahr = Lake; Deir = Convent; El = The; Eski = Old; Geul = Lake; Hissar = Castle or stronghold; Irmak = River; Kalaat, Kale = castle or stronghold; Kara = Black; Kizil = Red; Shehr = Town; Su = Water; Yeni = New.
Bagdad, German, 1903
" under construction or projected
British 1923
Anatolian, German, 1888
British
French
Russian
Turkish
" , under constr. or proj.
Egyptian state
Under construction or projected
Railways with dates of opening
The British Haidar Pasha - Ismid line became part of the Anatolian Railway in 1888, and Mersina - Adana line of the Bagdad Railway in 1908. The French Smyrna - Cassaba line passed to German control in 1899.
Caravan routes; Limit of British river navigation concessions. Deserts; Swamps; Pass; Ruins; Oil wells and seepages; Northern limit of concession to the Anglo - Persian Oil Company, 1909, 1919; Coal; Copper; Chrome.
Christian mission stations are underlined thus: Mosul; Sites of important events thus: (•)
S.S.R. = Soviet Socialist Republic
S (RUSSIA)
CASPIAN SEA
Makhach Kala
Derbend
Shemakha
Azerbaijan
Baku
Tabriz
Turkmanchay
Enzeli
Resht
Ashurada
Russian naval station, 1847
Barfurush
Astrabad
Kazvin
ELBURZ MTS.
Teheran
Semnan
Hamadan
Kermanshah
Kum
Kashan
Isfahan (Ispahan)
TURCOMAN S.S.R.
Gök-tepe
Askabad
Merv
Transcaspian District
Atrek R.
Kuchan
Sarakhs
Sabzawar
Meshed
Penjdeh
Kushk
Khaf
Herat
Heri Rud
AFGHANISTAN
Great Salt Desert
Kakh
Tun
Khur
PERSIA
Birjand
Limit of Russian Sphere
Yezd
Bafk
Nikh
Seistan
L. Hilmend
Arabistan
Shushtar
Maidan-i-Naphtun
Amara
Hamar
Basra
Zubeir
Khurma
Oil Pipe line
Abbadan I.
Shatt-el-Arab R.
Kuwait (Koweit)
Beibahan
Zeitun
Abadeh
Shuras R.
Kerman
Limit of British Sphere
Persepolis
Shiraz
L. Niriz or Bakhtegan
Kheir
Niriz
Darab
Bushire
Ahram
Yezdi Chast
Bam
Dosab
To Quetta
BALUCHISTAN
Khanu
Bampur
Bandar Abbas
Ormuz
Lingah
Strait of Ormuz
Kasrkand
Mekran
PERSIAN GULF
El Hasa
El Katif
Bahrein Is.
Ajer
Hofuf
Riad (Riadh)
Trucial Oman
GULF OF OMAN
Sohar
Maskat (Muscat)
OMAN
Scale 1 : 11000000
Miles
enwich

The Near East II.

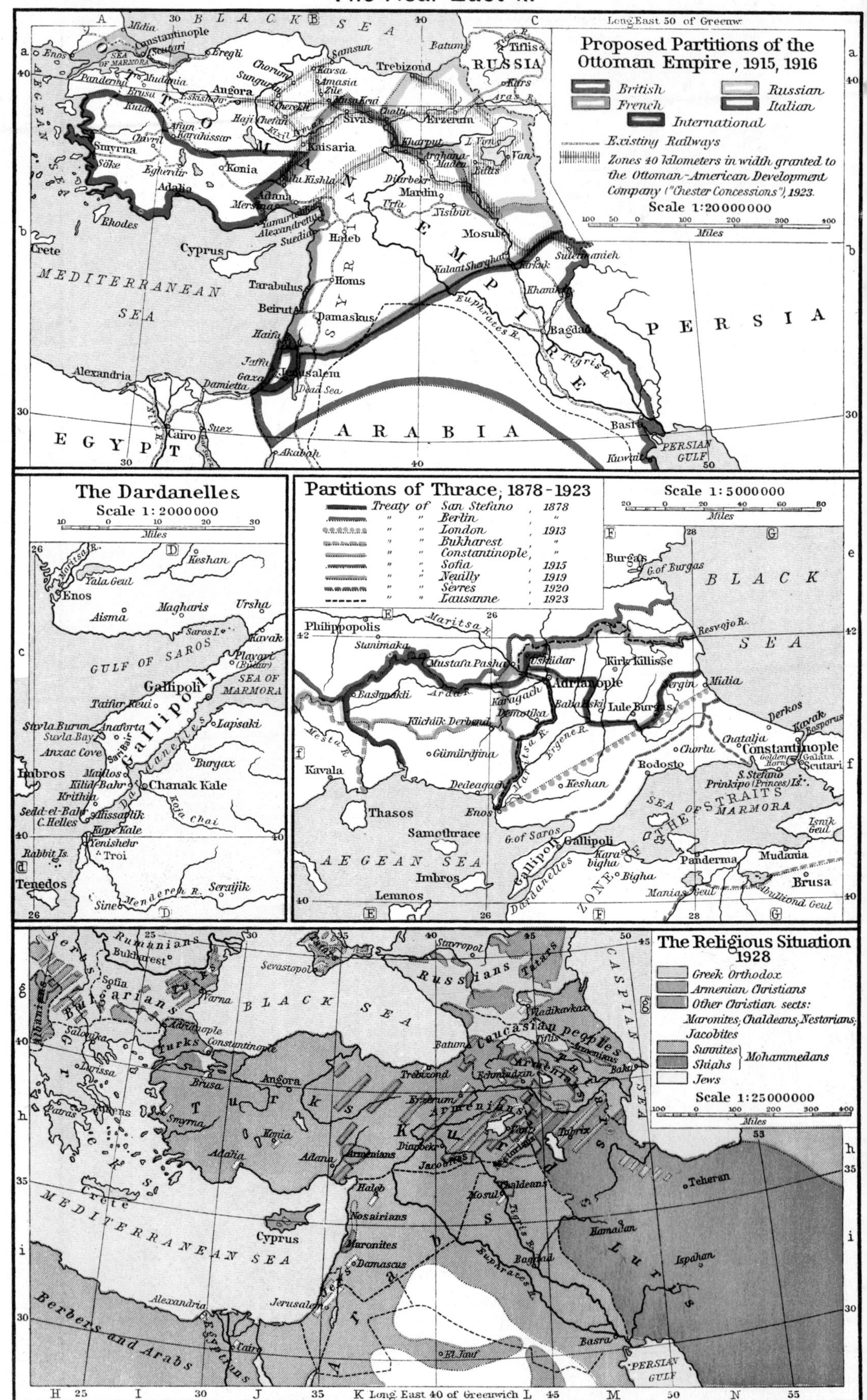

The Growth of European and Japar

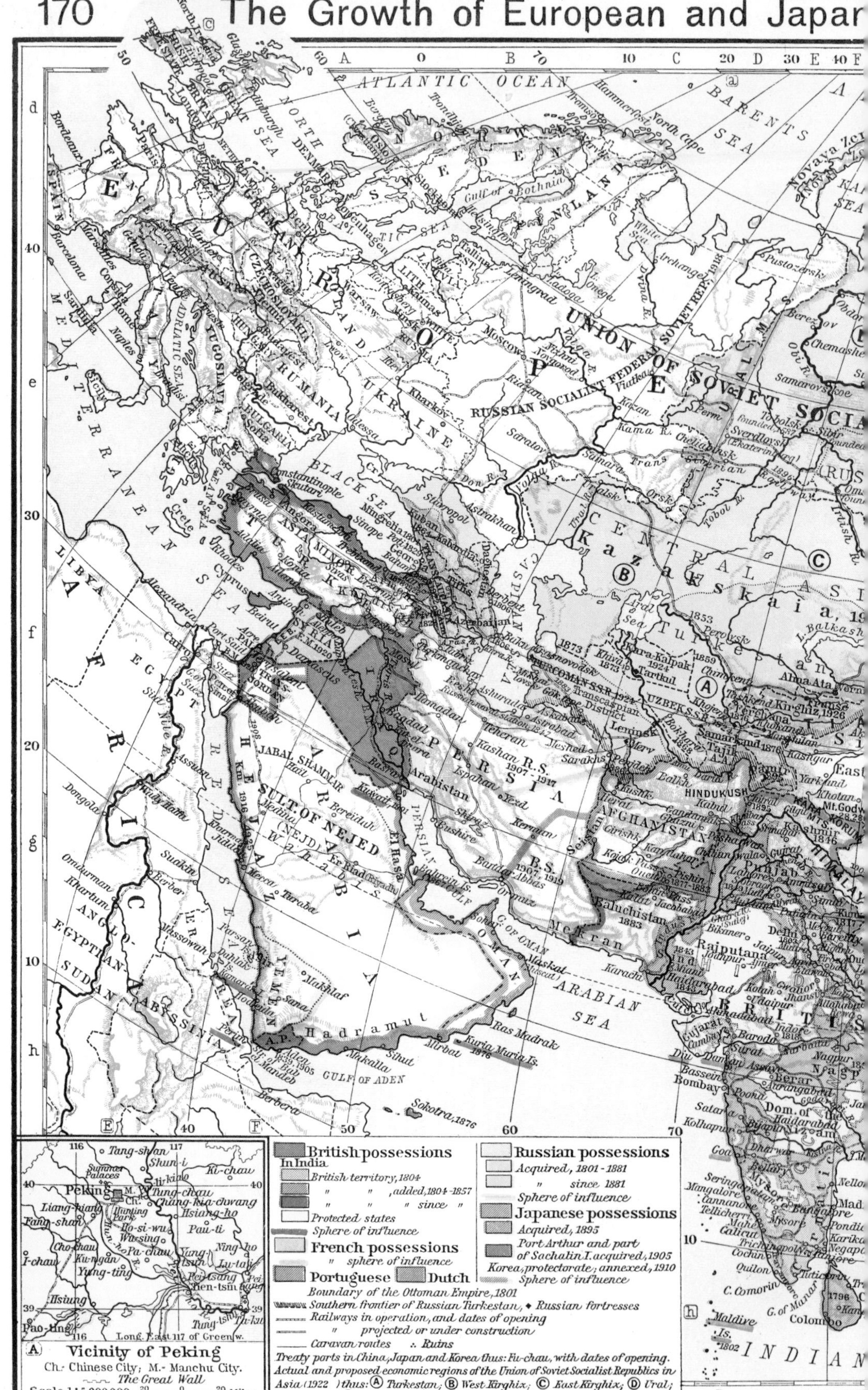

Abbreviations: A.A.=*Autonomous (Socialist Soviet) Area*; A.P.=*Aden Protectorate*; A.R.=*Autonomous (Socialist Soviet) Republic*; ALB.=*Albanie*
EST.=*Estonia*; E.M.S=*Federated Malay States*; F.M.=*French Mandate*; J.=*Japan*; LEB.=*Lebanon*; LITH.=*Lithuania*; PAL.=*Palestine*; R.=*Russio*

M.= British Mandate; Bur. Mong.= Buryato Mongolia; Cr.= Crimea; Dom.= Dominions; ...ere; REP.= Republic; S.S.R.= Socialist Soviet Republic; SULT.= Sultanate.

Scale 1:40000000 — 200 0 200 400 600 Miles

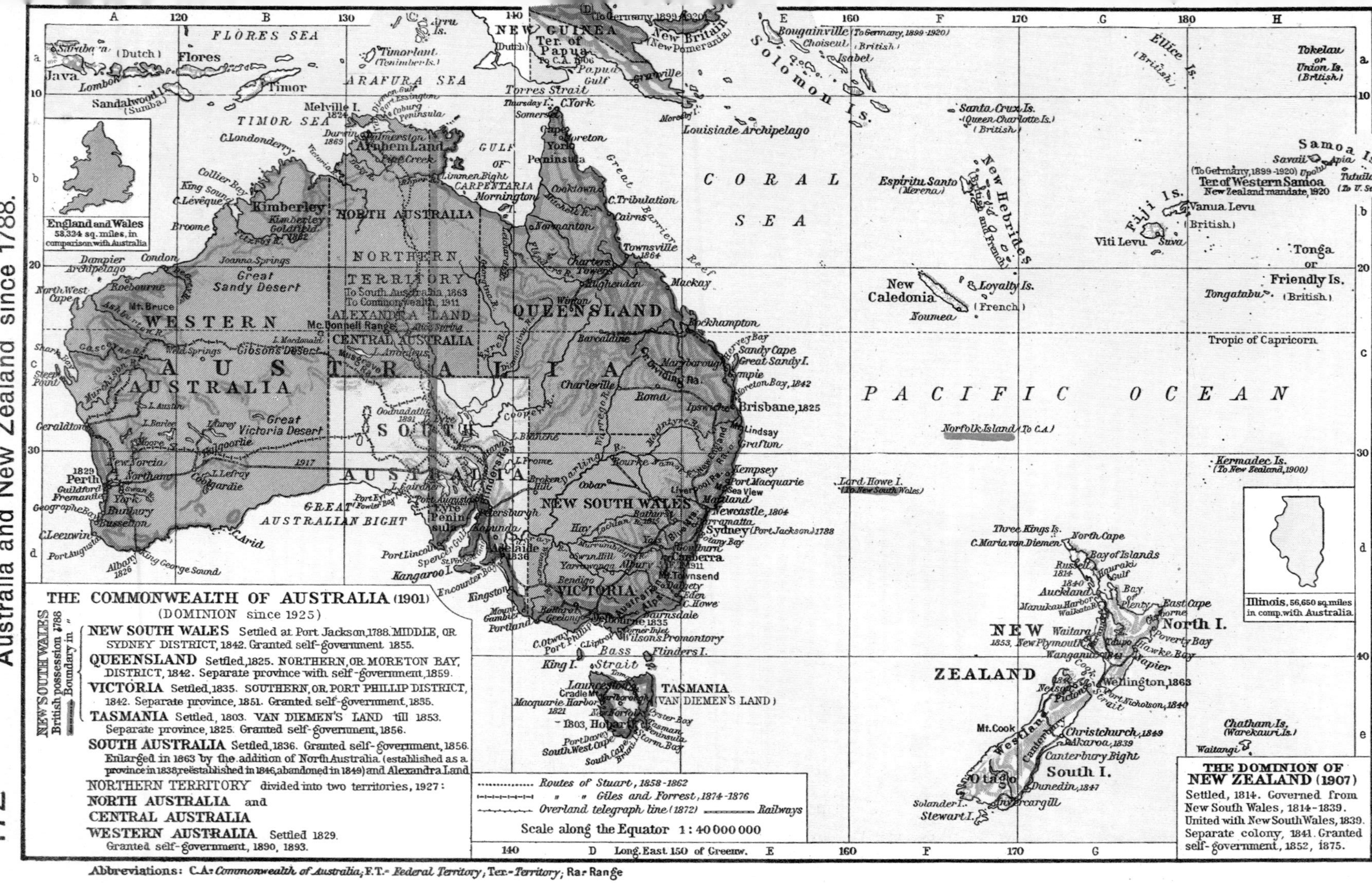
THE COMMONWEALTH OF AUSTRALIA (1901)
(DOMINION since 1925)
NEW SOUTH WALES British possession 1788 Boundary in "
NEW SOUTH WALES Settled at Port Jackson, 1788. MIDDLE, OR SYDNEY DISTRICT, 1842. Granted self-government 1855.
QUEENSLAND Settled, 1825. NORTHERN, OR MORETON BAY, DISTRICT, 1842. Separate province with self-government, 1859.
VICTORIA Settled, 1835. SOUTHERN, OR PORT PHILLIP DISTRICT, 1842. Separate province, 1851. Granted self-government, 1855.
TASMANIA Settled, 1803. VAN DIEMEN'S LAND till 1853. Separate province, 1825. Granted self-government, 1856.
SOUTH AUSTRALIA Settled, 1836. Granted self-government, 1856. Enlarged in 1863 by the addition of North Australia (established as a province in 1838, reëstablished in 1846, abandoned in 1849) and Alexandra Land
NORTHERN TERRITORY divided into two territories, 1927: NORTH AUSTRALIA and CENTRAL AUSTRALIA
WESTERN AUSTRALIA Settled 1829. Granted self-government, 1890, 1893.
Routes of Stuart, 1858-1862
" " Giles and Forrest, 1874-1876
Overland telegraph line (1872)
Railways
Scale along the Equator 1 : 40 000 000
THE DOMINION OF NEW ZEALAND (1907)
Settled, 1814. Governed from New South Wales, 1814-1839. United with New South Wales, 1839. Separate colony, 1841. Granted self-government, 1852, 1875.
England and Wales 58,324 sq. miles, in comparison with Australia
Illinois, 56,650 sq. miles in comp. with Australia
Long. East 150 of Greenw.
WESTERN AUSTRALIA
SOUTH AUSTRALIA
NORTH AUSTRALIA
NORTHERN TERRITORY
To South Australia, 1863
To Commonwealth, 1911
ALEXANDRA LAND
CENTRAL AUSTRALIA
QUEENSLAND
NEW SOUTH WALES
VICTORIA
TASMANIA
(VAN DIEMEN'S LAND)
NEW ZEALAND
North I.
South I.
PACIFIC OCEAN
CORAL SEA
ARAFURA SEA
TIMOR SEA
FLORES SEA
GREAT AUSTRALIAN BIGHT
Tropic of Capricorn
Great Sandy Desert
Great Victoria Desert
Gibsons Desert
Kimberley
Arnhem Land
Perth 1829
Adelaide 1836
Melbourne, 1835
Sydney (Port Jackson) 1788
Brisbane, 1825
Newcastle, 1804
Canberra
Hobart
Wellington, 1863
Auckland
Christchurch, 1849
Dunedin, 1847
NEW GUINEA
Ter. of Papua
To C.A. 1906
Solomon Is.
New Hebrides
New Caledonia (French)
Fiji Is. (British)
Samoa Is.
Ter. of Western Samoa
New Zealand mandate, 1920
Tonga or Friendly Is. (British)
Norfolk Island (To C.A.)
Lord Howe I. (To New South Wales)
Kermadec Is. (To New Zealand, 1900)
Chatham Is. (Warekauri Is.)
Abbreviations: C.A.= Commonwealth of Australia; F.T.= Federal Territory; Ter.= Territory; Ra.= Range

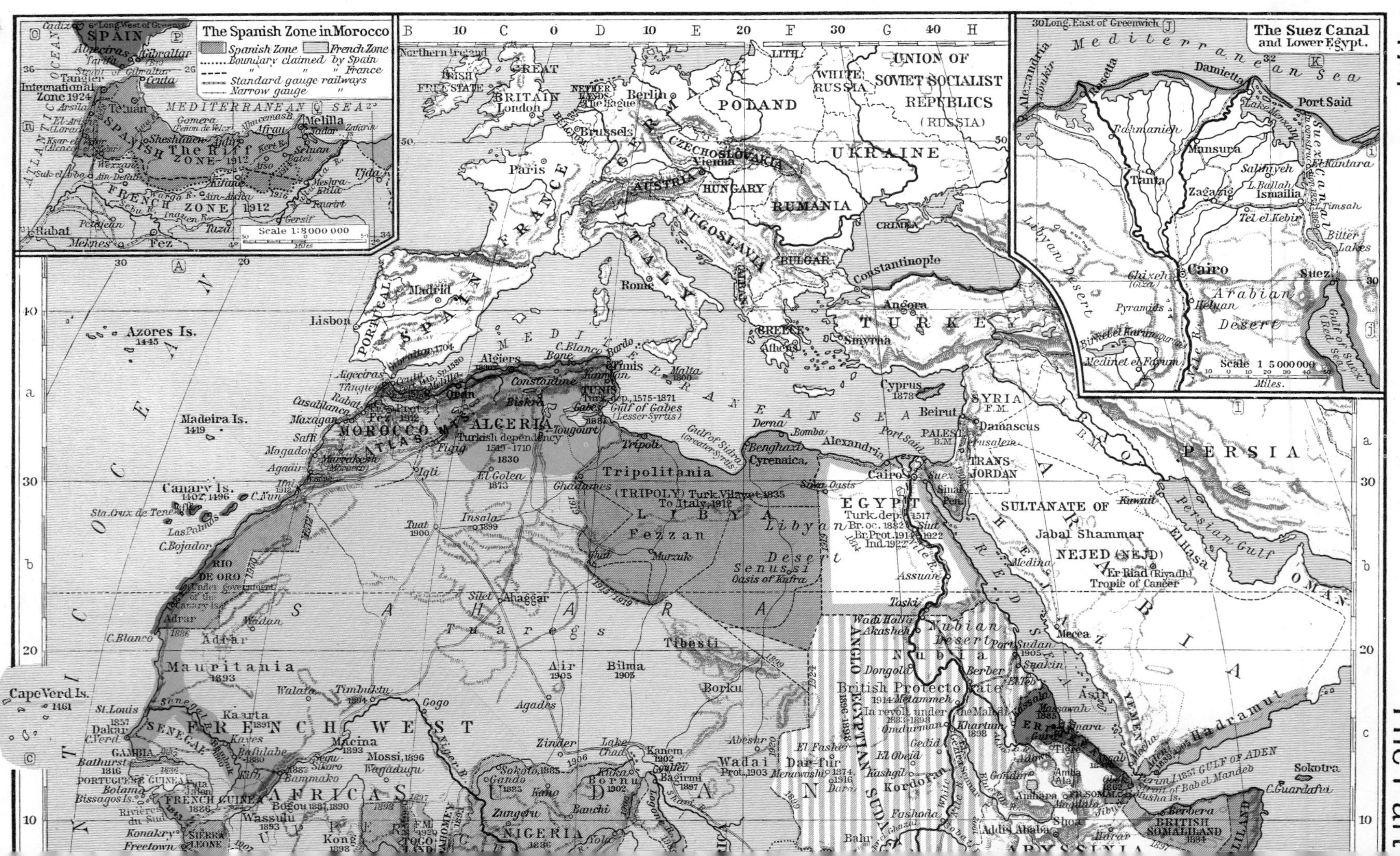
The Spanish Zone in Morocco
The Suez Canal and Lower Egypt.

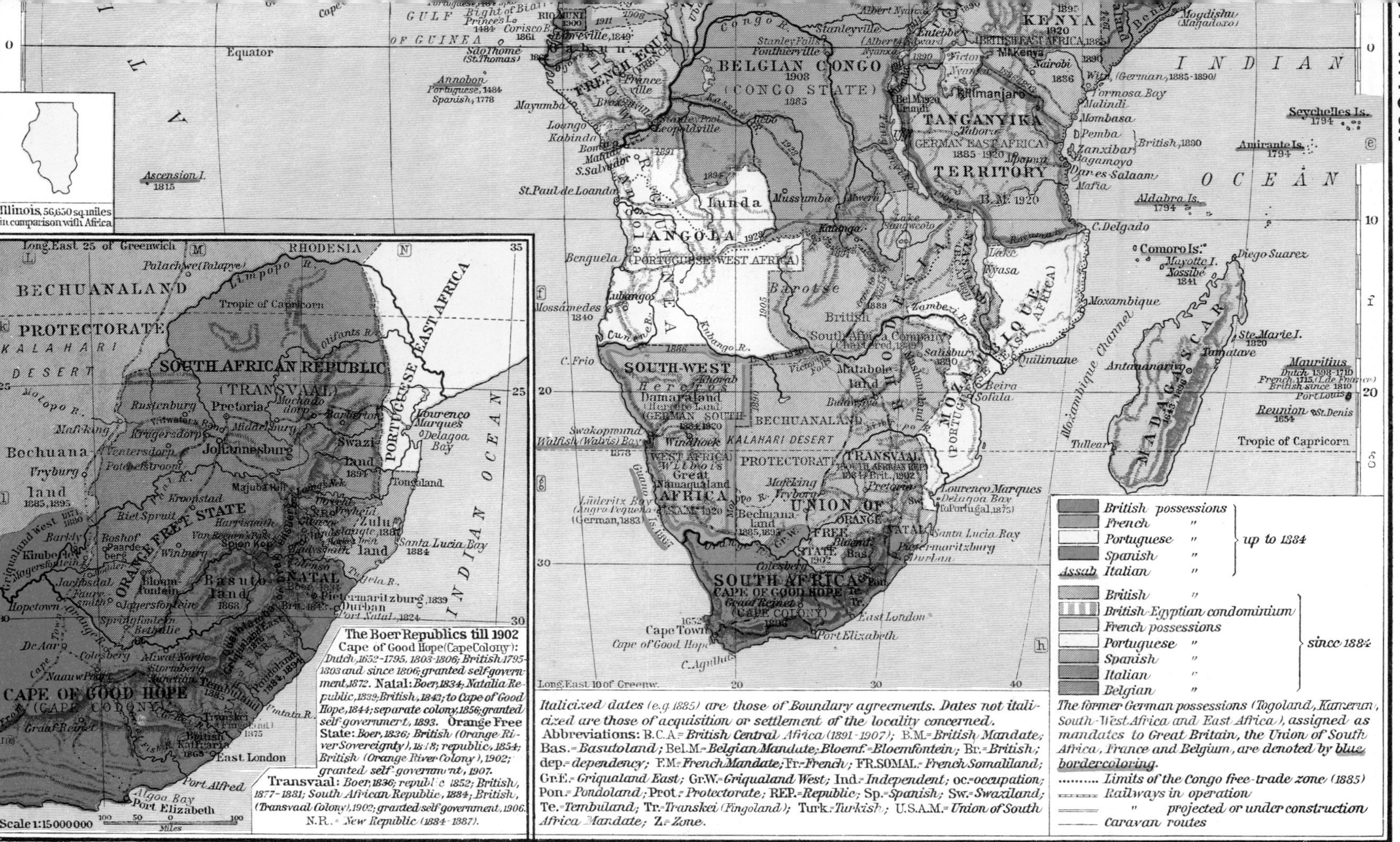
Illinois, 56,650 sq. miles in comparison with Africa
The Boer Republics till 1902
Cape of Good Hope (Cape Colony): Dutch, 1652-1795, 1803-1806; British 1795-1803 and since 1806; granted self-government, 1872. Natal: Boer, 1834; Natalia Republic, 1839; British, 1843; to Cape of Good Hope, 1844; separate colony, 1856; granted self-government, 1893. Orange Free State: Boer, 1836; British (Orange River Sovereignty), 1848; republic, 1854; British (Orange River Colony), 1902; granted self-government, 1907.
Transvaal: Boer, 1836; republic 1852; British, 1877-1881; South African Republic, 1884; British, (Transvaal Colony), 1902; granted self government, 1906.
N.R. = New Republic (1884-1887).
Scale 1:15000000
Italicized dates (e.g. 1885) are those of Boundary agreements. Dates not italicized are those of acquisition or settlement of the locality concerned.
Abbreviations: B.C.A. = British Central Africa (1891-1907); B.M. = British Mandate; Bas. = Basutoland; Bel.M. = Belgian Mandate; Bloemf. = Bloemfontein; Br. = British; dep. = dependency; F.M. = French Mandate; Fr. = French; FR.SOMAL. = French Somaliland; Gr.E. = Griqualand East; Gr.W. = Griqualand West; Ind. = Independent; oc. = occupation; Pon. = Pondoland; Prot. = Protectorate; REP. = Republic; Sp. = Spanish; Sw. = Swaziland; Te. = Tembuland; Tr. = Transkei (Fingoland); Turk. = Turkish; U.S.A.M. = Union of South Africa Mandate; Z. = Zone.
British possessions, French, Portuguese, Spanish, Italian — up to 1884
British, British-Egyptian condominium, French possessions, Portuguese, Spanish, Italian, Belgian — since 1884
The former German possessions (Togoland, Kamerun, South-West Africa and East Africa), assigned as mandates to Great Britain, the Union of South Africa, France and Belgium, are denoted by blue bordercoloring.
Limits of the Congo free-trade zone (1885)
Railways in operation
" projected or under construction
Caravan routes
Scale 1:40000000
Miles

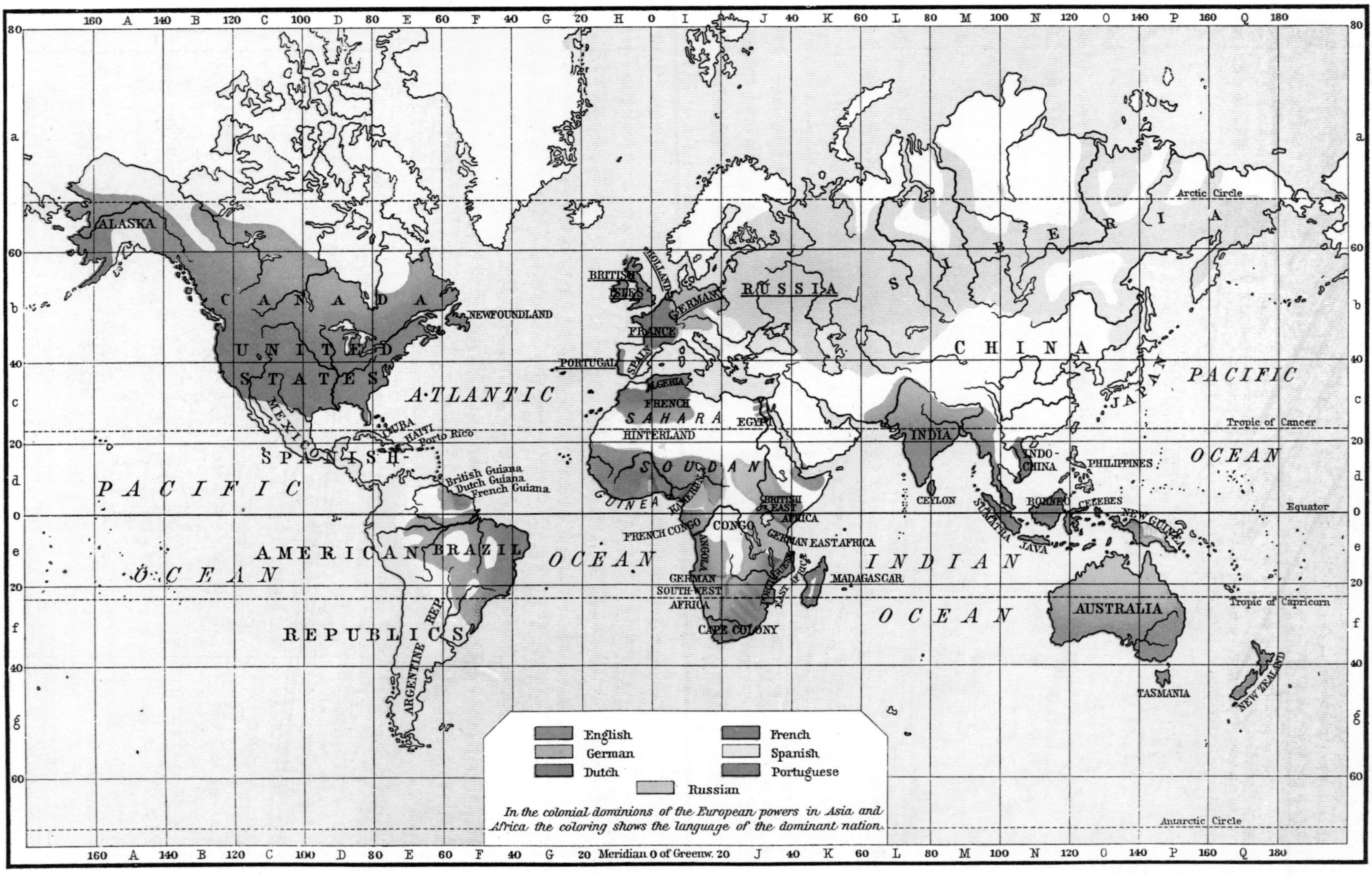
Arctic Circle
Tropic of Cancer
Equator
Tropic of Capricorn
Antarctic Circle
ALASKA
CANADA
UNITED STATES
NEWFOUNDLAND
MEXICO
CUBA
HAITI
Porto Rico
SPANISH-AMERICAN REPUBLICS
British Guiana
Dutch Guiana
French Guiana
BRAZIL
ARGENTINE REP.
PACIFIC OCEAN
ATLANTIC OCEAN
BRITISH ISLES
HOLLAND
GERMANY
FRANCE
PORTUGAL
SPAIN
RUSSIA
SIBERIA
CHINA
JAPAN
PACIFIC OCEAN
ALGERIA
FRENCH SAHARA HINTERLAND
EGYPT
SOUDAN
GUINEA
KAMERUN
FRENCH CONGO
CONGO
ANGOLA
GERMAN SOUTH-WEST AFRICA
CAPE COLONY
BRITISH EAST AFRICA
GERMAN EAST AFRICA
PORTUGUESE EAST AFRICA
MADAGASCAR
INDIA
CEYLON
INDO-CHINA
PHILIPPINES
SUMATRA
BORNEO
CELEBES
JAVA
NEW GUINEA
INDIAN OCEAN
AUSTRALIA
TASMANIA
NEW ZEALAND
English
German
Dutch
French
Spanish
Portuguese
Russian
In the colonial dominions of the European powers in Asia and Africa the coloring shows the language of the dominant nation.
Meridian 0 of Greenw.

Possessions of Great Britain
" " France
" " Russia
" " Portugal

Possessions of Spain
" " Denmark
" " the United States
" " Germany till 1920

Possessions of Japan
" " the Netherlands
" " Italy
" " Belgium

Nations not members of the League of Nations (53) in 1928: Afghanistan; Brazil; Costarica; Ecuador; Egypt; Mexico; Spain; Union of Soviet Socialist Republics (Russia); Turkey; United States.
Names of territories administered under mandate of the League ar underlined thus: South West Africa.
Figures placed in connection with names of islands, sea ports etc. give the date of acquisition by the nation concerned.
Former or alternate names are put in parentheses.

UNION OF SOVIET SOCIALIST REPUBLICS (RUSSIA)

Principal railway lines — " steamship " — " telegraph "
principal ocean cables — " wireless stations — " caravan routes
principal coal fields — " iron " — " oil "

Figures placed along the steamship lines give the number of nautical miles; Roman numerals at the top of the ma… the hours on various meridians when it is noon at Greenwich.

Abbreviations

A.M.= Australian Mandate; **ALB.= Albania**; Arch.= Archipelago; **Arm.= Armenia**; Aus.= Australia; **AUST.= Austri…** **Azerb.= Azerbaijan**; B.M.= British Mandate; **BEL.= Belgium**; Bel.M.= Belgian Mandate; *Bloemf.= Bloemfontei…* Br. Brit.= British; **CZEC.= Czechoslovakia**; **D.R.= Dominican Republic**; **EST.= Estonia**; F.M.= French Mandate; **F.M… Federated Malay States**; Fr.= French; *G.= Guatemala*; **H.= Haiti**; **HUNG.= Hungary**; **LITH.= Lithuania**; **M.= Monteneg…** N.Z.M.= New Zealand Mandate; **NETHS.= Netherlands**; **PAL.= Palestine**; **Pr.= Prince**; **SS.= Straits Settlements**; **SER.= Serbia**; St.= State; **SW.= Switzerland**; Ter.= Territory; **W.= Western**; **U.S.= United States**; U.S.A.M.= Union of South Africa Mandate; **YUGOSL.= Yugoslavia**.

Scale along the Equator 1:80 000 000

500 0 500 1000 1500 2000 2500 3000

Miles

European, African and Asiatic Migration.

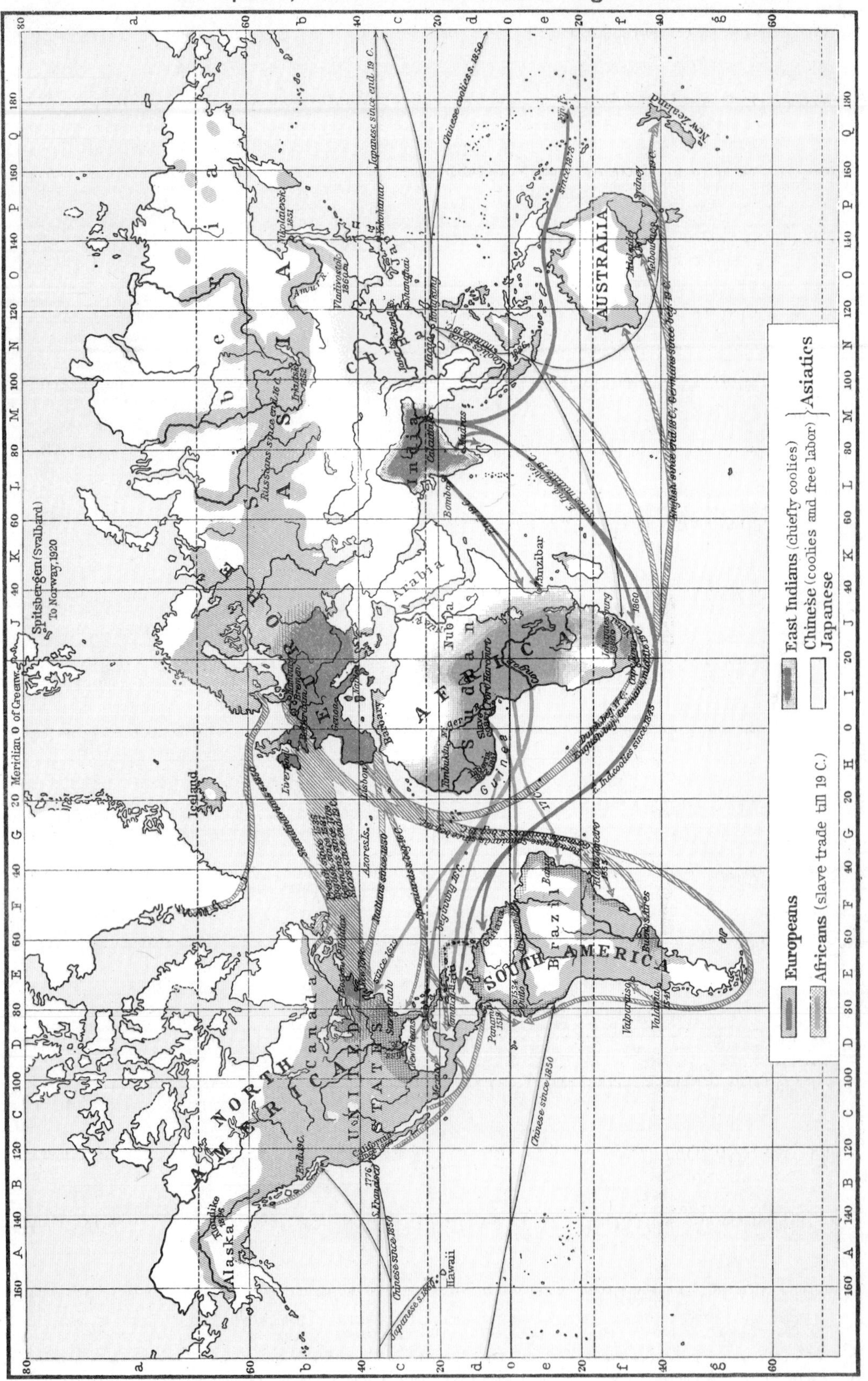

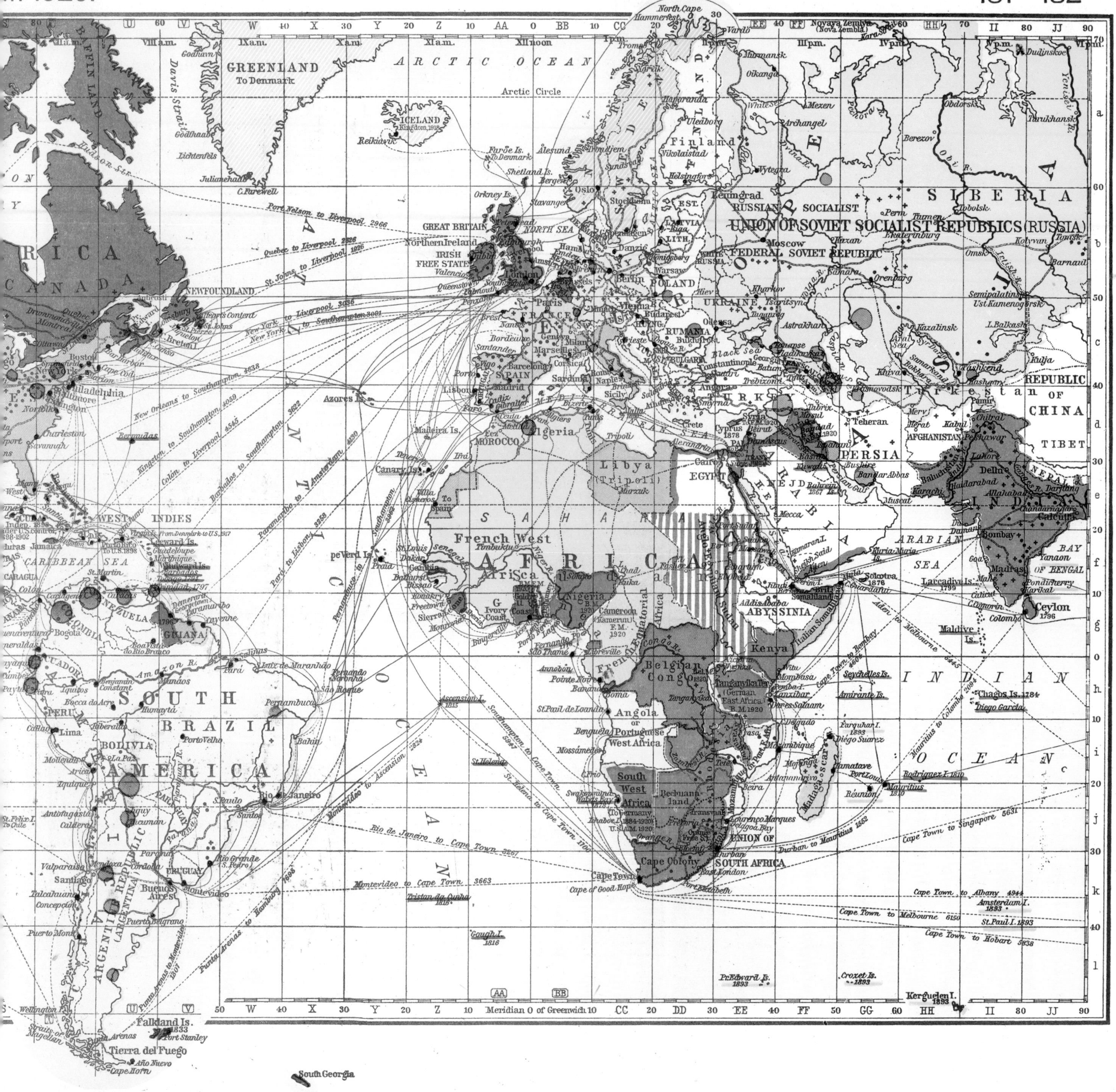

GREENLAND
To Denmark

ARCTIC OCEAN

Arctic Circle

ICELAND
Kingdom, 1918

Reikiavik

Finland

SWEDEN

NORWAY

Faroe Is. To Denmark

Shetland Is.

Orkney Is.

GREAT BRITAIN

Northern Ireland

IRISH FREE STATE

NORTH SEA

London

Paris

FRANCE

SPAIN

Madrid

Lisbon

Azores Is.

Madeira Is.

Canary Is.

MOROCCO

Algeria

Tunis

Tripoli

Libya (Tripoli)

EGYPT

Cairo

Moscow

RUSSIAN SOCIALIST FEDERAL SOVIET REPUBLIC

UNION OF SOVIET SOCIALIST REPUBLICS (RUSSIA)

UKRAINE

SIBERIA

Turkestan

REPUBLIC OF CHINA

TIBET

NEPAL

INDIA

Bombay

Calcutta

Delhi

Madras

BAY OF BENGAL

Ceylon 1796

Colombo

AFGHANISTAN

PERSIA

Teheran

ARABIA

NEJD

ARABIAN SEA

TURKEY

Black Sea

Constantinople

POLAND

Warsaw

Berlin

RUMANIA

BULGARIA

SAHARA

French West Africa

AFRICA

Nigeria

Gold Coast

Ivory Coast

Cameroon

French Equatorial Africa

Belgian Congo

ABYSSINIA

Kenya

Italian Somaliland

Tanganyika Ter. (German East Africa) B.M. 1920

Angola or Portuguese West Africa

South West Africa (To Germany 1884-1920) U.S.A.M. 1920

Bechuanaland

Madagascar

Mauritius

Réunion

UNION OF SOUTH AFRICA

Cape Colony

Cape Town

Cape of Good Hope

Durban

St. Helena

Ascension I.

Tristan da Cunha

Gough I.

INDIAN OCEAN

Seychelles Is.

Chagos Is. 1784

Diego Garcia

Maldive Is.

Laccadive Is.

Kerguelen I.

Amsterdam I.

St. Paul I.

Pr. Edward Is.

Croxet Is.

CANADA

NEWFOUNDLAND

Quebec

Montreal

Boston

New York

Philadelphia

Bermudas

WEST INDIES

CARIBBEAN SEA

Jamaica

VENEZUELA

GUIANA

COLOMBIA

ECUADOR

PERU

Lima

BOLIVIA

SOUTH AMERICA

BRAZIL

Amazon R.

Rio de Janeiro

Santos

URUGUAY

Montevideo

Buenos Aires

ARGENTINE REPUBLIC (ARGENTINA)

CHILE

Santiago

Valparaiso

Falkland Is. 1833

Tierra del Fuego

Cape Horn

South Georgia

ATLANTIC OCEAN

Port Nelson to Liverpool 2966

Quebec to Liverpool 2626

St. Johns to Liverpool 1926

New York to Liverpool 3036

New York to Southampton 3091

New Orleans to Southampton 4059

Kingston to Southampton 3622

Colón to Liverpool 4545

Barbados to Southampton

Paramaribo to Amsterdam

Pará to Lisbon

Rio de Janeiro to Cape Town 3267

Montevideo to Cape Town 3663

Southampton to Cape Town 5987

Cape Town to Albany 4944

Cape Town to Melbourne 6150

Cape Town to Hobart 5938

Cape Town to Singapore 5631

Durban to Mauritius 1552

Aden to Melbourne 6445

Cape Town to Bombay

Meridian 0 of Greenwich

Localities in Western Europe, connected with American History

Localities in England, connected with American History.

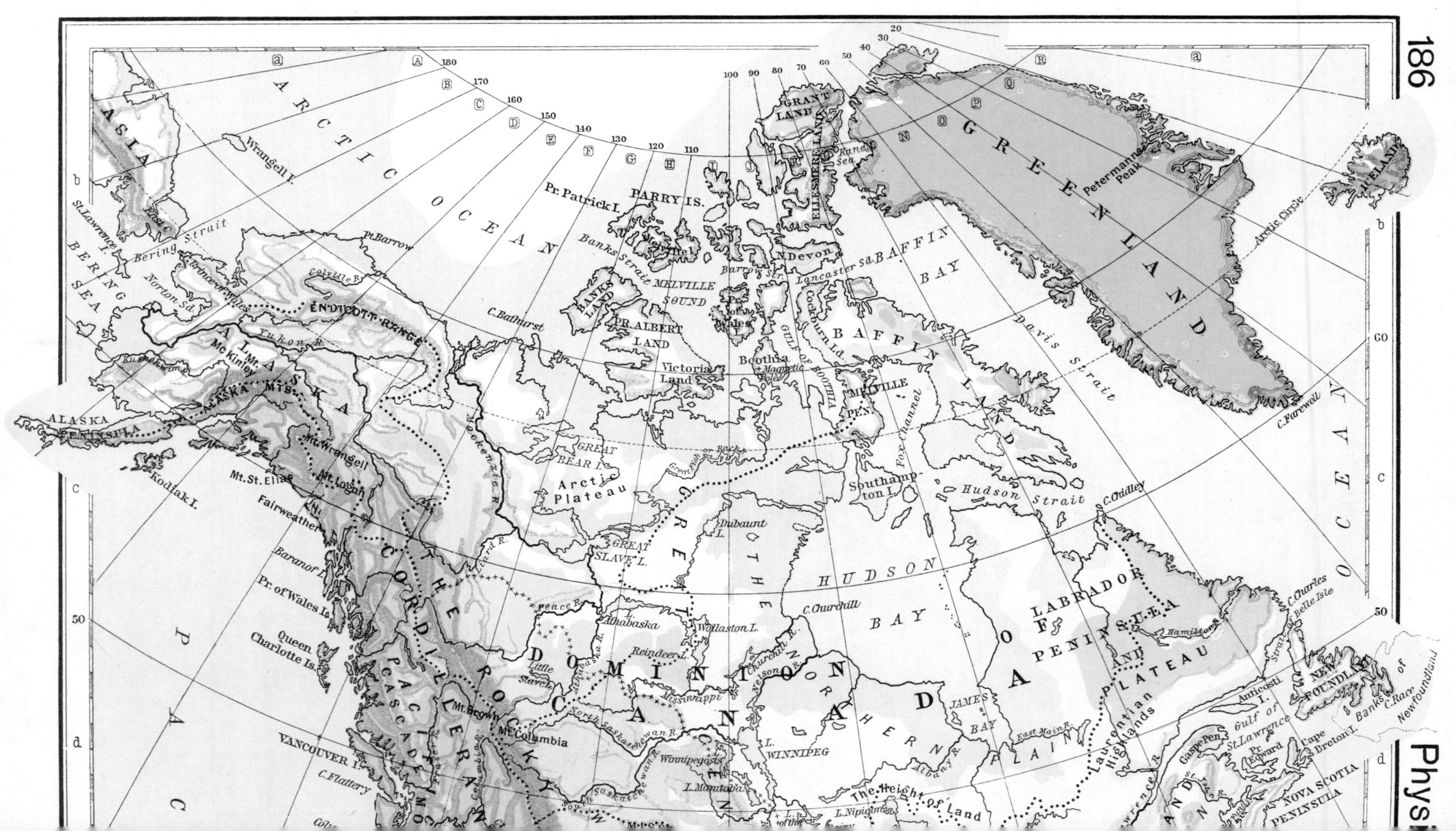
ASIA
ARCTIC OCEAN
Wrangell I.
St. Lawrence I.
Bering Strait
BERING SEA
Norton Sd.
Pt. Barrow
ENDICOTT RANGE
Yukon R.
ALASKA
Mt. McKinley
ALASKA MTS.
ALASKA PENINSULA
Kodiak I.
Mt. Wrangell
Mt. Logan
Mt. St. Elias
Fairweather
Baranof I.
Pr. of Wales I.
Queen Charlotte Is.
VANCOUVER I.
C. Flattery
Pr. Patrick I.
PARRY IS.
Banks Strait
MELVILLE SOUND
BANKS LAND
PR. ALBERT LAND
Victoria Land
C. Bathurst
Mackenzie R.
GREAT BEAR L.
Arctic Plateau
GREAT SLAVE L.
L. Athabaska
Peace R.
Little Slave L.
Reindeer L.
Wollaston L.
Dubaunt L.
GRANT LAND
ELLESMERE LAND
Kane Sea
N. Devon
Barrow Str.
Lancaster Sd.
BAFFIN BAY
Cockburn Ld.
GULF OF BOOTHIA
Boothia
Magnetic Pole
MELVILLE PEN.
BAFFIN LAND
Fox Channel
Southampton I.
Hudson Strait
C. Chidley
GREENLAND
Petermann Peak
Davis Strait
Arctic Circle
C. Farewell
ICELAND
OCEAN
HUDSON BAY
C. Churchill
JAMES BAY
East Main R.
Albany R.
LABRADOR PENINSULA
PLATEAU
Hamilton R.
Laurentian Highlands
C. Charles
Strait of Belle Isle
NEWFOUNDLAND
C. Race
Banks of Newfoundland
Anticosti I.
Gulf of St. Lawrence
Gaspe Pen.
Pr. Edward I.
Cape Breton I.
NOVA SCOTIA PENINSULA
THE GREAT
DOMINION OF CANADA
NORTHERN PLAIN
L. WINNIPEG
Winnipegosis
L. Manitoba
North Saskatchewan R.
Nelson R.
Churchill R.
The Height of Land
L. Nipigon
THE ROCKY
CORDILLERA
PACIFIC
CASCADE
Mt. Brown
Mt. Columbia
P A C

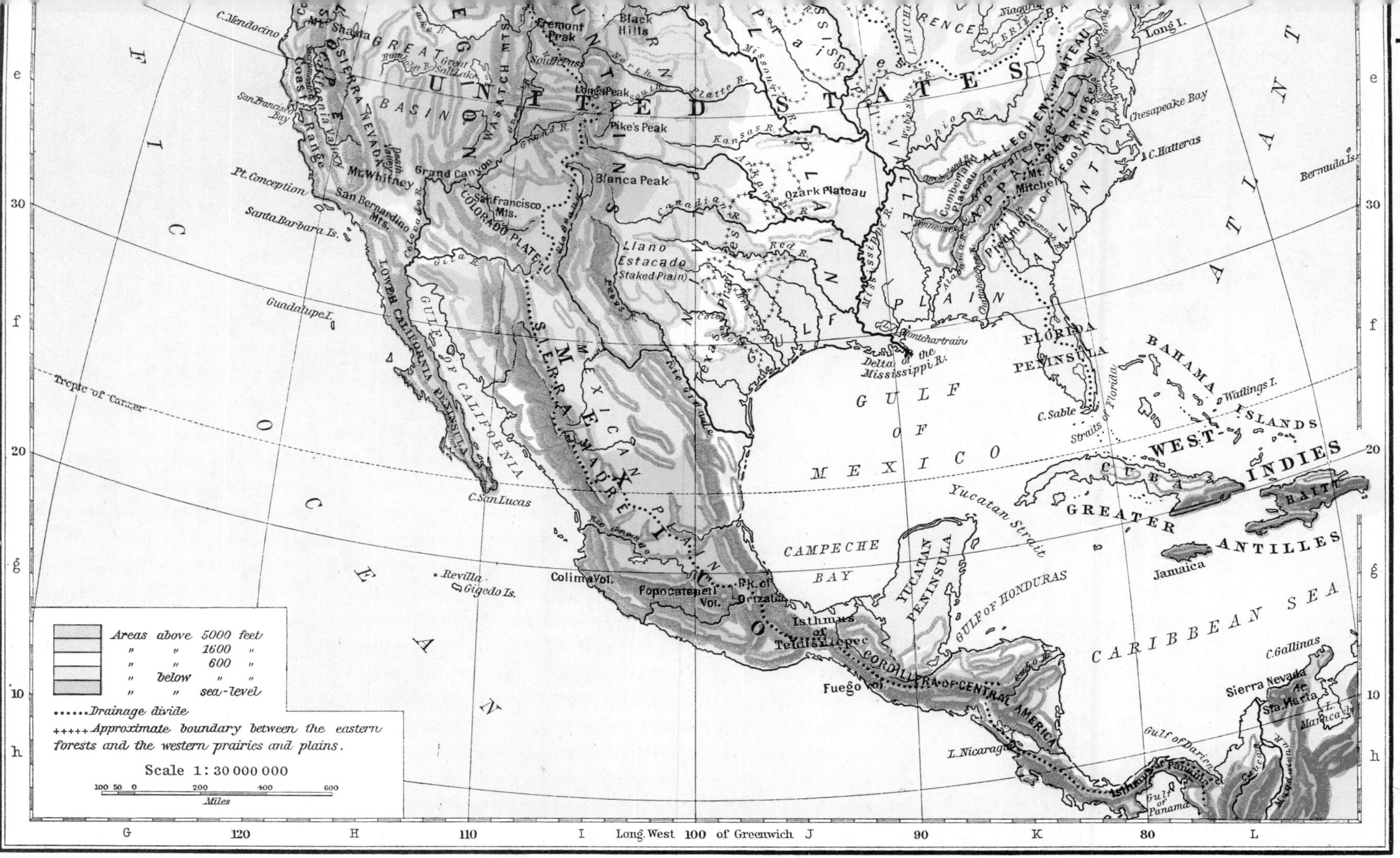
Areas above 5000 feet
" " 1600 "
" " 600 "
" below " "
" " sea-level
Drainage divide
Approximate boundary between the eastern forests and the western prairies and plains.
Scale 1: 30 000 000
Miles
Long. West 100 of Greenwich
ATLANTIC
PACIFIC OCEAN
GULF OF MEXICO
CARIBBEAN SEA
WEST INDIES
BAHAMA ISLANDS
GREATER ANTILLES
CUBA
HAITI
Jamaica
YUCATAN PENINSULA
Yucatan Strait
GULF OF HONDURAS
CAMPECHE BAY
CORDILLERA OF CENTRAL AMERICA
Isthmus of Tehuantepec
MEXICAN PLAIN
SIERRA MADRE
GULF OF CALIFORNIA
LOWER CALIFORNIA PENINSULA
C. San Lucas
Revilla Gigedo Is.
Colima Vol.
Popocatepetl Vol.
Pk. of Orizaba
Fuego
L. Nicaragua
Gulf of Darien
Gulf of Panama
Sierra Nevada de Sta. Maria
C. Gallinas
Tropic of Cancer
UNITED STATES
GREAT BASIN
SIERRA NEVADA
WASATCH MTS.
COLORADO PLATEAU
Grand Canyon
Mt. Whitney
Fremont Peak
Black Hills
Longs Peak
Pike's Peak
Blanca Peak
Llano Estacado (Staked Plain)
Ozark Plateau
Delta of the Mississippi R.
FLORIDA PENINSULA
C. Sable
Straits of Florida
Watlings I.
C. Hatteras
Chesapeake Bay
Long I.
Bermuda Is.
San Francisco Bay
Coast Range
Pt. Conception
Santa Barbara Is.
San Bernardino Mts.
Guadalupe I.
C. Mendocino

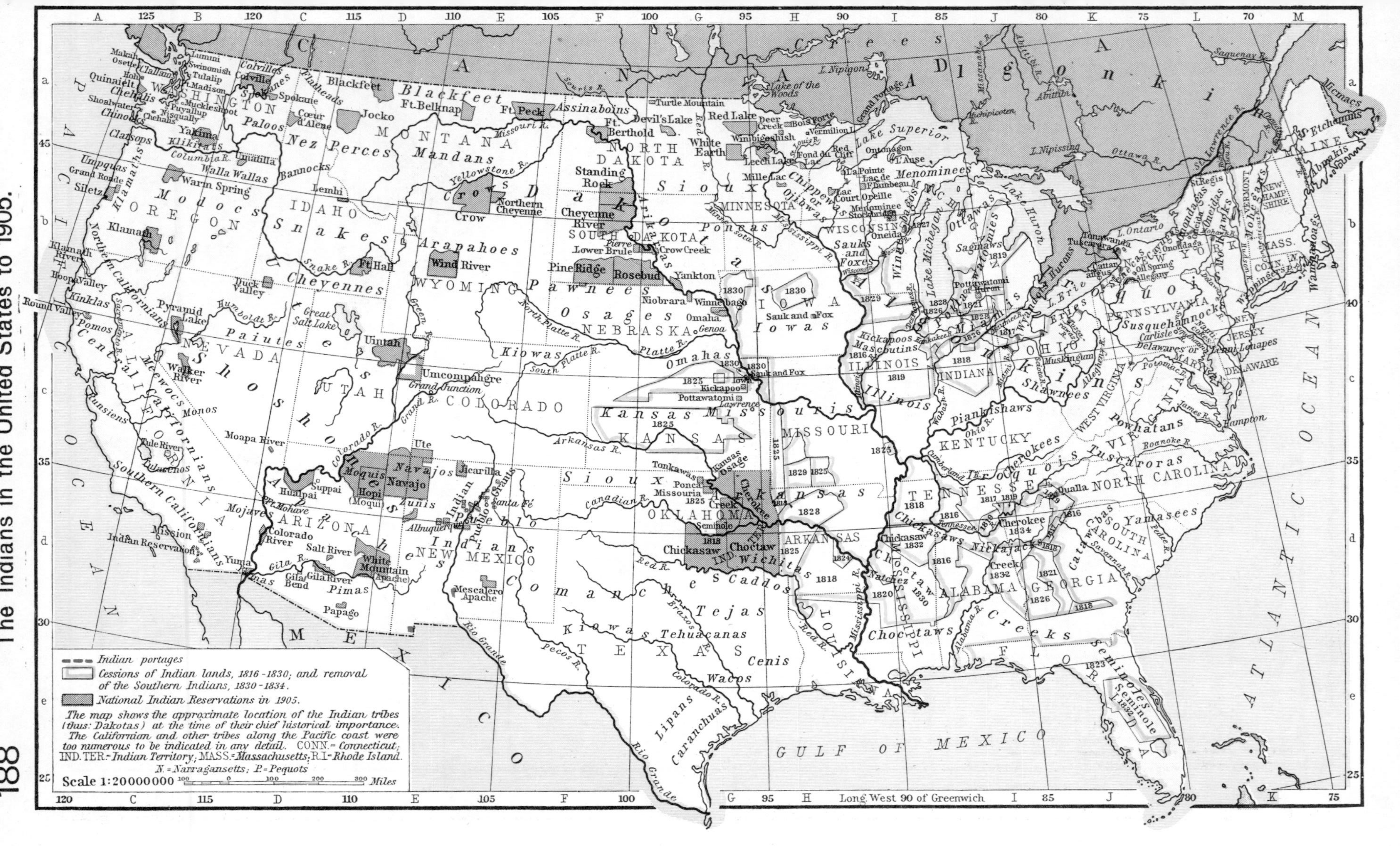
Indian portages
Cessions of Indian lands, 1816-1830; and removal of the Southern Indians, 1830-1834.
National Indian Reservations in 1905.
The map shows the approximate location of the Indian tribes (thus: Dakotas) at the time of their chief historical importance. The Californian and other tribes along the Pacific coast were too numerous to be indicated in any detail. CONN.-Connecticut; IND.TER.-Indian Territory; MASS.-Massachusetts; R.I.-Rhode Island.
N.-Narragansetts; P.-Pequots
Scale 1:20000000
Miles
Long. West 90 of Greenwich
GULF OF MEXICO
ATLANTIC OCEAN
PACIFIC OCEAN
MEXICO
CANADA
Algonkin
Dakotas
Shoshones
Comanches
Iroquois
Blackfeet
Crees
WASHINGTON
OREGON
CALIFORNIA
NEVADA
IDAHO
MONTANA
WYOMING
UTAH
ARIZONA
NEW MEXICO
COLORADO
NORTH DAKOTA
SOUTH DAKOTA
NEBRASKA
KANSAS
OKLAHOMA
TEXAS
MINNESOTA
IOWA
MISSOURI
ARKANSAS
LOUISIANA
WISCONSIN
ILLINOIS
INDIANA
OHIO
KENTUCKY
TENNESSEE
MISSISSIPPI
ALABAMA
GEORGIA
FLORIDA
SOUTH CAROLINA
NORTH CAROLINA
VIRGINIA
WEST VIRGINIA
PENNSYLVANIA
NEW YORK
MAINE

Reference Map of the New England Colonies, 1607—1760.

English possessions about 1750
Approximate area of settlement in 1660
" " " " " 1750
" frontier of the "New England Confederation", 1643-1684
Dutch possessions, 1613-1664, 1673-1674
French possessions about 1750

MASSACHUSETTS BAY
Corporate colony under patent from the Council for New England, 1628, and under royal charter, 1629; charter annulled, 1684; royal Province under new charter, 1691; charter practically abrogated by Parliament, 1774.

New Plymouth
Corporate colony under patent from the London Company, 1620, and from the Council for New England, 1621, 1630; added to Massachusetts Bay, 1691.

MAINE: *(between the Merrimac and Kennebec Rivers)-*
Proprietary colony under patent from the Council for New England, 1622

" : *(between the Piscataqua and Kennebec Rivers)-*
Proprietary colony under royal charter, 1637; held by Massachusetts Bay, 1651-1665, 1667-1679; nominally a royal province, but actually held by Massachusetts Bay, 1679-1686, 1689-1696

" : *(between the Kennebec and St. Croix Rivers)-*
Proprietary colony under royal charter, 1664-1691.

" : *(between the Piscataqua and St. Croix Rivers)-*
Added to Massachusetts Bay, 1691.

NEW HAMPSHIRE
Proprietary colony (part of MAINE*) under patent from the Council for New England, 1622; proprietary colony of* New Hampshire *(between the Merrimac and Piscataqua Rivers) under patent from the Council for New England, 1629; held by Massachusetts Bay, 1641-1679, 1690-1692; royal province, 1679-1690, 1692-1698; under same governor as Massachusetts Bay, 1698-1741; separate province, 1741-*

CONNECTICUT
Corporate colony under royal charter, 1662.

New Haven
United with Connecticut, 1664.

RHODE ISLAND
Corporate colony under charter from Parliament, 1644, and under royal charter, 1663.

Massachusetts Bay and the area in Maine subject to its control	1686-1689	under the rule of a royal governor-general
New Plymouth	"	
New Hampshire	"	
Rhode Island	"	
Connecticut	1687-1689	
New York	1688-1689	
East and West New Jersey	"	

The map is designed to serve as an index to localities in the New England Colonies which for lack of space could not be inserted in the map of European Exploration and Settlement in the United States, 1513-1776 (pages 190-191). The list of names given is not exhaustive. For names of Indian tribes, see page 188.

Dates associated with the names of localities having the sign (⊙ o) are those of settlement, or of change of name, e.g.: Agawam, 1633; Ipswich, 1634. In the case of Corlaer or Schenectady, Agamenticus, Casco or Ft. Loyal, Pemaquid, and Penobscot or Ft. Pentagöet, the dates of settlement are underlined.

✦ Fort, with date of construction. × Site of event in colonial warfare (1689-1760), with date of occurence. Other localities and dates of importance during the period of warfare in question are: Quebec, 1690, 1759; Port Royal (Acadia), 1690, 1707, 1710; Grand Pré, 1704; Canso, 1744; Louisburg, 1745, 1758; and St. Johns (Newfoundland), 1696, 1705, 1709. See p. 194.

To the extent shown in the map, the artificial boundaries (..........) are those of the present States of Massachusetts, New Hampshire, Connecticut and Rhode Island. Boundary disputes are not indicated. For the extent of the various grants by royal charter, see pp. 190-191 (inset).

Abbreviations: *C.-To Connecticut till 1664; Dart.-Dartmouth; Ki.-Kittery, 1624; M.B.-To Massachusetts Bay; Mid.-Middleborough; N.Hv.-To New Haven till 1664; Nor-Norwich; Rich.-Richmond I.; Salisb.-Salisbury; S.B.-South Berwick; Sudb.-Sudbury; Th.R.-Thames R.*

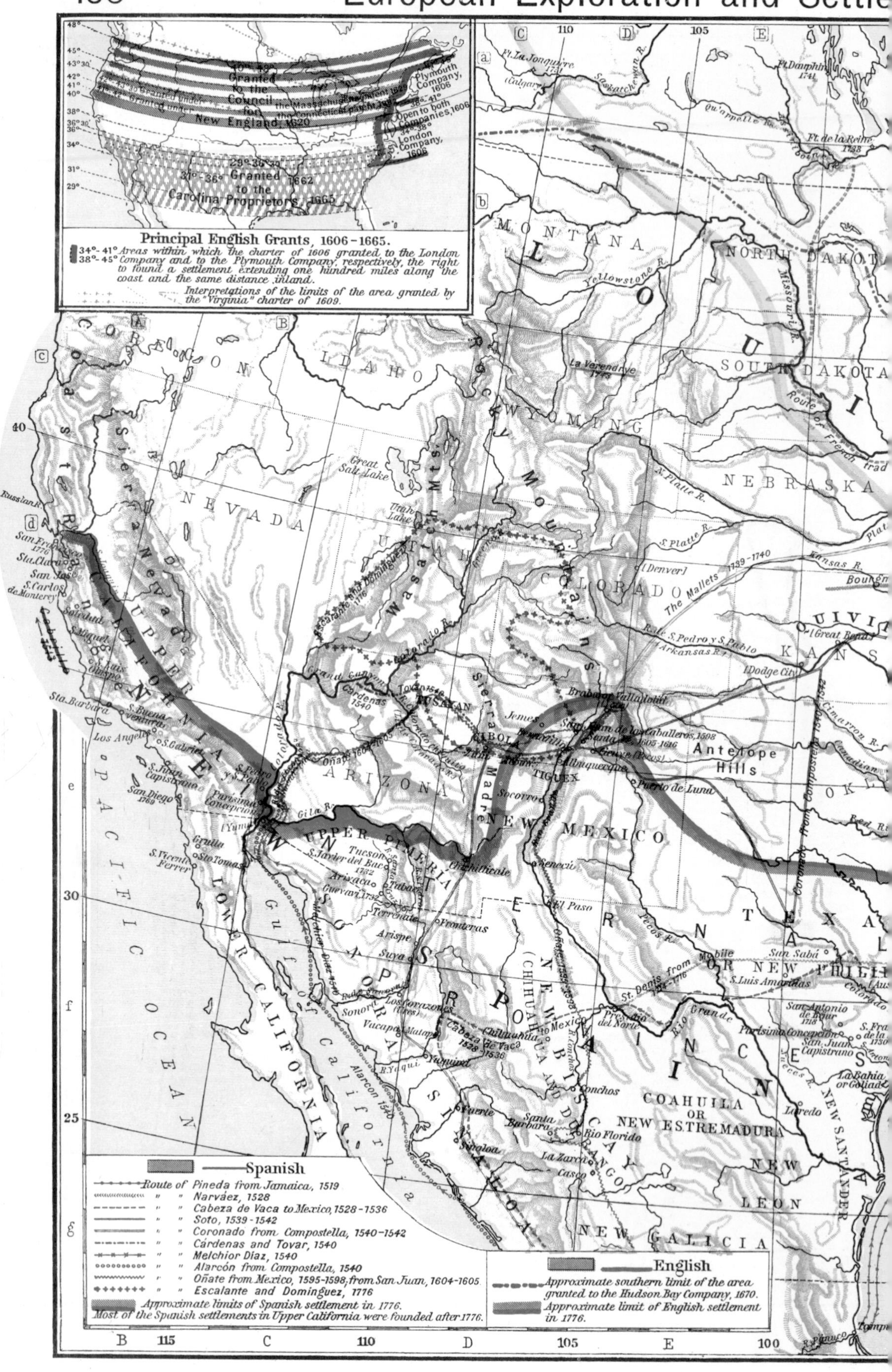
Principal English Grants, 1606-1665.
34°-41° 38°-45° Areas within which the charter of 1606 granted to the London Company and to the Plymouth Company, respectively, the right to found a settlement extending one hundred miles along the coast and the same distance inland.
Interpretations of the limits of the area granted by the "Virginia" charter of 1609.
40°-48° Granted to the Council for New England, 1620
Plymouth Company, 1606
Open to both Companies, 1606
London Company, 1606
29°-36°30' 31°-36° Granted to the Carolina Proprietors, 1662 1665
Spanish
Route of Pineda from Jamaica, 1519
" " Narváez, 1528
" " Cabeza de Vaca to Mexico, 1528-1536
" " Soto, 1539-1542
" " Coronado from Compostella, 1540-1542
" " Cárdenas and Tovar, 1540
" " Melchior Díaz, 1540
" " Alarcón from Compostella, 1540
" " Oñate from Mexico, 1595-1598; from San Juan, 1604-1605
" " Escalante and Domínguez, 1776
Approximate limits of Spanish settlement in 1776.
Most of the Spanish settlements in Upper California were founded after 1776.
English
Approximate southern limit of the area granted to the Hudson Bay Company, 1670.
Approximate limit of English settlement in 1776.
MONTANA
NORTH DAKOTA
SOUTH DAKOTA
IDAHO
OREGON
WYOMING
NEVADA
UTAH
COLORADO
NEBRASKA
KANSAS
ARIZONA
NEW MEXICO
TEXAS
UPPER CALIFORNIA
LOWER CALIFORNIA
PACIFIC OCEAN
Gulf of California
Great Salt Lake
Sierra Nevada
Rocky Mountains
Wasatch Mts.
Sierra Madre
UPPER PIMERIA
SONORA
CHIHUAHUA
NEW BISCAY
COAHUILA OR NEW ESTREMADURA
NEW LEON
NEW SANTANDER
NEW GALICIA
NEW SPAIN
Antelope Hills
QUIVIRA
CIBOLA
TUSAYAN
TIGUEX
San Francisco 1776
Santa Fe 1605-1616
El Paso
San Diego 1769
San Antonio de Bexar 1718
Route of French trade
The Mallets 1739-1740
La Verendrye 1743
St. Denis from Mobile 1714-1716
Escalante and Dominguez 1776
Coronado from Compostella
Alarcon 1540
B 115 C 110 D 105 E 100

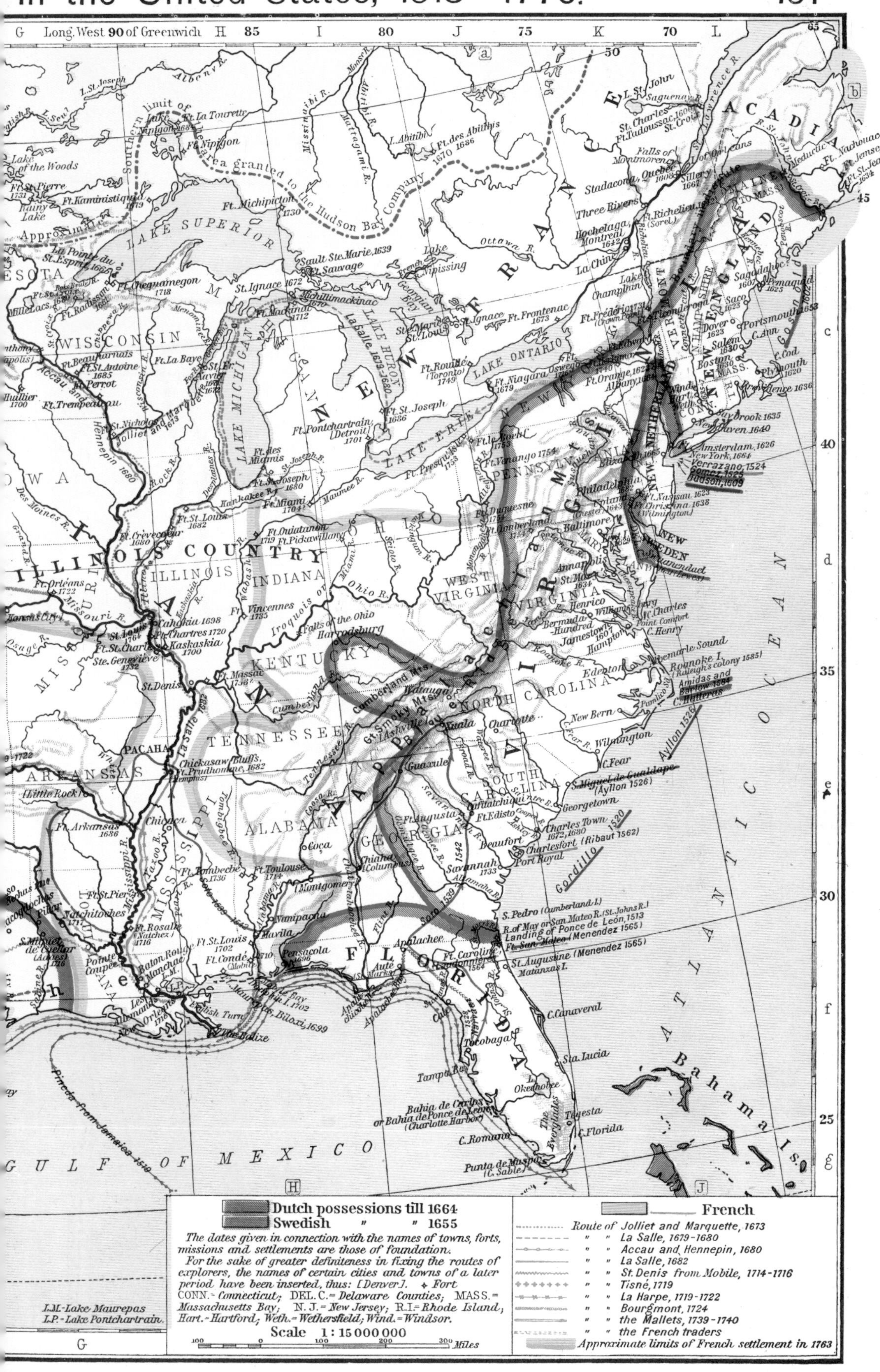
Long. West 90 of Greenwich
NEW FRANCE
ACADIA
NEW ENGLAND
NEW NETHERLAND
NEW SWEDEN
ILLINOIS COUNTRY
LOUISIANA
FLORIDA
APPALACHIAN MTS.
LAKE SUPERIOR
LAKE MICHIGAN
LAKE HURON
LAKE ONTARIO
LAKE ERIE
Southern limit of the area granted to the Hudson Bay Company
WISCONSIN
ILLINOIS
INDIANA
OHIO
KENTUCKY
TENNESSEE
WEST VIRGINIA
VIRGINIA
NORTH CAROLINA
SOUTH CAROLINA
GEORGIA
ALABAMA
MISSISSIPPI
ARKANSAS
PENNSYLVANIA
VERMONT
NEW HAMPSHIRE
MAINE
MASS.
CONN.
ATLANTIC OCEAN
GULF OF MEXICO
Bahama Is.
Quebec 1608
Montreal 1642
Three Rivers
Ft. Frontenac 1673
Ft. Niagara 1679
Ft. Pontchartrain (Detroit) 1701
Ft. Duquesne 1754
Philadelphia
Baltimore
Annapolis
Jamestown 1607
Charles Town 1672, 1680
Savannah 1733
St. Augustine (Menendez 1565)
Pensacola 1696
New Orleans 1718
Biloxi 1699
Kaskaskia 1700
Cahokia 1698
Ft. Chartres 1720
New Amsterdam 1626
New York 1664
Boston 1630
Plymouth 1620
Roanoke I. (Raleigh's colony 1585)
Dutch possessions till 1664
Swedish " " 1655
The dates given in connection with the names of towns, forts, missions and settlements are those of foundation.
For the sake of greater definiteness in fixing the routes of explorers, the names of certain cities and towns of a later period have been inserted, thus: [Denver]. ✦ Fort
CONN. = Connecticut; DEL. C. = Delaware Counties; MASS. = Massachusetts Bay; N. J. = New Jersey; R. I. = Rhode Island; Hart. = Hartford; Weth. = Wethersfield; Wind. = Windsor.
Scale 1 : 15 000 000
100 0 100 200 300 Miles
French
Route of Jolliet and Marquette, 1673
" " La Salle, 1679-1680
" " Accau and Hennepin, 1680
" " La Salle, 1682
" " St. Denis from Mobile, 1714-1716
" " Tisné, 1719
" " La Harpe, 1719-1722
" " Bourgmont, 1724
" " the Mallets, 1739-1740
" " the French traders
Approximate limits of French settlement in 1763
L.M. = Lake Maurepas
L.P. = Lake Pontchartrain.

Reference Map of the Middle Colonies, 1607—1760.

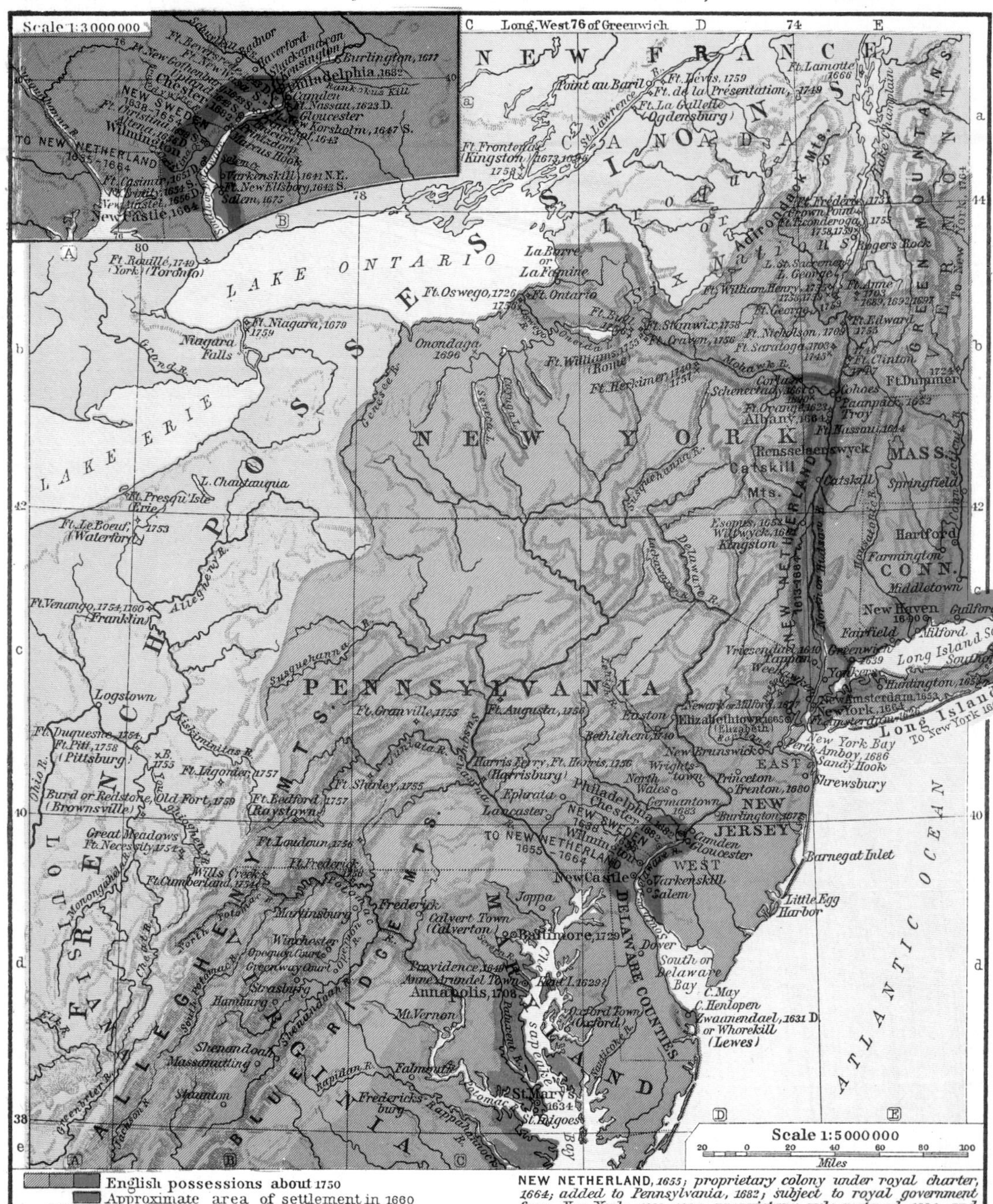

English possessions about 1750
Approximate area of settlement in 1660
" " " " " 1750
Line of the "Walking Purchase," 1737
Dutch possessions 1613-1664, 1655-1664, 1673-1674
Swedish possessions 1638-1655
French possessions about 1750

NEW YORK *As* NEW NETHERLAND, *under Dutch rule, 1623-1664, 1673-1674; proprietary colony under royal charter, 1664-1685; royal province, 1685-1688; united with the New England colonies under royal governor-general, 1688-1689; separate province, 1689-*

NEW JERSEY *Proprietary colony under royal charter, 1664, and under patent from the Duke of York, 1664-1674; divided into East New Jersey and West New Jersey, 1676; united with the New England colonies under royal governor-general, 1688-1689; proprietary colonies of East New Jersey and West New Jersey, 1689-1702; royal province of New Jersey, 1702; under same governor as New York, 1702-1738; separate province, 1738-*

PENNSYLVANIA *Proprietary colony under royal charter, 1681; subject to royal government from New York, 1692-1694; proprietary rule restored, 1694, and maintained till 1776*

DELAWARE COUNTIES (The Three Lower Counties on the Delaware) *As* NEW SWEDEN, *under Swedish rule, 1638-1655; annexed to* NEW NETHERLAND, *1655; proprietary colony under royal charter, 1664; added to Pennsylvania, 1682; subject to royal government from New York, 1692-1694; proprietary rule restored, 1694, and maintained over the Delaware Counties as a separate colony, 1704-1776.*

MARYLAND *Proprietary colony under royal charter, 1632; subject to royal government, 1692-1715; proprietary rule restored, 1715, and maintained till 1776.*

The map is designed to serve as an index to localities in the Middle Colonies which for lack of space could not be inserted in the map of European Exploration and Settlement in the United States, 1513-1776 (pages 190/191). The list of names given is not exhaustive. For names of Indian tribes, see p. 188.

Dates associated with the names of localities having the sign (⊙ o) are those of settlement, or of change of name.

✧ Fort, with date of construction. × Site of event in colonial warfare (1689-1760), with date of occurrence.

To the extent shown in the map, the artificial boundaries (..........) are those of the present States of New York, New Jersey, Pennsylvania, Delaware and Maryland. Boundary disputes are not indicated. For the extent of the various grants by royal charter, see p. 190 (inset).

Abbreviations: *B.=Site of Braddock's defeat;* **CONN.=CONNECTICUT,** D.=*Founded or renamed by the Dutch;* **MASS.=MASSACHUSETTS;** N.E.=*Settled from New England;* S.=*Founded or renamed by the Swedes.*

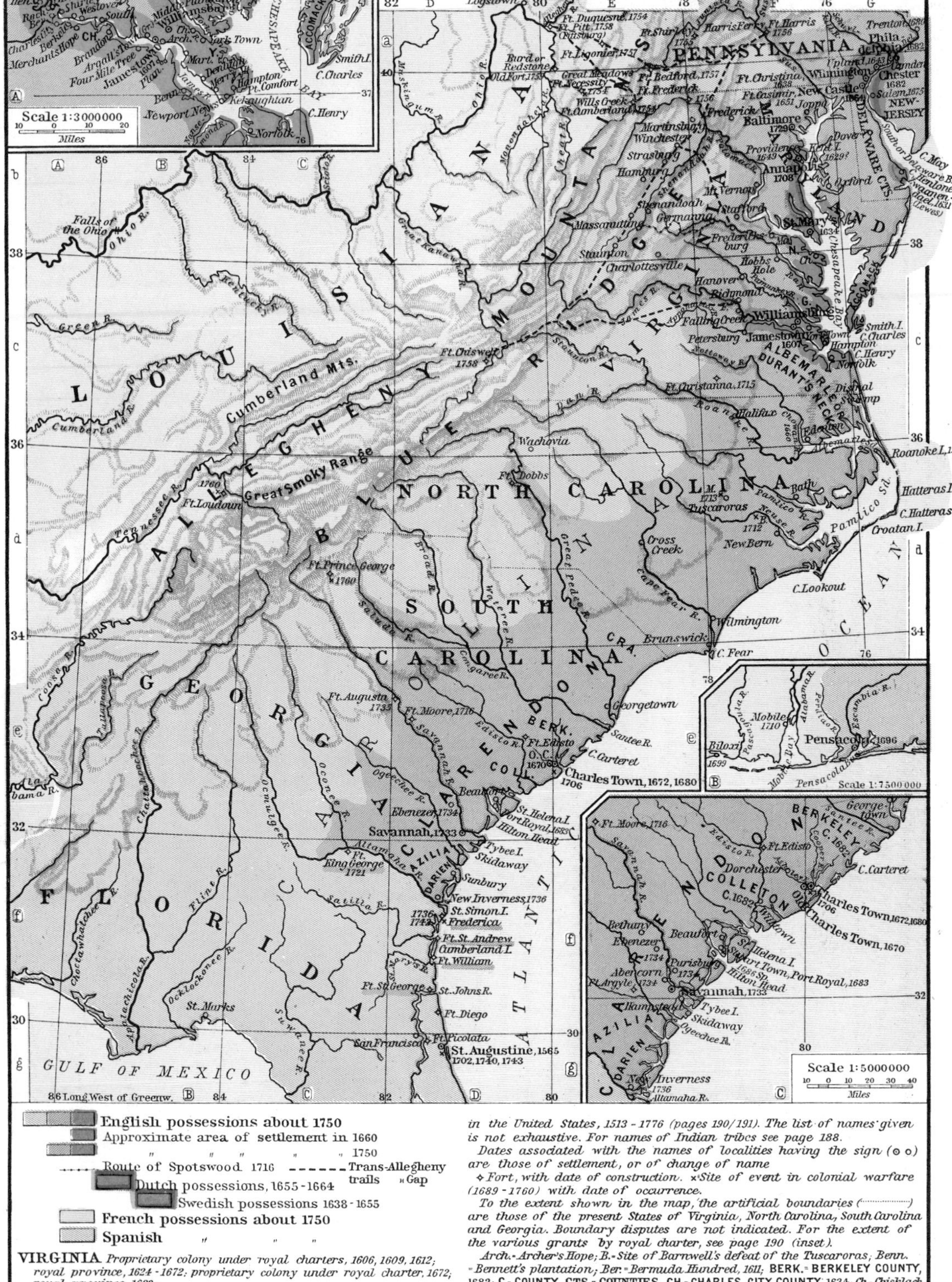

English possessions about 1750

Approximate area of settlement in 1660

" " " " " 1750

Route of Spotswood 1716 — Trans-Allegheny trails „Gap

Dutch possessions, 1655-1664

Swedish possessions 1638-1655

French possessions about 1750

Spanish " " "

VIRGINIA *Proprietary colony under royal charters, 1606, 1609, 1612; royal province, 1624-1672; proprietary colony under royal charter, 1672; royal province, 1683-*

NORTH CAROLINA *As part of Carolina, proprietary colony under royal charters, 1663, 1665; separate colony, 1713; proprietary rights surrendered to the Crown, 1729; royal province, 1731-*

SOUTH CAROLINA *As part of Carolina, proprietary colony under royal charters, 1663, 1665; separate colony, 1713; royal province, 1719-; proprietary rights surrendered to the Crown, 1729.*

GEORGIA *Proprietary colony under royal charter, 1732; royal province, 1752, 1754-*

The map is designed to serve as an index to localities in the Southern Colonies which for lack of space could not be inserted in the map of European Exploration and Settlement in the United States, 1513-1776 (pages 190/191). The list of names given is not exhaustive. For names of Indian tribes see page 188.

Dates associated with the names of localities having the sign (⊙ ○) are those of settlement, or of change of name

✧ Fort, with date of construction. × Site of event in colonial warfare (1689-1760) with date of occurrence.

To the extent shown in the map, the artificial boundaries (⋯⋯) are those of the present States of Virginia, North Carolina, South Carolina and Georgia. Boundary disputes are not indicated. For the extent of the various grants by royal charter, see page 190 (inset).

Arch. - *Archer's Hope*; *B.* - *Site of Barnwell's defeat of the Tuscaroras*; *Benn.* - *Bennett's plantation*; *Ber.* - *Bermuda Hundred, 1611*; BERK. - BERKELEY COUNTY, 1682; C. - COUNTY; CTS. - COUNTIES; CH. - CHARLES CITY COUNTY, 1634; *Ch.* - *Chisklack or Chiskiak*; *Chi.* - *Chicacoan* COLL. - COLLETON COUNTY, 1682; CRA. - CRAVEN COUNTY, 1682; *Cur.* - *Curles*; *Del.* - *Delaware River*; *F.* - *The Falls*; G. - GLOUCESTER COUNTY, 1651; *Gr.* - *Greenspring*; *Hen.* - *Henrico, 1611*; *M.* - *Site of Moore's defeat of the Tuscaroras*; *Ma.* - *Mattox*; *Mart.* - *Martin's Hundred*; N. - NORTHUMBERLAND COUNTY, 1648; O.C. - *Site of* Old Charles Town; *Plan.* - *Plantations across the water*; *Rap.* - *Rappahannock River*; *Roch.* - *Rochdale Hundred*; *South.* - *Southampton Hundred*; *Sus.* - *Susquehanna River*; Sp. - *Attacked by the Spaniards*; Y. - YORK COUNTY, 1634; *Y.* - *York River*

Scale 1: 7500000

20 0 20 40 60 80 100 120 140 160 180

Miles

The British Colonies in North America, 1763—1775.

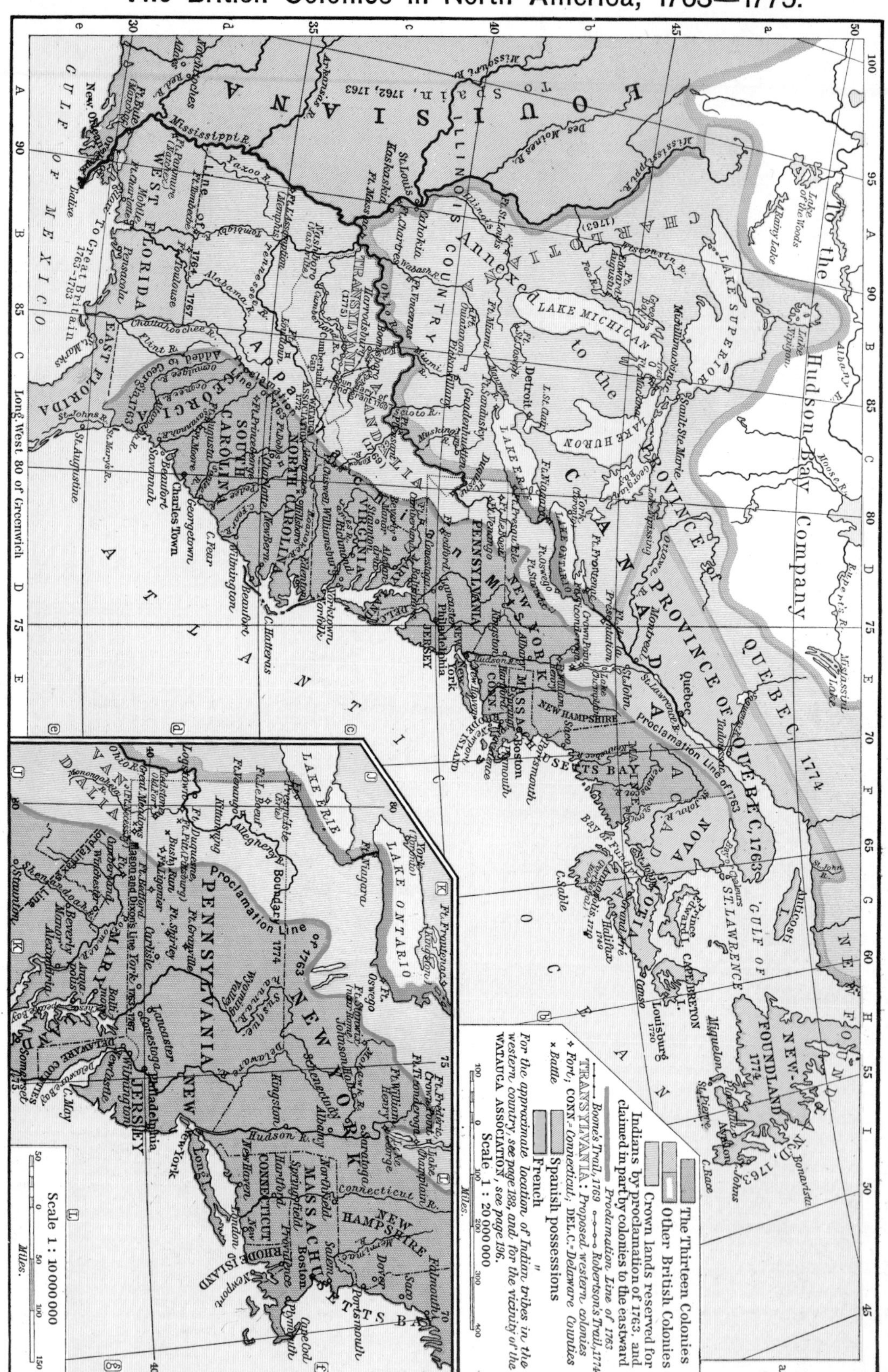

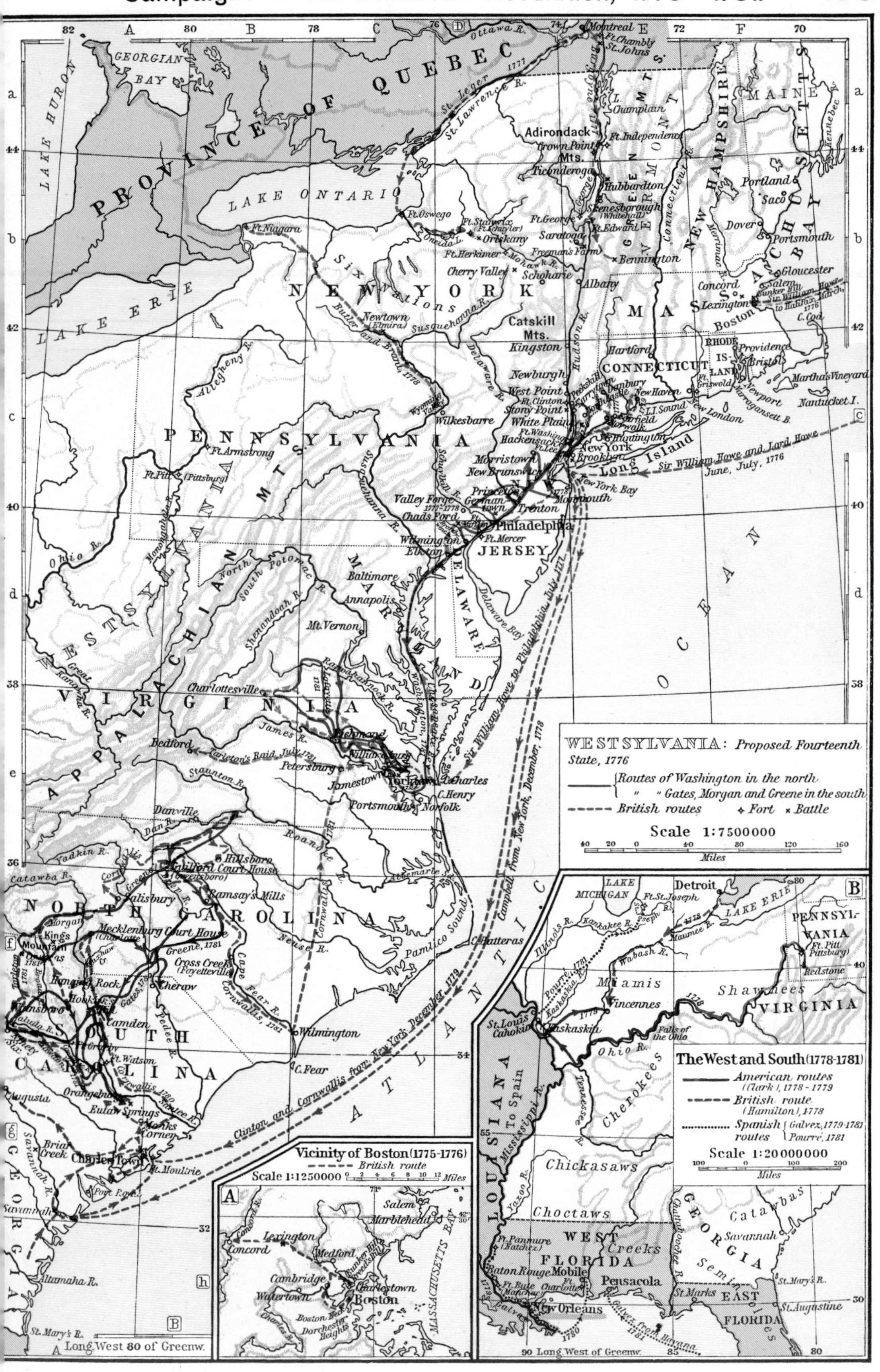
WESTSYLVANIA: Proposed Fourteenth State, 1776
Routes of Washington in the north
" " Gates, Morgan and Greene in the south
British routes
Fort
Battle
Scale 1:7500000
Miles
Vicinity of Boston (1775-1776)
British route
Scale 1:1250000
The West and South (1778-1781)
American routes (Clark), 1778-1779
British route (Hamilton), 1778
Spanish routes { Galvez, 1779-1781 Pourré, 1781
Scale 1:20000000
Miles
PROVINCE OF QUEBEC
NEW YORK
PENNSYLVANIA
VIRGINIA
NORTH CAROLINA
SOUTH CAROLINA
GEORGIA
MARYLAND
DELAWARE
JERSEY
CONNECTICUT
MASSACHUSETTS
NEW HAMPSHIRE
MAINE
VERMONT
ATLANTIC OCEAN
LAKE ONTARIO
LAKE ERIE
LAKE HURON
Sir William Howe and Lord Howe June, July, 1776
Sir William Howe to Philadelphia, July 1777
Campbell from New York, December, 1778
Clinton and Cornwallis from New York, December 1779
Long. West 80 of Greenw.
90 Long. West of Greenw.

The United States, 1783—1803.

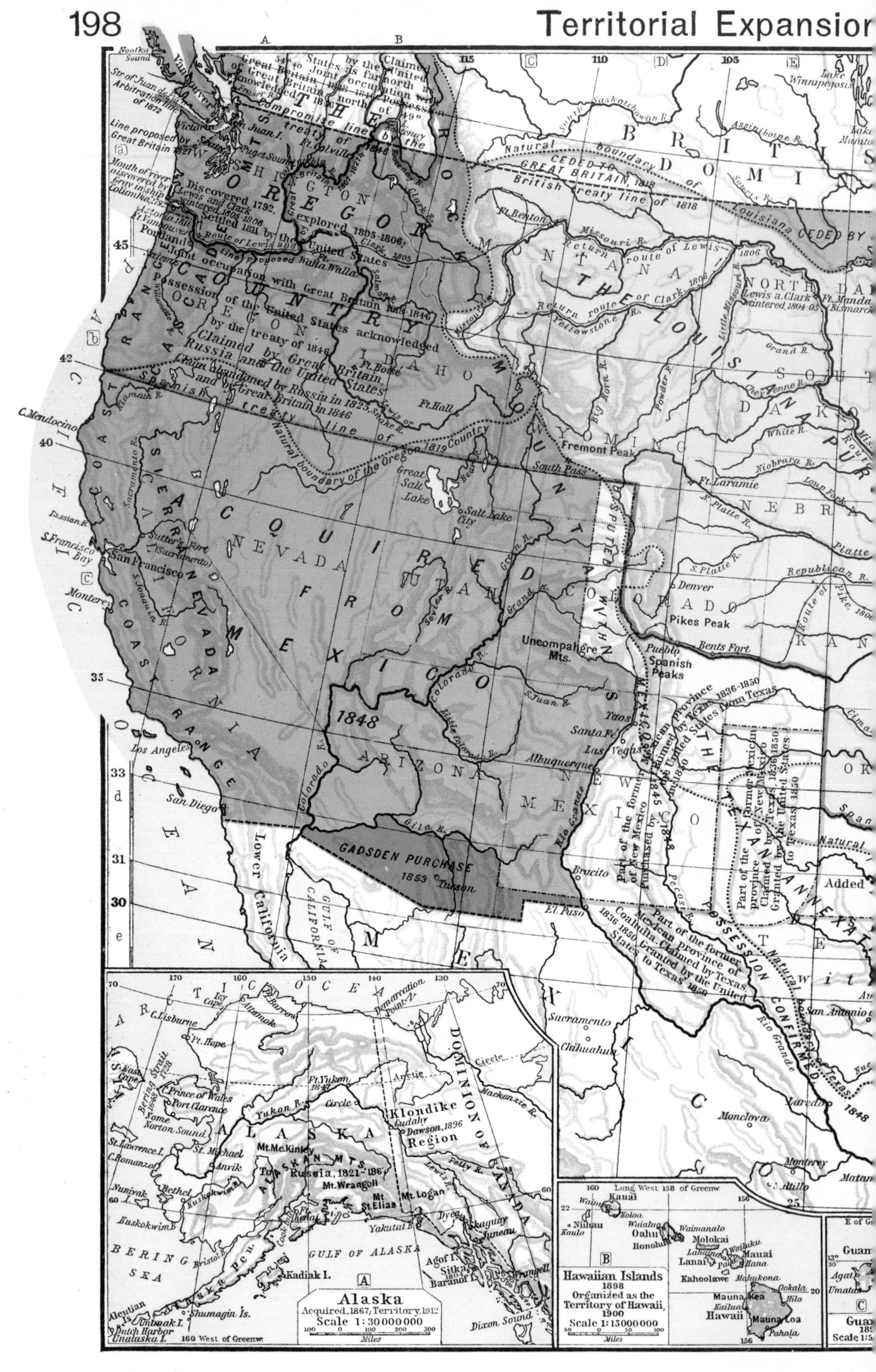

OREGON COUNTRY
ACQUIRED FROM MEXICO 1848
GADSDEN PURCHASE 1853
THE LOUISIANA PURCHASE
TEXAN ANNEXATION
ROCKY MOUNTAINS
Alaska
Acquired, 1867; Territory, 1912
Scale 1: 30 000 000
Hawaiian Islands
1898
Organized as the Territory of Hawaii, 1900
Scale 1: 15 000 000

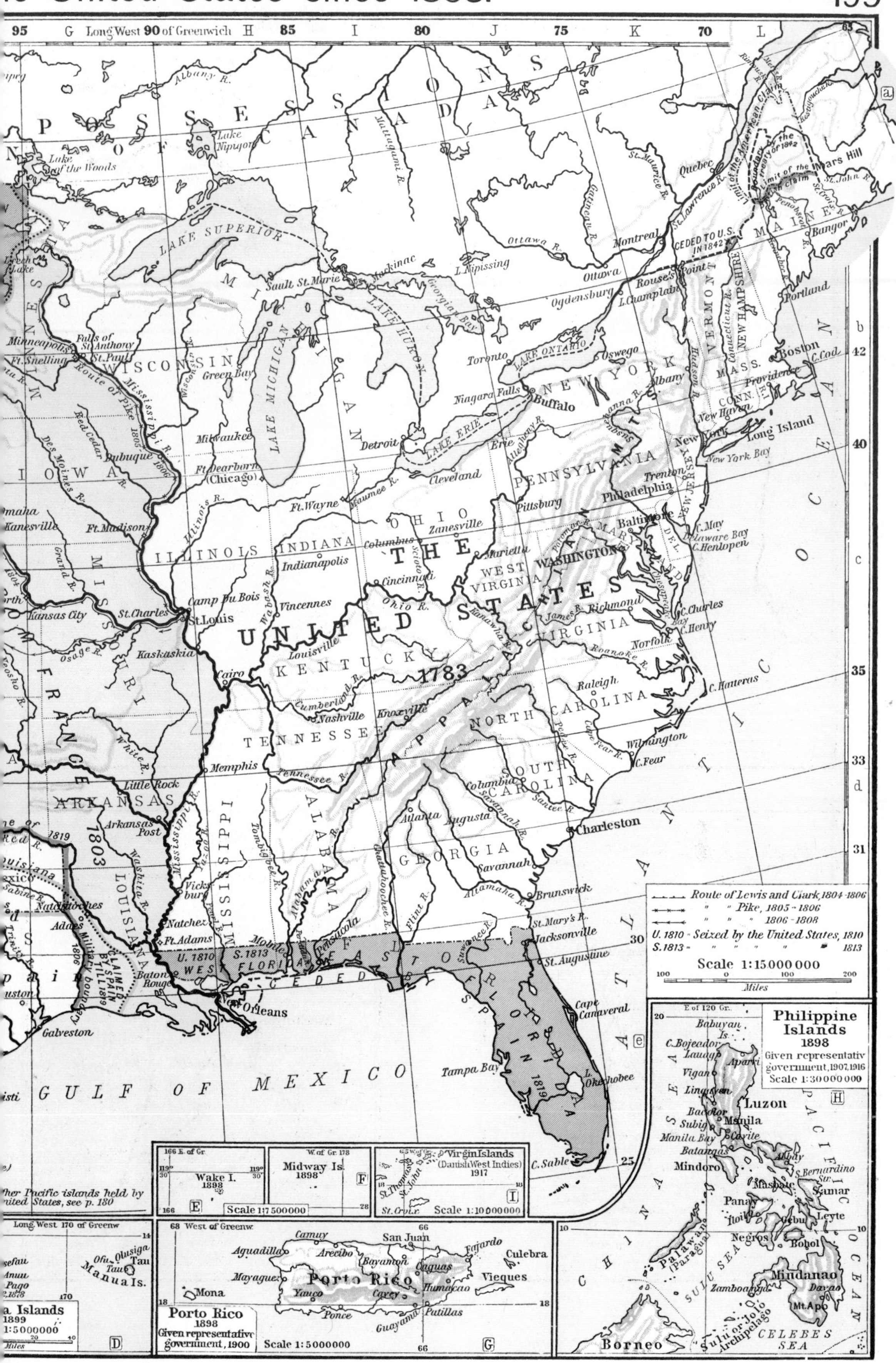

Campaigns of the War of 1812.

Campaigns of the War of 1812

Hull's route, 1812
Harrison's " 1813
Dearborn's " 1812-1813
Wilkinson's " 1813

Scale 1 : 7 500 000

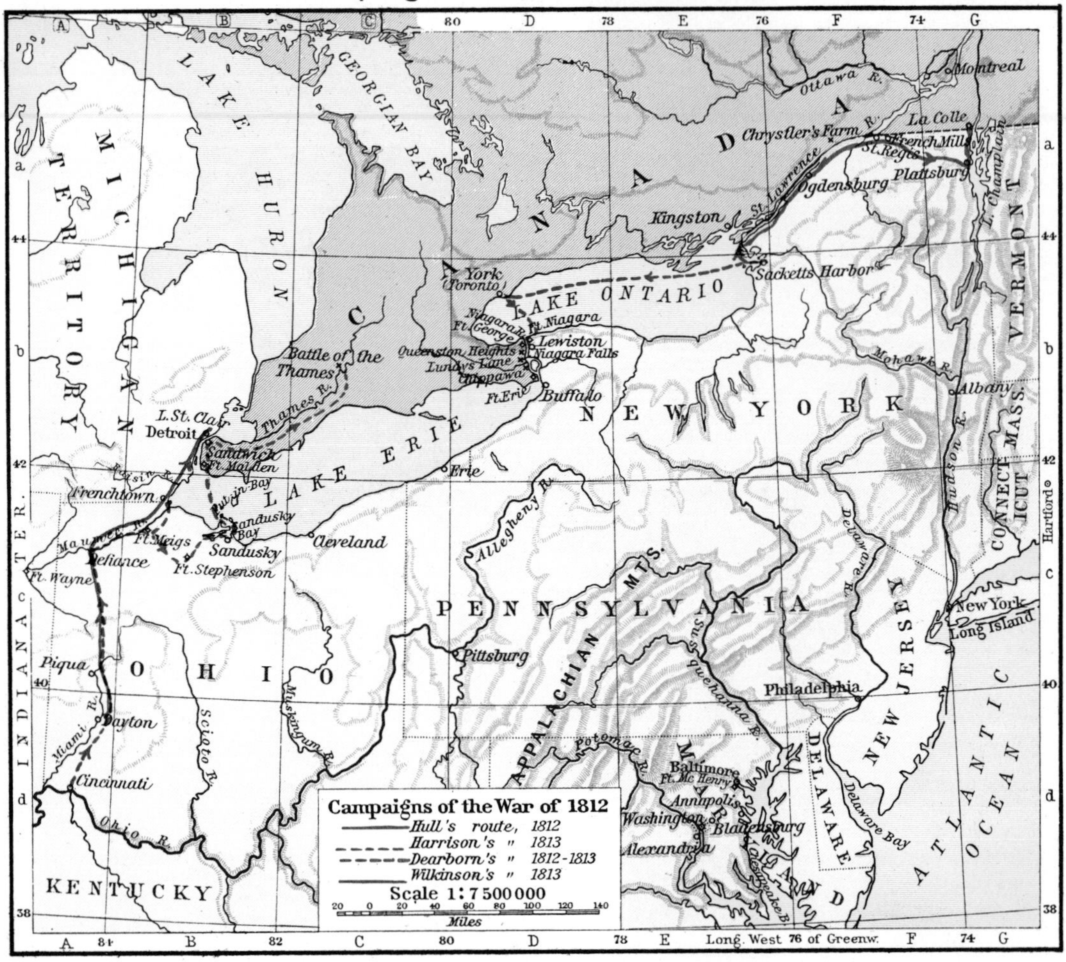

MASS.= MASSACHUSETTS; TER.= TERRITORY. ⋄ *Fort* × *Battle*

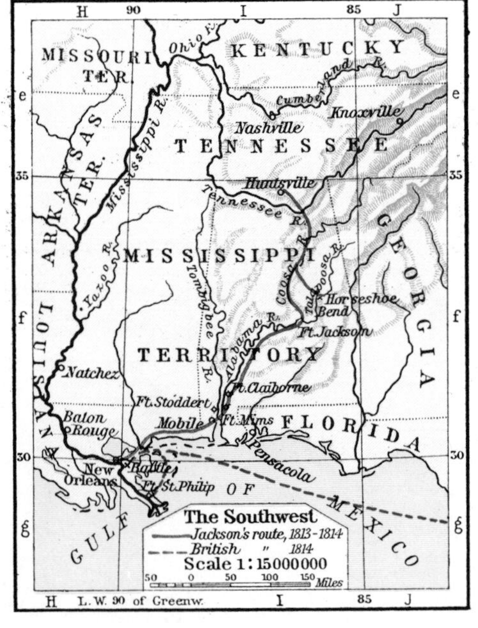

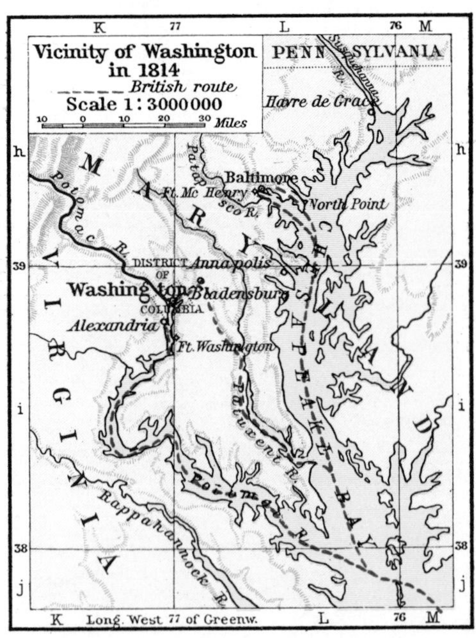

Campaigns of the Mexican War, 1846—1847.

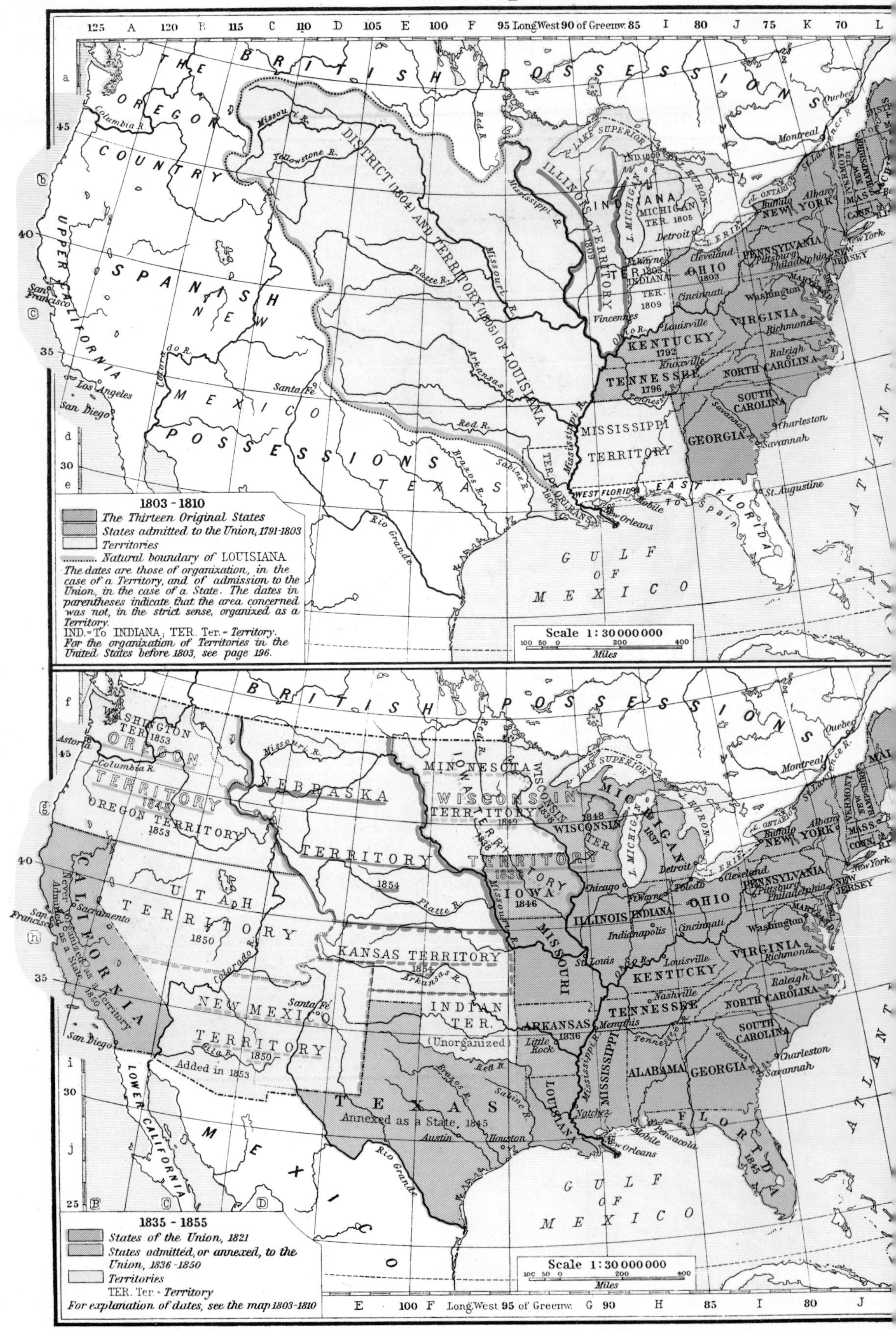
1803 - 1810
The Thirteen Original States
States admitted to the Union, 1791-1803
Territories
Natural boundary of LOUISIANA
The dates are those of organization, in the case of a Territory, and of admission to the Union, in the case of a State. The dates in parentheses indicate that the area concerned was not, in the strict sense, organized as a Territory.
IND. = To INDIANA; TER. Ter. = Territory.
For the organization of Territories in the United States before 1803, see page 196.
Scale 1: 30 000 000
Miles
BRITISH POSSESSIONS
THE OREGON COUNTRY
UPPER CALIFORNIA
SPANISH NEW MEXICO
MEXICO POSSESSIONS
TEXAS
DISTRICT (1804) AND TERRITORY (1805) OF LOUISIANA
ILLINOIS TERRITORY 1809
INDIANA TER. 1809
MICHIGAN TER. 1805
OHIO 1803
KENTUCKY 1792
TENNESSEE 1796
MISSISSIPPI TERRITORY
TER. OF ORLEANS 1804
WEST FLORIDA
EAST FLORIDA
To Spain
PENNSYLVANIA
NEW YORK
NEW JERSEY
MARYLAND
VIRGINIA
NORTH CAROLINA
SOUTH CAROLINA
GEORGIA
GULF OF MEXICO
1835 - 1855
States of the Union, 1821
States admitted, or annexed, to the Union, 1836-1850
Territories
TER. Ter. = Territory
For explanation of dates, see the map 1803-1810
Scale 1: 30 000 000
Miles
BRITISH POSSESSIONS
WASHINGTON TER. 1853
OREGON TERRITORY 1848
OREGON TERRITORY 1853
CALIFORNIA
Never Organized as a Territory Admitted as a State 1850
UTAH TERRITORY 1850
NEBRASKA TERRITORY 1854
KANSAS TERRITORY 1854
NEW MEXICO TERRITORY 1850
Added in 1853
MINNESOTA TERRITORY 1849
WISCONSIN TERRITORY 1836
IOWA TERRITORY 1838
IOWA 1846
WISCONSIN 1848
MICHIGAN 1837
MISSOURI
INDIAN TER. (Unorganized)
ARKANSAS 1836
TEXAS Annexed as a State, 1845
LOUISIANA
MISSISSIPPI
ALABAMA
FLORIDA 1845
ILLINOIS
INDIANA
OHIO
KENTUCKY
TENNESSEE
LOWER CALIFORNIA
MEXICO
GULF OF MEXICO

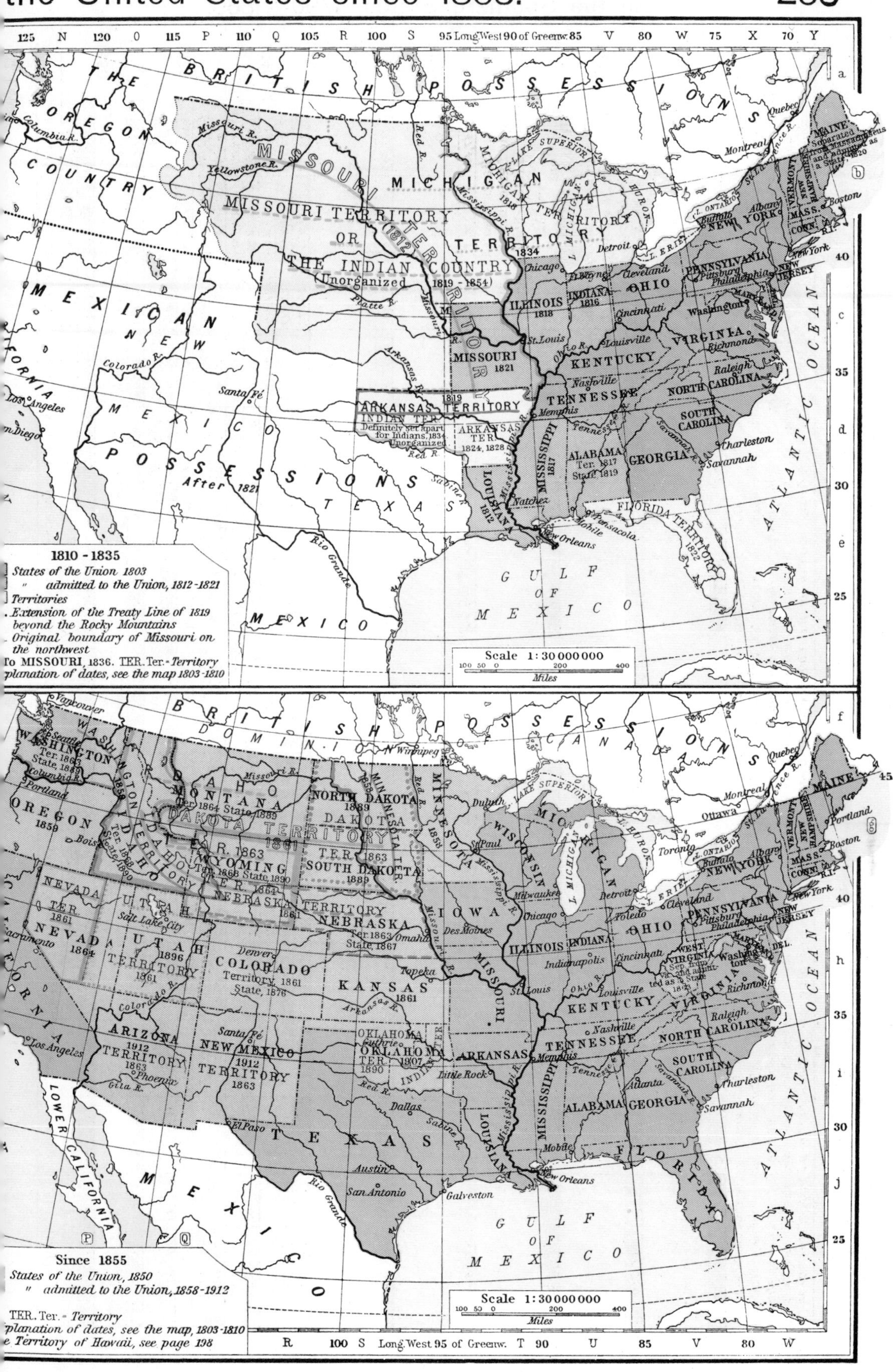
1810 - 1835
States of the Union 1803
" admitted to the Union, 1812-1821
Territories
Extension of the Treaty Line of 1819 beyond the Rocky Mountains
Original boundary of Missouri on the northwest
To MISSOURI, 1836. TER. Ter. = Territory
planation of dates, see the map 1803-1810
Scale 1: 30 000 000
Miles
THE BRITISH POSSESSIONS
OREGON COUNTRY
MISSOURI TERRITORY
MICHIGAN TERRITORY
MISSOURI TERRITORY OR THE INDIAN COUNTRY (Unorganized 1819-1854)
MEXICAN POSSESSIONS After 1821
NEW MEXICO
TEXAS
ARKANSAS TERRITORY 1819
INDIAN TER. Definitely set apart for Indians, 1834. Unorganized
ARKANSAS TER. 1824, 1828
ILLINOIS 1818
INDIANA 1816
OHIO
MISSOURI 1821
KENTUCKY
TENNESSEE
MISSISSIPPI 1817
ALABAMA Ter. 1817 State 1819
LOUISIANA 1812
GEORGIA
FLORIDA TERRITORY 1822
GULF OF MEXICO
ATLANTIC OCEAN
Since 1855
States of the Union, 1850
" admitted to the Union, 1858-1912
TER. Ter. = Territory
planation of dates, see the map, 1803-1810
e Territory of Hawaii, see page 198
Scale 1: 30 000 000
Miles
BRITISH POSSESSIONS
DOMINION OF CANADA
WASHINGTON Ter. 1853 State 1889
OREGON 1859
IDAHO Ter. 1863 State 1890
MONTANA Ter. 1864 State 1889
DAKOTA TERRITORY 1861
NORTH DAKOTA 1889
SOUTH DAKOTA 1889
WYOMING Ter. 1868 State 1890
NEBRASKA TERRITORY 1854
NEBRASKA Ter. 1863 State 1867
NEVADA TER. 1861
NEVADA 1864
UTAH 1896
UTAH TERRITORY 1861
COLORADO Territory 1861 State 1876
KANSAS 1861
MINNESOTA 1858
WISCONSIN
MICHIGAN
IOWA
MISSOURI
ILLINOIS
INDIANA
OHIO
KENTUCKY
WEST VIRGINIA
VIRGINIA
TENNESSEE
ARKANSAS
MISSISSIPPI
ALABAMA
GEORGIA
LOUISIANA
FLORIDA
OKLAHOMA 1907
OKLAHOMA TER. 1890
INDIAN TER.
ARIZONA 1912 TERRITORY 1863
NEW MEXICO 1912 TERRITORY 1863
TEXAS
LOWER CALIFORNIA
MEXICO
GULF OF MEXICO
ATLANTIC OCEAN

Slavery and the Staple Agricultural Products in the Southern States, 1790—1860.

	ALABAMA	ARKANSAS	FLORIDA	GEORGIA	KENTUCKY	LOUISIANA	MARYLAND	MISSISSIPPI	MISSOURI	N.CAROLINA	S.CAROLINA	TENNESSEE	TEXAS	VIRGINIA	Totals
1860	395,982,000	146,957,200	26,061,200	280,736,000		311,095,200		481,002,800	16,475,200	58,205,600	141,364,800	118,585,600	172,585,200	5,090,800	2,154,141,600
	232,914	989,980	828,815	919,318	108,126,840	39,940	38,410,965	159,141	25,086,196	32,853,250	104,412	43,448,097	97,914	123,968,312	375,266,094
	493,465	16,831	223,704	52,507,652		6,331,257		809,082	9,767	7,593,796	119,100,528	40,372	26,031	8,325	187,160,710
	175,000		1,669,000	1,167,000		221,726,000		506,000	402,000	38,000	198,000	2,000	5,099,000		230,982,000
	435,080	111,115	61,745	462,198	225,483	331,726	87,189	436,631	114,931	331,059	402,406	275,719	182,566	490,865	3,948,713
1850	225,775,600	26,137,600	18,052,400	199,636,400	303,200	71,494,800		193,716,800		29,538,000	120,360,400	77,812,800	23,228,800	1,578,800	987,635,600
	164,990	218,936	998,614	423,924	55,601,196	26,878	21,407,497	49,960	17,113,784	11,984,786	74,285	20,148,932	66,897	56,803,227	185,083,906
	2,312,252	63,179	1,075,090	38,950,691	5,688	4,425,349		2,719,856	700	5,465,868	159,930,613	258,854	88,203	17,154	215,313,397
	8,242,000		2,750,000	1,642,000	284,000	226,001,000		388,000			671,000	248,000	7,351,000		247,583,000
	342,844	47,100	39,310	381,682	210,981	244,809	90,368	309,878	87,422	288,548	384,984	239,459	58,161	472,528	3,198,074
1840	117,138,823	6,028,042	12,110,533	163,392,396	691,456	152,555,368	5,673	193,401,577	121,121	51,926,190	61,710,274	27,701,277		3,494,483	790,277,213
	273,302	148,439	75,274	162,894	53,436,909	119,824	24,816,012	83,471	9,067,913	16,772,359	51,519	29,550,432		75,347,106	209,905,454
	149,019	5,454	481,420	12,384,732	16,736	3,604,534		777,195	50	2,820,388	60,590,861	7,977		2,956	80,841,322
	10,143	1,542	275,317	329,744	1,377,835	119,947,720	36,266	77	274,853	17,163	30,000	258,073		1,541,833	124,100,566
	253,532	19,935	25,717	280,944	182,258	168,452	89,737	195,211	58,240	245,817	327,038	183,059		449,087	2,479,027
1830	117,549	4,576	15,501	217,531	165,213	109,588	102,994	65,659	25,091	245,601	315,401	141,603		469,757	1,996,065
1820	47,439	1,617		149,656	126,732	69,064	107,398	32,814	10,222	205,017	258,475	80,107		425,153	1,513,694
1810				105,218	80,561	34,660	111,502	17,088	3,011	168,824	196,365	44,535		392,518	1,154,282
1800				59,404	40,343		105,635	3,489		133,296	146,151	13,584		345,796	847,698
1790				29,264	11,830		103,036			100,572	107,094	3,417		293,427	648,640

Slavery and the Staple Agricultural Products in the Southern States, 1790-1860

Slaves
Cotton — Rice
Tobacco — Sugar-cane

By reference to the figures in each column, it will be seen that the colored strips extending from one vertical line to another indicate the maximum number of slaves, or of pounds of a certain agricultural product, recorded during any of the decennial years. The shorter strips are proportioned in size to this representation of the maximum number. In the absence of any strip, the figures alone mean that the number of slaves, or of pounds of a certain agricultural product, was less than one tenth of the maximum.

The purpose of this chart is to suggest a possible relation between the sectionalization of slavery and the growth of the staple agricultural products in the Southern States. Unfortunately the Reports of the Census Bureau of the United States, from which the figures are taken, do not supply agricultural statistics before 1840. – Although a slave-holding State, Delaware is not included in the list, because the amount of any of the staple agricultural products raised there was too small for the purpose of comparison.

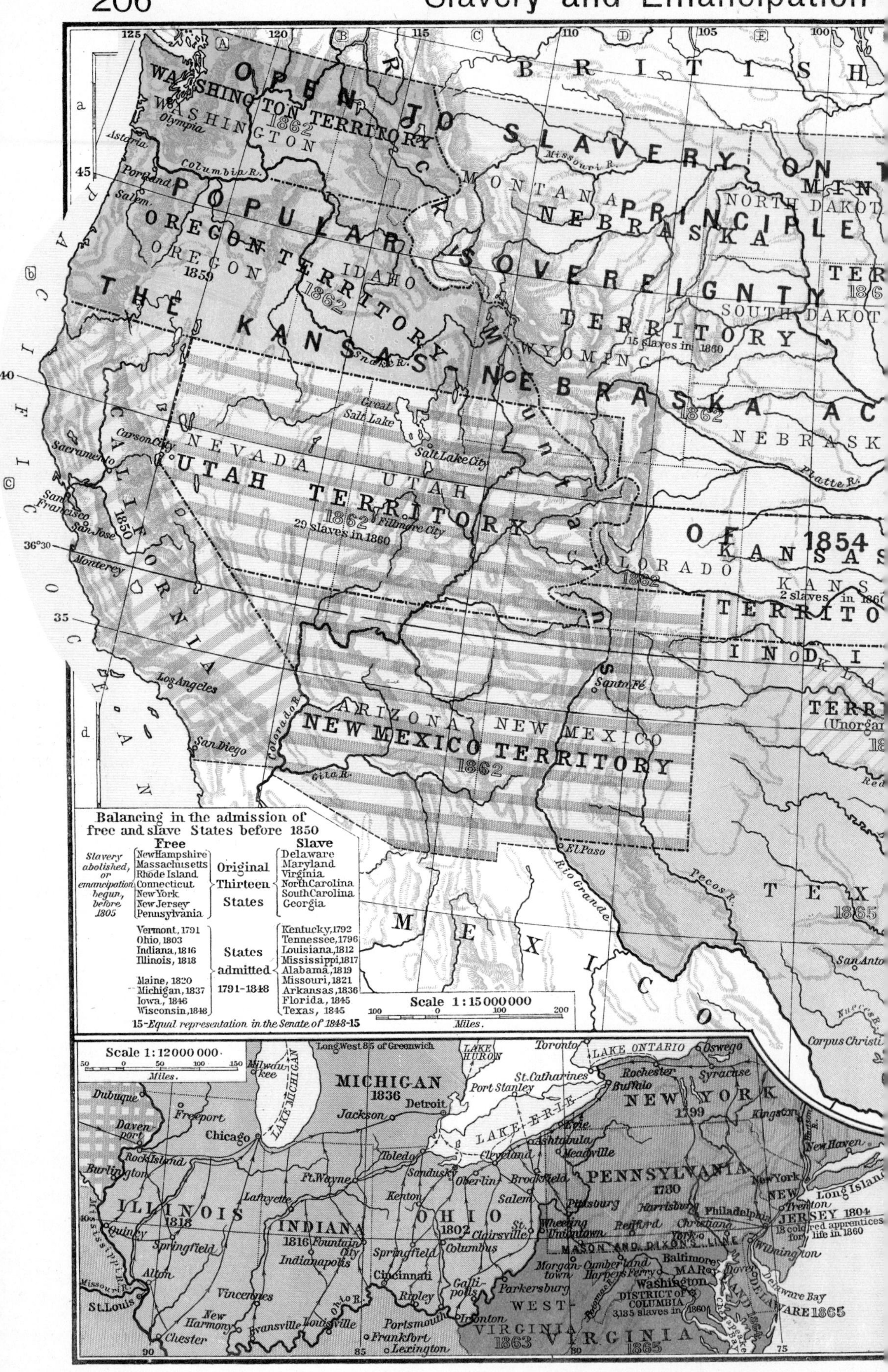

OPEN TO SLAVERY ON THE PRINCIPLE OF POPULAR SOVEREIGNTY
THE KANSAS-NEBRASKA ACT OF 1854
BRITISH
WASHINGTON TERRITORY
WASHINGTON 1862
Olympia
Astoria
Portland
Salem
Columbia R.
OREGON TERRITORY
OREGON 1859
IDAHO 1862
MONTANA
Missouri R.
NEBRASKA TERRITORY
NORTH DAKOTA
SOUTH DAKOTA
15 slaves in 1860
WYOMING
NEBRASKA 1862
Platte R.
Snake R.
Great Salt Lake
Salt Lake City
Carson City
Sacramento
San Francisco
San Jose
Monterey
Los Angeles
San Diego
CALIFORNIA 1850
NEVADA
UTAH
UTAH TERRITORY 1862
29 slaves in 1860
Fillmore City
COLORADO 1862
KANSAS
KANSAS TERRITORY
2 slaves in 1860
INDIAN TERRITORY (Unorganized)
OKLAHOMA
Santa Fé
ARIZONA
NEW MEXICO
NEW MEXICO TERRITORY 1862
Colorado R.
Gila R.
El Paso
Rio Grande
Pecos R.
TEXAS 1865
San Antonio
Nueces R.
Corpus Christi
MEXICO
PACIFIC OCEAN
Rocky Mountains
Balancing in the admission of free and slave States before 1850
Free
Slave
Slavery abolished, or emancipation begun, before 1805
New Hampshire
Massachusetts
Rhode Island
Connecticut
New York
New Jersey
Pennsylvania
Original Thirteen States
Delaware
Maryland
Virginia
North Carolina
South Carolina
Georgia
Vermont, 1791
Ohio, 1803
Indiana, 1816
Illinois, 1818
Maine, 1820
Michigan, 1837
Iowa, 1846
Wisconsin, 1848
States admitted 1791-1848
Kentucky, 1792
Tennessee, 1796
Louisiana, 1812
Mississippi, 1817
Alabama, 1819
Missouri, 1821
Arkansas, 1836
Florida, 1845
Texas, 1845
15-Equal representation in the Senate of 1848-15
Scale 1:15 000 000
Miles
Scale 1:12 000 000
Miles
Long. West 85 of Greenwich
LAKE HURON
LAKE MICHIGAN
LAKE ONTARIO
LAKE ERIE
Toronto
Oswego
St. Catharines
Port Stanley
Rochester
Syracuse
Buffalo
NEW YORK 1799
Kingston
New Haven
Long Island
MICHIGAN 1836
Detroit
Jackson
Milwaukee
Dubuque
Freeport
Davenport
Chicago
Rock Island
Burlington
Toledo
Sandusky
Cleveland
Erie
Ashtabula
Meadville
Ft. Wayne
Oberlin
Brookfield
Kenton
Salem
Lafayette
PENNSYLVANIA 1780
New York
NEW JERSEY 1804
18 colored apprentices for life in 1860
Trenton
Philadelphia
Harrisburg
Pittsburg
ILLINOIS 1818
INDIANA 1816
OHIO 1802
Quincy
Springfield
Fountain City
Indianapolis
Columbus
St. Clairsville
Wheeling
Uniontown
Bedford
Christiana
York
MASON AND DIXON'S LINE
Wilmington
Alton
Cincinnati
Morgantown
Cumberland
Harpers Ferry
Baltimore
Washington
DISTRICT OF COLUMBIA 3185 slaves in 1860
MARYLAND 1864
Dover
DELAWARE 1865
Delaware Bay
Chesapeake Bay
Potomac R.
Mississippi R.
Missouri R.
St. Louis
Vincennes
New Harmony
Evansville
Louisville
Ohio R.
Ripley
Gallipolis
Parkersburg
Portsmouth
Ironton
Chester
Frankfort
Lexington
WEST VIRGINIA 1863
VIRGINIA 1865

Long. West 85 of Greenwich
POSSESSIONS
LAKE SUPERIOR
LAKE MICHIGAN
LAKE HURON
LAKE ONTARIO
LAKE ERIE
MICHIGAN 1836
WISCONSIN 1848
IOWA 1846
ILLINOIS 1818
INDIANA 1816
OHIO 1802
MISSOURI 1864
KENTUCKY 1865
TENNESSEE 1865
ARKANSAS 1865
MISSISSIPPI 1865
ALABAMA 1865
GEORGIA 1865
LOUISIANA 1865
FLORIDA 1865
SOUTH CAROLINA 1865
NORTH CAROLINA 1865
VIRGINIA 1865
WEST VIRGINIA 1863
MARYLAND
DELAWARE 1865
PENNSYLVANIA 1780
NEW JERSEY 1804
NEW YORK 1799
CONN. 1784
RHODE ISLAND, 1784
MASS. 1780
VERMONT 1793
NEW HAMPSHIRE 1783
MAINE 1780
NEW BRUNSWICK
MASON AND DIXON'S LINE
Appalachian Mts.
ATLANTIC OCEAN
GULF OF MEXICO
Bahama Is.
Area of the Original Thirteen States
Slave
Free
…ng part of the Union before
…admitted as States until later
before 1850
…e States …rkansas) …1792-1845
Free territory by the Ordinance of 1787 (held by the courts not to free pre-existent slaves), supplemented by territorial Acts of Congress and by State constitutions
…e State …on, 1845.
Free territory by Act of Congress annexing Texas
Free territory by the Missouri Compromise, 1820
Free State admitted from the area subject to the Missouri Compromise
Free by the Missouri Compromise; slave by addition to Missouri in 1836
Slave State admitted from the area subject to the Missouri Compromise
Open to slavery by the Missouri Compromise
Free by the Missouri Compromise; but opened to slavery by the Compromise of 1850
Territory acquired from Mexico in 1848; free by Mexican law, but opened to slavery by the Compromise of 1850
Free State admitted from the territory acquired from Mexico
Free territory by act of organization, 1848
The areas opened to slavery under the principle of the Kansas-Nebraska Act of 1854 are indicated by the red lettering. The territorial organization shown in the map is that of 1854.
… dates of immediate abolition or of the beginnings of gradual emancipation by State action before 1861 are printed thus: 1780;
…e of immediate abolition by State or national action between 1861 and 1865 are printed thus: 1863.
…reference is made to the "Dred Scott dicta" of 1857, or to the Emancipation Proclamation of 1863; because, legally, the one did not authorize …uction of slavery into the Territories any more than the other effected the abolition of slavery in the Southern States.
Land } routes of the Sea } slave trade
"Underground" routes of fugitive slaves } land } water
The area east of the present State of Oregon formed part of Washington Territory in 1862. The names printed in thin capitals are those of States admitted subsequent to 1854

Seat of the Civil War, 1861—1865.

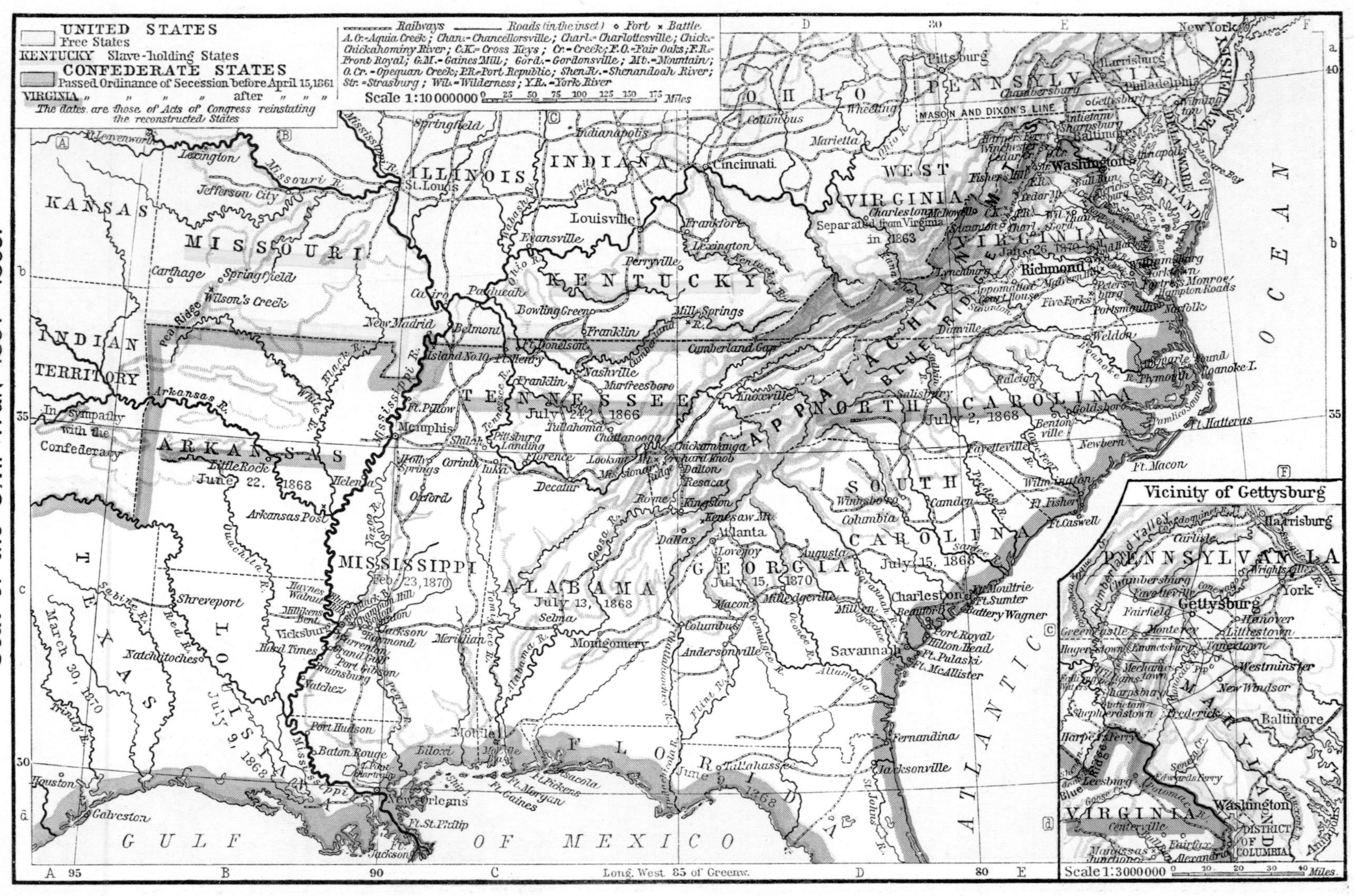

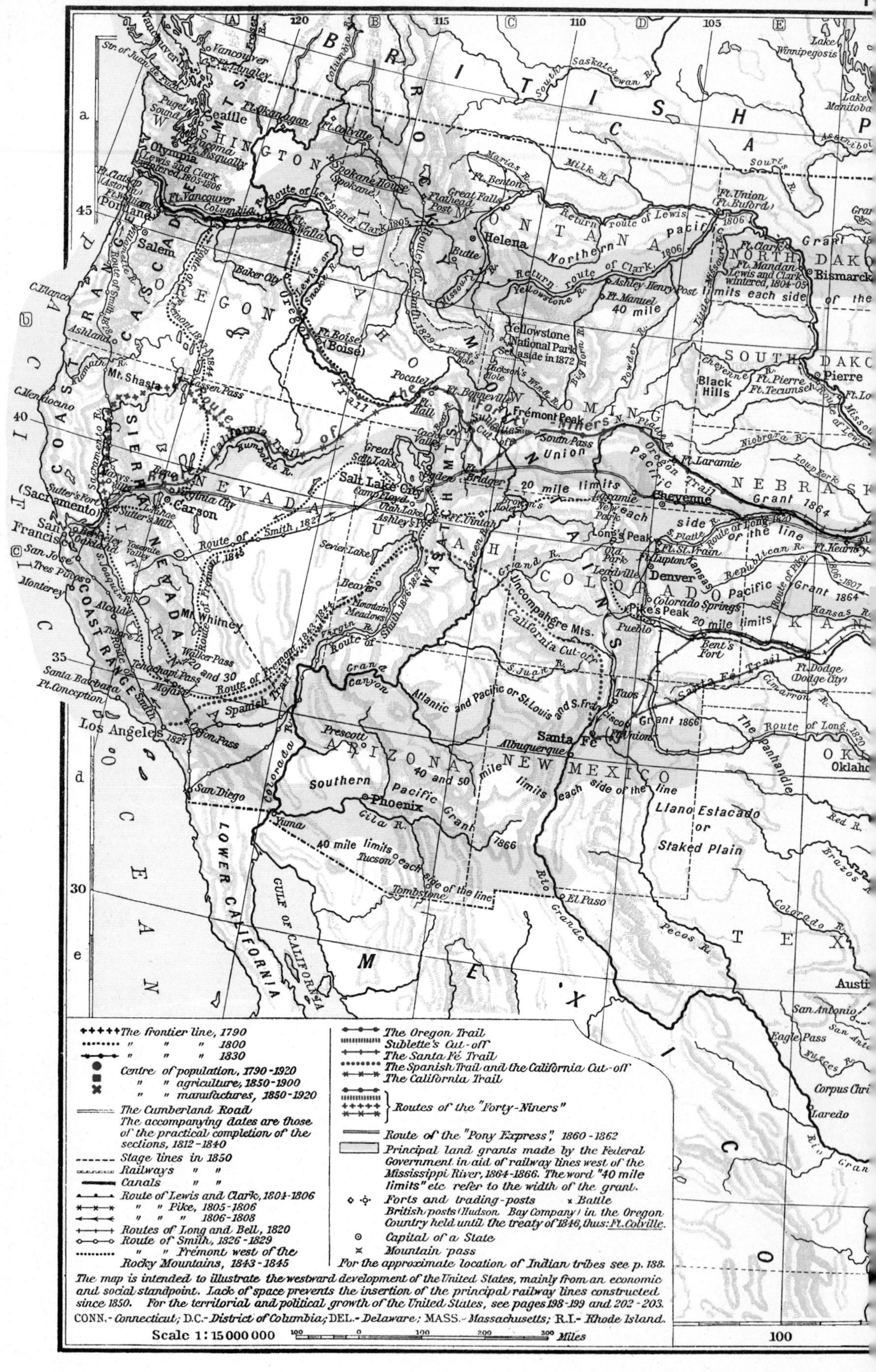
The frontier line, 1790
" " " 1800
" " " 1830
Centre of population, 1790-1920
" " agriculture, 1850-1900
" " manufactures, 1850-1920
The Cumberland Road
The accompanying dates are those of the practical completion of the sections, 1812-1840
Stage lines in 1850
Railways " "
Canals " "
Route of Lewis and Clark, 1804-1806
" " Pike, 1805-1806
" " 1806-1808
Routes of Long and Bell, 1820
Route of Smith, 1826-1829
" " Frémont west of the Rocky Mountains, 1843-1845
The Oregon Trail
Sublette's Cut-off
The Santa Fé Trail
The Spanish Trail and the California Cut-off
The California Trail
Routes of the "Forty-Niners"
Route of the "Pony Express", 1860-1862
Principal land grants made by the Federal Government in aid of railway lines west of the Mississippi River, 1864-1866. The word "40 mile limits" etc refer to the width of the grant.
Forts and trading-posts
Battle
British posts (Hudson Bay Company) in the Oregon Country held until the treaty of 1846, thus: Ft. Colville.
Capital of a State
Mountain pass
For the approximate location of Indian tribes see p. 188.
The map is intended to illustrate the westward development of the United States, mainly from an economic and social standpoint. Lack of space prevents the insertion of the principal railway lines constructed since 1850. For the territorial and political growth of the United States, see pages 198-199 and 202-203.
CONN.-Connecticut; D.C.-District of Columbia; DEL.-Delaware; MASS.-Massachusetts; R.I.-Rhode Island.
Scale 1: 15 000 000
Miles
BRITISH
WASHINGTON
OREGON
IDAHO
MONTANA
WYOMING
NEVADA
UTAH
COLORADO
ARIZONA
NEW MEXICO
NEBRASKA
SOUTH DAKO
NORTH DAKO
LOWER CALIFORNIA
GULF OF CALIFORNIA
MEXICO
PACIFIC OCEAN
CASCADE MTS.
SIERRA NEVADA
COAST RANGE
WASATCH MTS.
Seattle
Olympia
Salem
Helena
Butte
Bismarck
Pierre
Salt Lake City
Carson
(Sacramento)
San Francisco
Los Angeles
San Diego
Santa Fé
Denver
Cheyenne
Phoenix
Tucson
El Paso
Oregon Trail
California Trail
Santa Fé Trail
Spanish Trail
Northern Pacific
Southern Pacific
Atlantic and Pacific or St. Louis and S. Francisco
Union Pacific
Llano Estacado or Staked Plain
Yellowstone National Park Set aside in 1872

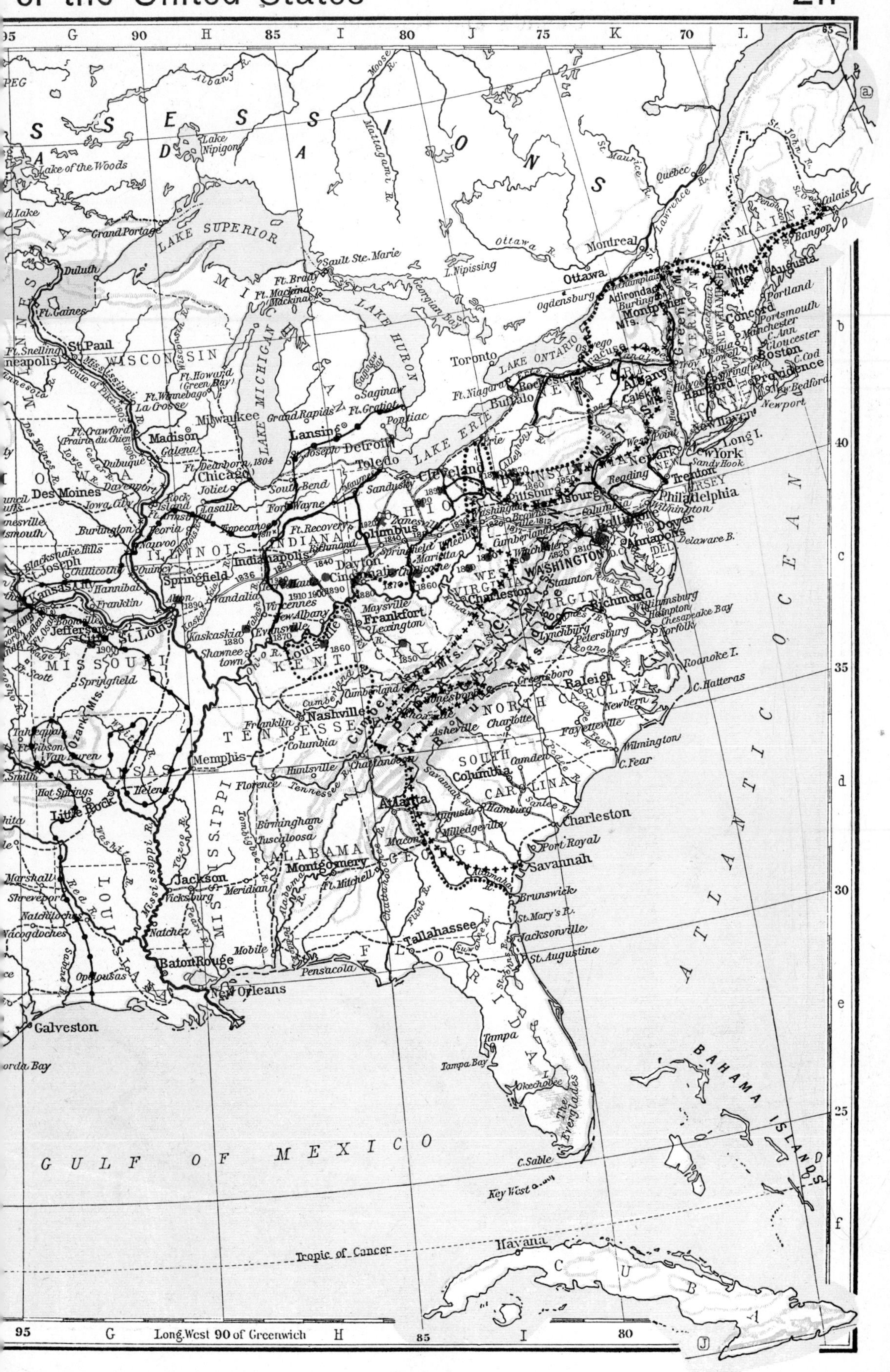
LAKE SUPERIOR
LAKE MICHIGAN
LAKE HURON
LAKE ERIE
LAKE ONTARIO
GULF OF MEXICO
ATLANTIC OCEAN
BAHAMA ISLANDS
CUBA
Tropic of Cancer
Long. West 90 of Greenwich

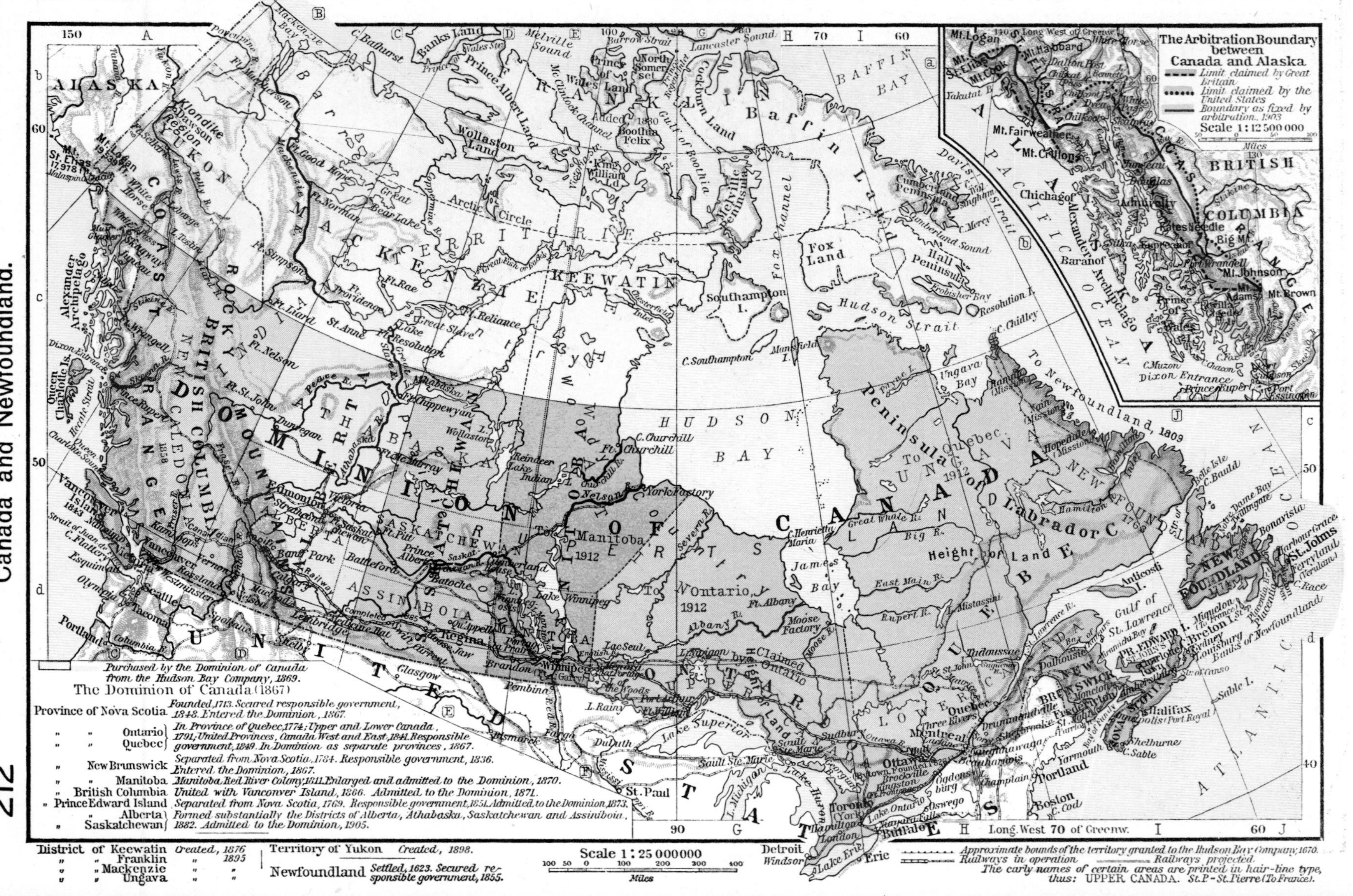
The Arbitration Boundary between Canada and Alaska
Limit claimed by Great Britain
Limit claimed by the United States
Boundary as fixed by arbitration, 1903
Scale 1: 12 500 000
Purchased by the Dominion of Canada from the Hudson Bay Company, 1869.
The Dominion of Canada (1867)
Province of Nova Scotia Founded, 1713. Secured responsible government, 1848. Entered the Dominion, 1867.
" " Ontario } " " Quebec } In Province of Quebec, 1774; Upper and Lower Canada, 1791; United Provinces, Canada West and East, 1841. Responsible government, 1849. In Dominion as separate provinces, 1867.
" New Brunswick Separated from Nova Scotia, 1784. Responsible government, 1836. Entered the Dominion, 1867.
" Manitoba Manitoba, Red River Colony, 1811. Enlarged and admitted to the Dominion, 1870.
" British Columbia United with Vancouver Island, 1866. Admitted to the Dominion, 1871.
" Prince Edward Island Separated from Nova Scotia, 1769. Responsible government, 1851. Admitted to the Dominion, 1873.
" Alberta } " Saskatchewan } Formed substantially the Districts of Alberta, Athabaska, Saskatchewan and Assiniboia, 1882. Admitted to the Dominion, 1905.
District of Keewatin Created, 1876
" " Franklin " 1895
" " Mackenzie " "
" " Ungava " "
Territory of Yukon Created, 1898.
Newfoundland Settled, 1623. Secured responsible government, 1855.
Scale 1: 25 000 000
Miles
Approximate bounds of the territory granted to the Hudson Bay Company, 1670.
Railways in operation
Railways projected
The early names of certain areas are printed in hair-line type, thus: UPPER CANADA. St.P - St. Pierre (To France).
Long. West 70 of Greenw.
DOMINION OF CANADA
UNITED STATES
ALASKA
YUKON
MACKENZIE
KEEWATIN
FRANKLIN
UNGAVA
BRITISH COLUMBIA
ALBERTA
SASKATCHEWAN
MANITOBA
ONTARIO
QUEBEC
NEW BRUNSWICK
NOVA SCOTIA
NEWFOUNDLAND
Labrador
Baffin Land
HUDSON BAY
James Bay
Hudson Strait
Fox Channel
BAFFIN BAY
Gulf of St. Lawrence
ATLANTIC OCEAN
PACIFIC OCEAN
To Newfoundland, 1809

British possessions in Central America and the West Indies
Possessions of the United States
French possessions in the West Indies
Dutch " " " " "
The dates connected with the names of islands in the West Indies are those of acquisition by the power concerned.
The names in block-line type, viz: CAPTAINCY GENERAL OF CUBA, CAPTAINCY GENERAL OF GUATEMALA, Presidency of Guadalajara, Audiencia of Mexico and Audiencia of Santo Domingo are those of the chief political divisions of the Viceroyalty of New Spain about 1790.
Mexico (United Mexican States): Independent, 1821; Republic, 1821-1822; Empire, 1822-1824; Republic, 1824-1863; Empire, 1863-1867; Republic since 1867
Central America: Guatemala, Honduras, Salvador, Nicaragua, Costa Rica: Independent, 1821; United with Mexico, 1821-1823; United Provinces of Central America, 1823-1839; Separate republics since 1839
Railways in operation
" projected or under construction
Line of the proposed Intercontinental (Pan American) Railway
× Battle of the Spanish-American War, 1898 E.C.=El Caney,
S.J.=San Juan Hill. Virtual protectorate of the United States, thus: CUBA
Abbreviations:
Br.=British; D.=Dutch; Fr.=French; Indep.=Independent; MOR.=MORELOS; Rep.=Republic; Sw.=Swedish; U.S.=United States
Scale 1:25 000 000
Miles
Scale 1:12 500 000
Miles
Long. West 90 of Greenwich
UNITED STATES
GULF OF MEXICO
ATLANTIC OCEAN
Tropic of Cancer
WEST INDIES
GREATER ANTILLES
Lesser Antilles
CARIBBEAN SEA
CENTRAL AMERICA
PACIFIC OCEAN
VENEZUELA
COLOMBIA
MICHOACAN
HIDALGO
GUERRERO
OAJACA
VERA CRUZ

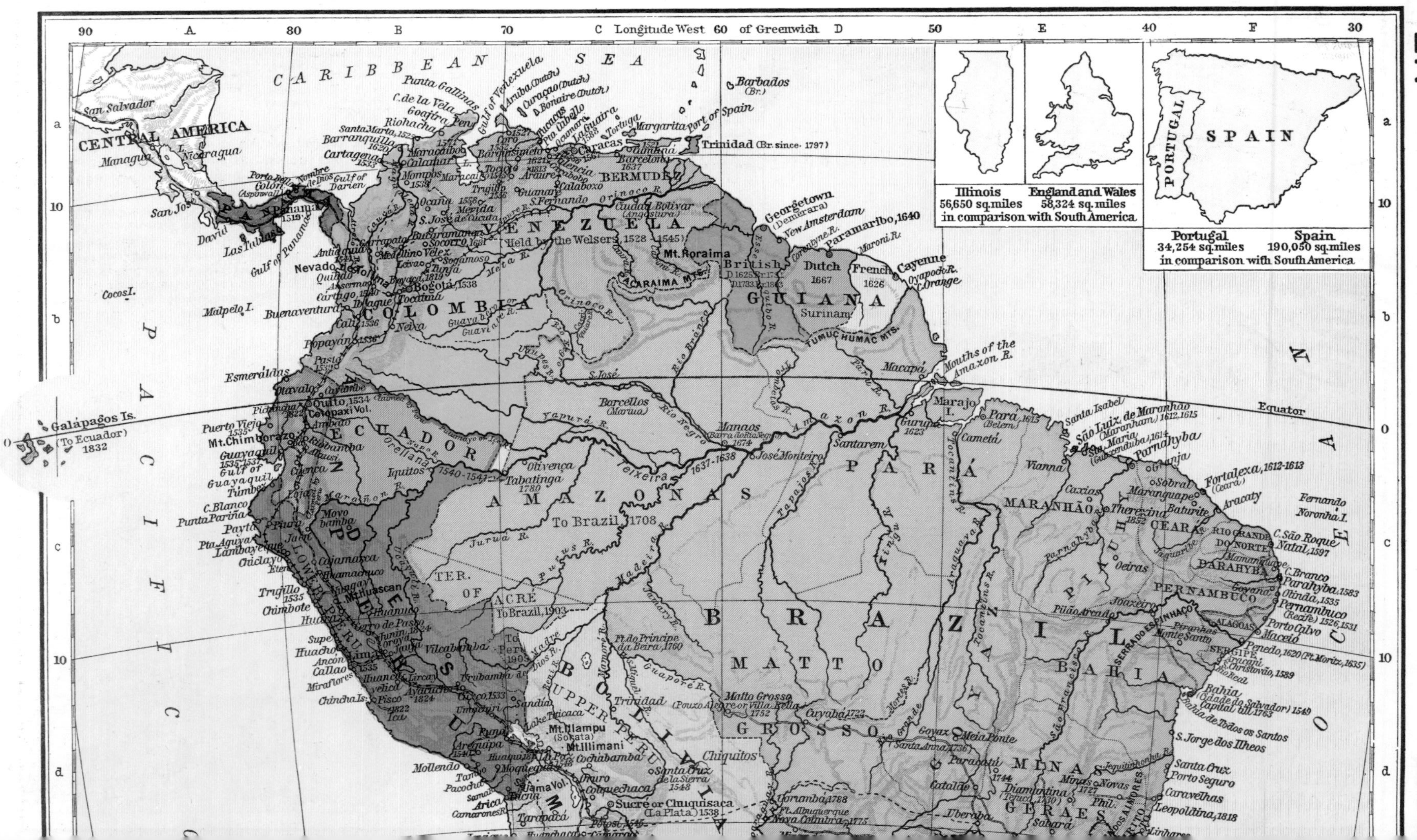
C Longitude West 60 of Greenwich D
C A R I B B E A N S E A
P A C I F I C
Equator
CENTRAL AMERICA
Trinidad (Br. since 1797)
Barbados (Br.)
Port of Spain
VENEZUELA
Held by the Welsers, 1528-1545
Mt. Roraima
PACARAIMA MTS.
TUMUC HUMAC MTS.
G U I A N A
British
Dutch 1667
French 1626
Surinam
Georgetown (Demerara)
New Amsterdam
Paramaribo, 1640
Cayenne
COLOMBIA
ECUADOR
Galápagos Is. (To Ecuador) 1832
Cocos I.
Malpelo I.
Mt. Chimborazo
Cotopaxi Vol.
A M A Z O N A S
To Brazil 1708
P A R Á
MARANHÃO
PIAUHY
CEARÁ
RIO GRANDE DO NORTE
PARAHYBA
PERNAMBUCO
ALAGOAS
SERGIPE
B A H I A
B R A Z I L
M A T T O G R O S S O
M I N A S G E R A E S
TER. OF ACRE
To Brazil, 1903
UPPER PERU
LOWER PERU
BOLIVIA
Mt. Illampu (Sorata)
Mt. Illimani
Mt. Huascan
Mouths of the Amazon R.
Illinois
56,650 sq.miles
England and Wales
58,324 sq.miles
in comparison with South America
PORTUGAL
SPAIN
Portugal
34,254 sq.miles
Spain
190,050 sq.miles
in comparison with South America

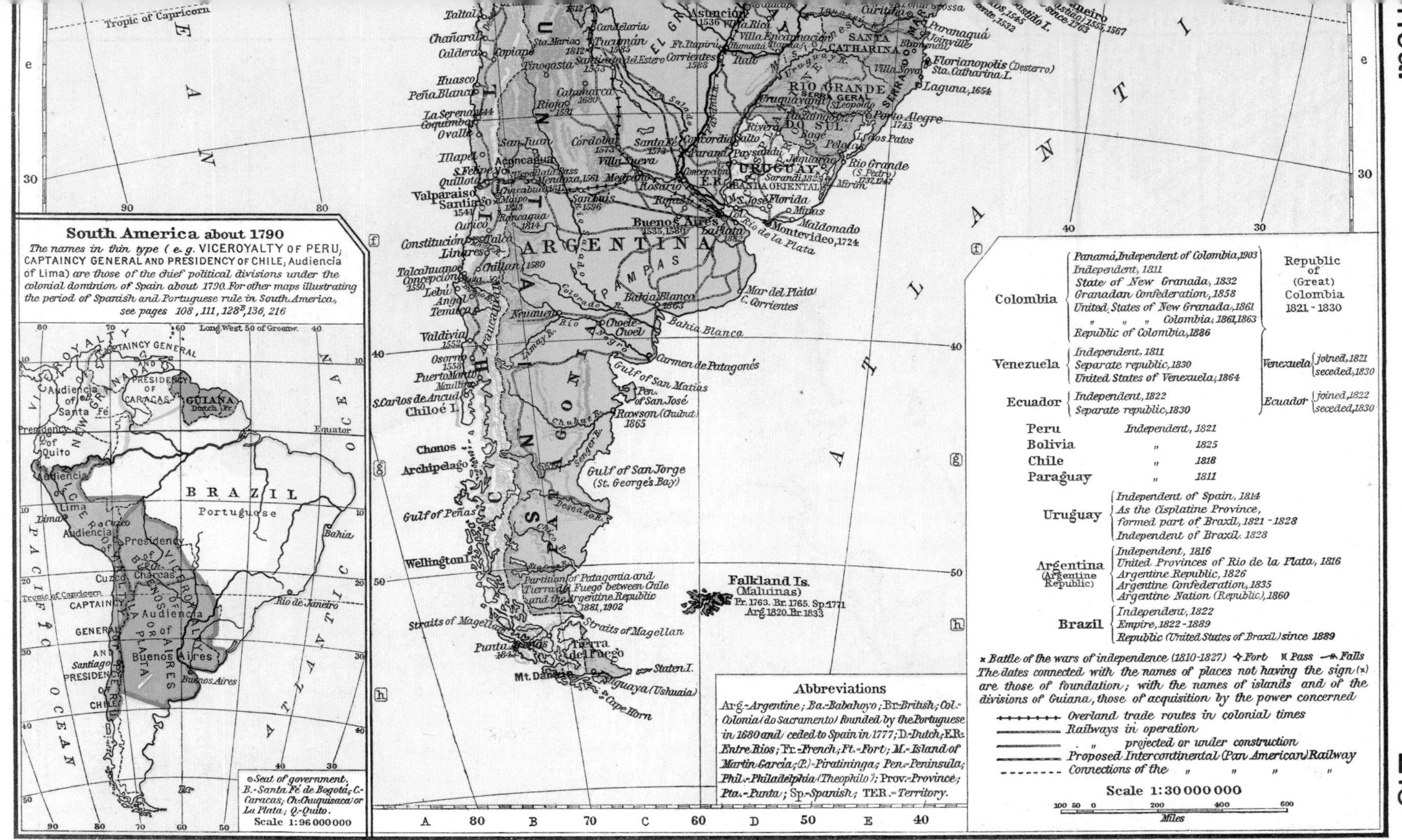
South America about 1790
The names in thin type (e.g. VICEROYALTY OF PERU; CAPTAINCY GENERAL AND PRESIDENCY OF CHILE; Audiencia of Lima) are those of the chief political divisions under the colonial dominion of Spain about 1790. For other maps illustrating the period of Spanish and Portuguese rule in South America, see pages 108, 111, 128B, 136, 216
⊙ Seat of government. B.-Santa Fé de Bogotá; C.-Caracas; Ch.-Chuquisaca or La Plata; Q.-Quito.
Scale 1:96 000 000
Colombia
Panamá, Independent of Colombia, 1903
Independent, 1811
State of New Granada, 1832
Granadan Confederation, 1858
United States of New Granada, 1861
" " " Colombia, 1861, 1863
Republic of Colombia, 1886
Republic of (Great) Colombia 1821 - 1830
Venezuela
Independent, 1811
Separate republic, 1830
United States of Venezuela, 1864
Venezuela joined, 1821 seceded, 1830
Ecuador
Independent, 1822
Separate republic, 1830
Ecuador joined, 1822 seceded, 1830
Peru Independent, 1821
Bolivia " 1825
Chile " 1818
Paraguay " 1811
Uruguay
Independent of Spain, 1814
As the Cisplatine Province, formed part of Brazil, 1821 - 1828
Independent of Brazil. 1828
Argentina (Argentine Republic)
Independent, 1816
United Provinces of Rio de la Plata, 1816
Argentine Republic, 1826
Argentine Confederation, 1835
Argentine Nation (Republic), 1860
Brazil
Independent, 1822
Empire, 1822 - 1889
Republic (United States of Brazil) since 1889
× Battle of the wars of independence (1810-1827) ✧ Fort)(Pass ⟶ Falls
The dates connected with the names of places not having the sign (×) are those of foundation; with the names of islands and of the divisions of Guiana, those of acquisition by the power concerned
Overland trade routes in colonial times
Railways in operation
" projected or under construction
Proposed Intercontinental (Pan American) Railway
Connections of the " " "
Scale 1:30 000 000
Miles
Abbreviations
Arg.-Argentine; Ba.-Babahoyo; Br.-British; Col.-Colonia (do Sacramento) founded by the Portuguese in 1680 and ceded to Spain in 1777; D.-Dutch; E.R.-Entre Rios; Fr.-French; Ft.-Fort; M.-Island of Martin Garcia; (P.)-Piratininga; Pen.-Peninsula; Phil.-Philadelphia (Theophilo); Prov.-Province; Pta.-Punta; Sp.-Spanish; TER.-Territory.
Falkland Is. (Malvinas) Fr. 1763. Br. 1765. Sp. 1771 Arg. 1820. Br. 1833
Partition of Patagonia and Tierra del Fuego between Chile and the Argentine Republic 1881, 1902
ARGENTINA
PAMPAS
URUGUAY
BRAZIL
Buenos Aires 1535, 1580
Montevideo, 1724
Tropic of Capricorn

Hispanic America, 1828—1929.

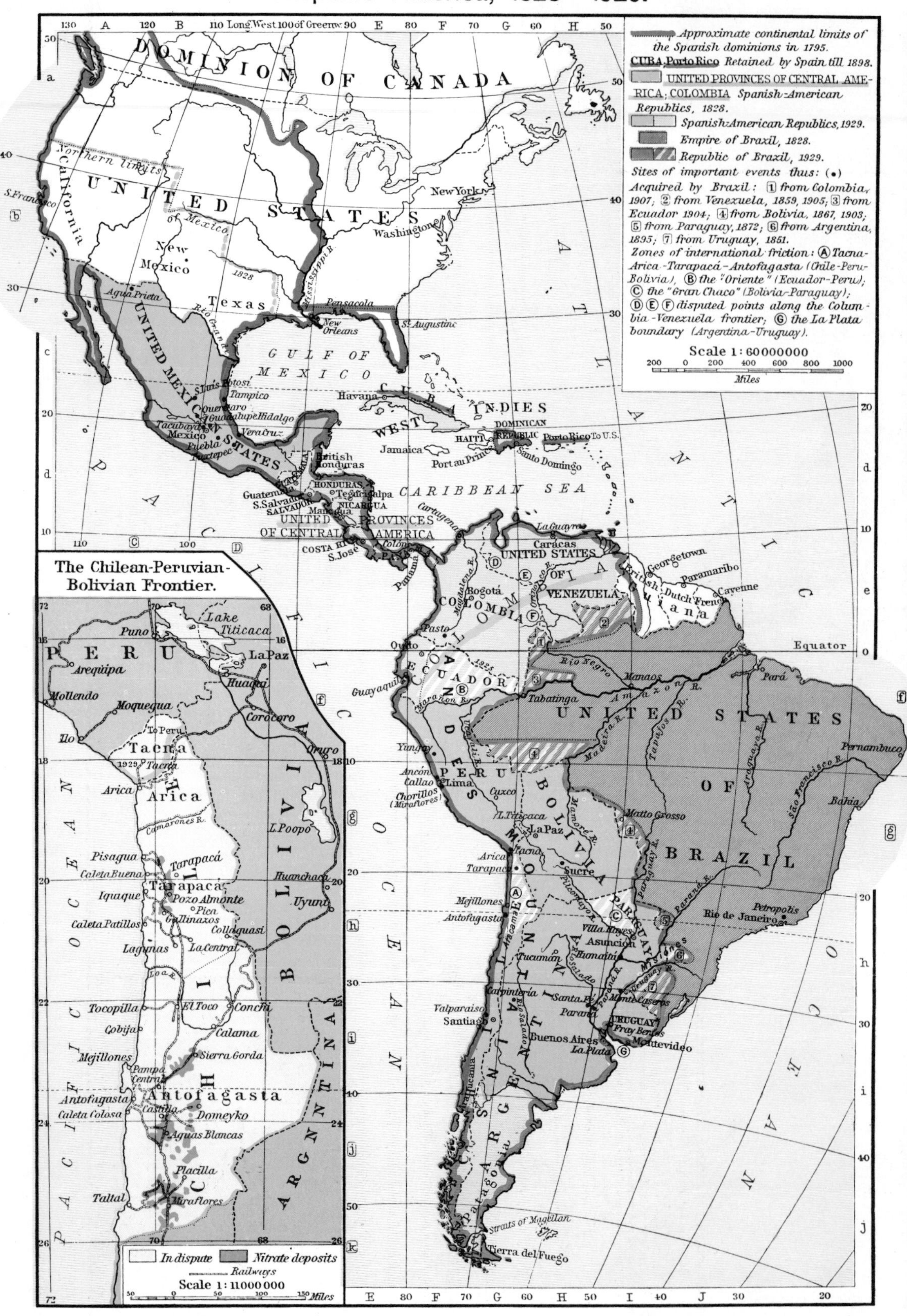

MAPS SINCE 1929

PREPARED BY C. S. HAMMOND & COMPANY

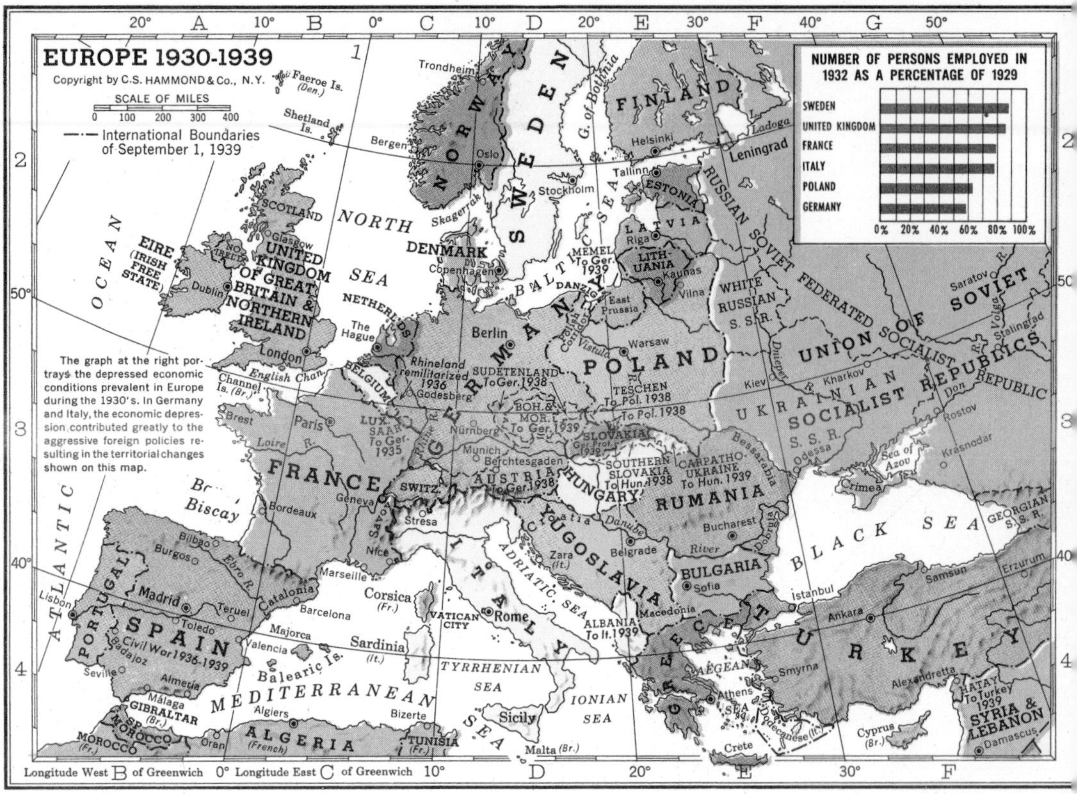

EUROPE 1930-1939

SCALE OF MILES
0 100 200 300 400

—·— International Boundaries of September 1, 1939

NUMBER OF PERSONS EMPLOYED IN 1932 AS A PERCENTAGE OF 1929

SWEDEN
UNITED KINGDOM
FRANCE
ITALY
POLAND
GERMANY

0% 20% 40% 60% 80% 100%

The graph at the right portrays the depressed economic conditions prevalent in Europe during the 1930's. In Germany and Italy, the economic depression contributed greatly to the aggressive foreign policies resulting in the territorial changes shown on this map.

Longitude West B of Greenwich 0° Longitude East C of Greenwich 10° D 20° E 30° F

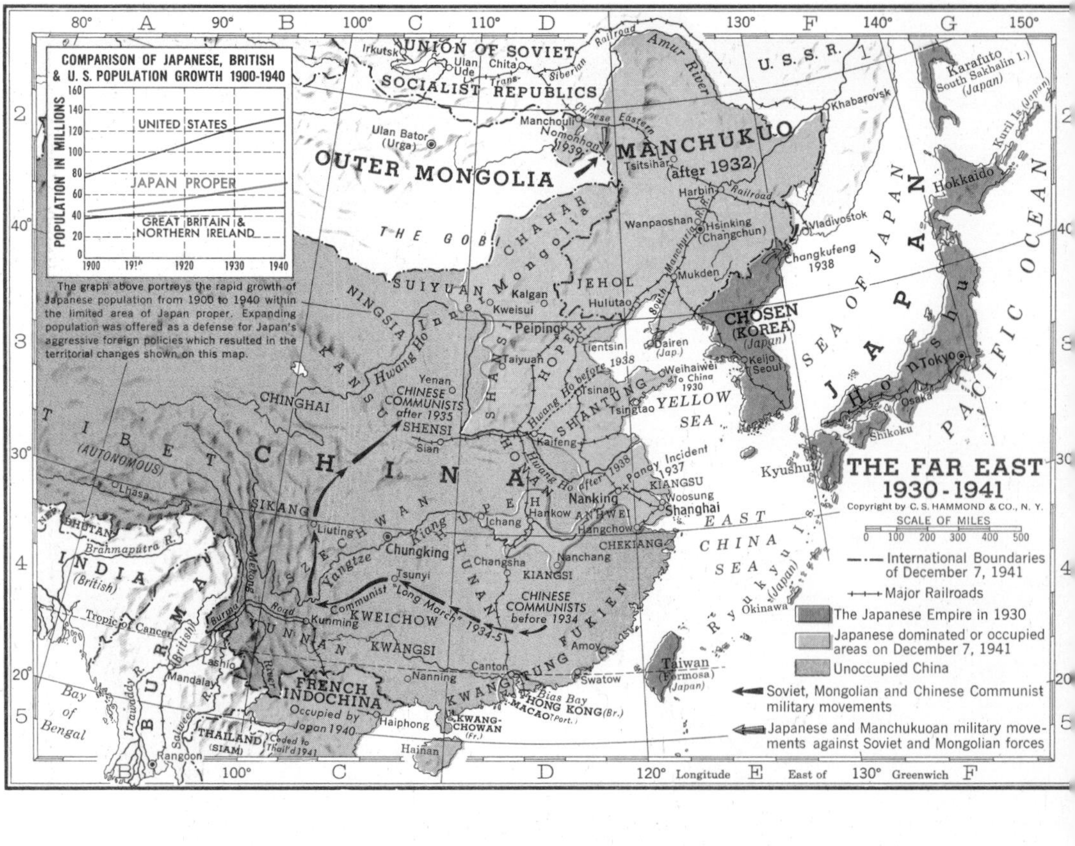

THE FAR EAST 1930-1941

SCALE OF MILES
0 100 200 300 400 500

—·— International Boundaries of December 7, 1941
+—+—+ Major Railroads

The Japanese Empire in 1930
Japanese dominated or occupied areas on December 7, 1941
Unoccupied China
Soviet, Mongolian and Chinese Communist military movements
Japanese and Manchukuoan military movements against Soviet and Mongolian forces

COMPARISON OF JAPANESE, BRITISH & U.S. POPULATION GROWTH 1900-1940

POPULATION IN MILLIONS: 0 20 40 60 80 100 120 140 160
1900 1910 1920 1930 1940

UNITED STATES
JAPAN PROPER
GREAT BRITAIN & NORTHERN IRELAND

The graph above portrays the rapid growth of Japanese population from 1900 to 1940 within the limited area of Japan proper. Expanding population was offered as a defense for Japan's aggressive foreign policies which resulted in the territorial changes shown on this map.

100° C D 120° Longitude E East of 130° Greenwich F

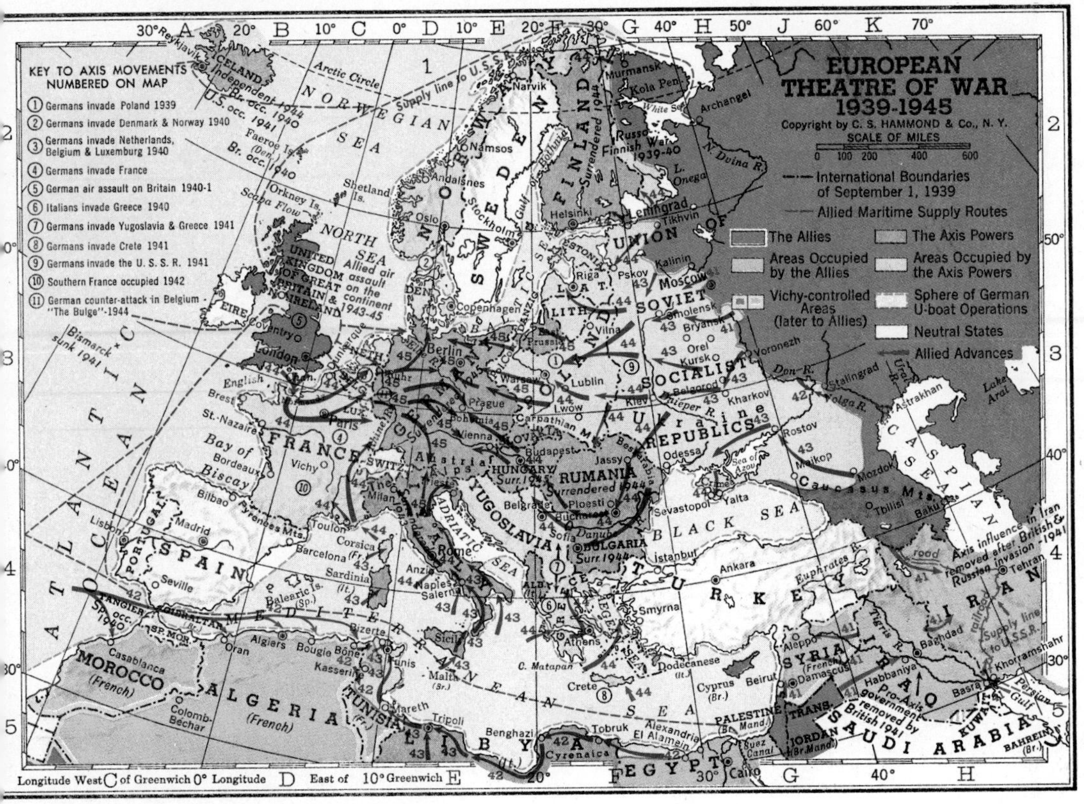

EUROPEAN THEATRE OF WAR 1939-1945

Copyright by C. S. Hammond & Co., N. Y.

SCALE OF MILES 0 100 200 400 600

KEY TO AXIS MOVEMENTS NUMBERED ON MAP

1. Germans invade Poland 1939
2. Germans invade Denmark & Norway 1940
3. Germans invade Netherlands, Belgium & Luxemburg 1940
4. Germans invade France
5. German air assault on Britain 1940-1
6. Italians invade Greece 1940
7. Germans invade Yugoslavia & Greece 1941
8. Germans invade Crete 1941
9. Germans invade the U. S. S. R. 1941
10. Southern France occupied 1942
11. German counter-attack in Belgium - "The Bulge"-1944

- International Boundaries of September 1, 1939
- Allied Maritime Supply Routes
- The Allies
- The Axis Powers
- Areas Occupied by the Allies
- Areas Occupied by the Axis Powers
- Vichy-controlled Areas (later to Allies)
- Sphere of German U-boat Operations
- Neutral States
- Allied Advances

Longitude West of Greenwich 0° Longitude East of 10° Greenwich

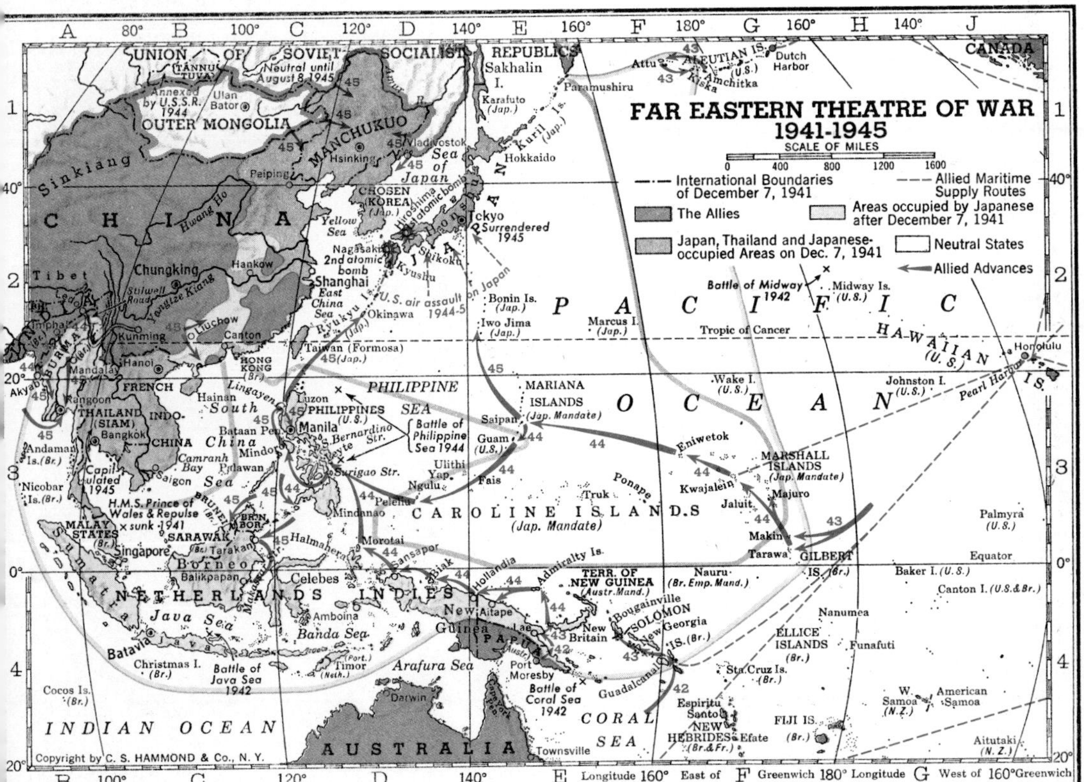

FAR EASTERN THEATRE OF WAR 1941-1945

SCALE OF MILES 0 400 800 1200 1600

- International Boundaries of December 7, 1941
- Allied Maritime Supply Routes
- The Allies
- Areas occupied by Japanese after December 7, 1941
- Japan, Thailand and Japanese-occupied Areas on Dec. 7, 1941
- Neutral States
- Allied Advances

Longitude 160° East of Greenwich 180° Longitude West of 160° Greenwich

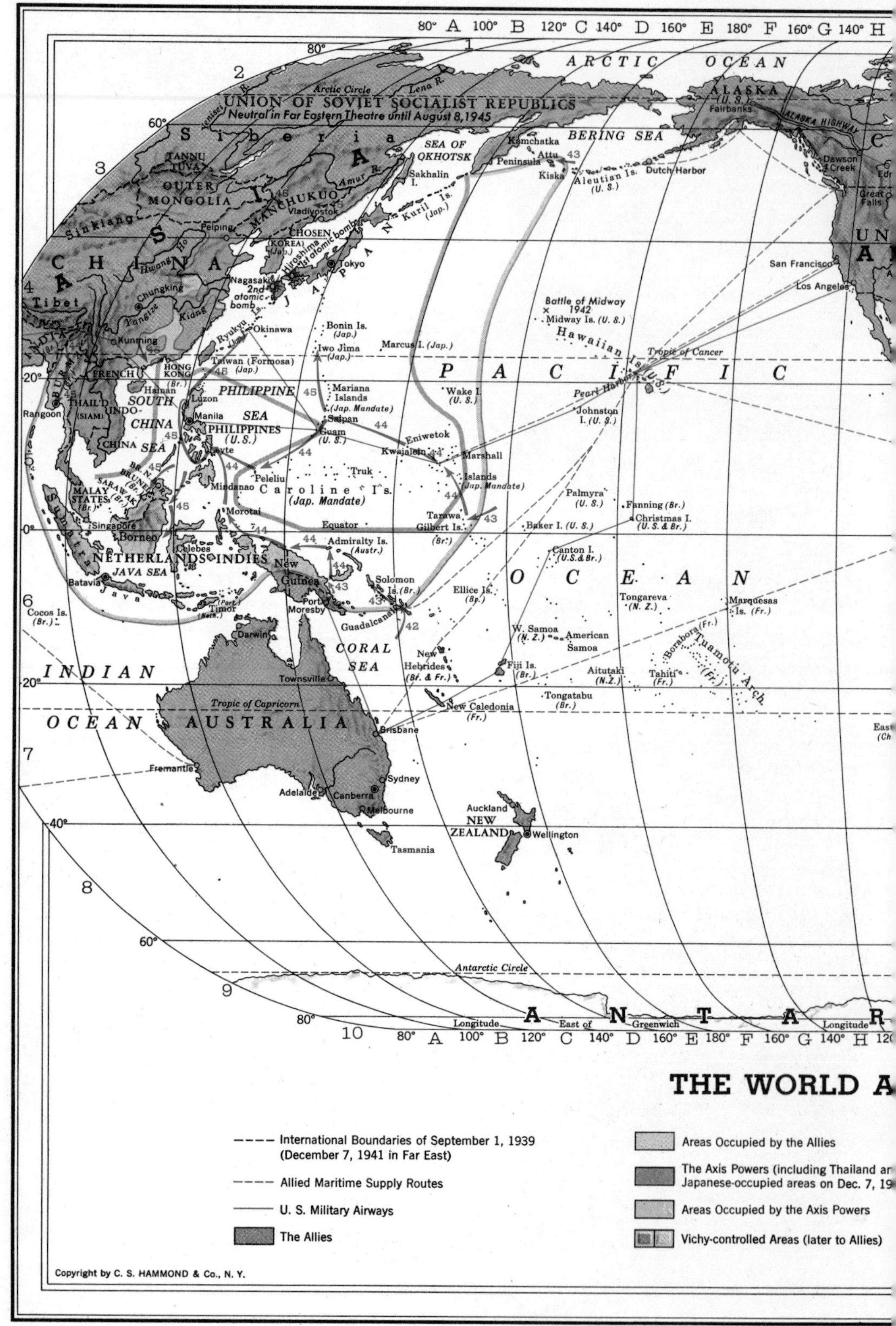
ARCTIC OCEAN
UNION OF SOVIET SOCIALIST REPUBLICS
Neutral in Far Eastern Theatre until August 8,1945
Siberia
ALASKA (U. S.)
Fairbanks
ALASKA HIGHWAY
BERING SEA
SEA OF OKHOTSK
Kamchatka Peninsula
Attu
Kiska
Aleutian Is. (U. S.)
Dutch Harbor
Sakhalin I.
Kuril Is. (Jap.)
TANNU TUVA
OUTER MONGOLIA
MANCHUKUO
Vladivostok
Sinkiang
Peiping
CHOSEN (KOREA) (Jap.)
Hiroshima 1st atomic bomb
Tokyo
JAPAN
Nagasaki 2nd atomic bomb
CHINA
Tibet
Chungking
Kunming
HONG KONG (Br.)
Taiwan (Formosa) (Jap.)
Ryukyu Is. (Jap.)
Okinawa
Bonin Is. (Jap.)
Iwo Jima (Jap.)
Marcus I. (Jap.)
Battle of Midway 1942
Midway Is. (U. S.)
Hawaiian Is. (U.S.)
Pearl Harbor
Tropic of Cancer
PACIFIC
OCEAN
FRENCH INDO-CHINA
Hainan
Rangoon
THAIL'D (SIAM)
SOUTH CHINA SEA
PHILIPPINE SEA
Luzon
Manila
PHILIPPINES (U. S.)
Leyte
Mindanao
Mariana Islands (Jap. Mandate)
Saipan
Guam (U. S.)
Wake I. (U. S.)
Johnston I. (U. S.)
Eniwetok
Kwajalein
Marshall Islands (Jap. Mandate)
Truk
Peleliu
Caroline Is. (Jap. Mandate)
Palmyra (U. S.)
Fanning (Br.)
Christmas I. (U. S. & Br.)
Baker I. (U. S.)
Tarawa
Gilbert Is. (Br.)
Equator
Morotai
MALAY STATES (Br.)
Singapore
Sumatra
Borneo
Celebes
NETHERLANDS INDIES
JAVA SEA
Batavia
Java
Timor (Port.)
Admiralty Is. (Austr.)
New Guinea
Port Moresby
Solomon Is. (Br.)
Guadalcanal
Canton I. (U.S.& Br.)
Ellice Is. (Br.)
Tongareva (N. Z.)
Marquesas Is. (Fr.)
W. Samoa (N. Z.)
American Samoa
Tuamotu Arch. (Fr.)
Tahiti (Fr.)
Aitutaki (N.Z.)
Fiji Is. (Br.)
Tongatabu (Br.)
New Hebrides (Br. & Fr.)
New Caledonia (Fr.)
Cocos Is. (Br.)
Darwin
CORAL SEA
Townsville
INDIAN OCEAN
Tropic of Capricorn
AUSTRALIA
Brisbane
Fremantle
Sydney
Adelaide
Canberra
Melbourne
Tasmania
Auckland
NEW ZEALAND
Wellington
San Francisco
Los Angeles
Dawson Creek
Antarctic Circle
ANTARCTICA
Longitude East of Greenwich
THE WORLD A
International Boundaries of September 1, 1939 (December 7, 1941 in Far East)
Allied Maritime Supply Routes
U. S. Military Airways
The Allies
Areas Occupied by the Allies
The Axis Powers (including Thailand ar Japanese-occupied areas on Dec. 7, 19
Areas Occupied by the Axis Powers
Vichy-controlled Areas (later to Allies)
Copyright by C. S. HAMMOND & Co., N. Y.

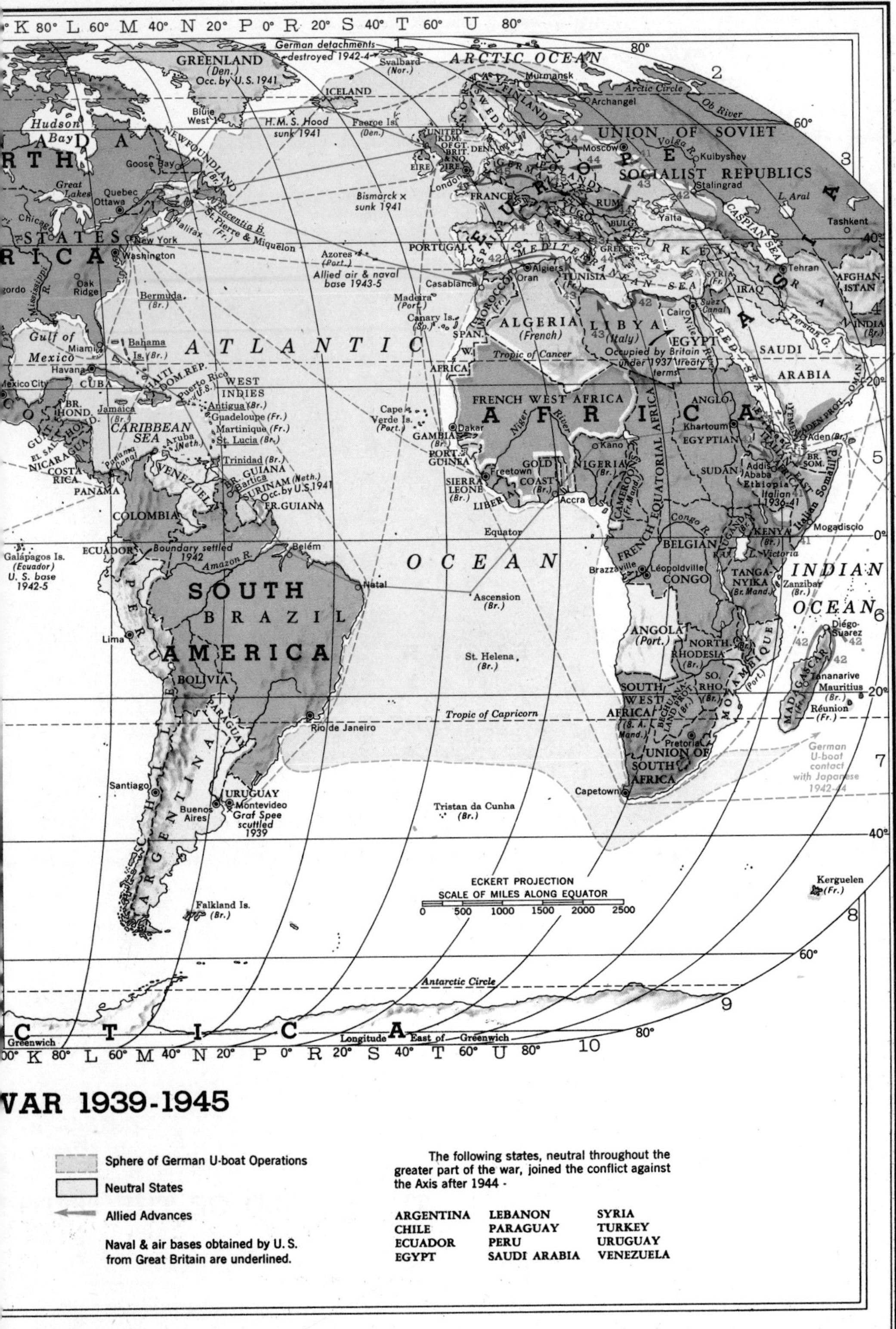

VAR 1939-1945

- Sphere of German U-boat Operations
- Neutral States
- Allied Advances

Naval & air bases obtained by U. S. from Great Britain are underlined.

The following states, neutral throughout the greater part of the war, joined the conflict against the Axis after 1944 -

ARGENTINA	LEBANON	SYRIA
CHILE	PARAGUAY	TURKEY
ECUADOR	PERU	URUGUAY
EGYPT	SAUDI ARABIA	VENEZUELA

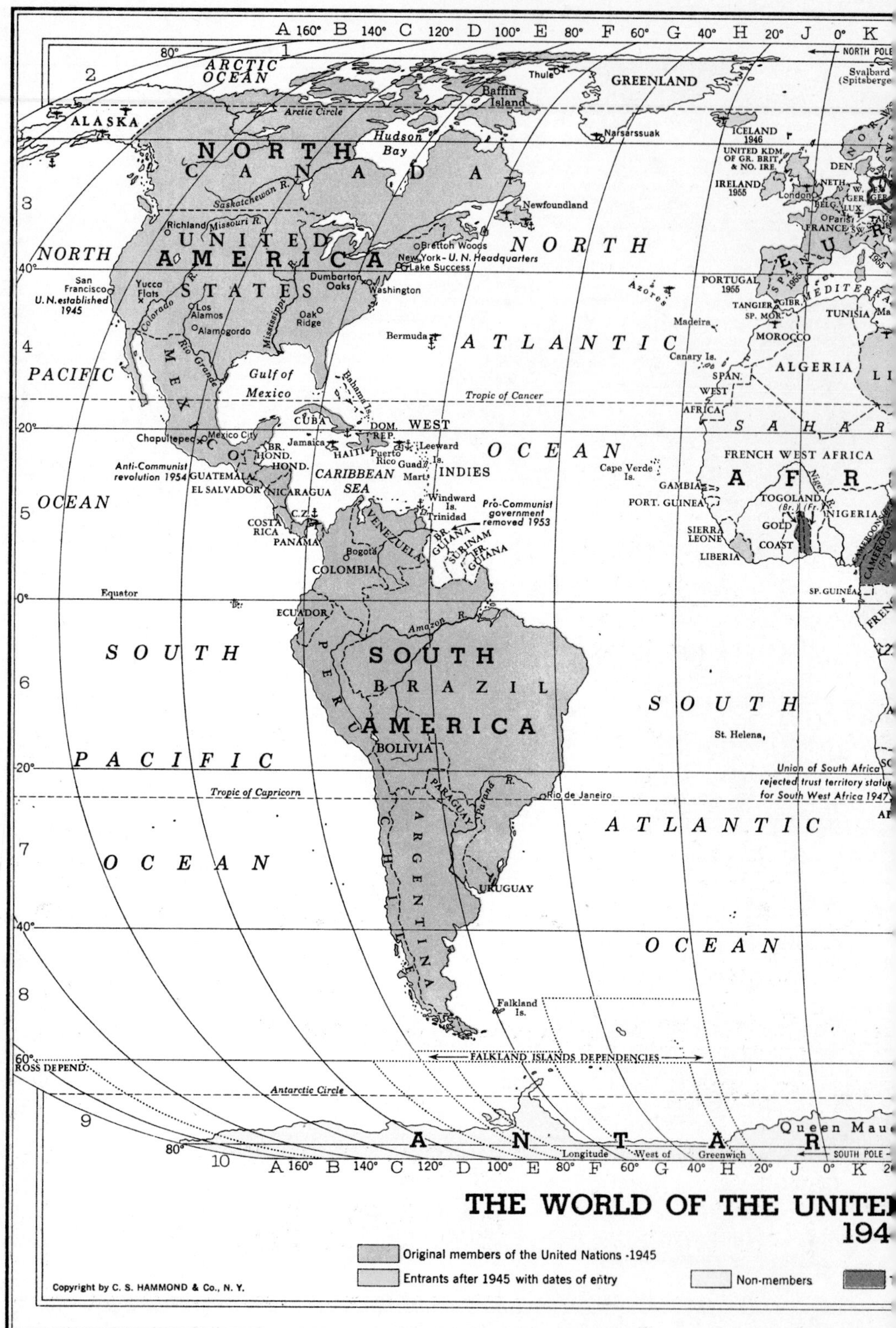
ARCTIC OCEAN
ALASKA
Arctic Circle
Thule
GREENLAND
Baffin Island
Hudson Bay
Narsarssuak
ICELAND 1946
UNITED KDM. OF GR. BRIT. & NO. IRE.
IRELAND 1955
London
NORTH AMERICA
CANADA
Saskatchewan R.
Newfoundland
Richland
Missouri R.
UNITED STATES
Bretton Woods
New York - U. N. Headquarters
Lake Success
NORTH
San Francisco
U. N. established 1945
Yucca Flats
Colorado R.
Los Alamos
Alamogordo
Mississippi R.
Dumbarton Oaks
Washington
Oak Ridge
PORTUGAL 1955
SPAIN 1955
TANGIER
GIBR.
SP. MOR.
MOROCCO
TUNISIA
ALGERIA
Madeira
Azores
Bermuda
ATLANTIC
Canary Is.
SPAN. WEST AFRICA
PACIFIC
MEXICO
Rio Grande
Gulf of Mexico
Bahama Is.
Tropic of Cancer
CUBA
DOM. REP.
HAITI
Jamaica
Puerto Rico
Leeward Is.
Guad.
Mart.
WEST INDIES
OCEAN
Mexico City
Chapultepec
BR. HOND.
HOND.
Anti-Communist revolution 1954
GUATEMALA
EL SALVADOR
NICARAGUA
CARIBBEAN SEA
Windward Is.
Trinidad
Pro-Communist government removed 1953
Cape Verde Is.
GAMBIA
PORT. GUINEA
SIERRA LEONE
LIBERIA
FRENCH WEST AFRICA
AFR
TOGOLAND (Br.) (Fr.)
GOLD COAST
NIGERIA
Niger R.
OCEAN
COSTA RICA
C.Z.
PANAMA
Bogotá
VENEZUELA
BR. GUIANA
SURINAM
FR. GUIANA
COLOMBIA
Equator
ECUADOR
Amazon R.
SP. GUINEA
SOUTH
PERU
SOUTH AMERICA
BRAZIL
BOLIVIA
SOUTH
St. Helena
PACIFIC
Union of South Africa rejected trust territory status for South West Africa 1947
Tropic of Capricorn
PARAGUAY
Paraná R.
Rio de Janeiro
ATLANTIC
OCEAN
CHILE
ARGENTINA
URUGUAY
OCEAN
Falkland Is.
FALKLAND ISLANDS DEPENDENCIES
ROSS DEPEND.
Antarctic Circle
Queen Mau
ANTAR
Longitude West of Greenwich
NORTH POLE
SOUTH POLE
Svalbard (Spitsberge
THE WORLD OF THE UNITE
194
Original members of the United Nations - 1945
Entrants after 1945 with dates of entry
Non-members
Copyright by C. S. HAMMOND & Co., N. Y.

ARCTIC OCEAN
Arctic Circle
Yenisei R.
Lena R.
Ob R.
UNION OF SOVIET SOCIALIST REPUBLICS
Moscow
L. Baikal
ASIA
L. Aral
Amu Darya
CASPIAN SEA
BLACK SEA
OUTER MONGOLIA
Manchuria
Inner Mongolia
Sinkiang
COMMUNIST CHINA
Civil War 1945-50
Peiping
Yenan
Nanking
Yangtze Kiang
Tibet
Jammu & Kashmir
AFGHANISTAN 1946
PAKISTAN 1947
NEPAL
SIKKIM
BHUTAN
Ganges R.
INDIA
PORT. INDIA
Bay of Bengal
ARABIAN SEA
BURMA 1948
THAILAND 1946
CAMBODIA 1955
VIETNAM
Dienbienphu
Indochinese hostilities 1946-54
Hainan
MACAO
HONG KONG
SOUTH CHINA SEA
CEYLON 1955
Communist guerrilla warfare 1948
FED. OF MALAYA
SING.
BRUNEI
SARAWAK
NORTH BORNEO
Borneo
Sumatra
Java
INDONESIA 1950
PORT. TIMOR
REPUBLIC OF THE PHILIPPINES
Taipei
NATIONALIST CHINA (FORMOSA)
EAST CHINA SEA
Okinawa
Ryukyu Is.
Nagasaki
Hiroshima
JAPAN
Hokkaido
NORTH KOREA
SOUTH KOREA
38°
Korean War 1950-3
SEA OF OKHOTSK
Sakhalin I.
Kuril Is.
Kamchatka Peninsula
BERING SEA
Aleutian Is.
South Sakhalin I. & Kuril Is. occupied by U.S.S.R. in 1945
NORTH PACIFIC OCEAN
Tropic of Cancer
Mariana Islands
Guam
Wake I.
Bikini
Eniwetok
Marshall Is.
TERRITORY OF Caroline Is. THE PACIFIC ISLANDS (United States)
Equator
NAURU (Austr., N. Z. & Br.)
NETH. NEW GUINEA
TERR. OF NEW GUINEA (Australia)
PAPUA TERR.
Solomon Is.
CORAL SEA
New Hebrides
New Caledonia
WESTERN SAMOA (New Zealand)
AUSTRALIA
Monte Bello Is.
Woomera
Darling R.
Tasmania
NEW ZEALAND
Tropic of Capricorn
INDIAN OCEAN
Maldive Is.
Seychelles Is.
Comoro Is.
MADAGASCAR
Réunion
Mauritius
TURKEY
Civil War 1946-9
Cyprus
SYRIA
LEBANON
ISRAEL
IRAQ
IRAN
Tehran
Azerbaijan
Soviet occupation 1945-6
Yalta
JORDAN 1955
KUWAIT
SAUDI ARABIA
QATAR
TR. OMAN
ADEN
YEMEN 1947
EGYPT
Cairo
Nile R.
RED SEA
Eritrea
FR. SOM.
BR. SOM.
ETHIOPIA
SOMALILAND (Italy)
KENYA
UGANDA
L. Victoria
RUANDA-URUNDI (Belgium)
TANGANYIKA (Br.)
Zanzibar
FED. OF RHODESIA AND NYASALAND
MOZAMBIQUE
SWAZILAND
BASUTOLAND
ECKERT PROJECTION
SCALE OF MILES ALONG EQUATOR
0 500 1000 1500 2000 2500
AUSTRALIAN ANTARCTIC TERRITORY
AUST. ANT. TERR.
ROSS DEPENDENCY
Antarctic Circle
Adélie Coast
ANTARCTICA
Longitude East of Greenwich
40° M 60° N 80° P 100° R 120° S 140° T 160° U 180° V
1 2 3 4 5 6 7 8 9 10
ATIONS AND THE COLD WAR
955
tories
The Soviet Union and Soviet dominated states
Overseas air bases of the United States
Overseas naval bases of the United States

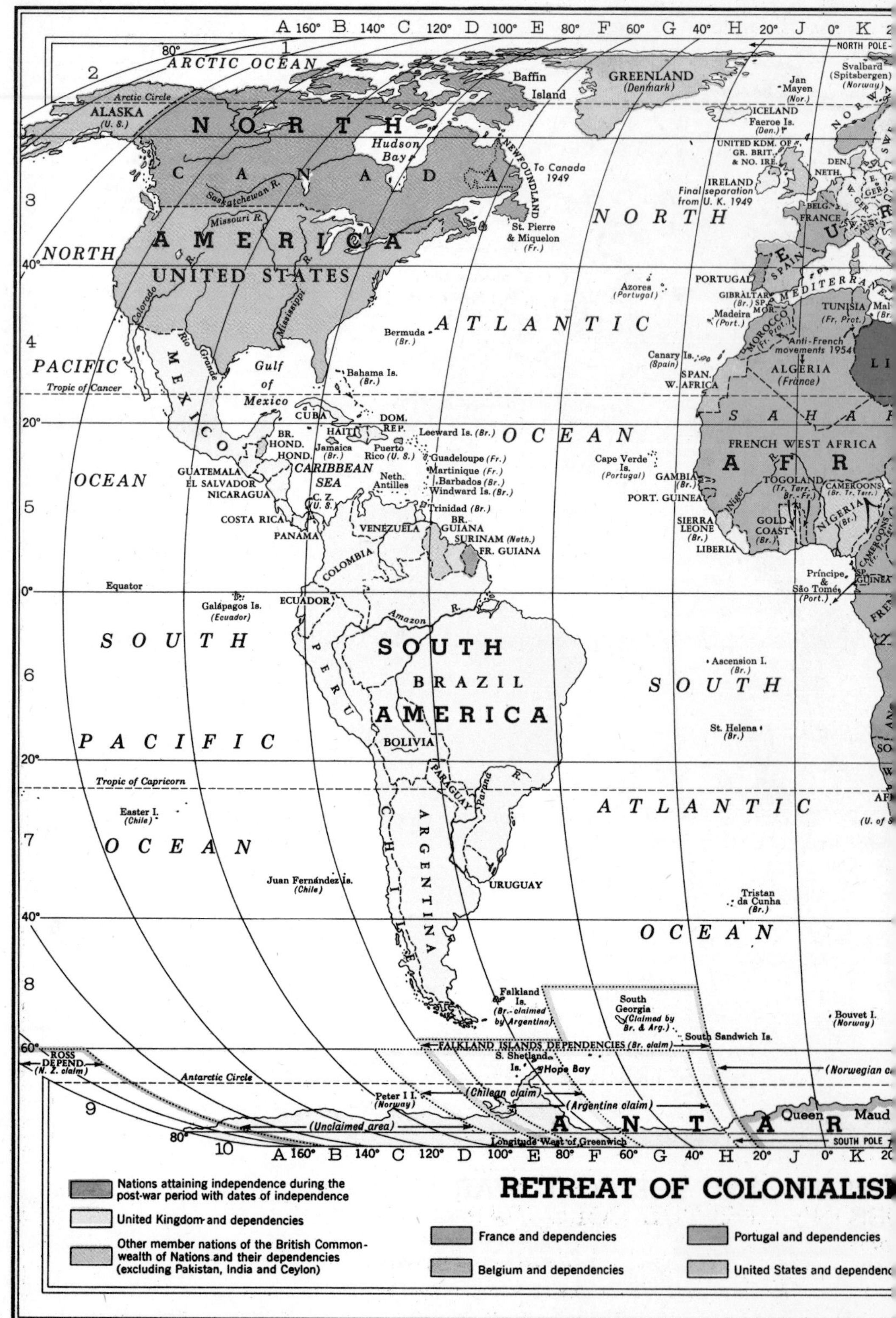
ARCTIC OCEAN
GREENLAND (Denmark)
Baffin Island
ALASKA (U. S.)
NORTH AMERICA
CANADA
Hudson Bay
NEWFOUNDLAND
To Canada 1949
St. Pierre & Miquelon (Fr.)
UNITED STATES
MEXICO
Gulf of Mexico
Bermuda (Br.)
Bahama Is. (Br.)
CUBA
HAITI
DOM. REP.
Jamaica (Br.)
Puerto Rico (U. S.)
CARIBBEAN SEA
Leeward Is. (Br.)
Guadeloupe (Fr.)
Martinique (Fr.)
Barbados (Br.)
Windward Is. (Br.)
Trinidad (Br.)
Neth. Antilles
BR. HOND.
GUATEMALA
EL SALVADOR
HOND.
NICARAGUA
COSTA RICA
PANAMA
C. Z. (U. S.)
VENEZUELA
BR. GUIANA
SURINAM (Neth.)
FR. GUIANA
COLOMBIA
ECUADOR
Galápagos Is. (Ecuador)
PERU
SOUTH AMERICA
BRAZIL
BOLIVIA
PARAGUAY
ARGENTINA
CHILE
URUGUAY
Juan Fernández Is. (Chile)
Easter I. (Chile)
Falkland Is. (Br.-claimed by Argentina)
South Georgia (Claimed by Br. & Arg.)
South Sandwich Is.
FALKLAND ISLANDS DEPENDENCIES (Br. claim)
S. Shetland Is.
Hope Bay
Peter I I. (Norway)
(Chilean claim)
(Argentine claim)
(Unclaimed area)
ROSS DEPEND. (N. Z. claim)
Antarctic Circle
(Norwegian c
Queen Maud
Bouvet I. (Norway)
Tristan da Cunha (Br.)
St. Helena (Br.)
Ascension I. (Br.)
Cape Verde Is. (Portugal)
Canary Is. (Spain)
Azores (Portugal)
Madeira (Port.)
SPAN. W. AFRICA
GAMBIA (Br.)
PORT. GUINEA
SIERRA LEONE (Br.)
LIBERIA
FRENCH WEST AFRICA
TOGOLAND (Tr. Terr. Br.-Fr.)
GOLD COAST (Br.)
NIGERIA (Br.)
CAMEROONS (Br. Tr. Terr.)
Príncipe & São Tomé (Port.)
SP. GUINEA
ALGERIA (France)
MOROCCO (Fr. Prot.)
SP. MOR.
Anti-French movements 1954
TUNISIA (Fr. Prot.)
PORTUGAL
SPAIN
GIBRALTAR (Br.)
FRANCE
BELG.
NETH.
DEN.
UNITED KDM. OF GR. BRIT. & NO. IRE.
IRELAND
Final separation from U. K. 1949
ICELAND
Faeroe Is. (Den.)
Jan Mayen (Nor.)
Svalbard (Spitsbergen) (Norway)
NORTH ATLANTIC OCEAN
SOUTH ATLANTIC OCEAN
NORTH PACIFIC OCEAN
SOUTH PACIFIC OCEAN
Tropic of Cancer
Tropic of Capricorn
Equator
Arctic Circle
NORTH POLE
SOUTH POLE
Longitude West of Greenwich
RETREAT OF COLONIALISM
Nations attaining independence during the post-war period with dates of independence
United Kingdom and dependencies
Other member nations of the British Commonwealth of Nations and their dependencies (excluding Pakistan, India and Ceylon)
France and dependencies
Belgium and dependencies
Portugal and dependencies
United States and dependenc

THE POST-WAR PERIOD

Netherlands and dependencies
Spain and dependencies
Italy and dependency
Denmark and dependency
Norway and dependencies
Other countries
Areas of the Soviet Union in which Great Russians constitute a majority of the population. Names of other peoples are underlined.

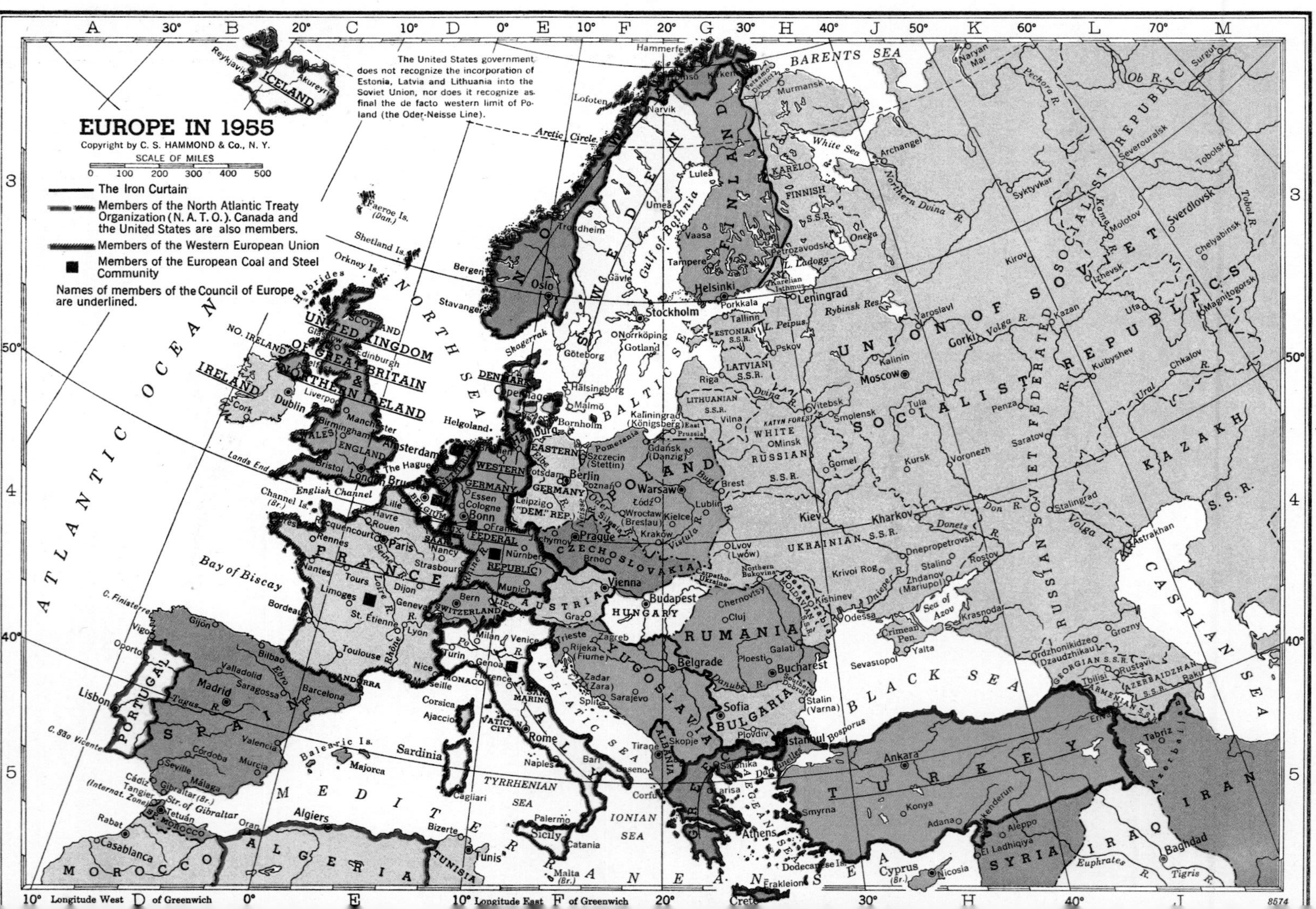
EUROPE IN 1955
Copyright by C. S. HAMMOND & Co., N. Y.
SCALE OF MILES
0 100 200 300 400 500
The Iron Curtain
Members of the North Atlantic Treaty Organization (N. A. T. O.). Canada and the United States are also members.
Members of the Western European Union
Members of the European Coal and Steel Community
Names of members of the Council of Europe are underlined.
The United States government does not recognize the incorporation of Estonia, Latvia and Lithuania into the Soviet Union, nor does it recognize as final the de facto western limit of Poland (the Oder-Neisse Line).
ATLANTIC OCEAN
NORTH SEA
BALTIC SEA
BARENTS SEA
BLACK SEA
CASPIAN SEA
MEDITERRANEAN SEA
ADRIATIC SEA
TYRRHENIAN SEA
IONIAN SEA
Bay of Biscay
UNION OF SOVIET SOCIALIST REPUBLICS
RUSSIAN SOVIET FEDERATED SOCIALIST REPUBLIC
UKRAINIAN S.S.R.
WHITE RUSSIAN S.S.R.
KAZAKH S.S.R.
ICELAND
IRELAND
UNITED KINGDOM OF GREAT BRITAIN & NORTHERN IRELAND
NORWAY
SWEDEN
FINLAND
DENMARK
POLAND
CZECHOSLOVAKIA
HUNGARY
AUSTRIA
SWITZERLAND
FRANCE
SPAIN
PORTUGAL
ITALY
YUGOSLAVIA
ALBANIA
RUMANIA
BULGARIA
GREECE
TURKEY
SYRIA
IRAQ
IRAN
MOROCCO
ALGERIA
TUNISIA
10° Longitude West of Greenwich
10° Longitude East of Greenwich
8574

INDEX

UNLESS otherwise indicated, the names given are those of towns. The Index does not furnish a complete set of references to the more important countries at successive periods of time. The maps needful for this purpose may be found by consulting the Table of Contents.

Modern names of ancient localities and different spellings of the same name are sometimes inclosed in parentheses, sometimes noted by cross-references. Though not appearing on the maps themselves, a considerable number of classical and medieval Latin names, and of different spellings of the same name, have been inserted in the Index with the proper cross-reference to the modern or customary form of such names.

If not accompanied by the letters B. C., the dates cited are A. D.

The number following a name refers to the page on which the name appears. The capital letter or letters following this number usually refer to a strip on that page inclosed by lines of longitude, and the small letter or letters, to a strip inclosed by lines of latitude. The name itself lies within the block formed by the intersection of the two strips. Thus the name *Madrid* 83 K g will be found on page 83, within the block formed by the intersection of the strip lettered K and the strip lettered g. In some cases, however, the letter or letters refer to a particular plan or inset on the page concerned.

Names which appear in the original Index without indication of the block in which they lie, are repeated with full information in the Index-Supplement. Names contained in the maps for the period 1911-1929 also appear in the Index-Supplement, as well as a number of names for the old maps which were omitted in the original Index.

ABBREVIATIONS

ab. = abbacy
abp. = archbishopric
Arg. Rep. = Argentine Republic
Aug. Reg. = Augustan Region
auton. = autonomous
bldg. = building
bp. = bishopric
Cal. = California
calif. = califate
cap. = captaincy
cent. = century
ch. = church
col. = colony
Conn. = Connecticut
cty. = county
cy. = city
dept. = department
desp. = despotat
dioc. = diocese
dist. = district
dom. = dominion(s)
E. = East
elect. = electorate
emir. = emirate
emp. = empire
exarch. = exarchate
fam. = family or clan
for. off. = foreign office
Frank. = Frankish
gen. = general or generality
gouv. = gouvernement
gov. = government
gr. = grand
Hanse. = Hanseatic
imp. = imperial
Ind. Res. = Indian Reservation
ins. = inset
isl. = island(s)
khan. = khanate
km. = kingdom
landgr. = landgraviate
leg. = legend
loc. = locality
margr. = margravate
marq. = marquisate
Mass. = Massachusetts
Miss. = Mississippi
mon. = monastery
mt., mts. = mountain(s)
N. = North
Ore. = Oregon
Pa. = Pennsylvania
palat. = palatinate
parl. bor. = parliamentary borough
patr. = patriarchate
pen. = peninsula
poss. = possessions
pref. = prefecture
pres. = presidency
princ. = principality
proc. = proconsultate
prom. = promontory
prot. = protectorate
prov. = province
R. = River
reg. = region
rep. = republic
Rom. = Roman
S. = South
satr. = satrapy
S. C. = South Carolina
seign. = seigniory
sen. = senatorial
set. = settlement
str. = strait
ter. = territory
univ. = university
U. S. = United States
Va. = Virginia
viscty. = viscounty
vol. = volcano
W. = West or Western

I

Aach 142 C e
Aachen (Aix-la-Chapelle) 55 Q i
Aalborg 88 C c
Aalen 143 J h
Aalesund 166 G c
Aarau 91 Q k
Aardenburg 117 B c
Aar or Aare River 91 Q k
Aargau, distr. 91 Q k
Aargau, region 62 D e
Abacaenum 30 E d
Abæ 11 D d
Aballo, see Avallon
Abalus (Helgoland), isl. 38 D b
Abana River 6 E a
Abarim, Mountains of 7 D f
Abaris, promontory 9 B c
Abasgi, people 35 M e
Abasgians, people 50 L d
Abbassids, Calif. of the 55 K h
Abbeville 76 D a
Abbotsbury, mon. 97 O k
Abdera, in Spain 12 C c
Abdera, in Thrace 12 H b
Abejar 82 B a
Abel 6 D b
Abel-Keramin 7 D e
Abella 30 D b
Abellinum 30 D b
Abensberg 154 F d
Abercorn, in Georgia 193 ins. C
Abercorn, in Scotland 185 C b
Aberdeen
Aberdeen, bp. 97 K b
Aberdeen, cty.
Aberdeen, univ. 100 E c
Aberffraw
Abergavenny
Abergavenny, mon. 97 O j
Aberystwith, parl. bor.
Abeshr 174 F c
Abia 14 C c
Abila, in Gilead 6 D c
Abila, in Mauretania 38 A e
Abila, in Syria 6 E a
Abingdon, in England 98 ins. A
Abingdon, mon. 97 P j
Abingdon, parl. bor. 163 M f (Ab.)
Abingdon, in Virginia 196 ins. A
Abittibi, lake 188 J a
Abittibi, river 188 J a
Abkhasia, reg. 119 L e
Abkoude 117 C b
Abnakis, people 188 M b
Abnoba Mountains 38 D c
Åbo 120 J d
Abodrites, people 55 R i
Abomey 174 D d
Abrincas or Abrincates, see Avranche
Abruzzi, dist. 90 D c
Abruzzo, bp. 95 E c
Absalom, Tomb of 6 ins. A
Abukir 174 J i
Abukir Bay 150 A a
Abus, mt. 20 I c
Abus Fluvius (Humber River).
Abu Simbel 4 F d
Abusina 38 E c
Abydos, in Egypt 4 F d
Abydos, on the Hellespont
Abyssinia, reg. 109 U g
Abyssinia, cty. 174 G d
Acadia, reg. 194 F a
Acalán, reg. 105 B c
Acalander River 31 F b
Acamas, prom. 20 E e
Acambaro 213 ins.
Acampsis River 20 I b
Acanthian Gulf 11 E b
Acanthus 11 E b
Acapulco 107, 108 H f
Acarnania, reg. 10 B d
Accau, route of 191 G c
Acci 38 B e
Accia 148 C c
Accomack, cty. 193 ins. A
Accra 175 C d
Aceldama, loc. near Jerusalem 6 ins. A
Acelum 26 F b
Acerenza 64 C b
Acerenza, abp. 95 F c
Acerra, bp. 95 ins.
Acerræ, in Campania 30 D b
Acerræ, in Venetia 26 D b
Aceruntia 30 E b
Acervo 27 I b
Acesines River, in India 19 L d
Acesines River, in Sicily 30 E e
Achaia, dioc. 43 G f
Achaia, princ. 89 B c
Achaia, prov. 35 I f
Achaia, reg. 14 B a
Achaia (Phtiotis), reg. 11 D c
Achaia, state 13 B b
Achaian, League 19 ins. A
Achaian Mountains 10 D d
Achalm, castle 62 E d
Achalm, ruin 143 H h
Acharnae 15 D a
Acharnian Gate 23 D
Achelous River 10 C d
Achern 142 B c
Acheron River 10 B c
Acherusia, lake in Campania 31 ins. A
Acherusia, lake in Epirus 10 B c
Achilles, Burial mound of
Achilleum
Achillis Island 18 D a
Achin 112 C c
Achonry, bp. 97 C b
Achradina, quarter in Syracuse 31 ins. B
Achrida 59 I e
Achshaph 6 C b
Achzib 6 C b
Acilii, Gardens of the 22 A
Aciris (Agri) River 31 F b
Acium 30 E e
Acla 105 E e
Acoma 190 D e
Aconcagua, mt. 215 C f
Acqui 90 I h
Acqui, bp. 95 D c
Acræ 30 D e
Acraephia 11 E d
Acragas (Girgenti) 30 C e
Acre, see Saint Jean d'Acre 73 G d
Acre, ter. 214 B c
Acriæ 15 C c
Acritas, mt. 14 B c
Acritas, prom. 14 B c
Acroceraunia, prom. 31 I b
Acroceraunia, reg. 17 A a
Acroceraunian Mountains 10 A b
Acrocorinthus 15 C b
Acropolis of Athens, plan of the 23 C
Acroria, reg. 14 B b
Acrothoi 11 F b
Acte, reg. in Argolis 15 D b
Acte, reg. in Attica 16 D c
Acte, reg. in Chalcidice 11 F b
Actium 10 B d
Aculco 213 ins.
Adadah 7 C f
Adaes 191 G e
Adalia 77 K e
Adams, Fort, in Mississippi 199 G d
Adams, Fort, in Ohio 196 ins. B
Adams, mt. 212 ins.
Adamawa, Adamaua, reg. 174 E d
Adana 20 F d
Ad Aquilam 27 F d
Ad Castores 26 E b
Adda River 90 I h
Addis Abeba
Addua (Adda) River 26 D a
Adelaide 172 C d
Adelberg, mon. 143 I h
Adelmannsfelden 143 I h
Adelsberg 159 H f
Adelsheim 142 D b
Adelsreuthe 142 E e
Aden
Aden, Gulf of 170 F g
Aden Protectorate 170 F g (A.P.)
Ad Fines
Adiabene, reg. 20 J e
Adige River 90 J h
Adirondack Mountains 192 D b
Adis Ababa
Admiralty Island 212 ins.
Admont, mon. 80 D h
Ad Novas, on Lake Sabatinus 35 ins. B
Ad Novas, near L. Trasimenus 27 F d
Adoraim 7 C e
Adour River 76 C e
Adowa 174 G c
Ad Padum 27 G c
Adra 82 B b
Adraha 6 E c
Adramyttium
Adramyttium, Gulf of
Adrana River 39 J h
Adrar, reg. 174 B b
Adratum 68 C c
Adria 64 B a
Adria, bp. 95 E b
Adrianople 43 H e
Adrianopolis 35 J e
Adrianus River 27 F b
Adriatic Sea 2 E d
Ad Sabatum 31 F c
Adsalluta River 27 I a
Ad Sextum 27 F d
Ad Statuas 35 ins. B
Adua see Adowa
Aduatuca 39 H h
Aduatuci, people 39 H h
Adula, mt. 26 C a
Adullam 7 B e
Adwalton Moor 127 X m
Æane 10 C b
Æas River 10 A b
Æcæ 30 E a
Æclanum 30 D a
Ædepsus 11 E d
Ædro, Portus 27 G b
Ædui, see Autun
Ædui, people 38 C c
Æfula 35 ins. B
Ægæ, in Achaia 14 C a
Ægæ, in Euboea 11 E d
Ægæ or Agææ, in Macedonia 10 D b
Ægaleos, mountain in Attica 16 B b
Ægaleus, mountain in Messenia 14 B b
Ægates, isl. 30 B d
Æge 11 E c
Ægeae 20 F d
Ægean Islands, Theme of the 59 I f
Ægean Sea 2 G e
Ægiæ 14 C c
Ægialea, reg. 14 B a
Ægilia, in Attica 16 B b
Ægilia, island near Crete 15 D d
Ægilia, island near Euboea 15 E a
Ægilips, isl. 10 B d
Ægilos, isl. 26 D d
Ægina 15 D b
Ægina, isl. 15 D b
Æginium 10 C c
Ægira 14 C a
Ægitium 10 D d
Ægium 14 C a
Ægospotami River
Ægosthena 15 D a
Ægusa, isl. 30 B e
Ægyptus, Rom. prov., see Egypt 35 J h
Ægys 14 C b
Ælana 35 K h
Ælia Capitolina (Jerusalem) 35 L g
Ælian Bridge 22 A
Ælmere, bay, see Zuider Zee

Æmilia, reg. 26 E c
Æmilia, Rom. prov. 42 E e (2)
Æmilia, Basilica, bldg. 24 B
Æmilian Bridge 24 A
Æmilian Portico 22 A
Æmilian Way, road 26 C c
Æmilian Way of Scaurus, road 26 D c
Ænaria, (Ischia), isl. 30 C b
Ænea 11 D b
Æneum, prom. 11 D b
Æniania, reg. 10 D d
Ænis, reg. 8 N h
Ænona 27 J c
Ænus
Ænus, mt. 10 B d
Ænus (Inn) River 38 E c
Ænyra 11 F b
Æoli, (Stromboli), isl. 30 E d
Æoliæ, (Lipari), isl. 30 D d
Æolian Islands 90 E e
Æolians, people 8 O h
Æolis, reg. 8 Q h
Æpea 14 B c
Æqui, people 27 H e
Æquians, people
Æquimelium 24 A
Æquum Tuticum 30 E a
Ærarium, bldg. in Rome
Aëre 6 E b
Æsar River 31 G c
Æsculapius, Temple of, in Carthage 34 ins. A (5)
Æsculapius, Temple of, in Rome 22 A
Æsepus River
Æsernia 30 D a
Æsis 27 H d
Æsis (Esino) River 27 H d
Æsium, see Jesi
Æson River 11 D b
Æstui, people 38 G a
Æthalia, (Elba), isl. 26 E e
Æthices, people 10 C c
Ætna 30 D e
Ætna, mt., see Etna
Ætolia, reg. 10 C d
Ætolian League 19 ins. A
Æxone 16 B b
Afghanistan, cty. 170 H e
Afghans, people
Africa, continent 174, 175
Africa, dioc. 42
Africa, exarch. 52 I f
Africa, Proconsular, Rom. prov. 34 F f
Africa, prov. 38 D e
Agade 4 G c
Agades 174 D c
Agalassa 19 L d
Agamenticus 189 C c
Agaña 198 ins. C
Agaraci, people 35 L g
Agat 198 ins. C
Agatha, Agathe (Agde) 12 D b
Agathyrnum 30 D b
Agawam (Ipswich, Mass.) 189 C c
Agawam (Springfield, Mass.) 189 B c
Agde 61 E e
Agedincum (Sens) 38 C c
Agen 46 G e
Agen, bp. 94 C c
Agen, cty. 69 D d
Agenais, cty. 61 D d
Agennum, see Agde
Agenorium 18 ins. B
Ager Gallicus, dist. 27 G d
Ager Romanus, dist. 35 ins. B
Ager Solonius, dist. 35 ins. B
Ager Vaticanus, dist. 22 A
Aggershuus (Christiania)
Aghadoe, bp. 97 B d
Aghlabids, Dom. of the 54 G g
Agida 27 H b
Agincourt 81 M g
Aginnum (Agen) 38 C d
Agnadello 90 I h
Agnus 16 B b
Agogna River 90 I h
Agora (Lysimachia)
Agordo 90 J g
Agostinho, Cape 108 R i
Agra 137 C c
Agræ 16 B b
Agræ, reg. 23 D
Agræi, people 10 C d
Agræna 6 E c
Agram 72 D b
Agram, bp. 95 F b
Agrianes, people 18 B b
Agri Decumates (Tithe Lands), distr. 39 J i
Agrigentum (Girgenti) 30 C e
Agrinium 10 C d
Agrippa, Baths of 22 A
Agrippa, Field of 22 A
Agrippa, Monument of
Agrippa's Bridge 22 A
Agrippina, Gardens of 22 A
Agryle 16 B b
Aguadilla 199 ins. G
Aguantum 27 G a
Aguarico River 111 B b
Agua Salud River
Aguas Blancas 215 B e
Aguas Calientes 213 ins.
Aguilar 83 K g
Aguilas 82 B b
Aguinum 30 C a
Agulhas, Cape 175 E h
Aguya, Punta 214 A c
Agyrium 30 D e
Ahausen 122 F d
Ahmadabad 137 B d
Ahmadnagar 137 B e
Ahorca Lagarto
Ahremberg 117 E d
Ahwaz 99 M g
Ai 7 C e
Aianteion, quarter 93 G e
Aianteum
Aibar 83 K g
Aidin 164 D c
Aidin, reg. 77 J e
Aigle 91 P l
Aigues-mortes 73 A b
Aiguillon 76 D d
Aigun 171 N c
Aimores, Serra dos 214 E d
Ain, dept. 148 F e
Ain River 126 D c
Ainay, mon. 148 B b
Aini 99 L e
Ainos 12 I b
Ain-Tab 68 C b
Aiquebelle, mon. 95 D c
Air, reg. 174 D c
Airaines 76 D b
Aird's Moss
Aire 126 C a
Aire, bp. 94 B c
Aire River 127 X m
Airebolu 165 E c
Airolo 91 Q l
Aisne, dept. 148 E e
Aisne River 126 C b
Aix 61 F e
Aix, (Aix-les-Bains) 130 N i
Aix, abp. 95 D c
Aix, gen. 147 F c
Aix, univ. 100 G f
Aix-la-Chapelle (Aachen) 55 Q i
Aix-la-Chapelle, imp. cy. 78 D c
Ajaccio 72 B c
Ajaccio, bp. 95 D c
Ajalon 7 C e
Ajana, reg.
Ajax, Burial mound of
Ajmere 137 B c
Akabah 99 K h
Akabah, Gulf of 99 J h
Akaroa 172 G e
Akasheh 174 F b
Ake 6 C c
Akerman 99 J d
Akhalzikh 164 G b
Akhsi
Akkad, reg. 4 G c
Akko 6 C c
Akkrum 117 D a
Akra 6 ins. A
Akrabbi 7 C d
Akrabbim, mts. 7 B g
Akserai 89 J g
Akshehr 93 D c
Akshi-Kioi
Aksu
Akureyri 166 B b
Alabama River 187 K e
Alabama, state 203 U d
Alabama, ter. 203 U d
Alabanda 20 C d
Alagoas, state 214 F c
Alagonia 14 C c
Alais 76 E d
Alalcomenæ 10 B d
Alalia 12 E b
Alamance, battle 194 D c
Alamanni, people in 486 50 E c
Alamanni, people about 900 57 E d
Alamannia, duchy about 1000 58 F d
Alamannia, Frank. prov. 53 N h
Alamannia, reg. 54 F d
Álamo, battle 201 F d
Álamos 213 B b
Álamos de Catorce 213 B b
Alamut 92 F d
Alancione, see Alençon
Åland Islands 120 I d
Alans, people in Russia
Alans, people in France 48 F d
Alans, people in Spain 45 C e
Alara River 39 J g
Alarcon 82 B b
Alarcon, route of 190 C f
Alashehr 93 C c
Alaska, Gulf of 198 ins. A
Alaska, dist. 186 D b
Alaska Mountains 186 D b
Alaska Peninsula 186 D c
Alatri, bp. 95 E c
Alausi 214 B c
Álava, cty. 82 B a
Álava, reg. 83 K g
Alazones, people 35 K d
Alba River, see Aube River
Alba 90 I h
Alba, bp. 95 D c
Albacete 83 K h
Alba Fucens 27 H e
Alba Longa 35 ins. B
Alba Mountains 38 D c
Albana 35 N e
Albania, princ. 93 A b
Albania, reg. in Caucasia 19 G b
Albania, reg. in Epirus 73 E b
Albanian Principalities 77 I d
Albanians, people 165 leg.
Albano 64 ins.
Albano, bp. 96 B b
Albanum, bp. 96 B b
Albanus, lake 35 ins. B
Albanus, mt. 30 B a
Albany, in W. Australia 172 A d
Albany, in New York 192 D b
Albany, Fort 212 G c
Albany, New 211 H c
Albany River 186 K c
Alba Pompeia 26 C c
Albara 68 C b
Albarracin 82 B a
Albarracin, emir. 83 E c
Albasin 171 N c
Albay 199 ins. H
Albemarle 184 D c

1*

Albemarle, reg. 193 F c
Albemarle Sound 193 F c
Albenga 90 B b
Albenga, bp. 95 D c
Albert 81 M g
Alberta, prov. 212 D c
Albert Edward Nyanza lake, see Edward Nyanza
Albert Nyanza, lake 175 F d
Albi 61 E e
Albi, abp. 148 B c
Albi, bp. 94 C c
Albi, viscty. 61 E e
Albici, people 38 D d
Albiga (Albi) 38 C d
Albigeois, cty. 69 E e
Albingaunum 26 C c
Albinia River 27 F e
Albintimilium 26 B d
Albion, name applied at first to Britain, later to England
Albis (Elbe) River 38 E b
Albon, cty. 69 F d
Albret, castle 76 C d
Albret, duchy 126 A d
Albret, seign. 69 C d
Albuera 130 B f
Albula Pass 91 R l
Albuquerque, in New Mexico 188 E d
Albuquerque, in Spain 83 J h
Albuquerque, duchy 83 J h
Albuquerque, Fort 214 D d
Albuquerque, route of 109 X h, 110 BB h
Alburnus, mt. 30 E b
Albury 172 D d
Alcácer do Sal 82 A b
Alcácer es Seguir 83 J h
Alcalá de Henares 82 B a
Alcalá de Henares, univ. 100 E f
Alcalá la Real 82 B b
Alcalde 210 A c
Alcañiz 82 B a
Alcántara 82 A b
Alcantarilla 82 B b
Alcaráz 82 B b
Alcázar 82 H f
Alcluyd
Alcmona River, see Altmühl R.
Alcobaça, mon. 94 A d
Alcoraz 66 F e
Alcyonian Gulf 15 D a
Aldabra Islands 175 H e
Aldan River
Aldborough, parl. bor. 163 M c
Aldeburgh, parl. bor. 163 P e
Alderney, isl. 69 B b
Aldersbach, mon. 95 E b
Aldersgate, in London 75 G g
Aldgate, in London 75 G g
Aldobrandeschi, fam. 90 L j
Alea 14 C b
Alemtejo, reg. 82 G f
Alençon 76 D b
Alençon, cty. 76 D b
Alençon, duchy 84 D e
Alençon, gen. 147 D b
Alençon, reg. 81 L h
Alençon, seign. 69 H f
Aleppo 68 C b
Alerheim 122 F d
Aleria 26 D e
Aleria, bp. 148 C c
Aleshki 131 J d
Alesia 38 C c
Alesium 14 B b
Alessandria 78 F f
Alessandria, bp. 95 D c
Alet 61 C b
Alet, bp. 94 C c
Aletium 31 H b
Aletrium 30 C a
Aletum, see Alet
Aleutian Islands 179 I b
Alexander Archipelago 212 ins.
Alexander's Mole 18 ins. B
Alexandra Land, reg. 172 C c
Alexandretta 68 C b
Alexandria, in Babylonia 19 G d
Alexandria, in Egypt 4 ins.
Alexandria, in India Superior 19 L d
Alexandria, near Parapanisus Mts. 19 K c
Alexandria, in Rumania 165 D b
Alexandria, in Syria (Iscanderum) 20 G d
Alexandria, in Virginia 194 K g
Alexandria, plan of 34 ins. C
Alexandria, patr. 52 K f
Alexandria Arachosiorum 19 K d
Alexandria Ariorum 19 J d
Alexandria eschata 19 K b
Alexandria Margiana 19 J c
Alexandria minor (Alexandretta) 68 C b
Alexandria Opiana 19 L e
Alexandria Oxiana
Alexandria Sogdiana 19 K e
Alexandria Troas
Alexandrine Aqueduct 35 ins. B
Alexinatz 164 C b
Alfdorf 143 I h
Alford
Algarve, dist. 82 G f
Algarve, Spanish, dist. 83 J h
Algarve de Aquem Mar, dist. 83 J h
Algeciras 82 A b
Algeria, col. 174 D a
Algeria, reg.
Algeria, state 118 E g
Algerian Plateaus 2 E e
Algerian Sahara 2 E e
Algidus, mt. 35 ins. B
Algiers 58 E f
Algoa Bay 175 M m
Algonkins, tribes 188 I b
Alhama, near Granada 82 B b
Alhama, near Murcia 82 B b
Alibunar 159 K f
Alicante 82 B b
Alice Spring Station 172 C c
Alife 64 B b
Alife, bp. 95 ins.
Aligarh 170 I f
Aliphera 14 B b
Aliso 39 I h and J h
Aliwal 170 I e
Aliwal North 175 M m
Aljubarrota 83 J h
Alkmaar 117 C b
Allahabad 137 D c
Allaine River 143 ins. F
Allegany, Ind. Res. 188 K b
Allegheny Mountains 193 B d-E a
Allegheny Plateau 187 K e
Allegheny River 192 B c
Allenstein 155 K b
Allerheiligen, mon. 142 B c
Alle River (Allaine R.) 143 ins. F
Alle River (Prussia) 115 K a
Aller River 78 F b
All Hallows, church in London 75 G g (26.30)
Allier, dept. 148 E e
Allier River 76 E d
Allifae 30 D a
Allobroges, people 26 A b
Allstedt 63 F c
Almada 82 A b
Almagro 83 K h
Almagro, route of 108 K i
Almalik 92 I c
Almansa 130 C f
Alma River 164 J f
Almazan 184 C d
Almeida 214 F d
Almendingen 143 I i
Almería 82 B b
Almería, bp. 94 B d
Almirante, Bahia del, bay 105 D e
Almissa, bp. 95 F c
Almodóvar del Campo 82 B b
Almohads, Dom. of the 70 H g
Almopia 10 D b
Almopia, reg. 10 D b
Almoravids, Dom. of the
Almuñecar 82 B b
Alnwick
Alnwick, mon. 97 P f
Alonæ 12 C c
Alope, in Locris 11 D d
Alope, in Phthiotis 11 D d
Alopece 16 B b
Alorus 11 D b
Alost 117 B d
Alpeni 16 F e
Alpheus River 14 B b
Alpirsbach 143 F i
Alpirsbach, mon. 95 D b
Alpis Graia, pass 26 A b
Alpis Poenina, pass 26 B b
Alpnach 91 Q l
Alps, The, mts. 2 E d
Alpuente 83 E d
Alpujarras, mts. 83 K h
Alresford 127 X o
Alresford, parl. bor.
Alsace, gen. 147 F b
Alsace, gouv. 146 C b
Alsace, prov. 148 F e
Alsace-Lorraine, imp. ter. 161 B c
Alsek River 212 ins.
Alsen, isl. 114 F a
Alsietinus, lake 35 ins. B
Alsietine Aqueduct 35 ins. B
Alsium
Altai Mountains 102 I c
Altamaha River 193 C f
Altamura 90 F d
Alta Ripa 39 J i
Alta Semita, loc. in Rome 22 A
Alt-Breisach 142 A d
Altdorf, near Nuremberg 114 F d
Altdorf, in Swabia 143 I j
Altdorf, in Switzerland 91 Q l
Alteföhr 123 G a
Alteia 39 I i
Altena (Wilmington) 192 ins.
Altenburg, in Hungary 72 D b
Altenburg, in Thuringia 72 C a
Altenburg, mon. in Austria 95 F b
Altenkirchen 134 D c
Altenstadt 143 I h
Altensteig 143 G h
Altensteig, lordship 143 G h
Altenzaun 154 F b
Altenzella, mon., near Würzburg 95 D b
Altenzelle, mon., near Meissen 85 G e
Alternus River 27 H e
Altheim, Hohen- 62 F d
Altinum 27 G b
Altis, loc. in Olympia
Alt-Lussheim 142 C b
Altmark, reg. 79 G b
Altmühl River 62 F d
Altomünster, mon. 95 E b
Alton, in England 127 Y o
Alton, in Illinois 211 G c
Alton, parl. bor.
Altona 122 E b
Altorf (Altdorf), in Switzerland 150 E c
Alt-Ötting 123 G d
Altötting, mon. 95 E b
Altranstädt 135 G c
Altshausen 143 I j
Altsohl 159 J d
Aluta River 73 E a
Alutus River (Aluta R.) 39 M l
Alvarado 213 ins.
Alvarado, route of 105 B c
Alvaro de Saavedra, route of 110 I f
Alvona 27 I b
Alwar 137 C c

Alyzia 10 B d
Amadeus, lake 172 C c
Amalekites, people 7 ins. C
Amalfi 64 B b
Amalfi, abp. 95 E c
Amalphis, see Amalfi
Amanus Mountains 20 G d
Amapuemecan
Amardi, people 19 H c
Amardians, people 8 D b
Amasea 35 L e
Amaserah 93 D b
Amasia 20 F b
Amastra 59 K e
Amastris 47 M e
Amatha 6 D c
Amathus, in Cyprus 20 E e
Amathus, in Peræa 7 D d
Amaya 82 H e
Amazonas, state 214 C c
Amazon River 214 D c
Amba Alaji, mt. 174 G c
Ambacia, see Amboise
Ambala 137 C b
Ambarri, people 38 C c
Ambato 214 B c
Amberg 122 F d
Ambérieu 130 N i
Ambert 76 E d
Ambiani or Ambianis, see Amiens
Amboise 69 H g
Amboyna, isl. 112 F d
Ambracia (Arta) 10 C c
Ambracia, state 13 B b
Ambracian Gulf (Gulf of Arta) 10 B d
Ambracus 10 B c
Ambras, castle 122 F e
Ambrières 65 F f
Ambrysus 11 D d
Ameland, isl. 117 D a
Amelia Island 207 I d
Ameria 27 G e
America, name on Waldseemüller map 108 K j
America, Central, reg. 213 D c
America, North, continent 186, 187
America, South, continent 214, 215
Amersfœrt 189 ins. C
Amersfoort 117 D b
Amersham, parl. bor. 163 N f (Am.)
Amesbury 127 X o
Amesbury, mon. 97 P j
Amestratus 30 D e
Amhara, reg. 174 G c
Amherstburg 212 I d
Amichel, reg. 191 F f
Amid or Amida (Diarbekr) 4 G c
Amida, abp. 43 K f
Amidas, route of 191 J d
Amiens 46 G d
Amiens, bp. 94 C b
Amiens, cty. 69 I f
Amiens, gen. 147 E b
Amirante Islands 175 I e
Amisia (Ems) River 38 D b
Amisus 20 G b
Amiternum 27 H e
Amjhera
Ammon, reg. 4 F c
Ammonites, people 7 ins. D
Ammonium 18 C e
Amnias River 20 F b
Amol, in Persia
Amol, in Turkestan
Amöneburg 134 E c
Amöneburg, mon. 95 D a
Amorbach 142 D a
Amorbach, mon. 95 D b
Amorgos, isl. 4 C b
Amorgus 13 D c
Amorium 20 D c
Amoy 171 M f
Ampelus, prom. in Chalcidice 11 E c
Ampelus, prom. in Crete 14 ins.
Ampfing 79 H d
Amphaxitis, reg. in Mygdonia 11 D b
Amphaxitis, reg. in Pæonia
Amphia 14 C b
Amphiale, prom. 16 B b
Amphiaræum 16 B a
Amphicæa 11 D d
Amphictionium 16 F e
Amphilochia, reg. 10 C c
Amphipagus, prom. 10 A c
Amphipolis 11 E b
Amphissa 11 D d
Amphitrope 16 C b
Amposta 83 L g
Ampsivarii, people 38 D b
Amritsar 137 B b
Amselfeld, battle 93 B b
Amsteg 91 Q l
Amsterdam 117 C b
Amsterdam, Hanse. cy. 99 ins. B
Amsterdam, Fort (New York) 189 ins. C
Amsterdam, New, in Dutch Guiana 214 D b
Amsterdam, New (New York) 189 ins. C
Amu-Daria River
Amur District 171 N c
Amur River
Amyclæ 14 C b
Amygdolon, Pool of 6 ins. A (6)
Amyrus 11 D c
Amyrus River 11 D c
Anab 7 B f
Anacæa 16 B a
Anactorium 10 B d
Anæa 17 E c
Anagni 90 D d
Anagni, bp. 95 E c
Anagnia (Anagni) 30 C a
Anagyrus 16 B b
Anah 99 L g
Anahuac, Plateau of 106 C a
Anam
Anamari, people 26 D c
Anamis River 19 I e
Anaphe, isl. 13 D c
Anaphlystus 15 D b
Anapus River, in Acarnania 10 C d
Anapus River, in Sicily 30 E e
Anas (Guadiana) River 38 A e
Anathoth 7 C e
Anatolia, reg. 99 I f
Anatolic Theme 59 K f
Anaua 20 C d
Anauni, people 26 E a
Anaunium 26 E a
Anazarbus 43 J f
Anbar 99 L g
Ancenis 84 C f
Anchedive Island
Anchesmus, mt. 16 B a
Anchialus 43 H e
Ancón 214 B d
Ancona 27 H d
Ancona, bp. 95 E c
Ancona, march 72 C c
Ancúd, San Carlos de 215 B g
Ancyra, in Galatia 20 E c
Ancyra, in Mysia 20 C c
Andaca 19 L d
Andagoya, route of 108 J g
Andahan
Andalos, reg. 53 B b
Andalusia, reg. 83 J h
Andaman Islands 103 J f
Andania 14 C b
Andaraba
Andecavi, see Angers
Andecavi, people 38 B c
Andechs, castle 72 C b
Andechs, mon. 95 E b
Andegavis, see Angers
Andelfingen, castle 91 Q k
Andelaus, see Andelot
Andelot 53 N h
Andelys 69 H f
Andematunnum 39 H j
Andenne 117 D d
Anderida or Anderidæ (Pevensey) 51 Q i
Anderitum, see Javols
Andermatt 150 E c
Andernach 62 D c
Andersonville 208 D c
Andes 26 E b
Andes Mountains 214 B bg
Andijan
Andlau, mon. 148 C b
Andorra 82 C a
Andover, in Mass. 189 C c
Andover, deanery, in England 100 A a
Andover, mon. 100 A a
Andover, parl. bor. 163 M f (And.)
Andoverpis, see Antwerp
Andros 15 E b
Andros, isl., Cyclades 15 E b
Andros Islands, Bahama Is. 213 E b
Androscoggin River 189 C b
Andrussov 138 D e
Andújar 82 B d
Andwell, mon. 100 B a
Anemas, Prison of 93 G e (9)
Anemo River 27 F c
Anemoria 11 D d
Anemurium, prom. 20 E d
Angara River
Angele 16 B b
Angerburg 155 K a
Angeriacus, see Saint Jean-d'Angély
Angermünde 85 D b
Angers 61 C c
Angers, bp. 94 B b
Angers, univ. 100 E e
Anghiari 90 M j
Angites River 11 E b
Angles, people, in Britain 51 R k
Angles, people, in Holstein 38 D b
Angles, people, about 900 57 E c
Anglesey, isl. 49 D e
Anglesey, cty. 127 U m
Anglesey, parl. dist. 163 J d
Anglo-Egyptian Sudan, reg. 174 F c
Anglo-Saxon kingdom, about 1000
Anglo-Saxon kingdoms, about 814 54 D c
Angol 215 B f
Angola, dist. 175 E e
Angora 55 K f
Angostura 214 C b
Angoulême 61 D d
Angoulême, bp. 94 C b
Angoulême, cty. 69 D d
Angoumois, cty. 61 C d
Angoumois, prov. 148 D e
Angra das Voltas 108 S j
Angra Pequena, bay 175 E g
Angria, reg. 62 E b
Angrians, people 55 Q i
Angrivarii, people 39 J g
Anguilla, isl. 213 F c
Angus, cty.
Angus, reg.
Anhalt, castle 71 S j
Anhalt, princ. 79 G c
Anhausen, mon. 143 J h
Anholt 117 E c
Ani 67 O e
Aniane, mon. 94 C c
Anicium, see Le Puy
Aniene River 96 B b
Anio River 27 G f
Anio novus, aqueduct 35 ins. B
Anisus River, see Enns River
Anjou, cty. 61 C c
Anjou, duchy 78 B e
Anjou, gouv. 146 A b
Anjou, prov. 148 D e
Anklam 87 I b
Anklam, Hanse. cy. 99 ins. B

Ann, Cape 189 C c
Annaburg, castle 115 ins. B
Annandale, reg.
Annapolis, in Maryland 192 C d
Annapolis, in Nova Scotia 212 I d
Anne, Fort 192 E b
Anne Arundel Town 192 C d
Annecy 130 O i
Anneianum, in Etruria 27 F d
Anneianum, in Venetia 27 F b
Annobon, isl. 175 D e
Anopæa Mountains 16 F e
Ansbach 114 F d
Ansbach, princ. 114 F d
Anserma 214 B b
Antaki
Antananarivo 175 H f
Antandrus
Antaradus 20 F e
Antelope Hills 190 E d
Antemnæ 35 ins. B
Antequera 82 B b
Anthedon, in Bœotia 11 E d
Anthedon, in Philistæa 7 A e
Anthela 16 F e
Anthemus 11 E b
Anthemus, reg. 11 E b
Anthemusias 35 L f
Anthena 15 C b
Antian Way, road 35 ins. B
Antibes 126 E e
Anticosti, isl. 186 M d
Anticyra, in Locris Ozolis 10 D d
Anticyra, in Malis 11 D d
Anticyra, in Phocis 11 D d
Antietam, battle 208 ins.
Antietam River 208 ins.
Antigonia, in Arcadia 14 C b
Antigonia, in Chalcidice 11 E b
Antigonia, in Epirus 10 A b
Antigua, isl. 105 H c
Antigua, Rio de la, river 106 D a
Anti-Lebanon Mountains 6 E a
Antinoë 43 I h
Antinum 27 H f
Antioch, in Phrygia 20 D c
Antioch, in Syria 20 G d
Antioch, patr. 52 L f
Antioch, princ. about 1140 68 C b
Antioch, princ. about 1190 71 N f
Antioch, theme 59 L f
Antiochia, in Asia Minor 43 I f
Antiochia, in Margiana 19 J c
Antioquia 214 B b
Antipatria 10 A b
Antipatris 7 B d
Antipodes Islands 179 I l
Antipolis 26 B d
Antirrhium, prom. 10 C d
Antirrhodus, isl. 34 ins. C (2)
Antissa 13 D b
Antitaurus Mountains 20 I c
Antium 30 B a
Antivari 164 B b
Antivari, abp. 95 F c
Antofagasta 215 B e
Antonine, Wall of 51 O g
Antoninus Pius, Column of 22 A
Antonius, Temple of 24 B (19)
Antrim, cty. 127 K f
Antron 11 E d
Antunnacum 39 I h
Antwerp 117 C c
Antwerp, Hanse. for. cy. 99 ins. B
Antwerp, marg. 117 C c
Anuu, isl. 199 ins. D
Anvik 198 ins. A
Anxa 31 G b
Anxanum 27 I e
Anxia 30 E b
Anxur (Terracina) 30 C a
Anydrus, mt. 16 B b
Anzican, reg. 109 S h
Aomori 171 P d
Aornus, in Bactria 19 K c
Aornus, in India 19 L d
Aorsi, people 35 N d
Aosta 90 A b
Aosta, bp. 95 D b
Aous, mt. 20 E e
Aous River 10 A b
Apache, Ind. Res. 188 E d
Apaches, tribe 188 D c
Apalachee 191 I e
Apalachee Bay 191 I f
Apalachicola River 193 B f
Apamea, in Osrhoëne 20 G d
Apamea, in Syria 20 G e
Apamea Cibotus 20 D c
Aparri 199 ins. H
Apenestae 31 F a
Apennines, mts. 2 F d
Aperanti, people 10 C d
Aperantia 10 C d
Aperopia (Doko), isl. 15 D b
Aphek
Aphetæ 11 E c
Aphidnæ 16 B a
Aphnitis Lake
Aphrodisias 43 H f
Aphrodisium 16 D c (4)
Aphytis 11 E b
Apia 172 H b
Apidanus River 10 D c
Apo, mt. 199 ins. H
Apodoti, people 10 C d
Apollo, Cave of 23 C
Apollo, Temple of 24 A
Apollon, Allée d' 149 A
Apollonia, in Illyricum 31 I b
Apollonia, in Mysia
Apollonia, in Palestine 7 B d
Apollonia, in Pieria 11 F b
Apollonia, in Sicily 30 D d
Apollonia, in Thrace 12 I b
Apollonia Chalcidice 11 E b
Apollonia Mygdonia 11 E b
Aponus 26 F b
Apostles, Church of the 93 G e
Appalachian Highland 187 K e
Appenweier 142 A c
Appenzell 91 R k
Appenzell, canton 91 R k
Appian Aqueduct 35 ins. B (3)
Appian Gate 22 A
Appian Way, road 30 B a
Appian Way, Old, road 35 ins. B
Appleby 127 W l
Appleby, dist. 84 B b
Appomattox Court House 208 E b
Appomattox River 193 E c
Appuldurcombe, mon. 100 A b
Apsinthii, people
Apsorus 27 I c
Apsorus, isl. 27 I c
Apsus 31 I b
Apsus River 10 A b
Apt, bp. 95 D c
Apta or Apta Iulia, see Apt
Apuani, people 26 D c
Apulia, cty. 64 C b
Apulia, duchy 70 I e
Apulia, reg. 30 E a
Apulia and Calabria, Aug. Reg. 38 F d (2)
Apulia and Calabria, prov. 42 F e (5)
Apulum 35 I d
Apure River 214 C b
Apurimac River 111 C d
Aquæ, see Aquæ Sextiæ
Aquæ, see Dax
Aquæ 39 J j
Aquæ Albulæ 35 ins. B
Aquæ Apollinares 35 ins. B
Aquæ Aureliæ 39 J i
Aquæ Bormiæ 26 E a
Aquæ Cutiliæ 27 G e
Aquæ Grani or Aquæ Granni, see Aix-la-Chapelle
Aquæ Mattiacæ 39 J h
Aquæ Pisanæ 26 E d
Aquæ Populoniæ 26 E d
Aquæ Sextiæ (Aix) 38 D d
Aquæ Solis or Aquæ Sulis (Bath) 51 O i
Aquæ Statiellæ 26 C c
Aquæ Volaterranæ 26 E d
Aquia Creek 208 E b (A. Cr.)
Aquidaban River 215 D e
Aquidneck Island 189 ins. A
Aquila 90 D c
Aquileia, in Germany 39 J i
Aquileia, in Venetia 27 H b
Aquileia, abp. 95 E b
Aquileia, march 64 B a
Aquileia, patr. 79 H e
Aquilonia, in E. Samnium
Aquilonia, in W. Samnium
Aquilo River 30 E a
Aquincum (Budapest) 38 F c
Aquino, bp. 95 E c
Aquis, see Aquæ Sextiæ (Aix)
Aquis, see Dax
Aquis Granum, see Aix-la-Chapelle
Aquitaine, duchy, 11 cent. 61 C c d
Aquitaine, duchy, 14 cent. 77 D d
Aquitaine, reg., about 814 54 E d
Aquitaine (Aquitania), Rom. prov. 38 C c (5)
Aquitaine I, Rom. prov. 42 C d (10)
Aquitaine II, Rom. prov. 42 B d (11)
Aquitania (Aquitaine), Rom. prov. 38 C c (5)
Aquitania Propria, reg. 38 B d
Arabah Valley 7 D e
Arabia, Rom. prov. 43 Y g (15)
Arabia, pen. 170 F f
Arabia, Rom. prov. 35 K g
Arabia, reg. 53 G d
Arabia, table land 3 I f
Arabia Deserta, reg. 20 H f
Arabian Desert, in Egypt 150 B b
Arabian Sea
Arabii, people 19 K c
Arabius River 19 K e
Arab raids, 9 cent. 45 G d
Arabs, people, in Arabia 4 G d
Arabs, people, in North Africa 45 D I-f
Arabs, people, in Sicily 45 G e
Arabs, people, in S. France 45 EF d
Arabs, people, in Spain, 711 45 D e
Arabs, people, in Spain, about 900 57 B f
Aracajú 214 F d
Aracan 136 N c
Aracan, reg. 112 C a
Aracaty 214 F c
Arachnæus, mt. 15 C b
Arachosia, prov. 19 K d
Arachosia, satr. 18 R h
Arachotus 8 E b
Arachotus River 19 K d
Arachthus River 10 C c
Aracynthus, mt. 10 C d
Arad, in Hungary 77 I c
Arad, in Palestine 7 C f
Arad, reg. 53 G b
Araden 14 ins.
Aradus 12 K d
Aræ Flaviæ 39 J i
Aræthyrea 14 C b
Arafura Sea 172 C a
Aragon, km., 12 cent. 82 H e
Aragon, km., 13—15 cent. 83 L g
Aragon, distr. 82 H e
Araguaya River 214 E c
Arakan, reg. 92 J e
Aral Sea 3 J d
Aramæans, people 7 ins. D
Ara Maxima 24 A
Aran Islands 127 H h
Arantia 14 C b
Arapahoes, tribe 188 E b
Araphen 15 E a

Ararat, mt. 3 I e
Arar River 38 C c
Araris River, see Aar or Aare River
Aras River 73 J c
Araucanians, people 215 B f
Araure 214 C b
Arausio or Arausione (Orange) 38 D d
Aravalli Hills 137 B c
Araxes River, in Armenia 5 D b
Araxes River, in Mesopotamia 20 I e
Araxes River, in Persis 19 H d
Araxus prom. 14 B a
Arba, isl. 27 I c
Arbe, bp. 95 E c
Arbela 4 G c
Arbela, abp. 43 K f
Arboga 88 F b
Arbor Felix 39 J j
Arc 81 N h
Arcadia, Rom. prov. 43 I h (5)
Arcadia, reg. 14 C b
Arcadia, state 13 B c
Arcadius, Column of 93 Ge (13)
Archangel 138 F c
Archas 68 C c
Archelaïs (Akserai), in Cappadocia 20 F c
Archelaïs, in Palestine 7 C d
Archers Hope 103 ins. A (Arch.)
Archidona 82 B b
Arcis-sur-Aube 154 C d
Arcole 150 F d
Arcos 82 A b
Arcot 137 C f
Arctic Ocean 2 E a
Arctic Plateau 186 H b
Ardabil 92 E d
Ardagh, bp. 97 D c
Ardea 30 B a
Ardea Gate 22 A
Ardèche, dept. 148 E f
Arden, forest 49 F e
Ardenne, mon. 94 B b
Ardennes, dept. 148 E e
Ardennes, mts. 62 C d
Ardettus, mt. 23 D
Ardfert, bp. 97 B d
Ardmore 210 F d
Ardstraw, bp. 97 D b
Arduenna Forest 39 H i
Arebrigium 26 B b
Arecibo 199 ins. G
Arelate 38 C d
Arelate (Arles), km. 62 D f
Aremberg, dist. 151 H f
Aremorica, reg. 38 B c
Arenacum 39 H f
Arenas, Punta, in Chile 215 B l
Arenas, Punta, in Costa Rica 213 D d
Arendal 130 E b
Arenenberg, castle 158 E e
Arensburg 119 I b
Areopagus (Mars Hill)
Areopolis 7 D f
Arequipa 214 B d
Arethon River 10 C c
Arethusa 11 E b
Arevaci, people 38 B d
Arezzo 90 L j
Arezzo, bp. 95 E c
Arezzo, univ. 100 H f (Ar.)
Argæus, mt. 20 F c
Argall's Town 193 ins. A
Argen River 143 I j
Argen River, Lower 143 I j
Argen River, Upper 143 I j
Argentan 76 C b
Argentarius, mt. 27 F e
Argenteus River 26 A d
Argentina, see Argentoratum (Strasburg)
Argentina, or the Argentine Republic, cty. 215 Cef
Argenton 126 B c
Argentoratum (Strasburg) 39 I i
Argiletum, street 22 A
Argilus 11 E b
Arginussæ Islands 17 E b
Argithea 10 C c
Argob, reg.
Argolic Gulf 4 B b
Argolis, reg. 15 C b
Argonauts, Portico of the 22 A
Argonnes, mts. 134 C d
Argos 14 C b
Argos Amphilochicum 10 C d
Argos Oresticum 10 C b
Argous Portus 26 E e
Arguin, isl.
Argun Islands 108 P e
Argun River 92 L b
Argura 11 D c
Argyle, bp. in Scotland
Argyle, cty.
Argyle, dist.
Argyle, Fort 193 ins. C
Argyrus (Argyrokastron) 10 B b
Aria, prov. 19 J d
Aria, reg. 8 E b
Aria, satr. 18 R h
Arialbinnum, see Basel
Ariana, reg. 19 H d
Ariano, bp. 95 F c
Arica 214 B d
Aricia 30 B a
Arid, Cape 172 A d
Ariège, dept. 148 E f
Arikaras, tribe 188 G b
Arilica 26 E b
Arimathea 7 C d
Ariminum 27 G c
Ariminus River 27 G c
Ariola 39 H i
Ariolica, in Gaul 39 I j
Ariolica, in Italy 26 B b
Arisbe
Arispe 190 C e
Aristonautæ 14 C a
Arius, lake 19 J d
Arius River 19 J d
Arivaca 190 C e
Arizona, ter. 203 P h
Arkansas, Fort 191 G e
Arkansas, tribe 188 G c
Arkansas, state 202 G h
Arkansas, ter. 1819 203 S c
Arkansas, ter. 1824 203 T d
Arkansas Post 199 G d
Arkansas Post, battle 208 B c
Arkansas River 190 E d
Arklow
Arkona 63 G a
Arles 61 F e
Arles, abp. 94 C c
Arles, km., about 1035 61 F d
Arles, km., 13 cent. 72 B b
Arlon 117 D e
Armagh
Armagh, abp. 97 D c
Armagh, cty. 127 K g
Armagnac, cty. 12 cent. 69 C e (Arm.)
Armagnac, cty. 14 cent. 76 D e
Armagnac, cty. 17 cent. 126 B e
Armagnac, dist. 81 M i
Armavir, Armavira 20 J b
Armenia, km., about 1140 68 C b
Armenia, km., 13 cent.
Armenia, km., 14 cent.
Armenia, reg., about 600 B. C. 8 C b
Armenia, reg., about 750 53 G c
Armenia, reg., about 1097 67 O f
Armenia, satr. 8 I e
Armenia I, Rom. prov. 43 J f (10)
Armenia II, Rom. prov. 43 J f (11)
Armenia, Great, reg. 99 L e
Armenia, Lesser, reg. in Cilicia 99 J f
Armenia, Lesser, reg. in Pontus 35 L f
Armenia minor, reg. 20 H c
Armeniac Theme 59 L e
Armenian Highlands 3 I d
Armenians, people
Armenta River 27 F e
Armentières 117 A d
Armstrong, Fort, in Illinois 211 G b
Armstrong, Fort, in Pa. 195 B c
Arnay-le-Duc 126 D c
Arne 10 D c
Arneburg 63 F b
Arnheim 117 D b
Arnhem, Hanse. cy. 99 ins. B
Arnhem Land, reg. 172 C b
Arnissa, in Illyricum 31 I b
Arnissa, in Macedonia 10 C b
Arno River 90 L j
Arnon River 7 D f
Arnsberg 62 D c
Arnshaugk 85 F e
Arnstadt 62 F c
Arnus (Arno) River 26 E d
Aro River 27 G f
Aroania, mt. 14 C b
Aroanius River 14 C b
Aroe 14 B a
Aroer, in Idumæa 7 C f
Aroer, in Peræa 7 D f
Arogas River 31 F c
Arolla 91 P l
Arolsen 154 E c
Arona 90 I h
Arouaise, mon. 94 C a
Arpad (Tel-Erfâd)
Arpi 30 E a
Arpinum (Arpino) 30 C a
Arquebuse 149 B
Arquennes 156 A a
Arques, castle 76 D b
Arrabo River, see Raab River
Arrabona 38 F c
Arran, isl.
Arras 117 A d
Arras, bp. 94 C a
Arraticum, see Arras
Arretium (Arezzo) 27 F d
Arru Islands 172 C a
Arsacids, Kingdom of the, about 200 B. C. 19 X k
Arsacids, Kingdom of the, about 90 B. C. 33 N f
Arsamosata 20 H c
Arsanias River 20 I c
Arsia (Arsa) River 27 I b
Arsian Forest 35 ins. B
Arsinoë, in Cyrenaica 34 H g
Arsinoë, on L. Mœris 4 ins.
Arsinoë, on the Red Sea 35 K g
Arsissa Lake 20 J c
Arsuf 68 ins. A
Arta 73 E c
Artabri, people 38 A d
Artacana 19 H d
Artace
Artacoana 19 J d
Artaki 165 E c
Artasium 68 C b
Artaxata 20 K c
Artemis, Temple of 31 ins. B (3)
Artemis Agrotera, temple 23 D
Artemis Brauronia, temple 23 C (3)
Artemisium, prom. 11 E c
Artemisius, mt. 14 C b
Artemita 35 M g
Artemita, isl. 10 C d
Artena 35 ins. B
Artlenburg 122 F b
Artois, cty. 14 cent. 76 E a
Artois, cty. 16 cent. 117 A d
Artois, gouv. 146 B a
Artois, prov. 148 E d
Artynia Lake
Aruba, isl. 214 C a
Arundel 127 Y p

Arundel, castle 65 F e
Arundel, mon. 74 E f
Arundel, parl. bor. 163 N g
Arupium 27 J c
Arurius (Aar or Aare) River 39 I j
Arvad 4 F c
Arverni, see Clermont-Ferrand
Arverni, people 38 C c
Arx (citadel) on Capitoline Mt. 24 A
Arx (citadel) on the Janiculum 22 A
Arx Regia, in Tyre 18 ins. B
Asabara 7 D e
Asalmanus Mountains 6 F c
Asamon Mountains 6 C c
Asbach, mon. 95 E b
Ascalon
Ascania Lake
Ascanian Domains 71 ins.
Ascension Island 108 P h
Aschaffenburg 86 G d
Aschaffenburg, princ. 151 K j (A)
Aschersleben, Hanse. cy. 99 ins. B
Asciburgium 39 I h
Asciburgius Mountains 38 F b
Asclepieum 23 C
Ascoli Piceno 64 B b
Ascoli Piceno, bp. 95 E c
Ascoli Satriano 64 C b
Ascoli Satriano, bp. 95 F c
Ascordus River 11 D b
Ascra 11 E d
Asculum (Ascoli Piceno) 27 H e
Ascuris 11 D c
Asea 14 C b
Ashanti, reg. 174 C d
Ashburton, parl. bor 163 K g
Ashburton River 172 A c
Ashby de la Zouch 127 X n
Ashdod 7 B e
Ashdown
Asher 7 C d
Asher, tribe 7 ins. D
Asheville 211 I c
Ashland 210 A b
Ashley River 193 ins. C
Ashley-Henry Post 210 D a
Ashley's Post 210 C c
Ashtabula 206 ins.
Ashtaroth-Karnaim 6 E c
Ashton, parl. bor 163 L d
Ashurada 170 G e
Asia, continent 170, 171
Asia, Rom. dioc. 43 I f
Asia, East Rom. prov. 43 H f
Asia, Rom. prov. 35 J f
Asia Minor, reg. 20
Asia Minor, table-land 3 H e
Asiana, reg. 50 I e
Asinarian Gate 22 A
Asine, in Argolis 15 C b
Asine, in Messenia 14 B c
Asines River 30 E e
Asir, reg. 170 F g
Asisium 27 G d
Askabad
Asmak River
Asmara 174 G c
Asmonæan Palace 6 ins. A
Asola 90 J h
Asopus 15 C c
Asopus River, in Bœotia 11 E d
Asopus River, in Corinth 14 C b
Asopus River, in Malis 14 D d
Aspadana (Ispahan) 19 H d
Aspara
Aspern 155 I d
Aspinwall
Aspisii, people 19 J a
Aspledon 11 D d
Aspona
Aspromonte, mt. 161 K h
Assa 11 E b
Assab 174 H c
Assaba 174 D d
Assaceni, people 19 L d
Assalt 68 ins. A
Assam, prov. 171 K f
Assam, reg. 92 J e
Assandun 64 E e
Assassins, sect, in Persia 92 F d
Assassins, sect, in Syria 68 C b
Assaye 137 C d
Assen 117 E a
Assenisipia, proposed state in U. S. 196 B b
Assens 88 D d
Assera 11 E b
Asseria 27 J c
Asseritis, reg. 11 E b
Assinaboins, tribe 188 F a
Assinarus River 30 E e
Assiniboia, prov. 212 E c
Assiniboine River
Assisi 90 D c
Assisi, bp. 95 E c
Assisium, see Assisi
Assorus 30 D e
Assuan 174 G b
Assur 4 G c
Assus
Assyria, prov. 18 F c
Assyria, reg. 8 C b
Assyria, satr. 8 I e
Assyrian Empire 5
Asta, see Asti
Astacus, in Acarnania 10 C d
Astacus, in Bithynia 9 E c
Astacus, bay of 9 E c
Astæ, people 9 D b
Astapa 38 B e
Astarac, cty. 76 D e
Astauene, reg. 19 I c
Asteris, isl. 10 B d
Asthala, isl. 19 J d
Asti 90 I h
Asti, bp. 95 D b
Aston Manor 162 E e
Astorga 82 A a
Astorga, abp. 42 A e
Astorga, bp. 94 A c
Astoria 198 A a
Astrabad
Astrabad, reg. 139 H h
Astrakhan 139 G f
Astrakhan, Khanate of 139 F f
Astroni, crater 31 ins. A
Astura 30 B a
Astures, people 38 A d
Asturias, cty. 82 A a
Asturias, Kingdom of 54 C e
Asturias, princ. 83 D c
Asturias, reg. 58 C e
Austurica Augusta (Astorga) 38 A d
Astypalæa, isl. 13 E c
Astypalæa, prom. 16 B b
Astyra
Asunción 215 D e
Asylum 24 A
Atabeks, Dom. of the 68 C c
Atabeks, Ildijiz, dom. 71 P f
Atabeks, Zengid, dom. 71 O f
Atabeks of Irbil, dom. 71 O f
Atacama, Desert of 215 C e
Atacama, reg. 108 K j
Atalante 11 D a
Atalante, isl. near Locris Opuntia 11 E d
Atalante, isl. near Salamis 16 B b
Atalia 26 D e
Atapuerca 83 E c
Atarneus
Ataroth 7 D e
Atbara River 174 G c
Atchison 210 F c
Atella, in Basilicata 90 E d
Atella, in Campania 30 D b
Aternum (Pescara) 27 I e
Aternus (Pescara) River 27 H e
Ateste (Este) 26 F b
Ath 117 B d
Athabaska, lake 186 H c
Athabaska, prov. 212 D c
Athabaska River 186 H c
Athamania, reg. 10 C c
Athelney
Athelney, mon. 97 O j
Athena 20 I b
Athena, Temple of, in Athens 23 C (1)
Athenæ 16 B b
Athenæ Diades 11 E d
Athenæum, in Arcadia 14 C b
Athenæum, in Epirus 10 C c
Athene, Temple of, in Syracuse 31 ins. B (2)
Athene Promachos, monument 23 C (5)
Athenian Empire 13
Athenopolis 26 A d
Athens, in Attica 15 D b
Athens, bp. 43 G f
Athens, duchy, 13 cent. 73 E c
Athens, duchy, 15 cent. 93 B c
Athens, plan of ancient 23 D
Athens, plan of modern 23 D
Athesis (Adige) River 26 E a
Athlone
Athmonum 16 B a
Athol, reg.
Athos, mt. 11 F b
Athyras River
Atienza 82 B a
Atina, in Latium 30 C a
Atina, in Lucania 30 E b
Atintania, reg. 10 B b
Atkinson, Fort 210 F b
Atlanta 211 I d
Atlantic and Pacific Railroad Grant 210 C c
Atlantic Ocean 108 Nc-Pk
Atlantic Plain 187 K e
Atlas Mountains 2 D e
Atmeidan 93 G e
Atoyac River
Atrans 27 I a
Atrato River 105 E e
Atrax 11 D c
Atrebates or Atrebatis, see Arras
Atrebates, people, in Britain 51 P i
Atrebates, people, in Gaul 38 C b
Atrectian Alps, mts. 26 B b
Atri 90 D c
Atri, bp. 95 E c
Atria 26 F b
Atropatene, Media, reg. 35 N f
Atropatene, Media, satr. 18 P h
Attalea 59 K f
Attalia 20 D d
Attalids, Kingdom of the 33 legend
Attalus, Stoa of 23 D
Attamok 198 ins. A
Attica, reg. 16
Attidium 27 G d
Attila, Empire of 48 F L b
Attilla, Palace of 48 I c
Attinghausen 91 Q l
Attium, prom. 26 C e
Attock 137 B b
Atur or Aturius (Adour) River 38 B d
Atwood Cay 105 F b
Aube, dept. 148 E e
Aube River 69 I f
Aubenas 126 D d
Aubeterre, mon. 94 B b
Aubusson 76 E d
Auch 61 D e
Auch, abp. 94 B c
Auch, gen. 147 D c
Auchi-les-Moines, mon 94 C a
Auckland 172 G d
Aude, dept. 148 E f
Aude River 126 C e
Audincourt 143 ins. F
Auerstädt 154 F c
Aufidena, in Apulia 31 F a
Aufidena, in Samnium 31 D a

Aufidus, Bridge of . . . . 30 E a
Aufidus (Ofanto) River . . . . . 31 F a
Aufinum . . . . 27 H e
Aughrim . . . . 127 I h
Augila . . . . 18 B e
Augsburg . . . . 62 F d
Augsburg, bp. . . . . 79 G e
Augsburg, imp. city . . . . 79 G d
Augusta, in Cilicia . . . . 20 F d
Augusta, in Maine . . . . 211 L b
Augusta, in Sicily . . . . 131 G f
Augusta, in S. C. . . . . 196 C d
Augusta, Asturica (Astorga) . . 38 A d
Augusta, Bracara (Braga) . . . . 38 A d
Augusta, Emerita (Mérida) . . . 38 A e
Augusta, Fort, in Georgia . . . 193 D e
Augusta, Fort, in Pa. . . . . . . 192 C c
Augusta Bagiennorum (Bene) . 26 B c
Augusta Prætoria (Aosta) . . . . 26 B b
Augusta Rauricorum (Augst) . . 39 I j
Augusta Suessionum, see Soissons
Augusta Taurinorum (Turin) . 26 B b
Augusta Treverorum (Trèves) . 39 I i
Augusta Vindelicorum (Augsburg) 38 E c
Augustamnica, Rom. prov. . . . 43 I g (6)
Augustan Canal . . . . 27 G c
Augustanus, Vicus . . . . 35 ins. B
Augusti, Lucus (Luc-en-Die) . 38 D d
Augusti, Lucus (Lugo) . . . . . 38 A d
Augusti, Portus . . . . 27 G f
Augustine Friars, mon. of . . . 75 G g
Augustobona (Troyes) . . . . . . 38 C c
Augustobriga (Talavera la Vieja) 38 B e
Augustodunum (Autun) . . . . . 38 C c
Augustodurum (Bayeux) . . . . 38 B c
Augustonemetum (Clermont-Ferrand) . . . . 38 C c
Augustoritum (Limoges) . . . . . 38 C c
Augustowo . . . . 155 L b
Augustus, Arch of . . . .
Augustus, Forum of . . . . 24 B
Augustus, Mausoleum of . . . . 22 A
Augustus, Naumachia of . . . . 22 A
Augustus, Palace of . . . . 24 B
Augustus, Port of . . . . 35 ins. B
Augustus, Temple of . . . . . .
Aujila . . . . 99 H h
Auldearn . . . . 127 Q g
Aulendorf . . . . 143 I j
Aulerci Cenomani, people . . . 38 B c
Aulis . . . . 11 E d
Aulnay . . . . 76 C c
Aulnay, mon. . . . . 94 B b
Aulon . . . . 31 I b
Aulon, valley in Laconia . . . . 14 C c
Aulon, valley in Macedonia . . 11 E b
Aulon, valley in Palestine . . . 7 D d
Aumale . . . . 76 D b
Aumône, L', mon. . . . . 94 C b
Auneau . . . . 126 B b
Aunis, gouv. . . . . 146 A b
Aunis, prov. . . . . 148 D e
Aurangabad . . . . 137 C e
Auranitis, reg. . . . . 7 E d
Auray . . . . 76 B c
Aureus, Mt. . . . . 26 C e
Aurelian Bridge . . . . 22 A
Aurelian Gate . . . . 22 A
Aurelian Gate, New . . . . 22 A
Aurelian Wall . . . . 22 A
Aurelian Way, road . . . . 26 E d
Aureliani or Aurelianis (Orléans) 38 C c
Aurelii, Forum . . . . 27 F e
Aureoli, Pons . . . . 26 D b
Aurich . . . . 158 D b
Aurillac . . . . 69 E d
Aurillac, mon. . . . . 94 C c
Aurunci, people . . . . 30 C a
Ausava . . . . 39 I h
Auscii or Ausciis, see Auch
Ausculum . . . . 30 E a
Ausetani, people . . . . 38 C d
Auser River . . . . 26 E c
Ausonians, people . . . . 29 C d
Aussig . . . . 87 J c
Austerfield . . . . 185 E d
Austerlitz . . . . 155 I d
Austin . . . . 210 F d
Austin, Lake . . . . 172 A c
Austral Islands . . . . 180 M j
Australia, continent 172
Australia, North, reg . . . . . . 172 C b
Australian Alps . . . . 172 D d
Australian Bight, Great . . . . . 172 B d
Austrasia, reg. . . . . 54 F c
Austria, archduchy . . . . 87 J d
Austria, duchy, 12 cent. . . . . 72 D b
Austria, duchy, 13 cent. . . . . 79 I d
Austria, empire, 1806 . . . . . . 151 M j
Austria, empire, 1812 . . . . . . 155 ins.
Austria, empire, 1815 . . . . . . 158—159
Austria, march . . . . 59 H d
Austria, margr. . . . . 63 I d
Austria, Lower, dist . . . . 159 H d
Austria, Upper, dist . . . . 159 H d
Austrian Netherlands, prov. . . 134 B c
Austrian Silesia, dist. . . . . . . 135 I c
Ausugum . . . . 27 F a
Autariatæ, people . . . . 39 L l
Auté . . . . 191 I e
Autessiodurum or Autissiodurum, see Auxerre
Autricum (Chartres) . . . . 38 C c
Autrigones, people . . . . 38 B d
Autun . . . . 61 F c
Autun, bp. . . . . 94 C b
Auvergne, cty. . . . . 61 E d
Auvergne, duchy . . . . 78 C f
Auvergne, gouv. . . . . 146 B b
Auvergne, prov. . . . . 148 E e
Auxerre . . . . 69 E c
Auxerre, bp. . . . . 69 I g
Auxerre, cty. . . . . 76 E c
Auxerre, dist. . . . . 84 E f
Auximum (Osimo) . . . . 27 H d
Auxonne . . . . 126 D c
Ava . . . . 103 J e
Ava, reg. . . . . 102 J e
Avah . . . . 99 M f
Avallon, Avallone . . . . 76 F c
Avalon Peninsula . . . . 212 J d
Avaricum (Bourges) . . . . 38 C c
Avars, people . . . . 54 H d
Avasgians, people . . . . 55 M e
Aveia . . . . 27 H e
Aveiro . . . . 82 A a
Avellino . . . . 90 E d
Avellino, bp. . . . . 95 ins.
Avendo . . . . 27 J c
Avenio or Avenione, see Avignon
Avens River . . . . 27 H e
Aventicum (Avenches) . . . . . . 39 I j
Aventine, quarter . . . . 96 A
Aventine, Augustan, Region of Rome . . . . 22 A
Aventine Mount . . . . 22 A
Avenue de Paris, Versailles . . 149 A
Avenue de Saint Cloud, Versailles . . . . 149 A
Avenue de Trianon, Versailles 149 A
Averni, see Clermont, in Auvergne
Avernus Lake . . . . 31 ins. A
Aversa . . . . 90 E d
Aversa, bp. . . . . 95 ins.
Aversa, cty. . . . . 64 B b
Avesica . . . . 27 H b
Avesnes . . . . 69 F a
Avesnes, mon. . . . . 148 B a
Aveyron, dept. . . . . 148 E f
Avezzano . . . . 64 ins.
Avignon . . . . 61 F d
Avignon, bp. . . . . 94 C c
Avignon, papal dom. . . . . . . 78 D f
Avignon, univ. . . . . 100 F f
Avila . . . . 82 B a
Avila, bp. . . . . 94 B c
Avilés . . . . 82 A a
Aviones, people . . . . 38 D a
Aviz . . . . 94 A d
Avlona . . . . 164 B b
Avola . . . . 90 E f
Avona River . . . . 38 B b
Avon River . . . . 127 W n
Avranches . . . . 61 C b
Avranches, bp. . . . . 94 B b
Avranches, cty. . . . . 69 C b
Axbridge, parl. bor. . . . .
Axel . . . . 117 B c
Axima . . . . 26 A b
Axiupolis . . . . 43 H e
Axius (Vardar) River . . . . . . 11 D b
Axminster . . . . 127 V p
Axona River, see Aisne River
Axtopolis . . . . 47 L e
Axuenna . . . . 39 H i
Axuenna River, see Aisne River
Ayacucho, battle . . . . 214 B d
Ayamonte . . . . 83 J h
Ayas . . . . 99 K f
Ayerbe . . . . 82 B a
Aylesbury, parl. bor. . . . . 163 N f (Ayl.)
Aylesbury, parl. dist . . . . 163 N f (Ayl.)
Ayllon, route of . . . . 191 J e
Ayotta . . . . 201 H g
Ayr . . . .
Ayr, cty. . . . . 127 P i
Ayr, reg. . . . .
Ayuthia . . . .
Ayutla . . . . 213 C c
Ayyubids, Dominion of the . . 73 H d
Azania, reg. . . . . 14 B b
Azenia . . . . 16 B b
Azerbijan, reg. . . . .
Azetium . . . . 31 F b
Azilia, dist. . . . . 193 ins. C
Aziris . . . . 18 B d
Azores Islands . . . . 175 A a
Azorus . . . . 10 D c
Azotus . . . . 7 B e
Azov . . . . 139 E f
Azov, Sea of . . . . 3 H d
Aztecs, Dominion of the . . . . 107 G e
Azzo Visconti, Dominion of . . 90 I h

Baalbec . . . . 6 E a
Baal Gad . . . . 6 D b
Baar, landgr. . . . . 142 B e
Babadagh . . . . 131 I e
Babahoyo . . . . 214 B c (Ba)
Baba Mahal, reg. . . . .
Bab el Mandeb, strait . . . . . 170 F g
Babenberg, see Bamberg . . . . 62 F d
Babuyan Islands . . . . 171 N g
Babylon . . . . 4 G c
Babylonia, prov. . . . . 18 G d
Babylonia, reg. . . . . 8 C b
Babylonia, satr. . . . . 8 I e
Bacallaos, Tierra de los . . . . 108 L c
Bacanore . . . .
Bacca . . . . 77 L e
Bacenis Forest . . . . 39 J h
Backnang . . . . 143 H h
Back's River . . . . 212 E b
Bac-ninh . . . . 171 L f
Bacolor . . . . 199 ins. H
Bacs, reg. . . . .
Baotra . . . . 8 E b
Bactria, prov. . . . . 19 K c
Bactria, reg. . . . . 8 E b
Bactria, satr. . . . . 8 K e
Bactrians, Kingdom of the . . . 19 Y k
Badajóz . . . . 83 D d
Badajóz, bp. . . . . 94 A d
Badajóz, emir. . . . . 83 D d
Badakshan, reg. . . . .
Baddesley, preceptory . . . . . 100 A b
Baden, in Baden . . . . 142 B c
Baden, in Switzerland . . . . . 91 Q k
Baden, near Vienna . . . . 79 J c
Baden, castle . . . . 62 E d
Baden, elect. . . . . 151 H g

Baden, gr. duchy 151 K j
Baden, margr. 86 G d
Badenoch, reg.
Badenweiler 142 A e
Badenweiler, lordship 142 A e
Badiæ 46 H g
Bæbiani 30 D a
Bæcula 38 B e
Bæterræ, see Béziers
Bætica, West Rom. prov. 42 A f(1)
Bætica, Farther, senat. prov. 34 C f
Bætica (Farther Spain) Augustan prov. 38 A e(3)
Bætica, Hither, senat. prov. 34 D f
Bætis River (Guadalquivir) 38 A e
Bæto 38 A e
Bæza 82 B b
Baffin Bay 186 L a
Baffin Land 186 L a
Bafulabe 174 B c
Bagæ 42 D f
Bagamoyo 175 G e
Bagdad 53 G c
Bagdad, calif. 73 I d
Bagé, in Brazil 215 D f
Bagé, in France 130 M h
Bagienni, people 26 B c
Bagirmi, reg. 174 E c
Bagistana (Behistun)
Bagno di Romagna 90 M j
Bagnolo 90 J h
Bagnorea, bp. 95 E c
Bagradas River 38 D e
Bahama Islands 105 E b
Bahawalpur 137 B c
Bahawalpur, reg. 137 B c
Bahia 214 F d
Bahia, cap. 108 M i
Bahia, state 214 E d
Bahia Blanca 215 C f
Bahia Blanca, bay 215 C f
Bahia del Almirante, bay 105 D e
Bahia de Todos os Santos, bay 214 F d
Bahmanid Sultanate 92 H f
Bahrein, isl.
Bahr el Ghazal, reg. 174 F d
Bahr el Ghazal, R. 174 F d
Baiæ 31 ins. A
Baikal, lake
Baila Monos River
Bailén 130 C f
Baindt, ab. 143 I j
Baisan 68 ins. A
Bajazet, Mosque of 93 G e(5)
Bajocas or Bajocasses, see Bayeux
Baker City 210 B b
Baker Island 180 J h
Bakkar
Bakony Wald, mts. 159 I e
Baktchiserai 93 D b
Baku 139 G g
Balabac Strait 171 M h
Balabo, mt. 30 E b
Balaklava 164 J f
Balasor
Balaton, lake
Balboa, route of 105 E e
Balbus, Crypta of 22 A
Balbus, Theatre of 22 A
Baldern 143 J h
Bâle, see Basel
Balearic Islands 2 E e
Balearic Isles, Rom. prov. 42 C f(7)
Balearic Sea 38 C e
Balesium 31 H b
Bali, isl. 112 E d
Balingen 143 G i
Balize 191 H f
Balkan Mountains 2 G d
Balkan Peninsula 2 G d
Balkash, lake
Balkh
Balkh, reg. 137 A a
Balla 11 D b
Ballaarat 172 D d
Ballah, lake 174 K i
Ballenstedt 62 F c
Ballinaslœ 98 B c
Ballyshannon 127 I g
Balsas, Rio de las, R. 213 ins.
Balta 139 C f
Baltic Port 120 J e
Baltic Sea 2 F c
Baltimore, in Ireland 184 B b
Baltimore, in Maryland 192 C d
Baltischport (Baltic Port) 120 J e
Baluches, people 92 G e
Baluchistan, state 170 H f
Balyra River 14 B b
Bamberg 62 F d
Bamberg, bp. 79 G d
Bamborough
Bamborough, parl. bor.
Bambuk, reg. 174 B c
Bamian 102 G d
Bammako 174 C c
Banat, reg. 159 K f
Banbury, parl. bor. 163 M e
Banda, isl.
Banda Oriental, prov. 215 D f
Bandar Abbas 170 G f
Bandusia, Fount of 30 E b
Banff, cty.
Banff Park, town 212 D c
Bangalore 137 C f
Bangkok 171 K g
Bangor, in Maine 199 L b
Bangor, in Wales
Bangor, bp. 97 M h
Bangweolo, lake 175 F f
Banialuka 159 I f
Banias 68 ins. A
Banjermassin, reg. 112 E d
Banks Land, isl. 186 G a
Banks Strait 186 G a
Bann River 49 C d
Bannocks, people 188 C a
Bañolas 82 C a
Baños de Ledesma 82 C a
Bantam 112 D d
Bantia 31 F b
Bantry Bay 127 G j
Banz, mon. 95 E a
Bauli 31 ins. A
Bapaume 117 A d
Baphyras River 11 D b
Bar (Antivari) 164 B b
Bar, in Podolia 131 I d
Bar-le-Duc 84 F e
Bar-sur-Aube 61 F b
Bar-sur-Aube, cty. 69 J f
Bar-sur-Seine 69 J f
Bar, duchy, 14 cent. 76 F b
Bar, duchy, 15 cent. 84 F e
Bar, duchy, 17 and 18 cent. 126 D b
Bar, dist., 18 cent. 134 C d
Baranof Island 212 ins.
Baraque, La 156 B a
Barathrum, mt. 23 D
Barataria Bay 207 G e
Barbados, isl. 213 F c
Barbary, reg. 108 Q d
Barbary States 118 D g
Barbastro 82 C a
Barberton 175 N l
Barbuda, isl. 213 F c
Barca 8 G e
Barca, reg. 66 K g
Barcaldine 172 D c
Barcellos 214 C c
Barcelona, in Spain 82 C a
Barcelona, in Venezuela 214 C b
Barcelona, bp. 94 C c
Barcelona, cty. 82 C a
Barcelona, univ. 100 F f
Barcelonette 126 E d
Barchin
Barchinona or Barcino (Barcelona) 38 C d
Bard, Fort 150 D d
Bardenwick, see Bardowiek
Bardney, mon. 97 Q h
Bardo
Bardowiek 62 F b
Bardstown 196 B c
Barduli 31 F a
Bardulia, cty. 82 B a
Barea 38 B e
Bareilly 137 C c
Bärenburg, castle 91 R l
Barfleur 65 F f
Barga 90 L i
Bargu, reg.
Bargylia 17 E c
Bari 64 C b
Bari, abp. 95 F c
Baris 31 H c
Barium 31 F a
Barka Plateau 2 G e
Barkhalikend
Barking 75 J h
Barking, mon. 97 R j
Barkly 175 L l
Barkul
Barlee, lake 172 A c
Barletta 90 F d
Barlings, mon. 97 Q h
Barlow, route of 191 J d
Barnegat Inlet 192 D d
Barnet 75 I h
Barnim, reg. 80 ins
Barnsley 162 E d
Barnstable 189 C d
Barnstaple 65 D e
Barnstaple, parl. bor. 163 J f
Barnus, mt. 10 C b
Barnwell, mon. 97 R i
Barroch
Baroda 137 B d
Baros 112 C c
Barotse, people 175 F f
Barquisimeto 105 G d
Barra do Rio Negro 214 D c
Barra Island
Barranquilla 214 B a
Barre, La 192 C b
Barren Country, reg. 212 C b
Barrios, Puerto 213 D c
Barrois mouvant, dist. 126 D b
Barrow, Point 186 D a
Barrow River 49 C e
Barrow Strait 186 J a
Barrum, see Bar-le-Duc and Bar-sur-Aube
Bartenstein, in Prussia 155 K a
Bartenstein, in Wurtemberg 143 I g
Bartfeld 131 H d
Barton, priory 100 A b
Barton-on-Humber, parl. bor.
Baruth 85 G d
Bärwalde 123 H b
Basel 91 P k
Basel, bp. 78 E e
Basel, canton 91 P k
Basel, imp. cy. 78 E e
Basel, univ. 100 G e
Basentus (Busento) River 31 F c
Bashan, reg. 6 E c
Bashkirs, people 139 H e
Basilica Æmilia, bldg 24 B
Basilica Julia, bldg. 24 B
Basilica Porcia, bldg.
Basilica Sempronia, bldg. 24 A
Basilica Ulpia, bldg. 24 B
Basilicata, dist. 90 E d
Basilia, see Basel
Basingstoke 127 X o
Basingstoke, college 100 A a (33)
Basingstoke, deanery 100 A a
Basingstoke, hospital 100 A a (29)
Basingstoke, parl. bor.
Basingwerk, mon. 97 N h
Basle, see Basel
Basman 112 C c

Basques, people 57 C e
Basra 53 G c
Bas-Rhin, dept. 148 F e
Bassam, Grand 175 C d
Bassania 31 I a
Bassano 72 C b
Basse-Fontaine, mon. 94 C b (B. F.)
Bassein 112 A b
Basses-Alps, dept. 148 F f
Basses-Pyrénées, dept. 148 D f
Bassignano 130 Q j
Bassigny, dist. 126 D c
Bass Strait 172 D d
Bastarnæ, people 35 I c
Bastetani, people 38 B e
Basti 38 B e
Bastia 77 F d
Bastidas, route of 105 E d
Bastille, bldg. 149 B
Basutoland, col. 175 M l
Bastogne 117 D d
Batalha 83 J h
Batalha, mon. 94 A d
Batanæa, reg. 6 E c
Batanga, Gross
Batangas 171 N g
Batava, Castra (Passau) 38 E c
Batavian Republic 151 H f
Batavians, people 38 C b
Batavodurum 39 H g
Bate 16 B a
Bateia
Bath, in England
Bath, in N. Carolina 193 F d
Bath, bp. 97 O j
Bath, parl. bor. 163 L f
Bathurst, in Gambia 174 B c
Bathurst, in N. S. Wales 172 D d
Bathurst, Cape 212 C a
Baticala 112 A b
Batinus River 27 I e
Batnæ 20 H d
Batoche 212 E c
Baton Rouge 191 G e
Battas, people
Battersea 75 I i
Battery Wagner, fort 208 E c
Battikalva 112 B c
Battle, mon. 97 R k
Battleford 212 E c
Baturin 131 J c
Baturite 214 F c
Bau 158 E a
Bauconia 39 J i
Baudemont 156 A a
Baugé, in Anjou 70 C c
Baugé, in Bresse 126 D c
Bauld, Cape 212 J c
Baume-les-Dames, mon. 95 D b
Baumgartenberg, mon. 95 E b
Bautzen 63 H c
Bautzen-Görlitz, dist. 85 D c
Bauzanum 27 F a
Bavaria, duchy, 10 cent. 63 G e
Bavaria, duchy, 13 cent. 72 C b
Bavaria, duchy, 16 cent. 115 G d
Bavaria, elect. 123 G d
Bavaria, Frank. prov., 8 cent. 53 O h
Bavaria, Frank. prov., 9 cent. 54 G d
Bavaria, km., 1806 151 L j
Bavaria, km., 1812 154 F d
Bavaria, km., 1815—1866 158 F d
Bavaria, km., since 1866 161 C c
Bavaria-Landshut, duchy 79 H d
Bavaria-Munich, duchy 79 G e
Bavaria-Straubing, duchy 79 H d
Bavarian East March (Ostmark) 63 H d
Bavarians, people 46 I d
Bawiti 150 A b
Bawtry 185 E d
Bayamon 199 ins. G
Bayeux 61 C b
Bayeux, bp. 94 B b
Baymen, people 136 ins. A
Bay of Chaleurs 212 I d
Bayona 82 A a
Bayonne 58 D e
Bayonne, bp. 94 B c
Bayou Pierre, R. 196 A d
Bayreuth 114 F d
Bayreuth, princ. 114 F d
Baza 82 B b
Bazadais, dist. 69 C d
Bazas 61 C d
Bazas, bp. 94 B c
Beachy Head 127 Z p
Bear River 198 C b
Béarn, gouv. 146 A c
Béarn, prov. 148 D f
Béarn, viscty. 76 C e
Bearroc Wood 49 F f
Beata, isl. 105 F c
Beaucaire 126 D e
Beauce, dist. 69 H f
Beau-Chêne 156 C c
Beaufort 193 ins. C
Beaugency 69 H g
Beaugency, mon.
Beauharnais, Fort 191 G c
Beauharnois 212 H d
Beaujeu 76 F c
Beaujeu, seign. 69 F c
Beaulieu, ab. 100 A b
Beaulieu, castle 76 D c
Beaulieu, mon., near Tours 94 C b
Beaulieu, mon., near Tulle 94 C b
Beaumaris, parl. bor. 163 J d
Beaumont, in Anjou 76 C b
Beaumont, in Hainaut 157 ins.
Beaumont, in Normandy 65 G f
Beaumont, on the Oise 76 E b
Beaumont, cty., in Normandy 76 D b
Beauvais 61 E b
Beauvais, bp. 94 C b
Beauvais, cty. 61 E b
Beauvale, mon. 97 P h
Beaver 210 C c
Bebenhausen, mon 143 H h
Bec 65 G f
Bec, mon. 94 C b
Bechuanaland, dist. 175 F g
Bechuanaland, prot., col. 175 F g
Beda 39 I i
Beddington 75 I i
Bedesis (Ronco) River 27 E d
Bedford, in England
Bedford, in Virginia 195 B e
Bedford, cty. 127 Y n
Bedford, Fort 192 B c
Bedford, New 211 K b
Bedford, parl. bor. 163 N e
Bedlington
Bedwyn, parl. bor.
Beejapore 137 C e
Beerfelden 142 C a
Beer Alston, parl. bor.
Beersheba 7 B f
Beeskow 85 H d
Beeston Castle 127 W m
Behar 137 E c
Behar, reg. 137 D d
Beichlingen 85 F e
Beilan 164 F c
Beilstein 143 H g
Beinheim 142 B c
Beira 175 G f
Beira, Fort do Principe da 214 C d
Beirut 68 C c
Beja 82 A b
Beka, The, reg. 6 D a
Bekes 168 G c
Belbek River 164 J f
Belbina, isl. 15 D b
Belbuck, mon. 80 D d
Belecke, castle 62 E c
Beleigh, mon. 97 R j
Belem, in Brazil 214 E c
Belem, in Portugal 83 J h
Belem, mon. 94 A d
Belemina 14 C b
Belen 105 D e
Belesme 65 G f
Belfast 127 L g
Belfort, in the Sundgau 122 D e
Belfort, in Syria, castle 68 ins. A
Belgæ, people 51 O i
Belgard 63 H b
Belgern 63 G c
Belgian Congo, col. 175 F e
Belgica 39 I h
Belgica, Rom. prov. 38 D c (3)
Belgica I, Rom. prov. 42 D d (5)
Belgica II, Rom. prov. 42 C c (6)
Belgium, km. 158 C c
Belgrade 43 G e
Belgrade, bp. 95 G c
Belize 213 D c
Belkesheim, dist. 63 F b
Belknap, Fort, Ind. Res. 188 D a
Bell, route of 210 F c
Bellac 69 D c
Bellagio see Bellaggio 90 I h
Bellary 137 C e
Belle-Alliance, La, farm 156 C c
Bellecombe, mon. 94 C c
Belle Ile, isl. 69 B c
Belle Isle 148 A b
Belle Isle, Strait of 186 N c
Bellême, seign. 69 H f
Belleville, mon. 94 C b
Belley 69 F d
Belley, bp. 95 D b
Belli, people 38 B d
Bellinzona 91 R l
Bellona, Temple of 24 A
Bellovaci or Bellovacis, see Beauvais
Bellovaci, people 38 C c
Belluno 63 G e
Belluno, bp. 95 E b
Bellunum 27 G a
Belmont 208 C b
Belrain 69 J f
Belt, Great, str. 88 D d
Belt, Little, str. 88 C d
Beltana 172 C d
Belts 59 I c
Belus River 6 C c
Belvoir, in Syria, castle 68 ins. A
Belvoir Castle, in England 127 Y n
Belzig 85 G d
Benacus (Garda), lake 26 E b
Benadir, reg. 175 H d
Benafrum, see Venafrum (Venafro)
Benares 137 D c
Benavente 83 J g
Bencoolen
Bender
Bendigo 172 D d
Benediktbeuren, mon. 95 E b
Beneschau 135 H d
Benevento 46 I e
Benevento, abp. 95 E c
Benevento, duchy 54 G e
Benevento, princ. 64 B b
Beneventum (Benevento) 30 D a
Bengal, dist.
Bengal, prov. 137 E d
Bengal, Bay of 112 B b
Benghazi 174 F a
Benguela 175 E f
Benguela, reg. 109 S i
Beni River 214 C d
Benin 174 D d
Benin, Bight of 174 D d
Benin, reg. 108 R g
Bénisson-Dieu, La, mon. 94 C b
Beni-Suef 150 B b
Benjamin, tribe 7 ins. D
Bennet, lake 212 ins.
Bennett's Plantation 193 ins. A (Benn.)
Ben Nevis, mt. 49 D c

Bennington 195 E b
Bentheim 62 D b
Bentheim, cty. 134 D b
Benton, Fort 198 C a
Bentonville 208 E b
Bent's Fort 198 E c
Benue River 174 D d
Berar, dist. 137 C d
Berar, prov. 170 I f
Berar, Rajah of, princ.
Berat 165 A c
Berber 174 G c
Berbera 174 H c
Berbers, people 53 B-D c-d
Berchtesgaden 79 H e
Berchtesgaden, ab. 79 H e
Berchtesgaden, mon. 72 C b
Berdera 175 H d
Berditchev 131 I d
Berea 7 C e
Bereïdah 170 F f
Berenice 34 H g
Beresina River 153 N g
Berezov 170 H b
Berg, cty. 78 E c
Berg, duchy 86 F c
Berg, gr. duchy 154 D c
Bergalei, people 26 D a
Berga 82 C a
Bergama 77 J e
Bergamo 90 I h
Bergamo, bp. 95 D b
Berge, in Macedonia 11 E b
Berge, mon. near Magdeburg 95 E a
Bergen, near Frankfort 134 E c
Bergen, in Netherlands 134 C b
Bergen, in New Jersey 189 ins. C
Bergen, in Norway 166 F c
Bergen, on Rugen Island 123 G a
Bergen, Hanse. for. off. 98 D a
Bergen, mon., on Rugen I. 80 C d
Bergen op Zoom 117 C c
Bergerac 69 D d
Bergerac, castle 76 D d
Bergomum (Bergamo) 26 D b
Bergues 126 C a
Bergula
Bergzabern 142 B b
Berhampur 171 J f
Bering Sea 179 I b
Bering Strait 186 C b
Beritini, people 26 A d
Berkeley, in California 210 A c
Berkeley, in England 185 D f
Berkeley, in Virginia 193 ins. A
Berkeley, castle
Berkeley County 193 ins. C
Berkhampstead 65 F e
Berkhampstead, parl. bor. 163
Berks, parl. dist. 163 M f
Berkshire, cty. 60 M i
Berlichingen 143 I g
Berlichingen, castle 114 E d
Berlin 85 C b
Berlin, Hanse. cy. 99 ins. B
Bermejo River 215 C e
Bermius, mt. 10 C b
Bermondsey, mon. 97 Q j
Bermuda, isl. 108 K d
Bermuda Hundred 191 J d
Bermudez, state 214 C b
Bermudez, route of 108 K d
Bernalillo 190 D d
Bernardino River
Bernburg 154 F c
Berne 91 P l
Berne, canton 91 P l
Berne, New (Newbern) 193 F d
Berneck, castle 143 G h
Bernhardin Pass 150 E c
Bernicia, dist.
Bernicians, people
Bernina Pass 91 S l
Bernkastel 142 ins. A
Bernstein 85 D b
Berœa, in Macedonia 10 D b
Berœa, in Syria 20 G d
Berœa, in Thrace 39 N l
Berones, people 38 B d
Berothai 6 D a
Berrhœa 10 D b
Berry, duchy 78 C e
Berry, gouv. 146 B b
Berry, prov. 148 E e
Berthold, Fort, Ind. Res. 188 F a
Bertinoro, bp. 95 E c
Bertiscus, mt. 11 E b
Berwick, in England
Berwick, in New Hampshire 189 C c
Berwick, cty.
Berwick on Tweed, parl. bor. 163 M b
Berwick, South 189 C c (S. B.)
Berytus (Beirut) 6 D a
Besa 16 C b
Besalú, mon. 94 C c
Besançon 62 D e
Besançon, abp. 95 D b
Besançon, gen. 147 F b
Besançon, imp. cy. 78 E e
Besançon, univ. 100 G e
Beshicktash, quarter
Besigheim 143 H g
Besika Bay
Besor River 7 B f
Bessapara 39 M l
Bessarabia, dist. in the Ottoman Empire
Bessarabia, dist. in Russia 139 C f
Bessi, people 39 M l
Bethany, in Georgia 193 ins. C
Bethany, in Palestine 7 C e
Bethar 7 B d
Betharbel
Beth-Aven 7 C e
Bethel, in Alaska 198 ins. A
Bethel, in Palestine 7 C e
Bethelea 7 A e
Bethencourt, route of 108 O e
Bethesda, Pool of 6 ins. A
Beth-Haran 7 D e
Beth-Horon 7 C e
Beth-Jeshimoth 7 D e
Bethlehem, in Palestine 7 C e
Bethlehem, in Pennsylv. 192 D c
Bethlen Gabor, route of 121 F c
Beth-Markaboth 7 C f
Beth-Meon
Beth-Nimrah 7 D e
Beth-Peor 7 D e
Bethsaida 6 D c
Bethshean 7 C d
Beth-Shemesh 7 B e
Bethso 6 ins. A
Bethulie 175 M m
Béthune 117 A d
Bethzur 7 C e
Betifulus
Betogabra 7 B e
Betonim 7 D e
Betriacum 26 E b
Beuil, Le, mon. 94 C b
Beutelsbach 143 H h
Beuthen 115 J c
Beveland, South, isl. 117 B c
Beverley 127 Y m
Beverley, parl. bor. 163 N d
Beverly Manor 194 K g
Bevern 134 E c
Beversrede, Fort 192 ins.
Beverswyck 189 A c
Bewdley, parl. bor. 163 L e
Bezabde 20 J d
Bézenas 126 C e
Bezetha 6 ins. A
Bezetha, Hill of 6 ins. A
Béziers 76 E e
Béziers, bp. 94 C c
Bhamo 171 K f
Bhartpur
Bhatkal 112 A b
Bhawalpore 137 B c
Bhawalpore, dist. 137 B c
Bhootan, Bhutan, princ. 137 E c
Bhopal 137 C d
Bhotan, Bhutan, princ. 171 K f
Bhurtpore
Biafra, reg. 109 I g
Biafra, bight 175 D d
Bialystok 138 B e
Biana
Biandrate 72 B b
Biar 82 H f
Bias River
Biasca 91 Q l
Biberach 142 E d
Biberach, imp. cy. 143 I i
Bibracte 38 C c
Bibrax 38 C c
Bibrich 117 E e
Bibroci, people
Bicocca 90 I h
Bidar
Bidassoa River 130 C e
Biel
Bielefeld 154 E b
Bielefeld, Hanse. cy. 99 ins. B
Bielgorod 139 E e
Bielgorod, gov. 131 K e
Bielitz 135 J d
Biella 90 I h
Bielosersk 138 E c
Bielsk 159 L b
Bienne 91 P k
Bierges 156 B a
Bieringen 143 G i
Big Mountain 212 ins.
Big River 212 H c
Big Black River 208 B c
Big Black River, battle 208 B c
Bigha 77 J d
Big Horn River 198 D b
Bigorre, cty. 76 C e
Bigorre, dist. 147 D c (Big.)
Bigorritis, lake 10 C b
Big Sioux River 198 F b
Bihacs 119 H e
Bijapur 137 C e
Bikaner 170 I f
Bikaner, dist. 137 B c
Bilbao 83 K g
Bilbilis 38 B d
Bilitio 26 C a
Billæus River 20 E b
Billingsgate, loc. in London 75 G g
Billungs, Lands of the 62 F b
Billungs, March of the 63 F b
Biloxi 191 H f
Bima
Bimlipatam
Binche 156 A b
Binchester
Bingen 62 D d
Bingerville 174 C d
Bingium (Bingen) 39 I i
Binn 91 Q l
Binsdorf 143 G i
Bintang, isl.
Biobio River 215 B f
Birkenfeld 142 ins. A
Birkel-el-Kerun, lake
Birket Israel 6 ins. A
Birmingham, in Alabama 211 H d
Birmingham, in England 127 X n
Birmingham, parl. bor. 163 M e
Birs River 91 P k
Birten 62 D c
Bisaltia 11 E b
Bisaltia, reg. 11 E b
Bisanthe
Biscay, Bay of 2 D d
Bisceglie 90 F d
Bischoflack 135 H e

Bischofsheim 142 E a
Bischofsheim, mon. 95 D b
Bischofswerda 155 H c
Bischofszell 142 D e
Biserta 58 F f
Bishbalk (Urumtsi)
Bishop-Auckland, mon. 97 P g
Bishop's Castle, parl. bor.
Bishopsgate, loc. in London 75 G g
Bishops Stortford, parl. bor. 163 O f (Bish. St.)
Bisignano 98 G f
Biskra 174 D a
Bismarck 210 E a
Bismarck Archipelago 179 F h
Bissagos Islands 174 B c
Bistritz
Bitburg 117 E d
Biterræ, see Béziers
Bitervium, see Viterbo
Bithynia, dist. 20 D b
Bithynia, East Rom. prov. 43 He(1.)
Bithynia, reg. 8 B a
Bithynia, Rom. prov. 35 K e
Bithynium 20 D b
Bitolia 164 C b
Bitonto 90 F d
Bitsch, fortress 154 D d
Bitter Lakes 174 K i
Bitterne 51 P i
Biturgia 27 F d
Bituriges or Biturigis, see Bourges
Bituriges, people 38 C c
Bivium 35 ins. B
Bizerta
Bizye 39 N l
Björneborg 120 J d
Blachernæ, palace 93 G e
Blackburn, parl. bor. 163 L d
Blackfeet, Ind. Res. 188 D a
Blackfeet, tribe 188 D a
Black Forest, mts. 62 D e
Black Friars, mon. in London 75 G g
Blackheath 75 J i
Black Hills 210 E b
Black River 208 B b
Black Russia, reg. 139 C e
Black Sea 3 H d
Blacksnake Hills, fort 211 G b
Blackwall 75 J h
Blackwater River
Bladensburg 200 L i
Blagovestchensk
Blakeney, parl. bor.
Blamont 143 ins. F
Blamont, lordship 143 ins. F
Blanca Peak 187 I e
Blanche, lake 172 D c
Blanche Garde, castle 68 ins. A
Blanchelande 65 F f
Blanchelande, mon. 94 B b
Blanco, Cape, in Guinea 174 B b
Blanco, Cape, in Oregon 210 A b
Blanco, Cape, in Peru 111 A b
Blanco, Cape, in Tunis 174 D a
Blanda, in Italy 30 E c
Blanda, in Spain 38 C d
Blandford, parl. bor.
Blankenberghe 117 B c
Blankenheim 117 E d
Blanmont 156 B a
Blariacum 39 H h
Blaubeuren 143 I i
Blaubeuren, mon. 95 D b
Blaye 76 C d
Bleiburg 115 H e
Bleichfeld 62 F d
Blekinge, dist. 88 F c
Bléneau 126 C c
Blenheim 129 F c
Blennerhasset's Island 196 C c
Blera, in Apulia 31 F b
Blera, in Etruria 27 G e
Blesum, see Blois
Bletchingley, parl. bor. 163 N f (Blet.)
Blindheim 134 F d
Block Island 189 C d
Bloemfontein 175 M l
Blois 61 D c
Blois, cty. 61 D c
Blore Heath 84 B c
Bluefields 213 D c
Blue Horde, people
Blue Licks 196 C c
Blue Mountains 172 D d
Blue Nile River 174 G c
Blue Ridge, mts. 193 C d — E b
Blumegg 142 B e
Blumenau, in Brazil 215 E e
Blumenau, in Hungary 159 I d
Blumenfeld 142 C e
Boactes River 26 D c
Bobbio 90 I h
Bobbio, bp. 95 D c
Bober River 63 H c
Bobium Castrum (Bobbio) 26 D c
Böblingen 143 H h
Bobruisk 167 K e
Boca del Dragón, str. 105 H d
Boca del Sierpe, str. 105 H d
Boca del Toro, bay 213 D d
Bocca Tigris 171 M f
Bocchetta Pass, La 150 E d
Bochnia 123 K c
Bocholt 117 E c
Böckelheim, castle 62 D d
Bode River 85 F e
Boderiæ Æstuarium (Firth of Forth) 38 B a
Bodetia 26 D c
Bodfeld, castle 62 F c
Bödigheim 142 D b
Bodmann 62 E e
Bodmin, mon. 97 M k
Bodmin, parl. bor. 163 J g
Bodonitza 89 B c
Bodotria Æstuarium (Firth of Forth) 51 O g
Bœæ 15 D c
Bœæ, Bay of 15 D c
Bœbe 11 D c
Bœbeis, lake 11 D c
Bœotia, reg. 11 E d
Bœum 11 D d
Bogesund 88 E c
Bogotá 214 B b
Bohemia, duchy 63 H d
Bohemia, km. 72 C b
Bohemia, plain of 2 F d
Bohemia, reg. 54 G d
Bohemian March 55 R j
Bohemians, people
Bohio
Böhmer Wald, mts. 63 G d
Böhmisch-Brod 87 J c
Bohol, isl. 199 ins. H
Bohus, dist. 88 D b
Boii, people, in Italy 26 E c
Boii, people, in Pannonia 38 F c
Bois Brulé River 191 G b
Boisé 210 B b
Boisé, Fort 198 B a
Bois Forte, Ind. Res. 188 H a
Bois-le-Duc 114 C c
Boissière, La, mon. 94 C b
Boïus, mt. 10 B b
Bojador, Cape 174 B b
Bojano, bp. 95 ins.
Bojeador, Cape 199 ins. H
Bojohæmum (Bohemia), reg 38 E c
Bokhara
Bokhara, emir.
Bola 35 ins. B
Bolama 174 B c
Bolan Pass 170 H f
Bolar 99 N c
Bolbe, lake 11 E b
Bolghars, people
Boli 89 J f
Bolkhov 139 E e
Bolivia, country 214 C d
Bologna 90 C b
Bologna, bp. 95 E c
Bologna, univ. 100 H f
Bolsena, lake 90 L j
Bolsward 117 D a
Bolton, in England 127 W m
Bolton, in Mississippi 208 B c
Bolton, mon. 97 P h
Bolton, parl. bor. 163 L d
Bolton Abbey 127 X l
Bolton Castle 127 X l
Boma 175 E e
Bomarsund 131 H a
Bombay 137 B e
Bona 66 H f
Bona Dea, Temple of 22 A
Bonaire, isl. 214 C a
Bonavista 212 J d
Bonavista, Cape 194 I a
Bone 174 D a
Bonifacio 72 B c
Bonn 62 D c
Bonna (Bonn) 39 I h
Bonndorf 142 B e
Bonndorf, cty. 142 B e
Bonneval, mon. 94 C b
Bonnes Vaux, mon. 94 C b
Bonnevaux, mon. 95 D b
Bonneville, Fort 210 C b
Bönnigheim 143 H g
Bononia (Bologna) 27 F c
Bononia (Boulogne) 38 C b
Bontobrica 39 I h
Boonesboro 194 C c
Boone's Trail 194 C c
Boonville 211 G c
Boothia, Gulf of 186 K b
Boothia, isl. 186 J a
Boothia Felix, pen. 212 F a
Bopfingen, imp. cy. 143 J h
Boppard 62 D c
Bora, mt. 10 C a
Borbetomagus (Worms) 39 J i
Borborus, lake 11 D b
Borculo 117 E b
Bordeaux 61 C d
Bordeaux, abp. 94 B b
Bordeaux, gen. 147 D c
Bordeaux, univ. 100 E f
Bordelais, dist. 76 C d
Bordesley, mon. 97 P i
Borgo San Donnino 90 J h
Borgo San Lorenzo 90 L j
Borgo San Sepolcro 90 M j
Borgo Sesia 130 Q i
Boriquen, isl. 105 G c
Borisov
Borkeloo 117 E b
Borku, reg. 174 E c
Borkum, isl. 117 E a
Bormio 90 J g
Borneo, isl.
Bornholm, isl. 88 F d
Bornhöved 72 C a
Bornu, reg. 174 E c
Borobodor
Borodino 131 K b
Boroughbridge 65 F c
Boroughbridge, parl. bor. 163 M c
Borovsk 153 P f
Borsippa 4 G c
Borysthenes (Dnieper) River 35 K d
Boscaudun, mon. 95 D c
Boshof 175 M l
Bosna River 159 J f
Bosnia, reg.
Bosnia, km. 93 A b
Bosnia, prov. in the Ottoman Empire 124 C b
Bosnia, prov. in Austria 164 B b
Bosporus, Bosphorus, strait 2 G d
Bosporus, Kingdom of the Cimmerian 35 K e
Bosrah 6 F c

Bossiney, parl. bor. 163 J g
Boston, in England 127 Y m
Boston, Hanse. for. cy. 98 ins. A
Boston, parl. bor. 163 O d
Boston, in Mass. 189 ins. B
Boston Neck, pen. 195 ins. A
Bostra 6 F c
Bostrenus River 6 C a
Bosworth 84 C c
Botany Bay 172 E d
Bothnia, Gulf of 2 G b
Bothwell
Botroun 68 C c
Bottiæis, reg. 11 D b
Bottice, reg. 11 E b
Bottwar, Gross 143 H h
Botzen 62 F e
Bouchain 117 B d
Bouches-du-Rhône, dept. 148 E f
Bouet, Port 175 C d
Bougainville, isl. 172 E a
Bougie 66 G f
Bouillon 117 D e
Bouillon, duchy 117 D e
Boulers 156 A a
Boulevard de la Reine, in Versailles 149 A
Boulevard du Roi, in Versailles 149 A
Boulogne 61 D a
Bounty Islands 179 I l
Bouras, mon. 94 C b
Bourbon 61 E c
Bourbon, cty 61 E c
Bourbon, duchy 76 E c
Bourbon, isl.
Bourbon, Palais, bldg. in Paris 149 B
Bourbon, seign. 69 E c
Bourbon-Lancy 69 I g
Bourbon-l'Archambault 76 E c
Bourbonnais, gouv. 146 B b
Bourbonnais, prov. 148 E e
Bourbonnais, seign. 69 E c
Bourbourg, mon. 148 B a
Bourg, in Bresse 126 D c
Bourg, in Saintonge 76 C d
Bourgachard, mon. 148 B b
Bourges 61 E c
Bourges, abp. 94 C b
Bourges, gen. 147 E b
Bourges, univ. 100 F e
Bourges, viscty. 69 D c
Bourgmont, route of 190 F d
Bourke 172 D d
Bourn, mon. 97 Q i
Bournet, mon. 94 B b
Boussac 69 D c
Bousval 156 A a
Bouvignes 117 C d
Bouvines 69 E a
Bouxières-aux-Dames, mon. 148 C b
Boves 81 M h
Bovianum Undecumanorum 30 D a
Bovianum vetus
Bovillæ 35 ins. B
Bovino 64 C b
Bovino, bp. 95 F c
Bow Church, in London 75 G g (5)
Bowling Green 208 C b
Boxberg 142 E b
Boxley, mon. 97 R j
Boxtel 117 D c
Boyacá, battle 214 B b
Boyen, fortress 159 K a
Boyne River 127 J h
Brà 90 H h
Braba 190 D d
Brabant, dist. 62 B c
Brabant, duchy, 12 cent. 72 A a
Brabant, duchy, 14 cent. 78 D c
Brabant, duchy, 16 cent. 117 C c
Bracara Augusta (Braga) 38 A d
Bracciano, lake 96 B a
Bracito 198 D d
Brackenheim 143 H g
Brackley, parl. bor. 163 M e
Bradanus (Bradano) River 31 F b
Braden Forest 49 E f
Bradenstoke, mon. 97 P j
Bradford, in Wiltshire
Bradford, in Yorkshire 127 X m
Bradninch, parl. bor.
Bradock Down 127 U p
Brady, Fort 211 H a
Braga 82 A a
Braga, abp. 94 A c
Braganza 82 A a
Brahe River 115 I b
Braila 93 C a
Braine-l'Alleud
Braine-le-Château 156 A a
Braine-le-Comte 156 A a
Braintree 189 C c
Brake 158 E b
Bramber and Steyning, parl. bor. 163 N g
Branco, Cape 214 F c
Brandeis 123 H c
Brandenburg 63 G b
Brandenburg, bp. 79 H b
Brandenburg, castle 143 J i
Brandenburg, Hanse. cy. 99 ins. B
Brandenburg, march 85
Brandenburg, margr. 71 S j
Brandenburg, prov. 158 G b
Brandenburg, Neu 123 G b
Brandon, in Manitoba 212 F d
Brandon, in Virginia 193 ins. A
Brandywine River 192 ins.
Branford 189 B d
Brannkirka 88 G b
Branodunum (Brancaster) 51 Q h
Brant, route of 195 C c
Brantôme, mon. 94 C b
Braschimov
Bratzlav 139 C f
Braunau, in Austria 135 G d
Braunau, in Bavaria 115 G d
Braunau, in Bohemia 123 I c
Bräunlingen 142 B e
Braunsberg 79 L a
Braunsberg, Hanse. cy. 99 H c
Brauron 15 D b
Brava 109 V g
Bray 69 I f
Brazen Gate 6 ins. A
Brazil, col. 108 M i
Brazil, country 214 D d
Brazos River 191 F f
Brazos Santiago 201 F d
Brazza, isl. 90 F c
Brazzaville 175 E e
Breadalbane, dist.
Bread Street, in London 75 G g
Breamore, priory 100 A b
Brechin, bp. 97 K c
Brecknock, cty. 127 V n
Brecknock, mon. 97 N i
Brecknock, parl. dist. 163 K e
Brecon, parl. bor. 163 K f
Breda 117 C c
Brede Fiord 166 A b
Breed's Hill 195 ins. A
Brege River 142 B d
Bregenz 134 E e
Brehna, cty. 85 G e
Breisach 62 D e
Breisach, Alt (Old) 142 A d
Breisach, New 134 D e
Breisgau, dist. 142 B e
Breitenfeld 123 G c
Breitenwang 72 C b
Brema, see Bremen
Bremberg 55 R j
Breme, mon. 95 D b
Bremen 62 E b
Bremen, abp. 95 D a
Bremen, duchy 134 E b
Bremen, Hanse. cy. 99 ins. B
Bremen, imp. cy. 78 F b
Bremerhaven 158 E b
Bremetennacum, see Ribchester
Brenner, pass 63 F e
Brenneville 69 H f
Brennus, mt. 26 E b
Brent River 75 I h
Brenta River 63 F f
Brentford 75 I i
Brentwood 75 J h
Brenz 143 J h
Brenz River 143 J h
Brescello 64 B b
Brescia 90 J h
Brescia, bp. 95 E b
Breslau 72 D a
Breslau, bp. 95 F a
Breslau, Hanse. cy. 99 ins. B
Bresse, dist. 126 D c
Brest, in France 69 A b
Brest, in Poland
Brest Litovsk
Breteuil, near Amiens 69 I f
Breteuil, in Normandy 76 D b
Brétigny 76 D b
Breton, Cape 108 K c
Bretones, Tierra de los 108 L c
Bretones, people
Bretten 142 C b
Breuckelen (Brooklyn) 189 ins. C
Briançon 84 G g
Briansk 139 D e
Briantica, reg.
Briar Creek 195 A g
Bridewell Palace, in London 75 G g
Bridgenorth 65 E d
Bridgeport 189 B d
Bridges, Fort 210 C b
Bridgetown 213 F c
Bridgnorth 127 W n
Bridgnorth, parl. bor. 163 L e
Bridgwater 84 B d
Bridgwater, parl. bor. 163 K f
Bridlington, mon. 97 Q g
Bridport, parl. bor. 163 L g
Brie, dist. 69 I f
Brieg 79 J c
Brieg, princ. 79 J c
Briel 117 C c
Briel, Hanse. cy. 99 ins. B
Brienne 76 F b
Brienz 91 P l
Brienz, lake 91 P l
Brig 91 Q l
Brigach River 142 B d
Brigæcium 38 A d
Brigantes, people, in England
Brigantes, people, in Ireland 38 A b
Brigantinus, lake 39 J j
Brigantio 26 A c
Brigantium (Bregenz), in Rætia 39 J j
Brigantium (Corunna), in Spain 38 A d
Brigetio 38 F c
Brighton 127 Y p
Brighton, parl. bor. 163 N g
Brignais 81 M h
Brignolles 126 E e
Brilessus, mt. 15 D a
Brill 117 C c
Brindisi 90 G d
Brindisi, abp. 95 F c
Brinta River 27 F b
Brionne 76 D b
Brioude 76 E d
Brioude, mon. 148 B b
Brisbane 172 E c
Bristol, in England
Bristol, in Rhode Island 189 ins. A
Bristol, castle
Bristol, parl. bor. 163 L f
Bristol Bay 198 ins. A
Bristol Channel 49 D f
Bristol Coalfield 162 D f
Britain, West Rom. dioc. 42 B c
Britain, Rom. prov. 34 D c

Britain I, West Rom. prov. . . . . 42 B c (3
Britain II, West Rom. prov. . . . 42 B c (4)
Britain, about 410 and 600 . . . 51
Britain, Lower, Rom. prov. . . . 38 B b (2)
Britain, Upper, Rom. prov. . . . 38 B b (1)
Britannia, Rom. prov., see Britain 34 D c
Britannia I, II, Rom. prov. . . . 38 B b
British Central Africa, see Nyasaland . . . . 175 G f
British Columbia, prov. . . . . . 212 C c
British East Africa, col. . . . . . 175 G d
British Guiana, col. . . . . 214 D b
British Honduras, col. . . . . . . 213 D c
British India, emp. . . . . 170 I f
British Isles . . . . 2 C c
British Kaffraria, dist. . . . . . . 175 M m
British New Guinea, col. . . . . . 172 D a
British Somaliland, col. . . . . . 174 H d
British South Africa Company 175 F f
Brito . . . . 213 D c
Britons, people . . . .
Brittany, cty. . . . . 61 B b
Brittany, duchy . . . . 76 B c
Brittany, gouv. . . . . 146 A b
Brittany, march . . . . 54 D d
Brittany, prov. . . . . 148 E d
Brittany, reg. . . . . 52 B b
Brivas, see Brioude
Brixellum . . . .
Brixen . . . . 63 F e
Brixen, bp. . . . . 79 G e
Brixham . . . . 127 V p
Brixia (Brescia) . . . . 26 E b
Broach . . . . 137 B d
Broad River . . . . 193 D d
Broad Way, street in Rome . . 22 A
Brocavium (Brougham) . . . . .
Brockville . . . . 212 H d
Brod, Böhmisch . . . . 87 I c
Brod, Deutsch . . . . 87 I d
Brode, mon. . . . . 80 C e
Brody . . . . 139 C c
Brogne, mon. . . . . 94 C a
Broken Hill . . . . 172 D d
Bromberg . . . . 79 J b
Bromberg Canal . . . . . . 135 I b (Br. C.)
Bromiscus . . . . 11 E b
Bromley . . . . 75 J i
Brömsebro . . . . 120 I e
Bromsgrove, parl. bor. . . . . . .
Bromyard, parl. bor. . . . .
Bronzell . . . . 158 E c
Brookfield, in Mass. . . . . 189 B c
Brookfield, in Ohio . . . . 206 ins.
Brooklyn . . . . 189 ins. C
Broome . . . . 172 B b
Broos . . . . 159 L f
Brou . . . . 69 H f
Brouage . . . . 126 A d
Brouwershaven . . . . 117 B c
Brown, mt., in Coast Range . . 212 ins.
Brown, mt., in Rocky Mts. . . . 186 H c
Brown, Fort . . . . 201 F d
Brown's Hole, dist. . . . . 210 D b
Brownsville, Pa. . . . . 192 B c
Brownsville, Texas . . . . 201 F d
Bruanium . . . . 10 C a
Bruce, mt. . . . . 172 A c
Bruchium, quarter in Alexandria 34 ins. C
Bruchsal . . . . 142 C b
Bruck, on the Leitha R. . . . . 159 I d
Bruck, on the Mur R. . . . . . . 87 J e
Bructeri, people . . . . 39 I h
Bruges . . . . 117 B c
Bruges, Hanse. for. off. . . . . . 99 ins. B
Brugg . . . . 91 Q k
Brügge (Bruges) . . . . 117 B c
Brugnato, bp. . . . . 95 D c
Bruinsburg . . . . 208 B c
Bruja Point . . . .
Brundisium or Brundusium (Brindisi) . . . . 31 G b
Brundulum . . . . 27 G b
Brunei . . . .
Bruni Island . . . . 172 D e
Brünig Pass . . . . 91 Q l
Brunkeberg, mt. . . . . 88 H b
Brünn . . . . 63 I d
Brunnen . . . . 91 Q l
Brunswick, in Germany . . . . . 62 F b
Brunswick, in Georgia . . . . . 199 I d
Brunswick, in Maine . . . . 189 C b
Brunswick, duchy, 14 cent. . . . 79 G b
Brunswick, duchy, 18 cent. . . . 134 F c
Brunswick, duchy, 19 cent. . . . 158 F c
Brunswick, Hanse. cy. . . . . . . 99 ins. B
Brunswick-Grubenhagen, duchy 79 G c
Brunswick-Kalenberg, duchy . 86 G b
Brunswick-Lüneburg, duchy . . 79 G b
Brunswick-Wolfenbüttel, duchy 114 F b
Brusa . . . . 77 J d
Brussels . . . . 117 C d
Bruton, mon. . . . . 97 O j
Bruttia and Lucania, West Rom. prov. . . . . 42 F f (6)
Bruttium, reg. . . . . 31 F d
Brüx . . . . 63 G c
Brye . . . . 156 B a
Bryges, people . . . . 17 B a
Bryseæ . . . . 14 C c
Bubastis or Bubastus (Tel Basta) 4 ins.
Buca . . . . 27 I e
Bucaramanga . . . . 214 B b
Buccaneers, head quarters of the
Bucellarian Theme . . . . 59 K e
Bucephala . . . . 19 L d
Bucephala, prom. . . . . 15 D b
Buch, captalat . . . . 69 C d
Buch, mon. . . . . 95 E a
Buchan, dist. . . . .
Buchau, ab. . . . . 143 I i
Buchau, imp. cy. . . . . 143 I i
Buchau, mon. . . . . 95 D b
Buchegg, castle . . . . 91 P k
Buchen . . . . 142 D a
Buchenberg . . . . 122 E d
Buchetium . . . . 10 B c
Buchhorn, imp. cy. . . . . 143 I j
Buckfastleigh, mon. . . . . 97 N k
Buckingham . . . .
Buckingham, cty. . . . . 127 Y o
Buckingham, parl. bor. . . . . . 163 N f
Buckland, mon. . . . . 97 M k
Bucks, cty. . . . . 163 N f
Bucoleon Palace . . . . 93 G e
Buda (Ofen) . . . . 66 J d
Buda, univ. . . . . 100 I e
Budamer . . . . 159 K d
Budapest . . . . 166 I f
Budatin . . . . 159 J d
Budini, people . . . . 35 K c
Budorus River . . . . 11 E d
Budshaja (Bougie) . . . . 66 G f
Budua, bp. . . . . 95 F c
Budweis . . . . 79 I d
Budziak . . . . 131 I d
Buea . . . . 175 D d
Buena Guia, Rio de, R. . . . . . 190 C e
Buenaventura . . . . 214 B b
Buena Vista, battle . . . . 201 E e
Buenos Ayres . . . . 215 D f
Buenos Ayres, audiencia . . . . 215 ins.
Buenos Ayres, viceroyalty . . . 215 ins.
Buffalo . . . . 196 D b
Buford, Fort . . . . 210 E a
Bug River, in Podolia . . . . . . 139 D f
Bug River, in Poland . . . . . . 99 H c
Bugey, dist. . . . . 126 D d
Bühl . . . . 142 B c
Buitrago, pass . . . . 82 B a
Bukharest . . . . 93 C b
Bukowina, dist. . . . . 139 C f
Bülach . . . . 91 Q k
Bulawayo . . . . 175 F g
Buleuterium . . . .
Bulgar . . . . 77 N b
Bulgaria, princ., about 1000 . . 59 I e
Bulgaria, km., 1203 . . . . 73 E b
Bulgaria, km., 1265 . . . . 89 B b
Bulgaria, km., 14 cent. . . . . . 89 H f
Bulgaria, km., 1909 . . . . 164 C b
Bulgaria, prov., 15 cent. . . . . 93 B b
Bulgaria, reg., 11 cent. . . . . . 67 K e
Bulgarians, people, about 900 . 57 H e
Bulgarians, people, about 1190 71 K e
Bulgarians, people, 19 cent. . .
Bulgarians, Kama-, people . . . 71 P b
Bulis . . . . 11 D d
Bull, Fort . . . . 192 D b
Bulla . . . . 38 D e
Bulle . . . . 91 P l
Bull Run, battle . . . . 208 ins.
Bulotus River . . . . 31 F d
Bulun . . . . 171 N a
Bumodus River . . . . 20 J d
Bunarbashi . . . .
Bunarbashi Brook, canal . . . .
Bunbury . . . . 172 A d
Bundelcund, reg. . . . . 137 C d
Bundelkhand, reg. . . . . 137 C d
Bunker Hill, battle . . . . 195 ins. A
Bunzelwitz . . . . 135 I c
Bunzlau, in Bohemia . . . . 63 H c
Bunzlau, in Silesia . . . . 155 H c
Buonconvento . . . . 72 C c
Buporthmus, prom. . . . . 15 D b
Buprasion . . . . 14 B a
Bura . . . . 14 C a
Büraburg . . . . 55 Q i
Buraicus River . . . . 14 C a
Burchana . . . . 38 D b
Burd . . . . 192 B c
Burdegala, Burdigala (Bordeaux) 38 B d
Büren, castle . . . . 62 E d
Burford . . . . 60 F e
Burford, parl. bor. . . . . .
Burgau . . . . 143 J i
Burgau, margr. . . . . 79 G d
Burghas . . . .
Bürglen . . . . 91 Q l
Burgos . . . . 83 E a
Burgos, abp. . . . . 94 B c
Burgoyne, route of . . . . 195 E a
Burgrieden . . . . 143 I i
Burgsdorf . . . . 91 P k
Burgundarholm (Bornholm), isl. 38 E a
Burgundians, Kingdom of the . 50 D c
Burgundians, people . . . . 45 H b, E c
Burgundy, cty. . . . . 61 F c
Burgundy, duchy . . . . 58 E d
Burgundy, gouv. . . . . 146 B b
Burgundy, km. . . . . 58 F de
Burgundy, prov. . . . . 148 E e
Burgundy, Cisjurane (Arles) . . 56 CD cd
Burgundy, Free County of, 14 cent. 78 D e
Burgundy, Free County of, 17 cent. 126 D e
Burgundy, Lower, dist. . . . . . 62 C f
Burgundy, Transjurane or Upper, km. . . . . 56 D c
Burgundy, Upper, dist. . . . . . 62 D e
Buri, people . . . . 34 H d
Burkersdorf . . . . 135 I c
Burlington, in Iowa . . . . 211 G b
Burlington, in New Jersey . . . 192 D c
Burlington, in Vermont . . . . . 211 K b
Burlyuk . . . . 164 J f
Burma, reg. . . . .
Burma, Lower, prov. . . . . 171 K g
Burma, Upper, prov. . . . . 171 K f
Burnum . . . . 38 F c
Burriana . . . . 82 B b
Burrough, route of . . . . 109 W a
Bursfelde, mon. . . . . 95 D a
Burshena see Purchena . . . . . 83 K h
Burton-on-Trent, mon. . . . . . 97 P i
Bury, parl. bor. . . . . 163 L d
Bury Saint Edmunds . . . . . .
Bury Saint Edmunds, mon. . . .
Bury St. Edmunds, parl. bor. . 163 O e
Burzenland, dist. . . . . 80 I i
Busaco . . . . 130 B e
Busento River . . . . 50 G e

Bushire . . . 170 G f
Bushwick . . . 189 ins. C (Bush.)
Bushy Run, battle . . . 194 K f
Busiris . . . 4 ins.
Busk . . . 159 K c
Busselton . . . 172 A d
Bussière, La, mon. . . . 94 C b
Busuluk . . . 139 H e
Bute, cty. . . .
Bute, Fort . . . 195 ins. B
Buthrotum (Butrinto) . . . 10 B c
Butler, route of . . . 195 C b
Butlers, The, fam. . . .
Butley, mon. . . . 97 S i
Buto . . . 4 ins.
Butonti . . .
Bütow . . . 115 I a
Butrinto . . . 93 A c
Butte . . . 210 C a
Buxar . . . 137 D c
Buxentum . . . 30 E b
Buxentum, prom. . . . 30 E c
Buxentus River . . . 30 E c
Buxtehude . . . 62 E b
Buxtehude, Hanse. cy. . . . 99 ins. B
Buzzards Bay . . . 189 C d
Byblus . . . 4 F c
Byland, mon. . . . 97 P g
Byllis . . . 31 I b
Byrsa, citadel . . . 34 ins. A (4)
Bytown (Ottawa) . . . 212 H d
Byzacium, reg. . . . 38 D e
Byzacium, West Rom. prov. . . . 42 D g (1)
Byzantine Empire, about 814 54-55 F f
Byzantine Empire, about 1000 . 59 H-L f
Byzantine Empire, 12 cent. . . . 71 K e
Byzantine Empire, in 1265 . . . 89
Byzantine Empire, in 1355 . . . 89
Byzantine Empire, in 1451 . . . 93 C b
Byzantium (Constantinople) . .

Caacupe . . . 215 D e
Cabalia, reg. . . . 20 C d
Cabasa . . . 43 I g
Cabellio or Cabellione, see Cavaillon
Cabes . . .
Cabeza de Vaca, route of . . . 190 D f
Cabillonum or Cabilonum (Chalon) . . . 39 H j
Cabira . . . 20 G b
Cabo das Corrientes, cape . . . 109 U j
Cabot, John, route of . . . 108 O b, M c
Cabot, Sebastian, route of . . . 108 L k
Cabra . . . 82 B b
Cabral, route of . . . 108 O h, Q j
Cabrillo, route of . . . 107 E d
Cabul (Kabul), in Afghanistan 53 I c
Cabul, in Palestine . . . 6 C c
Cabura (Kabul in Afghanistan) 19 K d
Caburrum . . . 26 B c
Cáceres . . . 82 A b
Cache Valley, dist. . . . 210 C b
Cacyparis River . . . 30 E e
Caddos, tribe . . . 188 G d
Cadiz . . . 82 A b
Cadiz, bp. . . . 94 A d
Cadore . . . 90 D a
Cadouin, mon. . . . 94 C c
Cadurci or Cadurcis, see Cahors
Cadurci, people . . . 38 C d
Cadusii (Cadusians), people . . 19 G c
Cæcina River . . . 26 E d
Cæcinus River . . . 30 E e
Cæcuban Territory . . . 30 C a
Cælemontane Gate . . . 23 B
Cælia, in Apulia . . . 31 F a
Cælia, in Calabria . . . 31 G b
Cælian Mount . . . 22 A
Cælian, quarter . . . 96 A
Cælimontium, Aug. Reg. of Rome . . . 22 A
Caen . . . 69 C b
Caen, gen. . . . 147 D b
Caen, mon. . . . 94 B b
Caen, univ. . . . 100 E e
Cænæ . . . 20 J e
Cænepolis . . . 14 C c
Cænia, mt. . . . 26 A c
Cænys, prom. . . . 31 E d
Cære . . . 27 G e
Cærleon-upon-Usk . . . 42 B c
Cærwent . . .
Cæsar, Statue of . . . 24 B (12)
Cæsar, Gardens of . . . 22 A
Cæsaraugusta (Saragossa) . . . 38 B d
Cæsarea, in Cappadocia (Kaisarieh) . . . 20 F c
Cæsarea, in Mauretania . . . 38 C e
Cæsarea, in Samaria . . . 6 B c
Cæsarea Philippi . . . 6 D b
Cæsarea, isl. (Jersey) . . . 38 B c
Cæsarobriga (Talavera de la Reina) . . . 38 B d
Cæsarodunum (Tours) . . . 38 C c
Cæsaromagus, see Beauvais
Cæsar's Forum . . . 24 B
Cæsena . . . 27 G c
Cagli, bp. . . . 95 E c (C.)
Cagliari . . . 42 D f
Cagliari, abp. . . . 95 D d
Caguas . . . 199 ins. G
Cahokia . . . 191 H d
Cahors . . . 91 D d
Cahors, bp. . . . 94 C c
Cahors, univ. . . . 100 F f
Cahorsin, cty. . . . 76 D d
Caiatia . . . 30 D a
Caicos Islands . . . 213 E b
Caicus River . . .
Caieta (Gaëta) . . . 30 C a
Caieta, bay . . . 30 C a
Cailac . . .
Cailloux, farm . . .
Caimitillo River . . .
Caino or Cainone, see Chinon
Cairns . . . 172 D b
Cairo, in Egypt . . . 67 M h
Cairo, in Illinois . . . 199 H c
Cairo, in Italy . . . 130 Q j
Cairo, calif. . . .
Caithness, bp. . . . 97 I a
Caithness, cty. . . .
Caithness, dist. . . .
Caius Cestius, Tomb of . . . 22 A
Cajamarca . . . 111 B c
Cajon Pass . . . 210 B d
Calabar . . . 175 D d
Calabozo . . . 214 C b
Calabria, dist., in Rom. times . 31 G b
Calabria, dist., 15 cent. . . . 90 F e
Calabria, duchy, 11 cent. . . . 66 J f
Calabria, theme, 10 cent. . . . 59 H f
Caladunum, see Châlons
Calaf . . . 82 C a
Calagurris (Calahorra) . . . 38 B d
Calahorra . . . 82 B a
Calahorra, bp. . . . 94 B c
Calais, in France . . . 76 D a
Calais, in Maine . . . 211 L a
Calama, in Algeria . . . 42 D f
Calama, in Chile . . . 215 C e
Calamar . . . 214 B a
Calamine, dist. . . . 10 B c
Calanicum . . . 26 C c
Calatafimi . . . 161 I i
Calatayud . . . 82 B a
Calatha . . . 38 D e
Calatia . . . 30 D a
Calatrava . . . 82 B b
Calatrava, mon. . . . 94 B d
Calauria, isl. . . . 15 D b
Calaurus, mt. . . . 11 E b
Calcaria, see Tadcaster
Calchedon . . .
Calchu . . . 5 D b
Calcutta . . . 137 E d
Caldera . . . 215 B e
Calderon . . . 213 ins.
Caldiero . . . 150 F d
Cale . . . 191 I f
Cale, Portus (Oporto) . . . 38 A d
Caleacte . . . 30 D e
Cale acte, Cape . . . 15 E a
Caledonia (Scotland) . . . 38 B a
Caledonia, New, isl. . . . 172 F c
Caledonii, people . . . 38 B a
Cales (Calvi), in Campania . . . 30 D a
Cales, in Umbria . . . 27 G d
Caletes, people . . .
Calgary . . . 212 D c
Calhoun, Fort . . . 210 F b
Cali . . . 111 B a
Calicut . . . 137 C f
Califate, emp. . . .
Califate, reg. . . . 71 O g
California, Gulf of . . . 187 H f
California, state . . . 202 A h
California, Lower, pen. . . . 187 H e-f
California, Lower, prov. . 107—108 F d e
California, Upper, prov. . . . 190 AB de
California Cut-off, route . . . 210 D c
California Trail . . . 210 B b
California Valley . . . 187 G e
Caligula, Palace of . . . 24 B
Calindœa . . .
Call, parl. bor. . . . 163 J g
Callao . . . 214 B d
Callas River . . . 11 E c
Callatis . . . 39 N l
Calleva (Silchester) . . .
Callidromus, mt. . . . 11 D e
Callipolis, in Calabria . . . 31 G b
Callipolis, in Thrace . . . 39 N l
Callirrhoe . . . 23 D
Callium . . . 10 D d
Calliupolis . . .
Callone . . . 18 G d
Calmar . . . 88 G c
Calmar, Hanse. for. cy. . . . 98 G b
Calne, parl. bor. . . . 163 L f
Calor River . . . 30 D a
Calpe, in Bithynia . . . 20 D b
Calpe, in Spain . . . 12 B c
Calpulalpan . . .
Caltanisetta . . . 90 D f
Caluso . . . 130 P i
Calvados, dept. . . . 148 D e
Calverton . . . 192 C d
Calvert Town . . . 192 C d
Calvi, bp. . . . 95 ins.
Calw . . . 143 G h
Calw, cty. . . . 143 G h
Calycadnus River . . . 20 E d
Calydon . . . 10 C d
Calydon, Gulf of . . . 14 B a
Calymna, isl. . . . 17 E c
Calynda . . . 20 C d
Cam, Diogo, route of . . . 108 R h
Camaldoli . . . 90 L j
Camaldoli, mon. . . . 95 E c
Camaracus, see Cambray
Camargo, in Bolivia . . . 214 C e
Camargo, in Mexico . . . 201 F d
Camarina . . . 30 D e
Camarones River . . . 214 B d
Cambalec (Peking) . . .
Cambay . . . 137 B d
Cambay, Gulf of . . . 137 B d
Cambete . . . 39 I j
Cambodia, reg. . . .
Cambodunum, in Britain . . . 51 P h
Cambodunum, in Rætia . . . 39 K j
Camboricum (Cambridge) . . .
Cambray . . .
Cambray, bp. . . . 117 B d
Cambrésis, cty. . . . 117 B d
Cambrian Mountains . . . 49 E e
Cambridge, in England . . .
Cambridge, in Mass. . . . 189 ins. B
Cambridge, castle . . . 65 G d

Entry	Page	Ref.
Cambridge, cty.	127	Z n
Cambridge, mon.	97	R i
Cambridge, parl. bor.	163	O e
Cambridge, parl. dist.	163	O e
Cambridge, shire		
Cambridge, univ.	100	F d
Cambridge, univ., parl. bor.	163	O e
Cambunian Mountains	10	C c
Cambuskenneth	84	B a
Camden, in N. S. Wales		
Camden, in New Jersey	192	D d
Camden, in S. Carolina	195	A f
Camelford, parl. bor.	163	J g
Cameria	35	ins. B
Camerino	90	D c
Camerino, bp.	95	E c
Camerino, march	64	B b
Camerinum	27	H d
Camerons, fam.	97	H c
Cameroons, see Kamerun		
Cameta	214	E c
Camexa		
Camillomagus	26	D b
Camirus	13	E c
Camisards, people	129	D d
Campagna, dist.	64	ins.
Campanha	214	E e
Campania, dist.	30	D b
Campania, Rom. prov.	42	E e(1)
Campbell, route of	195	D f
Campbells, fam.	97	H c
Camp du Bois	199	H c
Campeche	213	C c
Campeche, state	213	C c
Campeche Bay	187	J f
Camperdown	153	E b
Camp Floyd	210	C b
Campidona, see Kempten		
Campi Raudii or Raudian Plain, dist.	26	C b
Campobasso	90	E d
Campos	214	E e
Campo Vitale	62	F f
Campsey Ash, mon.	97	S i
Campus Martius, loc. in Rome	22	A
Campus Sceleratus, loc. in Rome	23	B
Campylus River	10	C c
Camulodunum (Colchester)		
Camunni, people	26	E b
Camuy	199	ins. G
Cana	6	C c
Cana River	7	B d
Canaan	207	L b
Canaan, reg.	4	F c
Canaanites, people	7	ins. D
Canada, col.	194	Cb, Ea
Canada, Dominion of	212	H c
Canadian Pacific Railway	212	D c
Canadian River	190	F d
Canal du Midi	130	D e
Canal Zone, dist.		
Cananea, bay of	108	M j
Caña Quebrada, R.		
Canary Islands	174	B b
Canastræum, prom.	11	E c
Canatha	6	F c
Canaveral, Cape	191	I f
Canbury	55	R i
Cancellaria	96	A
Candahar	137	A b
Candavia	10	B a
Candavian Mountains	10	B a
Candelaria	215	C e
Canea	77	I e
Cangas de Onis	82	A a
Canigou, mon.	94	C c
Cannæ	31	F a
Cannanore	137	C f
Canne	64	C b
Canninefates, people	39	H g
Cannock Chase	49	E e
Cannon Gate	93	G e
Cannstadt	143	H h
Canonicut Island	189	C d

Entry	Page	Ref.
Canopic Gate	34	ins. C
Canopus	4	ins.
Canossa	64	B b
Canso	194	G a
Canso, strait of	212	J d
Cantabri, people	38	B d
Cantabria, reg.	82	B a
Cantabrian Mountains	2	D d
Cantal, dept.	148	E e
Canterbury, in Conn.	207	L b
Canterbury, in England		
Canterbury, abp.	97	N i
Canterbury, dist. in N. Zealand	172	G e
Canterbury, Hanse. for. cy.	98	ins. A
Canterbury, parl. bor.	163	P f
Canterbury Bight	172	G e
Cantharus Port	16	D c
Cantii, people	51	Q i
Cantillana	82	A b
Canton	171	M f
Cantuaria, see Canterbury		
Canusium	31	F a
Cany	76	D b
Caononabo, chieftain	105	F c
Caorle, bp.	95	E b
Capara	38	A d
Capdenac	126	C d
Cape Ann	189	C c
Cape Coast Castle	175	C d
Cape Cod Bay	189	C d
Cape Colony, col.	175	F h
Cape Fear River	193	E d
Cape Haitien	213	E c
Capena	27	G e
Capena Gate, in Rome	23	B
Capena Gate, Aug. Reg., Rome	22	A
Cape of Good Hope, cape	175	E h
Cape of Good Hope, col.	175	F h
Cape of Storms	109	S k
Cape Porpoise	189	C c
Capernaum	6	D c
Cape Town	175	E h
Cape Verd	174	B c
Cape Verd Islands	174	A c
Cape York Peninsula	172	D b
Caphereus, prom.	15	E a
Caphyæ	14	C b
Capitanata, dist.	90	E d
Capitolias	6	D c
Capitoline, quarter	96	A
Capitoline Mount	24	A
Capo d'Istria		
Capo d'Istria, bp.	95	E b
Cappadocia, dist.	20	F c
Cappadocia, imp. prov.	35	L f
Cappadocia, prov.	18	D c
Cappadocia, reg.	8	B b
Cappadocia, satr.	8	H d
Cappadocia, theme	59	K f
Cappadocia I, East Rom. prov.	43	I f(6)
Cappadocia II, East Rom. prov.	43	I f(7)
Capraria, isl., near Corsica	26	D e
Capraria, isl., Balearic Is.	38	C e
Caprasia	31	F c
Capreæ (Capri), isl.	30	D b
Caprera, isl.	161	G g
Capri, bp.	95	ins.
Capri, isl.	90	E d
Caprus	11	E b
Capsa	34	F g
Capua (ancient)	30	D a
Capua (modern)	90	E d
Capua, abp.	95	E c
Capua, princ.	64	B b
Capucines, The, ch.		
Caput Africæ	22	A
Caputvada	52	D c
Caqueta River	111	C b
Carabaros	105	D e
Carabobo, battle	214	C b
Caracalla, Baths of	22	A
Caracarum or Karakorum		
Caracas	214	C a
Caracas, cap. gen. and pres.	215	ins.

Entry	Page	Ref.
Caraceni, people	27	I f
Caracuel	82	B b
Caradeña, mon.	94	B e
Caralis (Cagliari)	12	B c
Caramagna, mon.	95	D e
Caramoran River		
Carana	20	I c
Caranchuas, tribe	188	G e
Caraques, Bahia de, bay	111	A b
Caravaggio	90	B b
Caravellas	214	F d
Carbonera	82	B b
Carcaso, Carcasona or Carcasso (Carcassonne)	38	C d
Carcassonne	76	E e
Carcassonne, bp.	94	C c
Carchemish	4	F c
Carcinus River	31	F e
Cardamyle	14	C c
Cárdenas	213	D b
Cárdenas, route of	190	C d
Cardenas River		
Cardia		
Cardiff	65	E e
Cardiff, parl. bor.	163	K f
Cardigan, castle	74	C e
Cardigan, cty.	127	U n
Cardigan, parl. bor.	163	J e
Cardigan, parl. dist.	163	J e
Cardigan Bay		
Cardona	130	D e
Careiæ	35	ins. B
Carentan	76	C b
Carentonus River, see Charente River		
Careta	105	E e
Carey, lake	172	B c
Caria, dist.	20	C d
Caria, East Rom. prov.	43	H f(3)
Caria, reg.	5	B b
Caria, satr.	18	N h
Cariæ	14	C b
Cariari	105	D d
Caribbean Sea	187	L g
Carical		
Carinæ	22	A
Carinthia, duchy, about 1000	63	H e
Carinthia, duchy, 14 cent.	79	I e
Carinthia, march	63	H e
Carinthia, reg.	54	G d
Carioli	35	ins. B
Carisbrooke		
Carisbrooke, mon.	100	A b
Carisbrooke Castle	127	X p
Carisiacus, see Kiersy		
Carlat	76	E d
Carlat, viscty.	76	E d
Carlingford		
Carlisle, in England		
Carlisle, in Pa.	188	K b
Carlisle, bp.	97	O g
Carlisle, parl. bor.	163	L c
Carlos, Bahia de, bay	191	I f
Carlow		
Carlow, cty.	127	K i
Carlowitz	159	J f
Carlsbad	79	H c
Carlskrona	131	G b
Carlsruhe	142	B b
Carlstein, castle	79	H c
Carmagnola	130	P j
Carmalas River	20	F d
Carmana (Kirman)	19	I d
Carmania (Kirman), prov.	19	I e
Carmania, satr.	18	Q i
Carmanians, people	8	J e
Carmarthen, castle		
Carmarthen, cty.	127	U o
Carmarthen, mon.	97	M j
Carmarthen, parl. bor.	163	J f
Carmarthen, parl. dist.	163	J f
Carmel	7	C f
Carmel, mt.	6	C e
Carmelites, mon. in London	75	G g
Carmelites, The, mon. in Paris	149	B

Carmen 213 C c
Carmen de Patagonés 215 C g
Carmenta Gate 24 A
Carmona 82 A b
Carnarvon, castle
Carnarvon, cty. 127 U n
Carnarvon, parl. bor. 163 J d
Carnarvon, parl. dist. 163 J e
Carnatic, reg. 112 A b
Carni, people 27 H a
Carnic Alps, mts. 27 G a
Carnicum Julium 27 G a
Carniola, duchy 79 I f
Carniola, march 63 H f
Carniola, reg. 56 E c
Carnsore Point 127 K i
Carnuntum 38 F c
Carnus, isl. 10 B d
Carnotes or Carnutes, see Chartres
Carnutes, people 38 C c
Carolina, col. 193 C f-E e
Carolina, North, col. 193 E d
Carolina, North, state 196 C c
Carolina, South, col. 193 D d
Carolina, South, state 196 C d
Carolina Proprietors, Grants to the 190 ins.
Caroline, Fort 191 I e
Caroline Island 180 M h
Caroline Islands 179 F g
Caroline River 214 C b
Carolingian Empire 54
Carpathian Mountains 2 G d
Carpathian Sea 17 E d
Carpathos, isl. 4 C b
Carpentaria, Gulf of 172 C b
Carpentoracte, see Carpentras
Carpentras, bp. 95 D c
Carpetani, people 38 B d
Carpi 131 F e
Carpi, people 38 F i
Carpis 46 I f
Carrara, near Pisa 90 L i
Carrara, near Venice 90 J h
Carrara, dist. 79 G f
Carrea Potentia 26 B c
Carrhæ 20 H d
Carrick, dist.
Carrickfergus
Carrión de los Condes 83 K g
Carsioli 27 H e
Carson 210 B c
Carson City 206 A c
Carsulæ 27 G e
Cartagena, in Colombia 214 B a
Cartagena, in Spain 82 B b
Cártago, in Colombia 214 B b
Cártago, in Costa Rica 213 D d
Carteia 38 A e
Cartenna 38 C e
Carteret, Cape 193 ins. C
Carthæa 15 E b
Carthage (ancient) 38 E e
Carthage, in Missouri 207 G c
Carthage, New (Cartagena) 38 B e
Carthage, plan of 34 ins. A
Carthaginiensis, West Rom. prov. 42 B f(5)
Carthago 12 E c
Carthusian Priory of the Salutation 75 G g
Carthusians, The, mon. in Paris 149 B
Cartier, routes of 108 M b, O c
Caruanca, mt. 27 I a
Carus River, see Cher River
Carystus, in Eubœa 15 E a
Carystus, in Laconia 14 C b
Casablanca 174 C a
Casale 90 I h
Cascadas, Las
Cascade Mountains 186 G c
Casco, in Maine 189 C c
Casco, in Mexico 190 E f
Casco Bay 189 C c
Caserta 90 E d
Caserta, bp. 95 ins.
Cashel
Cashel, abp. 97 C d
Cashmere or Kashmir, reg.
Casilinum 30 D a
Casimir, Fort 192 ins.
Casinum 30 C a
Casmenæ 30 D e
Caspe 83 L g
Caspian Depression, plain 3 I d
Caspian Gates, pass 19 H c
Caspian Sea 3 I d
Caspians, people 8 I d
Cassander, Kingdom of 18
Cassandrea 11 E b
Cassano 134 E f
Cassano, bp. 95 F d
Cassel, in Flanders 117 A d
Cassel, in Hesse 62 E c
Cassian Way, road 27 F e
Cassii, Forum 27 G e
Cassim Pasha, quarter
Cassinelle 130 Q j
Cassiope 10 A c
Cassiquiare River 214 C b
Cassiterides Islands 34 C c
Cassope 10 B c
Cassopia, reg. 10 B c
Casteldelfino 130 O j
Castelfidardo 161 I f
Casteljaloux 126 B d
Castell 122 F d
Castellammare 161 J g
Castellaneta 90 F d
Castello Branco 94 A d
Castellón de la Plana 83 E a
Castellum (Kastel) 39 J h
Castellum Felicitatis, see Città di Castello
Castellum Firmanum 27 H d
Castellum Flevum 39 H g
Castelnaudary 69 D e
Castelnuovo 125 G d
Castelsagrat 126 B d
Castets 126 A d
Casthanæa 11 D c
Castiglione, in Calabria 90 F e
Castiglione, near Florence 90 L j
Castiglione, near Mantua 150 F d
Castiglione dalla Pescaja 90 L j
Castile, cty. 82 B a
Castile, km., 11 cent. 83 E c
Castile, km., 12 cent. 82 H e
Castile, km., 15 cent. 83 K g
Castilla del Oro, reg. 105 D e
Castillon 76 C d
Castine 189 D b
Castle Acre, mon. 97 R i
Castle Jacob 68 ins. A
Castle of the Seven Towers 93 G e
Castle Rising, parl. bor. 163 O e
Castor, near Norwich 51 Q h
Castor, Temple of
Castor and Pollux, Temple of
Castores, Ad 26 E b
Castoria 59 I e
Castra Batava (Passau) 38 E c
Castra Hannibalis 31 F d
Castra Sarræ 39 H i
Castra Vetera 39 I h
Castres 76 E e
Castres, bp. 94 C c (Cast.)
Castres, cty. 84 E h
Castres, seign. 76 E e
Castrimœnium 35 ins. B
Castriota, Dominion of 93 A b
Castro, bp. 95 E c
Castrogiovanni 64 B c
Castrovillari 90 F e
Castrum Bobium (Bobbio) 26 D c
Castrum Gordonis, see Sancerre
Castrum Minervæ 31 H b
Castrum Nantonis, see Château-Landon
Castrum novum, in Etruria 27 F e
Castrum novum, in Picenum 27 I e
Castrum Peregrinorum 68 ins. A
Castrum Truentinum 27 H e
Castulo 38 B e
Castulo, bp. 42 B f
Castulonensis, Saltus, mts. 38 B e
Casuentus (Basento) River 31 F b
Casus, isl. 17 E d
Caswell, Fort 208 E c
Catacombs of Saint Callistus 96 A
Catalão 214 E d
Catalauni or Catalaunis, see Châlons
Catalaunian Fields 48 E c
Catalonia, princ. 83 L g
Catalonia, reg. 82 I e
Catamarca 215 C e
Catana 30 E e
Catania 90 E f
Catania, bp. 95 F d
Catania, univ. 100 I g
Catanzaro 90 F e
Catanzaro, bp. 95 F d
Cataractonium (Catterick) 51 P g
Catawba River 195 A f
Catawbas, tribe 188 J d
Cateau-Cambrésis 117 B d
Cathay (China), cty. 92 K d
Catholic Hennersdorf 135 H c
Catillus, mt. 35 ins. B
Cat Island 105 E b
Catoche, Cape 105 C b
Catskill 192 E b
Catskill Mountains 192 D b
Cattaraugus, Ind. Res. 188 K b
Cattaro 90 G c
Cattaro, abp. 95 F c
Caturiges 39 H i
Caturiges, people 26 A c
Catuvellauni, people
Caub 154 D c
Cauca 38 B d
Cauca River 214 B b
Caucasians, people 57 K e
Caucasus Mountains 3 I d
Cauci, people 38 A b
Caudebec 126 B b
Caudine Forks, passes, near Caudium
Caudini, people 30 D a
Caudium 30 D a
Caughnawaga 212 H d
Caulonia 31 F d
Caunus 20 C d
Caura River 214 C b
Causannæ 51 P h
Caux, dist. 69 H f
Caux, Chef de, cape 81 L h
Cava, La, mon. 95 ins.
Cavaillon 76 F e
Cavaillon, bp. 95 D c
Cavan, cty. 127 J g
Cavite 199 ins. H
Cavore, mon. 95 D c
Cavour 130 P j
Cawnpur, Cawnpore 137 D c
Caxamarca 111 B c
Caxias 214 E c
Cayambe 214 B b
Cayenne 214 D b
Cayay 199 ins. G
Cayos, Los, isl. 105 E b
Cayphas 68 ins. A
Cayster River 13 E b
Caystrupedium
Cayuga Lake 192 C b
Cayugas, tribe 188 K b
Cazalla de la Sierra 82 A b
Cazlona 46 F f
Cé, Pont de 130 C d
Ceará 214 F c
Ceará, state 214 F c
Ceba 26 C c

Cebenna Mountains . . . . 38 C d
Cebrene . . . .
Cebu . . . . 112 F b
Cebu, isl. . . . . 110 D D f
Cecryphalæ, isl. . . . .
Cedar Creek, battle . . . . . . 208 E b
Cedar Keys . . . . 213 D b
Cedar Mountain, battle . . . . 208 E b
Cedar River . . . . 211 G b
Cedron, Vale of . . . . 6 ins. A
Cefalù . . . . 90 E e
Cefalù, bp. . . . . 95 E d
Ceiriadæ, deme . . . . 23 D
Celadussæ, isl. . . . . 27 J d
Celebes, isl. . . . .
Celebes Sea . . . . 171 N h
Celeia . . . . 27 J a
Celenderis . . . . 15 D b
Celetrum . . . . 10 C b
Céligny . . . . 91 O l
Cellæ . . . . 10 C b
Celle . . . . 79 G b
Celtiberians, people . . . . . . 32 A c
Celtic Gaul . . . . 38 ins.
Celtici, people . . . . 38 A e
Celts, people . . . . 5 A a
Cemenelum . . . . 26 B d
Cempoalla . . . . 106 D a
Cenabum (Orléans) . . . . 38 C c
Cenæum, prom. . . . . 11 D d
Cenchreæ, near Argos . . . . . 14 C b
Cenchreæ, near Corinth . . . . 15 D b
Ceneda, bp. . . . . 95 E b
Ceneda . . . . 27 G b
Cenis, Mont, pass . . . . 26 A b
Cenis, people . . . . 188 G d
Cenomani or Cenomanis see Le Mans
Cenomani, people . . . . 26 E b
Centerville . . . . 208 ins.
Central Africa, British, see Nyasaland 175 G f
Central America, reg. . . . . . 213 D c
Central America, Cordillera of 187 K g
Central Asia, reg. . . . . 170 G I d
Central Californians, tribes . . 188 B c
Central German Commercial Union . . . . 160 D c
Centripæ . . . . 30 D e
Centula or Centulum (Saint Riquier), mon. . . . . 94 C a
Centumcellæ (Civitavecchia) . . 27 F e
Centum Gradus . . . . 24 A
Centurinum . . . . 26 D e
Ceos (Cea), isl. . . . . 15 E b
Cephale . . . . 16 B b
Cephalenia, theme . . . . 59 H f
Cephallenia (Cephalonia), isl. . 10 B d
Cephalonia, cty. . . . . 73 D c
Cephalonia, isl. . . . . 89 H g
Cephalonia, palat. . . . . 89 A c
Cephalœdium . . . . 30 D d
Cephisia . . . . 16 B a
Cephisus River, in Attica . . . 16 B a
Cephisus River, in Bœotia . . . 11 D d
Ceprano . . . . 72 C c
Ceramic Gulf . . . . 17 E c
Ceramicus, Inner, quarter . . . 23 D
Ceramicus, Outer, quarter . . . 23 D
Ceramon-agora . . . . 20 C c
Cerasus . . . . 20 H b
Ceraunii Mountains . . . .
Cerbalus River . . . . 30 E a
Cercamp, mon. . . . . 94 C a
Certetius, mt. . . . . 10 C c
Cercina, isl. . . . . 38 E f
Cercinitis, lake . . . . 11 E b
Cerdagne, reg. . . . . 83 F c
Cerdylium . . . . 11 E b
Cereatæ . . . . 30 C a
Ceredigion, reg. . . . .
Ceres, Temple of . . . . 24 B
Ceresius (Lugano) lake . . . . 26 C a
Ceretani, people . . . . 38 C d
Cereus River . . . . 11 E d
Cerignola . . . . 90 E d
Cerigo, isl. . . . . 89 B c
Cerillæ . . . . 30 E c
Cerinthus . . . . 11 E d
Cérisy, mon. . . . . 94 B b
Cerlier, castle . . . . 91 P k
Cermalus, quarter . . . .
Cerne, Ilha do, isl. . . . . . . 109 W j
Cerne, mon. . . . . 97 O k
Cerro Columbia, hill . . . . . .
Cerro Comboy, hill . . . .
Cerro Culebra, hill . . . .
Cerro de Cabras, hill . . . . .
Cerro de los Harmigueros, hill
Cerro de Pasco . . . . 214 B d
Cerro de San Juan, hill . . . .
Cerro Gordo, battle . . . . . . 201 H g
Cerro Mitra, hill . . . .
Certosa, mon. . . . . 95 D b
Ceruglio . . . . 90 L j
Cervia . . . . 90 M i
Cervia, bp. . . . . 95 E c
Cerynia . . . . 14 C a
Cesena . . . . 90 D b
Cesena, bp. . . . . 95 E c
Cessetani, people . . . . 38 C d
Cestian Bridge . . . . 22 A
Cestrine, reg. . . . . 10 B c
Cestrus River . . . . 20 D d
Cettigne . . . . 166 I g
Ceuta . . . .
Ceutrones, people . . . . 26 A b
Ceva . . . . 90 I h
Ceylon, isl. . . . . 137 D g
Chablais, dist. . . . . 91 O l
Chaboras River . . . . 20 I e
Chacabuco, battle . . . . 215 B f
Chachapoyas . . . . 111 B c
Chacon, Cape . . . . 212 ins.
Chad, lake . . . . 174 E c
Chads Ford, battle . . . . 195 C c
Chæronea . . . . 11 D d
Chagatai, khan. . . . .
Chagos Islands . . . . 182 II h
Chagres . . . .
Chagres River . . . .
Chaibasa, reg. . . . . 137 E d
Chaillot . . . . 149 B
Chaise-Dieu, La, mon. . . . . . 94 C b
Chalæum . . . . 11 D d
Chalastra . . . . 11 D b
Chalcedon . . . .
Chalcidice, reg. . . . . 11 E b
Chalcis, in Ætolia . . . . 10 C d
Chalcis, in Epirus . . . . 10 C c
Chalcis, in Eubœa . . . . 11 E d
Chalcis, in Syria . . . . 6 D a
Chalco . . . . 106 B a
Chalco, lake . . . . 106 B a
Chaldæi, people . . . . 18 G d
Chaldea, reg. . . . . 4 G c
Chaldean Empire 8
Chaldeans, people . . . .
Chaldia, theme . . . . 59 L e
Chaldiran . . . .
Chales, mon. . . . . 94 C b
Chaleurs, Bay of . . . . 194 G a
Chalgrove . . . . 127 X o
Chalia . . . . 11 E d
Chalish (Karashar) . . . .
Chalivoy, mon. . . . . 94 C b
Chaloché, mon. . . . . 94 B b
Chalon . . . . 61 F c
Chalon, cty. . . . . 69 J f
Chalon, sur-Saône, bp. . . . . 94 C b
Châlons . . . . 61 F b
Châlons, cty. . . . . 61 F b
Châlons, duchy . . . . 76 F b
Châlons, gen. . . . . 147 E b
Châlons-sur-Marne, bp. . . . . 94 C b
Chalus, castle . . . . 69 D d
Cham . . . . 63 G d
Chamavi, people . . . . 39 I g
Chambal River . . . . 137 C c
Chambersburg . . . . 208 ins.
Chambéry . . . . 130 N i
Chambly, Fort . . . . 189 B b
Chambord . . . . 126 B c
Champa . . . .
Champa, reg. . . . .
Champagne, cty. 11 cent. . . . . 61 E b
Champagne, cty. 12 cent. 69
Champagne, cty. 14 cent. . . . . 76 F b
Champagne, prov. . . . . 148 E e
Champagne and Brie, gouv. . . 146 B b
Champ de Mars, loc. in Paris . 149 B
Champaubert . . . . 154 B d
Champion Hill . . . . 208 B c
Champlain, lake . . . . 189 B b
Champs Elysées, loc. in Paris . 149 B
Champtoceaux . . . . 81 L h
Chanar . . . . 187 D c
Chañaral . . . . 215 B e
Chancellade, mon. . . . . 94 C b
Chancellerie, Rue de la, street in Versailles . . . . 149 A
Chancellor, route of . . . . . . 109 Ub, Va
Chancellorsville . . . . 208 E b (Chan.)
Chanda . . . . 137 C d
Chandarnagar . . . . 137 E d
Chandax . . . . 59 J f
Chanderi . . . .
Chandernagore . . . . 137 E d
Changanor . . . .
Chang-chau . . . . 171 M f
Chang-chau-fu . . . .
Chang-kia-chwang . . . . 170 ins. A
Chang-sha . . . . 171 M f
Channel Islands . . . . 49 E g
Chaoni, people . . . .
Chaonia, dist. . . . . 10 A b
Chapelle-Saint-Lambert . . . .
Chapultepec, castle . . . . 201 H g
Charadra . . . . 10 B c
Charadrus . . . . 11 F b
Charadrus River . . . . 14 C b
Charcas, pres. . . . . 215 ins.
Chard . . . . 127 V p
Chard, parl. bor. . . . .
Chardjui . . . .
Charente, dept. . . . . 148 E e
Charente River . . . . 76 C d
Charente-Inférieure, dept. . . . 148 D e
Charenton . . . . 126 C b
Charidemi, prom. . . . . 38 B e
Charikar . . . .
Charing Cross, loc. in London 75 G g
Charisius, gate . . . . 93 G e
Charité, La, near Nevers . . . . 126 C c
Charité, La, in Paris . . . . . . 149 B
Charkov . . . .
Charlemont . . . . 126 D a
Charleroi . . . . 117 C d
Charles, Cape, in Labrador . . . 186 N c
Charles, Cape, in Virginia . . . 193 ins. A
Charles X., route of . . . . . . 121 D a
Charles City . . . . 193 ins. A
Charles City County . . . . 193 ins. A (Ch.)
Charlesfort . . . . 191 I e
Charles River . . . . 189 ins. B
Charleston, in S. C. . . . . . . 211 J d
Charleston, in W. Va. . . . . . 211 I c
Charlestown, near Boston . . . . 189 ins. B
Charles Town, in S. Carolina . 193 ins. C
Charleville . . . . 172 D c
Charlotiana, proposed col. in U.S. 194 A a
Charlotte . . . . 191 I d
Charlotte, Fort . . . . 195 ins. B
Charlotte Harbor . . . . 191 I f
Charlottenburg . . . . 135 G b
Charlottesville . . . . 193 E c
Charlottetown . . . . 212 I d
Charolais, cty. . . . . 126 D c
Charolais, dist. . . . . 81 M h
Charolles . . . . 76 F c
Charolles, cty. . . . . 114 C e
Charroux, mon. . . . . 94 C b
Charsianon, theme . . . . 59 K f

Charter House, bldg. in London 75 G g
Charters Towers 172 D b
Chartres 61 D b
Chartres, bp. 94 C b
Chartres, Fort 191 G d
Chartreuse, mon. 69 F d
Charudes, people 38 D a
Chassaigne, La, mon. 95 D b (L. Ch.)
Chastel Blanc, castle 68 C bc
Chastel Rouge, castle 68 C c
Châteaubriant, castle 76 C c
Château-Chalon, mon. 148 C b
Château Chinon 76 F c
Château Dauphin 126 E d
Château de Joux 126 E c
Château d'If 126 D e
Château d'Œx 91 P l
Châteaudun 61 D b
Châteaudun, bp. 94 C b (Chât.)
Château Gaillard, castle 76 D b
Château-Landon 61 E b
Châteauneuf, in Angoumois 126 B d
Châteauneuf, in Perche 76 D b
Château-Porcien 69 F b
Château-Renard 69 I g
Châteauroux 76 D c
Châteauroux, seign. 69 H g
Château-Thierry 69 I f
Châtelet, near Charleroi 117 C d
Châtelet, loc. in Paris 149 B
Châtellerault 76 D c
Châtellerault, viscty. 76 D c
Chatelot 143 ins. F
Chatelot, lordship 143 ins. F
Chatham, parl. bor. 163 O f
Chatham Islands 172 H e
Châtillon, on the Marne R. 69 I f
Châtillon, near Nevers 126 C c
Châtillon, in Savoy 91 P m
Châtillon, on the Seine R. 76 F c
Chattahoochee River 193 B e
Chattanooga 208 C b
Chatti, people 39 J h
Chauci, people 38 D b
Chaudière River 188 L a
Chaul
Chaumont, in Champagne 76 F b
Chaumont, in Vexin 76 E b
Chauon 18 F c
Chaussée, la 154 C d
Chautauqua, lake 192 B b
Chauvigny 76 D c
Chaves 82 A a
Cheadle 127 X n
Cheap, loc. in London 75 G g (35)
Cheat River 192 B d
Chef de Caux, Cape 81 L h
Chehalis, Ind. Res. 188 B a
Chehalis, tribe 188 B a
Che-kiang, prov. 171 M f
Cheliabinsk 170 H c
Chelidoniæ Islands 20 D d
Cheliff, or Sheliff, River 118 E f
Chelmsford 127 Z o
Chelmsford, parl. bor.
Chelonatas Gulf 14 B b
Chelonatas, prom. 14 B b
Chelsea 75 I i
Cheltenham, parl. bor. 163 L f (Chelt.)
Chemashevskoe 170 H b
Cheminon, mon. 94 C b
Chemmis 18 D e
Chemnitz 85 G e
Chemulpo 171 N e
Chenab River 137 C b
Cheng-tu-fu
Chen-si
Chepstow 127 W o
Chequamegon, Fort
Cher, dept. 148 E e
Cher River 69 H g
Cherasco 90 H h
Cheraw 195 B f
Cherbourg 76 C b
Cheremissians, people 138 G d
Cheribon
Chernaia River 164 J f
Cherokee, Ind. Res. 188 G c
Cherokee, Ind. Res. 1834 188 I d
Cherokees, tribe 188 J c
Cherronesus, proposed state in U. S.
Cherry Valley 195 D b
Cherson, in the Crimea 43 I e
Cherson, on the Dnieper
Cherson, theme 59 K e
Chersonese, Thracian, pen. 13 E a
Chersonese, Tauric, pen. 35 K d
Chersonesus, prom. 11 F d
Chertsey 75 H i
Chertsey mon.
Cherusci, people 38 J h
Chesapeake Bay 193 F c
Cheshire, cty. 127 W m
Chester, in England
Chester, in Illinois 207 H c
Chester, in Pa. 192 D d
Chester, bp. 97 O h
Chester, castle
Chester, cty. 162 D d
Chester, cty. palat.
Chester, parl. bor. 163 L d
Chesterfield Inlet 212 F b
Cheval-de-Bois
Cheviot Hills 49 E d
Chèvremont, castle 62 C c
Cheyenne 210 E b
Cheyenne River 198 E b
Cheyenne River, Ind. Res. 188 F a
Cheyennes, tribe 188 D b
Chezal-Benoît, mon. 94 C b
Chiaha 191 I e
Chiapa 105 B c
Chiapas, state 213 C c
Chiari 130 E d
Chiavari 90 I h
Chiavenna 91 R l
Chicaça 191 G e
Chicacoan 193 F c (Chi.)
Chicago 211 H b
Chichagof Island 212 ins.
Chichester
Chichester, bp. 97 Q k
Chichester, parl. bor. 163 N g
Chichilticale 190 D e
Chiclayo 214 A c
Chickamauga 208 D b
Chickasaw, Ind. Res. 188 G d
Chickasaw, Ind. Res. 1832 188 I d
Chickasaw Bluffs 191 H d
Chickasaws, tribe 188 I d
Chico River 215 B g
Chidley, Cape 186 M b
Chiemsee, bp. 95 E b
Chienti, bp. 95 F c
Chieri 130 P i
Chiers River 62 C d
Chieti 90 E c
Chieti, bp. 95 E c
Chièvres 117 B d
Chi-fu 171 N e
Chihuahua 213 B b
Chihuahua, prov. 190 D f
Chihuahua, state 213 B b
Chilau
Chile, capt. gen. and pres. 215 ins.
Chile, cty. 215 B g e
Chilenfu
Chilianwala 170 I e
Chilkat Pass 212 ins.
Chilcoot 212 ins.
Chilcoot Pass 212 ins.
Chillan 215 B f
Chillicothe, in Missouri 211 G c
Chillicothe, in Ohio 196 ins. B
Chillon, castle 91 O l
Chiloé Island 215 B g
Chilpancingo 213 B c
Chiltern Hills 49 F i
Chimalhuacan
Chimay 117 B d
Chimborazo, mt. 214 A c
Chimbote 214 B c
Chimerium 10 B c
Chimkent
Chimu 111 B c
China, country 171 L e
China Sea 112 E b
Chinalaph River, see Cheliff River
Chincha 111 B d
Chincha Islands 214 B d
Chinchilla 82 B b
Chinese City, loc. in Peking 170 ins. A
Chinese Empire 171 J M e
Chinilla River
Chin-kiang 171 M e
Chinon 69 H g
Chinon, castle 76 D c
Chinooks, tribe 188 B a
Chinsura 137 E d
Chintabor
Chiny
Chioggia 72 C b
Chioggia, bp. 95 E b
Chios, isl. 13 D b
Chipangu, empire (Japan)
Chippawa, battle 200 D b
Chippenham
Chippenham, parl. bor. 163 L f (Chipp.)
Chippewa River 191 G c
Chippewas, tribe 188 H a
Chippewyan, Fort 212 D c
Chipping Norton, parl. bor.
Chipping Wycombe, parl. bor. 163 N f (Ch. Wyc.)
Chiquitos, tribe 214 C d
Chira, Rio de la, river 111 A b
Chiremai, mt. 112 D d
Chiriqui Lagoon 105 D e
Chisey 76 C c
Chiskiak or Chisklack 193 ins. A (Ch.)
Chiswell, Fort 193 D c
Chita 171 M c
Chitral 170 I e
Chitral, reg. 137 B a
Chittagong 137 F d
Chiusi 90 L j
Chiusi, bp. 95 E c
Chivasso 130 P i
Chlum 159 H c
Chmielnik 92 C b
Choarene, reg. 19 H c
Choaspes River 19 L c
Choaspis River 19 G d
Cho-chau 170 ins. A
Choctaw, Ind. Res. 188 G d
Choctaw, Ind. Res. 1830 188 I d
Choctawhatchee River 193 B f
Choctaws, tribe 188 H d
Chœle-Chœl 215 C f
Chœrades Islands, in Eleusinian Gulf 16 B a
Chœrades Islands, in Gulf of Tarentum 31 G b
Choiseul, isl. 172 E a
Cholet 130 C d
Cholm 159 L c
Cholula 106 B a
Choluteca 213 D c
Chonos Archipelago 215 B g
Chorasmii, people 19 I b
Chorazin 6 D c
Chorin, mon. 79 H b
Chorsia(e) 11 D d
Chotin 131 I d
Chouteau's Landing 210 F c
Chotusitz 135 H d
Chowan River 193 F c
Christanna, Fort 193 F c
Christchurch, in New Zealand 172 G e
Christchurch, parl. bor. 163 M g
Christchurch, priory 100 A b

Christian IV., route of 121 C b
Christiana 206 ins.
Christiania (Aggershuus)
Christiansand 166 G c
Christiansborg
Christina, Fort 192 ins.
Christmas I., Indian Ocean 179 B i
Christmas I., Pacific Ocean 180 L g
Christophsthal 143 F i
Chrobatia, reg. 59 I c
Chrysas River 30 D e
Chrysea, isl. 14 ins.
Chrysokeras (Golden Horn) str. 93 G e
Chrysopolis
Chrysorrhoas River 6 E a
Chrystler's Farm, battle 200 F a
Chubut 215 C g
Chubut River 215 C g
Chudes, people 138 B d
Chumbi 171 J f
Chundah 137 C e
Chung-kiang 171 L f
Chuquisaca 214 C d
Chur, see Coire
Church, States of the, 9 cent. 56 E d
Church, States of the, 13 cent. 73 C b
Church, States of the, see also Papal States and Patrimony of Saint Peter
Churchill, Cape 186 J c
Churchill, Fort 212 F c
Churchill River 212 F c
Churubusco, battle 201 H g
Churwalchen 62 E e
Chusan, Islands 171 N e
Chuvashes, people 138 G d
Chylemath River 38 C e
Ciabrus River 39 M l
Ciando
Cibalis
Cibao, reg. 105 F c
Cibola, reg. 190 D d
Cibotus, Harbor of 34 ins. C (4)
Cibyra 20 C d
Cibyrrhæots, Theme of the 59 K f
Cicero, House of 24 A
Cichyrus 10 B c
Cicuye 190 D d
Cicynethus, isl. 11 E c
Cidade do Salvador (Bahia) 214 F d
Ciechanow 155 K b
Cienfuegos 213 D b
Cierium 10 D c
Cilicia, imp. prov. 35 K f
Cilicia, Macedonian prov. 18 D c
Cilicia, reg. 4 F c
Cilicia, Rom. prov.
Cilicia, satr. 18 O h
Cilicia, Strait of 20 E e
Cilicia, theme 59 L f
Cilicia I, E. Rom. prov. 43 I f (4)
Cilicia II, E. Rom. prov. 43 I f (13)
Cilli 72 D b
Cimarron River 190 F d
Cimbebas, people 109 S i
Cimbric Chersonese (Denmark) 38 D a
Ciminius, lake 27 G e
Cimmerian Bosporus, km. 33 L d
Cimolus (Kimolo), isl. 15 E c
Cincinnati 211 I c
Cinga River 38 C d
Cingulum 27 H d
Cintra 82 A b
Cipango, emp. (Japan)
Circæum, prom. 30 B a
Circars, reg. 137 D e
Circassia, reg.
Circassian Mamelukes, Dom. of the 93 E c
Circassians, people 139 E g
Circei or Circeii (San Felice) 30 C a
Circesium 20 I e
Circidius River 26 C e
Circle 198 ins. A
Circus Maximus, loc. in Rome 24 B
Circus Maximus, Aug. Reg., Rome 22 A
Cirencester 51 P i
Cirencester, mon. 97 O j
Cirencester, parl. bor. 163 M f (Cirenc.)
Cirphis, mt. 11 D d
Cirrha 11 D d
Cirta 38 D e
Cisa, La, pass 26 D c
Cisalpine Gaul, reg. 38 ins.
Cisalpine Republic 151 H g
Cisjurane Burgundy, km. 56 C d
Cisoing, mon. 94 C a
Cispadane Gaul, reg. 26 E c
Cispadane Gaul, Aug. Reg. 38 E d (8)
Cispius, mt. 22 A
Cisplatine Province 215 D f
Cissia, prov. 19 G d
Cissus 11 E b
Cissus, mt. 11 E b
Cité, Paris 149 B
Citeaux, mon. 95 D b
Cithæron Mountains 11 E d
Citium, in Cyprus 4 F c
Citium, in Macedonia 10 D b
Citlaltepec 106 A a
Citlaltepetl, mt. 106 C a
Citracan (Astrakhan) 99 M d
Città di Castello 90 D c
Città di Castello, bp. 95 E c
Cittanuova, bp. 95 E b
Cittavecchia, bp. 95 F c
City of Salt 7 C f
Ciudad Bolivar 214 C b
Ciudad de los Reyes 111 B d
Ciudadela, bp. 94 C d
Ciudad Guzman 213 ins.
Ciudad Juarez (El Paso del Norte) 213 B a
Ciudad Porfirio Diaz 213 B b
Ciudad Real 130 C f
Ciudad Rodrigo 82 G e
Ciudad Rodrigo, bp. 94 A c
Cius
Cius, Bay of
Cividale 90 D a
Civitá Castellana 96 B a
Civitate 64 C b
Civitavecchia 64 ins.
Civitella 90 D c
Civray 126 B c
Clackmannan, cty.
Cladeus River 14 B b
Clagny, Parc de, loc. in Versailles 149 A
Claiborne, Fort 200 I f
Clairac 126 B d
Clairac, mon. 94 C c
Clairets, Les, mon. 94 C b
Clairlieu, mon. 95 D b
Clairvaux 69 J f
Clairvaux, mon. 94 C b
Clallams, people 188 B a
Clampetia 31 F c
Clanis (Chiana) River 27 G e
Clanius River 30 C b
Clare, cty. 127 H i
Clarendon 69 B a
Clarendon, castle
Clarendon, dist. 193 ins. C
Clark, Fort 210 E a
Clark, route of 210 B a and D a
Clarke River 186 H d
Clarksville 210 F d
Clarus Mons, see Clermont-Ferrand
Clasis River 27 G d
Classes 27 G c
Clastidium 26 D c
Claterna 27 F c
Clatsop, Fort 210 A a
Clatsops, tribe 188 B a
Claudian Aqueduct 35 ins. B
Claudian Augustan Way, road 27 G b
Claudian Valerian Way, road 27 H e
Claudiopolis 20 D b
Claudius, Arch of 22 A
Clausentum (Bitterne) 51 P i
Clavenna (Chiavenna) 26 D a
Claverack 189 B c
Clazomenæ 13 E b
Clear, Cape 49 B f
Cleeve, mon. 97 N j
Clemont 143 ins. F
Clemont, lordship 143 ins. F
Cleonæ, on Acte Pen. 11 F b
Cleonæ, in Argolis 15 C b
Clepsydra, Spring of 23 C (4)
Clerf 117 E d
Clerkenwell, loc. in London 75 G g
Clermont, in Auvergne 61 E d
Clermont-en-Beauvoisis 76 E b
Clermont, bp. 94 C b
Clermont, cty. 76 E b
Clermont-en-Argonne 126 D b
Clermont-Ferrand 134 B f
Clesis River 26 E b
Cleveland 196 ins. B
Cleves 78 E c
Cleves, cty. 78 E c
Cleves, duchy 114 D c
Clew Bay 127 H h
Clifton 127 W l
Clinch River 196 ins. A
Clinton 208 B c
Clinton, Fort, near Saratoga 192 E b
Clinton, Fort, near West Point 195 D c
Clinton, route of 195 B g
Clipperton Island 180 P f
Clisius River 26 B c
Clitæ, people 20 E d
Cliternia 30 E a
Clitor 14 C b
Clitumnus River 27 G e
Clivus Argentarius, loc. in Rome 24 A
Clivus Capitolinus, loc. in Rome 24 A
Clivus Scauri, loc. in Rome 22 A
Clivus Victoriæ, loc. in Rome 24 A
Cloaca Maxima, loc. in Rome 24 A
Clodiana 31 I a
Clodian Way, road 27 F e
Clodius, Port of 35 ins. B
Clodii, Forum, near L. Sabatinus 35 ins. B
Clodii, Forum, near Luca 26 E d
Clogher, bp. 97 D b
Clomnacnoise, bp.
Clone, bp.
Clonfert, bp. 97 C c
Clonmel
Closter-Seven
Clota Æstuarium (Firth of Clyde) 38 A a
Cloyne, bp. 97 C e
Cluentus River 27 H d
Clugia, see Chioggia
Clunia, in Rætia 39 J j
Clunia, in Spain 38 B d
Cluny, mon. 94 C b
Clusium (Chiusi) 27 F d
Cluviæ 27 I f
Clyde, Firth of 49 D d
Clyde River 49 D e
Clydesdale, dist.
Cnemides 11 D d
Cnemis, mt. 11 D d
Cnidus 12 I c
Cnossus 14 ins.
Coahuila, prov. 190 E f
Coahuila, state 213 B b
Coast District 171 O d
Coast Range, mts., California 187 G d
Coast Range, mts., Canada 212 B b
Coatepec 106 B a
Coatzacoalco River 105 B c
Coatzacoalcos 213 C c
Coban 213 C c
Cobar 172 D d
Cobija 214 B e
Coblenz 62 D c
Coburg 85 F e
Coburg, Pflege, dist. 85 F e
Coburg Peninsula 172 C b

Coca . . . . 191 H e
Coca River . . . . 111 B b
Cocala . . . . 19 K e
Coccium (Ribchester) . . . . . .
Cocconato . . . . 130 Q i (Co.)
Cochaba . . . . 6 E b
Cochabamba . . . . 214 C d
Cocheco . . . . 189 B c
Cochin . . . . 137 C g
Cochin-China, country . . . . . 171 L g
Cockburn Land . . . . 186 K a
Cockermouth, parl. bor. . . . . . 163 K c
Cockersand, mon. . . . . 97 O h
Coco River . . . . 213 D c
Cocos I., Pacific Ocean . . . . . 214 A b
Cocos Is., Indian Ocean . . . . 179 A i
Cocynthum, prom. . . . . 31 F d
Cocytus River . . . . 10 B c
Cod, Cape . . . . 186 M d
Codfish Land . . . . 108 L c
Cœle, Deme of . . . .
Cœle, reg. . . . . 14 B b
Cœel Syria, reg. . . . .
Cœletæ, people . . . . 39 N l
Cœnyra . . . . 11 F b
Cœur d'Alene, Ind. Res. . . . . 188 C a
Coggeshall, mon. . . . . 97 R j
Cognac . . . . 76 C d
Cogolla, San Millan de la, mon. 94 B c
Cohœs . . . . 192 E b
Coiba, isl. . . . . 105 D e
Coimbatore . . . . 137 C f
Coimbra . . . . 82 G e
Coimbra, bp. . . . . 94 A c
Coimbra, univ. . . . . 100 D f
Coire . . . . 91 R l
Coire, bp. . . . . 78 F e
Colapis River . . . . 27 J b
Colatio . . . . 27 J a
Colberg . . . .
Colchester . . . .
Colchester, parl. bor. . . . . . . 163 O f
Colchis, reg. . . . . 20 J a
Colchis, satr. . . . . 8 I d
Cold Harbor, battle . . . . 208 E b
Col di Tenda Pass . . . . 130 P j
Coleman Street, in London . . . 75 G g
Colendonck . . . . 89 ins. C
Colenso . . . . 175 M l
Colesberg . . . . 175 M m
Colias, prom. . . . . 16 B b
Coligny . . . . 126 D c
Colima . . . . 213 ins.
Colima, vol. . . . . 187 I g
Collatia . . . . 35 ins. B
Colle . . . . 90 L j
Colle, La . . . . 200 G a
Colleton County . . . . 193 ins. C
Collier Bay . . . . 172 B b
Colline Gate . . . . 22 A
Collingwood . . . . 207 I b
Colmar . . . . 143 ins. D
Colmar, imp. city . . . . 78 E d
Colmenar de Oreja . . . . 82 H e
Cöln, see Cologne
Colnbrook . . . . 75 H i
Colne River . . . . 75 H h
Cologne (Cöln) . . . . 62 D c
Cologne, abp. . . . . 78 E c
Cologne, Hanse. cy. . . . . . . 99 ins. B
Cologne, imp. city . . . . 78 E c
Cologne, univ. . . . . 100 G d
Colombe, La, mon. . . . . 94 C b
Colombia, cty. . . . . 214 B b
Colombo . . . . 137 C g
Colón . . . . 214 A b
Colonea . . . . 59 L e
Colonea, theme . . . . 59 L f
Colonia Agrippina (Cologne) . 39 I h
Colonia Copia . . . . . . 31 F c (Col. Copia)
Colonia do Sacramento . . .
Colonia Neptunia 31 G b (Col. Neptunia)
Colonia Traiana . . . . 39 I h
Colonides . . . . 14 B c
Colonna, Cape . . . . 64 C c
Colonna, Piazza . . . . 22 A
Colonus . . . . 16 B b
Colonus, Deme of . . . .
Colorado, ter. . . . . 203 Q h
Colorado, state . . . . 203 Q h
Colorado Chiquito, R. . . . . . . 190 C d
Colorado Plateau . . . . 187 H e
Colorado River, flowing into G. of Mexico . . . . 187 J e
Colorado River, flowing into G. of California . . . . 187 H e
Colorado River, in Arg. Rep. . 215 C f
Colorado River, Little . . . . . . 190 C d
Colorado River, Ind. Res. . . . 188 D d
Colorado Springs . . . . 210 E c
Colossæ . . . . 20 C d
Colosseum, bldg. in Rome . . . 24 B
Colquechaca . . . . 214 C d
Columbia, in Ohio . . . . 196 ins. B
Columbia, in Pa. . . . . 211 J c
Columbia, in S. Carolina . . . . 211 I d
Columbia, in Tennessee . . . . 211 H c
Columbia, District of . . . . . . 208 ins.
Columbia, mt. . . . . 186 H c
Columbia Plateau . . . . 187 H d
Columbia River . . . . 186 G d
Columbus, in Georgia . . . . . . 191 I e
Columbus, in Ohio . . . . 199 I c
Columbus, voyages of . . 105, 108 M N e f
Columna Rhegium . . . . 30 E d
Colville, Fort . . . . 198 B a
Colville, Ind. Res. . . . . 188 C a
Colville River . . . . 186 D b
Colvilles, tribe . . . . 188 C a
Comacchio . . . . 90 K h
Comacchio, bp. . . . . 95 E c
Comacenus, lake . . . . 26 D a
Comaclum, see Comacchio
Comana, in Cappadocia . . . . . 20 G c
Comana, in Pontus . . . . 20 G b
Comanches, tribe . . . . 188 F d
Comayagua . . . . 213 D c
Combe, mon. . . . . 97 P i
Combermere, mon. . . . . 97 O i
Combrailles, cty. . . . . 76 E c
Comburg, castle . . . . 143 I g
Comfort, Point . . . . 193 ins. A
Cominges, cty. . . . . 76 D e
Comitium, loc. in Rome . . . . 24 A
Commagene, reg. . . . . 20 G d
Commendah . . . .
Comminges, bp. . . . . 94 C c
Common Lands, dist. . . . . .
Communipaw . . . . 189 ins. C
Como . . . . 90 I h
Como, bp. . . . . 95 D b
Como, lake . . . . 90 I h
Comorin, Cape . . . . 137 C g
Comoro Islands . . . . 175 H f
Compendium, see Compiègne
Compiègne . . . . 126 C b
Compludo, mon. . . . . 94 A c
Complutum . . . . 38 B d
Compostella, Santiago de . . . .
Compostella, Santiago de, abp.
Compsa . . . . 30 E b
Compton, Little . . . . 189 ins. A
Comum (Como) . . . . 26 D b
Concepción, in Arg. Rep. . . . 215 D f
Concepción, in Chile . . . . . . 215 B f
Concepción, in Paraguay . . . . 215 D e
Conception, Point . . . . 187 G e
Conception Island . . . . 108 P h
Conchos . . . . 190 D f
Conchos River . . . . 191 D f
Conciergerie, bldg. in Paris . . 149 B
Concord, Massachusetts . . . . . 189 ins. B
Concord, New Hampshire . . . 211 K b
Concord, Temple of . . . .
Concord River . . . . 195 ins. A
Concordia, in Arg. Rep. . . . . 215 D f
Concordia, in Upper Germany 39 I i
Concordia, in Venetia . . . . . . 27 G b
Concordia, bp. . . . . 95 E b
Condé . . . . 126 C a
Condevincum or Condivincum (Nantes) . . . . 38 B c
Condom, bp. . . . . 94 C c
Condrusi, people . . . . 39 H h
Conedoquinet River . . . . 208 ins.
Conegliano . . . . 150 G d
Conembriga . . . . 38 A d
Conestoga . . . . 194 K f
Conewago Creek . . . .
Confederation of the Rhine . . 155 leg.
Conflans, cty. . . . . 69 E e
Conflans, dist. . . . . 126 C e
Confluens, see Münster
Confluentes or Confluentia (Coblenz) . . . . 39 I h
Congaree River . . . . 193 D e
Congo, reg. . . . . 109 S h
Congo, Belgian, col. . . . . 175 F e
Congo, French, col. . . . . 175 E d
Congo River . . . . 175 F d
Congo State . . . . 175 F e
Congress Lands . . . . 196 ins. B
Conii, people . . . . 38 A e
Connaught, prov. . . . .
Connecticut, col. . . . . 189 B d
Connecticut, state . . . . 211 K b (Conn.)
Connecticut River . . . . 189 B c
Connor, bp. . . . . 97 E b
Conococheague Creek . . . . . . 208 ins.
Conope . . . . 10 C d
Conovium (Conway) . . . . 51 O h
Conques, mon., near Evreux . . 94 C b
Conques, mon., near Rodez . . 94 C c
Conrad III., crusade of . . . . . 70 I d
Consentia (Cosenza) . . . . . . 31 F c
Conserans, bp. . . . . 94 C c
Constance . . . . 62 E e
Constance, bp. . . . . 142 D e
Constance, imp. cy. . . . . 78 F e
Constantia (Constance) . . . . . 39 J j
Constantia, see Coutances
Constantia, in Cyprus . . . . . . 43 I f
Constantina . . . . 82 A b
Constantine . . . . 70 H f
Constantine, Arch of . . . . . . 24 B
Constantine, Basilica of . . . . 24 B
Constantine, Baths of . . . . . . 22 A
Constantine, Burnt Column of 93 G e (4)
Constantine, Church of . . . . . 23 D
Constantine, Statue of. . . . . .
Constantine, Forum of . . . . . 93 G e
Constantine, Wall of. . . . . . . 93 G e
Constantinople . . . . 43 H e
Constantinople, patr. . . . . . . 52 L f
Constantinople, plan of . . . . . 93 G e
Constantinople, Emp. of . . . . 73 F b
Constanz (Constance), bp. . . . 95 D b
Constanza . . . . 164 D b
Constitución . . . . 215 B f
Contestani, people . . . . 38 B e
Contrebia . . . . 38 B d
Contreras, battle . . . . 201 H g
Conway . . . .
Conway, parl. bor. . . . .
Conz, bridge of . . . . 122 D d
Conza, abp. . . . . 95 F c
Cooch Behar, reg. . . . . 137 E c
Cook, mt., in Alaska . . . . . . 212 ins.
Cook, mt., in New Zealand . . 172 F e
Cook Inlet . . . . 198 ins. A
Cook Islands . . . . 180 L i
Cook Strait . . . . 172 G e
Cooktown . . . . 172 D b
Coolgardie . . . . 172 B d
Cooper River, in Australia . . . 172 D c
Cooper River, in S. Carolina . 193 ins. C
Coorg, reg. . . . . 137 C f
Coosa River . . . . 208 C c
Copæ . . . . 11 E d
Copais, lake . . . . 11 E d
Copan . . . . 105 C d
Copenhagen . . . . 77 G a

Copenhagen, Hanse. for. cy. . . 98 F b
Copenhagen, univ. . . . . 100 H c
Cophen River . . . . 19 L d
Cophos Port . . . . 16 D c
Copia, col. . . . . 31 F c
Copiapó . . . . 215 B e
Coppermine River . . . . 212 D b
Coquimbo . . . . 215 B f
Cora . . . . 35 ins. B
Coracesium . . . . 20 E d
Corah . . . . 137 D c
Coral Islands . . . . 110 FF g
Coral Sea . . . . 172 E b
Corax, mt. . . . . 11 D d
Corbais . . . . 156 B a
Corbeia, see Corbie
Corbeil . . . . 61 E b
Corbie, mon. . . . . 55 P k
Corbridge . . . .
Corbridge, parl. bor. . . . .
Corcora River, in Noricum 27 I a
Corcora River, in Pannonia . 27 J b
Corcyra (Corfu), isl. . . . . . 10 A c
Corcyra Nigra . . . . 38 F d
Cordilleran Region . . . . . . 186 G c
Córdoba, in Arg. Rep . . . . . 215 C f
Córdoba, in Mexico . . . . . . 213 ins.
Cordova, in Spain . . . . 82 B b
Cordova, by. . . . . 94 B d
Cordova, calif. . . . . 58 C f
Cordova, emir. . . . . 54 D f
Cordova, km. . . . . 83 J h
Corduba (Cordova) . . . . . . 38 A e
Corduëne, reg. . . . . 20 J c
Corentine River . . . . 214 D b
Coressus . . . . 15 E b
Corfe Castle . . . . 127 W p
Corfinium . . . . 27 H e
Corfu, isl. . . . . 77 H e
Coria . . . . 82 A a
Coria, bp. . . . . 94 A d
Coria del Rio . . . . 82 A b
Corinium (Cirencester) . . . . 51 P i
Corinth, in Greece . . . . 15 C b
Corinth, in Mississippi . . . . 208 C c
Corinth, Gulf of . . . . 14 C a
Corinth, Isthmus of . . . . . . 2 G e
Corinthian Gate . . . . 6 ins. A
Coriovallum . . . . 39 H h
Coris . . . . 68 C b
Corisco Bay . . . . 175 D d
Coritani, people . . . . 51 P h
Cork . . . .
Cork, bp. . . . . 97 C e
Cork, cty. . . . . 127 I i
Corlær . . . . 192 D b
Cormons . . . . 161 I e
Cornavii, people . . . .
Cornelimünster, mon. . . . . . 95 D a
Corner Gate . . . . 6 ins. A
Corner Inlet . . . . 172 D d
Corneto . . . . 64 ins.
Corneto, bp. . . . . 95 E c
Corneville, mon. . . . . 94 E b (Cornev.)
Cornhill, in London . . . . . . 75 G g
Corniculum . . . . 35 ins. B
Corn Market, in London . . . 75 G g (34)
Cornouailles, cty. . . . . 69 B b
Cornwall, cty. . . . . 127 T p
Cornwall, reg. . . . .
Cornwallis, route of . . . 195 A g, B f, C f
Coro . . . . 105 G d
Corobilium, see Corbeil
Coromandel Coast . . . . 137 D f
Coron . . . .
Coronado, route of . . . . 190 F e
Corone . . . . 14 B c
Corone, Cape . . . . 16 C b
Coronea, in Bœotia . . . . . . 11 D d
Coronea, in Thessaly . . . . . 11 D c
Coronea, lake . . . . 11 E b
Corope . . . . 11 E c
Corozal . . . .
Corpus Christi . . . . 201 F d
Correggio . . . . 90 J h
Corrèze, dept. . . . . 148 E e
Corrientes . . . . 215 D e
Corrientes, Cabo das, cape in Africa . . . . 109 U j
Corrientes, cape, in Arg. Rep. . 215 D f
Corrientes, Cape, in Mexico . . 213 B b
Corsica, isl. . . . . 2 E d
Corsica, gen. . . . . 147 F c
Corsica, gouv. . . . . 146 C c
Corsica, French prov. . . . . . 148 F f
Corsica, W. Rom. prov. . . . . 42 D e (9)
Corsote . . . . 20 I e
Corso Umberto I, street in Rome 22 A
Corstopitum (Corbridge) . . . . 51 O g
Corte . . . . 146 C c
Cortemiglia . . . . 130 Q j
Cortenuova . . . . 72 B b
Cortereal, route of . . . . 108 L b
Cortez, routes of 105, 106
Cortil-Noirmont . . . . 156 B a
Cortona . . . . 27 G d
Cortona, bp. . . . . 95 E c
Cortoriacus or Corturiacus, see Courtrai
Corumbá . . . . 214 D d
Corunna . . . . 82 G e
Corvey . . . . 151 H f
Corvey, mon. . . . . 95 D a
Corycium, prom. . . . . 20 B c
Corydalus . . . . 16 B b
Corydalus, mt. . . . . 16 B b
Coryphasium, prom. . . . . . . 14 B c
Cos . . . . 13 E c
Cos, isl. . . . . 13 E c
Cosa . . . . 27 F e
Cosa, route of . . . . 108 M g
Cosedia, see Coutances
Cosenza . . . . 90 F e
Cosenza, abp. . . . . 95 F d
Cosmidion, quarter . . . .
Cosmin . . . .
Cosmo y Damiano, Saints, mon. 94 A c
Cossium, see Bazas
Cosne . . . . 76 E c
Cossacks of the Don, people . 139 F f
Cossacks of the Terek, people . 139 G g
Cossacks, Uralian, people . . . 139 H e
Cossack, Zaporogian, people . . 139 D f
Cossæi, people . . . . 19 G d
Cosseans, people . . . . 8 C b
Cossonay . . . . 130 O h
Cossyra, isl. . . . . 38 E e
Costa Rica, reg. . . . . 105 C d
Costa Rica, country . . . . . . 213 D c
Costnitz, (Constance), bp. . . . 95 D b
Cotaxtla, river . . . . 106 D b
Côte-d'Or, dept. . . . . 148 E e
Côte-d'Or, mts. . . . . 148 E e
Cotentin, dist. . . . . 81 L h
Côtes-du-Nord, dept. . . . . . 148 D e
Cotini, people . . . . 38 F c
Cotopaxi. mt. . . . . 111 B b
Cotrone . . . . 90 F e
Cotrone, bp. . . . . 95 F d
Cotswold Hills . . . . 49 E f
Cottbus . . . . 155 H c
Cottian Alps, mts. . . . . 26 B c
Cottian Alps, W. Rom. prov. . . 42 D e (5)
Cottius, Kingdom of . . . . . . 26 A c
Cotyaëum . . . . 20 C c
Cotyora . . . . 20 G b
Coucou, le . . . . 156 C c
Coucy . . . . 76 E b
Coucy, seign. . . . . 69 I f
Coulommiers . . . . 126 C b
Council Bluffs . . . . 211 F b
Council House, bldg. in Jerusalem 6 ins. A
Courland, duchy . . . . 88 J c
Courland, reg. . . . . 138 B d
Courmayeur . . . . 91 O m
Couronne, La, mon. . . . . . . 94 C b
Courtenay . . . . 69 I f
Courtrai . . . . 117 B d
Couserans, cty. . . . . 69 D e
Couserans, dist. . . . . 147 E c (Cous.)
Coutances . . . . 61 C b
Coutances, bp. . . . . 94 B b
Coutances, cty. . . . . 69 C b
Coutras . . . . 126 A d
Couvin . . . . 117 C d
Covadonga, cave . . . . 82 A a
Covadonga, mon. . . . . 94 A c
Coventry . . . .
Coventry, bp. . . . . 97 P i
Coventry, parl. bor. . . . . . . 163 M e
Coverham, mon. . . . . 97 P g
Cowpens, battle . . . . 195 A f
Coyohuacan . . . .
Cozumel, isl. . . . . 105 C b
Crac des Chevaliers, castle . . 68 C c
Cracow . . . . 70 J c
Cracow, bp. . . . . 95 F a
Cracow, Hanse. cy. . . . . 98 G c
Cracow, rep. . . . . 159 J c
Cracow, univ. . . . . 100 I d
Cradle Mount . . . . 172 D e
Crailsheim . . . . 143 J g
Craiova . . . . 164 C b
Cranæa . . . . 10 B c
Cranganore . . . .
Crania, mt. . . . . 10 B c
Cranii . . . . 10 B d
Crannon . . . . 11 D c
Craon . . . . 76 C c
Craon, castle . . . . 69 C c
Craonne . . . . 154 B d
Craterus, route of . . . . 19 I d
Crathis, mt. . . . . 14 C a
Crathis River, in Achaia . . . . 14 C a
Crathis (Crati) River, in Bruttium 31 F c
Crato . . . . 83 J h
Craven County . . . . 193 E e (Cra.)
Craven, Fort . . . . 192 D b
Crawford, Fort . . . . 211 G b
Crayford . . . . 75 J i
Crécy . . . . 76 D a
Crediton . . . .
Crediton, parl. bor. . . . .
Creek, Ind. Res. . . . . 188 G c
Creek, Ind. Res. 1832 . . . . . 188 I d
Creeks, tribe . . . . 188 I d
Crefeld . . . . 117 E c
Creglingen . . . . 143 J g
Crema . . . . 90 I h
Cremera River . . . . 35 ins. B
Cremisa, see Krems
Cremona . . . . 26 E b
Cremona, bp. . . . . 95 E b
Crenæ . . . . 10 C d
Crenides . . . . 11 F a
Crépy, near Laon . . . . 126 C b
Crépy, in Valois . . . . 69 I f
Crescentino . . . . 130 Q i (Cr.)
Crespy . . . . 114 B d
Crestonia, reg. . . . . 11 E b
Cretan Sea . . . . 15 D c
Crete, isl. . . . . 14 ins.
Crete, East Rom. prov. . . . . . 43 H f (2)
Crete, Rom. prov. . . . . 35 I g
Crete, theme . . . . 59 J g
Creuse, dept. . . . . 148 E e
Creuse River . . . . 76 D c
Creusis . . . . 11 E d
Creussen, castle . . . . 63 F d
Crevacuore . . . . 130 Q i
Crévant . . . . 76 E c
Crèvecœur, Fort . . . . 191 H c
Crewe . . . . 162 D d
Crewkerne . . . . 127 W p
Crexa . . . . 27 I c
Crexi, isl. . . . . 27 I c
Cricklade, parl. bor. . . . 163 M f (Crick.)
Crillon, mt. . . . . 212 ins.
Crimea, Khan of the . . . .
Crimea, pen. . . . . 3 H d
Crimisa . . . . 31 G c
Crimisa, prom. . . . . 31 G c

Crimisius River 30 C e
Cripplegate, in London 75 G g
Crisa or Crissa 11 D d
Crisa or Crissa (Salona), Gulf of 11 D d
Crisenon, mon. 94 C b
Crithote, prom. 10 B d
Criumetopon, prom. 14 ins.
Crius River 14 C a
Crixia 26 C c
Croatan Island 193 G d
Croatia, dist. 159 H f
Croatia, km. 59 H e
Croatia, reg. 54 H e
Croatian Military Frontier 159 H f
Croats, people 53 P i
Croceæ 14 C c
Crocian Field 11 D c
Crocylia, isl. 10 B d
Cromarty, cty.
Crommyon 15 D b
Cronos Hill
Crooked Island 105 F b
Cropredy Bridge 127 X n
Cross, Cape 109 S k
Crossæa, reg. 11 E b
Cross Creek 195 B f
Cross Keys 208 E b (C. K.)
Crotalus River 31 F c
Croton 31 G c
Crow, Ind. Res. 188 E b
Crow Creek, Ind. Res. 188 G b
Crowland
Crown Point 192 E h
Crows, tribe 188 E a
Croxton, mon. 97 Q i
Croydon 75 I i
Croyland, mon.
Crozet Island 182 GG l
Crusade, fourth 73
Crusade of Conrad III. 70
Crusade of Frederick Barbarossa 70
Crusade of Frederick II. 73
Crusade of Louis VII. 70
Crusade of Louis IX. 73
Crusade of Philip II. (Augustus) 70
Crusade of Richard I. 70
Crusis, reg. 11 E b
Crustumerium 35 ins. B
Crustumium River 27 G d
Crutched Friars, mon. in London 75 G g
Cruzblanca 201 H g
Cruz del Marqués 106 A a
Csanad, bp. 95 G b
Csepel Island 159 J e
Csik-Sereda 159 M e
Csongrád 159 J e
Csorna 159 I e
Csucsa 159 L e
Ctesiphon 20 K f
Ctimene 10 D c
Cuarius River 11 D c
Cuba, Capt. Gen. of 213 C/F a/c
Cuba, isl. 105 E b
Cubagua, isl. 105 H d
Cuch Behar, reg. 137 E c
Cuco River 187 K g
Cudahy 198 ins. A
Cuddalore
Cuenca, in Ecuador 111 B b
Cuenca, in Spain 82 B a
Cuernavaca 106 A b
Cufitatchiqui 191 I e
Cugerni, people 39 H h
Cuitlahuac 106 B a
Cujavia, reg. 138 A e
Cularo (Grenoble) 38 D c
Culebra
Culebra, isl. 199 ins. G
Culenborg 117 D c
Culhuacan
Culiacan 213 B b
Cullera 82 B b
Culloden Moor
Cumæ 31 ins. A
Cumaná 105 H d
Cumaná, reg. 105 H e
Cumania, reg.
Cumans, people 71 L d
Cumberland 211 J c
Cumberland, cty.
Cumberland, Fort 192 B d
Cumberland District 196 B c (C. D.)
Cumberland Gap, pass 194 C c
Cumberland House 212 E c
Cumberland Island 193 D f
Cumberland Mountains 193 C c
Cumberland Peninsula 212 I b
Cumberland Plateau 187 K e
Cumberland River 191 H d
Cumberland Road, see legend 210
Cumberland Sound 212 I b
Cumberland Valley 208 ins.
Cumbria, reg.
Cumbrian Mountains 49 E d
Cume 12 F b
Cumeoberg, mt. 54 H d
Cunaxa 20 J f
Cunene River 175 E f
Cuneo 90 H h
Cunerum, prom. 27 H d
Cuneus aureus
Cupra Maritima 27 H d
Curaçao, isl. 214 C a
Curalius River 10 C c
Curca 99 J f
Curetes, people 10 B d
Curia (Coire) 39 J j
Curia Hostilia 24 A
Curico 215 B f
Curicum 27 I b
Curitiba 215 E e
Curium 20 E e
Curles 193 ins. A (Cur.)
Curictæ, isl. 27 I b
Curta 99 J f
Curus 27 G e
Curzola, bp. 95 F c
Curzola, isl. 90 F c
Cusentia, see Consentia (Cosenza)
Cush, reg. 4 F e
Customs-Union of Bavaria and Wurtemberg 160 D c
Custoza 158 F f
Cutch, Gulf of 137 A d
Cutch, reg. 137 A d
Cutiliæ, Aquæ 27 G e
Cuttack 137 E d
Cuttiæ 26 C b
Cuttyhunk Island 189 C d
Cuxhaven 134 E b
Cuyabá 214 D d
Cuyahoga River 196 ins. B
Cuyk 117 D c
Cuyk, Land of 117 D c
Cuzco 111 C d
Cuzco, audiencia 215 ins.
Cyamosorus River 30 D e
Cyana, Shrine of 31 ins. B
Cyane River 31 ins. B
Cyathus River 10 C d
Cyclades, isl. 4 B b
Cycloborus River 23 D
Cydathenæum, deme 23 D
Cydnus (Tersus) River 20 F d
Cydonia 14 ins.
Cyllene 14 B b
Cyllene, gulf 14 B a
Cyllene, mt. 14 C b
Cyme, in Eubœa 11 F d
Cyme, in Italy 5 A a
Cymmer, mon. 97 N i
Cynætha 14 C a
Cynetes, people 38 A e
Cynkalan (Canton)
Cynkali
Cynosarges, loc. near Athens 23 D
Cynoscephalæ, mts. 11 D c
Cynosura, prom. in Diacria 16 C a
Cynosura, prom. in Salamis 16 B b
Cyntia, lake 10 C d
Cynuria, dist. in Arcadia 14 B b
Cynuria, dist. in Argolis 14 C b
Cynus 11 E d
Cyparisseis River 14 B b
Cyparissia 15 C c
Cyparissiæ 14 B b
Cyparissian Gulf (Gulf of Arcadia) 14 B b
Cyparissium, prom. 14 B b
Cyphanta 15 D c
Cyprus, isl. 20 E e
Cyprus, km. 71 M g
Cyprus, East Rom. prov. 43 I g (5)
Cyprus, Rom. prov. 35 K g
Cyprus, theme 59 K g
Cypsela 9 B c
Cyrene 12 H d
Cyrenaica, reg. 12 H d
Cyrenaica, Rom. prov. 35 I g
Cyreschata 19 K c
Cyretiæ 10 D c
Cyropolis 8 K e
Cyrrhus, in Macedonia 11 D b
Cyrrhus, in Syria 20 G d
Cyrus River (Kur R.) 18 G b
Cythera 15 D c
Cythera (Cerigo), isl. 15 C c
Cythnus 15 E b
Cythnus (Termia), isl. 15 E b
Cytinium 11 D d
Cyzicus
Czaslau 135 H d
Czechs, people 56 E c
Czegléd 159 J e
Czenstochowa 79 K c
Czenstochowa, mon. 95 F a
Czernowitz 131 I d

Dabayba, reg. 105 E e
Dacca 137 F d
Dacia, Rom. prov. 35 I d
Dacia, East Rom. dioc. 43 G e
Dacia Apulensis, Rom. prov. 39 M k
Dacia Maluensis, Rom. prov. 39 M l
Dacia mediterranea, East Rom. prov. 43 G e (1)
Dacia ripensis, East Rom. prov. 50 H d
Daghestan, reg. 139 G g
Dagö, isl. 88 I b
Dagupan 171 N g
Dahæ, people 19 I c
Dahbul 112 A b
Dahlak Islands 170 F g
Dahomey, col. 174 D d
Daibul
Dakar 174 B c
Dakota, ter. 1861 203 P f
Dakota, ter. 1863 203 R f
Dakota, North, state 203 R f
Dakota, South, state 203 R g
Dakota River 198 F b
Dakotas, tribe 188 F a
Dalaminzians, people 63 G c
Dalecarlia, reg. 88 F a
Dalgety 172 D d
Dalhem 117 D d
Dalhousie 212 I d
Dalias 82 B b
Dalkeith 84 B b
Dalkey Island 127 K h
Dallas, in Georgia 208 D c
Dallas, in Texas 210 F d
Dalmatia, imp. prov. 34 H e
Dalmatia, reg. 56 F d
Dalmatia, theme 59 H e
Dalmatia, West Rom. prov. 43 F e (11)
Dalny 171 N e
Dalon, mon. 94 C b
Dalriada, km.
Dal River 88 F a
Dalton 208 D c
Daly River 172 C b

Damaraland, reg. . . . . 175 E g
Damariscotta . . . . 189 D b
Damascene, reg. . . . . 6 E b
Damascus . . . . 5 C b
Damascus, emir. . . . . 68 C c
Damgarten . . . . 154 G a
Damghan . . . .
Damietta . . . . 150 B a
Damm . . . . 123 H b
Dammartin . . . . 76 E b
Dammeshek (Damascus) . . . . . 6 E a
Damnii, people . . . . 38 B a
Dampier Archipelago . . . . . . 172 A b
Dampierre . . . . 143 ins. F
Damvillers . . . . 126 D b
Dan . . . . 6 D b
Dan River . . . . 193 E c
Dan, tribe . . . . 7 ins. D
Danbury . . . . 195 E c
Danelaw, The, reg. . . . .
Danes, people . . . . 46 H b
Danes, people, in England . . . 57 C c
Danewerk, wall . . . . 63 E a
Danish Kingdom . . . . 54 F b
Danish March . . . . 58 F c (D.M.)
Danish Mercia, reg. . . . . . .
Danish Northumbria, reg. . . . .
Dankov . . . . 139 E e
Dannenberg . . . . 79 G b
Dantzic . . . . 63 J a
Dantzic, Hanse. cy. . . . . 98 G c
Dantzic, rep. . . . . 155 J a
Danube River . . . . 2 F d
Danuvius (Danube) River . . . . 34 G d
Danville . . . . 195 B e
Daphne . . . . 4 ins.
Daphnus . . . . 11 D d
Daphnus River . . . . 10 C d
Dara, in Dar-fur . . . . 174 F c
Dara, in Mesopotamia . . . . . . 20 I d
Darantasia . . . . 26 A b
Daras . . . . 52 M f
Dardanelles, str. . . . . 2 G e
Dardani, people . . . . 39 M l
Dardania, reg. . . . .
Dardania, East Rom. prov. . . . 43 G e (4)
Dardanus . . . .
Dar-es-Salaam . . . . 175 G e
Darent River . . . . 75 J i
Dar-fur, reg. . . . . 174 F c
Dargun, mon. . . . . 80 C e
Darien, Gulf of . . . . 105 E e
Darien, reg., in Colombia, see Urabá . . . . 105 E e
Darien, dist., in Georgia . . . . 193 ins. C
Darini, people . . . . 38 A b
Dariorigum, see Vannes
Darley, mon. . . . . 97 P i
Darling River . . . . 172 D d
Darlington . . . . 162 E c
Darmstadt . . . . 114 E d
Darnis . . . . 43 G g
Daroca . . . . 82 B a
Daron . . . . 68 ins. A
Dartford . . . . 75 J i
Dartfort, mon. . . . . 97 R j
Dartmoor . . . . 49 D f
Dartmouth, in England . . . . . 84 B d
Dartmouth, parl. bor. . . . . . . 163 K g
Dartmouth, in Mass. . . . . 189 C d (Dart.)
Darwin, mt. . . . . 215 B h
Dascon . . . . 31 ins. B
Dascylium . . . .
Dassaretæ, people . . . . 10 B b
Dassel . . . . 72 B a
Datis' fleet, route of . . . . . . 13 D c
Datum . . . . 11 F b
Daulatabad . . . .
Daulis . . . . 11 D d
Daunii, people . . . . 30 E a
Daunus River . . . . 30 E a
Dauphin, Fort . . . .
Dauphin, isl. . . . . 191 H e
Dauphin, Place du, Paris . . . . 149 B
Dauphiny, gouv. . . . . 146 C c
Dauphiny, prov. . . . . 148 F f
Davao . . . . 199 ins. H
Davenport . . . . 211 G b
Daventry . . . . 127 X n
Davey, Port . . . . 172 D e
David . . . . 214 A b
David, Street of . . . . 68 ins. B
David, Tomb(s) of . . . . 6 ins. A
David and Solomon, Wall of . . 6 ins. A
David Comnenus, Dom. of . . . 73 G b
David's Gate . . . . 68 ins. B
Davids house, Jerusalem . . . . 6 ins. A (3)
Davids Tower . . . . 68 ins. B
Davis Islands . . . . 108 L l
Davis, routes of . . . . 108 P b
Davis Strait . . . . 186 N b
Davos . . . . 91 R l
Dawson . . . . 212 B b
Dax . . . . 69 C e
Dax, bp. . . . . 94 B c
Dayton . . . . 200 A d
De Aar . . . . 175 L m
Dead Sea . . . . 7 C f
Dean, Forest of . . . . 49 E f
Dearborn, Fort (Chicago) . . . . 199 H b
Dearborn, route of . . . . 200 C d
Death Valley . . . . 187 H e
Debeltum . . . . 43 H e
Debreczin . . . .
Decastadium . . . . 30 E e
Decatur . . . . 208 C c
Deccan, reg. . . . . 137 C f
Decelea . . . . 15 D a
Decempagi . . . . 39 I i
Deciates, people . . . . 26 A d
Decise . . . . 126 C c
Decius, Baths of . . . .
Decuman Gate . . . . 22 A
Deddington, parl. bor. . . .
Dedham . . . . 189 ins. B
Deer Creek, Ind. Res. . . . . . . 188 H a
Deerfield, battle . . . . 189 B c
Deep River . . . . 195 B f
Dee River, in England . . . .
Dee River, in Scotland . . . . .
Dees . . . . 159 L e
Defiance . . . . 200 A c
Defiance, Fort . . . . 196 ins. B
Dego . . . . 150 E d
De Grey River . . . . 172 B c
Deheubarth, reg. . . . .
Dehkergan . . . .
Dei Consentes, Portico of the.
Deiotarus, Kingdom of . . . . . 35 K e
Deira, reg. . . . .
Deirades . . . . 16 C b
Deirans, people . . . .
Dekapolis, dist. . . . . 7 D d
Delagoa Bay . . . . 175 G g
Delaware, state . . . . 199 J c (Del.)
Delaware Bay . . . . 192 D d
Delaware Counties, col. . . . . . 192 D d
Delaware River . . . . 192 D c
Delawares, tribe . . . . 188 K c
Deleus . . . .
Delft . . . . 117 C b
Delftshaven . . . . 184 D b
Delfzyl . . . . 117 E a
Delgado, Cape . . . . 175 H f
Delhi . . . . 137 C c
Delhi, Empire of the Sultans of
Delian Amphictyony . . . . 8 P i
Delium . . . . 11 E d
Della Scala Dominions . . . . . 79 G f
Delle . . . . 143 ins. F
Delminium . . . . 38 F d
Delos . . . . 15 F b
Délos, isl. . . . . 8 P i
Delphi (Kastri) . . . . 11 D d
Delphic Amphictyony . . . 8 O h legend
Delphini, Portus . . . . 26 D c
Demarcation Point, cape . . . . 198 ins. A
Demerara . . . . 214 D b
Demetæ, people . . . . 51 N i
Demeter, Temple of . . . . 31 ins. B (12)
Demetrias . . . . 11 E c
Demmin . . . . 63 G b
Demmin, Hanse. cy. . . . . . . 99 ins. B
Demonesi Islands . . . .
Demotika . . . . 131 I e
Denain . . . . 134 B c
Denain, mon. . . . . 148 B a
Denbigh, in Virginia . . . . . . 193 ins. A
Denbigh, cty. in Wales . . . . . 127 V m
Denbigh, parl. bor. . . . . 163 K d
Denbigh, parl. dist. . . . . 163 K d
Dendera . . . . 4 F d
Dendermonde . . . . 117 C c
Denia . . . . 82 C b
Denkendorf . . . . 143 H h
Denmark, kingdom, about 1000 58 G b
Denmark, kingdom, 19 cent. . . 158 F a
Denmark and Norway, km. in 1812 155 ins.
Dennewitz . . . . 154 G c
Dennis, East . . . . 207 M b
Dentheletæ, people . . . . 39 M l
Dentheliatis, dist. . . . . 14 C c
Denver . . . . 210 E c
Deogir, reg. . . . .
Déols . . . . 61 D c
Déols, castle . . . . 76 D c
Déols, seign. . . . . 61 D c
Deorham . . . .
Deptford . . . . 75 I i
Dera Ghazi Khan . . . . 137 B b
Dera Ismail Khan . . . . 137 B b
Derbe . . . . 20 E d
Derbend . . . .
Derbiccans, people . . . . 8 J e
Derby . . . .
Derby, cty. . . . .
Derby, parl. bor. . . . . 163 M e
Derby, shire . . . .
Derg, Lough, lake . . . . 127 I h
Derindeh . . . . 124 G c
Derkos . . . . 165 F c
Dermbach . . . . 158 E c
Derrhis, prom. . . . . 11 E c
Derry, bp. . . . . 97 D b
Dertona . . . . 26 C c
Dertosa (Tortosa) . . . . 38 C d
Desastre, Rio del, river . . . . . 105 D d
Deseado, Cape . . . . 108 J l
Deseado River . . . . 215 C g
Deseret, see Utah . . . . 211 C b c
Des Moines . . . . 211 G b
Des Moines River . . . . 191 G c
Desna River . . . . 139 D e
Desplaines River . . . . 191 H c
Dessau . . . . 79 H c
Desterro . . . . 215 E e
Detmold . . . . 62 E c
Detroit, fort . . . . 191 I c
Detroit . . . . 199 I b
Dettingen . . . . 134 E c
Deulino . . . . 138 E d
Deuriopes, people . . . . 10 C a
Deutsch-Brod . . . . 87 J d
Deutsch-Krone . . . . 115 I b
Deutz . . . . 55 Q i
Deux Ponts (Zweibrücken) . . . 86 F d
Deux Ponts, princ. . . . . 134 D d
Deux-Sèvres, dept. . . . . 148 D e
Deva (Chester) . . . . 51 O h
Deva, in Transylvania . . . . . . 159 L f
Deventer . . . . 117 E b
Deventer, Hanse. cy. . . . . . . 99 ins. B
Deventer, mon. . . . . 95 D a
Devil's Lake, Ind. Res. . . . . . 188 G a
Devizes . . . . 65 F e
Devizes, castle . . . .
Devizes, parl. bor. . . . . 163 M f
Devol . . . . 67 K e
Devon, cty. . . . .
Devon, shire . . . .
Devonport, parl. bor. . . . . . . 163 J g

De Vries, route of
Deynze 117 B d
Dhar
Dharwar 137 C e
Dia, isl. 14 ins.
Diacira 20 J f
Diacria, dist. 16 B a
Diadochi, Kingdoms of the, about 200 B. C. 19
Diadochi, Kingdoms of the, 301 B. C. 18
Diagon River 14 B b
Dialas River 18 G c
Diamantina 214 E d
Diamantine River 172 C c
Diamond, Cape 112 C c
Diana, Grove of 35 ins. B
Diana, Temple of 22 A
Dianium 38 C e
Dianium, isl. 26 F e
Diarbekir, reg.
Diarbekr 99 L f
Diaz, Bartholomew, route of 108 Q g
Diaz, Melchior, route of 190 C f
Dibio, see Dijon
Dibon 7 D f
Dicæa 13 J d
Dicæarchia 31 ins. A
Dickrich 117 E e
Dicte 4 C b
Dicte, mt. 14 ins.
Didyma, mt. 15 D b
Didyme, isl. 30 D d
Die 61 F d
Die, bp. 95 D c
Diedenhofen (Thionville) 62 C d
Diego, Fort 193 D f
Diego Garcia, isl 182 II h
Diego Rodriguez, isl. 109 X i
Diego Suarez 175 H f
Diekirch 117 E e
Diepenow-Schanze, fort 123 H a
Diepholz 86 G b
Diepholz, cty. 86 G b
Dieppe 76 D a
Dieppe, Hanse. for. cy. 98 D d
Diessenhofen 142 C e
Diest 117 C d
Dieulacres, mon. 97 O h
Dieveren 117 E b
Digentia River 35 ins. B
Digne 69 G d
Digne, bp. 95 D c
Dijon 61 F c
Dijon, gen. 147 E b
Dillenburg 114 D c
Dillingen 114 F d
Dinan 76 B b
Dinant 117 C d
Dinant, Hanse. cy. 98 D d
Dinapur 137 E c
Dinaretium, prom. 20 F e
Dindigal, Dindigul, dist. 137 C g
Dindymus, mt. near Cyzicus
Dindymus, mt. near Sardis 20 C c
Dine, isl. 15 C b
Dinerof 117 E e
Dingle Bay 127 G i
Dinia, see Digne
Diocæsarea 6 C c
Diochares Gate 23 D
Dioclea 59 H e
Diocletian, Baths of 22 A
Diogenium 23 D
Diois, dist. 126 D d
Diomean Gate 23 D
Dion-le-Mont 156 B a
Dionysiades, isl. 14 ins.
Dionysius, Citadel of 31 ins. B (4)
Dionysopolis 39 N l
Dionysus, Temple of
Dionysus, Theatre of 23 C
Dioryctus 10 B d
Dioscurias 12 L b
Dioscurias, prom. 31 G d
Diospolis, in Bithynia 20 D b
Diospolis, in Egypt 4 F d
Diospolis, in Palestine 7 B e
Dipæa 14 C b
Diplokionion, quarter 93 G e
Dipylum 23 D
Diribitorium, loc. in Rome 24 B
Dirphys, mt. 11 E d
Dirschau 123 J a
Disentis, ab. 78 F e
Disentis, mon. 91 Q l
Disibodenberg, mon. 95 D b (Dis.)
Dismal Swamp 193 F c
District of Columbia 211 J c (D. C.)
Dithmarschen (Ditmarsh) reg. 62 E a
Dittani, people 38 B d
Diu 137 B d
Dium, in Chalcidice 11 F b
Dium, in Eubœa 11 D d
Dium, in Macedonia 11 D b
Dium, in Syria 6 D c
Divini, Portus 38 B e
Divione, see Dijon
Divirigi 99 K f
Divitia 39 I h
Divodurum (Metz) 39 I i
Divona, see Cahors
Divus Augustus, Temple of 24 B
Divus Claudius, Portico of 22 A
Divus Claudius, Temple of 22 A
Divus Julius, Temple of
Divus Romulus, Temple of
Divus Trajanus, Temple of 24 B
Dixcove
Dixmuide
Dixmuyden 117 A c
Dixon Entrance 212 ins.
Dixon Sound 198 ins. A
Dmietrov 71 N b
Dnieper River
Dniester River 139 C f
Dobbs, Fort 193 D d
Doberan, mon. 80 B d
Doberus 17 E a
Dobrilugk 63 G c
Dobritch, Dobrudja, Dobrudsha, dist. 119 J e
Dobrzyn 79 K b
Dobuni, people 51 O i
Doclea 39 L l
Dodendorf 154 F b
Dodge, Fort 210 E c
Dodge City 210 E c
Dodona 10 B c
Dœtinchem 117 E c
Doffingen 143 G h
Dohna 85 G e
Dohna, castle 63 G c
Dokkum 117 D a
Dol 61 C b
Dol, bp. 94 B b
Dolceacqua 130 P k
Dôle 114 C e
Dôle, univ. 100 G e
Doliche 10 D b
Doliche, isl. 10 C d
Dollart, The, bay 78 E b
Dolma Baghtcheh
Dolopes, people, in Scyrus 11 F d
Dolopes, people, in Thessaly 8 N h
Dolopia, reg. 10 C c
Dolores Hidalgo 213 ins.
Dolyani, bp. 95 F c
Domana 20 H b
Dombes, gen. 147 F b
Domfront 69 C b
Domine quo vadis, loc. near Rome 96 A
Dominguez, route of 190 C d
Dominica, isl., Antilles 105 H c
Dominica, isl., Marquesas 107 D h
Dominican Republic, country 213 E c
Dominion of Canada 212 C c
Domitian, Gardens of 22 A
Domitian, Palace of 24 B
Domitian, Stadium of 22 A
Dömitz 122 F b
Domo d'Ossola 90 I g
Domremy 81 N h
Domstadtl 135 I d
Don, Cossacks of the, people 139 F f
Donajec River 159 K d
Donaueschingen 142 B e
Donauwörth, imp. cy. 79 G d
Doncaster
Doncaster, parl. bor.
Donegal 127 J g
Donegal, cty. 127 J g
Donegal Bay 49 B d
Donelson, Fort 208 C b
Donetz River 139 F f
Dongola 174 F c
Donnington Castle 127 X o
Donnybrook, fair in Dublin 98 ins. A
Don River 139 F f
Donzy 76 E c
Dor, Dora 6 B c
Dora Baltea River 130 P i
Dora Ripaira River 130 O i
Dorat 126 B c
Dorchester, in Dorsetshire
Dorchester, in Oxfordshire
Dorchester, in Conn. 189 B d
Dorchester, in Mass. 189 ins. B
Dorchester, bp. 97 P j
Dorchester, parl. bor. 163 L g
Dorchester Heights 195 ins. A
Dordogne, dept. 148 E e
Dordogne River 76 D d
Dordrecht 117 C c
Dordrecht, Hanse. cy. 99 ins. B
Dorians, people
Doris, region, in Asia Minor 8 Q i
Doris, state, in Greece 13 C b
Doriscus
Dorium 14 B b
Dorking 75 I i
Dormition, loc. in Jerusalem 6 ins. A
Dornach, castle 91 P k
Dornhan 143 G i
Dornonia, see Dordogne
Dornstetten 143 G i
Dorocas, see Dreux
Dorogobusch
Dorogobuzh 153 O g
Dorostorium 43 H e
Dorpat 71 L b
Dorpat, Hanse. cy. 99 I b
Dorsætas, people
Dorset, cty.
Dorset, parl. dist. 163 L g
Dorset, shire
Dort 117 C c
Dortmund 62 D c
Dortmund, Hanse. cy. 99 ins. B
Dortmund, imp. city 78 E c
Dorylæum 20 D c
Dörzbach 143 I g
Dossenbach 158 E e
Dothan 7 C d
Dotian Field 11 D c
Dotternhausen 143 G i
Douai 117 B d
Doubs River 62 D e
Doubs, dept. 148 F e
Douglas 212 ins.
Douglas, castle 118 D b
Douglas, fam.
Doullens 117 A d
Dour 157 ins.
Douro (Duero) River 82 G e
Dover, in England
Dover, castle 65 G e
Dover, mon. 97 S j
Dover, parl. bor. 163 P f
Dover, in Delaware 192 D d
Dover, in New Hampshire 189 C c

Dovre Field . . . . 166 G c
Downgate, in London . . . . . . 75 G g
Down, bp. . . . . 97 E b
Down, cty. . . . . 127 K g
Downpatrick, bp. . . . . 97 F b
Downs, North, dist. . . . . 49 G f
Downs, South, dist. . . . . 49 F f
Downton, parl. bor. . . . . 163 M g
Drabescus. . . . . 11 F a
Dragashan . . . . 164 C b
Dragon's Mouth, str. . . . . 105 H d
Dragovitches, people . . . . 71 K c
Draguignan. . . . . 148 F f
Draheim. . . . . 123 I b
Drake, route of . . . . 107 C e
108 M k
109 I j
110 II f
Drake's Bay . . . . 107 E d
Drakenburg. . . . . 114 E b
Drakensberg, mts. . . . . 175 M l
Dramburg . . . . 85 D b
Drangiana, prov. . . . . 19 J d
Drangiana, satr. . . . . 8 K e
Drapsaca . . . . 19 K c
Drave River . . . . 63 I f
Dravus (Drave) River . . . . . . 38 E c
Dred Scott „dicta", see legend 207
Dreisam River . . . . 142 A e
Drenthe, cty. . . . . 117 E b
Drepanum, in Asia Minor . . .
Drepanum, in Sicily . . . . 30 B e
Drepanum, prom. . . . . 14 B a
Dresden . . . . 85 G e
Dreux . . . . 61 D b
Driesen . . . . 85 D b
Drilon River . . . . 17 B a
Drina River . . . . 89 G f
Drinus River . . . . 39 L l
Drissa . . . . 153 N f
Drišti, bp. . . . . 95 F c
Drobetæ . . . . 39 M l
Drogheda . . . .
Drohiczin . . . . 155 L b
Droitwich, parl. bor. . . . . 163 L e
Drokinsford, deanery . . . . . . 100 A b
Drôme, dept. . . . . 148 F f
Drömling, dist. . . . . 62 F b
Dromore, bp. . . . . 97 E b
Dromos, in Alexandria . . . . . 34 ins. C
Drübeck . . . . 122 F c
Druentia (Durance) River . . . 26 A c
Drummondville . . . . 212 H d
Drusi, Pons, bridge . . . . 27 F a
Drusus, Arch of . . . . 22 A
Drusus, Canal of . . . . 39 I h
Drymæa . . . . 11 D d
Dryopes, people. . . . . 15 E a
Dry Tortugas, isl. . . . . 213 D b
Dubaunt Lake . . . . 186 I b
Düben . . . . 123 G c
Dubienka . . . . 139 B e
Dubis (Doubs) River . . . . 39 I j
Dubitza . . . . 131 G d
Dublin . . . .
Dublin, abp. . . . . 97 E d
Dublin, cty. . . . . 127 K h
Dublin Bay . . . . 127 K h
Dubra, see Dubræ
Dubræ (Dover) . . . . 51 Q i
Dubrovna . . . . 153 O g
Dubuque . . . . 199 G b
Ducal Saxony . . . . 85 G d
Duck Valley, Ind. Res. . . . . . . 188 C b
Dudeldorf . . . . 117 E d
Duderstadt . . . . 62 F c
Dudinskœ . . . . 171 J b
Dudley, parl. bor. . . . . 163 L e
Duero (Douro) River . . . . . . 82 A a
Dufile . . . . 175 G d
Duisburg, in Belgium . . . . . . 50 D b
Duisburg, in Germany . . . . . . 62 D c
Duisburg, Hanse. cy. . . . . 99 ins. B
Dukla . . . . 159 K d

Dulcigno, bp. . . . . 95 F c
Dulcis Portus, bay . . . . 10 B c
Duluth . . . . 211 G a
Dumah. . . . . 7 B f
Dumbarton . . . .
Dumbarton, cty. . . . .
Dumbarton, dist. . . . .
Dumbrek, R. . . . .
Dumfries . . . .
Dumfries, cty. . . . .
Dumfries, reg. . . . .
Dumio, mon. . . . . 94 A c
Dummer, Fort . . . . 189 B c
Dumnonii, people . . . . 51 N i
Dünaburg . . . . 88 L c
Düna River . . . . 138 C d
Dunbar . . . .
Dunblaine, bp. . . . .
Duncansby Head . . . .
Dundalk . . . .
Dundalk Bay . . . . 127 K h
Dundee . . . .
Dundra Head, cape . . . .
Dunedin . . . . 172 G e
Dunfermline . . . .
Dung Gate, loc. in Jerusalem . 6 ins. A
Dunkeld . . . .
Dunkeld, bp. . . . . 97 J c
Dunkeswell, mon. . . . . 97 N k
Dunkirk . . . . 117 A c
Dunmow, Little, mon. . . . . . . 97 R j
Dunnottar Castle . . . .
Dunois, cty. . . . . 84 D e
Dunstable, castle
Dunstable, mon. . . . . 97 Q j
Dunstable, parl. bor. . . . .
Dunster, parl. bor. . . . .
Dunum, see Châteaudun
Dunwich . . . .
Dunwich, parl. bor. . . . . 163 P e
Düppel . . . . 158 E a
Duquesne, Fort . . . . 192 A c
Dura in Assyria . . . . 20 J e
Dura in Mesopotamia . . . . . . 20 I e
Durance River . . . . 69 F e
Durango . . . . 213 B b
Durango, prov. . . . . 190 D f
Durango, state . . . . 213 B b
Duranius (Dordogne) River . . . 38 C d
Durant's Neck, dist. . . . . 193 F c
Durazzo . . . . 42 F e
Durazzo, abp. . . . . 95 F c
Durban . . . . 175 N l
Durbuy . . . . 117 D d
Durham . . . .
Durham, battle . . . . 189 C c
Durham, bp. . . . . 97 P g
Durham, castle . . . . 65 F c
Durham, cty. . . . . 127 X l
Durham, palat. . . . .
Durham, shire . . . .
Duria Major (Dora Baltea) River 26 B b
Duria Minor River . . . . 26 B b
Dur-Ilu . . . . 5 D b
Durius (Douro) River . . . . . . 38 A d
Dur Kurigalzu . . . . 4 G c
Durlach . . . . 142 B c
Durnkrut . . . . 79 J d
Durnomagus . . . . 39 I h
Durnovaria (Dorchester) . . . . . 51 O i
Durobrivæ (Castor) . . . . 51 P h
Durobrivae (Rochester) . . . . . 51 Q i
Durocasses, see Dreux
Durocatalaunum, see Châlons
Durocornovium, see Corinium (Cirencester)
Durocortorum (Reims) . . . . . . 38 C c
Durolipons . . . .
Durostorum (Silistria) . . . . . . 39 N l
Durotriges, people . . . . 51 O i
Durovernum (Canterbury) . . . . 51 Q i
Dürrenstein, castle . . . . 72 D b
Dur-Samand, reg. . . . .
Dur-Sharukin (Khorsabad) . . . 5 D b

Düsseldorf . . . . 86 F c
Dutch Guiana . . . . 214 D b
Dutch Harbor . . . . 198 ins. A
Duxbury, in England . . . . 185 D d
Duxbury, in Mass. . . . . 189 C c
Dwara-Samudra . . . .
Dwina, Gulf . . . .
Dwina River . . . .
Dyea . . . . 212 ins.
Dyle River . . . . 62 C c
Dyme . . . . 14 B a
Dynevwor . . . .
Dyras River . . . . 16 E e
Dyrrhachium (Durazzo) . . . . . 31 I a
Dyrrhachium, theme . . . . 59 H e
Dyrta . . . . 19 L c
Dyscus . . . . 11 F d
Dysoron, mt. . . . . 11 E a

Eagle Pass . . . . 210 E e
East, Dioc. of the . . . . 43 J g
East, Pref. of the . . . . 43 I h
East Africa, British, col. . . . .
East Africa, German, col. . . . .
East Africa, Portuquese, col. . .
East Africa Company, German
East Africa Company, Imperial British . . . .
East Angles, people . . . . 51 S k
East Anglia, km. . . . .
East Anglia Heights . . . . 49 G e
East Cape, in Asia . . . . 171 T b
East Cape, in New Zealand . . 172 G d
Eastcheap, in London . . . . . . 75 G g
East Cornwall, parl. dist. . . . . 163 J g
East Cumberland, parl. dist. . . 163 L c
East Dennis . . . . 207 M b
Easter Island . . . . 180 Q j
Eastern Euphrates River . . . . 20 H c
Eastern Ghats, mts. . . . . 112 B b
Eastern Rumelia, prov. . . . . . 164 C b
Eastern Sea . . . . 171 N f
East Florida, col. . . . . 194 C de
East Franconia, duchy . . . . . . 62 E d
East Frankish Kingdom . . . . . 56 C b
East Friesland, cty. . . . . 122 D b
East Friesland, dist. . . . . 86 F b
East Friesland, princ. . . . . . . 134 D b
East Gloucester, parl. dist. . . . 163 L f
East Göthland, reg. . . . .
East Goths, Kingdom of the . . 52 D b
East Goths, people, in Asia Minor, in 382 . . . .
East Goths, people, on the Dnieper, in 200 . . . . 45 K c
East Goths, people, in Italy, in 493 45 G d
East Goths, people, in Pannonia, in 454 . . . . 45 H c
East Greenwich . . . . 189 ins. A
East Grinstead, parl. bor. . . . . 163 O f
Eastham . . . . 189 D d
Easthampton . . . . 189 B d
East Indies, reg. . . 109, 110 X-D D, e-h
East Kent, parl. dist. . . . . 163 O f
East London . . . . 175 M m
East Looe, parl. bor. . . . . 163 J g
East Main River . . . . 186 L c
East March, Bavarian . . . . . . 63 H d
East March, in Scotland . . . .
East Marches, in Northumberland . . . .
East New Jersey, col. . . . . . . 192 D c
East Norfolk, parl. dist. . . . . . 163 P e
Easton . . . . 192 D c
Eastphalia, dist. . . . . 62 F b
Eastphalians, people . . . . 55 R i
East Prussia, prov. . . . . 159 K a
East Prussia, reg. . . . . 135 K a
East Retfort, parl. dist. . . . . . 163 N d
East Riding, dist. . . . . 162 F d
East Riding, parl. dist. . . . . . 163 N d
East Roman Empire about 395 43
East Roman Empire in 486 50—51
East Roman Empire, 6 cent. . . 52

East Roman Empire, in 750 . . 53
East Saxons, people . . . . 51 R k
East Somerset, parl. dist. . . . . 163 L f
East Suffolk, parl. dist. . . . . 163 P e
East Surrey, parl. dist. . . . 163 N f (E.S.)
East Sussex, parl. dist. . . . . 163 O g
East Turkestan, reg. . . . . . . 170 I e
East Voorne, isl. . . . . 117 B c
East Worcester, parl. dist. . . . 163 L e
Eause (Eauze) . . . . 94 C c
Ebal, mt. . . . . 7 C d
Ebelsberg . . . . 155 H d
Ebenezer, in Georgia . . . . . . 193 ins. C
Ebenezer, in Judæa . . . . . . 7 B e
Eberbach . . . . 142 C b
Eberbach, mon. . . . . 95 D a
Ebernburg, castle . . . . 114 D d
Ebersberg, castle . . . . 63 F d
Eberstein, castle . . . . 142 B c
Eberstein, cty. . . . . 142 B c
Ebgate, in London . . . . 75 G g
Ebingen . . . . 143 H i
Eblana . . . . 34 C c
Eboracum or Eburacum (York in England) . . . . 51 P h
Ebrach, mon. . . . . 95 E b
Ebrodunum, see Embrun
Ebroicas, see Evreux
Ebro River . . . . 82 B a
Ebron . . . . 6 C c
Ebudae Islands (The Hebrides) 34 C b
Eburacum or Eboracum (York in England) . . . . 38 B b
Eburodunum (Embrum) . . . . . 26 A c
Eburodunum (Yverdon) . . . . . 39 I j
Eburones, people . . . . 39 H h
Eburovices, see Evreux
Eburovices, people . . . . 38 C c
Eburum . . . . 30 E b
Ebusus, isl. . . . . 38 C e
Ecbatana (Hamadan) . . . . 5 D b
Ecdippa . . . . 6 C b
Ecetra . . . . 30 C a
Echallens . . . . 91 O l
Echedamia . . . . 11 D d
Echedorus River . . . . 11 D b
Echinades, isl. . . . . 10 B d
Echinus . . . . 11 D d
Echternach . . . . 117 E e
Echternach, mon. . . . . 95 D b
Écija . . . . 82 A b
Eckernförde . . . . 158 F a
Ecnomus, mt. . . . . 30 C e
Ecolesima, see Angoulême
Ecuador, country . . . . 214 B c
Écuries, Grandes, in Versailles 149 A
Écuries, Petites, in Versailles . 149 A
Écuries de la Reine, in Versailles 149 A
Edam . . . . 117 D b
Edenton . . . . 193 F c
Edessa, in Macedonia . . . . . . 10 D b
Edessa, in Mesopotamia . . . . 20 H d
Edessa, cty. . . . . 68 C b
Edgartown . . . . 189 C d
Edgecote . . . . 84 C c
Edge Hill . . . . 49 F e
Edge Hill, village . . . . 127 X n
Edinburgh . . . .
Edinburgh, cty. . . . . . .
Edisto, Fort . . . . 193 ins. C
Edisto River . . . . 193 D e
Edmonton . . . . 212 D c
Edom, reg. . . . . 5 C b
Edomites, people . . . . 7 ins. D
Edones, people . . . . 11 E b
Edrei . . . . 6 E c
Edrisids, Dom. of the . . . . . . 83 E d
Edrum . . . . 26 E b
Edward, Fort . . . . 192 E b
Edward Augustus, Fort . . . . . 194 B b
Edward Nyanza, lake . . . . . . 175 G d
Edwards Ferry . . . . 208 ins.
Eetionea . . . . 16 D c
Eferding . . . . 123 G d
Eger . . . . 72 C a
Egerland, dist. . . . . 79 ins.
Eger River . . . . 63 G c
Egersund . . . . 166 G d
Egg Harbor, Little . . . . 192 D d
Eggmühl . . . . 154 G d
Egham . . . . 75 H i
Eghezée . . . . 156 B a
Egisheim . . . . 62 D d
Eglaim . . . . 7 D f
Eglingen . . . . 143 H i
Eglingen, lordship . . . . 143 J h
Eglisau, castle . . . . 91 Q k
Eglofs, cty. . . . . 143 I j
Eglon . . . . 7 B e
Egmond, castle . . . . 62 C b
Egmond, mon. . . . . 94 C a
Egnatia . . . . 31 G b
Egnatian Way . . . .
Egremont, parl. bor. . . . . . .
Egrigaia . . . .
Egypt, emp. . . . . 4 F d
Egypt, Rom. prov. . . . . 35 J h
Egypt, East Rom. dioc. . . . . . 43 H h
Egypt, East Rom. prov. . . . . . 43 I g (4)
Egypt, prov. 12 cent. . . . . . . 71 M h
Egypt, state . . . . 174 F b
Egypt, Port of . . . . 18 ins. B
Ehingen . . . . 143 I i
Ehnheim, Ober- . . . . 122 D d
Ehrenberger Klause Pass . . . . 114 F e
Ehrenbreitstein . . . . 122 D c
Eichsfeld, dist. . . . . 114 F c
Eichstädt . . . .
Eichstädt, bp. . . . .
Eider River . . . . 62 E a
Eiham, mon. . . . . 94 C a
Eilenburg . . . . 85 G e
Einbeck . . . . 114 F c
Einbeck, Hanse. cy. . . . . 99 ins. B
Eindhoven . . . . 117 D c
Einsiedeln, mon. . . . . 91 Q k
Eïon . . . . 11 E b
Eipel River . . . . 115 J d
Eisack River . . . . 62 F e
Eisenach . . . . 85 F e
Eisenberg . . . . 115 ins. B
Eisenburg . . . . 123 I e
Eiserntor Pass . . . . 159 L f
Eisleben . . . . 114 F c
Eislingen . . . . 143 I h
Ekaterinburg . . . . 138 J d
Ekaterinodar . . . . 167 M g
Ekaterinoslav . . . . 139 D f
Ekron (Akir) . . . . 7 B e
Elæa . . . . 10 B c
Elæatis, reg. . . . . 10 B c
Elæum, mt. . . . . 14 B b
Elæus, in Ætolia . . . . 10 C d
Elæus, in Argolis . . . . 14 C b
Elæus, in Epirus . . . . 10 B b
Elæus, in Thrace . . . .
Elæussa Island . . . . 16 B b
Elam, reg. . . . . 4 G c
Elandslaagte . . . . 175 N l
El Araish . . . . 118 C f
El Arish . . . .
Elatea, in Bœotia . . . . 11 D d
Elath . . . . 5 C c
Elatia . . . . 11 D c
Elatria . . . . 10 B c
Elatus, mt. . . . . 14 A b
Elaver (Allier) River . . . . . . 38 C c
Elba, isl. . . . . 90 L j
Elbassan . . . .
Elbe River . . . . 62 F b
Elberfeld . . . . 158 D c
Elbeuf . . . . 76 D b
Elbing . . . . 72 D a
Elbing, Hanse. cy. . . . . 98 G c
Elbruz, mt. . . . . 3 I d
Elburg . . . . 117 D b
Elburg, Hanse. cy. . . . . 99 ins. B
Elburz Mountains . . . . 3 J e
Elcano, route of . . . . 109 W k
Elche . . . . 82 B b
Elchingen, ab. . . . . 143 J i
Elchingen, mon. . . . . 143 J i
Eldena, mon. . . . . 80 C e
Elea . . . . 30 E b
Elealah . . . . 7 D e
Electoral Archchancellor, Ter. of the . . . . 151 H f (E.A.)
Electoral Hesse, state . . . . . . 158 E c
Electoral Saxony, state . . . . . 85 G d
Electorates, The Seven . . . . . 78 leg.
Elen . . . . 214 B c
Eleon . . . . 11 E d
Elephantine Island (Gezeret-Assuan) . . . . 4 F d
Eleusinian Gulf . . . . 16 B a
Eleusis (Levsina) . . . . 15 D a
Eleutheræ . . . . 15 D a
Eleuthernæ . . . . 14 ins.
Eleutheropolis . . . . 7 B e
Eleutherus River . . . . 30 C e
El Fasher . . . . 174 F c
Elgin . . . .
Elgin, bp. . . . . 97 J b
Elgin, cty. . . . .
El Golea . . . . 174 D a
El Gran Chaco, region . . . . . 215 C e
El Hasa, reg. . . . .
El Hejas, Hedjaz, reg. . . . . . . 170 E f
Elim . . . . 68 C d
Elimea . . . . 10 C b
Elimea, reg. . . . . 10 C b
Elis . . . . 14 B b
Elis, reg. . . . . 14 B b
Elis, state . . . . 13 B c
Elizabetgrad . . . . 167 L f
Elizabeth . . . . 192 D c
Elizabeth, Cape . . . . 189 C c
Elizabethtown . . . . 192 D c
El Jesireh, reg. . . . . 67 O f
El Kantara . . . . 174 K i
El Katif . . . .
Elk River . . . . 192 A d
Elkton . . . . 195 C d
El Kufa . . . . 73 I d
Ellesmere . . . . 162 D e
Ellesmere Land . . . . 186 K a
Ellice Islands . . . . 172 G a
Ellichpur . . . . 137 C d
Ellingham, mon. . . . . 100 A b
Ellomenon . . . . 10 B d
Ellwangen . . . . 143 J h
Ellwangen, mon. . . . . 95 E b
Ellwangen, provostry . . . . 143 J h
El-Mahdiya . . . . 73 C c
Elmet, Forest of . . . . 49 F e
Elmet, dist. . . . .
Elmham . . . .
Elmina . . . .
Elmira . . . . 195 C b
Elne, bp. . . . . 94 C c
El Obeid . . . . 174 F c
Elosa or Elusa, see Eause (Eauze)
El Pardo, castle . . . . 130 C e
El Paso . . . . 190 D e
El Paso del Norte . . . . 213 B a
Elphin, bp. . . . . 97 C c
Elsfleth . . . . 122 E b
Elsing Spital, bldg. in London . 75 G g
Elster, Schwarze, river . . . . . 85 G e
Elster, Weisse, river . . . . . . 85 G e
Elstow, mon. . . . . 97 Q i
El Teb . . . . 174 G c
Eltham . . . . 75 J i
Eltville . . . . 78 F c
Elusa, in France, see Eause (Eauze)
Elusa, in Palestine . . . . 7 B f
Elvas . . . . 82 A b
El Viejo . . . . 213 D c
Elvira . . . . 42 B f
Ely, in England . . . .
Ely, in India . . . .
Ely, bp. . . . . 97 R i

Ely, Isle of, dist.
Ely, parl. bor.
El Yemamah
Elymæi, people 19 G d
Elymi, people 30 B e
Elymia 14 C b
Elymians, people
Ely Place, loc. in London 75 G g
Elz River 142 A d
Elzach 142 B d
Emathia, reg. 11 D b
Embrun 69 G d
Embrun, abp. 95 D c
Emden 78 E b
Emerita Augusta (Mérida) 38 A e
Emesa 35 L g
Emilia, dist. 90 C b
Emly, bp. 97 C d
Emmaus 7 B e
Emmendingen 142 A d
Emmerich, in Germany 122 D c
Emmerich, in Transylvania 119 I d
Emmetsburg 208 ins.
Emona (Laibach) 27 I a
Emperador
Empire, The 81 H c
Empire of the French 155 ins.
Empire of the Sultans of Delhi
Emporiæ 38 C d
Emporium, loc. in Rome 22 A
Emporium, in Spain 12 D b
Empulum 35 ins. B
Ems 134 D c
Ems River 62 D b
Enaghdune, bp.
Enchelei, people 31 I a
Encounter Bay 172 C d
Endicott Range 186 D b
Endidæ 27 F a
Endor 6 C c
En-Eglaim 7 C e
Engadine, valley 91 S l
Enganna 7 D d
Engannim 7 C d
Engaño, Cape 171 N g
Engaño, Punta del, cape 107 F e
Engeddi 7 C f
Engelberg, mon. 91 Q l
Engen 142 C e
Enghien 117 C d
England, km. 66 F c
English, people
English Channel 2 D d
English Grants in North America 190 ins.
English Kingdom, 9 cent. 56 B b
English Marches, dist.
English Mercia, reg.
English Northumbria, km.
English Pale, The, dist.
English River 212 F c
English Turn, loc. on Miss. R. 191 H f
Engstingen 143 H i
Engyum 30 D e
Enipeus River, in Elis 14 B b
Enipeus River, in Macedonia 11 D b
Enipeus River, in Thessaly 11 D c
Enkhuizen 117 D b
Enkhuizen, Hanse. cy. 99 ins. B
Enna 72 C d
En-Nasirah 150 C a
Enniskillen 127 J g
Enns 115 H d
Enns River 63 H e
Enos 165 E c
Enschede 117 E b
Ensisheim 86 F e
Entella 30 C e
Entre Minho e Douro, reg. 83 J g
Entre Rios, prov., in Argentina 215 D f (E. R.)
Entre Tejo e Guadiana, reg. 83 J h
Enzberg, lordship 143 G i
Enzheim 122 D d
Enz River 143 H h
Eordæa, reg. 10 C b
Eordaïcus River 10 B b
Eordi, people
Epamantodurum
Eperies 159 K d
Épernay 69 I f
Épernay, mon. 94 C b
Ephesus 17 E c
Ephraim, Gate of 6 ins. A
Ephraim, mt. 7 C d
Ephraim, tribe 7 ins. D
Ephrata 192 C c
Ephyra, in Elis 14 B b
Ephyra, in Epirus 10 B c
Ephyra, isl., near Melos 15 E c
Ephyra, isl., near Argolis 15 C b
Epidamnus (Durazzo) 12 G b
Epidaurum 38 F d
Epidaurus, in Argolis 15 D b
Epidaurus Limera 15 D c
Epidelium, prom. 15 D c
Epila 83 K g
Épinal 78 E d
Épinal, mon. 95 D b
Épineuil 69 I g
Epiphania 20 G e
Epipolæ, quarter in Syracuse 31 ins. B
Epirus, country 10 B b
Epirus, desp., 13 cent. 73 E c
Epirus, desp., 15 cent. 93 B c
Epirus, Rom. prov. 35 I f
Epirus, state 13 B b
Epirus nova, East Rom. prov. 43 G e(5)
Epirus vetus, East Rom. prov. 43 G f(4)
Epitalium 14 B b
Epium 14 B b
Epizephyrii, Locri 31 F d
Epoissum 39 H i
Epopeus, mt. 30 C b
Eporedia (Ivrea) 26 B b
Eppenstein, castle 63 H e
Eppingen 142 C b
Epping Forest 49 F f
Epsom 75 I i
Epternacus, see Echternach
Epworth, mon. 97 Q h
Equatorial Provinces under Emin Pascha 1878—1889 174 F d
Equius
Erasinus River, in Arcadia 14 C b
Erasinus River, in Attica 16 C b
Eratyra 10 C b
Erbach, in Hesse 142 C a
Erbach, in Wurtemberg 143 I i
Erbstetten 143 I i
Ercavica
Erchia 16 B b
Ercte, mt. 30 C d
Erechtheum
Eresburg, stronghold 55 Q i
Eretria, in Eubœa 11 E d
Eretria, in Thessaly 11 D c
Eretum 27 G e
Erfurt 62 F c
Erfurt, mon. 95 E a
Erfurt, univ. 100 H d
Ergines River
Erginul, Erginur
Ergitium 30 E a
Ericinium 10 D c
Ericussa, isl. 30 D d
Eridanus River, see Po River
Eridu (Abu Shahrein) 4 G c
Erie 199 I b
Erie, Fort 200 D b
Erie, lake 187 K d
Erie Canal 211 J b
Eries, tribe 188 J b
Erigon River 10 C b
Erineus, in Achaia 14 B a
Erineus, in Doris 11 D d
Erith 75 J i
Eritium 10 D c
Eritrea, Italian col. 174 G c
Erivan
Erivan, reg.
Erlach, castle 91 P k
Erlangen 122 F d
Erlau 77 I c
Erlau, bp. 95 G b
Ermeland, reg. 87 M a
Ermeland, bp. 115 K a
Ermes 88 K c
Ermine Street, road 51 P g
Erms River 143 H h
Ernage 156 B a
Erolzheim 143 J i
Erpisfurt, see Erfurt
Er Riad
Er Rimmon 7 B f
Erstein, castle 62 D d
Eryces River 30 D e
Erymanthus mt. 14 B b
Erymanthus River 14 B b
Erythræ, in Ionia 13 E b
Erythræ, in Locris 10 D d
Eryx 30 B d
Erzerum 71 O f
Erzgebirge, mts., in Germany 2 F c
Erz Gebirge, mts., in Hungary 159 J d
Erzinjan 77 L e
Escalante, route of 190 C d
Escambia River 193 ins. B
Escaut River, see Scheldt River
Esch 117 D e
Eschwege 62 E c
Escondido, Rio 105 D d
Escorial, San Lorenzo del, mon. 94 B c
Escurial, see Escorial
Esdrælon
Eshcol, vale 7 C e
Esher 75 I i
Eskishehr 164 E c
Esmeraldas 214 B b
Esmeraldas River 111 A a
Esmûn, Temple of 34 ins. A (5)
Esopus 192 D c
Española, isl. 105 F c
Esparza 213 D d
Espinhaço, Serra do, mts. 214 E d
Espinosa 130 C e
Espinosa, route of 105 D e
Espirito Santo 214 E e
Espirito Santo, state 214 E d
Espiritu Santo, isl. 172 F b
Espiritu Santo, Rio del (Mobile R.) 107 I d
Esplechin 81 M g
Esquiliæ, Aug. Reg. of Rome 22 A
Esquiline, quarter 96 A
Esquiline Gate 22 A
Esquiline Mount 22 A
Esquimalt 212 C d
Es-Salihiyeh 150 B a
Esseg
Essen 158 D c
Essen, mon. 95 D a
Essequibo River 214 D b
Essex, cty.
Essex, km.
Essex, shire
Essington, Port 212 ins.
Essling 155 I d
Esslingen, imp. city 143 H h
Este 90 J h
Este, duchy 90 C b
Estella 82 H e
Esthonia, reg., 9 cent. 55 I c
Esthonia, reg., 14 cent. 88 K b
Esthonians, people 59 I b
Estoy 82 A b
Estremadura, reg. 83 J h
Estrun, mon. 94 C a
Etalle 117 D e
Etam 7 C e
Étampes 76 E b
Etawah 170 I f
Etchemins, tribe 188 M a

Eteocretes, people . . . . 14 ins.
Ether . . . .
Ethiopia, reg., Egyptian emp. . 4 F d
Ethiopia, reg., Sudan . . . . . . 109 S U g
Etna, mt. . . . . 36 E e
Étoges . . . . 154 C d
Étoile, L', mon. . . . . 94 C b
Eton . . . . 75 H i
Etropol . . . . 164 C b
Etruria, Aug. Reg. . . . . 38 E d (7)
Etruria, reg. . . . . 27 F d
Etruscans, people . . . .
Ettenheim . . . . 142 A d
Ettenheimmünster, mon. . . . . 142 A d
Ettlingen . . . . 142 B c
Etymander River . . . . 19 J d
Eu . . . . 61 D a
Eu, cty. . . . . 76 D a
Eubœa (Negropont), isl. . . . . . 4 B b
Eubœa, state . . . . 13 C b
Euboic Gulf . . . . 11 E d
Eudemia, isl. . . . . 11 F c
Euenus River . . . . 10 C d
Eufratensis, E. Rom. prov. . . . 43 J f (9)
Euganei, people . . . . 26 E b
Eugubium, see Gubbio
Euhydrium . . . . 11 D c
Eumenes, Stoa of . . . . 23 C
Eumenia . . . . 20 C c
Eunostus, Portus . . . . 34 ins. C
Euonymus, isl. . . . . 30 E d
Eupalium . . . . 10 C d
Eupatoria, in Crimea . . . . . . 139 D f
Eupatoria, in Pontus . . . . . . 33 U h
Euphrates River . . . . 18 F d
Eupilis, lake . . . . 26 D b
Euporia . . . . 11 E b
Eure, dept. . . . . 148 E e
Eure-et-Loir, dept . . . . 148 E e
Euripus, strait . . . . 11 E d
Eurœa . . . . 10 B c
Europe, continent . . . . . . 2—3, 166—167
Europe, E. Rom. prov. . . . . . 43 H e (1)
Europus, in Almopia . . . . . . 10 D b
Europus, in Emathia . . . . 11 D a
Europus, in Syria . . . . 52 L f
Europus River . . . . 10 D c
Eurotas (Iri) River . . . . 14 C b
Euryalus . . . . 31 ins. B
Eurychorus . . . . 18 ins. B
Eurymedon River . . . . 20 D d
Eurymenæ . . . . 11 D c
Eurytanes, people . . . . 10 C d
Eutæa . . . . 14 C b
Eutaw Springs, battle . . . . . 195 A g
Eutin . . . . 114 F a
Eutresia, reg. . . . . 14 C b
Evangelista, isl. . . . . 105 D b
Evansville . . . . 208 C b
Evaux . . . . 126 C c
Everest, mt. . . . . 171 J f
Everglades, The, swamp . . . . 191 I f
Evesham . . . . 127 X n
Evesham, mon. . . . . 97 P i
Evesham, parl. bor. . . . . 163 M e
Evora . . . . 82 A b
Evora, abp. . . . . 94 A d
Évreux . . . . 61 D b
Évreux, bp. . . . . 94 C b
Évreux, cty. . . . . 76 D b
Evron, mon. . . . . 94 B b
Ewell . . . . 75 I i
Exarchate of Italy . . . . 53 D b
Exeter, in England . . . . 127 V p
Exeter, bp. . . . . 97 N k
Exeter, castle . . . . 65 E e
Exeter, parl. bor. . . . . 163 K g
Exeter, in New Hampshire . . . 189 C c
Exeter, in Rhode Island . . . . 189 ins. A
Exilles . . . . 126 E d
Exmes . . . . 76 D b
Exmoor . . . . 49 E f
Eyach River . . . . 143 G i
Eydtkuhnen . . . . 159 L a
Eye, mon. . . . . 97 S i
Eye, parl. bor. . . . . 163 P e
Eyerland, isl. . . . . 117 C a
Eylau . . . . 155 K a
Eynesford . . . . 75 J i
Eynsham, mon. . . . . 97 P j
Eyoub, mosque . . . .
Eyoub, quarter . . . .
Eyre, lake . . . . 172 C c
Eyre Peninsula . . . . 172 C d
Eyre River . . . . 172 C c
Ezion-Geber . . . . 5 C c

Fabrateria nova . . . . 30 C a
Fabrician Bridge . . . . 22 A
Faenza . . . . 90 J h
Faenza, bp. . . . . 95 E c
Fæsulæ (Fiesole) . . . . 27 F d
Fagifulæ . . . . 30 D a
Fagundes, route of . . . . 108 L c
Fagutal . . . . 22 A
Fairfax . . . . 208 ins.
Fairfield, in Conn. . . . . 192 E c
Fairfield, in Pa. . . . . 208 ins.
Fair Oaks, battle . . . . . . 208 E b (F. O.)
Fairweather, mt. . . . . 212 ins.
Faizabad . . . . 137 D c
Fajardo . . . . 199 ins. G
Faknur . . . .
Falaise . . . . 65 F f
Falempin, mon. . . . . 94 C a (Fal.)
Falerii . . . . 27 G e
Falerio . . . . 27 H d
Falernian District . . . . 30 D a
Falesia . . . . 26 E e
Falkenstein, castle . . . . 62 E d
Falkirk . . . .
Falkland Islands . . . . 215 D h
Fallen Timber, battle . . . . . . 196 ins. B
Falling Creek . . . . 193 F c
Falling Waters, falls . . . . . . 208 ins.
Falls of the Ohio . . . . 193 B b
Falmouth, in Maine . . . . . . 189 C c
Falmouth, in Virginia . . . . . . 192 C d
Falmouth, parl. bor. . . . . . . 163 J g
Falster, isl. . . . . 114 F a
Falsterbo, Hanse. for. cy. . . . 98 F b
Falun . . . . 88 F a
Famagusta . . . . 68 B b
Famine, La . . . . 192 C b
Fanestris, Julia . . . . 27 H d
Fang-shan . . . . 170 ins. A
Fanning Island . . . . 180 L g
Fano . . . . 90 M j
Fano, bp. . . . . 95 E c
Fansur . . . .
Fanum or Fanum Fortunæ (Fano) 27 H d
Farah . . . .
Farama . . . . 99 J g
Farentia . . . . 27 F c
Farewell, Cape . . . . 186 O c
Farfa . . . . 64 ins.
Farfa, mon. . . . . 96 B a
Fargo . . . . 210 F a
Farmington . . . . 192 E c
Farnborough . . . . 75 J i
Farnham, parl. bor. . . . .
Farningham . . . . 75 J i
Farnsburg, castle . . . . 91 P k
Faro . . . . 82 A b
Faroe Islands . . . . 2 D b
Farquhar Island . . . . 182 G G i
Fars, reg. . . . .
Farsan Islands . . . . 170 F g
Farther India, reg. . . . .
Farther Pomerania, dist. . . . . 123 H b
Farther Rhine River . . . . 91 R l
Farther Spain, prov. . . . . . . 38 A e (3)
Fasher, El- . . . . 174 F c
Fashoda . . . . 174 G c
Fatimite, dynasty, about 1097 . 67 M g
Fatimites, Dom. of the, about 1000 58 D F f
Faubourg du Temple, quarter in Paris . . . . 149 B
Faubourg Montmartre, quarter in Paris . . . . 149 B
Faubourg Saint Antoine, quarter in Paris . . . . 149 B
Faubourg Saint Denis, quarter in Paris . . . . 149 B
Faubourg Saint Germain, quarter in Paris . . . . 149 B
Faubourg Saint Honoré, quarter in Paris . . . . 149 B
Faubourg Saint Honoré, Rue du, street in Paris . . . . 149 B
Faubourg Saint Jacques, quarter in Paris . . . . 149 B
Faubourg Saint Marcel, quarter in Paris . . . . 149 B
Faubourg Saint Martin, quarter in Paris . . . . 149 B
Faubourg Saint Michel, quarter in Paris . . . . 149 B
Faubourg Saint Victor, quarter in Paris . . . . 149 B
Faucigny . . . . 130 O h
Fauresmith . . . . 175 L l
Faustina, Temple of . . . .
Faventia, see Faenza
Faverney, mon. . . . . 95 D b
Faversham, mon. . . . . 97 R j
Faversham, parl. bor. . . . . . .
Favianæ . . . . 50 G c
Faxa Fiord . . . . 166 A c
Fayetteville, in N. Carolina . . 193 E d
Fayetteville, in Pa. . . . . 208 ins.
Fayum, reg. . . . . 4 ins.
Fear, Cape . . . . 191 J e
Fécamp . . . . 65 G f
Fécamp mon. . . . . 94 C b
Fecht River . . . . 143 ins. D
Feder, lake . . . . 143 I i
Fehmern, isl. . . . . 114 F a
Fehrbellin . . . . 123 G b
Feldkirch . . . . 78 F e
Felicitas Julia . . . . 38 A e
Felsina . . . . 27 F c
Feltre . . . . 63 F e f
Feltre, bp. . . . . 95 E b
Feltria (Feltre) . . . . 27 F a
Fenestrelle . . . . 126 E d
Fenni, people . . . . 35 I a
Fens, The, dist. . . . . 49 F e
Feodosia . . . . 89 E b
Ferdi, see Verden
Fère-Champenoise . . . . 154 B d
Ferentinian Grove . . . . 35 ins. B (4)
Ferentino . . . . 72 C c
Ferentinum, in Etruria . . . . . 27 G e
Ferentinum, in Latium . . . . . 30 C a
Ferghana, reg. . . . .
Ferlech . . . .
Fermanagh, cty. . . . . 127 J g
Fermo . . . . 90 D c
Fermo, bp. . . . . 95 E c
Fernandina . . . . 208 D c
Fernandina, isl. . . . . 105 F b
Fernando Noronha Island . . . 214 F c
Fernando Po, isl. . . . . 175 D d
Ferns, bp. . . . . 97 E d
Feronia . . . . 27 G e
Ferrara . . . . 90 J h
Ferrara, bp. . . . . 95 E c
Ferrara, duchy, 15 cent. . . . . 90 C b
Ferrara, univ. . . . . 100 H f
Ferraria, see Ferrara
Ferrières, mon. . . . . 94 C b
Ferro, Bay of . . . . 118 C e
Ferryland . . . . 212 J d
Ferté-sur-Grône, La, mon. . . . 94 C b
Fertur River . . . . 30 D a
Feuillants, The, mon. in Paris 149 B
Feurs . . . . 76 F d
Fez . . . . 70 E g
Fez, state . . . . 118 C g
Fezensac, dist. . . . . 126 B e
Fezenzac, cty. . . . . 69 D e (Fez)

Fezzan, Oases of 2 F f
Fezzan, reg. 174 E b
Ficulea 35 ins. B
Fidenæ 27 G f
Fidentia 26 E c
Field of Blood, loc. near Jerusalem 6 ins. A
Fierbois 76 D c
Fiesole 52 J e
Fiesole, bp. 95 E c
Fife, cty.
Figeac 126 C d
Figig 174 C a
Fiji Islands 172 G b
Filehne 155 I b
Filles Saint Thomas, mon. in Paris 149 B
Fillmore City 206 C c
Fils River 143 I h
Fines, near Divodurum 39 H i
Fines, Ad-, near Florentia 27 F d
Fingoland, reg. 175 M m
Finisterre, Cape 83 J g
Finistère, dept. 148 D e
Finland, Gulf of 138 C d
Finland, prov. 167 K c
Finland, reg. 138 C c
Finns, people 138 B c
Finow Canal 123 G b
Finsbury, parl. bor. 163 N f (Finsb.)
Finstermünz 134 F e
Fiorentino, castle 72 D c
Firebr
Fire Lands, dist. 196 ins. B
Firenzuola 90 L i
Firmanum, Castellum 27 H d
Firmum (Fermo) 27 H d
Firozabad 170 I f
Fiscannum, see Fécamp
Fischa River 63 I d e
Fischbach 142 B d
Fischhausen 80 F d
Fischingen, mon. 91 Q k
Fiscellus, mt. 27 H e
Fisher, Fort 208 E c
Fisher's Hill, battle 208 E b
Fish Gate 6 ins. A
Fish River. Great 175 M m
Fitchburg 207 L b
Fitero, mon. 94 B c
Fitzgeralds, The, fam.
Fitzroy River 172 B b
Fiume 135 H f
Five Forks, battle 208 E b
Fivizzano 90 C b
Fixtuinum, see Meaux, in France
Fladungen 62 E c
Flamborough
Flamenco Island
Fläming, mts. 80 ins.
Flaminia and Picenum Annonarium, West. Rom. prov. 42 E e (4)
Flaminian Circus 24 A
Flaminian Circus, Aug. Reg. of Rome 22 A
Flaminian Gate 22 A
Flaminian Way, road 27 G e
Flaminian Way, Old, road 27 G e
Flanders, cty. 61 E a
Flanders, duchy, about 1000 58 E c
Flanders, prov. 148 E d
Flanders and Artois, gen. 147 E a
Flanders and Hainaut, gouv. 146 B a
Flandrina
Flanola, Gulf of. 27 I c
Flanona 27 I b
Flarchheim 62 F c
Flatbush 189 ins. C
Flathead Post 210 C a
Flatheads, tribe 188 C a
Flatlands 189 ins. C
Flattery, Cape 186 G d
Flatow 79 J b
Flavia Cæsariensis, West. Rom. prov. 42 B c (5)
Flaviæ, Aræ 39 J i
Flavian Amphitheatre 24 B
Flavian Canal 27 G c
Flavian Way, road 27 H b
Flavigny, mon. 94 C b
Flaviobriga 38 B d
Fleet River, in London 75 G g
Fleet Street, in London 75 G g
Flensborg, Hanse. for. cy.
Flensburg 86 G a
Fleurus 156 B b
Fleury, mon. 94 C b
Flevo, lake (Zuider Zee) 39 H g
Flinders Range 172 C d
Flinders River 172 D b
Flinders Island 172 D d
Flint, cty. 127 V m
Flint, parl. bor. 163 K d
Flint, parl. dist. 163 K d
Flint River 193 B f
Flochberg, castle 72 C b
Flodden 118 D b
Flora, Temple of 23 B
Florence, in Alabama 211 H d
Florence, in Italy 64 B b
Florence, abp. 95 E c
Florence, rep. 90 M j
Florence, univ. 100 H f (Fl.)
Florentia (Florence, in Italy) 27 F d
Florentiola 26 D c
Flores 213 C c
Flores, isl. 112 F d
Flores Sea 172 B a
Floriacus, see Fleury
Florianopolis 215 E e
Florida 215 D f
Florida, Cape 191 I f
Florida, pen. 187 K f
Florida, col. 191 I e f
Florida, state 211 I e
Florida, Straits of 187 L f
Florida, ter. 203 V d
Florida, East, col. 194 C d e
Florida, West, col. 194 B d
Floyd, Camp 210 C b
Fluela Pass 91 R l
Flüelen 91 Q l
Fluorn 123 F i
Flushing, in Holland 117 B c
Flushing, in New York 189 ins. C
Flusor River 27 H d
Fobbing 98 ins. A
Fogaras 159 M f
Foggia 90 E d
Foggia Nuova 99 I f
Foligno, bp. 95 E c
Foix 61 D e
Foix, cty. 76 D e
Foix, gouv. 146 B c
Foix, prov. 148 E f
Fokchani 131 I d
Fo-kien, prov. 171 M f
Földvar 159 J e
Foligno 90 D c
Fond du Lac, Ind. Res. 188 H a
Fondi 90 D d
Fondi, bp. 95 E c
Fontainebleau 126 C b
Fontaine de Bèze, La, mon. 95 D b
Fontaine Française 126 D c
Fontanelle, mon. 94 C b (St. Van.)
Fontenay, in Auxerrois 56 C c
Fontenay, in Poitou 69 C c
Fontenay, castle 76 C c
Fontenay, mon. 94 B b (Font.)
Fontenay-le-Comte 84 C f
Fontenay, seign. 69 C c
Fontenoy, near Tournay 134 B a
Fontevrault 69 H g
Fontevrault, mon. 94 B b
Font-Marigny, mon. 94 C b
Fontus, Gate of
Foo-chau 92 M e
Foot Hills 187 L e
Forbach 142 B c
Forcalquier 69 F e
Forcalquier, cty. 69 F d
Forchheim 55 R j
Forchheim, mon. 95 E b
Ford, mon. 97 O k
Fordingbridge, deanery 100 A b
Fordingbridge, hospital 100 A b
Forentum 30 E b
Forest Cantons, Three 91 S k
Forez, cty. 61 F d
Forfar, cty.
Forli, in Romagna 90 C b
Forli, bp., in Romagna 95 E c
Forli, bp., in Venetia 95 E b
Forlimpopoli, bp. 95 E c (F.)
Formentera, isl. 83 L h
Formiæ 30 C a
Formigny 76 C b
Formio River 27 H b
Formosa, isl. 171 N f
Formosa Bay 175 H e
Fornix Fabianus 24 A
Fornovo 90 B b
Forest, routes of 172 leg.
Fors Fortuna, Temple of 22 A
Fort Adams, in Miss. 199 G d
Fort Adams, in Ohio 196 ins. B
Fort Albany 212 G c
Fort Albuquerque 214 D d
Fortaleza 214 F c
Fort Amsterdam (New York) 189 ins. C
Fort Anne 192 E b
Fort Argyle 193 ins. C
Fort Arkansas 191 G e
Fort Armstrong, in Illinois 211 G b
Fort Armstrong, in Pa. 195 B c
Fort Atkinson 210 F b
Fort Augusta, in Georgia 193 C e
Fort Augusta, in Pa. 192 C c
Fort Bard 150 D d
Fort Beauharnais 191 G c
Fort Bedford 192 B c
Fort Belknap, Ind. Res. 188 D a
Fort Benton 198 C a
Fort Berthold, Ind. Res. 188 F a
Fort Beversrede 192 ins.
Fort Boisé 198 B a
Fort Bonneville 210 C b
Fort Brady 211 H a
Fort Bridger 210 C b
Fort Brown 201 F d
Fort Buford 210 E a
Fort Bull 192 D b
Fort Bute 195 ins. B
Fort Calhoun 210 F b
Fort Caroline 191 I e
Fort Casimir 192 ins.
Fort Caswell 208 E c
Fort Chambly 189 B b
Fort Charlotte 195 ins. B
Fort Chartres 191 G d
Fort Chequamegon
Fort Chippewyan 212 D c
Fort Chiswell 193 D c
Fort Christanna 193 F c
Fort Christina 192 ins.
Fort Churchill 212 F c
Fort Claiborne 200 I f
Fort Clark 210 E a
Fort Clatsop 210 A a
Fort Clinton, near Saratoga 192 E b
Fort Clinton, near West Point 195 D c
Fort Colville 198 B a
Fort Craven 192 D b
Fort Crawford 211 G b
Fort Crèvecœur 191 H c
Fort Cumberland 192 B d
Fort Dauphin
Fort Dearborn 199 H b
Fort de la Présentation 192 D a
Fort Defiance 196 ins. B
Fort d'Huillier 191 G c
Fort Diego 193 D f

Fort Dobbs 193 D d
Fort Dodge 210 E c
Fort Donelson 208 C b
Fort do Principe da Beira 214 C d
Fort Dummer 189 B c
Fort Duquesne 192 A c
Fort Edisto 193 ins. C
Fort Edward 192 C b
Fort Edward Augustus 194 B b
Fort Erie 196 D b
Fort Fisher 208 E c
Fort Frédéric 192 E a
Fort Frederick 192 C d
Fort Frontenac 192 C a
Fort Gaines, in Alabama 208 C c
Fort Gaines, in Minnesota 211 G a
Fort George, in Canada 200 D b
Fort George, in Maine 189 D c
Fort George, in New York 192 E b
Fort Good Hope 212 C b
Fort Gibson 211 G c
Fort Granby 195 A g
Fort Granville 192 C c
Fort Gratiot 211 I b
Fort Greenville 196 ins. B
Fort Griswold 195 F c
Forth, Firth of 49 E c
Fort Hall 198 C b
Fort Hall, Ind. Res. 188 D b
Fort Halifax 189 D b
Fort Harmar 196 ins. B
Fort Hatteras 208 E b
Fort Henry 208 C b
Fort Herkimer 192 D b
Fort Howard 211 H b
Fort Independence 195 E a
Fort Jackson, in Louisiana 208 C d
Fort Jackson, in Mississippi 200 I f
Fort James
Fort Kaministiquia 191 G b
Fort Kearney 210 F b
Fort Kenai 198 ins. A
Fort King George 193 C f
Fort La Baye 191 H c
Fort Lac Pepin
Fort La Gallette 192 D a
Fort La Jonquière 190 C a
Fort Lamotte 189 B b
Fort Langley 210 A a
Fort Laramie 198 E b
Fort La Reine 190 F b
Fort L'Assomption 194 B c
Fort Leavenworth 198 F c
Fort Le Bœuf 192 A c
Fort Lee 195 D c
Fort Lévis 192 D a
Fort Liard 212 C b
Fort Ligonier 192 B c
Fort Lisa 210 F b
Fort Loudoun, in Pa. 192 B d
Fort Loudoun, in Tennessee 193 B d
Fort Louis 154 D d
Fort Lupton 210 E c
Fort Loyal 189 D c
Fort Mac Allister 208 D c
Fort Mac Henry 200 L h
Fort Mackinac 194 C a
Fort Mac Murray 212 D c
Fort Macon 208 E c
Fort Macpherson 212 B b
Fort Madison 199 G b
Fort Madison, Ind. Res. 188 B a
Fort Malden 200 B b
Fort Mandan 210 E a
Fort Manuel 210 D a
Fort Massac 194 B c
Fort Maurepas, in Mississippi 191 H e
Fort Maurepas, on L. Winnipeg 191 F a
Fort Meigs 200 B c
Fort Mercer 195 D d
Fort Miami 196 ins. B
Fort Mifflin 195 D d
Fort Mims 200 I f
Fort Mitchell 211 H d
Fort Mohave 188 D c
Fort Moore 193 ins. C
Fort Morgan 208 C c
Fort Moritz 214 F d
Fort Moultrie 195 B g
Fort Nassau, in New Jersey 191 K d
Fort Nassau, in New York 192 E b
Fort Necessity 192 B d
Fort Nelson 212 C b
Fort New Elfsborg 192 ins.
Fort New Gothenburg 192 ins.
Fort New Korsholm 192 ins.
Fort New Wasa 192 ins.
Fort Niagara 192 B b
Fort Nicholson 192 E b
Fort Nipigon 191 H b
Fort Nisqually 210 A a
Fort Norman 212 C b
Fort Okanagan 210 B a
Fort Ontario 192 C b
Fort Orange 192 D b
Fort Orleans 191 G d
Fortore River, see Frento River
Fort Osage 211 G c
Fort Oswegatchie 196 D b
Fort Oswego 192 C b
Fort Ouiatanon 191 H c
Fort Panmure 194 A d
Fort Peck, Ind. Res. 188 E a
Fort Pejepscort 189 C b
Fort Pentagöet 189 D b
Fort Pickens 208 C c
Fort Picolata 193 D g
Fort Pierre 210 E b
Fort Pillow 208 C b
Fort Pitt 212 E c
Fort Pontchartrain 191 I c
Fort Presqu'Isle 192 B b
Fort Prince George 193 C d
Fort Providence 212 D b
Fort Prudhomme 191 H d
Fort Pulaski 208 D c
Fort Rae 212 D b
Fort Recovery 196 ins. B
Fort Reliance 212 E b
Fort Resolution 212 D b
Fortress Monroe 208 E b
Fort Richelieu 189 B a
Fort Rosalie 191 G e
Fort Rouge
Fort Rouillé 192 B b
Fort Saint Andrew 193 D f
Fort Saint Charles, or Kaskaskia 191 G d
Fort Saint Charles, near Lake of the Woods 191 F b
Fort Saint David (Cuddalore) 137 C f
Fort Saint Thérèse 189 B b
Fort Saint George, in Florida 193 D f
Fort Saint George (Madras) 137 D f
Fort Saint John, in Brit. Columbia 212 C b
Fort Saint John, on Richelieu R. 189 B b
Fort Saint Joseph 191 H c
Fort Saint Louis, in Illinois Country 191 H c
Fort Saint Louis, in Texas 190 F f
Fort Saint Philip 200 I g
Fort Saint Pierre 191 G b
Fort Saint Vrein 210 E b
Fort Sandusky 194 C b
Fort San Mateo 191 I e
Fort Saratoga 192 E b
Fort Saskatchewan 212 D c
Fort Schuyler, near Montreal 189 B b
Fort Schuyler (Oriskany) 195 D b
Fort Scott 211 G c
Fort Selkirk 212 B b
Fort Shirley 192 C c
Fort Simpson 212 C b
Fort Smith 211 G c
Fort Snelling 199 G b
Fort Stanwix 192 D b
Fort Stephenson 200 B c
Fort Steuben 196 ins. B
Fort Stoddert 196 B d
Fort Sumter 208 E c
Fort Tecumseh 210 E b
Fort Ticonderoga 192 E b
Fort Tombecbé 191 H e
Fort Toulouse 191 H e
Fort Trinity 192 ins.
Fortuna, Temple of 22 A
Fortuna, Fanum 27 H d
Fortunæ, Tres 23 B
Fort Union, in New Mexico 210 D c
Fort Union, in North Dakota 210 E a
Fort Uintah 210 C b
Fort Vancouver 210 A a
Fort Venango 192 A c
Fort Vincennes 194 B c
Fort Walla Walla 198 B a
Fort Washington (Cincinnati) 196 ins. B
Fort Washington, in Maryland 200 L i
Fort Washington, near New York 195 D c
Fort Washita 210 F d
Fort Watson 195 A g
Fort Wayne 196 B b
Fort Western 189 D b
Fort William (Calcutta) 137 E d
Fort William, in Florida 193 D f
Fort William, in Ontario 212 F d
Fort William (Portland, Ore.) 210 A a
Fort William Henry 192 D b
Fort Williams 192 D b
Fort Winnebago 211 H b
Fort Wrangell 212 ins.
Forty-Niners, route of 210 legend
Fort York
Fort Yukon 198 ins. A
Foruli 27 H e
Forum, loc. in Carthage 34 ins. A (3)
Forum, loc. in Rome 24 A and B
Forum Aurelii 27 F e
Forum Boarium, loc. in Rome 24 A
Forum Cassii 27 G e
Forum Clodii, near L. Sabatinus 35 ins. B
Forum Clodii, near Luca 26 E d
Forum Cornelii 27 F c
Forum Fulvii
Forum Gallorum 27 F c
Forum Germanorum 26 B c
Forum Holitorium, loc. in Rome 24 A
Forum Julii (Fréjus), in Gaul 26 A d
Forum Julii (Cividale), in Venetia 27 H a
Forum Livii (Forli) 27 F c
Forum novum 26 E c
Forum Popilii (Forlimpopoli), in Cispadane Gaul 27 G c
Forum Popilii, in Lucania 30 E b
Forum Sempronii 27 G d
Forum Vibii 26 B c
Forum Vulcani (Solfatara), vol. 31 ins. A
Fossæ Papirianæ 26 E d
Fossalta 72 C c
Fossano 150 D d
Fossanuova, mon. 96 C b
Fosse Way, road 51 P h
Fossombrone, bp. 95 E c (Fo.)
Fotheringhay 127 Y n
Fougères 69 C b
Fougères, castle 76 C b
Fountain City 206 ins.
Fountains, mon. 97 P g
Four Mile Tree 193 ins. A
Fowey 127 U p
Fowey, parl. bor. 163 J g
Fowler Bay 172 C d
Fox, Cape 212 ins.
Fox, Sauk and, Ind. Res. 188 H b
Fox Land 212 H b
Fox Channel 186 K b
Fox River 188 I b
Foxes, tribe 188 H b
Foyle, lake 127 J f
Fraga 82 C a
Francavilla 131 F f
France, km., 11 cent. 58 E d
France, km., 12 cent. 70 G d

France, km., 18 cent. 130 D d
France, rep. 166 F f
France, Plain of. 2 E d
Franceville 175 E e
Franche Comté, gouv. 146 C b
Franche Comté, prov. 148 F e
Franche Comté, see also Free County of Burgundy
Francia, duchy, about 1000 58 E d
Francia, reg. 53 M h
Franconia, Frankish prov., 9 cent. 56 D b
Franconia, duchy, 12 cent. 71 R k
Franconia, E., duchy 62 E c d
Franconia, W., duchy 62 E c d
Franconofurt, see Frankfort-on-the-Main and Frankfurt-on-the-Oder
Frankenhausen 114 F c
Frankenthal 122 E d
Frankfort, in Kentucky 196 C c
Frankfort-on-the-Main 55 Q i
Frankfort-on-the-Oder 79 I b
Frankfort-on-the-Oder, Hanse. cy. 99 ins. B
Frankfort-on-the-Oder, univ. 100 H d
Frankfort, gr. duchy 154 E c
Frankfort, imp. cy. 78 F c
Fränkische Saale, river 158 E c
Franklin, in Kentucky 208 C b
Franklin, in Pa. 192 A c
Franklin, in Tennessee 208 C b
Franklin, dist. in Canada 212 E a
Franklin, proposed state in U.S. 196 ins. A
Franks, Kingdom of the, 486 50 D c
Franks, Kingdom of the, 526—600 52 C b
Franks, Kingdom of the, 6 cent. 52 I e
Franks, people in France, 486-496 45 E c
Franks, people in Italy, 774 45 G d
Franks, people, about 900 57 D E c
Franzensfeste 158 F e
Franzens Canal 159 J f
Frascati, see Tusculum 64 ins.
Frascati, bp. 96 B b
Fraser River 212 C c
Frasnes 156 A a
Frastanz 91 R k
Fraubrunnen 91 P k
Frauenalb, ab. 142 B c
Frauenburg 115 J a
Frauenburg, bp. 95 F a
Frauenfeld 91 Q k
Fraustadt 135 I c
Fraxinet or Fraxinetum (Garde-Frainet) 56 D d
Frazers, fam. 97 I b
Frédéric, Fort 192 E a
Frederica 193 D f
Fredericia 158 E a
Frederick 192 C d
Frederick, Fort 192 B d
Frederick Barbarossa, crusade of 70 I d
Fredericksburg 193 F b
Frederick William Canal 135 H b (Fr. W. C.)
Fredericton 212 I d
Frederikshamn
Frederiksholm, castle 120 H e
Free County of Burgundy, 14 cent. 78 D e
Free County of Burgundy, 17 cent. 126 D c
Freeman's Farm, battle 195 E b
Freeport 207 H b
Freetown 174 B d
Fregellæ 30 C a
Fregenæ 27 G f
Freiberg 85 G e
Freiburg, in Breisgau 78 E e
Freiburg, in Breisgau, univ. 100 G e
Freiburg, in Switzerland, see Fribourg 91 P l
Freiburg, canton, see Fribourg 91 P l
Freising 63 F d
Freising, bp. 79 G d
Freyburg, on the Unstrut R. 85 F e
Fréjus 69 G e
Fréjus, bp. 95 D c
Fremantle 172 A d
Fremington, parl. bor.
Fremont 210 F b
Frémont, routes of 210 leg.
Fremont Peak 187 I d
French, empire of the, 1806 151 K j
French, people, about 900
French Bay 105 ins.
French Broad River 196 ins. A
French Congo, col. 175 E e
French Frigate Island 180 J e
French Guiana, col. 214 D b
French Guinea, col. 174 B c
French Indo-China, col. 171 L g
French Mills 200 F a
French Republic 151 H g
French Somaliland, col. 174 H c (Fr. Somal.)
Frenchtown 200 B c
French West Africa, col. 174 C c
Frentani, people 27 I e
Frentanians, people
Frento (Fortore) River 30 E a
Fresnaye 76 D b
Fresnillo 213 B b
Fréteval 69 H g
Fretum Gallicum (Strait of Dover) 51 Q i
Freudenberg 142 D a
Freudenstadt 143 F i
Fribourg 91 P l
Fribourg, canton 91 P l
Frichemont
Friday Street, in London 75 G g
Friedberg, in Swabia 143 H j
Friedberg, on the Taunus 122 E c
Friedewald 114 E c
Friedland, in Bohemia 123 H c
Friedland, in Moravia 123 I d
Friedland, in Prussia 155 K a
Friedrichshafen, imp. city 143 I j
Friedrichstadt 158 E a
Friedrich Wilhelm Canal 123 H b
Friendly Islands 172 H c
Friesach 63 H e
Friesack 85 C b
Friesack, castle 72 C a
Friesians, people 38 D b
Friesland, reg., 9 cent. 56 C b
Friesland, reg., 13 cent. 72 B a
Friesland, reg., 14 cent. 78 E b
Friesland lordship, 16 cent. 117 D a
Friesland, East, reg. 86 F b
Friesland, West, dist. 117 C b
Frigidus River 27 H b
Frijoles
Friniates, people 26 E c
Frio, Cape, in Brazil 215 E e
Frio, Cape, in Africa 175 E f
Frisches Haff, bay 123 J a
Frisians, people, see Friesians
Frisinga, see Freising
Fritzlar 55 Q i
Fritzlar, mon. 95 D a
Friuli, March of. 54 G d
Friuli, people 52 J e
Friuli, dist. 63 G e
Frobisher, route of 108 L b
Frobisher Bay 212 I b
Froburg, castle 91 P k
Frohse 63 F b
Frohsdorf 159 I e
Frome, lake 172 D d
Frome, parl. bor. 163 L f
Fronsac, castle 76 C d
Frontenac, Fort 192 C a
Fronteras 190 D e
Frontiacus, see Fronsac
Front Royal 208 E b (F.R.)
Frutigen, castle 91 P l
Fruttuaria, mon. 95 D b
Fucens, Alba 27 H e
Fu-chau
Fucino, lake 96 C a
Fucinus (Fucino) lake 27 H f
Fuego, Tierra del, isl. 215 C h
Fuego, volcano 187 J g
Fuenterrabia 83 K g
Fuentes de Oñoro 130 B e
Fuentidueña 82 B a
Fuerte 190 D f
Fugger, lordship 143 J i
Fugui
Fulda 72 B a
Fulda, ab. 78 F c
Fulda, bp. 122 E c
Fulda, mon. 55 Q i
Fulginium (Foligno)
Fulham
Fulvii, Forum 26 C c
Fundi 30 C a
Fundoukli, quarter 93 G e
Fundy, Bay of 186 M d
Fünfkirchen 72 D b
Fünfkirchen, bp. 95 F b
Fünfkirchen, univ. 100 I e
Fünen, isl.
Furculæ Caudinæ, passes, see Caudine Forks
Furka Pass 91 Q l
Furlo Pass 27 G d
Furnes 69 E a
Furness, mon. 97 N g
Furth, in Bavaria 123 G d
Fürth, in Ansbach 122 F d
Fürstenau, castle 91 R l
Fürstenberg 142 C e
Fürstenberg, cty. 122 E e
Fürstenberg, princ. 142 B e
Fürstenfeld, mon. 95 E b
Fürstenwalde 79 I b
Fürstenwalde, bp. 95 E a
Furtwangen 142 B d
Fusan 171 N e
Füssen 134 F e
Futa, la-, Pass 27 F c
Futa Jalon, reg. 174 B c
Fuzo
Fyriswall 59 H b
Fyzabad 137 D c

Gabales or Gabalis, see Javols
Gabara 6 C c
Gabardan, dist. 147 E c (Gab.)
Gabarret 76 D d
Gabel 159 H c
Gabes 174 D a
Gabes, Gulf of 174 E a
Gabii 27 G f
Gabun, reg. 175 D e
Gad, tribe 7 ins. D
Gadara
Gadda 7 E d
Gadebusch 134 F b
Gades (Cadiz) 38 A e
Gadsden Purchase, reg. 1853 198 C d
Gaëta 90 D d
Gaëta, bp. 95 E c
Gaëtulia, reg. 34 F g
Gaikwar, Dom. of the 137 B d
Gaildorf 143 I g
Gaillac, mon. 94 C c (Gaill.)
Gaillard, castle 76 D b
Gaillon 76 D b
Gainas, people 51 F
Gaines, Fort, in Alabama 208 C c
Gaines, Fort, in Minnesota 211 G a
Gaines' Mill, battle 208 E b (G.M.)
Gainsborough 127 Y m
Gairdner, lake 172 C d
Galaaditis, reg. 7 D d
Galapagos Islands 214 A b
Galata, dist. in Constantinople 93 G e
Galatia, E. Rom. prov. 43 I f (2)
Galatia, Rom. prov.
Galatia Salutaris, E. Rom. prov. 43 I e (5)
Galatz 131 I d
Galeazzo Visconti, Dom. of 90
Galena 211 G b

5

Galepsus, in Pieria 11 F b
Galepsus, in Sithonia 11 E b
Galera 118 D f
Galicia, cty. in Spain 82 A a
Galicia, dist. in Austria-Hungary 159 K d
Galicia, dist. in Poland 139 B f
Galicia, km. in Spain 83 J g
Galicia, W. Rom. prov. 42 A e (3)
Galilee, dist. 6 C c
Galilee, Sea of 6 D c
Galitch
Gallæci, people 38 A d
Gallæcia, reg. 34 C e
Gallette, La, Fort 192 D a
Gallia, see Gaul 34 E d
Gallia Belgica, see Belgica 38 D c (3)
Gallia Cisalpina, see Cispadane and Transpadane Gaul 26
Gallia Cispadana, see Cispadane Gaul 26 E c
Gallia Lugdunensis, see Lugdunensis 38 C c (4)
Gallia Narbonensis, see Narbonensis 38 D d (6)
Gallia Transalpina, see Gaul 34 E d
Gallia Transpadana, see Transpadane Gaul 26 C b
Gallienus, Arch of 22 A
Gallinas, Cape 187 L g
Gallinas, Punta, cape 214 B a
Gallipoli, in Italy 90 F d
Gallipoli, in Thrace 71 L e
Gallipolis, in Ohio 196 ins. B
Gallo, Isla del, isl. 111 B a
Galloway, bp. 97 I e
Galloway, dist.
Galtelli 72 B c
Galveston 199 G e
Galvez, route of 195 ins. B
Galway
Galway, cty. 127 H h
Galway Bay 49 B e
Gamala 6 D c
Gambia, col. 174 B c
Gambia River 108 P f
Gambier Islands 180 N j
Gambrium
Gams 91 R k
Gandamak 170 H e
Gandavum, see Ghent
Gander River 212 J d
Gandersheim, mon. 95 D a
Gandia
Gando 174 D c
Gangani, people 38 A b
Ganges River 137 E c
Gangra 20 E b
Ganjam 137 E e
Gänserndorf 159 I d
Gap 126 E d
Gap, bp. 95 D c
Gard, dept. 148 E f
Garda 90 J h
Garda, lake 90 J h
Garde-Frainet, see Fraxinet or Fraxinetum
Gardelegen 85 B b
Gardiner's Island 189 C d
Gard Meuble, loc. in Versailles 149 A
Garendon, mon. 97 P i
Garessio 130 Q j
Gargano, mt. 64 C b
Garganum. prom. 31 F a
Garganus (Gargano), mt. 30 E a
Gargara
Gargettus 16 B a
Garigliano River 90 D d
Garmantes, people 35 G h
Garonne, Haute, dept. 148 E f
Garonne River 61 D d
Garrapata 214 B b
Garsaura 20 F c
Gartach, Gross 142 D b
Garts 123 H b
Garumna (Garonne) River 38 B d
Garz 63 H b
Gascony, dist. 50 C d
Gascony, duchy 61 C e
Gascony, prov. 148 D f
Gascoyne River 172 A c
Gaspé Peninsula 186 M d
Gastein 158 G e
Gates, route of 195 A f
Gateshead, parl. bor. 163 M c
Gath 7 B e
Gath Rimmon 7 B e
Gatheæ 14 C b
Gâtinais, dist. 69 I f
Gatineau River 199 J a
Gattinara 118 F d
Gatton, parl. bor. 163 N f (Gat.)
Gatun
Gatun River
Gaudus, isl. 14 ins.
Gaugamela 20 J d
Gaul, reg. 12 D a
Gaul, W. Rom. dioc. 42 C d
Gaul, W. Rom. pref. 42
Gaul, Cisalpine, reg. 38 ins.
Gaul, Cispadane, reg. 27 E c
Gaul, Transalpine, reg. 34 E d (Gaul)
Gaul, Transpadane reg. 26 C b
Gaur 92 I e
Gaure, dist. 126 B e
Gaurium 15 E b
Gaurus, mt. 31 ins. A
Gaya 137 E d
Gaza
Gazaca 35 N f
Gazaria, reg.
Gaziura 20 G b
Geba 7 C d
Gebal 6 D a
Gebal, reg.
Gebu, isl. 199 ins. H
Gederoth 7 B e
Gedid 174 G c
Gedrosia, prov. 19 J e
Gedrosia, satr. 8 K f
Geelong 172 G d
Geertsbergen 117 B d
Gefle 88 G a
Geislingen 143 I h
Geismar 55 Q i
Gela 30 D e
Gelas River 30 D e
Geldern 78 E e
Gelderland, Upper, dist. 117 E c
Gelderland, duchy 117 D b
Gelduba 39 I h
Gelnhausen 72 B a
Gelnhausen, imp. cy. 78 F c
Gembloux 156 B a
Gembloux, mon. 94 C a
Gemelli Hills 30 C e
Gemeticum, see Jumièges
Geminiacum (Gembloux) 39 H h
Gemioncourt 156 A a
Gemmingen 142 D b
Gemmi Pass 91 P l
Genappe 156 A a
Genava (Geneva) 26 A a
Generality Lands, see Common Lands
Genesee River 192 C b
Geneva 91 O l
Geneva, bp. 95 D b
Geneva, cty. 69 G d
Geneva, dist. 91 O l
Geneva, lake 39 I j
Genèvre, Mont, pass 26 A c
Genf, see Geneva 91 O l
Genfer See, see L. Geneva 91 O l
Gengenbach 142 B d
Gennath Gate 6 ins. A
Gennesaret, Lake of 6 D c
Gennesaret, Plain of 6 D c
Genoa, in Italy 90 I h
Genoa, abp. 95 D c
Genoa, Gulf of 26 C d
Genoa, rep. 90 B b
Genoa, in Nebraska 188 G b
Gentinnes 156 B a
Genua (Genoa) 26 C c
Genusia 31 F b
Genusus River 10 B a
Geographe Bay 172 A d
Geographer's Line 196 ins. B
George, Fort, in Canada 200 D b
George, Fort, in Maine 189 D c
George, Fort, in New York 192 E b
George, lake 192 E b
Georgeana 189 D c
Georgenthal, mon. 95 E a (G.)
Georgetown, in Brit. Guiana 214 D b
Georgetown, in Pulo Penang 171 K h
Georgetown, in S. Carolina 193 E e
Georgia, col. 193 C e
Georgia, km. 73 I b
Georgia, prov. 139 F g
Georgia, reg. 67 O e
Georgia, state 199 I d
Georgian Bay 191 I b
Georgina River 172 C c
Gepidæ, people 35 I d
Gepids, people 50 H c
Gera 87 I c
Gera River 85 F e
Gerabronn 143 I g
Gerace 90 F e
Gerace, bp. 95 F d
Geræstus, prom. 15 E b
Geraldton 172 A c
Gerania, mt. 15 D a
Gerasa 7 D d
Gerata, mt.
Gerberoy, castle 69 H f
Gerenia
Gergesa 6 D c
Gergithes 9 C c
Gergovia 38 C c
Geringswalde, mon. 80 ins.
Gerizim, mt. 7 C d
Germalus, mt. 23 B
German Confederation 157 C b
German East Africa, col.
German East Africa Company
German Empire
German South-West Africa, col.
Germania reg., see Germany
Germania I, West Rom. prov. 42 D d (3)
Germania II, West Rom. prov. 42 D c (4)
Germania Inferior, Rom. prov., see Lower Germany
Germania Superior, Rom. prov., see Upper Germany
Germanic Peoples, about 900 57
Germanicopolis 20 E b
Germanna 193 F b
German Ocean
Germanorum, Forum 26 B c
Germantown 192 D c
Germany, country, see German Empire
Germany, reg. 34 G c
Germany, Greater, reg.
Germany, km. 70 I d
Germany, Lower, Rom. prov.
Germany, Upper, Rom. prov.
German Zollverein, customs-union 160 D c
Germersheim 78 F d
Gernsbach 142 B c
Gerstungen
Geroldseck, castle 154 D d
Geroldseck, cty. 158 E d
Gerolstein 117 E d
Gerona 82 C a
Gerona, bp. 94 C c
Gerona, duchy 83 L g
Gerónimo de Yuste, San, mon. 94 A c
Geronthræ 14 C c

Gerontia, isl. 11 F c
Gerresheim, mon. 95 D a
Gerrha 19 H e
Gerrhæi, people 19 G e
Gers, dept. 148 E f
Gersau 91 Q k
Gersoriacum, see Boulogne
Gertruydenberg 117 C c
Gerunium 30 E a
Geshur, reg. 6 D c
Gesoriacum 38 C b
Getæ, people 18 B b
Gethsemane, loc. near Jerusalem 6 ins. A
Gettysburg 208 ins.
Gévaudan, cty. 61 E d
Gévaudan, dist. 84 E g
Gex, dist. 130 N h
Gezer 7 B e
Ghadames 174 D b
Ghara River 137 B b
Ghassanids, Dom. of the 52 L f
Ghazal, Bahr el, reg. 174 F d
Ghazal, Bahr el, R. 174 F d
Ghazni 170 H e
Gheel 117 D c
Ghent 117 B c
Ghent, Hanse. for. cy. 99 ins. B
Gherardesca 90 L j
Ghilan, reg. 139 G h
Gian Galeazzo Visconti, Dom. of 90
Giangtse 171 K f
Giants, Stoa of the
Gibeah
Gibellum 68 C b
Gibeon 7 C e
Gibilet 68 C c
Gibraltar 82 A b
Gibraltar, strait of 2 D e
Gibson, Fort 211 G c
Gibson's Desert 172 B c
Giebichenstein, castle 63 F c
Gien 76 E c
Giengen, imp. cy. 79 G d
Giessen 114 E c
Giglio Island 90 L j
Gigny, mon. 148 C b
Gigonus 11 E b
Gijón 82 A a
Gila Bend, Ind. Res. 188 D d
Gila River 187 H e
Gila River, Ind. Res. 188 D d
Gilbert Islands 179 I g
Gilboa 7 C d
Gilboa, mt. 6 C c
Gilead, mts. 7 D d
Gilead, dist.
Giles, routes of 172 leg.
Gilgal, near Jericho
Gilgal, near Ramathaim
Gilgal, in Samaria 7 B d
Gilgit 170 I e
Gilly 156 A b
Gilolo, isl. 112 F c
Gimoës, cty. 76 D e (Gim.)
Ginœa
Giornico 91 Q l
Giovanni Visconti, Dom. of 90 I h
Giovi, pass 26 D c
Giovinazzo 90 F d
Girgeh 150 B b
Girgenti 90 D f
Girgenti, bp. 95 E d
Girishk 170 H e
Gironde, dept. 148 D f
Gisborne 172 G d
Giseh 150 B a
Gishiga 171 R b
Gislikon
Gisors 69 H f
Gitana 10 B c
Gitschin 159 H c
Gitta 7 C d
Giurgevo 93 C b
Givet 117 C d
Gizeh
Glabais 156 A a
Glacier Bay 212 ins.
Glamorgan, cty. 127 V o
Glamorgan, parl. dist. 163 K f
Glandève, bp. 95 D c
Glaphyræ 11 D c
Glarus 91 R k
Glarus, canton 91 R l
Glasgow
Glasgow, abp. 97 G b
Glasgow, univ. 100 E c
Glastonbury 60 E e
Glastonbury, mon. 97 O j
Glastonbury, parl. bor. 163 L f
Glatz 63 I c
Glatz, cty. 87 K c
Glaucus River, in Achaia 14 B a
Glaucus River, in Armenia 20 I b
Gleichen, castle 115 ins. B
Glen Coe, in Scotland
Glencoe, in Natal 175 N l
Glengarry
Glen Shiel
Glevum (Gloucester) 51 O i
Glisas 11 E d
Globukoie
Glogau 63 I c
Glogau, princ. 79 I c
Glom River 166 H c
Glommen River 120 H d
Gloucester, in England
Gloucester, castle
Gloucester, cty.
Gloucester, mon.
Gloucester, parl. bor. 163 L f
Gloucester, shire
Gloucester, in Mass. 189 D c
Gloucester, in New Jersey 192 D d
Gloucester, cty. in Virginia 193 F c (G.)
Glücksburg 158 E a
Glückstadt 122 E b
Glurns
Glykys Limen, bay 10 B c
Glympeis 15 C b
Gmünd, imp. cy. 143 I h
Gmunden 123 G e
Gnadenhuetten 194 C b
Gnatia 31 G b
Gnesen
Gnesen, abp.
Gnevin 63 G c
Goa 137 B e
Goajíra Peninsula 214 B a
Gobæum, prom. 38 A c
Gobannium (Abergavenny) 51 O i
Gobi, desert 92 K c
Goch 117 E c
Gochsheim 142 C b
Godavari River 137 C e
Godmundingham
Gödöllö 159 J e
Gods, Portico of the 24 B
God's House, League of, dist. 91 R l
Godstow, mon. 97 P j
Godwin Austen, mt. 170 I e
Gogana 19 H e
Gogo, in Africa 174 D c
Gogo, in India
Gogo, reg. 108 R f
Göhrde 154 F b
Goito 161 H e
Gök-tepe 170 G e
Golan 6 D c
Golan, reg. 6 D c
Golconda 137 C e
Goldberg 123 H c
Gold Coast, col. 174 C d
Golden Castile, reg. 105 D e
Golden Gate, in Constantinople 93 G e
Golden Gate, The, in Jerusalem 68 ins. B
Golden Horde, khan. of the 77 M c
Golden Horn, bay 93 G e
Goldenkron, mon. 80 D g
Golden Mile-stone, in Rome
Goldsboro 208 E b
Golea, El 174 D a
Golfo Dulce 105 C c
Golgatha, loc. near Jerusalem 6 ins. A
Goliad 198 F e
Göllheim 78 E d
Gollnow 135 H b
Gollnow, Hanse. cy. 99 ins. B
Golo, dept. 148 F f
Golowczyn 131 I c
Golymin 155 K b
Gomaringen 143 H i
Gomel 139 D e
Gomera, isl. 108 P e
Gomez, route of 108 J c
Gommern 85 F d
Gomphi 10 C c
Gondar 174 G c
Gonnus 11 D c
Gonzaga, fam. 79 G f
Gonzales de Avila, route of 105 C d
Good Hope, Cape of 109 S k
Good Hope, Fort 212 C b
Goole 162 F d
Goor 117 E b
Goose Creek 208 ins.
Gophna 7 C e
Göppingen 143 I h
Gora 155 K c
Gordieum 20 D c
Gordillo, route of 191 J e
Gordons, fam.
Gordonsville 208 E b (Gord.)
Gorée
Gorgiana 189 D c
Gorgon, isl. 26 D d
Gorgona
Gorgona Island 111 B a
Gorinchem 117 C c
Goritza 165 B c
Görlitz 63 H c
Gortyna
Gortys 14 C b
Görz 72 C b
Görz, cty. 79 H f
Gorze, mon. 95 D b
Gorzno 123 J b
Goshen, reg. 4 ins.
Goslar 62 F c
Goslar, Hanse. cy. 99 ins. B
Goslar, imp. cy. 79 G c
Gosnold, route of 191 L c
Göss, mon. 80 D h
Gosselies 156 A b
Göteborg
Gotha 85 F e
Götha River
Götheborg
Gothenburg
Gothia, dist. 46 I b
Gothia, marq. 61 E e
Gothland, dist. 66 I b
Gothland, isl.
Göthland, E., dist.
Göthland, W., dist.
Goths, people, in Dacia 47 K d
Goths, people, in Scandia 38 E a
Gotland, see Gothland and Göthland
Gottenburg 184 F a
Gottesgab 115 ins. B
Gotteshausbund, dist. 91 R l
Gotthard, Sankt 131 G d
Göttingen 78 F c
Göttingen, Hanse. cy. 99 ins. B
Gottlieben, castle 86 G e
Gottorp, castle 114 E a
Gottschee 80 D h
Göttweig, mon. 80 D g
Gough Island 181 A A l
Goulas 4 B b
Goulburn 172 E d
Gourdon 76 D d

Gournay . . . 126 B b
Govola River . . . 26 D e
Goyana . . . 214 F c
Goyaz . . . 214 D d
Goyaz, state . . . 214 E d
Gozo, isl. . . . 131 F f
Graaf Reinet . . . 175 L m
Grabow . . . 85 B b
Graçay . . . 76 D c
Gracias á Dios, Cape . . . 105 D c
Grado . . . 63 G f
Gradus Monetæ . . . 24 A
Græcia, Magna, reg. . . . 29 E e
Græcostasis, in Rome . . .
Grafton . . . 172 E c
Graham Harbor . . . 105 ins.
Graia, Alpis, pass . . . 26 A b
Graian Alps, mts. . . . 26 B b
Graïce, dist. . . . 16 B a
Grain Coast, reg. . . . 174 B d
Graioceli, people . . . 26 A b
Grammont . . . 117 B d
Grampian Mountains . . . 49 D c
Grampound, parl. bor. . . .
Gramzow, mon. . . . 80 ins.
Gran . . . 59 H d
Gran, abp. . . . 95 F b
Gran River . . . 63 J d
Granada, in Nicaragua . . . 105 C d
Granada, in Spain . . . 83 E d
Granada, abp. . . . 94 B d
Granada, emir. . . . 83 E d
Granada, km. . . . 83 K h
Granby, Fort . . . 195 A g
Gran Chaco, El, reg. . . . 215 C e
Grand Bassam . . . 175 C d
Grand Canyon . . . 187 H e
Grande Chartreuse, La, mon. . . 95 D b
Grande Gete River . . . 156 B a
Grande Ronde, Ind. Res. . . . 188 B b
Grandes Écuries, in Versailles 149 A
Grand Forks . . . 210 F a
Grand Gulf . . . 208 B c
Grand Junction . . . 188 E c
Grand Portage . . . 211 G a
Grand Portage, Ind. Res. . . . 188 I a
Grandpré, in France . . .
Grand Pré, in Nova Scotia . . . 194 G b
Grand Rapids . . . 211 H b
Grand River, in Missouri . . . 199 G b
Grand River, in Utah . . . 198 D c
Grand River, in S. Dakota . . . 198 E a
Grand Selve, mon. . . . 94 C c
Grandson . . . 91 O l
Grand Trianon, in Versailles . 149 A
Grandvilliers . . . 76 E b
Granges . . . 143 ins. F
Granges, lordship . . . 143 ins. F
Granicus River . . .
Granja . . . 214 E c
Granja, La, castle . . . 130 C e
Granson . . . 130 O h
Grantham . . . 127 Y n
Grantham, parl. bor. . . . 163 N e
Grant Land . . . 186 L a
Granville . . . 172 D a
Granville, Fort . . . 192 C c
Grasburg, castle . . . 91 P l
Grasse . . . 126 E e
Grasse, bp. . . . 95 D c
Gratianopolis, see Grenoble
Gratiot, Fort . . . 211 I b
Gratz . . . 72 D b
Graubünden (Grisons), dist. . . 91 R l
Graudenz . . . 115 J b
Gravelines . . . 126 C a
Gravelle . . . 76 C b
Grävenstein, castle . . . 142 ins. B
Grävenstein, lordship . . . 142 ins. B
Gravesend, in Kent . . . 75 J i
Gravesend, in Long Island . . . 189 ins. C
Graviscæ . . . 27 F e
Great Armenia, reg. . . . 99 L e
Great Australian Bight . . . 172 B d
Great Barrier Reef . . . 172 D b
Great Barrington . . . 196 E b
Great Basin . . . 187 H d
Great Bear Lake . . . 186 H b
Great Belt, str. . . . 88 D d
Great Bend . . . 190 F d
Great Bulgaria, reg. . . . 77 N b
Great Canal . . .
Great Cayman, isl. . . . 105 D c
Great Central Plain . . . 186 I b
Great Desert . . .
Greater Antilles, isl. . . . 187 L g
Greater Armenia, reg. . . . 33 N e
Greater Germany, reg. . . .
Greater Phrygia, satr. . . . 18 O h
Greater Syrtis, gulf . . . 51 G f
Great Exuma, isl. . . . 105 E b
Great Falls . . . 210 C a
Great Fish River, in Canada . 186 I b
Great Fish River, in Cape Col. 175 M m
Great Grimsby, parl. bor. . . . 163 N d
Great Harbor . . . 189 C d
Great Inagua, isl. . . . 213 E b
Great Kanawha River . . . 193 D b
Great Kei River . . . 175 M m
Great Khan, Empire of the . . .
Great Lakes, The . . . 186 K d
Great Lowland Plain . . . 2 E c
Great Malvern, mon. . . . 97 O i
Great Marlow, parl. bor. . 163 N f (Gr. M.)
Great Meadows, battle . . . 192 B d
Great Miami River . . . 196 ins. B
Great Namaqualand, reg. . . . 175 E g
Great Northern Coalfields, England . . . 162 E b
Great Oasis . . . 4 E d
Great Ouse River . . . 49 F e
Great Pedee River . . . 193 E d
Great Poland, reg. . . . 131 G c
Great Redan, Fort . . . 164 L g
Great Russia, see Muscovy
Great Russians, people . . . 139 E e
Great Saint Bernard Pass . . . 91 P m
Great Salt Lake . . . 190 C c
Great Sandy Desert . . . 172 B c
Great Sandy Island . . . 172 E c
Great Siberian Plain . . . 3 K c
Great Slave Lake . . . 186 H b
Great Slave River . . . 212 D b
Great Smoky Range . . . 193 C d
Great South Wales Coalfield . 162 C f
Great Valley . . . 187 K e
Great Victoria Desert . . . 172 B b
Great Wall . . .
Great Wallachia, reg. . . . 89 C b
Great Wahle River . . . 212 H c
Great Yarmouth, parl. bor. . . . 163 P e
Grecian Peninsula . . . 2 G e
Greece, km. . . . 164 C c
Greece, reg. . . . 4 B b
Greek Patriarchate . . . 93 G e (8)
Greeks, people . . . 165 leg.
Green Bay . . . 191 H c
Green Bay, cy. . . . 199 H b
Greenbrier River . . . 192 A d
Greencastle . . .
Greene, route of . . . 195 B f
Greenland, isl. . . . 186 O a
Green Mountains . . . 192 E b
Green River, in Kentucky . . . 193 A c
Green River, in Utah . . . 190 D d
Greensboro . . . 211 J c
Greenspring . . . 193 ins. A (Gr.)
Greenville . . . 196 ins. A
Greenville, Fort . . . 196 ins. B
Greenway Court . . . 192 B d
Greenwich, in Conn. . . . 192 E c
Greenwich, in England . . . 75 I i
Greenwich, parl. bor. . . . 163 O f
Greenwich, E. . . . 189 ins. A
Greetsiel . . . 122 D b
Greifenhagen . . . 123 H b
Greifensee, castle . . . 91 Q k
Greifswald . . . 80 C d
Greifswald, Hanse. cy. . . . 99 ins. B
Greifswald, univ. . . . 100 H d
Greiz . . . 135 G c
Grenade, isl. . . . 213 F c
Grenadines, isl. . . . 213 F c
Grenoble . . . 61 F d
Grenoble, bp. . . . 95 D b
Grenoble, gen. . . . 147 F c
Grenoble, univ. . . . 100 G e
Greutungs, people . . . 50 I c
Grève, Place de, Paris . . . 149 B
Grève, Quai de la, Paris . . . 149 B
Grevenmacher . . . 117 E e
Grey Friars, mon. in London . 75 G g
Greytown . . . 213 D c
Grèzes . . . 76 E d
Gries Pass . . . 91 Q l
Grignan . . . 126 D d
Grijalva River . . . 213 C c
Grijalva, route of . . . 105 B c
Grimma . . . 85 G e
Grimsby, Hanse. for. cy. . . . 98 ins. A
Grinsel Pass . . .
Grinnell . . . 207 G b
Gripsholm, castle . . . 120 I e
Griqualand East, dist. . . . 175 M m
Griqualand, West, dist. . . . 175 L l
Grisons, dist. . . . 91 R l
Griswold, Fort . . . 195 F c
Grobe, mon. . . . 80 D d
Grodno . . . 138 B e
Groenlo . . . 117 E b
Groitzsch . . . 63 G c
Grol . . . 117 E b
Grone, castle . . . 62 E c
Groningen . . . 117 E a
Groningen, Hanse. cy. . . . 99 ins. B
Groningen, lordship . . . 117 E a
Gross Batanga . . .
Gross Beeren . . . 154 G b
Gross Bottwar . . . 143 H h
Grossenhain . . . 85 G e
Grosseto . . . 90 L j
Grosseto, bp. . . . 95 E c
Gross Friedrichsburg . . .
Gross Gartach . . . 142 D b
Gross Görschen . . . 154 G c (Gr. G.)
Gross Jägersdorf . . . 135 K a
Gross Mariazell, mon. . . . 95 F b
Gross Sachsenheim . . . 143 H h
Gross Scheuern . . . 159 M f
Groton, in Conn. . . . 189 C d
Groton, in England . . . 185 G e
Groton, in Mass. . . . 189 C c
Grotzko . . .
Grubenhagen, castle . . . 122 F c
Grulla . . . 190 B e
Grumbach, castle . . . 114 E d
Grumentum . . . 30 E b
Grumum . . . 31 F b
Grünberg . . . 123 H c
Grünhain, mon. . . . 80 ins.
Grünsfeld . . . 142 E a
Grünwettersbach . . . 143 G h
Grussenheim . . . 143 ins. D
Gruyères . . . 91 P l
Gryneum . . . 17 E b
Guadalajara, in Spain . . . 82 B e
Guadalajara, in Mexico . . . 213 ins.
Guadalajara, pres. . . . 213 B b
Guadalquivir River . . . 82 A b
Guadalupe . . . 214 C e
Guadalupe, isl., Antilles . . . 105 H c
Guadalupe, isl. off Lower Cal. . 187 H f
Guadalupe, mon. . . . 94 A d
Guadalupe Hidalgo . . . 201 F f
Guadeloupe, isl. . . . 105 H c
Guadiana River . . . 82 A b
Guadix . . . 82 B b
Guadix, bp. . . . 94 B d
Guaira . . . 108 L j
Guaira, La, see Guayra, La
Gualtieri . . . 90 J h
Guam, isl. . . . 179 F f

Guanahani, isl. 105 F b
Guanajuato 213 ins.
Guanare 214 C b
Guangja, isl. 105 D c
Guano Islands 175 E g
Guantánamo 213 E b
Guapore River 214 C d
Guarda, bp. 94 A c
Guardafui, Cape 174 I c
Guardia, bp. 95 F c
Guarionex, chieftain 105 F c
Guastalla 90 C b
Guastalla, duchy 151 L k
Guatemala 105 B d
Guatemala, capt. gen. and pres. 213 D c
Guatemala, country 213 C c
Guatemala, reg. 105 B d
Guaviare River 214 B b
Guaxenduba 214 E c
Guaxule 191 I e
Guayabero River 214 B b
Guayama 199 ins. G
Guayaquil 111 B b
Guayaquil, Gulf of 111 A b
Guaymas 213 A b
Guayra, La 214 C a
Gubbio 90 D c
Gubbio, bp. 95 E c
Guben 85 H e
Guelf Domains 71 ins.
Guerande 76 B c
Guéret 69 E c
Guernsey, isl. 69 B b
Guerrero, state 213 ins.
Guevara, route of 108 J j
Guevari 190 C e
Güglingen 143 G g
Guiana, British, col. 214 D b
Guiana, Dutch, col. 214 D b
Guiana, French, col. 214 D b
Guiana, reg.
Guidi, fam. 90 L j
Guienne, dist. 84 C g
Guienne, duchy, 11 cent. 61 D d
Guienne, duchy, 14 cent. 76 D d
Guienne, prov. 148 D f
Guienne and Gascony, gouv. 146 A c
Guildford, in England 75 H i
Guildford, parl. bor. 163 N f (Guildf.)
Guildford, in W. Australia 172 A d
Guildhall, bldg. in London 75 G g
Guild of the Holy Ghost, college 100 A a (33)
Guilfort, in Conn. 192 E c
Guilford Court House 195 B e
Guinea, Gulf of 175 D d
Guinea, reg. 108 Q g
Guinea, French, col. 174 B c
Guinea, Lower, reg. 175 E e
Guinea, Portuguese, col. 174 B c
Guinea, Upper, reg. 174 C d
Guinegate 114 B c
Guines 69 D a
Guines, cty. 69 D a
Guingamp, castle 76 B b
Guingamp, mon. 94 B b
Guipúzcoa, dist. 83 K g
Guise 76 E b
Guîtres, mon. 94 B b
Gujarat, reg. 137 B d
Gujrat 170 I e
Gulf Plain 187 J f
Gumbinnen 159 L a
Gum Coast 108 P e
Gumush Maden 165 E d
Gundelfingen 143 H i
Gundelfingen, lordship 143 H i
Gundelsheim 143 H g
Güns 115 I e
Günsburg 154 F d
Günthersthal, mon. 142 A e
Guntia 39 K i
Guntoor, Guntur 137 D e
Günz River 143 J i
Gura 174 G c
Gurgures Mountains 27 G e
Guriev 139 H f
Gurk 80 D h
Gurk, bp. 95 E b
Gurupa 214 D c
Gustavus Adolphus, route of 121 D b
Güstrow 79 H b
Güstrow, princ. 79 H b
Gutenberg, castle
Gutenstein 142 D d
Gutenstein, lordship 142 D d
Gutensell, ab. 143 J i
Guthrie 210 F c
Guthrum's Kingdom
Gutones, people 38 F b
Guzerat, reg., see Gujarat
Guzman, route of 107 G e
Gwalior 137 C c
Gwent, dist.
Gwynedd, dist.
Gyarus, isl. 15 E b
Gympie 172 E c
Gyöngyös 159 J e
Gyrton 11 D c
Gythium 14 C c
Gzhatsk 153 O f

Haarlem 117 C b
Habbard, mt. 212 ins.
Habitancium (Risingham)
Habsburg, see Hapsburg
Habsburg (Hapsburg), castle 62 E e
Hackensack 189 ins. C
Hacsány 131 G d
Hadad-Rimmon 6 C c
Haddeby 62 E a
Haddington, cty. 127 R i (HA.)
Hadeln, Land, dist. 86 G b
Hadley 189 B c
Hadramut, Hadramaut, reg. 53 G e
Hadranus River 30 D e
Hadranum 30 D e
Hadria 27 I e
Hadrian, Mausoleum of 22 A
Hadrian, Wall of, in Athens 23 D
Hadrian, Wall of, in Britain 42 B c
Hadrian, Stoa of 23 D
Hadrianopolis, in Epirus 10 B c
Hadrianopolis, in Thrace 39 N l
Hadrian's Circus 22 A
Hadrian's Gate 23 D
Hadrian's Mole 96 A
Hadrian's Villa 35 ins. B (7)
Hadrian's Wall 51 O g
Hadrumetum 38 E e
Haegsted, see Eichstädt
Hæmimont, theme 59 J e
Hæmimontium, E. Rom. prov. 43 H e (3)
Hæmus Mons (Mountains) 39 M l
Haff, Kurisches, bay 155 K a
Haff, Stettiner, bay 155 H b
Hafsids, dynasty 77 F e
Hagelberg 154 G b
Hagenau 72 B b
Hagerstown 208 ins.
Hague, de la, Cape, battle off
Hague, The 117 C b
Haidarabad, in Deccan 137 C e
Haidarabad, in Sind 137 A c
Haigerloch 143 G i
Haïl 170 F f
Hain River
Hai-nan, isl.
Hainau 155 H c
Hainault Forest 49 G f
Hainaut, cty. 117 B d
Hainaut, dist. 62 B c
Hainaut and Cambrésis, gen. 147 E a
Hainburg 63 I d
Haine River 156 A b
Haiti, isl. 187 L g
Haiti, rep. 213 E c
Hakodate 171 P d
Hal 156 A a
Halæ 11 E d
Halæ Araphenides 16 C b
Halæ Æxonides 16 B b
Halæsa 30 D d
Halberstadt 62 F c
Halberstadt, bp. 95 E a
Halberstadt, Hanse. cy. 99 ins. B
Halberstadt, princ. 122 F c
Haldensleben 72 C a
Haldenstein, castle 91 R l
Hales, mon. 97 P i
Hales Owen, mon. 97 O i
Hales River 30 E b
Halex River 30 E e
Haliacmon River 10 D b
Haliartus 11 E d
Halica 15 D b
Halicarnassus 13 E c
Halicyæ 30 B e
Halicz 59 I d
Halicz, princ. 71 K d
Halidon Hill
Halieis 15 D b
Halifax, in England 162 E d
Halifax, parl. bor. 163 M d
Halifax, in Nova Scotia 212 I d
Halifax, Fort 189 D b
Halil-Eli
Halimus 16 B b
Halipedon, dist. 16 D c
Haliussa Island 15 D b
Hall, in Tyrol 154 F e
Hall, imp. cy., in Wurtemberg 143 I g
Hall, Fort 198 C b
Hall, Fort, Ind. Res. 188 D b
Hall Peninsula 212 I b
Halland, dist. 88 E c
Halle 63 G c
Halle, Hanse. cy. 99 ins. B
Halles, loc. in Paris 149 B
Hallstadt
Halmahera, isl. 112 F c
Halmstad 120 H e
Halonnesus, isl. 11 F c
Haluntium 30 D d
Halus 11 D c
Halycus River 30 C e
Halys River 20 F b
Ham 117 B e
Hamadan
Hamah 68 C b
Hamar 131 F a
Hamath, on Lake of Gennesaret 6 D c
Hamath, on the Orontes R. 4 F c
Hamaxitos, road 23 D
Hambach 158 E d
Hamble, mon. 100 A b
Hamburg, in Germany 62 F b
Hamburg, Hanse. cy. 99 ins. B
Hamburg, imp. cy. 78 F b
Hamburg, in S. Carolina 211 I d
Hamburg, in Virginia 193 E b
Hamdanids, Dom. of the 59 L f
Hameln 122 E b
Hameln, Hanse. cy. 99 ins. B
Hami
Hamid, reg. 89 J g
Hamilton, in Canada 212 G d
Hamilton, in Scotland
Hamilton Inlet 212 J c
Hamilton River 212 I c
Hamiltons, fam. 97 I d
Hamme 156 B a
Hammerfest 167 J a
Hammerstein, castle 62 D c
Hammon 6 C b
Hamont 117 D c
Hampshire, cty.
Hampstead, in England 75 I h
Hampstead, in Georgia 193 ins. C
Hampton, in England 75 I i
Hampton, in N. Hampshire 189 C c
Hampton, in Virginia 193 ins. A
Hampton Court, castle 75 I i

Hampton Roads, harbor . . . . . 208 E b
Hana . . . . 198 ins. B
Hanau . . . . 122 E c
Hang-chau-fu . . . .
Hanging Rock, battle . . . . . . 195 A f
Hangö, isl. . . . . 131 H b
Hannibal . . . . 211 G c
Hannibalis, Castra . . . . 31 F d
Ha-noi . . . . 171 L f
Hanolelet . . . .
Hanover, in Germany . . . . . . 86 G b
Hanover, Hanse. cy. . . . . 99 ins. B
Hanover, elect. . . . . 134 E b
Hanover, km. . . . . 158 E b
Hanover, in Pa. . . . . 208 ins.
Hanover, in Virginia . . . . 193 F c
Hansi . . . .
Hanwell . . . . 75 I h
Hanworth . . . . 75 I i
Haparanda . . . . 167 J b
Happiness, Temple of . . . . . . 24 A
Hapsburg, castle . . . . 91 Q k
Haran . . . . 5 C b
Harar . . . . 174 H d
Harbin . . . . 171 N d
Harbour Grace . . . . 212 J d
Harburg . . . . 134 E b
Hardanger Field . . . . 166 G c
Harderwyk . . . . 117 D b
Harderwyk, Hanse. cy. . . . . . 99 ins. B
Hardheim . . . . 142 D a
Hard Times . . . . 208 B c
Harfleur . . . . 76 D b
Harfleur, Hanse. for. cy. . . . . 98 D d
Harlech, castle . . . .
Harlingen . . . . 117 D a
Harmakut, mts. . . . .
Harmar, Fort . . . . 196 ins. B
Harmene . . . . 20 F a
Harmersbach . . . . 142 B d
Harmony, New . . . . 206 ins.
Harmozia . . . . 8 D c
Harmozica . . . . 20 K b
Harpers Ferry . . . . 208 ins.
Harplea . . . .
Harran . . . . 67 N f
Harris, dist. . . . . 127 N g
Harris, Fort . . . . 192 C c
Harrisburg . . . . 196 D b
Harris Ferry . . . . 192 C c
Harrismith . . . . 175 M l
Harrison, route of . . . . 200 C d
Harrodsburg . . . . 191 I d
Harrow-on-the-Hill . . . . 75 I h
Harsany . . . . 164 B a
Hartford, in Conn. . . . . 189 B d
Hartford, in England . . . . . . 185 D d
Hartland, mon. . . . . 97 M k
Harvard . . . . 189 C c
Harwich . . . . 127 A A o
Harwich, parl. bor. . . . . 163 P f
Harz, mts. . . . . 62 F c
Harzburg, castle . . . . 62 F c
Hasa, El, reg. . . . .
Haslach . . . . 142 B d
Haslemere, parl. bor. . . . . . . 163 N f
Hasle Thal, valley . . . . 91 Q l
Hasnon, mon. . . . . 94 C a
Hasselt, in Liège . . . . 117 D d
Hasselt, in Overyssel . . . . . . 117 E b
Hasta, in Liguria . . . . 26 C c
Hasta, in Spain . . . . 38 A e
Hastenbeck . . . . 134 E b
Hastings . . . .
Hastings, parl. bor. . . . . 163 O g
Hatera . . . . 11 D b
Hatfield, in England . . . .
Hatfield, in Mass. . . . . 189 B c
Hatita . . . . 7 E d
Hatra . . . . 20 J e
Hatria, see Atria . . . . 27 G b
Hatria, see Hadria . . . . 27 I e
Hatteras, Cape . . . . 193 G d
Hatteras, Fort . . . . 208 E b
Hatteras Island . . . . 193 G d
Hattin . . . . 68 ins. A
Hatvan . . . . 159 J e
Hauara . . . . 18 E e
Hauenstein . . . . 142 B e
Hauenstein, cty. . . . . 142 B e
Hauran, reg. . . . . 6 E c
Hauraki Gulf . . . . 172 G d
Hausach . . . . 142 B d
Hausbergen . . . . 72 B b
Hausen, lordship . . . . 142 B d
Haute-Crête, mon. . . . . 95 D b
Hauteford, castle . . . . 76 D d
Haute-Garonne, dept. . . . . . . 148 E f
Haute-Loire, dept. . . . . 148 E e
Haute-Marne, dept. . . . . 148 E e
Hauterive, mon. . . . . 95 D b
Hautes-Alps, dept. . . . . 148 F f
Haute-Saône, dept. . . . . 148 F e
Hautes-Pyrénées, dept. . . . . . 148 D f
Haute-Vienne, dept. . . . . 148 E e
Hauteville . . . . 65 F f
Haut-Rhin, dept. . . . . 148 F e
Hautvillers, mon. . . . . 94 C b (Hv.)
Havana . . . . 105 D b
Havel River . . . . 63 G b
Havelberg . . . . 63 G b
Havelberg, bp. . . . . 95 E a
Havelberg, Hanse. cy. . . . . . . 99 ins. B
Haverford . . . . 192 ins.
Haverfordwest, mon. . . . . 97 M j
Haverfordwest, parl. bor. . . . . 163 I f
Haverhill . . . . 189 C c
Havering-atte-Bower . . . . 75 J h
Havre . . . . 69 H f
Havre de Grace, in France . . . 126 B b
Havre de Grace, in Maryland . . 200 L h
Hawaii, isl. . . . . 198 ins. B
Hawaii, ter. . . . . 198 ins. B
Hawaiian Islands . . . . 198 ins. B
Hawke Bay . . . . 172 G d
Haye, la, farm . . . .
Haye Sainte, la, farm . . . . . .
Hayling, mon. . . . . 100 B b
Haynes Bluff . . . . 208 B c
Hazah, reg. . . . . 99 M f
Hazor, near Asamon Mts. . . . . 6 C c
Hazor, near Ashdod . . . . 7 B e
Hazor, near waters of Merom . . 6 D b
Heathfield . . . .
Hebdomon, palace . . . . 93 G e
Hebrides, The, isl. . . . . 49 C c
Hebrides, New, isl. . . . . 172 F b
Hebron . . . . 7 C e
Hebrus River . . . . 39 N l
Hebulae Islands (The Hebrides) 38 A a
Hecate Strait . . . . 212 B c
Hecatompylus . . . . 19 I c
Hechingen . . . . 143 G i
Hecla, mt. . . . . 166 B c
Hedjaz, El Hejas, reg. . . . . . .
Hedon, parl. bor. . . . . 163 N d
Heemstede . . . . 189 B d
Heggbach, ab. . . . . 143 I i
Hegyes . . . . 159 J f
Heide . . . . 114 E a
Heidelberg . . . . 142 C b
Heidelberg, univ. . . . . 100 G e
Heidelsheim . . . . 142 C b
Heidenheim . . . . 143 J h
Heidenheim, lordship . . . . . . 143 J h
Heidenheim, mon. . . . . 95 E b
Height of Land, The . . . . 186 K c
Heilbronn . . . . 72 B b
Heilbronn, imp. cy. . . . . 143 H g
Heiligenbeil . . . . 123 K a
Heiligenberg . . . . 142 D e
Heiligenberg, cty. . . . . 142 D e
Heiligenhafen . . . . 122 F a
Heiligenkreuz, mon. . . . . 80 E h
Heiligerlee . . . . 117 E a
Heiligkreuzthal, ab. . . . . 143 H i
Heilsberg . . . . 80 G d
Heimsheim . . . . 143 G h
Heinrichau, mon. . . . . 95 F a
Heisterbach, mon. . . . . 95 D b
Heitersheim . . . . 142 A e
Hejas, El, Hedjaz, reg. . . . . .
Hela . . . . 115 J a
Hela, pen. . . . . 88 H d
Helbon . . . . 6 E a
Helder . . . . 117 C b
Heldua . . . . 6 C a
Helena, Baths of . . . . 22 A
Helena, in Arkansas . . . . 208 B c
Helena, in France, see Elne
Helena, in Montana . . . . 210 C a
Helena, isl. . . . . 15 E b
Helenopontus, East Rom. prov. 43 J e (8)
Helfenstein, castle . . . . 114 E d
Helfenstein, ruin . . . . 143 I h
Helgoland, isl. . . . . 62 D a
Helice . . . . 14 C a
Helicon, mt. . . . . 11 D d
Helicon River . . . . 11 D b
Helicranum . . . . 10 B c
Heliopolis, in Egypt . . . . 4 F c
Heliopolis, in Syria . . . . 6 E a
Heliopolis, ruins of . . . . 150 B a
Helisson River . . . . 14 C b
Hellas, seg. . . . . 8 A b
Hellas, theme . . . . 59 I f
Helleporus River . . . . 31 F d
Hellespont (Dardanelles), strait
Hellespontine Phrygia, satr. . .
Hellespontus, dioc. . . . . 43 H f
Hellopia, dist. . . . . 10 B c
Helme River . . . . 85 F e
Helmern, castle . . . . 62 E c
Helmond . . . . 117 D c
Helmstedt . . . . 114 F b
Helmstedt, Hanse. cy. . . . . . . 99 ins. B
Helorine Way . . . . 31 ins. B
Helorus . . . . 30 E e
Helorus River . . . . 30 D e
Helos . . . . 15 C c
Helsingborg . . . . 120 H e
Helsingborg, Hanse. for. cy. . . 98 F b
Helsingfors . . . . 119 J a
Helsingör . . . . 120 H e
Helsingör, Hanse. for. cy. . . . 98 F b
Helston, parl. bor. . . . . 163 I g
Heluan . . . . 174 J j
Helvetian Republic . . . . 151 H g
Helvetii, people . . . . 38 D c
Helvii, people . . . . 38 C d
Helvillum . . . . 27 G d
Helvinus River . . . . 27 I e
Hemeroscopium . . . . 12 C c
Hemesa . . . . 20 G e
Hemmingstedt . . . . 86 G a
Hempstead . . . . 189 B d
Hengstburg . . . . 63 H e
Heniochi, people . . . . 35 L e
Henlopen, Cape . . . . 192 D d
Henna . . . . 30 D e
Henneberg, castle . . . . 85 F e
Henneberg, cty. . . . . 114 F c
Hennebont, castle . . . . 76 B c
Hennegau, see Hainaut
Hennepin, route of . . . . 191 G c
Hennersdorf, Catholic . . . . . . 135 H c
Henrichemont . . . . 126 C c
Henrico . . . . 193 ins. A (Hen.)
Henrico County . . . . 207 K c
Henrietta Maria, Cape . . . . . . 212 G c
Henry, Cape . . . . 193 ins. A
Henry, Fort . . . . 208 C b
Henry the Illustrious, Poss. of 85
Henton, mon. . . . . 97 O j
Hepha . . . . 6 B c
Heppenheim . . . . 142 C a
Heptastadium, loc. in Alexandria 34 ins. C
Heraclea, in Acarnania . . . . . 10 C d
Heraclea, in Cappadocia . . . . 67 M f
Heraclea, in Elis . . . . 14 B b
Heraclea, in Epirus . . . . 10 C c
Heraclea, in Lucania . . . . . . 31 F b

Heraclea, in Macedonia . . . . . 10 C a
Heraclea (Perinthus) . . . .
Heraclea Chersonesus . . . . . . 12 J b
Heraclea Minoa . . . . 30 C e
Heraclea Pontica . . . . 20 D b
Heraclea Trachinia . . . . 11 D d
Heracleopolis . . . . 4 ins.
Heracleum, in Athens . . . . . . 23 D
Heracleum, in Syracuse . . . . 31 ins. B (10)
Heracleum, cy. in Macedonia . 11 D b
Heraclius, Wall of . . . . 93 G e
Heræa . . . . 14 B b
Heræan Mountains . . . . 30 D e
Heræum, cy. in Thrace . . . . .
Heræum, temple, in Olympia .
Heræum, prom. . . . . 15 C a
Herat . . . .
Hérault, dept. . . . . 148 E f
Herault River . . . . 148 E f
Herbertshöhe . . . . 172 E a
Herbita . . . . 30 D e
Herbrechtigen . . . . 122 F d
Herck . . . . 117 D d
Herculaneum . . . . 30 D b
Hercules, isl. . . . . 18 ins. B
Hercules, Pillars of, (Calpe, or Gibraltar, and Abila), promontories . . . . 38 B e
Hercules, prom. . . . . 31 F e
Hercules, Temple of . . . . 24 A
Hercules Custor, Temple of . .
Herculian Way . . . . 30 E a
Herculis Monœci, Portus (Monaco) . . . . 26 B d
Hercynian Forest, mts. . . . . . 38 E b
Herdoniæ . . . . 30 E a
Hereford . . . .
Hereford, bp. . . . . 97 O i
Hereford, castle . . . . 65 E d
Hereford, cty. . . . .
Hereford, parl. bor. . . . . 163 L e
Hereford, parl. dist. . . . . 163 L e
Hereford, shire . . . .
Herenthals . . . . 117 C c
Herford . . . . 122 E b
Herford, Hanse. cy. . . . . 99 ins. B
Herford, mon. . . . . 95 D a
Héricourt . . . . 143 ins. F
Héricourt, lordship . . . . 143 ins. F
Heristal . . . . 53 N g
Herjedalen, dist. . . . . 120 H d
Herkimer, Fort . . . . 192 D b
Hermanitz . . . . 123 H c
Hermannstadt . . . . 80 I i
Herminius, mt. . . . . 38 A d
Herminones, people . . . . 38 E b
Hermione . . . . 15 D b
Hermon, mts. . . . . 6 D b
Hermopolis (Eshmun) . . . . . . 18 D e
Hermosillo . . . . 213 A b
Hermunduri, people . . . . 38 E b
Hermus . . . . 16 B a
Hermus River . . . . 20 C c
Hernad River . . . . 115 K d
Hernandez de Cordova, route of 105 C b
Hernici, people . . . . 27 H f
Hernösand . . . . 166 I c
Herod, Tomb of . . . . 6 ins. A
Herod Agrippa, Wall of . . . . 6 ins. A
Herodes Atticus, Exedra of . .
Herodes Atticus, Odeum of . . 23 C
Herodium . . . . 7 C e
Herod's Palace, in Jerusalem . 6 ins. A
Heroopolis . . . . 4 ins.
Herrenalb, mon. . . . . 95 D b
Herrenberg . . . . 143 G h
Herrenbreitungen, mon. . . . . 95 E a
Herrenhausen, castle . . . . . . 134 E b
Herrero Land, reg. . . . . 175 E g
Herrstein . . . . 142 ins. A
Herrstein, lordship . . . . 142 ins. A
Hersfeld . . . . 56 D b
Hersfeld, ab. . . . . 78 F c
Hersfeld, mon. . . . . 95 D a
Hersfeld, princ. . . . . 122 E c
Hertford . . . .
Hertford, cty. . . . .
Hertford, parl. bor. . . . . 163 O f
Hertford, parl. dist. . . . . 163 N f
Hertford, shire . . . .
Herulians, people, in Denmark 38 E a
Herulians, people, in Hungary 50 G c
Hervey Bay . . . . 172 E c
Hervey Islands . . . . 180 K i
Herzogenbuchsee . . . . 91 P k
Herzogenrath . . . . 117 E d
Herzegovina, dist., 15 cent. . . . 93 A b
Herzegovina, dist., 20 cent. . . . 164 B b
Hesdin . . . . 117 A d
Heshbon . . . . 7 D e
Hesperis . . . . 12 G d
Hesse, dist. . . . . 62 E c
Hesse, gr. duchy, 1812 . . . . . 154 E c
Hesse, gr. duchy, 1866 . . . . . 158 E c
Hesse, landgr. . . . . 78 F c
Hesse, people . . . . 55 Q i
Hesse, Electoral, state . . . . . 158 E c
Hesse-Cassel, landgr. . . . . . . 122 E c
Hesse-Darmstadt, landgr. . . . . 122 E c
Hestia, Temple of . . . . 16 D c (2)
Histiæotis, dist. . . . .
Heubach . . . . 143 I h
Heubach, Klein . . . . 142 D a
Heusden . . . . 117 C c
Hevellians, people . . . . 63 G b
Hexamilion . . . .
Hexapylum, loc. in Syracuse 31 ins. B (11)
Hexham . . . .
Hexham, mon. . . . .
Hexham, dist. . . . .
Heyst . . . . 117 C c
Heystesbury, parl. bor. . . . 163 L f (Heyt.)
Hezekiah, Pool of . . . . 6 ins. A (6)
Hezekiah, Wall of . . . . 6 ins. A
Hibernia (Ireland) . . . . 34 C c
Hibernii, people . . . . 38 A b
Hiberus River, see Ebro River
Hildalgo, state . . . . 213 ins.
Hiera, isl., Ægates Island . . . . 30 B e
Hiera, isl., Liparææ Island . . . 30 E d
Hierapolis, in Asia Minor . . .
Hierapolis, in Syria . . . . 20 G d
Hierapytna . . . . 14 ins.
Hieromyces River . . . . 6 D c
Hieron Æsculapii . . . . 15 D b
Hierosolyma (Jerusalem) . . . . 35 L g
Higham Ferrers, parl. bor. . . . 163 N e
Highlanders, people . . . . 184 C a
Highlands, reg. . . . . 49 D c
Highworth, parl. bor. . . . .
Higuey, reg. . . . . 105 G c
Hilara River . . . . 39 J i
Hildburghausen . . . . 134 F c
Hildesheim . . . . 62 E b
Hildesheim, bp. . . . . 95 D a
Hildesheim, Hanse. cy. . . . . . 99 ins. B
Hilerda, see Lérida
Hili . . . .
Hill of Evil Counsel . . . . 6 ins. A
Hill of the Muses . . . . 23 D
Hill of the Nymphs . . . . 23 D
Hillsboro . . . . 195 B e
Hilo . . . . 198 ins. B
Hilsbach . . . . 142 C b
Hilton Head, cape . . . . 193 ins. C
Hilton Head, cy. . . . . 208 D c
Himalaya Mountains . . . . 170 I e
Himella River . . . . 27 H e
Himera . . . . 30 C e
Himera River, N. . . . . 30 C e
Himera River, S. . . . . 30 D e
Himmelpforte, mon. . . . . 80 ins.
Himmelpforten . . . . 122 E b
Hims, see Homs . . . . 59 L g
Hindon . . . . 127 W o
Hindon, parl. bor. . . . . . 163 L f (Hind.)
Hindukush, mts. . . . .
Hindustan, reg. . . . . 137 B-E c
Hingham . . . . 189 ins. B
Hinnom, valley . . . . 6 ins. A
Hinter-Rhein, see Farther Rhine River . . . . 91 R l
Hinterpommern, see Farther Pomerania . . . . 123 H b
Hiogo . . . .
Hippicus Tower . . . . 6 ins. A
Hippodamea . . . . 16 D c
Hippodrome, loc. in Rome . . . 24 B
Hippola . . . . 14 C c
Hipponiates, gulf . . . . 31 F d
Hipponium (Vibo) . . . . 31 F d
Hippo Regius . . . . 38 D e
Hippo Zarytus . . . . 38 D e
Hippus . . . . 6 D c
Hiram's Grave . . . . 6 C b
Hirato, isl. . . . .
Hiroshima . . . . 171 O e
Hirpini, people . . . . 30 D b
Hirrlingen . . . . 143 G i
Hirsau, mon. . . . . 95 D b
Hirschberg . . . . 123 H c
Hisn Keifa, on the Euphrates . 68 C b
Hisn Keifa, on the Tigris . . . 71 O f
Hispalis (Seville) . . . . 38 A e
Hispania, see Spain
Hispania Bætica, prov. . . . . . 38 A e (3)
Hispania Lusitania, prov. . . . 38 A d (2)
Hispania Tarraconensis, prov. . 38 B d (1)
Hispaniola, isl. . . . . 105 F c
Hispellum . . . . 27 G c
Hissar, in India . . . . 137 C c
Hissar, in Turkestan . . . .
Hissarlik . . . .
Histiæa . . . . 11 E d
Histiæotis, dist. . . . . 11 E d
Histonium . . . . 27 I e
Histria, reg., see Istria . . . . . 27 H b
Hither Pomerania, dist. . . . . 123 G a
Hither Rhine River . . . . 91 R l
Hither Spain, prov. . . . . 38 B d (1)
Hittites, people . . . . 4 F c
Hlidbeki, see Lübeck
Hoang-ho, R. . . . .
Hobart . . . . 172 D e
Hobkirks Hill, battle . . . . . . 195 A f
Hoboken . . . . 189 ins. C
Hochberg, castle . . . . 142 A d
Hochberg, margr. . . . . 142 A d
Hochdorf . . . . 143 G h
Hochelaga . . . . 191 K b
Hochkirch . . . . 135 H c
Höchst, S. of Frankfort . . . . 122 E c
Höchst, W. of Frankfort . . . . 62 E c
Höchstädt . . . . 134 F d
Hodeida . . . . 170 F g
Hof . . . . 154 F c
Hogland, isl. . . . . 131 I a
Hogue or Hougue, la, see Saint Vaast-de-la-Hougue
Hoh, Ind. Res. . . . . 188 B a
Hohen-Altheim . . . . 62 F d
Hohenasperg . . . . 143 H h
Hohenberg, ruin . . . . 143 G i
Hohenberg, Lower, cty. . . . . . 143 G i
Hohenberg, Upper, cty. . . . . . 143 G i
Hohenburg, in Alsace . . . . . . 72 B b
Hohenburg, in Bavaria . . . . . 63 F d
Hohenems . . . . 72 B b
Hohenfriedeberg . . . . 135 I c
Hohengeroldseck, cty. . . . . . . 142 A d
Hohengeroldseck, mon. . . . . . 142 A d
Hohenhöwen, castle . . . . 142 C e
Hohenkarpfen, ruin . . . . 143 G i
Hohenlinden . . . . 135 G d
Hohenlohe, princ. . . . . 143 I g
Hohen-Mölsen . . . . 63 G c
Hohenneuffen, ruin . . . . 143 H h
Hohenrechberg, ruin . . . . . . 143 I h
Hohenstaufen, castle . . . . . . 114 E d
Hohenstaufen, ruin . . . . 143 I h
Hohenstaufen Domains 71
Hohentwiel, castle . . . . 114 E c

Hohen Urach, ruin . . . . 143 H i
Hohenzollern, castle . . . . 154 G b
Hohenzollern, princ. . . . . 143 H i
Hohnstein. . . . . 122 F c
Hojeda, route of . . . . 105 G d, 108 M g
Hole Bourn, loc. near London . 75 G g
Holebourn Bridge . . . . 75 G g
Holkar, Dom. of. . . . . 137 C c
Hollabrunn . . . . 155 I d
Holland, cty. . . . . 117 C c
Holland, dist. . . . .
Holland, km., 1806 . . . . 151 K i
Holland, km., 1831 . . . . 158 C b
Höllental, valley . . . . 134 E e
Holly Springs . . . . 208 C c
Holmby House . . . . 127 X n
Holme Cultram, mon. . . . . . . 97 N g
Holmiæ, prom. . . . . 15 C a
Holstein, cty. . . . . 72 B a
Holstein, dist. . . . . 62 E a
Holstein, duchy, 15 cent. . . . . 86 G b
Holstein, duchy, 19 cent. . . . . 151 H f
Holston River . . . . 196 ins. A
Holwan . . . .
Holyoke . . . . 211 K b
Holy Rock, loc. in Jerusalem . 6 ins. A (1)
Holy Roman Empire about 1000 58, 59
Holy Roman Empire, 1138—1254 72
Holy Sepulchre, Church of the 6 ins. A
Holy Sepulchre, street of the . 68 ins. B
Holy Trinity the less, ch. in London. . . . . 75 G g (22)
Homberg . . . . 114 E c
Homblières, mon. . . . . . 94 C b (Hombl.)
Homburg, in Bavarian Palatinate 142 ins. B
Homburg, in Hesse . . . . 158 E c
Homolium . . . . 11 D c
Homs . . . . 68 C c
Ho-nan, prov. . . . . 171 M e
Honawar . . . . 137 B f
Hondo, isl. . . . . 171 O e
Honduras, Cape . . . . 105 C c
Honduras, country . . . . 213 D c
Honduras, reg. . . . . 105 C d
Honduras, Gulf of . . . . 105 C c
Hondschoote . . . . 134 B c
Honfleur . . . . 76 D b
Hongkong . . . . 171 M f
Honiton . . . . 127 V p
Honiton, parl. bor. . . . . 163 K g
Honolulu . . . . 198 ins. B
Honor, Temple of . . . . 22 A
Honore . . . . 137 B f
Honorias, E. Rom. prov. . . . . 43 I e (4)
Hood, mt. . . . . 187 G d
Hoogly . . . .
Hoogly River . . . .
Hoogstraeten . . . . 72 B a
Hoogwoud . . . . 72 A a
Hoopa Valley, Ind. Res. . . . . 188 B b
Hoorn . . . . 117 D b
Hoorn, cty. . . . . 117 D c
Hope, Temple of . . . .
Hopedale . . . . 212 I c
Hopetown . . . . 175 L l
Hopi, Ind. Res. . . . . 188 D c
Hopton Heath . . . . 127 W n
Horace, Villa of. . . . . 35 ins. B
Horb . . . . 143 G i
Horburg . . . . 143 ins. D
Horburg, cty. . . . . 143 ins. D
Horgen . . . . 91 Q k
Horma . . . .
Horn . . . . 123 H d
Horn, Cape, in Iceland . . . . . 166 A b
Horn, Cape, in S. America . . . 215 C h
Hornachos . . . . 82 A b
Hornbach, mon. . . . . 95 D b
Hornberg . . . . 142 B d
Horncastle . . . . 98 ins. A
Horneck . . . . 143 H g
Hornisgrinde, pass . . . . 134 E d
Horologium, in Athens . . . . . 23 D
Horrea . . . . 26 A d
Horrea, loc. in Rome . . . . . . 23 A
Horse Gate . . . . 6 ins. A
Horseham, parl. bor. . . . .
Horsens . . . . 158 E a
Horseshoe Bend, battle . . . . . 200 I f
Horsham, mon. . . . . 97 S i
Horta . . . . 27 G e
Ho-si-wu . . . . 170 ins. A
Hostilia . . . . 26 F b
Hôtel des Invalides, in Paris . 149 B
Hôtel de Ville, in Paris . . . . 149 B
Hôtel Dieu . . . . 149 B
Hôtel du Grand Maître in Versailles . . . . 149 A
Hôtels, Rue des, street in Versailles . . . . 149 A
Hot Springs . . . . 211 G d
Hottentots, people . . . . 109 S k
Houffalize . . . . 117 D d
Hougomont, castle . . . .
Hougue, La . . . . 130 C d
Hounslow . . . . 75 I i
Housatonic River . . . . 189 B c
House of Hope . . . . 189 B d
House of the Mighty Men, in Jerusalem . . . . 6 ins. A (4)
Houston . . . . 198 F d
Houtain . . . . 156 A a
Howard, Fort . . . . 211 H b
Howe, Cape . . . . 172 E d
Howe, route of Lord . . . . . . 195 F c
Howe, route of Sir William 105 F c, D e
Höwen, lordship . . . . 142 C e
Howland Island . . . . 180 J g
Höxter . . . . 55 Q i
Höxter, mon. . . . . 95 D a
Höxter, Hanse. cy. . . . . 99 ins. B
Hoya . . . . 78 F b
Hoya, cty. . . . . 78 F b
Hoyerswerda . . . . 155 H c
Hradisch, mon. . . . . 80 E g
Hsiang-ho . . . . 170 ins. A
Hsiang-yang . . . .
Hsiung . . . . 170 ins. A
Huacho . . . . 214 B d
Huallaga River . . . . 111 B c
Hualpai, Ind. Res. . . . . 188 D c
Huamachuco . . . . 111 B c
Huamanga . . . . 111 C d
Huancabamba . . . . 111 B c
Huancavelica . . . . 214 B d
Huanchaca . . . . 214 C e
Huanuco nuevo . . . . 111 B c
Huanuco viejo . . . . 111 B c
Huaqui . . . . 214 C d
Huaraz . . . . 111 B c
Huascan (Huascaran), mt. . . . 214 B c
Huasco . . . . 215 B e
Hubbardton . . . . 195 E b
Hubermont, Farm . . . .
Hubermont, Woods of. . . . . .
Hubert, Saint . . . . 117 D d
Hubertusburg . . . . 135 G c
Huddersfield, parl. bor. . . 163 M d (Hudd.)
Hude, mon. . . . . 95 D a
Hudson, route of . .
Hudson Bay . . . . 186 K b
Hudson River . . . . 189 B d
Hudson Strait . . . . 186 L b
Hudson's Bay Company . . . . .
Hué . . . . 171 L g
Huejotlipan . . . .
Huejotzingo . . . .
Huelgas, mon. . . . . 94 B c
Huelva . . . . 82 A b
Huesca . . . . 82 B a
Huesca, bp. . . . . 94 B c
Huesca, univ. . . . . 100 E f
Huescar . . . . 82 H f
Huete . . . . 82 B a
Hughenden . . . . 172 D c
Hugli . . . . 137 E d
Hugli River . . . . 137 E d
Hühnerwasser . . . . 159 H c
Huillier, Fort d' . . . . 191 G c
Hull, in Canada . . . . 212 H d
Hull, in England . . . . 127 Y m
Hull, Hanse. for. cy. . . . . 98 ins. A
Hull, parl. bor. . . . . 163 N d
Hull, in Massachus . . . . 189 ins. B
Hull, route of . . . . 200 C d
Hulst . . . . 117 C c
Hulwan . . . . 99 M g
Humacao . . . . 199 ins. G
Humaitá . . . . 215 D e
Humber River . . . . 49 G e
Humboldt River . . . . 187 H d
Huna Floi . . . . 166 A b
Hu-nan, prov. . . . . 171 M f
Hundheim . . . . 158 E d
Hungarian Plain . . . . 2 F d
Hungarians, people, on the Dniester . . . . 55 J d
Hungarians, people, on the Theiss 168 G c
Hungary, km., about 1000 . . . 59 H-I d
Hungary, km., about 1190 . . . 70 K d
Hungary, km., part of the Ottoman Empire . . . . 119 H d
Hungary, km., about 1740 . . . 131 H d
Hungary, km., 19 cent. . . . . . 159 J e
Hungerford . . . . 127 X o
Hun-ho, R. . . . . 170 ins. A
Hüningen . . . . 122 D e
Hunkiar Skelessi . . . . 164 D b
Hunnic (Attila's) Empire . . . . 48 F-L b
Huns, people, on the Volga R.
Huns, people, in Hungary . . .
Hunte River . . . . 114 E b
Huntingdon . . . . 127 Y n
Huntingdon, castle . . . . 65 F d
Huntingdon, cty. . . . .
Huntingdon, mon. . . . . 97 Q i
Huntingdon, parl. bor. . . . . . 163 N e
Huntingdon, parl. dist. . . . . . 163 N e
Huntingdon, shire . . . .
Huntington . . . . 192 E c
Huntsville . . . . 211 H d
Hu-pei, prov. . . . . 171 M e
Huriel . . . . 69 I g
Huron, lake . . . . 187 K d
Hurons, tribe . . . . 188 J b
Hurst Castle . . . . 127 X p
Hushi . . . . 131 I d
Hussinetz . . . . 79 H d
Huy . . . . 117 D d
Hwang-chau . . . .
Hwiccas, people . . . .
Hyampolis . . . . 11 D d
Hybla Heræa . . . . 30 D e
Hybla Maior . . . . 30 D e
Hyblæus River . . . . 30 D e
Hyccara . . . . 30 C d
Hydaspes River . . . . 19 L d
Hyderabad, in Deccan . . . . . 137 C e
Hyderabad, in Sind . . . . 137 A c
Hydraotes River . . . . 19 L d
Hydrea (Hydra), isl. . . . . 15 D b
Hydruntum (Otranto) . . . . . . 31 H b
Hydrusa, isl. . . . . 16 B b
Hyeres, isl. . . . . 126 E e
Hilæthus River . . . . 11 D d
Hyle . . . . 11 E d
Hylias River . . . . 31 F c
Hylice, lake . . . . 11 E d
Hymettus, mt. . . . . 15 D b
Hypæpa . . . . 20 B c
Hypanis River (Bug R.) . . . . 18 D a
Hypanis River (Kuban R.) . . . 18 E a
Hypata . . . . 10 D d
Hypatus, mt. . . . . 11 E d
Hyphasis River . . . . 19 D d
Hyphormus, Port of . . . . 16 B b
Hypsas River . . . . 30 B e
Hyrcania, reg. . . . . 19 H c
Hyrcania, satr. . . . . 8 J e
Hyria, lake . . . . 10 C d
Hyrmine . . . . 14 B a
Hyrminus River . . . . 30 D e

Hyrtacina . . . . 14 ins.
Hysiæ . . . . 14 C b
Hythe . . . .
Hythe, parl. bor. . . . . 163 P f

Iaccetani, people . . . . 38 C d
Iader . . . . 27 J c
Ialysus . . . . 4 C b
Iamo . . . . 38 C e
Iamnia . . . . 7 B e
Iamnia maritima. . . . 7 B e
Iamzai . . . .
Ianiculum, mt. . . . . 22 A
Iapis River . . . . 16 A a
Iapydes, people . . . . 27 I b
Iapygians, people . . . . 29 E d
Iapygium, prom. . . . . 31 H c
Iardanus River, in Crete . . . . 14 ins.
Iardanus River, in Elis . . . . 14 B b
Iassus . . . . 13 E c
Iazyges Metanastæ, people . . . 38 F c
Ibagué . . . . 214 B b
Ibebin . . . .
Iberia, reg. (Caucasia) . . . . 18 F b
Iberia, reg. (Spain) . . . . 12 B c
Iberian Peninsula . . . . 2 D d
Iberian Sea. . . . . 38 B e
Iberus River, see Ebro River
Ibir-Sibir, reg. . . . . 102 G b
Iburg, mon. . . . . 95 D a
Ica, battle . . . . 214 B d
Iça River . . . .
Icaria . . . . 16 B a
Icaria, isl. . . . . 13 E c
Icaros, see Icaria . . . . 17 E c
Icauna or Icaunus River, see Yonne River
Ice Cape . . . . 170 I a
Iceland, isl. . . . . 166 B c
Iceni, people . . . . 51 Q h
I-chang . . . . 171 M e
I-chau . . . . 170 ins. A
Ichnæ . . . . 11 D b
Ichtershausen, mon. . . . . 95 E a
Ichthyophagi, people . . . . 19 J e
Ichthys, prom. . . . . 14 B b
Iciodurum, see Issoire
Icknield Way, road . . . . 51 P i
Icolmkill, isl. . . . .
Iconium (Konieh) . . . . 20 E d
Iconium, sultanate, 12 cent. . . 68 B b
Iconium, sultanate, 13 cent. . . 73 H c
Icorigium . . . . 39 I h
Icosium . . . . 12 D c
Iculisna, see Angoulême
Icus . . . . 11 E c
Icus (Khiliodromia), isl. . . . . 11 E c
Icy Cape . . . . 198 ins. A
Ida, mt., in Crete . . . . 14 ins.
Idaho, state . . . . 210 B a
Idaho, ter. 1863 . . . . 203 P f
Idaho, ter. 1864 . . . . 203 P g
Idaho, ter. 1868 . . . . 203 O g
Ida Mountains, in Troas . . . .
Idanha . . . . 82 A b
Idar . . . . 142 ins. A
Idex River . . . . 27 F c
Idistaviso . . . . 39 J g
Idomene . . . .
Idrisids, dom. of the . . . . 54 E f
Idstedt . . . . 158 E a
Idubeda Mountains . . . . 38 B d
Idumæa, reg. . . . . 7 B f
Ieracia, isl. . . . .
Ierne (Ireland), isl. . . . . 38 A b
Igilgilis . . . . 38 D e
Igilium, isl. . . . . 26 E e
Iglau . . . . 79 I d
Igli . . . . 174 C a
Iglo . . . . 159 K d
Iguala . . . . 213 ins.
Iguassú, river and falls . . . . 215 D e
Iguvium . . . . 27 G d
Ilanz . . . . 91 R l
Ilchester, parl. bor. . . . . 163 L g
Ildijis Atabeks, people . . . . 71 P f
Ile du Palais, loc. in Paris . . . 149 B
Ilei . . . . 15 D b
Ilerda (Lérida) . . . . 38 C d
Ilergetes, people . . . . 38 B d
Ilfeld, mon. . . . . 95 E a
Ilheos, cap. . . . . 108 M i
Ili River . . . . 92 H c
Ilici . . . . 38 B e
Ilipula Mountains . . . . 38 B e
Ilissus River . . . . 16 B b
Ilium (Troy) . . . .
Ilium, in Epirus . . . . 10 B c
Il-Khans of Persia, Dom. of the
Illampu, Mount . . . . 214 C d
Illapel . . . . 215 B f
Ille-et-Vilaine, dept. . . . . 148 D e
Iller River . . . . 62 F d
Illiberi or Illiberis (Elvira) in Spain 38 B e
Illiberis, in France, see Elne
Illimani, Mount . . . . 214 C d
Illinoia, proposed stale in U. S.
Illinois, tribe . . . . 188 H c
Illinois Country, reg. . . . . 191 G H c
Illinois, ter. 1809 . . . . 202 G a
Illinois, state . . . . 203 T b
Illinois River . . . . 191 G d
Illiturgi . . . . 38 B e
Illkirch . . . . 122 D d
Illurgavonenses, people . . . . 38 C d
Illyria, reg. . . . . 12 G b
Illyria, km. . . . . 159 H e
Illyrian Provinces . . . . 155 G e
Illyrians, people . . . . 5 A a
Illyricum, reg., 1st cent. . . . . 34 H e
Illyricum, reg., 5 cent. . . . . 50 H d
Illyricum, E. Rom. pref. . . . . 43 G f
Illyrii, people . . . . 17 B a
Illyris, dist. . . . . 10 B b
Ilm River . . . . 85 F e
Ilmen, lake . . . . 59 K b
Iloilo . . . . 199 ins. H
Iluro, see Oloron
Ilus, Burial mound of . . . .
Ilva (Elba), isl. . . . . 26 E e
Imbros, isl. . . . .
Imil . . . .
Immenstadt . . . . 143 J j
Imola . . . . 90 J h
Imola, bp. . . . . 95 E c
Imperial Canal . . . . 171 M e
Inachus River, in Æniania . . . 10 D d
Inachus River, in Argolis . . . . 14 C b
Inachus River, in Epirus . . . . 10 C c
Inagua, isl. . . . . 105 F b
Incas, Dom. of the . . . . 108 J h K j
In Castello . . . . 27 F c
Incia River . . . . 26 E c
Inda, mon. . . . . 95 D a
Independence, in Missouri . . . 211 G c
Independence, in Texas . . . . 210 F d
Independence, Fort, in Vermont 195 E a
India, emp. 137
India, reg. . . . . 112 A b
India Inferior, prov. . . . . 19 K e
India infra terram, reg. . . . . 99 M g
Indiana, ter. 1803 . . . . 202 H b
Indiana, ter. 1809 . . . . 202 H b
Indiana, state . . . . 203 U b
Indianapolis . . . . 199 H c
Indian Country, reg. 1819 . . . . 203 R b
Indian Lake . . . . 212 F c
Indian Ocean . . . . 109 W-A A h
Indian Pueblo Grants . . . . 188 E c
India Superior, prov. . . . . 19 L d
Indian Territories, in Canada . 212 C c
Indian Territory, in the U. S. . 203 S c
Indians in the United States . . 188
Indigetes, people . . . . 38 C d
Indies, E., reg. . . . 109, 110 X-D D e-h
Indies, The, reg. . . . 107, 108, leg.
Indien, W., reg. . . . 107, 108 E-O, a-l
Indo-China, French col. . . . . 171 L g
Indore . . . . 137 C d
Indragiri . . . .
Indre, dept. . . . . 148 E e
Indre-et-Loire, dept. . . . . 148 E e
Indus River, in Caria . . . . 20 C d
Indus River, in India . . . . 137 A c
Industria . . . . 26 C b
Inessa . . . . 30 D e
Infantado, duchy . . . . 83 K g
Infante, Rio del, R. . . . . 109 T k
Ingævones, people . . . . 38 D b
Ingauni, people . . . . 26 C c
Ingelfingen . . . . 143 I g
Ingelheim . . . . 62 D d
Ingerkingen . . . . 143 I i
Ingermanland, reg. . . . . 138 C d
Ingolstadt . . . . 79 G d
Ingolstadt, univ. . . . . 100 H e
Ingria, reg. . . . . 138 C d
Iniada . . . . 165 F c
Inkerman . . . . 164 J f
Inland India, reg. . . . . 99 M g
Inn River . . . . 63 G d
Innichen . . . . 54 G d
Innichen, mon. . . . . 80 C h
Inn Quarter, dist. . . . . 135 G d
Innsbruck . . . . 72 C b
Innviertel, dist. . . . . 157 C c
Inowraclaw (Hohensalza) . . . . 135 J b
In Portu . . . . 26 E d
Insala . . . . 174 D b
Insterburg . . . . 155 K a
Insubres, people . . . . 26 C b
Interamna or Interamne (Terni), in Umbria . . . . 27 G e
Interamna Lirenas (Termini), in Latium . . . . 30 C a
Interamnia, in Picenum . . . . 27 H e
Interamnium . . . . 31 F c
Interlaken . . . . 91 P l
Internal Provinces, New Spain 190 B F e f
Interocrium . . . . 27 H e
Interpromium . . . . 27 H e
Intimilii, people . . . . 26 B d
Inverary . . . .
Invercargill . . . . 172 F e
Inverloch . . . .
Inverness . . . .
Inverness, cty. . . . .
Inycum . . . . 30 C e
Iol . . . . 38 C e
Iolcus . . . . 11 D c
Ion River . . . . 10 C c
Iona, bp. . . . . 97 G c
Iona, isl. . . . . 49 C c
Ionia, reg. . . . . 8 Q h
Ionia, satr. . . . . 8 G e
Ionian Islands . . . . 164 B c
Ionians, people . . . .
Ionian Sea . . . . 5 A b
Ios . . . . 13 D c
Iovavum (Salzburg), see Iuvavum
Ioventio, pass . . . . 26 D c
Iowa City . . . . 211 G b
Iowa, Ind. Res. . . . . 188 G c
Iowa, ter. 1838 . . . . 202 F f
Iowa, state . . . . 202 G g
Iowa River . . . . 211 G b
Iowa, tribe . . . . 188 H b
Ipni Promontorium. . . . . 11 E c
Ipoly-Ságh . . . . 159 J d
Ipsus . . . . 20 D c
Ipswich, in England . . . .
Ipswich, Hanse. for. cy. . . . . 98 ins. A
Ipswich, parl. bor. . . . . 163 P e
Ipswich, in Mass. . . . . 189 D c
Ipswich, in Queensland . . . . 172 E c
Iquique . . . . 214 B e
Iquitos . . . . 214 B c
Ira . . . . 14 B b
Ira River . . . . 26 D c
Irak, reg. . . . .
Irak Ajemi, reg. . . . .
Irak Arabi, reg. . . . .

Iran, Plateau of . . . 3 J f
Irawadi River . . .
Irbil . . . 71 O f
Ireland, isl. . . .
Iria . . . 26 C b
Irish, people, about 900 . . .
Irish Sea . . . 49 D e
Iris River . . . 20 G b
Irkutsk . . . 171 L c
Iron . . . 6 C b
Iron Bridge, over the Orontes R. 68 C b
Ironton . . . 206 ins.
Iroquois, tribes . . . 192 D a
Iroquois River . . . 191 H
Irrhesia, isl. . . . 11 F c
Irtish River . . .
Is (Hit) . . . 18 F d
Isabel, isl. . . . 172 E a
Isabella . . . 105 F c
Isabella, isl. . . . 105 F b
Isar River . . . 63 G d
Isara, see Pontoise
Isara River (Isère R.) . . . 38 D c
Isara River (Oise R.) . . . 38 C c
Isarci, people . . . 27 F a
Isarcus River . . . 27 F a
Isaszeg . . . 159 J e
Isatis (Yezd) . . . 19 H d
Isaura . . . 20 E d
Isauria, reg. . . .
Isauria, E. Rom. prov. . . . 43 I f (14)
Isauria, Rom. prov. . . .
Isca Dumnoniorum (Exeter) . . 51 O i
Isca Silurum (Caerleon-upon-Usk) . . . 51 O i
Ischia, bp. . . . 95 ins.
Ischia, isl. . . . 90 D d
Ischl . . . 158 G e
Isel-Berg, mt. . . . 154 F e
Isenburg, princ. . . . 154 E c
Iser River . . . 115 H c
Isère, dept. . . . 148 F e
Isère River . . . 84 F g
Isernia . . . 161 J g
Isernia, bp. . . . 95 E c
Iseum . . . 22 A
Ishim River . . .
Ishmaelites, people . . . 7 ins. C
Isis, Temple of . . . 22 A
Isis and Serapis, Aug. Reg. of Rome . . . 22 A
Isker . . . 138 K d
Isker River . . . 168 H e
Iskut River . . . 212 ins.
Isla del Gallo, isl. . . . 111 B a
Isla de Pinos, isl. . . . 105 C c
Isla de Sacrificios, isl. . . . 106 D a
Isla de Términos, isl. . . . 105 B c
Islamabad . . . 137 C b
Island No. 10, fort . . . 208 C b
Islands, Bay of . . . 172 G d
Isla Santa, isl., off coast of Perú 111 B c
Isla Santa, i. e. South America 105 F e
Islay, isl. . . . 49 C d
Isle de France, isl. . . . 175 I f
Isle of France, gouv. . . . 146 B b
Isle of France, prov. . . . 148 E e
Isle of Wight . . . 100 A b
Isle of Wight, parl. dist. . . . 163 M g
Isles, The, bp. . . . 97 G c
Islington . . . 75 I h
Islip Bridge . . . 127 X o
Ismail . . . 131 I d
Ismailia . . . 174 K i
Ismenus River . . . 11 E d
Ismid . . . 77 K d
Ismilan . . . 165 D c
Isnik . . . 89 I f
Isny . . . 114 F e
Isny, imp. city . . . 143 J j
Isocum . . . 38 C e
Isontus River, see Salzach River
Isonzo River . . . 50 F c
Ispahan . . . 53 H c
Israel, Kingdom of . . . 6 ins. B
Issachar, tribe . . . 7 ins. D
Issoire . . . 126 C d
Issoudun . . . 61 E c
Issoudun, castle . . . 76 E c
Issoudun, seign. . . . 61 D c
Issus . . . 20 G d
Issus, Gulf of . . . 20 F d
Issyk-kul, lake . . .
Istævones, people . . . 38 D b
Ister (Danube) River . . . 35 I e
Istib . . .
Istone, mt. . . . 10 A c
Istria, reg. . . . 27 H b
Istria, march . . . 63 G f
Istropolis . . . 39 N l
Istrus . . . 12 I b
Istvæones, see Istævones
Isurium (Aldborough) . . . 51 P g
Italia, dist. in Bruttium . . . 30 E d
Italia, see Italy
Italians, people . . .
Italian Peninsula . . . 2 F d
Italian Republic . . . 151 H g
Italian Somaliland, col. . . . 174 H d
Italica . . . 38 A e
Italy, reg. . . . 12 F b
Italy, West. Rom. dioc. . . . 42 E d
Italy, exarch. of . . . 52 J e
Italy, km., 9 cent. . . . 56 E d
Italy, km., 12 cent. . . . 70 I e
Italy, km., 19 cent. . . . 154 F f
Itanus . . . 14 ins.
Itapirú, Fort . . . 215 D e
Itapua . . . 215 D e
Itasca, lake . . . 186 J d
Itati . . . 215 D e
Ithaca . . . 10 B d
Ithaca, isl. . . . 10 B d
Ithaca (Leucas), isl. . . . 10 B d
Ithome . . . 10 C c
Ithome, mt. . . . 14 B b
Ithoria . . . 10 C d
Itil (Astrakhan) . . . 99 M d
Itius, Portus, bay . . . 38 C b
Itonus . . . 11 D c
Ituna Æstuarium (Solway Firth) 51 O g
Iturea, dist. . . . 6 D a
Ituzaingó, battle . . . 215 D f
Ityke . . . 12 F c
Itzehoe . . . 55 Q i
Iuenna . . . 27 I a
Iuka . . . 208 C c
Iuliabriga . . . 38 B d
Iuliacum (Jülich) . . . 39 I h
Iulia Fanestris . . . 27 H d
Iuliobona . . . 38 B c
Iuliomagus (Angers) . . . 38 B c
Iulis . . . 15 E b
Iulius, Vicus . . . 39 J i
Iulium Carnicum . . . 27 G a
Iunonia Falisca . . . 27 G e
Iuvanum . . . 27 I f
Iuvavum (Salzburg) . . . 38 E c
Ivangorod, in Ingria . . . 138 C d
Ivangorod, in Poland . . . 159 L c
Ivanitza . . . 165 B b
Ivanovo Vosnessensk . . .
Iviza, bp. . . . 94 C d
Iviza, isl. . . . 82 C b
Ivois, castle . . . 62 C d
Ivory Coast, French col. . . . 174 C d
Ivrea . . . 90 A b
Ivrea, bp. . . . 95 D b
Ivrea, marq. . . . 64 A a
Ivry . . . 76 D b
Ixtacamaxtitlan . . .
Ixworth, mon. . . . 97 R i
Izium . . . 139 E f
Iznalloz . . . 82 B b
Iztaban . . . 105 B c
Iztaccihuatl, volcano of . . . 106 B a
Iztapalapan . . .
Iztaplatzinco . . .
Jabalpur, Jubbulpore . . . 137 C d
Jabbok River . . . 7 D d
Jabesh-Gilead . . .
Jablunkau . . . 123 J d
Jabneel, in Galilee . . . 6 D c
Jabneel, in Philistæa . . . 7 B e
Jaca . . . 82 B a
Jackson, in Michigan . . . 207 I b
Jackson, in Mississippi . . . 211 G d
Jackson, Fort, in Alabama . . . 200 I f
Jackson, Fort, in Louisiana . . 208 C d
Jackson, route of . . . 200 I g
Jackson's Hole, dist. . . . 210 C b
Jacksonville . . . 199 I d
Jacob, castle . . . 68 ins. A
Jacobins, The, bldg. in Paris . 149 B
Jacobsdal . . . 175 L l
Jadera . . . 54 H e
Jaén, in Peru . . . 214 B c
Jaén, in Spain . . . 82 B b
Jaén, bp. . . . 94 B d
Jaén, km. . . . 83 K h
Jaffa . . . 68 ins. A
Jafna . . . 112 B c
Jafnapatam . . . 112 B c
Jagannath . . . 137 E e
Jägerndorf . . . 115 I c
Jägerndorf, princ. . . . 115 I c
Jagersfontein . . . 175 M l
Jagst River . . . 143 J g
Jagstberg . . . 143 I g
Jagstheim . . . 143 H g
Jagstzell . . . 143 J g
Jaguarão . . . 215 D f
Jaguaribe River . . . 214 F c
Jahna, castle . . . 63 G c
Jaipur, in Madras . . . 170 J g
Jaipur, in Rajputana . . . 170 I f
Jaipur, Jaypore, dist. . . . 137 C c
Jaisalmer, dist. . . . 137 B c
Jaitza . . .
Jalalabad . . . 137 B b
Jalapa . . . 106 D a
Jalayrs, Dom. of the . . . 77 N f
Jaligny . . . 69 E c
Jalisco, state . . . 213 ins.
Jamaica . . . 189 ins. C
Jamaica, isl. . . . 105 E c
Jamapa, R. . . . 106 D a
Jamary River . . . 214 C d
Jambi . . .
James, Fort . . . 132 J h
James Bay . . . 186 K c
James River . . . 188 K c
Jamestown . . . 193 ins. A
Janiculan citadel . . . 23 B
Janina . . .
Janitza . . . 165 C c
Janizary Quarter, Old, in Constantinople . . . 93 G e
Jankau . . . 123 H d
Jan Mayen, isl. . . . 166 D a
Janus, Temple of, in Rome . .
Janus quadrifrons, in Rome . . 24 B
Japan, emp. . . .
Japan Sea . . .
Jargeau . . . 76 E c
Jarmuth Ramoth . . . 7 C d
Jarnac . . . 126 A d
Jaroslaw . . . 159 L c
Jarrow . . .
Jarrow, mon. . . . 97 P g
Jassy . . . 139 C f
Játiva . . . 82 B b
Jauer . . . 79 I c
Jauja . . . 111 B d
Java, isl. . . .
Javols, about forty miles northeast of Rodez
Jaxartes River (Syr-Daria) . . . 19 J a
Jazer . . . 7 D e
Jean-Loo . . .
Jeba . . . 6 B c
Jeblaam . . . 7 C d

Jedburgh
Jefferson City 211 G c
Jehlam 137 B b
Jehol 171 M d
Jehoshaphat, gate, in Jerusalem 68 ins. B
Jehoshaphat, street 68 ins. B
Jehoshaphat, Tomb of 6 ins. A
Jehoshaphat, Valley of 6 ins. A
Jelairs, people
Jemappas 134 B c
Jemes 190 D d
Jemmingen 114 D b
Jemtland, dist. 120 E d
Jena 114 F c
Jeni-Kivi
Jeni-Shehr
Jenkinson, route of 108 R a
Jequitinhonha River 214 E d
Jerba, isl. 73 C d
Jerez de la Frontera 82 G f
Jerez de los Caballeros 82 G f
Jericho 7 C e
Jerichow 85 C b
Jerichow, mon. 80 ins.
Jersey, isl. 69 B b
Jersey City 189 ins. C
Jerusalem 7 C e
Jerusalem, plan of ancient 6 ins. A
Jerusalem, plan of mediaeval 68 ins. B
Jerusalem, km., 12 cent. 68 C c
Jerusalem, km., 13 cent. 73 G d
Jerusalem, patr. 52 L f
Jervaulx, mon. 97 P g
Jeshua 7 B f
Jesi 90 D c
Jesi, bp. 95 E c
Jesireh, El, see El Jesireh
Jesulmere, reg. 137 B c
Jever 114 D b
Jever, lordship 122 D b
Jeypore, Jaipur, dist. 137 C c
Jezreel 6 C c
Jezreel, Plain of 6 C c
Jhansi 137 C c
Jheelum
Jibuti 174 H c
Jicarilla, Ind. Res. 188 E c
Jiddah
Jimena 82 A b
Jiphtha 6 C c
Jitomir 139 C e
Joachimsthal 115 G c
Joanna Springs 172 B b
Joazeiro 214 E c
Jocko, Ind. Res. 188 D a
Jodhpur 137 B c
Jodoigne 156 B a
Johann Georgenstadt 123 G c
Johannesburg 175 M l
John Cabot, route of 108 O b M c
John of Pian de Carpine, route of
Johnson, mt. 212 ins.
Johnson Hall 194 L f
Johnstones, fam. 97 J d
Johnston Islands 180 K f
Joigny 61 E c
Joinville, in Brazil 215 E e
Joinville, in France 76 F b
Joinville, seign. 69 J f
Jokneam 6 C c
Joli-Bois
Joliet 211 H b
Jolliet, route of 191 G c
Joló Archipelago 199 ins. H
Jomsburg 63 H b
Jonesboro 196 ins. A
Jönköping 120 H e
Joppa, in Maryland 192 C d
Joppa, in Palestine 7 B d
Joppe 7 B d
Jordan River 7 D d
Josefstadt 159 I c
José Monteiro 214 D c
Joug-Dieu, Le, mon. 94 C b
Jouy, mon. 94 C b
Juana (Cuba), isl. 105 D b
Juan de Fuca, Strait of 198 A a
Juan Fernandez Island 107 I k
Juba River 175 H d
Jubbulpore, Jabalpur 137 C d
Judæa, reg. 7 B e
Judah, Kingdom of 6 ins. B
Judah, tribe 7 ins. D
Judah, Mountains of 7 C e
Judah, Wilderness of 7 C e
Judenburg 123 H a
Judith, Point, cape 189 ins. A
Juggernaut 137 E e
Juist, isl. 117 E a
Jujuy 215 C e
Julian Alps, mts. 27 H a
Julian Aqueduct 22 A
Julian Augustan Way, road 26 B d
Julias 6 D c
Julica, Basilia, bldg. in Rome 24 B
Jülich 62 D c
Jülich, duchy 78 E c
Jülich-Cleves-Berg, prov. 158 D c
Julier, pass 26 D a
Jumet 156 A b
Jumièges 65 G f
Jumièges, mon. 94 C b
Jumna River
Junction City 210 F c
Juneau 212 ins.
Jungaria, reg. 92 I c
Jung-Bunzlau 115 H c
Juniata River 192 C c
Junin, battle 214 B d
Junkseylon 112 C c
Juno Lucina, Temple of 22 A
Juno Moneta, Temple of 24 A
Juno Regina, Temple of 22 A
Jupiter Capitolinus, Temple of 24 A
Jupiter Dolichenus, Temple of 22 A
Jupiter Latiaris, Temple of 35 ins. B (5)
Jupiter Stator, Temple of 24 A
Jupiter Victor, Temple of 24 A
Jura, dept. 148 F e
Jura Mountains 38 D c
Jurjan 102 F d
Juruá River 214 B c
Jussy 91 O l
Justingen 143 I i
Justingen, lordship 143 I i
Justinian, Statue of 93 G e (2)
Jüterbog 63 G c
Jutes, people, 5 cent.
Jutes, people, about 900
Jutigalpa 213 D c
Jutland, reg. 70 H b
Juttah 7 C f
Juturna, Lake of
Kaaden 79 H c
Kabarda, reg.
Kabinda 175 E e
Kabul 137 A b
Kadesh 4 F c
Kadesh Barnea 7 ins. C
Kadesh Naphtali 6 ins. B
Kadesia 53 G d
Kadiak, isl. 198 ins. A
Kadikeui 93 G e
Kafche-kué, reg.
Kaffa 73 H a
Kaffraria, reg. 175 M m
Kaffraria, British, dist. 175 M m
Kafiristan, reg. 137 B a
Kafr Embabeh
Kagoshima 171 O e
Kahlen Berg, mt. 123 I d
Kahoolawe, isl. 198 ins. B
Kai-fong-fu
Kail
Kailua 198 ins. B
Kaindu
Kairwan 53 C c
Kais, isl.
Kaisarieh
Kaisersberg 126 E b
Kaiserslautern 122 D d
Kaiserstuhl 142 B e
Kaiserswerth 62 D c
Kaiserswerth, mon. 55 Q i
Kaiser Wilhelms Land, col. 179 F h
Kaisheim, mon. 95 E b
Kalahari Desert 175 F g
Kalamata 164 C c
Kalenberg, Brunswick-, duchy 86 G b
Kalgan 171 M d
Kalhat
Kalifati
Kalinga, reg.
Kalisz, Kalisch 79 K c
Kallundborg, Hanse. for. cy. 98 F b
Kalmucks, people 139 F f
Kalocsa 168 F c
Kalocsa, abp. 95 F c
Kalpi 170 I f
Kaluga 139 E e
Kalw 62 E d
Kama-Bulgarians, people 71 P b
Kama River 138 H d
Kamakura
Kamaran Island 170 F g
Kamba 62 E d
Kamburg 63 F c
Kamen 153 N f
Kamens 80 ins.
Kamerun, Cameroons, German col. 174 E d
Kaminiets Podolski 119 J d
Kaministiquia, Fort 191 G b
Kamloops 212 C c
Kammin 72 D a
Kammin, bp. 79 J a
Kammin, Hanse. cy. 99 ins. B
Kamp, mon. 95 D a
Kampen 117 D b
Kampen, Hanse. cy. 99 ins. B
Kamrup, reg.
Kamtchatka, pen.
Kanah 6 C b
Kanara, reg. 137 B f
Kanata 6 E c
Kanauj
Kanawha River, Great 193 D b
Kan-chau-fu
Kandahar
Kandalakskaya 167 L b
Kandern 142 A e
Kandy 137 D g
Kané
Kane Sea 186 L a
Kanem, reg. 174 E c
Kanesville 199 F c
Kangaroo Island 172 C d
Kanin Peninsula 167 N b
Kankakee River 191 H c
Kanklis, reg.
Kano 174 D c
Kansan
Kansas, tribe 188 F c
Kansas, state 203 S h
Kansas, ter. 1854 202 E h
Kansas City 211 G c
Kansas Osage, Ind. Res. 188 G c
Kansas Pacific Grant 210 E c
Kansas River 198 F c
Kan-su, prov. 171 L e
Kantara, El 174 K i
Kaoli, reg. (Korea)
Kao-tai
Kapfenburg, castle 143 J h
Kaphar Saba 7 B d
Kapolna 159 K e
Kappel 91 Q k
Kappenberg, mon. 95 D a
Kapunda 172 C d
Karabunar 165 D b

Karachal, mts.
Karachi 137 A c
Kara Dagh, mts. 99 M f
Karahissar 89 K f
Karajang
Karajang, reg.
Karakhitai, reg. 92 H c
Karakodja
Karakoram (Karakorum) Mountains
Karakorum, Caracarum 92 K c
Kara-Kuyunli, people 77 L e
Karaman 93 D c
Karaman, princ. 93 D c
Karaman, reg. 89 J g
Kara Sea 170 H a
Karashar
Karasi, reg. 89 I g
Karatova 165 C b
Karchedon (Carthage) 5 A b
Kardis
Karelia, reg. 138 C c
Karikal 137 D f
Karlsburg, near Bremen 122 E b
Karlsburg, in Transylvania 159 L e
Karlstadt 155 H f
Karnak 4 F d
Karnata, reg.
Karnul 137 C e
Kars 67 O e
Kartha 6 B c
Kasbek, mt. 167 O g
Kaschau
Kashan
Kashgar
Kashgil 174 F c
Kashmir, Cashmere, reg.
Kaskaskia 191 H d
Kaskaskia River 191 H d
Kasr el Kebir 118 C g
Kassai River 175 E e
Kassites, people 5 D b
Kassogs, people 71 O e
Kastamuni 77 K d
Kastamuni, dist. 77 K d
Kastelberg, lordship 142 B d
Kastellaun 142 ins. A
Kastoria 71 K e
Katcha River 164 J f
Kates Needle, mt. 212 ins.
Kathiawar, Kattiwar, dist. 137 B d
Katieh 150 B a
Katif, El
Kattegat, str. 88 D c
Katwyk 117 C b
Katzbach River 155 I c
Kauai, isl. 198 ins. B
Kaufbeuren, imp. city 79 G e
Kaula, isl. 198 ins. B
Kavala 131 H e
Kaveri River
Kawar, oasis 2 F g
Kay 135 H b
Kayalik
Kayeli
Kayes 174 B c
Kayna 72 C a
Kaysersberg 143 ins. D
Kazan 138 G d
Kazan, khan. 139 G e
Kazerun
Kazvin
Kearney, Fort 210 F b
Kearney, route of 201 legend
Kecskemét 159 J e
Kedah
Kedesh Naphtali 6 D b
Keeling Islands 179 A i
Keewatin, dist. 212 F b
Kehl 142 A c
Keilah 7 B e
Kei River, Great 175 M m
Kekaughtan 193 ins. A
Kelat 67 O f
Kelat, reg. 73 I c
Kehlheim 122 F d
Kells 127 K h
Kelso
Kem 138 D c
Kemkemjuts, people
Kempsey 172 E d
Kempten, ab. 79 G e
Kempten, mon. 95 E b
Kenai, Fort 198 ins. A
Kenath 6 F c
Kendal 127 W l
Kendal, parl. bor. 163 L c
Kendal, reg. 84 B b
Keneh 150 B b
Kenesaw Mount, battle 208 D c
Kenia, mt. 175 G e
Kenilworth
Kenilworth, castle
Kenilworth, mon. 97 P i
Kenites, people 7 ins. D
Kenmare Bay 127 G j
Kennebec River 189 D b
Kennedys, fam.
Kensington, in Pa. 192 ins.
Kensington, castle, in England 75 I h
Kent, cty.
Kent, kingdom
Kentishmen, people
Kent Island 192 C d
Kenton 206 ins.
Kentucky, dist. 196 B c
Kentucky, state 211 H c
Kentucky River 193 B c
Kenzingen 142 A d
Keraits, people
Kerak 68 ins. A
Kerbela 77 M f
Kerguelen Islands 182 H H l
Kerith River 7 C c
Kerko Porta 93 G e
Kermadec Islands 172 H d
Kermian, reg. 89 I g
Kerry, cty. 127 H j
Kertch
Kerulen River
Kerun, Birket el, lake
Kesho
Kesmacoran, reg.
Kessel, dist. 117 D c
Kesselsdorf 135 G c
Kessin 63 F a
Kesteven and Holland, parl. dist. 163 N d
Ketsch 142 C b
Kexholm 138 D c
Keynsham, mon. 97 O j
Key West 211 I f
Khabarovka 171 O d
Khaibar Pass 170 I e
Khair-ed-Din Barbarossa, Tomb of 93 G e (12)
Khairpur 137 A c
Khalkas, people
Khalman (Aleppo) 5 C b
Khamil
Khanate of the Golden Horde
Khanbalig (Peking)
Khandesh, reg. 137 B d
Kharesm
Kharesm, Khuwarizm, reg.
Kharesmians, people 8 K d
Kharezmians, dynasty 73 I d
Kharkov 139 E e
Kharluks, people
Khartum 174 G c
Khatanga River
Khatangskoe 171 L a
Khatmandu 171 J f
Khazars, people 55 K c
Khelat
Kherson 139 D f
Khingan Mountains
Khitans, people
Khiva 170 G d
Khiva, khan.
Khojent
Khokand
Kholm 131 J b
Kholmogory 138 F c
Khorasan, reg. 53 H c
Khorat 171 L g
Khoritza 139 D f
Khorsabad 5 D b
Khotan
Khuram
Khuwarizm, Kharesm, reg.
Khuzistan, reg.
Khyrpore 137 A c
Kiakhta
Kiang-si, prov. 171 M f
Kiang-su, prov. 171 M e
Kiao-chau 171 N e
Kia-yu-kwan
Kiburg, castle 62 E e
Ki-chau 170 ins. A
Kickapoo, Ind. Res. 188 G c
Kickapoos, tribe 188 H b
Kichinev 139 C f
Kidderminster, parl. bor. 163 L e (Kidderm.)
Kiel 79 G a
Kiel, Hanse. cy. 99 ins. B
Kielce 159 K c
Kien-chang-fu
Kiersy 56 C c
Kieselbronn 142 C c
Kiev 71 M c
Kiev, prov. 131 J c
Kiev, dist. 71 L c
Kievits Hoeck 189 B d
Kiffhausen, castle 72 C a
Kij Mekran, reg.
Kikinda 159 K f
Kilburn 75 I h
Kildare, bp. 97 E c
Kildare, cty. 127 K h
Kilfenora, bp. 97 B d
Kilia 164 D a
Kilia, mouth of the Danube R. 164 D a
Kilimandjaro, mt. 175 G e
Kilkenny
Kilkenny, bp. 97 D d
Kilkenny, cty. 127 J i
Killala, bp. 97 B b
Killaloe, bp. 97 C d
Killarney 127 H i
Killiecrankie
Kilmacduagh, bp. 97 C c
Kilmore, bp. 97 D c
Kilsyth
Ki-lung 171 N f
Kilwa 109 U h
Kimberley, in Africa 175 L l
Kimberley, dist. in Australia 172 B b
Kimberley Goldfield 172 B b
Kinburn 139 D f
Kincardine, cty.
Kincardine, dist.
Kinchat
Kingdom of the Two Sicilies, 15 cent. 90 E e
King George, Fort 193 C f
King George Sound 172 A d
King Island 172 D e
King of Jerusalem, Palace of the 68 ins. B (7)
King's County 127 J h
King's Garden, isl. 105 E b
Kings Lynn, parl. bor. 163 O e
Kings Mountain, battle 195 A f
King Sound 172 B b
Kingston, in Canada 200 E a
Kingston, in Georgia 208 D c
Kingston, in Jamaica 213 E c
Kingston, in New York 192 D c
Kingston, in S. Australia 172 C d
Kingston, South, Rhode Island 189 ins. A
Kingston-upon-Hull, mon. 97 Q h

Kingston-upon-Thames . . . . . 75 I i
Kingswood, mon. . . . . 97 O j
King William Land . . . . . . 212 F b
Kinklas, tribe . . . . 188 B b
Kinross, cty. . . . .
Kinross, dist. . . . .
Kinsai (Hang-chau-fu) . . . . .
Kinsale . . . .
Kinzig Pass . . . . 134 E e
Kinzig River . . . . 142 A d
Kiovia, dist. . . . . 139 C e
Kiowas, tribe, in Colorado . . 188 E b
Kiowas, tribe, in Texas . . . . 188 F d
Kipchak, khan. . . . .
Kirchberg, on the Hunsrück Mts. . . . . 142 ins. A
Kirchberg, on the Jagst R. . . . 143 I g
Kirchheim . . . . 143 H h
Kirghiz, people, in Turkestan . 92 G c
Kirghiz, people, on the Yenisei R.
Kirghiz Steppe . . . . 3 J d
Kiriathaim . . . . 7 D e
Kirin . . . . 171 N d
Kirjath-Jearim . . . . 7 C e
Kirkcudbright . . . .
Kirkcudbright, cty. . . . .
Kirkcudbright, dist. . . . .
Kirkham, mon. . . . . 97 Q g
Kirkstall, mon. . . . . 97 P h
Kirkstead, mon. . . . . 97 Q h
Kirkwall, seat of bishopric . . 97 Ka leg.
Kirman . . . .
Kirman, reg. . . . . 53 H d
Kirn . . . . 142 ins. A
Kir of Moab . . . . 7 D f
Kish . . . .
Kishm, isl. . . . .
Kishon River . . . . 6 C c
Kiskiminitas River . . . . . . 192 B c
Kissingen . . . . 158 F c
Kisslegg . . . . 143 I j
Kistna River . . . . 112 A b
Kittanning . . . . 194 K f
Kittery . . . . 189 C c (Ki.)
Kitzen . . . . 154 G c (Ki.)
Kitzingen . . . . 72 C b
Kitzingen, mon. . . . . 95 E b
Kiung-chau . . . . 171 M g
Kiushiu, isl. . . . .
Kiutayeh . . . . 164 D c
Kiverova Gora . . . . 138 C d
Kizil Irmak River . . . . 93 D b
Kladrau . . . . 79 H d
Kladrau, mon. . . . . 95 E b
Klagenfurt . . . . 79 I e
Klamath, Ind. Res. . . . . . . 188 B b
Klamath River . . . . 198 A b
Klamath River, Ind. Res. . . . 188 B b
Klamaths, tribe . . . . 188 B b
Klar River . . . . 88 E a
Klause Pass . . . . 72 C b
Klausen Pass . . . . 91 Q l
Klausenburg . . . . 80 H h
Klein-Heubach . . . . 142 D a
Klein-Mariazell, mon. . . . . . 95 F b
Klein-Schnellendorf . . . . . . 135 I c
Klephts, people . . . . 164 C c
Klettgau, landgr. . . . . 142 B e
Klissow . . . .
Klikitats, tribe . . . . 188 B a
Klondike Region . . . . 212 B b
Klostergrab . . . . 123 G c
Klosterneuburg, mon. . . . . 80 E g
Knaered . . . . 120 H e
Knaresborough . . . . 127 X l
Knaresborough, parl. bor. . . . 163 M d
Kniebis Pass . . . . 142 B d
Knights of Saint John, Dom. of the . . . . 89 I g
Knights of Saint John, Hospital of the . . . . 68 ins. B (2)
Knin . . . . 131 G e
Knin, bp. . . . . 95 F c
Knittelfeld . . . . 155 H e
Knittlingen . . . . 143 G g
Knocke . . . . 134 B c
Knoxville . . . . 196 ins. A
Kobdo . . . . 171 K d
Kobdo, Plateau of . . . . . . 3 N d
Kobe . . . . 171 O e
Kocher River . . . . 143 J g
Kodiak, isl. . . . . 186 D c
Koesfeld, Hanse. cy. . . . . . 99 ins. B
Koevorden . . . . 117 E b
Koevorden, lordship . . . . . . 117 E b
Koil . . . .
Kojak Pass . . . . 170 H e
Kokel River . . . . 159 M e
Koko-nor, lake . . . .
Koksherev . . . . 71 P b
Kola . . . . 138 D b
Kola Peninsula . . . . 3 H b
Kolachel . . . .
Kolapore . . . .
Kolbatz, mon. . . . . 80 ins.
Kolberg . . . . 63 H a
Kolberg, Hanse. cy. . . . . . . 99 ins. B
Kolberger Heide, dist. . . . . . 122 F a
Kolding . . . . 154 E a
Kolditz . . . . 154 G c
Kolguiev, isl. . . . . 138 H b
Kolhapur . . . . 137 B e
Kolimsk, Nijne . . . .
Kolimsk, Sredne . . . . 171 Q b
Kolin . . . . 79 I c
Kölln, on the Spree . . . . . . 85 C b
Kölln, Hanse. cy. . . . . 99 ins. B
Kolmar . . . . 62 D d
Köln, see Cologne
Koloa . . . . 198 ins. B
Kolomna . . . . 138 E d
Kolonos . . . . 16 E e
Komorn . . . . 159 J e
Konakry . . . . 174 B d
Kongsberg . . . . 88 C b
Konieh . . . .
Königgrätz . . . . 135 H c
Königinhof . . . . 159 H c
Königsberg, in Prussia . . . . . 79 L a
Königsberg, Hanse. cy. . . . . 99 H c
Königsberg, imp. cy. in Franconia . . . . 114 F c
Königsbronn . . . . 122 F d
Königseck, castle . . . . 143 H j
Königseck, cty. . . . . 143 H j
Königsfelden, mon. . . . . . . 91 Q k
Königshofen . . . . 142 E a
Königslutter, mon. . . . . 95 E a
Königstein . . . . 123 H c
Königswartha . . . . 155 H c
Königs-Wusterhausen . . . . . 135 G b
Konin . . . . 123 J b
Koningsveld, mon. . . . . 94 C a
Konitz . . . . 135 I b
Konkan, reg. . . . .
Konkan-tana . . . .
Konstanz, see Constance
Konzenberg . . . . 142 C d
Kootenay, lake . . . . 198 B a
Kootenay River . . . . 198 B a
Köpenick . . . . 123 G b
Koporiye . . . .
Koppenstein, castle . . . . . . 142 ins. A
Korb . . . . 143 H g
Kordofan, reg. . . . . 174 F c
Korea, Jap. prot. . . . . 171 N e
Korea, reg. . . . .
Körmend . . . . 155 I e
Körmöczbanya . . . .
Korneuburg . . . . 123 I d
Körös River . . . . 159 K e
Korsör . . . . 158 F a
Kortrijk . . . . 122 B c
Koschmin . . . . 159 I c
Kosel . . . . 123 J c
Köslin . . . . 123 I a
Koslov . . . . 139 F e
Kosseir . . . . 150 B b
Kossovopolje, valley . . . . . . 93 B b
Kostnitz, see Constance
Kostroma . . . . 138 F d
Kotah . . . . 170 I f
Kotah, reg. . . . . 137 C c
Kota Rajah . . . . 171 K h
Kotchak Bay . . . . 167 P f
Kottbus . . . . 72 C a
Köthen . . . . 154 F c
Kötzschenbroda . . . . 123 G c
Kovel . . . . 159 M c
Kovno . . . . 77 I a
Kovno, Hanse. for. cy. . . . . . 99 H b
Koweyt . . . .
Kraich River . . . . 142 C b
Krainburg . . . . 123 H e
Krajova . . . .
Krasnoi . . . . 153 O g
Krasnoi-Yar . . . . 139 G f
Krasnovodsk . . . . 170 G d
Krasnoyarsk . . . . 171 K c
Krasny . . . . 71 M c
Krautheim . . . . 142 E b
Krementchug . . . .
Kremmen . . . . 85 C b
Kremnitz . . . . 80 F g
Krems . . . . 63 H d
Kremsier . . . .
Kremsmünster, mon. . . . . . . 80 D h
Kreuzberg, pass . . . . 27 G a
Kreuznach . . . . 122 D d
Kriechingen . . . . 134 D d
Kroia . . . .
Kroia, bp. . . . . 95 F c
Kroissenbrunn . . . . 72 D b
Kronstadt, in Russia . . . . . . 138 C c
Kronstadt, in Transylvania . . .
Kroonstad . . . . 175 M l
Krossen . . . . 63 H b
Krugersdorp . . . . 175 M l
Krumau . . . . 135 H d
Kuban, dist. . . . . 170 E d
Kuban, reg. . . . . 77 L c
Kuban River . . . . 73 H a
Kubango River . . . . 175 E f
Kuchar . . . .
Kuen-lun Mountains . . . . .
Kufstein . . . . 115 G e
Kufra, oases . . . . 2 G f
Kughi . . . .
Kuinder . . . . 117 D b
Kuinre . . . . 117 D b
Kuka, Kukawa . . . . 174 E c
Kulbarga . . . . 92 H f
Kuldja . . . .
Kulevdcha . . . .
Kulikovo . . . . 92 D b
Kulm, in Bohemia . . . . 72 C a
Kulm, in Prussia . . . . 72 D a
Kulm, bp. . . . . 95 F a
Kulm, Hanse. cy. . . . . 98 G c
Kulmbach . . . . 87 H c
Kulmerland, dist. . . . . 72 D a
Kulmsee, seat of bishopric . . . 95 F a
Kuma River . . . . 99 M e
Kumaon, reg. . . . . 170 I e
Kumassi . . . . 174 C d
Kum-Kale . . . .
Kum-Kioi . . . .
Kunde . . . . 174 E d
Kunduz . . . .
Kunersdorf . . . . 135 H b
Ku-ngan . . . . 170 ins. A
Künzelsau . . . . 143 I g
Kuopio . . . . 167 K c
Kupiansk . . . . 139 E f
Kupreanof Island . . . . 212 ins.
Kur River . . . .
Kura River . . . .
Kurachee . . . . 137 A c
Kuraiyat . . . .
Kurdistan, reg. . . . . 67 O f
Kurdistan Highlands . . . . . . 3 I e
Kurds, people . . . .

Kuria Muria Islands 170 G g
Kurile Islands 171 P d
Kurisches Haff, bay 155 K a
Kürnbach 142 C b
Kurnegalle
Kursk 139 E e
Kushk 170 H e
Kuskokwim River 186 C b
Küssnacht 91 Q k
Kustendji
Küstrin 79 I b
Kutais 167 N g
Kutchuk Kainardji
Kutha (Tel Ibrahim) 4 G c
Kuttenberg 79 I d
Kwang-chau-wan 171 M f
Kwang-si, prov. 171 L f
Kwang-tung, prov. 171 M f
Kwei-chau, prov. 171 L f
Kwei-lin-fu
Kwei-yang 171 L f
Kyburg, castle 91 Q k
Kyle, dist.
Kymmene River 120 K d
Kyoto 171 O e
Kyritz, Hanse. cy. 99 ins. B

Láa 123 I d
Laach, mon. 95 D a
Laaland, isl. 114 F a
La Bahia 190 F f
La Baraque 156 B a
La Barre 192 C b
La Baye, Fort 191 H c
Labdalum 31 ins. B
Labeates Lake 39 L l
La Belle-Alliance, farm
La Bénisson-Dieu, mon. 94 C b
Labiau 131 H c
Labican Way, road 35 ins. B
Labicum 35 ins. B
La Boca
La Bocchetta Pass 150 E d
La Boissière, mon. 94 C b
Labourd, dist. 147 D c (Lab.)
Labrador Peninsula 186 L c
Labrador Plateau 186 L c
Labranda 13 E c
Labuan 171 M h
La Bussière, mon. 94 C b
La Cava, mon. 95 ins.
Laccadive Islands 137 B f
Lac Court Oreille, Ind. Res. 188 H a
Lac de Flambeau, Ind. Res. 188 I a
Lacedæmon 14 C b
Lacedæmonia, state 14 C b
Laceria 11 D c
La Chaise-Dieu, mon. 94 C b
La Charité, on the Loire R. 126 C c
La Charité, in Paris 149 B
La Chassaigne, mon. 95 D b (L. Ch.)
La Chaussée 154 C d
La Chine, Lachine 191 K b
Lachine Rapids 189 A b
Lachish 7 B e
Lachlan River 172 D d
Laciadæ, deme 23 D
Lacinium, prom. 31 G c
La Cisa, Pass 26 D c
Lackawaxen River 192 D c
Lacmus, mt. 10 C c
La Colle 200 G a
La Colombe, mon. 94 C b
Laconia, reg. 14 C c
Laconia, gulf of 14 C c
La Couronne, mon. 94 C b
Lac Pepin, Fort G c
La Crosse 211 G b
Lac Seul, lake 212 F c
Lactarius, mt. 52 D b
Lactora, see Lectoure
Lacus Asphaltites (Dead Sea) 7 C f
Lade, isl. 13 E c
Ladenburg 142 C b
Lado 174 G d
Ladoga 138 D c
Ladoga, lake 138 D c
Ladon River, in Arcadia 14 B b
Ladon River, in Elis 14 B b
Ladrones, isl. 110 FF f
Ladysmith 175 M l
Laebactes 27 G a
Laevi, people 26 D b
La Famine 192 C b
Lafayette 206 ins.
La Ferté-Bernard 76 D b
La Ferté-sur-Grône, mon. 94 C b
La Flèche 126 A c
La Fontaine de Bèze, mon. 95 D b
La Force, bldg. in Paris 149 B
La Gallette, Fort 192 D a
Lagash 4 G c
Lagina River 39 J g
Lagny 76 E b
Lago Maggiore, lake 90 I h
Lagos, in Nigeria 174 D d
Lagos, in Portugal 82 J h
Lagos, dist. 174 D d
La Grande Chartreuse, mon. 95 D b
La Granja, castle 130 C e
La Guayra, La Guaira 214 C a
Laguna 215 E e
Laguna das Patos, lake 215 D f
Lagussa, isl. 15 F c
La Hague, Cape de, battle off 125 C c
Lahaina 198 ins. B
Lahari
La Harpe, route of 191 F e
La Haye, farm 156 C c
La Haye Sainte, farm
Lahn River 62 D c
La Hogue or La Hougue, see Saint Vaast-de-la-Hougue
Lahore 137 B b
La Hougue 130 C d
Lahr 142 A d
La Huerta, isl. 105 D d
La Hulpe 156 A a
Laibach 63 H f
Laietani, people 38 C d
Laino 90 E e
Laish 6 D b
Lajazzo 99 K f
La Jonquière, Fort 190 C a
Lake Country 49 E d
Lake of the Woods 191 G b
Lake Region 2 G b
Laknaoti
La Levette, farm
La Lusern, mon. 94 B b
La Maison-du-Roi 156 C c
La Mancha, dist. 83 K h
La Marche or Marche, cty. 61 D c
La Marche or Marche, gouv. 146 B b
La Marche or Marche, prov. 148 E e
Lambach, mon. 80 C g
Lambaesis 38 D e
Lambayeque 111 B c
Lambeth 75 I i
Lambeth, parl. bor. 163 N f (Lamb.)
Lambethmoor, dist. 75 G g
Lambrus River 26 D b
Lamego 82 A a
Lamego, bp. 94 A c
Lametus River 31 F d
Lamia 11 D d
Laminium 38 B e
Lamotte, Fort 189 B b
Lampsacus 5 B a
Lamptræ inferior 16 B b
Lamptræ superior 16 B b
Lanai, isl. 198 ins. B
Lanark 127
Lanark, cty. 127
Lanark, dist.
Lancashire, cty.
Lancaster, in England
Lancaster, cty. palat.
Lancaster, parl. bor. 163 L c
Lancaster, in Mass. 189 C c
Lancaster, in Ohio 196 ins. B
Lancaster, in Pa. 192 C c
Lancaster Sound 186 K a
Lancastrian Estates 84
Lan-chau-fu
Lancia 38 A d
Lanciano 64 B b
Landau 114 E d
Landeck 79 G e
Landen 117 D d
Landes, dept. 148 D f
Landeshut, in Silesia 135 H c
Landrecies 126 C a (Land.)
Landsberg, in Styria 135 H e
Landsberg, on the Warthe 80 ins.
Landsberg, march 85 G e
Land's End, cape 49 C f
Landshut, in Bavaria 115 G d
Landskrona 123 J d
Landstuhl 114 D d
Lanercost, mon.
Lang Bourn, in London 75 G g
Langenargen 143 I j
Langenau 143 J h
Langenburg 143 I g
Langensalza 158 F c
Langley 75 H h
Langley, Fort 210 A a
Langport 127 W o
Langport, parl. bor.
Langres 61 F c
Langres, bp. 95 D b
Langres, cty. 61 F c
Langres, duchy 76 F c
Langside 118 D b
Langs Nek
Lang-soi
Languedoc, dist. 69 E e
Languedoc, gouv. 146 B c
Languedoc, prov. 148 E f
Lankavi Island
Lansdown 127 X o
L'Anse, Ind. Res. 188 I a
Lansing 211 H b
Lanuvium 35 ins. B
Laodicea, in Coele-Syria 20 G e
Laodicea, in Lycaonia 20 E c
Laodicea, in Phrygia 20 C d
Laodicea, in Syria 20 F e
Lao-kai 171 L f
Laon 61 E b
Laon, bp. 94 C b
Laon, cty. 61 E b
La Part-Dieu, mon. 91 O l
Lapathus 11 D c
La Paz, in Bolivia 214 C d
La Paz, in Lower Cal. 213 A b
Lapis Niger, in Rome
Lapithas, mt. 14 B b
Lapland, reg. 167 J b
La Plata, in the Arg. Rep. 215 D f
La Plata, in Bolivia 214 C d
La Plata, viceroyalty 215 ins.
La Pointe, Ind. Res. 188 H a
La Pointe du Saint Esprit 191 G b
La Pola de Gordon 82 A a
Lappa 14 ins.
Lapps, people 138 B b
La Prairie 189 B b
La Pré-sur-Arnon, mon. 94 C b
Lapurdum, see Bayonne
La Rábida 184 B e
Laramie 210 D b
Laramie, Fort 198 E b
Laranda 71 M f
Laredo, in Spain
Laredo, in Texas 198 F e
La Reine, Fort 190 F b
La Réole, castle 76 D d
Larga 39 I j
Larino 64 B b
Larino, bp. 95 E c

Larinum 30 D a
Larisa, see Larissa
Larissa, in Assyria 20 J d
Larissa, in Thessaly 11 D c
Larissa Cremaste 11 D d
Larisus River 14 B a
Larius (Como), lake 26 D a
Larix 27 H a
La Roche, in Burgundy 143 ins. F
Laroche, in Luxemburg 117 D d
La Roche, cty. 69 F a (L. R.)
La Rochelle 130 C d
La Rochelle, gen. 147 D b
Laron 76 D d
La Rothière 154 C d
Larsa or Larsam (Senkereh) 4 G c
Larymna 11 E d
Las 14 C c
Lasalle, in France 184 D d
Lasalle, in Illinois 211 H b
La Salle, routes of 191 H d, I c, F d
Las Cascadas
Las Cruces
La Serena 215 B e
Lasion 14 B b
Las Navas de Tolosa 83 K h
Lasne
Lasne River 156 A a
Las Palmas 174 B b
Las Salinas 108 J i
Lassen Pass 214 B b
L'Assomption, Fort 194 B c
Las Tabbas 214 A b
Las Vegas 198 D c
Las Vigas 201 H g
Lateran, Palace 22 A
Laterani, Palace of the 22 A
La Teste de Buch 76 C d
Latham House 127 W m
Latin Empire 73 E c
Latin Gate 22 A
Latini or Latins, people 30 B a
Latin Way, road 30 B a
Latis River 26 B c
Latium, reg. 30 B a
Latium and Campania, Aug. Reg. of Rome 38 E d (1)
Latomiæ, loc. in Syracuse 31 ins. B (7)
La Tour 69 E d
Latovici, people 27 I b
Latovicorum Prætorium 27 I b
La Trappe 126 B b
La Trappe, mon. 94 C b
La Tremouille 81 M h
Lauag 199 ins. H
Lauban 80 ins.
Lauchert River 143 H i
Lauchheim 143 J h
Laudonnière, set. of 191 I e
Lauenburg, on the Elbe 72 C a
Lauenburg, in Pomerania 123 I a
Lauenburg, duchy 87 H b
Lauffen 143 H g
Laumellum 26 C b
L'Aumône, mon. 94 C b
Launceston, in England 127 U p
Launceston, mon. 97 M k
Launceston, parl. bor. 163 J g
Launceston, in Tasmania 172 D e
Laund, mon. 97 Q i
Laupen 91 P l
Lanpheim 143 I i
Laurentian Highlands 186 L d
Laurentum 35 ins. B
Lauresham, see Lorch, mon.
Lauriacum, (Lorch, in Austria) 38 E c
Laurium, mt. 16 C b
Laurvik 166 G d
Laus 30 E c
Laus, Pompeia 26 D b
Laus, bay 30 E c
Laus (Lao) River 30 E c
Lausanne 91 O l
Lausanne, bp. 95 D b
Lausitz, march 58 G c
Lausitz, margr. see Lusatia 79 I c
Lausitz, Nieder. margr. see Lusatia, Lower 87 I c
Lausitz, Ober, margr. see Lusatia, Upper 87 I c
Lausonna, see Lausanne
Lautern 72 B b
Lautrec 76 E e
Lautulæ 30 C a
Lautumiæ 24 A
Lauzelle 156 B a
Laval 76 C b
Lavant 80 D h
Lavant, bp. 95 E b
Lavant River 63 H e
Lavatræ
Lavaur 76 D e
Lavaur, bp. 94 C c
La Vérendrye, route of 190 D c
Laverna, Gate of 23 B
Lavinium 30 B a
Lawrence 206 F c
Laxenburg, castle
Laybach, see Laibach
Laycock, mon. 97 O j
La Zarca 190 E f
Lea River 75 I h
Leadenhall Street, in London 75 G g
Leadville 210 D c
League of God's House, dist. 91 R l
League of Ten Jurisdictions, dist. 91 R l
Leander, Tower of 93 G e
Leavenworth, Fort 198 F c
Leba 123 I a
Lebadea 11 D d
Lebanon, House of 6 ins. A
Lebanon Mountains 6 D a
Lebarge, lake 212 B b
Lebedos 13 E b
Le Beuil, mon. 94 C b
Lebinthus, isl. 17 E c
Le Boeuf, Fort 192 A c
Lebonah 7 C d
Lebú 215 B f
Lebus 63 H b
Lebus, bp. 79 I b
Lebus, dist. 85 D b
Lebusa, castle 63 G c
Lecce 90 G d
Lecco 150 E d
Lech River 62 F e
Lechæum 15 C b
Lechfeld, dist. 62 F d
Leck River 117 D c
Lecompton 206 F c
Le Coucou
Lectoure 76 D e
Lectoure, bp. 94 C c
Lectum, prom. 17 D b
Ledbury, parl. bor.
Ledesma 82 A a
Lee, Fort 195 D c
Lee River 127 H j
Leech Lake 199 G a
Leech Lake, Ind. Res. 188 H a
Leeds, in Yorkshire 127 X m
Leeds, mon. in Kent 97 R j
Leeds, parl. bor. 163 M d
Leesburg 208 ins.
Leeuwarden 117 D a
Leeuwin, Cape 172 A d
Leeward Islands 213 F c
Le Fleix 126 B d
Lefroy, lake 172 B d
Legæ, people 35 N e
Legedia, see Avranches
Leghorn 90 L j
Legnago 150 F d
Legnano 72 B b
Le Havre 126 B b
Lehigh River 192 D c
Lehnin, mon. 72 C a
Leicester
Leicester, cty.
Leicester, parl. bor. 163 M e
Leicester, shire
Leichardt River 172 C b
Leighlin, bp. 97 D d
Lein River 143 I h
Leine River 158 E b
Leiningen, princ. 142 D a
Leinster, prov.
Leinstetten 143 G i
Leipheim 143 J i
Leipnik 123 I d
Leipsic, Leipzig
Leipsic, Leipzig, univ.
Leiria 82 G f
Leisnig 85 G e
Leiston, mon. 97 S i
Leith
Leitha River 63 I e
Leitmeritz 63 H c
Leitomischl 63 H d
Leitrim, cty. 127 I g
Leitzkau 63 F b
Leitzkau, mon. 80 ins.
Leiva 214 B b
Le Jafs, farm
Le Joug-Dieu, mon. 94 C b
Lelantian Fields 11 E d
Lelantus River 11 E d
Le Maire, route of
Le Mans 61 C b
Le Mans, bp. 94 C b
Lemanus (Geneva), lake 26 A a
Lemanus Portus (Lymne) 38 C b
Lemberg 139 B f
Le Mesnil
Lemgo, Hanse. cy. 99 ins. B
Lemhi, Ind. Res. 188 D a
Lemnos, isl. 13 D b
Lemovices or Lemovicis, see Limoges
Lemovices, people 38 C c
Lemovii, people 38 F b
Lena River 171 N b
Lenczyca 135 J b
Lenni-Lenapes, tribe 188 K c
Lennox, dist.
Lens 117 A d
Lenton, mon. 97 P i
Lenzen 63 F b
Lenzin
Leo IV, Wall of Pope 96 A
Leoben 135 H e
Leodicum, see Liège
Leominster, mon. 97 O i
Leominster, parl. bor. 163 L e
Léon, in France 61 B b
León, in Mexico 213 ins.
León, in Nicaragua 105 C d
León, in Spain 82 A a
León, bp. 94 A c
Léon, dist. 81 L h
Léon, km. 82 A a, G e
Léon, viscty. 69 A b
Leonberg 143 H h
Leone 199 ins. D
Leonidæum
Leonine City, in Rome 96 A
Leontine Way 31 ins. B
Leontini 30 D e
Leontium 14 B a
Leontopolis 43 I g
Leopoldina 214 F d
Leopoldstadt 155 I d
Leopoldville 175 E e
Lepanto 89 H g
Le Paraclet, mon. 94 C b
Lepel 153 N g
Lepelletier 149 B
Lepidum, Regium 26 E c
Le Pin, mon. 94 C b
Lepontii, people 26 C a
Lepontine Alps, mts. 90 B a

Lepreum . . . . 14 B b
Lepsydrium . . . . 16 B a
Leptis maior or magna . . . . 34 G g
Leptis minor . . . . 38 E e
Le Puiset . . . . 69 H f
Le Puy . . . . 61 E d
Le Puy, bp. . . . . 94 C b
Le Quesnoy . . . . 117 B d
Lérida . . . . 82 C a
Lérida, bp. . . . . 94 C c
Lérida, univ. . . . . 100 F f
Lérins, mon. . . . . 95 D c
Lerma, lake . . . . 106 A a
Lerna . . . . 14 C b
Leros, isl. . . . . 16 B b
Le Roussart . . . .
Lerus . . . . 13 E c
Lerus, isl., Sporades . . . . 13 E c
Les Allemands . . . . 191 G f
Lesbos, isl. . . . . 13 D b
Lescar . . . . 61 C e
Lescar, bp. . . . . 94 B c
Les Clairets, mon. . . . . 94 C b
Lesina, bp. . . . . 95 F c
Lesina, isl. . . . . 90 F c
Lesje . . . . 130 E a
Lesna . . . . 131 J c
Lessa . . . . 15 D b
Lesser Antilles, isl. . . . . 213 F c
Lesser Armenia, reg. in Pontus . . . . 33 M e
Lesser Armenia, reg. in Syria . . . . 99 J f
Lesser Scythia, reg. . . . . 39 N l
Lesser Syrtis, gulf . . . . 51 F f
Lete . . . . 11 D d
Lethæus River, in Crete . . . . 14 ins.
Lethæus River, in Thessaly . . 10 C c
Lethbridge . . . . 212 D d
Letoa, isl. . . . . 14 ins.
Letocetum . . . . 51 P h
L'Etoile, mon. . . . . 94 C b
Letrini . . . . 14 B b
Letts, people . . . . 57 H c
Leubus, mon. . . . . 80 E f
Leuca . . . . 31 H c
Leuca, mt. . . . . 14 ins.
Leucadia, isl. . . . . 89 H g
Leucæ Islands . . . . 14 ins.
Leucas . . . .
Leucas (Santa Maura), isl. . . .
Leucate, prom. . . . .
Leuce, isl. . . . . 18 D a
Leuce acte . . . . 15 E b
Leuceræ . . . . 26 D b
Leuchtenberg . . . . 63 G d
Leuci, see Toul
Leuci, people . . . . 38 D c
Leucimma, prom. . . . . 10 B c
Leucopetra, prom. . . . . 30 E d
Leuctra . . . . 11 E d
Leuctrum . . . . 14 C c
Leuk . . . . 91 P l
Leuthen . . . . 135 I c
Leutkirch, imp. cy. . . . . 143 J j
Leutkircher Heide, dist. . . . . 143 J j
Leutschau . . . .
Levadia, reg. . . . . 131 H f
Leventina, valley . . . . 91 Q l
Lévêque, cape . . . . 172 B b
Levette, la, farm . . . . 156 C c
Lévis, Fort . . . . 192 D a
Lewes, in England . . . .
Lewes, castle . . . .
Lewes, mon. . . . . 97 Q k
Lewes, parl. bor. . . . . 163 O g
Lewes, in Delaware . . . . 192 D d
Lewis, dist. . . . . 127 N f
Lewis River, in Canada . . . . 198 ins. A
Lewis River, in Idaho . . . . 198 C b
Lewis and Clark, routes of . . 198, 199
Lewiston . . . . 200 D b
Lexington, in Kentucky . . . . 208 D b
Lexington, in Mass. . . . . 195 ins. A
Lexington, in Missouri . . . . 208 B b
Lexington, in Virginia . . . . 207 K c
Lexovii or Lexoviis, see Lisieux
Leyden . . . . 117 C b
Leyre, mon. . . . . 94 B c
Leyte, isl. . . . . 199 ins. H
Lezat, mon. . . . . 94 C c
Lhasa . . . . 92 J d
Liamone, dept. . . . . 148 F f
Liang-hiang . . . . 170 ins. A
Liao-yang . . . . 171 N d
Liard, Fort . . . . 212 C b
Liard River . . . . 212 C c
Liau-ho, R. . . . .
Liau-tung, pen. . . . .
Libarna . . . . 26 C c
Libau . . . . 77 I a
Libau, Hanse. cy. . . . . 99 H b
Liberia, country . . . . 174 C d
Libici, people . . . . 26 C b
Libisonis, Turris . . . . 38 D d
Libreville . . . . 175 D d
Liburnia, reg. . . . . 27 I b
Libya, reg. . . . . 18 C d
Libyan Desert . . . . 2 G f
Lichades Islands . . . . 11 D d
Lichfield . . . . 65 F d
Lichfield, bp. . . . . 97 P i
Lichfield, parl. bor. . . . . 163 M e
Lichtenau . . . . 142 A c
Lichtenberg, princ. . . . . 158 D d
Lichtenstein, castle . . . . 143 H i
Lichtenthal, ab. . . . . 142 B c
Licking River . . . . 196 ins. B
Licus (Gail) River . . . . 27 H a
Licus (Lech) River . . . . 39 K j
Lidford, parl. bor. . . . .
Liebenwalde . . . . 85 C b
Liebenzell . . . . 143 G h
Liechtenstein . . . . 154 E e
Liechtenstein, princ. . . . . 150 E c
Liège . . . . 117 D d
Liège, bp. . . . . 117 D d
Liegnitz . . . . 63 I c
Liegnitz, princ. . . . . 79 J c
Lienz . . . . 115 G e
Lierre . . . . 117 C c
Lies, Field of . . . . 56 D c
Liestal . . . . 142 A e
Liger (Loire) River . . . . 38 C c
Ligny . . . . 156 B a
Ligonier, Fort . . . . 192 B c
Ligures Baebiani . . . . 30 D a
Liguria, Aug. Reg. . . . . 39 D d (9)
Liguria, reg. . . . . 26 B c
Liguria, French prov. . . . . 152 B e
Liguria, West Rom. prov. . 42 D d (3)
Ligurian Alps, mts. . . . . 90 B b
Ligurian Republic . . . . 151 H h
Ligurian Sea . . . . 150 E e
Ligurians, people . . . . 12 E b
Lilæa . . . . 11 D d
Lilienfeld, mon. . . . . 95 F b
Lille . . . . 117 B d
Lilleshall, mon. . . . . 97 O i
Lillois . . . . 156 A a
Lilybæum . . . . 30 B e
Lima . . . . 214 B d
Lima, audiencia . . . . 215 ins.
Limal . . . . 156 B a
Limasol . . . . 68 B c
Limay River . . . . 215 C f
Limburg . . . . 117 E d
Limburg, castle in Lower Lorraine . . . . 62 D c
Limburg, castle in Swabia . 62 E d
Limburg, castle in W. Franconia . . . . 62 E c
Limburg, duchy . . . . 117 D d
Limburg, prov. . . . . 158 C c
Limburg-on-the-Hardt, mon. . 95 D b
Limburg-on-the-Lahn, mon. . . 95 D a
Limelette . . . . 156 B a
Limerick . . . . 74 A e
Limerick, bp. . . . . 97 C d
Limerick, cty. . . . . 127 H i
Limes (Roman Wall) . . . . 38 D c
Limestone . . . . 196 ins. B
Limia, dist. . . . . 83 J g
Limmen Bight . . . . 172 C b
Limnæ, in Athens . . . . 23 D
Limnæ, in Messenia . . . . 14 C b
Limonum, see Poitiers
Limousin, prov. . . . . 148 E e
Limpurg, castle . . . . 143 I g
Limpurg, cty. . . . . 143 I h
Linares . . . . 215 B f
Lin-ching . . . .
Lincoln, in England . . . .
Lincoln, bp. . . . . 97 Q h
Lincoln, castle . . . . 65 F d
Lincoln, cty. . . . .
Lincoln, parl. bor. . . . . 163 N d
Lincoln, shire . . . .
Lincoln, in Nebraska . . . . 210 F b
Lincoln Heights . . . . 49 F e
Lincoln Wolds . . . . 49 F e
Lindau . . . . 62 E e
Lindau, imp. cy. . . . . 78 F e
Lindau, mon. . . . . 95 D b
Lindenfels . . . . 142 C a
Lindisfarne, mon. . . . . 97 P f
Lindisfarne Island . . . .
Lindiswaras, people . . . .
Lindsay, mt. . . . . 172 E c
Lindsey, parl. dist. . . . . 163 N d
Lindum (Lincoln) . . . . 51 P h
Lindus . . . . 13 F c
Lingayen . . . . 199 ins. H
Lingen . . . . 62 D b
Lingones, see Langres
Lingones, people, in Gaul . . . 38 D c
Lingones, people, in Italy . . . 27 F c
Linhares . . . . 214 F d
Linköping . . . . 46 J b
Linlithgow . . . .
Linlithgow, cty. . . . .
Linones, people . . . . 55 R i
Lindsays, fam. . . . . 97 K d
Linth River . . . . 150 E c
Linththal . . . . 91 R l
Lin-tsing-chau . . . .
Linz . . . . 63 H d
Lion Hill, village . . . .
Lipans, people . . . . 188 G e
Lipara . . . . 30 E d
Liparææ (Æolin or Lipari) Islands . . . . 30 D d
Lipari Islands . . . . 90 E e
Lippe, cty. . . . . 114 C e
Lippe, princ. . . . . 134 E c
Lippe, reg. . . . . 86 G c
Lippe River . . . . 62 D c
Lippe-Detmold, princ. . . 154 E b (L.D.)
Lippeham . . . . 55 Q i
Lippstadt . . . . 158 E c
Liptrap, Cape . . . . 172 D d
Liquentia River . . . . 27 G b
Liques, mon. . . . . 94 C a
Lircay . . . . 214 B d
Liria . . . . 82 B b
Liris (Garigliano) River . . . . 30 C a
Lisa, Fort . . . . 210 F b
Lisaine River . . . . 143 ins. F
Lisbon . . . . 82 A b
Lisbon, abp. . . . . 94 A d
Lisbon, univ. . . . . 100 D g
Lisburne, Cape . . . . 198 ins. A
Lisieux . . . . 69 D b
Lisieux, bp. . . . . 94 C b
Liskeard, parl. bor. . . . . 163 J g (Lisk.)
L'Isle . . . . 143 ins. F
L'Isle Jourdan . . . . 126 B e
Lismore, bp. in Ireland . . . . 97 D d
Lismore, bp. in Scotland . . . . 97 H c
Lissa . . . . 115 I c
Lissa, island, off Spalato . . . . 90 F c
Lissa, island, off Zara . . . . 27 J c

Lissa Island 161 J f
Lissabon, see Lisbon
Lissus 31 I a
Lissus, prom. 14 ins.
Lita River
Litani River
Liternum 30 C b
Lithuania, gr. princ. 119 J c
Lithuania, reg., about 1190 71 K b
Lithuania, reg., about 1360 77 J b
Lithuanians, people 59 I b
Littanum 27 G a
Little Belt, strait 88 C d
Little Burgundy, duchy 69 G c
Little Cayman, isl. 105 D c
Little Colorado River 198 C c
Little Compton 189 ins. A
Little Dunmow, mon. 97 R j
Little Egg Harbor 192 D d
Little Harbour 189 C c
Little Miami River 196 ins. B
Little Missouri River 198 E a
Little Oasis 4 E d
Little Poland, reg. 131 H c
Little Redan, fort 164 L g
Little Rock 211 G d
Little Russia, reg. 139 C e
Little Russians, people 139 C e
Little Saint Bernard Pass 130 O i
Little Slave Lake 186 H c
Littlestown 208 ins.
Little Tatary, reg. 139 D f
Little Wallachia, reg. 131 H d
Little Yarmouth, parl. bor.
Littorale, reg. 123 G f
Litus Saxonicum (Saxon Shore) 51 Q i
Liu-kiu Islands 171 N f
Liutizians, people 63 G b
Liverpool 127 V m
Liverpool, parl. bor. 163 K d
Liverpool Range 172 E d
Livia, Palace of 24 B
Livia, Portico of 22 A
Livno 164 B b
Livny 139 E e
Livonia, reg., 9—14 cent. 80 I c
Livonia, reg., 14—16 cent. 88 K c
Livonia, reg., 17—18 cent. 138 C d
Livonia, Polish, reg. 131 I b
Livonians, people 59 I b
Livorno, see Leghorn 90 L j
Livraimont, farm
Lixus 38 A e
Lizard Head 127 T p
Llamas del Moro 82 A a
Llandaff
Llandaff, bp. 97 N j
Llangollen 162 C e
Llano Estacado, plain 210 E d
Llanthony, mon. 97 N j
Llerena 82 A b
Loa River 214 B e
Loampo 110 D D e
Loanda, Saint Paul de 175 E e
Loana 130 Q j
Loango 175 E e
Löbau, in Lusatia 115 H c
Löbau, in Prussia 115 J b
Löbau, dist. 72 D a
Lobbes, mon. 94 C a
Lobetani, people 38 B e
Lobos, isl. 201 F e
Lobositz 135 G c
Locarno 91 Q l
Locca, see Loches
Loccum, mon. 95 D a
Locedia, mon. 95 D b
Lochaber, dist.
Lochau 115 ins. B
Loches 61 D c
Lochias 34 ins. C
Lochleven 118 D b
Locoritum 39 J h
Locras River 26 C f
Locris Epicnemidia, dist. 11 D d
Locris Epizephyrii, dist. 31 F d
Locris Opuntia, dist. 11 E d
Locris Ozolis, dist. 10 D d
Lod 7 B e
Lodève 76 E e
Lodève, bp. 94 C c
Lodi 90 I h
Lodi, bp. 95 D b
Lodz 159 J c
Lofoten Islands 2 E b
Logan, mt. 186 F b
Logroño 82 B a
Logstown 192 A c
Loidis
Loir River 76 C c
Loire, dept. 148 E e
Loire River 61 C c
Loire-Inférieure, dept. 148 D e
Loiret, dept. 148 E e
Loir-et-Cher, dept. 148 E e
Loja, in Ecuador 214 B c
Loja, in Spain 82 H f
Lomagne, dist. 126 B e
Lomas de Ahorca Lagarto, hills
Lomas de Palenquillo, hills
Lombards, Kingdom of the 53 O i
Lombards, people 45 F b, G d
Lombard Street, in London 75 G g
Lombardy, Plain of 2 F d
Lombardy, prov. 158 E f
Lombardy, reg. 58 F d
Lombardy, theme 59 H e
Lombez, bp. 94 C c
Lombok, isl. 172 A a
Lome 174 D d
Lomellina, dist. 161 G e
Lomello 90 I h
Lomond, loch, lake 49 D c
Lomzha
Lonato 150 F d
Londinium (London) 51 P i
London, in Canada 212 G d
London, in England
London, plan, about 1300 75 G g
London, bp. 97 Q j
London, Hanse. for. off. 98 ins. A
London, parl. bor. 163 O f
London, New 189 B d
London Bridge 75 G g
London Compagny, Grants to the 190 ins.
Londonderry, in Ireland 127 J f
Londonderry, in N. Hampshire 189 C c
Londonderry, cty. 127 J g
Londonderry, Cape 172 B b
Long, route of 210 E b
Longaticum 27 I b
Longford, cty. 127 J h
Long Island, in the Bahamas 105 F b
Long Island, off New York 189 B d
Long Island Sound 189 B d
Longjumeau 126 C b
Long's Peak 210 D b
Longueville 76 D b
Longula 30 B a
Longvilliers, mon. 94 C a
Longwy 114 C d
Lonicum 27 H a
Lons-le-Saunier 69 J f
Lons-le-Saunier, mon. 148 C b
Loo, mon. 94 C a
Lookout, Cape 193 F d
Lookout, Fort 210 F b
Lookout Mountain, battle 203 C c
Looz 117 D d
Lop
Lopadusa 34 G f
Lopez de Sequeira, route of 109 Y g
Lop-nor, lake 92 I c
Lopodunum 39 J i
Lora del Rio 82 A b
Lorca 82 B b
Lorch, in Austria 42 E d
Lorch, in Wurtemberg 143 I h
Lorch, mon. 95 D b
Lord Fairfax's Line 194 K g
Lord Howe, route of 195 F c
Lord Howe Island 172 F d
Lorenzo Marques
L'Orient 130 C d
Lorne, dist.
Lorne, Firth of 49 C c
Lörrach 142 A e
Lorraine, duchy 126 E b
Lorraine, gouv. 146 C b
Lorraine, prov. 148 F e
Lorraine, Lower, duchy 62 C c
Lorraine, Upper, duchy 62 D d
Lorraine and Barrois, gen. 147 F b
Lorris 98 D d
Lorsch, mon. 95 D b
Los Angeles 190 B e
Losantiville (Cincinnati) 196 ins. B
Los Cayos, isl. 105 E b
Los Corazones 190 C f
Losoncz 159 J d
Lostwithiel 127 U p
Lostwithiel, parl. bor. 163 J g
Lot, dept. 148 E f
Lot River 76 E d
Lota 215 B f
Lot-et-Garonne, dept. 148 E f
Lotharingia, duchy 56 D b
Lothbury 75 G g
Lothian, dist.
Lothian
Loudoun, Fort, in Pa. 192 B d
Loudoun, Fort, in Tennessee 193 B d
Loudun, in France 61 D c
Lough Corrib, lake 127 H h
Lough Derg, lake 127 I h
Lough Erne, lake 127 J g
Lough Mask, lake 127 H h
Lough Neagh, lake 127 K g
Lough Ree, lake
Louis VII., crusade of 70 H d
Louis, Fort 191 H e
Louisbourg 212 J d
Louisiade Archipelago 172 E b
Louisiana, dist. 202 G c
Louisiana, reg. 190 D b — H e
Louisiana, state 203 T d
Louisiana, ter. 202 G c
Louisville 199 H c
Loup Fork, R. 198 E b
Louroux, mon. 94 C b
Lousonna (Lausanne) 26 A a
Louth, cty. in Ireland 127 K h
Louth, parl. bor. in England
Louvain 117 C d
Louvain, univ. 100 F d
Louvier, Ile 149 B
Louviers 126 B b
Louvre, The, palace, in Paris 149 B
Louvre, Quai du, in Paris 149 B
Lovat River 88 N c
Lovejoy 208 D c
Low Archipelago 180 N i
Lowell 211 K b
Löwen, see Louvain
Löwenstein 143 H g
Löwenstein, cty. 143 H g
Löwenstein-Wertheim, cty. 142 D a
Lower Argen River 143 I j
Lower Bavaria, dist. 123 G d
Lower Britain, prov. 38 B b (2)
Lower Brule, Ind. Res. 188 F b
Lower Burgundy, dist. 62 C f
Lower Burma, reg. 171 K g
Lower California, pen. 187 H e
Lower California, reg. 190 C f
Lower California, ter. 213 A b
Lower Canade, reg. 212 H d
Lower Dacia, prov. 39 N k (1 b)
Lower Egypt, reg.
Lower Germany, prov.
Lower Gihon, well 6 ins. A
Lower Guinea, reg. 175 E c

Lower Libya, East Rom. prov. 43 H g (2)
Lower Lorraine, duchy 62 C c
Lower Lusatia, dist. 85 H e
Lower Lusatia, margr. 87 J c
Lower Moesia, prov. 35 J e
Lower Pannonia, prov. 34 H d
Lower Peru, reg. 214 B c
Lower Rhenish Province 158 D c
Lower Silesia, dist. 72 D a
Lower Tunguska River
Lowlands, reg. 49 D d
Loyalty Islands 172 F c
Lo-yang
Loyola 94 B c
Lozère, dept. 148 E f
Loznitza 165 A a
Lübbecke 55 Q i
Lübben 115 G c
Lübeck 62 F b
Lübeck, bp. 95 E a
Lübeck, Hanse. cy. 99 ins. B
Lübeck, imp. cy. 79 G b
Lublin 139 B e
Luca (Lucca) 26 E d
Lucania, reg. 30 E b
Lucania and Bruttium, Aug. Reg. 38 F e (3)
Lucca 90 L j
Lucca, bp. 95 E c
Lucca, duchy 161 G f
Lucca, princ. 151 K j
Lucca, rep. 150 F e
Lucena 82 B b
Lucens 91 O l
Lucentum 38 B e
Lucera 64 C b
Luceria 30 E a
Luceria, bp. 95 F c
Lucerne 91 Q k
Lucerne, canton 91 Q k
Lucerne, Lake of 91 Q l
Lucignano 118 G e
Lucka 79 H c
Luckau 85 C c
Lucknow, see Luknow
Luçon 76 C c
Luçon, bp. 94 B b
Lucretilis, mt. 35 ins. B
Lucrinus Lake 31 ins. A
Lucullus, Gardens of 23 B
Lucus. Augusti (Luc-en-Die) 38 D d
Lucus Augusti (Lugo) 38 A d
Lüderitz Bay 175 E g
Lüderitzbucht, see Lüderitz Bay
Ludgate, loc. in London 75 G g
Ludgershall, parl. bor.
Ludias River 11 D b
Ludlow 127 W n
Ludlow, parl. bor. 163 L e
Ludomeria, dist.
Ludwigsburg 143 H h
Lueg, pass 154 G e
Lugano 91 Q l
Lugano, lake 91 Q m
Lugansk 167 M f
Lugdunensis, Rom. prov. 38 C c (4)
Lugdunensis, West Rom. prov. 42 C d (2)
Lugdunum (Bagnères de Luchon) 38 C d
Lugdunum, see Laon
Lügenfeld (Field of Lies) 56 D c
Lugeus, lake 27 I b
Lugii, people 38 F c
Lugo 82 A a
Lugo, bp. 94 A c
Lugos 131 H d
Lugudunensis, prov. 34 D d
Lugudunum (Lyons) 38 C c
Lugudunum Batavorum (Leyden) 38 C b
Luguvallium (Carlisle) 51 O g
Luith
Lu-kiang, R. 171 K f
Lukmanier Pass 91 Q l
Luknow, Lucknow 137 D c
Lule River 166 I b
Luleå 167 J b
Lummi, Ind. Res. 188 B a
Luna 26 E c
Lunæ Portus (Gulf of Spezia) 26 D d
Lund 46 I b
Lund, abp. 95 D a
Lundenburg 168 E b
Lundy's Lane, battle 200 D b
Lüneburg 62 F b
Lüneburg, duchy 122 E b
Lüneburg, Hanse. cy. 99 ins. B
Lunéville 62 D d
Lung-chau 171 L f
Luni 64 B b
Luni River 137 B c
Lupercal, grotto 24 A
Lupfen, ruin 143 G i
Lupia (Lippe) River 39 I h
Lupiæ 31 H b
Lupton, Fort 210 E c
Lure, mon. 148 C b
Lurgan 127 K g
Luristan, reg. 99 M g
Lusatia, march 62 H c
Lusatia, margr. 76 C a
Lusatia, Lower, margr. 87 J c
Lusatia, Upper, margr. 87 J c
Lusatians, people 63 G c
Lusern, La, mon. 94 B b
Lusignan 126 B c
Lusignan, castle 76 D c
Lusignan, seign. 69 D c
Lusignans, dynasty 73 G c
Lusitani, people 38 A e
Lusitania, prov. 38 A d (2)
Lusitania, reg. 82 A b
Lusitania, West Rom. prov. 42 A e (2)
Lusones 38 B d
Lussheim, Alt 142 C b
Lustenau 143 J g
Lu-tai 170 ins. A
Lutetia (Paris) 38 C c
Luteva, see Lodève
Lutter am Barenberge 122 F c
Lutterberg 134 E c
Lutterworth, about thirtheen miles north-east of Coventry 97 P i
Lüttich, see Liège
Lützelburg 62 C d
Lützen 123 G c
Lutzk 139 C e
Luxembourg, palace 149 B
Luxemburg 117 D e
Luxemburg, duchy 78 D d
Luxemburg, gr. duchy 158 C d
Luxeuil, mon. 95 D b
Luxor 4 F d
Luxovium (Luxeuil) 39 I j
Luzern, see Lucerne
Luzon, isl. 199 ins. H
Luzy 69 I g
Lycabettus, mt. 23 D
Lycæus, mt. 14 B b
Lycaonia, East Rom. prov. 43 I f (5)
Lycaonia, Macedonian prov. 18 D c
Lycaonia, Rom. prov.
Lycandos, theme 59 L f
Lyceum, quarter 23 D
Lychnidus 10 B a
Lychnites, lake, in Epirus 10 B a
Lychnitis, lake, in Armenia 20 K b
Lycia, East Rom. prov. 43 H f (4)
Lycia, Macedonian prov. 18 C c
Lycia, reg. 8 A b
Lycia, Rom. prov. 20 C d
Lycia, satr. 18 N h
Lyck 155 L b
Lycosura 14 C b
Lycus River, in Phœnicia 6 D a
Lycus River, in Pontus 20 H b
Lycus, The, river, in Constantinople 93 G e
Lydda 7 B e
Lydia, East Rom. prov. 43 H f (2)
Lydia, Macedon. prov. 18 C c
Lydia, reg. 8 A b
Lydia, Rom. prov. 20 C c
Lydia, satr. 18 N h
Lydian Kingdom 5 B b
Lyme Regis 127 W p
Lyme Regis, parl. bor. 163 L g
Lymington, parl. bor. 163 M g
Lyncestis, dist. 10 C a
Lynchburg 208 E b
Lyncus, mt. 10 C c
Lynn, in England 65 G d
Lynn, Hanse. for. cy. 98 ins. A
Lynn, in Mass. 189 ins. B
Lynn Canal 212 ins.
Lyonnais, cty. 69 F d
Lyonnais, gouv. 146 B b
Lyonnais, prov. 148 E e
Lyons 70 G d
Lyons, abp. 94 C b
Lyons, gen. 147 E b
Lyons, Gulf of 38 C d
Lyrcea 14 C b
Lys River 117 A d
Lysikrates, Monument of
Lysimachia, in Ætolia 10 C d
Lysimachia, on the Propontis
Lysimachus, Kingdom of 18
Lysimelian Marsh 31 ins. B
Lystra 20 E d
Lyttus 14 ins.

Maacha, reg. 6 D b
Ma'bar, reg. 102 H f
McAllister, Fort 208 D c
Macao 110 CC e
Macapá 214 D b
Macara 30 C e
Macaria, dist. 14 C b
Macassar
Macassar, Strait of 171 M h
Macclesfield 127 W m
Macclesfield, parl. bor. 163 L d
McClintock Channel 212 E a
Macdonald, lake 172 B c
MacDonalds, fam.
McDonnell Range 172 C c
McDowell 208 E b
Macedonia, East Rom. dioc. 43 G e
Macedonia, East Rom. prov. 43 Ge(1.)
Macedonia, reg. 10 C b
Macedonia, Rom. imp. prov. 39 M l(4.)
Macedonia, Rom. sen. prov. 35 I e
Macedonia, state 18 B b
Macedonia, theme 59 J e
Macedonia Salutaris, East Rom. prov. 43 Ge (6.)
Macedonian Empire, The 18, 19
Maceió 214 F c
Macellum Liviae, in Rome 22 A
Macellum magnum, in Rome 22 A
Macerata 90 D c
Macerata, bp. 95 E c
Macestus River
Maceta, Cape 19 I e
McGillivray's Town 196 B d
Machadodorp 175 N e
Machærus 7 D e
McHenry, Fort 200 L h
Machias 189 E b
Macijowice
MacIntoshes, fam.
Macintyre River 172 D c
Macistus 14 B b
Macistus, mt. 11 E d
Mackay 172 D c
MacKays, fam.
Mackenzie, dist. 212 C b
MacKenzies, fam.
Mackenzie Bay 212 B b
Mackenzie River 186 G b
Mackinac 211 H a
Mackinac, Fort 194 C a
McKinley, mt. 186 D b

MacLeans, fam. . . . .
Macleod . . . . 212 D d
MacLeods, fam. . . . .
McMurray, Fort . . . . 212 D c
Macomades . . . . 46 H f
Mâcon, in France . . . . 61 F c
Mâcon, bp. . . . . 94 C b
Macon, in Georgia . . . . 208 D c
Macon, Fort, in N. Carolina . . 208 E c
MacPhersons, fam. . . . .
Macpherson, Fort . . . . 212 B b
Macquarie Harbor . . . . 172 D e
Macra River . . . . 26 D c
Mactan, isl. . . . . 110 D D g
Macynia . . . . 10 C d
Madagascar, isl. . . . . 175 H g
Madaura . . . . 38 D e
Madeira Islands . . . . 174 B a
Madeira River . . . . 214 C c
Madeket . . . . 189 C d
Madeleine, The, church, in Paris 149 B
Mâdion, mon. . . . . 94 B b
Madison . . . . 211 H b
Madison, Fort . . . . 199 G b
Madison, Fort, Ind. Res. . . . . 188 B a
Madrak, Ras . . . . 170 G g
Madras . . . . 137 D f
Madre de Dios River . . . . . . 214 C d
Madrid . . . . 83 K g
Madura . . . . 137 C g
Madytus . . . .
Mæander (Mendere) River . . . 20 C d
Mæcenas, Gardens of . . . . . 22 A
Mædi, people . . . . 39 M l
Mæetae, people . . . . 35 L d
Mænalus . . . . 14 C b
Mænalus, mt. . . . . 14 C b
Mænan, mon. . . . . 97 N h
Mæotis, lake (Sea of Azov) . . 12 K a
Maeseyck . . . . 117 D c
Maestricht . . . . 117 D d
Mafeking . . . . 175 F g
Mafia, isl. . . . . 175 H e
Magadaburg, see Magdeburg
Magadoxo . . . . 175 H d
Magalhães (Magellan) Strait . . 108 K l
Magalhães, route of, see Magellan . . . . 107—110 leg.
Magalia, quarter in Carthage . 34 ins. A
Magdala, in Abyssinia . . . . . 174 G c
Magdala, in Palestine . . . . . 6 D c
Magdalen, Postern of the . . . 68 ins. B
Magdalena . . . . 213 A a
Magdalena, isl. . . . . 107 D i
Magdalena Bay . . . . 111 B a
Magdalena River . . . . 214 B b
Magdeburg . . . . 63 F b
Magdeburg, abp. . . . . 95 E a
Magdeburg, duchy . . . . 122 F b
Magdeburg, Hanse. cy. . . . . 99 ins. B
Magdiel . . . . 6 B c
Magdolum . . . . 4 ins.
Magellan, route of . . . . 107 Ah, 108 Ng, 110 DDg
Magellan, Straits of . . . . . . 215 B h
Magenta . . . . 158 E f
Mägerkingen . . . . 143 H i
Magersfontein . . . . 175 L l
Magetobriga . . . . 39 H j
Maggia . . . . 91 Q l
Maggiore, Lake . . . . 91 Q m
Magia . . . . 39 J j
Magna Charta Island . . . . . . 75 H i
Magna Græcia, reg. . . . . . . 29 E e
Magna Mater, Temple of . . . . 24 A
Magnano . . . . 150 F d
Magnesia (Manissa) . . . . . . 93 C c
Magnesia, reg. . . . . 11 D c
Magnetic Pole, Northern . . . . 186 J a
Mago . . . . 38 C e
Magoras River . . . . 6 D a
Magrib, reg. . . . . 98 C g
Maguelonne, bp. . . . . 94 C c
Magyars, people, 800 . . . . . .
Magyars, people, about 900 . .
Mahanadi River . . . . 137 E d
Mahanaim . . . . 7 D d
Mahanuddy River . . . . 137 E d
Mahé . . . . 137 C f
Mahedia . . . . 70 I f
Mahlberg . . . . 142 A d
Mahlberg, lordship . . . . . . 142 A d
Mahmoud Bridge . . . . 93 Ge (10.)
Maholm . . . . 88 L b
Mahon . . . . 83 L h
Mahra, reg. . . . . 53 H e
Mahratta Confederacy . . . . . 137 B d
Mahukona . . . . 198 ins. B
Maidstone, in England . . . . 127 Z o
Maidstone, parl. bor. . . . . . 163 O f
Maidstone (Easthampton), in New York . . . . 189 C d
Maienfeld . . . . 91 R k
Mail, Plaine du, Versailles . . . 149 A
Mailand, see Milan
Mailapur . . . .
Mailberg . . . . 63 H d
Maillezais, bp. . . . . 94 B b
Mailly . . . . 69 I g
Maimatchin . . . . 171 L d
Mainau, isl. . . . . 142 D e
Maine, cty., in France . . . . . 61 D b
Maine, gouv., in France . . . . 146 A b
Maine, prov., in France . . . . 148 D e
Maine, col., in U. S. . . . . . 189 C c
Maine, dist., in U. S. . . . . . 196 F b
Maine, state, in U. S. . . . . . 203 Y a
Maine-et-Loire, dept. . . . . . 148 D e
Mainots, people . . . . 164 C c
Main River . . . . 62 F c
Main River, East . . . . 186 L c
Maintenon . . . . 126 B b
Maintenon, castle . . . . 130 D d
Mainz, see Mayence
Maior (Majorca), isl. . . . . . 38 C e
Maipo, battle . . . . 215 B f
Maison-du-Roi, la . . . . 156 C c
Maitland . . . . 172 E d
Majapahit . . . . 112 E d
Majar . . . . 99 L e
Majella, Mount, mon. . . . . . 95 E c
Majorca, bp. . . . . 94 C d
Majorca, isl. . . . . 82 C b
Majorca and Roussillon, km. . . 83 L g
Majuba Hill, mt. . . . . 175 M l
Majumas . . . . 7 A e
Makah, Ind. Res. . . . . 188 A a
Makalla . . . . 170 F g
Makarska, bp. . . . . 95 F c
Makhlaf . . . . 170 F g
Makri . . . . 99 I f
Makua River . . . . 175 F d
Malabar, reg. . . . . 137 C f
Malabar Coast . . . . 137 B e
Malaca (Málaga) . . . . 38 B e
Malacca . . . . 112 D c
Malacca, pen. . . . . 112 D c
Málaga . . . . 82 B b
Málaga, bp. . . . . 94 B d
Malakoff, Fort . . . . 164 L g
Mälar, lake . . . . 119 H b
Malaspina, fam. . . . . 90 L i
Malaspina Glacier . . . . 212 A c
Malatia . . . . 99 K f
Malatieh . . . .
Malay Peninsula . . . . 171 L h
Malborn . . . . 142 ins. A
Malden . . . . 189 ins. B
Malden, Fort . . . . 200 B b
Malden Island . . . . 180 L h
Maldive Islands . . . . 112 A c
Maldon . . . . 65 G e
Maldon, parl. bor. . . . . 163 O f
Maldonado . . . . 215 D f
Malea, prom. in Laconia . . . . 15 D c
Malea, prom. in Lesbos . . . .
Malécites, mission . . . . 189 E a
Malian Gulf . . . . 11 D d
Malian Plain . . . . 16 E e
Malindi . . . . 175 H e
Malines, abp. . . . . 148 B a
Malin Head . . . . 127 J f
Malis, dist. . . . . 11 D d
Mallets, route of the . . . . . 190 E d
Malli, people . . . . 19 L d
Mallianum, bp. . . . . 96 B a
Malling, mon. . . . . 97 R j
Malmedy . . . . 117 E d
Malmedy, mon. . . . . 95 D a
Malmesbury . . . .
Malmesbury, mon . . . .
Malmesbury, parl. bor. 163 L f (Malm.)
Malmö . . . . 88 E d
Malmö, Hanse. for. cy. . . . . 98 F b
Mallœa . . . . 10 D c
Maloja Pass . . . . 91 R l
Maloyaroslavets . . . . 153 P g
Malpelo Island . . . . 214 A b
Malplaquet . . . . 134 B c
Malta, isl. . . . . 50 F e
Malton, parl. bor. . . . . 163 N c
Maluentum . . . . 30 D a
Maluinas (Falkland), isl. . . . 215 D h
Malvasia . . . . 124 D c
Malvern, Great, mon. . . . . . 97 O i
Malvern Hill, in Virginia . . . 208 E b
Malvern Hills, in England . . . 49 E e
Malwa, reg. . . . . 137 C c
Mamanguape . . . . 214 F c
Mamei . . . .
Mamelukes, Dom. of the . . . 73 H d
Mameluke Sultanates . . . . . 77 I e
Mamertium . . . . 31 F d
Mamistra . . . . 68 C b
Mamoré River . . . . 214 C d
Man, Isle of . . . . 49 D d
Manado . . . .
Managua . . . . 213 D c
Manahiki Islands . . . . 180 L i
Manaos . . . . 214 D c
Manar, Gulf of . . . . 137 C g
Manassas Junction . . . . . . 208 ins.
Manasseh, tribe . . . . 7 ins. D
Manbij . . . . 68 C b
Mancha, La, dist. . . . . 83 K h
Manchac . . . . 191 G e
Manche, dept. . . . . 148 D e
Manchester, in England . . . . 127 W m
Manchester, parl. bor. . . . . 163 L d
Manchester, in New Hampshire 211 K b
Manchester, in Ohio . . . . . . 196 ins. B
Manchu City, in Peking . . . . 170 ins. A
Manchuria, reg. . . . . 171 N c d
Manchus, people . . . .
Mancunium (Manchester) . . .
Mandalay . . . . 171 K f
Mandans, tribe . . . . 188 D a
Mandan, Fort . . . . 210 E a
Manderscheid . . . . 117 E d
Mandeure . . . . 143 ins. F
Mandingo River . . . .
Mandræ . . . .
Mandu . . . . 112 A a
Mandubii, people . . . . 38 C c
Manduessedum . . . .
Manduria . . . . 31 G b
Manfredonia (Siponto) . . . . 90 F d
Mangalore . . . . 137 B f
Mangarewa Island . . . . 180 O j
Mangaseya . . . .
Manhardsberg, mt. . . . . . . 54 H d
Manhattan . . . . 189 ins. C
Manhattan Island . . . . 189 ins. C
Manila . . . . 171 N g
Manila Bay . . . . 171 N g
Manipur . . . . 171 K f
Manissa (Magnesia) . . . . . . 93 C c
Manitoba, lake . . . . 186 I c
Manitoba, prov. . . . . 212 F c
Mannheim . . . . 142 B a
Manosque . . . . 126 D c

Manosque, mon. . . . . . . 148 C c (Man.)
Manresa . . . .
Mans, Le . . . . 61 C b
Mans, Le, bp. . . . . 94 C b
Mansfeld . . . . 62 F c
Mansfeld, cty. . . . . 114 F c
Mansfeld, Ernest of, route . . . 121 C c
Mansfield Island . . . . 212 G b
Mansura, in Egypt . . . . 174 J i
Mansurah, in India . . . . . . 53 I d
Mantes . . . . 69 H f
Manthyrea . . . . 14 C b
Mantinea nova . . . . 14 C b
Mantinea vetus . . . . 14 C b
Mantinum . . . . 26 D e
Mantua . . . . 26 E b
Mantua, bp. . . . . 95 E b
Mantua, duchy . . . . 150 F d
Mantua, marq. . . . . 90 C b
Manua Islands . . . . 199 ins. D
Manuel, Fort . . . . 210 D a
Manukau Harbor . . . . 172 G d
Manytch River . . . . 164 G a
Manzanillo . . . . 213 B c
Manzanillo, Bay of . . . . . .
Manzi, reg. . . . . 92 L e
Manzikert . . . . 67 O f
Maon . . . . 7 C f
Maqueda . . . . 82 B a
Mar, dist. . . . .
Maracaibo . . . . 214 B a
Maracaibo Lake . . . . 105 F e
Maracanda . . . . 19 K c
Maragha . . . . 73 J c
Marajo Island . . . . 214 E c
Marakesh (Morocco) . . . . . . 174 C a
Maranguape . . . . 214 F c
Maranham . . . . 214 E c
Maranhão, state . . . . 214 E c
Marañon River . . . . 214 B c
Marans . . . . 126 A c
Maransart . . . .
Marash . . . . 68 C b
Marash, reg. . . . . 124 G c
Marathon . . . . 15 D a
Marathon, Plain of . . . . 16 B a
Marbach . . . . 143 H h
Marbais . . . . 156 B a
Marbella . . . . 82 B b
Marblehead . . . . 189 ins. B
Marburg . . . . 123 H e
Marcellus, Theatre of . . . . . . 22 A
March River . . . . 63 I d
Marche, or La Marche, cty. . . 61 D c
Marche, or La Marche, gouv. . 146 B b
Marche, or La Marche, prov. . 148 E e
Marches, The, dist. . . . . . . 90 D c
Marchfeld, dist. . . . . 79 J d
Marchienne . . . . 156 A b
Marchthal, ab. . . . . 143 I i
Marchthal, mon. . . . . 143 I i
Marcian Aqueduct . . . . 35 ins. B
Marcianopolis . . . . 39 N l
Marcinelle . . . . 156 A b
Marcodurum . . . . 39 I h
Marcomagus . . . . 39 I h
Marcomanni, people . . . . . . 38 E c
Marco Polo, route of . . . . .
Marcus Aurelius, Arch of . . . . 22 A
Marcus Aurelius, Column of . . 22 A
Marcus Aurelius, Temple of . . 22 A
Marcus Hook . . . . 192 ins.
Mar del Norte (Caribbean Sea) 108 J f
Mar del Plata . . . . 215 D f
Mar del Sur (South Sea or Pacific Ocean) . . . . 107 F H g
Mardin . . . . 68 D b
Mardocho . . . . 6 F c
Mardonius' Fleet, route of . . . 13 D b
Mardyck . . . . 122 B c
Marengo . . . . 150 E d
Mareotis, lake . . . . 4 ins.
Margalæ . . . . 14 B b
Margam, mon. . . . . 97 N j
Margarita, isl. . . . . 105 H d
Margat . . . . 68 C b
Marghilan . . . . 170 I e
Margiana, prov. . . . . 19 J c
Margus River (Morava R.) . . . 39 M l
Margus River (Murgab R.) . . 19 J c
Maria Galante, isl. . . . . . . 105 H c
Mariamne . . . . 6 ins. A
Mariampol . . . . 155 L a
Mariana . . . . 26 D e
Marianne Islands . . . . 110 F F f
Marias River . . . . 210 C a
Maria Theresiopel . . . . 159 J e
Maria van Diemen, Cape . . . . 172 G d
Mariazell, Gross, mon. . . . . . 95 F b
Mariazell, Klein, mon. . . . . . 95 F b
Marici, people . . . . 26 D b
Maridunum (Carmarthen) . . . . 51 N i
Marie Galante, isl. . . . . . . 213 F c
Marienbourg . . . . 117 C d
Marienburg . . . . 79 K b
Marienburg, Hanse. cy. . . . . 98 G c
Marienstern, mon. . . . . 95 E a
Marienthal, mon. . . . . 95 E a
Marienwalde, mon. . . . . 80 ins.
Marienwerder . . . . 72 D a
Marienwerder, bp. . . . . 95 F a
Marietta . . . . 196 ins. B
Marignano . . . . 90 I h
Mariguana, isl. . . . . 105 F b
Marinids, dynasty . . . . 77 C f
Mario, Monte . . . . 96 A
Mariposa . . . . 201 B b
Maritima, isl. . . . . 30 A e
Maritime Alps, mts. . . . . . . 26 B c
Maritime Alps, West Rom. prov. 42 D e (7)
Maritza River . . . . 89 C b
Mariua . . . . 214 C c
Mariupol . . . . 139 E f
Mark, cty. . . . . 78 E c
Mark, see Brandenburg
Market Harborough . . . . 98 ins. A
Markgröningen . . . . 143 H h
Markovo . . . . 171 S b
Marlborough, in England . . . . 127 X o
Marlborough, parl. bor. 163 M f (Marlb.)
Marlborough, route of . . . . . 129 leg.
Marlborough, in Tasmania . . . 172 D e
Marle . . . . 69 I f
Marmande . . . . 126 B d
Marmarica, dist. . . . . 35 I g
Marmarium . . . . 15 E a
Marmora, Sea of . . . . 3 H d
Marmoutier, mon. . . . . 94 C b
Marne, dept. . . . . 148 E e
Marne River . . . . 69 I f
Maroneus, mt. . . . . 30 D e
Maronia . . . . 13 D a
Maroni River . . . . 214 D b
Maros River . . . . 73 E a
Maros-Vasarhely . . . . 159 M e
Marpessa, mt. . . . . 15 F b
Marquesas de Mendoza, isl. . . 107 D h
Marquesas Islands . . . . 180 M h
Marquette, route of . . . . . . 191 H c
Marra . . . . 68 C b
Marrucini, people . . . . 27 I e
Marruvium . . . . 27 H f
Mars, Temple of . . . . 22 A
Mars the Avenger, Temple of 24 B
Marsala . . . . 90 D f
Marsalquivir . . . . 130 C f
Marsan, dist. . . . . 147 D c
Marsan, viscty. . . . . 84 C g
Marsdiep, strait . . . . 117 C b
Marseilles . . . . 61 F e
Marseilles, bp. . . . . 95 D c
Marshall . . . . 211 G d
Marshall Islands . . . . 179 I f
Mars' Hill, (Areopagus) in Athens . . . .
Mars Hill, mt. in Maine . . . . 199 L a
Marsi, people, in Germany . . 39 I h
Marsi, Marsians, people, in Italy
Marsico, bp. . . . . 95 F c
Marston Moor . . . . 127 X m
Martaban . . . .
Marta River . . . . 27 F e
Martel . . . . 76 D d
Martha's Vineyard, isl. . . . . . 189 C d
Martigny . . . . 91 P l
Martin Garcia, Island of . . 215 D f (M.)
Martinino (Martinique), isl. . . . 105 H d
Martinique, isl. . . . . 213 F c
Martinsbruck . . . . 150 F e
Martinsburg . . . . 193 F b
Martin's Hundred . . . 193 ins. A (Mart.)
Martinstein . . . . 142 ins. A
Martinstein, lordship . . . . . . 142 ins. A
Martinswand . . . . 87 H e
Martirano . . . . 72 D d
Marton, mon. . . . . 97 Q g
Martyropolis . . . . 52 M f
Marusium . . . . 31 I b
Marus River (March R.) . . . . 38 F c
Marvejols . . . . 126 C d
Marwar, dist. . . . . 137 B c
Marwell, college . . . . 100 A b
Maryborough . . . . 172 E c
Maryland, col. . . . . 192 C d
Maryland, state . . . . 211 J c
Mary-le-bone, parl. bor.
Marysville . . . . 210 A c
Masada . . . . 7 C f
Masampo, Masampho . . . . . . 171 N e
Masbate, isl. . . . . 199 ins. H
Mascara . . . . 130 D f
Mascarenhas, isl. . . . . 109 W i
Mascoutins, tribe . . . . 188 H b
Masefau . . . . 199 ins. D
Maserfield (Oswestry) . . . . . .
Mases . . . . 15 D b
Mashonaland, dist. . . . . 175 G f
Masis, mt. . . . . 18 F c
Masius Mountains . . . . 20 I d
Maskat . . . . 170 G f
Mason and Dixon's Line . . . . 194 K g
Mason and Gorges' Claim . . . 189 C c
Masovia, dist. . . . . 138 B e
Massa . . . . 90 L j
Massa, bp. . . . . 95 E c
Massa Marittima . . . . 90 L j
Massa Veternensis . . . . 26 E d
Massac, Fort . . . . 194 B c
Massaca . . . . 19 L d
Massachusetts, state, till 1820 . 202 K b
Massachusetts, state, since 1820 203 X b
Massachusetts Bay . . . . 189 C c
Massachusetts Bay, col. . . . . 189 C c
Massagetæ, Massagetans, people . . . . 19 J b
Massanutting . . . . 193 E b
Massaua or Massawa, see Massowah
Masserano . . . . 130 Q i
Massicus, mt. . . . . 30 C a
Massilia (Marseilles) . . . . . . 38 D d
Massowah . . . . 174 G c
Massylii, people . . . . 38 D e
Mastanli . . . . 165 D c
Masulipatam . . . . 137 D e
Matabeleland, reg. . . . . 175 F f
Matachin . . . .
Matagorda Bay . . . . 190 F f
Matamoros . . . . 201 F d
Matanzas . . . . 213 D b
Matanzas Island . . . . 191 I f
Matapan, Cape . . . . 167 J h
Matape . . . . 190 D f
Matatane . . . . 109 V j
Matelots, Allée des, Versailles 149 A
Matera . . . . 64 C b
Matera, abp. . . . . 95 F c
Maternum . . . . 27 F e
Mathia, mt. . . . . 14 B c
Mathis River . . . . 31 I a
Mathraval . . . .
Matianus, lake . . . . 18 G c

Matifu, Cape . . . . 118 E f
Matilica . . . . 27 H d
Matinum . . . . 31 F a
Matisco or Matiscone (Mâcon, in France) . . . . 39 H j
Matrega, Matriga . . . . 73 H b
Matrinum . . . . 27 I e
Matrona, Mount (Mt. Genèvre), pass . . . . 26 A c
Matrona (Marne) River . . . . . 38 C c
Mattagami River . . . . 211 I a
Mattium . . . . 39 J h
Matto Grosso (Villa Bella) . . . 214 D d
Matto Grosso, state . . . . . . 214 D d
Mattox . . . . 193 F b (Ma.)
Mauai, isl. . . . . 198 ins. B
Maubeuge . . . . 117 B d
Maubeuge, mon. . . . . 148 B a
Maugio . . . . 76 F e
Maulbronn, ab. . . . . 143 G h
Maulbronn, mon. . . . . 143 G g
Maule River . . . . 215 B f
Mauléon . . . . 126 A e
Maullin . . . . 215 B g
Maultasch, castle . . . . 79 G e
Maumee River . . . . 200 A c
Mauna Kea, mt. . . . . 198 ins. B
Mauna Loa, mt. . . . . 198 ins. B
Maupertuis . . . . 81 M h
Maurepas, lake . . . . . 191 G e (L. M.)
Maurepas, Fort (Biloxi) . . . . . 191 H e
Maurepas, Fort (on Winnipeg L.) 191 F a
Mauretania, reg. . . . . 46 F g
Mauretania Cæsariensis, prov. . 34 D g
Mauretania Cæsariensis, West Rom. prov. . . . . 42 C f (5.)
Mauretania Sitifensis, West Rom. prov. . . . . 42 C f (4.)
Mauretania Tingitana, imp. prov. 34 C g
Mauretania Tingitana, West Rom. prov. . . . . 42 B g (6.)
Mauretanians, people . . . . . . 51 C f
Mauriac . . . . 126 C d
Maurici, Portus . . . . 26 C d
Maurienne, bp. . . . . 95 D b
Mauritius, isl. . . . . 175 I f
Mauritsstad . . . .
Maursmünster, mon. . . . . 95 D b
Mauvezin . . . . 126 B e
Mauze, castle . . . . 69 C c
Mavila . . . . 191 H e
Maxen . . . . 135 G c
Maxima Cæsariensis, West Rom. prov. . . . . 42 B c (1.)
Maxima Sequanorum, West Rom. prov. . . . . 42 D d (9.)
Maximianopolis . . . . 6 C c
May, Cape . . . . 192 D d
May, River of . . . . 191 I e
Maya . . . . 82 B a
Mayaguana, isl. . . . . 105 F b
Mayaguez . . . . 199 ins. G
Mayas, people . . . . 105 C c
Mayence . . . . 62 E d
Mayence, abp. . . . . 95 D b
Mayence, univ. . . . . 100 G d
Mayenne . . . . 76 C b
Mayenne, dept. . . . . 148 D e
Mayo, bp. . . . . 97 B c
Mayo, cty. . . . . 127 H h
Mayotte Island . . . . 175 H f
Maysi, Cape . . . . 105 F c
Maysville . . . . 211 I c
Mayumba . . . . 175 D e
Mazaca (Kaisarieh) . . . . 20 F c
Mazagan . . . . 108 P d
Mazamet . . . . 126 C e
Mazan, mon. . . . . 94 C c
Mazanderan, reg. . . . . 139 H h
Mazara . . . . 30 B e
Mazatlan . . . . 213 B b
Mazovia, reg. . . . . 59 I c
Mazzara . . . . 90 D f
Mazzara, bp. . . . . 95 E d
Mazzo . . . . 91 S l
McCarthys, The, fam. . . . . .
McGuires, The, fam. . . . . . .
McMahons, The, fam. . . . . .
McMurroughs, The, fam. . . . .
Meadville . . . . 206 ins.
Meara . . . . 6 D a
Mearns, dist. . . . .
Meath, bp. . . . . 97 E c
Meath, cty. . . . . 127 K h
Meath, dist. . . . .
Meat Market, in London . . 75 G g (33.)
Meauléon . . . . 76 C e
Meaux, in France . . . . 61 E b
Meaux, bp. . . . . 94 C b
Meaux, mon., in England . . . . 97 Q h
Mecca . . . .
Mechanicstown . . . . 208 ins.
Mechlin . . . . 76 F b
Mechlin, abp. . . . . 148 B a
Mechlin, lordship . . . . 117 C d
Mecklenburg . . . . 55 R i
Mecklenburg, castle . . . . 63 F b
Mecklenburg, dist. . . . . 79 G b
Mecklenburg, duchy . . . . 87 H b
Mecklenburg Court House . . . 195 A f
Mecklenburg-Güstrow, duchy . 123 G b
Mecklenburg-Schwerin, duchy . 122 F b
Mecklenburg-Schwerin, gr. duchy 158 F b
Mecklenburg-Strelitz, duchy . . 135 G b
Mecklenburg-Strelitz, gr. duchy 158 G b
Mecyberna . . . . 11 E b
Medama . . . . 12 G c
Medeba . . . .
Medellin, in Columbia . . . . . 214 B b
Medellin, in Mexico . . . . 106 D a
Medellin, in Spain . . . . 82 A b
Medemblik . . . . 117 D b
Medeon . . . . 10 C d
Medes, people . . . . 5 D b
Medeshamstead . . . .
Medford . . . . 189 ins. B
Medgyes . . . . 159 M e
Media, prov. . . . . 19 G c
Media, reg. . . . . 8 C b
Media, satr. . . . . 8 I e
Media Atropatene, reg. . . . . 35 N f
Media Atropatene, satr. . . . . 18 P h
Media Magna, satr. . . . . 18 P h
Median Empire 8
Median Wall . . . . 18 F d
Mediasch . . . . 159 M e
Medicine Hat . . . . 212 D d
Medina . . . .
Medinaceli . . . . 82 B a
Medina del Campo . . . . 83 K g
Medina de Pomar . . . . 82 B a
Medina de Rioseco . . . .
Medina Sidonia . . . . 82 A b
Medinet el Fayum . . . . 174 J j
Mediolanium, Mediolanum (Milan) 26 D b
Mediolanum, see Evreux
Mediolanum, see Saintes
Mediomatrici, see Metz
Mediomatrici, people . . . . . . 38 D c
Mediterranean Sea . . . . 2 E e
Medjidie . . . . 165 F a
Medma . . . . 30 E d
Medma River . . . . 31 F d
Medrano . . . . 215 C f
Meduacus (Brenta) River . . . . 27 F b
Medulli, people . . . . 26 A b
Medullia . . . . 35 ins. B
Meenen . . . .
Meersberg . . . . 142 D e
Meerut . . . . 137 C c
Meewocs, tribe . . . . 188 B c
Megalopolis . . . . 14 C b
Megara, in Greece . . . . 15 D a
Megara, quarter in Carthage . 34 ins. A
Megara Hyblæa . . . . 30 E e
Megaris, dist. . . . . 15 D a
Megaris, isl. . . . . 31 ins. A
Megiddo . . . . 6 C c
Mehadia . . . . 159 L f
Mehaigne River . . . . 156 B a
Meia Ponte . . . . 214 E d
Meigs, Fort . . . . 200 B c
Meiningen . . . . 154 F c
Meiringen . . . . 91 Q l
Meisenheim . . . . 158 D d
Meissen . . . . 63 G c
Meissen, bp. . . . . 95 E a
Meissen, march . . . . 85 G e
Me-Jarkon . . . . 7 B d
Mejillones . . . . 215 B e
Mekong River . . . .
Mekran, reg. . . . . 170 H f
Melænæ . . . . 16 B a
Melæneæ . . . . 14 B b
Melas, gulf . . . .
Melas River . . . . 16 E e
Melbourne . . . . 172 D d
Melcart, Island of . . . . 18 ins. B
Melchior Diaz, route of . . . . . 190 C f
Melchthal . . . . 91 Q l
Melcombe Regis, parl. bor. . . 163 L g
Meldæ or Meldis, see Meaux
Meldorf . . . . 62 E a
Meleda, isl. . . . . 90 F c
Meledunum, see Melodunum
Melencze . . . . 159 K f
Melfi . . . . 90 E d
Melfi, bp. . . . . 95 F c
Melgueil, cty. . . . . 69 E e
Melibocus Mountains . . . . . . 39 K h
Meliboea . . . . 11 D c
Melilla . . . . 118 D f
Melinde . . . .
Melita (Malta), isl. . . . . 34 G f
Melita (Meleda), isl. . . . . . . 38 F d
Melitæa . . . . 11 D c
Melite, deme of . . . . 23 D
Melite, lake . . . . 10 C d
Melitean Gate . . . . 23 D
Melitene (Malatieh) . . . . 20 H c
Melk . . . . 63 H d
Melk, mon. . . . . 95 F b
Mella River . . . . 26 E b
Melli . . . . 108 Q f
Mellrichstadt . . . . 62 F c
Melnik . . . . 63 H c
Melno, lake . . . . 88 H e
Melodunum (Melun) . . . . 38 C c
Melon, mon. . . . . 94 A c
Meloria, isl. . . . . 72 C c
Melos . . . . 15 E c
Melos (Milo), isl. . . . . 15 E c
Melpes River . . . . 30 E c
Melrose . . . .
Melton Mowbray, parl. bor. . .
Melun . . . . 76 E b
Mellville Island, off Australian coast . . . . 172 B b
Melville Island, Parry Is. . . . . 186 H a
Melville Peninsula . . . . 212 G b
Melville Sound . . . . 186 H a
Memel . . . . 80 G d
Memleben . . . . 63 F c
Memleben, mon. . . . . 95 E a
Memmingen . . . . 79 G d
Memphis, in Egypt . . . . 4 ins.
Memphis, in Tennessee . . . . . 199 H c
Menæum . . . . 30 D e
Menam River . . . . 171 K g
Menapii, people . . . . 39 H h
Menat, mon. . . . . 94 C b
Menawaski . . . . 174 F c
Mendana, route of . . . . 110 HH h
Mende, in Chalcidice . . . . . . 11 E c
Mende, in France . . . . 61 E d
Mande, bp. . . . . 94 C c
Mendere River (Scamander R.)
Mendere River (Mæander R.)
Mendes . . . . 4 ins.
Mendip Hills . . . . 49 E f
Mendocino, Cape . . . . 187 G d
Mendon . . . . 189 C c

Mendoza . . . . . 215 C f
Mendoza, route of . . . . . 107 G f
Mendrisio . . . . . 91 Q m
Menendez, set. of . . . . . 191 J e
Mengen . . . . . 143 H i
Meng-tsze . . . . .
Menin . . . . . 117 B d
Meninx . . . . . 34 G d
Men-nofer (Memphis) . . . . . 4 F d
Menominee, Ind. Res. . . . . . 188 I a
Menominee River . . . . . 191 H b
Menominees, tribe . . . . . 188 I a
Mentana . . . . . 161 I f
Menteith, dist. . . . . .
Mentesa . . . . . 82 H f
Mentesha, reg. . . . . . 89 I g
Mentone . . . . . 130 P k
Mentorides, isl. . . . . . 27 I c
Mentz, see Mayence
Menzaleh, lake . . . . .
Meonwara, people . . . . .
Meppel . . . . . 117 E b
Meppen . . . . . 122 D b
Meppen, mon. . . . . . 95 D a
Mequinenza . . . . . 82 C a
Meran . . . . . 114 F e
Meran, mon. . . . . . 95 E b
Merash . . . . .
Merbe Braine . . . . .
Mercer, Fort . . . . . 195 D d
Merchant's Hope . . . . . 193 ins. A
Mercia, Kingdom . . . . .
Mercia, Danish, reg. . . . . .
Mercia, English, reg. . . . . .
Mercians, people . . . . . 51 R k
Mercoeur, castle . . . . . 69 E d
Mercurii, prom. . . . . . 38 E e
Mercury, Temple of . . . . . 22 A
Mercy, Cape . . . . . 212 I b
Mere, parl. bor. . . . . .
Merena, isl. . . . . . 172 F b
Merevale, mon. . . . . . 97 P i
Mergens, Pitinum . . . . . 27 G d
Mergentheim . . . . . 143 I g
Mergen . . . . . 112 A b
Mérida, in Spain . . . . . 82 A b
Mérida in Venezuela . . . . . 214 B b
Mérida, in Yucatan . . . . . 213 D b
Meridian . . . . . 208 C c
Mérindol . . . . . 126 D e
Mering . . . . . 62 F d
Merinum . . . . . 31 F a
Merioneth, cty. . . . . . 74 D e
Merioneth, parl. dist. . . . . . 163 K e
Merkits, people . . . . .
Merom . . . . . 6 C c
Merom, Waters of . . . . . 6 D b
Merrimac River . . . . . 189 C c
Merry Mount, in Mass. . . . . . 189 C c
Merry Mount, in Virginia . . . . . 193 ins. A
Merse, dist. . . . . .
Merseburg . . . . . 63 G c
Merseburg, bp. . . . . . 95 E a
Merseburg, Hanse. cy. . . . . . 99 ins. B
Merseburg, march . . . . . 63 G c
Mersen . . . . . 55 Q i
Mersey River . . . . . 127 W m
Merthyr Tydfil, parl. bor. . . . . . 163 K f
Merry Mount, village . . . . . 189 C c
Mertola . . . . . 82 A b
Merton . . . . . 75 I i
Merton, mon. . . . . . 97 Q j
Merv . . . . . 53 I c
Méry . . . . . 45 E c
Mesambria, on the Ægean Sea 17 D a
Mesambria, Mesembria, on the Black Sea . . . . . 12 I b
Mescalero Apache, Ind. Res. . 188 E d
Meseritz . . . . . 155 H b
Meseritz, mon. . . . . . 95 F a
Meshed . . . . .
Meshed-Ali . . . . . 99 L g
Mesogæa, dist. . . . . . 15 D b
Mesopotamia, Rom. prov. . . . 35 M f
Mesopotamia, East Rom. prov 43 J f (12.)
Mesopotamia, reg. . . . . . 4 G c
Mesopotamia, satr. . . . . . 18 P h
Mesopotamia, theme . . . . . 59 L f
Mesopotamia Plains . . . . . 3 I e
Messa . . . . . 14 C c
Messana (Messina) . . . . . 30 E d
Messapii, Messapians, people . 31 G b
Messene . . . . . 14 B b
Messenia, Gulf of . . . . . 14 C c
Messenia,, state . . . . . 14 B b
Messina . . . . . 90 E e
Messina, abp. . . . . . 95 E d
Messina, Strait of . . . . . 30 E d
Messkirch . . . . . 142 D d
Messkirch, lordship . . . . . 142 D d
Meta River . . . . . 214 B b
Metammeh . . . . . 174 G c
Metanastæ, Jazyges, people . . 38 F c
Metapontum, Metapontium . . . 31 F a
Metaris Æstuarium (The Wash) 51 Q h
Meta sudans, in Rome . . . . . 24 B
Metauro River . . . . . 90 M j
Metaurus River, in Bruttium . . 30 E d
Metaurus River, in Umbria . . 27 G d
Methana . . . . . 15 D b
Methone, in Macedonia . . . . . 11 D b
Methone, in Magnesia . . . . . 11 E c
Methone (Modoni), in Messenia 14 B c
Methydrium . . . . . 14 E b
Methymna . . . . .
Metis River . . . . . 199 L a
Metropolis, in Acarnania . . . 10 C d
Metropolis, in Epirus . . . . . 10 C d
Metropolis, in Pelasgiotis . . . . 11 D c
Metropolis, in Thessaliotis . . . 10 C c
Metropotamia, proposed state in U. S. . . . . .
Metroum . . . . .
Metrovian Gate . . . . . 22 A
Metsovo . . . . .
Mettis (Metz) . . . . . 39 I i
Metulum . . . . . 27 J b
Metz . . . . . 62 D d
Metz, bp. . . . . . 78 E d
Metz, imp. cy. . . . . . 78 E d
Metz and Verdun, gouv. . . . . 146 C b
Metzingen . . . . . 143 H h
Meulant, castle . . . . . 76 D b
Meung . . . . . 76 D c
Meurs . . . . . 117 E c
Meurthe, dept. . . . . . 148 F e
Meuse, dept. . . . . . 148 F e
Meuse River . . . . . 62 C c
Mevania . . . . . 27 G e
Mevaniola . . . . . 27 F c
Mewar, dist. . . . . . 137 B d
Mexicaltzinco . . . . .
Mexican Plain . . . . . 187 I f
Mexico . . . . . 106 A a
Mexico, audiencia . . . . . 213 C c
Mexico, viceroyalty, see New Spain
Mexico, country . . . . . A — D a — c
Mexico, Gulf of . . . . . 187 J f
Mexico, New, ter. . . . . . 203 Q h
Meymac, mon. . . . . . 94 C b
Mezen . . . . . 167 N b
Mézières . . . . . 69 J f
Miami . . . . . 213 D b
Miami, Fort . . . . .
Miami River . . . . . 191 I d
Miamis, tribe . . . . . 188 I b
Miana . . . . .
Miani . . . . . 170 H f
Miantonomo . . . . . 189 ins. A
Michael, parl. bor. . . . . .
Michaelovsk . . . . .
Michigan, lake . . . . . 187 K d
Michigan, state . . . . . 202 H f
Michigan, ter. 1805 . . . . . 202 H b
Michigan, ter. 1818 . . . . . 203 T a
Michigan, ter. 1834 . . . . . 203 S a
Michigania, proposed state in U. S. . . . . .
Michilimackinac, or Michillimackinac . . . . . 191 I b
Michipicoten . . . . .
Michipicoten River . . . . . 188 J a
Michmash . . . . . 7 C e
Michoacan, state . . . . . 213 ins.
Mickleham, mon. . . . . . 97 R k
Micmacs, tribe . . . . . 188 M a
Middelburg, in Holland . . . . . 117 B c
Middelburg, Hanse. cv. . . . . . 99 ins. B
Middelburg, in Transvaal . . . . 175 M l
Middelfart . . . . . 88 C d
Middle Angles, people . . . . . 51 R k
Middleborough . . . . . 189 C d (Mid.)
Middle District, New South Wales . . . . . 172 leg.
Middle Empire, see Chagatai .
Middle March, dist. . . . . .
Middle Plantation . . . . . 193 ins. A
Middle Saxons, people . . . . .
Middlesbrough . . . . . 162 E c
Middlesex, cty. . . . . .
Middlesex, dist. . . . . .
Mindlesex, parl. dist. . . .
Middletown . . . . . 189 B d
Midea . . . . . 15 C b
Midhurst, parl. bor. . . . . . 163 N f
Midi, Canal du . . . . . 130 D e
Midia . . . . . 165 F c
Midian, dist. . . . . . 4 F d
Midianites, people . . . . . 7 ins. C
Midnapur . . . . . 137 E d
Midway Islands . . . . . 180 J e
Midwout . . . . . 189 ins. C
Mien . . . . .
Mien, reg. . . . . . 109 A A e
Mies . . . . . 87 I d
Mifflin, Fort . . . . . 195 D d
Migdol . . . . . 4 ins.
Milan . . . . . 90 B b
Milan, abp. . . . . . 95 D b
Milan, duchy, 1395 . . . . . 78 F f
Milan, duchy, 1494 . . . . . 90 B b
Milan, duchy, 1796. . . . . . 150 E d
Milanese, The, dist., 1339–1402 90 H-K g-h
Milassa (Miletus) . . . . .
Milazzo . . . . . 161 J h
Milborne Post, parl. bor.
Mile End Meadow . . . . . 75 I h
Miletopolis . . . . .
Miletus . . . . . 20 B d
Mileve . . . . . 42 D f
Milford, in Conn. . . . . . 192 E c
Milford, in New Jersey . . . . . 192 D c
Milford, in Wales . . . . . 70 E c
Milford Haven . . . . . 84 A d
Milhaud . . . . . 76 E d
Milhaud, viscty. . . . . . 69 E d
Milid (Maladieh) . . . . . 5 C b
Military boundary, 1806 . . . . . 199 G e
Military Bounty Lands . . . . . 196 ins. B
Military Frontier, Croatian, Slavonian and Banat . . . . . 159 H-L f
Milk River . . . . . 210 D a
Milledgeville . . . . . 208 D c
Mille Lac, Ind. Res. . . . . . 188 H a
Millen . . . . . 208 D c
Millesimo . . . . . 130 Q j
Millikens Bend, point on Miss. R. 208 B c
Mill Springs, battle . . . . . 208 D b
Miloslaw . . . . . 159 I b
Miltenberg . . . . . 142 D a
Milton Abbas, mon. . . . . . 97 O k
Milvian Bridge . . . . . 96 A
Milwaukee . . . . . 199 H b
Milyana . . . . . 73 A c
Milyas, dist. . . . . . 20 D d
Milzienians, people . . . . . 63 H c
Mimate, see Mende
Mimigerniford, see Münster
Mims, Fort . . . . . 200 I f
Minagara . . . . . 18 R i
Minas . . . . . 215 D f

Minas Geraes, state . . . . . . 214 E d
Minas Novas . . . . 214 E d
Minch, The, strait . . . . 49 C c
Mincio River . . . . 150 F d
Mincius (Mincio) River . . . . . 26 E b
Minda, see Minden
Mindanao, isl. . . . . 199 ins. H
Mindel River . . . . 143 J i
Minden . . . . 62 E b
Minden, bp. . . . . 95 D a
Minden, Hanse, cy. . . . . 99 ins. B
Minden, princ. . . . . 122 E b
Mindi . . . .
Mindoro, isl. . . . . 199 ins. H
Minehead, parl. bor. . . . . . . 163 K f
Minerva, Temple of, on the Aventine Mt. . . . 22 A
Minerva, Temple of, in the Forum . . . . 24 B
Minerva, Temple of, on Sunium Promontory . . . 16 C b
Minerva, prom. . . . . 30 D b
Minerva Archegetis . . . . 23 D
Minervæ, Castrum . . . . 31 H b
Minervia, see Scolacium (Squillace)
Mingio . . . . 103 M e
Mingrelia, reg. . . . . 164 G b
Minhla . . . . 171 K g
Minho River . . . . 82 A a
Minibar, reg. . . . .
Minieh . . . . 150 B b
Minio River . . . . 27 F e
Minius (Minho) River . . . . . . 38 A d
Minneapolis . . . . 199 G a
Minnesota, state . . . . 203 S f
Minnesota, ter. . . . . 202 F f
Minnesota River . . . . 198 F b
Minnith . . . . 7 D e
Minnodunum . . . . 39 I j
Minoa, in Laconia . . . . 15 D c
Minoa, on Siphnus I. . . . . . .
Minoa, isl. . . . .
Minor (Minorca), isl. . . . . . . 38 C d
Minorca, bp. . . . . 94 C d
Minorca, isl. . . . . 82 C b
Minsk . . . . 138 C e
Minthe, mt. . . . . 14 B b
Minturnæ . . . . 30 C a
Minucian Portico . . . . 22 A
Minyæ, people . . . . 11 D d
Miquelon, isl. . . . . 212 J d
Mirabel, in France . . . . 69 D d
Mirabel, castle in Palestine . . 68 ins. A
Miraflores, in Panamá . . . . .
Miraflores, in Perú . . . . 214 B d
Miramichi Bay . . . . 212 I d
Miranda . . . . 214 D e
Miranda de Corvo . . . . 82 G e
Miranda do Douro . . . . 83 J g
Miranda de Ebro . . . . 82 B a
Mirande, in France . . . . 126 B e
Mirandola . . . . 90 J h
Miravet . . . . 82 C a
Mirbat . . . . 170 G g
Mirebeau . . . . 69 H g
Mirebeau, castle . . . . 76 D c
Mirepoix . . . . 76 D e
Mirepoix, bp. . . . . 94 C c
Mirepoix, seign. . . . . 76 D e
Mirim, lake . . . . 215 D f
Miriquidi, mts. . . . . 63 G c
Miró, District of . . . . . 196 B c (C. D.)
Miscus River . . . .
Misenum, harbor of . . . . 31 ins. A
Misenum, prom. . . . . 30 C b
Mishawum . . . . 189 ins. B
Misiones, dist. . . . . 215 D e
Miskolcz . . . . 159 K d
Miso River . . . . 27 H d
Misquamicut . . . . 189 ins. A
Missanabie River . . . .
Missema . . . . 6 E b
Missenden, mon. . . . . 97 Q j
Missinnippi River . . . . 186 I c
Mission Indian Reservation . . . 188 C d
Missionary Ridge, battle . . . . 208 C c
Mississippi, state . . . . 203 U d
Mississippi, ter. . . . . 202 H d
Mississippi River . . . . 191 G e
Mississippi River, Delta of the 187 J f
Mississippi Valley . . . . 187 J d
Missolonghi . . . . 164 C c
Missouri, state . . . . 203 F c
Missouri, ter. 1812 . . . . . . 203 Q a
Missouri, ter. 1819 . . . . . . 203 Q b
Missouri Plateau . . . . 186 I d
Missouri River . . . . 187 J d
Missouri River, Little . . . . . 198 E a
Missouria, Ind. Res. . . . . . . 188 G c
Missouris, tribe . . . . 188 G c
Missunde . . . . 158 E a
Mistassini, lake . . . . 212 H c
Mistra . . . . 89 B c
Mistra, desp. . . . . 93 B c
Mitau . . . . 88 J c
Mitchell, Fort . . . . 211 H d
Mitchell, mt. . . . . 187 K e
Mitchell, parl. bor. . . . . . . 163 I g
Mitchell River . . . . 172 D b
Mithradates VI., Kingdom of . 33 leg.
Mitla . . . . 213 C c
Mitrovitza, in Slavonia . . . .
Mitrovitza, in Turkey . . . . .
Mittelmark, dist. . . . . 85 C b
Mitys River . . . . 11 D b
Mizpah, N. of Jerusalem . . . . 7 C e
Mizpah, W. of Jerusalem . . . . 7 B e
Mizpah, mt. . . . .
Mizpah, Valley of . . . . 6 D a
Mizquiz . . . .
Mława . . . . 155 K b
Moab, dist. . . . . 7 D f
Moabites, people . . . . 7 ins. D
Moapa River, Ind. Res. . . . . . 188 C c
Mobar, reg. . . . .
Mobile . . . . 191 H e
Mobile Bay . . . . 191 H e
Mocha . . . . 174 H c
Möckern, near Leipsic . . . . . 154 G c
Möckern, near Magdeburg . . . 154 G b
Möckmühl . . . . 143 H g
Mocsa . . . . 159 J e
Modbury, parl. bor. . . . . . .
Modder River . . . . 175 M l
Modena . . . . 90 J h
Modena, bp. . . . . 95 E c
Modena, duchy . . . . 90 C b
Modicia . . . . 26 D b
Modigliana . . . . 90 L i
Modin . . . . 7 C e
Modlin . . . . 155 K b
Modocs, tribe . . . . 188 B b
Modon . . . .
Modrush, bp. . . . .
Möen, isl. . . . . 115 G a
Mœnus (Main) River . . . . . . 38 D b
Mœris, lake . . . . 4 ins.
Mœsia, reg. . . . . 47 K e
Mœsia, Lower, imp. prov. . . . 35 J e
Mœsia, Upper, imp. prov. . . . 35 I e
Mœsia I, East Roman prov. 43 F e (2.)
Mœsia II, East Roman prov. 43 H e (5.)
Mogadisho . . . . 175 H d
Mogador . . . . 174 B a
Mogaung . . . .
Möggingen . . . . 142 D e
Moghan, plain . . . . 99 M f
Moghilev . . . .
Mogul Empire in 1700 . . . . . 137 leg.
Mogontia or Mogontiacum (Mayence) . . . . . . 39 J i
Mohammed Artin, Dom. of . . 77 L e
Mohammed II., mosque . . . . 93 G e
Mohammedans . . . . 67 ins., leg.
Mohave, Mojave . . . . 210 B d
Mohave, Fort . . . . 188 D c
Mohaves, Mojaves, tribe . . . . 188 C d
Mohawk River . . . . 192 D b
Mohawks, tribe . . . . 188 L b
Mohegans, tribe . . . . 188 L b
Mohi . . . . 92 C c
Möhra . . . . 114 F c
Möhringen . . . . 143 H h
Mohrungen . . . . 155 J b
Moidart . . . .
Moissac, mon. . . . . 94 C c
Mola . . . . 90 F d
Moldau River . . . . 63 H d
Moldavia, dist. 19 cent. . . . . 164 D a
Moldavia, princ. 16 cent. . . . 119 J d
Moldavia, reg., 14 cent. . . . . 77 J c
Moldavia, reg., 18 cent. . . . . 131 I d
Mole River . . . . 75 I i
Molesme, mon. . . . . 94 C b
Molina . . . . 83 K g
Molina, barony . . . . 83 K g
Molino del Rey, battle . . . . . 201 H g
Molinos, R. . . . . 106 B b
Molise, dist. . . . . 90 E d
Mollendo . . . . 214 B d
Mollwitz . . . . 135 I c
Molodechno . . . . 153 N g
Molokai, isl. . . . . 198 ins. B
Molopo River . . . . 175 E g
Molossi, people . . . .
Molossis, dist. . . . . 10 B c
Moluccas, isl. . . . . 112 F d
Molycria . . . . 10 C d
Mombasa . . . . 175 H e
Momemphis . . . . 8 B b
Mömpelgard . . . . 143 ins. F
Mömpelgard, cty., see Montbéliard . . . . 86 F e
Mömpelgard, princ. cty. . . . . 143 ins. F
Mompos . . . . 214 B b
Mona (Anglesey), isl. . . . . . 51 N h
Mona, isl., West Indies . . . . 105 G c
Monaco . . . . 90 A c
Monaco, princ. . . . . 161 F f
Mona Passage, str. . . . . 213 F c
Monaghan, cty. . . . . 127 K g
Monapia (Isle of Man) . . . . . 51 N g
Monastir . . . . 164 C b
Moncalieri . . . . 130 P j
Monchique . . . . 83 J h
Monclova . . . . 213 B b
Moncontour . . . . 76 D c
Moncton . . . . 212 I d
Mondego River . . . . 82 G e
Mondoñedo . . . . 82 A a
Mondoñedo, bp. . . . . 94 A c
Mondovi . . . . 90 H h
Mandovi, bp. . . . . 95 D c
Mondsee, mon. . . . . 95 E b
Monemvasia . . . . 89 B c
Monflanquin . . . . 126 B d
Monforte, mon. . . . . 94 A c
Monghyr, Mongheer . . . . . . 137 E c
Mongolia, reg. . . . . 92 K c
Mongols, Khanate of the . . .
Mongols, people . . . .
Monhegan Island . . . . 189 D c
Monilia . . . . 26 D c
Monk-Bretton, mon. . . . . . . 97 P h
Monkey Hill, village 216
Monk Sherborne, mon. . . . . . 100 A a
Monks Corner . . . . 195 B g
Monkton Farleigh, mon. . . . . 97 O j
Monmouth, in England . . . . .
Monmouth, cty. . . . . 127 W o
Monmouth, parl. bor. . . . . . . 163 L f
Monmouth, parl. dist. . . . . . 163 K f
Monmouth, in New Jersey . . . 195 D c
Monnikendam . . . . 117 D b
Monocacy River . . . . 208 ins.
Monœcus (Monaco) . . . . 26 B d
Monongahela River . . . . 192 A d
Monopoli . . . . 90 F d
Monos, tribe . . . . 188 C c
Mon Plaisir, farm . . . .
Monreale, abp. . . . . 95 E d

Monroe, Fortress . . . . 208 E b
Monrovia . . . . 174 B d
Mons, in Hainaut . . . . 117 C d
Mons Brisiacus (Breisach) . . . 39 I i
Mons Casinus, see Monte Cassino
Monserrate, isl. . . . . 105 H c
Mons Ferrandus, castle . . . . 68 C c
Mons Gaudii, mt. . . . . 96 A
Mons Regalis, see Montreal, in Syria . . . . 68 C c
Montacute, parl. bor. . . . . .
Montafon Valley . . . . 91 R k
Montaigu . . . . 69 C c
Montaigu, seign. . . . . 69 C c
Montalcino, bp. . . . . . . 95 E c (Mo.)
Montana, ter. 1864 . . . . 203 P f
Montana, state . . . . 203 P f
Montaperto . . . . 90 L j
Montargis . . . . 69 I f
Montauban . . . . 76 D d
Montauban bp. . . . . 94 C c
Montauban, gen. . . . . 147 E c
Montbard . . . . 69 J f
Montbéliard . . . . 143 ins. F
Montbéliard, cty. . . . . 86 F e
Montbéliard, princ.-cty. . . . . 143 ins. F
Mont Blanc, mt. . . . . 2 E d
Montbrison . . . . 69 E d
Mont Cenis Pass . . . . 130 O i
Montcontour . . . . 118 D d
Mont-de-Marsan . . . . 148 D f
Montdidier . . . . 126 C b
Montebello . . . . 150 E d
Montebourg, mon. . . . . 94 B b
Montecarlo, near Pisa . . . . . 90 L j
Monte Cassino . . . . 64 B b
Monte Cassino, bp. . . . . 95 E c
Monte Cassino, mon. . . . . . . 95 E c
Montechiaro, near Asti . . . . . 130 Q j
Montechiaro, near Brescia . . . 90 J h
Montefeltro . . . . 64 B b
Monteleone . . . . 161 K h
Montélimart . . . . 126 D d
Monte Mario . . . . 96 A
Montemór, near Coimbra . . . . 82 A a
Montemór, near Evora . . . . . 83 J h
Montendre . . . . 126 A d
Montenegro, princ. . . . . 164 B b
Montenegro, reg. . . . . 93 A b
Montenotte . . . . 150 E d
Monte Nuovo, mt. . . . . 31 ins. A
Montepulciano . . . . 90 L j
Montereau . . . . 154 B d
Monterey, in California . . . . . 198 A c
Monterey, in Mexico . . . . . . 201 E d
Monterey, in Pa. . . . . 208 ins.
Monte Rosa, mt. . . . . 2 E d
Monte Santo, town . . . . 214 F d
Montesha, reg. . . . . 77 J e
Montes Serrorum (Transylvanian Alps) . . . . 39 M k
Monte Testaccio . . . . 22 A
Montevideo . . . . 215 D f
Montfaucon, mon. . . . . 95 D b
Montferrat, marq. . . . . 90 B b
Montfort, in France . . . .
Montfort, in Syria . . . . 68 ins. A
Montfort, castle, in France . . . 69 H f
Montfort, castle, in Vorarlberg 78 F e
Montfort, cty., in France . . . . 76 D b
Montfort, cty., in Swabia . . . . 143 I j
Mont Genèvre Pass . . . . 130 O j
Montgomery, in Alabama . . . 211 H d
Montgomery, in Wales . . . . . 127 V n
Montgomery, castle . . . .
Montgomery, cty. . . . . 127 V n
Montgomery, parl. bor. . . . . . 163 K e
Montgomery, parl. dist. . . . . 163 K e
Montiel . . . . 83 K h
Montigny, mon. . . . . 148 C b
Montlaur . . . . 76 E d
Montlhéry . . . . 76 E b
Montlucon . . . . 69 I g
Montluel . . . . 130 N i
Montmartre, Faubourg, quarter in Paris . . . . 149 B
Montmartre, mt. . . . . 62 B d
Montmédy . . . . 126 D b
Montmirail, in Champagne . . . 154 B d
Montmirail, in Perche . . . . . . 76 D b
Montmorency . . . . 69 I f (Montm.)
Montmorency, Falls of . . . . . 191 K b
Montpelier . . . . 211 K b
Montpellier . . . . 76 E e
Montpellier, gen. . . . . 147 E c
Montpellier, univ. . . . . 100 F f
Montpensier . . . . 76 E c
Montreal, in Canada . . . . . . 189 B b
Montreal, in Syria . . . . 68 C c
Montreuil . . . . 61 D a
Montreuillon . . . . 69 I g
Montriond . . . . 62 D e
Montrose . . . .
Mont-Saint-Guibert . . . . 156 B a
Mont-Saint-Jean, farm . . . . . .
Mont-Saint-Jean, village . . . .
Mont-Saint-Michel, mon. . . . . 94 B b
Montserrat, isl. . . . . 213 F c
Montserrat, mon. . . . . 94 C c
Monza . . . . 90 I h
Mook . . . . 117 D c
Mooltan . . . . 137 B b
Moon, Gate of the, in Alexandria . . . . 34 ins. C
Moon, Temple of the, in Rome 24 B
Moore, Fort . . . . 193 ins. C
Moore, lake . . . . 172 A c
Moorfields, in London . . . . . 75 G g
Moorgate, in London . . . . . . 75 G g
Moorish States, in Spain . . . . 82 B a
Moors, people, in Spain . . . . 57 C f
Moorshedabad . . . . 137 E d
Moose Factory . . . . 212 G c
Moose Jaw, post . . . . 212 E c
Moose River . . . . 212 G c
Mopsium . . . . 11 D c
Mopsuestia, Mopsuhestia . . . . 20 F d
Moquegua . . . . 214 B d
Moqui, Ind. Res. . . . . 188 D c
Moquis, tribe . . . . 188 D c
Mor . . . . 159 J e
Mora . . . . 88 F a
Moradabad . . . . 137 C c
Morat . . . . 91 P l
Morava River . . . . 119 I e
Moravia, march, about 1000 . . 59 H d
Moravia, march, 12 cent. . . . . 72 D b
Moravian Kingdom, 9 cent. . . 56 F c
Moravians, people, about 900 . 57 G d
Moray, bp. . . . . 97 I b
Moray, dist. . . . .
Moray Firth . . . . 49 E c
Morbegno . . . . 91 R l
Morbihan, dept. . . . . 148 D e
Mordvins, people . . . . 139 G e
Morea Peninsula . . . . 2 G e
Morecambe Bay . . . . 127 V m
Morelia . . . . 213 ins.
Morella . . . . 82 B a
Morelos, state . . . . 213 ins.
Moresby Island . . . . 172 E b
Moreton . . . . 172 D b
Moreton Bay . . . . 172 E c
Moreton Bay District . . . . . . 172 leg.
Morgan, Fort . . . . 208 C c
Morgan, route of . . . . 195 A f
Morgantina . . . . 30 D e
Morgantown . . . . 206 ins.
Morgarten . . . . 91 Q k
Moriah, mt. . . . . 68 ins. B
Moril . . . . 91 Q l
Morimont, mon. . . . . 148 C b
Morini, see Thérouanne
Morini, people . . . . 38 C b
Moritz, Fort . . . . 214 F d
Mornington Island . . . . 172 C b
Morocco . . . . 174 C a
Morocco, reg., 14 cent. . . . . 77 C f
Morocco, state, 16 cent. . . . . 118 C g
Morocco, state, 20 cent. . . . . 174 C a
Morón . . . . 82 A b
Morontobara . . . . 19 K f
Morpeth, parl. bor. . . . . 163 M b
Morristown . . . . 195 D c
Mortagne . . . . 61 D b
Mortain . . . . 69 C b
Mortain, cty. . . . . 69 C b
Mortara . . . . 130 Q i
Mortemer . . . . 65 G f
Mortemer, mon. . . . . . . 94 C b (Mort.)
Mortes River . . . . 214 D d
Mortimers Cross . . . . 84 B c
Mosa (Meuse) River . . . . 38 D b
Mosbach . . . . 142 D b
Mosbach, Palatine, princ. . . . 87 H d
Moschi, people . . . . 35 M e
Moscow . . . . 138 E d
Moscow, princ. . . . . 77 L a
Moscow, gov. . . . . 131 K b
Mosella (Moselle) River . . . . . 38 D c
Moselle, dept. . . . . 148 F e
Moselle River . . . . 62 D d
Moskva River . . . . 153 P f
Mosomagus . . . . 39 H i
Mosquito Coast . . . . 213 D c
Moss . . . . 131 F b
Mossámedes . . . . 175 E f
Mostar . . . . 93 A b
Mosul . . . . 67 O f
Mosul, Dominion of . . . . 67 O f
Mosyr . . . . 167 K e
Motola . . . . 90 F d
Motrone . . . . 90 L j
Mottisfont, priory . . . . 100 A a
Motupe . . . . 111 B c
Motyca . . . . 30 D e
Motye . . . . 30 B e
Moulins . . . . 76 E c
Moulins, gen. . . . . 147 E b
Moulmein . . . . 171 K g
Moultrie, Fort . . . . 195 B g
Mount Desert Island . . . . . . 189 D b
Mount Gambier, town . . . . . 172 C d
Mount Grace, mon. . . . . 97 P g
Mount Hope, town . . . . 189 ins. A
Mount Majella, mon. . . . . . . 95 E c
Mount of Offense . . . . 6 ins. A
Mount of Olives . . . . 6 ins. A
Mount Sinai, mon. of . . . . . . 150 B b
Mount Vernon, town . . . . . . 193 F b
Mount Wollaston, village . . . . 189 C c
Mount Zion, Street of . . . . . . 68 ins. B
Moura . . . . 83 J h
Moureille, mon. . . . . 94 B b
Mouse River, see Souris River
Moutier-Ramey, mon. . . . 94 C b (M. R.)
Moutiers . . . . 130 O i
Mouzon . . . . 76 F b
Mouzon, mon. . . . . 95 D b
Moyobamba . . . . 214 B c
Moys . . . . 135 H c
Mozambique . . . . 175 H f
Mozambique, see Portuguese East Africa
Mozambique Channel . . . . . . 175 H g
Mozhaisk . . . . 138 E d
Mozufferpore . . . . 137 D c
Mpapwa . . . . 175 G e
Muchelney, mon. . . . . 97 O k
Much Wenloch, parl. bor. . . . 163 L e
Muckleshoot, Ind. Res. . . . . . 188 B a
Mudki . . . . 170 I e
Mugonian Gate . . . . 24 A
Mühlberg . . . . 115 G c
Mühldorf . . . . 79 H d
Mühlenbach . . . . 159 L f
Mühlhausen, in Thuringia . . . 62 F c
Mühlhausen, in Thuringia, imp. cy. . . . . 79 G c
Mühlheim, on the Danube R . . 143 G i
Muiden . . . . 117 D b
Muir Glacier . . . . 212 B c

Mukden . . . . 171 N d
Mukdishu . . . . 175 H d
Mula . . . . 82 B b
Mulde River . . . . 85 G e
Mülhausen, in Alsace, imp. cy. 78 E f
Mul-Java (Malacca), pen. . . . .
Mull, isl. . . . .
Multan . . . . 137 B b
Mulucha River . . . . 38 B e
Müncheberg . . . . 80 ins.
München, see Munich
Münchengrätz . . . . 159 H c
Müdnen . . . . 134 E c
Munderkingen . . . . 143 I i
Munich . . . . 72 C b
Munkacs . . . . 131 H d
Münsingen . . . . 143 I i
Munster, in Ireland, prov. . . .
Münster, in Alsace . . . . 126 E b
Münster, in Bp. of Basel . . . . 91 P k
Münster, in Westphalia . . . . 62 D c
Münster, bp. . . . . 78 E c
Münster, Hanse. cy. . . . . 99 ins. B
Münsterberg . . . . 79 J c
Münsterberg, princ. . . . . 79 J c
Münster Thal, valley . . . . 91 S l
Munychia, dist. . . . . 16 D c
Munychia Port . . . . 16 D c
Muota Tal, valley . . . . 150 E c
Mur River . . . . 63 I e
Muranum . . . . 31 F c
Murat, viscty. . . . . 69 E d
Murbach, ab. . . . . 78 E e
Murbach, mon. . . . . 95 D b
Murbogi, people . . . . 38 B d
Murchison River . . . . 172 A c
Murcia . . . . 82 B b
Murcia, bp. . . . . 94 B d
Murcia, Km. . . . . 83 K h
Muret . . . . 76 D e
Murfreesboro . . . . 208 C b
Murg River . . . . 142 B c
Murshidabad . . . . 137 E d
Muri, mon. . . . . 91 Q k
Murom . . . . 138 F d
Murr River . . . . 143 H d
Murray River . . . . 172 D d
Murrays, fam. . . . . 97 I c
Murrhardt . . . . 143 I h
Murrumbidgee River . . . . 172 D d
Mursa . . . . 42 F d
Murten . . . . 91 P l
Murus (Mur) River . . . . 38 E c
Murviedro . . . . 82 B b
Musarna . . . . 19 J d
Muscat . . . .
Musciacus, see Moissac
Muscle Shoals . . . . 196 B d
Muscovite Dominions, 16 cent. 119 K b
Muscovy, reg. . . . . 109 U b
Musgrave Range . . . . 172 C c
Musha Islands . . . . 174 H c
Mushki, people . . . . 5 C b
Muskingum River . . . . 196 ins. B
Muskingum, tribe . . . . 188 J c
Muspa, Punta de, cape . . . . 191 I f
Mussidan . . . . 126 B d
Mussumba . . . . 175 F e
Musulami, people . . . . 38 D e
Mutapili . . . .
Muthul River . . . . 38 D e
Mutilum . . . . 27 G c
Mutina (Modena) . . . . 26 E c
Muttra . . . . 170 I f
Muwahhids, Dom of the . . . . 73 C d
Muzaffarpur . . . . 137 D c
Muzon, Cape . . . . 212 ins.
Mweru, lake . . . . 175 F e
Mycale, mt. . . . . 13 E c
Mycalessus . . . . 11 E d
Mycenæ . . . . 15 C b
Mycenean Greece . . . . 4 B b
Mygdonia, dist., in Macedonia 11 D b
Mygdonia, dist., in Mesopotamia 20 I d
Mykonos . . . . 13 D c
Mylæ, in Sicily . . . . 30 E d
Mylæ, in Thessaly . . . . 10 D c
Mylasa . . . . 17 E c
Myndus . . . . 17 E c
Mynyw (Saint Davids) . . . . 60 D e
Myonia . . . . 11 D d
Myonnesus . . . . 20 B c
Myra . . . . 20 D d
Myrcinus . . . . 11 E b
Myriandrus . . . . 18 E c
Myrina . . . . 17 E b
Myrmex . . . . 34 ins. C
Myrrhinus . . . . 16 B b
Myrtea . . . . 9 D c
Myrto, isl. . . . . 15 E b
Myrtoum Sea . . . . 15 D b
Myrtuntium . . . . 14 B b
Myrtuntium, lake . . . . 10 B d
Mysia, Macedonian prov. . . . . 18 C c
Mysia, Rom. prov. . . . . 20 B c
Mysia, reg. . . . . 8 G e
Mysore . . . . 137 C f
Mysore, reg. . . . . 137 C f
Mystic . . . . 189 C d
Mystic River . . . . 189 ins. B
Mytilene . . . .
Mytilene, isl. . . . .
Myus . . . . 13 E c

Naarath . . . . 7 C e
Naarden . . . . 117 D b
Naas . . . . 127 K h
Naauw Poort . . . . 175 L m
Nab River . . . . 63 G d
Nabatæi, people . . . . 35 L h
Nabburg . . . . 63 G d
Nablus, see Neapolis . . . . 68 ins. A
Nachod . . . . 159 C c
Nacogdoches . . . . 191 G e
Naqjivan . . . . 99 M f
Nævian Gate . . . . 23 B
Näfels . . . . 91 R k
Nagasaki . . . . 171 N e
Nagold . . . . 143 G h
Nagold River . . . . 143 G h
Nagpur, Nagpore . . . . 137 C d
Nagpur, state . . . . 170 I f
Nagy-Kanizsa . . . . 159 I e
Nagy Sallo . . . . 159 J d
Nahe River . . . . 62 D d
Naimans, people . . . .
Nain, in Galilee . . . . 6 C c
Nain, in Labrador . . . . 212 I c
Nairi, people . . . .
Nairn, cty. . . . .
Naissus . . . . 39 M l
Nájera . . . . 82 B a
Nakel . . . . 63 I b
Namaqualand, Great, dist. . . . 175 E g
Namnetes, see Nantes
Namnetes, people . . . . 38 B c
Namnetum, isl. . . . . 38 B c
Namnetum, Portus (Nantes) . . 38 B c
Namoi River . . . . 172 D d
Namugum, see Namur
Namur . . . . 117 C d
Namur, cty. . . . . 117 C d
Nan-chan-fu . . . .
Nancy . . . . 84 G e
Nandurbar . . . .
Nangis . . . . 154 B d
Nanipacna . . . . 191 H e
Nanking . . . .
Nanrantsouck Mission . . . . 189 D b
Nansemond River . . . . 193 ins. A
Nantasket . . . . 189 ins. B
Nantes . . . . 61 C c
Nantes, bp. . . . . 94 B b
Nantes, cty. . . . . 69 C c
Nantes, univ. . . . . 100 E e
Nanteuil, mon. . . . . 94 B b
Nanticoke River . . . . 192 D d
Nanticokes, tribe . . . . 188 K b
Nantuates, people . . . . 26 A a
Nantucket, isl. . . . . 189 D d
Nantwich . . . . 127 W m
Napata (Jebel Barkal) . . . . 4 F e
Naphtali, Mountains of . . . . 6 C c
Naphtali, tribe . . . . 7 ins. D
Napier . . . . 172 G e
Naples . . . . 90 E d
Naples, abp. . . . . 95 E c
Naples, Bay of . . . . 30 D b
Naples, km., 14 cent. . . . . 81 I d
Naples, km., 16 cent. . . . . 119 H e
Naples, km., 1812 . . . . 152 D e
Naples, theme . . . . 58 G e
Naples, univ. . . . . 100 H f
Napo River . . . . 111 B b
Napoca . . . . 35 I d
Napoleonshöhe, castle . . 154 E c (N.)
Nar River . . . . 27 H e
Naragarra . . . . 38 D e
Narbada River . . . . 137 C d
Narbata . . . . 6 B c
Narbo Martius (Narbonne) . . . 38 C d
Narbonensis, Rom. prov. . . 38 D d (6)
Narbonne . . . . 61 E e
Narbonne, abp. . . . . 94 C c
Narbonne, viscty. . . . . 76 E e
Narbonnensis I, West Rom. prov. . . . . 42 C e (13)
Narbonnensis II, West Rom. prov. . . . . 42 D e (14)
Narew River . . . . 87 M b
Narni . . . . 90 D c
Narnia . . . . 27 G e
Narona . . . . 38 F d
Narova River . . . . 88 L b
Narragansett Bay . . . . 189 ins. A
Narragansetts, tribe . . . . 189 ins. A
Narthacius, mt. . . . . 11 D c
Narva . . . . 88 M b
Narva, Hanse. cy. . . . . 99 I b
Narvaez, route of . . . . 191 I f
Naseby . . . . 127 Y n
Nashboro . . . . 194 B c
Nashua . . . . 211 K b
Nashville . . . . 199 H c
Nasium . . . . 39 H i
Nasos, quarter in Syracuse . . 31 ins. B
Nass River . . . . 212 ins.
Nassau, Bahama Is. . . . . 213 E b
Nassau, in Germany . . . . 72 B a
Nassau, cty. . . . . 78 F c
Nassau, duchy . . . . 154 E c
Nassau, princ. . . . . 122 E c
Nassau, Fort, in New York . . 192 E b
Nassau, Fort in Pa. . . . . 192 ins.
Natal . . . . 214 F c
Natal, col. . . . . 175 N l
Natchez . . . . 208 B c
Natchez, tribe . . . . 188 H d
Natchitoches . . . . 191 G e
Natick . . . . 189 C d
Natiso River . . . . 27 H b
Natuna, isl. . . . .
Naucratis . . . . 4 ins.
Nauen . . . . 85 C b
Naugard . . . . 155 H b
Naulinco . . . . 106 C a
Naulochus . . . . 30 E d
Naumachia of Augustus . . . . 22 A
Naumburg . . . . 63 F c
Naumburg, bp. . . . . 95 E a
Naumkeag . . . . 189 ins. B
Naupactus . . . . 10 C d
Nauplia . . . . 15 C b
Nauportus . . . . 27 I b
Nautaca . . . . 19 K c
Nauvoo . . . . 211 G b
Nava River . . . . 39 I i
Navajo, Ind. Res. . . . . 188 E c
Navajos, tribe . . . . 188 E c
Navalia (shipyards in Rome) . 22 A
Navalia River . . . . 39 I g
Navari, people . . . . 35 J d

Navarre, dist. 56 B d
Navarre, km. 82 H e
Navarre and Béarn, km. 126 A e
Navarrete 83 K g
Navas de Tolosa, Las 83 K h
Navidad 105 F c
Navigator Islands 180 K i
Nawsett 189 D d
Naxos 13 D c
Naxos, duchy 89 C c
Naxos, isl. 13 D c
Naxua 99 M f
Naxus
Nay 126 A e
Nazareth, in Palestine 6 C c
Nazareth, abp. in Italy 95 F c
Nazas, Rio de, R. 213 B b
Nazianzus 20 F c
Nazli 165 F d
Neæ, isl.
Neæthus (Neto) River 31 F c
Neagh, lough, lake 49 C d
Neapel, see Naples
Neapolis, in Africa 38 E e
Neapolis, in Apulia 31 G a
Neapolis, in Campania (Naples) 30 D b
Neapolis, in Chalcidice 11 E b
Neapolis, in Istria 27 H b
Neapolis, in Macedonia 11 F b
Neapolis, in Palestine 7 C d
Neapolis, in Sardinia 38 D e
Neapolis, quarter in Syracuse 31 ins. B
Nearchus, route of 19 H e
Neath, mon. 97 N j
Nebbio 148 C c
Nebelhöhle 143 H i
Nebo, mt. 7 D e
Nebouzan, reg. 146 B f
Nebraska City 206 F b
Nebraska, state 203 R g
Nebraska, ter. 1854 202 C f
Nebraska, ter. 1861 203 Q g
Nebraska, ter. 1863 203 R g
Nebrodes Mountains 30 D e
Necessity, Fort 192 B d
Neckar River 62 E d
Neckar-Bischofsheim 142 C b
Neckargemünd 142 C b
Neckarsulm 143 H g
Necropolis, dist. 16 D c
Nectansmere
Neda River 14 B b
Nedad River 50 G c
Nedjed, reg.
Nedjef
Nedon River 14 C b
Neerwinden 122 C c
Neetum 30 E e
Negapatam 137 D f
Nègrepelisse 126 B d
Negro, Cabo, cape 108 R i
Negropont, isl. 89 H g
Negros, isl. 199 ins. H
Neidenburg 115 K b
Neïus, mt. 10 B d
Neipperg 143 H g
Neisse 115 I c
Neisse River, Glatzer 63 I c
Neisse River, Görlitzer 63 H c
Neiva 214 B b
Nelea 11 E c
Neleus River 11 E d
Nellenburg, castle 142 C e
Nellenburg, landgr. 142 C e
Nellore 137 D f
Nelson, in Alberta 212 D d
Nelson, in New Zealand 172 G e
Nelson, Fort 212 C c
Nelson River 186 J c
Nemara 6 F c
Nemausus (Nîmes) 38 C d
Nemea 15 C b
Nemetacus, see Arras
Nemetes, see Spires
Nemetes, people 39 I i
Nemorensis, lake 35 ins. B
Nemossus 38 C c
Nemours 69 I f
Nemours, duchy 84 E e
Nen River 127 Y n
Neocæsarea 20 G b
Neosho River 198 F c
Nepal, Nepaul, state 171 J f
Nepete 27 G e
Nepi, bp. 95 E c
Nepomuk, mon. 95 E b
Neponset River 189 ins. B
Nepos, Dom. of emperor 50 G d
Neptune, Basilica of 22 A
Neptune, Mts. of 30 E d
Neptune, Temple of 34 ins. C (8)
Neptunia, Colonia (Taranto) 31 G b
Nequinum 27 G e
Nérac 126 B d
Nerbudda River 137 C d
Neresheim 143 J h
Neresheim, ab. 143 J h
Neretum 31 G b
Neris 14 C b
Nēritus, mt. 10 B d
Nerium, prom. 38 A d
Nero, Aqueduct of 22 A
Nero, Baths of 22 A
Nero, Circus of 22 A
Nero, Colossus of 24 B
Nero, Villa of 22 A
Neronian Meadows 96 A
Nerós house, in Olympia
Nertchinsk
Nertobriga 38 B d
Nerulum 31 F c
Nerva, Forum of 24 B
Nervii, people 38 C b
Nesactium 27 H c
Nesis, isl. 31 ins. A
Nesle 69 I f
Ness, loch, lake 49 D c
Nesselwang 114 F e
Nessonis, lake 11 D c
Nestorians, sect 67 X m
Nestus River 11 F b
Netherlands, Austrian, prov. 134 B c
Netherlands, Kingdom of the 158 C c
Netherlands, Spanish, prov. 122 B c
Netherlands, The, reg. 117
Netherlands, United, country 122 C b
Netley, ab. 100 A b
Netolitz 63 G d
Netze District 135 I b
Netze River 63 I b
Neu-Brandenburg 123 G b
Neubreisach 154 D e
Neuburg 62 F d
Neuburg, palat. 122 F d
Neuburg, princ. 134 F d
Neuchâtel 91 O l
Neuchâtel, dist. 91 O l
Neuchâtel, lake 91 O l
Neuchâtel, princ. 151 K j
Neudenau 142 D b
Neuenburg, in Baden 142 A e
Neuenburg, in Switzerland 91 O l
Neuenburg, (Neuchâtel) princ. 134 D e
Neuenstadt 143 H g
Neuenstein 143 I g
Neufchâteau 117 D e
Neuffen 143 H h
Neufra 143 H i
Neuhaldensleben 122 F b
Neuhaus 154 F b
Neuhäusel 131 G d
Neukamp 123 G a
Neumark, dist. 85 D b
Neumarkt, in Bavaria 154 F d
Neumarkt, in Galicia 135 K d
Neumarkt, in Styria 135 H e
Neumünster 72 B a
Neuquen 215 C f
Neu-Ravensburg 143 I j
Neu-Ruppin 158 G b
Neu-Sandec 159 K d
Neusatz 159 J f
Neuse River 193 F d
Neusohl 159 J d
Neuss 62 D c
Neuss, Hanse. cy. 99 ins. B
Neustadt, in the Black Forest 142 B e
Neustadt, on the Hardt 142 B b
Neustadt, in Moravia 135 I d
Neustadt, on the Orla 114 F c
Neustadtl 123 H f
Neu-Stettin 123 I b
Neu-Strelitz 123 G b
Neustria, reg. 54 E d
Neutra 72 D b
Neutra, bp. 95 F b
Neutra River 159 J d
Neuzelle, mon. 80 ins.
Neva, lake 71 M a
Nevada, state 203 O h
Nevada, ter. 203 O g
Nevada, Sierra, mts. 187 H e
Nevado de Tolima, mt. 214 B b
Neve 6 E c
Nevers 61 E c
Nevers, bp. 94 C b
Nevers, cty. 61 E c
Nevilles Cross
Nevirnum, see Nevers
Nevis, isl. 213 F c
New Albany 211 H c
New Abbey of Saint Mary of Grace Cisterciana 75 G g
New Amstel 192 ins.
New Amsterdam, in Dutch Guiana 214 D b
New Amsterdam (New York) 189 ins. C
New Amsterdam Island 182 II k
New Andalusia, reg. 105 E e
Newark, in England 74 E e
Newark, parl. bor. 163 N d
Newark, in New Jersey 192 D c
New Athens 23 D
New Aurelian Gate 22 A
New Bedford 211 K b
New Berne, Newbern
New Biscay, prov. 190 D f
Newborough, parl. bor.
New Breisach 134 D e
New Brunswick, in New Jersey 192 D c
New Brunswick, col. 212 I d
Newburgh, in New York 195 D c
Newburgh, mon. in England 97 P g
Newburn 127 X k
Newbury, in England 127 X o
Newbury, parl. bor.
Newbury, in Mass. 189 C c
New Caledonia, isl. 172 F c
New Caledonia, reg. 212 C c
New Carthage (Cartagena) 38 B e
New Castle, (Newcastle), in Delaware 192 D d
Newcastle, New South Wales 172 E d
Newcastle-on-Tyne 65 F c
Newcastle, parl. bor. 163 M b
Newcastle-under-Lyme, parl. bor. 163 L d
New Castile, km., in Spain 83 K h
New Castile (Peru), reg.
New Claudian Way 27 H e
New East Prussia, dist. 138 B e
New Elfsborg, Fort 192 ins.
New England Colonies, The 189
New England Confederation, see 189 leg.
New England Range 172 E d
Newenham, mon. in Bedford 97 Q i
Newenham, mon. in Devon 97 N k
New Estremadura (Chile), reg. 108 J k
New Estremadura, prov. in Mexico 190 E f
New Forest, The 49 F f

Newfoundland, col. 212 I c
New France, reg. 191 I c K b
New Galicia, prov.
Newgate, loc. in London 75 G g
New Gothenburg, Fort 192 ins.
New Granada, reg. 108 J g
New Granada, viceroyalty 215 ins.
New Guinea, isl. 110 F F h
New Hampshire, col. 189 C c
New Hampshire, state 199 K b
New Harmony 206 ins.
New Haven, in Conn. 189 B d
Newhaven, in England 185 G g
New Haven, col. 189 B d
New Hebrides, isl. 172 F b
New Inverness 193 ins. C
New Jersey, col. 192 D c
New Jersey, East, col. 192 D c
New Jersey, West, col. 192 D d
New Jersey, state 199 K c
New Korsholm, Fort 192 ins.
New León, prov. 190 E f
New London 189 B d
New Madrid 208 C b
Newmarket 127 Z n
New Mecklenburg, isl. 179 G h
New Mexico, prov. 190 D e
New Mexico, ter. 1850 202 C h
New Mexico, ter. 1863 203 Q h
Newminster, mon. 97 P f
New Netherland, col. 192 D c
New Norcia 172 A d
New Norfolk 172 D e
New Orleans 191 G f
New Park, dist. 210 D b
New Philippines, prov. 190 F e
New Plymouth, col. 189 C d
New Plymouth, in New Zealand 172 G d
New Pomerania, isl. 172 E a
Newport, parl. bor. in Cornwall 163 J g
Newport, in I. of Wight 127 X p
Newport, parl. bor., I. of Wight 163 M g
Newport, in Rhode Island 189 ins. A
Newport News 193 ins. A
New Providence 213 E b
New Romney, parl. bor. 163 P g
Newry 127 K g
New Santander, prov. 190 F f
New Seraglio, loc. in Constantinople 93 G e
New Seraglio, Wall of the 93 G e
Newsham, mon. 97 Q h
New Shops, loc. in Rome
New Shoreham, parl. bor. 163 N g
New Shoreham, parl. dist. 163 N g
New Silesia, dist. 135 J c
New Siberia Islands 171 O a
New Spain, viceroyalty 213 leg.
New South Wales, col. 172 leg.
New South Wales, state 172 D d
Newstead, mon. 97 P h
New Sweden, col. 192 ins.
New Toggenburg, castle 91 R k
Newton, parl. bor. 163 L d
Newton Abbot 127 V p
Newtown, in Conn. 189 B d
Newtown, in Mass. 189 ins. B
Newtown, in New York 195 C b
Newtown, in Wales 162 C e
Newtown, parl. bor., I. of Wight 163 M g
New Utrecht 189 ins. C
New Wasa, Fort 192 ins.
New White Russia, reg. 138 C d
New Windsor, in Maryland 208 ins.
New Windsor, parl. bor. in England 163 N f
New Woodstock, parl. bor. 163 M f (New. Wood.)
New York 189 ins. C
New York, col. 192 D b
New York, state 199 J b
New York Bay 189 ins. C
New Zealand, col.
Nez Percés, tribe 188 C a
Ngan-hwei, prov. 171 M e
Nganking
Niagara, Fort 192 B b
Niagara Falls 192 B b
Niagara River 200 D b
Nicæa, in Bithynia 20 C b
Nicæa, in India 19 L d
Nicæa (Nice), in Liguria 26 B d
Nicæa, in Locris 16 F e
Nicæa, Empire of 73 G c
Nicaragua, lake 105 C d
Nicaragua, country 213 D c
Nicaragua, reg. 105 C d
Nice 61 G e
Nice, bp. 95 D c
Nicephorium 20 H e
Nicer (Neckar) River 39 J i
Nicholson, Fort 192 E b
Nickajacks, tribe 188 I d
Nicobar Islands
Nicomedia 20 C b
Nicopolis, in Epirus 10 B c
Nicopolis, in Mœsia 39 N l
Nicopolis, in Palestine 7 B e
Nicopolis, in Pontus 20 H b
Nicopolis, on the Danube
Nicopolis, theme 59 I f
Nicosia 68 B b
Nicotera 30 E d
Nicoya 213 D c
Nicoya, Gulf of 105 D e
Nictheroy 215 E e
Nida 39 J h
Nidum (Neath)
Niebla 82 A b
Nieder Schopfheim 142 A d
Niederstetten 143 I g
Niemitsch 63 H c
Niemen River 138 B e
Nienburg, on the Saale 63 F c
Nienburg, on the Weser 134 E b
Nienburg, mon. 95 E a
Nieuport 117 A c
Nieuwstad 117 D c
Nièvre, dept. 148 E e
Niezhin 167 L e
Niger River 174 D c
Nigeria, col. 174 D d
Nigritia, reg. 108 Q f
Niigata 171 O e
Niihau, isl. 198 ins. B
Nijne Kolimsk
Nijni Novgorod 138 F d
Nike, Temple of 23 C (7)
Niklashausen 86 G d
Nikolaiev 139 D f
Nikolaievsk 171 O c
Nikolaistad 138 B c
Nikolsburg 159 I d
Nikolskaya 171 O d
Nikopol
Nile, Delta of the 4 ins.
Nile River 174 G b
Nile River, Blue 174 G c
Nile River, White 174 G c
Nil-Saint-Vincent 156 B a
Nimbschen, mon. 80 ins.
Nimburg 63 H c
Nimeguen, see Nimwegen
Nîmes 76 F e
Nîmes, bp. 94 C c
Nimptsch 63 I c
Nimwegen 117 D c
Nimwegen, Hanse. cy. 99 ins. B
Ninety Six 195 A f
Nineveh 4 G c
Ning-hia
Ning-ho 170 ins. A
Ning-po 171 N f
Ningus River 27 H b
Ninus 20 J d
Niobrara, Ind. Res. 188 G b
Niobrara River 198 E b
Niort 69 C c
Nipigon, Fort 191 H b
Nipigon, lake 191 H a
Nipissing, lake 191 I b
Nippon (Japan), empire
Nippur (Niffer) 4 G c
Nisæa 15 D b
Nisæa, dist. 18 R h
Nisæan Plain 19 G c
Nish 93 B b
Nishapur
Nisibin
Nisibis 5 D b
Nisqually, Fort 210 A a
Nisqually, Ind. Res. 188 B a
Nissa (Nish) 59 I e
Nisyrus, isl. 17 E c
Nithsdale, dist.
Nitiobroges, people 38 C d
Niuche, people 103 M c
Niu-chwang 171 N d
Niumaga, see Nimwegen
Nivelles 117 C d
Nivelles, mon. 94 C a
Nivernais, gouv. 146 B b
Nivernais, prov. 148 E e
Nivernis, see Nevers
Nizam, Dom. of the 137 C e
Nizib 164 F c
Nizza, see Nice
Nizza della Paglia 130 Q j
Noas Island 216
Noce River 91 S l
Nocera 90 E d
Nocera, bp. in Campania 95 ins.
Nocera, bp. in Umbria 95 E c
Nogaians, people 139 E f
Nogales 213 A a
Nogays, people 77 L c
Nogent 69 I f
Nogent-le-Rotrou 69 H f
Noirmoutier, isl. 69 B c
Noisy, Allée de, in Versailles 149 A
Nola 30 D b
Nola, bp. 95 ins.
Noli, bp. 95 D c
Nollendorf 155 H c
Nombre de Dios 105 E e
Nome 198 ins. A
Nomentan Gate 22 A
Nomentan Way, road 35 ins. B
Nomentum 27 G e
Nomia, mt. 14 B b
Nona, bp. 95 F c
Nonacris 14 C a
Nonantola 64 B b
Nonantola, mon. 95 E c
Nonnenweier 142 A d
Nonsuch, castle 75 I i
Nora, in Cappadocia 18 O h
Nora, in Sardinia 38 D e
Norba 35 ins. B
Norba Cæsarea 38 A e
Norbona, see Narbo Martius (Narbonne)
Narcia, New 172 A d
Nord, dept 148 E d
Nordalbingia, dist. 55 Q i
Norddeutscher Bund, see North German Federation
Norden 62 D b
Nordgau, dist. 55 R j
Nordgau, margr. 63 F d
Nordhausen 62 F c
Nordhausen, imp. cy. 79 G c
Nordheim, mon. 95 E a
Nördlingen 62 F d
Nördlingen, imp. cy. 79 G d
Nordmark, march 63 G b
Noreia 38 E c
Norfolk, in Virginia 193 ins. A
Norfolk, cty. in England
Norfolk, shire
Norfolk Island 172 F c
Norfolk, New 172 D e

Norham
Noricum, Rom. prov. 38 E c
Noricum mediterraneum, West Rom. prov. 42 E d (12)
Noricum ripense, West Rom. prov. 42 E d (13)
Norman, Fort 212 C b
Norman Principalities 66 I f
Normandy, duchy 61 D b
Normandy, gouv. 146 A b
Normandy, prov. 148 D e
Normanton 172 D b
Normans, people, in England 45 D b
Normans, people, in France 45 D c
Normans, people, in Italy 45 H e
Norridgewock 189 C b
Norrköping 131 G b
Northallerton 65 F c
North Allerton, parl. bor.
Northam, in N. Hampshire 189 C c
Northam, in W. Australia 172 A d
North America, continent, 186 187
Northampton, in England
Northampton, cty.
Northampton, mon. 97 Q i
Northampton, parl. bor. 163 N e
Nordhamptan, shire
Northampton, in Mass. 189 B c
North Australia, reg.
North Borneo, col. 171 M h
North Cape, in Europe 2 G a
North Cape, in New Zealand 172 G d
North Channel. 49 C d
North Carolina, col. 193 E d
North Carolina, state 199 I c
North Castle 195 E c
North Chester, parl. dist. 163 L d
North Dakota, state 203 R f
North Derby, parl. dist. 163 M d
North Devon, isl. 186 K a
North Devon, parl. dist. 163 J g
Nord Downs, dist. 49 G f
North Durham, parl. dist. 163 M c
Northeim 62 E c
Northern Californians, tribes 188 B b
Northern Cheyenne, Ind. Res. 188 E a
Northern District, Queensland 172 leg.
Northern Dwina River 3 I b
Northern Ghats, mts. 112 A a
Northern Pacific Grant 210 D a
Northern Plain, The 186 J c
Northern Territory, S. Australia 172 C b
North Essex, parl. dist. 163 O f
Northfield 189 B c
Northfleet 75 J i
North Folk (Angles), people 51 S k
North Fort, Sevastopol 164 L g
North Gate, in Olympia
North German Federation 161 D c
North Hants, parl. dist. 163 M f
North Humbrians, people
North Isles (Hebrides)
North Island, New Zealand 172 G d
North Lancaster, parl. dist. 163 L c
North Leicester, parl. dist. 163 M e
North March, dist. 58 G c
Northmen, people, in Scandinavia 45 F a
Northmen, people, in Russia 45 K b
North Northampton, parl. dist. 163 N e
North Northumberland, parl. dist. 163 L b
North Nottingham, parl. dist. 163 M d
North Platte River 190 E c
North Point, in Maryland 200 L h
North Potomac River 192 B d
North Riding, parl. dist. 163 M c
North (Hudson) River 189 B d
North Salop, parl. bor. 163 L e
North Saskatchewan River 186 H c
North Sea 2 E c
North Somerset, isl. 212 F a
North Sporades, isl.
North Stafford, parl. dist. 163 L e
Northumberland, cty., in England
Northumberland County, in Virginia 193 F b (N.)
Northumberland, shire
Northumbria, km.
Northumbria, Danish, reg.
Northumbria, English, km.
North Wales, town in Pa. 192 D c
North Wales, dist.
North Warwick, parl. dist. 163 M e
North West Cape, Australia 172 A c
North West Territories, Canada
Northwest Territory, in U. S., 1787 196 B b
Northwest Territory, in U. S., 1800—1802 196 C b
Northwich 162 D d
North Wilts, parl. dist. 163 L f
Norton, mon. 97 O h
Norton Folgate 75 G g
Norton Sound 186 C b
Norwalk 189 B d
Norway, km., about 1000 58 F a
Norway, km. 1910 166 G d—I b
Norwegians, people 46 H a
Norwich, in Conn. 189 B d (Nor.)
Norwich, in England 84 D c
Norwich, bp. 97 S i
Norwich, castle 65 G d
Norwich, Hanse. for. cy. 98 ins. A
Norwich, parl. bor. 163 P e
Nossen 85 G e
Nossi Bé, isl.
Nostell, mon. 97 P h
Noteborg 119 K b
Notium 17 E c
Notium, prom. 38 A b
Notre Dame, church, Paris 149 B
Notre Dame, bridge, Paris 149 B
Notre Dame, church, Versailles 149 A
Notre Dame Bay 212 J c
Notre-Dame-de-la-Grasse, mon. 94 C c
Nottingham
Nottingham, castle 65 F d
Nottingham, cty.
Nottingham, parl. bor. 163 M e
Nottingham, shire
Nottoway River 193 F c
Noumea 172 F c
Nouvion, le 117 B e
Nova Coimbra 214 D d
Novæ 39 N l
Novæsium 39 I h
Nova Friburgo 215 E e
Novantæ, people 38 B a
Novara 90 I h
Novara, bp. 95 D b
Novaria 26 C b
Novas, Ad, on the Clanis R. 27 F d
Novas, Ad, on L. Sabatinus 35 ins. B
Nova Scotia, prov. 212 I d
Nova Scotia Peninsula 186 M d
Novaya Zemlya (Nova Zembla) islands 170 G a
Novempopulana 42 B e (12)
Novgorod 57 J b
Novgorod, gov. 131 J b
Novgorod, Hanse. for. off. 99 J b
Novgorod, reg. 138 D d
Novgorod, rep. 92 D b
Novgorod, ter. 71 N a
Novgorod Seversk 77 K b
Novi, in Bosnia
Novi, in Italy 90 I h
Novi Bazar 119 I e
Noviodunum, in Aquitania 38 C c
Noviodunum, in Lugdunensis 38 B c
Noviodunum, in Mœsia 39 N k
Noviodunum, in Pannonia
Noviomagus, see Lisieux
Noviomagus (Neufchâteau), on the Meuse 39 H i
Noviomagus (Neumagen), near the Moselle 39 I i
Noviomagus (Nimwegen), on the Waal 39 H h
Noviomagus, see Noyon
Noviomagus (Spires), on the Rhine 39 J i
Noviomum, see Noyon
Novo-Georgievsk 155 K b
Novogrudek 119 J c
Novo-Tscherkask
Novum Castrum 29 D c
Noyers 126 D c
Noyon 61 E b
Noyon, bp. 94 C b
Noyon, cty. 61 E b
Nubia, reg. 174 G c
Nubian Desert 3 H f
Nuceria Alfaterna 30 D b
Nuceria Camellaria 27 G d
Nudionnum, see Sées
Nueces River 190 F f
Nuevitas 213 E b
Nuevo León, state 213 B b
Numana 27 H d
Numantia 38 B d
Numicus River 35 ins. B
Numidia, reg. 38 D e
Numidia, Rom. prov. 34 F f
Numidia, West Rom. prov. 42 D f (2)
Numistro 30 E b
Nun, Cape 174 B b
Nunivak, isl. 198 ins. A
Nur 159 L b
Nure River 26 D c
Nuremberg 62 F d
Nuremberg, burgraviate 79 G d
Nuremberg, imp. cy. 79 G d
Nursia 27 H e
Nürtingen 143 H h
Nusco, bp. 95 F c
Nussbaum 142 C c
Nutmeg Islands
Nyasa, lake 175 G f
Nyasaland, col. 175 G f
Nykerk 117 D b
Nyköping 131 G b
Nymphæum, loc. in Rome 22 A
Nymphæum, prom. 11 F b
Nymphenburg, castle 134 F d
Nysa 17 F c
Nyssa 20 F c
Nystad 138 B c

Oahu, isl. 198 ins. B
Oajaca 213 C c
Oajaca, state 213 C c
Oakala 198 ins. B
Oak forest, near Mizpah 7 B e
Oakland 210 A c
Oaracta, isl. 19 I e
Oatlands, castle 75 I i
Oaxas
Oaxes River 14 ins.
Obdorsk 170 H b
O Becse 159 K f
Obeid, El 174 F c
Oberalp Pass 91 Q l
Ober-Ehnheim 122 D d
Oberlahnstein 78 E c
Oberlin 206 ins.
Oberndorf 143 G i
Oberried, mon. 142 A e
Oberried, provostry 142 A e
Ober-Sontheim 143 I g
Oberstenfeld 143 H g
Obi, Gulf of 138 L b
Obi River
Obilinnum 26 A b
Obispo
Obok 174 H c
O'Brennans, The, fam.
O'Briens, The, fam.
Observatory Inlet 212 ins.
Ocaña, in Colombia 214 B b
Ocaña, in Spain 82 H f

Oceanus Britannicus (English Channel) . . . 51 O i
Oceanus Germanicus (North Sea) . . . 51 Q g
Oceanus Hibernicus (Irish Sea) 51 N h
Ocelum . . . 26 B b
Ocha, mt. . . . 15 E a
Ochrida . . .
Ochsenfurt . . . 62 F d
Ochsenfurt, mon. . . . 95 E b
Ochsenhausen, ab. . . . 143 I i
Ochus River . . . 19 J c
Ockley . . .
Ocklockonee River . . . 193 B f
Ocmulgee River . . . 193 C e
Oconee River . . . 193 C e
O'Connels, The, fam. . . .
O'Connors, The, fam. . . .
Ocra, mt. . . . 27 I b
Ocriculum . . . 27 G e
Octavia, Portico of . . . 24 B
Octovius, Portico of . . . 22 A
Octodurus . . . 26 B a
Octagesa . . . 38 C d
Octogon, in Olympia . . .
Ocumare . . . 214 C a
O'Dempseys, The, fam. . . .
Ödenburg (Sopron) . . . 63 I e
Odenheim, mon. . . . 142 C b
Odenheim, princ. . . . 142 C b
Odense . . . 154 F a
Odéon, bldg. in Paris . . . 149 B
Oderberg . . . 115 J d
Oder River . . . 63 H b
Odessa . . . 139 D f
Odessus . . . 39 N l
Odeum vetustissimum, bldg. in Athens . . . 23 D
Odeypore . . . 137 B d
Odiham, parl. bor. . . .
Odoacer, Kingdom of . . . 50 F d
Odomanti, people . . . 11 E a
O'Donnells, The, fam. . . .
O'Donoghues, The, fam. . . .
O'Doughertys, The, fam. . . .
Odrysæ, people . . . 39 N l
O'Dwyers, The, fam. . . .
Oea . . . 34 G g
Oeanthea . . . 11 D d
Oechalia, in Ætolia . . . 10 C d
Oechalia, in Messenia . . . 14 B b
Oedenburg, see Ödenburg
Oee . . . 16 B a
Oeiras . . . 214 E c
Oeneon . . . 10 C d
Oeniadæ . . . 10 C d
Oenoë, in Argolis . . . 14 C b
Oenoë, near Cythæron Mts. . 16 A a
Oenoë, in Elis . . . 14 B b
Oenoë, on the Istmus of Corinth 15 D a
Oenoë, near Marathon . . . 16 B a
Oenophyta . . . 11 E d
Oenotrians, people . . . 29 D e
Oenus (Inn) River . . . 14 C b
Oenussæ Island . . . 14 B c
Oëroë River . . . 11 E d
Oescus . . . 39 M l
Oescus River (Isker R.) . . . 39 M l
Oesyme . . . 11 F b
Oeta, mt. . . . 11 D d
Oetæa, dist. . . . 10 D d
Oetylus . . . 14 C c
Oeum . . .
O'Farrells, The, fam. . . .
Ofen (Buda) . . . 63 J e
Ofen (Buda) univ. . . . 100 I e
Ofen Pass . . . 91 S l
Offa's Dike . . .
Offenburg . . . 142 A d
Öfingen . . . 142 C e
O'Flahertys, The, fam. . . .
Ofu, isl. . . . 199 ins. D
Ogden . . . 210 C b
Ogdensburg . . . 192 D a
Ogeechee River . . . 193 C e
Oglasa, isl. . . . 26 E e
Oglio River . . . 90 J h
Ogowe River . . . 175 E e
Ohain . . .
Ohain, Woods of . . .
Ohain River . . .
O'Hanlons, The, fam. . . .
O'Haras, The, fam. . . .
Ohiv Company . . . 196 ins. B
Ohio, Falls of the . . . 196 B c
Ohio, state . . . 202 I b
Ohio, ter. . . . 196 C b
Ohio River . . . 187 K e
Ohrdruf, mon. . . . 95 E a
Ohre River . . . 85 F d
Öhringen . . . 143 H g
Oil River, dist. . . . 174 D d
Oil Spring, Ind. Res. . . . 188 K b
Oise dept. . . . 148 E e
Oise River . . . 126 C b
Ojibwas, Chippewas, tribe . . . 188 H a
Okanagan, Fort . . . 210 B a
Oka River . . . 139 E e
Okechobee, lake . . . 191 I f
Okehampton, parl. bor. . . . 163 J g
O'Kellys, The, fam. . . .
Okhotsk . . . 171 P c
Okhotsk, Sea of . . . 171 P c
Oklahoma . . . 210 F c
Oklahoma, state . . . 203 S h
Oklahoma, ter. . . . 203 S h
Olana River . . . 27 F c
Öland, isl. . . . 77 H a
Olbia, in Gaul . . . 12 E b
Olbia, in Sardinia . . . 38 D d
Olbia, in Sarmatia . . . 35 K d
Old Appian Way, road . . . 35 ins. B
Old Basing . . . 127 X o
Old Castile, km. . . . 83 K g
Old Celtic Church, area under influence of the . . . 46 E c
Olp Charles Town . . . 193 ins. C
Old Dean's Lane, in London 75 G g (32)
Oldenburg, in Holstein . . . 62 F a
Oldenburg, in Oldenburg . . . 72 B a
Oldenburg, cty. . . . 78 F b
Oldenburg, duchy . . . 134 E b
Oldenburg, gr. duchy . . . 158 E b
Oldenesche . . . 72 B a
Oldesloe . . . 72 C a
Old Fish Street, in London . . 75 G g
Old Flaminian Way, road . . . 27 G e
Old Gate, in Jerusalem . . . 6 ins. A
Oldham, parl. bor. . . . 163 L d
Old Park, dist. . . . 210 D c
Old Sarum . . .
Old Sarum, parl. bor. 163 M f (Old S.)
Old Seraglio, loc. i. Constantinople 93 G e
Old Shops, loc. in Rome . . .
Old Toggenburg, castle . . . 91 R k
Old Tyre . . . 18 ins. B
Old Versailles . . . 149 A
Olenus . . . 14 B a
Oléron, isl. . . . 76 C d
Oliarus (Antiparos), isl. . . . 15 F b
Olid, route of . . . 105 D c
Olifants River . . . 175 N k
Oligyrtus, mt. . . . 14 C b
Olinda . . . 214 F c
Olisipo (Lisbon) . . . 38 A e
Olite . . . 83 K g
Oliva, mon. . . . 95 F a
Olivença, in Brazil . . . 214 C c
Olivenza, in Portugal . . . 83 J h
Olives, Mount of . . . 68 ins. B
Olizon . . . 11 E c
Ollius River . . . 26 E b
Olmedo . . . 83 K g
Olmütz . . . 63 I d
Olmütz, bp. . . . 95 F b
Olocáu . . . 82 B b
Oloosson . . . 10 D c
Olophyxus . . . 11 F b
Oloron . . . 76 C e
Oloron, bp. . . . 94 B c
Olorone, see Oloron
Olpæ . . . 10 C d
Öls . . . 79 J c
Öls, princ. . . . 79 J c
Oltenitza . . . 164 D b
Oltis (Lot) River . . . 38 C d
Olubria River . . . 26 C c
Olusiga, isl. . . . 199 ins. D
Olympia, in Elis . . . 14 B b
Olympia, Plan of . . . 9
Olympia, in Washington . . . 210 A a
Olympieum, in Athens . . . 23 D
Olympieum, in Syracuse . . . 31 ins. B
Olympus, mt., in Attica . . . 16 B b
Olympus, mt., in Cyprus . . . 20 E e
Olympus, mt., in Macedonia . . 11 D b
Olympus Mysius, mt. . . .
Olynthus . . . 11 E b
Omagh . . . 127 J g
Omaha . . . 198 F c
Omaha, Ind. Res. . . . 188 G b
Omahas, tribe . . . 188 G b
O'Malleys, The, fam. . . .
Oman, Gulf of . . .
Oman, reg. . . .
Oman, Sea of . . .
Ombrone River . . . 90 L j
Omdurman . . . 174 G c
Omekonsk . . . 171 P b
Omercote . . . 137 A c
Ommiad Emirate of Cordova . 54 C e
Omoa . . . 213 D c
Omont . . . 61 F b
O'Mores, The, fam. . . .
Omphalium . . . 10 B b
Omsk . . . 170 I c
On . . . 4 F d
Oñate, routes of . . . 190 C e, D e
Onchesmus . . . 10 B c
Onchestus River . . . 11 D c
Onea, mt. . . . 15 C b
Onega, Gulf of . . . 167 M c
Onega, lake . . . 138 E c
Oneglia . . . 130 Q k
Oneida Ind. Res. . . . 188 I b, K b
Oneida Lake . . . 192 D b
Oneidas, tribe . . . 188 L b
O'Neills, The, fam. . . .
Onis, Cangas de . . . 82 A a
Ono . . . 7 B d
Onochonus River . . . 10 D c
Onondaga, battle . . . 192 C b
Onondaga, Ind. Res. . . . 188 K b
Onondagas, tribe . . . 188 K b
Onon River . . .
Ontario, Fort . . . 192 C b
Ontario, lake . . . 187 L d
Ontario, prov. . . . 212 G d
Ontonagon, Ind. Res. . . . 188 I a
Onugnathos, prom. . . . 15 C c
Oodnadatta . . . 172 C c
Oostburg . . . 117 B c
Opelousas . . . 211 G d
Opequan Creek . . . 208 E b (O. Cr.)
Opequon Court . . . 192 B d
Opequon River . . . 192 B d
Ophel . . . 6 ins. A
Ophiones, people . . . 10 C d
Ophis River . . . 14 C b
Ophiussa, isl. . . . 38 C e
Ophrah . . . 7 C e
Ophrynium . . .
Opis . . . 20 K f
Opisthomarathus . . . 11 D d
Opitergium . . . 27 G b
Oporto . . . 82 A a
Oporto, bisp. . . . 94 A c
Oppeln . . . 79 K c
Oppeln, princ. . . . 79 K c
Oppenau . . . 142 B d
Oppenheim . . . 62 E d
Oppius, mt. . . . 22 A

Opsician Theme . . . . 59 J f
Opslo . . . . 88 D b
Optimaton, Theme of the. . . . 59 K e
Opus . . . . 11 E d
Opus, prom. . . . . 11 D d
Oraculum Fauni, loc. near Rome 35 ins. B
Oräfa Jökul, mt. . . . . 166 B c
Oran, in Algeria . . . . 174 C a
Orán, in Arg. Rep. . . . . 215 C e
Orange . . . . 61 F d
Orange, bp.. . . . . 94 C c
Orange, Cape . . . . 214 D b
Orange, Fort. . . . . 192 D b
Orange, princ.. . . . . 114 ins. A
Orange, univ. . . . . 100 F f
Orangeburg. . . . . 195 A g
Orange Free State, rep.. . . . . 175 M l
Orangerie, Rue de l', street in Versailles. . . . . 149 A
Orange River . . . . 175 E g
Orange River Colony . . . . . . 175 F g
Orbais, mon. . . . . 94 C b
Orbe . . . . 91 O l
Orbelus, mt. . . . . 11 F a
Orbetello . . . . 90 L j
Orcades Islands (Orkneys) . . . 34 D b
Orchard Knob, battle . . . . . . 208 C b
Orchies . . . . 117 B d
Orchimont . . . . 117 C e
Orchoë . . . . 18 G d
Orchomenus, in Arcadia . . . . 14 C b
Orchomenus, in Bœotia . . . . . 11 D d
Ordessus River . . . . 39 N l
Ordovices, people . . . .
Örebro. . . . . 88 F b
Oregon Country, The . . . . . . 198 A a
Oregon, state . . . . 203 N g
Oregon, ter. 1848 . . . . 202 A f
Oregon, ter. 1853 . . . . 202 A g
Oregon Trail, route . . . . . . 210 B b
O'Reillys, The, fam. . . . . . .
Orel . . . . 139 E e
Orellana, route of . . . . 214 B c
Orenburg . . . . 139 I e
Orense . . . . 82 A a
Orense, bp.. . . . . 94 A c
Oreshek . . . .
Oresticum . . . . 10 C b
Orestis, dist. . . . . 10 C b
Oretani, people . . . . 38 B e
Oretum . . . . 38 B e
Oreus . . . . 11 E d
Orfani . . . . 165 D c
Orford, parl. bor. . . . . 165 P e
Orgellis, see Urgel
Orgus River . . . . 26 B b
Oria . . . . 90 F d
Oricum . . . . 31 I b
Orient, L' . . . . 130 C d
Origny, mon.. . . . . 94 C b
Orihuela . . . . 82 B b
Orinoco River. . . . . 214 C b
Oriskany, battle . . . . 195 D b
Orissa, reg. . . . . 137 D d
Oristano, abp. . . . . 95 D d
Oritæ, people . . . . 19 K e
Orizaba . . . . 106 C b
Orizaba, vol. . . . . 106 C b
Orkhon River . . . .
Orkney, bp. . . . . 97 J a
Orkney Islands . . . . 49 E b
Orlamünde . . . . 85 F e
Orléanais, gouv.. . . . . 146 B b
Orléanais, prov. . . . . 148 E e
Orléans . . . . 61 E c
Orléans, bp. . . . . 94 C b
Orléans, duchy . . . . 84 D f
Orléans, gen.. . . . . 147 E b
Orléans, univ. . . . . 100 F e
Orleans, ter. . . . . 202 G d
Orleans, Fort . . . . 191 G d
Orleans, Island of, Mississippi R. 194 A e
Orleans, Island of, St. Lawrence R. . . . . 191 K b
Orlov, Cape . . . . 167 N b
Ormea . . . . 130 P j
Ormenium . . . .
Ormskirk . . . . 98 ins. A
Ormuz, isl. . . . .
Ormuz, km. . . . .
Ornas . . . .
Orne, dept. . . . . 148 D e
Orne River, in Belgium . . . . . 156 B a
Orne River, in France . . . . . 148 D e
Orneæ . . . . 14 C b
Orneau River . . . . 156 B a
Oro, Rio de, dist. . . . . 174 B b
Orobiæ . . . . 11 E d
Orolaunum . . . . 39 H i
Orontes River . . . . 68 C b
Oropus . . . . 15 D a
Oropus River . . . . 10 B c
O'Rorkes, The, fam. . . . . . .
Oroya . . . . 214 B d
Orsha . . . . 153 O g
Orsini, fam. . . . . 90 L j
Orsk . . . . 139 I e
Orsovo. . . . . 71 K e
Orte, bp. . . . . 95 E c
Ortegal, Cape . . . . 166 D g
Ortenau, dist. . . . . 142 A c
Ortez de Retes, route of . . . .
Orthez . . . . 126 A e
Orthokids, people. . . . . 75 I c
Orthospana (Kabul). . . . . . . 19 K d
Ortona. . . . . 27 I e
Ortopla . . . . 27 I c
Ortospana, see Orthospana
Ortygia, quarter in Syracuse . . 31 ins. B
Orumbovii, people . . . . 26 D b
Oruro . . . . 214 C d
Orval. . . . . 69 I g
Orval, mon.. . . . . 95 D b
Orvieto . . . . 90 M j
Orvieto, bp. . . . . 95 E c
Oryxis, mt. . . . . 14 C b
Osage, Fort. . . . . 211 G c
Osage River . . . . 191 G d
Osages, tribe. . . . . 188 F b
Osaka . . . . 171 O e
Osawatomie . . . . 206 F c
Osca (Huesca) . . . . 38 B d
Oscela . . . . 26 C a
Öschelbronn . . . . 142 C c
Ösel, isl. . . . . 138 B d
Osenay, mon. . . . . 97 P j
Osette, Ind. Res. . . . . 188 A a
O'Shaugnessys, The, fam.. . . .
Oshmiany . . . . 153 N g
Osi, people . . . . 38 F c
Osimii, people. . . . . 38 B c
Osimo . . . . 90 D c
Osma. . . . . 82 B a
Osma, bp.. . . . . 94 B c
Osmanli (Ottoman Turks), Dom. of the . . . . 89 I g
Osnabrück . . . . 62 D b
Osnabrück, bp. . . . . 78 F b
Osnabrück, Hanse. cy. . . . . . 99 ins. B
Osoppo . . . . 158 G e
Osopus . . . . 27 H a
Osorno . . . . 215 B g
Osrhoëne, dist. . . . . 20 H d
Osrhoëne, prov. . . . . 43 J f (11)
Ossa, mt. . . . . 11 D c
Ossawatomie, see Osawatomie
Osse . . . . 126 A e
Osseg, in Bohemia . . . . 123 G c
Osseg, on the Vistula R. . . . .
Osseg, mon. . . . . 80 ins.
Ossero, bp. . . . . 95 E c
Ossola, val d', valley. . . . . . 91 Q l
Ossory, bp. . . . . 97 D d
Ostend . . . . 117 A c
Ostend, mon.. . . . . 94 C a
Osteodes, isl. . . . . 30 C d
Osterburken . . . . 142 D b
Osterland, margr. . . . . 79 H c
Osterland, dist. . . . . 85 G e
Osterode . . . . 155 K b
Ostia. . . . . 27 G f
Ostia, bp. . . . . 96 B b
Ostiaks, people . . . .
Ostian Gate . . . . 22 A
Ostian Way, road . . . . 35 ins. B
Ostmark (Austria), march . . . . 63 H d
Ostmark, march. in Brandenburg 63 G c
Ostrach . . . . 134 E e
Ostrog . . . . 119 J c
Ostrogoths, Dom. of the . . . . 50 G c
Ostrolenka . . . . 155 K b
Ostrov . . . . 138 C d
Ostrovno . . . . 153 N f
Ostrowo . . . . 135 I c
O'Sullivans, The, fam. . . . . .
Osuna . . . . 82 A b
Oswegatchie, Fort . . . . 196 D b
Oswego . . . . 196 D b
Oswego, Fort . . . . 192 C b
Oswego River . . . . 192 C b
Oswestry . . . . 127 V n
Otago, prov. . . . . 172 F e
Otaheite, isl. . . . . 136 ins. B
Otalini, people . . . . 38 B a
Otavalo . . . . 214 B b
Otchakov . . . . 139 D f
Otford . . . .
Othrys, mt. . . . . 11 D c
Otochatz, bp. . . . .
O'Tooles, The, fam. . . . . . .
Otranto . . . . 90 G d
Otranto, abp. . . . . 95 F c
Otrar . . . .
Otryne . . . . 16 C a
Ottawa. . . . . 212 H d
Ottawa River . . . . 199 J a
Ottawas, tribe . . . . 188 I b
Ottenbourg . . . . 156 B a
Ottensen . . . . 154 E b
Ottignies . . . . 156 B a
Ottilienberg, mon. . . . . 95 D b
Ötting, Alt . . . . 123 G d
Öttingen . . . . 122 F d
Öttingen, princ. . . . . 143 J h
Ottobeuren, mon. . . . . 95 E b
Ottocar of Bohemia, Dom. of . 79 ins.
Ottoman (Turkish) Empire, 1451—1481 93
Ottoman (Turkish) Empire, 1481—1683 124
Ottoman (Turkish) Empire, since 1683 164
Ottoman Turks, Dom. of the, 14 cent. . . . . 89 I g
Ottoman Turks, Dom. of the, early 15 cent. . . . . 92 C d
Otumba . . . . 106 B a
Otway, Cape . . . . 172 D d
Oudenarde . . . . 117 B d
Oudh, Oude, reg. . . . . 137 D c
Ouiatanon, Fort . . . . 191 H c
Ourique . . . . 82 G f
Ouro Prereto . . . . 214 E e
Ourthe River . . . . 117 D d
Ouse River, R. . . . . 49 F d
Ouse River, Great . . . . 49 F e
Ovalle . . . . 215 B f
Oven Tower, loc. in Jerusalem 6 ins. A
Översee . . . . 158 E a
Overton, parl. bor. . . . .
Overyssel, Lordship of . . . . . 117 E b
Oviedo . . . . 82 A a
Oviedo, bp. . . . . 94 A c
Ovilava . . . . 38 E c
Ovile (Sæpta) . . . . 23 B
Owen . . . . 143 H h
Öwisheim, Unter . . . . 142 C b
Owston, mon. . . . . 97 Q i
Oxford, in England . . . . 127 X o
Oxford, castle . . . . 94 E f
Oxford, cty. . . . . 127 X o
Oxford, mon.. . . . . 97 P j

Oxford, parl. bor. 163 M f
Oxford, parl. dist. 163 M f
Oxford, univ. 100 E d
Oxford University, parl. bor. 163 M f
Oxford, in Maryland 192 C d
Oxford, in Mass. 189 C c
Oxford, in Miss. 208 C c
Oxford Town 192 C d
Oxus (Amu-Daria) River 92 G d
Oxybii, people 26 A d
Oxynia 10 C c
Oxyrhynchus
Oyapock River 214 D b
Oyster Bay, town in New York 189 B d
Oyster Bay 172 D e
Ozark Mountains 211 G c
Ozark Plateau 187 J e
Ozora 159 J e

Paanpack 192 E b
Paardeberg, mt. 175 M l
Pacaha, reg. 191 G d
Pacaraima Mountains 214 C b
Pacasmayo 111 B c
Pachacamac 111 B d
Pa-chau 170 ins. A
Pachuca 213 ins.
Pachynus, prom. 30 E e
Pacific Ocean 179—180
Pacific Slope 186 G c
Pacocha 214 B d
Pactolus River 20 B c
Pactyans, people 8 E b
Pactye
Paderborn 62 E c
Paderborn, bp. 95 D a
Paderborn, Hanse. cy. 99 ins. B
Padrabrunna, see Paderborn
Padrão, Rio do, river 108 R h
Padrón 82 A a
Padua 90 J h
Padua, bp. 95 E b
Padua, univ. 100 H e (Pa.)
Paducah 208 C b
Padum, Ad 27 G c
Padus River, see Po River
Padusa River 27 F c
Pæania 16 B b
Pædagogium, loc. in Rome 24 B
Pæligni, people 27 H e
Pæmani, people 39 H h
Pæonia, dist. 17 B a
Pæonidæ 16 B a
Pæstum 30 D b
Pæstum, Bay of 30 D b
Pagæ 15 D a
Pagan
Pagasæ 11 D c
Pagasæan Gulf 11 D c
Pageh Islands
Pago Pago 199 ins. D
Pagus Ianiculensis, dist. in Rome 22 A
Pahala 198 ins. B
Paia 198 ins. B
Paiutes, Piutes, tribe 188 C b
Paja River
Pajajaran 112 D d
Pajeau
Pak-hoi 171 L f
Paks 159 J e
Palachwe 175 M k
Palæbyblus 6 D a
Palæo-Kastro
Palæopolis 31 ins. A
Polærus 10 B d
Palæstra
Palætyrus 6 C b
Palais Bourbon, bldg. in Paris 149 B
Palais Royal, bldg. in Paris 149 B
Palam
Palatinate, see Rhenish Bavaria 158 D d
Palatinate, Bavarian, dist. 142 C b
Palatinate, Upper, dist. 79 G d
Palatinate of the Rhine, elect. 78 F d
Palatinate-Saxony 85 F e
Palatine, quarter in Rome 96 A
Palatine, Aug. Reg. of Rome 22 A
Palatine Library, bldg. in Rome 24 B
Palatine Mosbach, princ. 87 H d
Palatine Mount 24 A
Palatine Simmern, princ. 86 F d
Palatine Zweibrücken, princ. 86 F d
Palau Islands 179 E g
Palawan, isl. 112 E c
Palazzo Borghese, bldg. in Rome 96 A
Palazzo Colonna, bldg. in Rome 96 A
Palazzo di Venezia, bldg. in Rome 96 A
Palazzo Farnese, bldg. in Rome 96 A
Palazzo Massimi, bldg. in Rome 96 A
Palazzo Orsini Savelli, bldg. in Rome 96 A
Pale 10 B d
Pale, The English, dist.
Palea 14 B a
Palembang
Palencia 82 B a
Palencia, bp. 94 B c
Palencia, univ. 100 E f
Palenque 105 B c
Palermo 90 D e
Palermo, abp. 95 E d
Palestine, reg. 6—7
Palestine I, East Rom. prov. 43 I g (1)
Palestine II, East Rom. prov. 43 J g (6)
Palestine (Salutaris), East Rom. prov. 43 I h (7)
Palestrina 64 ins.
Palestrina, bp. 96 B b
Palice 30 D e
Pa-li-kioa 170 ins. A
Palinurus, prom. 30 E c
Pallacopas Canal 18 G d
Pallantia 38 B d
Pallantium 14 C b
Pallanum 27 I e
Pallanza 90 I h
Pallas, Gardens of 22 A
Pallene, in Attica 16 B a
Pallene, pen. 11 E b
Pallia River 27 F e
Palma 38 C e
Palma, bp. 94 C d
Palma, univ. 100 F g
Palmanova 158 G f
Palmaria, isl. 30 B b
Palmas, Cape 175 C d
Palmas, Las 174 B b
Palmerston 172 C b
Palmyra 20 H e
Palmyra Island 180 K g
Palo Alto, battle
Paloos, tribe 188 C a
Palos 83 J h
Pambotis, lake 10 B c
Pamiers 126 B e
Pamiers, bp. 94 C c
Pamier, plateau 3 L e
Pamir, reg. 170 I e
Pamisus River, in Messenia 14 B b
Pamisus River, in Thessaly 10 C c
Pamlico River 193 F d
Pamlico Sound 193 F d
Pamodus 27 I c
Pampeluna, see Pamplona
Pamphia 10 C d
Pamphylia, Macedonian prov. 18 D c
Pamphylia, Rom. prov. 35 K f
Pamphylia, East Rom. prov. 43 I f (1)
Pamphylia, reg. 20 D d
Pamphylia, satr. 8 H e
Pamphylians, people 5 C b
Pamplona 82 B a
Pamplona, bp. 94 B c
Pamunkey River 193 F c
Pan, Cave of 23 C
Panachaicus, mt. 14 B a
Panactum 16 B a
Panætolius, mt. 10 C d
Panamá
Panamá, Bay of
Panamá, Gulf of 213 E d
Panamá, country 214 A b
Panay, isl. 199 ins. H
Pancalieri 130 P j
Pancsova 159 K f
Pandarani
Pandateria, isl. 30 C b
Pandosia, in Epirus 10 B c
Pandosia, in Lucania 31 F b
Paneas 6 D b
Pangæus, mt. 11 E b
Panhandle, The, reg. 210 E c
Panionium 13 E c
Panipat, Paniput 137 C c
Panixer Pass 150 E c
Panjdeh 170 H e
Panmure, Fort 194 A d
Pannonia, reg. 38 F c
Pannonia I, West Rom. prov. 42 F d (10)
Pannonia II, West Rom. prov. 42 F d (8)
Pannonia, Lower, Rom. prov. 34 H d
Pannonia, Upper, Rom. prov. 34 H d
Pannonian March 54 H d
Panopeus 11 D d
Panopolis (Chemmis) 18 D e
Panormus, in Peparethus 11 E c
Panormus (Palermo), in Sicily 30 C d
Panormus, port, in Epirus 10 A b
Pantanus, lake 30 E a
Pantelleria Island 161 H i
Pantheon, bldg. in Rome 22 A
Panticapæum (Kertch) 12 K a
Pánuco River 201 F e
Paons, Allée des, Versailles 149 A
Pao-ting 170 ins. A
Papago, Ind. Res. 188 D d
Papal States 131 F e
Papelotte, farm
Paphlagonia, Macedonian prov. 18 D b
Paphlagonia, reg. 8 B a
Paphlagonia, Rom. prov. 20 E b
Paphlagonia, East Rom. prov. 43 I e (3)
Paphlagonia, satr. 18 O g
Paphlagonia, theme 59 K e
Paphos 20 E e
Papia (Pavia) 26 D b
Papirianæ, Fossæ 26 E d
Pappua, mt. 52 C c
Papua, col., see British New Guinea
Papua Gulf 172 D a
Pará 214 E c
Pará, state 214 D c
Paracatú 214 E d
Paraclet, Le, mon. 94 C b
Paradies, mon. 95 F a
Paraetacene, reg. 19 K c
Paraetaceni, people 19 H d
Parætonium 18 C d
Paragua, isl. 199 ins. H
Paraguay, country 215 D e
Paraguay River 21 D d
Parahyba 214 F c
Parahyba, state 214 F c
Parahyba River 214 E e
Paraiso 216
Paralia, dist. 15 D b
Paramanga 111 B d
Paramaribo 214 D b
Paraná 215 C f
Paraná, state 215 D e
Paraná River 214 D e
Paranaguá 215 E e
Paranapema River 215 D e
Parapanisadæ, people 19 K d
Parapanisus Mountains 19 K c
Parapotamii 11 D d
Parauæa, dist. 10 B b
Parchim 158 F b
Pardiac, cty. 69 D e (P.)
Pardo, El, castle 130 C c

Pardubitz 159 H d
Parentium (Parenzo) 27 H b
Parenzo 90 D b
Parenzo, bp. 95 E b
Parga 93 B c
Paria, Gulf of 105 H d
Paria, reg. 105 H d
Paricanii, Paricanians, people 19 K e
Pariña, Punta, cape 111 A b
Paris 61 E b
Paris in 1789, plan of 149 B
Paris, bp. 94 C b
Paris, gen. 147 E b
Paris, univ. 100 F e
Parisii or Parisius, see Paris
Parisii, people 38 C c
Parita, reg. 105 D e
Parium
Parkersburg 206 ins.
Parma 26 E c
Parma, bp. 95 E c
Parma, duchy 150 E d
Parma River 26 E c
Parnahyba 214 E c
Parnahyba River 214 E c
Parnassus, mt. 11 D d
Parnes Mountains 15 D a
Parnon Mountains 14 C b
Paroisse, Rue de la, street in Versailles 149 A
Paros 15 F b
Paros, isl. 15 F b
Parramatta 172 E d
Parrhasia, reg. 14 B b
Parrtown 212 I d
Parry Islands 186 H a
Parsdorf 134 F d
Part-Dieu, La, mon. 91 O l
Partenkirchen 72 C b
Partenkirchen, mon. 95 E b
Parthanum 38 E c
Parthenay 69 C c
Parthenius, mt. 14 C b
Parthenius River 20 E b
Parthenon, bldg. in Athens 23 C
Parthenopæan Republic 151 I h
Parthenope (Naples) 5 A a
Parthia, prov. 19 I c
Parthia, reg. 8 D b
Parthia, satr. 18 Q h
Parthians, Empire of the 35 N g
Paru River 214 D b
Paryadres Mountains 20 H b
Pasado, Cape 111 A b
Pasargadæ 19 H d, H e
Pasargadæ, people 8 D c
Pas-de-Calais, dept. 148 E d
Paseir 112 C c
Pasewalk 85 C b
Pashat
Pasitigris River 19 G d
Passaic River 189 ins. C
Passarge River 155 J a
Passaro, Cape 131 G f
Passaron 10 B c
Passarowitz
Passau 63 G d
Passau, bp. 95 E b
Passavant, castle 143 ins. F
Passavant, lordship 143 ins. F
Passeier Tal, valley 154 F e (Pa.)
Pastaza River 111 B b
Pasto 214 B b
Patagonia, reg. 215 C g
Patani
Patapsco River 200 L h
Patara 20 C d
Patavia, see Passau
Patavium (Padua) 26 F b
Patay 76 D b
Paterno 64 ins.
Paternum 31 G c
Patiala 137 C b
Patillas 199 ins. G
Patmos, isl. 13 E c
Patna 137 D c
Patos, Laguna dos 215 D f
Patræ 14 B a
Patras 89 H g
Patras, desp. 93 B c
Patriarchates, 593—600 52
Patrimony of Saint Peter (States of the Church), 9 cent.
Patrimony of Saint Peter (States of the Church), 12 cent. 70 I e
Patrimony of Saint Peter (States of the Church), 15 cent. 90 C c
Patroclus, Burial mound of
Patroclus Island 15 D b
Pattala 19 K e
Pattan Somnath
Patti, bp. 95 E d
Patuca River 105 D c
Patuxent River 192 C d
Patzinaks or Petchenegs, people
Pátzcuaro 213 ins.
Pau 69 C e
Pau and Bayonne, gen. 147 D c
Paul, journeys of the Apostle 46, 47 leg.
Paulinzella, mon. 95 E a
Paulus Hoeck 189 ins. C
Paumotu, isl. 180 M i
Paus 14 B b
Pausilypum 31 ins. A
Pausulæ 27 H d
Pau-ti 170 ins. A
Pavia 90 I h
Pavia, bp. 95 D b
Pavia, univ. 100 G e
Pavonia 189 ins. C
Pawnees, tribe 188 F b
Pawtucket 189 ins. A
Pawtuxed 189 ins. A
Pax Iulia 38 A e
Paxo, isl. 157 D e
Paxus, isl. 10 B c
Payerne 91 O l
Payne Lake 212 H c
Paysandú 215 D f
Payta 111 A c
Paz, La 214 C d
Peace, Altar of 22 A
Peace, Temple of 24 B
Peace River 186 H c
Peakland, dist.
Pea Ridge, mts. 208 B b
Pearl Coast 105 G d
Pearl River 191 H e
Pe-chi-li, gulf 171 M e
Pe-chi-li, prov. 171 M e
Pechora, River 3 J b
Peck, Fort, Ind. Res. 188 E a
Pecos 190 E d
Pecos River 190 E e
Pedasus (Methoni) 14 B c
Pedee River, Great 193 E d
Pediæus River 20 E e
Pedias, dist. 15 D a
Pedion, dist. 16 B b
Pedir 112 C c
Pedo 26 B c
Pedroche 82 B b
Pedro Miguel 216
Pedum 35 ins. B
Peebles, cty.
Peebles, dist.
Peekskill 195 E c
Peene River 63 G b
Peenemünder Schanze, fort 123 G a
Peer 117 D c
Pegau, mon. 80 ins.
Pegu
Pegu, reg.
Pei-ho, R. 170 ins. A
Peipus, lake 88 L b
Peishwa, Doms. of the 137 B e
Pei-tang 170 ins. A
Pei-tsang 170 ins. A
Pejepscot, Fort 189 C b
Peking
Pelagonia 10 C a
Pelagonia, dist. 17 B a
Pelasgiotis, dist. 11 D c
Pelendones, people 38 B d
Pelew Islands 179 E g
Pelican Point, cape 108 R j
Pelinnæum 10 C c
Pelion, mt. 11 E c
Pelisipia, proposed state in U. S.
Pelium 10 B b
Pella, in Gilead 7 D d
Pella, in Macedonia 11 D b
Pellana 14 C b
Pellene 14 C a
Pelly River 212 B b
Pelopium
Peloponnesus, Byzantine prov. 89 B c
Peloponnesus, pen. 13 C c
Peloponnesus, theme 59 I f
Pelorus, prom. 30 E d
Pelotas 215 D f
Pelplin, mon. 95 F a
Peltuinum 27 H e
Pelusium 4 ins.
Pelusium, ruins of 150 B a
Pemaquid 189 D c
Pemba, isl. 175 H e
Pembroke 84 A d
Pembroke, castle
Pembroke, cty. 127 U o
Pembroke, parl. bor. 163 J f
Pembroke, parl. dist. 163 J f
Peña Blanca 215 B e
Penas (Peñas) Gulf of 215 B g
Penay 91 N l
Pendennis Castle 127 T p
Penedo 214 F d
Peneus River, in Elis 14 B b
Peneus River, in Thessaly 11 D c
Peñiscola 82 C a
Penjhir
Pennar River
Penneloci 26 A a
Pennine Alps, mts. 26 B a
Pennine Chain, mts. 49 E d
Pennine Valley 26 B a
Pennine and Graian Alps, West Rom. prov. 42 D d (8)
Pennsylvania, col. 192 C c
Pennsylvania, state 199 J b
Penobscot 189 D b
Penobscot Bay 189 D b
Penobscot River 189 D b
Peñon de Velez 130 C f
Penrhyn Islands 180 L i
Penryn and Falmouth, parl. bor. 163 I g
Penrith 127 W l
Pensacola 191 H e
Pensacola Bay 193 ins. B
Pentagöet, Fort 189 D b
Pentapolis, dist., in Cyrenaica 43 G g
Pentapolis, dist., in Italy 64 B b
Pentapylum 31 ins. B (5)
Pentele 16 B a
Pentelicus, mt. 16 B a
Penthièvre, cty. 69 B b
Pentney, mon. 97 R i
Pentri, people 30 D a
Penuel 7 D d
Penza 139 G e
Peoria 212 G b
Peparethus, isl. 11 E c
Pephnos 14 C c
Pequots, tribe 189 C d
Pera 93 G e
Peræa, dist., in Palestine 7 D e
Peræa, dist., in Greece 15 C a
Perche, cty. 69 H f
Perche-Gouet, dist. 76 D b (P. G.)
Percote
Perdido River 193 ins. B
Pered 159 J d

Perekop . . . 139 D f
Perekop, Isthmus of . . . 3 H d
Pereslawl . . . 138 E d
Pergamum . . .
Pergamum, km. . . . 33 C b
Pergamus . . . 11 F b
Perge . . . 43 I f
Périgord, cty. . . . 61 D d
Périgueux . . . 61 D d
Périgueux, bp. . . . 94 C b
Perim Island . . . 174 H c
Perinthus . . .
Peristhlava . . . 59 J e
Perlas, Isla de, isl. . . . 105 E e
Perlasz . . . 159 K f
Perleberg . . . 154 G b
Perm . . . 138 I d
Permians, people . . . 138 H d
Pernambuco or Recife . . . 214 F c
Pernambuco, state . . . 214 F c
Pernau . . . 88 K b
Pernau, Hanse. cy. . . . 99 H b
Péronne . . . 76 E b
Perosa . . . 130 P j
Perote . . . 106 C a
Perote, Cofre de, mt. . . . 106 C a
Perovsk . . . 170 H d
Perpignan . . . 61 E e
Perpignan, gen. . . . 147 E c
Perpignan, univ. . . . 100 F f
Perrhæbi, people . . . 10 C c
Perrhæbia, dist. . . . 10 C c
Perryville . . . 208 C b
Persante River . . . 159 I b
Perseigne, mon. . . . 94 C b
Persephone, Temple of . . . 31 ins. B (12)
Persepolis . . . 8 J f
Pershore, mon . . . 97 O i
Pershore, parl. bor. . . .
Persia, country . . . 170 G e
Persia, khan. . . .
Persia, reg. . . .
Persian Empire, about 500 B. C. 8
Persian Gulf . . . 3 I f
Persis, prov. . . . 19 H e
Persis, reg. . . . 8 D b
Persis, satr. . . . 8 J f
Perth, in Australia . . . 172 A d
Perth, in Scotland . . .
Perth, cty. . . .
Perth, dist. . . .
Perth Amboy . . . 192 D c
Peru, Conquest of . . . 111
Peru, reg. . . . 111 B c
Peru, rep. . . . 214 B c
Peru, viceroyalty . . . 215 ins.
Peru, Lower, reg. . . . 214 B c
Peru, Upper, reg. . . . 214 C d
Perugia . . . 90 D c
Perugia, bp. . . . 95 E c
Perugia, univ. . . . 100 H f
Perusia (Perugia) . . . 27 G d
Perwez . . . 156 B a
Pesaro . . . 90 D c
Pesaro, bp. . . . 95 E c
Pescado River . . .
Pescadores, isl. . . . 171 M f
Pescara . . . 90 E c
Peschiera . . . 90 C b
Peshawar, Peshawur . . . 137 B b
Pessinus . . . 20 D c
Petaliæ Islands . . . 15 E b
Petchenegs or Patzinaks, people
Petchora River . . .
Petelia . . . 31 G c
Peten, isl. . . . 105 B c
Petenisca . . . 39 I j
Peterborough . . .
Peterborough, mon. . . .
Peterborough, parl. bor. . . . 163 N e
Peterborough, soke and abbey of
Peterhead . . .
Peterhof . . . 131 I b
Peterlingen, mon. . . . 95 D b
Petermann's Peak . . . 186 P a
Petersberg, mon. . . . 85 G e
Petersburg, in Virginia . . . 193 F c
Petersburg, Saint, in Russia . . 138 D c
Petersburgh, in S. Australia . . 172 C d
Petersfield, parl. bor. 163 M g (Petersf.)
Petersham . . . 196 E b
Petershausen, ab. . . . 142 D e
Peterwardein . . . 159 K f
Petitarus River . . . 10 C d
Petites Écuries, loc. in Versailles 149 A
Petite Venise, loc. in Versailles 149 A
Petite Venise, Allée de la, in Versailles . . . 149 A
Petit Rœulx . . . 156 A a
Petit Trianon, loc. in Versailles 149 A
Petra, in Arabia . . . 18 E d
Petra, in Macedonia . . . 11 D b
Petra, in Sicily . . . 30 D e
Petracoris, see Périgueux
Petræantheatre . . . 16 D c (3)
Petro-Alexandrovsk . . . 170 H d
Petrocorii, see Périgueux
Petronell . . . 54 H d
Petropavlovsk . . . 171 Q c
Petropolis . . . 215 E e
Petrovsk . . . 167 O g
Petrozavodsk . . . 138 D c
Pettau . . . 54 H d
Petten . . . 117 C b
Petty Armenian States . . . 67 N f
Peuce Island . . . 18 C a
Peucelaotis . . . 19 L d
Peucetii, people . . . 31 F b
Pevensey . . .
Pfaffenhofen . . . 134 F d
Pfalzburg . . . 158 D d
Pfävers, mon. . . . 91 R l
Pfeddersheim . . . 142 B a
Pfinz River . . . 142 C c
Pflege Coburg, dist. . . . 85 F e
Pforta, mon. . . . 95 E a
Pforzheim . . . 142 C c
Pfullendorf . . . 142 D e
Pfullingen . . . 143 H i
Phacium . . . 10 D c
Phæca . . . 10 C c
Phæna . . . 6 E b
Phæstus, in Crete . . . 14 ins.
Phæstus, in Locris . . . 11 D d
Phæstus, in Thessaly . . . 10 D c
Phagres . . . 11 E b
Phalacrum, prom. in Corcyra . 10 A c
Phalacrum, prom. in Sicily . . . 30 E d
Phalæsiæ . . . 14 C b
Phalanna . . . 11 D c
Phalara . . . 11 D d
Phalasia, prom. . . . 11 E d
Phalerum . . . 15 D b
Phaliga . . . 20 I e
Phaloria . . . 10 C c
Phanagoria . . . 12 K a
Phanariote Quarter, in Constantinople . . . 93 G e
Phanote . . . 10 A b
Phara . . . 10 B d
Pharæ, in Achaia . . . 14 B a
Pharæ, in Messenia . . . 14 C b
Pharcadon . . . 10 C c
Pharis . . . 14 C b
Pharmacussa, isl. . . . 16 B b
Pharnacia . . . 20 H b
Pharpar River . . . 6 E b
Pharos, isl. . . . 12 G b
Pharos, lighthouse . . . 34 ins. C
Pharsalus (Pharsala) . . . 11 D c
Pharus, isl. . . . 38 F d
Phaura, isl. . . .
Phasael . . . 6 ins. A
Phasaëlis . . . 7 C d
Phaselis . . . 20 D d
Phasis . . . 12 L b
Phasis River . . . 20 J a
Phea . . . 14 B b
Pheasants, Isle of . . . 126 A e
Pheneus . . . 14 C b
Pheræ . . . 11 D c
Phigæa . . . 16 B b
Phigalia . . . 14 B b
Phila . . . 11 D c
Philadelphia, in Asia Minor . . 20 C c
Philadelphia, in Brazil . . 214 E d (Phil.)
Philadelphia, in Pa. . . . 192 D c
Philadelphia, in Syria . . . 7 D e
Philæ Island . . . 4 F d
Philiphaugh . . .
Philippeum, in Olympia . . .
Philippeville . . . 117 C d
Philippi . . . 11 F a
Philippine Islands . . . 199 ins. H
Philippopolis, in Syria . . . 6 F c
Philippopolis, in Thrace . . . 39 M l
Philippopolis, in Bulgaria . . . 167 J g
Philippsburg . . . 142 B b
Philippus, Portico of . . . 22 A
Philistæa, dist. . . . 7 A f
Philistines, people . . . 7 ins. D
Philomelium . . . 67 M f
Philopappus, Monument of . . . 23 D
Phinopolis . . .
Phintias . . . 30 C e
Phlegra, pen. . . . 11 E c
Phlegræan Fields . . . 31 ins. A
Phlius . . . 14 C b
Phlya . . . 16 B a
Phlygonium . . . 11 D d
Phocæa . . . 12 I c
Phocian Wall . . . 16 F e
Phocis, state . . . 11 D d
Phœnice . . . 10 B c
Phœnicia, country . . . 6 C c
Phœnicia, East Rom. prov. . . . 43 J g (2)
Phœnicia, reg. . . . 4 F c
Phœnicia Libani, East Rom. prov. 43 J g (8)
Phœnicians, people . . . 7 ins. D
Phœnicus, in Cythera . . . 15 D c
Phœnicus Port, in Messenia . . 14 B c
Phœnicussa, isl. . . . 30 D d
Phœnix . . . 210 C d
Phœnix Islands . . . 180 J h
Phœnix River, in Achaia . . . 14 B a
Phœnix River, in Malis . . . 16 F e
Pholegandrus, isl. . . . 15 E c
Pholoë, mt. . . . 14 B b
Phorbantia, isl. . . . 30 B d
Phoron, Port of . . . 16 B b
Photice . . . 10 B c
Phra . . . 19 J d
Phrixa . . . 14 B b
Phrygia, reg. . . . 20 D c
Phrygia, Macedonian prov. . . . 18 D c
Phrygia Pacatiana, East Rom. prov. . . . 43 H f (7)
Phrygia Salutaris, East Rom. prov. . . . 43 I f (8)
Phrygians, people . . . 5 C b
Phthiotis, reg. . . . 11 D c
Phylacæ, in Macedonia . . . 10 D b
Phylace, in Epirus . . . 10 B c
Phylace, in Thessaly . . . 11 D c
Phyle . . . 15 D a
Phyllus . . . 10 D c
Phytia . . . 10 C d
Piacenza . . . 90 I h
Piacenza, bp. . . . 95 D c
Piacenza, univ. . . . 100 G f
Pialia . . . 10 C c
Pian de Carpine, John of, route of . . .
Piankishaws, tribe . . . 188 I c
Piauhy, state . . . 214 E c
Piave River . . . 90 D b
Picardy, gouv. . . . 146 B b
Picardy, prov. . . . 148 E d
Picentes, Picentians, people . .
Picentia . . . 30 D b
Picentini, people . . . 30 D b
Picenum, dist. . . . 27 H d

Picenum Suburbicarium, West Rom. prov. 42 E e (3)
Pichincha, battle 214 B c
Pickawillany 194 C b
Pickens, Fort 208 C c
Pickering, parl. bor.
Picolata, Fort 193 D g
Pictavi, see Poitiers
Pictavi, people 38 B c
Pictland (Scotland), reg.
Picton 172 G e
Picts, people, 5 cent. 50 C a
Picts, people, 9 cent. 54 D b
Piedmont, dist. 90 A b
Piedmont, princ. 150 D d
Piedmont Hills 187 K e
Piedra, mon. 94 B c
Piedras Negras 213 B b
Pieria, dist., on the Strymonic Gulf 11 F b
Pieria, dist., on the Thermaic Gulf 11 D b
Pierre 210 F b
Pierre, Fort 210 E b
Pierre's Hole, dist. 210 C b
Pierus, mt. 10 D b
Pierus River 14 B a
Pietas Iulia, col. 27 H c
Pietermaritzburg 175 N e
Piéton River 156 A a
Pietramala 90 L i
Pietra Santa 90 C c
Pigeon Creek 105 ins.
Pike, route of 198 F c, 199 G b
Pike's Peak 198 E c
Pilar 191 G e
Pilate, House of 68 ins. B (16)
Pilcomayo River 214 C e
Pilica River 87 M c
Pillars of Hercules (Calpe, or Gibraltar, and Abila), prom. 12 B c
Pillau 115 J a
Pillnitz, castle 135 G c
Pillow, Fort 208 C b
Pilsen 63 G d
Pilten 88 I c
Pimas, tribe 188 D d
Pimería, Upper, dist. 190 C e
Pin, Le, mon. 94 C b
Pinacotheca, bldg. in Athens 23 C
Pinar del Rio 213 D b
Pinciacus, see Poissy
Pincian, qnarter in Rome 96 A
Pincian Gate 22 A
Pincian Mount 22 A
Pincian Way 22 A
Pinczow 123 K c
Pindus 11 D d
Pindus Mountains 10 C c
Pine Creek 172 C b
Pineda, route of 191 G f
Pine Ridge, Ind. Res. 188 F b
Pinerolo 90 A b
Pines, Isle of 105 D b
Ping-yang, in China
Ping-yang, in Corea 171 N e
Pinhel 94 A c
Pinkie 118 D b
Pinna 27 H e
Pinos Puente 184 C e
Pinsk 139 C e
Pinto, route of
Pinzgau, valley 115 G e
Pinzon, route of, 1499 108 N g
Pinzon, route of, 1508 105 D c
Piombino 90 L j
Piombino, princ. 151 L k
Piotrkow 159 J c
Pipe Creek, stream 208 ins.
Pipewell, mon. 97 Q i
Piqua 200 A c
Piquentum 27 H b
Piræus, The 16 B b
Piræus, harbor of the 16 D c
Piraic Gate 23 D
Piranhas 214 F c
Piranum 27 H b
Piratininga 215 E e (P.)
Piresiæ 10 D c
Pirmasens 134 D d
Pirna 115 G c
Pirot 164 C b
Pirus River 14 B a
Pisa, ruins, in Elis 14 B b
Pisa, in Italy 90 L j
Pisa, abp. 95 E c
Pisa, univ. 100 H f
Pisæ (Pisa, in Italy) 26 E d
Pisanus, Portus 26 E d
Pisatis, dist. 14 B b
Pisaurum (Pesaro) 27 G d
Pisaurus River 27 G d
Piscataqua 189 C c
Piscina Publica, in Rome 23 B
Piscina Publica, Aug. Reg. of Rome 22 A
Pisco 214 B d
Pisek 79 H d
Pisgah, mt. 7 D e
Pishin 170 H e
Pisidia, E. Rom. prov. 43 I f (6)
Pisidia, Macedonian prov. 18 D c
Pisidia, reg. 20 D d
Pisino, bp. 95 E b
Pisistratus, Aqueduct of 23 D
Piski 159 L f
Pistoja
Pistoriæ (Pistoja) 26 E d
Pistum 31 I a
Pistyrus 11 F b
Pisura, Punta, cape 111 A c
Pitcairn Island 180 O j
Pithecussæ, isl. 30 C b
Pithom 4 ins.
Pitinum Mergens 27 G d
Pitinum Pisaurense 27 G d
Pitt, Fort, in Canada 212 E c
Pitt, Fort, in Pa. 192 A c
Pittsburg 195 B c
Pittsburg Landing 208 C b
Pityus 12 L b
Pityusæ, isl. 38 C e
Pityussa, isl. 15 D b
Piura 111 A c
Piura River 111 A c
Pizarro, route of 111
Place d'Armes, in Versailles 149 A
Place de Grève, in Paris 149 B
Place de Louis XV., in Paris 149 B
Place des Victoires, in Paris 149 B
Place du Carrousel, in Paris 149 B
Place du Dauphin, in Paris 149 B
Place Vendôme, in Paris 149 B
Placentia (Piacenza), in Italy 26 D b
Placentia, in Newfoundland 212 J d
Placentia Bay 212 J d
Placilla 215 C e
Plaine de la Ménagerie, loc. in Versailles 149 A
Plaine de Trianon, loc. in Versailles 149 A
Plaine du Mail, loc. in Versailles 149 A
Plaine Saint Antoine, loc. in Versailles 149 A
Plaine-Selve, mon. 94 B b
Planasia, isl. 26 E e
Planchenoit
Plantations across the Water 193 ins. A (Plan.)
Plasencia 83 J g
Plasencia, bp. 94 A c
Plassey 137 E d
Plata, La, in the Arg. Rep. 215 D f
Plata, La, in Bolivia 214 C d
Plata, La, viceroyalty 215 ins.
Platææ 11 E d
Platamodes, prom. 14 B b
Platanistus, prom. 15 C c
Platte River 190 F c
Platte River, North 190 E c
Platte River, South 190 E c
Plattsburg 200 G a
Plattsmouth 210 F b
Plaue 85 C b
Plauen 85 G e
Plauer Canal 135 G b
Plavis (Piave) River 85 G e
Pleissnerland, dist. 85 G e
Plemmyrium, dist. 31 ins. B
Plemmyrium, prom. 30 E e
Plenty, Bay of 172 G d
Pleskau 88 M c
Pless 135 J d
Plessis-les-Tours 126 B c
Plestinus, lake 27 G d
Pleuron 10 C d
Plevlie 164 B d
Plevna 164 C b
Plistus River 11 D d
Plock 115 J b
Plock, bp. 95 F a
Ploërmel 76 B c
Ploesti 165 D a
Plökenpass 27 G a
Plombières-les-Bains 158 D e
Plothia 16 B a
Plymouth, in England
Plymouth, parl. bor. 163 J g
Plymouth, in Mass. 189 C d
Plymouth, in N. Carolina 208 E b
Plymouth, New, col. in Mass. 189 C d
Plymouth, New, New Zealand 172 G d
PlymouthCompany, Grants to the 190 ins.
Plympton, mon. 97 M k
Plympton, parl. bor. 163 K g
Pnom-Penh 171 L g
Pnyx, loc. in Athens 23 D
Poblet, mon. 94 C c
Pocasset 189 ins. A
Pocatello 210 C b
Pöchlarn 63 H d
Podandus 59 K f
Podgoritza 164 B b
Podiebrad 87 J c
Podlesia, dist. 139 C e
Podolia, dist. 139 C f
Podolsk 153 P f
Pœcilus, mt. 16 B a
Pœdiculi, people 31 F a
Pœessa 15 E b
Poel, isl. 122 F a
Pœnina, Alpis, pass 26 B b
Pœtovio 42 F d
Pöhlde 62 F c
Point au Baril 192 D a
Point au Fer 196 E b
Point Comfort, cape 193 ins. A
Pointe Coupée 191 G e
Point de Galle, cape 112 B c
Point Pleasant, battle 194 C c
Poischwitz 155 H c
Poissy 76 E b
Poitiers 61 D c
Poitiers, bp. 94 C b
Poitiers, gen. 147 D b
Poitiers, univ. 100 F e
Poitou, cty. 61 C c
Poitou, gouv. 146 A b
Poitou, prov. 148 D e
Pojang Lake
Pola 27 H c
Pola, bp. 95 E c
Pola de Gordon, La 82 A a
Polabians, people 62 F b
Poland, duchy 59 H c
Poland, km., 11 cent. 63 I c
Poland, km., 12 cent. 70 J c
Poland, km., 16 cent. 119 I c
Poland, km., 18 cent. 131 I c
Poland, km., 19 cent. 159 J b
Poland, Great, dist. 139 A e
Poland, Little, dist. 139 B e
Polati, bp. 95 F c
Polaticum, prom. 27 H c

Polden Hills 49 E f
Poles, people 57 H c
Polesina, dist. 90 C b
Policastro 90 E e
Policastro, bp. 95 F c
Polichne, quarter in Syracuse. 31 ins. B
Poligny 126 D c
Polillo, isl. 171 N g
Polish Livonia, dist. 131 I b
Pollentia, Balearic Is. 38 C e
Pollentia, in Liguria 26 B c
Pollenza 50 E d
Polling 62 F e
Polling-places, loc. in Rome 24 B
Polo, Marco, route of
Polotsk 71 L b
Polotsk, princ. 71 L b
Polovzians, people 71 N d
Poltava 139 D f
Polyægus, isl. 15 E c
Polypotamia, proposed state in U. S.
Polyrrhenia 14 ins.
Polytimetus River 19 K b
Pombia 62 E f
Pomerania, dist. 59 H c
Pomerania, Farther, dist. 123 H b
Pomerania, Hither, dist. 123 G b
Pomerania, duchy, 12 cent. 72 D a
Pomerania, duchy, 15 cent. 87 J b
Pomerania, prov. 159 H b
Pomerania, Swedish, dist. 154 G a
Pomeranians, Bp. of the 95 E a
Pomeranians, people 46 J c
Pomerelia, dist. 72 D a
Pomoria, dist. 138 D b
Pomos, tribe 188 B c
Pompadour 126 B d
Pompælo (Pamplona) 38 B d
Pompeii 30 D b
Pompeiopolis, in Cilicia 20 F d
Pompeiopolis, in Paphlagonia 20 F b
Pompey, Gardens of 23 B
Pompey, Portico of 22 A
Pompey, Senate-house of 22 A
Pompey, Theatre of 22 A
Pompey's Pillar 34 ins. C (7)
Pomptine Marshes 30 B a
Ponca, Ind. Res. 188 G c
Poncas, tribe 188 G b
Ponce 199 ins. G
Ponce de León, Bahia de, bay 191 I f
Ponce de León, landing-place of 191 I e
Pondicherry 137 C f
Pondoland, dist. 175 M m
Pons, castle 76 C d
Pons Ælii (Newcastle)
Pons Aureoli 26 D b
Pons Drusi 27 F a
Pons Ferri (Iron Bridge) 68 C b
Pons Saravi 39 I i
Ponta Grossa
Pontafel Pass 135 G e
Pontarlier 122 D e
Pont au Change, loc. in Paris. 149 B
Pont Audemer 76 D b
Pontchartrain, Fort 191 I c
Pontchartrain, lake 208 B c
Pont de Cé 126 A c
Pont de l'Arche 76 D b
Ponteamas
Pontecorvo 90 D d
Pontecorvo, princ. 151 L k
Pontefract 65 F d
Pontefract, mon. 97 P h
Pontefract, parl. bor. 163 M d
Ponte Molle, loc. in Rome 96 A
Ponte Sant' Angelo, loc. in Rome 96 A
Ponthieu, cty. 76 D a
Pontiac 211 I b
Pontiæ, isl. 30 B b
Pontiæ Islands 30 C b
Pontica, reg. 50 J d
Ponticus, lake 19 J d
Pontifex Maximus, House of the 24 A
Pontigny 69 I g
Pontigny, mon. 94 C b
Pont Notre Dame, loc. in Paris 149 B
Pont Neuf, loc. in Paris 149 B
Pontoise 126 C b
Pontremoli 90 I h
Pontresina 91 R l
Pont Royal, loc. in Paris 149 B
Pont Saint Michel, loc. in Paris 149 B
Pontus, East Rom. dioc. 43 J f
Pontus, reg.
Pontus, Rom. prov.
Pontus Euxinus (Black Sea) 12 J b
Pontus Polemoniacus, East Rom. prov. 43 J e (9)
Pony Express, route of the 210 F b
Ponzone 130 Q j
Pool of the Aqueduct 6 ins. A (5)
Poole 127 X p
Poole, parl. bor. 163 L g
Poona 137 B e
Popayan 111 B a
Poperinghe 117 A d
Popilian Way, road 27 G c, 31 F d
Popocatepetl, vol. 106 B a
Popotlan
Poppi 90 L j
Populoniæ, Aquæ 26 E d
Populonium 26 E e
Po River 90 J h
Porchester
Porcien, cty. 69 J f
Porcobera River 26 C c
Porcupine River 212 A b
Porfirio Diaz, Ciudad 213 B b
Porhoët, castle 76 B b
Porhoët, cty. 76 B b
Porman 82 B b
Porphyrion 6 C a
Porpoise, Cape 189 C c
Porta Appia, loc. in Rome 96 A
Porta aurea, loc. in Jerusalem. 68 ins. B
Portæ Caspiæ, pass, see Caspian Gates 19 H c
Portæ Caucasiæ, pass, see Caucasian Gates 18 F b
Porta Flaminia, loc. in Rome 96 A
Portage la Prairie 212 F c
Porta Latina, loc. in Rome 96 A
Portalegre 94 A d
Porta Pia, loc. in Rome 96 A
Port Arthur, in Canada 212 F d
Port Arthur, in Asia 171 N e
Porta Salaria, loc. in Rome 96 A
Porta San Pancrazio, loc. in Rome 96 A
Porta San Paolo, loc. in Rome 96 A
Porta Tiburtina, loc. in Rome. 96 A
Port Augusta, S. Australia 172 C d
Port Augusta, W. Australia 172 A d
Port au Prince 213 E c
Port Bouet 175 C d
Port Clarence 198 ins. A
Port Darwin 172 B b
Port Davey 172 D e
Port Elizabeth 175 M m
Porte Saint Denis, loc. in Paris 149 B
Porte Saint Martin, loc. in Paris 149 B
Portese, Porta, loc. in Rome 22 A
Port Essington, in Australia 172 C b
Port Essington, in Canada 212 ins. A
Port Eyre 172 C d
Port Gibson 208 B c
Port Hamilton 171 N e
Porthmus 11 F d
Port Hope 198 ins. A
Port Hudson 208 B c
Portico of the Gods, loc. in Rome 24 B
Port Jackson 172 E d
Portland, in Australia 172 D d
Portland, in England 127 W p
Portland, in Maine 179 K b
Portland, in Oregon 198 A a
Portland Canal 212 ins.
Port Lincoln 172 C d
Port Louis 175 I g
Port Macquarie 172 E d
Port Natal 175 N l
Port Nicholson 172 G e
Porto, bp. 96 B b
Porto Alegre 215 D e
Porto Bello 105 E e
Porto Cabello, see Puerto Cabello
Porto Calvo 214 F c
Port of Spain 214 C a
Porto Maurizio 90 B c
Porto Novo 174 D d
Porto Rico, col.
Porto Rico, isl. 199 ins. G
Porto Santo 108 P d
Porto Seguro 214 F d
Porto Viejo
Port Phillip 172 G d
Port Phillip District 172 leg.
Port Republic 208 E b (P.R.)
Port Royal, in Jamaica
Port Royal, in Nova Scotia 212 I d
Port Royal, loc. in Paris 149 B
Port Royal, near Paris 126 B b
Port Royal, in S. C. 193 ins. C
Port Said 174 K i
Port Simpson 212 ins.
Portsmouth, in England 69 C a
Portsmouth, parl. bor.
Portsmouth, hospital 100 A b
Portsmouth, in N. Hampshire 189 C c
Portsmouth, in Ohio 206 ins.
Portsmouth, in Rhode Island 189 ins. A
Portsmouth, in Virginia 207 K c
Portsmouth Harbor 51 P i
Port Stanley 206 ins.
Port Sudan 174 G b
Portugal, cty. 83 D c
Portugal, km., 12 cent. 82 G e
Portugal, km., 15 cent. 83 J g
Portuguese, people
Portuguese East Africa, col. 175 G g
Portuguese Guinea, col. 174 B c
Portuguese West Africa, col. 175 E f
Portunata, isl. 27 I c
Portunus, Temple of 24 A
Portus, bp. 96 B b
Portus Ædro 27 G b
Portus Augusti 27 G f
Portus Cale (Oporto) 38 A d
Portus Delphini 26 D c
Portus Divini 38 B e
Portus Eunostus 34 ins. C
Portus Herculis Monœci (Monaco) 26 B d
Portus Itius 38 C b
Portus Lemanus (Lymne) 38 C b
Portus Magnus (Portsmouth Harbor)
Portus Maurici (Porto Maurizio) 26 C d
Portus Namnetum (Nantes) 38 B c
Portus Pisanus 26 E d
Portus Traianus 26 E e
Portus Veneris 26 D e
Port Way, road 35 ins. B
Poschiavo 91 S l
Posen 63 I b
Posen, bp. 95 F a
Posen, prov. 159 I b
Posidium, near Alexandria 34 ins. C
Posidium, near Corinth 15 D b
Posidium, prom., Acanthian Gulf 11 E b
Posidium, prom., Bay of Pæstum 30 D b
Posidium, prom., Phthiotis 11 E c
Posidium, prom., Propontis
Posidium, prom., Thermaic Gulf 11 E c
Posidonia 12 F b
Posilipo, mt. 31 ins. A
Pospol, farm
Postern, loc. in London 75 G g
Postumian Way, in Liguria, road 26 C c
Postumian Way, in Venetia, road 27 G b
Poswol 131 H b

Potaïssa 35 I d
Potamii 16 C b
Potchefstroom 175 M l
Potentia, in Lucania 30 E b
Potentia, in Picenum 27 H d
Potenza 90 E d
Poti 99 L e
Potidæa 11 E b
Potomac River 187 L e
Potosí 214 C d
Potsdam 123 G b
Pottawatomi, Ind. Res. 188 G c
Pottawatomi of Huron, Ind. Res. 188 I b
Pottawatomies, tribe 188 I b
Poultry, loc. in London 75 G g (36)
Pourré, route of 195 ins. B
Poussay, mon. 148 C b
Pouzo Alegre 214 D d
Poverty Bay 172 G d
Powder River 198 D b
Powell River 196 ins. A
Powhatans, tribes 188 J c
Pozhega 159 I f
Pozzuoli 46 I e
Pozzuoli, bp. 95 ins.
Præneste 27 G f
Præneste, bp. 96 B b
Prænestine Gate 22 A
Prænestine Way, road 35 ins. B
Prætorian Camp, loc. in Rome 22 A
Prætorian Gate 22 A
Prætorium Latovicorum 27 I b
Prætuttii, people 27 H e
Prævalitana, prov. 43 F e (3)
Praga 115 K b
Pragel Pass 150 E c
Prague 63 H c
Prague, abp. 95 E b
Prague, univ. 100 H d
Prairie, La, battle 189 B b
Prairie du Chien 211 G b
Prasiæ, in Attica 16 C b
Prasiæ, in Laconia 15 C b
Prata Quinctia, loc. in Rome 22 A
Prato, near Florence 90 L j
Prattigau, valley 91 R l
Pratzen 155 I d
Právia 82 A a
Pré-sur-Arnon, La, mon. 94 C b
Préaux, mon. 94 C b
Prechthal 142 B d
Pregel River 87 M a
Prela 130 P k
Prémontré 69 I f (Prém.)
Prémontré, mon. 94 C b
Prenzlau 79 H b
Prenzlau, Hanse. cy 99 ins. B
Preobrazhensk 138 E d
Prepesinthus, isl. 15 E c
Presburg 63 I d
Presburg, univ. 100 I e
Prescott 210 C d
Présentation, Fort de la 194 D b
Presidio del Norte 190 E f
Presidio, State of the 151 I h
Presqu'Isle, Fort 192 B b
Presteign, parl. bor.
Preston 127 V m
Preston, parl. bor. 163 L d
Prestonpans
Pretoria 175 M l
Preussisch-Eylau 153 I b
Prevesa 93 B c
Priapus
Pribilof Islands 180 K b
Priene 13 E c
Prignitz, dist. 85 B b
Prilip 89 B b
Prilius, lake 26 E e
Prince Albert, town 212 E c
Prince Albert Land 186 H a
Prince Edward Island, Canada 186 M d
Prince Edward Island, Ind. Oc. 182 E E l
Prince George, Fort 193 C d
Prince of Wales, Cape 186 C b
Prince of Wales Island, Arctic Ocean 186 J a
Prince of Wales Island, Pacific Ocean 212 ins.
Prince of Wales Land 212 F a
Prince of Wales Strait 212 D a
Prince Patrick, isl. 186 G a
Prince Regent Inlet 212 F a
Prince Rupert, town 212 ins.
Prince's Island 175 D d
Princeton 192 D c
Principati, dist. 90 E d
Principe da Beira, Fort do 214 C d
Printzdorp 192 ins.
Printzhof 192 ins.
Pripet, Marshes of the 2 G c
Pripet River 139 C e
Prishtina 89 B b
Prison Gate, in Jerusalem 6 ins. A
Prisrend 77 I d
Prittlewell, mon. 97 R j
Pritzwalk, Hanse. cy. 99 ins. B
Privas 126 D d
Privernum 30 C a
Prizlawa 63 G b
Probalinthus 16 B a
Probus, Bridge of 22 A
Prochyta, isl. 30 C b
Procida, isl. 90 D d
Proclamation Line of 1763 194 C d, E a
Proconnesus
Proconnesus, isl.
Proconsular Africa, Rom. prov. 34 F f
Proërna 11 D c
Progreso 213 D b
Prome
Promontorium pulchrum, cape 15 E a
Pronni 10 B d
Pronsk 71 N c
Propaxus, isl. 10 B c
Prophthasia 19 J d
Propylæa, bldg. in Athens 23 C (6)
Propylæum, bldg. in Olympia
Propontis (Sea of Marmora)
Proschium 10 C d
Propopis 4 ins.
Prospalta 16 B b
Prote, isl. 14 B b
Provence, cty., 11 cent. 61 F e
Provence, cty., 12 cent. 69 G e
Provence, cty., 15 cent. 84 F h
Provence, gouv. 146 C c
Provence, marq. 69 F d
Provence, prov. 148 F f
Providence, in Rhode Island 189 ins. A
Providence, in Maryland 192 C d
Providence, Fort 212 D b
Providence Islands
Provins 76 E b
Prudhomme, Fort 191 H d
Prüm 117 E d
Prüm, mon. 95 D a
Pruntrut
Prusa
Prussia, dist. 77 I b
Prussia, duchy 88 I d
Prussia, km., 1701 135 K a
Prussia, km., 1812 155 J a
Prussia, km., 1815—1866 158—159
Prussia, km., 1910 161 B-E b
Prussian Customs-Union 160 D c
Prussian Hessian Customs-Union 160 D c
Prussians, people, about 1000 59 I c
Pruth River 59 J d
Pruvinum, see Provins
Prytaneum, bldg. in Athens 23 D
Prytaneum, bldg. in Olympia
Przemyśl 159 L d
Psacum, prom. 15 D d
Psamathus Port 14 C c
Psaphara 11 E b
Psaphis 15 D a
Psephinus Tower, in Jerusalem 6 ins. A
Pskov 88 M c
Pskov, Hanse. for. cy. 99 I b
Psophis 14 B b
Psyra, isl. 13 D b
Psyttalea, isl. 16 B b
Pteleum 11 D c
Ptolemaïs, in Cyrenaica 35 I g
Ptolemaïs, in Egypt 47 M k
Ptolemaïs (Acre), in Phœnicia 6 C c
Ptolemies, Kingdom of the 19 U l
Ptolemy, Kingdom of 18 P i, leg.
Ptoon, mt. 11 E d
Ptychia, isl. 10 A c
Pucinum 27 H b
Puebla de los Ángeles (Puebla) 106 B a
Pueblo 198 E c
Pueblo Indians, tribe 188 E c
Puerto Barrios 213 D c
Puerto Bello, see Porto Bello 214 B b
Puerto Cabello 214 C a
Puerto de Bastimentos 105 E e
Puerto de Caballos 105 C c
Puerto de Luna 190 E e
Puerto de Retrete 105 E e
Puerto de Santa Gloria 105 E c
Puerto Limon 213 D c
Puerto Mexico, see Coatzacoalcos
Puerto Montt 215 B g
Puerto Principe 213 E b
Puerto Plata 213 E c
Puerto viejo 111 A b
Puget Sound 198 A a
Puig 82 B b
Puigcerda 82 C a
Puiset, Le 69 H f
Pukapuka, isl. 107 D i
Pulaski, Fort 208 D c
Pulicat
Pullaria 27 H c
Pulo Condore, isl.
Pulo Penang, isl. 171 K h
Pultusk 87 M b
Puna, see Poona
Puna Island 111 A b
Punakha 171 K f
Punicum 27 F e
Punitz 135 I c
Punjab, Punjaub, reg. 137 B b
Puno 214 B d
Punta Arenas, in Chile 215 B h
Punta Arenas, in Costa Rica 213 D d
Punta Bernal 106 D a
Puntarenas, see Punta Arenas, in Costa Rica
Pura 19 J e
Purchena 83 K h
Puri 137 E e
Purísima Concepción, in California 190 C e
Purísima Concepción, in Texas 190 F f
Purus River 214 C c
Purysbourg 193 ins. C
Pustertal, valley 115 G e
Pustozersk 138 H b
Puteoli 31 ins. A
Put-in-Bay 200 B c
Putlam
Putlitz 85 C b
Putney 75 I i
Putten, isl. 117 C c
Puttiala 137 C b
Putzig 123 J a
Puy, Le 61 E d
Puy, Le, bp. 94 C b
Puy-de-Dôme, dept. 148 E e
Puyallup, Ind. Res. 188 B a
Puylaurens 126 C e
Pydna 11 D b
Pydna vetus 11 D b
Pylæ Caucasiæ, pass, see Caucasian Gates 18 F b
Pylene 10 C d
Pylos or Pylus, in Messenia 14 B c
Pylus, in Elis

Pyramid Lake, Ind. Res. 188 C b
Pyramids, in Egypt 174 J j
Pyramus River 20 F d
Pyrasus 11 D c
Pyrenæum, prom. 38 C d
Pyrenees Mountains 38 B d
Pyrénées, Hautes, dept. 148 D f
Pyrénées Orientales, dept. 148 E f
Pyrgi, in Greece
Pyrgi, in Italy
Pyritz 63 H b
Pyrmont 158 E b
Pyrrha
Pyrrha, prom. 11 D c
Pyrrhichus 14 C c
Pythium, in Athens 23 D
Pythium, in Thessaly 11 D b
Pyxus 30 E b
Pyxus River 30 E c

Quadi, people 38 F c
Quadratæ 26 C b
Quai de la Grève, loc. in Paris 149 B
Quai du Louvre, loc. in Paris 149 B
Quakenbrück 122 E b
Qualla, Ind. Res. 188 J c
Qu'Appelle 212 E c
Quarr, ab. 100 A b
Quathlamba, mts. 175 M m
Quatres Bras 156 A a
Quatre Vallées, dist. 147 E c (Q. V.)
Quatre Vallées, viscty 76 D e
Quauhtitlan
Quebec 191 K b
Quebec, prov. 1763 194 E a
Quebec, prov. 1774 194 E a
Quebec, prov. 1910 212 H d
Quebrancha River
Quedlinburg 62 F c
Quedlinburg, mon. 95 E a
Queenborough, parl. bor. 163 O f
Queen Charlotte Islands, near British Columbia 186 F c
Queen Charlotte Islands (Santa Cruz Island) north east of Queensland 172 F b
Queen Charlotte Sound 212 C c
Queenhithe, loc. in London 75 G g
Queen's County 127 J i
Queen's Garden, isl. 105 E b
Queensland, state 172 D c
Queenston Heights, battle 200 D b
Queenstown 127 I j
Queis River 85 H e
Quelpart, isl. 171 N e
Quengian
Quercy, cty. 61 D d
Querétaro 213 ins.
Querquetulan Gate 23 B
Querquetulum 35 ins. B
Quesada 82 B b
Quesnoy, le 117 B d
Quetta 170 H e
Quezaltenango 105 B d
Quiaca 214 C e
Quibdo 214 B b
Quiberon 130 C d
Quiberon Bay 132 B c
Quierzy, see Kiersy
Quilimane 175 G f
Quillota 215 B f
Quiloa 109 U h
Quilon
Quimper 76 A b
Quimper, bp. 94 B b
Quimperlé 76 B c
Quimperlé, mon. 94 B b
Quinaielt, Ind. Res. 188 B a
Quincy 211 G c
Quinsai (Hang-chau-fu)
Quirinal, palace 96 A
Quirinal Gate 23 B
Quirinal Hill 22 A
Quirinus, Temple of 22 A
Quiros, discoveries of
Quito 111 B b
Quito, pres. 215 ins.
Quito, reg. 111 C b
Quitzow 85 B b
Quivira, reg. 190 F d

Raab
Raab, bp. 95 F b
Raab River 159 I e
Raba River, see Raab River
Rabat 174 C a
Rabba 99 K g
Rabbath Ammon 7 D e
Rabbath Moab 7 D f
Rabida, La 184 B e
Racca
Radkersburg 135 I e
Radnor, in Pa. 192 ins.
Radnor, in Wales 163 K e
Radnor, cty. 127 V n
Radnor, parl. bor. 163 K e
Radnor, parl. dist. 163 K e
Radolfzell 142 C e
Radom 87 M c
Radstadt 123 G e
Radusculan Gate 23 B
Radziejewo
Radzin 131 H c
Rae, Fort 212 D b
Raetia, dist. 62 E e
Rætia, prov. 38 D c
Rætia I, prov. 42 E d (6)
Rætia II, prov. 42 E d (7)
Rætian Alps, mts. 26 D a
Ragaba 7 D d
Ragaz 91 R k
Raglan Castle 127 W o
Ragusa, in Dalmatia 73 D b
Ragusa, abp. 95 F c
Ragusa, rep. 131 G e
Ragusa, in Sicily 90 E f
Ragy
Rahin River 143 ins. F
Rahmanieh or Rahmaniyeh 174 J i
Rai
Rain 122 F d
Rainham 75 J h
Rainier, mt. 186 G d
Rainy Lake 191 G b
Raipur 137 D d
Rais, dist. 81 L h
Rais, seign. 69 C c
Raisin River 200 B c
Rajamahendri 112 B b
Rajpootana or Rajputana, dist. 137 B c
Rajputs, people 92 H e
Rakka 99 K f
Rakosfeld, dist. 159 J e
Raleigh 211 J c
Raleigh's col. 191 J d
Rama, dist. 72 D c
Ramadan, reg.
Ramah, in Galilee 6 C c
Ramah, in Judæa 7 C e
Rahmah, in Labrador 212 I c
Ramah, in Phœnicia 6 C b
Ramathaim 7 C d
Rambacia 19 K e
Ramillies 134 C c
Ramleh 68 ins. A
Ramoth-Gilead
Ramsay's Mills 195 B f
Ramsey, mon. 97 Q i
Rancagua 215 B f
Rangoon 171 K g
Rankokus Kill, stream 192 ins.
Ransbecke
Rapallo 130 R j
Rapidan River 192 B d
Raphia 7 A f
Raphoe, bp. 97 D b
Rappahannock River 193 F c (Rap.)
Rapperswyl, castle 91 Q k
Rappoltsweiler 143 ins. D
Rara 62 E d, F c
Raritan River 192 D c
Raron 91 P l
Rasa
Ras Madrak 170 G g
Rastatt 142 B c
Ratæ (Leicester) 51 P h
Ratanpura
Rathenow 85 C b
Rathlure, bp. 97 D b
Ratiaria 39 M l
Ratibor 79 K c
Ratibor, princ. 79 K c
Ratisbon 63 G d
Ratisbon, bp. 79 H d
Ratisbon, imp. cy. 79 G d
Ratkau 154 F a
Rat Portage 212 F d
Ratzeburg 62 F b
Ratzeburg, bp. 79 G b
Raudii, or Raudian Plain, Campi, dist. 26 C b
Raurici, people 39 I j
Rauricorum, Augusta (Augst) 39 I j
Ravendal
Ravenna 27 G c
Ravenna, abp. 95 E c
Ravensburg 72 B b
Ravensburg, cty. 86 G b
Ravensburg, imp. cy. 143 I j
Ravensburg, Neu 143 I j
Ravenspur 84 D c
Ravenstein 117 D c
Rawa 135 K c
Rawalpindi 137 B b
Rawdon, route of 195 A g
Rawicz
Rawka 135 J c
Rawson 215 C g
Rawulpindee, see Rawalpindi
Raymond 208 B c
Raystown 192 B c
Razlawice 135 K c
Räzüns 91 R l
Ré, isl. 76 C c
Reading, in England
Reading, mon. 97 Q j
Reading, parl. bor. 163 N f (Read.)
Reading, in Mass. 189 ins. B
Reading, in Pa. 196 D b
Reate 27 G e
Rechberg, Hohen, ruin 143 I h
Rechberg, lordship 143 I h
Recife, or Pernambuco 214 F c
Reckheim 117 D d
Recknitz River 63 G a
Recovery, Fort 196 ins. B
Reculver
Red Lake 211 F a
Red Lake, Ind. Res. 188 G a
Red River, in southern U. S. 211 G d
Red River, in Tongking 171 L g
Red River of the North, in U. S. and Canada 210 F a
Redan, Great and Little, forts 164 L g
Redarians, people 63 G b
Red Cedar River 199 G b
Red Cliff, Ind. Res. 188 H a
Redesdale, dist.
Redones, people 38 B c
Redonis, see Rennes
Red Russia, reg. 139 B e
Red Sea 3 H f
Redstone, Old, Fort 195 ins. B
Reepsholt, mon. 95 D a
Reganesburg, see Ratisbon
Regen River 63 G d
Regensburg, see Ratisbon
Reggio, in Calabria 90 E e
Reggio, abp. 95 F d
Reggio, in Emilia 90 J h
Reggio, bp. 95 E c
Reggio, univ. 100 H f

Regia, in Rome
Regia, quarter in Alexandria . 34 ins. C
Regillus, lake 35 ins. B
Regina, in Saskatchewan 212 E c
Regina castra (Ratisbon) 38 E c
Regium (Reggio in Emilia) 26 E c
Regium, see Riez
Regni, people 51 P i
Regnitz River 62 F d
Regnum (Chichester) 51 P i
Regulbium (Reculver) 51 Q i
Rehoboth, in Mass. 189 ins. A
Rehoboth, in Palestine 7 B f
Reichenau, ab. 142 D e
Reichenau, mon. 95 D b
Reichenbach 135 I c
Reichenbach, mon. 143 F h
Reichenberg 135 H c
Reichenweier 143 ins. D
Reichenweier, lordship 143 ins. D
Reichersberg, mon. 95 E b
Reigate 75 I i
Reigate, parl. bor. 163 N f
Reims 61 F b
Reims, abp. 94 C b
Reims, cty. 61 F b
Reims, duchy 76 F b
Rein, mon. 95 F b
Reindeer Lake 212 E c
Reinhardsbrunn, mon. 95 E a
Rejaf 175 G d
Rejang 112 D d
Reliance, Fort 212 E b
Remesiana 43 G e
Remi or Remis, see Reims
Remi, people 38 C c
Remich 117 E e
Remiremont, mon. 148 C b
Rems River 143 I h
Remuria, in Rome 23 B
Renaix 117 B d
Rench River 142 B d
Rendsburg 78 F a
Renfrew, cty.
Rennes 61 C c
Rennes, bp. 94 B b
Rennes, cty. 69 C b
Rennes, gen. 147 D b
Rennsteig, road 62 F c
Reno 210 B c
Reno River 150 F d
Rense 78 E c
Rensselærswyck, dist. 192 D b
Renus (Reno) River 27 F c
Rephaim, Valley of 6 ins. A
Republican River 198 E c
Resaca, battle 208 D c
Resaca de la Palma, battle 201 F d
Resaina 20 H d
Reschen-Scheideck Pass 91 S l
Resengo
Reseph 6 ins. C
Réservoirs, Rue des, street in Versailles 149 A
Resht 170 F e
Resolution, Fort 212 D b
Resolution Island 212 I b
Rest, House of, in Jerusalem 68 ins. B (15)
Restigouche River 199 L a
Retford, parl. bor. 163 N d
Rethel 69 J f
Rethel, cty. 76 F b
Retimo 164 C c
Retovium 26 D c
Retz, duchy 126 A c
Retz, seign. 76 C c
Reuben, tribe 7 ins. D
Reunion, isl. 175 I g
Reuss, cty. 114 F c
Reuss River 91 Q l
Reutlingen, imp. cy. 78 F d
Reval 88 K b
Reval, Hanse. cy. 99 H b
Revesby, mon. 97 R h
Revilla Gigedo Island, Alaska 212 ins.
Revilla Gigedo Islands, to Mexico 213 A c
Revin 117 C e
Rewa 170 J f
Rewa, dist. 137 D d
Rewley, mon. 97 P j
Reyes, Ciudad de los (Lima) 111 B d
Reykjavik
Rha (Volga) River 35 N d
Rhætian Wall 39 K i
Rhagæ 8 D b
Rhakotis, quarter in Alexandria 34 ins. C
Rhamnus 15 E a
Rheba
Rhegium (Reggio in Calabria) 30 E d
Rhein River, see Rhine River
Rheinau 142 A d
Rheinau, mon. 91 Q k
Rheinberg 117 E c
Rheinbund, see Confederation of the Rhine
Rheinfelden 91 P k
Rheinfelden, lordship 142 A e
Rheinsberg 135 G b
Rheinwald, valley 91 R l
Rheitoi, lake 16 B a
Rheneia, isl. 15 F b
Rhenish Prussia, prov. 158 D c
Rhense, see Rense
Rhenus (Rhine) River 34 F c
Rhesus River
Rhetra 63 G b
Rhin, Bas, dept. 148 F e
Rhin, Haut, dept. 148 F e
Rhine River 2 E c
Rhinocolura 47 M g
Rhion 14 B c
Rhium, prom., in Corsica 26 C e
Rhium, prom., in Greece 14 B a
Rhizus, in Magnesia 11 D c
Rhizus, in Pontus 20 I b
Rhitymna 14 ins.
Rhoda or Rhodæ, in Spain 38 C d
Rhodanus River, see Rhône River
Rhode, in Belgium 156 A a
Rhode Island, col. 189 C d
Rhode Island, isl. 189 ins. A
Rhode Island, state 199 K b (K I)
Rhodes, state 33 C b
Rhodes, isl. 4 C b
Rhodes, Knights of 77 J e
Rhodesia, prot. 175 F f
Rhodius River
Rhodope, mt. 39 M l
Rhodope, Rom. prov. 43 H e (4)
Rhodt 142 B b
Rhodus 43 H f
Rhœdias River 10 D b
Rhœteum
Rhœteum, prom.
Rhône, dept. 148 E e
Rhône River 61 F d
Rhotanus River 26 D e
Rhyndacus River
Rhypes 14 C a
Riade 62 F c, 63 G c
Riadh
Riazan 139 E e
Ribagorza, dist. 83 F c
Ribaut, set. by 191 J e
Ribble River 127 V m
Ribchester
Ribe 158 E a
Ribemont 56 C c
Riblah 6 ins. C
Ribnitz 123 G a
Ricciacum 39 I i
Richelieu, in France 126 B c
Richelieu, Fort, in Canada 189 B a
Richelieu River 189 B b
Richelieu, Rue de, street in Paris 149 B
Richmond, in England
Richmond, parl. bor. 163 M c
Richmond, in Indiana 211 H b
Richmond, in Virginia 193 F c
Richmond, castle, near London 75 I i
Richmond Island 189 C c (Rich.)
Ricina 27 H d
Ricomagus, see Riom
Riddagshausen, mon. 95 E a
Riding Rocks, cape 105 ins.
Ried 135 G d
Riedlingen 143 H i
Rienzi, so-called House of 96 A
Riesa 135 G c
Riesa, mon. 95 E a
Riesenberg, castle 87 I d
Rieti 161 I f
Rieti, bp. 95 E c
Riet Spruit 175 M l
Rieux, bp. 94 C c
Riez, bp. 95 D c
Riffins, isl. 112 G c
Riga 138 B d
Riga, abp. 95 F a
Riga, Hanse. cy. 99 H b
Riga, Gulf of 80 H c
Rigomagus, on the Po R. 26 C b
Rigomagus (Remagen), on the Rhine R. 39 I h
Rigodulum 39 I i
Rijnsburg 62 B b
Rimac River 111 B d
Rimini 90 M i
Rimini, bp. 95 E c
Rimmon, in Galilee 6 C c
Rimmon, in Judæa 7 C e
Rimouski River 199 L a
Rinteln 122 E b
Riobamba 111 B b
Rio Blanco, in Mexico 106 D b
Rio Branco, in Brazil 214 C b
Rio Colorado Chiquito, R. 190 C d
Rio das Boas Sinaes, R. 108 U i
Rio de Janeiro 215 E e
Rio de Janeiro, state 215 E e
Rio de la Antigua, R. 106 D a
Rio de la Buena Guia, R. 190 C e
Rio de la Chira, R. 111 A b
Rio de la Plata, R. 215 D f
Rio de las Balsas, R. 213 ins.
Rio de Nazas, R. 213 B b
Rio de Oro, dist. 175 B b
Rio Dulce (delta of the Orinoco R.) 105 H e
Rio Florido 190 D f
Rio Grande, cty. in Brazil 215 D f
Rio Grande, river, in south central Brazil 214 D d
Rio Grande, river, in south-eastern Brazil 214 E e
Rio Grande, river, between Mexico and U. S. 187 I f
Rio Grande, river, in Panamá 216
Rio Grande de Santiago, river, in Mexico 213 B b
Rio Grande do Norte, state 214 F c
Rio Grande do Sul, state 215 D e
Riohacha 214 B a
Rioja 215 C e
Rioja, dist. 82 B a
Riom 76 E d
Riom, gen. 147 E b
Riomum, see Riom
Rio Muni, dist. 175 D d
Rio Negro, river, in Arg. Rep. 215 C f
Rio Negro, river, in Brazil 214 C c
Rions, castle 76 C d
Rio Real, R. 214 F d
Rio Salado, river, northern Arg. Rep. 215 C e
Rio Salado, river, southern Arg. Rep. 215 C f
Ripa, Alta 39 J i
Ripaille, mon. 86 F e

Ripley . . . 206 ins.
Ripoll, mon. . . . 94 C c
Ripon . . . 65 F c
Ripon, mon. . . . 97 P g
Ripon, parl. bor. . . . 163 M c
Rippoldsau, mon. . . . 142 B d
Ripuarians, people . . . 50 E c
Risano, bp. . . . 95 F c
Risingham . . .
Risinum . . . 38 F d
Riss River . . . 143 I i
Ritzebüttel . . . 114 E b
Riu-kiu (Liu-kiu) Islands . . . 171 N f
Riva . . . 134 F f
Rivaulx, mon. . . . 97 Q g
Rivera . . . 215 D f
River Gate . . .
Rivières du Sud, dist. . . . 174 B c
Rivoli, near Turin . . . 130 P i
Rivoli, near Verona . . . 150 F d
Roanne . . . 76 E c
Roanoke Island . . . 193 G d
Roanoke River . . . 193 F c
Robertsbridge, mon. . . . 97 R k
Robertsons, fam. . . .
Robertson's Trail, route . . . 194 B c
Roberval . . . 184 D c
Rocca San Casciano . . . 90 L i
Roccasecca . . . 90 D d
Rochdale, parl. bor. . . . 163 L d
Roche, mon., in England . . . 97 P h
Roche, la, in Belgium . . . 76 F a
Roche, la, in France . . . 143 ins. F
Roche, la, cty. . . . 69 F a
Rochedale Hundred . . 193 ins. A (Roch.)
Rochefort, in Belgium . . . 117 D d
Rochefort, in France . . . 84 C g
Rochelle, La . . . 76 C c
Rochelle, La, gen. . . . 147 D b
Rochester, in England . . . 127 Z o
Rochester, bp. . . . 97 R j
Rochester, castle and mon. . . 74 F f
Rochester, Hanse. for. cy. . . .
Rochester, parl. bor. . . . 163 O f
Rochester, in New York . . . 211 J b
Rochlitz . . . 115 G c
Rock Island . . . 211 G b
Rock River . . . 191 H c
Rockhampton . . . 172 E c
Rockingham . . . 65 F d
Rocky Mountains, The . . . 186 H c
Rocoux . . . 134 C c
Rocroy . . . 157 ins.
Rodalben . . . 142 ins. B
Rodez . . . 76 E d
Rodez, bp. . . . 94 C c
Roding River . . . 75 J h
Rodomum, see Rouen
Rodosto . . . 93 C b
Rodriguez Island . . . 182 HHi
Roebourne . . . 172 A c
Roer River . . . 117 E d
Roermond . . . 117 E c
Roermond, Hanse. cy. . . . 99 ins. B
Roeskilde . . . 58 G b
Roeskilde, Hanse. for. cy. . . . 98 F b
Rœulx . . . 156 A a
Rogalin . . . 159 I b
Rogel, Well of . . . 6 ins. A
Rohan . . . 69 B c
Rohilcund, Rohilkhand, dist. . . 137 C c
Roidomna, see Roanne
Rojas . . . 215 C f
Roma, Temple of . . .
Roma, in Queensland . . . 172 D c
Roma, see Rome, in Italy
Roma quadrata, loc. in Rome, Italy . . . 23 B
Romagna, dist. . . . 90 D b
Roman Empire about 395 . . . 42, 43
Roman Empire of the German Nation about 1000 . . . 58, 59
Roman Empire of the German Nation, 1138—1254 . . . 72
Roman Empire, Holy, about 1000 58, 59
Roman Empire, Holy, 1138—1254 72
Roman Forum, The . . . 24 B
Roman Forum, Aug. Reg. of Rome . . . 22 A
Roman Gate, in Olympia . . .
Romania, desp. . . . 93 A c
Romania, emp. . . . 73 F b
Romano, Cape . . . 191 I f
Roman Republic, 1803 . . . 151 I h
Romans . . . 126 D d
Romanula Gate . . . 24 A
Roman Wall, in England . . .
Roman Wall, in Hungary . . . 159 J f
Romanzof, Cape . . . 198 ins. A
Rome, in Georgia . . . 208 C c
Rome, in Italy . . . 27 G f
Rome, abp. . . . 95 E c
Rome, ancient imperial, plan of 22 A
Rome, ancient republican, plan of 23 B
Rome, medieval, plan of . . . 96 A
Rome, modern, plan of . . . 22 A
Rome, patr. . . . 52 J f
Rome, territorial expansion of 34, 35
Rome, univ. . . . 100 H f
Rome, vicinity of ancient . . . 35 ins. B
Rome, in New York . . . 192 D b
Rome, Temple of . . . 24 B
Rome, City of, Rom. dioc. . . . 42 E e
Romford . . . 75 J h
Romney . . .
Romont, castle . . . 91 O l
Romorantin . . . 126 B c
Romorantin, castle . . . 76 D c
Romsey, ab. . . . 100 A b
Romulus, Grave of . . .
Romulus, Hut of . . . 24 A
Roncaglia . . . 72 B c
Roncesvalles . . . 82 B a
Roncesvalles, mon. . . . 94 B c
Ronda . . . 82 A b
Ronnenberg . . . 52 C a
Ronsse . . . 117 B d
Roosbeke . . .
Roosendaal . . . 117 C c
Roper River . . . 172 C b
Ropicum . . . 26 C e
Roraima, mt. . . . 214 C b
Rorkes Drift . . . 175 N l
Rorschach . . . 142 D e
Rosalie, Fort . . . 191 G e
Rosario, in Arg. Rep. . . . 215 C f
Rosario, in Mexico . . . 213 B b
Rosasna . . . 153 O g
Roscianum . . . 31 F c
Roscommon, bp. . . . 97 C c
Roscommon, cty. . . . 127 I h
Rosebud, Ind. Res. . . . 188 F b
Roselle . . . 64 B b
Rosenfeld . . . 143 G i
Rosemarkie, bp. . . .
Rosetta . . . 174 J i
Rosheim . . . 126 E b
Rosières . . . 156 B a
Ross, bp., in Ireland . . . 97 B e
Ross, bp., in Scotland . . . 97 H b
Ross, cty. . . .
Ross, parl. bor. . . .
Ross, dist. . . .
Rossano . . . 64 C c
Rossano, abp. . . . 95 F d
Rossbach . . . 134 F c
Rossbühl Pass . . . 134 E d
Rossieny . . . 159 L a
Rossland . . . 212 D d
Rosslau . . . 123 G c
Rossomme, farm . . . 156 C c
Rossstall . . . 62 F d
Rosstock, mt. . . . 150 E c
Rostock, Hanse. cy. . . . 99 ins. B
Rostock, univ. . . . 100 H d
Rostov, on the Don R. . . . 71 N d
Rostov, north-east of Moscow 138 E d
Rostra, loc. in Rome . . . 24 A (6)
Rostra Julia, loc. in Rome . . . 24 B (15)
Rostro Hermoso . . . 108 N h
Röteln, lordship . . . 142 A e
Rotenturm Pass . . . 159 M f
Roth, ab. . . . 143 J j
Roth River, flowing into Danube R. . . . 143 I i
Roth River, flowing into Kocher River . . . 143 J g
Rothenburg, imp. cy. on the Tauber . . . 143 J g
Rothenfels, ruin . . . 143 J j
Rotherham . . . 162 E d
Rotherhithe . . . 75 I i
Rothesay . . .
Rothière, La . . . 154 C d
Rotomagus (Rouen) . . . 38 C c
Rottenburg . . . 143 G i
Rottenmünster, ab. . . . 143 G i
Rotterdam . . . 117 C c
Rottumeroog, isl. . . . 117 E a
Rottweil, imp. cy. . . . 143 G i
Roucy . . . 69 I f
Roucy, cty. . . . 69 I f
Rouen . . . 61 D b
Rouen, abp. . . . 94 B b
Rouen, gen. . . . 147 E b
Rouergue, cty. . . . 61 E d
Rouge, Fort . . .
Rouillé, Fort . . . 192 B b
Roulers . . . 117 B d
Roum, sultanate . . . 67 M f
Round Valley . . . 188 B c
Rouse's Point . . . 199 K b
Roussart, Le . . . 156 C c
Rousselaere . . . 117 B d
Roussillon . . . 126 D d
Roussillon, cty. . . . 61 E e
Roussillon, gouv. . . . 146 B c
Roussillon, prov. . . . 148 E f
Roussy . . . 69 J f
Rouvray . . . 76 E b
Rovereto . . . 114 F f
Rovigno . . . 90 D b
Rovigo . . . 90 J h
Rovuma River . . . 175 G f
Roxburgh . . .
Roxbury . . . 189 ins. B
Roxolani or Roxolans, people . 35 L d
Royal Canal . . . 126 B e
Royal Castle, in Athens . . . 23 D
Royal Niger Company . . . 174 D c
Royan . . . 76 C d
Rubi . . . 31 F a
Rubicon River . . . 27 G c
Rubruck or Rubruquis, William of, route of . . .
Rudau . . . 79 L a
Ruden, isl. . . . 123 G a
Rudiæ . . . 31 H b
Rudnia . . . 153 O f
Rudolf, lake . . . 175 G d
Rudolstadt . . . 62 F c
Rueda . . . 82 A a
Rue de la Chancellerie, street in Versailles . . . 149 A
Rue de la Paroisse, street in Versailles . . . 149 A
Rue de la Surintendance, street in Versailles . . . 149 A
Rue de l'Orangerie, street in Versailles . . . 149 A
Rue de Richelieu, street in Paris 149 B
Rue des Hôtels, street in Versailles . . . 149 A
Rue des Réservoirs, street in Versailles . . . 149 A
Rue de Faubourg Saint Honoré, street in Paris . . . 149 B
Rue du Temple, street in Paris 149 B
Rue Saint Antoine, street in Paris 149 B
Rue Saint Denis, street in Paris 149 B
Rue Saint Honoré, street in Paris 149 B
Rue Saint Jacques, street in Paris 149 B

Rue Saint Martin, street in Paris 149 B
Rue Saint Martin, street in Versailles 149 A
Rue Vivienne, street in Paris 149 B
Rufford, mon. 97 P h
Rugeley 162 D e
Rügen, isl. 63 G a
Rügen, princ. 79 I a
Rügenwalde 135 I a
Rügenwalde, Hanse. cy. 98 G c
Rugia (Rugen), isl. 38 E b
Rugians or Rugii, people
Ruginium (Rovigno) 27 H b
Ruha 77 L e
Ruhr River 62 D c
Ruith 142 C b
Rûm, sultanate, see Roum
Rumania, km. 164 D b
Rumania, princ. 164 D b
Rumanians, people 165 leg.
Rum Cay, isl. 105 F b
Rumelia, dist. 93 B b
Rumelia, Eastern, prov. 164 C b
Rumigny 69 J f
Runnymede 75 H i
Runsiens, people 188 B c
Rupert River 212 H c
Rupert's Land
Ruppin 79 H b
Ruppin, cty. 87 I b
Rura (Ruhr) River 39 I h
Rusa 138 E d
Rusaddir 38 B e
Rusellæ 27 F e
Rusicade 38 D e
Ruspæ or Ruspe 12 F c
Ruspina 38 E e
Russell 172 G d
Russia, reg., about 1000 59 J L c
Russia, reg., about 1190 71 L c
Russian Empire, about 1740 131 J b
Russian Empire, 14—18 cent. 138/139
Russian Empire, 1910 170 F/O c
Russians, people 47 L c
Russian States, 14 cent. 77 K a
Russo 71 M b
Rustchuk
Rustdorp 189 ins. C
Rustenburg 175 M l
Ruteni or Rutenis, see Rodez
Ruteni, people 38 C d
Ruthenians, people 168 leg.
Rutland, cty. 127 Y n
Rutland, parl. dist. 163 N e
Rütli 91 Q l
Rutuba River 26 B d
Rutuli, people 35 ins. B
Rutupiæ (Richborough) 51 Q i
Ruvo 90 F d
Rybinsk 167 M d
Rye 189 D c
Rye, parl. bor. 163 O g
Rypin 159 J b
Ryswick 122 C b
Rzhev 138 D d

Saale River, flowing into Elbe R. 63 F c
Saale River, flowing into Main R. 62 E c
Saalfeld 63 F c
Saalkreis, dist. 122 F c
Saanen 91 P l
Saane River 150 D c
Saarbrücken 62 D d
Saarlouis 122 D d
Saar River 114 D d
Saarwerden 114 D d
Saavedra, route of 107 B f, 110 F F g
Saaz 63 G c
Sabará 214 E d
Sabaria 42 F d
Sabate 27 G e
Sabatia, Vada 26 C c
Sabatinus, lake 27 G e
Sabatus River, in Bruttium 31 F c
Sabatus River, in Samnium 30 D b
Sabatum, Ad 31 F c
Sabellians, people 39 C c
Sabina, bp. 96 B a
Sabina, dist. 90 D c
Sabine River 211 G d
Sabini, people, west of L. Benacus 26 E b
Sabines, or Sabini, north-east of Rome 27 G e
Sabino 189 D c
Sabis River 39 H h
Sablé 76 C c
Sable, Cape, in Florida 187 K f
Sable, Cape, in Nova Scotia 186 M d
Sable Island 212 J d
Sabrata 12 F d
Sabrina (Severn) River 38 B b
Sabrina Æstuarium (Bristol Channel) 51 O i
Sabutum
Sacæ, Sacans, people 18 S h
Sacaraucæ, people 19 H b
Sacasene, dist. 35 N e
Sacaseni, people 18 G b
Sacer River 26 D e
Sachion
Sachsenburg, in Carinthia 135 G e
Sachsenburg, castle in Thuringia 115 ins. B
Sachsenhausen 78 F c
Sachsenheim, Gross 143 H h
Sachsenklemme, pass 154 F e
Sacile 154 G f
Sacketts Harbor 200 E b
Säckingen 142 A e
Säckingen, mon. 95 D b
Saco 189 C c
Saco River 189 C b
Sacramento, in Cal. 210 A c
Sacramento, in Mexico 198 D e
Sacramento River 210 A c
Sacra Urbs, Temple of 24 B
Sacred Mount 35 ins. B
Sacred Gate 23 D
Sacred Way, street in Athen 23 C
Sacred Way, street in Rome 24 A, B
Sacrificios, Isla de, isl. 106 D a
Sacriportus 35 ins. B
Sacrum, prom., in Corsica 26 D d
Sacrum, prom., in Portugal 38 A e
Sadowa 159 H c
Sæpinum 30 D a
Sæpta Julia, loc. in Rome 24 B
Sætabis 38 B e
Sævo, mt. 34 F a
Safed 68 ins. A
Sagadahoc 191 L c
Sagadahoc River 189 D b
Sagan 85 H e
Sagan, duchy 115 H c
Sagar 137 C d
Sagartians, people 8 D b
Sagartii 19 I d
Sagii, see Sées
Saginaw 211 I b
Saginaw Bay 211 I b
Saginaws, tribe 188 I b
Sagis River 27 G c
Sagone 148 C c
Sagra River 31 F d
Sagres 82 A b
Sagrus (Sangro) River 27 I e
Saguenay River 212 H d
Saguntum 38 C e
Sahagun 82 B a
Sahagun, mon. 94 A c
Sahara, desert 175 C b
Saigon 171 L g
Saint, see also Sankt
Saint-Affrique see Saint-Frique 126 C e
Saint Alban, church in London 75 G g (10)
Saint Albans, in England
Saint Albans, mon.
Saint Albans, parl. bor. 163 N f
Saint Albans, in Vermont 207 L b
Saint-Amand 156 B a
Saint-Amand-la-Haye 156 B a
Saint Andrew, church in London, near Holebourn Bridge 75 G g
Saint Andrew, church in London, on Leadenhall Street 75 G g (13)
Saint Andrew, Fort, in Georgia 193 D f
Saint Andrews, in Scotland
Saint Andrews, abp. 97 I b
Saint Andrews, univ. 100 E c
Saint Anne, in Mackenzie Ter. 212 D b
Saint Anne, church in Jerusalem 68 ins. B (14)
Saint Anthony, Falls of 191 G a
Saint-Antoine, near Paris 122 B d
Saint-Antoine, Faubourg, quarter in Paris 149 B
Saint-Antoine, mon. 148 C b
Saint-Antoine, Plaine, loc. in Versailles 149 A
Saint-Antoine, Rue, street in Paris 149 B
Saint Asaph, bp. 97 N h
Saint Augustine, in Florida 193 D g
Saint Augustine, church in London 75 G g (4)
Saint-Avit, mon. 94 C b
Saint Barthélemy, isl., in West India 213 F c
Saint Bartholomew, priory in London 75 G g
Saint Bartholomew's Spital, in London 75 G g
Saint Benets-at-Hulme, mon.
Saint-Benoit-sur-Loire, mon. 94 C b
Saint-Bernard, mon. 95 D b (S. B.)
Saint Bernard, Great, pass 26 B b
Saint Bernard, Little, pass 26 A b
Saint Bernardino, pass 26 D a
Saint Blaise, ab. 142 B e
Saint Blaise, mon. 142 B e
Saint Botolph, church near Aldgate, in London 75 G g
Saint Botolph, church near Bishopsgate, in London 75 G g
Saint Botolph, church near London Bridge, in London 75 G g (28)
Saint Bride, church in London 75 G g (2)
Saint-Brieuc 61 B b
Saint-Brieuc, bp. 94 B b
Saint-Bris 126 A d
Saint Callistus, Catacombs of 96 A
Saint Catharines 207 I b
Saint Charles, in Missouri 199 G c
Saint Charles, Fort, in Illinois 191 G d
Saint Charles, Fort, in Manitoba 191 F b
Saint-Chef, mon. 148 C b
Saint Christopher (St. Kitts), isl. 213 F c
Saint Clair, lake 200 B b
Saint Clairsville 206 ins.
Saint Clare, abbey in London 75 G g
Saint-Claude 126 D c
Saint-Claude, mon. 148 C b
Saint Clement's Danes, church in London 75 G g
Saint Clement's Well, loc. in London 75 G g
Saint-Cloud 114 B d
Saint-Cloud, Avenue de, in Versailles 149 A
Saint Croix, isl. 105 H c
Saint Croix River, between Minnesota and Wisconsin 191 G b
Saint Croix River, eastern boundary of Maine 191 L b
Saint Cross, mon. 100 A b
Saint Cyril 138 E d
Saint David, Fort (Cuddalore) 137 C f
Saint Davids (Mynyw)
Saint Davids, bp. 97 L j
Saint Demetrius, loc. near ancient Troy
Saint Denis, in Illinois 191 H d
Saint-Denis, near Paris 76 E b
Saint-Denis, mon. 94 C b

Saint Denis, on Réunion I. . . 175 I g
Saint-Denis, Faubourg, quarter in Paris . . . . 149 B
Saint-Denis, Porte, loc. in Paris 149 B
Saint-Denis, route of . . . . . . 190 E e
Saint-Denis, Rue, street in Paris 149 B
Saint-Dié, mon. . . . . 95 D b
Saint Dimitri, quarter in Constantinople . . . . 93 G e
Saint-Dizier . . . . 134 C d
Saint Domingue, col. . . . . . .
Saint Dunstan, in the East, church in London . . . . 75 G g (29)
Saint Dunstan, in the West, church in London . . . . 75 G g
Saint Edmund the King, church in London . . . . 75 G g (16)
Sainte-Foy . . . . 126 B d
Sainte-Geneviève . . . . 191 G d
Sainte-Geneviève, church in Paris . . . . 149 B
Saint Elias, mt. . . . . 186 E b
Saint Elias Range . . . . 212 ins.
Sainte-Marguerite, isl. . . . . . 126 E e
Sainte-Marie . . . . 191 I c
Sainte-Marie, isl. . . . . 175 I f
Sainte-Menehould . . . . 134 C d
Saintes . . . . 76 C d
Saintes, bp. . . . . 94 B b
Saint Ethelburga, church in London . . . . 75 G g
Sainte-Thérèse, Fort . . . . . . 189 B b
Saint-Étienne . . . . 76 F d
Saint-Étienne-de-Vaux, mon. 94 B b
Saint-Eustache, Saint Eustatius, isl. . . . . 213 F c
Saint Fagans . . . . 127 V o
Saint-Flour . . . . 76 E d
Saint-Flour, bp. . . . . 94 C b
Saint Francis River . . . . 189 B b
Saint-François-de-Sales . . . . 189 C a
Saint-Frique . . . . 126 C e
Saint-Fuscien, mon. . . . . 94 C b
Saint Gall . . . . 56 D c
Saint Gall, mon. . . . . 95 D b
Sainte-Geneviève, church in Paris . . . . 149 B
Saint George, Fort, in Florida 193 D f
Saint George, Fort (Madras) . . 137 D f
Saint George Mouth, Danube R. 164 D b
Saint Georges, in Maine . . . . 189 D c
Saint George's Bay . . . . 215 C g
Saint George's Channel . . . . . 49 C f
Saint-Germain-en-Laye . . . . 126 C b
Saint-Germain, Faubourg, quarter in Paris . . . . 149 B
Saint-Germain-des-Prés, church in Paris . . . . 149 B
Saint Germans, mon. . . . . 97 M k
Saint Germans, parl. bor. . . . 163 J g
Saint-Gildas-de-Ruis, mon. . 94 B b
Saint-Gildas-de-Bois, mon. . . 94 B b
Saint Giles, church in Jerusalem . . . . 68 ins. B (5)
Saint-Gilles, mon. . . . . 94 C c
Saint Gotthard Pass . . . . 91 Q l
Saint Helena, isl., in the Atlantic Ocean . . . . 108 Q i
Saint Helena Island, off S. C. . 193 ins. C
Saint Helens, mon. . . . . 100 A b
Saint Helen's Priory, in London 75 G g
Saint-Hippolyte . . . . 143 ins. F
Saint-Honorat, isl. . . . . 126 E e
Saint-Honoré, Faubourg, quarter in Paris . . . . 149 B
Saint-Honoré, Rue, street in Paris . . . . 149 B
Saint-Honoré, Rue du Faubourg, street in Paris . . . . 149 B
Saint-Hubert . . . . 117 D d
Saint-Hubert, ab. of . . . . 117 D e
Saint-Hubert, mon. . . . . 95 D a
Saint-Ignace, in Canada . . . . 191 J c
Saint-Ignace, in Michigan . . . 191 H b
Saint Inigoes . . . . 192 C d
Saint Ives . . . . 98 ins. A
Saint Ives, parl. bor. . . . . 163 I g
Saint-Jaques, Faubourg, quarter in Paris . . . . 149 B
Saint-Jaques, Rue, street in Paris 149 B
Saint James, church, in London 75 G g (23)
Saint James the Elder, church, in Jerusalem . . . . 68 ins. B (11)
Saint James the Less, chapel, in Jerusalem . . . . 68 ins. B (6)
Saint-Jean-d'Acre . . . . 68 ins. A
Saint-Jean-d'Angély . . . . 76 C c
Saint-Jean-d'Angély, mon. . . . 94 B b
Saint-Jean-de-Losne . . . . . . 69 J g
Saint-Jean-de-Maurienne . . . 130 O i
Saint-Jean-Pied-de-Port . . . 126 A e
Saint John, in Quebec . . . . . 194 E a
Saint John, in New Brunswick 212 I d
Saint John, Fort, on Peace R. 212 C c
Saint John, Fort, on Richelieu R. 189 B b
Saint John, Knights of . . . . . 73 F c
Saint John, lake . . . . 212 H d
Saint John, priory in London . 75 G g
Saint John River . . . . 211 L a
Saint John Lateran, ch. . . . . . 96 A
Saint John the Baptist, ch. . . 68 ins. B (4)
Saint Johns, in Newfoundland 212 J d
Saint Johns-at-Colchester, mon. 97 R j
Saint John's Field . . . . 75 I h
Saint John's Island (Prince Edward Island) . . . . 212 I d
Saint Johns River . . . . 211 I e
Saint Joseph, in Missouri . . . 211 G c
Saint Joseph, in Michigan . . . 211 H b
Saint Joseph, Fort . . . .
Saint Joseph River . . . . 191 H c
Saint-Josse . . . . 76 D a
Saint-Jouin-de-Marnes, mon. . 94 B b
Saint Julian, Port . . . . 108 K l
Saint Katherine, hospital in London . . . . 75 G g
Saint Katherine Cree, bldg. in London . . . . 75 G g (14)
Saint Kitts (St. Christopher), isl. 213 F c
Saint Ladre, postern, gate in Jerusalem . . . . 68 ins. B
Saint-Laurent, mon. . . . . 94 C b
Saint Laurentius Island . . . . . 109 V j
Saint Lawrence, church in London . . . . 75 G g (11)
Saint Lawrence, Gulf of . . . . 186 M d
Saint Lawrence Basin . . . . . . 187 K-L d
Saint Lawrence Island . . . . . 180 J a
Saint Lawrence River . . . . . . 186 L d
Saint-Lazare, ch. . . . . 149 B
Saint Lazarus Islands . . . . . . 212 F b
Saint Leger, route of . . . . . . 195 D a
Saint-Lô . . . . 76 C b
Saint-Lô, mon. . . . . 94 B b
Saint-Lomer-le-Moutier, mon. 94 C b
Saint Louis, in Canada . . . . . 191 I c
Saint Louis, in Missouri . . . . 191 G d
Saint Louis, in Senegal . . . . . 174 B c
Saint Louis, Fort, in Illinois Country . . . . 191 H c
Saint Louis, Fort, in Texas . . 190 F f
Saint-Louis, Ile, isl. . . . . 149 B
Saint Louis River . . . . 188 H a
Saint Louis and San Francisco Grant . . . . 210 D c
Saint Lucia, isl. . . . . 213 F c
Saint Magnus, church in London 75 G g (27)
Saint-Maixent . . . . 126 A c
Saint-Maixent, mon. . . . . 94 B b
Saint-Malo . . . . 76 B b
Saint-Malo, bp. . . . . 94 B b
Saint-Marcel, Faubourg, quarter in Paris . . . . 149 B
Saint-Marcel, mon. . . . . 94 C c
Saint Margarets Church, London 75 G g
Saint Marks . . . . 193 B f
Saint-Martin, near Ligny . . . . 156 B b
Saint Martin, ch. . . . . 68 ins. B (10)
Saint-Martin, Faubourg, quarter in Paris . . . . 149 B
Saint Martin, isl. . . . . 213 F c
Saint-Martin, Porte, loc. in Paris 149 B
Saint-Martin, Rue, street in Paris . . . . 149 B
Saint-Martin, Rue, street in Versailles . . . . 149 A
Saint Martin le Grand, church in London . . . . 75 G g
Saint Martin of Tours, mon. . . 94 C b
Saint Martin Outwich, church in London . . . . 75 G g (12)
Saint Mary Aldermary, church in London . . . . 75 G g (19)
Saint Mary Bothaw, church in London . . . . 75 G g (25)
Saint Mary Magdalen, church in Jerusalem . . . . 68 ins. B (13)
Saint Mary Magdalene, church in London, east of St. Pauls 75 G g (7)
Saint Mary Magdalene, church in London, south of St. Pauls 75 G g (20)
Saint Mary of Grace, abbey in London . . . . 75 G g
Saint Mary of the Germans, hospital . . . . 68 ins. B (9)
Saint Mary of the Latins, ch. 68 ins. B (3)
Saint Mary Overey's Priory, in London . . . . 75 G g
Saint Mary Spital, bldg. in London . . . . 75 G g
Saint Mary's-at-York, mon. . . 97 Q h
Saint Mary's, in Maryland . . . 192 C d
Saint Mary Somerset, church in London . . . . 75 G g (21)
Saint Mary's River . . . . 193 D f
Saint-Maur-des-Fossées, mon. 94 C b
Saint-Maur-sur-Loire, mon. . 94 B b
Saint-Maurice, mon. . . . . 91 O l
Saint Maurice River . . . . 212 H d
Saint Mawes, parl. bor. . . . . . 163 J g
Saint Maximin, mon. . . . . 95 D b
Saint Michael, in Alaska . . . . 198 ins. A
Saint Michael, church in London . . . . 75 G g (15)
Saint Michael le Querne, church in London . . . . 75 G g (9)
Saint Michael Paternoster, church in London . . . . 75 G g (24)
Saint-Michel, Faubourg, quarter in Paris . . . . 149 B
Saint-Michel, Pont, loc. in Paris 149 B
Saint-Mihiel . . . . 184 E c
Saint Neots, mon. . . . . 97 Q i
Saint Nicolas . . . . 117 C c
Saint Olave, church in London 75 G g
Saint-Omer . . . . 76 E a
Saint-Omer, mon. . . . . 94 C a
Saintonge, cty. . . . . 61 C d
Saintonge, prov. . . . . 148 D e
Saintonge and Angumois, gouv. 146 A b
Saint-Papoul . . . . 94 C c
Saint-Paul, near Nice . . . . . . 126 E e
Saint Paul, in Minnesota . . . . 199 G b
Saint-Paul, bp., near Orange . 94 C c
Saint Paul Island . . . . 182 II k
Saint Paul de Loanda . . . . . . 175 E e
Saint Paul's, church in London 75 G g
Saint Paul's Bakehouse, in London . . . . 75 G g (31)
Saint Paul's Cross, in London 75 G g (3)
Saint Peter in Gallicantem, church in Jerusalem . . . . . . 68 ins. B
Saint Peter, church in Cheapside, London . . . . 75 G g (8)
Saint Peter, church in Cornhill, London . . . . 75 G g
Saint Peter, church in Jerusalem 68 ins. B (12)
Saint Peter, Patrimony of (States of the Church) . . . . 64 ins.
Saint Peter's, church in Rome 22 A, 96 A
Saint Petersburg . . . . 138 D c
Saint Peters' Yard, Hanse. for. off. . . . . 88 N b

Saint Philip, Fort . . . 200 I g
Saint-Pierre, Fort . . . 191 G b
Saint-Pierre, isl. . . . 212 J d (St. P.)
Saint-Pol . . . 76 E a
Saint-Pol-de-Leon . . . 76 A b
Saint-Pol-de-Leon, bp. . . . 94 B b
Saint-Pons, bp. . . . 94 C c
Saint-Pourçain, mon. . . . 94 C b
Saint-Quentin . . . 61 E b
Saint-Rambert, mon. . . . 95 D b
Saint Regis . . . 200 F a
Saint Regis, Ind. Res. . . . 188 L b
Saint-Riquier, mon. . . . 94 C a
Saint-Roch, church in Paris . 149 B
Saint Romanus, Late of . . . .
Saint-Sacrement, lake . . . 192 E b
Saint-Sauveur . . . 69 I g
Saint-Seine, mon. . . . 95 C b
Saint-Seurin, mon. . . . 94 B c
Saint-Sever, castle . . . 76 C e
Saint-Sever, mon. . . . 94 C c
Saint Simeon . . . 68 C b
Saint Simon Island . . . 193 D f
Saint Sophia, church in Constantinople . . . 93 G e (1)
Saint Stephen, church in London 75 G e (17)
Saint Stephen, gate . . . 68 ins. B
Saint Stephen, street . . . 68 ins. B
Saint-Sulpice, mon. . . . 95 D b
Saint Swithin, church in London 75 G g (18)
Saint-Thierry, mon. . . . 94 C b (S. T.)
Saint Thomas, isl., Gulf of Guinea . . . 175 D e
Saint Thomas, isl., West Indies 213 F c
Saint Thomas of Acon, church in London . . . 75 G g (6)
Saint-Trond . . . 117 C d
Saint-Trond, mon. . . . 95 D a
Saint Trudpert, mon. . . . 95 D b
Saint-Urbain, mon., in France 95 D b
Saint Urban, mon., in Switzerland . . . 91 P k
Saint-Vaast, mon., near Arras . 94 C a
Saint-Vaast-de-la-Hougue . . 126 A b
Saint-Valery, mon. . . . 94 C a
Saint-Vandrille, mon. . 94 C b (St. Van.)
Saint-Victor, Faubourg, quarter in Paris . . . 149 B
Saint Vincent, cape . . . 83 J h
Saint Vincent, isl. . . . 213 F c
Saint Vincent Gulf . . . 172 C d
Saint-Vrain, Fort . . . 210 E b
Saint Xavier . . . 191 H c
Saint-Wandrille, mon. see Saint-Vandrille
Saint-Yrieux . . . 126 B d
Sairam . . .
Sais . . . 4 F c
Sajama, volcano . . . 214 C d
Sajo River . . . 115 K d
Sakaria River . . . 93 C b
Sakhalin, isl. . . . 171 P c
Sala (Saale) River . . . 38 E b
Saladin, Dom. of . . . 71 M g
Salamanca . . . 82 A a
Salamanca, bp. . . . 94 A c
Salamanca, univ. . . . 100 D f
Salamis, in Attica . . . 16 B b
Salamis, on Cyprus I. . . . 47 M f
Salamis, isl. . . . 15 D b
Salapia . . . 31 F a
Salapia, lake . . . 31 F a
Salarian Gate . . . 22 A
Salarian Way, road . . . 27 H e
Salassi, people . . . 26 B b
Saldæ . . . 38 C e
Saldaña . . . 82 B a
Salem, in Mass. . . . 189 ins. B
Salem, in New Jersey . . . 192 D d
Salem, in Ohio . . . 207 I b
Salem, in Oregon . . . 198 A b
Salem, in Palestine . . . 7 C d
Salem Creek . . . 192 ins.
Salemi . . . 161 I i
Saleph River . . . 67 M f
Salerno . . . 90 E d
Salerno, abp. . . . 95 F e
Salerno, princ. . . . 64 C b
Salerno, univ. . . . 100 H f
Salernum (Salerno) . . . 30 D b
Saletio . . . 39 J i
Salford . . . 162 D d
Salford, parl. bor. . . . 163 L d (Salf.)
Salians, people . . . 50 D b
Salihiyeh . . . 174 J i
Salina Cruz . . . 213 C c
Salinæ (Castellane) . . . 26 A d
Salins . . . 69 J f
Salinus (Saline) River . . . 27 I e
Salisbury, in England . . . .
Salisbury, bp. . . . 97 P j
Salisbury, parl. bor. . . 163 M f (Salisb.)
Salisbury, in Mass. . . . 189 C c (Salisb.)
Salisbury, in N. Carolina . . . 195 A f
Salisbury, in Rhodesia . . . 175 G f
Salisbury Plain . . . 49 F f
Salkhat . . . 6 F c
Sallentini . . . 31 G b
Sallentinum, prom. . . . 31 H c
Sallust, Gardens of . . . 22 A
Salm, in the Ardennes . . . 62 C c
Salm, in the Vosges . . . 126 E b
Salm, cty. in the Vosges . . . 134 D d
Salm, cty., in Westphalia . . . 151 H f
Salmansweiler, ab. . . . 142 D e
Salmantica (Salamanca) . . . 38 A d
Salmon Falls, town . . . 189 C c
Salmon River . . . 198 B a
Salmydessus . . . 39 N l
Salò . . . 150 F d
Salobreña . . . 82 B b
Salodurum (Solothurn) . . . 39 I j
Salofo, reg. . . . 108 P f
Salona, in Dalmatia . . . 42 F e
Salona, in Greece . . . 89 B c
Salonæ (Salona, in Dalmatia) . 38 F d
Salonica or Saloniki . . . 59 I e
Salsette Island . . . 137 B e (S.)
Salt River, Ind. Res. . . . 188 D d
Salta . . . 215 C e
Saltanovka . . . 153 O g
Saltillo . . . 201 E d
Salt Lake City . . . 198 C b
Salto . . . 215 D f
Saltus Castulonensis, mts. . . . 38 B e
Saluda River . . . 193 C d
Salurnis . . . 27 F a
Salus, Gate of . . . 23 B
Salus, Temple of . . . 22 A
Saluzzo . . . 90 H h
Saluzzo, marq. . . . 126 E d
Salvador, country . . . 213 D c
Salvatierra . . . 213 ins.
Salwin River . . .
Salz . . . 55 R i
Salza . . . 72 C a
Salzach River . . . 63 G e
Salzburg . . . 63 G e
Salzburg, abp. . . . 95 E b
Salzburg, elect. . . . 157 I g
Salzungen . . . 62 E c
Salzungen, mon. . . . 95 E a
Salzwedel . . . 62 F b
Salzwedel, Hanse. cy. . . . 99 ins. B
Sama River . . . 214 B d
Samag . . . 99 M e
Samalanga . . . 112 C c
Samana, cape . . . 105 G c
Samana, isl. . . . 105 F b
Samar, isl. . . . 199 ins. H
Samara . . . 139 H e
Samara River, see Sambre River and Somme River
Samaria . . . 7 C d
Samaria, dist. . . . 7 C d
Samarcand or Samarkand . . . 92 G d
Samarobriva (Amiens) . . . 38 C c
Samaron . . . 99 M e
Samarovskoe . . . 170 H b
Sambalpur . . . 137 D d
Sambhal . . .
Sambhal, reg. . . .
Sambor . . .
Sambracitan Gulf . . . 26 A d
Sambre River . . . 62 C c
Sambreffe . . . 156 B a
Same . . . 10 B d
Samicum . . . 14 B b
Samme River . . . 156 A a
Samnites, people . . .
Samnium, reg. . . . 30 D a
Samnium, Rom. prov. . . . 42 E e (7)
Samoa Islands . . . 199 ins. D
Samogitia, reg. . . . 88 J d
Samonium, prom. . . . 14 ins.
Samos . . . 13 E c
Samos, isl. . . . 13 E c
Samos, theme . . . 59 J f
Samosata . . . 20 H d
Samothrace, isl. . . .
Samsun . . . 89 K f
Samoyedes, people . . . .
San River . . . 159 L d
Sana . . .
Sanabria, dist. . . . 83 J g
San Agostinho, Cabo, cape . .
San Antonio . . . 210 F e
San Antonio, Cape . . . 105 D b
San Antonio River . . . 190 F f
San Antonio de Béjar . . . 190 F f
San Bernardino, pass, see Saint Bernardino
San Bernardino Mountains . . . 187 H e
San Bernardino Strait . . . 199 ins. H
San Bernardo, isl. . . . 107 A h
San Blas . . . 213 B b
San Buenaventura . . . 190 B e
San Carlos de Ancud . . . 215 B g
San Carlos de Monterey . . . 190 A d
Sancerre . . . 76 E c
Sancerre, cty. . . . 76 E c
San Cesareo, ch. . . . 96 A
San Clemente, ch. . . . 96 A
San Crisogono, ch. . . . 96 A
San Cristóbal . . . 213 C c
San Cristóbal, isl. . . . 110 HH i
Sanctus Ægidius, see Saint-Gilles
Sanctus Dionysius, see Saint-Denis
Sanctus Gallus, see Saint Gall
Sancus, Gate of . . . 23 B
Sand . . . 154 F e
Sandal Castle . . . 127 X m
Sandalwood Island . . . 172 A b
Sandau . . . 154 G b
Sandía . . . 214 C d
San Diego . . . 190 B e
Sandomierz . . . 87 M c
Sandrocotta, Kingdom of . . . 18 S h
Sandu . . .
Sandusky . . . 200 B c
Sandusky, Fort . . . 194 C b
Sandusky Bay . . . 200 B c
Sandwich, in Canada . . . 200 B b
Sandwich, in England . . . .
Sandwich, parl. bor. . . . 163 P f
Sandwich, in Mass. . . . 189 C d
Sandy Cape . . . 172 E c
Sandy Desert, Great . . . 172 B c
Sandy Hook, cape . . . 192 E c
Sandy Island, Great . . . 172 E c
Sandy Sea, desert . . .
Sane, in Acte . . . 11 E b
Sane, in Pallene . . . 11 E b
San Estéban . . .
Sanf, reg. . . .
San Felipe . . . 215 B f
San Fernando . . . 214 C b
San Francisco, in California . 190 A d
San Francisco, in Florida . . 193 D g
San Francisco, Cape . . . 111 A a

San Francisco Bay . . . . 187 G e
San Francisco Mountains. . . . 187 H e
San Francisco de la Espada. . 190 F f
San Francisco de los Nechas . 191 F e
San Francisco de los Tejas . . 191 F e
Sanga River . . . . 175 E d
San Gabriel . . . . 190 B e
Sangala . . . . 19 L d
Sangarius (Sakaria) River . . . 20 D b
San Germano . . . . 72 C c
San Gerónimo de Yuste, mon. 94 A c
San Gimignano . . . . 90 L j
San Giovanni, Porta, gate . . . 22 A
San Giovanni in Fiori, mon. . 95 F d (S. G. i. F.)
San Giusto, mon. . . . . 95 D b
Sangpo River . . . .
San Gregorio Magno, mon. . . 96 A
San Ildefonso . . . . 184 C d
San Ildefonso, castle . . . . . . 130 C e
Sanitium, see Senez
San Javier del Bac . . . . 190 C e
San Joaquin River . . . . 198 A c
San Jorge, Gulf of. . . . . 215 C g
San Jorge da Mina. . . . . . .
San Jorge da Minha, see San Jorge da Mina
San José, in California . . . . . 190 A d
San José, in Costa Rica . . . . 213 D d
San José, in Guatemala . . . . 213 C c
San José, in Uruguay . . . . . . 215 D f
San José, pen. . . . . 215 C g
San José de Cúcuta . . . . 214 B b
San Juan, in Arg. Rep.. . . . . 215 C f
San Juan, in Porto Rico . . . . 199 ins. G
San Juan Island . . . . 198 A a
San Juan River, in Ecuador . 111 B a
San Juan River, in New Mexico 198 D c
San Juan River, in Nicaragua. 213 D c
San Juan Bautista, in Mexico . 213 C c
San Juan Bautista (Porto Rico), isl. . . . . 105 G c
San Juan Capistrano, in California . . . . 190 B e
San Juan Capistrano, in Texas 190 F f
San Juan de la Peña, mon. . . 94 B c
San Juan del Norte . . . . 213 D c
San Juan de los Caballeros . . 190 D d
San Juan de Ulúa, Fort . . . . 106 D a
Sankt-Blasien, see Saint Blaise
Sankt-Florian, mon. . . . . 95 E b
Sankt-Gallen, see Saint Gall
Sankt-Georgen . . . . 142 B d
Sankt-Goar . . . . 62 D c
Sankt-Goar, mon. . . . . 95 D a
Sankt-Gotthard Pass . . . . . . 91 Q l
Sankt-Gotthard, in Hungary . 123 I e
Sankt-Jacob . . . . 91 P k
Sankt-Lambrecht, mon. . . . . . 80 D h
Sankt-Leonhardt . . . . 154 F e
Sankt-Luziensteig, pass . . . . 150 E c
Sankt-Märgen, mon. . . . . 142 B d
Sankt-Maximin, mon. . . . . . . 95 D b
Sankt-Peter, ab. . . . . 142 B d
Sankt-Pölten . . . . 63 H d
Sankt-Pölten, mon. . . . . 80 D g
Sankt-Trudpert, ab. . . . . 142 A e
Sankt-Trudpert, mon. . . . . . . 95 D b
Sankt-Urban, mon. . . . . 91 P k
Sankt-Vith . . . . 117 E d
Sankt-Wendel . . . . 154 D d
San Leo . . . . 64 B b
San Leo, bp. . . . . 95 E c
San Lorenzo del Escorial, mon. 94 B c
San Lorenzo in Damaso, ch.. . 96 A
San Lorenzo in Lucina, ch. . . 96 A
San Lorenzo fuori le Mura, ch. 96 A
San Lucar de Barrameda . . . . 83 J h
San Lucas, Cape . . . . 187 H f
San Luis, in Arg. Rep. . . . . . 215 C f
San Luis Amarillas. . . . . 190 F e
San Luis Obispo . . . . 190 A d
San Luis Potosí . . . . 201 E e
San Luis Potosí, state . . . . . 213 B b
San Marco, in Calabria . . . . . 90 F e
San Marco, bp. . . . . 95 F d
San Marco, church in Rome . . 96 A
San Marino, rep. . . . . 90 D c
San Martin, isl. . . . . 105 H c
San Martin, mon. . . . . 94 C d
San Mateo, Bahia de, bay . . . 111 B a
San Mateo, Fort. . . . . 191 I e
San Mateo River . . . . 191 I e
San Matias, Gulf of . . . . 215 C g
San Michele . . . . 64 C b
San Michele, mon. . . . . 95 F c
San Miguel, in California . . . . 190 A d
San Miguel (Piura). . . . . 111 A c
San Miguel, in Salvador . . . . 213 D c
San Miguel (Tangarara). . . . . 111 A b
San Miguel Allende . . . . 213 ins.
San Miguel de Cuellar . . . . . 191 G e
San Miguel de Gualdape . . . . 191 J e
San Miguel, Cape. . . . . 105 F c
San Miguel, Gulf of . . . . 105 E e
San Miguel River. . . . . 214 C d
San Millan de la Cogolla, mon. 94 B c
San Miniato al Tedesco. . . . . 90 L j
San-mun Bay . . . .
San Pablo. 216
San Pablo, isl. . . . . 107 D i
San Pancrazio, ch. . . . . 96 A
San Pancrazio, Porta, gate . . . 22 A
San Paola, Porta, gate. . . . . . 22 A
San Paolo fuori le Mura, ch. . 96 A
San Pedro . . . . 191 I e
San Pedro, Rio, R. . . . . 190 C e
San Pedro y San Pablo, Rio de (Arkansas R.) . . . . 190 E d
San Pietro, Piazza di, loc. in Rome 22 A
San Pietro in Vincoli, ch. . . . . 96 A
San Remo . . . . 130 P k
San Roman, Cape . . . . 105 F d
San Roque, Cape . . . .
San Sabá . . . . 190 F e
San Salvador, in Angola . . . . 175 E e
San Salvador (Bahia) . . . . . .
San Salvador, in Salvador . . . 105 C d
San Salvador, isl. . . . . 105 F b
San Sebastian, in Columbia . . 105 E e
San Sebastian, in Spain . . . . . 82 H e
San Sebastiano, ch. . . . . 96 A
San Sebastiano, Porta, gate . . 22 A
San Sebastiano, Via di Porta, street . . . . 22 A
San Severino . . . . 90 E d
San Severo . . . . 90 E d
San Silvestro, mon. . . . . 95 E c
San Silvestro in Capite, ch. . . 96 A
San Sisto, ch. . . . . 96 A
San Stefano, near Constantinople 164 D b
San Stefano Rotondo, ch. . . . 96 A
Santa Anna (Goyaz) . . . . 214 D d
Santa Balbina, ch. . . . . 96 A
Santa Bárbara, in California . . 190 B e
Santa Bárbara, in Mexico . . . 190 D f
Santa Bárbara Islands . . . . . . 187 H e
Santa Catalina Island . . . . . . 108 M j
Santa Catharina, state . . . . . 215 D e
Santa Catharina Island . . . . . 215 E e
Santa Cecilia in Trastevere, ch. 96 A
Santa Clara, in California . . . 190 A d
Santa Clara, in Cuba . . . . . . 213 D b
Santa Clara Island . . . . 111 A b
Santa Croce in Gerusalemme, ch. 96 A
Santa Cruz, in Brazil . . . . . . 214 F d
Santa Cruz de la Sierra . . . . . 214 C d
Santa Cruz de Teneriffe . . . . 174 B b
Santa Cruz Quiché. . . . . 105 B c
Santa Cruz, Cape . . . . 105 E c
Santa Cruz, Rio, R. . . . . 190 C e
Santa Cruz, Terra de (Brazil) . 108 M i
Santa Cruz, isl., Atlantic Ocean 105 H c
Santa Cruz Islands, Pacific Ocean 172 F b
Santa Cruz River, in Patagonia 215 B g
Santa Elena, Punta, cape. . . . 111 A b
Santa Fé, in Arg. Rep. . . . . . 215 C f
Santa Fé, in New Mexico . . . 190 D d
Santa Fé, in Spain . . . . 184 C e
Santa Fé, audiencia . . . . 215 ins.
Santa Fé, mon. in Spain . . . . 94 B d
Santa Fé Trail, route . . . . . . 210 E c
Sant'Agata in Suburra, ch.. . . 96 A
Sant'Agata, bp. . . . . 95 ins.
Santa Gloria, Puerto de. . . . . 105 E c
Sant'Agnese fuori le Mura, ch. 96 A
Sant'Agostino, ch. . . . . 96 A
Santa Isabel . . . . 214 E c
Santa Isabel de la Estrella, isl. 110 G G h
Sant'Alessio . . . . 96 A
Santa Lucia, in Italy . . . . . . 161 H e
Santa Lucia, in Florida. . . . . 191 I f
Santa Lucia Bay . . . . 175 N l
Santa Maria, in Arg. Rep. . . . 215 C e
Santa Maria, in Brazil . . . . . . 214 E c
Santa Maria Aventinese, ch. . . 96 A
Santa Maria de la Concepción, isl. . . . . 105 F b
Santa Maria della Pace, ch. . . 96 A
Santa Maria in Cosmedin, ch.. 96 A
Santa Maria in Domnica, ch. . 96 A
Santa Maria in Trastevere, ch. 96 A
Santa Maria la Antigua del Darien . . . . 105 E e
Santa Maria Maggiore, ch. . . . 96 A
Santa Maria Rotonda, ch. . . . . 22 A
Santa Marta . . . . 105 F d
Santander. . . . . 82 B a
Santander, bp. . . . . 94 B c
Sant'Andrea, mon. . . . . 96 A
Sant'Angelo, castle. . . . . 96 A
Sant'Apollinare in Classe, mon. 95 E e
Santa Prassede, ch.. . . . . 96 A
Santa Prisca, ch. . . . . 96 A
Santa Pudenziana, ch. . . . . . . 96 A
Santarem, in Brazil. . . . . 214 D c
Santarem, in Portugal . . . . . . 82 A b
Santa Rosalia . . . . 213 B b
Santa Sabina, ch. . . . . 96 A
Santas Creus, mon. . . . . 94 C c
Santa Severina, in Calabria . . 90 F e
Santa Severina, abp. . . . . 95 F d
Santa Susanna, ch. . . . . 96 A
Santee River . . . . 193 E e
San Teodore, ch. . . . . 96 A
Santhià . . . . 130 Q i
San Thomé. . . . . 112 B b
San Thomé, Cape . . . .
Santiago, in Chile . . . . 215 B f
Santiago de Compostella . . . .
Santiago de Compostella, abp. .
Santiago de Cuba. . . . . 213 E c
Santiago del Estero . . . . 215 C e
Santiago, isl. (Jamaica) . . . . . 105 E c
Santiago River. . . . . 111 B a
Santi Apostoli, ch. . . . . 96 A
Santi Cosma e Damiano, ch. . . 96 A
Santi Giovanni e Paolo, ch. . . 96 A
Santillana . . . . 82 B a
Santi Quattro Coronati, ch. . . 96 A
Santistéban . . . . 82 B b
Santo Colmado, mon. . . . . . . 94 A c
Santo Domingo . . . . 105 G c
Santo Domingo, rep. . . . . 213 E c
Santo Domingo, Audiencia of. 213 E b
Santones, see Saintes
Santones, people . . . . 38 B c
Sant'Onofrio, ch. . . . . 22 A
Santos, city in Brazil . . . . . . 215 E e
Santos Cosmoy Damiano, mon. 94 A c
Santo Spirito, mon. . . . . 95 E c
Santo Stefano . . . . 164 D b
Santo Tomas, in Guatemala . . 213 D c
Santo Tomas, in Lower Cal. . . 190 B e
San Vicente Ferrer . . . . 190 B e
San Vitale, ch. . . . . 96 A
San Zoilo, mon. . . . . 94 B c
Sanzumata . . . .
São Christovão . . . . 214 F d
São Francisco River . . . . 214 E d
São João, in Minas Geraes . . 214 E e
São João da Barra . . . . 214 E e

São Jorge dos Ilheos 214 F d
São José, in Amazonas 214 C b
São Leopoldo 215 D e
São Luiz de Maranhão 214 E c
Saona, isl. 105 G c
Saône River 62 C e
Saône, Haute, dept. 148 F e
Saône-et-Loire, dept. 148 E e
São Paulo 215 E e
São Paulo, state 214 D e
São Pedro (Rio Grande) 215 D f
São Salvador 214 F e
São Sebastião 215 E e
São Sebastião Island 215 E e
São Thomé, cape, see San Thomé
São Thomé, isl. 108 R h
São Vicente, in Brazil 215 E e
São Vicente, mon., in Portugal 94 A d
Sapera
Sapis River 27 F d
Sapphe 20 J d
Saracano 99 N d
Saracenic poss. 58 D F f
Saracens, people, see Arabs 45 leg.
Saragossa 82 B a
Saragossa, abp. 94 B c
Saragossa, emir. 83 E c
Saragossa, univ. 100 E f
Sarai 92 E c
Saraitchikovsk
Sarakhs
Sarandi 215 D f
Sarangians, people 8 E b
Saransk 139 G e
Saratoga 194 L f
Saratoga, proposed state in U.S.
Saratoga, Fort 192 E b
Saratov 139 G e
Saravus (Saar) River 39 I i
Sarawak, col. 171 M h
Sardica 39 M l
Sardinia, isl. 2 E d
Sardinia, km., 16 cent. 118 F e
Sardinia, km., 18 cent. 130 E e
Sardinia, km., 19 cent. 161 F e
Sardinia, Rom. prov. 34 F e
Sardinia, W. Rom. prov. 42 D e (8)
Sardis 13 F b
Sared River 7 D f
Sarepta 6 C b
Sari
Sarius (Serio) River 26 D b
Sarlat 76 D d
Sarlat, mon. 94 C c
Sarmatæ, people 18 F a
Sarmatia, reg. 35 J c
Sarmizegetusa 39 M k
Sarnen 91 Q l
Sarni 26 F b
Sarnia, isl. 38 B c
Sarnius (Atrek) River 19 H c
Sarno, bp. 95 ins.
Sarnus (Sarno) River 30 D b
Saronic Gulf 15 D b
Sarpedon, prom. 33 D b
Sarsina 27 G d
Sarsina, bp. 95 E c
Sarta River, see Sarthe River
Sartaba, mt. 7 C d
Sarthe, dept. 148 D e
Sarthe River 69 C c
Sarukhan, reg. 89 I g
Sarum, Old 60 F e
Sarus River 20 F d
Sarzana 90 L i
Sarzana, bp. 95 D c
Sasbach, near Achern 142 B c
Sasbach, near Alt-Breisach 142 A d
Sashiversk 171 P b
Saskatchewan, Fort 212 D c
Saskatchewan, prov. 212 E c
Saskatchewan River 186 I c
Saskatchewan River, North 186 I c
Saskatchewan River, South 186 I c
Sason 31 I b
Saspirans, people 8 I d
Sassanids, Dom. of the 43 K g
Sassari 77 F d
Sassula 35 ins. B
Saszvaros 159 L f
Satara 137 B e
Saternus (Santerno) River 27 F c
Satganw
Saticula 30 D a
Satilla River 193 C f
Satpura Mountains 137 C d
Satricum 30 B a
Sattagydans, people 8 K e
Saturn, Temple of
Saturnia 27 F e
Saucourt 56 C b
Sauer River 117 E e
Saufeld 62 F c
Saugona River, see Saône River
Saugus River 189 ins. B
Sauk and Fox, Ind. Res. 188 H b
Sauks and Foxes, tribes 188 H b
Saulgau 143 H i
Sault Sainte Marie, in Michigan 191 I b
Sault Sainte Marie, in Ontario 212 G d
Saumur 76 C c
Saumurois, gouv. 146 B b
Sausenberg, landgr. 142 A e
Sauvenière 156 B a
Savah
Savaii, isl. 172 H b
Savannah 193 ins. C
Savannah River 193 D e
Savaria 38 F c
Save River 87 J e
Savia, West Rom. prov. 42 F d (9)
Savigliano, mon. 95 D c
Savigny, mon. 94 B b
Savo 26 C c
Savo River 30 C a
Savona 90 I h
Savona, bp. 95 D c
Savoy, cty. 69 G d
Savoy, duchy 86 F f
Savoy, growth of, 1418—1748 130 ins.
Savoy, neutral dist. 161 F e
Savoy, The, bldg. in London 75 G g
Savus (Save) River 38 F c
Saxa Rubra 35 ins. B
Saxon March 58 G c (Sax. M.)
Saxons, people, before fifth cent. 38 D b
Saxons, people, in Britain 51 R k
Saxons, people, in Germany 45 F b
Saxon Shore, dist. 51 Q i
Saxony, Frankish prov., 9 cent. 56 D b
Saxony, duchy, 10 cent. 62 E b
Saxony, duchy, 13 cent. 72 B a
Saxony, elect., 14 cent. 79 H c
Saxony, elect., 16 cent. 115 G c
Saxony, elect., 17—18 cent. 123 G c
Saxony, km., 1812 154 G c
Saxony, km., 1815 158 G c
Saxony, prov. of Prussia 158 F c
Saxony-Lauenburg, dist. 79 G b
Sayansk Mountains 171 K c
Saybrook 189 B d
Scalæ Caci, loc. in Rome 24 A
Scalæ Gemoniæ, loc. in Rome.
Scala Santa, loc. in Rome 96 A
Scaldis (Scheldt) River 38 C b
Scallabis 38 A e
Scamander River
Scambonidæ, deme 23 D
Scampa 10 B a
Scandea 15 D c
Scandia (Scandinavia), reg. 38 E a
Scandile, isl. 11 F c
Scandinavian Highlands 2 E b
Scandinavian Peninsula 2 F c
Scania, dist. 88 E c
Scapsa 11 D b
Scara
Scarbantia (Ödenburg) 38 F c
Scarborough 60 J g
Scarborough, parl. bor. 163 N c
Scardona 38 F d
Scardona, bp. 95 F c
Scardus, mt. 39 M l
Scarphea 11 D d
Scarpona 39 H i
Scepsis
Schächen Tal, valley 150 E c
Schaffhausen 91 Q k
Schaffhausen, canton 91 Q k
Schaffhausen, imp. cy. 78 F e
Schaftersheim 122 F d
Schalksburg 62 E b
Schärding 79 H d
Scharnitz, fort 154 F e
Scharnitz Pass 134 F e
Schässburg 159 M e
Schauenburg, castle 142 B b
Schaumburg, castle 72 B a
Schaumburg-Lippe, princ. 155 E b (S. L.)
Scheer 143 H i
Scheer, princ. cty. 143 H i
Scheidungen 63 F c
Scheldt River 117 B d
Schelklingen 143 I i
Schemnitz 155 J d
Schenectady 192 D b
Schenkenschanz 122 D c
Schesel 55 R i
Scheyern, castle 62 F d
Schiermonnikoog, isl. 117 D a
Schillingsfürst, castle 143 J g
Schiltach 142 B d
Schivelbein 85 D b
Schladming 115 G e
Schlawe 85 E a
Schlei, inlet 62 E a
Schleiden 117 E d
Schleiz 154 F c
Schleswig 62 E a
Schleswig, bp. 95 D a
Schleswig, duchy 158 E a
Schleswig, march 62 E a
Schleswig-Holstein, prov. 161 B b
Schlettstadt 126 E b
Schlettstadt, imp. cy. 78 E d
Schliengen 142 A e
Schluchtern 142 D b
Schlüsselburg 138 D d
Schmalkalden 114 F c
Schneidemühl 159 I b
Schœnus 15 D b
Schoharie 195 D b
Schokland, isl. 117 D b
Schönau 142 A e
Schönbrunn, castle 135 I d
Schönbuch, dist. 143 H h
Schonen, dist., see Scania
Schönhausen 158 F b
Schönthal, ab. 143 H g
Schopfheim 142 A e
Schopfheim, Nieder 142 A d
Schorndorf 143 I h
Schouten, route of
Schouwen, isl. 117 B c
Schramberg 143 F i
Schroda 159 I b
Schussen River 143 I j
Schussenried, ab. 143 I i
Schütt Island 159 I e
Schuyler, Fort 189 B b
Schuylkill River 195 D c
Schwabach 114 F d
Schwaigern 143 H g
Schwarzach, in Bavaria 114 F d
Schwarzach, mon. in Baden 142 B c
Schwarzburg, castle 79 G c
Schwarzburg, principalities 154 F c (S.)
Schwarze Elster, R. 85 G e
Schwarzenburg, in Switzerland 91 P l
Schwarzenberg, lordship in Baden 142 A d
Schwaz 154 F e

Schwechat . . . . 159 I d
Schwedt . . . . 85 D b
Schweidnitz . . . . 63 I c
Schweinfurt . . . . 62 F c
Schweinfurt, imp. cy. . . . . . . 79 G c
Schweinschädel . . . .
Schwerin, in Mecklenburg . . . 62 F b
Schwerin, on the Warthe R. . . 79 I b
Schwerin, bp. . . . . 95 E a
Schwerin, duchy . . . . 79 G b
Schwetz . . . . 87 L b
Schwetzingen . . . . 142 C b
Schwiebus . . . . 115 H b
Schwyz . . . . 91 Q k
Schwyz, canton . . . . 91 Q k
Schyl River . . . . 168 H d
Sciathus. . . . . 11 E c
Sciathus, isl. . . . . 11 E c
Scidrus . . . . 30 E b
Scillus . . . . 14 B b
Scilly Islands . . . . 130 B d
Scingomagus . . . . 26 A b
Scione . . . . 11 E c
Scioto Company, grant . . . . . 196 ins. B
Scioto River . . . . 196 ins. B
Scipios, Tomb of the . . . . . . 22 A
Scipio's camp . . . . 34 ins. A
Scipio's mole . . . . 34 ins. A
Sciri, people . . . .
Sciritis, dist. . . . . 14 C b
Scituate . . . . 189 ins. B
Scodra (Scutari in Albania) . . 39 L l
Scolacium (Squillace) . . . . . . 31 F d
Scollis, mt. . . . . 14 B b
Scolus, in Bœotia . . . . 11 E d
Scolus, in Chalcidice . . . . . . 11 E b
Scomius, mt. . . . . 39 M l
Scone . . . .
Scopia (Uskub) . . . . 73 E b
Scordisci, people . . . . 39 L k
Scotch, people . . . .
Scotland, km. . . . . 58 D b
Scotland Yard, in London . . . 75 G g
Scots, people . . . . 54 C c
Scots, people in Ireland . . . .
Scott, Fort . . . . 211 G c
Scott, route of . . . . 201 leg.
Scott, fam. . . . .
Scotussa . . . . 11 D c
Scrooby . . . . 185 E d
Scultenna (Panaro) River . . . 27 F c
Scupi (Uskub) . . . . 39 M l
Scutari, in Albania . . . . 93 A b
Scutari, on the Bosporus . . . . 93 G e
Scutari, bp. . . . . 95 F c
Scylla . . . . 90 E e
Scylacium (Squillace) . . . . . . 31 F d
Scylacium, gulf . . . . 31 F d
Scyllæum . . . . 30 E d
Scyllæum, prom., in Greece . . 15 D b
Scyllæum, prom., in Italy . . . 30 E d
Scylletium (Squillace) . . . . . . 31 F d
Scyrians, people . . . . 50 F c
Scyrus . . . . 11 F d
Scyrus (Skyros), isl. . . . . . . 11 F d
Scythia, East Rom. prov. . . . . 43 H e (6)
Scythia, Lesser, reg. . . . . 39 N l
Scythians, people, in Asia . . . 8 J d, L e
Scythians, people. in Europe . 18 D a
Scythopolis . . . . 7 C d
Seaford, parl. bor. . . . . 163 O g
Sea of the Indies (Arabian Sea)
Seattle . . . . 210 A a
Sea View, mt. . . . . 172 E d
Sebago, lake . . . . 189 C c
Sebaste, in Palestine . . . . . . 7 C d
Sebaste, in Pontus . . . . 43 J f
Sebastea . . . . 59 L f
Sebastea, theme . . . . 59 L f
Sebastia . . . . 20 G c
Sebastian Cabot, route of . . . 108 L k
Sebastopolis (Phasis) . . . . . . 20 I a
Seben . . . . 62 F e
Sebenico . . . . 90 E c
Sebenico, bp. . . . . 95 F c
Sebennytos . . . . 4 ins.
Sebinus (Iseo), lake . . . . 26 E b
Sebzewar . . . . 92 F d
Secia (Secchia) River . . . . . . 26 E c
Seckau . . . . 80 D h
Seckau, bp. . . . . 95 E b
Seckenheim . . . . 142 C b
Secondee . . . .
Secunderabad . . . . 137 C e
Sedan . . . . 126 D b
Sedetani, people . . . . 38 B d
Sedge Moor, dist. . . . . 49 E f
Sedgemoor . . . . 127 W o
Seduni, people . . . . 26 B a
Sedunum (Sion) . . . . 26 B a
Seehausen, Hanse. cy. . . . . . 99 ins. B
Seekonk . . . . 189 ins. A
Sées . . . . 76 D b
Sées, bp. . . . . 94 C b
Segeberg . . . . 72 C a
Segeberg, mon. . . . . 95 D a
Segedunum . . . . 38 B a
Segesta, in Liguria . . . . 26 D c
Segesta, in Sicily . . . . 30 B e
Segni . . . . 64 ins.
Segni, bp. . . . . 96 C b
Segobodium . . . . 39 H j
Segobriga . . . .
Segodunum, see Rodez
Segontia (Sigüenza) . . . . 38 B e
Segontium (Carnarvon) . . . . . 51 N h
Segor . . . . 68 ins. A
Segorbe . . . . 82 H f
Segorbe, bp. . . . . 94 B d
Segovia . . . . 38 B d
Segovia, bp. . . . . 94 B c
Segovia River . . . . 213 D c
Segura, near Murcia . . . . . . 82 B b
Segura, near Saragossa . . . . . 82 B a
Segura de la Frontera . . . . . 106 C b
Seguro, captaincy . . . . 108 M i
Segusio (Susa) . . . . 26 A b
Segustero or Segusterone, see Sisteron
Sehwan . . . .
Seine-et-Marne, dept. . . . . . 148 E e
Seine-et-Oise, dept. . . . . . . 148 E e
Seine-Inférieure, dept. . . . . . 148 E e
Seine River . . . . 61 D b
Seistan, reg. . . . .
Selas River . . . . 14 B b
Selborne, priory . . . . 100 B a
Selby . . . . 127 X m
Selby, mon. . . . . 97 P h
Selefke . . . . 93 D c
Selenga River . . . .
Seleucia, in Babylonia . . . . . 18 P h
Seleucia, in Cilicia . . . . 20 E d
Seleucia, in Syria . . . . 20 F d
Seleucia, theme . . . . 59 K f
Seleucids, Kingdom of the . . 19 W k
Seleucus, Kingdom of . . . . . 18 P i
Selge . . . . 20 D d
Selgovæ, people . . . . 38 B a
Seligenstadt, mon. . . . . 95 D a
Selinus, in Cilicia . . . . 20 E d
Selinus, in Laconia . . . . 14 C b
Selinus, in Sicily . . . . 30 B e
Selinus River . . . . 14 C a
Seljuk Turks, Dom. of the . . . 67 O f
Seljuk Turks, people . . . . . . 77 K e
Selkirk . . . .
Selkirk, cty. . . . .
Selkirk, dist. . . . .
Selkirk, Fort . . . . 212 B b
Selkirk Forest . . . . 49 F d
Sella . . . . 98 G h
Sellasia . . . . 14 C b
Selleis River . . . . 14 B b
Selles . . . . 69 H g
Selma . . . . 208 C c
Selsey . . . .
Selwood . . . . 49 E f
Selymbria . . . .
Selz . . . . 142 B c
Selz, mon. . . . . 95 D b
Semana (Thuringian) Forest . . 39 K h
Semendria . . . . 93 B b
Semenud . . . . 150 B a
Semgallia, dist. . . . .
Seminara . . . . 90 E e
Seminole, Ind. Res. . . . . 118 G c
Seminoles, tribe . . . . 188 J e
Semipalatinsk . . . . 170 J c
Semlin . . . .
Semlov . . . . 153 O f
Semmering Pass . . . . 135 H e
Semnones, people . . . . 38 E b
Semo Sancus, Temple of . . . . 23 B
Sempronii, Forum . . . . 27 G d
Sempach . . . . 91 Q k
Sempronia Basilica, bldg. in Rome . . . . 24 A
Senaculum, bldg. in Rome . . .
Sena Gallica (Sinigaglia) . . . . 27 H d
Sena Iulia . . . . 27 F d
Sena (Cesano) River . . . . 27 H d
Senate House, in Rome . . . . . 24 B
Seneca Creek . . . . 208 ins.
Seneca Lake . . . . 192 C b
Senecas, tribe . . . . 188 K b
Senécu . . . . 190 D e
Seneffe . . . . 156 A a
Senegal, col. . . . . 174 B c
Senegal River . . . . 174 B c
Senez, bp. . . . . 95 D c
Senger River . . . . 215 C g
Senia . . . . 27 I c
Senigallia, see Sinigaglia . . . . 90 M j
Senlis . . . . 61 E b
Senlis, bp. . . . . 94 C b
Senlac . . . . 65 F G e
Sennabrin . . . .
Sennar, dist. . . . . 174 G c
Senne River . . . . 156 A a
Sennette River . . . . 156 A a
Senones (Sens) . . . . 38 C c
Senones, people, in Gaul . . . . 38 C c
Senones, people, in Italy . . . . 27 G d
Sens . . . . 61 E b
Sens, abp. . . . . 94 C b
Sens, cty. . . . . 69 I f
Sentinum . . . . 27 G d
Seoul . . . . 171 N e
Seph . . . . 6 C c
Sepharvaim, see Sippar
Sepias, prom. . . . . 11 E c
Sepphoris . . . . 6 C c
Sepsi-Szent-György . . . . 159 M e
Septem peda . . . . 27 H d
Septimania, reg. . . . . 53 M i
Septimer, Pass . . . . 26 D a
Septimian Gate . . . . 22 A
Septimius Severus, Arch of . .
Septimius Severus, Palace of . 24 B
Septizonium, loc. in Rome . . . 22 A
Septs-Fonts, mon. . . . . 94 C b
Sepulcretum, loc. in Rome . . . 24 A
Sepulveda . . . . 94 B c
Sequana (Seine) River . . . . . 38 C c
Sequani, people . . . . 38 D c
Seraglio, New and Old, in Constantinople . . . . 93 G e
Seraglio Point . . . . 93 G e
Serai . . . . 77 N c
Serajevo . . . . 119 H e
Serapeum, loc. in Alexandria 34 ins. C (7)
Serapeum, loc. in Rome . . . . 22 A
Serapis, Temple of . . . . 22 A
Serbs, people . . . . 57 G e
Serena, La . . . . 215 B e
Seres . . . . 93 B b
Sergievski . . . . 138 E d
Sergipe, state . . . . 214 F d
Seringapatam . . . . 137 C f
Seriphus (Serpho) . . . . 15 E b
Seriphus (Sériphos), isl. . . . . 15 E b

Sermyle . . . 11 E b
Serpa . . . 38 A e
Serpent Column, in Constantinople . . . 93 G e (3)
Serpent Pool, in Jerusalem . . . 6 ins. A
Serpent's Mouth, str. . . . 105 H e
Serra do Espinhaço, mts. . . . 214 E d
Serra do Mar, mts. . . . 215 E e
Serra dos Aimores, mts. . . . 214 E d
Serra Geral, mts. . . . 215 D e
Serran . . . 111 B c
Serra parda, Cabo, cape . . . 108 R j
Serravalle . . . 90 K h
Serrhæ . . . 11 E a
Serrhium, prom. . . .
Serrorum Montes (Transylvanian Alps), mts. . . . 39 M k
Servia, reg. . . . 54 H e
Servia, km., 13 cent. . . . 89 B b
Servia, km., 14 cent. . . . 89 H f
Servia, km., 15 cent. . . . 93 B b
Servia, km., 19 cent. . . . 164 C b
Servia, princ., 19 cent. . . . 164 C b
Servia, prov. of Ottoman Empire
Servian Principalities, 14 cent. 77 I d
Servians, people . . .
Servian Wall . . . 23 B
Sesamus . . . 20 E b
Sesia River . . . 130 Q i
Sesites River . . . 26 C b
Sessa . . . 90 E d
Sessa, bp. . . . 95 ins.
Sessorium . . . 22 A
Sestinum . . . 27 G d
Sestus . . .
Setauket . . . 189 B d
Setia . . . 30 C a
Setif . . . 70 H f
Setons, fam. . . . 97 J d
Setu, isl. . . .
Setúbal . . . 83 J h
Seul, see Seoul . . . 171 N e
Seurre . . . 126 D c
Sevastopol, in the Crimea . . .
Sevastopol, plan of . . . 164 L g
Sevastopoli, in Abkhasia . . . 99 L e
Seven Basilicas, churches . 96 A
Seven Lakes . . . 27 F c
Sevenoaks, battle . . . 75 J i
Seven Ranges, The, dist. . . . 196 ins. B
Seven Towers, Castle of the . . 93 G e
Severia, dist. . . . 139 D e
Severians, people . . . 71 M c
Severian Way, road . . . 35 ins. B
Severin . . . 77 I d
Severin, banat . . . 89 B b
Severn River, in England . . . 49 E e
Severn River, in Canada . . . 212 G c
Severus, wall of . . . 34 E b
Sevier, lake . . . 210 C c
Sevier River . . . 198 C c
Seville . . . 82 A b
Seville, abp. . . . 94 A d
Seville, emir. . . . 83 D d
Seville, km. . . . 83 J h
Seville, univ. . . . 100 D g
Sevre River . . . 148 D e
Sewan-hacky (Long Island) . . 189 B d
Sexi . . . 38 B e
Sextum, Ad . . . 27 F d
Seybothenreuth . . . 158 F d
Seychelles Islands . . . 175 I e
Sfax . . . 73 C d
Sha-chau . . .
Shackamaxon . . . 192 ins.
Shaftesbury . . .
Shaftesbury, mon. . . .
Shaftesbury, parl. bor. . . . 163 L g
Shahr Zor . . . 67 P f
Shahrzur, reg. . . .
Shah-Armen, Dom. of . . . 71 O f
Shaliyat . . .
Shanghai . . . 171 N e
Shangtu . . .
Shan-hai-kwan . . . 171 M d
Shannon River . . . 49 B e
Shan-si, prov. . . . 171 M e
Shan-tung, prov. . . . 171 M e
Shap, mon. . . . 97 O g
Shari River . . . 174 E c
Shark Bay . . . 172 A c
Shark's Island . . . 107 C i
Sharmakhi . . . 99 M e
Sharon, Plain of . . . 7 B d
Sharpness . . . 162 D f
Sharpsburg . . . 208 ins.
Shasta, mt. . . . 210 A b
Shau-hsien . . . 171 N f
Shavly . . . 131 H b
Shaw . . . 127 X o
Shawmut . . . 189 ins. B
Shawnee Mission . . . 206 F c
Shawnees, tribe . . . 188 J c
Shawneetown . . . 211 H c
Shawomet . . . 189 ins. A
Shechem . . . 7 C d
Sheen, mon. . . . 97 Q j
Sheep Gate, in Jerusalem . . . 6 ins. A
Sheffield . . . 162 E d
Sheffield, parl. bor. . . . 163 M d
Sheik-ul-Islam, loc. in Constantinople . . . 93 G e
Shelburne . . . 212 I d
Sheliff River . . . 125 D e
Shelter Island . . . 192 E c
Shelton . . . 127 W n
Shenandoah . . . 193 E b
Shenandoah River . . . 193 E b
Shen-si, prov. . . . 171 L e
Shephela, Plain of . . . 7 B e
Shepherdstown . . . 208 ins.
Sheppey, isl. . . .
Sherborne . . . 65 E e
Sherborne, mon. . . . 97 O k
Sherborne, parl. bor. . . . 163 L g (Sherb.)
Sherboro, Island . . . 174 B d
Sherbrooke . . . 212 H d
Sheriffmuir . . .
s'Hertogenbosch . . . 117 D c
Sherwood Forest . . . 49 F e
Shetland Islands . . . 49 F a
Shigansk . . . 171 N b
Shikoku, isl. . . . 171 O e
Shilka River . . .
Shiloh, in Palestine . . . 7 C d
Shiloh, in Tennessee . . . 208 C b
Shimoda . . . 171 O e
Shimonoseki . . . 171 O e
Ship Island . . . 208 C c
Shipka Pass . . . 164 C b
Shipyards, loc. in Rome . . . 22 A
Shiraz . . .
Shirley . . . 193 ins. A
Shirley, Fort . . . 192 C c
Shirpurla . . . 4 G c
Shirvan, reg. . . .
Shoa, dist. . . . 174 G d
Shoalwater, Ind. Res. . . . 188 B a
Shoebury . . .
Shomron . . . 7 C d
Shoreditch . . . 75 I h
Shoreditch, street in London . 75 G g
Shoreham . . .
Shoshones, tribe . . . 188 C c
Shreveport . . . 208 B c
Shrewsbury, in England . . .
Shrewsbury, castle . . .
Shrewsbury, mon. . . . 97 O i
Shrewsbury, parl. bor. . . . 163 L e
Shrewsbury, in New Jersey . . 192 E c
Shropshire, cty. . . .
Shropshire, shire . . .
Shtiplie . . . 164 C b
Shubra Kheit . . .
Shumagin Islands . . . 198 ins. A
Shumla . . . 131 I e
Shunem . . . 6 C c
Shun-i . . . 170 ins. A
Shuri, isl. . . . 171 N f
Shuster . . .
Sialkot . . . 137 B b
Siam, km. . . . 171 L g
Siam, Gulf of . . . 171 L h
Siam, reg. . . .
Siberia, khan. of . . . 138 J d
Siberia, reg. . . . 171 J-R b
Sibir . . .
Sibir, khan. . . . 92 H b
Sibir, reg. . . . 109 X b
Sibota Islands . . . 10 B c
Sibton, mon. . . . 97 S i
Sicani or Sicanians, people . . 30 C e
Sicca . . . 42 D f
Sicels, people . . .
Sicilia, see Sicily
Sicilian Sea . . . 34 H f
Sicilies, Kingdom of the Two . 72 C d
Sicily, Rom. prov. . . . 30 C d
Sicily, isl. . . . 2 F e
Sicily, km. . . . 77 G d
Sicily, West Rom. prov. . . . 42 E f (4)
Sicinus (Sikinos), isl. . . . 15 F c
Sickingen, castle . . . 114 E d
Sicoris River . . . 38 C d
Siculi, people . . . 30 D e
Sicyon . . . 14 C b
Side, in Laconia . . . 15 D c
Side, in Pamphylia . . . 18 D c
Sidicinum, Teanum . . . 30 D a
Sidodone . . . 19 H e
Sidon . . . 6 C a
Sidon, Port of, in Tyre . . . 18 ins. B
Sidra, Gulf of . . . 174 E a
Sidus . . . 15 D b
Siedlce . . . 155 L b
Siegburg, mon. . . . 95 D a
Siegen . . . 158 E c
Siena . . . 90 L j
Siena, abp. . . . 95 E c
Siena, univ. . . . 100 H f
Sierra de Piña, mts. . . .
Sierra Leone, col. . . . 174 B d
Sierra Madre, mts. in Mexico . 187 I f
Sierra Madre, mts. in New Mexico . . . 190 D d
Sierra Mindi, mts. . . .
Sierra Morena, mts. . . . 2 D e
Sierra Nevada, mts. in Spain . 2 D e
Sierra Nevada, mts. in California . . . 190 A d
Sierra Nevada de Santa Marta, mts. . . . 187 L g
Sierra Quebrancha, mts. . . .
Sievershausen . . . 114 F b
Siga . . . 38 B e
Sigeum . . .
Sigeum, prom. . . . 9 A a
Sigiburg . . . 55 Q i
Sigmaringen . . . 143 H i
Sigmaringen, castle . . . 62 E d
Signau, castle . . . 91 P l
Signia . . . 35 ins. B
Signia, bp. . . . 96 C b
Signy, mon. . . . 94 C b
Sigtuna . . . 46 J b
Sigüenza . . . 83 K g
Sigüenza, bp. . . . 94 B c
Sigüenza, univ. . . . 100 E f
Sihuatan, Puerto . . . 107 G f
Sihut . . . 170 G g
Sikanderabad . . .
Sikhim . . .
Sikh States . . .
Si-kiang, R. . . .
Sila Mountains . . . 31 F d
Silarus River, in Æmilia . . . 27 F c
Silarus River, in Campania . . 30 D b
Silberberg, fortress . . . 155 I c
Silesia, dist. . . . 59 H c
Silesia, duchy . . . 72 D a
Silesia, Austrian, dist. . . . 159 I c
Silesia, Lower, dist. . . . 72 D a

Silesia, Prussian, prov. 159 I c
Silesia, Upper, dist. 72 D a
Siletz, Ind. Res. 188 B b
Silingæ, people 38 F b
Silis River 19 K b
Silistria 73 F b
Siloam, Pool of 6 ins. A
Silures, people 51 O i
Silves 82 A b
Silves, bp. 94 A d
Silvium 31 F b
Simancas 82 B a
Simbach 135 G d
Simbirsk 139 G e
Simeon, tribe 7 ins. D
Simferopol 139 D g
Simla 170 I e
Simmern 86 F d
Simmern, princ. 86 F d
Simœis River (Dumbrek R.)
Simplon Pass 91 Q l
Simpson, Fort 212 C b
Simpson, Port 212 ins.
Sinaes, Rio das boas, R. 108 U i
Sinai, mt. 3 H f
Sinai Peninsula 150 B b
Sinaloa 190 D f
Sinaloa, prov. 190 D f
Sinaloa, state 213 B b
Sinclairs, fam.
Sind, reg. in 8 cent. 53 I c
Sind, reg. in 18 cent. 137 A c
Sindelfingen 114 E d
Sindi, people 35 L e
Sindia, Dom. of 137 C c
Sindomana 19 K e
Sindringen 143 H g
Sindus 11 D b
Si-ngan-fu
Singapore
Singara 20 I d
Singidunum (Belgrade) 50 H d
Singitic Gulf (Gulf of Monte Santo) 11 E b
Sing-ngan 171 L e
Singus 11 E b
Sinigaglia 90 M j
Sinigaglia, bp. 95 E c
Si-ning-fu
Sinjar
Sin-kiang, prov. 171 J d
Sinnius River 27 F c
Sinonia, isl. 30 C b
Sinope (Sinub) 20 F a
Sinsheim 142 C b
Sintleozesavia, see Reichenau
Sinuessa (Mondragone) 30 C a
Sion 91 P l
Sion, bp. 95 D b
Sion, mon. 75 I i
Sioux, tribe 188 F c, G a
Sioux City 210 F b
Sioux Falls, town 210 F b
Sioux River, Big 198 F b
Siphæ 11 E d
Siphnus 15 E c
Siphnus (Siphnos), isl. 15 E c
Siponto 64 C b
Siponto, abp. 95 F c
Sipontum (Manfredonia) 30 E a
Sippar (Abu Habba) 4 G c
Sippara 20 J f
Sipylus, mt. 20 B c
Siraca 19 J c
Siracæ, people 35 M e
Siraf
Sirgune River 72 D a
Siris, in Lucania 31 F b
Siris, in Macedonia 11 E a
Siris River 31 F b
Sirmio (Sermione) 26 E b
Sirmium (Mitrovitza) 38 F d
Sirt 98 G g
Sis 73 H c
Sisal 213 C b
Sisapon 38 A e
Siscia 38 F c
Sisia 68 C b
Sissek 54 H d
Sisteron 126 D d
Sisteron, bp. 95 D c
Sistova 93 C b
Sit River 92 D b
Sitacus River 19 H e
Sithiu, see Saint-Omer
Sithonia, pen. 11 E b
Sitifis 38 D e
Sitka 198 ins. A
Sitomagus
Sitones, people 34 G a
Sittace 20 K f
Sitten, see, Sion 91 P l
Siugui
Siut 174 G b
Sivas 89 E c
Siwah Oasis
Six Nations, tribes 192 D b
Sixt, mon. 95 D b
Skaga Fiord 166 B b
Skager Rak, str. 88 C c
Skagway 198 ins. A
Skalitz 159 I c
Skåne, dist. 88 E d
Skanör, Hanse. for. cy. 98 F b
Skeena River 212 C c
Skenesborough 195 E b
Skidaway 193 ins. C
Skipton 127 V m
Skopia (Uskub), see Scopia
Skye, isl. 49 C c
Slamat, mt.
Slankamen 131 H d
Slatoust 167 Q d
Slave Coast, reg. 174 D d
Slaviansk 167 M f
Slavic Peoples about 900 57 leg.
Slavinia, reg. 58 G c
Slavonia, reg. 70 J d
Slavonian Military Frontier 159 I f
Sligo 127 I g
Sligo, cty. 127 I g
Sligo Bay 49 B d
Sliven 165 E b
Slivnitza 164 C b
Sloboneva 153 O f
Slonim 139 C e
Slovaks, people 168 leg.
Slovenes, people, about 900
Slovenes, people, 1910
Sluys 117 B c
Sluys, Hanse. for. cy. 99 ins. B
Smaland, dist. 88 F c
Smederevo 93 B b
Smenus River 14 C c
Smith, Fort, town 211 G c
Smith, routes of 210 B c
Smithfield, loc. near London 75 G g
Smith Island 193 ins. A
Smohain
Smoky Range, Great 193 C d
Smolensk 153 O g
Smolensk, gov. 131 J b
Smoothfield (Smithfield), loc. near London 75 G g
Smyrna 20 B c
Smyrna vetus 20 B c
Snake River 198 C b
Snakes, tribe 188 C b
Snelling, Fort 199 G b
Snowdon, mt. 49 E e
Soana 64 ins.
Soana, bp. 95 E c
Sobat River 174 G d
Sobernheim 142 ins. A
Sobral 214 E c
Sobràon 170 I e
Sobrarbe, dist. 83 E c
Society Islands 180 L i
Socoh, in Idumæa 7 B f
Socoh, in Judæa 7 B e
Soconusco, reg. 105 B c
Socorro, in Colombia 214 B b
Socorro, in New Mexico 190 D e
Socorro Island 213 A c
Socotra, isl., see Sokotra
Socrates, Prison of, in Athens 23 D
Söderhamn 166 I c
Söderköping 88 G b
Soest 62 E c
Soest, Hanse. cy. 99 ins. B
Sofia 93 B b
Soflingen 143 I i
Soflingen, ab. 143 I i
Sogamoso 214 B b
Sogd, reg.
Sogdiana, prov. 19 K c
Sogdiana, satr. 18 R h
Sogne Fiord 166 G c
Sohar 170 G f
Soignes, Forest of 156 A a
Soignies 117 C d
Soissons 61 E b
Soissons, bp. 94 C b
Soissons, gen. 147 E b
Sokoto 174 D c
Sokotra, isl. 174 I c
Solander Island 172 F e
Soldaia (Sudak) 99 K e
Soldau 123 K b
Soledad 190 A d
Solent, str. 49 F f
Solfatara, vol. 31 ins. A
Solferino 158 F f
Solignac, mon. 94 C b
Solikamsk 138 I d
Solimariaca 39 H i
Solis, route of 105 D d
Solis River (Rio de la Plata) 108 L k
Solitaria, isl. 107 A i
Sollium 10 B d
Solmona 64 B b
Solomon, Palace of, in ancient Jerusalem 6 ins. A
Solomon, Palace of, in medieval Jerusalem 68 ins. B (7)
Solomon Islands 172 E a
Solomon's Pool, in ancient Jerusalem 6 ins. A (2)
Solona 27 F c
Solothurn 91 P k
Solothurn, canton 91 P k
Solovets 138 E c
Solsona 82 C a
Solsona, bp. 94 C c
Soluntum, or Solus 30 C d
Solway Firth
Solway Moor 118 D c
Solway Moss
Solygea 15 D b
Somah 165 E d
Somaliland, British, col. 174 H d
Somaliland, Italian, col. 174 H d
Somborne, deanery 100 A a
Somberete 213 B b
Sombrero, isl. 213 F c
Somena River, see Somme River
Somersætas, people
Somerset, in Maryland 194 K g
Somerset, in Queensland 172 D b
Somerset, cty. in England
Somerset, shire
Somerset House, in London 75 G g
Somme, dept. 148 E e
Somme River 76 E b
Sommerschenburg 85 B b
Sommerschenburg, castle 72 C a
Sommières 126 D e
Somnath, Pattan
Somosierra 130 C e
Sonderburg 88 C d
Sondershausen 134 F c
Sondrio 91 R l

Songhar . . . .
Song-ka River . . . .
Sonoma . . . . 201 A b
Sonora. . . . . 190 C f
Sonora, prov. . . . . 190 C e
Sonora, Rio de, R. . . . . 190 C f
Sonora, state . . . . 213 A b
Son-tai . . . . 171 L f
Sontheim, Ober . . . . 143 I g
Sontius (Isonzo) River . . . . . . 27 H b
Soor . . . . 135 H c
Sophene, reg. . . . . 20 H c
Sophia . . . .
Sopianæ. . . . . 38 F c
Sopron (Ödenburg) . . . . 63 I e
Sora . . . . 30 C a
Sora, bp. . . . . 95 E c
Soracte, mon. . . . . 95 E c
Soracte, mt. . . . . 27 G e
Sorata, mt. . . . . 214 C d
Sorau . . . . 79 I c
Sorbian March . . . . 55 R i
Sorbiodunum (Old Sarum) . . .
Sorbiodurum (Straubing) . . . . 38 E c
Sorbonne, bldg. in Paris . . . . 149 B
Sorbs, people . . . . 53 O g
Sorek River . . . . 7 B e
Sorel. . . . . 189 B b
Soria. . . . . 82 H e
Sorocaba . . . . 215 E e
Soros. . . . . 16 B a
Sorrento. . . . . 90 E d
Sorrento, abp. . . . . 95 E c
Soto, route of . . . . 191 H e, I e
Soubise, near La Rochelle . . . 126 A d
Soubise, loc. in Paris . . . . . . 149 B
Soule, dist. . . . . 147 D c
Soule, viscty. . . . . 76 C e
Souna, dist. . . . . 63 H e
Sound, The, strait . . . . 88 E d
Souris River . . . . 198 E a
South Africa Company, British 175 F f
South African Republic . . . . 175 M k
South America, continent . . . 214, 115
Southampton, in England . . . .
Southampton, deanery . . . . . 100 A b
Southampton, hospitals . . . . . 100 A b
Southampton, mon. . . . . 100 A b
Southampton, parl. bor. . . . . 163 M g
Southampton, on Long Island . 189 B d
Southampton, Cape, in Canada 212 G b
Southampton County, in Virginia 207 K c
Southampton Hundred 193 ins. A (South.)
Southampton Island . . . . 212 G b
South Angles, people . . . . . .
South Australia, state . . . . . 172 C c
South (Delaware) Bay . . . . . . 192 D d
South Bend, tower . . . . 211 H b
South Berwick. . . . . 189 C c (S. B.)
South Beveland, isl. . . . . 117 B c
South Cape, Tasmania . . . . . . 172 D e
South Carolina, col. . . . . 193 D e
South Carolina, state . . . . . . 199 I d
South Carolina Yazoo Company 196 A d
South Chester, parl. dist. . . . 163 L d
South Dakota, state . . . . 210 E b
South Derby, parl. dist. . . . . 163 M d
South Devon, parl. dist. . . . . 163 K g
South Downs, dist. . . . . 49 F f
South Durham, parl. dist. . . . 163 M c
Southern Californians, tribes . 188 C d
Southern District, Victoria . . . 172 leg.
Southern Pacific Grant . . . . . 210 C d
Southern Uplands, Scotland . . 49 E d
South Essex, parl. dist. . . . . . 163 O f
South Folk (Angles), people . .
South Hants, parl. dist. . . . . 163 M g
South Island, New Zealand . . . 172 G e
South Isles, Scotland . . . .
South Kingston . . . . 189 ins. A
South Lancaster, parl. dist. . . 163 L d
South Leicester, parl. dist. . . . 163 M e
South Molton, parl. bor. 163
South Northampton, parl. dist. 163 N e
South Northumberland, parl. dist. . . . . 163 L b
South Nottingham, parl. dist. . 163 N d
Southold . . . . 189 B d
South Pass . . . . 210 D b
South Platte River . . . . 210 E b
South Potomac River . . . . . . 192 B d
South Prussia, dist. . . . . 135 I c
South (Delaware) River . . . . . 192 D d
South Salop, parl. dist. . . . . . 163 L e
South Saskatchewan River . . . 186 H c
South Saxons, people . . . . . . 51 R k
South Sea (Pacific Ocean) . . . 107 F h
South Shields, parl. bor. . . . . 163 M c
South Sporades, isl. . . . . 164 D c
South Stafford, parl. dist. . . . 163 L e
South Stafford Coalfield . . . . 162 D e
South Voorne, isl. . . . . 117 C c
South Wales Coalfield, Great . 162 C f
Southwark, suburb of London . 75 G g
Southwark, parl. bor. . 163 N f (Southw.)
South Warwick, parl. dist. . . . 163 M e
South West Africa, German, col.
South West Cape, Tasmania . . 172 D e
Southwest Gate, in Olympia . .
Southwick, priory . . . . 100 A b
South Wilts, parl. dist. . . . . . 163 L f
Söul, see Seoul . . . . 171 N e
Souvigny, mon. . . . . 94 C b
Sox, castle . . . . 91 R k
Sozopolis, in Asia Minor . . . . 71 M f
Sozopolis, in Bulgaria . . . . . . 73 F b
Spaichingen . . . . 143 G i
Spain, country, 910—1492 . . . 82, 83
Spain, km., about 1560 . . . . 118 D e
Spain, km., about 1740 . . . . . 130 C f
Spain, reg., in Roman times . . 34 C e
Spain, Rom. dioc. . . . . 42 B e
Spalato . . . . 90 F c
Spalato, abp. . . . . 95 F c
Spalauthræ . . . . 11 E c
Spalding, mon. . . . . 97 Q i
Spalding, parl. bor. . . . .
Spalt . . . . 114 F d
Spandau . . . . 85 C b
Spanish Algarve, dist. . . . . . 83 J h
Spanish March, 8 cent. . . . . . 53 L i
Spanish March, 9 cent. . . . . . 56 C d
Spanish Netherlands, prov. . . . 122 B c
Spanish Peaks . . . . 198 D c
Spanish Plateau . . . . 2 D d
Spanish Town . . . . 213 E c
Spanish Trail, route . . . . 210 B d
Sparnacus, see Épernay
Sparta . . . . 14 C b
Spartel, Cape . . . . 2 D e
Spartolus . . . . 11 E b
Speen . . . .
Spencer Gulf . . . . 172 C d
Spercheus River . . . . 10 D d
Spes Vetus, Temple of . . . . . 22 A
Speyer, see Spires
Spey River . . . .
Spezia . . . . 90 B b
Spezzia, isl. . . . . 164 C c
Sphacteria, isl. . . . . 14 B c
Sphagia, isl. . . . . 14 B c
Sphendale . . . . 16 B a
Sphettus . . . . 16 B b
Spice Islands . . . . 112 F d
Spielberg, castle . . . . 159 I d
Spier . . . . 62 F c
Spina . . . . 27 G c
Spinæ (Speen) . . . .
Spineticum Ostium, mouth of Po R. . . . . 27 G c
Spion Kop, mt. . . . . 175 M l
Spiræum, prom. . . . . 15 D b
Spira (Spires) . . . . 39 J i
Spires . . . . 62 E d
Spires, bp. . . . . 78 F d
Spires, imp. cy. . . . . 78 F d
Splügen . . . . 91 R l
Splügen Pass . . . . 91 R l
Spokane, or Spokane House . 210 B a
Spokane, Ind. Res. . . . . 188 C a
Spokanes, tribe . . . . 188 C a
Spoletium (Spoleto) . . . . 27 G e
Spoleto . . . . 90 D c
Spoleto, bp. . . . . 95 E c
Spoleto, duchy . . . . 54 G e
Sponheim, castle . . . . 142 ins. A
Sponheim, cty. . . . . 114 D d
Sponheim, mon. . . . . 95 D b
Sporades, isl. . . . . 13 E c
Spree River . . . . 85 G d
Spremberg . . . . 85 H e
Sprimont . . . . 117 D d
Springfield, in Illinois . . . . . 211 H c
Springfield, in Mass. . . . . . . 189 B c
Springfield, in Missouri . . . . . 211 G c
Springfield, in Ohio . . . . 211 I c
Sprinfontein . . . . 175 M m
Squillace . . . . 90 F e
Squillace, bp. . . . . 95 F d
Sredne Kolimsk . . . . 171 Q b
Stabiæ . . . . 30 D b
Stabulaus, see Stavelot
Stadaconá (Quebec) . . . . 191 K b
Stade . . . . 62 E b
Stade, Hanse. cy. . . . . 99 ins. B
Stadion, castle and town . . . . 143 I i
Stadtlohn . . . . 122 D b
Staffarda . . . . 130 P j
Staffis . . . . 91 O l
Stafford, in England . . . . 127 W m
Stafford, in Virginia . . . . 193 F b
Stafford, cty. . . . . 127 W n
Stafford, parl. bor. . . . . 163 L l
Staggia . . . . 90 L j
Stagira, or Stagirus . . . . 11 E b
Stagno, bp. . . . . 95 F c
Stagnum Tuneticum (Bay of Tunis) . . . . 34 ins. A
Stahremberg, castle . . . .
Staines . . . . 75 H i
Stainforth . . . . 162 F d
Staked Plain . . . . 210 E d
Stalida, isl. . . . . 16 D c
Stamford, in Connecticut . . . . 189 B d
Stamford, in England . . . . . . 127 Y n
Stamford, castle . . . . 65 F d
Stamford, parl. bor. . . . . 163 N e
Stamford Bridge . . . . 65 F d
Stampæ, see Étampes
Standing Rock, Ind. Res. . . . . 188 F a
Standish . . . . 185 D d
Stanislau . . . . 168 I b
Stanislawow . . . . 159 M d
Stanley, mon. . . . . 97 O j
Stanley Falls . . . . 175 F d
Stanley Pool, lake . . . . 175 E e
Stanleyville . . . . 175 F d
Stanovoi Mountains . . . . 171 Q b
Stanwix, Fort . . . . 192 D b
Stanz . . . . 91 Q l
Starbuck Island . . . . 180 L h
Star Fort . . . . 164 L g
Stargard, in Mecklenburg . . . 79 H b
Stargard, duchy . . . . 79 H b
Stargard, in Pomerania . . . . . 79 I b
Stargard, Hanse cy. . . . . 99 ins. B
Starkenburg, castle, in Hesse . 142 C a
Starkenburg, castle, on the Moselle R. . . . . 142 ins. A
Starodub . . . . 139 D e
Staten Island, South America . 215 C h
Staten Island, U. S. . . . . 189 ins. C
States of the Church, 9 cent. . 56 E d
States of the Church, 13 cent. 73 C b
States of the Church, see also Papal States and Patrimony of St. Peter
State Treasury, in Rome . . . .
Statilii, Tomb of the . . . . . . 22 A
Statonia . . . . 27 F e
Statuas, Ad . . . . 35 ins. B
Staufen, in Baden . . . . 142 A e

Staufen, lordship . . . . 142 A e
Staufen or Hohenstaufen, castle in Wurtemberg . . . . 62 E d
Staufenberg, castle . . . . 142 B d
Staufenberg, lordship . . . . . . 142 B d
Staunton . . . . 193 E b
Staunton River . . . . 193 E c
Stavanger . . . . 88 A b
Stavelot . . . . 117 D d
Stavelot, ab. . . . . 117 D d
Stavelot, mon. . . . . 95 D a
Stavoren . . . . 117 D b
Stavoren, Hanse. cy. . . . . 99 ins. B
Stavropol . . . . 139 F f
Steckelberg, castle . . . . 86 G c
Stecknitz Canal . . . . 79 G b
Stedingen, dist. . . . . 72 B a
Steelyard, The, loc. in London 98 ins. A
Steenbergen . . . . 117 C c
Steenkerque . . . . 122 C c
Steenwyk . . . . 117 E b
Steep Point, cape . . . . 172 A c
Stegeborg . . . . 119 H b
Steier, castle . . . . 63 H d
Stein . . . . 91 Q k
Steinamanger . . . . 135 I e
Steinau . . . . 123 I c
Steinfeld . . . . 142 E a
Steinfurt . . . . 122 D b
Steinhuder Lake . . . . 39 J g
Stelvio Pass . . . . 91 S l
Stenay . . . . 126 D b
Stendal . . . . 72 C a
Stendal, Hanse. cy. . . . . 99 ins. B
Stenimakhos . . . . 165 D c
Stenyclarus . . . . 14 B b
Stephenson, Fort . . . . 200 B c
Sternberg, dist. . . . . 85 D b
Sterzing . . . . 154 F e
Steterburg . . . . 62 F b
Steterburg, mon. . . . . 95 Ea (St.)
Stetten . . . . 142 D d
Stetten, lordship . . . . 142 D d
Stettenfels, castle . . . . 143 H g
Stettenfels, lordship . . . . 143 H g
Stettin . . . . 63 H b
Stettin, duchy, 14 cent. . . . . . 79 I b
Stettin, duchy, 16 cent. . . . . . 115 I a
Stettin, Hanse. cy. . . . . 99 ins. B
Stettin, Neu . . . . 123 I b
Steuben, Fort . . . . 196 ins. B
Steuerverein (Tax-Union) . . . . 160 I f
Steusslingen . . . . 143 I i
Stewart Island . . . . 172 F e
Stewarts, fam. . . . .
Steyning, parl. bor. . . . . 163 N g
Steyr, in Austria . . . . 135 H e
Stikine River . . . . 212 ins.
Stiklestad . . . . 64 F d
Stilfser Joch, pass . . . . 26 E a
Stiria . . . . 16 C b
Stiris . . . . 11 D d
Stirling . . . .
Stirling, cty. . . . .
Stobi . . . . 39 M l
Stockach . . . . 142 D e
Stockbridge, Ind. Res. . . . . . . 188 I a
Stockelsdorf . . . . 88 D e
Stockholm . . . . 77 H a
Stockholm, Hanse. for. cy. . . . 98 G b
Stockport . . . . 127 W m
Stockport, parl. bor. . . . . 163 L d
Stocks Market, in London . . . 75 G g (37)
Stockton . . . . 162 E c
Stoddert, Fort . . . . 200 I f
Stœni, people . . . . 26 E b
Stoke-upon-Trent, parl. bor. . 163 L d
Stoke-Courcy, parl. bor. . . . . .
Stolbovo . . . . 138 D d
Stollhofen . . . . 134 D d
Stollhofen Lines, military dist. 129 E c
Stolp . . . . 123 I a
Stolp, Hanse. cy. . . . . 98 G c
Stolpen . . . . 115 H c

Stoneleigh, mon. . . . . 97 P i
Stonington . . . . 189 C d
Stony Point, on Hudson R. . . 195 D c
Stork Tower, in Jerusalem . . . 6 ins. A
Storkyro . . . . 131 H a
Stormarn, dist. . . . . 62 E b
Storm Bay . . . . 172 D e
Stormberg Junction . . . . 175 M m
Storms, Cape of . . . . 109 S k
Stoss, Pass . . . . 91 R k
Stotzingen . . . . 143 J h
Stour River . . . . 49 G e
Stourbridge . . . . 98 ins. A
Stourport . . . . 162 D e
Stow-on-the-Wold . . . . 127 X o
Stradella . . . . 130 R i
Straits Settlements, col. . . . . . 171 L h
Stralsund . . . . 79 H a
Stralsund, Hanse. cy. . . . . 99 ins. B
Strand, street in London . . . . 75 G g
Strasburg, in Alsace . . . . 62 D d
Strasburg, bp. . . . . 78 E d
Strasburg, imp. cy. . . . . 78 E d
Strasburg, in Virginia . . . . . . 193 E b
Strata Florida, mon. . . . . 97 N i
Stratford, near London . . . . . 75 J h
Stratford, in Connecticut . . . . 189 B d
Stratford Langthorne, mon. . . 97 R j
Strathclyde, km. . . . .
Strathcona . . . . 212 D c
Strathearn, dist. . . . .
Strathnaver, dist. . . . .
Stratonicea . . . . 11 E b
Straton's Tower in Jerusalem . 6 B d
Strättligen, castle . . . . 91 P l
Stratton . . . . 127 U p
Stratus . . . . 10 C d
Straubing . . . . 79 H d
Strausberg . . . . 85 D b
Strawberry Bank, village . . . . 189 D c
Strehla . . . . 63 G c
Strehlen . . . . 135 I c
Strengnäs . . . . 119 H b
Stresow . . . . 135 G a
Stretensk . . . . 171 M c
Streu River . . . . 62 F c
Stridon . . . . 42 F e
Striegau . . . . 135 I c
Strivali Islands . . . . 157 E e
Strogonov, Colony of . . . . . .
Strongyle, isl. . . . . 30 E d
Strood . . . . 98 ins. A
Strophades Islands . . . . 14 B b
Stroud, parl. bor. . . . . 163 L f
Stryme . . . .
Strymon River . . . . 11 E a
Strymonic Gulf . . . . 11 F b
Stuart, routes of . . . . 172 leg.
Stuart Town . . . . 193 ins. C
Studzianka . . . . 153 N g
Stühlingen . . . . 142 B e
Stühlingen, landgr. . . . . 142 B e
Stuhlweissenburg . . . . 159 J e
Stuhmsdorf . . . . 123 J b
Stura River (Stura di Demonte) 26 B c
Stura River (Stura di Lanzo) . 26 B b
Sturni . . . . 31 G b
Stuttgart . . . . 143 H h
Styberra . . . . 10 C a
Stymphalus . . . . 14 C b
Styra . . . . 15 E a
Styria, duchy, 12 cent. . . . . . . 72 D b
Styria, duchy, 14 cent. . . . . . . 79 I e
Styria, march, 11 cent. . . . . . . 63 H e
Styx River . . . . 14 C b
Suakin . . . . 174 G c
Suana . . . . 27 F e
Suanetes, people . . . . 26 D a
Subiaco . . . . 64 ins.
Subiaco, mon. . . . . 96 C b
Subig . . . . 199 ins. H
Sublaqueum (Subiaco) . . . . . . 27 H f
Sublavio (Seben) . . . . 27 F a
Sublette's Cut-off, route . . . . 210 C b

Sublician Bridge, Rome . . . . . 24 A
Sublime Porte, loc. in Constantinople . . . . 93 G e
Subura, quarter in Rome . . . . 22 A
Succoth . . . . 7 D d
Succur . . . .
Su-chau, in Kan-su . . . . 171 K e
Su-chau, in Kiang-su . . . . . . 171 N e
Suchester . . . .
Sucré . . . . 214 C d
Sucro River (Júcar R.) . . . . . 38 B e
Suczawa . . . . 168 J c
Sudak . . . . 99 K e
Sudan, reg. . . . . 174 C c
Sudan, Anglo-Egyptian, reg. . . 174 F c
Sudbury, in England . . . . 163 O e
Sudbury, parl. bor. . . . . 163 O e
Sudbury, in Mass. . . . . . . 189 C c (Sudb.)
Sudbury, in Ontario . . . . 212 G d
Sudermania, dist. . . . . 119 H b
Sudetes, mts. . . . . 166 I e
Sudeti Mountains . . . . 38 E b
Sueones, people . . . . 38 E a
Suessa Aurunca or Suessa (Sessa) 30 C a
Suessa Pometia . . . . 30 B a
Suessiones or Suessionis, see Soissons
Suessiones, people . . . . 38 C c
Suessula (Torre di Sessola) . . 30 D a
Sueves, people, in Germany . . 45 G b
Sueves, people, in Spain 45 C d, 50 B d, 52 H e
Suez . . . . 174 K i
Suez, Gulf of . . . . 174 K j
Suez, Isthmus of . . . . 3 H e
Suez Canal . . . . 174 K i
Sufes . . . . 42 D f
Suffolk, cty. . . . . 127 Z n
Sugambri, people . . . . 39 I h
Suhar . . . .
Suhl . . . . 154 F c
Suhlingen . . . . 154 E b
Sui-chau-fu . . . .
Suindinum, see Le Mans
Suipacha . . . . 214 C e
Sukadana . . . . 112 E d
Sukhona River . . . . 167 N c
Sukhum Kaleh . . . . 164 G b
Sulby, mon. . . . . 97 Q i
Sulci . . . . 38 D e
Suleïman, mosque . . . . 93 G e
Sulina . . . . 165 F a
Sulina Mouth of Danube . . . . 164 D a
Suliots, people . . . . 164 C c
Sully . . . . 126 C c
Sulmo . . . . 27 H e
Sulmone . . . . 90 E c
Sultaniyeh . . . . 99 M f
Sultan's Pool . . . . 6 ins. A
Sultan Valideh, mosque . . . . . 93 G e (6)
Sulu, isl. . . . .
Suluan, isl. . . . . 110 D D g
Sulu Archipelago . . . . 199 ins. H
Sulu Sea . . . . 199 ins. H
Sulz . . . . 143 G i
Sulzbach, in Bavaria . . . . 79 G d
Sulzbach, in Wurtemberg . . . . 143 I g
Sulzbach, palat. . . . . 123 G d
Sumatium . . . .
Sumatra, isl. . . . . 112 C c
Sumba, isl. . . . . 172 A b
Sumbal . . . .
Sumbal, reg. . . . .
Sumbawa, isl. . . . .
Sumelocenna . . . . 39 J i
Sumer, reg. . . . . 4 G c
Sumiswald, castle . . . . 91 P k
Summo lacu . . . . 26 D a
Summus Pœninus, see Great Saint Bernard
Sumter, Fort . . . . 208 E c
Sun, Gate of the, in Alexandria 34 ins. C
Sunarganw . . . .
Sunderland, parl. bor. . . . . . . 163 M c
Sundgau, dist. . . . . 114 D e

Sundhofen . . . . 143 ins. D
Sun Dial, in Rome . . . . 22 A
Sundswall . . . . 166 I c
Sungari River . . . .
Sumian Gate, in Athens . . . .
Suntar . . . . 171 M b
Süntel, mts. . . . . 55 Q i
Supe . . . . 214 B d
Superior, lake . . . . 186 K d
Suppai, Ind. Res. . . . . 188 D c
Süpplingenburg, castle . . . . . 62 F b
Sura, Baths of . . . .
Surabaja . . . . 172 A a
Surat . . . . 137 B d
Surgut . . . . 170 I b
Surinam, col. . . . . 214 D b
Surintendance, Rue de la, street in Versailles . . . . 149 A
Surrentum (Sorrento) . . . . . . 30 D b
Surrey, cty. . . . . 127 Y o
Surreymen, people . . . .
Sursee . . . . 91 Q k
Surt . . . .
Susa, in Italy . . . . 90 A b
Susa, marq. . . . . 64 A a
Susa, in Persia . . . . 19 G d
Susia . . . . 19 I c
Susiana, prov. . . . . 19 G d
Susiana, reg. . . . . 8 C b
Susiana, satr. . . . . 18 P h
Susquehanna River . . . . 192 C c
Susquehannocks, tribe . . . . . . 188 K b
Sussex, cty. . . . . 127 Y p
Sussex, km. . . . .
Sutherland, cty. . . . .
Sutherland, dist. . . . .
Sutherlands, fam. . . . . 97 I a
Sutley River . . . . 137 B a
Sutri . . . . 64 ins.
Sutri, bp. . . . . 95 E c
Sutrium (Sutri) . . . . 27 G e
Sutter's Fort (Sacramento) . . . 198 A c
Sutter's Mill . . . . 210 A c
Suva . . . . 172 G b
Suwali . . . .
Suwanee River . . . . 193 C f
Suya . . . . 190 C e
Suzdal . . . . 138 F d
Sveaborg, fortress . . . . 131 H a
Svendborg . . . . 88 D d
Svendborg, Hanse. for. cy. . . . 98 E b
Svenigrod . . . . 71 L d
Sventziany . . . . 153 N f
Svir River . . . . 167 L c
Swaanendael see Zwaanendael . 191 J d
Swabia, Frank. prov., 9 cent. . 56 D c
Swabia, duchy, about 1000 . . . 58 F d
Swabia, duchy, 11 cent. . . . . 62 E e
Swabia, duchy, 12 cent. . . . . 72 B b
Swabia, Lower, "landvogtei" . . 143 I j
Swabia, Upper, "landvogtei" . . 143 I j
Swabians, people . . . . 57 E d
Swakopmund . . . . 175 E g
Swale River . . . . 127 X l
Swan Hill, town . . . . 172 D d
Swan River . . . . 172 A d
Swanscombe . . . . 75 J i
Swansea . . . . 189 ins. A
Swansea, parl. bor. . . . . 163 J f
Swaziland, reg. . . . . 175 N l
Sweet Waters, Valley of the, loc. in Constantinople . . . . 93 G e
Sweden, km., about 1000 . . . . 59 H b
Sweden, km., about 1097 . . . . 66 J b
Sweden, km., about 1190 . . . . 70 J a
Sweden, km., about 1569 . . . . 119 I a
Sweden, km., about 1658 . . . . 120 leg.
Sweden, km., about 1740 . . . . 131 H a
Sweden, km., about 1812 . . . . 155 ins.
Sweden, km., 1910 . . . . 166 H d
Swedes, people . . . . 46 I b
Swedish Pomerania, dist. . . . . 154 G a
Swift Current, town . . . . 212 E d
Swinemünde . . . . 135 H b
Swineshead, mon. . . . . 97 Q i
Swinomish, Ind. Res. . . . . . . 188 B a
Swiss Confederation, 14—18 cent. 91
Syagrius, km. of . . . . 33 M h
Sybaris . . . . 31 F c
Sybaris River . . . . 31 F c
Sycæ . . . . 93 G e
Sycaminon . . . . 6 B c
Sycurium . . . . 11 D c
Sydney, on Cape Breton I. . . . 212 J d
Sydney, in New South Wales . 172 E d
Sydney District . . . . 172 leg.
Syene (Assuan) . . . . 4 F d
Sylhet . . . . 137 F c
Sylt, isl. . . . . 114 E a
Sylvania, proposed state in U. S.
Symæthus River . . . . 30 D e
Syme, isl. . . . . 13 E c
Symmes Purchase, dist. . . . . . 196 ins. B
Synnada . . . . 20 D c
Sypalettus . . . . 16 B a
Syracusæ, see Syracuse, in Sicily
Syracuse, in New York . . . . . 196 D b
Syracuse, in Sicily . . . . 30 E e
Syracuse, bp. . . . . 95 F d
Syracuse, plan of . . . . 31 ins. B
Syra Orda . . . .
Syrastrene, reg. . . . . 19 L f
Syr Daria, River . . . .
Syria, km. . . . . 33 E b
Syria, Macedon. prov. . . . . . 18 E d
Syria, reg. . . . . 67 N g
Syria, Rom. prov. . . . . 35 L g
Syria, satr. . . . . 18 O h
Syria I, E. Rom. prov. . . . . . 43 J f (3)
Syrian Desert . . . . 3 H e
Syria Salutaris, Rom. prov. . . 43 J f (10)
Syrias, prom. . . . . 20 F a
Syros, isl. . . . . 15 E b
Syrtis, Greater, gulf . . . . . . 174 E a
Syrtis, Lesser, gulf . . . . 174 E a
Syrtis Maior (Greater Syrtis), gulf 34 H g
Syrtis Minor (Lesser Syrtis), gulf 34 G g
Sys River, in Achaia . . . . . . 14 C b
Sys River, in Macedonia . . . . 11 D c
Sythas River . . . . 14 C b
Szamos Rirer . . . . 159 L e
Szamos-Ujvar . . . . 159 M e
Szasz-Regen . . . . 159 M e
Szathmar . . . .
Sze-chwan, prov. . . . . 171 L e
Szentes . . . . 159 K e
Szent Imre . . . . 119 I d
Szent Tamas . . . . 159 J f
Szolnok . . . . 159 K e
Szöreg . . . . 159 K e

Taanach . . . . 6 C c
Tabæ, in Asia Minor . . . . . . 47 L f
Tabæ, in Palestine . . . . 6 D c
Tabæ, in Persia . . . . 19 I d
Tabard, The, inn, near London 75 G g
Tabasco . . . . 107 H f
Tabasco, reg. . . . . 105 B c
Tabasco River . . . . 105 B c
Tabasco, state . . . . 213 C c
Tabatinga . . . . 214 C c
Tabbas, Las . . . . 214 A b
Tabernæ (Zabern) . . . . 39 I i
Tabernæ (Rheinzabern) . . . . . 39 J i
Taberna frigida . . . . 26 E d
Tabernas . . . . 82 B b
Tabernilla . . . .
Tabor, in Bohemia . . . . 87 J d
Tabor, in Iowa . . . . 206 F b
Tabor, mt. . . . . 6 C c
Tabora . . . . 175 G e
Tabriz . . . . 139 G H
Tabularium (Record Office) in Rome . . . . 24 A
Taburi, people . . . . 19 H c
Tacape . . . . 12 F d
Tacna . . . . 214 B d
Tacoma . . . . 210 A a
Tacubaya . . . . 106 A a
Tadcaster . . . . 127 X m
Tadmor . . . . 20 H e
Tadousac . . . . 212 H d
Tænarum . . . . 14 C c
Tænarum, prom. (Cape Matapan) 14 C c
Tænia . . . . 34 ins. A
Tæzalorum, prom. . . . . 38 B a
Taff River . . . .
Tafilet . . . . 98 C g
Taganrog . . . . 139 E f
Tagaste . . . . 42 D f
Tagernauseo, see Tegernsee
Taghaza . . . . 108 Q e
Taginæ . . . . 52 D b
Tagliacozzo . . . . 72 C c
Tagliamento River . . . . 135 G e
Tagong . . . .
Tagus River . . . . 82 A b
Tahiti, isl. . . . . 180 M i
Tahlequah . . . . 211 G c
Tahoe, lake . . . . 210 B c
Taido (Peking) . . . .
Taillebourg . . . . 69 C d
Taillebourg, castle . . . . 76 C d
Taimur Peninsula . . . . 171 K a
Tai-wan . . . . 171 N f
Tai-yuen-fu . . . .
Taiza . . . . 105 C c
Ta-ku . . . . 170 ins. A
Taku River . . . . 212 ins.
Talabriga . . . . 38 A d
Talamone . . . . 72 C c
Talas . . . .
Talavera de la Reina . . . . . . 82 A a
Talay River . . . .
Talca . . . . 215 B f
Talcahuano . . . . 212 B f
Ta-lien-wan . . . . 171 N e
Ta-li-fu . . . .
Tallahassee . . . . 211 I d
Tallapoosa River . . . . 193 B e
Talley, mon. . . . . 97 N j
Talmont . . . . 69 C c
Talmont, seign. . . . . 69 C c
Taltal . . . . 215 B e
Talva, see Tarbes
Taman . . . . 93 E a
Tamar . . . . 7 C f
Tamar River, in Cornwall . . .
Tamar River, in Tasmania . . . 172 D e
Tamara . . . . 83 E c
Tamarus River . . . . 30 D a
Tamatave . . . . 175 H f
Tamaulipas, state . . . . 213 C b
Tambo, near Cuzco . . . . 111 C d
Tambo, near Mollendo . . . . . 214 B d
Tambov . . . . 139 F e
Tamesa (Thames) River . . . . . 38 C b
Tampico . . . . 201 F e
Tammerfors . . . . 131 H a
Tampa . . . . 211 I e
Tampa Bay . . . . 211 I e
Tampico . . . . 107 H f
Tamworth . . . . 127 X n
Tamworth, parl. bor. . . . . . . 163 M e
Tamynæ . . . . 11 F d
Tamyras River . . . . 6 C a
Tana (Azov) . . . . 77 M c
Tanager River . . . . 30 E b
Tanagra . . . . 11 E d
Tanaïs . . . . 35 L d
Tanaïs (Don) River . . . . 35 M d
Tanana River . . . . 212 A b
Tanarus (Tanaro) River . . . . . 26 C c
Tanatis Island . . . . 38 C b
Tancred's Tower, in Jerusalem 68 ins. B
Tanegashima Island . . . . 110 E E e
Taneytown . . . . 208 ins.
Tangarara . . . . 111 A b
Tanganyika, lake . . . . 175 F e
Tangermünde . . . . 85 B b
Tangermünde, Hanse. cy. . . . . 99 ins. B
Tangier . . . . 174 C a

Tang-shan 170 ins. A
Tangut, reg.
Tanis 4 ins.
Tanjore 137 C f
Tannenberg 87 L b
Tanners, Postern of the, loc. in Jerusalem 68 ins. B
Tannetum 26 E c
Tan-sui 171 N f
Tanta 150 B a
Tantalam Island 171 L h
Tanus River 14 C b
Taormina 90 E f
Taos 190 D d
Tapajos River 214 D c
Tophiæ Islands 10 B d
Taphus, isl. 10 B d
Tappahannock 193 F c
Tappan 192 D c
Tapti River 137 C d
Taranaki, prov. 172 G d
Taranto 90 F d
Taranto, abp. 95 F c
Tarapacá 214 C d
Taras (Taranto) 31 G b
Tarascon, in Foix 69 D e
Tarascon, in Provence 72 A c
Tarasp 122 F e
Tarazona 82 B a
Tarazona, bp. 94 B c
Tarbes 61 C e
Tarbes, bp. 94 C c
Tarentaise 61 G d
Tarentaise, abp. 95 D b
Tarentum (Taranto) 31 G b
Tarentum, dist. in Rome 23 B
Tarentum, Gulf of 31 G c
Targovitza 131 J d
Tarifa 82 A b
Tarifa, Cape 166 D h
Tarija 214 C e
Tarim River
Tarleton, raid of 195 B e
Tarleton, route of 195 A f
Tarma 111 B d
Tarn, dept. 148 E f
Tarn River 76 E d
Tarn-et-Garonne, dept. 148 E f
Tarnaiæ 26 A a
Tarnis River, see Tarn River
Tarnopol 139 C f
Tarnow 87 M c
Taro River 150 E d
Tarphe 16 F e
Tarquinii 27 F e
Tarracina (Terracina) 30 C a
Tarraco (Tarragona) 38 C d
Tarraconensis, Rom. prov. 38 B d (1)
Tarraconensis, West Rom. prov. 42 B e (4)
Tarragona 82 C a
Tarragona, abp. 94 C c
Tarrant, mon. 97 O k
Tarrytown 195 E c
Tarsatica 27 I b
Tarshish, reg. 12 B c
Tarsi, people
Tarsius River
Tarsus 20 F d
Tartars or Tatars, people, north of Black Sea 93 D a
Tartars or Tatars, people in eastern Asia
Tartars or Tatars, people in eastern Russia 138 H d
Tartarus River 27 F b
Tartary or Tatary, reg. 109 W-BB c
Tartary or Tatary, Little, reg. 139 D f
Tartas 76 C e
Tarua 8 D c
Taruana or Taruenna, see Thérouanne
Tarus (Taro) River 26 E c
Tarvis 135 G e
Tarvisium (Treviso) 27 G b
Tashkent
Tasman, route of
Tasman Peninsula 172 D e
Tasmania, state 172 D e
Tatars, see Tartars
Tatary, reg., see Tartary
Tatra, mts. 166 I f
Tatta 137 A d
Tatta, lake 20 E c
Tau 199 ins. D
Tau, isl. 199 ins. D
Tauber River 114 E d
Tauberbischofsheim 158 E d
Taulantii, people 10 A b
Taungu
Taungu, reg.
Taunton, in England 127 V p
Taunton, mon. 97 N k
Taunton, parl. bor. 163 K f
Taunton, in Mass. 189 ins. A
Taunus Mountains 39 J h
Taupo, lake 172 G d
Taurasia (Turin) 26 B b
Tauresium 52 K e
Taurianum, prom. 30 E d
Tauric Chersonese (Crimea) 35 K d
Taurida, reg. 139 D f
Taurini, people 26 B c
Taurinum, see Turin
Taurisci, people 38 E c
Tauroggen 131 H b
Tauromenium 30 E e
Taurus Mountains 3 H e
Taurus, prom. 30 E e
Taus 87 I d
Tavan 119 K d
Tavastehus 119 I a
Tavira 82 A b
Tavoy
Tavoy, reg.
Tavistock, mon. 97 M k
Tavistock, parl. bor. 163 J g
Tavium 20 F c
Tawali, isl. 112 F d
Tawalisi, people
Tawi-Tawi, isl. 112 F c
Taxila 19 L d
Taxis, castle 143 J h
Taxis, princ. 143 J h
Tay River 49 D c
Taygetus Mountains 14 C b
Taylor, route of 201 leg.
Tcheragan Palace
Tcherkasy 139 D f
Tchernigov 139 D e
Tchernoi-Yar 139 G f
Tchesme 164 D c
Tchigrin 139 D f
Tchirmen 93 C b
Tchorgun 164 J f
Tchuds, people 71 K b
Tchuguiev 139 E f
Teano, bp. 95 ins.
Teanum Apulum 30 E a
Teanum Sidicinum 30 D a
Teate, Apulum 30 E a
Teate, Marrucinum (Chieti) 27 I e
Teb, El 174 G c
Tebuk 99 K h
Teck, duchy 143 H h
Teck, ruin 143 H h
Tecklenburg 78 E b
Tecklenburg, cty. 78 E b
Tecmon 10 B c
Tecumseh, Fort 210 E b
Tees River 49 F d
Tegea 14 C b
Tegernsee, mon. 95 E b
Tegesta 191 I f
Tegianum 30 E b
Tegucigalpa 213 D c
Tehachapi Pass 210 B c
Teheran 170 G e
Tehuacan 213 ins.
Tehuacanas, tribe 188 G d
Tehuantepec 105 A c
Tehuantepec, Gulf of 213 C c
Tehuantepec, Isthmus of 213 C c
Teixeira, route of 214 C c
Tejada 46 F f
Tejas, tribe 188 G d
Tejuco 214 E d
Tekfour Serai, loc. in Constantinople 93 G e
Tekka, reg. 89 J g
Tekoa 7 C e
Tela 20 H d
Telamon 27 F e
Telesia 30 D a
Telethrius, mt. 11 E d
Telium 26 E a
Tell, The, reg. 2 E e
Tellicherri 137 C f
Tell el Kebir
Tellena
Tellus, Temple of, Rome 22 A
Telmessus, Telmissus 20 C d
Telo Martius (Toulon) 38 D d
Telshi 125 H a
Telus 13 E c
Tembuland, reg. 175 M m
Temenites 31 ins. B
Temenium 15 C b
Temes River 159 K f
Tempe, valley 11 D c
Templars, House of the, Jerusalem 68 ins. B (8)
Temple, Faubourg du, quarter in Paris 149 B
Temple, Rue du, street in Paris 149 B
Temple, Inner, Middle and Outer, loc. in London 75 G g
Temple, The, in Jerusalem 68 ins. B
Temple, Rue du, street in Paris 149 B
Temple, Street of the, Jerusalem 68 ins. B
Temple, The, bldg. in Paris 149 B
Temple, Vieille, Rue du, street in Paris 149 B
Temple Church, in London 75 G g (1)
Temple of Peace, Aug. Reg. of Rome 22 A
Tempsa 31 F c
Temrink 119 L d
Temuco 215 B f
Tenancingo 106 A a
Tenasserim
Tenasserim, prov. 171 K g
Tenby 65 D e
Tencteri, people 38 D b
Tenda 130 P j
Tenda, Col di, pass 150 D d
Tenduc, people
Tenea 15 C b
Tenebrium, prom. 38 C e
Tenedos 13 E b
Tenedos, isl. 13 E b
Teneriffe, isl. 108 P e
Teneriffe, Santa Cruz de 174 B b
Tenes 66 G f
Tenimber Islands 172 C a
Ten Jurisdictions, League of, dist. 91 R l
Tenneberg 85 F e
Tennessee, state 202 H c
Tennessee River 211 H d
Tennessee Yazoo Company 196 A d
Tennis Court, loc. in Versailles 149 A
Tenochtillan 106 A a
Tenos 15 F b
Tenos, isl. 15 F b
Tentura or Tentyris (Dendera) 4 F d
Teodosia 124 G b
Teos 13 E b
Teotihuacan 106 B a
Tepeaca 106 C b
Tepexacac
Tepfenhardt 142 D e
Tepic 213 B b

Tepic, ter. 213 B b
Tepl, mon. 95 E a
Teplitz 154 G c
Tepotzotlan 106 A a
Tepulaw Aqueduct 22 A
Teramo 90 D c
Teramo, bp. 95 E c
Teredon 19 G d
Terek River 139 G g
Terek, Cossacks of the, people 139 G g
Tergeste (Trieste) 27 H b
Tergeste, Gulf of 27 H b
Tergovist 77 J c
Terina 31 F d
Terjan 93 E c
Ter la Haye
Termes 38 B d
Termini 90 D f
Termoli 90 E c
Termoli, bp. 95 E c
Termonde 117 C c
Ternate, isl. 112 F c
Terni 90 D c
Terni, bp. 95 E c
Ternodurum, see Tonnerre
Terracina 90 D d
Terracina, bp. 95 E c
Terranova, in Calabria 90 F e
Terranova, in Sicily 90 E f
Terre Haute 211 H c
Terrenate 190 C e
Terrington, parl. bor.
Terschelling, isl. 117 D a
Teruel 82 H e
Terventum
Teschen 79 K d
Teschen, princ. 79 K d
Teslin, lake 212 B b
Tessin (Ticino) River 78 F f
Tessin, dist., see Ticino 91 Q l
Testaccio, Monte, Rome 22 A
Teste de Buch, la 76 C d
Testry 55 P j
Tetrica, mt. 27 H e
Tetschen 123 H c
Tettnang 143 I j
Tetuan 70 E f
Teufelsbrücke, bridge 150 E c
Teumessus 11 E d
Teurnia 27 H a
Teuthrania, dist.
Teuthrone 14 C c
Teutoburger Forest, Teutoburgiensis Saltus, mts. 39 J g
Teutones, people 34 F c
Teutonic Order, Dom. of the, 14 cent. 77 H b
Teutonic Order, Dom. of the, 16 cent. 119 J b
Teviotdale, dist.
Tewkesbury 84 B d
Tewkesbury, mon. 97 O j
Tewkesbury, parl. bor. 163 L f (Tewkesb.)
Texas, prov. 190 F e
Texas, state 202 E i
Texas Prairies, reg. 187 J f
Texel, isl. 117 C a
Textricum, see Testry
Texuandri, people 39 H h
Tezcuco
Tezcuco, lake
Thabraca 46 H f
Thagines River 31 F c
Thala 38 D e
Thamatha 7 D e
Thame, mon. 97 Q j
Thames River, in Canada 200 B b
Thames River, in Connecticut 189 B d (Th.R.)
Thames River, in England 49 F f
Thames, Battle of the 200 C b
Thamesis Æsturianum (Thames River) 51 Q i
Thana
Thanet, island of 51 S k
Thann 154 G d
Thannheim 143 J i
Thantia 7 E d
Thapsacus 20 H e
Thapsus, in Algeria 12 E c
Thapsus, in Sicily 30 E e
Thapsus, in Tunis 38 E e
Thara 19 H c
Thasos 11 F b
Thasos, isl. 11 F b
Thaumaci 11 D c
Thaya River 63 I d
Theanum, see Teano
Thebæ Phthiotides 11 D c
Thebais, Rom. prov. 43 I h (3)
Thebes, in Bœotia 11 E d
Thebes, in Egypt 4 F d
Thebez, in Samaria 7 C d
The Close, loc. in London 75 G g
The Danelaw, reg.
The Downs, roadstead 185 H f
The Filder, dist. 143 H h
The Free Land, reg. 117 A c
Theganussa, isl. 14 B c
The Hague 117 C b
The Isles, bp. 97 G c
Theiss River 73 D a
Thelepte 34 F g
Thelpusa 14 B b
Themiscyra 20 G b
Themistocles, Grave of 16 D c
Themistocles, Wall of 23 D
Thenæ 34 G g
The Naze, cape 166 G d
Thengen 142 C e
Thengen, cty. 142 C e
Theocoleum
Theodonis Villa, see Thionville
Theodosia 12 K a
Theodosiopolis (Erzerum) 20 I c
Theodosius II., Wall of, Constantinople 93 G e
Theophilo 214 E d (Phil.)
Theotmelli, see Detmold
Thera 13 D c
Thera, isl. 13 D c
Therambus 11 E c
Therapne 14 C b
Theres, castle 62 F c
Therezina 214 E c
Therma (Salonika) 11 D b
Thermæ Himeræ 30 C e
Thermæ Selinuntiæ 30 C e
Thermaic Gulf 11 D b
Therme
Thermessa, isl. 30 E d
Thermodon River 20 G b
Thermopylæ, pass 11 D d
Thermopylæ, plan of 16
Thermum, in Ætolia 10 C d
Thérouanne, bp. 94 C a
Thervings, people 50 I d
Theseum, loc. in Athens 23 D
Theseum, loc. in the Pyræus 16 D c
Thespiæ 11 E d
Thesprotia, dist. 10 B c
Thesprotian Gulf 10 B c
Thessaliotis, dist. 10 D c
Thessalonica (Salonika) 11 D b
Thessalonica, km. 73 E b
Thessalonica, theme 59 I e
Thessaly, Rom. prov. 43 G f (3)
Thessaly, Turkish prov. 164 C c
Thessaly, reg. 10 C c
Thessaly, Wallachian, princ. 89 B c
Thestium 10 C d
Thetford
Thetford, castle 65 G d
Thetford, mon. 97 R i
Thetford, parl. bor. 163 O e
Theudoria 10 C c
Theveste 38 D e
Thiengen, near Freiburg in Breisgau 142 A e
Thiengen, near Waldshut in Baden 142 B e
Thiers 69 E d
Thiers, mon. 94 C b
Thierstein, castle 91 P k
Thieves Islands 110 GG f
Thilabus 20 J e
Thimnathah
Thines 156 A a
Thines River 156 A a
Thionville, or Diedenhofen 62 C d
Thirsk, parl. bor. 163 M c
This 4 F d
Thisbæ
Thisoa 14 C b
Thoire 76 F c
Tholen 117 C c
Tholey 157 ins.
Thoræ 15 D b
Thoricus 15 E b
Thorigny 76 C b
Thorn, in the Netherlands 117 D c
Thôrn, in Prussia 72 D a
Thorn, Hanse. cy. 98 G c
Thorney, mon. 97 R i
Thornton-upon-Humber, mon. 97 Q h
Thospitis, lake 20 J c
Thouars 61 C c
Thouars, viscty. 76 C c
Thourout, mon. 94 C a
Thrace, East Rom. prov. 43 G e (2)
Thrace, reg. 8 A a
Thrace, Rom. dioc. 43 H e
Thrace, Rom. prov. 35 I e
Thrace, theme 59 J e
Thracesian Theme 59 J f
Thracian Bosporus, str.
Thracian Chersonese, pen. 17 E a
Thracian Sea 17 C b
Three Bishoprics, gen. 147 F b
Three Kings Islands 172 G d
Three Points, cape
Three Rivers, town 191 K b
Thremhall, mon. 97 R j
Thria 16 B a
Thriasian Plain 16 B a
Thronium 11 D d
Thuin 117 C d
Thun 150 D c
Thun, lake of 91 P l
Thun, stronghold 91 P l
Thurgarton, mon. 97 Q h
Thurgau, dist. 62 E e
Thurii 31 F c
Thüringer Wald (Thuringian Forest), mts. 62 F c
Thuringia, dist. 62 F c
Thuringia, landgr. 85 F e
Thuringia, march 63 G c
Thuringians, people 45 F b
Thurrock 75 J i
Thursday Island 172 D b
Thyamis (Kalamas) River 10 B c
Thyamus, mt. 10 C d
Thyatira 20 C c
Thyle River 156 B a
Thymbra
Thymbrius River
Thymœtadæ 16 B b
Thynias, prom. 20 C b
Thyreum 10 C d
Thyrides, prom. 14 C c
Thyssagetæ, people 19 G a
Thyssus 11 F b
Tian-shan Mountains
Tiber River 64 B b
Tiber Island 22 A
Tiberias 6 D c
Tiberine Way, road 35 ins. B
Tiberinum 27 G d
Tiberis River, see Tiber River
Tiberius, Arch of, on the Campus Martius 22 A
Tiberius, Arch of, in the Forum

Tiberius, Palace of . . . . 24 B
Tibesti, reg. . . . . 174 E b
Tibet, reg. . . . .
Tibiscus River . . . . 39 M k
Tibur (Tivoli) . . . . 27 G f
Tiburon, Cape . . . . 105 F c
Tiburones, Isla de los, isl. . . . 107 C h
Tiburtian Way, road . . . . 35 ins. B
Tiburtine Gate . . . . 22 A
Ticino, dist. . . . . 91 Q l
Ticino River . . . . 130 Q i
Ticinum (Pavia) . . . . 26 D b
Ticinus (Ticino) River . . . . . 26 C a
Tickhill, parl. bor. . . . .
Ticonderoga . . . . 196 E b
Ticonderoga, Fort . . . . 192 E b
Tidore, isl. . . . . 112 F c
Tiel . . . . 117 D c
Tie-ling, see Tie Pass . . . . . 171 N d
Tienen . . . . 117 C d
Tien-tsin . . . . 170 ins. A
Tie Pass . . . . 171 N d
Tierra del Fuego, isl. . . . . . . 215 C h
Tierra de los Bacallaos, reg. . . 108 L c
Tierra de los Bretones, reg. . . 108 L c
Tierra Firme, reg. . . . . 105 G e
Tieté River . . . . 214 D e
Tifata, mt. . . . . 30 D a
Tifernum . . . . 27 G d
Tifernus, mt. . . . . 30 D a
Tifernus (Biferno) River . . . . 27 I f
Tiflis . . . . 67 O e
Tiger Hill, village 216
Tigisis, in Mauretania . . . . . . 42 C f
Tigisis, in Numidia . . . . 46 H f
Tigranocerta . . . .
Tigre, dist. . . . . 174 G c
Tigris River . . . . 5 D b
Tiguex, reg. . . . . 190 D e
Ti-hwa (Urumtsi) . . . . 171 J d
Tilburg . . . . 117 D c
Tilburg, castle . . . . 75 J i
Tilingana . . . .
Tiliventus (Tagliamento) River 27 G a
Tilleda . . . . 62 F c
Tilly . . . . 156 B a
Tilox, prom. . . . . 26 D e
Tilsit . . . . 88 I d
Tilty, mon. . . . . 97 R j
Timan Mountains . . . . 3 I b
Timavus (Timavo) River . . . . 27 H b
Timbuktu . . . . 174 C c
Timnah . . . . 7 B e
Timonium . . . . 34 ins. C (3)
Timor, isl. . . . . 112 F d
Timor Sea . . . . 172 B b
Timorlaut, isl. . . . . 172 C e
Timsah, lake . . . . 174 K i
Timur, Dom. of . . . .
Tinchebrai . . . . 65 F f
Tinetio . . . . 26 D a
Tingis (Tangier) . . . . 38 A e
Tinia River . . . . 27 G d
Tinicum Island . . . . 192 ins.
Tinna River . . . . 27 H d
Tinnevelli . . . .
Tinogasta . . . . 215 C e
Tintern, mon. . . . . 97 O j
Tiphsach . . . . 6 ins. C
Tippecanoe, battle . . . . 211 H b
Tipperah, dist. . . . . 137 F d
Tipperary, cty. . . . . 127 I i
Tippermuir . . . .
Tippoo, Dominions of . . . . . . 137 C f
Tirano . . . . 91 S l
Tirhut, reg. . . . .
Tirlemont . . . . 117 C d
Tirmidh . . . .
Tirnova . . . . 59 J e
Tiron, mon. . . . . 94 C b
Tiryns . . . . 15 C b
Tirzah . . . . 7 C d
Tisæus, mt. . . . . 11 E c
Tisia (Theiss) River . . . . 35 I d
Tisné, route of . . . . 190 F d
Tisza, River, see Theiss River 43 G d
Tisza-Füred . . . . 159 K e
Titane . . . . 14 C b
Titanus, mt. . . . . 10 D c
Titaresius River . . . . 10 D c
Titarius, mt. . . . . 10 D b
Titchfield, ab. . . . . 100 A b
Titel . . . . 159 K f
Tithe Lands, dist. . . . . 39 J i
Tithorea . . . . 11 D d
Tithronium . . . . 11 D d
Titicaca, lake . . . . 214 C d
Titulcia . . . . 38 B d
Titus, Arch of . . . . 24 B
Titus, Baths of . . . . 22 A
Tium . . . . 20 E b
Tiumen . . . . 138 K d
Tiveden, dist. . . . . 88 F b
Tiverton . . . . 189 C d
Tiverton, parl. bor. . . . . 163 K g
Tivoli . . . . 96 B b
Tivoli, bp. . . . . 95 E c
Tizón, Rio del, R. . . . . 190 C e
Tlacopan . . . .
Tlalmanalco . . . . 106 B a
Tlalpan . . . . 201 H g
Tlascala, Tlaxcala . . . . 106 B a
Tlemsen . . . . 66 F g
Tlemsen, dist. . . . . 118 D g
t'Loo . . . . 117 D b
Tmolus, mt. . . . . 20 C c
Toarcis, see Thouars
Tobago, isl. . . . . 105 H d
Tobitschau . . . . 159 I d
Tobol River . . . .
Tobolsk . . . . 170 H c
Tocaima . . . . 214 B b
Tocantins River . . . . 214 E c
Tocci, Dom. of the . . . . 93 B c
Tocobaga . . . . 191 I f
Tocopilla . . . . 214 B e
Tocuyo . . . . 214 C b
Todi . . . . 64 ins.
Todi, bp. . . . . 95 E c
Todos os Santos, Bahia de, bay 214 F d
Todtnau . . . . 142 A e
Toggenburg, dist. . . . . 91 R k
Toggenburg, New, castle . . . . 91 R k
Toggenburg, Old, castle . . . . . 91 R k
Togoland, German col. . . . . .
Tokay . . . . 159 K d
Tokelau Islands . . . . 172 H a
Tokyo . . . . 171 O e
Tolbiacum . . . . 39 I h
Toledo, in Ohio . . . . 211 I b
Toledo, in Spain . . . . 82 B b
Toledo, abp. . . . . 94 A c
Toledo, emir. . . . . 83 E d
Tolentino . . . . 151 I h
Tolenus (Turano) River . . . . . 27 G e
Toleria . . . . 35 ins. B
Tolerus (Sacco) River . . . . . . 30 C a
Toletum (Toledo) . . . . 38 B e
Tolima, Nevada de, mt. . . . . . 214 B b
Tolna . . . . 159 J e
Tolone, see Toulon
Tolophon . . . . 10 D d
Tolosa (Toulouse) . . . . 38 C d
Toluca . . . . 106 A a
Tomarus, mt. in Epirus . . . . . 10 B c
Tomarus, mt. in Illyris . . . . . 10 B b
Tombecbé, Fort . . . . 191 H e
Tombigbee River . . . . 191 H e
Tombs of the kings, in Jerusalem 6 ins. A
Tombstone . . . . 210 C d
Tomebamba . . . . 111 B b
Tomi . . . . 39 N l
Tomis . . . . 35 J e
Tömös Pass . . . . 159 M f
Tomsk . . . . 171 J c
Tonala . . . . 213 C c
Tonawanda, Ind. Res. . . . . . . 188 K b
Tondern . . . . 80 A d
Tonga Islands . . . . 180 J i
Tongaland, dist. . . . . 175 N l
Tongatabu, isl. . . . . 172 H c
Tongking, reg. . . . . 92 K e
Tongres . . . . 117 D d
Tongrinne . . . . 156 B a
Tonk . . . . 137 C c
Tonkawas, Ind. Res. . . . . 188 G c
Tonnerre . . . . 61 E c
Tonnerre, cty. . . . . 76 F c
Tönning . . . . 134 E a
Toongabuddra River . . . . 137 C e
Topeka . . . . 198 F c
Tophane, quarter in Constantinople . . . . 93 G e
Tor, mon. . . . . 97 N k
Tor Bay . . . . 127 V p
Torcello, bp. . . . . 95 E b
Tordesillas . . . .
Torgau . . . . 115 G c
Torinna, see Turenne
Torksey, castle . . . . 65 F d
Torne River . . . . 167 J b
Torneå . . . . 167 J b
Tornodorum, see Tonnerre
Toro . . . . 82 A a
Toron . . . . 68 ins. A
Toronaic Gulf . . . . 11 E b
Torone . . . . 11 E b
Toronto . . . . 199 J b
Toropetz . . . . 71 M b
Torre di Faro . . . . 161 J h
Torrens, lake . . . . 172 C d
Torreon . . . . 213 B b
Torres, abp. . . . . 95 D c
Torres Strait . . . . 172 D a
Torres Vedras . . . . 130 B f
Torrington . . . . 127 U p
Torris . . . . 72 B c
Tortona . . . . 90 I h
Tortona, bp. . . . . 95 D c
Tortosa, in Spain . . . . 82 C a
Tortosa, bp. . . . . 94 C c
Tortosa, in Syria . . . . 68 C c
Tortuga, isl., near Haiti . . . . 105 F b
Tortuga, isl., near Venezuela . 105 G d
Toryne . . . . 10 B c
Törzburger Pass . . . . 159 M f
Torzhok . . . . 99 J b
Toskih . . . .
Totnes . . . . 127 V p
Tottenham . . . . 75 I h
Toul . . . . 62 C d
Toul, bp. . . . . 95 D b
Toul, gouv. . . . . 146 C b
Toul, imp. cy. . . . . 78 D d
Toulon . . . . 69 F e
Toulon, bp. . . . . 95 D c
Toulouse, in France . . . . 61 D e
Toulouse, abp. . . . . 148 B c
Toulouse, cty. about 1000 . . . 58 E e
Toulouse, cty. 12 cent. . . . . . 69 E e
Toulouse, cty. 15 cent. . . . . . 84 D h
Toulouse, gen. . . . . 147 E c
Toulouse, univ. . . . . 100 F f
Toulouse, Fort, in Alabama . . 191 H e
Touques . . . . 146 G e
Touraine, cty. . . . . 69 H g
Touraine, duchy . . . . 78 B e
Touraine, gouv. . . . . 146 B b
Touraine, prov. . . . . 148 E e
Tourcoing . . . . 134 B c
Tourinnes . . . . 156 B a
Tournai . . . . 117 B d
Tournai, bp. . . . . 94 C a
Tournai, cty. . . . . 61 E a
Tourneppe . . . . 156 A a
Tournon . . . . 76 F d
Tours . . . . 61 D c
Tours, abp. . . . . 94 B b
Tours, cty. . . . . 69 H g
Tours, gen. . . . . 147 D b
Tovar, route of . . . . 190 C d
Tovin . . . . 73 I b

Tower, in London . . . . 75 G g
Tower of Leander, in Constantinople . . . . 93 G e
Tower of the Winds, in Athens 23 D
Tower Hamlets, parl. bor. . . . 163 O f
Tower Street, in London . . . . 75 G g
Townsend, mt. . . . . 172 D d
Townsville . . . . 172 D b
Towton . . . . 84 C c
Toxandria, dist. . . . . 62 C c
Tozan, people . . . .
Trachea, dist. . . . . 33 L e
Trachenberg . . . . 154 I c
Trachinia . . . . 11 D d
Trachinian Cliffs . . . . 16 F e
Trachis . . . . 16 E e
Trachonitis, dist. . . . . 6 E c
Trachselwald, castle . . . . . . 91 P l
Trafalgar, Cape . . . . 130 B f
Tragia, isl. . . . . 20 B d
Traiana, Colonia . . . . 39 I h
Traianopolis, in Cilicia . . . . . 20 E d
Traianopolis, in Thrace . . . . . 39 N l
Traianus, Portus . . . . 26 E e
Traiectum (Utrecht, in the Netherlands) . . . . 39 H g
Traiectus, see Maestricht
Traietto . . . . 90 D d
Trais River . . . . 31 F c
Traisen River . . . . 63 H d e
Trajan, Caths of . . . . 22 A
Trajan, Port of . . . . 35 ins. B
Trajan, Statue of . . . . 24 B
Trajan's Aqueduct . . . . 35 ins. B (6)
Trajan's Column . . . . 22 A (14)
Trajan's Forum . . . . 24 B
Trajan's Way, road . . . . 30 E a
Traktir . . . . 164 J f
Tralles . . . . 17 E c
Tramin . . . . 150 F c
Trancoso . . . . 83 J g
Trani . . . . 90 F d
Trani, abp. . . . . 65 F c
Transalpine Gaul, reg. . . . 34 E d (Gaul)
Trans Baikal Province . . . . . 171 M c
Transcaspian District . . . . . . 170 G e
Transjurane Burgundy, km. . . 56 D c
Transkei, reg. . . . . 175 M m
Transpadane Gaul, reg. . . . . . 26 B b
Trans Siberian Railway . . . . . 170 G c
Trans Tiberim, Aug. Reg of Rome 22 A
Transvaal Colony . . . .
Transvaal, rep. . . . . 175 M l
Transylvania, gr. prim. in Hungary . . . . 131 H d
Transylvania, princ. . . . . . . 119 I d
Transylvania, reg. . . . . 59 I d
Transylvania, proposed col. in U. S. . . . . 194 B c
Transylvanian Alps, mts. . . . . 39 M l
Trapani . . . . 90 D f
Trapezus, in Arcadia . . . . . . 14 C b
Trapezus, in Pontus (Trebizond) 20 H b
Trappe, La, mon. . . . . 94 C b
Trarbach . . . . 134 D d
Trasimenus (Trasimeno), lake . 27 G d
Trastamare, cty. . . . . 83 J g
Trastevere, quarter . . . . 96 A
Trasyllus, Monument of . . . . 23 C (9)
Traú, bp. . . . . 95 F c
Trauchburg, ruin . . . . 143 J j
Traungau, dist. . . . . 63 G e
Trausnitz, castle . . . . 79 H d
Trautenau . . . . 135 H c
Travancore, reg. . . . . 137 C g
Travendal, castle . . . . 134 F b
Travemünde . . . . 154 E a
Traz os Montes, dist. . . . . . . 83 J g
Trea . . . . 27 H d
Treba . . . . 27 H f
Trebia . . . . 27 G e
Trebia (Trebbia) River . . . . . 26 D c
Trebizond . . . . 67 N e
Trebizond, empire, 13 cent. . . 73 H b
Trebizond, empire, 14 cent. . . 89 K l
Trebizond, empire, 15 cent. . . 93 E b
Trebnitz, mon. . . . . 80 E f
Trebujena . . . . 82 A b
Trebula, in Samnium . . . . . . 30 D a
Trebula Mutuesca . . . . 27 G e
Trecas, see Troyes
Tre Fontane, mon. . . . . 96 B b
Tregony, parl. bor. . . . . 163 J g
Tréguier . . . . 61 B b
Tréguier, bp. . . . . 94 B b
Trémoins . . . . 143 ins. F
Tremouille, La . . . . 81 M h
Trencsin . . . .
Trent . . . . 62 F e
Trent, bp. . . . . 79 G e
Trent River . . . . 49 F e
Trenton . . . . 192 D c
Tréport, mon. . . . . 94 C a
Trerus River, see Tolerus R. . 30 C a
Tres Pinos . . . . 210 A c
Treuenbrietzen . . . . 85 C b
Treveri or Treveris, see Trèves
Treveri, people . . . . 38 D c
Trèves . . . . 62 D d
Trèves, abp. . . . . 95 D b
Trèves, univ. . . . . 100 G d
Treviso . . . . 90 K h
Treviso, bp. . . . . 95 E b
Treviso, univ . . . . 100 H e
Trévoux . . . . 147 F b
Triaditza . . . . 59 I e
Triana . . . . 82 A b
Trianon, Avenue de, in Versailles 149 A
Trianon, Grand, loc. in Versailles 149 A
Trianon, Petit, loc. in Versailles 149 A
Trianon, Plaine de, loc. in Versailles . . . . 149 A
Triballi, people . . . . 39 M l
Triberg . . . . 142 B d
Triberg, lordship . . . . 142 B d
Triboci, people . . . . 39 I i
Tribulation, Cape . . . . 172 D b
Tribur . . . . 62 E d
Tricameron . . . . 52 C c
Tricasses, see Troyes
Tricca (Trikala) . . . . 10 C c
Trichinopoly . . . . 137 C f
Trichonis, lake . . . . 10 C d
Trichonium . . . . 10 C d
Tricorythus . . . . 16 C a
Tricrana, isl. . . . . 15 D b
Tridentine Alps . . . . 27 F a
Tridentini, people . . . . 27 F a
Tridentum (Trent) . . . . 27 F a
Trient, see Trent
Trier, see Trèves
Trieste . . . . 63 G f
Trieste, bp. . . . . 95 E b
Trifanum . . . . 30 C a
Trifels, castle . . . . 62 D d
Trigemina Gate . . . . 23 B
Trikala . . . . 89 B c
Trileucum, prom. . . . . 38 A d
Trim, bp. . . . . 97 E c
Trimenia . . . . 16 B a
Trinacria, km. . . . . 77 G e
Trincomalee . . . . 137 D g
Trinidad, in Bolivia . . . . 214 C d
Trinidad, in Cuba . . . . 213 E b
Trinidad, isl. . . . . 105 H d
Trinidad River . . . .
Trinity, Fort . . . . 192 ins.
Trinity River . . . . 191 G e
Trinius River . . . . 27 I f
Trinkomali . . . .
Trino . . . . 130 Q i
Trinobantes, people . . . .
Triopium, prom. . . . . 20 B d
Triparadisus . . . . 18 O h
Triphylia, dist., in Elis . . . . . 14 B b
Triphylia, dist., in Epirus . . . 10 B c
Tripodiscus . . . . 15 D a
Tripoli, in Africa . . . . 53 D c
Tripoli, reg. . . . . 77 G i
Tripoli, vilayet . . . . 174 E a
Tripoli, in Syria . . . . 68 C c
Tripoli, cty. . . . . 68 C b
Tripolis, in Phœnicia . . . . . . 20 F e
Tripolis, in Pontus . . . . 20 H b
Tripolis, dist., in Thessaly . . . 10 D b
Tripolis, reg., in Africa . . . . . 34 G g
Tripolitana, W. Rom. prov. . . 42 E g (3)
Tripolitza . . . . 131 H f
Tristan da Cunha, isl. . . . . . . 108 P k
Tritæa, in Achaia . . . .
Tritæa, in Locris . . . . 11 D d
Triumphal Way, road . . . . . . 35 ins. B
Trivandrum . . . . 137 C g
Trivento, bp . . . . 95 E c
Troarn . . . . 76 C b
Troarn, mon. . . . . 94 B b (Tr.)
Troas, reg. . . . . 9 B d
Trochtelfingen . . . . 143 H i
Trœsmis . . . . 39 N l
Trœzen . . . . 15 D b
Trogen . . . . 91 R k
Trogilus Port . . . . 31 ins. B
Troglodytes, people . . . . 4 F d
Troian Plain . . . .
Trois Fontaines, mon. . . . . . . 94 C b
Troitsa . . . . 138 E d
Troitski . . . . 171 J b
Troitzkoi, mon. . . . . 131 K b
Troja, in Asia Minor, see Ilium
Troja, in Italy . . . . 90 E d
Troja, bp. . . . . 95 F c
Trombetas River . . . . 214 D c
Tromsoe . . . . 166 I b
Tropea, bp. . . . . 95 F d
Troppau . . . . 79 J d
Troppau, princ. . . . . 79 J d
Troy, in Asia Minor . . . .
Troy, in New York . . . . 192 E b
Troyes . . . . 61 E b
Troyes, bp. . . . . 94 C b
Troyes, cty. . . . . 61 E b
Troyland, reg. . . . .
Trubchevsk . . . . 131 J c
Truentus (Tronto) River . . . . 27 I e
Trujillo, in Honduras . . . . . . 213 D c
Trujillo, in Peru . . . . 111 B c
Trujillo, in Spain . . . . 82 A b
Trujillo, in Venezuela . . . . . . 214 B b
Trumplini, people . . . . 26 E b
Truro . . . . 127 T p
Truxillo (Trujillo, in Honduras) 105 C c
Tsanpu River . . . . 171 J f
Tshiblak . . . .
Tsi-nan . . . . 171 M e
Tsi-ning-chau . . . .
Tsitsihar . . . . 171 N d
Tsuen-chau-fu . . . . 103 L e
Tuam, abp. . . . . 97 C c
Tuamotu, isl. . . . . 180 N i
Tuat, oasis . . . . 2 D f
Tubac . . . . 190 C e
Tubantes, people . . . . 39 I g
Tubariyeh . . . .
Tübingen . . . . 143 H h
Tübingen, palat. . . . . 143 G h
Tübingen, univ. . . . . 100 G e
Tublinum . . . . 26 E a
Tubuai Islands . . . . 180 M j
Tucacas . . . . 214 C a
Tucci . . . . 42 B f
Tuchcov . . . . 131 I d
Tucson . . . . 190 C e
Tucumán . . . . 215 C e
Tuder . . . . 27 G e
Tugela River . . . . 175 N l
Tuileries, The, loc. in Paris . . 149 B
Tula . . . . 139 E e
Tulalip, Ind. Res. . . . . 188 B a
Tulare, lake . . . . 210 B c
Tularenos, tribe . . . . 188 C c
Tule River, Ind. Res. . . . . . . 188 C c
Tullahoma . . . . 208 C b

Tulle . . . . 84 D g
Tulle, bp. . . . . 94 C b
Tullear . . . . 175 H g
Tullianum . . . . 24 A (3)
Tulln . . . . 63 I d
Tullum (Toul) . . . . 39 H i
Tultcha . . . . 164 D a
Tumbez . . . . 111 A b
Tumuc Humac Mountains . . . 214 D b
Tumut . . . .
Tunbridge, parl. bor. . . . . . .
Tunes (Tunis) . . . . 38 E e
Tungabhadra River . . . . 137 C e
Tung-chang . . . . 171 M e
Tung-chau . . . . 170 ins. A
Tungri, people . . . . 39 H h
Tung-tshu . . . . 170 ins. A
Tunguses, people . . . .
Tunguska River, Lower . . . . .
Tunguska River, Upper . . . . .
Tunis . . . . 53 D c
Tunis, bay of . . . . 34 ins. A
Tunis, French dependency . . . 174 D a
Tunis, reg. . . . . 54 F f
Tunis, state . . . . 77 F e
Tunjá . . . . 214 B b
Tunsberg . . . . 58 F b
Tupiza . . . . 214 C e
Turan, khan. . . . . 92 G b
Turcilingians, people . . . . .
Turcomans, people . . . . 170 G e
Turdetani, or Turdetanians, people . . . . 38 A e
Turduli, people . . . . 38 B e
Turenne . . . . 61 D d
Turenne, castle . . . . 76 D d
Turenne, viscty. . . . . 78 B f
Turenum (Trani) . . . . 31 F a
Turfan . . . .
Turholz, mon. . . . . 94 C a
Turicum (Zurich) . . . . 39 J j
Turin . . . . 90 H h
Turin, univ. . . . . 100 G e
Türkheim . . . . 126 E b
Türkheim, imp. cy. . . . . 122 D d
Turkestan, reg. . . . . 170 H d
Turkestan, E., reg. . . . . 170 I e
Turkish (Ottoman) Empire, 1451—1481 93
Turkish (Ottoman) Empire, 1481—1683 124
Turkish (Ottoman) Empire, since 1683 164
Turkmanchai . . . . 170 F e
Turkomans, people . . . . 77 L e
Turks, people . . . . 165 leg.
Turks Islands . . . . 213 E b
Turner's Falls, village . . . . . 189 B c
Turnhout . . . . 117 C c
Turones, see Tours
Turones, people, in Gaul . . . . 38 C c
Turones, people, in Germany . 38 E c
Turoqua . . . . 38 A d
Turriff . . . .
Turris Libisonis . . . . 38 D d
Tursan, viscty. . . . . 69 C e
Turtle Mountain, Ind. Res. . . . 188 G a
Turukhansk . . . . 171 J b
Tusayan, reg. . . . . 100 C d
Tuscaloosa . . . . 211 H d
Tuscan Presidios, dist. . . . . . 118 G e
Tuscan Street, in Rome . . . . . 24 A
Tuscana . . . . 27 F e
Tuscany, gr. duchy . . . . 161 H f
Tuscany, dist. . . . . 64 B b
Tuscany and Umbria, West Rom. prov. . . . . 42 E e (2)
Tuscarawas River . . . . 188 J b
Tuscarora, Ind. Res. . . . . 188 J b
Tuscaroras . . . . 193 F d
Tuscaroras, tribe . . . . 188 J c
Tuscia, dist. . . . . 27 F d
Tusculum . . . . 35 ins. B
Tusculum, bp. . . . . 96 B b
Tuskegee . . . . 207 H d
Tutbury . . . . 118 D c
Tutbury, mon. . . . . 97 P i
Tutela, see Tudela
Tutikorin . . . . 170 I h
Tuttlingen . . . . 143 G j
Tutuila, isl. . . . . 199 ins. D
Tuxtla . . . . 213 C c
Tuy . . . . 82 A a
Tuy, bp. . . . . 94 A c
Tver . . . . 138 E d
Twann . . . . 91 P k
Twat, reg. . . . . 53 B d
Tweed River . . . . 49 E d
Tweeddale, dist. . . . .
Twickenham . . . . 75 I i
Twiel, castle . . . . 62 E e
Twillingate, isl. . . . . 212 J d
Two Sicilies, km., 12 cent. . . . 72 C d
Two Sicilies, km., 15 cent. . . . 90 E e
Tyana . . . . 20 F d
Tybee Island . . . . 193 ins. C
Tyburn . . . . 75 I h
Tycha, quarter in Syracuse . . 31 ins. B
Tykocin . . . . 159 L b
Tylus Island . . . . 19 H e
Tymphæa, dist. . . . . 10 C b
Tymphe, mt. . . . . 10 C b
Tymphrestus, mt. . . . . 10 C d
Tyndale, dist. . . . .
Tyndaris . . . . 30 E d
Tyne River . . . . 49 E d
Tynemouth, mon. . . . . 97 P f
Tynemouth, parl. bor. . . . . . . 163 M b
Typhrestus, mt. . . . . 10 C d
Tyra . . . . 35 K d
Tyras River . . . . 35 J d
Tyrconnel, cty. . . . . 127 I g
Tyre . . . . 6 C b
Tyre, Ladder of, cape . . . . . 6 C b
Tyre, plan of . . . . 18 ins. B
Tyrissa . . . . 10 C b
Tyrnau . . . . 115 I d
Tyrol, castle . . . . 72 C b
Tyrol, cty. . . . . 79 G e
Tyrol, princ. cty. . . . . 150 F c
Tyrone, cty. . . . . 127 J g
Tyropœon Valley . . . . 6 ins. A
Tyrrhenian Sea . . . . 29 B d
Tyrus (Tyre), in Phœnicia . . . 6 C b
Tyrus, in Laconia . . . . 15 C b
Tyrus, in Peræa . . . . 7 D e
Tzaritzyn . . . . 139 F f

Uaupes River . . . . 214 C b
Ubangi River . . . . 175 E d
Úbeda . . . . 82 B b
Uberaba . . . . 214 E d
Uberi, people . . . . 26 B a
Überlingen, imp. cy. . . . . 142 D e
Ubii, people . . . . 39 I h
Ubulla . . . . 99 M g
Ucaca . . . . 99 M c
Ucayali River . . . . 111 C c
Uceda . . . . 83 E c
Ucetium, see Uzès
Uclés . . . . 82 B b
Udaipur . . . . 137 B d
Udine . . . . 90 D a
Udine, bp. . . . . 95 E b
Ufa . . . . 139 I e
Uffnau, isl. . . . . 91 Q k
Uganda, prot. . . . . 175 G d
Ugernum, see Beaucaire
Uglitch . . . .
Ugrians, people . . . .
Uigurs, people . . . .
Uintah, Fort . . . . 210 C b
Uintah, Ind. Res. . . . . 188 D b
Uirats, people . . . .
Ujjain . . . .
Ukak . . . . 99 M c
Uker River . . . . 154 G b
Ukermark, dist . . . . 85 C b
Ukraine, reg. . . . . 139 D f
Ukrians, people . . . . 63 G b
Ulatha, dist. . . . . 6 D b
Uleåborg . . . . 138 C c
Uliarus (Oléron), isl. . . . . 38 B c
Uliassutai . . . .
Ulloa, route of, 1537 . . . . . . 107 F e
Ulm . . . . 62 E d
Ulm, imp. cy. . . . . 143 I h
Ulpia (Sardica) . . . . 39 M l
Ulpia, Basilica, bldg. in Rome 24 B
Ulpia Traiana . . . . 39 M k
Ulpiana . . . . 39 M l
Ulrichen . . . . 91 Q l
Ulster, prov. . . . .
Ulu-kem River . . . .
Ulwar . . . . 137 C c
Ülzen, Hanse. cy. . . . . 99 ins. B
Umachiri . . . . 214 B d
Uman . . . . 139 D f
Uman, reg. . . . .
Umarkot . . . . 137 A c
Umatas . . . . 198 ins. C
Umatilla, Ind. Res. . . . . 188 C a
Umballa . . . . 137 C b
Umber, lake . . . . 27 G d
Umbilicus, loc. in Rome . . . .
Umbria, Aug. Reg. . . . . 27 G e
Umbria, dist., 15 cent. . . . . . . 90 D c
Umbrians, people . . . . 29 C c
Umbro (Ombrone) River . . . . 27 F e
Umeå . . . . 166 I c
Umpquas, tribe . . . . 188 B b
Umtata River . . . . 175 M m
Unalaska, isl. . . . . 198 ins. A
Uncompahgre Mountains . . . . 198 D c
Uncompahgre, Ind. Res. . . . . . 188 E c
Unestrudis River, see Unstrut River
Ungarisch Altenburg . . . . 155 I e
Ungava, dist. . . . . 212 H c
Ungava Bay . . . . 212 I c
Unghvar . . . . 168 H b
Unimak, isl. . . . . 198 ins. A
Union, Fort, in New Mexico . . 210 D c
Union, Fort, in N. Dakota . . . 210 E a
Union Islands . . . . 172 H a
Union Pacific Grant . . . . 210 D b
Uniontown . . . . 206 ins.
United Netherlands, country . . 122 C b
United States, 1783 196
United States, 1910 . . . . 198, 199
Unna River . . . . 155 I f
Unstrut River . . . . 62 F c
Unter-Öwisheim . . . . 142 C b
Unterwalden, canton . . . . 91 Q l
Upi . . . . 4 G c
Upland (Chester, in Pa.) . . . . 192 ins.
Upminster . . . . 75 J h
Upolu, isl. . . . . 172 H b
Upper Alsace, landgr. . . . . . . 114 D e
Upper Argen River . . . . 143 I j
Upper Bavaria, dist. . . . . 122 F e
Upper Britain, prov. . . . . 38 B b (1)
Upper Burgundy, dist. . . . . . . 62 C e
Upper Burgundy, km. . . . . 56 D c
Upper Burma, prov. . . . . 171 K f
Upper California, prov. . . . . . 190 B d
Upper Canada, prov. . . . . 212 G d
Upper Dacia, prov. . . . . 39 M k (1 a)
Upper Egypt, reg. . . . .
Upper Gelderland . . . . 117 E c
Upper Germany, prov. . . . . . .
Upper Gihon, well . . . . 6 ins. A
Upper Guinea, reg. . . . . 174 C d
Upper Libya, East Rom. prov. . 43 G g (1)
Upper Lorraine, duchy . . . . . 62 C d
Upper Lusatia, dist. . . . . 80 ins.
Upper Lusatia, margr. . . . . . . 87 J c
Upper Mœsia, prov. . . . . 39 M l (2 a)
Upper Palatinate, dist. . . . . . . 79 G d
Upper Pannonia, prov. . . . . . 34 H d
Upper Peru, reg. . . . . 214 C d
Upper Pimería, dist. . . . . 190 C e

Upper Silesia, dist. 72 D a
Upper Tunguska River
Upsala 88 G b
Upsala, univ. 100 I c
Ur (Mugheir) 4 G c
Urabá, Gulf of 105 E e
Urabá, reg. 105 E e
Urach 143 H h
Urach, castle 62 E d
Urach, cty. 143 H i
Urach, Hohen, ruin 143 H i
Ural Mountains 138 I c
Ural River 139 H e
Uralian Cossacks, people 139 H e
Uralsk 139 H e
Urba (Orbe) 39 I j
Urban VIII, Wall of Pope 96 A
Urbevetum, see Orvieto
Urbino 90 M j
Urbino, bp. 95 E c
Urbinum (Urbino) 27 G d
Urbs Salvia 27 H d
Urci
Urcinium 26 C e
Urés 213 B b
Urga 171 L d
Urgel 82 C a
Urgel, bp. 94 C c
Urgenj
Urgo, isl. 26 D d
Uri, canton 91 Q l
Uri, dist. 71 R k
Uria 31 G b
Uria, lake 10 C d
Urias Bay 30 E a
Uriconium (Wroxeter) 51 O h
Urium 30 E a
Urk, isl. 117 D b
Ursberg, mon. 95 E b
Urseren 91 Q l
Urspring, mon. 143 I i
Urubamba 214 B d
Urubamba River 111 C d
Uruguay, country 215 D f
Uruguay River 215 D e
Uruguayana 215 D e
Uruk (Warka) 4 G c
Urumiah
Urumiah, lake
Urumtsi
Uscosium 27 I f
Usedom 63 G b
Usellis 38 D e
Ush
Ushuaia 215 C h
Usipetes, people 38 D b
Usk River
Uskub 77 I d
Uspallata Pass 215 C f
Ussuri River
Ustica, isl. 30 C d
Ustrina 22 A
Ust Maiskaya 171 O b
Ust Sysolsk 167 P c
Ust-Urt, reg. 139 H g
Ust Yansk 171 O a
Ust Zylma 138 H b
Usuguaya 215 C h
Utah, state 210 C c
Utah, ter. 1850 202 C g
Utah, ter. 1861 203 P g
Utah Lake 190 C c
Ute, Ind. Res. 188 E c
Utelle 150 D e
Utes, tribe 188 C b
Utians, people 8 D c
Utica, in Afrika 38 D e
Utica, in New York 207 K b
Utii, people 35 N e
Utinum, see Udine
Utis River 27 F c
Utrecht, in the Netherlands 117 D b
Utrecht, bp. 95 D a
Utrecht, lordship 114 C b
Utrecht, in Transvaal 175 N l
Utrecht, New, in New York 189 ins. C
Uxbridge 75 I h
Uxellodunum
Uxentis, isl. 38 A c
Üxküll 80 I c
Uyuni 214 C e
Uzentum 31 H c
Uzès 76 F d
Uzès, bp. 94 C c
Uzgent
Uzi, people
Uznach, castle 91 Q k

Vaal River 175 M l
Vabres, bp. 94 C c
Vacalus River 39 H h
Vacapa 190 C f
Vaccæi, people 38 B d
Vaccanæ 35 ins. B
Vada Sabatia 26 C c
Vada Volaterrana 26 E d
Vadimonis, lake 27 G e
Vaduz 134 E e
Vaduz, castle 91 R k
Vaga 46 H f
Vaigatch, isl. 138 J a
Vaihingen 143 G h
Vaison, bp. 95 D c
Valais, dist. 91 P l
Valais, rep. 151 H g
Valangin, castle 91 O k
Valcour 157 ins.
Valdai 131 J b
Valdai Hills 167 L d
Val de Grâce, church in Paris 149 B
Valdivia 215 B f
Val d'Ossola 91 Q l
Valence 61 F d
Valence, bp. 94 C c
Valence, univ. 100 F f
Valencia, in Spain 82 B b
Valencia, abp. 94 B d
Valencia, emir. 83 E d
Valencia, km. 83 K h
Valencia, univ. 100 E g
Valencia, in Venezuela 214 C a
Valencia de Don Juan 82 A a
Valenciennes 117 B d
Valens, Aqueduct of 93 G e
Valentia, see Vibo
Valentia (Valence, in France) 38 D c
Valentia (Valencia, in Spain) 38 B e
Valentia, Rom. prov., in southern Scotland 38 B a (3)
Valentia (Wales), Rom. prov. 42 B c (2)
Valentia Island 166 C e
Valentianæ, see Valenciennes
Valentinois, cty. 76 F d
Valentinois, dist. 126 D d
Valenza 90 I h
Vale of the Camenæ (Muses), loc. in Rome 22 A
Valera de Abajo 82 B b
Valeria, Rom. prov. 42 E e (10)
Valeria ripensis, Rom. prov. 42 F d (14)
Valeria Way, in Italy, road 27 H e
Valerian Way, in Sicily, road 30 D d
Valerius Asiaticus, Gardens of 22 A
Vale Royal, mon. 97 O h
Val-ès-Dunes 65 F f
Valetium 31 H b
Valideh Bridge 93 G e (11)
Valkenburg 117 D d
Valladolid, in Michoacan, Mexico 213 ins.
Valladolid, in New Mexico 190 D d
Valladolid, in Spain 82 H e
Valladolid, bp. 94 B c
Valladolid, univ. 100 E f
Valladolid, in Yucatan, Mexico 213 D b
Vallæ 11 D b
Valle Crucis, mon. 97 N h
Val Leventina, valley 91 Q l
Valley 72 C b
Valley Forge 195 C c
Valley Gate 6 ins. A
Valley of the Sweet Waters
Vallombrosa 64 B b
Vallombrosa, mon. 95 E c
Valmont, mon. 94 C b
Valmy 134 C d
Valognes 76 C b
Valois, cty. 76 E b
Valois, duchy 84 E e
Valona, bp. 95 F c
Valparaiso 215 B f
Valromey 126 D d
Val Sainte, mon. 91 P l
Val-Secret, mon. 94 C b (V. S.)
Valsers, mon. 94 C b (Val.)
Valtellina, dist. 91 R l
Valvata 26 E d
Van 20 J c
Van, lake 99 L f
Van Buren 211 G c
Vancouver 212 C d
Vancouver, Fort 198 A a
Vancouver, isl. 186 G d
Vandalia 211 H c
Vandalia, proposed col. in U. S. 194 C c
Vandals, kingdom of the, 5 cent. 50 E e
Vandals, kingdom of the, 6 cent. 52 C c
Vandals, people 45 H b, C e, F e
Van Diemen Gulf 172 C b
Van Diemen's Land, isl. 172 D e
Vandili, people 38 F b
Vangrones, people 39 J i
Vannes 61 B c
Vannes, bp. 94 B b
Van Reenen's Pass 175 M l
Vanua Levu, isl. 172 H b
Vapincum, see Gap
Var, dept. 148 F f
Var (Vara) River 130 O k
Varallo 130 Q i
Varanger Fiord 167 L a
Varangians, people 45 J d
Varangians, route of the 59 I b
Vararis Æstuarium (Moray Firth) 38 B a
Varaville 65 F f
Varch Bosna 72 D c
Vardar River 119 I e
Varduli, people 38 B d
Varennes 134 C d
Varese 161 G e
Varia
Varini, people 38 E b
Varkenskill 192 D d
Varna 59 J e
Varnitza 131 I d
Varus (Var) River 26 A d
Vasa 138 B c
Vasates, see Bazas
Vasco da Gama, route of 108 Q i
109 W g
Vascones, people 38 B d
Vasio or Vasione, see Vaison
Vassy 114 C d
Vasvar 123 I e
Vatican, palace in Rome 22 A
Vatican Bridge 96 A
Vatrenus (Santerno) River 27 F c
Vaucelles 118 D d
Vauclair, mon. 94 C b
Vaucluse, dept. 148 F f
Vaucouleurs 69 J f
Vaud, dist. 91 O l
Vaudemont 86 E d
Vauluisant, mon. 94 C b
Vauxchamps 154 B d
Vazerol 91 R l
Veamini, people 26 A c
Vecht River 117 E b
Vectilii, Palace of the 22 A
Vectis, isl. (I. of Wight) 51 P i
Vediantii, people 26 A d
Vegia 27 J c
Veglia, bp. 95 E b

Veii . . . . 27 G e
Veile . . . . 158 E a
Vela, Cape de la . . . . 105 F d
Velabrum, quarter in Rome . . 24 A
Velay, cty. . . . . 61 E d
Veldenz . . . . 122 D d
Veldidena . . . . 38 E c
Veleia . . . . 26 D c
Veleiates, people . . . . 26 D c
Velencze . . . . 159 J e
Vélez . . . . 214 B b
Velez, Peñon de . . . . 130 C f
Veleze . . . . 165 B c
Vélez Málaga . . . . 82 B b
Velia, in Lucania . . . . 30 D b
Velia, quarter in Rome . . . . . 24 A
Veliki Luki . . . . 138 D d
Velinus, lake . . . . 27 G e
Velitræ (Velletri) . . . . 35 ins. B
Velitræ, bp. . . . . 96 B b
Vellberg . . . . 143 I g
Velletri . . . . 90 D d
Velletry, bp. . . . . 96 B b
Vellinghausen . . . . 134 D c
Vellore . . . . 137 C f
Veltæ, people . . . . 38 G b
Veltlin, dist., see Valtellina . . . 91 R l
Venafri, bp. . . . . 95 ins.
Venafrum (Venafro) . . . . 30 D a
Venaissin, cty. . . . . 69 F d
Venaissin, prov. . . . . 148 F f
Venango, Fort . . . . 192 A c
Vence, mon. . . . . 148 C c
Vendée, dept. . . . . 148 D e
Vendée, dist. . . . . 130 C d
Vendôme . . . . 69 H g
Vendôme, cty. . . . . 69 H g
Vendôme, Place, loc. in Paris . 149 B
Venedæ, people . . . . 38 F b
Venedic Bay . . . . 38 F b
Venelli, people . . . . 38 B c
Veneris, Portus . . . . 26 D c
Venetes or Venetis, see Vannes
Veneti, people, in Brittany . . . 38 B c
Veneti or Venetians, people, in Italy . . . . 27 F b
Venetia, see Venice
Venetia, dist. in Roman times . 27 F b
Venetia, prov., 19 cent. . . . . . 158 F f
Venetia and Istria, prov. . . . . 42 E d (1)
Venetia and Istria, reg. . . . . . 38 E c (10)
Venetian Alps, mts. . . . . 27 H a
Venetian Republic, 11 cent. . . 64 B a
Venetian Republic, 14 cent. . . 79 H f
Venetian Republic, 15 cent. . . 90 C b
Venetian Republic, 16 cent. . . 118 G d
Venetian Republic, 18 cent. . . 131 F d
Venetus, lake . . . . 39 J j
Venezia, Piazza, loc. in Rome . 22 A
Venezuela, Gulf of . . . . 105 F d
Venezuela, reg. . . . . 105 F d
Venezuela, rep. . . . . 214 C b
Venice . . . . 56 E c
Venice, abp. . . . . 95 E b
Venice, duchy . . . . 63 G f
Venise, Petite, loc. in Versailles 149 A
Venlo . . . . 117 E c
Venlo, Hanse. cy. . . . . 99 ins. B
Venonæ . . . . 51 P h
Venonetes, people . . . . 26 D a
Venosa . . . . 90 E d
Venostes, Venostæ, people . . . 26 E a
Venta Belgarum (Winchester) . 51 P i
Ventadour . . . . 69 E d
Ventadour, castle . . . . 76 E d
Ventadour, cty. . . . . 78 C f
Venta Icenorum (Castor near Norwich) . . . .
Venta Silurum (Cærwent) . . . . 51 O i
Ventersdorp . . . . 175 M l
Ventimiglia . . . . 90 A c
Ventimiglia, bp. . . . . 95 D e
Venus, Temple of, on Mt. Ægaleos 16 B a
Venus and Rome, Temple of . 24 B
Venus Cloacina, Temple of . . 24 A (9)
Venus Erycina, Temple of . . . 22 A
Venus Genetrix, Temple of . 22 A
Venus Victrix, Temple of . . . 22 A
Venusia . . . . 30 E b
Veprik . . . . 131 J c
Vera . . . . 82 B b
Vera Cruz, modern site of . . . 106 D a
Vera Cruz, Villa Rica de la . . 106 D a
Vera Cruz, la Antigua . . . . . 106 D a
Vera Cruz, state . . . . 213 ins.
Veragri, people . . . . 26 B a
Veragua, reg. . . . . 105 D e
Veramin . . . .
Verbanus (Maggiore), lake . . . 26 C a
Vercellæ (Vercelli) . . . . 26 C b
Vercelli . . . . 90 I h
Vercelli, bp. . . . . 95 D b
Vercelli, univ. . . . . 100 G e
Vercheres . . . . 189 B b
Verd, Cape . . . . 174 B c
Verden . . . . 62 E b
Verden, bp. . . . . 95 D a
Verden, princ. . . . . 122 E b
Verdun . . . . 62 C d
Verdun, bp. . . . . 78 D d
Verelä . . . . 131 I a
Veretum . . . . 31 H c
Vereya . . . . 153 P f
Vergil's Grave . . . . 31 ins. A
Veria . . . . 165 C c
Veringen . . . . 143 H i
Verkhoyansk . . . . 171 O b
Vermandois, cty. . . . . 61 E b
Vermilion Lake, Ind. Res. . . . 188 H a
Vermont, dist. . . . . 189 B c
Vermont, state . . . . 199 K b
Verneuil . . . . 69 H f
Verneuil, castle . . . . 76 D b
Verni . . . . 170 I d
Vernio . . . . 90 L i
Vernon, in British Columbia . . 212 D c
Vernon, in France . . . . 69 H f
Vernon, Mount, town in Virginia 193 F b
Verodunum, see Verdun
Veroli, bp. . . . . 95 E c
Verona . . . . 26 F b
Verona, bp. . . . . 93 E b
Verona, march . . . . 72 C b
Verona and Aquileia, march . . 64 B a
Verrazano, route of . . . . 108 M d
Versailles . . . . 126 C b
Versailles, in 1789, plan . . . . 149 A
Versailles, Old . . . . 149 A
Versecz . . . . 168 G d
Verteræ . . . . 51 O g
Vertus . . . . 76 F b
Veruela, mon. . . . . 94 B c
Verulæ . . . . 30 C a
Verulam (Ferryland) . . . . 212 J d
Verulamium (Saint Albans, in England) . . . . 51 P i
Vervins . . . . 114 B d
Vesontio, see Visontio
Vesoul . . . . 122 D e
Vespasian, Forum of . . . . 24 B
Vespasian, Temple of . . . . . .
Vespucci, route of . . . 105 G d, 108 L k
Vesta, Grove of . . . . 24 A
Vesta, Temple of . . . . 24 A
Vestals, House of the . . . . . . 24 A
Vestini, people . . . . 27 H e
Vesubia River . . . . 26 B d
Vesulus, mt. . . . . 26 A c
Vesunna (Périgueux) . . . . 38 C c
Vesuvius, mt. . . . . 30 D b
Veszprim . . . .
Veszprim, bp. . . . .
Vettona . . . . 27 G d
Vettones, people . . . . 38 A d
Vetulonium . . . . 26 E e
Veurne (Furnes) . . . .
Vexin, dist. . . . . 69 H f
Vézelay . . . . 69 I g
Vézelay, mon. . . . . 94 C b
Via Æmilia (Æmilian Way), road 26 E c
Via Æmilia Scauri (Æmilian Way of Scaurus), road . . . . 26 D c
Via Antiana (Antian Way), road 35 ins. B
Via Appia (Appian Way), road 31 F b
Via Appia vetus (Old Appian Way), road . . . . 35 ins. B
Via Aurelia (Aurelian Way), road 26 E d
Via Cassia (Cassian Way), road 27 F e
Via Claudia Augusta (Claudian Augustan Way), road . . . . . 27 G b
Via Claudia Valeria (Claudian Valerian Way), road . . . . . 27 H e
Via Clodia (Clodian Way), road 27 F e
Via di Ripetta, street in Rome 22 A
Via Dolorosa, in Jerusalem . . 68 ins. B
Viadua (Oder) River . . . . 38 F b
Via Flaminia (Flaminian Way), road . . . . 27 G e
Via Flaminia vetus (Old Flaminian Way), road . . . . 27 G e
Via Flavia (Flavian Way), road 27 H b
Via Julia Augusta (Julian Augustan Way), road . . . . 26 B d
Via Labicana (Labican Way), road 35 ins. B
Via Lata, Aug. Reg. of Rome . 22 A
Via lata (Broad Way), street in Rome . . . . 22 A
Via Latina (Latin Way), road . 30 B a
Viale Aventino, street in Rome 22 A
Viale Giulio Cesare, street in Rome . . . . 22 A
Via mala, pass . . . . 150 E c
Via Merulana, street in Rome . 22 A
Viana . . . . 214 E c
Via Nomentana (Nomentan Way), road . . . . 35 ins. B
Via Ostiensis (Ostian Way), road 35 ins. B
Via Popilia (Popilian Way), road 31 F d
Via Portuensis (Port Way), road 35 ins. B
Via Postumia (Postumian Way, in Liguria), road . . . . 26 C c
Via Postumia (Postumian Way, in Venetia), road . . . . 27 G b
Via Prænestina (Prænestine Way), road . . . . 35 ins. B
Via Sacra (Sacred Way), street in Rome . . . . 23 A, B
Via Salaria (Salarian Way), road 27 H e
Via Severiana (Severian Way), road . . . . 35 ins. B
Viasma or Vyasma . . . . 138 D d
Via Tiberina (Tiberine Way), road . . . . 35 ins. B
Via Tiburtina (Tiburtian Way), road . . . . 35 ins. B
Viatka or Vyatka . . . . 138 G d
Viatka, dist. . . . . 71 P b
Via Traiana (Trajan's Way), road 30 E a
Via Triumphalis (Triumphal Way), road . . . . 35 ins. B
Via Valeria (Valerian Way, in Italy), road . . . . 27 H e
Via Valeria (Valerian Way, in Sicily), road . . . . 30 D d
Vibii, Forum . . . . 26 B c
Vibinum . . . . 30 E a
Vibo, Gulf of . . . . 31 F d
Vibo Valentia . . . . 31 F d
Viborg, in Denmark . . . . 88 C c
Viborg, in Finland . . . . 138 C c
Vic . . . . 76 E d
Vicenza . . . . 90 J h
Vicenza, univ. . . . . 100 H e (Vic.)
Vicetia (Vicenza) . . . . 26 F b
Vich . . . . 82 C a
Vich, bp. . . . . 94 C c
Vicinonia River, see Vilaine River
Vicksburg . . . . 208 B c
Vico, lake . . . . 96 B a
Victoria, in Alberta . . . . 212 D c
Victoria, in Brazil . . . . 214 F e
Victoria, in Vancouver . . . . . 198 A a

Victoria, state 172 D d
Victoria Desert, Great 172 B c
Victoria Falls 175 F f
Victoria Land 186 I a
Victoria Nyanza, lake 175 G e
Victoria River 172 B b
Victoria Strait 212 E b
Victoriæ, Clivus, loc. in Rome 24 A
Victrix Julia Tarraconensis(Tarragona) 38 C d
Victumulæ 26 C b
Vicus Augustanus 35 ins. B
Vicus Aurelii 39 J i
Vicus Iulius 39 J i
Vicus Jugarius, street in Rome 24 A
Vicus Tuscus, street in Rome 24 A
Vidin 164 C b
Vidrus (Vecht) River 39 I g
Viejo, el 213 D c
Vielsalm 117 D d
Vienna (Vienne), in France 38 C c
Vienna 63 I d
Vienna, univ. 100 I e
Vienne, in France 69 F d
Vienne, abp. 95 D b
Vienne, dept. 148 E e
Vienne River 69 D c
Viennensis, Rom. prov. 42 D e (1)
Viennois, Dauphiny of, dist. 76 F d
Viennois, dist. 126 D d
Vieques, isl. 199 ins. G
Viersen 117 E c
Vierwaldstätter See, see Lucerne, lake 91 Q l
Vierzon 69 I g
Vieux-Amis
Vigan 199 ins. H
Vigas, las 201 H g
Vigenna, see Vienne
Vigevano 90 B b
Vigo 130 B e
Vijayanagar, Kingdom of 112 A b
Viktring, mon. 95 E b
Vilaine River 148 D e
Vilcobamba 214 B d
Vilija River 159 M a
Vilini River
Vilkomir 159 M a
Villa Albani, loc. in Rome 96 A
Villa Bella 214 D d
Villa Borghese, loc. in Rome 96 A
Villach 63 G e
Villa Encarnación 215 D e
Villa Farnesina, loc. in Rome 96 A
Villafranca 158 F f
Villagos
Villa Ludovisi, loc. in Rome 96 A
Villa Madama, loc. in Rome 96 A
Villa Nova, in Santa Catharina 215 E e
Villa Nueva, in Arg. Rep. 215 C f
Villa Publica, loc. in Rome 24 A
Villa Rica, in Paraguay 215 D e
Villa Rica de la Vera Cruz
Villa rica la Vieja
Villars, in Provence 126 E e
Villars-sur-Ecot 143 ins. F
Villa Umberto I, loc. in Rome 22 A
Villaviciosa, in Asturias 83 J g
Villaviciosa, in Castile 130 C e
Villa Viçoza, in Brazil 108 N i
Villefranche 76 E d
Villegaignon Island 108 M j
Villemur 76 D e
Villena, marq. 83 K h
Villeneuve 126 B d
Villingen 142 B d
Vilna 138 C e
Vilvorde 117 C d
Vimeiro 130 B f
Viminacium 39 M l
Viminal, quarter in Rome 96 A
Viminal Gate 22 A
Viminal Hill 22 A
Vincennes
Vinciacus, see Vinchy
Vinchy 55 P i
Vindava, see Windau
Vindelicia, dist. 38 E c
Vindhya Mountains 137 C d
Vindilis, isl. 38 B c
Vindobona (Vienna in Austria) 38 F c
Vindocinum, see Vendôme
Vindogladia
Vindonissa (Windisch) 39 J j
Vinegar Hill 127 K i
Vinnitsa 139 C f
Vinovia (Binchester) 51 P g
Vintium 26 B d
Vintodurnum, see Winterthur
Vipsanian Portico 22 A
Virballen 159 L a
Virère, Woods of
Virgin Aqueduct 35 ins. B (2)
Virginia City 210 B c
Virginia, col. 193 E c
Virginia, reg.
Virginia, state, 1788 202 I c
Virginia, state, 1863 203 V h
Virginia Military Lands 196 ins. B
Virginia, West, state 203 V h
Virginia Yazoo Company 196 A d
Virgin Islands 105 H c
Virgin River 210 C c
Virgin's Well 6 ins. A
Viriballum, prom. 26 C e
Virneburg 122 D c
Viroconium (Wroxeter)
Virodunum (Verdun) 39 H i
Viromandis, see Saint-Quentin
Virton 117 D e
Virtue, Temple of 22 A
Viru 111 B c
Virunum 39 E c
Visa 165 E c
Visconti, Dom. of the 78 F f
Visconti, Milanese under the 90
Visé 117 D d
Visentium 27 F e
Visontio (Besançon) 39 H j
Visp 91 P l
Vistula River 159 J b
Visurgis (Weser) River 38 D b
Vita 42 E f
Vitebsk 138 D d
Viterbo 90 D c
Viterbo, bp. 95 E c
Vith, Sankt 117 E d
Viti Levu, isl. 172 G b
Vitim River
Vitodurum 39 J j
Vitoria 82 B a
Vitricium 26 B b
Vitry
Vittorio Emanuele, Corso, street in Rome 22 A
Vittorio Emanuele, Piazza, loc. in Rome 22 A
Vivarais, dist. 76 F d
Vivarium, see Viviers
Vivienne, Rue, street in Paris 149 B
Viviers 78 D f
Viviers, bp. 94 C c
Viviers, cty. 69 F d
Viviscus 26 A a
Vizagapatam 137 D e
Vizakna 159 L f
Vizcaya, dist., see also Biscay 83 K g
Vizéu 82 A a
Vizéu, bp. 94 A c
Vizianagram 137 D e
Vlaardingen 62 C c
Vladikavkas 167 O g
Vladimir 138 F d
Vladimir Volynsk 139 B e
Vladivostok 171 O d
Vlieland, isl. 117 C a
Vlissingen (Flushing), in Holland 117 B c
Vlissingen (Flushing), in New York 189 ins. C
Vöcklabruck 123 G d
Voclade, see Vouillé
Vocontii, people 38 D d
Vogtland, dist. 85 G e
Vogules, people
Volane River 27 F c
Volaterræ 26 E d
Volcæ Arecomici, people 38 C d
Volcæ Tectosages, people 38 C d
Volcei 30 E b
Volcera 27 I b
Volci 27 F e
Volerius River 26 D e
Volga River 139 G f
Volhynia, dist. 139 C e
Volkerode, mon. 95 E a
Volkhov River 88 N b
Volkovisk 155 M b
Vollenhove 117 D b
Vollmaringen 143 G h
Volo 164 C c
Vologda 138 E d
Vologesia 20 K f
Volsci, people 30 C a
Volsiniensis, lake 27 F e
Volsinii novi 27 G e
Volsinii veteres 27 G e
Volta 161 H e
Volta River 128 ins. D
Volterra 90 L j
Volterra, bp. 95 E c
Voltri 150 E d
Volturara, bp. 95 F c
Volturnum 30 C b
Volturnus (Volturno) River 30 D a
Vomanus River 27 I e
Von der Leyen, princ. 154 E d
Vonitsa 131 H f
Voorne, East, isl. 117 B c
Voorne, South, isl. 117 C c
Voorne, West, isl. 117 B c
Vorarlberg, dist. 114 E e
Vorder-Rhein, see Hither Rhine River 91 R l
Voronezh 139 E e
Voronezh, gov. 131 K c
Voronov 153 P f
Vorsfelde 85 B b
Vorskla River 92 D c
Vosges, dept. 148 F e
Vosges Mountains 38 D c
Vosolvia 39 I h
Vossem 122 C c
Votyaks, people 138 H d
Vouillé 50 D c
Voullon 50 D c
Vratza 165 C b
Vredeland 189 ins. C
Vriesendael 192 D c
Vryburg 175 F g
Vryheid 175 N l
Vuelta, Cabo de la, cape 111 A b
Vulcan Island 30 E d
Vulcaniæ (Æolian, Lipari) Islands 30 E d
Vultur, mt. 30 E b
Vyasma or Viasma 138 D d
Vyatka or Viatka 138 G d
Vychegda River

Waadt, dist., see Vaud 91 O l
Waag River 63 J d
Waal River 117 D c
Wabash River 191 H d
Wacos, tribe 188 G d
Wadai, sultanate 174 E c
Wadan 174 B b
Wadelai 175 G d
Wadi Natrun, reg. 150 B a
Wadstena 88 F b
Wady Halfa
Wagadugu 174 C c
Waghäusel 158 E d

Wagnelée . . . 156 A a
Wagner, Battery, fort . . . 208 E c
Wagram . . . 155 I d
Wagrians, people . . . 62 F a
Wahlstatt . . . 155 I c
Wahlstatt, mon. . . . 72 D a
Wahlwies . . . 62 E e
Waialua . . . 198 ins. B
Waiblingen . . . 143 H h
Waibstadt . . . 142 C b
Waidhofen . . . 115 H e
Waikato River . . . 172 G d
Wailuku . . . 198 ins. B
Waimanalo . . . 198 ins. B
Waimea . . . 198 ins. B
Wain . . . 143 J i
Wain, lordship . . . 143 J i
Wainganga River . . . 137 C d
Waitangi . . . 172 H e
Waitara . . . 172 G d
Waitzen . . . 159 J e
Waitzen, bp. . . . 95 F b
Wakefield, in England . . . 127 X m
Wakefield, parl. bor. . . . 163 M d
Wakefield, in Miss. . . . 196 B d
Wake Island . . . 179 H f
Walata . . . 174 C c
Walbeck . . . 62 F b
Walcheren, isl. . . . 117 B c
Walck . . . 131 I b
Waldangeloch . . . 143 G g
Waldburg . . . 143 I j
Waldburg, cty. . . . 143 I j
Waldeck, cty. . . . 114 E c
Waldeck, dist. . . . 86 G c
Waldeck, princ. . . . 134 E c
Walden, mon. . . . 97 R i
Waldenburg . . . 143 I g
Waldkirch . . . 142 A d
Waldsassen, mon. . . . 95 E b
Waldsee . . . 143 I j
Waldshut . . . 142 B e
Waldstein, castle . . . 123 H c
Waldstetten . . . 143 I h
Wales, dist. . . .
Wales, march . . .
Wales, princ. about 1300 . . .
Wales, princ. 17 cent. . . . 127 V n
Wales, North, dist. . . .
Wales, West, dist. . . .
Walfisch Bay . . . 175 E g
Walhain . . . 156 B a
Walkenried . . . 122 F c
Walkenried, mon. . . . 95 E a
Walker Pass . . . 210 B c
Walker River, Ind. Res. . . . 188 C c
Walkers . . . 196 B c
Wallachia, dist. . . . 77 I d
Wallachia, princ. . . . 119 I e
Wallachia, Great, dist. . . . 89 C b
Wallachia, Little, dist. . . . 89 B b
Wallachian Plain . . . 2 G d
Wallachian Thessaly, princ. . . 89 B c
Walla Walla, Fort . . . 198 B a
Walla, Wallas, tribe . . . 188 C a
Wall Brook, in London . . . 75 G g
Wallenstein, route of . . . 121 D c
Wallerstein . . . 143 J h
Wallhausen . . . 63 F c
Wallingford . . .
Wallingford, castle . . .
Wallingford, parl. bor. . . 163 M f (Wall.)
Wallis, dist., see Valais . . . 91 P l
Walloons, people . . . 184 D b
Wallnut Hills, village . . . 208 B c
Wallnut Hills, Fort . . . 196 A d
Walsall, parl. bor. . . . 163 M e
Walsingham, Cape . . . 212 I b
Walsingham, mon. . . . 97 S i
Walsleben . . . 63 F b
Waltham, mon. . . . 97 R j
Waltham Abbey . . . 75 J h
Walton . . . 75 I i
Wampanoags, tribe . . . 189 C d
Wandewash or Wandiwash . . . 137 C f
Wanganui . . . 172 G d
Wangen, imp. cy. . . . 143 I j
Wangenies . . . 156 B b
Wantage . . .
Wappingers, tribe . . . 188 L b
Warangal . . .
Warasdin . . . 159 I e
Warberg, in Sweden . . . 88 E c
Warberg, Hanse. for. cy. . . . 98 F b
Warburg, Hanse. cy. in Germany . . . 99 ins. B
Warden, mon. . . . 97 Q i
Wardour Castle . . . 127 W o
Warego River . . . 172 D c
Wareham, in England . . . 127 W p
Wareham, castle . . . 65 E e
Wareham, barl. bor. . . . 163 L g
Wareham, in Mass. . . . 207 L b
Warekauri Islands . . . 172 H e
Waren . . . 79 H b
Waren, princ. . . . 79 H b
Wargla, oasis . . . 2 E e
Warka . . . 159 K c
Warley . . . 75 J h
Warm Spring, Ind. Res. . . . 188 B b
Warnabians, people . . . 63 F b
Warneton . . . 117 A d
Warns, people . . . 50 F b
Warnstedt . . . 62 F c
Warren . . . 189 ins. A
Warrenton . . . 208 B c
Warrington . . . 127 W m
Warrington, parl. bor. . . 163 L d (Warr.)
Warsaw . . . 79 L b
Warsaw, duchy . . . 155 K b
Warsaw, gr. duchy . . . 152 D c
Warta River, see Warthe River
Wartau, castle . . . 91 R k
Wartburg, castle . . . 62 F c
Wartenberg, in Silesia . . . 123 I c
Wartenburg, in Saxony . . . 154 G c
Warthausen . . . 143 I i
Warthe . . . 63 I c
Warthe River . . . 63 I b
Warwick, in England . . . 127 X n
Warwick, castle . . . 65 F d
Warwick, cty. . . .
Warwick, parl. bor. . . . 163 M e
Warwick, shire . . .
Warwick, in Rhode Island . . . 189 ins. A
Warwick Lane, street in London . . . 75 G g (32)
Wasatch Mountains . . . 187 H e
Wash, The, bay . . . 49 G e
Washington, in District of Columbia . . . 208 ins.
Washington, in Miss. . . . 196 A d
Washington, in Pa. . . . 211 I b
Washington, Fort, in Maryland 200 L i
Washington, Fort, in New York 195 D c
Washington, Fort, in Ohio . . . 196 ins. B
Washington, route of . . .
Washington, proposed state . .
Washington, state . . . 210 A a
Washington, ter. 1853 . . . 202 A f
Washington, ter. 1859 . . . 203 O f
Washington, ter. 1863 . . . 203 N f
Washita, River . . . 199 G d
Washita Fort . . . 210 F d
Wasit . . . 99 M g
Wassenberg . . . 72 B a
Wasseralfingen . . . 143 J h
Watauga . . . 191 I d
Watauga Association . . . 194 C c
Watauga River . . . 196 ins. A
Watauga Settlements . . . 196 ins. A
Watchet, parl. bor. . . .
Wateree River . . . 193 D d
Waterford, in Ireland . . .
Waterford, bp. . . . 97 D d
Waterford, cty. . . . 127 J i
Waterford, in Pa. . . . 192 A c
Water Gate . . . 6 ins. A
Waterloo . . .
Watertown . . . 189 ins. B
Watling's Island . . . 105 ins.
Watling Street, road in England . . . 51 P h
Watling Street, in London . . . 75 G g
Watson, Fort . . . 195 A g
Wattignies . . . 134 B c
Waverley, mon. . . . 97 Q j
Wavre . . . 156 B a
Waxhaw Creek . . . 195 A f
Wayne, Fort . . . 196 B b
Wayne's Treaty Line . . . 196 ins. B
Ways . . . 156 A a
Weald, The, forest . . . 49 F f
Weare, parl. bor. . . .
Wearmouth . . .
Wearmouth, mon . . . 97 P g
Wedmore . . .
Weehawken . . . 192 D c
Wehlau . . . 123 K a
Weibertreu, ruin . . . 143 H g
Weichsel River, see Vistula River
Weiden . . . 123 G d
Wei-hai-wei . . . 171 N e
Weikersheim . . . 143 I f
Weilburg . . . 114 E c
Weilburg, castle . . . 62 E c
Weil der Stadt, imp. cy. . . . 143 G h
Weiler . . . 143 H g
Weilheim . . . 143 I h
Weiltingen . . . 143 J g
Weimar . . . 85 F e
Weinfelden . . . 142 D e
Weingarten, ab. . . . 143 I j
Weingarten, mon. . . . 95 D b
Weinheim . . . 142 C a
Weinsberg . . . 143 H g
Weinsberg, lordship . . . 143 H g
Weisse Elster River . . . 63 G c
Weissenau, ab. . . . 143 I j
Weissenburg, imp. cy., in Alsace 78 E d
Weissenburg, mon. . . . 95 D b
Weissenburg, imp. cy., in Bavaria . . . 79 G d
Weissenburg, castle, in Switzerland . . . 91 P l
Weissenburg, in Transylvania .
Weissenfels . . . 135 G c
Weissenhorn . . . 143 J i
Weissenstein . . . 143 I h
Weisser Berg, mt. . . . 123 H c
Weisses Meer, see Kara Sea . . 170 H a
Weisskirchen . . . 159 K f
Weisweil . . . 142 A d
Welbeck, mon. . . . 97 P h
Weldon . . . 208 E b
Weld Springs, village . . . 172 B c
Welehrad, mon. . . . 95 F b
Welfesholz . . . 63 F c
Welland River . . . 127 Y n
Well Gate . . . 6 ins. A
Wellington . . . 172 G e
Wellington Island . . . 215 B g
Wells, in England . . .
Wells, bp. . . . 97 O j
Wells, parl. bor. . . . 163 L f
Wells, in New Hampshire . . . 189 C c
Wels, in Austria . . . 63 G d
Welsh, people . . .
Wels Mountains . . .
Welzheim . . . 143 I h
Welzheim, lordship . . . 143 I h
Wen-chau . . . 171 N f
Wenden . . . 88 K c
Wendish March, dist. . . . 77 I f
Wendover, parl. bor. . . . 163 N f (We.)
Wends, people, in Austria . . . 54 G d
Wends, people, in Germany . . 46 I c
Wener, lake . . . 88 E b
Wenersborg . . . 88 F b
Wennington . . . 75 J h
Weobley, parl. bor. . . . 163 L e

Werben . . . . 63 F b
Werden, mon. . . . . 95 D a
Werdenberg, castle . . . . . . 91 R k
Werl . . . . 62 D c
Werla, castle . . . . 62 F b
Werra River . . . . 79 G c
Werschitz . . . . 159 K f
Wertheim . . . . 142 D a
Werwick . . . . 117 A d
Wesel . . . . 114 D c
Wesel, Hanse. cy. . . . . . . 99 ins. B
Wesen . . . . 91 R k
Weser River . . . . 62 E b
Wessagussett . . . . 189 ins. B
Wessex, km. . . . .
Wessobrunn, mon. . . . . 95 E b
Westacre, mon. . . . . 97 R i
West Africa, French, col. . . . 174 C c
West Africa, Portuguese, col. . 175 E f
West Bromwich . . . . 162 D e
Westbury, parl. bor. . . . . . . 163 L f
Westchester . . . . 189 ins. C
West Cornwall, parl. dist. . . . 163 I g
West Cumberland, parl. dist. . 163 K c
West Dereham, mon. . . . . . . 97 R i
Westerås . . . . 88 G b
Westerham . . . . 75 J i
Westerly . . . . 189 ins. A
Western, Fort . . . . 189 D b
Western Australia, state . . . . 172 C c
Western Ghats, mts. . . . . . . 112 A b
Western Plain . . . . 187 I d
Western Reserve of Connecticut, dist. . . . . 196 ins. B
West Fiord . . . . 166 H b
West Florida, col. . . . . 194 B d
West Frankish Kingdom . . . . 56 B c
West Franconia, duchy . . . . . 62 E d
West Friesland, dist. . . . . . . 117 C b
West Galicia, dist. . . . . 139 B e
West Gloucester, parl. dist. . 163 L f
West Göthland, dist. . . . . .
West Goths, Kingdom of the, 486 . . . . 50 D d
West Goths, Kingdom of the, 6 cent. 52
West Goths, people . . . . . . 45 I c, D d
West Indies, reg. . . . 107, 108 E-O, a-l
West Indies, isl. . . . . 187 L f
West Kent, parl. dist. . . . . . 163 O f
Westland, dist. . . . . 172 F e
West Love, parl. bor. . . . . . 163 J g
West Marches, dist., in England
West March, dist., in Scotland
West Meath, cty. . . . . 127 J h
Westminster, in England . . . . 65 F e
Westminster, mon. . . . . 97 Q j
Westminster, parl. bor. 163 N f (Westm.)
Westminster, in Maryland . . . 208 ins.
Westminster, New, in British Columbia . . . . 212 C d
Westminster Hall, in London . 75 G g
Westmoreland, cty. . . . .
Westmoreland, parl. dist. . . .
Westmoreland, shire . . . . . .
West New Jersey, col. . . . . . 192 D d
West Norfolk, parl. dist. . . . 163 O e
Westover . . . . 193 ins. A
Westphalia, dist. . . . . 62 D b c
Westphalia, duchy . . . . 78 F c
Westphalia, km. . . . . 154 E c
Westphalia, prov. . . . . 158 E c
Westphalians, people . . . . . . 55 Q i
West Point . . . . 195 D c
Westport . . . . 210 F c
West Prussia, dist. . . . . 135 I b
West Prussia, prov. . . . . . . 159 I b
West Riding, parl dist. . . . . 163 M d
West Roman Empire . . . . . 42 A-F e
West Saxons, people . . . . . .
West Somerset, parl. dist. . . . 163 K f
West Suffolk, parl. dist. . . . . 163 O e
West Surrey, parl. dist. . . . . 163 N f
West Sussex, parl dist. . . . . 163 N g
Westsylvania, proposed state in U S. . . . . 195 A d
West Turkistan, Plains of . . . 3 K d
West Virginia, state . . . . . . 211 I c
West Voorne, isl. . . . . 117 B c
West Wales, dist. . . . .
West Worcester, parl. dist. . . 163 L e
Wethersfield, in Connecticut . 189 B d
Wethersfield, in England . . . . 185 G f
Wetter, lake . . . . 88 F b
Wettin, castle . . . . 63 F c
Wettin, cty. . . . . 85 F e
Wettin Lands 85
Wettingen, mon. . . . . 95 D b
Wetzlar . . . . 62 E c
Wetzlar, imp. cy. . . . . 78 F c
Wexford . . . .
Wexford, cty. . . . . 127 K i
Weybridge . . . . 75 I i
Weymouth, in England . . . . 84 B d
Weymouth, parl. bor. . . . . . . 163 L g
Weymuoth, in Mass. . . . . . . 189 ins. B
Wey River, in Hereford . . . . 127 W n
Wey River, in Surrey . . . . . . 75 H i
Wezet . . . . 117 D d
Whalley, mon. . . . . 97 O h
Wheeling . . . . 196 C b
Wherwell, ab. . . . . 100 A a
Whitby . . . .
Whitby, mon. . . . . 97 Q g
Whitby, parl. bor. . . . . 163 N c
Whitchurch, parl. bor. . . . . . 163 M f
White Chapel, loc. near. London 75 I h
White Earth, Ind. Res. . . . . . 188 G a
White Friars, mon. . . . . 75 G g
Whitehall, loc. in London . . . 75 G g
Whitehall, in New York . . . . 195 E b
Whitehaven, parl. bor. . . . . . 163 K c
White Horde, people . . . . . .
White Horse, village . . . . . . 212 ins.
White Mountain, in Bohemia . . 123 H c
White Mountain,Ind. Res. . . . 188 D d
White Mountains, in N. Hampshire . . . . 189 C b
White Nile River . . . . 174 G c
White Pass . . . . 212 ins.
White Plains, town . . . . 195 D c
White River, in Arkansas . . . 191 G d
White River, in Indiana . . . . 208 C b
White River, in S. Dakota . . . 198 E b
White Russia, reg. . . . . 138 C e
White Russians, people . . . . . 138 C e
White Sea . . . . 138 E b
Whithorn, bp. . . . . 97 I e
Whitney, mt. . . . . 210 B c
Whorekill (Lewes, in Delaware) 192 D d
Whydah . . . . 174 D d
Wiblingen, ab. in Wurtemberg . 143 I i
Wiblingen, mon. . . . . 143 J i
Wichita . . . . 210 F c
Wichitas, tribe . . . . 188 G d
Wicklow . . . . 127 K i
Wicklow, cty. . . . . 127 K i
Widdern . . . . 143 H g
Widin, see Vidin
Wieblingen, in Baden . . . . . 142 C b
Wieliczka . . . . 115 I d
Wielun . . . .
Wien, see Vienna in Austria
Wiener Neustadt . . . . 115 H e
Wieprz River . . . . 159 L c
Wieringen, isl. . . . . 117 D b
Wieselburg . . . . 159 I e
Wiesensteig . . . . 143 I h
Wiesensteig, lordship . . . . . . 143 I h
Wiese River . . . . 142 A e
Wiesloch . . . . 142 C b
Wigan . . . . 127 W m
Wigan, parl. bor. . . . . 163 L d
Wight, Isle of . . . . 49 F f
Wight, Isle of, parl. dist. . . . 163 M g
Wigmore, mon. . . . . 97 O i
Wigtown . . . .
Wigtown, cty. . . . .
Wigtown, dist. . . . .
Wi-ju . . . . 171 N e
Wildbad . . . . 143 G h
Wildberg, in Wurtemberg . . . 143 G h
Wildberg, castle, in Austria . . 79 I d
Wildenstein . . . . 143 J g
Wilderness, battle . . . . . 208 E b (Wil.)
Wildeshausen . . . . 62 E b
Wildhaus . . . . 91 R k
Wilhelmshaven . . . . 158 D b
Wilhelmstein, Fort . . . . 134 E b
Wilhelmsthal . . . . 134 E c
Wilkesbarre . . . . 195 D c
Wilkinson, route of . . . . 200 C d
Willamette River . . . . 198 A b
William, Fort (Calcutta) . . . . 137 E d
William, Fort, in Florida . . . . 193 D f
William, Fort (Portland) . . . . 210 A a
William, Fort, in Ontario . . . 212 F d
William Henry, Fort . . . . . . 192 D b
William of Rubruck, route of .
Williams, Fort, in New York . 192 D b
Williamsburg . . . . 193 ins. A
Williamsport . . . . 208 ins.
Willoughby, route of . . . . . . 108 R a
Willow Brook . . . . 6 ins. B
Wills Creek, Fort . . . . 192 B d
Wilmington, in Delaware . . . 192 D d
Wilmington, in N. Carolina . . 193 F d
Wilsaetas, people . . . .
Wilsnack . . . . 87 H b
Wilson's Creek, battle . . . . . 208 B b
Wilson's Promontory . . . . . . 172 D d
Wilten . . . . 63 F e
Wilton . . . .
Wilton, mon. . . . . 97 O j
Wilton, parl. bor. . . . . 163 M f
Wiltshire, cty. . . . .
Wiltwyck . . . . 192 D c
Wiltz . . . . 117 D e
Wilzi or Wilzians, people . . . 63 G b
Wimbledon . . . . 75 I i
Wimmera River . . . . 172 D d
Wimmis, castle . . . . 91 P l
Wimpfen . . . . 62 E d
Wimpfen, imp. cy. . . . . 142 D b
Winburg . . . . 175 M l
Wincanton . . . . 127 W o
Winceby . . . . 127 Y m
Winchcombe, mon. . . . . 97 P j
Winchelsea, parl. bor. . . . . . 163 O g
Winchester, in England . . . . .
Winchester, bp. . . . . 97 P j
Winchester, castle . . . . 65 F e
Winchester, college . . . . . . 100 A a
Winchester, deanery . . . . . . 100 A a
Winchester, hospitals . . . . . 100 A a
Winchester, mon. . . . . 100 A a
Winchester, parl. bor. . 163 M f (Winch.)
Winchester, in Virginia . . . . 193 E b
Windau, Hanse. cy. . . . . . . 99 H b
Windhoek, or Windhuk . . . . 175 E g
Wind River . . . . 210 D b
Wind River, Ind. Res. . . . . . 188 E b
Windsheim . . . . 114 F d
Windsor, in Canada . . . . 212 G d
Windsor, in Connecticut . . . . 189 B d
Windsor, in England . . . . . . 75 H i
Windsor, castle . . . .
Windsor, New, in Maryland . . 208 ins.
Windward Channel . . . . 213 E c
Windward Islands . . . . 213 F c
Winibigoshish, Ind. Res. . . . 188 H a
Winnebago, Fort . . . . 211 H b
Winnebago, Ind. Res. . . . . . 188 G b
Winnebagos, tribe . . . . 188 I b
Winnenden . . . . 143 H h
Winnepesaukee, lake . . . . . . 189 C c
Winnington Bridge . . . . 127 W m
Winnipeg . . . . 212 F d
Winnipeg, lake . . . . 212 F c
Winnipegosis, lake . . . . 186 I c
Winnsboro . . . . 195 A f
Winschoten . . . . 117 E a

Winterburg . . . 142 ins. A
Winterstetten . . . 143 I i
Winterthur . . . 91 Q k
Wintney, priory . . . 100 B a
Winton . . . 172 D c
Winwaedsfield . . .
Wirtemberg, ruin . . . 143 H h
Wirzaburg, see Würzburg
Wisbech, parl. bor. . . . 163 O e
Wisby . . . 88 H c
Wisby, Hanse. cy. . . . 98 G b
Wischehrad . . .
Wisconsin, state . . . 211 G b
Wisconsin, ter. 1836 . . . 202 F f
Wisconsin, ter. 1838 . . . 202 G f
Wisconsin River . . . 199 H b
Wisera River, see Weser River
Wismar . . . 80 B e
Wismar, Hanse. cy. . . . 99 ins. B
Witham, mon. . . . 97 O j
Witney, parl. bor. . . .
Wittelsbach, castle . . . 72 C b
Wittenberg . . . 72 C a
Wittenberg, univ. . . . 100 H d
Wittstock . . . 123 G b
Witu . . . 175 H e
Witwaters Rand, mts. . . . 175 M l
Wloclawek . . . 159 J b
Wloclawek, bp. . . . 95 F a
Włodawa . . . 155 L c
Woburn . . . 189 ins. B
Woburn, mon. . . . 97 Q j
Wogastisburg . . . 55 R j
Wohlau . . . 115 I c
Wohlau, princ. . . . 115 I c
Woiwodina, dist. . . . 159 J f
Wola . . . 135 K b
Wolfach . . . 142 B d
Wolfegg . . . 143 I j
Wolfenbüttel . . . 79 G b
Wolfenbüttel, duchy . . . 122 E c
Wolfsegg . . . 123 G d
Wolgast . . . 63 G a
Wolgast, duchy . . . 115 G b
Wolgast, Hanse. cy. . . . 99 ins. B
Wollaston, Mount, village . . . 189 C c
Wollaston Lake . . . 186 I c
Wollaston Land . . . 212 D b
Wollin . . . 63 H b
Wolmirstedt . . . 85 B b
Wolvega . . . 117 D b
Wolverhampton, parl. bor. 163 L e (Wolv.)
Women's Tower, loc. in Jerusalem . . . 6 ins. A
Won-san . . . 171 N e
Woods, Lake of the . . . 191 G b
Wood Street, in London . . . 75 G g
Woodstock . . . 127 X o
Woodstock, New 163 M f (New Wood.)
Woolwich . . . 75 J i
Wootton Bassett, parl. bor. 163 M f (W. B.)
Worcester, in England . . .
Worcester, bp. . . . 97 O i
Worcester, cty. . . .
Worcester, parl. bor. . . 163 L e (Worc.)
Worcester, shire . . .
Worcester, in Mass. . . . 189 C c
Wörgl . . . 154 G e
Worksop, mon. . . . 97 P h
Workum . . . 117 D b
Wormatia, see Worms, on the Rhine River
Worms, on the Rhine River . . 62 E d
Worms, bp. . . . 95 D b
Worms, imp. cy. . . . 78 F d
Worms (Bormio), on the Adda . 122 F e
Worndorf . . . 142 C e
Wörnitz River . . . 143 J g
Worringen . . . 78 E c
Wrangell . . . 198 ins. A
Wrangell, Fort . . . 212 ins.
Wrangell, mt. . . . 186 E b
Wreschen . . . 159 I b
Wrexham parl. bor. . . . 163 K d
Wrightstown . . . 192 D c
Wrightsville . . . 208 ins.
Wroxeter . . . 51 O h
Wu-chau . . . 171 M f
Wu-hu . . . 171 M e
Wurm River . . . 143 G h
Wurtemberg, castle . . . 62 E d
Wurtemberg, cty. . . . 78 F d
Wurtemberg, elect. . . . 151 H g
Wurtemberg, km. . . . 151 K j
Wurzach . . . 143 I j
Würzburg . . . 62 E d
Würzburg, bp. . . . 95 D b
Würzburg, gr. duchy . . . 154 E d
Würzburg, elect. . . . 151 K j
Würzburg, univ. . . . 100 G e
Wurzen . . . 85 G e
Wu-sing . . . 170 ins. A
Wutach River . . . 142 B e
Wyandots, tribe . . . 188 J b
Wychwood . . . 49 F f
Wye River . . . 49 E e
Wyk, in Holland . . . 117 C b
Wyk by Duurstede . . . 117 D b
Wymondham, mon. . . . 97 S i
Wyoming . . . 196 D b
Wyoming, state . . . 210 D b
Wyoming, ter. . . . 203 Q g
Wyoming Valley . . . 195 C c
Wyre, Forest of . . . 49 E e
Wyschehrad, castle . . .

Xaltocan . . . 106 A a
Xaltocan, lake . . . 106 B a
Xanten . . . 62 D c
Xanthus . . . 20 C d
Xanthus River . . . 20 C d
Xaragua, reg. . . . 105 F c
Xauxa (Jauja) . . . 111 B d
Xerxes Canal . . . 11 E b
Xerxes, route of fleet of . . . 13 D a
Xico . . . 106 B a
Xingu River . . . 214 D c
Xions . . . 159 I b
Xochicalco . . . 106 A b
Xochimilco . . . 106 A a
Xuala . . . 191 I d
Xyniæ . . . 11 D c
Xynias, lake . . . 11 D c
Xypete . . . 16 B b
Xystus . . . 6 ins. A

Yablonoi Mountains . . . 171 M c
Yacki . . .
Yadkin River . . . 195 A e
Yakima, Ind. Res. . . . 188 B a
Yakutat Bay . . . 198 ins. A
Yakutsk . . . 171 N b
Yalta . . . 164 K f
Ya-lu River . . . 171 N d
Yama . . . 119 J b
Yamasees, tribe . . . 188 J d
Yamburg . . . 119 K b
Yanaon . . . 137 D e
Yandabo . . .
Yang-tse-kiang, R. . . .
Yang-tun . . .
Yangui . . .
Yankton, Ind. Res. . . . 188 G b
Yap, isl. . . . 179 E g
Yapura River . . . 214 C c
Yaqui, Rio, R. . . . 190 C f
Yaquimi . . . 190 D f
Yarkand . . .
Yarm, parl. bor.
Yarmouth, in England . . . 65 G d
Yarmouth, Hanse. for. cy. . . . 98 ins. A
Yarmouth, parl. bor. . . . 163 M g
Yarmouth, in Mass. . . . 189 C d
Yarmouth, in Nova Scotia . . . 212 I d
Yarmouth River . . . 6 D c
Yaroslavl . . . 138 E d
Yarrawonga . . . 172 D d
Yass . . . 172 D d
Yatwegs, people . . . 71 K c
Yauco . . . 199 ins. G
Yautepec, R. . . . 106 B b
Yazoo Company . . . 196 A d
Yazoo River . . . 208 B c
Yedi Kouleh, castle . . . 93 G e
Yedisan, reg. . . . 139 C f
Yedo . . . 171 P e
Yeletz . . . 139 E e
Yellow Sea . . . 171 N e
Yellowstone National Park . . 210 C b
Yellowstone River . . . 210 D a
Yelnia . . . 153 O g
Yemamah, el . . .
Yemen, reg. . . . 170 F g
Yenikale . . . 164 F a
Yenisei River . . .
Yeniseisk . . . 171 K c
Yeni Shehr, quarter in Constantinople . . . 93 G e
Yeovil . . . 127 W p
Yeu, isl. . . . 84 B f
Yezd . . .
Yezo, isl. . . . 171 P d
Yildiz Kiosk . . . 93 G e
Ylst . . . 117 D b
Yokohama . . . 171 P e
Yola . . . 174 E d
Yonkers . . . 192 E c
Yonne, dept. . . . 148 E e
Yonne River . . . 62 B e
York (Toronto), in Canada . . . 194 D b
York, in England . . .
York, abp. . . . 97 N g
York, castle . . . 65 F d
York, cty. . . .
York, Hanse. for. cy. . . . 98 ins. A
York, in New Hampshire . . . 189 C c
York, in Pa. . . . 208 ins.
York, in Western Australia . . 172 A d
York, Cape . . . 172 D b
York, Fort, in Sumatra . . . 136 O e
York, Vale of . . . 49 F d
York County . . . 193 ins. A
York Factory, post . . . 212 F c
York River . . . 193 ins. A
York Town (Yorktown) . . . 193 ins. A
York Wolds, dist. . . . 49 F d
Yorkist estates . . . 84
Yorkshire Coalfield . . . 162 E d
Yosemite Valley . . . 210 A c
Yoshino . . .
Youghal . . .
Youghiogheny River . . . 192 B c
Ypres . . . 117 A d
Ypres, Hanse. for. cy. . . . 99 ins. B
Yssel River . . . 117 E b
Ysselstein . . . 117 C b
Yucatan, pen. . . . 105 C c
Yucatan, state . . . 213 D b
Yucatan Strait . . . 187 K f
Yukon, ter. . . . 212 B b
Yukon River . . . 186 D b
Yuma . . . 210 C d
Yuma, Ind. Res. . . . 188 C d
Yumas, tribe . . . 188 D d
Yü-mon-kwan, pass . . . 92 J c
Yun-nan, prov. . . . 171 K f
Yun-nan, reg. . . . 92 J e
Yun-nan-fu . . . 171 L f
Yungay . . . 214 B c
Yung-ning, in Kwang-si . . . 171 M f
Yung-ning-fu, in Yun-nan . . .
Yung-ting . . . 170 ins. A
Yuste, mon., see San Gerónimo de Yuste
Yverdon . . . 91 O l
Yvetot . . . 126 B b
Yvoix . . . 117 D e

Zaandam . . . 122 C b
Zabatus River . . . 20 J d
Zabeda . . . 6 E a
Zabern . . . 114 D d

Zabern, castle . . . . 62 D d
Zacatecas . . . . 213 B b
Zacatecas, state . . . . 213 B b
Zacatula . . . . 213 ins.
Zacharias, Tomb of . . . . 68 ins. B
Zacynthus, in Greece . . . . . . 14 A b
Zacynthus, isl. . . . . 14 A b
Zacynthus, in Spain . . . . . . 12 C c
Zadracarta . . . . 19 H c
Zafa, reg. . . . .
Zafra . . . . 82 A b
Zagazig . . . . 174 J i
Zagrab . . . .
Zahara . . . . 83 J h
Zähringen, castle . . . . 142 A d
Zaitun (Tsuen-chau-fu) . . . . .
Zalaca . . . . 82 A b
Zalmon Mountains . . . . 6 F c
Zama regia . . . . 38 D e
Zamboanga . . . . 199 ins. H
Zambesi River . . . . 175 G f
Zamora, in Mexico . . . . 213 ins.
Zamora, in Spain . . . . 82 A a
Zamora, bp. . . . . 94 A c
Zamosc . . . . 139 B e
Zampa, reg. . . . .
Zancle (Messina) . . . . 30 E d
Zandvliet . . . . 117 C c
Zane's Trace, road . . . . . . 196 ins. B
Zanesville . . . . 196 C c
Zante, isl. . . . . 89 H g
Zanzibar . . . . 175 H e
Zanzibar, isl. . . . . 175 H e
Zaporogian Cossacks . . . . . . 139 D f
Zara . . . . 90 E b
Zara, abp. . . . . 95 E c
Zaradrus River . . . . 19 L d
Zarax . . . . 15 D c
Zarax, mt. . . . . 15 D c
Zardandan, reg. . . . .
Zarephath (Sarepta) . . . . . . 6 C b
Zaretra . . . . 11 F d
Zariaspa . . . . 19 K c
Zarnow . . . . 123 K c
Zea Port . . . . 16 D c
Zealand Island . . . . 154 F a
Zealand, New, col. . . . . 172 F d
Zebid . . . .
Zebulon, Plain of . . . . 6 C c
Zebulon, tribe . . . . 7 ins. D
Zeeland, cty. . . . . 117 B c
Zeeland, dist. . . . . 78 C c
Zehdenick, mon. . . . . 80 ins.
Zehngerichtebund (League of Ten Jurisdictions), dist. . . . 91 R l
Zeil, castle . . . . 143 I j
Zeila . . . . 109 V g
Zeirids, people . . . . 66 H f
Zeithain . . . . 135 G c
Zeitz . . . . 63 G c
Zeitz, march . . . . 63 G c
Zela . . . . 20 F b
Zelea . . . .
Zell, on the Harmersbach, imp. cy. . . . . 142 B d
Zell, on the Moselle R. . . . . 142 ins. A
Zell, on the Wiese R. . . . . . 142 A e
Zell, on the Ziller R. . . . . . 154 G e
Zemaun Shah, Dom. of . . . .
Zengg . . . . 72 D c
Zengg, bp. . . . . 95 F b
Zengid Atabeks, people . . . . 71 O f
Zenobia . . . . 20 H e
Zenta . . . . 131 G d
Zephyrium, prom. . . . . 31 F d
Zerbst . . . . 63 G c
Zerdan . . . . 68 C b
Zerenj . . . .
Zermatt . . . . 91 P l
Zeugitana, reg. . . . . 38 D e
Zeugma . . . . 20 G d
Zeus, Altar of . . . .
Zeus, Temple of . . . .
Zeus Soter, Temple of . . . . . 16 D c (1)
Zevenaar . . . . 117 E c
Zhagubitza . . . .
Zianids, dynasty . . . . 77 E e
Zichi, or Zichians, people . . . 35 L e
Zichia, reg. . . . . 99 K e
Zidon . . . . 6 C a
Zierikzee . . . . 78 C c
Zierikzee, Hanse. cy. . . . . . 99 ins. B
Zigana . . . . 20 H b
Zilis . . . . 12 B c
Ziller Tal, valley in Tyrol . . . 114 F e
Zillerthal, in Silesia . . . . . . 159 H c
Zinder . . . . 174 D c
Zinjar . . . .
Zinna, mon. . . . . 80 ins.
Zion, cy., see Jerusalem
Zion, Gate of . . . . 68 ins. B
Zion, mt. . . . . 68 ins. B
Zion, quarter in Jerusalem . . . 6 ins. A
Ziph . . . . 7 C f
Zips, dist. . . . . 80 G g
Ziskaberg, mt. . . . . 87 J c
Zitácuaro . . . . 213 ins.
Zittau, in Bohemia . . . . 79 I c
Zittau, in Lusatia . . . . 115 H c
Zituni . . . . 89 H g
Znaym . . . .
Zoar . . . . 7 C f
Zollern, castle . . . . 62 E d
Zollern, cty. . . . . 86 G d
Zollverein, German, (Customs-Union) . . . . 160 D c
Zolyom . . . .
Zombor . . . . 159 J f
Zor (Tyre) . . . . 6 C b
Zorah . . . . 7 B e
Zorndorf . . . . 135 H b
Zoroa . . . . 6 E c
Zoster, prom. . . . . 15 D b
Zschillen, mon. . . . . 80 ins.
Zsibo . . . . 159 L e
Zsibo Pass . . . . 129 H c
Zug . . . . 91 Q k
Zug, canton . . . . 91 Q k
Zug, lake . . . . 91 Q k
Zuider Zee, bay . . . . 117 D b
Züllichau . . . . 123 H b
Zülpich . . . . 62 D c
Zultepec . . . . 106 B a
Zululand, reg. . . . . 175 N l
Zumpango . . . . 106 A a
Zumpango, lake of . . . . 106 A a
Zungaria, reg. . . . .
Zungeru . . . . 174 D d
Zuñi . . . . 190 D d
Zuñis, tribe . . . . 188 E c
Zurich . . . . 91 Q k
Zurich, canton . . . . 91 Q k
Zurich, lake of . . . . 91 Q k
Zurich, mon. . . . . 95 D b
Zurichgau, dist. . . . . 62 E e
Zurita . . . . 82 H e
Zusmarshausen . . . . 122 F d
Zutfen, Hanse. cy. . . . . 99 ins. B
Zutphen . . . . 117 E b
Zutphen, cty. . . . . 117 E b
Zwaanendael . . . . 192 D d
Zweibrücken . . . . 86 F d
Zweibrücken, princ. . . . . . . 134 D d
Zwettl, mon. . . . . 95 F b
Zwickau . . . . 85 G e
Zwiefalten, ab . . . . 143 H i
Zwiefalten, mon. . . . . 143 H i
Zwingenberg . . . . 142 C a
Zwinguri, Fort . . . . 91 Q l
Zwittau . . . . 168 E b
Zwolle . . . . 117 E b
Zwolle, Hanse. cy. . . . . 99 ins. B
Zwornik . . . . 119 H e

INDEX-SUPPLEMENT

Aalst (Alost) . . . 86 D c
Aarhus . . . 88 D c
Abadeh . . . 168K F c
Abash, reg. . . . 104B D f
Abbadan, isl. . . . 168K E d
Abdon . . . 6 C b
Abel ha Sittim . . . 7 D e
Abel Mehola . . . 7 D d
Abercorn, bp. . . . 60 C b
Aberdeen . . . 128 F c
Aberdeen, cty. . . . 128 F c
Aberffraw . . . 60 G c
Abergavenny . . . 74 J h
Aberystwith . . . 74 J g
Abitibi, lake . . . 191 I b
Abitibi River . . . 191 I a
Abitibis, Fort des . . . 191 J b
Abkhasia, auton. rep. . . . 168G M/N g
Abrettene, reg. . . . 9 F e
Abrittus . . . 39 N l
Abrushum, R. . . . 168K G b
Abulliond Geul . . . 168J A a
Abus Aestuarium . . . 51 Q h
Abusir, Pyramids of . . . 4 ins.
Abydus . . . 9 D d
Academy of Science, bldg. in Athens . . . 23 D
Academy Street, in Athens . 23 D
Acarnanians, people . . . 8 N h
Accra . . . 128C ins. D
Achaeans (Achaians), people 8 N h
Achaia, Proconsulate of . . 43 G f
Achilles, Burial mound of . 9 A b
Achilleum . . . 9 A b
Achonry . . . 74 B a
Acilius, Compitum of . . . 24 B
Acre . . . 168J B c
Acton Burnell . . . 74 K g
Adabazar . . . 168J B a
Adalia, Gulf of . . . 168J B b
Adam's Peak . . . 137 D g
Addis Ababa . . . 174 G d
Aden . . . 104B E f
Ad Fines, near Florencia . . 27 F d
Ad Fines, near Volaterrae . 26 E d
Adida . . . 7 B e
Adonis River . . . 6 D a
Adramyttium . . . 9 D e
Adramyttium, Gulf of . . . 9 D e
Adranos River . . . 168J A b
Adyge Cherkises, auton. area . . . 168F leg.
Adyge Cherkises, people . 168J C a
Aegaei Mountains . . . 14 ins.
Aegospotami River . . . 9 D d
Aegusae Islands . . . 30 B d
Aena . . . 7 D g
Aenianians, people . . . 8 N h
Aenus . . . 9 D d
Aeolians, people . . . 14 leg.
Aerarium, bldg. in Rome . . 24 A (15)
Aesepus River . . . 9 E e
Aethiopia, reg., Egyptian emp. 4 F d
Aetolians, people . . . 8 N h
Afghan Dominions . . . 137 A b
Afiun Karahissar . . . 164 E c
Afrau . . . 174 Q n
Africa, Proconsulate of . . . 42 D f
African Sea . . . 29 B f
Afso . . . 174 Q n
Agdir, reg. . . . 45 F a
Agora (Lysimachia) . . . 9 D d
Agrae Hills . . . 23 D
Agreda . . . 83 K g
Agrianes River . . . 9 D c
Aguas Blancas . . . 216 ins.
Aguatulco . . . 107 E d
Agylla . . . 27 G f
Ahaggar, reg. . . . 174 D b
Ahaus . . . 78 E b
Ahram . . . 168K F d
Aianteum . . . 9 B a
Aigues-Mortes . . . 102 G g
Ain-Aicha . . . 174 P n
Ain-Defali . . . 174 P n
Ain-Tab . . . 168J C b
Airds Moss . . . 128 D e
Aire River, in France . . 104A C c
Airobol . . . 165 E c
Aisma . . . 168L D c
Ajax, Burial mound of . . . 9 B b
Ajdir . . . 174 Q n
Ajlun . . . 168J C c
Ajudia . . . 128C N e
Akershuus (Christiania) . . . 88 D b
Akhsi . . . 104B H c
Ak Mechet . . . 168G L f
Akrabatta . . . 7 C d
Akshi-Kioi . . . 9 B b
Ak-su . . . 104B I c
Ala . . . 154 F f
Ala Kul . . . 104B I c
Alans, people in Russia . . 45 M d
Alashia (Cyprus) . . . 4 F c
Alba Julia (Karlsburg) . . . 159 L e
Albanians, people, about 900 57 G-H e
Albanians, people, in 1929 168H E d
Albarracin Mountains . . . 82 B a
Albreda . . . 136 I d (A.)
Alcacer-el-Kebir . . . 174 O n
Alcimus, prom. . . . 16 D c
Alclyde . . . 60 B b
Alcoraz . . . 82 H e
Aldan River . . . 104C M b
Aldborough (Isurium) . . . 51 P g
Aleppo (Haleb) . . . 68 C b
Alesund . . . 181B B a
Alexander's Port . . . 19 K f
Alexandria Troas . . . 9 D e
Alexandropol (Leninakan) . 168J D a
Alexandrovsk (Caspian sea) 168G P g
Alford . . . 128 F c
Alhucemas Bay . . . 174 Q n
Aller . . . 60 H d
Alma Ata (Verni) . . . 170 I d
Almenara . . . 83 K h
Almonacid . . . 153 D c
Almoravids, Dom. of the . . 66 E g
Alnwick . . . 74 L d
Alopeconnesus . . . 9 D d
Alpis Iulia . . . 27 I b
Altai Mountains . . . 104B I c
Altenberg (in Saxony) . . . 87 I c
Altendorf (Stará Ves) . . . 79 L d
Altis, loc. in Olympia . . . 9 H f
Altkirch . . . 91 P k
Alto Adige, reg. . . . 168H ins.
Altsohl (Svolen) . . . 79 K d
Alt-Zella, mon. . . . 85 G e
Alula . . . 182G G f
Amadia . . . 168J D b
Amalion, bldg. in Athens . . 23 D
Amance . . . 104A D c
Amara . . . 168K E c
Amardus (Kizil Uzen) River 44 G c
Ambly . . . 104A C b
Amboina, isl. . . . 128C ins. C.
Ambrones . . . 38 D a
Amecameca . . . 106 B a
Amerongen . . . 168D B c
Amjhera . . . 104B R i
Ammon, dist. . . . 7 D e
Amol, on Caspian Sea . . 104B F d
Amol, on the Amu-Daria R. 104B G d
Amor, dist. . . . 4 F c
Amoun Derness, dist. . . . 60 H c
Ampelus, in Crete . . . 14 ins.
Amphipyrgos, prom. . . . 10 B c
Amsterdam, isl. . . . 128C M g
Amsterdam (Carmentine) 128C ins. D
Amu-Daria River . . . 104B G d
Amur River . . . 104C M b
Anaforta . . . 168L D c
Anapa . . . 139 E g
Anavio . . . 51 P h
Anchedive Island . . . 104B R j
Anchialus . . . 39 N l
Ancient Prytaneum, in Athens 23 D (10)
Ancient Wall of Athens . . 23 D
Ancyle, deme . . . 23 D
Andaman (Angaman) Islands . . . 104C J f
Andaraba . . . 104B G d
Andijan . . . 104B H c
Angaman (Andaman) Islands . . . 104C J f
Angara River . . . 104C K b
Anglo-Norman Colonies & Earldoms . . . 70 E c
Anglo-Saxons, people, about 900 . . . 57 C c
Angus, dist. . . . 128 F d
Anim . . . 7 C f
Annaghdown, bp. . . . 97 B c
Annam . . . 171 L g
Annan . . . 128 E f
Annandale, dist . . . 128 E e
Annopol . . . 103 O c
Año Nuevo . . . 181 U l
Anshan, dist. . . . 4 G c
Antakia (Antioch) . . . 168J C b
Antandrus . . . 9 D e
Antioch, princ. in 1265 . . . 89 E c
Antofagasta, prov. . . . 216 ins.
Antoninus and Faustina, Temple of . . . 24 B (22)
Anzac Cove . . . 168L D c
Apán . . . 106 B a
Aphek, near Gebal . . . 6 D a
Aphek, near Joppa . . . 7 B d
Aphnitis Lake . . . 9 E d
Aphrodisias . . . 9 D d
Aphroditopolis . . . 4 F d
Apollonia, in Cyrenaica . . . 35 I g
Apollonia, in Guinea . . 128C ins. D
Apollonia, in Mysia . . . 9 F d
Apollo Patroos, in Athens . 23 D (5)
Apremont . . . 104A C b
Apremont-Dun, seign. . . 104A C b
Apsinthii, people . . . 9 D d
Aptera . . . 14 ins.
Apuli, people . . . 29 D d
Aquae, in Britain . . . 51 P h

Aquae Flaviae 38 A d
Aquae Tarbellicae 38 B d
Aqueduct of Hadrian, in Athens 23 D
Aqueduct of Pisistratus, in Athens 23 D
Arabian Sea 104 B G f
Arabia Sebba, reg. 104 B E f
Arabistan, reg. 168 K E c
Arabs, people 168 L K i
Aracan, reg. 171 K e-f
Aragon, march 45 D d (Ar)
Aragon River 82 B a
Aramatha 6 E c
Aramu, people 4 F c
Aranjuez 130 C e
Ararat, mt. 168 J D b
Aras River 139 G h
Arbedo 86 G e
Arbela (Beth Arbeel) 6 D c
Arbil 99 L f
Arbocala 38 A d
Arcadians, people 8 N i
Arcadians, people 14 leg.
Archelais, in Palestine 7 C e
Archelaus, Dominions of 7
Arches, near Épinal 104 A D c
Arcis-sur-Aube 104 A B c
Arctonnesus, isl. 9 E d
Arda, R. 168 L E f
Ardabil 139 G h
Ardahan 139 F g
Ardasa 168 J C a
Ardstraw 74 C a
Arganthonius, mt. 9 F d
Argennum, prom. 9 D e
Argentaria 39 I i
Argentorate (Strasburg) 39 I i
Arghana Maden 168 J D b
Argob, reg. 6 D c
Argonne Forest 168 C C c
Arguin, isl. 128 B H d
Argyll and Tarbet, cty. 128 C d
Aribi, people 5 C b
Arica, reg. 216 ins.
Arisba, in Lesbos 9 D e
Arisbe, in Troas 9 D d
Arklow 74 C b
Arlberg Pass 87 H e
Armagaon 128 B ins. B
Armagh 74 C a
Armalec 104 B I c
Armenia, auton. rep. 168 G N-O g
Armenia, Lesser, km., in 1265 89 D c
Armenia, Lesser, km., in 1355 89 J g
Armenian Christians 168 L leg.
Armenians, people 168 L L h
Ar Moab 7 D f
Aror 53 I d
Arpad (Tel-Erfâd) 4 F c
Arran, isl. 128 C e
Arrancy 104 A C b
Arrö, isl. 87 H a
Arsakion, bldg. in Athens 23 D
Arsila 174 O n
Artace 9 E d
Artemea 9 E d
Artynia Lake 9 F d
Arve River, in Savoy 91 O l
Arx, in Munychia 16 D c
Ascalon 7 B e
Ascania Lake 9 G d
Asch 79 H c
Ashburton 74 J i
Ashdown 60 I d
Ashdown, dist. 60 D d
Asia, Proconsulate of 43 H f
Asia, Rom. prov. under Trajan 20 C c (I)
Asiago 168 H ins.
Askabad 104 B F d
Asmak River 9 B b
Asolo near Feltre 87 H f
Aspara 104 B H c
Aspinwall (Colón) 214 A b
Assiniboine River 190 E a
Assus 9 D e
Assyrian Empire 5
Assyrian trade-routes 44 leg.
Astacus, in Bithynia 9 G d
Astacus, Bay of 9 G d
Astae, people 9 F c
Astaroth 6 E c
Astrabad 104 B F d
Astrabad, reg. 139 H h
Astyra 9 D e
Åsunden, lake 88 E c
Atalaya 106 C a
Atarneus 9 D e
Athena Street, in Athens 23 D
Athene, Altar of 23 C
Athene Hygiaea, in Athens 23 C (4)
Athenry 74 B b
Athlone 74 C b
Atholl, dist. 128 E d
Athyras River 9 F c
Atrek River 139 I h
Augustobriga 38 A e
Augustus, Arch of 24 B (18)
Auldearn 128 E c
Aulon, str., on Andros I. 15 E b
Auschwitz (Oswiecim) 87 L c
Aust 60 C d
Austeravia, isl. 38 D b
Austerfield 60 D c
Austria, rep. 168 F H-I f
Ava 104 C J e
Ava, reg. 104 C J e
Avaris 4 ins.
Avars, people, in Hungary 45 H c
Avars, people, on the Don R. 45 M c
Avignon, abp. 94 C c (A.)
Avioth 104 A C b (Av.)
Avon River 60 D c
Awanui 179 I k
Awarua 179 H l
Axbridge 60 H d
Axim 128 C ins. D
Axos (Oaxus) 14 ins.
Ayana, reg. 109 V g
Aylesborough = Aylesb. 60 D d
Ayotzingo 106 B a
Ayr 128 D e
Ayr River 128 D e
Ayyub, Mosque of 93 G e
Ayyub, quarter 93 G e
Azcopatzalco 106 A a
Azerbaijan, auton. rep. 168 G O g
Azerbaijan, reg. 67 P f
Aziziyah 168 J A b
Azjer 168 K F d

Baal Hazor 7 C e
Baal Meon 7 D e
Baal Salisa 7 C d
Baba Eski 168 L F f
Babilu (Babylon) 4 G c
Babylon (Cairo) 99 J h
Babylonian trade-routes 44 leg.
Bacanore 104 B R j
Baccanae 35 ins. B
Bacharach 102 H c
Bactrus River 19 K c
Badakshan, reg. 104 B H d
Badenoch, dist. 128 D c
Bafk 168 K G c
Baghché 168 J C b
Bagistana (Behistun) 5 D b
Bahrein, isl. 104 B F e
Baikal, lake 104 C K b
Bairnsdale 172 D d
Baither 7 C e
Bakchiserai 139 D g
Bakewell 60 I c
Bakhtegan (Niriz), lake 168 K F d
Bakkar 104 B G e
Baku, Sea of 99 N f
Balasore 137 E d
Balaton, lake (Platten-See) 87 K e
Balga, castle 87 M a
Balkash, lake 104 B H c
Balkh 104 B G d
Ballarat 172 D d
Ballyk 9 B b
Bam 168 K G d
Bambilonia (Cairo) 99 J h
Bamborough 60 D b
Bamian 104 B G d
Bampur 168 K H d
Banana 182 CC h
Banda Islands 104 C M h
Banff, cty. 128 E c
Bangor, in Wales 60 G c
Banjaluka (Banialuka) 159 I f
Banjarmasin, reg. 104 C L h
Bankot 137 B e
Bannaventa 51 P h
Baňská Bystrica (Neusohl) 103 N d
Baňská Štiavnica (Schemnitz) 103 N d
Bar (Antivari) abp. 95 F c
Baramahal, reg. 137 C f
Barberini, Palazzo, bldg. in Rome 22 A
Barcelona, march 45 E d (B)
Barchin 104 B G c
Barda'a 99 M f
Bardney, abbey 74 M f
Bardo, in Posen 159 J b
Bardo, in Tunis 174 E a
Bardonis, mt. 26 D c
Barfurush 168 K F b
Bargu, reg. 104 C L b
Bar Harbor 181 U c
Barkhalikend 104 B H c
Barkul 104 C J c
Baroch 104 B R i
Barra, isl. (Calabria) 31 H b
Barra, isl. (Hebrides) 128 A c
Barrow-in-Furness 162 C c
Baselus (Besor) River 7 B f
Bashkir, auton. rep. 168 G Q e
Bashmakli 168 L E f
Basileus, Stoa 23 D (3)
Basilica Argentaria, bldg. in Rome 24 A
Basilica Fulvia, bldg. in Rome 24 A
Basilica Opimia, bldg. in Rome 24 A (6)
Basilica Porcia, bldg. in Rome 24 A (5)
Basing 60 I d
Bassae 14 B b
Batanga, Great- 174 E d
Batavia 128 C N f
Bateia 9 B b
Batel 174 Q n
Bath, in England 60 H d
Battas, people 104 C J g
Battle, abbey 74 N i
Batum 139 F g
Bauchi 174 E c
Bauske 88 K c
Bayazid 168 J D b
Beaufort, near Stenay 104 A C b
Beaumont, near Sedan 158 D d
Beaumont-en-Argonne 104 A B b
Beaune-la-Rolande 158 B d
Bedford, in England 60 I c
Bedmar 83 K h
Bedr 53 F d
Bedwin (Bedwyn) 74 L h
Bedwyn (Bedwin), Great-, parl. bor. 163 M f
Beer Elim 7 D e
Behistun (Bagistana) 5 D b
Beibahan 168 K F c
Belbeis 150 B a

Belleau Wood 168 C B c
Bellefontaine 104 A C b
Bellenz (Bellinzona) 91 R l
Benbecula, isl. 128 A c
Bencoolen (Benkulen) 104 C K h
Benešov (Beneschau) 135 H d
Benevento, march 45 H d (Be)
Benfleet 60 J d
Bengala, reg. 104 B I e
Benjamin Constant 181 U h
Bennamarim 7 D f
Bensington 60 D d
Beograd (Belgrade) 89 B b
Berar, prov., 18 cent. 137 D d
Beraun River 135 G d
Berbice 128 B ins. A
Bere, castle 74 J g
Bere Alston. parl. bor. 163 J g (B.A.)
Bereku 128 C ins. D
Berenice, in Egypt 4 F d
Berga, in Macedonia 11 E b
Bergreichenstein 103 K d
Bergulae 9 E c
Berkeley, castle 74 K h
Berlin, Treaty of 168 L leg.
Bermudas, isl. 128 B E d
Bernau 103 K b
Bernicia, dist. 60 C b
Berwick 128 G e
Berwick, cty. 128 F e
Besace, La- 104 A B b (L.B.)
Besbicus, isl. 9 F d
Besika Bay 9 A b
Besika Tepe 9 A b
Besztercze (Bistritz) 159 M e
Beszterczebanya (Neusohl) 159 J d
Beth Anoth 7 C e
Beth Arbeel 6 D c
Beth Emek 6 C c
Beth Gamul 7 D f
Beth Garma 99 L f
Beth Hagla 7 C e
Beth Maacha 6 D b
Bethramphtha 7 D e
Beth Rehob 6 D b
Beth Thappuah 7 C e
Betifuli 27 H f
Beuthen, castle, in Brandenburg 85 C b
Beyshehr 168 J B b
Bezek 7 C d
Bharatpur (Bhurtpore) 137 C c
Biana 104 B H e
Bias River 14 B c
Bidar 104 B R j
Biel 91 P k
Bielaia River 99 O c
Bielostok (Bialystok) 168 G J e
Bielsko (Bielitz) 155 J d
Bièvres 104 A C b (Bi.)
Bihach (Bihač) 87 J f
Bilin 82 J c
Bilin, castle 79 H c
Bilma, reg. 174 E c
Bima, isl. 128 C ins. C
Bimlipatam 104 B S j
Birjan 168 K G c
Birkenhead 162 C d
Birket el Karun (Qurun), lake 174 J j
Birmingport 181 S d
Birze 138 B d
Bisanthe 9 E c
Bishbalk (Urumtsi) 104 B I c
Bissao 181 Z f
Bistonis Lake 9 C c
Bistrița (Bistritz) 159 M e
Bithynia and Pontus, Rom. prov. 20 D b (II)
Bitolj (Monastir) 165 B c
Bit-Yakin, reg. 5 D b
Blackpool 162 C d
Black Sea Basin 168 J B b
Blackwater River, in Ireland 74 B b
Blagny 104 A C b
Blagoveschensk 171 N c
Blair Atholl 128 E d
Blancheville 104 A C c
Blatobulgium 51 O g
Bleiberg 103 K e
Blemmyes, people 4 F d
Bletchingley 74 M h
Bne Barak 7 B d
Boa Vista do Rio Branco 181 U g
Bocca do Acre 181 U h
Bochum 168 E E b
Bodensee (Lake of Constance) 103 I e
Bodmin 74 I i
Boeotians, people 14 leg.
Boer Republics, the 175 N m
Boghaz-koi 4 F c
Bogou, reg. 174 C c
Bohun, dist. 74 J h
Bokhara 104 B G d
Bolerium, prom. 38 A b
Bolinas 180 O d
Bolingbroke 74 M f
Bolzano (Bozen) 103 J e
Bomba 174 F a
Bonin Islands 171 P f
Borgholm 88 G c
Borgo (di Valsugana) 168 H ins.
Borissow 153 N g
Bosham 60 I d
Bosnia, reg. 56 F d
Bosra 168 J C c
Botanical Garden, in Athens 23 D
Bothwell 128 E e
Boulevard des Italiens, in Paris 149 B
Bourbon, isl. 128 C K g
Bourdon 104 A C c
Bouresches 184 ins.
Bourgneuf, Bay of 102 C e
Bournemouth 162 E g
Bovianum vetus 30 D a
Bozanti 168 J B b
Brabant, duchy, 13 cent. 104 A B a
Bradford, battle 60 C d
Brahmanabad 53 I d
Brancepeth 74 L e
Branchidarum, Oppidum 19 K c
Bränkyrka 88 G b
Brașov, Brassó (Kronstadt) 159 M f
Bratislava (Presburg) 103 M d
Bravonium 51 O h
Brazhimov 71 P b
Breadalbane, dist. 128 D d
Brechin 128 F d
Brecknock, dist. 60 C c
Brecon 74 J h
Bremenium 51 O g
Bremetennacum 51 O h
Bressanone (Brixen) 168 H ins.
Brest-Kujawsk 88 H e
Brest-Litowsk 155 L b
Breux 104 A C b (Br.)
Briantica, reg. 13 D a
Bribiesca 83 K g
Bridport, English bor. 60 H d
Briey 168 E A c
Brigantes, people in England 51 O g
Brigobanne 39 J j
British North Borneo, col. 171 L h
Brixen (Bressanone) 168 H ins.
Brixillum 26 E c
Brno (Brünn) 87 K d
Brocavum 51 O g
Brocomagus 39 I i
Broumov (Braunau, in Bohemia) 135 I c
Brunanburh 60 H b
Bruneck (Brunico) 168 H ins.
Bruntál = Freudental 72 D b
Bruttii, people 29 E e
Bruyères, near Épinal 104 A D c
Bryges, people 10 C b
Brzesc (Brest Kujawsk) 135 J b
Brześć (Brest-Litowsk) 159 L b
Buccaneers, headquaters of the 128 B ins A
Buchan, dist. 128 F c
Buckingham, English bor. 60 I d
Budějovice (Budweis) 87 J d
Budorum, pen. 16 A b
Budva (Budua), bp. 95 F c
Buenos Aires 215 D f
Buenos Aires, audiencia 215 ins.
Buenos Aires, viceroyalty 215 ins.
Builth 74 J g
Bukharest, Treaty of 168 L leg.
Bulair (Playari) 168 L D c
Buleuterium, in Athens 23 D (8)
Buleuterium, in Olympia 9 H f (1)
Bulgaria, Khanate of 55 I e
Bulgaria, km. in 1929 168 G J-K g
Bulgarians, people, about 500 57 I d
Bulgarians, people in 1929 168 H F-G d; G c
Bulgars, people on the Upper Volga 59 N b
Bulgurlu 168 J B b
Bunarbashi 9 B b
Bunarbashi Brook, canal 9 A b
Bungay, castle 74 O g
Burdur 168 J B b
Burgas 168 L F e
Burgas, Gulf of 168 L F e
Burgenland, prov. 168 D D d
Burhanpur 128 B ins. B
Burma, reg. 104 C J e
Burtas, people 59 M c
Buryato Mongolia, Autonomous Socialist Soviet Republic 171 L c
Bury Saint Edmunds (Venta Icenorum) 51 Q h
Bury Saint Edmunds, abbey 74 N g
Bute, cty. 128 C e
Butifilis 104 B S j
Butler, fam. 74 C b
Butuntum 31 F a
Bydgoszcz (Bromberg) 87 K b
Byzantium 9 F c
Byzdry (Peisern) 79 J b
Cabyle 39 N l
Caconda 128 C I f
Caeni, people 9 D c
Caerleon, castle 74 J h
Caerphilly, castle 74 J h
Caesao 26 A c
Caesar, Statue of 24 B (23)
Café Corazza, in Paris 149 B
Cahul 139 C f
Caicus River 9 E e
Cailac 92 H c
Cairo, Calif. of 66 H g; 67 K h
Caistor (St. Edmund) 51 Q h
Caithness, dist. 128 E b
Calchedon 9 G d
Caledonia, reg. 128 B ins. A
Caledonia Bay 128 B ins. A (C. B.)
Caleta Buena 216 ins.
Caleta Colosa 216 ins.
Caleta Patillos 216 ins.
Caleti, people 38 C c
Calgary (Fort La Jonquière) 190 C a
Califate, The, emp. about 750 53
Calleva Atrebatum (Silchester) 51 P i
Calliupolis 9 D d
Calmar, Union of 77 leg.
Calpán, Ranchos de 106 B a
Calven, Pass 91 S l
Calydnae Islands 9 A b

Camanu, reg. 5 C b
Cambalec (Peking) 104 C L d
Cambambe, reg. 128 C I f
Cambodia, reg. 104 C K f
Cambrai (Cambray) 62 B c
Cambridge, in England 60 J c
Camerons, fam. 128 C d
Campbells, fam. 128 C d
Campo Formio 153 G c
Campo Militare, loc. in Rome 22 A
Camulodunum (Colchester) 51 Q i
Canary Islands 128 B H d
Canbalec (Peking) 103 L d
Canberra 172 D d
Candia 168 J A b
Cannes 157 B d
Canovium 51 O h
Cansay 92 M d
Canterbury, in England (Durovernum) 51 Q i
Canterbury, bp. 60 E d
Cantigny 168 C B c
Cantwara, people 51 S k
Cape Breton Island 212 I d
Cape Cod 181 U c
Cape Three Points 128 C ins. D
Caporetto 168 B F b
Cappadocia, Rom. prov. under Trajan 20 G c (IV)
Capuchins, The, ch. in Paris 149 B
Capuchins, The, mon. 149 B
Caracarum (Karakorum) 104 C K c
Carbisdale 128 D c
Carcer (Prison), in Rome 24 A (4)
Cardia 9 D d
Cardiff, castle 74 J h
Cardigan, dist. 60 G c
Carduniash, reg. 5 D b
Caresus River 9 E d
Carians, people 8 Q i
Carian Tributary 13 K f (IV)
Carlisle, in England 60 C b
Carlow 74 C b
Carmarthen, castle 74 I h
Carmelites, The, mon. in Paris 149 B
Carmentine 128 C ins. D
Carnarvon, castle 74 I f
Carpintería 216 G i
Carrick, dist. 128 D e
Carrion River 83 E c
Carthaginian trade-routes 44 leg.
Cascaes 83 J h
Casimirs (Kazimierz) 103 O c
Cassaba 168 J A b
Castellorizzo, isl. 168 J A b
Castel Sant' Elmo 153 G d
Castilla 216 ins.
Castlekevin 74 C b
Castleroe 74 C a
Castor and Pollux, Temple of 24 A (21)
Catalauni 38 C c
Cataonia, reg. 20 F d
Cathedral (Metropolitan Church), in Athens 23 D
Catterick, mon. 60 D b
Caucasian Gates, Pass 18 F b
Caucasian peoples 168 L L g
Cauvery River 137 C f
Cavour, Piazza, loc. in Rome 22 A
Cavour, Ponte, loc. in Rome 22 A
Cavour, Via, street in Rome 22 A
Caystrus 20 D c
Céa River 83 D c
Cebrene 9 D e
Cecryphalea, isl. 15 D b
Cedrius, mt. 14 ins.
Celestins, The, mon. in Paris 149 B
Celje (Cilli) 159 H e
Celtae, people 29 C a
B b
Celts, people, about 900 57 B d/c
Cembalo 99 J e
Cemetery, in Athens 23 D
Central Australia, state 172 C c
Central Black Earth, economic reg. 168 F leg
Central Industrial, economic reg. 168 F leg.
Cephisia Street, in Athens 23 D
Ceramus 13 K f
Cerata, mt. 16 A a
Ceraunii Mountains, in Epirus 17 A a
Ceraunii Mountains, in Italy 27 H e
Ceres, Temple of, in Athens 23 D
Ceressus 11 E d
Ceriadac, deme 23 D
Cernauţi (Czernowitz) 168 G K f
Česká Skalice (Skalitz) 159 I c
České Budějovice (Budweis) 103 L c
Cetinje 165 A b
Ceuta 174 P n
Chagatai, Khanate of 92 leg.
Chahar, reg. 171 M d
Chalcedon 9 G d
Chalco, lake 106 B a
Chaldea, in the Middle Ages 99 M g
Chaldeans, people 168 L L h
Chalish (Karashar) 104 C I c
Chalti 168 J A b
Chalybon 20 G d
Chamonix 91 O m
Champagne, cty., 13 cent. 104 A A c
Champe, reg. 104 C K f
Champigny 158 B d
Chanak Kale 168 L D c
Chanchalacas, R. 106 D a
Chanderi 104 B H e
Changanor 104 C L c
Changchun 179 D c
Chantraines 104 A C c
Chaones (Chaoni), people 8 M g
Chapultepec 106 A a
Charadra River 16 B a
Charax(-Spasinu) 44 F c
Charikar 104 B G d
Charkov (Kharkov) 139 E e
Charleville (Ardennes) 168 C C c
Charmouth 60 H d
Charny 104 A C b
Charshembe 168 J C a
Chatalja 168 L G f
Châtenois 104 A C c
Chatham 162 G f
Chatyn Deirmeni 9 A b
Chaul 104 B R j
Chaumont-devant-Damvillers 104 A C b
Cheb (Eger) 87 I c
Cheboksara 168 G O d
Chebreiss 150 B a
Chechen, auton. area 168 G O g (2), leg.
Chechen, isl. 168 G O g
Chelm 159 L c
Chełmno (Kulm) 135 J b
Chełmno (Kulm), bp. 95 F a
Chelmża (Kulmsee), seat of bishopric 95 F a
Chelsea 60 D d
Chemin des Dames 168 C B c
Chemmis 4 F d
Cheng-tu-fu 104 C K d
Chen-si 104 C J c
Chequamegon, Fort 191 G b
Cheragan Palace 93 G e
Cherekli 168 J B a
Cherkasy 139 D f
Chernigov 71 M c
Chernoi-Yar 139 G f
Cherso, isl. 161 J e
Chersonesus, in Crete 14 ins.
Chertsey, mon 60 D d
Chesme 165 E d
Chester, battle 60 C c
Chester, castle 60 H c
Chester, County Palatine of 74 K f
Chester, Palatine Earldom of 65 E d
Chichester, Engl. bor. 60 I d
Chico Viejo 106 D a
Chigrin 139 D f
Chilen-fu 104 C L d
Chillaw 104 B R k
Chilternsaete, people 60 D d
Chimkent 170 H d
Chin, Sea of 104 C M e
China, Republic of 171 J M e
Chintabor (Goa) 104 B R j
Chiny 104 A C b
Chiny, cty. 104 A C b
Chipangu, emp. (Japan) 104 C O d
Chippenham 60 H d
Chirbury 60 H c
Chisholms, fam. 128 C c
Chisinau (Kishinev) 168 G K f
Chitor 92 H e
Chivril 168 J A b
Chocim 139 C f
Chojnice (Konitz) 135 I b
Chomutov (Komotau) 87 I c
Chorillos 216 F g
Chorlu 168 L F f
Chorum 168 J B a
Choshi 179 E d
Christchurch, parl. bor. 163 M g (Chr.)
Christiania (Akershus) 88 D b
Christiansborg 128 C ins. D
Chrysopolis 9 G c
Chuguiev 139 E f
Chullu 44 B c
Churche, people 92 M c
Chu River 104 B G c
Chuvash, auton. rep. 168 G O d
Ciando (Shangtu) 104 C L c
Cibalae 39 F c
Cicones, people 9 C c
Cieszyn (Teschen) 159 J d
Cilicia, Rom. prov. under Trajan 20 F d (VI)
Cilician and Syrian Gates, pass 20 G d
Cilician Gates, pass 20 F d
Cilli, County of 87 J c
Cimbri, people 38 D a
Cimmerians, people 5 C a
Cimolus 15 E c
Circassia, reg. 164 F b
Cius 9 G d
Cius, Bay of 9 F d
Clackmannan, cty. 128 E d
Clanoventa 51 O g
Clare, dist. in Wales 74 J h
Clausentum (Southampton) 51 P i
Claverhouse 128 F d
Cleon, Wall of, in Athens 23 D
Cleveland, dist. in England 60 I b
Cleven (Chiavenna) 91 R l
Clitheroe 74 K f
Clonmel 74 C b
Cloppenburg 78 F b
Cluj (Klausenburg) 159 L e
Clun, castle 74 K g
Cluse, La 158 D e
Clydesdale, dist. 128 E e
Clysma 4 ins.
Coatlichán 106 B a
Cobh (Queenstown) 168 F D e
Coburg (Koburg) 79 G c
Coccium 51 O h
Cockermouth, castle 74 J e
Coelaletae, people 9 C c
Coelesyria, reg. 20 G f
Coilon (Quilon) 104 B H g
Colchester (Camulodunum) 51 Q i
Colchester, abbey 74 N h
Coleroon River 137 D f
Colisée, The, bldg. in Paris 149 B
Coll, isl. 128 B d

Collaguasi . . . . 216 ins.
Collège des Quatre Nations, bldg. in Paris . . . . 149 B
Collège Mazarin, bldg. in Paris . . . . 149 B
Collioure . . . . 83 L g
Collytus, deme . . . . 23 D
Colombey . . . . 158 D d
Colonae . . . . 9 D e
Colonia do Sacramento . 128 B F f
Colonia Falisca . . . . 27 G e
Colonus Agoraeus, deme . . 23 D
Colonus Hippius, deme . . 23 D
Colurnbum . . . . 104 B R k
Comedae, people . . . . 19 L c
Commenda . . . . 128 C ins. D
Compitum of Acilius . . . . 24 B
Complludo . . . . 83 K g
Compostela, Santiago de . . 82 A a
Compostela, Santiago de, abp. 94 A c
Conchi . . . . 216 ins.
Conchi, Land of . . . . 92 H b
Concord, Temple of . . . . . 24 A (7)
Conde, Fort (Mobile) . . . 191 H e
Connaught, prov. . . . . 74 B b
Consabura . . . . 38 B e
Constanța (Kustenje) . . . . 165 F a
Constantine, Statue of . . . 24 B (15)
Constantinople, Treaty of 168 L leg.
Conway . . . . 74 J f
Conway River . . . . 60 G c
Cophas . . . . 19 J e
Coptos . . . . 4 F d
Corameran River . . . . . 104 C K c
Corbilo (Nantes) . . . . 44 A b
Corbridge . . . . 60 H b
Cordeliers, The, mon. in Paris . . . . 149 B
Cordova, in Alaska . . . . 180 M a
Coreae . . . . 7 C d
Cork . . . . 74 B c
Coron (Koroni) . . . . 89 H g
Coronel . . . . 168 A F f
Corpilii, people . . . . 9 C c
Corrib, Lough, lake . . . . 127 H h
Corso d'Italia, street in Rome 22 A
Cortina (d'Ampezzo) . . 168 H ins.
Cortona, in Etruria . . . . . 27 G d
Cortona, in Spain . . . . . 38 C d
Cosmin . . . . 104 C J f
Côte Lorraine . . . . . . 168 C C c
Courland, bp. . . . . 88 J c
Courons, people . . . . 57 H b
Cours de la reine, in Paris 149 B
Coventry, abbey . . . . 74 L g
Coyoacán . . . . 106 A a
Cranganur (Cranganore) . 137 C f
Cravant . . . . 86 D e
Crediton . . . . 60 C d
Crediton, bp. . . . . 97 N k
Cricklade, bor. . . . . 60 H d
Crimea, auton. rep. . . . 168 G L f
Croats, people in 1929 . 168 H E c
Cromarty . . . . 128 D c
Cromarty, cty. . . . . 128 C b
Cronos Hill . . . . 9 H f
Crowland, mon. . . . . 60 I c
Cuantitlán . . . . 106 A a
Cuiavia (Kujavia), dist. . . . 79 K b
Culloden Moor . . . . 128 D c
Cumania, reg. . . . . 99 J d
Cumans, people, in Turkestan 53 H b
Cumberland, dist. in England 60 H b
Cumuhi (Cummuhi), reg. . . 5 C b
Cumukh . . . . 99 M e
Cunetio . . . . 51 P i
Cunningham, dist. . . . . . 128 D e
Cunus aureus . . . . 26 D a
Cupar . . . . 128 E d
Curia Julia . . . . 24 B
Cusus River, near Brigetio . 39 F c
Cusus River, near Lauriacum 39 E c
Cuyavia, reg. . . . . 87 L b

Cybistra . . . . 20 F d
Cydamus . . . . 44 C c
Cynia, lake . . . . 10 C d
Cynkali . . . . 104 B R k
Cypsela . . . . 9 D d
Cyrenaica, dist. . . . . . . 174 F a
Cyzicus . . . . 9 E d
Czechoslovakia, rep. . . . 168 G H/J f
Częstochowa . . . . 135 J c

Dabrath . . . . 6 C c
Dagasira . . . . 19 I e
Daghestan, auton. rep. . 168 G O g
Dahshur, Pyramids of . . . . 4 ins.
Daibul . . . . 104 B G e
Dai'am . . . . 99 N f
Dalarne (Dalecarlia), dist. . 88 F a
Dalriada, dist. . . . . 60 F b
Dalwhinnie . . . . 128 D d
Damascus, Kingdom of . . . 5 C b
Damghan . . . . 104 B F d
Damme, near Bruges . . . 102 F c
Danelagh (Danelaw), The . 60 leg.
Danishmend, reg. . . . . . . 67 N f
Danish Mercia . . . . 60 I c
Dannaba . . . . 7 D f
Dannewerk, wall . . . . . . 55 Q i
Darab . . . . 168 K F d
Dardania, reg. . . . . 17 B a
Dardanus . . . . 9 D d
Darien Colony . . . . . . 128 B ins. A
Dascylium . . . . 9 F d
Daulatabad . . . . 104 B R j
Dauphin, Fort . . . . 190 E a
Dawston (Degsastan) . . . . 60 C b
Deal . . . . 154 A c
Debir . . . . 7 B f
Dęblin (Ivangorod) . . . . . 159 K c
Debreczén . . . . 159 K e
Decapolis, dist. . . . . 7 leg.
Děčín (Tetschen) . . . . . . 135 H c
De Clare, earldom . . . . . 70 E c (De C.)
De Courcy, earldom . . . 70 E c (De Co.)
Deddington, castle . . . . . 74 L h
Dedeagach . . . . 164 D b
Deer . . . . 128 F c
Deerhurst . . . . 60 H d
Dee River, in Wales . . . . . 60 C c
Dee River, in Kirkcudbright 128 D f
Dee River, in Aberdeen . 128 F c
Degsastan (Dawston) . . . . 60 C b
Deheubarth, dist. . . . . . . 60 G c
Dei Consentes, Portico of the 24 B (7)
Deira, dist. . . . . 60 D b
Deir-ez-Zor . . . . 168 J D b
Dej (Dees) . . . . 159 L e
De Lacy, earldom . . . . . 70 E c (De L.)
Delcus . . . . 9 F c
Delhi, Empire of the Sultans of . . . . 104 B H e
Deligun Buldagha . . . . . 92 L b
Delta, reg. . . . . 4 F c (I)
Demonnesi Islands . . . . . . 9 F d
Demarchia, bldg. in Athens 23 D
Denbigh, castle . . . . 74 J f
Denisli . . . . 168 J A b
Deogir, reg. . . . . 104 B R i
Deorham (Dyrham) . . . . . . 60 C d
Derat . . . . 168 J C c
Derbent . . . . 139 G g
Derby, danish borough . . . 60 I c
Derby, cty. . . . . 74 L f
Derna . . . . 174 F a
Deshima, isl. . . . . 128 C O d
Desmond, dist. . . . . 74 B c
Deutschendorf . . . . 80 G g
Develtum . . . . 39 N l
Deveron River . . . . 128 F c
Devon, dist. . . . . 60 C d
De Vries, route of . . . . 128 C P c
Dhafar . . . . 104 B F f
Dhar . . . . 104 B R i
Dhibat al Mahal, isl. . . 104 B H g

Diagorgan . . . . 99 M f
Diala River . . . . 168 K E c
Didyma . . . . 13 E c
Dieppe, near Verdun . . 104 A C b
Dieuze . . . . 102 H d
Dindymus, mt. near Cyzicus 9 E d
Dinefwr . . . . 60 G d
Dinhaba . . . . 7 D f
Diomea, deme . . . . 23 D
Dionysium, Lenaeum and, in Athens . . . . 23 D (12)
Dirk Hartog, isl. . . . . . 128 C N g
Disna . . . . 88 M d
Disna River . . . . 88 L d
Dium, prom. . . . . 14 ins.
Dividing Range, Great . . . 172 D c
Divonum . . . . 38 C d
Divrik (Divirigi) . . . . . . 99 K f
Divus Julius, Temple of . . 24 B (17)
Divus Romulus, Temple of 24 B (21)
Dixcove . . . . 128 C ins. D
Dixmude . . . . 168 C B b
Dnieper River . . . . 139 D f
Doblen . . . . 88 J c
Doboj . . . . 87 L f
Dobruja, reg. . . . . 89 C b
Dodecanesia, isl. . . . . . . 165 E e
Dodekaschoenos, reg . . . . 4 F d (IV)
Dofar . . . . 104 B F f
Dogger Bank . . . . . 168 A J b (II leg.)
Doliones, people . . . . 9 E d
Doljani (Dolyani), bp . . . . 95 F c
Dolonci, people . . . . 9 D d
Domašov (Domstadtl) . . . 135 I d
Domeyko . . . . 216 ins.
Dominion of the Hammadites 66 G g
Dominion of the Karakhitai 92 H c
Dominions of Timur . . . . 92 leg.
Dompaire . . . . 104 A D c
Dondra Head . . . . 137 D g
Don River, Scotland . . . . 128 F c
Doorn . . . . 168 D B c
Doornik (Tournai) . . . . . . 86 D c
Dorchester . . . . 74 K i
Dore . . . . 60 I c
Dorestad . . . . 45 F b
Doria, Piazza, loc. in Rome 22 A
Dorians, people . . . . 14 leg.
Doriscus . . . . 9 D d
Dornoch . . . . 128 E c
Dorpat, bp. . . . . 88 L b
Dorset, cty. . . . . 74 K i
Dosab . . . . 168 K H d
Douaumont . . . . 168 C C c
Douglas, in Scotland . . . 128 E e
Dover . . . . 60 J d
Downpatrick . . . . 74 D a
Downton . . . . 74 L h
Drač = Durazzo . . . .
Drepanum, in Asia Minor . 9 G d
Drewenz River . . . . 135 J b
Dregoviches, people . . . . . 57 H-I c
Drevlians, people . . . . . . 57 I c
Drissa River . . . . 88 M d
Drogheda . . . . 74 C b
Droi, people . . . . 17 C a
Droitwich . . . . 74 K g
Drumclog . . . . 128 D e
Dubica (Dubitza) . . . . . . 164 B b
Dublin . . . . 60 F c
Dubrovnik (Ragusa) . . . . . 89 A b
Dubrovnik (Ragusa), abp. . 95 F c
Dukha, people . . . . 5 C b
Dulyebs, people . . . . 57 H c
Dumbarton . . . . 128 D e
Dumbarton, cty. . . . . . . 128 D d
Dumbrek, R. . . . . 9 B b
Dumfries . . . . 128 E e
Dumfries, cty. . . . . 128 E e
Dun (-sur-Meuse) . . . . . 104 A C b
Dunajec River . . . . 135 K d
Dunbar . . . . 128 F e
Dunblane . . . . 128 D d

Dunblane, bp. 97 J c
Dundalk 74 C b
Dundee 128 F d
Dundram, castle 74 C a
Dunfermline 128 E d
Dungarvan 74 C b
Dunkeld 128 E d
Dunnottar Castle 128 F d
Dunwich 74 O g
Dunwich, bp. 60 E c
Duos Lucos, Inter, loc. in Rome 24 A
Duressi = Durazzo
Durham, Palatinate of 74 L e
Düren 168 E B b
Dürnstein 155 H d
Durobrivae, near Lindum 51 P h
Durobrivae, near Londinium 51 Q i
Durocobrivae 51 P i
Dur-Samand, reg. 104 B R j
Dutch, people in 1929 168 H C b
Dutch East Indies, col. 179 B/E h
Duzje 168 J B a
Dvina, Gulf of 167 G M b
Dvina River 167 N c
Dwara-Samudra 104 B R j
Dyfed, dist. 60 B d
Dyrham (Deorham) 60 C d

Earn River 128 D d
East Africa, British = Kenya, col. and prot. 175 G d
East Africa, German, Brit. Mand. 175 G e
East Africa, Portuguese = Mozambique 175 G g
East Anglia, km. 60 J c
Eastbourne 162 G g
East Götland, dist. 88 F b
East-Kirghiz, economic reg. 170 leg.
East March, dist. 128 F e
East Scheldt, R. 168 C B b
East Sea 99 G b
Ebora 38 A e
Echmiadzin 139 F g
Echo Hall, in Olympia 9 H f
École Militaire, in Paris 149 B
Écuries, in Paris = 1 149 B
Eddisbury 60 H c
Edelsland, reg. 128 C N g
Edgcott 84 C c
Edinburgh 128 E e
Edinburgh, cty. 128 E e
Edington 60 H d
Edirne (Adrianople) 93 C b
Eendrachtsland, reg. 128 C N g
Eger (Erlau) 79 L e
Eger (Erlau), bp. 95 G b
Egesta 30 B e
Eggenburg 87 J d
Egherdir 168 J B b
Eglaim 7 D f
Egnatian Way 10 A a
D b
Egremont, castle 74 J e
Egrigaia 104 C K d
Egyptian Empire 4
Eichstätt 79 G d
Eichstätt, bp. 79 G d
Eiderstedt, reg. 86 G a
Eifel, mts. 168 C D b
Eigg, isl. 128 B d
Eisenerz 103 L e
Ekhmim 4 F d
Elaeus, in Thrace 9 D d
El-Arish, in Egypt 67 M g
El-Arish, in Morocco 174 O n
Elbasan 165 A c
El Caney 213 E b (E. C.)
Elde River 134 F b
Eleans, people 8 N i
Eleutherius, Port of 93 G e
Elfsborg 88 E c
El Gezira, reg. 174 G c
Elgin 128 E c
Elgin and Forres, cty. 128 E c
El Hasa, reg. 104 B E e
Elizabetpol 139 G g
El-Jauf 168 J C c
El Kab 4 F d
El Katif 104 B E e
El Katr, reg. 168 K F d
Ellandun 60 I d
Elmedsaete, people 60 D c
Elmham 60 E c
Elmina (São Jorge da Mina) 128 B H e
Elsinore (Helsingör) 103 K a
El Toco 216 ins.
Ely, mon., in England 60 E c
Ely (Hili), in India 104 B R j
Ely, Isle of, dist. 74 N g
El Yemamah 104 B E e
Embabeh 150 B a
Emmerich 168 E B b
Empinghan 74 M g
Empire of the Great Khan 92 leg.
Empire of the Sultans of Delhi 104 B H e
Emporium, loc. in Piraeus 16 D c
Enaghdun, bp. 74 B b
English Marches, dis. 74 K d
English Pale, The, dist. 74 C b
Enneakrounos, in Athens 23 D (11)
Enneapylon (Pelasgikon) in Athens 23 C
Entebbe 174 G d
Enzeli 168 G O h
Eord(ai)i, people 10 B a
Epamanduodurum 39 I j
Ephron (Ephrem) 7 C e
Epirots, people 8 N h
Eppan 72 C b
Equins 104 B H c
Erbil (Arbil) 99 M f
Ercavica 38 B d
Eregli (in Cilicia) 168 J B b
Eregli (Heraclea) 168 J B a
Eressus (Eresus) 9 C e
Ergene, riv. 168 L F f
Ergines River 9 D c
Erginul, Erginur 104 C K d
Eridanus, River, in Athens 23 D
Erivan 139 F g
Erne, Lough-, lake 127 J g
Er Riad 104 B E e
Ersekujvar (Neuhäusel) 135 J e
Esbus 7 D e
Esdrelon 6 C c
Esebon 7 D e
Eskdale, dist. 128 E e
Esla River 83 D c
Essek (Osjek) 77 H c
Essequibo 128 B ins. A
Esthaol 7 C e
Estonia, rep. 168 G J/K d
Estrella Mountains 82 A b
Esztergóm (Gran) 59 H d
Esztergóm (Gran), abp. 95 F b
Etaples 86 C c
Etea 14 ins.
Ether (Jattir) 7 C f
Ethiopia (Abyssinia), reg. 174 G d
Etropolje 165 C b
Etrusci, people 29 B c
Etsch River = Adige River 90 C b
Eudoses, people 38 D a
Euesperides = Hesperis 44 D c
Eule, in Bohemia 103 L d
Eupen 168 E A b
Eureka 180 O c
Euripides Street, in Athens 23 D
Europus, in Syria 20 G d
Evangelismos, bldg. in Athens 23 D
Ewst River 88 L c
Eynsham 60 D d
Eyoub (Ayyub), mosque 93 G e
Eyoub (Ayyub), quarter 93 G e

Fairbanks 180 M a
Fair Island 128 ins.
Faith, Temple of 24 A (1)
Faknur 104 B R j
Falkenstein, castle, in Swabia 62 E d
Falkenstein, castle, on the Selke R. 85 F e
Falkirk 128 E e
Fansur 104 C J g
Fao 168 K E c
Farah 104 B G d
Far-Eastern, economic reg. 170 leg.
Far Eastern Region 171 N Q c
Far Eastern Republic 171 O P c
Farquharsons, fam. 128 E d
Fars, reg. 104 B F e
Farther India, reg. 104 C J e
Faucigny, reg. 91 O m
Faucilles, Monts 168 C C c
Faustina, Temple of Antoninus and 24 B (22)
Federal Democratic Republic Transcaucasia 1917—1918 168 G N/O g
Federal Territory = F. T. 172 D d
Federated Malay States = F. M. S. 171 L h
Fehértemplon (Weisskirchen) 159 K f
Fehmarn, isl. 134 F a
Felden 79 H d
Fellin 88 K b
Ferentis 27 G e
Ferghana, reg. 104 B H c
Ferlech 104 C J g
Fern Pass 87 H e
Ferrières, near Joinville 104 A C c
Ferrol 83 J g
Feronian Grove 35 ins. B
Ferrybridge 74 L f
Fetlar, isl. 128 ins.
Fez, reg., 14 cent. 77 C f
Fidei Faith), Temple 24 A (1)
Findhorn River 128 E c
Fines, Ad, near Volaterrae 26 E d
Finland, rep. 168 G K b/c
Finmark, reg. 138 B b
Finns proper, people 57 H-I a
Firando (Hirado), isl. 128 C O d
Firebr 104 B G d
Firth of Clyde 128 C e
Firth of Forth 128 F d
Firth of Lorne 128 C d
Fismes 168 C B c
Fitzgerald, fam. 74 B b
Flandrina 104 B R j
Flaviae, Aquae 38 A d
Flemings, people in 1929 168 H B b
Flevum 38 C b
Flodden Field 128 F e
Florent 104 A B b
Flushing 168 C B b
Foča 87 L g
Focsani (Fokshani) 153 J c
Fojnica 103 M g
Fons, Gate of, in Rome 24 A
Fonseca Bay 213 D c
Fontanafredda 150 G c
Forbes, fam. 128 F c
Forfar, cty. 128 F d
Formartin, dist. 128 F c
Fornham 65 G d
Fort Albany 128 B D c
Fort Amsterdam 128 B E c
Fort Bliss 180 Q d
Fort Chequamegon 191 G b
Fort Condé (Mobile) 191 H e
Fort Dauphin, in Canada 190 E a
Fort Dauphin, in Madagascar 128 C K g

Fort de la Reine . . . . . . 190 F a
Fort des Abitibis . . . . . . 191 J b
Fort des Miamis . . . . . . 191 H c
Fort Edward . . . . 191 K c
Fort Garry (Winnipeg) . . 212 F d
Fort Gibbon . . . . 180 L a
Fort Hollandia . . . . 136 I d
Forth River . . . . 128 D d
Fort James, in Gambia . 128B H e
Fort Jemseg . . . . 191 L b
Fort La Tourette . . . . . . 191 H a
Fort Meductic . . . . 191 L b
Fort Miami . . . . 191 H c
Fort Michipicoten . . . . . 191 H b
Fort Nachouac . . . . 191 L b
Fort Perrot . . . . 191 G c
Fort Pickawillany . . . . . 191 I c
Fort Radisson . . . . 191 G b
Fortrose, bp. . . . . 97 I b
Fort Rouge . . . . 190 F b
Fort Rupert . . . . 128B E c
Fort Saint Antoine . . . . 191 G c
Fort Saint Croix . . . . . . 191 G b
Fort Saint Jean . . . . 191 L b
Fort Saint Joseph, L. Huron 191 I c
Fort Saint Louis, Alabama R. . . . . 191 H e
Fort Saint Nicholas . . . . 191 G c
Fort Saint Pierre, in Mississippi . . . . 191 G e
Fort Sauvage . . . . 191 I b
Fort Sill . . . . 180 R d
Fort Tadoussac . . . . 191 K b
Fort Trempealeau . . . . . 191 G c
Fortune, Temple of . . . . . 24 A
Fort Victoria . . . . 137 B e
Fort York (Bencoolen) . 128C ins. C
Fort Zelandia . . . . 128C O d
Forum Fulvii . . . . 26 C b
Forum Piscarium (Fish-market), in Rome . . . . 24 A
Foula, isl. . . . . 128 ins.
Fountain Gate, in Rome . . 24 A
Fraserburgh . . . . 128 G c
Frazers, fam. . . . . 128 D c
Fredrikshamn . . . . 138 C c
Freistadt, in Austria . . . . . 79 I d
Freiwaldau (Frývaldov) . . 103 M c
French River . . . . 191 I b
Freudental (Bruntál) . . . . . 72 D b
Friesians, people in 1929 168H C b
Friuli (Furlans), people in 1929 . . . . 168H D c
Frouard . . . . 104A D c
Frunse . . . . 170 I d
Fugui (Fu-chau) . . . . . 104C L e
Fulford . . . . 65 F d
Fulginiae (Foligno) . . . . . 27 G e
Fulham . . . . 60 I d
Fulvian Way . . . . 26 C c
Fünen (Fyen or Fyn), isl. . . 88 D d
Furness, dist. . . . . 60 H b
Fustat . . . . 53 F c
Fuzo (Fu-chau) . . . . . . 104C L e
Fyn (Fünen), isl. . . . . 88 D d
Fyvie . . . . 128 F c

Gadara, in Gilead . . . . . . 7 D d
Gadara, in Jair . . . . 6 D c
Gaina, reg. . . . . 51 R k
Galatia, Rom. prov. under Trajan . . . . 20 E c (III)
Galava . . . . 51 O g
Galich . . . . 138 F d
Galinds, people . . . . 57 H c
Galli, people . . . . 29 A b
Gallinazos . . . . 216 ins.
Gallipoli, pen. . . . . 168L D c
Galloway, dist. . . . . 60 G b
Galway . . . . 74 B b
Gambia, reg. . . . . 128B H e
Gambrium . . . . 9 E e
Gambron . . . . 128C K d
Gandia . . . . 88 K h
Ganfu . . . . 104C M d
Ganja (Gandja) . . . . 139 G g
Ganus . . . . 9 E d
Garamantes, people . . . . . 34 G h
Garanbi . . . . 179 D e
Garde Meuble, bldg. in Paris 149 B
Garde Meuble, bldg. in Versailles . . . . 149 A
Gardinas (Grodno) . . . . 168G J e
Gargamish . . . . 5 C b
Gargara . . . . 9 D e
Gariannonum . . . . 51 Q h
Garibaldi, Monument of, in Rome . . . . 22 A
Garioch, dist. . . . . 128 F c
Garma, Beth . . . . 99 L f
Garry, Fort (Winnipeg) . . 212 F d
Gata Mountains . . . . 82 A a
Gath Hepher . . . . 6 C c
Gaulanitis, reg. . . . . 6 D c
Gävle (Gefle) . . . . 88 G a
Gaza, in Judaea . . . . 7 A e
Gaza, in Sogdiana . . . . . . 19 K b
Gebalene . . . . 7 C g
Gebel Silsileh . . . . 4 F d
Gedor, in Gilead . . . . 7 D d
Gedor, in Jair . . . . 6 D c
Gelsenkirchen . . . . 168E B b
Gemauerthof . . . . 138 B d
Gembes . . . . 104A C a
Gemina, Legio VII . . . . . 38 A d
Gemona . . . . 154 G e
Genevois, reg. . . . . 91 O m
Georgia, auton. rep. . . . 168G N g
Gerbéviller . . . . 104A D c
Gerenia (Pylus) . . . . 14 B c
Gerlos Pass . . . . 87 H e
German East Africa, Late, Brit. Mand. . . . . 175 G e
Germania Inferior . . . . . . 39 H h
Germania Magna, reg. . . . . 38 D b
Germania Superior . . . . . . 39 H j
German Ocean . . . . 98 D b
German Republic on Volga . . . . 168G O e
German South-West Africa, Late . . . . 175 E g
Germany, rep. . . . . 166 H e
Germe . . . . 9 E e
Gérouville . . . . 104A C b
Gersif . . . . 174 Q n
Gerstungen . . . . 62 E c
Gesoriacum (Boulogne) . . . 38 C b
Gex . . . . 86 F e
Ghat . . . . 174 E b
Ghel (Ghelan), Sea of . . . . 99 M-N e
Gheluvelt . . . . 168C B b
Gheria . . . . 137 B e
Gherla (Szamos-Ujvar) . . 159 L e
Ghiseh (Ghizeh) . . . . 150 B a
Giants, Stoa of the, in Athens 23 D (2)
Gibeah of Benjamin . . . . . 7 C e
Gibeah of Saul . . . . 7 C e
Gilbert, route of . . . . . . 108 L c
Gilead . . . . 7 D d
Gilead, reg. . . . . 7 D d
Gilgal, near Jericho . . . . . 7 C e
Gilgal, near Joppa . . . . . . 7 B d
Gilgal, near Ramathaim . . . 7 C d
Gilgal, near Shechem . . . . 7 C d
Gilgenburg . . . . 87 M b'
Gilyan, reg. . . . . 139 G h
Gilyan, Sea of . . . . 99 N e
Gimso . . . . 7 B e
Ginaea . . . . 7 C d
Girba, isl. . . . . 44 C c
Giurgiu (Giurgevo) . . . . 165 D a
Giza (Ghizeh) . . . . 174 J j
Gjatsk . . . . 153 O f
Glamorgan, dist. . . . . 60 C d
Glasgow . . . . 128 D e
Glastonbury, ab. . . . . 74 K h
Glastonbury, mon. . . . . . . 60 H d
Glencoe, in Scotland . . . 128 C d
Glengarry . . . . 128 C c
Glenluce . . . . 128 D f
Glen Shiel . . . . 128 C c
Gloucester, in England . . . 60 H d
Gloucester, abbey . . . . . . 74 K h
Gloucester, cty. . . . . 74 K h
Glubokoie . . . . 153 N f
Glurns . . . . 91 S l
Gmünd, in Carinthia . . . . 87 I e
Gnesen (Gniezno) . . . . . . 63 I b
Gnesen (Gniezno), abp. . . . 95 F a
Gobelins, The, bldg. in Paris 149 B
Göding (Hodonin) . . . . . . 87 K d
Godmanham . . . . 60 D c
Gokcha, lake . . . . 168K E a
Goldap . . . . 155 L a
Golden Mile-stone, in Rome 24 B (9)
Goldingen . . . . 88 J c
Gollub . . . . 87 L b
Golzow . . . . 85 C b
Gomer (Cimmerians), people 5 C a
Gomera, bay . . . . 174 P n
Gomera, (Peñon de Velez) 136 I c (P.)
Goplo, lake . . . . 88 H e
Gorales, people in 1929 . 168H E c
Gordons, fam. . . . . 128 D e
Goree, isl. . . . . 128B H e
Gorizia (Görz) . . . . 103 K f
Gormaz, San Estéban de . . 82 B a
Gortscha (Koritza) . . . . . 165 B c
Gortyn . . . . 14 ins.
Gorze . . . . 78 E d
Göta River . . . . 88 E b
Göteborg (Gothenburg) . . . 88 E c
Gothia (Crimea) . . . . 99 J d
Gotland, isl. . . . . 88 H c
Gotland, East, dist. . . . . . 88 F b
Götland, West, dist. . . . . . 88 E b
Goulfeï . . . . 174 E c
Gower, dist. . . . . 60 G d
Gradisca . . . . 154 G f
Graecostasis, in Rome . . . 24 A (9)
Gran (Esztergom) . . . . 79 K e
Grand Arsenal, bldg. in Paris . . . . 149 B
Grand-Failly . . . . 104A C b
Grand Morin, R. . . . . . . 168C B c
Grandpré, in France . . 104A B b
Grandpré, cty. . . . . 104A B b
Granicus River . . . . 9 E d
Grants, fam. . . . . 128 E c
Grappa, Monte . . . . 168B F b
Graslitz . . . . 79 H c
Graupen . . . . 79 H c
Gravelotte . . . . 158 C d
Grave of Adam, mt. . . . 104B I g
Grave of Saint Thomas . 104B I f
Gray League . . . . 91 R l
Great Batanga . . . . 174 E d
Great Bedwin, parl. bor. . 163 M f
Great Belchen, mt. . . . . 168C D c
Great Canal, in China . . 104C L d
Great Desert . . . . 104C K c
Great Dividing Range . . . 172 D c
Greater (Black) Sea . . . . . 99 J e
Greater Zap River . . . . 168J D b
Great Gymnasium, in Olympia 9 H f
Great Hungary, reg. . . . . . 92 E b
Great Khan, Empire of the 92 leg.
Great Salt Desert . . . . 168K F c
Great Wall, in China . . 104C K d
Greece, rep. . . . . 168G J h
Greek Orthodox . . . . . 168L N g leg.
Greek trade-routes . . . . . . 44 leg.
Greencastle, in Ireland . . . 74 D a
Greencastle, in Pa. . . . . . 208 ins.
Greenland, reg. . . . . . . 128B F
Greenwich, East, in Rhode Island . . . . 189 ins. A
Grenada, isl. . . . . 136 ins. A
Grimsby . . . . 74 M f

Grimsel Pass . . . 91 Q l
Grójec . . . 135 K c
Grosser Belchen, mt. . . 168 C D c
Gross Friedrichsburg . . 128 B H e
Grozka (Grocka) . . . 139 B g
Grozny . . . 168 K E a
Grudziądz (Graudenz) . . . 135 J b
Grünberg, castle in Bohemia 87 I d
Guadalaviar River . . . 82 B a
Guadalcanal . . . 83 J h
Guadarrama Mountains . . . 82 B a
Guaira, La . . . 214 C a
Guaranis, reg. . . . 128 B F g
Guiana, reg. . . . 128 B F e
Guichet de Marigny, in Paris . . . 149 B (3)
Gümürdjina . . . 168 L E f
Güns (Köszeg) . . . 115 I e
Güssing, castle . . . 79 J e
Gwent, dist. . . . 60 C d
Gwynedd, ter. . . . 60 C c
Györ (Raab) . . . 87 K e
Györ (Raab), bp. . . . 95 F b
Gyrwe, people . . . 60 D c

Habayes, Les . . . 104 A C b
Habitancum . . . 51 O g
Haddington, cty. . . . 128 F e
Hadersleben (Haderslev) . . 88 C d
Hadid . . . 7 B e
Hadrian, Aqueduct of, in Athens . . . 23 D
Hadrianopolis, quarter in Athens . . . 23 D
Hadrianutherae . . . 9 E e
Hafir . . . 53 G d
Hafisfiord . . . 45 F a
Hagia Triada . . . 4 B b
Haidar Pasha . . . 168 J A a
Haifa . . . 150 B a
Haji Chefan . . . 168 L B b
Hala-l-Bedr . . . 4 F d
Haleb (Aleppo) . . . 4 F c
Halhul . . . 7 C e
Halidon Hill . . . 74 K d
Halil-Eli . . . 9 B b
Hallein . . . 79 H e
Hallstadt, near Bamberg . . 55 R j
Hallstatt, near Salzburg . . 103 K e
Halonnesos, isl. . . . 9 C e
Halwan, near Babylon . . . 5 D b
Halwan, near Bagdad . . . 99 M g
Hamadan . . . 53 G c
Hamar, in Iraq . . . 168 K E c
Hamar, in Norway . . . 131 F a
Hami . . . 104 C J c
Hamilton in Scotland . . . 128 D e
Hamm . . . 168 E B b
Hammadites, Dom. of the . 66 G g
Hang-chau-fu . . . 104 C L e
Hanifa, people . . . 53 G d
Hankau . . . 171 M e
Hanoi (Kesho) . . . 104 C K e
Hansi . . . 104 B H e
Hapharaim . . . 6 C c
Harah (Herat) . . . 104 B G d
Hardegg . . . 72 D b
Hardt Mountains . . . 168 C D c
Harlech . . . 74 I g
Harmakut, mts. . . . 104 B I e
Harpessus River . . . 9 C c
Harplea . . . 14 C c
Hartmannsweiler Kopf . . 168 C D c
Hasa, El-, reg. . . . 104 B E e
Hastings . . . 60 J d
Haunts of the Buccaneers 128 B ins. A
Hay . . . 74 K g
Haye Sainte, La . . . 156 A a
Heathfield . . . 60 D c
Heavenfield . . . 60 D b
Hecanas (Magesaete), people 60 C c
Hedon . . . 74 M f
Hejaz, reg. . . . 170 E i
Hekatompedon (Temple of Athena), in Athens . . . 23 C (1)
Helicon Mons, in Attica . . 23 D
Helif . . . 168 J D b
Helles, cape . . . 168 L D c
Hellespont (Dardanelles), str. 9 D d
Hellespontine Phrygia, satr. . 17 E b
Hellespontine Tributary . . . 13 K d (II)
Helmsdale . . . 128 E b
Hendrica, dist. . . . 60 D d
Hephaestia . . . 9 C e
Heptanomis, reg. . . . 4 F d (II)
Heraclea (Perinthus) . . . 9 E d
Heracleum, in Crete . . . 14 ins.
Heraeum, in Olympia . . . 9 H f (7)
Heraeum, in Thrace . . . 9 E c
Herat . . . 104 B G d
Hercules Custos, Temple of 22 A
Hercules Invictus, Temple of 24 A
Hercules Pompejanus, Temple of . . . 24 B
Hereford, Palatine earldom . 65 E d
Hereros, people . . . 175 E f
Heri-Rud, R. . . . 168 K H c
Herkend, Sea of . . . 104 B I f
Hermandad, Santa . . . 83 L h leg.
Hermes Street, in Athens . 23 D
Hermopolis, in Egypt. . . . 4 F d
Hermupolis, in Greece . . 165 D e
Herod Antipas, Principality of . . . 7
Herodes Atticus, Exedra of 9 H f (6)
Herodes Atticus, Tomb of . 23 D
Herstal . . . 104 A C a
Hertford . . . 60 D d
Hertogenbosch . . . 168 E A b
Hestiaeotis, dist. . . . 10 C c
Hexamilion . . . 9 D d
Hexham, mon. . . . 60 C b
Hielmar (Hjälmar), lake . . . 88 F b
Hieraconpolis . . . 4 F d
Hierapolis, in Asia Minor . 20 C d
Hili (Ely) . . . 104 B R j
Hilmend, lake . . . 168 K H c
Himyar, people . . . 53 G e
Hind . . . 104 B R j
Hindenburg Line . . . 168 C leg.
Hindukush Mountains . . 104 B G d
Hippodrome, in Olympia . 9 H f
Hirado (Firando), isl. . . . 128 C O d
Hispaniola, reg. . . . 128 B ins. A
Hissar, in Turkestan . . . 104 B G d
Hissarlik . . . 9 A b
Hittites, Kingdom of the . . 4 F c
Hixton Down . . . 60 G d
Hjälmar (Hielmar), lake . . . 88 F b
Hoang-ho, R. . . . 104 C L d
Hodonin (Göding) . . . 87 K d
Hohenzieritz . . . 154 G b
Holderness, dist. . . . 60 I c
Holland, dist. in England . 60 I c
Holland, dist. in Friesland . 62 C b
Holme . . . 60 I c
Holme Saint Benet, abbey . 74 O g
Holwan (Halwan) . . . 53 G c
Holy Brotherhood . . . 83 L h leg.
Holyhead . . . 60 G c
Hooghly . . . 137 E d
Hooghly River . . . 137 E d
Hope (Spes), Temple of . . 24 A
Hôpital Saint-Louis, in Paris 149 B
Hořice (Horschitz) . . . 87 J c
Horonaim . . . 7 D f
Horsham . . . 74 M h
Horsham, parl. bor. . . . 163 N f
Hôtel de Cluny, bldg. in Paris 149 B
Hôtel de Soubise, in Paris . 149 B
Hôtel Rambouillet, in Paris 149 B
House of Parliament, in Athens . . . 23 D
Hoy, isl. . . . 128 E b
Hradec Kralove (Königgrätz) . . . 87 J c
Hradec Kralove (Königgrätz), bp. . . . 95 F a
Hradisch (Hradiště) . . . 87 K d
Hsiang-yang . . . 104 C L d
Hudson, route of . . . 128 B D c
Hudson Bay Company . 128 B D c
Hudson Bay Territory . . . 133 L e
Huexotzingo . . . 106 B a
Hueyotlipán . . . 106 B a
Hulagu (Dominion of the Ilkhans) . . . 92 leg.
Humaytá, in Brazil . . . 181 U h
Hungarian Altenburg . . . 155 I e
Hungarians, people, on the Theiss R. . . . 45 I c
Hungary, rep. . . . 168 G I-J f
Huningue (Hüningen) . . . 157 B c
Hunkiar Iskelessi . . . 164 D b
Huns, people, in Hungary . 45 I c
Huns, people, on the Dnieper R. . . . 45 K c
Huns, people, on the Ural R. 45 N c
Hunsrück, mts. . . . 168 C D c
Huntingdon, Dan. bor. . . . 60 I c
Huntingdon, cty. . . . 74 M g
Hu-peh, reg. . . . 171 M e
Hushi (Huşi, Hush) . . . 131 I d
Huzuli, people in 1929 . 168 H F c
Hvar (Lesina), isl. . . . 90 F c
Hwang-Ho (Hoang-ho), R. . 92 M d
Hwicce, people . . . 51 R k
Hyères . . . 78 E g
Hyettus . . . 11 E d
Hyogo (Hiogo, Kobe) . . . 171 O e
Hythe . . . 74 O h

Iaca . . . 38 B d
Iacetani, people . . . 38 B d
Ibelim . . . 68 ins. A
Ibir-Sibir, reg. . . . 104 B G b
Iça River . . . 214 C c
Ida Mountains, in Troas . . 9 D e
Idle River . . . 60 D c
Idomene, in Epirus . . . 10 C c
Idomene, in Macedonia . . . 17 C a
Idria . . . 103 L e
Iglau, in Moravia (Jihlava) . 79 I d
Iglau, in Zips (Igló, Spišská Nová Ves) . . . 80 G g
Igló = Neudorf, in Zips . . 87 M d
Ilchester, bor. . . . 74 K h
Ilebo . . . 175 F e
Ile (Isle) Bourbon . . . 128 C K g
Ilipa . . . 38 A e
Ilium (Troy) . . . 9 B b
Ilkhans of Persia, Dominion of the . . . 92 leg.
Ilkley . . . 51 P h
Illyrii, people . . . 29 D b
17 B a
Ilus, Burial mound of . . . 9 A b
Imbros . . . 9 C d
Imbros, isl. . . . 9 C d
Imeritia, reg. . . . 139 F g
Imil . . . 104 B I c
Inauen River . . . 174 P n
Incurables, The, bldg. in Paris . . . 149 B
India, Farther, reg. . . . 104 C J e
Indian Islands, Sea of the 104 C K g
Indragiri . . . 128 C ins. C
Ineboli . . . 168 J B a
Ingushetiya, auton. area 168 F leg.
Inner Ceramicus, deme . . . 23 D
Inner Tibet reg. . . . 171 K e
Insulae Nudorum (Nicobar Islands) . . . 104 C J g
Insular Tributary . . . 13 J e (V)
Intercontinental Railway . 215 leg.
Inverary . . . 128 C d
Inverlochy . . . 128 C d
Inverness . . . 128 D c
Inverness, cty. . . . 128 B c

Seistan, reg. . . . . 104 B G d
Selenga River . . . . 104 C K c
Selestat (Schlettstadt) . . . 134 D d
Selke River . . . . 85 F e
Selkirk . . . . 128 F e
Selkirk, cty. . . . . 128 E e
Selmeczbánya (Schemnitz) . 87 L d
Selsey, bp. . . . . 60 D d
Seluan . . . . 174 Q n
Selymbria . . . . 9 F c
Selymbria, Gate of . . . . . 93 G e
Semender . . . . 45 N d
Semigallia, dist. . . . . . . 88 K c
Semigallians, people . . . . 57 I b
Semiscant (Samarkand) . 104 B G d
Semlin (Zemun) . . . . 87 M f
Semnan . . . . 168 K F b
Semneh . . . . 4 F d
Senaculum, bldg. in Rome . 24 A (8)
Senatorio, Palazzo, bldg. in Rome . . . . 22 A
Senj (Zengg) . . . . 72 D c
Senj (Zengg), bp. . . . . . . 95 F b
Senjirli . . . . 4 F c
Sennabris . . . . 6 D c
Senussi, people . . . . . . 174 F b
Septimius Severus, Arch of 24 B (11)
Seraijik . . . . 168 L D d
Serampur . . . . 128 B ins. B
Serbs, people in 1929 . . 168 H E d
Sergin . . . . 168 L F f
Serre River . . . . 104 A A b
Serrhium, prom. . . . . . . 9 C d
Sestus . . . . 9 D d
Sevastopol (Cherson) . . . . 89 J f
Severians, people about 900 57 J c, I e
Sèvres . . . . 168 D A d
Sèvres, Treaty of . . . . . 168 L leg.
Sézanne . . . . 104 A A c
Shabatz (Šabac) . . . . 87 L f
Sha-chau . . . . 104 C J c
Shadwan Island . . . . 150 B b
Shaftesbury . . . . 74 K i
Shaftesbury, mon. . . . . . . 97 O k
Shaliyat (Calicut) . . . . . 104 B R j
Shamaiten (Samogitia), reg. 88 J d
Shamir (Van) . . . . 99 L f
Shangtu . . . . 104 C L c
Shatt-el-Arab, R. . . . . . 168 K E d
Sheffield, castle . . . . . . 74 L f
Shemak (Shemakha) . . . . . 99 M e
Sheppey, Isle of . . . . . . 60 E d
Sherborne, bp. . . . . 60 C d
Sheriffmuir . . . . 128 E d
Sheshauen . . . . 174 P n
Shiahs, sect . . . . 168 L N g, leg.
Shiblak . . . . 9 B b
Shilka River . . . . 104 C L b
Shipyards, loc. in Rome . . 24 B
Shiraz . . . . 104 B F e
Shirvan, reg. . . . . 139 G g
Shkodra (Scutari), in Servia 89 A b
Shoreham . . . . 74 M i
Shrewsbury in England . . . 65 E d
Shrewsbury, abbey . . . . . 74 K g
Shrewsbury, Palatine earldom 65 E d
Shropshire, cty. . . . . 74 K g
Shusha . . . . 168 K E b
Shushtar (Shuster) . . . . . 99 M g
Šibenik (Sebenico) . . . . . 87 J g
Sibenik (Sebenico), bp. . . . 95 F c
Siberian, economic reg. . . 170 leg.
Sibir . . . . 104 B G b
Sibiu (Hermannstadt) . . . 159 M f
Sicelia, hill in Athens . . . 23 D
Sidini, people . . . . 38 E b
Sidnacaester, bp. . . . . . . 60 D c
Sieg River . . . . 134 D c
Sierra Gorda . . . . 216 ins.
Sierra Leone, reg. . . . . 128 B H e
Siewierz . . . . 79 K c
Sigeum . . . . 9 A b
Sighişoara (Schässburg) . . 159 M e
Sigrium, prom. . . . . 9 C e
Sikhs, people . . . . 137 B b
Si-kiang, R. . . . . 104 C K e
Sikkim . . . . 171 J f
Silberberg . . . . 103 M c
Silchester . . . . 51 P i
Silet . . . . 174 D b
Silian (Ceylon). isl. . . . 104 B S k
Silivri, Gate of . . . . 93 G e
Siljan, lake . . . . 88 F a
Silk-Route . . . . 104 B leg.
Sillein (Zsolna, Žilina) . . 155 J d
Sillerie . . . . 191 K b
Sil River . . . . 82 A a
Silsileh, Gebel . . . . 4 F d
Simoeis River (Dumbrek R.) 9 B b
Sin . . . . 104 C L d
Sin-al-Sin (Canton) . . . . 104 C L e
Sinclayrs, fam. . . . . 128 E b
Sine . . . . 168 L D d
Si-ngan-fu . . . . 104 C K d
Si-ning-fu . . . . 104 C K d
Sinkalan (Canton) . . . . 104 C L e
Sinob (Sinope) . . . . 89 K f
Sinti, people . . . . 17 C a
Sinub (Sinope) . . . . . . 168 J C a
Siraf . . . . 104 B F e
Siugui . . . . 104 C M d
Sivas . . . . 89 K g
Siwa Oasis . . . . 174 F b
Skara . . . . 46 I b
Skias (Tholos), in Athens . 23 D (7)
Skofja Loka (Bischoflack) 135 H e
Skoplje (Uskub) . . . . 89 H f
Skradin (Scardona), bp. . . 95 F c
Skutari . . . . 168 G K g
Slack . . . . 60 C c
Sleat Sound . . . . 128 C c
Slesvik . . . . 78 F a
Slesvik, Duchy of . . . . . . 78 F a
Slesvik (Schleswig), March of 62 E I
Sligo, castle . . . . 74 B a
Slovenes, poeple, about 900 57 I-J b
Slovenes, people in 1929 168 H Dc, Gd
Sochaczew (Sokhaczew) . . 135 K b
Södermanland, dist. . . . . . 88 G b
Soer . . . . 104 B F e
Sofala . . . . 128 C J g
Sofia, Treaty of . . . . . . 168 L leg.
Söke . . . . 168 J A b
Solangas, people . . . . 92 M c
Sole Bay . . . . 125 D b
Solingen . . . . 102 H c
Solon Street in Athens . . 23 D
Solovyeva . . . . 153 O g
Solvychegodsk . . . . 138 G c
Solway Firth . . . . 60 C b
Soma . . . . 165 E d
Somnath . . . . 104 B R i
Songhar . . . . 104 B R i
Songko River . . . . 171 L f
Sorbiodunum (Salisbury) . . 51 P i
Sous, Wadi . . . . 174 C a
Southampton in England . . 60 I d
Southern Country (Negeb) . 7 B f
Southern Long Wall in Athens 23 D
Southern Sung Dynasty . . . 92 K e
South Folk (East Angles), people . . . . 51 S k
South Mining, economic reg. 168 F leg.
South Osset, auton. area . 168 F leg.
South Osset, Territory . . 168 J D a
Southport . . . . 162 C d
South Sea Islands, Japan. Mand. . . . . 179 G f
South Uist, isl. . . . . . . 128 A c
Southwark, bor. . . . . 60 I d
Southwest, economic reg. . 168 F leg.
Spa . . . . 168 F G e
Spanish Main (Tierra Firme) . . . . 128 B ins. A
Spes (Hope), Temple of . . 24 A
Spey (Spay) River . . . . . 128 E c
Spichern . . . . 158 D d
Spišská Stará Ves (Altendorf) . . . . 79 L d
Spišská Nová Ves (Igló, Neudorf) . . . . 87 M d
Spithead . . . . 127 X p
Spits (Zips), dist. . . . . 168 D E d
Split (Spalato) . . . . 89 A b
Split (Spalato), abp. . . . . . 95 F c
Spoleto, march . . . . 45 G d (Sp)
Spring Gate . . . . 93 G e
Srebrenica . . . . 103 N f
Srebrenik . . . . 87 L f
Sredetz (Sofia) . . . . 89 B b
Środa (Schroda) . . . . . . 159 I b
Stadium, in Athens . . . . . 23 D
Stadium, in Olympia . . . . 9 H f
Stadium, street in Athens . 23 D
Stafford, bor. in England . . 60 H c
Stamford, in England, danish borough . . . . 60 I c
Stamford, mon. . . . . 60 D c
Stanimaka . . . . 165 D c
Stanislawow (Stanislau) . . 159 M d
Stará Ves (Spišská-, Altendorf) . . . . 79 L d
Stargard, in Holstein . . . 103 J a
Stargardt (in Pomerelia) . . 87 L b
Starhemberg, castle, near Wels . . . . 79 H d
Starhemberg, castle, near Wiener Neustadt . . . . . 123 I e
Stari Grad (Cittavecchia), bp. 95 F c
Statenland (New Zealand) 128 C Q h
State Treasury, in Rome . . 24 B (8)
Stato degli Presidii . . . . 151 I h
Stefano Rotondo, Santo, ch. in Rome . . . . 22 A
Stentoris Lake . . . . 9 D d
Stewarts, fam. . . . . 128 C d
Štiavnica (Baňská-, Schemnitz) . . . . 79 K d
Štip (Ištip) . . . . 165 C c
Stirling . . . . 128 D d
Stirling, cty. . . . . 128 D d
Stoa, on the Acropolis of Athens . . . . 23 C
Stoa Basileios, in Athens . 23 D (3)
Stoa of Attalus . . . . 23 D
Stoa of Eumenes, in Athens 23 C
Stoa of Hadrian . . . . 23 D
Stoa of Jupiter Eleutherus 23 D (4)
Stoa of the Giants, in Athens 23 D (2)
Stoa Poikile, in Athens . . 23 D (1)
Stockbridge, parl. bor. . . 163 M f
Stockerau . . . . 87 K d
Stolberg (in Harz) . . . . . . 87 H c
Stolpe River . . . . 135 I a
Strasburg, near Thorn . . . . 87 L b
Strathclyde, dist. . . . . . . 60 B b
Strathclyde, km. . . . . 60 G b
Strathearn, dist. . . . . . . 128 D d
Strathmore, dist . . . . . . 128 E d
Strathnaver, dist. . . . . . 128 D b
Streaneshalch (Whitby), mon. 60 D b
Street of Tombs, in Athens 23 D
Stříbro (Mies) . . . . 103 K d
Stroganov, Colony of . . . 138 I d
Stryme . . . . 9 C d
Stuhm . . . . 87 L b
Styr River . . . . 168 I a
Suamians, people . . . . . . 57 H-I a
Suardones, people . . . . . . 38 E b
Subeitala . . . . 53 C c
Subotica (Szabadka, Maria-Theresiopel) . . . . 168 F c
Succur (Su-chau) . . . . . 104 C J c
Su-chau (Siugui) . . . . . 104 C M d
Suedia . . . . 168 J C b
Suffolk, dist. . . . . 60 E c
Sugd, reg. . . . . 92 G c
Sui-chau-fu . . . . 104 C K e
Suiones (Sueones), people . 34 G b

Suiyan 171 M d
Suk-el Arba 174 O n
Sukhum-kaleh 164 G b
Sukkot 7 D d
Suleimanieh 168 K E b
Sulu, isl. 104 C M g
Sumatia 14 C b
Sumbal 104 B H e
Sumbal, reg. 104 B H e
Sumbawa, isl. 128 C ins. C
Šumen (Shumla) 165 E b
Sunarganw 104 C J e
Sungari River 104 C M c
Sung Dynasty 92 K d
Sung Dynasty, Southern 92 K e
Sungerlu 168 J B a
Sunian Gate, in Athens 23 D
Sunium, prom. 15 E b
Sunnites, sect 168 L leg.
Sunzumata 104 C L d
Surrounding Sea 104 C L g
Sutherland, cty. 128 D b
Sutherland, dist. 127 P f
Suthrige (Surrey), dist. 60 D d
Suvla Bay 168 L D c
Suvla Burun 168 L D c
Suwali 104 B R i
Svensksund 138 C c
Sverdlovsk (Ekaterinburg) 168 G R d
Svienta River 88 K d
Svitary (Zwittau, in Moravia) 168 E b
Swanage 60 I d
Swansea, castle, in Wales 74 J h
Swansea, in Mass. 189 ins. A
Sweden and Norway, km. 1815—1905 157 B a
Swenet (Syene) 4 F d
Swiecie (Schwetz) 135 J b
Syra, isl. 165 D e
Syra Orda 104 C K c
Syrian Gate 20 G d
Syrmia, dist. 87 L f
Szabadka (Maria Theresiopel) 159 J e
Szaszvaros (Broos) 159 L f
Szatmar Nemeti (Satu Mare) 80 H h
Szegedin (Szeged) 79 L e
Székesfehérvár (Stuhlweissenburg) 159 J e
Szendrö 87 M d
Szombathely (Steinamanger) 159 I e

Taanath-Shiloh 7 C d
Tabal, people 5 C b
Tabernae novae, bldg. in Rome 24 A (17)
Tabernae veteres, bldg. in Rome 24 A (16)
Tachau (Tachov) 87 I d
Tacna, prov. 216 ins.
Tacuba 106 A a
Tadoussac, Fort 191 K b
Tagong 104 C J e
Tahiti (Sagitaria), isl. 128 B A f
Taif 53 G d
Taifur Keui 168 L D c
Tain 128 D c
Tai-yuen-fu 104 C L d
Tajik, Autonomous Socialist Soviet Area 170 H e
Talas 104 B H c
Talay River 104 C K e
Ta-li-fu 104 C K e
Talish, reg. 164 H c
Tallinn (Reval) 168 D E b
Tamerlane (Timur), Dom. of 92 leg.
Tamworth, bp. 60 D c
Tanatus Island 51 Q i
Tanganyika Territory (Late German East Africa) 175 G e
Tangut 104 C J c
Tangut, reg. 104 C J d
Tannu-Tubin, rep. 170/171 K c
Tantamquerry 128 C ins. D
Taoce 19 H e
Tapiau 87 M a
Tarabulus (Tripoli) 168 J C c
Tarapacá, prov. 216 ins.
Tarbellicae, Aquae 38 B d
Targovicz (Targovitza 139 D f
Târgu Mureşului (Maros Vasarhely) 159 M e
Tarim River 104 B H d
Tarsi, people 104 B I c
Tarsius River 9 E e
Tartar, auton. rep. 168 G P d
Tartessus River 44 A c
Tartkul 170 H d
Tartu (Dorpat) 168 D F b
Tashkent 104 B G c
Tasman, route of 128 C O f
Tasmania (Van Diemen's Land) 128 C P h
Tasmanland, reg. 128 C O f
Tatar Dynasty in China 92 L d
Tatars, people in Azerbaijan 168 L M g
Tatars, people in eastern Asia 104 C L c
Tatars, people in Dobruja 168 H G d
Tauchira 44 D c
Taungu 104 C J f
Taungu, reg. 104 C J f
Taurirt 174 Q n
Tavoy 104 C J f
Tavoy, reg. 104 C J f
Tawalisi, people 104 C L g
Taydo (Peking) 104 C L c
Taza 174 P n
Tebez 7 C d
Tecoac 106 C a
Tegyra 11 E d
Tehennu, people 4 E c
Tejend, R. 168 K H b
Tekrit 168 J D c
Tel (Tell) el Kebir 174 J J i
Telingana, reg. 104 B R j
Tell el Amarna 4 F d
Tellenae 35 ins. B
Temesvar (Temisoara) 103 O f
Templin 87 I b
Tempsford 60 I c
Tenasserim 104 C J f
Tenduc, people 104 C L c
Tepeyac 106 A a
Teplice (Teplitz, in Bohemia) 159 G c
Teptunis 4 ins.
Teruentum 27 I f
Tešanj 87 K f
Teschen (czech Těšín) 79 K d
Teschen, (Těsín) princ. 79 K d
Teschen (polish Cieszyn) 168 F b
Tesmelucán 106 B a
Téte 182 E E i
Tettenhall 60 H c
Teuthrania, reg. 9 E e
Teutonic Order, 13 cent. 47 K c
Texcoco 106 B a
Texcoce, lake 106 B a
Thaema 44 E d
Thaenae 44 C c
Thana 104 B R j
Thebais, reg. 4 F d (III)
Theocoleum in Olympia 9 H f
Theodosius, Port of 93 G e
The Riff, reg. 174 P n
Thesmotheteum, in Athens 23 D (9)
Thesprots (Thesprotians), people 8 N h
Thessalians, people 14 leg.
Thimnath Serah 7 C e
Thirsk, castle 74 L e
Thisb(a)e 11 D d
Thisbe 7 D d
Thogarma, reg. 5 D b
Tholos (Skias), in Athens 23 D (7)
Thomar 83 J h
Thomond, km. 74 B b
Thonne le Thil 104 A C b (Th.)
Thonon 91 O l
Thourout, fair 99 ins.
Thracian Bosporus, str. 9 G c
Thracian Tributary 13 J d (I)
Thracians, people 8 P g
Thrasyllus, Monument of 23 C (10)
Three Points, cape 128 C ins. D
Thriasian Gate, in Athens 23 D
Thriplow (Triploe) Heath 127 Z n
Thsenthung (Tsuen-chau-fu) 104 C L e
Thule (Shetland) Islands 34 D a
Thuria 14 C b
Thuringia, state 168 D C c
Thurso 128 E b
Thymbra 9 B b
Thymbrius River 9 B b
Thyni, people 9 G d
Thyrea 14 C b
Tian-shan Mountains 104 B H d
Tiberius, Arch of, on the Forum 24 B (14)
Tibet, reg. 104 B I d
Tibet, Inner, reg. 171 K e
Tibet, Outer, reg. 170 J e
Tichiussa 17 E c
Tigranocerta 20 I c
Tihany, mon. 80 E h
Timişoara (Temesvar) 103 O f
Timna 7 C e
Timur, Dominions of 92 leg.
Tinnevelly 137 C g
Tintagel 74 I i
Tione 168 H ins.
Tippermuir 128 E d
Tiraspol 168 G K f
Tireboli 168 J C a
Tiree, isl. 128 A d
Tirmidh 104 B G d
Tirnovo (Tirnova) 93 C b
Tityrus, mt. 15 D d
Tivertzes, people 57 I d
Tobol River 104 B G b
Tokaj (Tokay) 87 M d
Tokat 168 J C a
Toledo, univ. 100 E g
Toledo Mountains 82 B b
Tönsberg 58 F b
Tor (Sinai Penins.) 150 B b
Torcy 168 C B c
Tordesillas 83 J g (Tordes.)
Torksey 60 I c
Torre (Tor), mon. 97 N k
Torrelobaton (Torrelob.) 83 J g
Torres, route of 128 C P f
Toruń (Thorn) 135 J b
Toski 174 G b
Touapse 182 E E c
Tougurt 174 D a
Tovačov (Tobitschau) 159 I d
Towcester 60 I c
Tozan, people 104 C K d
Tralee 74 B b
Tramin, castle 79 G e
Tranquebar 128 B ins. B
Transcaucasia, rep. 168 G N-O g
Transcaucasian Socialist Federal Soviet Republic (T.S.F.S.R.) 168 F leg.
Trans-Jordan, reg. 168 J C c
Transoxiana, reg. 53 I c
Transvaal (South African Republic) 175 M l
Trastevere Railway Station, in Rome 22 A
Traun River 135 G d
Trave River 134 F a
Treasuries in Olympia 9 H f
Trebbin, castle 85 C b
Trebiae 27 G e
Trebinje (Trebinye), bp. 94 F c

Trebitsch (Trebič) . . . . . . 87 J d
Tregony, bor. . . . . 74 I i
Trempealeau, Fort . . . . . 191 G c
Trenčin (Trencsén, Trentschin) . . . . 63 J d
Trentino, reg. . . . . . . 168 H ins.
Trikkala . . . . 89 B c
Trimontium . . . . 51 O g
Trincomali (Trincomalee) 137 D g
Trinovantes, people . . . . 51 Q i
Triocala . . . . 30 C e
Triploe (Thriplow) Heath 127 Z n
Tripods, Street of the, in Athens . . . . 23 C
Tripolitania, dist. . . . . . . 174 E a
Tripolitsa, in Greece . . . 165 C e
Tritaea, in Achaia . . . . . . 14 B b
Trnava (Tyrnau, Nagyszombat) . . . . 79 J d
Trnova (Tirnova) . . . . 93 C b
Troas, reg. . . . . 9 D e
Trocnov (Troznow) . . . . . 87 J d
Trogir (Traú), bp. . . . . . . 95 F c
Troian Plain . . . . 9 A b
Troitskaia . . . . 138 E d
Troki . . . . 88 K d
Tropaeum Augusti . . . . . . 26 B d
Troy in Asia Minor . . . . . 9 B b
Troyland, reg. . . . . 9 D e
Trucial Oman, reg. . . . 168 K F d
Truns . . . . 91 R l
Truro, mon. . . . . 97 L k
Trutnov (Trautenau) . . . 135 H c
Tsaribrod . . . . 168 G J g
Tsaritsyn . . . . 139 F f
Tsarskoe Selo . . . . . . 138 D d (T.S.)
Tscherlitz (Echallens) . . . . 91 O l
Tsi-ning-chau . . . . 104 C L d
Tsuen-chau-fu . . . . 104 C L e
Tuapse . . . . 168 J C a
Tuaregs, people . . . . . . 174 D b
Tuat . . . . 174 C b
Tüffer . . . . 72 D b
Tulcea (Tulcha) . . . . . . 165 F a
Tun . . . . 168 K G c
Tunguska River, Lower- 104 C J a
Tunguska River, Upper- 104 C J b
Turaba . . . . 170 F f
Turan, reg., in India . . . . 53 I d
Turcoman Socialist Soviet Republic . . . . 168 F leg.
Turfan . . . . 104 C I c
Turkestan, economic reg. 170 leg.
Turkestan, East, reg. . . . 170 I e
Turkey, Republic, 1923 . 168 J B b
Turkish (Ottoman) Empire, 1683—1913 164
Turkish (Ottoman) Empire, till 1920, 1922 . . 168 J B b
Turkoman Socialist Soviet Republic . . . . 170 G d-e
Turks, people, 8 cent. . . . . 53 H b
Turks, people, 14 cent. . . . 89 J g
Turks, people, in 1913 . . 165 leg.
Turriff . . . . 128 F c
Tus . . . . 99 L g
Tutbury, castle . . . . 74 L g
Tuticorin . . . . 170 I h
Tuxtepec . . . . 216 D d
Tuz Geul . . . . 168 J B b
Tuz-Khurmati . . . . 168 J D c
Tuzla . . . . 103 N f
Tweeddale, dist. . . . . . . 128 E e
Twyneham . . . . 60 I d
Tyche, Temple of . . . . . . 23 D
Tyrconell, ter. . . . . 74 B a
Tyre . . . . 168 J C c
Tyria . . . . 168 J A b
Tyrnau (Trnava, Nagyszombat) . . . . 79 J d
Tzompantzinco . . . . 106 B a
Udgir . . . . 137 C e
Uglich . . . . 138 E d
Ugrians, people . . . . . 104 B G a
Uigurs, people . . . . . . 104 C I c
Uirats, people . . . . 104 C J b
Uist, North and South, isl. 128 A c
Ujda . . . . 174 Q n
Ujek-Tepe . . . . 9 A b
Ujiji . . . . 175 F e
Ujjain . . . . 104 B R i
Ujvidék (Neusatz, Novi Sad) 168 F d
Ukrainian Socialist Soviet Republic (U.S.S.R.) . . 168 F leg.
Uladh (Ulster), dist. . . . . . 60 A b
Ulala . . . . 170 J c
Ulan-Butor-Khoto (Urga) . 171 L d
Ulcinj (Dulcigno) . . . . . 165 A e
Ulcinj, (Dulcigno), bp. . . . 95 F c
Uliasutai . . . . 171 K d
Uliches, people . . . . 57 J d
Ulster (Uladh), dist. . . . . . 60 A b
Ulster, prov. . . . . 74 C a
Ulu-kem River . . . . . . 104 C J b
Uman reg. . . . . 104 C J e
Umberto I, Ponte-, loc. in Rome . . . . 22 A
Umbilicus, in Rome . . . . . 24 B (10)
Umbri, people . . . . 29 C c
Ume River . . . . 98 G a
Una River . . . . 87 K f
Unie, isl. . . . . 168 F H g
Unghvár (Užhorod) . . . . . 168 H b
Union of South Africa . . 175 F g
Union of Soviet Socialist Republics (Russia) 168 G L-R d
Université, quarter in Paris 149 B
University, in Athens . . . . 23 D
University Street, in Athens 23 D
Unst, isl. . . . . 128 ins.
Upland, dist., in Sweden . . 88 G a
Upper Egypt, reg. . . . . . . 4 F d (III)
Upper Germans, people in 1929 . . . . 168 H C-E c
Upper (Gray) League . . . . 91 Q l
Upper Lorraine, duchy, 13 cent. . . . . 104 A C c
Upper Nairi Sea . . . . 5 D b
Upper Silesia, reg. . . . . 168 D D c
Upper Tunguska River . 104 C J b
Uppsala (Upsala) . . . . 88 G b
Ural, economic reg. . . . . 170 leg.
Uratu, dist. . . . . 4 G c
Urci . . . . 38 B e
Urci. bp. . . . . 42 B f
Urfa . . . . 168 J C b
Urgenj . . . . 104 B F c
Urmia . . . . 168 K E b
Urmia, Lake . . . . 99 M f
Ursha . . . . 168 L D c
Urumtsi . . . . 104 B J c
Urundi, reg. . . . . 175 F e
Ush . . . . 104 B H c
Usk, castle . . . . 74 K h
Usk, R. . . . . 60 H d
Uskub (Skoplje) . . . . 89 H f
Üsküdar . . . . 168 L F f
Ussa River . . . . 138 J b
Ussuri River . . . . 104 C N c
Ústí (Aussig) . . . . 135 G c
Uvejek . . . . 9 A b
Uxellodunum, in Britain . . 51 O g
Uxellodunum, in Gaul . . . 38 ins.
Uzbek Socialist Soviet Republic . . . . 170 H d
Uzes, people, on the Dnieper R. . . . . 99 J d
Uzes, people, on the Ural R. 53 H b
Uzgend . . . . 104 B H c
Užhorod (Unghvár) . . . . . 168 H b

Vaçcanae (Baccanae) . . . . 35 ins. B
Vács (Waitzen) . . . . 87 L e
Vács (Waitzen), bp. . . . . . 95 F b
Vadstena (Wadstena) . . . . 88 F b
Valencia Island, in Ireland 168 F C e
Vallay of Salt . . . . 7 B f
Valley of the Sweet Waters of Europe . . . . 93 G e
Val Pusteria . . . . 168 H ins.
Valona (Avlona) . . . . . . 164 B b
Val Venosta (Vintschgau), reg. . . . . 87 H e
Väner (Wener), lake . . . . 88 E b
Vangui (Yang-chau-fu) . 104 C M d
Varad, Nagy-(Grosswardein, Oradea Mare) . . . . . . 168 G c
Värälä . . . . 138 C c
Varberg (Warberg) . . . . . . 88 E c
Varini, people . . . . 38 D a
Värmland (Vermland), reg. 45 G a
Varvakion, bldg. in Athens 23 D
Västerås (Westerås) . . . . . . 88 G b
Vätter (Wetter), lake . . . . 88 F b
Vaudemont . . . . 104 A D c
Vaudemont, cty., 13 cent. 104 A D c
Vaux (-devant-Damloup) 168 C C c
Vaux-lès-Laferté . . . 104 A C b (V.l. L.)
Vaux-lès-Mouzon . . . 104 A C b (V.l. M.)
Vechta . . . . 78 F b
Veldes . . . . 79 I e
Veles . . . . 165 B c
Venta Icenorum (Caistor, Bury St. Edmunds) . . . . 51 Q h
Venus, Temple of, near Ardea 35 ins. B
Venus Cloacina, Temple of 24 A (14)
Venus Genetrix, Temple of 24 B (24)
Venzone . . . . 154 G e
Veps, people . . . . 59 L b
Veramin . . . . 104 B F d
Verbas River . . . . 87 K f
Verneuil (near Évreux) . . . 69 H f
Verneuil (near Montmédy) 104 A C b (Ve.)
Versecz (Werschetz, Vršac) 168 G d
Vesle River . . . . 104 A B b
Vespasian, Temple of . . . . 24 B (6)
Vesta, Temple of . . . . . . 24 A (19)
Veszprem . . . . 87 K e
Veszprem, bp. . . . . 95 F b
Veurne see Furnes . . . . 134 B c
Via Appia Nuova, street in Rome . . . . 22 A
Via Cavour, street in Rome 22 A
Via della Lungara, loc. in Rome . . . . 22 A
Via di Porta San Sebastiano, in Rome . . . . 22 A
Viale Ardeatino, in Rome . 22 A
Viale Ostiense, in Rome . . 22 A
Via Nazionale, street in Rome 22 A
Via Nomentana, street in Rome . . . . 22 A
Viatka . . . . 138 G d
Viatka River . . . . 138 G d
Viatka-Vetluga, economic reg. . . . . 168 F leg.
Via Venti Settembre, street in Rome . . . . 22 A
Viazma . . . . 138 D d
Viborg (Wiborg) . . . . 88 C c
Vieille Rue du Temple, street in Paris . . . . . . 149 B
Vielun (Wielun) . . . . 79 K c
Vienna, in Austria . . . . . . 63 I d
Vigneul-sous-Montmédy . 104 A C b (Vi)
Vijayadurg . . . . 137 B e
Vijayanagar, reg. . . . . 92 H f
Viking raids . . . . 45 E b
Világos . . . . 139 B f
Viliui River . . . . 104 C L a
Viliya (Wiliya) River . . . . 88 K d
Villa Cisneros . . . . 181 Z e
Villafranca (Villefranche) 102 H g
Villa Hayes . . . . 216 H h
Villalar . . . . 83 J g (Villal.)
Villanueva, in Spain . . . . 83 K g
Villa Medici, bldg. in Rome 22 A
Villareal . . . . 83 K h
Villa Rica de Vera Cruz 106 D a

Villa Rica la Vieja 106 D a
Villa Viçosa (Portugal) 83 J h
Ville, quarter in Paris 149 B
Villefranche (-de-Rouergue) 76 E d
Villefranche (-sur-Mer) 102 H g
Villers-lès-Mangiennes 104 A C b
Vilmanstrand 138 C c
Vilnius (Vilna) 168 D F c
Vimy Ridge, mt. 168 C B b
Vincennes, in France 86 D d
Vincennes, Fort-(Indiana) 191 H d
Vintschgau (Val Venosta), reg. 87 H e
Virbalis (Virballen) 159 L a
Virginia, reg. 191 I e-L b
Viroconium (Wroxeter) 51 O h
Virzjärv (Wirzjärw), lake 88 K b
Vis (Lissa), isl. 90 F c
Visborg (Wisborg), castle 88 H c
Visby (Wisby) 88 H c
Višegrad, in Bosnia 87 L g
Visegrad, castle in Hungary 87 L e
Visoko 89 A b
Vitim River 104 C L b
Vitry (-le-François) 154 C d
Vitry (-en-Perthois) 104 A B c
Vittorio Emanuele, Ponte, loc. in Rome 22 A
Vittório Véneto 168 B F b
Viza 165 E c
Vltava (Moldau), R. 168 D C d
Voguls, people 138 J c
Voivodina, reg. 159 J f
Vordernberg 79 I e
Vordingborg 87 H a
Voreda 51 O g
Vosprus 99 K d
Votiak, auton. area 168 G P d
Vots, people 57 I b
Vrana 87 J g
Vratza (Vraca) 165 C b
Vrbas River 161 K e
Vredenburg 128 C ins. D
Vrhbosna (Sarajevo) 87 L g
Vršac (Versecz, Werschetz) 168 G d
Vychegda River 138 G c
Vyschegrad (Wyszegrad), castle (near Bromberg) 79 K b
Vyšehrad (Wyschehrad), castle (near Prague) 79 I d
Vytegra 182 E E a

Wadgaon 137 B e
Wadi Halfa 174 G b
Wadi Sous 174 C a
Wagon Road (Hamaxitos) 23 D
Wahabis, people 170 F f
Waldenburg, in Saxony 79 H c
Waldenburg, in Wurtemberg 143 I g
Wales, princ. 8 cent. 60 C c
Wales, princ. 11 cent. 65 E d
Wales, princ., 1200-1450 74 I g
Wales in 1832 163
Wales, North-, dist. 60 H c
Wallingford 60 I d
Walloons, people in 1929 168 H B b
Walvis (Walfish) Bay 175 E g
Wanborough 60 D d
Wantage 60 I d
Warangal 104 B R j
Ware 127 Z o
Warga River 174 P n
Warszawa (Warsaw) 87 M b
Wartenberg, castle, in Bohemia 79 I c
Washington, routes of 195 C d
Wassulu, reg. 174 C d
Watchet, borough 60 H d
Waterford, in Ireland 74 C b
Waterloo 156 A a
Wawat, reg. 4 F d
Wedmore 60 H d
Weissenstein, castle, in Esthonia 88 K b
Weitenstein, castle 79 I e
Weitra 79 I d
Wells, in England 74 K h
Welsh Marcher Earldoms 70 F c (W.M.E.)
Welsh Mountains 2 D c
Welshpool 74 J g
Welsh Principalities 70 F c (W. P.)
Wends, people in 1929 168 H D b
Wenlock, mon. 60 C c
Werdenfelds, castle 79 G e
Werfen 87 I e
Werschetz (Versecz, Vršac) 168 G d
Weset 4 F d
Wessex, Kingdom of 60 leg.
West, economic reg. 168 F leg.
Westerna, dist. 60 C c
Western Euphrates River 18 E c
Western Samoa, Territory of 172 H b
Westerwald, mts. 168 C D b
West Götland, dist. 88 E b
West Hartlepool 162 E c
West Kirghiz, economic reg. 170 G d leg. (B)
Westmanland, dist. 88 F b
West March, dist. 128 E e
Westminster, abbey 74 M h
Westmorland, dist. 60 H b
Westmorland, cty. 74 K e
Westmorland, parl. dist. 163 L c
Westray, isl. 128 E a
West Riding, dist. 60 I c
West Samoa, Territory 180 J i
West Saxons, people 60 C-D d
West Scheldt, R. 168 C B b
West Sea (North Sea) 98 D c
West Wales, dist. 60 B d
Wexford 74 C b
Wezzan 174 P n
Whalsay, isl. 128 ins.
Wharfe River 60 D c
Whitby (Streaneshalch), mon. 60 D b
Whiterne (Whithorn), bp. 60 B b
White Russian Socialist Soviet Republic (W.R.S.S.R) 168 F leg.
Whithorn 128 D f
Whithorn (Whiterne), bp. 60 B b
Wick 128 E b
Wicklow, castle 74 C b
Wied, castle 78 E c
Wiek, dist. 88 J b
Wieringen 168 D A c
Wigmore, castle 74 K g
Wigtown 128 D f
Wigtown, cty. 128 D f
Wilimow 87 J d
Wiliya (Viliya) River 138 C e
William of Rubruck, Route of 104 B leg.
Willis Islets 179 F i
Wilno (Vilna) 159 M a
Wilton, battle 60 I d
Winchester in England (Venta Belgarum) 51 P i
Windau River 88 J c
Winds (Slovenes), people 56 E c
Wing 60 I d
Winnebah 128 C ins. D
Winnipeg River 190 F a
Winwaedsfield, battle 60 D c
Wirzjärw, lake 88 K b
Wisborg (Visborg), castle 88 H c
Wislica 87 M c
Witbois, people 175 E g
Witham, borough 60 J d
Witteland, reg. 128 C N g
Wittgenstein, castle 86 G c
Wkra River 135 K b
Woëvre Plain 168 C C c
Wolkowysk 155 M b
Wollin, bp. 95 E a
Wolmar 88 K c
Wolodomir 99 H c
Wolyn, dist. 139 C e
Woodstock, borough 74 L h
Worcester, bp. in England 60 C c
Wormser Joch, pass (Stelvio Pass) 86 H e
Wörth 158 D d
Wrath, cape 128 C b
Wreocensaete, people 60 C c
Wycombe 74 M h
Wye River 60 C c
Wyschehrad (Vyšehrad), castle 79 I d
Wyszegrad (Vyschegrad), castle 79 K b
Wytschaete Ridge 168 C B b (W.)

Xavier, Saint Fr(ancis) 191 H c
Xochimilco, lake 106 A a
Xocotla 106 C a
Xoïs 4 ins.

Yachi 104 C K e
Yakut, economic reg. 171 O b (G)
Yakutat 180 N b
Yakutsk, Autonomous Socialist Soviet Republic 171 M/P b
Yala Geul 168 L D c
Yamburg 88 M b
Yamurtalik 168 J C b
Yandabu 171 K f
Yang-chau-fu 104 C M d
Yang-tse-kiang, R. 104 C K e
Yang-tsun 170 ins. A
Yanina (Janina) 89 B c
Yarkand 104 B H d
Yarmouth, (I. of Wight) 74 L i
Yarmouth, Great- (Norfolk) 65 G d
Yarmouth, Great-, parl. bor. 163 P e
Yatnan (Cyprus), isl. 5 C b
Yatreb (Medina) 53 G d
Yatvegs, people 71 K c
Yazvings, people 57 H c
Yedlinsk (Jedlinsk) 155 K c
Yell, isl. 128 ins.
Yemama, reg. 53 G d
Yemamah, El- 104 B E e
Yenihan 168 J C b
Yeni Kioi 9 A b
Yenisei River 104 C I a
Yeni-Shehr 9 A b
Yerkessi 9 A b
Yezd 170 G e
Yezdi Chast 168 K F d
York, in England 60 D b
York, abbey 74 M f
York, Kingdom of 60 I b
Yoshino 104 C N d
Yozgad 168 J B b
Ypiranga 215 D e
Yrac, reg. 99 K f
Yser River 168 C B b
Ystad 103 K a
Yttingaford 60 I d
Yuan Dynasty 92 K e
Yu-ché, people 104 C M c
Yugoslavia, km. 168 F I-J g
Yung-ning-fu 104 C K e

Zab River 53 G c
Zadar (Zara) 168 D d
Zafarin Islands 174 Q n
Zagreb (Zagrab, Agram) 79 J f
Zagreb (Agram), bp. 95 F b
Zagros Mountains 168 K D b-E c
Žagubica 165 B a
Zaiton (Tsuen-chau-fu) 104 C L e
Zaječa 103 N f
Zamość 155 L c
Zampa, reg. 104 C K f
Zappeion, bldg. in Athens 23 D
Zardandan, reg. 104 C J e
Zarev 139 G f
Zarev, abp. 99 M d
Zarnowitz 87 L a

Žatec (Saaz) . . . . 87 I c
Zator . . . . 87 L d
Zebid . . . . 104 B E f
Zeebrugge . . . . 168 C B b
Zeitun . . . . 168 K F c
Zeitz, bp. (Naumburg-) . . . 95 E a
Zeklers, people in 1929 . 168 H G c
Zelea . . . . 9 E d
Zemun (Semlin, Zimony) . 168 G d
Zenda Rud, R. . . . . . . 168 K F c
Zengg (Senj) . . . . 168 D d
Žepče . . . . 87 L f
Zephat . . . . 6 C c
Zephyrium, prom., in Crete 14 ins.
Zerenj . . . . 104 B G d
Zeus, Temple of, in Olympia 9 H f (2)
Zhagubitza (Žagubica) . . 165 B a
Zhaia . . . . 104 B F f
Zhitomir . . . . 139 C e
Ziegenhain . . . . 78 F c
Ziklag . . . . 7 B f
Zile . . . . 168 J C a
Zimony (Zemun, Semlin) 168 G d
Zinjar . . . . 77 M e
Zipangu, emp. (Japan) . 104 C O d
Zips, County of . . . . 87 M d
Zircz, mon. . . . . 80 E h
Ziza . . . . 7 D e
Znaim (Znojmo) . . . . 87 K d
Zolyom (Zvolen, Altsohl) 159 J d
Zone of the Straits . . . 168 D F e
Zsolna (Sillein) . . . . 155 J d
Zubeir. . . . . 168 K E c
Zuhab . . . . 99 M g
Zvornik (Zwornik) . . . . . 87 L f
Zwettl . . . . 87 J d